ENCYCLOPEDIA OF POTTERY & PORCELAIN
The 19th & 20th Centuries

Encyclopedia of Pottery & Porcelain

The 19th & 20th Centuries

Elisabeth Cameron

faber and faber

LONDON · BOSTON

First published in 1986
by Faber & Faber Limited
3 Queen Square London WC1N 3AU

Printed in Great Britain by
R.J. Acford, Chichester, Sussex

Produced by Cameron Books, 2a Roman Way, London N7 8XG
Editor: Jill Hollis
Designer: Ian Cameron

British Library Cataloguing in Publication Data

Cameron, Elisabeth
  Encyclopedia of pottery and porcelain: the
  nineteenth and twentieth centuries.
  1. Pottery—19th century—Dictionaries
  2. Pottery—20th century—Dictionaries
  3. Porcelain—19th century—Dictionaries
  4. Porcelain—20th century—Dictionaries
  I. Title
  738.2′03′21   NK3770

  ISBN 0-571-11397-4

Acknowledgements

Editorial consultants:
Paul Atterbury
Emmanuel Cooper
T.A. Lockett
Hugo Morley-Fletcher
Susan H. Myers
Jennifer Opie
John Wade

Cameron Books wish particularly to acknowledge the help they have received from Susan H. Myers of the Smithsonian Institution, Washington, from John Wade of the Museum of Applied Arts and Sciences, Sydney, and from Paul Atterbury. We are indebted to R.J. Charleston for advice in the early stages of the book. We are also grateful to the picture librarians of Sotheby's, Christie's and Phillips in London, and of Royal Doulton in Stoke-on-Trent, and to Kenneth R. Trapp of the Cincinnati Art Museum for their help with pictures. For work on picture research, translation, text processing and production, we would like to thank Charles Alcock, Christine Chodun, Tim Davies, Alice Rugheimer, Maria Schleger, Simon Taylor, Donna Thynne, Tom Wesel and Sophie Zeman.

I have several people to thank for the book's production. Our consultants have given expert advice on the entries in their particular areas of specialization, and meticulous care has been taken over the accurate transformation of manuscript into print. The errors are therefore mine, and I should be glad to hear of any that readers may find.

Elisabeth Cameron
Leamington Spa
January 1986

About this Book

In this book, I have attempted to draw together published information on the makers of ceramics in the 19th and 20th centuries. I have on the whole omitted those whose important work was all in the 18th century even if their production continued in the first decade or so of the 19th. Modern makers have been included only if they have produced work, other than as students, before 1960. Where I have felt it helpful, I have defined materials, techniques and stylistic movements, but patterns are dealt with only in relation to the factories that used them, as in general are lines of ware. The main marks are mentioned and in some cases illustrated, particularly where they are difficult to describe adequately because they incorporate monograms or other devices. The important reservation here is that the appearance and feel of a pot, rather than the mark it bears, provide the truest guide to its maker. Where a factory or maker used many marks, only a selection are mentioned.

The length of an entry should not necessarily be taken as an indication of the subject's importance; it also represents the amount of published information that is available. In the current state of literature on ceramics, some artists' and manufacturers' work has been almost over-documented (and much exhibited), while other wares have escaped attention. The captions contain varying levels of information depending on the sources of the pictures.

I have tried to make best use of the space available by avoiding comment and evaluation (though I do not suppose that I have always kept personal preferences out of sight). Also, partly because of space considerations, the lists of examples are not comprehensive – if a workshop is said to have concentrated on utilitarian wares, it should not be assumed that no special pieces were ever produced there, and a potter who is best known for work of a particular range may have produced apparently uncharacteristic pieces at some time or another.

In the alphabetical arrangement of the book, names are taken to include any prefix as part of the surname, e.g. de Feure, Georges; Van Briggle, Artus; von Heider, Maximilian; when, even so, it is not clear where a name belongs, cross references are provided, e.g. for Bontjes van Beek, Jan. Entries appear in order of the uninverted part of the entry title. Company names including more than one surname appear after any entries containing the first surname alone, e.g. Doulton, Sir Henry; Doulton, John; Doulton & Co.; Doulton & Watts. Names that include a definite article are normally inverted in the entry heading, as are names that start with an indication of function or corporate status, e.g. Ram, Plateelbakkerij.

An asterisk in the text signifies that an entry may be found under the name indicated. Cases such as Meissen, Sèvres and the firm of Wedgwood, which appear frequently, have asterisks only when their entries contain further information on the subject in question.

The majority of entries conclude with a list of references. The lists for the best documented subjects are necessarily very selective, but an attempt has been made to include works that offer further bibliographical information. Titles that appear frequently have been abbreviated, usually to the author's surname, plus a date where a number of books by the same author have been cited. The list of abbreviations that appears at the back of the book is intended as just that and makes no attempt to be a full bibliography of 19th and 20th century ceramics.

Aaron, Michel (d 1856) and **Valin,** Jean-Baptiste. French porcelain makers. Aaron and the sculptor Valin, both formerly making bronzes in Paris, established a porcelain factory in 1832 at Limoges, working in a partnership, Michel & Valin, that lasted until Aaron left for *Chantilly in 1845. The company submitted a display at the Exposition de l'Industrie Française in 1844, winning a silver medal for decorative pieces which included clock cases representing equestrian subjects (Napoleon, François I) and romantic figures, as well as female portraits (Venus, Nôtre Dame des Victoires, and a woman lacing her bodice).

Continuing the firm alone, Valin specialized in decorative ware, noted for its lavish ornamentation of scrolls, flowers and small figures. He took a son-in-law named Berthoud into the firm in 1855. At the Exposition Universelle in Paris that year, his display included biscuit models of animals, equestrian figures, a madonna and child (one metre in height), two candelabra painted by his son, and a vase (two metres high) on which two life-sized storks formed the handles and a serpent appeared among reeds.

Valin was succeeded by Berthoud (1864-78) and the partnership Delotte & H. Tarnaud (1879-86), which gradually turned production over to tableware.
Refs: Chavagnac & Grollier; d'Albis & Romanet.

Abbot, Edgar. See G.D.A.

Abington, Leonard James (1785-1867). English potter born in London. Abington worked as a carver and modeller before moving in 1819 to Staffordshire, where he worked e.g. for Joseph Mayer (*see* Mayer, E., & Son) and as a partner of W.*Ridgway. He was editor of a Staffordshire paper, *The Pottery Mercury*, in 1824, and entered into partnership with Edward John Ridgway (*see* Ridgway Potteries Ltd) from the 1830s until c.1860 at the Church Works in Hanley, where their firm made earthenware and porcelain, including jugs with high-quality relief decoration.
Ref: Godden (1972).

Abino ware. See Buffalo Pottery.

Ablott, Richard. English porcelain painter, born in Canada during his father's military service in Manitoba. After the family's return to England, Ablott was apprenticed at the *Derby porcelain factory, where he worked from 1825, eventually specializing in landscapes, in a style resembling that of D.*Lucas. He left Derby in 1845 for Staffordshire, then worked at the *Coalport factory, and, c.1870-80, for *Davenport's. His painting included signed porcelain plaques.
Refs: Barrett & Thorpe; Lockett (1972); Twitchett (1980).

Aborigine. See Owens, John B.

Abraham, Robert Frederick (1827-95). English porcelain painter. Abraham studied in Paris and Antwerp, and exhibited historical scenes and portraits at the Royal Academy and British Institution between 1846 and 1853. He moved to *Coalport by 1855, working at the factory as art director until

1862. He painted panels on vases in Sèvres style shown at the International Exhibition, 1862. He worked at the Hill Pottery in Burslem, Staffordshire, and in 1865 succeeded G.*Eyre as art director for the firm of W.T.*Copeland, where he was employed until his death. Abraham's work was delicate, often in the style of William Etty, and included cupids and classical figures.
Refs: Blacker (1922a); Godden (1970); Jewitt; Rhead.

Abraham, Robert John (1850-1925). English pottery painter; son of R.F.*Abraham. He trained in art at the South Kensington Schools, London, Abraham subsequently designed and painted tiles for the firm of W.T.*Copeland with portraits, and in 1874-75 (with L.*Besche) a narrative series depicting Health, Strength, Courage and Fortitude, commissioned for the house built by Macfarlane, a maker of decorative ironwork. Abraham worked for a firm of ceramic decorators in Stoke-on-Trent, Staffordshire, in the 1880s.
Refs: Blacker (1922a); Rhead.

Abramtsevo. School established near Moscow by a businessman, Savva Mamontov, and his wife, to make art socially useful by providing employment and artistic expression for young peasants. The project was inspired by other workshops set up in 1884 by Elena Polonova. As well as running a private theatre, where they commissioned established artists to paint scenery, the Mamontovs founded a pottery in 1890, where artists including M.*Vrubel worked on the production of earthenware with coloured glazes, under the supervision of P. Vaulin. The workshop was transferred to Moscow in 1896 and became state property in 1918. Inspired by icons, Russian architecture and maiolica of the 17th and 18th centuries, the artists made vases, dishes, sculptural pieces and architectural ware. The work was exhibited, and small quantities were sold.

Mark (1890-1918): Abramtsevo in Cyrillic capitals.
Refs: Bubnova; Rheims.

acid gilding. See gilding.

Acme Pottery Co. See Hull Pottery.

Adamantine China. See Wheeling Pottery Co.

Adamesk ware. See Adams & Co.

Adamovich, Mikhail Mikhailovich (b 1884). Russian painter and porcelain decorator. Adamovich studied at the Stroganov Institute in his native Moscow, leaving as a Gold Medallist in 1907. He studied painting in Italy and returned to work as a painter in Moscow. In 1911, he worked in St Petersburg, notably on ecclesiastical decoration. Work carried out on mosaics in the vault of King George I for the Greek government was followed by military service in Russia

until 1917. Adamovich worked for the St Petersburg factory in 1918, when his porcelain painting included classical architectural studies, e.g. views of St Petersburg, ruins, monuments. After 1919, he painted revolutionary subjects and scenes of life in the Red Army, in which he served, 1919-21.
Ref: Gollerbach.

Adams, Harvey. English manufacturer of earthenware, stoneware and porcelain. Briefly a partner (1861-62) with J.B.*Shelley at the Dresden Works, Longton, Staffordshire, Adams then established the Sutherland Road Works, also in Longton, working for a short time in the firm Adams, Scrivener & Co. and subsequently in partnership with Titus Hammersley (d 1875), succeeded by Hammersley's son George Harris Hammersley. The firm, trading as Harvey Adams & Co. until 1885, made a wide range of table services, toilet sets and domestic utensils in earthenware, stoneware jugs, teapots, etc., as well as domestic and ornamental porcelain. The decoration included perforated borders, embossed leaf patterns, modelled flowers painted in natural colours, and silver gilding, either matt or brilliant, used as a ground for flower painting, as well as in highlights. The firm is credited with the introduction of *moustache cups. Under the art direction of flower painter John Marshall from 1881, there were new lines of ware inspired by Persian and oriental styles. After the retirement of Harvey Adams in

John Adams. Baluster vase painted with fish and water plants on ruby, coral and grey lustre. Marked Bernard Moore 1910 *with Adams's monogram. 41 cm high.*

1885, the firm continued as Hammersley & Co. until the 1930s, and subsequently operated as Hammersley & Co. (Longton) Ltd at the Alsager Pottery.

Printed mark: a crown with the initials H.A.&CO., 1870-75.
Refs: Jewitt; Watkins *et al.*

Adams, John (1882-1953). English potter and ceramic designer; born in Stoke-on-Trent. Adams started work at the age of 13 in the design studio of a local tileworks and studied at the art school in Hanley, Staffordshire. He subsequently worked as a painter of lustre ware for B.*Moore while studying on a scholarship and, for two years, teaching in London. In 1912, with three fellow ceramics students, Adams worked on tiles, stained glass and other decoration for the Palace of Peace at The Hague. He became head of the art school at Durban Technical College, South Africa (1914-20) and made pottery with his wife, T.*Carter. In 1921, Adams joined Charles Carter and H.*Stabler in founding *Carter, Stabler & Adams, and was managing director of the company until he retired in 1949, remaining as art director until the following year. He was concerned with glaze research, developing a range which included semi-matt and glossy glazes in blues, browns, black, orange and white. He based some experiments on contemporary achievements by studio potters, using wood ash and other natural ingredients. Chinese blues, tangerine and mirror black superseded lustres on the pottery's art wares. Adams designed many of the shapes made at the pottery, including the Streamline tableware (in production from 1936) and initiated fresh experimentation in glazes from c.1923.

Mark: for Moore, monogram of AJ in circle.
Refs: A. Dawson *Bernard Moore, Master Potter 1850-1935* (Richard Dennis, London, 1982); Hawkins; Myers; *Pottery Gazette* (obituary, September 1953).

Adams, Truda. *See* Carter, Truda.

Adams, William. *See* Adams family.

Adams & Co. English pottery at Scotswood-on-Tyne, initially a brick and tile works established c.1840 and trading as W.C. Gibson & Co. Ltd in 1880, when the premises passed into the hands of the Adams brothers, under the title Adams & Co., for the production of sanitary ware from local fireclay. Under the control of Moses J. Adams, the firm produced art pottery marketed as Adamesk and made 1904-14. The Adamesk range included decorative fern pots, vases, inkstands, bird baths, fonts, and monumental urns, made in a fireclay body and covered with leadless glazes coloured with salts of copper (green), cobalt (blue), titanium (yellow) and manganese/copper (bronze), which developed during slow firing in a muffle kiln at about 1200° C. The shapes were simple, often featuring

large or looped handles, and decorated in relief with Celtic-inspired designs. Animal figures were also made. Alan H. Adams joined the firm in 1912 as modeller and designer, becoming director in 1921, and introduced a further line of art pottery, Elanware, which has continued in production. The firm adopted the trade name of Adamsez Ltd.

Marks include ADAMESK, impressed; monogram MJA; the initials AHA impressed on Elanware.
Ref: Bell.

Adams family. Staffordshire potters directly descended from a potter working at Burslem in the late 14th and early 15th centuries. Three members of the family, all cousins named William Adams, were working in Staffordshire in the early 19th century.

William Adams (1746-1805) inherited his father's factory at Burslem, operated another at Newfield, Tunstall, and established the Greengates Pottery, also in Tunstall, in 1779, when he started the production of jasper ware, similar in quality to the work of the Wedgwood factory. He used the mark ADAMS on both dipped and solid jasper ware until 1805. The firm also made stoneware, including tankards, jugs and wine coolers, decorated in relief with sporting or drinking scenes, domestic creamware and, later, pearlware of good quality (painted or printed), as well as mocha ware, etc. Much of the work produced at Greengates was exported to France until the war with Napoleon, when the firm concentrated on sales in London. Adams's second son, Benjamin Adams (1787-1828), succeeded his father and older brother, William (1778-1805) and sold the factory in the early 1820s.

William Adams (1748-1831), after operating the Brick House Works, Burslem, from 1769, moved in 1774 to Cobridge, where he made printed tableware and probably some figures until the factory was let in 1813. He was also the owner of collieries near Cobridge and, from c.1800, a mill producing paper tissues for transfer printing.

William Adams (1772-1829), the son of Richard Adams (1739-1811), a maker of saltglaze and creamware at Cobridge, worked in partnership with his father-in-law, Lewis Heath, a potter at Hadderidge Works, Burslem, from the time of his marriage in 1793 until he established his own firm in 1804 at Upper Cliff Bank Works, Stoke-on-Trent. Adams acquired the main works at Cliff Bank in 1810 and by 1818 owned three further Stoke-on-Trent factories. His firm's main output consisted of tableware printed with American views as well as scenes showing buildings in London and the English countryside, much exported to North America. Adams's eldest son, also William Adams (1795-1865), opened a branch in New York under the title Adams Brothers, and succeeded his father in 1829. He opened a shipping office in Liverpool, 1832. In partnership with his brothers, Lewis (1805-50), Edward and Thomas, as

proprietors of five factories in Stoke-on-Trent, additionally in 1834 taking over the Greenfield Works at Tunstall from his father-in-law John Breeze, he made large quantities of earthenware for the home and export markets. In the 1840s, the firm started production of parian figures and groups. William Adams withdrew from the partnership in 1853, afterwards continuing the Greenfield Works, and became involved in several collieries. The Stoke-on-Trent factories passed out of the family's hands by 1863, after his brothers' deaths. In 1896, his son, William Adams (1833-1905), acquired the Greengates Works, Tunstall, sold earlier by Benjamin Adams, and operated both Greenfield and Greengates Potteries, succeeded by two of his sons.

Marks usually incorporate the name Adams. W. Adams & Son used WA & S or the firm's full name and a variety of printed backstamps which often incorporate the trade names of body or pattern.
Refs: W.L. Adams *A History of the Adams Family* (London, 1914); Blacker (1922a); Bunt; M. Deaton 'Adams of Greengates' in *Apollo* (April 1953); Hughes (1959); R. Nicholls *The Adams Family* (1928); D. Peel *A Pride of Potters* (Arthur Barker, London, 1959); Towner (1957); W. Turner *William Adams, an Old English Potter* (Chapman & Hall, London, 1904).

Adamsez Ltd. *See* Adams & Co.

Adderleys Ltd. Staffordshire manufacturers producing earthenware and ironstone china at the Daisy Bank Pottery in Longton, which had been occupied from 1851 by C.J. Mason (*see* Mason, G.M. and C.J.) and was later renamed the Gainsborough Works. In 1853 the lease of the premises passed to the partnership of Hulse, Nixon & Adderley, which traded as Hulse & Adderley from Nixon's death in 1869. William A. Adderley continued the pottery when Hulse died in 1873, trading under his own name from the following year. The output was mainly tableware of high quality for export and the home market. After 1906, when the firm became Adderleys Ltd, small decorative pieces were made, including commemorative models for World War I. The firm produced tea and dinner ware in bone china at the Paladin Works in Fenton and, for a time, the Gainsborough Works; flowers and small figures were made at another Longton factory, Adderley's Floral China Works. The firm combined with *Ridgway Potteries Ltd in 1952 and later formed part of Allied English Potteries Ltd (*see* Pearson, S.,& Sons Ltd).

Marks after 1876 include a circular printed mark depicting a three-masted ship. Marks normally incorporate the initials WAA (to 1905), or *Adderley* or *Adderleys*, and sometimes the name of a pattern.
Refs: Andrews; Bunt; Godden (1972); Jewitt.

Addison, Falconer & Co. *See* Newcastle Pottery.

Adelberg, Louise. *See* Rörstrand Porslins Fabriker.

Adler, Christian (1787-1850). German porcelain painter working at *Nymphenburg

Adderleys Ltd. Cup and saucer with over-glaze painted flowers and gilding by A. Wagg. Made by W.A. Adderley & Co. between 1890 and 1905. Saucer 12 cm in diameter.

from 1811 until his death; head of the painting workshop, 1815-38. Adler is noted for his copies of paintings in the collection of Ludwig, King of Bavaria, commissioned after 1827.
Refs: Danckert; Weiss.

aerography. A decorative technique in which colour is applied to pottery or porcelain by means of an atomizer. The method, developed by L.A.*Fry at the *Rookwood Pottery in 1884, allowed the even blending and shading of colours. The effect became a feature of Rookwood's standard ware and art lines made at the *Lonhuda Pottery; the technique soon came into general use in America as the means of applying underglaze ground colour and eventually glazes. In Britain, aerography was used for laying large areas of colour on low-priced porcelain and earthenware.

Aesthetic Movement. An informal artistic movement in England, 1860s to late 1880s, arising in part as a reaction against the examples of contemporary taste shown in the Great Exhibition in London, 1851, and characterized by a rejection of moral, social or other purposes in art. The movement helped to raise the status of design in relation to the fine arts.

Sources of inspiration for the movement include: Pre-Raphaelite painting, the principles of design and craftsmanship recommended by the *Arts & Crafts Movement, and the stylistic aims of James McNeill Whistler. William Morris's firm, Morris, Marshall, Faulkner & Co. (formed in 1861), aimed at improving design standards in domestic goods and decoration, and produced a small amount of pottery, mainly tiles. Whistler worked in Paris in the mid 1850s and settled in London by 1863. He drew on contemporary French painting and Japanese art, which became important

influences in the movement, and promoted the concept of Art for Art's Sake in his *Ten O'Clock Lecture* (1885) and *The Gentle Art of Making Enemies* (1890). Attitudes of the movement were espoused by Oscar Wilde (1854-1900) in the 1870s. In spite of derision by *Punch* in the 1880s and in Gilbert and Sullivan's *Patience*, he became influential in America with a series of lectures coinciding with performances of *Patience* in New York.

The ceramics emphasize fine design, and the making of high-quality individual pieces with inspiration from a variety of sources: *japonisme (*Mintons Ltd., J.*Wedgwood & Sons Ltd, *Worcester); medieval influences (expressed in slipware made by the *Watcombe Pottery and C.H.*Brannam, echoed by E.H.*Elton and E.*Bingham). C.*Dresser influenced a group of potteries in the Midlands and North of England; *Linthorpe Pottery was early among European potteries in imitating features of Pre-Columbian pottery. W.*Ault, *Burmantofts and *Bretby Art Pottery in turn inspired the work of the *Salopian Art Pottery and others.

The movement encouraged a fashion for decorative tiles and a rapid growth in the tile industry from the 1860s. Wall tiles, popular from the 1870s, were frequently decorated with such symbols as the lily, peacocks, sunflowers and Japanese scenes, figures and motifs. Notable examples were the work of W.B.*Simpson & Sons, *Maw & Co. (designs by W.*Crane, L.F.*Day) and W.*De Morgan's tiled porch in the London house of Alexander Ionides.

Agano ware. Japanese pottery made in or near Agano village in Fukuoka Prefecture from the early 17th century, using local clays from the slopes of Mount Fukuchi. Like *Takatori wares, the output was initiated by the feudal lord after Japanese military incursions into Korea during the late 16th century, and both kilns were among the seven sources of ware picked by the tea-master Kobori Enshu (1579-1647) as worthy of tea-ceremony use. Several generations of potters descended from the founder, a Korean potter called Sonkai (d 1646), adopted the name *Totoki and, under the administration

of feudal lords until 1868, were among potters making tea-ceremony wares and vessels (fully or partially glazed) for domestic use. They worked from 1625 at the main Agano kiln in the present-day Agano-Sarayama, Akaike Town, in Tagawa County. The Korean influence in style was modified from the early 19th century, after visits by the official potter, Totoki Mogozaemon, to study both in Tokyo and, from 1804, under a raku potter in Kyoto. Stylistic elements introduced under the influence of raku artists included the use of a reddish-purple glaze known as shiso-de, the trailing of yellow and bluish-green glazes on dark brown to form a three-colour (sansai) glaze, an effect of egg-yolk yellow (tamago-de) achieved by firing white clay with transparent glaze in an oxidizing atmosphere, and a surface texture resembling wood grain (mokume) achieved by working together red and white clays. A bluish-green copper glaze (rokusho) introduced in the late 18th century was allowed to run over a transparent glaze to give a flecked effect (rokusho-nagashi) on pieces which were mass-produced for sale throughout Japan in the 19th century. This glaze often occurs on the interior of bowls in buff clay, flowing in streaks to the centre, and sometimes used in contrast with a dark brown. Other decorative effects used on the Sarayama kiln's later wares were trailed streaks of feldspathic glaze (somen-nagashi); white slip, roughly applied with a hemp-fibre brush and covered with amber glaze—an effect known as ki-tataki (yellow paddling); kushime, the combing of slip with a toothed bamboo tool, a technique introduced by potters from nearby Takatori; white slip used as an inlay in incised or stamped patterns, or roughly brushed. The modern Agano studio potter, Agano Taira, is known for patterns of cranes in flight, etc., incised and inlaid with white slip. Early kiln sites have been excavated by *Kumagai and others.
Refs: Brinkley; Hannover; Jenyns (1965); Koyama; Kozuru *Agano & Takatori* (Kodansha International Ltd, Tokyo/New York/San Francisco, 1981); Munsterberg; Sanders.

agate ware. Earthenware made with a mixture of clays, either naturally coloured or stained with different colours, which resembles the striped gemstone, agate, in appearance. Unlike surface marbling with coloured stripes, agate ware has striations throughout the body.

In England, agate ware was known in Roman times and revived in Staffordshire by the mid 18th century. The ware was normally shaped in moulds until the late 19th century, when more plastic clay mixtures allowed wheel throwing. The colours blended on the surface, but were scraped after throwing to expose the variations in body colour before polishing and glazing.

Aho, Kaarina (b 1925). Finnish ceramic designer, born in Helsinki and trained at the school of industrial art. Aho worked for *Arabia from 1946, and designed wares in simple shapes for everyday use in a variety of materials, including porcelain, fine, white earthenware, and a dark body containing chamotte, with coloured glazes.
Ref: Aro.

Ahola, Hilkka-Liisa (b 1920). Finnish ceramic designer, born in Helsinki and trained at the school of industrial art. She joined *Arabia in 1947, and her work includes ornamental bowls, plaques, etc., in glazed earthenware with painted or *sgraffito* patterns, often of flowers.
Ref: Aro.

Ahrenfelt, Charles (c.1857-1934). French porcelain manufacturer. Ahrenfelt built a factory at Brègefort in the district of Montjovis, Limoges (Haute-Vienne), which was in operation from 1896. He employed his Zurich agent M. Grob as director until 1917. The output of high-quality porcelain won the Grand Prix at the Exposition Internationale des Arts Décoratifs et Industriels Modernes in Paris, 1925. The factory was enlarged in the following year. Ahrenfelt was succeeded by his widow, and their firm passed to a finance group in 1958. Production gradually diminished before the factory's closure in 1969.

Ahrenfelt's father, also Charles Ahrenfelt (1807-94), had been an exporter who enlarged the reputation of Limoges as a centre of porcelain production by developing a wide market, notably in North America.

Marks incorporate name, or monogram of CA.
Ref: d'Albis & Romanet.

Ainley Top Pottery. Yorkshire pottery established at Ainley Top near Huddersfield c.1826, and operated by the *Kitson family until its sale in 1890 and subsequent demolition. The firm produced bricks, tiles and, later, kitchen ware and miniature cradles and chests of drawers in reddish earthenware decorated with applied strips of white clay and patterns impressed with a roulette wheel.
Refs: Brears (1971a); Lawrence.

Aitchison & Co. *See* Caledonian Pottery.

Aitken, Russell Barnett (b 1910). American ceramist. Aitken studied in Vienna under M.*Powolny (1832-33) after graduating from R.G.*Cowan's ceramics course at the Cleveland School of Art in 1931, and exhibited regularly in Cleveland and New York during the 1930s. He made humorous, mock-heroic figures and groups (e.g. The Hunter, Student Singers, and a figure of Europa) in earthenware with brightly coloured lead glazes. Other sculptural pieces often feature animals or Western pioneer themes.
Refs: G. Archbold 'Ceramic Sculptures of Russell Aitken' in *Design* 36 (December 1934); Clark & Hughto; 'The Art with the Inferiority Complex' in *Fortune* 6 (1937).

Aizu. Japanese ceramic centre. A pottery, established on the site of a feudal kiln which opened in the mid 17th century at Hongo, in the Aizu district of what is now Fukushima prefecture, produced black-glazed ware for local sale from the early 18th century. During the 19th century, the original Aizu kiln and a number of other potteries nearby made either pottery or porcelain, mainly blue-painted, which was introduced to the area in the late 18th century and gradually replaced other wares until, after c.1926, the only remaining producer of Aizu-Hongo stoneware was the Munakata kiln, with an output

of domestic *mingei wares. The strong, simple forms are covered with ame glaze (containing iron, a warm amber when fired in an oxidizing atmosphere, or a darker shade under reduction), namako glaze (streaked with white, purple and deep blue), or white with decoration dripped in green glaze. Rectangular dishes are used locally for storing salted herring.
Refs: Mizuo; Munsterberg.

aka-e (Japanese, red painting). Polychrome overglaze painting of bold, simple patterns of birds, flowers, etc., in which red is the dominant colour, developed in China in the 16th century, and produced by the Imperial kilns at *Ching-tê chên in the Yung-Chêng period (1723-35) after a lapse in use in the 17th century, when it was superseded by the more complicated five-colour and nishikide designs. Aka-e was introduced directly from China into Japan, where it is thought to have been first produced by Sakaida Kakiemon (*see* Kakiemon family) in Arita in the 1640s, although similar patterns were used almost simultaneously in *Kutani and *Ninsei ware. It became a feature of certain *Nabeshima and *Imari wares. The red enamel, revived at the *Minzan and *Ono kilns and often accompanied in Kutani wares by gold and silver, was applied in a thin wash with matt effect. The technique made greater use of the white ground than *kinrande and the related ware developed by *Hachiroemon in Kutani. *Shuhei specialized in aka-e porcelain, which also featured in the work of *Shuntai. (*See also* gosu aka-e.)
Refs: Gorham; Jenyns (1965); Munsterberg; Nakagawa.

Akahada ware. Japanese ceramics made at Koriyama, near Gojo, in Nara Prefecture, in the late 16th and 17th centuries and again, after a lapse in production, from the 18th century until the present day. The kiln's output, after its revival under the patronage of the feudal lord of Koriyama, included earthenware with patterns in enamel, notably red, delicately painted over a buff or tan glaze, e.g. bowls with designs representing Mount Fuji; the same ornamental design was also used in relief. Glazes in green, olive, brown, grey and white were used alone, or with variegated effects; *flambé* and thick, light-coloured crackle glazes were also used. A group of raku-type ware was sometimes painted with flowers and other ornament in enamel or light-coloured slip on a gold ground in imitation of pieces by *Ninsei. *Mokuhaku made raku tea bowls at Akahada during the early 19th century.

Marks: Akahada (Chinese characters aka and hada, or three characters, aka, ha, da), in the 19th century; the seal Mokuhaku.
Refs: Audsley & Bowes; Brinkley; Gorham; Hannover; Hobson; Jenyns (1971); C. Mitsuoka 'Old Japanese Wares ...' in *Oriental Ceramics* IX, 4; Mizuo; Morse; Munsterberg.

akaji-kinga. *See* hachiro de.

Akashi. *See* Shigaraki ware.

Aki ware. Japanese porcelain made at Uchiharano in the city of Aki in Kochi prefecture, Shikoku, at a folk kiln established

in the 1820s by potters from *Nosoyama. The output of domestic ware included large rice bowls (goroshichi) and saké warmers (iraregan).
Ref: Okamura.

Akudo. Japanese folk kiln working from 1806 to the early 20th century at Shimoyuguchi in Aomori Prefecture in the north of Honshu. The ware included saké bottles, cylindrical containers for hot water, and fire containers with decoration trailed in slip.
Ref: Mizuo.

Albany slip. A suspension of fine, dark clay, rich in iron, associated with Albany, New York, where it is still dug. The clay was used, sometimes with lead added, in a slip glaze for the lining of American stonewares in the early 19th century and came into general use c.1840. It is also used in modern studio pottery.
Ref: Fournier.

Alberhill Coal & Clay Co. Clay producers from 1895 in the Alberhill-Corona district of California, formerly a coal-mining company. The firm employed A.W.*Robertson to experiment with local clays (1912-14). During this period, Robertson made wheel-thrown terracotta ware, mostly in light tones, though some pieces were red in colour; a limited number of pieces were glazed. Decoration consists of impressed classical motifs, e.g. in a band encircling the shoulders of a squat jar, or relief modelling, e.g. a single lizard on the side of vases, which are often angular in shape.

Marks include *A.C.C.Co. Cal.*, incised; *Alberhill* impressed; the initials of Robertson.
Ref: Evans.

Albert, Tobias. *See* Gera.

Alberti, Carl G. *See* Uhlstädt.

Albert Works. *See* Wild, T., & Co.

Albion Pottery. *See* Fisher, George; Ouseburn Bridge Pottery.

Albion ware. *See* Bennett, Edwin.

Albissola (Liguria). A centre of Italian maiolica production in the 17th and 18th centuries, which developed again as a source of ceramic production in the 1920s when many Futurist artists settled there to work. In 1927, Filippo Tommaso Marinetti started a collaboration with the Albissola potter, Tullio, on *Il Manifesto futurista ceramica e aeroceramica* (published 1938). L.*Fontana worked at the Tullio Mazzoti factory at Albissola in the 1930s. In the years after World War II, Albissola attracted sculptors, including members of the Cobra group, which was started by Surrealist artists from Copenhagen, Brussels and Amsterdam. Their work included ceramic panels.
Ref: Préaud & Gauthier.

Albouts, Wilhelm G. (1897-1971). German potter. Albouts worked as an apprentice in his native Krefeld under P. Dressler in 1921, also studying, 1921-22, at the ceramics school in Höhr-Grenzhausen. He was then manager of the Kammerburg pottery in

Lorch, on the Rhine, until his return to Höhr-Grenzhausen, 1925-26. After a time spent in Norway as manager of a pottery at Sandnes, 1926-29, he worked in a stoneware workshop at Höhr-Grenzhausen, 1930-31. After managing the ceramics department of Fontaine & Co., Frankfurt, 1939-59, he retired, but opened a workshop, Die Muschel, at the factory, where he continued his own work. Using porcelain paste, as well as clay from Westerwald and Kassel, he made bowls and vases, mainly thrown, but with the surface carefully smoothed of throwing lines. Albouts used very translucent glazes, sometimes with a layer trickled over the ground glaze. From 1966, he used an electric kiln for reduction firing.

Marks: A or ALBUS incised until 1945; later, applied relief mark with a shell impressed.
Refs: Bock; Klinge.

Alcock, Henry, & Co. *See* Robinson, Harold Taylor.

Alcock, Samuel (b c.1846). English porcelain painter, trained at the Royal Academy Schools, and employed by the firm of W.T. *Copeland from the 1880s until the early 20th century. Alcock was noted for paintings in a muted, delicate style of figures in classical or contemporary dress within elaborate gilt or jewelled borders on dessert services, etc. His work also included vases with allegorical figures, e.g. Morning and Night, the arts, and the seasons, painted on large, jewelled vases, or woodland scenes on more delicate dessert ware.
Mark: signature.
Refs: Godden (1961); Jewitt; Rhead.

Alcock, Samuel, & Co. Staffordshire pottery and porcelain manufacturers, working in Cobridge c.1828-53 and at the Hill Pottery, Burslem, 1830-59. The firm made basalt and stoneware, concentrating on porcelain after moving to the Hill Pottery, which Alcock rebuilt in 1839. The output included high-quality bone china, semi-porcelain and a wide range of blue-printed earthenware. As well as biscuit porcelain figures, the firm produced parian ware, including jugs decorated in relief with scenes depicting Naomi and her Daughters-in-Law (patented in 1847) and Daniel in the Lions' Den (1859). The stock and general estate were bought in 1860 by the earthenware manufacturers, Sir James Duke & Nephews.
Marks: SAML ALCOCK & CO printed or impressed with COBRIDGE c.1828-53, printed, impressed or moulded with BURSLEM c.1830-59. Other marks, printed, painted or impressed, incorporate the firm's initials or name and include the Royal Arms or a beehive device; sometimes initials or name alone c.1830-59.
Refs: Blacker (1922a); Cushion (1976); Godden (1963); P.A. Halfpenny 'Samuel Alcock & Co.' in *Journal of the Northern Ceramic Society* Vol II (1975-76); Jewitt.

Alcora. Spanish faience factory established 1726-27 near Valencia by the Count of Aranda. The factory produced faience, at first under the influence of French factories, especially Moustiers and Strasbourg, then turned to lustre ware, using formulae brought from Manises. Tableware and figures were also produced in porcelain; cream-coloured earthenware was made in English styles from c.1774. Ownership passed to the Dukes of Hijar in 1798. The later wares were simple and generally without decoration, though the factory produced a class of ware with green lead glaze. The Catalan industrialist, Ramon Girona, owner from 1858, introduced workmen from Staffordshire, and the politician Cristobal Aicart purchased the factory in 1895 in an unsuccessful attempt to restore production to 18th-century standards.
Marks (19th century): *Fabca de Aranda A*, in a circle; A, transfer-printed in red.
Refs: J.F. Riano *The Industrial Arts in Spain* (London 1879); B. Rackham *Catalogue of the Glaisher Collection* (Fitzwilliam Museum, Cambridge, 1930); Escriva de Romani *Conde de Casal—Historia de la Ceramica de Alcora* (Madrid, 1945).

Alexandra Porcelain Works. *See* Wahliss, Ernst.

Alexandria Pottery. American stoneware pottery established by John Swann at Alexandria, Virginia, and acquired in 1841 by Benedict Milburn, who operated it with his sons. The pottery's grey stoneware was decorated with leaves, flowers, etc., in cobalt blue.
Mark: ALEXANDRIA D.C. (Alexandria was retroceded to Virginia from 1846.)
Ref: Stradling.

Allan, Hugh. *See* Allander Pottery.

Allander Pottery. Scottish art pottery in operation at Milngavie, near Glasgow, 1904-08. The founder, Hugh Allan, produced vases relying for decoration on glazes coloured with metallic oxides and sometimes variegated. Allan also used some crystalline glazes.
Incised or painted mark with the name ALLANDER in script, and a date.
Refs: Coysh (1976); Hughes (1961).

Allard, James. *See* Cornwell, Alfred.

Allen, George. American potter, making white and yellow glazed ware, Rockingham ware and limited quantities of parian ware, 1857-58, in Philadelphia at a pottery formerly occupied by R.B.*Beech and later by stoneware potter, Richard Remmey (*see* Remmey family).
Ref: Barber (1976).

Allen, Harry (b c.1886). English ceramic decorator, apprenticed 1900 at *Doulton & Co., Burslem, Staffordshire, where he remained until 1950, after training under the supervision of his father R.*Allen and for ten years at Burslem School of Art. He was a painter of flowers, landscapes, working scenes, Arab desert villages and other Middle Eastern scenes, animals (e.g. a polar bear) and, notably, birds which included kingfishers, owls, nightingales, thrushes, storks, peacocks and toucans, in the decoration of Titanian wares. From the early 1920s, he specialized in painting modelled figures. Allen also executed hand painting over litho prints, which he signed with the pseudonym *Richmond*.
Refs: see Doulton & Co.

Allen, Robert. English ceramic decorator. After working briefly for *Mintons Ltd in his youth, Allen joined the firm of *Pinder, Bourne & Co. in 1870, and trained as a painter of flowers, birds, insects, nautical scenes, etc., both under John *Slater and at the Burslem School of Art. In 1882, Pinder, Bourne & Co. become part of Doulton & Co.. As head of a department producing the firm's choicest pieces, Allen worked from the early 1890s on the design of patterns in Italian Renaissance styles for execution in raised and etched gold to surround painting by other artists. He designed some Lactolian pieces and, with his son, H.*Allen, assisted in the artistic development of Titanian ware. He continued to work for Doulton & Co. until 1929.
Marks: signature (rare); initials RA on many decorative pieces produced in his department.
Refs: see Doulton & Co.

Allen, Thomas (1831-1915). English ceramic decorator and designer. Allen worked at the Minton factory (*see* Mintons Ltd) from c.1845 while studying in evening classes at the Stoke-on-Trent School of Art, Staffordshire. He painted figures (e.g. dancing Seasons) in panels on vases in the Sèvres style shown at the International Exhibition, London, 1851. With T.*Kirkby, he worked on reproductions of Italian tinglaze for the firm's range of majolica. Allen won a scholarship to the South Kensington Schools, 1852-53 (his diary, written at the time, is preserved in the Wedgwood Museum at Barlaston) and returned to Minton & Co., 1854-75. His work mainly consisted of figure subjects, occasionally flowers, and he was responsible for enamel paintings on panels and other architectural decorations formed of hexagonal *tesserae* in the South Kensington Museum (now the Victoria & Albert Museum).
After joining the Wedgwood factory in 1876, Allen took charge of the fine art studio, later becoming chief designer and, from 1880 until his retirement in 1905, art director. His designs comprised patterns for tableware, including Columbia, still in production, and more frequently figure subjects for the decoration of vases, e.g. a pair of vases shown in the Exposition Universelle, Paris (1878), painted with nymphs and cupids. In 1881, Allen decorated earthenware dishes and plaques with subjects from the works of Shakespeare.
Refs: Batkin; G. Godden in Atterbury (1980); G. Godden 'Victorian Ceramic Artists' in *Apollo* (August 1959); Haggar (1953); Rhead; *Staffordshire Evening Sentinel* (obituary, 13th October 1915).

Allen, W.H. *See* Harris family.

Allerton, Charles, & Sons. Staffordshire manufacturers of earthenware, semi-porcelain and bone china, working from 1831 at the Peak Works, Longton, and still under the control of grandsons of the founder,

Charles Allerton, in the early 20th century. The firm produced domestic ware and ornamental pieces, specializing in gold or silver lustre of high quality, and became Allertons Ltd in 1912, when taken over by Cauldon Potteries Ltd (*see* Brown-Westhead, Moore & Co.).

Marks, when used, incorporated the name or initials of the firm and, often, a crown.

Refs: Blacker (1922a); Godden (1964); Jewitt.

Allerton Bywater. *See* Gill, William.

Aller Vale Pottery. Devonshire pottery near Newton Abbot, originally a small workshop established in 1865 for the production of domestic earthenware and purchased by J.*Phillips in 1868. The pottery then produced architectural ware, terracotta and slip-painted ware including pitchers, jugs and other domestic articles, advertised in 1884 as Devonshire faience (with *sgraffito* designs of seaweed, shells, flowers, under glossy glazes), Aller Vale terracotta (plaques, vases and bottles, some of them black-glazed and decorated with flowers in oil paints) and domestic art pottery (pitchers, Toby jugs, stoneware jugs). The 'faience', normally a red earthenware body, thickly painted in slip with designs of scrolled leaves on a ground of cream, white or, later, occasionally green or blue, and often inscribed in *sgraffito* lettering, became characteristic of the pottery, for which Phillips adopted the name Aller Vale Pottery in 1887. Other painted designs include a daisy-like motif in buff, blue and green, which became known as the Abbots Kerswell pattern. A white body was used for painting with the foliate Sandringham pattern in blue, and other stylized leaves in a variety of colours. The glaze was normally clear and glossy, but Amber ware, usually undecorated, was coated in deep yellow translucent glaze, and a streaked or mottled effect was achieved by the use of slip in several colours brushed or splashed on the dark body.

After receiving the patronage of Queen Victoria's daughter, Princess Louise, in 1889, the firm traded as the Royal Aller Vale Pottery, and sold its ware through Liberty's. The store's catalogue of 1892 lists a wide range of domestic and ornamental ware decorated with stylized flower patterns derived from Isnik pottery. Aller Vale pieces were thrown, moulded or slip cast. Motto ware, characterized by a rhyme, aphorism or quotation in *sgraffito* lettering on a cream ground, often combined with a motif resembling a *fleur-de-lis* (known as 'Scandy') under a clear glaze, or the Abbots Kerswell daisy under a yellow glaze, was widely imitated by other potteries in the Torquay area. A group of vases was introduced in 1900 in a variety of shapes and decorated with crocus flowers and leaves in yellow and green against a dark blue ground. Normandy ware, with green glaze running down in streaks from the rim over a body coated in white slip, was introduced at the same time.

On Phillips's death in 1897, the works were sold to Hexter, Humpherson & Co., clay merchants and makers of tiles and sanitary ware at Kingsteignton, Devon, who bought the *Watcombe Pottery in 1901 and operated the combined business as Royal Aller Vale and Watcombe Pottery Co. The Aller Vale works closed in 1924.

Marks include ALLER VALE impressed 1887-1901. From 1901 ROYAL ALLER VALE impressed or printed.
Refs: Jewitt; Lloyd Thomas (1974, 1978); Wakefield.

Allied English Potteries. *See* Pearson, S., & Sons Ltd.

Allies, Edwin. *See* Bristol Pottery.

Allison's Pottery. *See* Hunslet New Pottery.

Alloa Pottery. Scottish earthenware pottery established 1790 by James Anderson and afterwards operated by William Gardiner, who added Rockingham-glazed teapots to the output of brown ware produced from local clay similar to that used at the *Dunmore Pottery. White earthenware was produced from 1841, with decoration generally painted over transfer-printed patterns. In 1855, the pottery was bought by the firm of W.& J.A. Bailey, who continued the output of brown-glazed teapots, adding basalt and majolica. Some pieces had engraved decoration of ferns, etc. The Baileys continued to operate the pottery until the 20th century; they were also glassmakers.
Refs: Hughes (1961); Jewitt; McVeigh.

Alluaud, Eugène (1866-1947). French landscape painter and porcelain decorator, the grandson of F.*Alluaud. In 1896, he took over a factory established in 1878 for the production of porcelain in rue Charpentier, Limoges (Haute-Vienne), where he worked for five years before establishing a decorating workshop at his home in rue Grange-Garat in 1901. His work included a series of six plates, designed in 1916, and made by Haviland & Co. (*see* Haviland, C.) with decoration commemorating World War I (titles: Un Blessé, 1915, La Guerre Aérienne, Le Poilu, Un Bleuet, La Croix de Guerre) printed and finished by hand, for sale in aid of army social work. In 1925, after returning to painting for nearly ten years, Alluaud carried out decoration for the firms of H.& A.*Balleroy Frères, L.*Bernardaud & Cie, and R.*Haviland, winning a prize at the Exposition Internationale des Arts Décoratifs in Paris.
Mark: signature, *E.Alluaud.*
Ref: d'Albis & Romanet.

Alluaud, François (1778-1866). French porcelain manufacturer, born in Limoges (Haute Vienne) and educated in Paris. He took over the porcelain factory established by his father, François Alluaud (1739-99) in rue des Anglais, Limoges, in the late 18th century, and adopted industrial techniques, cutting production costs by such measures as restricting the decoration on some pieces to simple bands of gilding. The firm, renowned for the quality of a fine, white paste perfected by Alluaud's father exhibited work in Limoges in 1803 and 1804, and displayed a group, Chevaux de Marly, in Paris, 1806. Alluaud formed the Société Alluaud in partnership with his brother Jean-Baptiste-Clément in 1805, and two years later rented a small works established by Léonard Monnerie and Jean Joubert in 1793, opening depots in Toulouse and Paris.

Alluaud took over the disused *Monnerie factory in Limoges in 1813. In the following year he formed Alluaud Frères, in which he worked with his brother as technical director until 1823. The firm's records of 1810-19 mention decoration of flower sprigs, wide gilded bands or armorial devices on plates; cups varied in shape, sometimes with beaded decoration; jugs were moulded with a cockerel, eagle or mythical animal. Ornamentation was in general sparing and included mythological or allegorical subjects, sometimes carried out *en grisaille*, and trophies. By 1819, the range of painting included classical landscapes, botanical studies, and designs from *Moeurs, Loix et Coûtumes des Sauvages du Canada* (published 1791). The output of high-quality pieces made for sale at moderate prices included table services, flower holders, vases and other decorative items. The firm used the newly developed chrome green in decoration from 1813. A brown ground containing diorite, developed in 1827 and used with decoration in biscuit reserves, was quickly imitated by other factories.

Alluaud opened a new factory in Casseaux, Limoges, which was in operation by 1817 and employed 150 workers in 1819. His family owned deposits of kaolin at Saint-Yrieix by 1820, supplying the Sèvres factory, among others. He became mayor of Limoges in the early 1830s, leaving the firm under his nephew, Paul Lacombe, who was joined by Alluaud's sons Victor (d 1876) and Amédée (d 1872), and their brother-in-law Amédée Vandemarcq between 1839 and 1845. Alluaud's successors increased the workforce of 181 in 1844 to 300 in 1864, and Vandemarcq took over direction on his death. In 1876, the factory passed to C.F. *Haviland, who had married François Alluaud's grand-daughter in 1858.

Marks include the initials FA and date.
Refs: Chavagnac & Grollier; d'Albis & Romanet; Ernould-Gandouet; C. Grellier *L'Industrie de la Porcelaine en Limousin* (Paris, 1909); A. Leroux *Histoire de la Porcelaine de Limoges* (Limoges, 1904).

Alpaugh & Magowan. *See* Coxon, Charles; Trenton Potteries Co.

Alpine. *See* Owens, John B.

Alpine Pink. *See* Wedgwood, Josiah, & Sons Ltd.

Altenburg. German earthenware factory established at Altenburg, Thuringia, by the brothers Doll, who were succeeded in 1806 by Heinrich Mühlberg.
Mark: A impressed.
Refs: Cushion (1980); Scherf.

Älteste Volkstedter Porzellanfabrik. *See* Unterweissbach; Volkstedt-Rudolstadt.

Altman, Johann Gottlieb. *See* Bunzlau.

Altrohlau. Bohemian creamware factory established at Altrohlau, near Karlsbad, in 1814 by Benedikt Hasslacher, formerly director of the *Dallwitz factory, who concentrated on the mass production of household ware. The factory was let to Andreas Schwengsbier from 1820 until its sale in 1823 to August Nowotny. By the following year, 100 workers were employed on the production of creamware with decoration inspired by patterns used at English and other Bohemian factories, and engravings by the Prague artist, Georg Döbler, of posies and bouquets, which were used on tea and coffee cups from the 1830s. Nowotny introduced the technique of transfer printing. The factory received an honourable mention for a display in the national exhibition of industrial products at Prague, 1829; pieces were decorated in monochrome or full colour with flowers (roses, tulips, carnations), landscapes or views of Prague. Porcelain, made in large quantities from the late 1830s, was exported to Austria and Hungary.

The firm remained in the hands of Nowotny's family until 1884, when it was purchased by the Prague banker Moritz Zdekauer.

Under C.M. Hutschenreuther (*see* Hutschenreuther family), owner from 1909, the firm continued to make domestic porcelains, becoming Starovsky Porcelan Narodni Podnik Stara Role in 1945.

Marks:(Hasslacher) monogram BH impressed or *Ha*; (Nowotny) A.H. NOWOTNY, or later *Nowotny & Co*; (Zdekauer) MZ; marks often incorporate the place name *Altrohau* or *Alten Rohlau* and a variety of borders or symbols.
Refs: Danckert; Meyer; Weiss.

Altwasser. German porcelain factory established at Altwasser, near Waldenburg, Silesia (now Poland) in 1845 by C. Tielsch (d 1882) for the production of hard-paste porcelain tableware. Tielsch afterwards bought another factory from an architect

Altwasser. Pair of plates entitled 'Love Restrained' and 'Love Encouraged', painted en grisaille *within brick-red borders, one marked with an eagle. Made by the Tielsch firm in the late 19th century. 29 cm and 29.5 cm in diameter.*

and businessman named Silber. He was succeeded by his son Egmont von Tielsch, who in 1882 operated a decorating workshop which was united with the main Tielsch factory in 1906. The works were then modernized with the addition of the first tunnel kiln to be used in Europe for the firing of porcelain. C.M. Hutschenreuther of *Arzberg took over the firm in 1918.

Marks usually incorporate the initials CT and ALTWASSER, with anchor, *fleur-de-lis* or, more often, an eagle; from 1918, an eagle with C.T./HUTSCHENREUTHER/ARZBERG/BAVARIA/GERMANY.
Refs: Danckert; Weiss.

Aluminia A.S. Danish pottery established 1863 at Smallegade, Copenhagen, for the production of earthenware at reasonable prices for everyday use. The firm amalgamated with the Royal *Copenhagen Porcelain factory in 1882, and moved it into the Aluminia premises in 1884 under the direction of P.*Schou, who began to improve the artistic standards in porcelain production, helped by artist A.*Krog and followed in earthenware production by F.*Dalgas, with painters Harald Slott-Moller and C.H. *Joachim. The factory's policy was to exploit the characteristics of earthenware rather than use it for the imitation of porcelain, giving designers freedom to choose the material better suited to their artistic aims. A large display at the St Louis World's Fair in 1904 included bowls, vases, etc., with underglaze decoration in a lush palette of browns, yellows, blues, greens and purple.

Marks: ALUMINIA in oval trom 1863; initial A with a device of three waves replacing the crossbar from 1903. Ironstone china was

Aluminia A.S. Vase painted with a lakeside scene in soft underglaze brown and blue-grey, c.1930. Marks: the decorator's painted signature, Arth Boesen, *and* Dahl Jensen, *(the designer), printed. 29 cm high.*

marked with the waves across the centre of a circle from 1929.
Refs: Danckert; Haslam (1977); Weiss.

Aluminite, L', S.A. *See* Frugier, René.

Amable, Baron Paul-Charles. French ceramist. Amable was the owner of a patent taken out in 1827 for glazed earthenware with relief decoration (*see* émaux ombrants).

American Encaustic Tiling Co. Terracotta tile plaque with a cherub and a ram, in low relief. With H.C.*Mueller's mark and the firm's name impressed. 15.2 x 40.6 cm.

He carried out research on this technique at the creamware pottery owned by the firm of Darte & Billèle in rue de la Roquette, Paris, until its closure in 1836, when he transferred his experiments to a pottery at Montreuil-sous-Bois (Seine), and later went into partnership with his friend A.*du Tremblay at Rubelles (Seine-et-Marne), hoping to make use of his patent; the partners took out a further fifteen-year patent on their process in 1842.
Ref: Lesur (1971).

Amberg. German faience factory established at Amberg, Bavaria, in 1759. The manufacture of cream-coloured earthenware started in the late 18th century, and everyday stoneware and porcelain in the 19th century. Porcelain was printed in black or blue under the glaze. In 1850, the firm acquired over 90 models from the Ludwigsburg factory, which had been sold to the Schwerdtner factory at Regensburg after the closure of Ludwigsburg in 1824. The factory remained in operation until 1910.
Marks include *Amberg*, impressed.
Refs: Danckert; Honey (1952); Weiss.

Amber ware. See Aller Vale Pottery.

AMB Pottery. See Boyd, Arthur.

ame glaze. See Aizu.

American Art Clay Works. Pottery established at Edgerton, Wisconsin, in 1892 by T.P.A.*Samson and L.*Ipson, who were joined by Samson's brother, Hans, formerly a language teacher. Their firm produced figures and busts made of local red or buff clays, either unglazed or with bronze-coloured finish. Early pieces included a bust of Grover Cleveland, and copies of the Venus de Milo and other sculptural pieces. The pottery was taken over and enlarged by Louis H. Towne, a local lawyer, in 1895, while remaining under the supervision of the previous owners until Ipson's return to Denmark in 1896, and traded as the Edgerton Art Clay Works. Artists who signed or initialled their work included sculptor Helen Farnsworth Mears and T.P.A. Samson's wife, Martina. After a

break in production, when part of the premises was used as a bottling works, Samson and Ipson briefly reopened the pottery in 1903, leaving again in the same year.
Marks, when used: *Samson Bros & Co* or *American Art Clay Works* (1892-95); *Edgerton Art Clay* or *Art Clay Works, Edgerton, Wis* (1895-1900); vase containing monogram of EACW (probably 1902-03).
Refs: Evans; Kovel & Kovel; E.M. Raney in *Rock County Chronicle* (Rock County Historical Society, Wisconsin, Spring, 1962).

American China Manufactory. See Tucker, William Ellis.

American Encaustic Tiling Co. Ohio firm founded at Zanesville in 1875 to manufacture tiles of sufficiently high quality to compete with imported English tiles. The company was incorporated in 1879. Among early commissions were the production and installation of tiled floors in a Zanesville courthouse (1877) and the New York State Capitol Building in Albany (1880). The firm initially produced encaustic tiles but introduced glazed tiles in 1880 and embossed tiles the following year. Inlaid tiles with geometrical designs were made either by moulding plastic clay or by compressing clay dust in automatic presses. H.*Mueller, designer of relief tiles from 1886, also created large panels depicting classical female figures, naked children, etc. K.*Langenbeck, in charge of the company's experimental department from 1890, left with Mueller to establish the *Mosaic Tile Co. in 1893. In 1892, the opening of a new factory (then the largest tileworks in the world) was celebrated by a special issue of tiles. Portraits and pictorial decoration were executed by flooding *intaglio* designs with coloured glaze, which settled more thickly in the sections that were more deeply carved, e.g. designs commemorating the presidential election of 1896. Other special issues of tiles included a series with W.*Crane's illustrations for *The Baby's Opera* and *The Baby's Own Aesop,* c.1891. C.*Nielson was modeller and designer, 1894-1902. L.V.*Solon, designer 1912-25, painted plaques and a series of animal cartoons. W.A.*Long was employed in 1914. H.M.*Northrup became head of casting, decorating and glazing after World War I. F.H.*Rhead took charge of research after the closure of his own art pottery in 1917, and made a small quantity of art ware while

carrying out experiments to find a porcelain suitable for bathroom furniture and decorative tiles. Rhead's work also included a series of tiles decorated with signs of the zodiac from designs by his second wife, Lois.

The firm introduced faience tiles by the 1920s. A plant in California and a New York City mosaic-cutting workshop were opened in 1919. The Californian plant was sold at the onset of financial difficulties in 1932. The main works in Zanesville ceased operation in 1935 and was reopened two years later by the *Shawnee Pottery.

Marks: versions of AETCO FAIENCE; AETCO; name in full on reverse of tiles; A.E. TILE Co./LIMITED. Mueller's work also bears monogram of HM.
Refs: Barber (1976); Barnard; Evans; Kovel & Kovel; Lehner; K.M. McClinton *Collecting American Victorian Antiques* (Charles Scribner's Sons, New York, 1966); L.& E. Purviance & N.F. Schneider *Zanesville Art Pottery in Color* (Mid-America Book Co., Leon, Iowa, 1968).

American faience. See McLaughlin, Mary Louise.

American Limoges. See Wheatley, Thomas Jerome.

American Limoges China Co. See Sterling China Co.

American Porcelain Manufacturing Co. Producers of soft-paste porcelain at Gloucester, New Jersey, 1854-57. The firm's work included tableware decorated with floral designs in relief. The firm's successor, the Gloucester China Co., formed in 1857, made domestic ware of an improved porcelain paste, but with poor finish and glazing; the decoration was restricted to moulded relief. The factory closed in 1860.
Mark: APM CO.
Ref: Barber (1976).

American Pottery Manufacturing Co. See Jersey City Pottery.

American Pottery Works. *See* Sebring Pottery Co.

American Terra Cotta & Ceramic Co. Pottery established in 1880 by W.D.*Gates for the manufacture of drainpipes, bricks and architectural terracotta at Terra Cotta, Illinois, and incorporated in 1887. The firm made art pottery experimentally from c.1895, and on a commercial scale from 1901. Marketed under the trade name Teco, the art ware consisted mainly of flower vases and was moulded or, occasionally, thrown in coloured clays obtained locally or from Brazil, Indiana. Early shapes, many designed by Gates, were often elaborate and incorporated plant forms—petals, leaves, stems and ears of corn, sometimes from specimens, especially aquatic plants, cultivated at the factory to provide inspiration—but, with increasing production, designs became simplified to cut the cost of workmanship. Similarly, the experimental glazes in varying shades of red, buff, or later brown, and sometimes with streaked or mottled effects (also used on the firm's glazed architectural ware) were abandoned in the early 20th century in favour of a matt green glaze with mossy crystalline effect on a body that resembles stoneware; this also appears on many of the firm's tiles. Glaze colours introduced later include platinum, blue, purple, red, yellow, browns, several shades of green and a number of crystalline effects. The art line was discontinued c.1922. Garden ornaments (in some cases very large, and often classical in design) and grey or pinkish glazed teasets were also sold under the Teco mark. Relief decoration and, from 1912, underglaze painting were used on tiles, which include mantel ornaments in green, blue, orange or grey, often featuring landscapes. Terracotta relief panels commemorating the life of Abraham Lincoln were made for the Lincoln Hall at the University of Illinois in Urbana. The factory, referred to in

American Terra Cotta & Ceramic Co. Earthenware vase with four handles, early 20th century. Marked with Teco, impressed, and a paper label. 34.5 cm high.

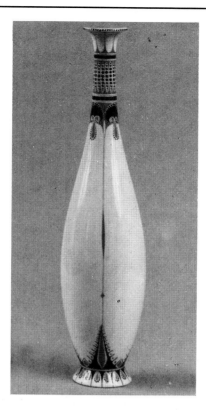

*Amphora (Oegstgeest-Lez-Leiden). Earthenware vase with decoration in black, designed by C.J.*van der Hoef, c.1913. 11.6 cm high.*

Teco advertisements as the Gates Potteries, was sold in 1930.

Teco

Mark: *T* containing *eco* vertically on the right of the vertical stroke, usually impressed.
Refs: Barber (1976); Evans; Kovel & Kovel.

Amirault, Paul. *See* Jouneau, Prosper.

Amphora. Dutch pottery and tileworks in operation 1908-33 at Oegstgeest-Lez-Leiden. The firm was influenced in style by porcelain made at the *Rozenburg factory, and the decorators S.*Schellink and R.*Sterken worked there before going to Rozenburg. Underglaze painting was carried out to designs by C.J.*van der Hoef.
Painted mark: AMPHORA/HOLLAND often with the designer's name or in circle with amphora motif.
Refs: Hakenjos; Singelenberg-van der Meer; van Straaten.

Amphora. Bohemian porcelain manufacturer established 1892 in Turn-Teplitz by Hans Riessner, Carl Riessner (d 1910), Eduard Stellmacher and Rudolf Kessel, former employees of Stellmacher's father, Alfred. The partnership produced stoneware and porcelain, including vases with

layered glazes, exhibited widely (Chicago and San Francisco, 1893; Antwerp, 1894; Leipzig, 1896, 1903; Düsseldorf and St Louis, 1904), and opened depots in Paris and Berlin. The factory of Riessner, Stellmacher & Kessel took the title 'Amphora' in 1903. Ivory porcelain and metallic lustre effects were in production by this time, and the output in 1905 included figures, pieces decorated with modelled flowers, model animals, jewelled ware, copies in ceramics of glass by E.*Gallé, and lines sold under the names Kutani (decorated with peacock-feather motifs) and Hokusai (with decoration after prints by the Japanese artist). In the following year, the firm marketed Gloriana faience (in blue, red and enamel colours), Heidland pottery (decorated with birds, roses and chrysanthemums), and wares which were inspired by country pottery.
Stellmacher left the partnership in 1904 to work independently, and the firm subsequently traded as Riessner & Kessel, remaining in operation until after 1945.
Marks include initials or monograms of R ST K; AMPHORA (from 1915) with *Turn, Austria*, or from c.1918 *Czechoslovakia*; a crown.
Ref: Neuwirth (1974b).

Amstel. Dutch porcelain factory, transferred from Oude Loosdrecht to Oude Amstel in 1784. The output included hard-paste porcelain of very high quality in styles copied from Meissen in polychrome enamel. In the case of Amstel, brown was prominent in painted decoration. Neo-classical elements became increasingly frequent in style. G. Donner & Co., owners from 1799, moved production to their chemical plant in Nieuwer Amstel, where it continued until 1820.
Marks: *Amstel*; *Amstel/M.O.L.*
Ref: Hannover.

Amphora (Teplitz). Stoneware vase painted over the glaze, c.1900. Marked with the initials NK over AMPHORA in relief. 44.5 cm high.

Amphora (Teplitz). Earthenware vases, the one on the left decorated with a portrait of a girl among tall, green leaves, and the other decorated in high and low relief with flowers and gold berries. Both marked Amphora. *The left-hand vase is 46 cm high.*

Amstelhoek. Workshops established in 1894 or 1895 at Omval, near Amsterdam, by the Dutch goldsmith W. Hoeker for the production of ceramics, metalwork and furniture. The designers of pottery included the sculptor, L. Zijl, and C.J.*van der Hoef. The studio's early work, in brownish clay with red or green glazes carefully applied, was simple in form. Thinly potted vases, etc., were decorated with wave patterns, birds and other animals, or abstract geometrical designs, carved out and inlaid with contrasting clay in black, white, green or blue against a yellowish or rust-coloured ground. The ceramic workshop merged with De *Distel in 1910.

Marks include monograms of AH in a circle or oval, sometimes with AMSTELHOEK/AMSTERDAM/HOLLAND.
Refs: Hakenjos; *Jugendstil aardewerk uit eigen bezit* (Centraal Museum, Utrecht, 1976); A.M. Marien-Dujardin 'Céramiques hollandaises et étrangères au Salons de la Libre Esthétique de 1900 et 1901' in *Mededelingenblad Vrienden van de Nederlandse Ceramiek* 84 (1976); E. Thovez 'The International Exhibition of Modern Decorative Art at Turin—the Dutch Section' in *The Studio* 26 (1902); van Straaten.

Anchor Works. *See* Boyle, John.

Ancy-le-Franc. French town, 18 kilometres from Tonnerre (Yonne), the site of two faience factories. The first was in operation as a pottery from c.1725 on the estate of F.-C. Tellier, Marquis de Courtanvaux, and was sometimes known as 'L'Usine du Château'. Faience was made from the mid 18th century. The workshop, sequestrated during the Revolution, was under the direction of Antoine Montenet, helped by his son François, in 1798. Another workshop was established in that year by Joseph-Adrien Dumortier, formerly director of the earlier factory and founder of the Faïencerie de *Vausse. He was succeeded in 1803 by a relative, Charles-Bernard-Bonaventure Foulnier, to whom he had let the Vausse workshop, and the workshop became known as 'L'Usine Foulnier'.

The output of the original factory included plates with raised rims, decorated at the centre with human figures or animals among foliage. Original designs, e.g. bottles in the form of female portrait busts, were imitated by the Domaine des *Cornes workshop. The range of colours, originally greytoned, was extended to include bright, clear blue, yellow and orange; red was used sparingly from its introduction in the late 18th century. Everyday wares were decorated in brown, pale green, and a much duller yellow.

Dumortier favoured mythological themes in decoration (e.g. the Judgement of Paris) and used a colour scheme in which light blue and violet were prominent. Foulnier introduced patterns inspired by faience made at Nevers, and made in a similar body, as well as copying the work of the earlier Ancy factory. The colours of this period lack shine and appear hard. Foulnier was succeeded by his son and grandson until the factory's closure c.1850. The earlier factory had already closed by the early 1840s.

Amstelhoek. Earthenware group depicting a country woman with a cow, decorated in green, blue, violet and red, c.1905. Marked Amstelhoek Amsterdam Holland *with the name of the designer, H.*Teixera de Mattos, *incised. 30 cm long.*

Painters who marked or initialled their work include Pierre Peigney, who trained and worked at Ancy, c.1804-20, and was later employed at Vausse.
Refs: Huillard; Lesur (1971).

Anderson & Co. *See* Prestonpans Pottery.

Andreson, Laura (b 1902). American artist potter and teacher. Born in San Bernardino, Laura Andreson studied until 1932 at the University of California, Los Angeles, subsequently teaching there each summer, while she studied painting at Columbia University, New York, until 1936. She ran a pottery course, initially working in glazed earthenware, sometimes with lustre effects, and began making stoneware in the late 1940s, porcelain in 1957. Her vases, bottles, bowls, etc., in simple, uncluttered forms influenced by Scandinavian ceramics are known for their clear, vivid colours.
Ref: Clark & Hughto.

Andrieux, Paul. *See* Jouhanneaud, Paul.

Angoulême. French faience factory established 1748 at Lhoumeau, near Angoulême (Charente), and until c.1840 under the direction of J.-B. Glaumont-Sazerac, son-in-law of the founder Bernard Sazerac (d 1774). The factory made a wide variety of traditional faience, including imitations of Rouen and Moustiers. Figures of animals (notably lions) resting a paw on a shield or cartouche were a speciality. The output of this and other local factories also included model shoes, tureens, armorial vases, bells, clock cases, as well as ecclesiastical and pharmacy wares. Some pieces were sparingly decorated (c.1850) with yellow foliage against a dark blue ground.

Potteries operating at Angoulême in the 19th century include faience works run by Jean and Henri Garrive (1806), known for bold, carefree decoration; Massié in 1848; Nicollet, Taffet and Gousse, all working in 1860. A firm owned in 1860 by Léon Durandeau was in the hands of Pineau & Patras, faïenciers, in 1888. The artist Alfred Renouleau was making earthenware and stoneware at Angoulême in 1922, using as a mark his initials or monogram.

Laura Andreson. Earthenware vase with red glaze, c.1944. 12.6 cm high.

Refs: Ernould-Gandouet; Fontaine; Garnier; Hannover; Lesur (1971); Tilmans (1954).

Annecy. Several French potters making everyday earthenware at Annecy (Haute-Savoie) in the early 19th century included P. Jacquet, formerly a drawing teacher at Annecy, who made rustic earthenware decorated with slip, at first with flowers, then geometrical designs.

Antoine Tripp, working at a pottery established in the late 18th century, made green and yellow glazed ware, sometimes marbled, including *écuelles*, draining dishes and flowerpots.

Hertz, a Saxon potter formerly working for Tripp, established a pottery in 1860 and made decorated dishes and jars as well as plain cooking ware, succeeded until 1940 by his son. The pottery continued to produce earthenware, yellow or ochre-glazed, and sometimes decorated with birds or other motifs.

White earthenware marked ANNECY was made c.1800-c.1808.
Refs: Ernould-Gandouet; Lesur (1971).

Annfield Pottery. Scottish earthenware pottery established c.1812 in Gallowgate, Glasgow, by John Thomson, who employed workers from Staffordshire to make and decorate fine pearlware, especially tea services. The decoration included oriental scenes transfer-printed in a deep purple. The firm exported much of its output to Australia and remained in production until the late 19th century.

Printed marks include J.T./ANNFIELD, and J.T. & SONS/GLASGOW, often with the pattern name (until 1884).
Refs: Fleming; Godden (1964); Jewitt; Hughes (1961).

Ansbach. German factory originally established for the production of faience, and making porcelain from the late 1750s under the control of the Duke Charles Alexander (1736-1806). Production moved in the early 1760s to the duke's estate at Brückberg. The factory, known for work in rococo style in the 1760s and 1770s, came under state ownership (by Prussia 1797 and by Bavaria, briefly, 1806-07) before becoming privately owned. Production ceased in 1864.
Refs: A. Bayer *Ansbacher Porzellan* (Ansbach, 1933); Danckert.

Anstett, Charles-A. (b 1771). French potter. One of a family of potters working in eastern France. In 1800, he established his own workshop at Colmar (Haut-Rhin) for the production of porcelain and, using clay from Pfaffenheim (Haut-Rhin), fine earthenware. He was among the earliest manufacturers in France to use underglaze transfer-printed decoration. In 1804, he was making stoves designed for economical use of wood fuel.

Mark: signature *Anstett* and sometimes *Colmar* in gold.
Refs: Lesur (1967, 1971); Weiss.

Anstice, Horton & Rose. *See* Rose, John.

Antheunis, Cornelis Eduard (1876-1943). Dutch potter, born in Bergen-op-Zoom. He began c.1919 in Gouda with the manufacture of earthenware and art pottery, which often

resembled the work of other Gouda firms, especially in decoration. After the closure of his business in 1933, Antheunis went to work for *Zuid-Holland.
Marks incorporate initials EA and GOUDA.
Ref: Scheen.

Antoine. *See* Islettes, Les.

Ao-Bizen ware. *See* Bizen ware.

Apátfalva. Hungarian pottery established at Apátfalva (Borsod) in the 1850s, initially making brown-glazed ware and later producing white earthenware stencilled with simple folk designs.
Marks: versions of the place name with a single digit and the names of lessees *Zs. & F. Nagy, Foldvary* or *Pruzsinsky*; 20th century marks incorporate APATFALVA or BEZAPATFALVA impressed in a circle surrounding monogram or cypher.
Ref: Csanyi.

Apoil, Suzanne-Estelle. *See* Béranger, Antoine.

Apostle jug. *See* relief-decorated jugs.

Apple Tree Lane Pottery. *See* O'Hara, Dorothea Warren.

Aprey (Haute-Marne). A centre for the production of traditional French faience throughout the 19th century. The most important makers include the Ollivier family, owners or managers of a factory established in the mid 18th century by Jacques Lallemant. Jacques-Marie Ollivier exchanged potteries with another local maker, Mme Caublot, in 1806, producing undecorated ware until 1832. His pottery was later taken over by A.*Girard, succeeded by a former employee, E. Jacotin, until its closure in 1885. In the last period, the output included *cachepots*, etc., in Louis XV style, with red body, unglazed and decorated in relief with foliage, flowers and fruits. Relief decoration was also used on the borders of dishes and plates. A wide variety of kitchen ware was produced.
Refs: Brunhammer (1959); Chavagnac & Grollier; Deveaux *Les Faïences d'Aprey* (Paris, 1908); Ernould-Gandouet; Fontaine; Garnier; Hannover; Honey (1952); Lane; Lesur (1971).

Apt (Vaucluse). French pottery centre noted for marbled ware made with local clay rich in iron, which ranged in colour from reddish brown to white tinged with yellow or green; earthenware was also coloured with a black derived from manganese. The variegated body was fashionable in the 18th century for figures and groups as well as useful wares, some of which were decorated with leaves, masks and scrollwork applied in light coloured clay.

A factory founded in 1728 by César Moulin remained in the family of his associate Joseph-Jacques Fouque (*see* Fouque-Arnoux) until 1852; the owner from 1798 was Fouque's sister, Claire Arnoux (1750). This factory and the one established by E.*Bonnet in 1799 continued the traditional agate ware, also making green, yellow or brown glazed wares.

Later potteries included that started by Joseph Bernard in 1875 (and continued to

*Arakawa Toyoso. Bamboo-shaped vase in the manner of yellow *Seto ware, c.1960.*

the present day by his family), and the Delacroix factory working by 1880, which produced small vases and other decorative pieces, brown-glazed and sent to Toulouse for decoration with flowers and foliage.
Refs: Ernould-Gandouet; Lesur (1971).

Aqua Verdi. *See* Owens, John B.

Arabia. The main firm of ceramic manufacturers in Finland, established 1874 at Helsinki, and working as a subsidiary of the Swedish firm of *Rörstrand until 1914. The firm's early designs mainly followed those of the parent factory, but tall vases in black or deep blue decorated with white or gold, shown in the local trade fair in 1876, became characteristic of the output of the 1880s. Under the artistic direction of Thure Öberg (from the late 19th century until 1931), the firm adopted, in about 1900, ideals that had been earlier expressed by the English Arts & Crafts Movement, with designs by Finnish industrial artist Axel Gallen-Kallela (1865-1931). The influence of A.W.*Finch, teacher at Helsinki's school of applied arts, is also apparent. The Rörstrand influence diminished after World War I, when Arabia came under Finnish ownership (1916), and the firm showed increasing awareness of contemporary developments in design.

The output of earthenware, stoneware and porcelain includes technical, sanitary and domestic ware and, notably, individual work by artist potters who are employed to complete their own designs, using facilities and materials provided at the Arabia factory. Artists include F.*Kjellberg (from 1924), A.*Siimes, T.*Muona, M.*Schilkin, B.*Kaipiainen (from the 1930s), who exhib-

ited work at the Paris Exposition in 1937. Under the direction of Kurt Ekholm (1931-48), the firm formed an art department in 1932, and followed it with other departments for the creation of models and decoration for hand-made ware in series of varying numbers). Design development was under the control of K.*Franck from 1945. The firm has been part of the Wärtsilä combine since 1948, working as O/Y Arabia A/B.

Marks usually incorporate the name *Arabia*; others include shields with a lion holding a dagger, and a castle with the initials P/AA.
Refs: Aro; Beard; Préaud & Gauthier.

Aragon & Vultury. *See* Jouhanneaud, Hippolyte.

Arakawa Toyoso (b 1894). Japanese potter working near his birthplace, Tajimi, in Gifu prefecture. Arakawa studied painting in Kyoto before training in pottery techniques under Tozan Miyanaga (1868-1941), for whom he worked as factory manager, becoming assistant to *Rosanjin in 1927. His discovery of a ruined kiln in the Okaya district of Gifu in 1930 showed Mino as the source of the 16th century production of *Shino and *Oribe wares, as well as yellow and black *Seto ware. After 1933, he built a kiln in the same style as the original, half-underground kiln which he found at Mudabora, where fine Shino ware had been made, and produced black and yellow Seto wares, also concentrating on the re-creation of the ancient Shino techniques. He is noted for the production of coarse-textured white pottery bowls for the tea ceremony, decorated with abstract or plant patterns under the glaze; his work also included flower vases, in which he exploited the body's tendency to split or distort, and saké bottles. Bowls are characteristically thrown and turned, with a hollowed-out foot. He was among the first artists to be designated a Holder of Intangible Cultural Properties in 1955, for his research into Shino and black Seto wares. In 1971, he received the Order of Cultural Merits.
Refs: Fujioka; Jenyns (1971); Koyama; Living National Treasures; Masterpieces; Munsterberg; Okada; Roberts; Sanders; Sugimura.

Architectural Pottery Co. Earthenware tile, painted with a raven in copper lustre, 1879. Stamped Architectural Pottery Co., Poole, Dorset. 10.2 cm square.

Arbenz, F.J.A. *See* Florentine Pottery Co.

Arboras-Grigny. Manufacturer of cream-coloured earthenware and, later, porcelain at the village of Arboras (Rhône) established in 1830 by the brothers Decaen, who took over another factory in 1839 in the township of Grigny, of which Arboras forms a part. Decaen Frères made everyday earthenware, at first very plain, including square dishes with lobed rims, and elegantly formed ewers. They later made decorative pieces after English models, woven baskets and silver lustre ware. Some work was painted sparsely with garlands in blue, resembling the floral decoration of Tournai porcelain. Series of plates with transfer-printed designs depict Roman or French history, Italian or Egyptian landscapes, or views of monuments (in black, beige, blue or violet) and pastoral scenes (in violet cameo). From the 1840s, *chinoiseries* in green or blue occur, probably inspired by those of *Creil-Montereau. The factory continued under various owners to the present day.
Refs: Ernould-Gandouet; Lesur (1971).

Arcadian. *See* Arkinstall & Sons.

Arcadian service. *See* Petri-Raben, Trude.

Arc-en-Ciel Pottery. American art pottery established 1903 in the former premises of A.*Radford at Zanesville, Ohio, by a company which included J.*Lessell, who became manager. The firm exhibited pottery covered with reddish gold lustre at St Louis in 1904, but art ware proved unprofitable and production was turned over in 1905 to a domestic line marketed as Brighton Cooking Ware: bowls and dishes in varying sizes, jars, pitchers, teapots and cooking ware with stippled blue, brown or green, or mottled brown and yellow glazes. The firm was renamed the Brighton Pottery Co. soon afterwards and continued working until 1907.

Marks: ARC-EN-CIEL (often mis-spelt, CEIL) between rainbow-shaped lines (impressed) or circular lines (printed).
Refs: Evans; Henzke; Kovel & Kovel.

Archangelskoye. Russian village, the site of a porcelain workshop established by Prince *Yusupov on his estate. An earthenware factory, built in 1825 and let to Lambert, a French painter employed by Yusupov, produced tableware, plaques and figures (e.g. a flower-patterned cow) from 1827 until its closure in 1838. The employment of local serfs as decorators was reflected in the painting, which is influenced by Russian folk art, although the forms are often inspired by Delftware.

Some pieces, including a flowered cup, are inscribed with the place name in Roman or Cyrillic characters.
Ref: Bubnova.

Architectural Pottery Co. Dorsetshire pottery established at Hamworthy, Poole, in 1854 by a group of potters who included J.*Ridgway. The output comprised a wide range of tiles, tin-glazed earthenware and terracotta for architectural use. The firm supplied biscuit tiles in the 1870s and, from the 1880s, bowls and dishes for decoration by W.*De Morgan. It was taken over by

*Carter & Co. in 1895 and continued the production of glazed earthenware and terracotta until c.1900, then took over the manufacture of tiles from the Carter & Co. works at East Quay, Poole, and was linked with a nearby factory purchased in 1901 for the making of white and cream-glazed tiles.
Refs: Hawkins; Jewitt; Myers.

Ardant, Henri (1828-83). French porcelain manufacturer. Ardant went into partnership with Pierre Poncet at the former royal factory in Limoges (Haute-Vienne) in 1854. The firm's work shown in the Paris exhibition, 1855, included vases made in one piece to a height of 1.4 metres. On Poncet's retirement in 1858, Ardant formed a new company, Henri Ardant & Cie, employing 150 workers at 6 rue Cruveilher and specializing in biscuit wares, notably sculptures, and such work as cabaret sets and tall jugs with relief decoration applied on a tinted paste in soft shades of grey, blue or green. A.-E.*Carrier-Belleuse modelled a number of figures in the 18th-century manner. The firm exhibited in London, 1862, Bayonne and Limoges, 1864, and Paris, 1867.
Ardant went into partnership with his son-in-law R.*Laporte in 1878. The factory was taken over by A.*Lanternier in 1890.
Ref: d'Albis & Romanet.

Arendts & Scotzniovsky. *See* Nymphenburg.

Arequipa Pottery. American pottery established in 1911 at the Arequipa Sanitorium at Fairfax, California, to provide occupational therapy for women undergoing treatment for tuberculosis. The patients took part in all aspects of production under the direction of F.H.*Rhead, who taught there (as did his first wife, Agnes) and carried out research in local clays. A commercial company, separate from the medical work, was incorporated in 1913, but went into voluntary liquidation two years later. Rhead was succeeded in 1913 by A.L.*Solon, under whose direction the pottery expanded. Much of the work was thrown in clay obtained nearby; larger pieces were press-moulded and some shapes were cast. Decoration was carved or painted (from designs by Solon and external artists) by patients who were trained as far as possible in their brief stays at the sanitorium, and initialled their work if it was of sufficiently high standard. Quality was uneven, though sometimes very high, and the style of the work was similarly varied.
Fred H. Wilde, an experienced potter, was appointed director in 1916 and, like Solon, introduced a number of new glazes. He also developed the production of handmade tiles, many of which were in styles adapted from Spanish examples. The pottery closed in 1918, though the sanitorium was in existence until 1957.

Marks generally comprise a vase or jug under a tree, impressed, incised or painted; others include a row of three jugs; most accompanied by AREQUIPA/CALIFORNIA; initials AP also occur; paper labels were

often used in addition.
Refs: Evans; Jervis; L.& E. Purviance & N.F. Scheider *Roseville Art Pottery In Color* (Wallace-Homestead, Des Moines, Iowa, 1970).

Arita. Japanese ceramic centre: the area surrounding Arita village in Saga prefecture on the island of Kyushu. Production of the first porcelain made in Japan was started in the early 17th century at Arita by the Korean Ri Sanpei after the discovery of a local source of kaolin. Blue and white porcelains exported through the port of Imari in the late 17th and early 18th centuries became very popular in Europe, where they were thought to represent Japanese taste, and were much imitated by European porcelain factories. By the mid 17th century, Sakaida Kakiemon, founder of the line of potters making *Kakiemon ware, had perfected the first Japanese overglaze enamel painting of porcelain in Arita. The *Fukagawa family became established as makers of porcelain in the mid 17th century.
Although some types of the local ware were made specifically for export in European shapes and designs, many lavishly decorated pieces were made for the Japanese market. Eggshell porcelain was made, probably not before the late 18th century, and decorated either in underglaze blue or, starting at a later date, with figures of warriors or courtesans in red, gold and sometimes light blue over the glaze. Wine cups, often sold in sets of three, five or seven, were protected by woven basketwork made in Nagasaki.
The export of three-colour and five-colour classes of enamelled *Imari ware continued until c.1830. Much of the work was carried out in small workshops using local clays, and fired in shared kilns. The potters frequently moved between workshops and usually left their work unmarked. Some painting was carried out by decorators who established themselves in communities known as aka-e mura (red painting village). The district's garden kilns, producing wares for presentation or personal use by feudal lords, included *Mikawachi and *Nabeshima.
In 1870, the ceramist Gottfried Wagner (1831-92) introduced European techniques of industrial production, and a number of Arita kilns started large-scale imitation of traditional wares (Imari, Kakiemon, Nabeshima).
From the 19th century, Arita was an important training ground for potters who took porcelain techniques to other parts of Japan, starting up numerous, often short-lived kilns. In the 1950s, there were some 180 factories employing about 3,500 workers, mainly in industrial production. The main factories now working in the area include *Koran-sha; that of *Imaizumi Imaemon (13th generation); the Fukagawa Porcelain Co., claiming establishment 1689; *Seijisha. Folk wares produced in the district surrounding Arita include the Takeo *Karatsu wares of *Osotoyama, decorated bowls and large storage jars made at Yumino, and the coiled and thrown pots of *Tataro.
Refs: Brinkley; Gorham; Hannover; Jenyns (1965, 1971); Munsterberg; Nakagawa; Sanders.

Arkinstall & Sons. Staffordshire porcelain manufacturers established 1904 by H.T.

*Robinson at the Trent Bridge Pottery, Stoke-on-Trent, for the production of souvenirs and novelties. The firm, using the trade name Arcadian, was among the largest British manufacturers of small commemorative pieces and crested wares over a long period. Many early pieces were copies of earlier shapes by W.H.*Goss or the small souvenir animals and grotesques imported from Germany. These were followed by miniature tanks, weapons, etc., for World War I; black cats, children and humorous items, and later female figures in the 1920s. The firm also made small vases, etc., printed with views and, in the early 1920s, advertised Nursery Rhyme ware. Much of the output was exported. The company merged with *Robinson & Leadbeater before becoming a branch of J.A. Robinson & Sons Ltd c.1912, and was taken over in 1925 by Cauldon Potteries Ltd (*see* Brown-Westhead, Moore & Co.).
Marks incorporate A & S and ARCADIAN or ARCADIAN CHINA until c.1924.
Refs: Andrews; Godden (1964).

Arledge, Caleb and Gus. *See* Donyatt.

Armstrong, Robert William (1824-84). British potter, previously an architect. Armstrong visited Ireland with W.H.*Kerr on a search for porcelain materials and in 1857 conceived the idea of using feldspar found near *Belleek to produce Irish porcelain. In partnership with D.*McBirney, he established the Belleek factory; he became sole proprietor in 1882. Armstrong designed many of the pieces based on marine forms which the firm produced, and devised his pottery's characteristic lustrous glazes, which remained a family secret.
Refs: Blacker (1922a); Collard; letter in *Country Life* (27th March 1958); Jewitt.

Arnhemsche Fayencefabrik, N.V. *See* Vet, Klaas and Jacob.

Arnold or **Lomas,** Gertrude (b 1919). Viennese sculptor and designer. She trained in various branches of modelling and design at the Vienna Kunstgewerbeschule, 1933-38, and worked for *Keramos in Vienna, the *Augarten factory, the firms of F.*Goldscheider, and E.*Schleiss and at Znaim. From 1947 she modelled work for interior decoration (fireplaces, coats of arms and relief panels), specializing in religious subjects.
Ref: Neuwirth (1974a).

Arnoldi, E.& F.C. German porcelain manufacturers producing everyday wares at Elgersburg, Saxe-Coburg, from 1808. The output became restricted to technical porcelain in the 20th century.

Marks include ACEF arranged down a vertical line or incorporate the device illustrated.
Refs: Danckert; Weiss.

Arnoux, Antoine. *See* Fouque-Arnoux.

Joseph-François-Léon Arnoux. Henri II ware in cream-coloured earthenware with painted and inlaid decoration by Arnoux, made by Mintons Ltd, 1859.

Arnoux, Joseph-François-Léon (1816-1902). Ceramic chemist and decorator, born in Toulouse (Haute-Garonne), son of Antoine Arnoux fils (*see* Fouque-Arnoux). Arnoux studied at l'Ecole des Arts et Manufactures in Paris, where he met A.*Brongniart, who made it possible for him to gain technical experience in the Sèvres depot in Paris. He went on to manage the Fouque factory in Valentine (Haute-Garonne). Arnoux worked in England, joining the firm of Minton & Co. (*see* Mintons Ltd) in 1848, initially to reproduce the formula of French hard-paste porcelain, and became art director in 1849. He was regarded as an important contributor to the firm's success in the Great Exhibition (1851). His technical achievements included the development of many Renaissance-inspired wares, including an earthenware body (1850) used for tiles, table and ornamental ware, sculptural pieces, etc., in imitation of early Hispano-Moresque and Italian tin-glazed ware, and, notably, the brightly coloured low-temperature glazes of majolica. Arnoux introduced Henri II ware, and developed agate and marbled wares in designs similar to those of the 18th century. After research into hard-paste porcelain, he made improvements in the bone china paste used at the Minton factory and achieved ground colours equivalent to some used at Sèvres, e.g. *rose Pompadour, bleu du roi*, and turquoise. In the 1870s Arnoux developed the Minton down-draught kiln.

Arnoux's work for Minton came at the start of a trend towards the large-scale employment of French and other European artists in England, which strongly affected the nature of ceramic design. His own decorative work included the painting of an earthenware plaque (1859) in Renaissance style after a design by A.*Stevens, and a signed reproduction of a Chinese vase with crackle glaze, displayed in the International Exhibition, London, 1862. In 1878, he received the Order of Francis Joseph and became Chevalier of the Légion d'Honneur for achievements as a ceramic chemist and documentarist. After his retirement as art director in 1892, Arnoux continued work as consultant to Minton until his death.

Mark (on very rare examples, especially of experimental work) L.A....X.
Refs: see Mintons Ltd.

Arsenal Pottery. American pottery operated in the late 19th century by the Mayer Pottery Manufacturing Co. at Trenton, New Jersey, with Joseph S. Mayer as president. The firm made porcelain and white ware, using enamel or underglaze decoration, and was also noted for the production of majolica. High-quality Toby jugs, in imitation of English originals, were included in the firm's display at the World's Columbian Exposition, Chicago, 1893.
Ref: Barber (1976).

Art China Co. *See* Lessell, John.

Art Deco. A group of styles in European design which reached a peak after the Exposition des Arts Décoratifs et Industriels Modernes in Paris (1925) and remained evident through the 1930s in the output of individual artists and industrial manufacturers. Drawing in part on the functional and more austere elements of Art Nouveau seen in the work of C.F.A.*Voysey and other British and German designers, Art Deco artists were also inspired by oriental designs for the Ballets Russes in Paris (from 1909) and various manifestations of modernism, e.g. classical and functional architecture, and paintings by cubist painters and the Union des Artistes Modernes.

The emphasis in decoration changed from ornament which would accentuate form to surface patterns which would negate it. Broken or interrupted contours were common in design. Primary colours and stark contrasts were used in situations where shaded pastel colours might formerly have been expected. Elements from other cultures, e.g. Egyptian scarabs, palmettes, pyramid shapes (after the opening of Tutankhamen's tomb in the early 1920s), and the stepped forms found in Central American art, bespoke an interest in cultures outside the artists' own. Treatment of these themes was often consciously naive and stylized.

The technical specialities of other countries were studied, e.g. oriental metal and lacquerwork. In the same way that new materials (chrome, nickel, bakelite) were enthusiastically taken up, scientific symbols provided a new vocabulary for decoration: arrows, lightning flashes, slip-stream diagrams, etc. Forms or decoration derived from racing cars, aeroplanes and other machinery represented attempts to create a bold dynamic style reflecting the atmosphere of the time.

Art Deco. La Soie, earthenware figure with crackle glaze and mottled gilt robe. Designed by Marcel Renard and made in Boulogne, probably c.1925. Gilt signature: Marcel Renard. 48.5 cm.

Folk art and simple, traditional, everyday crafts inspired the designers who sought reform and enabled them to create an output that could be mass produced.

Ceramics in the Art Deco idiom figured in the work of individual artists (e.g. E. *Decoeur, E.*Lenoble, J.*Mayodon, A. *Metthey and G.*Serré), producing unique pieces, and industrial manufacturers. Among retailers of decorative items, Atelier Primavera produced inexpensive ceramic pieces designed e.g. by Marcel Renard and C. *Guéden, and articles commissioned from the *Longwy factory. F.*Jourdain designed and sold ceramics at his own shop and Georges Rouard commissioned designs by M.*Goupy from T.*Haviland, also the producer of work by S.*Lalique. J.*Luce designed, produced and sold Art Deco pieces. The Sèvres factory exhibited in Paris (1925) porcelain decorated by R.*Dufy and Suzanne Lalique.

Art Deco design was not restricted to France. Work following similar stylistic principles was produced in Austria, after styles set by J.*Hoffmann, B.*Löffler and M.*Powolny. German ceramics were inspired by Bauhaus design; the producers include M.*Laeuger and *Rosenthal. Other Art Deco ceramics were made by the Royal *Copenhagen and *Bing & Grøndahl factories in Denmark, the *Zsolnay factory in Czechoslovakia, at the *Doccia factory in Italy, and by *Boch Frères in Belgium. In England, the Wedgwood factory produced designs by A.*Powell and D.*Makeig-Jones. Lustre patterns were among the work of S.*Cooper for A.E.*Gray & Co. Ltd. Work by C.*Cliff includes notable examples. Matt-glazed pottery was made by *Carter, Stabler & Adams and at Pilkington's Tile & Pottery Co. The artist Frank Brangwyn designed pottery for *Doulton & Co. Carlton ware was painted with floral designs in gold and bright enamels (*see* Wiltshaw & Robinson). Animal figures in Cubist style were produced to designs by the artist Louis Wain.

Refs: Baschet; Battersby (1969b, 1971); R. Bossaglia *Il 'Deco' Italiano Fisionomica dello Stile 1925* (Milan, 1975); Y. Brunhammer *1925 Exposition internationale des arts décoratifs et industriels modernes 1925, sources et consequences* (Paris, 1976); L. Deshairs *Modern French Decorative Art* (Architectural Press, London, 1926-30); Dowling; Bevis Hillier *The World of Art Deco* (Studio Vista, London, 1971); Kahle; McClinton; Theodore Menton (ed) *The Art Deco Style* (Dover, New York, 1972); Nikolaus Pevsner *Pioneers of Modern Design* (Pelican, London, 1960); K.-J. Sembach *Into the Thirties: Style and Design 1924-34* (Thames & Hudson, London, 1972); G. Veronesi *Stile 1925. Ascesa e caduta delle Arte deco* (Florence, 1966).

Arte della Ceramica, L'. *See* Chini, Galileo, Guido and Chino.

Artèl. Craft workshops established 1908 in Prague on the model of the Wiener Werkstätte for the production of work in leather, metal and other materials, including earthenware. The group's ceramic artists included Vlatislav Hofman (b 1884), who designed vases, either in fluted and ribbed shapes or constructed from interlocking triangles and painted with blocks of colour to accentuate the geometrical forms; Pavel Janák (b 1882), designer of vases and covered pots in fluted shapes, sometimes with stripes or repeating patterns in gold and black or brown on creamy, crackled glaze; Jaroslav Horejc (b 1886), who designed vases, often conical in shape with dark glazes and patches, or occasionally small repeating designs, in gold or white. Janák and Horejc were later to teach at the school of art in Prague. The group built workshops after becoming a limited company in 1919, and continued operation until 1935.

Mark: *Artel*.
Ref: Neuwirth (1974b).

Arthé, Faïencerie d'. French faience workshop established by the mid 18th century at Arthé, near Toucy (Yonne). Production of pottery made in local red clay, partly or wholly glazed in white, was interrupted from 1789 until 1792, when the workshop was reopened by the Tavernier family. André Tavernier, working in 1821, was succeeded soon after that year by Charles Tavernier (d 1844). Antoine Tavernier (b 1792) worked at Auxerre, leaving in 1817 to start work at Arthé three years later. He returned to Auxerre in 1835. The Taverniers used clear colours, including violet, blue, green and yellow, in decoration. Excavations at the site in 1938 revealed clay bodies ranging from red, through brown and grey to a yellowish white.

Marks found on occasional pieces include ANDRE TAVERNIER FABRICANT DE FAIENCE, *A.T.F. de faience, Artai*, each with date, and initials A.T., or L.T. (André Tavernier's daughter, Louise).
Refs: Huillard; Lesur (1971).

Arthur, Charles. *See* Victoria Pottery.

Artigas, Llorens (b 1892). Spanish-born potter. Artigas trained as a painter and ceramist in Barcelona and worked from 1922 in Paris, where he began his collaboration with painters, who included Albert Marquet (1933) and Georges Braque (from 1949). Artigas was particularly concerned with the development of a fine stoneware body and glazes. Working with Raoul Dufy (1922-30, and again 1937-39), he made vases painted with dancers and garlands of flowers or foliage, as well as fountains and indoor gardens. In 1927 Artigas and Dufy began an association with architect Nicolas Marubio, producing decorative pieces on architectural themes, or miniature landscapes containing growing plants. Artigas left Paris for Céret (Pyrénées Orientales) in 1939, returned to Barcelona in 1941 and later established a workshop in nearby Gallifa. He collaborated from the 1940s with the painter Joan Miró who had taught him in Barcelona, and worked with him on the production of sculptures, wall panels, and decorated vases in terracotta, tinglaze, or lead-glazed earthenware. Artigas visited Japan and returned in 1963 to build a new kiln at Gallifa on Japanese models. As well as working with painters, Artigas made stonework vases, etc., in simple shapes with fine glazes and shaded colours. His later work included large sculptural pieces made with Miró for the UNESCO building in Paris (1958), Harvard University (1960), the Guggenheim Museum in New York (1966), Barcelona Airport (1971) and the Paris Cinémathèque (1972).

Refs: Bénézit; Céramique française contemporaine; Faré; L.-P. Fourest 'Miró et Artigas' in *Cahiers de la céramique du verre et des arts du feu* 6 (Spring 1957); J. Pierre & J. Corredor-Matheos *Miró et Artigas: Céramiques* (Paris, 1974); Préaud & Gauthier.

Artistic Ceramics Cooperative. Group of Russian potters working from the 1930s to revive the ceramics of the *Gzhel area; they established a factory in 1934 at Turygino near Rechitsy. Under the chief technician, Zinaida Zhadina (*see* Zhadin family), the group produced household ware and figures, biscuit-fired at about 800°C before decoration by Tatyana Dunashova, or Tatyana Yeremina (whose work included intricate patterns gilded on a blue ground), both employed at the factory from 1935. The pieces, still made, are then glazed and re-fired at about 1300°C. Designers include Anna Fedyashin (*see* Fedyashin, I.), chief painter; some pieces, especially jugs, are made in shapes devised by N.*Bessabarova.
Ref: Ovsyannikov.

artist potters. Individual artists who use ceramics as a medium in which to express their creative aims. These include studio potters, taking full responsiblity for their work from design to completion and producing unique pieces, designers controlling the execution of work by others, and craftsmen engaged on the production of everyday ware in quantity. T.*Deck, regarded as a pioneer, made ornamental ware in Paris from 1856. Other early French artist potters include A.*Delaherche, E.*Chaplet, J.-C.*Cazin—who later worked with R.W. *Martin in England—and J.*Carriès. In England, the work of French potters with high-temperature glazes was echoed in the early 20th century, e.g. by B.*Moore and W.H.*Taylor. Other potters were encouraged by the development of craft teaching in regional colleges of art. D.*Billington studied and later taught at the Royal College of Art in South Kensington, London. R.*Fry, W.S.*Murray, C.*Vyse, and R.*Wells all received their early training at the Camberwell School of Art. B.*Leach established his studio, producing his own work and teaching other potters, e.g. M. *Cardew, K.*Pleydell-Bouverie, and N. *Braden. L.*Rie worked in London from the 1930s, after studying under M.*Powolny in Vienna. Powolny was followed by R. *Obsieger as teacher in the Vienna Kunstgewerbeschule. Hungarian artist potters include I.*Gador, M.*Kovács, and F. *Gorka. In Germany, the Bauhaus pottery encouraged artist potters, e.g. O.*Lindig, T.*Bogler, and M.*Friedlander under the direction of G.*Marcks. The *Rosenthal factory, although an industrial concern, applied the Bauhaus ideals in the use of designs produced by students. The *Arabia factory in Finland employed individual designers, e.g. T.*Muona (a former pupil of A.W.*Finch), A.*Siimes, F.*Kjellberg, B.*Kaipiainen and M.*Schilkin, providing them with facilities to carry out their own work. *Gustavsberg, *Rörstrand, and the Royal *Copenhagen factories followed a policy of encouraging individual potters. The Danish Saxbo pottery produced the combined work of E.*Staehr-Nielson and the founder, N.*Krebs. Dutch pottery was dominated by the work of L.*Nienhuis. Influences in the work of American artist potters include the ideals of the Bauhaus, as expressed in the work of e.g. Marguerite Friedlander and F.*Wildenhain in California, and early trends in France, e.g. in the work of C.*Volkmar. C.F.*Binns, working at Alfred University, New York, is regarded as important in developing the concept of the potter as an individual; his pupils include A.E.*Baggs and the English potter, T.*Haile.

Many artist potters have worked in association with artists in other fields, e.g. P.*Gauguin's use of Chaplet's workshop in making his pottery, work by A.*Metthey in the early 20th century, and the collaboration of L.*Artigas with Dufy, Pierre-Albert Marquet, and later, Joan Miró.

Refs: Beard; T. Birks *The Art of the Modern Potter* (Country Life, London, 1976); M. Casson *Pottery in Britain Today* (Tiranti, London, 1967); Clark & Hughto; Evans; Haslam (1975); Henzke; Hettes & Rada; Kovel & Kovel; E. Lewenstein & E. Cooper *New Ceramics* (Studio Vista, London, 1974); Préaud & Gauthier; Rose; Wingfield Digby.

Art Nouveau. A decorative style of the late 19th and 20th centuries in Europe and North America, at its height at the time of the Exposition Universelle in Paris, 1900, and combining many elements also found in European, Middle Eastern and Oriental

Art Nouveau. Vase designed by Hans Christiansen, maker unknown, c.1900.

Art Nouveau. Vase made in Austria, c.1910. 55 cm high.

decoration. The style is associated with the Galéries de l'Art Nouveau opened by S. *Bing in December 1895, at which he was to show works by artists from France and other countries, including ceramics by A.*Bigot, P.-A.*Dalpayrat, A.-L.*Dammouse, A. *Delaherche, C.*Massier, E.*Müller, etc. Art Nouveau was characterized by the use of coiled or meandering linear ornament (either in abstract arrangements or representing stylized plant forms, flowing hair, cloud formations, moving water, draped fabric, etc.) as well as glistening, iridescent surfaces, often with cloudy, shaded effects, and the prevalence of symbolic motifs (birds, plants, insects, serpents). The style had close affinities with both the Naturalist and Symbolist movements in fine art and literature. In ceramics, the style was widely adopted, and expressed in elongated, sometimes contorted shapes and shimmering or richly coloured glazes, as well as the patterns and motifs typical of Art Nouveau decoration.

F.*Bracquemond, among the forerunners of Art Nouveau, was inspired by Japanese prints from the 1850s. He designed plates for T.*Deck (whose own work was to include red-glazed pieces shown in the Exposition Universelle, 1878), and while in charge of C.*Haviland's workshop in Auteuil produced work that was influenced both by Japanese forms and techniques, and by an

Impressionist view of naturalistic decoration. P.*Gauguin, working in the 1880s, was among early painters and sculptors who turned to the decorative arts. Other designers include H.*van de Velde, L. Guimard and C.*Lévy-Dhurmer, who worked with C.*Massier, 1887-95; the sculptor Auguste Rodin created models for the Sèvres factory and for J.*Carriès, who was himself a sculptor and produced stoneware after 1878.

Art Nouveau porcelain was produced in Scandinavia, e.g. by A.*Krog of the Royal *Copenhagen Porcelain Factory, the *Bing & Grøndahl factory and the individual makers T.*Bindesbøll and A.W.*Finch. In Germany (where the style was developed by a group of contributors to the journal *Jugend*, and became known as Jugendstil, the established designers Peter Behrens, R.*Riemerschmid and H.C.*van de Velde created pieces for production at *Meissen, *Nymphenburg, etc.; M.*Laeuger and *Villeroy & Boch (at Mettlach) also produced Jugendstil wares. Austrian Jugendstil was affected by the functionalist principles of Otto Wagner, and decoration mainly took the form of abstract, linear ornament. J.*Hoffmann and Karl Klaus created ceramic designs, and *Wiener Keramik produced the work of founders M.*Powolny and B.*Löffler. In Hungary, the *Zsolnay factory made wares with iridescent glazes under V.*Wartha. Italian makers of Art Nouveau ware included U.*Cantagalli and the *Ginori family.

In American ceramics, the style is most clearly seen in the work of A.*Van Briggle, L.C.*Tiffany and W.H.*Grueby, but M.L. McLaughlin and other Cincinnati ceramists were strongly influenced by French pottery shown in the Philadelphia Centennial Exhibition, 1876. H.C.*Robertson worked on the development of iridescent, flown, bubbled and, notably, *sang-de-boeuf* glazes, and later T.*Doat taught ceramics at the *University City Pottery, where the work included *flambé* and crystalline glazes on porcelain.

Refs: M. Amaya *Art Nouveau* (Studio Vista London, Dutton New York, 1966); E. Aslin *The Aesthetic Movement: Prelude to Art Nouveau* (Elek, London, 1969); M. Battersby *The World of Art Nouveau,* (Arlington Books, London, 1968); S. Bing *Artistic America, Tiffany Glass, and Art Nouveau* ed. R. Koch (MIT Press, Cambridge, Massachusetts, 1970); Bossaglia; G. Bott *Kunsthandwerk um 1900: Jugendstil, Art Nouveau, Modern Style, Nieuwe Kunst* (Hessisches Landesmuseum, Darmstadt, 1973); *British Sources of Art Nouveau* (Whitworth Art Gallery, Manchester, n.d.); Brunhammer *et al* (1976); Camart *et al*; J. Cassou *et al Les Sources du XXe Siècle* (Musée Nationale d'Art Moderne, Paris, 1960-61); I. Cremona *Il Tempo dell'Art Nouveau* (Florence, 1964); D. Culot *Pionniers du XXe Siècle: Guimard, Horta, Van de Velde* (Musée des Arts Décoratifs, Paris, 1971); A., D. and G. Drexler *Introduction to Twentieth Century Design from the Collection of The Museum of Modern Art* (The Museum of Modern Art, New York, 1959); R.H. Guerrand *Art Nouveau in Europe,* (Plon, Paris, 1965); R. Koch 'Art Nouveau Bing' in *Gazette des Beaux-Arts* (March 1959); F.-C. Legrand *Symbolism in Belgium,* (Laconti, Brussels, 1972); H.F. Lenning *The Art Nouveau* (The

Hague, 1951); Madsen (1956, 1967); A. Michel *Histoire Générale de l'Art* (Librairie Armand Colin, Paris, 1929); N. Pevsner *Pioneers of the Modern Movement from William Morris to Walter Gropius* (Faber & Faber, London, 1936), *Pioneers of Modern Design* (Penguin, London, 1960), *Sources of Modern Architecture and Design* (Thames & Hudson, London, 1968); P. Portoghesi 'Art Nouveau in Italy' in *Italy the New Domestic Landscape* ed. E. Ambasz (The Museum of Modern Art, in collaboration with Centro Di, Florence, 1972); R. Puaux 'L'Art Nouveau Bing' in *Oeuvres de Georges de Feure* (L'Art Nouveau, Paris, 1903); M. Rheims *L'Objet 1900* (Arts et Métiers Graphiques, Paris, 1964), *The Age of Art Nouveau* (Thames & Hudson, London, 1966); P. Weisberg, a series of articles in *The Connoisseur* (October, December 1969, January 1971, March, April, May, June, November 1971); G.P. Woeckel *Jugendstilsammlung* (Staatliche Kunstsammlungen, Kassel, 1968).

Art Nouveau, L'. *See* Weller, Samuel A.

Artoisenet family. Faience manufacturers working in Brussels in the 18th and early 19th centuries. In 1765, Joseph-Philippe Artoisenet (d 1783) took over a faience factory established 1705 on rue de Laeken; he was succeeded by his widow until 1811 and subsequently by Jean-Baptiste-Morren Artoisenet until 1839. The factory had been noted for a copper green used in decoration, either for the painting of patterns or as a ground colour.

The rival De Moriaen factory, established by Jacques Artoisenet on rue de la Montagne, Brussels, in 1751, produced figures of animals, cupids, religious subjects, and groups of children, as well as wares with painted decoration adapted from Japanese porcelain, the work of the Sinceny factory, and faience from Rouen and Moustiers. The output also included stoves. After changes in ownership, the pottery closed in 1824.

Jean-Baptiste Artoisenet established a factory which operated near La Porte de Laeken, 1791-1866.
Refs: Hannover; J. Helbig *La Céramique Bruxelloise de bon vieux temps* (Brussels, 1946); A. Wauters 'Faïences et porcelaines de Bruxelles' in *L'Art ancien à l'Exposition Nationale Belge* (Brussels, 1882).

art pottery. In Britain, ceramics produced in response to changes in artistic standards that had taken place by the 1870s. By the mid 1850s much of Britain's ceramic output was industrially produced, but over the preceding 20 years principles of design had been evolving which depended mainly on the relationship of form to function, the choice of decoration to emphasize rather than obscure form, and an awareness of the characteristic properties of materials. In the 1850s, this tendency was reinforced by concern over the design of industrial wares, as seen, for example, in the Great Exhibition in London, 1851. John Ruskin rejected the aesthetic standards of factory-made goods and urged a return to those achieved only by individual craft workers who were able to express their creative aims freely, and both the *Arts & Crafts and *Aesthetic movements sought in their ways to improve standards of design. The demand for art pottery arose from attempts at artistic creation made by established manufacturers, in addition to their commercial output, or by new potteries established for the purpose. In the 1860s, a collaboration with the firm of *Doulton & Co. had enabled students of the Lambeth School of Art to decorate salt-glazed stoneware made at Doulton's Lambeth workshop in London, producing individual, signed pieces of work. Also making ornamental stoneware, the *Martin brothers worked from the early 1870s at Fulham and then Southall, sharing the tasks involved in production and retail. W.*De Morgan, friend of William Morris and closely associated with the Arts & Crafts Movement, carried out underglaze painting inspired by Near-Eastern pottery and revived lustre painting. Painted decoration, fashionable in France, developed in England with the employment of French artists, e.g. E.*Lessore and E.*Rischgitz, at the Minton factory in Stoke-on-Trent. *Minton's Art Pottery Studio opened (1871) in London for amateur and professional painters under the direction of W.S.*Coleman. Doulton introduced painted wares in 1873, followed by the art potteries in the late 1870s and 1880s. The *Watcombe Pottery (established 1869) used local clay decorated with enamel or turquoise glaze and often intricately modelled. C.H.*Brannam, working in Barnstaple, North Devon, combined elements of fashionable design with characteristics of traditional Devonshire slipware. The effects of glaze and colour were stressed in pottery made from 1880 at Linthorpe, Yorkshire, by H.*Tooth and designed by C.*Dresser. The partnership of Tooth and W.*Ault (1883-86), in the *Bretby Art Pottery produced ornamental ware with coloured glazes and applied decoration; later work was sometimes made in imitation of metal, bamboo, etc. Ault continued experiments with glazes at his own pottery at Swadlincote and, in the 1890s, used designs by Dresser. In the work of E.*Elton, raised floral motifs in coloured slip were used with streaked grounds predominantly in blue; he developed metallic, crackled glaze effects in the early 20th century. The *Della Robbia Pottery, established in the 1890s, produced work signed by individual artists.

By c.1900, the market was sufficiently well established to attract many commercial firms into the production of art pottery. W.*Moorcroft, responsible from 1898 for an art pottery department started by J.*Macintyre & Co., later established his own company. *Pilkington's Tile & Pottery Co., founded in the mid 1890s, was noted for lustre decoration (from 1903). Much work was carried out by independent designers, e.g. L.F.*Day, C.F.A.*Voysey, and W.*Crane. Pottery made from 1898 by W.H.*Taylor often relied for effect on high-temperature glazes.

In the early 20th century, art pottery gradually became eclipsed by the work of artist potters produced in studio conditions. Moorcroft, among the few who continued the manufacture of art pottery, was forced to introduce a variety of experimental lines. In America, the *Chelsea Keramic Art Works (established 1866) alone produced art pottery before 1879, making earthenware with barbotine decoration from 1876.

Work shown in the Philadelphia Centennial Exhibition (1876) inspired H.C.*Robertson to attempt the reproduction of oriental glazes. Several potteries established in the period 1879-89, centred on the area of Cincinnati, Ohio, but *Rookwood Pottery was notable in surviving after 1890. The pottery of W.A.*Long, founded at Steubenville, Ohio, in 1892, produced pottery resembling Rookwood's Standard Ware and eventually passed to S.A.*Weller. Long himself moved to Zanesville and, briefly at the J.B.*Owens Pottery Co., continued his use of underglaze decoration. Later, in Colorado, Long produced matt-glazed pottery decorated in Art Nouveau style. Rozane art ware was made at *Roseville Pottery Co. (established in 1892) and, by 1900, in Zanesville. The *Newcomb College Pottery, organized in 1897 to provide practical training in ceramics, also produced pottery inspired by Rookwood wares. W.H.*Grueby made pottery covered with matt enamel after seeing A.*Delaherche's dull-finish glaze at the World's Columbian Exposition in Chicago, and was imitated by other potters. A.*Van Briggle introduced matt glazes at Rookwood (1896) and later made art pottery in Colorado Springs.

In more general terms, art pottery refers to the work of *artist potters as opposed to industrial wares.

Arts & Crafts Movement. Artistic and social movement operating in Britain in the late 19th century, associated with the work and theories of William Morris, who urged a return to medieval standards of craft and design in a reaction to industrialization. Earlier influences had developed in the work of H.*Cole, A.W.N.*Pugin and the architect G.E. Street. John Ruskin decried mechanization and the division of labour, which separated designer and maker from their final output, and Morris developed and put into practice the ideals of good design and craftsmanship and fitness of purpose with his establishment of craft workshops and the revival of many traditional crafts. His firms, Morris, Marshall, Faulkner & Co. (1861) and the subsequent Morris & Co. designed and made decorative items and materials. The movement's ideals were embodied in the Art Workers' Guild formed in 1884 and the Arts & Crafts Exhibition Society (1886), of which designers such as L.F.*Day and W.*Crane were members.

In ceramics, the movement's ideals were expressed in the work of *artist potters in studio conditions, and such workshops as the *Aller Vale Pottery, *Bretby Art Pottery, *Burmantofts, the *Della Robbia Pottery, *Pilkington's Tile & Pottery Co. and W.H.*Taylor's Ruskin Pottery.

The American Art Workers' Guild was established c.1885 in Providence, Rhode Island, and the movement influenced work in America until c.1915, initially through Arts & Crafts exhibition societies, which started in Chicago and Boston, and a number of design periodicals which began publication in the 1890s (e.g. *The House Beautiful, International Studio, Brush and Pencil,* and *Keramic Studio*). Factories which answered the new demand for ceramics that in some measure maintained these standards of design included *Rookwood Pottery Co. and its later rivals opened by W.A.*Long,

Art Unions. Stoneware vase modelled by M.V.*Marshall for *Doulton & Co. with dark blue and green glazes, and detail in white slip, c.1905. Marked with the artist's initials, incised, Doulton's mark of a crown, lion and circle, impressed, and Art Union of London. 40.6 cm.

J.B.*Owens and S.A.*Weller, all producing slip-painted wares. The *Newcomb College Pottery was also known for painted decoration, and opened in 1895, the year in which S.G.*Frackelton's book on china-painting, *Tried by Fire*, went into a third edition.

In response to the taste for more simple design promoted by American followers of the Arts & Crafts movement (e.g. Gustav Stickley, Elbert Hubbard and Frank Lloyd Wright) artists such as H.C.*Robertson and C.*Volkmar turned to oriental ceramics for inspiration. A.*Grueby worked with matt glazes after seeing the work of A.*Delaherche in the World's Columbian Exposition in Chicago (1893).

L.C.*Tiffany's company, Associated Artists, had been established in 1879 after the model of Morris & Co., and he continued to follow Morris's principles, first exhibiting ceramics in St Louis (1904). H.C. *Mercer, a prizewinner in the St Louis exhibition, began his Moravian Pottery for the production of hand-made tiles to his own designs.
Refs: Anscombe & Gere; R. Banham *Theory and Design in the First Machine Age* (London, 1960); G. Bell *The Schools of Design* (Routledge & Kegan Paul, London, 1963); A. Briggs (ed) *William Morris, Selected Writings and Designs* (Penguin Books, Harmondsworth, 1968); Callen; Clark & Hughto; Eidelberg; Evans; M. Morris (ed) *Collected Works of William Morris* (Longman, London, 1910-15); M.

Morris *William Morris: artist, writer, socialist* (Basil Blackwell, Oxford, 1936); Naylor.

Art Tile Works. *See* Low, John Gardner.

Art Unions. Societies formed in England with encouragement from Albert, Prince Consort, to promote the sale of works of art. The Art Union of London, established in 1836, organized yearly lotteries of works of art among subscribers, who paid an annual subscription. After the legalization of draws (1846), the Art Unions commissioned limited editions of parian figures, e.g. from the Minton and Copeland factories, as prizes. Later Unions included the Crystal Palace Art Union (1865), the Royal Irish Art Union and the Art Union of Glasgow. Work was commissioned in many fields as well as porcelain, marked with the initials of the Unions or the Union's name, date and prize.

Art Vellum. *See* Brush-McCoy Pottery; Owens, John B.

Arzberg. A German centre of industrial porcelain manufacture. A works established by the firm of Acker in the 1830s was taken over by Carl Magnus Hutschenreuther (*see* Hutschenreuther family) in 1918. Other factories included those of Strebel, working in 1867; Carl Schumann, established 1881 for the production of decorated tableware (some with openwork) and novelty items; Theodor Lehmann, founded in 1886 for the manufacture of tea and coffee sets, vases, etc., under the control of *Kahla from 1927, and working as the Arzberg Porcelain Factory S.A. from the following year; Carl Auvera, who was making heads for tobacco pipes in the 1880s.

The Schumann factory was the first Bavarian works to adopt streamlined modern shapes for tableware, e.g. the services Arzberg 1382, designed by Hermann Gretsch (d 1950) and Arzberg 2000, designed by Heinrich Löffelhardt in 1954. Löffelhardt was to design another service, Arzberg 2075, with fluted cylindrical cups, teapot and other hollow ware in 1963.

The local factories have mainly been absorbed into the Hutschenreuther group

Arzberg. Coffee pot from the service Arzberg 1382 by Hermann Gretsch. Made at the Schumann factory, 1931.

and produce hotel ware, everyday porcelain and some original designs.

Hutschenreuther marks usually incorporate *Arzberg*. Schumann marks mainly include a shield and *Arzberg* or an arrangement of the letters CSA.
Refs: Danckert; Préaud & Gauthier; Weiss.

Asahi ware or **Yamashiro ware.** Japanese ware made from the 17th century at the Asahi kilns (one of the sources selected by the teamaster Kobori Enshu for tea-ceremony ware), near Uji, to the south of Kyoto in the former Yamashiro province. The kilns' main product consisted of teabowls of graceful shape in a soft, coarse, brown body, streaked with white slip which shows through translucent blue or green glazes; in some cases, a greenish glaze is spotted with brown. A white, feldspathic glaze occurs on pieces resembling *Karatsu and *Hagi wares in style and technique. Cups and other small pieces were also intended for tea-ceremony use. Production, after dying out c.1730, was revived in the 19th century by the potter Matsubayashi Chobei, who worked between 1830 and 1873, and provided inspiration for *Ito Tozan.
Refs: Brinkley; Gorham; Jenyns (1971); Mitsuoka; Morse; Munsterberg.

Asbury, Edward. Staffordshire potter. In 1866 Asbury joined the firm of Hammersley, Freeman & Co., producers of earthenware and porcelain at the Prince of Wales Pottery, Longton. He became a partner in 1870 on the retirement of Freeman, and proprietor in 1875 on the death of Hammersley, trading as Edward Asbury & Co. until 1925. His firm produced tea, coffee, dessert and toilet sets in porcelain, also making a speciality of pieces transfer-printed with views of spas and resorts for sale as souvenirs. The firm also produced a line of Charles Dickens ware—beakers, mugs, jugs and plates printed with drawings by the artist Hablot Knight Browne ('Phiz') and a small range of model animals, tanks, shoes, cartoon characters, etc. at the time of World War I.

Marks include Prince of Wales feathers, printed, and H & A, A & CO or ASBURY LONGTON.
Refs: Andrews; Godden (1964); Jewitt.

Aschach. German factory established in 1829 for the production of earthenware. The output included creamware with transfer printing in a style influenced by contemporary English ware. The factory continued under the founders, William Sattler and his son, until 1860.

Marks: WS & S ASCHACH, impressed.
Refs: Haggar (1960); Honey (1952).

Ashby Potters' Guild. English pottery established in 1909 at Woodville, Derbyshire, by the ceramic chemist, Pascoe Tunnicliffe, for the production of decorative and utilitarian earthenware, all thrown, with all pieces carried out from their own designs by individual makers. The pottery's leadless glazes, which included blue, moss green and flame red, were often used in combinations of two or more colours.

The firm was absorbed by W. Ault's pottery, which traded as Ault & Tunnicliffe from the following year.

Marks: ASHBY/GUILD within oval line,

impressed; artists' initials sometimes appear.
Refs: Coysh (1976); Godden (1964).

Ashtead Potters Ltd. English pottery established at Ashtead, Surrey, after World War I, to provide employment for disabled ex-servicemen, with assistance from established potters. The number engaged in production, initially 14, increased to 30 by the mid 1920s. The firm's output of tableware and small articles in earthenware, such as inkwells, was originally white-glazed; later, painted linear designs and landscapes were introduced. A range of nursery ware was decorated with E.H. Shepard's illustrations of Winnie the Pooh in the 1920s. In the 1930s the firm produced simply modelled figures with white glaze enlivened by touches of enamel colour (e.g. painted hair and headband) and garlands of flowers brightly enamelled in yellow, green, blue, maroon. Among designers of the figures were P. *Stabler.

Mark: printed tree and *Ashtead Potters* used 1926-36.
Refs: Godden (1964); Haslam (1977).

Ashworth, George Leach, Taylor and James. Staffordshire potters. Taylor Ashworth (b c.1839) worked for F.*Morley at the Broad Street works, Hanley, from 1857, becoming his partner in the following year, when the firm traded as Morley & Ashworth. Succeeding Morley on his retirement by 1862, Taylor Ashworth traded with his brothers as George L. Ashworth & Bros Ltd, and continued the production of ironstone china using the Mason patterns and models which Morley had acquired after C.J.*Mason's bankruptcy in 1848. The firm used a fine, white body, marketed as 'opaque porcelain', in the production of dessert services printed in colour (c.1870) with Return of the Gleaners and other farming scenes. Under the direction of Taylor Ashworth until its sale in 1883 (when his brothers suffered financial losses in the collapse of the Lancashire wool trade), the firm expanded to produce table, toilet and dessert sets, kitchen ware and decorative pieces in a number of earthenware bodies. Vases were lavishly gilded. The handles of jugs were often in the form of dragons or other creatures. The firm also manufactured stoneware from the moulds of the Meigh firm to which Morley had been successor. Other products included chemical, sanitary and electrical wares. In 1884, Taylor Ashworth took up a share in the management of the Old Hall Earthenware Co., previously owned by his father-in-law C. *Meigh. G.L. Ashworth & Bros continued to sell wares of the type made by Masons, mainly tableware, jugs and vases, with the traditional patterns, trading from 1968 as Mason's Ironstone China Ltd.
Refs: Bunt; Godden (1963); Haggar (1952); Rhead.

Asshoff, Bruno (b 1914) and Ingeborg (b 1919). German potters. After eleven years' military service, Bruno Asshoff began an apprenticeship in 1945 at a workshop producing lead-glazed earthenware at Fredelsloh, with his wife, who had studied sculpture in Düsseldorf. In 1947 they opened a workshop in Ingeborg Asshoff's home town, Bochum-Querenburg (in the Ruhr district),

Bruno and Ingeborg Asshoff. Vase with red stripes painted on tin glaze, made in earthenware fired at 1060-1100°C, c.1955. 27 cm high.

producing a variety of unique hand-built pieces which ranged from the solid and robust to the delicate and elegant. Initially producing earthenware, sometimes salt glazed, they soon started to make stoneware, fired at 1200°C, using a slip glaze containg ash. In the 1950s, the workshop produced thrown pieces, at first without decoration but from c.1955 with linear patterns in coloured glazes, and hollow ware which also features coloured or textured glazes. They became known for pieces of

large size. In the 1960s, the couple made figures and groups composed of cones of clay with limbs and other modelled details applied.

Marks: vase containing monogram of TA (Töpferei Asshoff) impressed (1948-c.1955); no mark 1956-66; *a* impressed from 1967.
Refs: Bock; Klein; Klinge.

Astbury & Maddock. *See* Maddock, Thomas, & Sons.

Astles, Samuel. English porcelain painter specializing in groups of flowers. Astles was a pupil of T.*Baxter and worked at the *Worcester porcelain factory of Flight, Barr & Barr c.1812-40. His painting was primarily on vases. He exhibited work at the Royal Academy in 1827.
Refs: Chaffers; Sandon (1978b).

Astley, Joseph. *See* Goss, William Henry.

Aston, Jabez (b c.1799). English porcelain maker, born at Ironbridge, Shropshire. Aston worked at the *Coalport factory as a painter of flowers and fruit in a delicate, naturalistic style, c.1820-75. Several plaques were signed and dated.
Refs: Godden (1970); Jewitt.

Athenian. *See* Beardmore, Frank, & Co.

Athens Pottery. *See* Clark, Nathan.

Atlas China Co. *See* Cambridge Art Pottery.

Atwood, Eugene R. *See* Grueby, William H.

Aubé, Jean-Paul (1837-1916 or 1920). French sculptor and ceramic modeller, born in Longwy (Meurthe-et-Moselle). After studying sculpture in Italy, Aubé first exhibited in the Salon of 1861; he later worked

Jean-Paul Aubé. Glazed earthenware jardinière, c.1878.

under F.*Bracquemond at C.*Haviland's studios in Auteuil, where he was employed with his son in 1882, and then at the rue Blomet studio. His work included vases with figures (1874).
Refs: Bénézit; Brunhammer *et al* (1976); d'Albis *et al*; Heuser & Heuser; Thieme & Becker.

Auckland, William. American potter. Auckland worked as a thrower for F.*Dallas before joining the Rookwood Pottery in 1881, and created the majority of early Rookwood shapes. His daughter, Fannie, then 12 years old, joined the pottery as a decorator in 1881. Her work, until she left Rookwood (by 1885), included incised ornament, and patterns of stamped motifs.
Refs: Evans; Kovel & Kovel; Peck.

Audley, Robert. *See* New Hall.

Auer, Anton (1778-1814). German porcelain painter working at Nymphenburg from 1795 and eventually becoming chief painter in 1809. His son, Max-Joseph Auer, also worked at Nymphenburg from 1823.
Ref: Danckert.

Auerbach factory. Russian earthenware factory established 1809 at the village of Domkino in Tver province by Friedrich Brinner with the help of two employees of the *Gardner factory. After it was acquired by Andrei Auerbach in 1810, the business quickly achieved a reputation for the high quality of its output of tableware, becoming one of Russia's largest ceramics factories, and receiving a state subsidy in 1819.

The work was simple in form with fresh, restrained decoration, usually garlands of flowers, or delicate, tendrilled plants freely

*William Auckland. Covered jar designed and thrown by Auckland with decoration attributed to A.R.*Valentien, made at the *Rookwood Pottery, 1883. 25.4 cm high with cover.*

painted in green and brown or black and blue over the glaze. Until the introduction of printed decoration between 1818 and 1820, landscape designs were painted at the centre of plates with floral ornament on the rim. After perfecting clear, detailed printing techniques, the factory mass produced tableware with monochrome printed patterns at the centre of plates, etc., framed with painted flowers at the rim.

By c.1820, the range of products included dishes, mugs, dinner and tea services, and individual items of tableware, painted or printed over a white glaze. After the transfer of the factory to the banks of the river Dankhovka at Kuznetsovo, still in the Korchovo district of Tver province, in 1829, the factory won a silver medal for tableware in the first exhibition of Russian manufacturers in 1829 and a gold medal in the second exhibition two years later. Two types of ware evolved at this time: printed wares with bold designs, and hand-painted ware in traditional Russian styles with free, delicate brushwork in a limited range of colours. Garlands painted in blue resemble the decoration of contemporary earthenware made in the *Gzhel area, and other painted designs include plants with many delicate tendrils, an all-over pattern of flowers, landscapes, and copies of popular prints. A service in elegant Empire-style forms, and painted in the factory's characteristic manner with garlands of foliage and flowers, in underglaze blue highlighted with a lighter shade of blue, was made in the 1820s for the Tsar's palace at Tver.

Printed designs include a caricature of Napoleon as a baby held by the devil (derived from a German cartoon of 1814) as well as landscapes, genre scenes, animals and, notably, military events, which were illustrated in large numbers from the 1840s. Printed decoration was sometimes accompanied by gilded designs.

The factory produced a small quantity of figures, e.g. paperweights in the form of lions, beer mugs in the form of German townsfolk wearing tricorne hats, and inkwells in the form of Napoleon's tomb, but these remained very much a sideline.

After financial difficulties in the 1850s, the factory's workforce was cut to 86 as a result of the liberation of the serfs, and the output was subsequently restricted mainly to cheap tableware decorated only with lines, and wavy-rimmed plates with leaves in relief. The factory won a prize at the All-Russia Industrial Exhibition (1870) for the quality and strength of its white earthenware for domestic use, and was sold the same year to the Kuznetsov combine (*see* Kuznetsov family).

Under the Kuznetsovs, the factory was reorganized with new buildings and equipment by the late 1870s. Kuznetsov introduced porcelain production c.1885 and added figures to the output; architectural and refractory wares were also made. *Trompe l'oeil* butter dishes, jugs, caviare dishes, tobacco pots, ashtrays, etc., became a speciality, realistically modelled and coloured in the form of fruit, vegetables, fish, birds, other animals, or such articles as a cap, a pile of pancakes, mushrooms, gnarled logs, etc. A popular revival of Russian art in the 1880s resulted in the production of large numbers of water cups closely imitating painted wood, and plates illustrating scenes

from Russian legends in the manner of early enamel ware. Relief decoration, generally accompanied by lavish painting and gilding, occurs on table services as finials in the form of ribbon bows; a 'faceted' service has a raised pattern of ovals covering the surface of large or small pieces. Figures and groups often served also as pencil holders, flower vases, etc., and their themes included genre subjects, the representation of paintings by Perov, Ghe, etc., costume studies, humorous treatment of children at play, drunken peasants and workers.

Marks: AUERBACH (1817) or AK (1817-33); *Auerbach* and arms of the State from 1833; Kuznetsov mark from 1872.
Refs: Bubnova; Ivanova; Ross.

Augarten, Wiener Porzellanmanufaktur. Viennese porcelain factory established at the Schloss Augarten in 1922 as a continuation of the Vienna State factory. The firm produced decorative wares which included a wide variety of figures—costume studios, portrait busts and humorous animals, as well as horses from the Lippizaner stud and

Augarten. Coffee pot in enamel-painted porcelain, made 1928. 21 cm high.

other animal models. Tableware included a service designed by J.*Hoffmann in 1928. The firm produced designs by artists including F.*Barwig, W.*Bosse, H.*Bucher, M.*Jacksch, B.*Kuhn, M.*Powolny, O.*Prutscher, K. and I.*Schwetz-Lehmann, and V.*Wieselthier.

Marks: *Augarten Austria* on a label shape; a shield with two horizontal lines, sometimes with a crown and/or *Augarten Wien*.
Refs: Danckert; Neuwirth (1974a); Weiss.

Auld Heather Ware. *See* Links Pottery.

Ault, William (b 1841). English potter, born in Burslem and trained in Staffordshire. He worked at a pottery in Church Gresley near Woodville, Derbyshire, from 1863, leaving in 1867 to study business and accountancy, before returning to work as pottery manager in the new earthenware works built by T.G. Green adjoining Church Gresley Pottery.

William Ault. Jardinière *with swirling relief pattern under raspberry-coloured glaze shading to lime green, c.1895. Moulded vase mark.*

He established the *Bretby Art Pottery in partnership with H.*Tooth before building his own pottery at Swadlincote, also near Woodville, in 1887 for the production of Ault Faience. (The title, which was applied to all the firm's output of lead-glazed earthenware was changed to Ault's English Art Pottery c.1910.) One of the pottery's specialities was ornately moulded *jardinières* and pedestals with flown or shaded glazes (some blending from one colour at the rim to another at the base); in some cases, relief decoration is highlighted with an additional colour. Ault's own research achieved a variety of glazes with splashed and broken effects. He also produced earthenware for domestic use, and a small number of hand-painted ornamental pieces.

A series of pieces designed by C.*Dresser c.1892-c.1896 included a vase with globular body, long cylindrical neck and small, right-angled handles, and a gourd-shaped vase with goat's head handles. Production of Dresser's designs continued after his death in 1904, and the pieces were sold with a range of glaze effects.

By the end of the 19th century, the pottery produced a wide variety of decorative ware, including plaques, busts, figures, models of animals, and vases with light-coloured figures in low relief against darker grounds. Many of the pieces were moulded or slip cast, although some were thrown or jolleyed. Large pieces included pedestals

and *jardinières*. The display in the World's Columbian Exposition in Chicago (1893) won the Higher Award for pottery.

The introduction of new decorative techniques continued in the early 20th century, often using shapes that were already in production. The lines included *sgraffito* vases with scrolled and floral designs incised under one of a range of glazes; vases and toilet sets with a single scrolled design (Creke pattern) on a red ground; named patterns of a single plant head, e.g. iris, honesty, anemone, bulrush, painted over a printed outline; Mauresque Ware vases and bottles with splashed and streaked glaze effects; and a series with pierrot figures in red, white and grey on a black, semi-matt glaze. Ault was assisted by two daughters, Gertrude and Clarissa (the painter of vases with designs of butterflies and flowers, which she initialled C.J.A.). The company amalgamated with the *Ashby Potters' Guild in 1922, trading as Ault & Tunnicliffe from the following year until 1937, when it became Ault Potteries Ltd. The firm has since specialized in decorated table and kitchen ware.

Marks: fluted vase (the first piece of Ault faience), moulded, 1887-1923; versions of monogram APL, printed or impressed, used from 1887 and by Ault Potteries Ltd. Ault & Tunnicliffe: printed or impressed in circular mark containing *ARLtd*; *Aultcliff* printed or impressed, 1923-27.
Refs: Blacker (1922a); Coysh (1976); Godden (1964); Lloyd Thomas (1974).

Aurelian ware. *See* Moorcroft, William; Weller, Samuel A.

Auroro. *See* Weller, Samuel A.

Austin, Jesse (1806-79). English pottery decorator, born in Longton, Staffordshire. Austin studied drawing at night school and became an apprentice at *Davenport's, where he learned copper plate engraving. Some multi-coloured prints produced by Davenport's, 1834-36, are thought to be his work. He worked independently as a designer and engraver of copper plates for printing on ceramics in Burslem, Staffordshire, 1826-40. Entering the firm of F.& R. Pratt & Co. in 1846 or early 1847, he made engravings of portraits, views, genre subjects, etc., from his own watercolours or from designs by other artists, for use on tableware, toilet sets and vases as well as pot lids. His engravings were at first printed in two colours for additional painting by hand, but Austin, who became noted for his skill as a colour analyst, later produced the full range of colour from a three-colour plate used with a key plate, which was often printed in brown. In 1859, Austin briefly joined the firm of *Brown-Westhead, Moore & Co.

returning to Pratt's within a year. His designs included boating scenes, bear pictures, portraits of the Royal Family and contemporary celebrities (1852-59), views of London (mainly 1864-73), his own watercolours and miniature copies of famous paintings. All Pratt's pot lids up to 1875 were apparently painted and engraved by Austin or under his supervision, and the firm's style changed after his death. Austin signed or initialled the plates from 43 designs, of which 36 were for pot lids. His last signed pattern was issued in 1873, and his marks were removed from the engraving of pictures issued by Pratt's after his death.

Marks: signature or initials.
Refs: H.G. Clarke *Underglaze Colour Picture Prints on Staffordshire Pottery* (Courier Press, London, 1970); Godden (1966); G. Godden in *Collector's Guide* (November 1971); Wakefield; Williams-Wood.

Austin, Peter. *See* Wear Pottery.

Austin, Reginald Harry (1890-1955). Porcelain painter working at the *Worcester Royal Porcelain factory from the early 20th century until the 1930s. Austin specialized in paintings of flowers and birds (sometimes on reproductions of earlier pieces with blue-scale ground) as well as fruit and more general subjects. He worked as a freelance designer with his brother W.H.*Austin and joined *Paragon China Ltd as a designer. His work there included patterns of marguerites, roses and lovebirds on ware commissioned to commemorate the birth of Princess Margaret. He returned to work independently in Worcester.
Ref: Sandon (1978a).

Austin, Walter Harold (1891-1971). English porcelain painter working at the *Worcester Royal Porcelain factory, with his brother, R.H.*Austin, from the early 20th century until the 1930s. He specialized in paintings of fish, flowers and fruit; some of his work was carried out on the firm's Sabrina ware. He worked with his brother as a freelance after leaving the factory, also carrying out many watercolour paintings, and worked part-time for a Worcester manufacturer, painting furniture, until c.1948.
Ref: Sandon (1978a).

Austin, William. *See* Dixon, Austin & Co.

Australian ceramics. Little early work by Australian potters survives that can be definitely attributed to the maker. The pots were for domestic use and not highly valued by the users. Samuel Skinner (d 1807), who emigrated to Sydney with his convict wife in 1801, is regarded as the first free potter to make a living by selling his work, of which little is known. Other early potters working in New South Wales include J. and A. *Moreton, J.*King and R. Turton, later employed by J.*Silcock. The *Lithgow Pottery started production of household wares in the early 1880, *Bakewell Bros in the 1890s, and the *Mashman Brothers added decorative wares to their output in the 1890s.

The first reference to Tasmanian pottery is in 1816, but the earliest known pieces were made by J.*Sherwin from c.1831. J.*McHugh established a pottery at Launceston c.1873. In 1876 A.*Cornwell opened a Tasmanian branch of his manufacture (which had started at Brunswick, Melbourne in 1861). In the Hobart area, A.*Worbey was working by 1882.

Victoria had a brickmaking industry by the mid 19th century at South Yarra. The Melbourne area developed as a centre of pottery making. Early potters included A. *Fritsch, H.*Emery, the *Chesterfield Pottery Co. The main potteries at Brunswick, a Melbourne suburb, were opened by Cornwell and L.*Nolan (also a director of the *Hoffman Brick Co.). The *Bendigo pottery was established in 1857.

In South Australia, the pottery industry established by the mid 19th century around Adelaide produced little household ware. Terracotta was made in the 1880s. The *Magill Pottery opened in 1868, W.*Holford was working in Adelaide in the 1880s, pottery was made at Longwood in the early 20th century and *Koster's Premier Pottery (Adelaide) remains active to the present day. G.*Reynell made ware with incised decoration in the 1920s.

In Queensland, D.*Fensom and G. *Fischer (succeeded by James Campbell) were among early potters. The industry developed to the south of Brisbane in the late 1880s and early 1890s at potteries that included C.A.*Stone's Bristol Pottery (c.1894) and in Ipswich at the *Dinmore Pottery and the *Reliance Pottery.

Styles were influenced by 19th-century English wares until World War I. Improvements were then made in techniques and marketing. Many potteries, however, maintained financial stability through the production of chemical and drainage ware, bricks, etc. The *Fowler family concentrated on these wares until the early 20th century. Rockingham-glazed and white earthenware had been made in Victoria from the 1870s. The only serious attempt to manufacture porcelain was at *Yarraville after 1880.

Later earthenware potteries, making colour-glazed figures, vases, etc., as well as domestic ware, included the *Premier Pottery (Melbourne), the *Disabled Soldiers' Pottery and the makers of *Bosley ware and *Rose Noble. The firm of *Wunderlich Ltd was involved in the production of wartime tableware at works formerly occupied by the *Calyx Porcelain and Paint Co. Ltd.

Studio potters include L.*Blakeborough, M.*Boyd, F.E.*Cox, M.*Douglas, I. *Englund, L.J.*Harvey, H.R.*Hughan, F. Ladells, N.*McCredie, M.*Poynter, G. *Reynell, W.*Ricketts, P. Rushforth, G. Deccombe. The influence of B.*Leach and M.*Cardew has been important in studio pottery through the work and teaching of I. *McMeekin.

Refs: Cooper; Graham; J.& T. Hooper *A Guide to Collecting Australiana* (Macmillan, 1978); C. Simpson *et al Australian Antiques First Fleet to Federation* (Golden Press/National Trust of Australia Women's Committee, New South Wales, 1977).

Australian Pottery. Yorkshire pottery, built in the 1850s on land adjoining the *Ferrybridge Pottery by its owners, the Woolf family, for the production of domestic ware, much of it transfer-printed. It was run by Sidney Woolf and bought in 1899 by Horn Brothers, from whom the Cooperative Wholesale Society bought it in 1920. The pottery was again sold in 1947 to T.H. Newsome Co. Ltd.

Marks: printed marks incorporating the title of a pattern, also contain initials L.W. or s.W. (Lewis Woolf or son, Sidney). *Refs:* Grabham; Lawrence.

Auteuil. *See* Chaplet, Ernest; Haviland, Charles.

Autumn Foliage. *See* Doulton & Co.

Auvillar (Tarn et Garonne). French pottery centre. Of faience workshops in operation in the early 19th century, the oldest had been established by potters from Ardus, c.1750. One of the original partners, Mathieu Rigal (d 1793), owner from 1789, was succeeded by his son Guillaume, and the pottery remained in the Rigal family until its sale in 1844. The 19th-century faience was painted simply with bouquets or sketchy landscapes, until c.1820, when decoration ceased. The workshops also produced pottery with a reddish lead glaze until operation ceased in 1875.

The twelve or so workshops in production in 1834 also include La Faïencerie du Port, established in 1788 on the banks of the Garonne by a thrower from Bruges, Henri-Joseph Landevert or Landaner (d 1812), who was succeeded until 1820 by his widow and son; the output included terracotta busts, and faience vases garlanded with flowers after the earlier work of Strasbourg and Marseilles, in green, violet and a dull yellow. The workshop was bought by Isidore Verdier, owner of another faience workshop in the area.

Joseph Castex (b c.1787), already owner of one factory, established production on rue de l'Argenterie in 1811. He was succeeded by his son, who continued work until c.1870, when other local workshops, Labou and Techiné, also closed.

The faience made in Auvillar workshops in general resembles the work of Rigal. The region also produced domestic earthenware, including jugs for oil, wine or water, with enamelled decoration. The work was not habitually marked.
Refs: Lesur (1971); Riff.

Auxerre. A pottery was established in a former Capuchin monastery at Auxerre (Yonne) in the late 1790s by Claude Boutet, who had formerly made faience at *Ancy-le-Franc. He produced white or red-bodied earthenware, sometimes influenced by the traditional faience of Nevers, with patriotic designs. Boutet's successor, Edmé-François Montenot (b 1770), owner of the pottery from c.1807 until the 1820s, used an improved white glaze, decorated with figures *en camaïeu* or with flowers, fruit, birds or medallions held by cupids, in a full range of colours, including a characteristic, clear blue. Soup tureens, oil jars, toys and a figure of a lion are among the known output. The painters included Pierre Peigney from *Ancy-Le-Franc, from 1822. After Montenot's departure the clear oranges and blues used by Boutet were revived and attempts were made to copy the work of earlier faience centres. Throughout its operation, the workshop produced brown or white pottery for kitchen use. A former employee of the pottery, André Tavernier, who also worked at *Arthé, returned to Auxerre c.1822 and produced earthenware wine bottles with touches of green decoration and lightly spotted brown ground until the mid 19th century.

Marks include *fayence d'Auxerre*; *Au Capucin*; MONTENOT, *fabricant à AUXERRE* Tavernier's initials or signature.
Refs: Ernould-Gandouet; Huillard; Lesur (1971).

Avalon ware. *See* Chesapeake Pottery.

Avenard, Etienne (1873-1952). French author and ceramist, born at Saint-Brieuc (Côtes-du-Nord). Seeking to renew the art of tinglaze in France, he threw or press-moulded a variety of forms, but especially covered bowls, in clay from his own Paris garden. He painted geometrical motifs or stylized designs inspired by plants (always adapting the ornament to the form of the piece) in yellows, blues, greens and red on a ground which ranged from pure white or cream to whites with a blue, green or rusty tinge. After World War I, he became director of a faience workshop at the Sèvres factory, showing faience at the Salon de l'Automne between 1920 and 1923, and later moving to Cannes (Alpes-Maritimes). A display of his work at Sèvres in 1930 included bowls, vases, and a powder box decorated in combinations of blue, red, green and yellow on white.

Mark: cypress tree, painted.
Refs: Baschet; Bénézit; Lesur (1971).

aventurine glaze. *See* crystalline glaze.

Avisseau, Charles-Jean (1796-1861). French potter, the first of many 19th-century makers of *Palissy ware. He worked, like his father, as a stonemason, before learning pottery techniques in earthenware workshops near his home town of Tours (Indre-et-Loire). He became foreman at the pottery of Grillet-Travaillard in Saint-Pierre-des-Corps, Tours, 1815, and in 1825 joined a pottery owned by Baron Beçenval at Beaumont-des-Autels (Eure-et-Loire), making stoneware hand-painted in the style of 18th-century Strasbourg faience. Inspired by the work of Bernard Palissy, which he studied at this time, he returned in 1829 to Tours, where he built his own pottery and worked to reproduce Palissy's techniques, achieving fully controlled results c.1840. He moulded from nature, ferns, fish, lizards, frogs, etc., using a similar white body and lead glaze coloured with metallic oxides, wider and lighter in range than Palissy's, but his treatment was more free, with attention to function and movement rather than simply to form. Avisseau's later pieces were further removed from Palissy's work, with *trompe l'oeil* and perforated decoration, e.g. baskets of fish. In 1852, Avisseau settled in Place de l'Archevêque, still in Tours. Other potters producing Palissy ware in the same area included several of Avisseau's relations: his son Edouard (1831-1911), who assisted, then succeeded him; his daughter Caroline and grandson E.-L.*Deschamps-Avisseau; his brother-in-law J.*Landais; pupils L. *Brard and A.*Chauvigné.

Marks: signature or monogram of AV, incised.

Charles-Jean Avisseau. Modelled earthenware plate, 19th century. 33 cm.

Refs: Bénézit; Céramique française contemporaine; Ernould-Gandouet; Hannover; Heuser & Heuser; Thieme & Becker.

Avon Faience Co. American firm, originally *Vance Faience operating at Tiltonville, Ohio, with the Avon name from 1902, under the management of W.P.*Jervis. F.H. *Rhead, who worked at the pottery in 1903, developed a line of underglaze-decorated ware with Art Nouveau designs in a variety of colours, sometimes outlined in the white slip that was later associated with the *Jap Birdimal ware that he developed for S.A. *Weller. Moulded ware with high-relief decoration was also made in the heavy earthenware used at the pottery. The output included vases, tobacco jars, *jardinières* and umbrella stands. The firm combined with the *Wheeling Pottery Co. and the nearby La Belle and Riverside potteries as part of the Wheeling Potteries Co. at the end of 1902. Production of the ware made at Tiltonville was transferred to Wheeling, West Virginia, in 1905, where a semi-porcelain body was used in place of earthenware, and the Avon plant reverted to the manufacture of sanitary ware, for which it had been used by the previous owners in the 1890s. Later, after the failure of the Wheeling Potteries Co. in 1908, the works became the Wheeling Sanitary Manufacturing Co.

Marks: *AVON F.Co/Tiltonville*, incised; *Avon*, over four wavy lines; *Avon/W. Pts. Co.* in a mark incorporating a building and two curved lines.
Refs: Barber (1976); Cox; Evans; Jervis; Kovel & Kovel; Lehner.

Avon Pottery. Short-lived American pottery established in Cincinnati, Ohio, in 1886 by K.*Langenbeck. The main range was thrown in white clay, which fired to a soft, ivory colour, and was decorated with shaded colours—pink, violet, blue, olive green and

brown—blended on the biscuit clay with an atomizer and covered with clear, glossy glaze. The only other decoration was on the handles, which were modelled in the shape of a curved ram's horn or, in the case of some covered jars, elephants' heads, although early experimental examples have painted designs. One line was thrown in yellow clay, with incised or modelled decoration under a dull-surfaced or smear glaze. The chief artist was James MacDonald, and A.*Van Briggle was employed as an apprentice until 1887. The pottery closed in the following year.

The only known mark is AVON.
Refs: Barber (1976); Evans; Kovel & Kovel; Lehner; C.J. Thorn *Handbook of Old Pottery and Porcelain Marks* (Tudor Publishing Co., New York, 1947).

Awaji wares. Japanese pottery and porcelain made at the village of Iganomura on Awaji island from 1831 at a kiln established by *Mimpei, who had learned the techniques of pottery in Kyoto and retained the influence of Kyoto potters. Mimpei started the production with a variety of glazes, notably green and yellow and purple, a palette similar to that of Kochi ware. He continued to make enamelled faience in the manner of *Awata, and was succeeded in 1870 by his son, Rikitaro, then still a child, his nephew, Sampei, and a pupil, Keyakada Zengoro. Sampei left to establish his own kiln, where he continued the production of dishes with yellow and green glazes. Rikitaro remained at his father's kiln; his work included bowls decorated in red with a prawn design. An additional workshop opened at Sumoto in 1883 under Tamura Kyuhei.
Refs: Brinkley; Gorham; Hannover; Jenyns (1965, 1971); Morse.

Awata. District of Kyoto, Japan, noted for the production of earthenware with enamelled decoration in the tradition of *Ninsei wares and *Kenzan wares. Work of kilns in the district, notably those of the *Kinkozan, *Hozan, *Taizan, *Bizan, and *Tanzan families, includes tea ware, saké bottles, incense burners and containers, vases and

figures and is characterized by high quality in style and finish, in keeping with other Kyoto wares. The decoration, painted over a yellow-tinged crackle glaze, predominantly in blue, bright green and lavender enamels and gold, with silver, red and white also occurring, represents a variety of plant forms, birds, landscapes and, rarely, figures. Enamelled earthenware was among the output of *Tomimoto, who moved to Kyoto in the 1940s.

The original Kyoto clay body, fired to an orange tinge and coated with finely crackled transparent glaze, allowed the use of white enamel in decoration; the effect has latterly been achieved by the use of white clay from Shigaraki with the addition of other clays and a lime glaze fired in an oxidizing atmosphere.
Refs: Brinkley; Jenyns (1965, 1971); Hannover; B. Leach *Kenzan and his Tradition* (Faber, London, 1966); Munsterberg.

Awerdick, Leon. *See* Halcyon Art Pottery.

Aynsley, H.J. *See* Paragon China Ltd.

Aynsley, John, & Sons. Staffordshire porcelain manufacturers established 1864 at the Portland works, Longton, by a descendant of John Aynsley (1752-1829), maker of creamware in Lane End. The owner, also John Aynsley, in 1869 bought part of the former *New Hall works, which he left to *Booths Ltd. In 1903, the firm advertised fancy porcelain items, plain or enamelled, and in the following year registered military models with crests as mementoes of the South African war. Domestic bone china included pieces transfer-printed with views in black.

Marks include AYNSLEY impressed from 1875; AYNSLEYS in ribbon over 8-pointed star, printed, 1875-90; subsequent printed marks incorporate a crown and AYNSLEY/ENGLAND.
Refs: Andrews; Godden (1963, 1964).

Ayrton, Harry (1905-1976). English porcelain painter working at the *Worcester Royal Porcelain factory from 1920 until his retirement in 1970, after which he continued to work part-time. He specialized in paintings of fruit until the mid 1930s, with a two-year break c.1930, when he was engaged in the colouring of printed castle views. Afterwards, he painted fish and horse models, as well as fruit studies.

His brother, James John Ayrton (1897-1918), was an apprentice at the Worcester factory from c.1913, and his work included signed still lifes. He left for war service in 1915.
Ref: Sandon (1978a).

Back, Doug. *See* Donyatt.

Badar, Balazs. Hungarian potter working at Mezőtúr, one of the oldest centres of peasant pottery in Hungary, from the late 19th century until the 1920s. He was noted for thrown jugs, narrow-necked vases and dishes. Badar's pupils included F.*Gorka.
Ref: I. Pataky-Brestyánszky *Modern Hungarian Ceramics* (Corvina, Budapest, 1961).

Baddeley, John and Edward. *See* Hicks, Richard.

Baddeley family. Staffordshire potters. William Baddeley was working at Eastwood, Hanley, until the early 19th century. He made earthenware and stoneware, and was succeeded by his son, also William Baddeley, who improved the pottery's output, producing creamware and fine stoneware (caneware, red stoneware and black basalt), which was marked with the firm's name, EASTWOOD, often indistinctly impressed and sometimes mistaken for the Wedgwood mark. After the sale of the Eastwood works, the second William Baddeley's son, Henry William Baddeley (b 1807), manufactured terracotta, tobacco pipes and earthenware finials for metal tea and coffee pots at Queen Street, Hanley, and moulded telegraph insulators at works in Market Lane. After moving to Wharf Street, Longton, in 1846, Baddeley started the manufacture of cutlery handles in imitation of horn and bone, but discontinued that output when Sheffield cutlers refused to use ceramic handles. He was succeeded in 1864 by his widow, who worked in Commerce Street, Longton, until 1875, producing figures and rustic pieces in terracotta. Their son, William Baddeley, began the manufacture of decorative plant holders, stands, inkpots, etc., in terracotta, finished to represent wood, bark and other materials, at Normacott Road, Longton, in 1862, also ceasing production in 1875.
Refs: Jewitt; Reilly & Savage.

Baecher or **Bacher**, Anthony W. (1824-89). Potter producing red ware and a little stoneware in the Shenandoah Valley. Born in Falkenberg, Bavaria, he went to America in 1848 and worked as assistant to a potter in Pennsylvania before entering into partnership with Jacob Lynn at Thurmont, Maryland. In 1868, Baecher built a pottery at Winchester, Virginia, operating both works until his withdrawal from the Thurmont pottery in 1880. He was noted for varied, original and technically skilful decorative work. Also a farmer, he made many model animals (goats, squirrels, bears, etc.) as well as some human figures. Applied decoration on vases, jugs, jar lids, etc., includes modelled birds, often holding a worm, perched on large flowers, which have leaves and stems also in applied relief. This decoration appears on a wall pocket with curling tip, a form copied by members of the *Bell family. Flower sprays, when forming the sole decoration, are often in high relief with delicately modelled petals. The handles on vases and other hollow ware are gracefully curved and end in a curl, or taper to a sharp V-point.
   Mark: at first *Bacher*, later *Baecher, Winchester, Va.* stamped; many pieces signed in script and dated.
Refs: Rice & Stoudt; Stradling; Wiltshire.

Baensch, Heinrich. German porcelain manufacturer working at Lettin, Saxony, from 1858. His firm, making ornamental and everyday wares, became VVB-Keramik in 1945.
   Marks incorporate the initial L and often the name or initials of Baensch.
Refs: Danckert; Weiss.

Baggaley, Ernest (b 1904). Staffordshire potter, trained in Stoke-on-Trent. Employed at *Carter, Stabler & Adams, 1936-45, Baggaley threw the first of J.*Adams's streamlined shapes, and worked on the development of a reliable body and glazes. He introduced semi-matt glazes with a vellum finish, which were again used after World War II. In 1945, Baggaley established a pottery where he made electrical components cast in earthenware and a translucent body containing feldspar. From 1956, he produced fine wares with hand-painted decoration at the Branksome China Works, Fordingbridge, Dorset, trading as E. Baggaley Ltd.
   Printed marks: *Branksome/Ceramics/ England; Branksome/Stoneware/England,* or *Branksome/China/England*, with a crown.
Refs: Godden (1964); Hawkins.

Baggott, Samuel and William. *See* Goodwin, John (d 1875).

Baggs, Arthur Eugene (1886-1947). American artist potter. Baggs studied under C.F.*Binns and, on his recommendation, became technical and artistic director of the *Marblehead Pottery from 1905. As owner from 1915 until its closure in 1936, Binns was responsible for the restrained style that became associated with the pottery. His decorative designs of stylized natural forms were carried out in few colours, often within incised outlines, on simple shapes; some pieces were decorated only with a muted matt glaze. Baggs developed a clay body which resembled porcelain, although low-fired, and was used in the making of bowls with rice-grain decoration. While remaining at Marblehead for some time each year, he continued his studies at the Art Students' League and Alfred University in New York, and taught ceramics in New York, 1913-20, at Cleveland School of Art, c.1925-28, and as Professor of Ceramic Arts at Ohio State University, Columbus, from 1928 until his death. He was among the artists associated with the pottery of R.G.*Cowan and, while teaching in Cleveland, worked (1925-28) for Cowan on the development of glazes, including Egyptian blue and Persian green. Salt-glazed stoneware, which he made during the 1930s, included a covered jar in a rounded shape with a double looped handle on the lid, winner of the first prize for pottery in the 7th Ceramic National Exhibition at Syracuse, New York. His educational principles echoed those of Binns in the wish to impart to his students technical and artistic knowledge, with stress on sound craftmanship, the integration of form and decoration, and careful use of glazes. His own work was simple in style and technically accomplished, with very varied glazes.
Refs: A.E. Baggs 'The Story of a Potter' in *The Handicrafter* 1, 2 (1929); Clark & Hughto; Cox; Donhauser; Eidelberg; Evans; Kovel & Kovel; Henzke; E. Levin 'Pioneers of American Ceramics: Arthur Baggs, Glen Lukens' in *Ceramics Monthly* 24 (January 1976); E. McSwiggan 'The Marblehead Pottery' in *Spinning Wheel* (26th March 1972).

Bagnall, Sampson. *See* Mason, Miles.

Bagnall, William. English porcelain painter working 1918-c.1930 at the *Worcester Royal Porcelain Factory. He specialized in the painting of fruit and still-life subjects. Bagnall left the factory to work in Guildford, Surrey, and later worked at the *Compton Pottery.
Ref: Sandon (1978a).

Baguley, Isaac (1794-1855). English ceramic decorator. Baguley was employed as a painter in Derby c.1822 and subsequently worked at the *Swinton Pottery, becoming manager of the painting and gilding department by 1829. He was known for his painting of birds. Baguley established a decorating studio at the pottery after its failure in 1842, using earthenware and porcelain obtained from other manufacturers. His best-known output is Rockingham-glazed ware with gilded patterns. The Swinton workshop was taken over on his death by his son Alfred Baguley (d 1891), who moved in 1865 to Mexborough, Yorkshire, where he continued to decorate white earthenware. Alfred Baguley passed Swinton's Rockingham glaze to a friend and employee, Bowman Heald of the *Kilnhurst Old Pottery.
   Mark: a version of the Rockingham griffin mark, with *Baguley/Rockingham Works.*
Refs: Jewitt; Lawrence; Rice.

Baignol factory. French porcelain manufacturers, established 1797 by Etienne Baignol (1750-1822) at Limoges (Haute-Vienne). The firm made luxury pieces, decorative vases or biscuit groups, but also made tea and tableware in the white porcelain associated with Limoges, notably with white beading on gilded rims, and decorative handles (e.g. terminating in modelled female heads). The founder was succeeded in 1817 by his son François Baignol (1791-1875), who established a factory at *Saint-Brice in 1825 and sold the Limoges works in 1834.
Refs: d'Albis & Romanet; Chavagnac & Grollier; Ernould-Gandouet; Grellier & Leroux.

Bailey, C.J.C. English potter, formerly a civil engineer. In 1865, Bailey acquired and enlarged the Fulham Pottery, which had been worked in the late 17th century by John Dwight. He extended the production to include domestic, sanitary and technical stoneware, as well as decorative vases, stoves and architectural ware made in light pink or red terracotta (sometimes using both shades on the same piece), and sold brown-ware cream and milk containers, dishes, basins, trays and other kitchen ware, lined with white glaze and marketed as Sunderland Ware. Bailey's production of stoneware with *sgraffito* designs, introduced in the 1860s, expanded in the following decade. Salt-glazed jugs and mugs incised or impressed with heraldic emblems or designs of Japanese inspiration were designed by J.-C.*Cazin, who joined the pottery in the early 1870s, and collaborated closely with R.W.*Martin, modeller and designer from 1872. E.*Kettle decorated jugs and vases with patterns of foliage, birds and other animals or medieval figures. Other pieces in saltglaze include *jardinières* incised with

C.J.C. Bailey. Stoneware vase with medallions of cherub musicians on a buff ground with floral scrolls in blue, green, and rust, 1880. Marked with the incised monogram of E. Bennet. 41.9 cm high.

foliage patterns, designed by the architect J.P. Seddon.

Pale, highly refined stoneware, made 1873-c.1887 from Dwight's formula, was used for vases, etc., with decoration incised and coloured under the glaze. The sculptor E. Bennet took artistic control of this branch of production.

Bailey's business failed in 1888 and the pottery was sold three years later to a firm which later traded as the *Fulham Pottery.

Marks: incised monogram of CJCB; several impressed or incised marks incorporating BAILEY and FULHAM; some pieces produced under Bennet were marked with his incised monogram.
Refs: Blacker (1922b); Haslam (1977); Jewitt; Oswald.

Bailey, Cuthbert. English ceramic chemist, trained in science at South Kensington, London. He joined his father, J.C.*Bailey,

*Joseph Bailey, Sr. Trial piece by Bailey, the decorator unknown, made at the *Rookwood Pottery, with crescent marks. 14.3 cm high.*

at the Burslem factory of *Doulton & Co. in 1900 and in the following year began his collaboration with consultant B.*Moore in continuing the firm's experiments with *flambé* glazes. He left the company in 1907, but returned to succeed his father as general manager of the Burslem factory in 1925.
Refs: Atterbury & Irvine; Dennis (1975); Eyles (1980).

Bailey, John Cuthbert (b c.1854). English potter. Bailey worked briefly for a pottery at Greengates, Tunstall, Staffordshire, at the age of 14, and then joined the firm of Bates, Elliott & Co. (*see* Mayer, T.J.& J.) as an apprentice, c.1870, subsequently working for *Pinder, Bourne & Co. After his appointment by H.*Doulton as general manager of the Burslem factory at the age of 23, Bailey set out initially to limit the range of products in the interests of artistic quality, but encouraged technical development, particularly concerning bodies and glazes, and was instrumental, with John *Slater, in the introduction of bone porcelain. He was a director of the firm from 1909 until his retirement from the board in 1928; his son, C.*Bailey, succeeded him as factory manager in 1925.
Refs: Atterbury & Irvine; Dennis (1975); Eyles (1980).

Bailey, Joseph, Sr (c.1826-98). English-born potter. Bailey left Staffordshire for America in 1848 and worked briefly for R.B.*Beech in Philadelphia in the same year, then at a pottery in East Liverpool, Ohio, before going to Cincinnati in 1850. As superintendent of F.*Dallas's pottery from 1865, he assisted M.L.*McLaughlin and the Cincinnati Pottery Club with research and work carried out at the pottery, 1879-81. Invited to join the *Rookwood Pottery on its formation in 1880, he delayed his move until after Dallas's death in the following year and maintained his connection with the

Dallas pottery until its closure. After his resignation from Rookwood, Bailey went to Chicago as supervisor in the establishment of a kiln by a pottery club which had been formed there in 1882. He returned to Rookwood after 1885 and worked there until his death in 1898. Bailey was known for his talent and experience with clay and glazes, and was regarded as influential in the establishment of pottery techniques at Rookwood through his son, Joseph Bailey Jr, who had been employed at the Dallas pottery and had joined Rookwood at his father's suggestion in 1880.
Refs: Barber (1976); Evans; Kovel & Kovel; Peck.

Bailey, W. *See* Billingsley, William.

Bailey, W.& J.A. *See* Alloa Pottery.

Bailey, Murray & Bremner. *See* Saracen Pottery.

Baker, Alfred. English ceramic modeller, trained at the works of *Brown-Westhead, Moore & Co., and working for *Doulton & Co. in Burslem, 1888-1928. His work included elaborately modelled vases and other ornamental pieces for exhibition display.
Refs: Atterbury & Irvine; Eyles (1980).

Bakewell Brothers. Australian potters at Erskineville, Sydney. The firm added architectural terracotta to an existing output of brick and pipes in the 1890s, and from 1891 made Bristol-glazed bottles, butterpots, jars and other domestic ware, including small rings ('safe stands') to hold water in which the feet of cupboards were stood for the protection of food from attack by ants. Advertisements of 1904-07 list stoneware with Bristol glaze, caneware, and sponged and majolica goods; some moulded tableware was left in the white. Bakewells were among early Australian producers (1905-c.1914) of transfer-printed earthenware for table use, patterned in green or sepia with Australian flora or English designs, but

Bakewell Brothers. Earthenware jug, transfer-printed with flannel flowers in green, c.1914. 16 cm high.

were unable to compete with imported wares, and by 1918 the firm was dealing in English transfer-printed ware. Art Deco elements in style which appeared in the 1930s were restricted to ornamental ware, mainly vases and jugs, rather than tableware, although sets consisting of slip-cast teapot, sugar bowl and jug, sometimes with a matching tray, were made with sharp winged or fluted designs in relief and shaded glaze. A Newtone range, produced c.1937, included hand-painted vases with bush landscapes in blue or natural colours and birds (including kookaburras). The firm also produced small moulded koala bears and kookaburras on pin dishes in the late 1930s and after World War II. Painted wares continued briefly after 1945 and included small dishes in the shape of Australia. The firm closed in 1955, but some moulds were subsequently used by a former employee working alone until the early 1960s.

Transfer-printed ware with the firm's mark (BB and a crown) up to the 1920s may have been commissioned from Staffordshire manufacturers.

Mark: NEWTONE stamped in a semi-circular arch.
Ref: Graham.

Baldwyn, Charles (1859-1943). Porcelain painter working at the *Worcester Royal Porcelain Factory from 1874 until the early 20th century. He specialized in studies of birds, including swans, from nature, frequently using a moonlit setting. He exhibited watercolours at the Royal Academy (1887-93), and worked as a watercolourist after leaving the factory.

Mark: BY.
Refs: Bénézit; Sandon (1978a).

Balfour, Alexander. *See* North British Pottery.

Ball, Edward. English landscape painter, working at the *Coalport factory in the 19th and early 20th centuries. His work, including misty river or lakeside scenes on Sèvres-style vases, was signed *E. Ball, E.O. Ball* or *T. [Ted] Ball.*
Ref: Godden (1970).

Ball, Ezra (b c.1872). English ceramic modeller and mouldmaker, employed by the *Adams family at Greengates Pottery and still active in the late 1950s. Ball was awarded the British Empire Medal for services to pottery in 1950.
Ref: D. Peel *A Pride of Potters* (Arthur Barker Ltd, London, 1957).

Ball, F. Carlton (b 1911). American artist potter and teacher. Born in California, he studied at the University of Southern California 1932-35, and then taught ceramics in California, Wisconsin and Washington. Ball's stoneware includes painted plates and other pieces noted for large size and textured surface.
Refs: F.C. Ball *Decorating Pottery with Clay, Slip and Glaze* (Professional Publications, Columbus, Ohio, 1967); 'Ceramics: Double Issue' in *Design Quarterly* 42-43 (1958); Clark & Hughto; J. Lovoos 'F. Carlton Ball, Master Potter' in *Ceramics Monthly* 13 (September 1965).

*Charles Baldwyn. Plaque painted by Baldwyn with tooled gold against a matt blue ground. Made at the *Worcester Royal Porcelain factory, 1902. 30.2 cm in diameter.*

Ball, William (b c.1842). English porcelain painter working in *Worcester. Ball was apprenticed to the firm of Kerr & Binns in 1857 and subsequently worked for the Worcester Royal Porcelain Co.
Ref: Sandon (1978a).

Ball Brothers. *See* Deptford Pottery.

Ballard,O.L.& A.K. *See* Nichols & Alford.

Ballard, Philip. *See* Randall, Thomas Martin.

Balleroy, H.& A., Frères. French porcelain manufacturers. Henri, a decorator, and Antoine Balleroy (d 1929), a modeller working in Limoges (Haute-Vienne), came from a family of porcelain painters. They joined a partnership, Société Immobilière, in 1901, using a porcelain factory in Limoges. The brothers left the partnership in 1908 and worked in temporary premises before, in

*Edward Ball. Small baluster vase made at *Coalport, with a view of Loch Fyne painted and signed E.O. Ball. The ground is deep blue and cream, the scrollwork gilt. 10.5 cm high.*

Elfriede Balzar-Kopp. Stoneware ewer in grey body with hoops containing wavy lines and spots, and vertical banding in deep blue, after 1927. Signed Balzar Kopp. 25 cm high.

1912, taking over a factory which had been established in 1860, also in Limoges. Antoine took charge of their production while Henri was responsible for decoration. Their work, mainly decorative pieces, was of high quality. The firm won a silver medal at the decorative arts exhibition in Paris, 1925, for tableware in Art Deco style. Henri Balleroy closed the factory in 1937.

Marks include LIMOGES/B & CIE/FRANCE; PORCELAINE HA BALLEROY FRERES LIMOGES.

Balon, E, Sr. *See* Besnard, Ulysse.

Balzar-Kopp, Elfriede (b 1904). German studio potter, born in Bendorf in the Westerwald region, Rhineland. After studying in Höhr-Grenzhausen (1924-26) and at the Staatliche Majolika-Manufaktur *Karlsruhe in 1926, she opened a workshop in Höhr-Grenzhausen in 1927. Initially working with W.*Mühlendyck, she made earthenware, some for architectural use, and grey salt-glazed stoneware in the local tradition, painted with cobalt blue, manganese purple, and a shaded brown (Kölnische Braun), which she used in painted designs or as a complete covering for the pot. Although she concentrated mainly on utilitarian ware in the 1930s and 1940s, Balzar-Kopp also made small salt-glazed animal figures (increasingly stylized) and ceramic sculptures. Her human figures and groups were often assembled from thrown components; a Madonna dating from the 1930s was influenced by her study at Karlsruhe, and other pieces showed the influence of M.*Laeuger. Some figures were large in size, e.g. a woman gardener carrying a dish on her head, about one metre high. In later years, she restricted her work to the design and decoration of pieces thrown for her in her workshop, which is run mainly by her daughter and son-in-law, who employ a number of assistants. Her son, Heiner Balzar (b 1937), trained at the workshop 1952-54, and in Höhr-Grenzhausen, under H.*Griemert 1956-58.

Mark: *Balzar-Kopp.*
Refs: Bock; Klinge.

Bampi, Richard (1899-1965). Studio potter, artist and sculptor, born in Amparo, Brazil, to Italian and German parents. Bampi grew up in Germany and did military service in World War I. After training in Munich, where he studied architecture, 1918, and at the *Bauhaus in the following year, Bampi travelled in Switzerland, Italy and Austria, 1920-23. He spent the next four years in Brazil, where he continued his work in woodcuts (first exhibited 1917 in Erfurt) and produced sculptures in Expressionist style, using marble and bronze. Having also made his first ceramics in Brazil, he returned to Germany in 1927 and, in close association with M.*Laeuger, opened a workshop, which was part of the Kandern factory. His work included vases with Cubist decoration. He exhibited examples of tin-glazed earthenware in Leipzig, 1928. He was inspired by Chinese ceramics shown in Berlin in 1929, and started lengthy research (his laboratory notes record 1052 experiments) into glazes. His stoneware showed a strong Chinese influence from 1942, when he first made use of feldspathic glazes on stoneware fired at 1200°C, produced alongside wares fired at about 1080°C through the 1940s. The glazes range from brilliant orange to delicate crackled turquoise, and some were applied in layers of varying thickness. Much of Bampi's work consists of bowls and vases. His decoration includes patterns recalling Japanese calligraphy. He made some asymmetrical pieces after c.1950, and became known for his use of crystalline glazes later

*Richard Bampi. Stoneware vase, 1959.
17.5 cm high.*

in the 1950s. Bampi specified that the proceeds of his estate after his death should provide an annual prize to assist the study or technical development of a potter under 30 years old, living in Germany. The prize was first awarded in 1969, and rises in the market value of Bampi's work enabled the trustees to extend it to three runners-up.

Marks include B, RB, *Bampi* and the oval mark illustrated (1944-65).
Refs: Bock; Klein.

Bancroft, Joseph (1796-1857). English porcelain decorator. He remained briefly at the porcelain factory in Nottingham Road, *Derby, after serving his apprenticeship there, then went to work in Staffordshire e.g. for J.& W.*Ridgway in the mid 1820s, and also possibly in Liverpool. By the autumn of 1831, he had become the principal painter of flowers, fruit and studies of feathers for *Mintons Ltd. Work by him mentioned in the Minton pattern books includes garlands of flowers in a style inspired by Sèvres (1837). He is thought to have remained at Mintons for the rest of his working life.
Refs: Aslin & Atterbury; Godden (1968), 1972); Haslem; Twitchett (1980).

Bare, Ruth. *See* Della Robbia Pottery.

Bankes, Henry. *See* Billingsley, William.

Bankfoot Pottery. Scottish pottery at Prestonpans, which was operated from the 1790s by Robert Gordon (d c. 1834) and his son, George Gordon. The firm made rounded jugs in bodies ranging from creamware to one which approached stoneware in hardness, usually with low-relief moulded decoration, and coloured under a lead glaze in a manner resembling Pratt ware; the themes include such subjects as The Sailor's Farewell and Scottish emblems or topical events. Moulded creamware jugs with relief decoration, and patterns painted both under the glaze and in enamel colours, date from c.1815-20; flower patterns, printed and hand painted, sometimes occur within the necks of jugs. The Gordons left Bankfoot in 1812, and were succeeded by C.*Belfield, who was already working at the pottery, probably as manager.

Rare marks include G raised, inside a pair of dividers and set square; GORDON; G.G.
Ref: McVeigh.

Banko ware. Japanese pottery inspired by the work of merchant and amateur potter, Numanami Shigenaga (1718-77), also named Rozan or Gozaemon, who used the seals 'banko' (everlasting) and 'fujiki' (changeless). Working at Kuwana village in the pre-Meiji province of Ise (Mie prefecture), he made a varied output, including copies of *raku, *Shino,* Oribe and *Karatsu wares, western designs (e.g. Delft ware), *Awata wares, and, under the patronage of the shogun Iyenari from 1785, red and green Ming export porcelain (*see* gosu aka-e) and

*Eliza Banks. Stoneware vase with flowers painted in thick slip and borders of beading and stylized foliage. Made by *Doulton & Co., Lambeth, 1879. 17.5 cm high.*

Chinese polychrome wares, all of high quality; he is noted particularly for floral decoration, landscapes etc., painted in enamel over brilliant glazes. The tall, slim-necked ewer form is characteristic.

The secrets of his technique were rediscovered in the 19th century by *Yusetsu Mori, who obtained from Rozan's grandson the banko seal, which was also used as a mark by many other Ise potters (21 exhibitors used this seal on work shown in the Exposition Universelle in Paris, 1878), and *Hansuke, who worked at Yokkaichi in Mie prefecture, which became the main centre of Banko ware with the opening of many small kilns.

In general, Banko ware is very thinly hand-built (not thrown or moulded) in a strong dull brown, red or fawn body fired at high temperature. Some pieces in clay of mixed colours are classed as mokume ('wood graining'). The strength of the body allows the use of perforated and finely-modelled decoration, and the setting of porcelain plaques in holes cut through the vessel walls. Teapots are often ornamented with fine-linked chains, or knobs which swivel in clay sockets; stamped and inlaid marks are characteristic. Enamel decoration, when used, is very thick and depicts birds, flowers and figures.

The kiln founded by Yusetsu continues the production of blue-painted porcelain, as well as bowls, bottles and plump wine-ewers in a soft, coarse clay body with cream, unevenly crackled glaze and decoration in underglaze blue or aka-e. Another group of Banko ware, made in large quantities, consists of fine, reddish stoneware teapots, with bamboo or plum and Chinese verse engraved on the body. Finials are in the form of domestic or mythical animals. Enamel designs of flowers, or medallions of blue-painted decoration also occur on a dark red

or bronze unglazed ground. The greyish white glaze used in these examples also appears with Chinese landscapes, carefully painted in underglaze blue as the lining for a lid (or the entire inside surface of a bowl) with the rest of the piece left unglazed.
Refs: Brinkley; Feddersen; Gorham; Jenyns (1971); Morse; Munsterberg; Woodhouse.

Banks, Eliza. English ceramic decorator. After training at the Lambeth School of Art, she joined the firm of *Doulton & Co. in 1873, and was among the first artists to carry out painting in thickly-applied slip, after experiments which started at the pottery in 1876-77. Her work is characterized by bold, fluent brushwork.
Ref: Callen.

Baptist Mills Pottery. *See* White, Frederick J.

Baranówka. Polish hard-paste porcelain factory established in 1804 at Baranów, near Volhynia, by Adam and Josephine Wallewski. Under the direction of Franz Mezer, succeeded by his brother, Michael, the factory became noted for the production of envelope-shaped snuff boxes and Easter eggs painted, e.g. with biblical scenes. Members of the Mezer family became owners, 1820-46. The factory continued in operation until shortly before the start of World War II.

Marks include *Baranówka* in Roman or Cyrillic characters; double-headed eagle; three stars, painted.
Refs: Danckert; Weiss.

Barbizet, Victor. French maker of *Palissy ware. After studying at the Ecole des Beaux-Arts in Chalon-sur-Saône (Saône-et-Loire), Barbizet established a workshop in Paris c.1851, where he worked until 1890, assisted by his son, Achille, who was responsible for much of the potting while his father developed and prepared the glazes. The workshop produced Palissy ware in very large quantities, specializing in plant pots, *jardinières*, figures and other ornaments for use in indoor gardens. The colours are less intense than those used by C.-J.*Avisseau and some glazes are inclined to flake.

Mark: initials, BV.
Refs: Ernould-Gandouet; Heuser & Heuser; Lesur (1971).

barbotine decoration. A decorative technique in which coloured slip is painted on the clay body in the manner of oils, with colours mixed to provide variations in tone. The method was developed by E.*Chaplet in the 1870s and frequently used until c.1890, but presented difficulties with flaking of the decoration in firing because of differences between the densities of body and slip. In America, M.L.*McLaughlin carried out successful experiments in barbotine decoration ('Cincinnati Limoges') after seeing the display of French wares in the Philadelphia Centennial Exhibition, 1876. The technique became characteristic of art wares made at the *Rookwood Pottery and by other Cincinnati producers, as well as W.A.*Long, J.B.*Owens and S.A.*Weller elsewhere. The name barbotine is also sometimes used to describe trailed slip.

barbotine ware. *See* Doulton & Co.

Baranówka. Cups and saucers painted in enamel colours and gold, c.1815-20. Marked with three stars in blue and Baranówka *in black. Cups 8.9 cm high; saucers 8.6 cm in diameter.*

Barcelona. Spanish porcelain factory established 1894 at Barcelona by the firm Berenguer & Canals for the production of decorated tea and coffee sets, and utilitarian wares. From 1921 the factory traded under the title of Manufactura Cerámicas.

Marks include a phoenix and a geometrical arrangement of two quadrilaterals topped by a triangle.

Also in Barcelona, the Hosta factory made porcelain in the late 1860s.
Refs: Danckert; Weiss.

Barck, Nils Ivan Joachim Graf (1863-1930). Painter and ceramist, born in Malmö, Sweden, and educated in Paris. Barck

N.I.J. Graf Barck. Stoneware vase with glazes in grey under flowing blue/green. Marked with Graf's signature.

studied pottery techniques at St-Amand-en-Puisaye (Nièvre) in the late 19th century, following the style of J.*Carriès, whose influence on local stoneware makers remained after his death in 1894. In 1915, Barck bought the Château de Montriveau and the workshop at St-Amand formerly used by Carriès, living there until his death.

Mark: signature, *de Barck* (or *Bark*), incised.
Refs: Bénézit; Heuser & Heuser; Lesur (1971); Thieme & Becker.

Bareuther & Co. German manufacturers of porcelain, table and utility ware established at Waldsassen, Upper Palatinate, in 1866.

Marks include a shield with *fleur-de-lis*; crossed arrows containing the initials BCPW; a crown with *Bareuther* and BAVARIA.
Refs: Danckert; Weiss.

barge, bargee or **Measham ware.** English earthenware with dark brown glaze and relief decoration of birds, flowers, applied in white clay and touched with green, blue and pink. Sold at Measham, Leicestershire, on the Ashby-de-la-Zouch canal, often to barge people, the ware was made c.1860-c.1910 at Church Gresley and nearby Woodville, Derbyshire, and included kettles,

barge ware. Teapot with applied decoration, probably made at Church Gresley, Derbyshire, c.1880.

chamber pots, jugs, tobacco jars, as well as large teapots (up to about eight litres in capacity) with a finial in the form of a similarly shaped miniature teapot; the pieces were sometimes inscribed and dated to order with printer's type pressed on an applied pad of white clay before firing. Makers included 'Bossy' *Mason, a potter working at the village of Jacks-in-the-Hole, near Midway.
Refs: Bedford; Lewis (1969).

Barker, David Wilson. *See* Worcester.

Barker, Ernest (1890-1956) English porcelain painter working for the *Worcester Royal Porcelain Co. from the early 20th century until shortly before his death. Barker trained under H.*Davis and specialized in paintings of sheep in Davis's style, but also painted flowers and garden birds. Some of his flower painting was carried out on the centres of plates in the style of early Worcester floral decoration. Other pieces included plaques and other ware intended for mounting in silver.
  Mark: signature, *B.A. Kerr*.
Ref: Sandon (1978a).

Barker, J.P. and S. *See* Mexborough.

Barker, Peter. *See* Low Pottery.

Barlach, Ernst (1870-1938). German sculptor, poet, graphic artist. Some of his designs were executed in ceramics. Barlach began an association with R.*Mutz with a commission for a commemorative plaque on the 25th anniversary of Hamburg museum in 1902 and modelled plaques and relief-decorated ware for the Mutz Workshop until 1904, when he became a teacher at the Fachschule für Keramik at Höhr-Grenzhausen. He subsequently collaborated with Richard Mutz in Berlin-Wilmersdorf. On his return from a visit to Russia in 1906, Barlach began to express the suffering of the peasants in sculptures which were cast in white porcelain and glazed at porcelain workshops in Schwarzburg c.1908-13, and in white porcelain and red stoneware by the Meissen

Ernst Barlach. Figure of a girl produced in porcelain by the Schwarzburger Werkstätten to Barlach's design, 1908. 23.5 cm high.

*Hannah Barlow. Salt-glazed beaker with incised and coloured decoration. Marked with HBB and LEE [Louisa E. Edwards]. Made by *Doulton & Co., 1875. 14 cm high.*

factory in the 1920s and 1930s. His book, *Keramik: Stoff und Form*, was published in 1908.
Refs: Bock; Pelka; K. Reutti *Mutz-Keramik* (catalogue, Ernst-Barlach-Hauses, Hamburg, 1966); Scheffler; W. Scheffler *Werke um 1900* (catalogue, Kunstgewerbemuseum, Berlin, 1966).

Barlow, Arthur B. (1845-79). English ceramic decorator. Barlow studied at the Lambeth School of Art before joining the *Doulton & Co. Lambeth studio, soon after his sister, H.B.*Barlow, in 1871. Despite his ill health, Barlow decorated and designed a great quantity of work. His designs were chiefly bold, stylized patterns of leaf scrolls characterized by a subtle use of colour. He adopted the use of all-over patterns, often repeating motifs of pointed leaves. Although he concentrated on surface decoration, Barlow sometimes used applied details, e.g. flower heads and border designs.
  Mark: incised monogram ABB.
Refs: Atterbury & Irvine; Blacker (1922b); Dennis (1971); Rhead.

Barlow, Florence E. (d 1909). English ceramic decorator. She worked at Doulton's Lambeth studio from 1873, initially executing incised designs of birds on stoneware in a technique similar to that of her sister, H.B. *Barlow, and also using incised patterns of scrolled leaves. Later, Florence Barlow painted birds, foliage, etc., in thick layers of coloured slip. She was among the artists engaged on the decoration of Doulton's Marqueterie ware.
  Marks: versions of monogram, FB or FEB.
Refs: Atterbury & Irvine; Blacker (1922b); Callen; Dennis (1971); Rhead.

Barlow, Hannah Bolton (1851-1916). English ceramic decorator. After the death of her

father, she started professional training in painting, modelling and design at the Lambeth School of Art in 1868, and after a brief period spent decorating at *Minton's Art Pottery Studio, joined *Doulton's Lambeth studio in 1871, initially as a freelance, the first female artist to work there. Hannah Barlow decorated the studio's salt-glazed stoneware with spirited, freehand sketches of horses, sheep, dogs and country scenes with children or farm workers, relying for effect on few lines, which were incised and filled with pigment. From c.1895, her drawing became more detailed and the borders a more prominent feature. Hannah Barlow also modelled animals in relief, and exhibited modelled terracotta placques at the Royal Academy in the 1880s. She also painted designs on *Lambeth Faience. Her assistants included her sister, Lucy, who worked at Doulton's Lambeth studio 1882-84.

Mark: monogram of HBB.
Refs: Atterbury & Irvine; Blacker (1922b); Callen; Dennis (1971); Rhead.

Barlow, James. English porcelain painter noted for his studies of birds and insects. Barlow worked at the factory in Nottingham Road, *Derby, in the last years of its operation and subsequently worked in Staffordshire. In 1876, he was employed as foreman by the firm of C.*Allerton & Sons.
  His father, also James Barlow (d 1842), was at the head of the department producing utilitarian wares at the Nottingham Road factory from 1837 until the year of his death.
Ref: Twitchett (1980).

Barluet & Cie. *See* Montereau.

Barmin Brothers. Russian potters, owners (c.1820-c.1831) of a factory producing earthenware and porcelain at Fryazevo in the *Gzhel area until 1918, after several changes in ownership. Their work included a teaset painted with scenes of houses, etc., within gold cartouches on a white ground, now preserved in the state museum of history.
  Marks often incorporate the Barmin name usually in Cyrillic characters in a circular or other shape.
Ref: Bubnova.

Barnard, Harry (1862-1933). English designer and ceramic modeller, born in London. While still a student in London, Barnard worked at *Doulton's Lambeth studio under M.V.*Marshall on the decoration of ornamental vases (with modelled dragons, low relief fish and water weed against a ground of rows of tadpoles, etc.) and commemorative jugs (with portrait medallions). By 1884 he had become under-manager of the studio. He also decorated some of the company's Burslem productions, e.g. a Spanish Ware bowl painted with iris flowers c.1890. In 1895 he left to join the firm of J.*Macintyre, where he introduced a form of *pâte-sur-pâte* decoration, which he called Gesso. Two years later, he joined J.*Wedgwood & Sons Ltd, where he worked as a decorator of bone porcelain, majolica and tiles, and became manager of the tile department in 1899. Barnard worked as manager of Wedgwood's London retail branch in 1902 and returned in 1919 to Etruria, where he worked on the expansion of the firm's museum under John Cook. He started experiments in the same year for the production of a new edition of the Portland Vase, achieving his first success in 1923 and several further examples in the following year. In 1927 he modelled a large black basalt panel about 135 cm square and 12.75 cm thick with a design of a potter at work, accompanied by a quotation from the *Rubaiyat of Omar Khayyam*, for a Canadian retailer of English ceramics. Barnard continued to make individual pieces for firing at the Wedgwood factory until his death. He was the author of *Chats on Wedgwood Ware* (1924).

Doulton mark: monogram of HB.
Refs: Atterbury & Irvine; Batkin; Blacker (1922a); Dennis (1971); Reilly & Savage.

Barnet, James. *See* Derby.

Barnsley, Grace. English ceramic decorator. Daughter of architect and designer Sidney Barnsley. In the 1920s and 1930s, she painted ware bought from the Wedgwood factory, where the work was returned for firing and glazing. On the return of her husband, O.*Davies, from a career at sea in 1934, she established with him the *Roeginga Pottery and took responsibility for decorating in enamel colours the output of matt-glazed earthenware.

Mark: painted monogram of GBD on Wedgwood wares painted by Mrs Davies.
Refs: Batkin; Reilly & Savage.

Baron, William Leonard. English designer and potter. Baron was employed by C.H. *Brannam in the production of Barum ware, 1885-93. In the late 1890s, he established his own pottery at Rolle Quay, Barnstaple, Devon, producing motto wares, vases, plaques and figures, that were similar in style to Barum ware, but with stronger colour contrasts. In 1902, Baron opened showrooms in Barnstaple. His son, Frederick Baron (d 1939), also employed by Brannam (c.1897-c.1910), took over his father's works c.1910 until the pottery was absorbed by Brannam's in 1939.

Marks: both Barons initialled their work for Brannam. Their pottery mark was *Baron/Barnstaple*, incised, until c.1938, or BARON. DEVON, impressed c.1905-c.1938.
Refs: Blacker (1922a); Coysh (1976); Lloyd Thomas (1974).

Baroni, Giovanni. *See* Nove.

Barr, Martin (1757-1813). Worcester businessman. Barr became a partner of J.*Flight in the *Worcester porcelain factory in 1792, and was particularly concerned with the improvement of paste formulae and firing processes. The firm traded as Flight & Barr until Barr's son Martin (c.1784-1848) became a partner when the firm's title changed to Barr, Flight & Barr, 1807-1813. On the death of the elder Martin Barr, his son George Barr (c.1788-1848) was admitted into the partnership (the firm becoming Flight, Barr & Barr) and managed the London showroom. After the amalgamation with Chamberlain's factory in 1840, the Barr

brothers ceased active participation in the production of porcelain, retaining only a minority interest. One of the brothers remained at the premises vacated by the porcelain firm, working with one of its directors, Fleming St John, on the production of encaustic tiles. The works were sold in 1850 to *Maw & Co., who moved production to Broseley in 1852.
Refs: Binns (1910); Jewitt; Sandon (1978b).

Barr, Flight & Barr. *See* Worcester.

Barratt, Robert (d 1940). English porcelain painter and watercolour artist. An apprentice at the Royal Crown *Derby factory in Osmaston Road c.1899, he also studied at art school for about fifteen years, and visited Australia with W.E.*Mosely in 1932. He painted flowers, e.g. bouquets featuring a large rose, signed *R. Barratt*. After leaving the factory to work as a civil servant, Barratt continued to paint in watercolours.
Refs: Gilhespy; Twitchett (1976).

Barré, Louis. *See* Sèvres.

Barron, Paul (b 1917). English studio potter trained at the Brighton School of Art from 1937 as a pupil of N.*Braden; he later attended the Royal College of Art in London. He joined H.F.*Hammond at the Farnham School of Art in 1950 and assisted in the development of a vocational course in ceramics. He also established his own studio at Bentley near Farnham, 1953. After making slipware, he turned in the early 1950s to stoneware, making some series wares but primarily individual pieces, with glazes containing wood ash and local minerals, reduction fired.

Mark: B in a rectangle with rounded ends.
Refs: Rose; Wingfield Digby.

Barum ware. *See* Brannam, Charles Hubert.

Barwig, Franz (1868-1931). Sculptor and modeller, born in Schönau and trained as a woodcarver at the Vienna Kunstgewerbeschule, where he returned to teach, 1910-22. He designed animal figures and groups independently for the Wiener Porzellanmanufaktur *Augarten and the Wienerberger Fabrik in the 1920s.

Marks: signature or initials, incised.
Ref: Neuwirth (1974a).

Basaltine. *See* Beardmore, Frank, & Co.

Basket weave. *See* Brush-McCoy Pottery.

Batavian ware. *See* Leeds Pottery.

Batenin factory. Russian porcelain factory established in 1812 at St Petersburg by a merchant, Sergei Batenin (d 1814), who was succeeded by his sons Filipp (d 1832) and Peter (d by 1829). The factory continued under the Batenins' executors until its sale to the *Kornilov firm in 1839. Using porcelain paste acquired from the nearby *St Petersburg factory, the Batenins produced a profitable line of low-priced teaware in naive, Russian provincial style, as well as luxury vases, presentation cups and table services, including some large pieces. Brightly painted decoration included flowers in large

bouquets, portraits of the Tsar, views of St Petersburg, copies of 18th and 19th century paintings, and arrangements of playing cards. Gilding was used, especially on vases, and matt gold grounds were characteristic. The Batenin family was unusual among Russian porcelain firms in producing no known figures.

C. 3. K. 6.

Marks (always impressed) include the initials of Sergei Batenin; initials of 'St Petersburg factory of the merchant Batenin' or initials of 'St Petersburg Heirs of Batenin' (all in Cyrillic characters). Impressed mark as illustrated, 1800-25.
Refs: B. Alekseev *Porcelain* (Moscow, 1958); Emme; Hare; Ivanova; Nikiforova; Ross; Rozembergh; Saltykov.

Bates, David. English porcelain painter of flower subjects working for the *Worcester Royal Porcelain Co. c.1855-80, and trained at the factory. He exhibited work at the Royal Academy between 1868 and 1893, becoming a landscape painter on leaving the factory.
Refs: Bénézit; Sandon (1978a).

Bates, Brown-Westhead & Co. *See* Brown-Westhead, Moore & Co.

Bateson family. Yorkshire potters working at Burton-in-Lonsdale. William Bateson (d 1887) succeeded John Bateson as proprietor of a pottery established in the mid 19th century at Burton-in-Lonsdale, making stoneware bottles, jars and cooking utensils. He was joined by his sons Henry (d 1922), Frank (d 1938) and Robert (d 1908). From 1887, the pottery traded as Waterside Pottery. The family also bought the Greta

*Franz Barwig. Model of a bear made at *Augarten, c.1926-27. Signed F. Barwig. 34 cm high.*

Bank Pottery at Barnawick, to the east of Burton-in-Lonsdale, in 1887. Robert left the partnership in 1902, later buying the *Greta Bank Pottery, which he ran until his death, succeeded by Henry and Frank Bateson, who continued the pottery until its closure in 1918. The main output consisted of stoneware bottles. The last of the potteries in the town was operated by a Richard Bateson until its closure in 1945.
Refs: Brears (1971a, 1974); Lawrence.

Batiz. Hungarian pottery established 1822 on the Nalaczy family estate at Batiz by the French potters, George d'André and his son, who was sole owner, 1850-58. The output, noted for its high quality, included black ware, sparingly decorated in silver, and a wide range of tableware and decorative items in white earthenware, with hard, durable glazes.

Marks: arms of the landowners, with a crown, until 1845; subsequently the place name, *Batiz*.
Ref: Csanyi.

Battam, Thomas (1810-64). English pottery and porcelain painter, trained in the London decorating workshop of his father, also Thomas Battam. Trading as Battam & Son in Gough Square, London, he specialized in painting Etruscan terracotta ware, mainly urns and vases, bought from *Blanchard & Co., with oil-based colour, fired at very low temperatures. His decoration of silhouette figures in black on a red or buff ground was inspired by historical, mythological or domestic scenes on specimens of Greek red-figure ware. His firm's display in the Great Exhibition of 1851 took the form of an Etruscan tomb, a grotto filled with decorative vases. His son continued the workshop until the 1870s. The output also included painting in the style of Limoges enamels. Thomas Battam, as art director of the Copeland factory from c.1835, painted ornamental and domestic ware in terracotta and bone porcelain, again in Etruscan-inspired style. Battam also made copies of oil paintings on large porcelain slabs, and is credited with the development of parian paste at the Copeland factory in the 1840s. After his return to London, he was founder of the Crystal Palace Art Union in 1858.

Workshop mark: initials BS flanking four dots.
Refs: Godden (1961); Hughes (1977); Wakefield.

Batty, Dora M. English designer, working for *Carter, Stabler & Adams c.1921-c.1925. Her work included a design of a girl carrying a basket of fish on her head, for tiles, and publicity material for Mac Fisheries, but she is known for studies of farmyard animals, ducks, rocking horses, etc., on nursery ware, and toys or scenes from nursery rhymes on tiles.
Refs: Coysh (1976); Hawkins.

Baudisch or **Baudisch-Wittke,** Gudrun (b 1907). Austrian ceramist born in Pöls, Steiermark. She worked 1926-30 in the ceramic design department of the *Wiener Werkstätte under J.*Hoffmann, and then with M. von Potoni at her own workshop in Vienna until 1936, when she left to work in Berlin, 1936-42. She established her own

*Gudrun Baudisch-Wittke. Vase made at the *Wiener Werkstätte, 1925. 23 cm high.*

workshop in Hallstadt, 1943, later collaborating with other artists in 'Keramik Hallstadt'. Her work at the Wiener Werkstätte included narrow, lobed vases and free-standing figures and groups, or dishes, lamps, etc., which incorporate flowers, figures or model animals. She continued to make vases, often in tall shapes, some hand-built in increasingly simple and often non-functional styles.

Marks: signature; GUDRUN BAUDISCH; GB/W; GBW with H in a circle.
Ref: Neuwirth (1974a).

Baudour. Porcelain manufacture established at Baudour, Belgium, on the purchase of a small workshop in 1842 by François Declercq, who had worked at the Meissen factory. From 1849 the workshop belonged to Nicòlas de Fuisseaux, succeeded by his widow and son, trading as Anciennes Usines de Fuisseaux. The output of hard-paste porcelain consisted of hotel ware, luxury pieces, figures and other decorative items. The factory passed to SA des Pavillons (1927) and the Société Belge de Céramique (Cérabel) in 1934.
Refs: La Porcelaine de Baudour (Palais des Beaux-Arts, Brussels, 1948); *Porcelaines de Baudour* (Palais des Beaux-Arts, Brussels, 1951).

Bauer family. Family of American potters making earthenware and stoneware for domestic use in Paducah, Kentucky, from 1885 until the pottery's closure in the early 20th century, following the death of John Bauer in 1898. The works were reopened and modernized after the incorporation of the company in 1905, and produced glazed stoneware for domestic and pharmaceutical

use, as well as flowerpots, filters, etc. In the same year, John A. Bauer opened a pottery in Los Angeles and, with a number of employees brought from Kentucky, produced utility ware, flowerpots and, by the time of the exhibition in San Diego in 1914, a line of moulded art pottery made in Californian clay, using machinery from the Paduca Works. Bauer's son, Edwin, entered the firm in 1914, and the works were enlarged in 1919. After its sale in the early 1920s, the pottery was incorporated as J.A. Bauer Pottery Co. Inc. and continued operation until the late 1950s. Production of art pottery ceased in 1920s.

Marks: name of the firm, moulded in art pottery, usually printed in blue on the other ware.
Refs: W.F. Dietrich *The Clay Resources and the Ceramic Industry of California* (California State Mining Bureau, Sacramento, 1928); Evans.

Bauer & Pfeiffer. German porcelain manufacturers working from 1904 at Schorndorf, Württemberg, on the production of tea and coffee sets, tableware, hotel porcelain. The firm is no longer in operation.

Marks often incorporate the initials WPM and a coronet; examples resembling marks of the earlier Ludwigsburg factory also occur.
Refs: Danckert; Weiss.

Bauhaus. German school of design established at Weimar 1919, and operating and operating under the direction of the architect Walter Gropius (1883-1969) until 1928.

The ceramics department at Dornburg was under the control of G.*Marcks, who, with technical help from a skilled potter, taught apprentices including O.*Lindig, T.*Bogler and M.*Friedlander; R.*Bampi was employed for a short time. At first using soft earthenware, the workshop introduced a harder body, fired at a higher temperature and often unglazed, in the production of functional wares in bold, simple shapes

Bauhaus. Coffee pot made at the Bauhaus pottery in Dornburg, 1921-25.

emphasizing the qualities of the material and consciously derived from traditional local pottery. The Bauhaus pottery was the first department to design work for industrial production, e.g. porcelain designs made by the *Berlin and *Volkstedt-Rudolstadt factories. When the school moved to Dessau in 1925, the Dornburg pottery was taken over by Lindig for his own work and the training of students until the 1930s. Marcks moved to Halle, where Friedlander took over the running of the workshop on the lines established at Dornburg, allowing him to concentrate on ceramic sculpture. Experimentation with porcelain was made possible by the loan of a kiln from the Berlin factory, and work continued until 1935.
Refs: Bock; G. Naylor *The Bauhaus* (Studio Vista, London, 1968); W. Scheidig *Weimar Crafts of the Bauhaus* (Studio Vista, London, 1967).

Baumann, Hans Theo. *See* Rosenthal.

Baumgart. *See* Sèvres.

Baumgarten, Adolf. *See* Weingarten,

Bäuml, Albert. *See* Nymphenburg.

Baumler, Joseph. *See* Zoarite Pottery.

Baury, Charles. *See* Gille.

Bauscher Brothers. German porcelain manufacturers, August Bauscher (1849-1917) and Conrad Bauscher (1853-1910), formerly a painter in the *Tirschenreuth factory working from 1881 at Weiden (Oberpfalz). Their firm produced tableware for hotel, railway, shipping and institutional use, as well as chemical wares and heat-proof cooking utensils. They also produced table services in modern style with straight-sided dishes by the architect and designer Peter Behrens (1868-1940) in the early 20th century. The firm, a joint stock company from 1911, merged in 1927 with the company owned by Lorenz *Hutschenreuther.
Marks usually incorporate B over W in a circle, often with BAUSCHER/WEIDEN in full. The mark LUZIFER denotes a heat-resistant porcelain used for kitchen ware.
Refs: Danckert; Weiss.

Bawo & Dotter. *See* Guérin, William.

Baxter, Thomas (1782-1821). English porcelain painter. Baxter studied at the Royal Academy schools and worked as an independent decorator with his father at Gough Square, Clerkenwell, and from 1814 in their home town, *Worcester, where he also taught porcelain painting to apprentices. Baxter's own work, then carried out mainly on Chamberlain's and *Coalport wares, included figures, notably in scenes from Shakespeare or Scott's novels, views of gardens, studies of flowers, feathers, seashells and birds. For the firm of Flight, Barr & Barr, he painted figures in classical style; two display plates depict Mrs Siddons as the Tragic Muse. Dancing figures appear on a service made in 1815 for the Nabob of Oude. In Swansea for about 18 months from the spring of 1816, he painted botanical flowers on porcelain developed by W.*Billingsley and S.*Walker at the *Cambrian Pottery.

Thomas Baxter. A plate made at Coalport, painted with spring onions and long radishes and a gilt border of palmettes and scrollwork, while Baxter was in London. Signed by Baxter and dated 1809. 24 cm in diameter.

Baxter's painting is characterized by careful detail and finish. His figure subjects were delicately stippled, often in sepia, and birds, flowers, etc., executed in natural colours. He returned to Worcester in 1819, working there until his death.
Refs: S.W. Fisher *The Decoration of English Porcelain* (Derek Verschoyle, London, 1954); Godden (1970); Hobson; W.B. Honey 'German and English Decoration of Chinese Porcelain' in *Antiques* (March 1932); John; Nance; B. Rackham 'Mr. F. Hurlbutt's Collection of Pottery and Porcelain' in *The Connoisseur* 72 (August 1925); Sandon (1978b); Turner.

Bayeux. A French porcelain factory operating from c.1810 in a former Benedictine priory at Bayeux (Calvados) under J.*Langlois, who was assisted and succeeded by his wife Yvette Langlois (1779-1847) and daughters, Jenny and Sophie, until 1849; his son Frédéric helped in the production. Local kaolin gave the porcelain paste a greyish-blue tinge and enabled it to bear heat well. The paste became whiter and less heavy c.1840. The Langlois family made industrial ware and chemical and laboratory equipment, and produced a range of machine parts, etc., previously made in other materials. Their output also included decorative ware, initially in Empire style and later inspired by Japanese decoration in red, blue and gold, sometimes with medallions or oriental scenes, large butterflies or fantastic birds. Joachim Langlois also made his own interpretations of Chinese pieces with heavy relief decoration.
Despite financial difficulties which demanded an increase in her output of laboratory equipment, his widow continued to produce everyday domestic ware and a few decorative pieces, in which she maintained the Korean or Japanese inspiration, with blue predominating, although the range of high temperature colours was extended. She reintroduced versions of the 18th-century French *décor à barbeaux* in blue, green and gold. Also characteristic of this period, and reminiscent of contemporary Paris styles in decoration, were subjects in full relief, for which Bayeux became noted. A little later, decoration, predominantly in blue and gold,

was again inspired by oriental wares. Sketchy figures and apple blossom, outlined in black, were distantly derived from Canton wares.
Jenny and Sophie Langlois continued simpler versions of their parents' oriental-inspired designs until their sale of the factory in 1849 to the Paris decorator François Gosse, succeeded briefly 1870-73 by his son, Paul. In decoration, François Gosse concentrated on mythological subjects or Egyptian motifs and introduced a design of apples executed in underglaze blue. Paul Gosse and his widow gradually discontinued the decorative ware, retaining only the apple design, patterns of daisies in blue, and cornflowers in blue with dark green foliage, together with underglaze blue patterns. Their successors, Jules Morlent and his family, produced only utilitarian and industrial wares until the sale of the factory in 1951.
Marks: Chinese-style seals, painted in underglaze blue; *J.L. Bayeux*, painted in red (1812-30). Several marks incorporating *Ve Langlois* or *Ve L* in underglaze blue or green enamel; impressed mark *Bayeux* with date. Gosse's marks incorporate his name or add G to a *Veuve Langlois* mark. Morlent: BX in black or green.
Refs: Chavagnac & Grollier; Danckert; Ernould-Gandouet; Lesur (1967).

Bayreuth. German faience works established 1714, acquired by Prince George Wilhelm of Bayreuth in 1724 and working until 1835. The factory was sold in 1806 to Christoph Friedrich Leers (b 1769), who was succeeded by his widow until her death in 1825, followed by Johann Christian Schmidt, producer of creamware and porcelain until 1835. The faience was known for fine decoration, which included armorial painting. Work was supplied for painting by outside decorators.
Mark: B.K.
Ref: Hüseler.

Beardmore, Evelyn Hope (c.1886-1972). English ceramic decorator, born in Stoke-on-Trent. Hope Beardmore (sometimes referred to in ceramic literature as Hilda) was engaged on the painting of powder-blue wares at the Wedgwood factory, later starting work for B.*Moore, probably during World War I. Her subjects include birds, fish, water plants, and scrolled or trailing foliage. Some patterns contain elements of Middle Eastern or oriental design, others resemble the work of W.*De Morgan.
Mark: painted monogram of HB.
Refs: Batkin; A. Dawson *Bernard Moore* (Richard Dennis, London, 1982).

Beardmore, Frank, & Co. Staffordshire earthenware manufacturers, working 1903-14 at the Sutherland Pottery, which had been established c.1884 at Fenton. The firm continued production of tableware and toilet sets of high quality in semi-porcelain or ivory-toned earthenware and used some shapes and patterns bought from the firm of W.E.*Brownfield, which failed in 1898. The output of art ware included two lines of Grecian inspiration: Basaltine (shapes copied from Greek originals, decorated with figures after Greek drawings against a dull, black ground) and Athenian (decorated with figures and coloured drapery on shapes which were taken to be Grecian in origin, but included an albarello). The decoration of a line marketed as Sutherland Art Ware includes simple designs from the work of Kate Greenaway, and a variety of subjects including girls bathing, windmills or floral patterns on elegant Art Nouveau shapes, advertised in 1906. A series decorated with country scenes featuring a cottage and elm trees by a stream with a red punt was entitled A Bit of Old Country.

Marks: several, printed or impressed, incorporating initials F.B. & CO.; Sutherland Art Ware marked with a dove in a circular band bearing the firm's full name and FENTON, over the name of the ware, printed.
Refs: Bedford; Blacker (1911); Godden (1974a); Jewitt.

bear jug. Pottery jug moulded in the shape of a bear, with detachable head acting as cup or lid. The animal is normally fighting with a dog, which may act as the jug's spout. Examples were made in Austria in the 16th century. In England, they were made in white or brown stoneware in the 18th century and in enamelled earthenware in the 18th and early 19th centuries, especially in Staffordshire and Yorkshire.

Beattie, William (1829-67) English sculptor and modeller; exhibitor at the Royal Academy, 1829-64. Beattie's work includes models for Mintons, Copeland and the *Adams family; for Wedgwood (1856-64), he modelled biblical and allegorical figures and groups. His work was in neo-classical style.
Ref: Batkin.

Beau et Porquer. *See* Loc Maria.

Beaver Falls Art Tile Co. American tile company formed in 1886 at Beaver Falls, Pennsylvania, by F.W. Walker, manager, who also undertook the development of glazes. Starting with plain, enamelled tiles, the company soon introduced relief decoration, making a speciality of stove tiles with high-quality glazes that withstood heat without crazing. Rich, transparent glazes in blue, greys tinged with purple or green, other pastel shades, dark brown, etc., were used of tiles showing portraits (often with relief border in contrasting colour) or on full-length figures. A profile of George Washington against a background of stars is well known. I.*Broome provided designs depicting Sappho, large panels representing music, poetry and painting, and several floral panels. M.*Morgan was employed as a modeller. The company was taken over in 1927 and closed three years later.

Mark: BEAVER FALLS/PA in relief or impressed; B.F.A.T.CO.
Refs: Barnard, Kovel & Kovel.

Bechyň, Fachschule für Thonindustrie. State-run trade school for ceramics founded at Bechyn, Czechoslovakia, in 1884 to train potters and provide services and further training for local potters. The work of students, in earthenware, stoneware and porcelain, with a wide range of decorative techniques, and first exhibited at the winter exhibition of the Oesterreichisches Museum für Kunst und Industrie in Vienna in 1898,

bear jug. Earthenware jug and cover in the form of a bear hugging a dog which forms the spout, mid 19th century. Marked J. Morris, Stoke, impressed. 31 cm high.

included figures, vases, and other ornamental wares, sometimes inspired by local folk wares. A display of pieces in Vienna, 1910, included pieces with *flambé*, *sang-de-boeuf* and crystalline glazes, as well as slip-painted wares.
Ref: Neuwirth (1974b).

Beck, Hatton (b 1901) and Lucy. Australian potters. Hatton Beck was born in Victoria and studied at Melbourne Technical College before taking up potting at home in 1927, while he was working as a tilemaker. In 1930, he began work for the *Fowler family at Thomastown. He married Lucy Boyd in 1939, and the same year established a pottery at Murrumbeena, which was sold to A.*Boyd after World War II. Beck was pottery instructor at Brisbane's Central Technical College, 1948-60. Since 1950, Lucy and Hatton Beck have been best known for their decorated ceramic tiles.

Beck, Josiah. *See* Womelsdorf.

Beckett's Pottery. *See* Winchcombe Pottery.

Beddow or **Beddowes,** George (b c.1790). Ceramic decorator, born in Swansea, Wales, where he worked until the 1830s in pottery and porcelain; he is believed to have painted landscapes. He was in Staffordshire, possibly working at the *Ridgway factory, in 1851.
Refs: Godden (1972); W. Scarratt *Old Times in the Potteries* (privately published, 1906).

Bedford Works. *See* Ridgway Potteries Ltd.

Bee, William. Porcelain painter working for the *Worcester Royal Porcelain Co. from his apprenticeship c.1918 until the 1930s, and specializing in studies of fruit.
Ref: Sandon (1978a).

Beech, Ralph Bagnall (1810-1857). London-born potter. Beech worked at the Wedgwood factory before emigrating to America

in 1842. He was employed by A.*Miller before establishing his own earthenware pottery in 1845 at Kensington, Philadelphia. He made vases, etc., with a ground of black or blue enamel decorated with mother-of-pearl inlaid by a process which Beech had patented in 1851. He also produced vases, often in panelled shapes, with enamelled portraits of prominent personalities. A relief pitcher portraying the head of Daniel O'Connell, Irish patriot, from an original made by Doulton & Co. in London, moulded in several sizes and glazed in yellow or brown, was produced at the *Haig Pottery after the closure of the Beech business. Beech retired in 1857 and set out for the Honduras, where he died of yellow fever soon after his arrival.

Marks: RALPH B. BEECH/KENSINGTON, P.A. impressed.
Ref: Barber (1976).

Beeley, W. *See* Billingsley, William.

Beerbower & Griffen. *See* Griffen, Smith & Hill.

Belding or **Belden,** David (b 1813). American stoneware potter, born in Whately, Massachusetts, and son-in-law of Thomas Crafts (*see* Crafts family). At Whately, he made a small stoneware churn impressed with *D. Belding* and the place name. He owned land in South Ashfield, Massachusetts, by 1837, and probably moved from there in the early 1840s. He worked with Walter Orcutt (1799-1854), a maker of stoneware (1848-50) at South Ashfield, distributing the pottery's wares as Orcutt, Belding & Co. Belding married a widow, Sybil Stanley, in 1845 and with his wife's brother, Wellington Hastings, owned Orcutt's share in the pottery, 1850-54. He produced one of the very few examples of New England stoneware to have relief decoration, which features a figure of George Washington flanked by floral sprays in cobalt blue. Hastings & Belding were succeeded in

David Belding. A wooden-lidded stoneware water cooler decorated with an applied figure of George Washington moulded from a cast-iron stove decoration, and sprays of fuchsia in cobalt blue, 1850-54. Stamped Hastings & Belding/Ashfield, Mass. *35 cm.*

John and Matthew Bell. Plate with decoration designed exclusively for export to South-East Asia, late 19th century.

1854 by an employee, Staats Van Loon, in partnership with George Washington Boyden (1830-58), and Orcutt's partner, the businessman, John Guildford, who had retained his third share in the firm, but the pottery closed in 1856. Stoneware was made at the pottery from New Jersey clay, fired to light brown, buff or bluish grey, and salt-glazed. Decoration was usually a flower spray trailed from a quill in cobalt blue or, occasionally, dashes of brown. Brown or black slip, used to line jugs, storage jars and churns, also frequently covered the entire surface of undecorated pieces. Figures include a moulded dog, completely covered under the glaze with cobalt blue and made by van Loon, a toy bank made as a gift for Belding's stepdaughter, and other presentation pieces. A water cooler made by Hastings & Belding features a low-relief design of Diana with a deer.

Marks stamped: *Orcutt, Guildford & Co* (1848-50); *Hastings & Belding* (1850-54); *Van Loon & Bouden* (1854-56). Makers' names often appear over *Ashfield, Mass.*; place name sometimes stamped alone.
Refs: Stradling; Watkins (1950).

Belfield, Charles (b 1788). Potter, working in Scotland. Belfield was an employee and, from 1812, owner of the *Bankfoot Pottery, where his firm produced creamware dinner and dessert services from clay obtained near Dalkeith. He followed Robert and George Gordon, former owners of Bankfoot pottery (for whom he was working in 1808) to their works at Cuttle when the Gordon estate was dissolved, and produced brown-glazed earthenware, including teapots in many shapes, as well as sanitary and drainage ware. The Cuttle pottery became associated with tableware decorated with leaves, or sometimes in leaf shapes, and with a range of lead glazes richly coloured with metallic oxides. Belfield was in partnership with his son James from 1836, trading as Charles Belfield & Son from the 1840s, and their firm remained in the hands of the Belfield family until the 1930s.
Refs: Fleming; McVeigh.

Bell, Isaac. *See* Ouseburn Bridge Pottery; Phoenix Pottery.

Bell, John (d 1880) and Perston, Matthew (d 1869). Scottish potters who established the Glasgow Pottery in the early 19th century for the production of fireclay and sanitary ware and garden pottery. Their firm made bone china, semi-porcelain and white earthenware from the 1840s and soon afterwards introduced parian ware and terracotta. Among the firm's display in the Great Exhibition (1851) were stoneware dinner services decorated with views of the Italian lakes printed in blue, or flower designs in mulberry with a blue border, teasets in stoneware and bone china, storage containers and wine coolers in drab stoneware, parian ware vases and jugs, and large vases in terracotta. Pieces in bone china were frequently painted with flowers, fruit or Scottish views, and some vases were decorated with Roman military subjects in raised white enamel on a black enamel ground. Late in its working life, the pottery produced granite ware and bone china tableware in large quantities, earthenware, including dessert services with hand-painted floral decoration enclosed in perforated borders, and parian vases decorated with figures in relief.

The founders' company was succeeded in 1910 by the partnership of Joseph Turner and John Weir, who continued until 1940.

Marks: a bell impressed or printed; after 1869, B or JB inside the bell; printed marks with bell inside a belt (c.1881-1928).
Refs: Blacker (1911); Godden (1964).

Bell, Thomas. *See* Fell, Thomas, & Co.

Bell, Vanessa (1879-1961). English painter and designer. In ceramics, she was primarily interested in decoration. She visited the workshop in Mitcham, Surrey, where R.*Fry first learned pottery techniques, and carried out abstract geometrical patterns or figure subjects on ceramics (probably among those made by *Carter & Co.) for the *Omega Workshops. With D.*Grant, she decorated slip-cast wares made by P.*Keyes in London in the 1920s and 1930s. She was among the artists commissioned by C.*Cliff and the firm of Wilkinson & Co. to decorate tableware which was exhibited in 1934.
Refs: Hawkins; Watkins *et al*; P. Wentworth-Shields & K. Johnson *Clarice Cliff* (L'Odeon, London, 1976).

Bell family. A family of potters working throughout the 19th century in the Shenandoah Valley in Virginia, Maryland and West Virginia. They produced red ware decorated with brightly coloured slips and glazes, and dark grey stoneware with decoration in cobalt blue with purplish tinge, or manganese brown.

Peter Bell (1775-1847) was the son of a German emigrant who had reached America from Wiesbaden by 1767; Bell was born in Hagerstown (then Elizabeth Town), Maryland, where he made pottery, selling earthenware by 1805. He ran a pottery at Winchester, Virginia, 1824-45, chiefly producing red ware for domestic use, but he introduced stoneware in 1832. Among his earliest known marked work is a wide bowl, banded and trailed on the interior and rim with coloured slips, and equipped with handles, which was of a shape and decorative treatment later used by other members of the family. His

sons, John, Samuel and Solomon, all worked at the Winchester pottery. When marked, his work was stamped *P. Bell*.

John Bell (1800-80), born in Hagerstown, accompanied his family to Winchester in 1824, then ran a pottery in Chambersburg, Pennsylvania, from 1827 and moved to Waynesboro in the same state in 1833. He made red ware and stoneware for household use; special pieces included an earthenware inkwell with pale glaze and brushed decoration in blue, marked *J. Bell* and made at his father's Winchester pottery in 1825; figures of animals, e.g. lions with strands of clay representing mane, tail tip and whiskers, spaniels closely resembling Staffordshire dogs, with dark, flowing glaze, or painted and sponged decoration in oil-based paint; a figure of a boy carrying fruit, entirely glazed with brown. He used the marks *J. Bell*, later *John Bell*, and then *John Bell, Waynesboro*, all stamped.

He was succeeded in 1880 by his eldest son, John W. Bell (d 1895), who made primarily useful wares (stamped mark, *John W. Bell, Waynesboro, Pa.*), and in 1895 by a younger son, Upton, who continued production of utilitarian wares (stamped *Upton Bell, Waynesboro*).

Samuel Bell (b 1811). Worked with his father, Peter Bell, before buying a pottery in Strasburg, Virginia, where he worked until his death. As well as continuing the output of everyday wares, he made many special pieces in red ware and stoneware, often for relatives and friends. He often used bands of small, impressed elliptical and circular motifs at rims, etc. A picture frame with modelled fruit and flowers is surmounted by an eagle, and his pottery was noted for small, moulded animal figures, especially dogs and cats. Large pieces include handled bowls and water coolers. Decorated stoneware has rich designs of plants, notably tulips, in cobalt blue; an unusual jar has four silhouettes of a horse, lightly stamped and filled with cobalt blue, as well as sprays of flowers brushed on in blue. Samuel Bell left production largely to his brother, Solomon, who joined the pottery in 1837, while himself concentrating on the pottery's business affairs. He was succeeded by his sons, Richard Franklin Bell (1845-1908) and Charles Forrest Bell (1864-1933).

Samuel Bell's marks include *S. Bell*, stamped, sometimes in raised letters; *S. Bell & Sons, Strasburg*, 1882-1904; *Bell*, impressed, 1904 until closure of the pottery in 1908.

Solomon Bell (1817-82), son of Peter Bell, joined his brother Samuel at the pottery in Strasburg, 1837. His work sometimes features lion motifs, e.g. lion's head handles on a red ware vase, or handles which end in an indentation made with a finger tip (especially on jugs, which are often inverted at the lip). His animal figures include a red ware whippet, made at Winchester and marked with his full name and the place, incised in script, lions made as gifts for relatives, and spaniel dogs moulded in red ware. A neo-classical figure of a woman in flowing robe (dated 1862) has head and neck coated in white slip, while the rest of the figure and the base are covered with dark brown oil-based paint. Solomon Bell's stoneware includes an elaborately decorated water cooler with modelled handles, incised

and applied motifs, and tulips painted in cobalt blue.
Refs: Barber (1976); Rice & Stoudt; Stradling; Webster; Wiltshire.

Belle, La. *See* Avon Faience Co.

Belleek factory. Irish porcelain factory established in 1857 on the River Erne in Co. Fermanagh, near its borders with Co. Donegal. The firm, originally trading as D. McBirney & Co., was noted for a thin, light porcelain paste containing feldspar (and thus a type of parian ware), rich ivory in colour, with iridescent glaze, which was used to make decorative tableware, mainly ornamented with elaborately modelled natural forms. The ware was developed with the assistance of W.*Bromley and other workmen from the factory of W.H.*Goss. A tea service made for Queen Victoria used shapes inspired by sea urchins, resting on pieces of branched coral, while a service for the Prince of Wales which was shown in the International Exhibition (1872) included fluted dishes supported by sea creatures (merpeople, white horses, dolphins) and shells. The delicate eggshell paste was tinted, gilt or left unglazed; matt and nacreous finishes sometimes appear on the same piece. Perforated decoration and woven parian basketwork may be further ornamented with applied flowers or shells in teasets. Some vases have painted decoration. Many of the original designs remain in production. The factory's other products included earthenware made from local clays, ironstone, coloured stonewares and white porcelain in a variety of styles, as well as laboratory and sanitary ware. Lithophanes were made and marked FERMANAGH/POTTERY until 1890.
    The factory's normal marks were BELLEEK CO. FERMANAGH, impressed or in relief, and a device comprising a wolfhound, a tower and a harp; occasionally a harp surmounted with a crown was impressed or printed.
Refs: Blacker (1922a); Collard; C. Eastlake *Hints on Household Taste* (1868); Godden (1961); Jewitt; J. Price, letter in *Country Life* (27th March 1958); G.M. Smith *Belleek Porcelain and Pottery* (Toucan Press, 1979).

Belleek ware. In America, delicate porcelain resembling ware produced at the *Belleek factory in Ireland. Makers included *Ott & Brewer in the mid 1880s, the *Ceramic Art Co., the *Columbian Art Pottery Co., the *Cook Pottery Co. and *Willet's Manufacturing Co.

Bellefroid, Edmond. *See* Regout, Petrus.

Belleview or **Bellevue Pottery.** Sussex pottery, established by F.*Mitchell at his home, Belleview, and in production from 1869. The output of ornamental earthenware, advertised as 'Sussex Rustic Ware', includes an extension of the green-glazed wares developed by Mitchell at his father's *Cadborough Pottery, and a line of vases, jugs, bowls, *jardinières*, etc., in brown clay, sometimes given a bark-like texture with a scattering of pigments that flowed in the glaze during firing; handles and other details were often green-glazed. The similar Hop Ware included candlesticks, jugs, jars, and

Belleek factory. Spill vases in the form of Irish potato pickers, with clothes in pink lustre and rockwork bases in green and brown lustre. Marked Belleek, Co. Fermanagh. 18 cm high.

vases in a speckled brown body with relief decoration of plant forms, mainly hops, glazed green.
    Frederick Mitchell was succeeded by his widow, who produced decorative pieces including imitations of Mycenean pottery (marketed as Trojan Ware) and other wares, jugs and vases in twisted shapes achieved by bending thrown pieces before firing, and models of carpenters' bags with tools. In 1882, she took into the business her nephew, Frederick T. Mitchell (1864-1920), who succeeded her on her death in 1895 and produced wares similar to those of his uncle, but characterized by sharper, more detailed modelling. Some examples of Hop Ware with relief designs on a buff body were sold in the biscuit state. He also produced jugs, vases and other items hand-modelled in miniature and usually glazed brown or green, jugs in the shape of pigs (traditional ale containers associated with Sussex since the 18th century), and beads and miniature items with iridescent glaze, usually in blue or yellow.
    The firm was sold by F.T. Mitchell's widow in 1930 and, after closing through the war years, reopened in 1947 under John C. and Walter V. Cole, who made slip-decorated or white-glazed wares with decoration in modern style, while continuing such lines as Sussex pigs.
    Marks: the initials S R W (on Sussex Rustic Ware) and *Rye* filling the angles made by two crossed lines or, on small articles, the place name, *Rye*, incised from 1869; impressed or printed marks used by the Cole company incorporate the name, *Rye*, or *Rye Pottery*.
Refs: Brears (1974); C. Dawson 'Sussex Pottery' in *Sussex Archaeological Collections* 46 (1903); Godden (1964); Jewitt; Lloyd Thomas (1974).

Belle Vue Pottery. Yorkshire pottery established 1802 in Hull by Joseph Hipwood and potters, James and Jeremiah Smith, all of Hull, with Job *Ridgway. The Smith brothers went bankrupt in 1806, assigning their interest to Job and his brother G.*Ridgway who together ran the pottery for a short time. The premises were taken over in 1826 by William Bell, who extended the pottery and

worked there until the closure of the works in 1841, exporting many of his products to Germany (through a Hamburg depot managed by his brother Edward) and the Netherlands. Earthenware for domestic use was printed with a variety of landscapes, etc., or banded with blue or brown slip and ornamented with swirls of trailed slip (usually in white, blue and dark brown) or mocha decoration; rims were sometimes engine turned. Painted decoration consisted of floral designs in blue, pink, yellow, orange and grey; some lustre colours were used. Teapots with high arched covers were characteristic from 1826.
    Marks include: BELLE VUE POTTERY HULL impressed or blue printed in a circle around two overlapping bells; the bells device without lettering; BELLE VUE. Much ware was unmarked.
Refs: Bartlett & Brooks *Hull Pottery* (Kingston-upon-Hull Museums Bulletin No 5); Grabham; Hurst; Jewitt; Lawrence; T. Sheppard 'The Belle Vue Pottery, Hull' in *The Transactions of the British Ceramic Society* Vol 40 (1941).

Belper Pottery. Derbyshire pottery established c.1740 for the production of brown saltglaze. Under William Bourne, proprietor from the 1770s, the pottery made a range of bottles, including pistol-shaped flasks, bottles for blacking, beer or mineral water, as well as mugs, jugs, loving-cups, punchbowls and, after 1820, cordial bottles, of which the top half was in the form of a human figure down to waist level, with its head pierced for the stopper. The owner was succeeded by his son J.*Bourne, who transferred the workforce and equipment to his pottery at Denby in 1834.
    Impressed marks usually incorporate BELPER—much work was unmarked.
Refs: Jewitt; Oswald.

Bemrose, H.W.& W. *See* Derby.

Bendigo Pottery. Australian pottery established 1857 (initially as the Epsom Pottery) at Bendigo, formerly Sandhurst, Victoria, by a Scottish potter, George Guthrie (c.1828-1910), who built up an output of kitchen and table ware, vases, etc., with Rockingham and other coloured glazes. The pottery also produced stoneware storage jars, etc. with Bristol glaze. Guthrie left for a time in the 1880s to return to Britain, but rejoined the pottery, with a partner, by 1898, when he introduced stylistic elements which resemble those of the *Alloa Pottery. The production of majolica and Rockingham-glazed ware, including teapots, jugs, tobacco jars and serving dishes, continued into the 20th century, alongside sanitary and drainage wares. White-bodied earthenware introduced in the early 20th century included decorated teaware. Much of the ware was moulded, and such pieces as jugs in the form of portraits of military leaders were sold in large quantities in World War I. Langley Ware, a line of brown glazed tableware for domestic and café use, continued in production until the 1930s. Sets consisting of teapot, sugarbowl and jug were made with mottled or shaded glazes in blues or beige, or uniform shades of blue, green or yellow. The pottery also made vases, flower bowls in the 1930s and 1950s under the name Waverley ware, and a small output of vases and bowls in agate ware, as well as household jugs with surface marbling in shades of brown. The pottery side of the business has been revived since 1968.

Mark: *Bendigo Pottery*, impressed.
Ref: Graham; P. Scholes *The Bendigo Pottery* (Kilmore, 1979).

Bengtsson, Hertha (b 1917). Swedish potter and designer. While working at the *Rörstrand factory, 1941-64, she created designs for everyday porcelain as well as boxes, bowls and other individual pieces in porcelain or stoneware. She is noted for her decorative use of the contrast between matt and glossy glazes. She left Rörstrand to work in partnership with John Andersson at Höganäs, near Elsinore (1965-69). Her tableware and unique pieces in stoneware won a gold medal at Faenza in 1966. Since 1969 she has worked as a freelance designer for the firm of *Rosenthal.
Refs: Hettes & Rada; *Rosenthal Hundert Jahre Porzellan* (catalogue, Kestner-Museum, Hannover, 1982); *Three Centuries of Swedish Pottery* (catalogue, Victoria & Albert Museum, London, 1959).

Benham, C. *See* Muncie Pottery.

Bennet, E. *See* Bailey, C.J.C.

Bennett, Edwin (1818-1908). English-born potter, working in America. He joined his brother James *Bennett in Ohio, 1841-44, and established a pottery in Baltimore, Maryland (1846), working from c.1848 with his brother, William, who retired c.1856; the partnership traded as E.& W. Bennett. The brothers produced unglazed porcelain jugs, coffee pots, vases, etc., in a hard grey-green or blue body with relief decoration. An earthenware teapot depicting Rebekah at the Well (1852) from a Staffordshire design, and initially produced with a Rockingham glaze, was among many jugs with decoration modelled by C.*Coxon (between 1850 and c.1862). The firm made large jugs with moulded decoration of fish, lobsters and shells, covered with a light blue glaze, busts (e.g. of George Washington), and *jardinières* with relief decoration and high-quality glazes in shades of blue, green and lemon yellow. Decorative vases, coffee pots, etc. have blue, brown or olive-green mottled glazes. Tableware was made in white earthenware or semi-porcelain after the enlargement of the pottery in 1869, sometimes with transfer-printed decoration. Parian porcelain and Belleek ware were made in the 1880s; parian plaques, modelled by Priestman, were produced in 1887. The firm became the Edwin Bennett Pottery Co. in 1890 and introduced porcelain tableware, tea and toilet sets, notably with underglaze decoration in blue, and gilding.

After the World's Columbian Exposition in Chicago (1893), Bennett's company started production of art wares. The Brubensul line of earthenware, named after Henry Brunt, manager, Bennett and another member of the firm called Sullivan and introduced in 1894, was a brilliantly glazed majolica— mainly *jardinières* and pedestals—with glazes in orange, crimson, blue, green and shades of brown which mingled in firing. Albion ware (1895-97) was decorated with slip in muted colours painted, generally on a

green ground, under a transparent glaze. Designs were hunting scenes in desert or jungle, featuring animals and parties of hunters, carried out notably by Kate DeWitt Berg, who trained at the School of Industrial Art of Pennsylvania Museum; other Albion ware was decorated by Annie Haslam Brinton. The pottery continued after Bennett's death, finally closing in 1936. His son, Edwin Houston Bennett, worked at the *Chesapeake Pottery, where he experimented with kilns and pottery techniques.

Marks include globe pierced by a sword through the United States and motto BONA FAMA EST MELIOR ZONA AUREA; E. BENNETT POTTERY Co. around year, with *Albion*; *E.B.P. Co.* in shield or diamond or in coronet surrounded by wreath; Brubensul marked with paper label including pierced globe.
Refs: Barber (1976); Evans; Kovel & Kovel; Lehner.

Bennett, James (1812-62). English-born potter, working in America after leaving Derbyshire in 1834. Bennett was employed at the *Jersey City Pottery until 1837, then by the Indiana Pottery Co., manufacturers of white ware in Troy, for one year. Finding the area bad for his health, he moved to East Liverpool, Ohio, and built a small pottery, among the first in the area, in 1839, producing mugs, pans and kitchen utensils in yellow ware made from local clay. He was joined in 1841 by his brothers, Daniel, William and Edwin, in a firm which then traded as Bennett & Brothers and started to produce Rockingham ware. In 1841, the firm built a larger factory at Birmingham (Pittsburgh), Pennsylvania, winning prizes for Rockingham and yellow wares in exhibitions in New York and (in 1846) Philadelphia. E.*Bennett left to build his own pottery in Baltimore in 1846, followed two years later by his brother William, and they subsequently traded as E.& W. Bennett.

Mark: *Bennett Bros* from 1844.
Refs: Barber (1976); Clement (1947); Evans; Kovel & Kovel; Lehner.

Bennett, John. English-born potter. Previously employed in Doulton's Lambeth faience workshop, Bennett moved to America in 1876, settling temporarily in New York City. He built a kiln in Lexington Avenue, where he carried out underglaze decoration, at first on biscuit ware imported from England, and then employing potters to make cream-coloured earthenware. He also used white ware made in Trenton, New Jersey. Bennett selected simple shapes for decoration, with flowers and foliage boldly sketched from natural specimens in a palette which included mustard yellow, dark blues and rust. The background was then laid in delicate shades, and the design outlined in black under a fine, glossy glaze. Bennett also decorated unglazed pieces with coloured slips in the style of the 'Limoges faience' made in Cincinnati. He moved in 1882 to Orange Mountains, New Jersey, but is thought to have completed little work there.

Marks: *J. Bennett NY*; later *West Orange NJ*.
Refs: Barber (1976); Kovel & Kovel.

Bennett's Pottery. Australian pottery established by Charles Bennett at Magill, South Australia, by 1868. The output of domestic stoneware included jugs and storage jars. After Bennett's death or retirement, the pottery traded as Charles Bennett & Sons from 1904, making household and farm ware, together with vases glazed in brown and other colours. Art lines were introduced in the 1930s. The pottery remains in the hands of the Bennett family to the present day.

Mark: Charles Bennett's name impressed; a variety of impressed marks incorporating *W.C. Bennett; Bennett/Adelaide* incised in script.
Ref: Graham.

Bennington. *See* Fenton, Christopher Webber; Norton, John; Norton, Julius; Norton, Luman.

Benthall Works. *See* Maw & Co.

Béranger, Antoine (1785-1867). French porcelain decorator; born in Sèvres (Seine-et-Oise). At first a painter of still-lifes and historical subjects, Béranger then painted porcelain at the Sèvres factory, 1807-46, notably figure subjects celebrating the victories of Napoleon. His daughter, Suzanne-Estelle Apoil (b 1825), was his pupil and a painter of flowers and fruit at the factory 1865-92.
Refs: Bénézit; Lesur (1967).

Berbas. *See* Porceleyne Fles, De.

Berg, Kate De Witt. *See* Bennett, Edwin.

Berger family. *See* Saint-Brice.

Berlage, Hendricus Petrus (1856-1934). Dutch architect, designer of ceramics, metalwork and furniture, born in Amsterdam. He studied in Zurich 1875-78, and under the architect, Gottfried Semper, in Dresden. He was a co-founder of 't *Binnenhuis in 1900 and in the same year designed tiles and dinner ware for the *Holland factory.

Mark: painted monogram.
Refs: *H.P. Berlage, bouwmeester 1856-1934* (catalogue, Gemeentesmuseum, The Hague, 1975); Haslam (1977); Scheen; Singelenberg-van der Meer; Thieme & Becker.

Berlin Königliche (later **Staatliche**) **Porzellan-Manufaktur**. German porcelain factory established by Frederick the Great in 1763, and continued under a Commission set up by King Friedrich Wilhelm III (1786-97). The neo-classical treatment which predominated in the factory's output from 1786 was replaced by elements of the Empire style before the French occupation of Prussia in 1806, which caused severe financial problems for the factory, but failed to halt technical developments in paste, glazes, etc. The defeat

Berlin. Display cup and saucer, painted with flowers and a sepia portrait, 1829. Marked with a sceptre, in blue. 14.5 cm.

Berlin. Group, Europa and the bull, modelled by Adolph Amberg, 1904-05, and produced at Berlin, 1913.

of Napoleon in 1815 was followed by a period of lavish decoration, with ceramic jewels, elaborate gilding and bronze effects, as well as borders in the style of mosaics used on table services, and vases in a new range of shapes. Services ordered as royal gifts, sometimes in honour of military generals, include a setting consisting of about 470 pieces designed for the Duke of Wellington with table decoration of an obelisk, and allegorical figures modelled by the sculptor Johann Gottfried Schadow, and one for the Russian Imperial court with a centrepiece inspired by the Flora Farnese in Rome.

Vases and plates were decorated with city views, buildings, etc., in the manner of oil paintings framed with lavish gilding. Botanical studies and still lifes of flowers and fruit also occurred frequently in painted decoration. Lithophanes were made from c.1830. Figures, all in biscuit porcelain polished with hardwood to resemble marble in texture, included models after classical statuary and marble busts of Prussian generals, etc. Portrait plaques were produced in large numbers.

From c.1840, the production of elaborate ornamental wares continued alongside an increasing output of porcelain made at a lower cost for a wide middle-class market.

Technical achievements were outstanding and stylistic elements were drawn from an increasing range of sources. A commission appointed by the Prussian parliament by 1878 criticised the factory's artistic values, also recommending a fresh approach in the development of pastes and glazes. The research director, H.*Seger, perfected a new paste, *Segerporzellan*, at this time, and soon afterwards developed *sang de boeuf* and crackle glazes. His assistant and successor, the chemist Albert Heinecke, achieved a crystalline glaze, based on titanium dioxide, which was later used on pieces in Art Nouveau styles. Vases in the 1880s often featured dark ground colours with relief ornament and flowers painted in enamels and gold. From 1902, T.*Schmuz-Baudiss created many new designs, often using underglaze pigments. His work includes the Ceres range of tableware, with a flowing design of two horns of plenty painted overglaze on the rims of plates, etc., and accompanied on some pieces by an arched, openwork design.

A series of figures entitled 'Wedding March' which incorporated 22 designs representing various nationalities in celebration of the Crown Prince's marriage in 1905 was produced 1908-10, a series of costume studies,

1908-14. Figures of children were designed by Hermann Hubatsch (in Berlin from 1903), and many animal models by Carl Wilhelm Robra (a factory artist) and A.*Puchegger.

Trading from 1918 as the National Porcelain Manufacture, the factory came under the control of Nicola Moufang (1925-28) and Count Günther von Pechmann (1928-38), who both fostered the artistic aims of the Deutscher Werkbund and the Bauhaus. In collaboration from 1929 with the School of Applied Arts in Halle, the factory produced functional designs by M.*Wildenhain and later H.*Griemert. The Urbino service designed by T.*Petri-Raben and characterized by simple oval forms gained the Grand Prix for the factory at the Paris Exposition in 1937. Painted decoration, produced in smaller quantities, included animals and flowers in Japanese style by Adolf Flad, geometrical patterns and stylized plants by Ernst Böhm, plants and fish by Else Mockel. In modelling, P.*Scheurich (from 1918) initiated a revival of rococo elements in style, and Richard Scheibe, Edwin Scharff and Ludwig Gies created figures (often abstract) and portrait plaques. M.A.*Pfeiffer was director of the factory, 1938-45. The buildings suffered bomb damage in 1943, and new works opened at Weiden (Oberpfalz) and Mayerhofen (near Karlsbad), while work also continued at the former Paul Müller factory at Selb from 1942, and a new Berlin factory. Production resumed in 1949 at enlarged premises on the original site, and the factory was reunited with the Selb branch in the mid 1950s. Many of the recent styles represent a return to the factory's earlier work, in response to market demands.

Marks include, in the mid 19th century, orb or eagle holding sceptre, printed, or sceptre, printed or impressed, both often

Berlin. Rectangular plaque depicting a harem. Marked with a sceptre and KPM *impressed, 1837-44. 20 x 32 cm.*

Berlin. Teapot, with painted cornflowers and gilding from a service made at the Berlin factory c.1850. Circular mark, Prussian eagle and sceptre.

Berlin. Porcelain vase with intaglio *decoration. Marked with a sceptre in blue and the designer's mark. 21.5 cm.*

with KPM or KOENIGLICHE PORZELLAN-MANUFAKTUR; printed sceptre from 1870.
Refs: J. Erzgraber *Königlich Berlin 1763 bis 1913* (Berlin, 1913); E. Köllmann *Berliner Porzellan 1763-1963* (Brunswick, 1966), *Berliner Porzellan,* (Brunswick, 1960); G. Lenz *Berliner Porzellan* (Berlin, 1913).

Bernard, François. *See* Islettes, Les.

Bernard, Joseph. *See* Apt (Vaucluse).

Bernardaud, L., & Cie. French porcelain manufacturers working in Limoges. Leonard Bernardaud worked for some years at the de la Taupinière factory (established 1863) before becoming a partner in the firm in 1895, and manager for the new proprietors from 1901. He opened a New York office (1911), to be run by his son, Jacques Bernardaud (b c.1888), and in 1919 bought the factory, taking his sons into the company: Michel Bernardaud (c.1896-1949) was technical director until his death, while his brother Jacques was administrator and artistic director. The firm's work included tableware with bands of decoration in gold with red, blue or black, and multicoloured designs of leaves, as well as vases and other ornamental pieces, shown in the Paris Exposition Internationale des Arts Décoratifs et Industriels Modernes in 1925.

In 1949, the firm installed the first effective tunnel kiln in Limoges. Jacques Bernardaud was president of the firm from its reorganization in 1955 until his retirement in 1962. He was succeeded by his nephew (and for twelve years assistant), Pierre.

Marks: B & CO/LIMOGES/FRANCE under the glaze; BERNARDAUD/LIMOGES/*France*, over the glaze.
Refs: Lesur (1967); d'Albis & Romanet.

Bernstiel, Liebfriede (b 1915). German potter born in Hamburg, where she studied at art school 1933-34. She then trained in ceramics under H.*Griemert in Halle-Giebichenstein, near Leipzig. Bernstiel worked with O.*Lindig in Dornburg, 1939-46, with G.*Marcks and S.*Möller at the state art school in Hamburg 1947-48, and collaborated with Marcks on the design of a teaset in 1948; she was assistant to Lindig at the art college in Hamburg, 1947-55. At her own workshop, established 1955 in Ahrensburg, near Hamburg, she continued work in the tradition of the Bauhaus and Halle. Her simple, utilitarian stoneware, mainly thrown, includes tableware, vases, bowls, boxes. She also produced wall panels.

Mark: B incised in a rectangle; painted torch-like device on important pieces.
Ref: Bock.

Berthoud. *See* Aaron, Michel and Valin, Jean-Baptiste.

Besche, Lucien (d 1901). French-born porcelain decorator. He worked for *Mintons Ltd in 1871, after his arrival in England, and then for the firm of W.T.*Copeland (c.1872-85). His work there included vases with paintings of figure subjects after Antoine Watteau, which won commendation at the Universal Exhibition in Vienna, 1873. With R.J.*Abraham, he worked on sporting murals commissioned from the Copeland factory in 1874-75. From 1885, he worked as painter, magazine illustrator and theatrical costume designer in London.
Mark: signature.
Ref: d'Albis & Romanet.

Besnard, Jean (b 1889). French painter and artist potter, born in Paris. He exhibited at the Salon des Tuileries from 1925 and the Salon d'Automne, 1927-37. Besnard was noted for simple, humorous forms, which

Jean Besnard. Stoneware vase with repeating pattern in relief and crackled glaze, 1930. Signed Jean Besnard, FRANCE. *29.1 cm high.*

Ulysse Besnard. Bottle decorated in white slip on a grey ground, 19th century. 21.5 cm high.

included jugs in the shape of human figures or small animals; he also made vases, lamp bases and ceramic jewellery. Often using light colours, heightened with gold, Besnard invented a white enamel glaze which contracted on firing to give a shark-skin effect, and experimented with lustres, combining gold and platinum with pink, white and black enamel effects, often in geometrical diaper patterns.
Refs: Baschet; Bénézit; Faré; Lesur (1971); Valotaire.

Besnard, Ulysse. French potter working, (under the name Ulysse), at Blois (Loir-et-Cher) from the 1850s. He made earthenware in imitation of 16th-century Italian maiolica, often with lustre designs. His partner, J. Tortat, withdrew in 1862 and established his own workshop ten years later. Ulysse became curator of the Blois museum in 1866. His pottery was later taken over by the Balon family, who continued to use the mark *Ulysse à Blois*, adding, in 1911, *E. Balon Sr.*
Other marks include: *Ulysse Besnard* or *Blois*. Marks usually incorporate a cross over a V, often on a scallop shell.
Ref: Lesur (1971).

Bessarabova, Natalya. Russian potter, formerly an interior decorator. Bessarabova joined the Research Institute of Industrial Arts and worked with the historian, Alexander Saltykov, in the documentation and revival of ceramics in the *Gzhel area. She made reproductions of 18th and early 19th century Gzhel wares after intensive study, and went on to make her own variations on the pieces, adapting the local style to make vases, jugs, teapots and mugs in forms and patterns suited to modern settings. Her prototypes are still in production at the *Artistic Ceramics Cooperative factory, where she taught painters. Bessarabova continued to live in the Gzhel area, where she worked until her retirement.
Ref: Ovsyannikov.

Beswick, John, Ltd. Staffordshire earthenware manufacturers. The firm operated at the Gold Street works, Longton, leased in 1897 and purchased in 1900 by John Wright Beswick (d 1921), formerly a coal owner, who traded as J.W. Beswick. He was joined by his son John (d 1936), who had trained at a Tunstall pottery. Their firm produced a steadily expanding output of transfer-printed tableware, toilet sets, invalid ware and ornamental pieces, including *jardinières* and pedestals, vases, Toby jugs and animal and human figures. After World War I, the firm specialized in decorative ware, most of it exported, including figures of horses and riders, dogs modelled from show-winners, and a wide range of birds, fish, domestic and wild animals, as well as salad bowls and other decorated pieces for domestic use. The firm traded as John Beswick Ltd from the 1930s and was still in the hands of the founder's family in the 1950s.

Early work unmarked; marks on later wares usually incorporate BESWICK/ENGLAND.
Refs: Bunt; Godden (1964).

Betteley, Herbert (b c.1860). English ceramic artist. After training at the Burslem School of Art and doing freelance work as a ceramic designer, he worked for *Doulton & Co. in Burslem 1886-1930. Betteley was known for delicate line drawings and gilded patterns, and his work featured in the World's Columbian Exposition in Chicago, 1893. He was responsible for the training of junior artists and headed a decorative department which operated alongside that run by R.*Allen. Betteley initialled work carried out under his supervision, HB.
Refs: Atterbury & Irvine; Eyles (1980).

Bevington, Ambrose, & Co. *See* New Hall.

Bevington, Timothy and John. English potters. Born in Stratford-upon-Avon, Timothy Bevington was employed as chief clerk and then works manager by L.W.*Dillwyn, while his son, John, worked as salesman and clerk. Both became partners in the *Cambrian Pottery in 1811, taking over the lease from Dillwyn in 1817 with partners George Haynes, his son, also George, and the Tamworth business man John Roby. They bought from Dillwyn the means of producing both earthenware and porcelain, including two of the paste formulae developed by W.*Billingsley and S.*Walker (the duck-egg green and 'trident' pastes), and the stock of undecorated porcelain, but concentrated on the production of earthenware. The lease reverted to Dillwyn in 1824.

Mark: BEVINGTON & CO., impressed, c.1817-24, and with SWANSEA (rare, mainly on earthenware), 1817-21.
Ref: Jenkins.

Beyer, Henri-Paul-Auguste (1873-1945). French glass artist and potter. One of a family of stained-glass artists who settled in Besançon (Doubs), and worked from c.1893 on cathedral glass before developing an interest in ceramics c.1905. Beyer went to Vallauris (Alpes-Maritimes) before working on his own research in Ain in Switzerland, and from 1914 in Lyons, where he developed his knowledge of salt-glazed stoneware. His salt-glazed stoneware included figures of saints, and of animals and birds, which he studied in their natural surroundings. Work-

Paul Beyer. Cockerel, 34 cm high.

ing from 1932 at a studio attached to the Sèvres factory, and moving in 1942 to La *Borne, Beyer produced pitchers, bowls, vases adapted from oriental shapes, bulbous jugs (sometimes in the form of human heads), and humorous, stylized figures (e.g. duckling, chicken) composed of thrown units, making use of the lines of throwing and sometimes added streaks of pigment, to represent the texture of feathers.

Beyer is noted for his efforts in reviving the production of salt-glazed stoneware in France. He was joined at La Borne by stoneware potters including V.*Ivanoff, E.*Joulia and J.*Lerat.
Refs: Céramique française contemporaine; Faré; Lesur (1971).

Beyrand, André (1887-1976). French ceramic painter and designer. After apprenticeship to the *Pouyat family, Beyrand joined the firm of C.*Ahrenfelt in 1919, creating numerous patterns. He taught painting in a school of ceramics from 1940, but continued to design for Ahrenfelt and other factories until his retirement in 1959.
Ref: d'Albis & Romanet.

Bézard, Aristide. French potter. Bézard made earthenware with slip painted under the glaze at a workshop established 1902 at Marlotte (Seine-et-Marne) with associate Emile Mousseux. Bézard's work includes vases, *jardinières*, cups, with designs of flowers and other subjects inspired by nature. He also painted panels with landscapes. After his death in World War I, the pottery was continued until the early 1930s by Mousseux, who made stoneware including vases and figures, using *flambé* glazes.

Marks: incised signature; painted factory mark, *B.M. Marlotte S.M.*; AB or EM with *Marlotte*.
Refs: Brunhammer *et al* (1976); Lesur (1971).

Bichweiler. German earthenware manufacturer working in the late 19th century at Hamburg in traditional styles. The work included moulded plates with a border of flowers and foliage enclosing a central panel

Alexandre Bigot. Gourd-shaped stoneware vase; green glaze flecked with black crystalline markings. Early 20th century. 17 cm high.

with such designs as a knight on horseback, and inscriptions in Gothic lettering.
Ref: World Ceramics.

Bigot, Alexandre (1862-1927). French ceramist, teacher of physics and chemistry in Alsace. Inspired by the display of oriental porcelain and stoneware in the Exposition Universelle (1889), Bigot carried out experiments in stoneware at his own workshop in his native town, Mer (Loir-et-Cher), abandoned teaching, and in 1894 exhibited his early work: small pieces thrown in simple shapes with matt glazes in yellow, green and buff. Stoneware plates with newts, frogs, mermaids, etc., applied in relief recall Palissy ware. He made a frieze decorated with lions from designs by the sculptor, Paul Jouve, for the entrance to the Exposition Universelle (1900), where he won a Grand Prize. Bigot opened a Paris workshop for the production of vases, figures, tiles and other decorative stoneware with *flambé* glazes, in order to make the beauty and durability of stoneware available to architects and interior decorators. His studio's

Bichweiler. Glazed earthenware plate with a horse and rider in relief, 1880.

output included a version in reduced scale of the frieze made for the exhibition gateway, other friezes in stoneware by designers including H.*Guimard, Pierre Roche, Henri Sauvage, Louis Majorelle, Louis Bigaud and H.*van de Velde, and the ceramics for the decoration of buildings designed by Jules Lavirotte and Guimard. Bigot made many pieces to his own designs, including a vase in the ribbed shape of a gourd, covered in grey glaze, streaked to represent veining and flecked with turquoise (the interior glazed yellow and green). Some pieces, e.g. a matt green glazed pitcher, dated 1895, are mounted with silver or silver gilt designed by E.*Colonna. Bigot sold work through S.*Bing's shop in Paris. He continued his own work after the closure of the Paris workshop in 1914. In 1902, he published a list of architectural commissions undertaken in collaboration with leading architects and designers: *Principales Applications executés depuis le mois de juillet 1898*. He read a paper on the distribution of heat in ceramic ovens to the English Ceramics Society in 1914.

Marks, incised: signature; a tower over GRES DE BIGOT, impressed.

Refs: Brunhammer *et al* (1976); A. Bigot 'Emaux pour grès' in *Le Moniteur de la Céramique et de la Verre* (1894), *Grès de Bigot* (2nd edition, Paris, 1902); A. Dawson *Bernard Moore* (Richard Dennis, London, 1982); Heuser & Heuser.

Billingsley (also Billenly, Billensley, Beeley or Bailey), William (1758-1828). Born in Derby, (the son of a flower painter at Chelsea) and apprenticed at the Derby porcelain factory in 1774, becoming the factory's principal flower painter by 1790. He developed a naturalistic style, using a heavily loaded brush to paint the petals, then wiping away the colour for highlights with a dry brush, and adding details and shading to create the impression of depth. He increased the variety in patterns by painting roses from various angles, arranging the flowers in bouquets which often spread from a rose (or other single flower) at the centre and often included a white or cream bloom; he used a slightly translucent green to paint leaves. His style was later widely followed, e.g. at the Worcester factory, by M.*Webster at Derby, and by other painters whom he trained. While carrying out the decoration of important services and commissioned pieces, Billingsley also conducted his own search for a porcelain to rival the soft paste made at Sèvres, basing his experiments on the paste used at Derby. During this period he adopted the name Beeley or Bailey.

Billingsley started work as manager of the newly formed *Pinxton porcelain factory, in which he was a partner in 1796, leaving in 1799 (when the venture failed financially) to work as an independent decorator in Mansfield, Nottinghamshire. He subsequently founded a porcelain works at Torksey, Lincolnshire, in 1802 in association with Henry Bankes, formerly a partner in the Pinxton works, who went bankrupt in 1803. The property passed to a group which included Billingsley and his son-in-law, S. *Walker, who both left abruptly, probably because of financial difficulties, in 1808. The few known pieces of their porcelain have decorations that include Japan patterns in red and blue, small views in cartouches, and a copy from an engraving of the Durham Ox.

Billingsley and Walker worked for Barr, Flight & Barr at Worcester 1808-13, continuing their research into pastes, although Billingsley was at Coalport briefly in 1811. He went with Walker to start work at *Nantgarw in November 1813 and succeeded in making a soft paste of very high quality by the following summer. In financial trouble because of high kiln losses, despite loans from their main backer, W.W.*Young, they applied unsuccessfully for Government aid in their experiments and moved to Swansea, joining L.W.*Dillwyn at the Cambrian Pottery by the autumn of 1814. There, Billingsley painted landscapes as well as the flowers for which he was celebrated, and taught several decorators in his own style while in charge of the painting department.

After Dillwyn's withdrawal from the porcelain works and pottery at Swansea in 1817, Billingsley and Walker returned to Nantgarw, where their experiments were backed by Young with ten other subscribers. The porcelain they produced in the following two years fulfilled Billingsley's hope of approaching the Sèvres paste in quality and was produced in styles derived from 18th-century and Empire French porcelains. Much of the output was sent to London for decoration and sale through dealers *Mortlock & Co. However, the losses were again high through collapse of the pieces in firing, and Billingsley and Walker left the works in early 1820, entering into a seven-year partnership with J.*Rose to manufacture their porcelains, moving moulds and equipment to Coalport.

Mark: signature on decoration at Mansfield and the porcelain of Swansea and Nantgarw.

Refs: Barrett & Thorpe; Charles; C.L. Exley *The Pinxton China Factory* (Trusley, Derby, 1963); Godden (1963, 1964); Haslem; Honey (1948a); Jewitt; W.D. John *William Billingsley* (Ceramic Book Co., Newport, 1968); Nance; Williams (1932a).

William Billingsley. Porcelain vase made in Derby and painted with roses in the style of Billingsley on a white ground below a band of roses modelled in parian paste. The rim and the foot are gilded. Early 19th century.

Billington, Dora May (1890-1968). English studio potter, teacher and painter. She studied at art school in Staffordshire and worked as a decorator for B.*Moore for about two years from 1912. Her work at Moore's pottery included flowers, foliage, dragons, and a galleon painted on vases and a covered jar. She went on to study in South Kensington, then taught and, in 1926, took charge of the pottery department at the Central School of Arts & Crafts in London. She made and decorated her own ceramics as well as designing for industrial firms, e.g. J.& G.*Meakin in the early 1930s. In her teaching, Dora Billington was aware of the breadth of ceramic tradition and encouraged her students to develop individual attitudes, interests and standards through experimentation with a wide variety of interests and techniques.

Marks: monogram of DMB painted on work for Bernard Moore, 1912-15; DB incised or painted on studio ware from 1920. *Refs:* D.M. Billington *The Art of the Potter* (Oxford University Press, 1937), *The Techniques of Pottery* (Batsford, London, 1962); Coysh (1976); A. Dawson *Bernard Moore* (Richard Dennis, London, 1982); J. Farleigh *The Creative Craftsman* (London, 1950); Godden (1964); Haslam (1977); Rose; Wingfield Digby.

Biloxi Art Pottery. *See* Ohr, George E.

Bilton, Louis. English ceramic artist, noted for his paintings of flowers and birds. He trained under W.*Mussill at Mintons, and travelled to Australia, where he painted watercolours of the native flora for publication in *The Picturesque Atlas*. He joined *Doulton & Co. in Burslem in 1892, and his flower paintings were shown on vases in the World's Columbian Exposition, Chicago, in the following year. Some flower drawings were litho-printed on tableware and remained in production over a long period. He also painted Spanish and Luscian wares, as well as providing patterns of children and Japanese women for printing in underglaze blue. *Refs:* Aslin & Atterbury; Atterbury & Irvine; Eyles (1980).

Bimini Werkstätten. Austrian company, incorporated as the Bimini Werkstatt für Kunstgewerbe Gesellschaft m.b.H., in Vienna in 1923 for the production and sale of decorative items (in a variety of materials), toys and small pieces of furniture. In practice, the output consisted mainly of ceramics and glass. Plaques, tiles, vases, candlesticks, covered jars and figures were among the ceramics, which were mainly produced by Bernadine Kuhn (b 1891), an artist born and trained in Vienna, who was at the workshop from 1926 until at least 1931. The pieces were carefully made and decorated. From 1926, the firm traded as Bimini Werkstätten Gesellschaft für angewandte Kunst m.b.H. It went into liquidation in 1928 and was afterwards run as a partnership by the founders David Rosenthal and Fritz Lampl, producing hand-crafted glass and decorative objects, and finally closed in 1940. *Ref:* Neuwirth (1974a).

Bindesbøll, Thorvald (1846-1908). Danish designer and ceramist. He trained as an architect but worked in a wide range of media:

Thorvald Bindesbøll. Vase painted thinly in black and white between sgraffito *outlines. Designed and decorated by Bindesbøll and made at Valby, Copenhagen. 71.7 cm high.*

furniture, silver, leatherwork and book binding, as well as ceramics. His earthenware was enamelled in blues, greens, browns, yellows, black, and cream, with *sgraffito* patterns, often flowers, etc. Bindesbøll worked in an apparently casual style, which remained consistent through the 1880s and 1890s, and was noted for its inventiveness. In decorating pottery, he often worked from his own watercolour designs. Some abstract schemes, introduced by 1886, included a motif resembling cloud formations. Bindesbøll's designs were produced between 1883 and 1890 at the factory of J. Wallmann (established 1867 at Utterslev) and other factories in the Copenhagen district.
Refs: Hettes & Rada; Hiort.

Bing, Samuel (1838-1905). German publisher, collector and art dealer, who, with the opening of his Paris gallery in 1895, made an important contribution to the development of French Art Nouveau. Initially employed at a ceramics factory in Hamburg (his home town), he worked in France from 1871. After travelling in China and Japan, he opened a shop selling oriental *objets d'art*, displayed his own collection of Japanese art at the Exposition Universelle in 1878 and (1888-91) published a monthly magazine, *Le Japon Artistique*, hoping to draw the attention of French industrial designers to the best in all branches of Japanese art. At his Salon de l'Art Nouveau, he featured ceramics by A.*Bigot, A.-L.*Dammouse, P.-A.*Dalpayrat, C.*Massier, A.*Delaherche, E.*Muller, as well as furniture and glass E.*Colonna and G.*de Feure were collaborators on the decoration of a complete interior for his pavilion in the Exposition Universelle of 1900; their ceramic designs for Bing were produced by Limoges firms, e.g. *G.D.A.
Refs:* S. Bing *Artistic America Tiffany Glass*

and Art Nouveau ed. R. Koch (MIT Press, Cambridge, Mass, 1970); R. Koch 'Art Nouveau Bing' in *Gazette des Beaux-Arts* (1959); G.P. Weisberg, series of articles on Bing in *The Connoisseur* 172 (1969), 175 (1970), 176, 177 and 178 (1971).

Bing & Grøndahl Porcelaensfabrik. Danish factory established 1853 in Copenhagen by the brothers M.H. and J. Harald Bing, local shop-owners, in partnership with porcelain modeller Frederik Grøndahl initially for the production of decorative porcelain, especially biscuit pieces after B.*Thorwaldsen. Dinner ware, introduced in the early years of the factory, was painted with flowers (often arranged in small bouquets) and lavishly gilded. The firm's art director, P.*Krohn, designed the Heron service (1888) with underglaze painted panels of herons standing or dancing contained within elaborate low-relief decoration on a scalloped rim, lavishly gilded. Under J.F.*Willumsen, art director 1897-1900, the factory developed the underglaze decorative technique started by Krohn. Willumsen encouraged individual artists to work imaginatively in the creation of unique pieces. Underglaze painting was combined with relief decoration in the openwork pieces designed by E. Hegermann-Lindencrone and Fannie Garde. It was also used on figures and animal models. Plates have been issued in limited editions as collectors' pieces each Christmas since 1895. Work by K.*Nielsen and J.*Gauguin was exhibited in Paris, 1900. From 1910, painting was carried out in a blue pigment which flowed into the glaze during firing, usually on porcelain, but sometimes, in the case of household ware, on stoneware (which was first exhibited in 1909). A subsidiary company, Norden Insulators Ltd, established in 1916, produced electrical

*Samuel Bing. Porcelain vase designed by G.*de Feure for production by Gérard Dufraisseix & Co. (see G.D.A.) in 1900 and commissioned by Bing. 28.4 cm high.*

Bing & Grøndahl. Porcelain group of a milkmaid watched by a cat, after a model by Axel Loecher, 20th century. Marked with a castle, printed in green. 23 cm high.

porcelain. In the 1920s, the output included ornamental porcelain, painted under the glaze, decorated in relief, or relying for effect on coloured glazes (sometimes matt), and figures by Nielson and Gauguin, who became known for sculptural work in a fire-clay body which was called *roche céramique*. The factory also introduced a soft-paste porcelain, achieved after extensive research and decorated in bright colours. Work shown in the exhibition, *Les Années '25* (1963), included a bottle made c.1925 and decorated with geometrical motifs in bands around the belly, and work that was Chinese in inspiration, coloured pink under a matt glaze, and decorated with three stylized flowers in black. In New York (1939), the firm exhibited work by Nielson and Gauguin, as well as figures depicting Hans Andersen characters modelled by Hans Tegner. During World War II, the firm made dinner ware for the Danish market. At the end of the war, a new factory for the manufacture of dinner ware was built in Valby, and the original plant, extended and rebuilt, became devoted to the production of art wares, which are now exported throughout the world. R.*Kjaeregaard and L.*Munch Petersen are among artists who have been engaged on experimental design work. The firm is still in operation.

Marks usually incorporate the initials B & G, and *Kjøbenhavn* or *Copenhagen* and three towers; *Danish China Works* also occurs.
Refs: Beard; J. Bing *Bing & Grøndahl Copenhagen Porcelain* (Bing & Grøndahl Porcelain Ltd, Copenhagen, c.1978).

Bingham, Edward (b 1829). English potter. Bingham learned pottery techniques at his father's red ware pottery (established c.1837) at Castle Hedingham, Essex, but was apprenticed until 1846 to a bookmaker. He continued to make pottery, and after 1851 produced only decorative ware, which he sold at a shop in Castle Hedingham, taking other employment (opening a school, 1856-64, and working as a sub-postmaster) to support his ceramic work. He took over the family pottery after his father's death in 1872 and, using the title Hedingham Art Pottery, continued the production of a wide range of ornamental ware, until his retirement in 1899. His earthenware, moulded in local clays, decorated with slip or applied relief designs (coats of arms, classical motifs, etc.) and finished with coloured glazes in grey, blue, green or brown, included imitations of English medieval pottery, German stoneware, *Palissy ware, and reproductions of Greek or Roman pottery. Imitations of wares from the 17th century sometimes bear dates from that period.

His son, Edward W. Bingham, sold the pottery in 1901 to a Devonshire firm, Hexter Humpherson, remaining as manager and trading as the Essex Art Pottery Co. until the pottery's closure in 1901. Bingham later followed his son to America, where he had emigrated with his family on closing the pottery.

Marks: small relief of Hedingham Castle over a scroll with E. BINGHAM; incised signature; ROYAL ESSEX ART POTTERY WORKS incised c.1901.
Refs: Blacker (1922a); Brears (1971a); R.J. Bradley 'The story of Castle Hedingham pottery' Parts I, II and III in *The Connoisseur* 167 (1968); Godden (1964); Jewitt.

Binnenhuis, 't. An association of architects, artists and designers in Holland, founded (1900) in Amsterdam by the architect, J. van der Bosch, and arising from a move in the late 19th century to reform Dutch design. Members and associates included Karel Petrus Cornelis de Bazel (1869-1923), Gerrit Willem Dijsselhof (1866-1924), C.A.*Lion-Cachet, Jan Eisenloeffel (1876-1957), J.*Toorop, and W.C.*Brouwer. The group worked in a wide range of media—building and interior decoration as well as glass, wood, metal, textiles, leather and ceramics. Members provided designs for several Dutch potteries, e.g. the work of Toorop for de *Porceleyne Fles and the *Rozenburg factory, and of a number of designers for the *Holland factory.

Binns, Charles Fergus (1857-1934). English-born ceramist and teacher, the son of R.W. *Binns. He was apprenticed at the Royal Worcester Porcelain Works when 14 years old, later studying chemistry in Birmingham; he returned to work in a laboratory newly set up to achieve stricter technical control of the factory's production and eventually became superintendent of the works. At this stage he wrote on technical subjects (clay, glazes, firing) for the journals *Pottery Gazette* and *Ceramic Technology*. Binns visited America on a lecture tour before settling in New Jersey, 1898; he became principal of the Technical School in Trenton, New Jersey, and from 1900 until his retirement in 1932, the first director of the *New York City School of Clay Working and Ceramics. He was a founder member and an officer of the American Ceramic Society, a member of the Boston Society of Arts & Crafts and the English Ceramic Society, and wrote monographs and papers for periodicals, as well as his books. Binns made simple, austere stoneware, noted for fine glazes and inspired by Korean and Chinese wares, especially those of the Ch'ing dynasty, using a coal-burning kiln at the school's pottery in Alfred University. His work was often thrown in sections, which were then turned to achieve precision in thickness and shape before assembly. He

Edward Bingham. Stoneware vase with low relief decoration against a mottled purple ground. Marked with a castle in relief and Edward Bingham, Castle Hedingham, Essex, 1888. 76 cm high.

described his search for technical perfection in the article, 'In Defense of Fire' (*Craftsman*, March 1903). He also supported the concept of the studio potter as responsible for the entire realization of his own designs and stressed the importance of an understanding of the science and technology of ceramics as well as the artistic aspects of the making of beautiful pottery. His pupils included: A.E. *Baggs, M.K.*Cable, P.E.*Cox, M.*French, E.G. Oberbeck, M.C.*Perry, F.E.*Walrath.
Refs: C.L. Avery 'A Memorial Exhibition of the Work of Charles F. Binns' in *Bulletin of the Metropolitan Museum of Art* 30; Barber (1976); C.F. Binns *Ceramic Technology* (Scott Greenwood, London, 1898), *The Story of the Potter* (G. Newnes, London, 1898), *The Potter's Craft* (Constable, London; Van Nostrand, New York, 1910), 'In Defense of Fire' in *Craftsman* (March 1903); Clark & Hughto; Donhauser; Evans; Henzke; Jervis; Kovel & Kovel; J.N. Norwood *Fifty Years of Ceramic Education at State College of Ceramics* (Alfred, New York, 1950).

Binns, Richard William (d 1900). English porcelain manufacturer. Binns worked in *Worcester in partnership with W.H.*Kerr 1851-62 and became director in charge of the artistic side of production in the joint stock company (Worcester Royal Porcelain Co.) formed in 1862. He was noted for his considerate treatment of the staff under his

control, sending young artists for training at the government school of design established in Worcester, 1851, and providing a recreational centre with training facilities in 1884. He opened the company's museum in 1879.

His son, Albert Binns (d 1882), decorated a plaque with a *sgraffito* design of a dog's head holding a rabbit, signed and dated in the year of his death at the age of 20. C.F. *Binns also worked at the Worcester factory and edited his father's book on its history before leaving on his first visit to America in 1897, the year of his father's retirement through serious illness. Binns was succeeded as the factory's art director by another son, William Moore Binns.
Ref: Binns (1865); Sandon (1978a); C.F. Binns (ed) *Worcester China: A Record of the Work of Forty-five Years 1852-1897* (Bernard Quaritch, London, 1897).

Binz, Heinrich. *See* Cambridge Art Tile Works.

Birbeck, Donald (retired early 1960s). English porcelain painter, trained at the Cauldon works, Shelton (*see* Brown-Westhead Moore & Co.), and one of a family of painters, some of whom worked at the *Coalport factory. Birbeck worked for 30 years in Shelton, painting animals and birds. In 1931, he joined the *Derby porcelain factory at Osmaston Road, where his work included services painted with game subjects and fish. He also executed sketches for three-dimensional models, e.g. a kingfisher.
Refs: see Derby.

Birbeck, Holland A. (d 1906). English ceramic decorator, working for the *Watcombe Pottery and for the *Torquay Terra-Cotta Co. in the late 19th century as a painter of flowers and birds.

His son, Harry Birbeck, also worked for the Watcombe Pottery and in 1915 at the Torquay Terra-Cotta Co. He signed work for H.E.*Crute in the 1920s.
Ref: Lloyd Thomas (1978).

Birbeck, Joseph (b c.1798). English ceramic decorator, born in Worcester and probably trained at the Chamberlain factory. Birbeck moved to *Coalport by the 1820s, where he decorated services, specializing in flower subjects, including roses, but also painting fruit. He became foreman c.1844 and was a supervisor of the works in 1861. His sons, Joseph (b 1831) and Thomas, were also porcelain painters. Other Coalport painters include Francis, Philip and W.*Birbeck.
Ref: Godden (1970).

Birbeck, Joseph (b 1862). English ceramic artist and naturalist. Birbeck worked for *Brown-Westhead, Moore & Co., and joined *Doulton & Co. in Burslem in 1900. Noted as a painter of game and fish, Birbeck also executed moor and woodland landscapes, exotic birds and flowers in the 18th-century styles of Bow and Chelsea porcelain decoration. His work included dessert services and other tableware.
Refs: Atterbury & Irvine; Eyles (1980); Godden (1972).

Birbeck, William (b c.1825). English porcelain painter, working at *Coalport from c.1840 until a visit to France in the 1850s. He returned to England by 1861 and subsequently worked at the Copeland factory. Birbeck specialized in landscapes, and his work for Coalport included views of Scotland. *Ref:* Godden (1970).

Birks, Alboine (1861-1941). Porcelain decorator, specializing in the technique of *pâte-sur-pâte* after training under L.-M.-E. *Solon at Mintons, where he worked from c.1873. Birks's work included designs of cherubs playing with hearts, masks, etc., that appear on tableware. His cousin, Lawrence Birks, was also a pupil of Solon and carried out *pâte-sur-pâte* decoration at the Minton factory c.1874-95.
Ref: Aslin & Atterbury.

Birks, L.A., & Co. or **Birks, Rawlings & Co.** Staffordshire manufacturers of earthenware and later porcelain, established 1896 as L.A. Birks & Co., and trading as Birks, Rawlings & Co., China Manufacturers, from 1900. The firm made household ware, including breakfast and teasets, some with perforated decoration. A range of porcelain miniatures for sale as souvenirs, introduced c.1910 under the trade name Savoy China, was among the firm's large output of novelty items. While working for the firm, F.A. *Rhead designed vases, plaques, etc., with coloured *pâte-sur-pâte*, including work shown in exhibitions at Turin (1911) and Ghent (1913). The company showed parian ware in the British Empire Exhibition of 1915 and merged with *Wiltshaw & Robinson in 1932.

Marks, all printed, usually incorporate the firm's name or initials and often a vine leaf and bunch of grapes or the trade name of the material (e.g. *Roseate Porcelain, Savoy China, Carlton China*).
Refs: Godden (1964); Watkins *et al.*

biscuit. Once-fired earthenware or porcelain paste. Biscuit porcelain as a medium for figures and groups was introduced at Vincennes in the mid 18th century and afterwards used at many European factories.

*Alboine Birks. Plate from a service made by *Mintons Ltd by Birks in pâte-sur-pâte and decorated with scenes of women and putti alternating on the border with panels of gilt urns and festoons of bell flowers on an ivory ground. The service was sold through Tiffany & Co. and the marks include Birks's initials. Early 20th century. 26 cm diameter.*

Bizen ware. Stoneware figure of Diakoku with brown glaze, the rice bales glazed grey-green, c.1870. 31 cm high.

Flowers and other modelled decoration were also made in biscuit porcelain. In England, biscuit figures and groups were produced at *Derby in the late 18th century. White and matt in appearance, the material is distinct from *parian ware, which is silky textured and marble-like.

Bishop & Stonier. *See* Robinson.

Bizan or **Gekka** (d 1838). Japanese potter, Hasegawa Kumenosuke, formerly a painter. Bizan worked for the 6th in line of the *Taizan family at *Awata from 1820 until his death. His successor, Yozaemon or Bizan II (c.1804-62), was noted for his painting of figures in official dress or No theatre costume, used in the decoration of a fine, hard earthenware body, with glossy crackle glaze. Bizan III (d 1887), who extended the workshop and built up a considerable export trade, was followed by a fourth member of the line.
Refs: Brinkley; Jenyns (1971).

Bizan. Earthenware plate, painted with scrolls showing a cockerel and a mountain landscape flanking a third showing three women, and lavishly gilded, c.1900. Painted mark, Bi-zan. 21.5 cm in diameter.

Bizen ware. Stoneware tiger, the fur marked in dark and light brown with incised detail, the teeth white, 19th century. 32 cm high.

Bizarre Ware. *See* Wilkinson, A.J., Ltd.

Bizen ware. Japanese stoneware of ancient origin made at or near Imbe village in the pre-Meiji province of Bizen (Okayama prefecture) on the island of Honshu. The traditional stoneware made for everyday domestic use in hard, fine-textured grey body was subjected to long firing at very high temperatures, which resulted in surface effects ranging from matt to glossy and often a reddish colour, without any artificial glaze. The shapes were simple (a wide-bellied grain jar with narrow neck is typical) and decoration was limited to the effects achieved in firing: pieces fired among pine needles were shaded with fine lines (matsuba kage); brine-dampened straw ropes wound around the clay body resulted in the red mottled coloration of Hidasuki ware; the glossy yellow spotting of sesame seed gloss (gomagusuri) developed from intense heat in the presence of pinewood ash, while the effect of Edo period Ao-Bizen ware in slate-coloured body with tones of blue and green resulted from interruption of the movement of air in the kiln. The output of Bizen includes tea-ceremony wares (vases, jars, containers, etc., but not teabowls) and roof tiles.

Of six main families of potters who worked in the area in close cooperation and following strict limitations on succession, the *Mori family remained active until the 20th century, and the Kanashige family was represented until 1967 by *Kanashige, the 78th generation. Relying on the properties of fine local clay, Bizen potters were relatively free from external influences in style, and followed traditional techniques, although the variety of firing effects diminished with improvements in the kilns. In the 18th and 19th centuries, they exploited the plastic properties of the clay in making elaborately modelled incense burners and figures of animals, deities, etc., which became popular with western collectors.

Imbe, near the main source of clay, was associated with a refined class of the local ware developed in the 19th century. After the

abolition of the feudal system, the Bizen kilns primarily produced utilitarian ware, and a large proportion of their output now consists of bricks and drainage pipes. *Fujiwara, working from 1932, makes mainly vases, plates, teabowls and water containers. The kiln established at *Mushiake by Kakatori Mori, was known for ware made c.1870 with red ground spotted in yellowish grey.
Refs: Brinkley; Feddersen; Gorham; Hannover; Hobson; Honey (1945); Jenyns (1971); Koyama; Munsterberg; Okada; Orange; Sanders.

Björnquist, Karen. *See* Gustavsberg.

black basalt. Hard stoneware developed by Josiah Wedgwood in the 18th century and coloured black, mainly with iron and manganese compounds. The fine-grained body can be turned and burnished, and has been used in tea ware as well as vases, busts, plaques and other ornamental pieces. The firm of Wedgwood has continued production to the present day. Other makers include the *Herculaneum and *Leeds potteries.
Refs: Godden (1966a); M.H. Grant *The Makers of Black Basaltes* (William Blackwood & Sons, 1910); Reilly & Savage.

Blake, Kitty. Porcelain painter working for the *Worcester Royal Porcelain Co., 1905-53. Kitty Blake painted flowers in the style developed by J.*Hadley. Her own designs included patterns of blackberries and buttercups and clover.
Ref: Sandon (1978a).

Blakebrough, Les (b 1928). Studio potter, originally a painter, working in Australia. Born in England, Blakeborough worked in a scene-painting workshop and, for one year, as a seaman before going to Australia in 1948. In Sydney (1951), he returned to painting and in 1955 started studies at the National Art School, East Sydney, which included ceramics (1956-57) taught by M. *Douglas. He worked with I.*McMeekin at Sturt Pottery, in a style influenced by the work of M.*Cardew, 1957-59, subsequently managing the pottery, 1960-72. On a visit to Japan in 1963, he spent some months in the workshop of *Kawai Kanjiro. His stoneware and porcelain, made with local materials for the Australian and New Zealand market, include large plates, jars, casseroles and other functional pieces, with relief decoration of stylized flowers, etc., brushwork or splashes of iron oxide, resist patterns and a variety of glazes, e.g. celadon, Chün or temmoku. Pieces in porcelain are often small, but include such decorative work as a screen of unglazed porcelain discs brushed with cobalt and iron oxides and joined together with wire. He now teaches glass and ceramics at the Tasmanian College of Advanced Education in Hobart.
Ref: Hood; P. Thompson *Twelve Australian Craftsmen* (Sydney, 1973).

Blakey, Thomas S. and John. *See* Stockton Art Pottery.

Blanchard & Co. English terracotta manufacturers established in 1839 by sculptor and modeller M.H. Blanchard in Blackfriars Road, London. The firm made vases, urns,

*black basalt. Krater vase with encaustic decoration in red and white, produced by J.*Wedgwood & Sons Ltd, c.1810. 33 cm in diameter.*

fountains, figures and groups, as well as garden ornaments and such architectural features as balustrades, pedestals and brackets, which were awarded medals at the Great Exhibition in 1851 and the International Exhibition in 1862. The firm moved to Bishop's Waltham, Hampshire, in the 1860s, exhibiting in the Paris Exposition Universelle, 1867.
Refs: Coysh (1976); Godden (1964); Jewitt; Wakefield.

Blankenhain. Thuringian porcelain and faience factory established at Blankenhain in 1790 by C.A.W. Speck (d 1830), who exhibited porcelain at Leipzig in 1798. Gustav Vogt, owner from 1830, sold the factory in 1836, but later bought it back. In 1841, the factory merged with that of Kästner in Weimar and turned to mass production. It was owned by the Fasolt family from 1848 and modernized under the direction of Max and Karl Fasolt. Subsequently, under the ownership of E. Eichler, the firm merged with his *Duxer Porzellan-Manufaktur and was purchased in 1918 by Ernst Carstens. It remained under the management of his heirs, C.& E.*Carstens, until it was nationalized in 1948. The trade name Weimar Porzellan has been in use since 1928. The factory is known for the production of high-quality tableware, tea, coffee and mocha sets, richly gilded vases and other display pieces. Blue-printed decoration includes the Meissen onion pattern (*Zwiebelmuster*). Modern designs were created by Georg Küspert (1948-50) and Sigrid Seitler (1956-59).
Marks, from c.1900, normally incorporate *Weimar* or *Weimar Porzellan*, on the city's shield, later with a crown and laurel wreath.
Refs: Cushion (1980); Danckert; Scherf.

Blau, N. Porcelain painter employed at the Royal *Copenhagen Porcelain Factory from 1791, becoming chief painter, 1818-20.
Ref: Danckert.

Blazys, Alexander. *See* Cowan, R. Guy.

Bleak Hill, Cobridge. *See* Warburton, Peter.

Bloch, Bernard. Porcelain manufacturer working in Bohemia. Bloch was owner of a firm, Vereinigte Siderolith und Majolika Fabriken, Hohenstein, manufacturing white earthenware and ironstone china in Hohenstein bei Teplitz in 1887. He was subsequently owner and manager of the Majolika und Fayence Fabrik, Eichwald, established c.1870 and making tableware, smokers' sets, inkstands, vases, figures and other ornamental pieces in earthenware with painted decoration or coloured glazes. In 1907, Bloch introduced porcelain tableware, tea and coffee services, toilet sets, covered jars, display plates, etc., with blue and white decoration following the styles of Copenhagen, Meissen and Vienna. A pattern known as 'Karlsbad Zwiebelmuster' is still in production at Eichwald. Under the direction of Oskar Bloch, the factory continued the manufacture of ornamental earthenware and produced ironstone tiles for stoves. Bernard Bloch returned to establish a factory at Hohenstein (1907) specializing in modern stoneware, but also producing a range of glazed and unglazed earthenwares.
Marks used at Eichwald include a crown with E and MADE IN CZECHOSLAVAKIA; *Bloch & Co/Eichwald/Czechoslovakia*, Bloch's initials, BB. Others refer to the pattern, e.g. ORIGINAL ZWIEBELMUSTER in oval; outlines; versions of the Vienna shield mark.
Refs: Danckert; Neuwirth (1974b); Weiss.

Blomet, rue. *See* Chaplet, Ernest.

Blondeau, Pierre. *See* Sazerat, Pierre-Léon.

Bloor, Robert (d 1846). English porcelain manufacturer. Bloor joined the factory in Nottingham Road, *Derby, as a clerk and in 1811 succeeded M.*Kean as proprietor. Bloor's business was handled by his representatives during an illness which lasted from 1828 until his death; it failed to prosper under the management of James Thomason, and was closed in 1848 by Alderman Clarke, husband of Bloor's grand-daughter.
Ref: Twitchett (1980).

Robert Bloor. Soup tureen from a dinner service made in *Derby by Robert Bloor & Co., with Cherry-Tree pattern in blue and iron red, c.1825. Marked with a crown, crossed batons and D marks in iron red.

Bloor, Ott & Booth. *See* Ott & Brewer.

Blore, Robert (1810-68). English potter and ceramic modeller. After his apprenticeship at the *Derby porcelain factory in Nottingham Road, Blore left to work briefly for *Mintons Ltd, but returned to set up his own workshop at his father's Derby home, where he modelled vases, ewers, figures and animals in porcelain. Blore worked for the firm of G.M.& C.J.*Mason from c.1835 and subsequently for the earthenware manufacturers Isaac Wilson & Co. in Middlesbrough, Yorkshire. Blore's figures in biscuit porcelain include a Sleeping Endymion now preserved in the Derby Museum.
Refs: Aslin & Atterbury; Twitchett (1980).

Blunt, Reginald. *See* De Morgan, William.

Blyth, John. *See* Denaby Pottery.

Boch, Anna (1848-1936). Belgian painter and ceramist, the daughter of Frederick Victor Boch, artistic director of *Boch Frères. In the 1860s and 1870s she painted pottery with designs of plants or landscapes with figures *en camaïeu.* From 1885, she was influenced in style by impressionist and neo-impressionist painters, and in the following year she became a member of Les Vingt. At her invitation, A.W.*Finch worked at her family's factory as decorator from 1890.
Refs: Brunhammer *et al* (1976); *De Art Nouveau* (catalogue, Museum voor Sierkunst, Ghent, 1979).

Boch, William. One of a family of German-born potters who worked in America. With his brother, Boch started a small pottery at Greenpoint, New York in the 1840s making door furniture, stair rods, etc., in porcelain. He showed work, which by then included decorated tableware, in the Crystal Palace Exhibition in New York in 1853. The work-

shop was sold in 1861 to T.C.*Smith, who called it the *Union Porcelain Works. Boch's involvement with a number of other factories included the reopening of the works of C.*Cartlidge in 1857, a year after its closure.
Ref: Barber (1976).

Boch Frères. Pottery manufacturers working in Belgium, Luxembourg and the Saar basin. A factory established at Sept-fontaines in Luxembourg in 1767 produced figures and other ornamental ware under Pierre-Joseph Boch (d 1818). Jean-François Boch (d 1858) trained in Paris from 1802 and established a factory in the former Benedictine abbey at Mettlach (Rhineland) by 1809. He also inherited the Sept-fontaines factory from his father. His son, Eugène Boch, took over direction of the firm in 1829 and amalgamated with N. Villeroy to form *Villeroy & Boch.

After the partition of Luxembourg and Belgium in 1839, Belgian members of the Boch family moved to La Louvière (Saint-Vaast), where they established the Keramis factory in 1841, trading as Boch Frères and producing a wide range of earthenware and stoneware, including white-bodied earthenware for household and table use and, from 1847, decorated earthenware which included pieces in imitation of Delft and Middle Eastern pottery. A.W.*Finch joined the firm in 1890 as a decorator at the invitation of A.*Boch.

Printed or impressed marks include a bare shield topped by a crown and flanked by the initials BF; the initials BFK; a wolf over KERAMIS/MADE IN BELGIUM; trade names *Keramis* or *Grès Keramis.*
Refs: Brunhammer *et al* (1976); Haslam (1977); T. Thomas *Villeroy & Boch Keramik vom Barock bis zur Neuen Sachlichkeit* (Munich, 1976).

Böck, Jos., Wiener Porzellan-Manufaktur. Viennese firm of porcelain manufacturers, initially dealers in earthenware (from 1828), which passed to the Böck family. Josef Böck, owner 1879-87, was succeeded by his son, also Josef Böck (d 1935), who opened a decorating workshop in 1893. From the late 1890s, the firm produced designs by students of the Wiener Kunstgewerbeschule and members of the Wiener Werkstätte. The output included tableware, tea sets, etc., designed by artists including J.*Hoffmann, B.*Löffler, glass artist, Karl Massanetz, Kolo Moser, D.*Peche, M.*Powolny, O.*Prutscher, J.*Sika, T.*Trethan, and V.*Wieselthier. From 1935, the firm was under the control of Ferdinand Böck (1896-1959) and Karl Böck, who had been in partnership with their father since 1922. Ferdinand Böck had worked for a year at the Wiener Kunstgewerbeschule under M.*Powolny (1920-21). The firm was sold to Haas & Cjzjek in 1960.

Printed marks include the initials WPM in an oval; with JOS. BÖCK/WIEN in a

Wiener Porzellan-Manufaktur Jos. Böck. Mocha service commissioned by the firm, designed by J.*Hoffmann, 1910, and made in Schlackenwerth by the firm of Pfeiffer & Löwenstein.

Gerd Bøgelund. Stoneware vases designed by Bøgelund for the Royal*Copenhagen porcelain factory, 1949. 30 cm, 18 cm high.

rectangle of dots; JB in monogram or in the outline of a bell.
Refs: Danckert; Neuwirth (1974a, 1974b).

Böckman, Edgar. Swedish potter known for his output of salt-glazed stoneware in the 1940s. Böckman uses delicate linear decoration engraved on simple shapes.
Ref: Lagercrantz.

Boehm, Edward Marshall (1912-69). American ceramic sculptor. He started a studio pottery in 1949 at Trenton, New Jersey, later working at Washington Crossing in the same state. Trained in animal husbandry, he modelled farm animals as well as figures (sometimes religious in theme) and flowers; he also made bowls and vases. He was primarily known for accurately detailed birds modelled in biscuit porcelain and realistically coloured, based on close ornithological

Møgens Bøggild. Stoneware group of roosting chickens modelled by Bøggild and decorated with coloured glazes. Produced by *Bing & Grøndahl in 1949.

Theodor Bogler. Teapot made by Bogler in earthenware at the *Bauhaus workshop in Dornburg, 1925.

observation. He established a firm trading as Osso Ceramics in the early 1950s and later as Edward Marshall Boehm Inc.
Ref: L.A. Boger *The Dictionary of World Pottery and Porcelain* (Scribner, New York, 1971).

Bogatay, Paul (1905-72). American potter and ceramic designer. Bogatay studied at the Cleveland School of Art in his home state of Ohio, under R.G.*Cowan. He went to Ohio State University at Columbus as a graduate student of A.E.*Baggs, under whom he had trained briefly in Cleveland, and himself taught ceramics at Columbus from the early 1930s until 1971. Bogatay provided designs for production by Cowan in limited editions, 1929-30, and continued to make figures in earthenware (e.g. Javanese Mother and Child, 1935).
Refs: Clark & Hughto; Evans; Kovel & Kovel.

Bøgelund, Gerd (b 1923). Danish ceramic artist, who worked for the Royal *Copenhagen Porcelain Factory, 1941-42, and again from 1946, and in N.*Krebs's Saxbo workshop 1943-45. She designed stoneware with decoration closely related to form and function, e.g. vases and jars with incised or low-relief repeating patterns resembling seeds or ears of wheat, with monochrome or subtly shaded glazes. She also designed porcelain with similar decoration of small repeating motifs in the manner of *blanc-de-chine*.
Refs: Hiort; W. Hull *Danish Ceramic Design* (Catalogue, Museum of Art Pennsylvania State University, 1981).

Bøggild, Mogens. Danish ceramic sculptor, who produced designs for the *Bing & Grøndahl factory c.1950. His work, in naturalistic style, includes a stoneware group depicting chickens perched on branches, combining coloured glazes representing plumage, etc., and unglazed portions for the bark.
Ref: Hiort.

Bogler, Theodor (1896-1968). German potter and designer. After military service in

World War I, Bogler studied architecture and history of art in Munich (1919) and at the *Bauhaus until 1920, going on to train as a potter at the Bauhaus ceramics department in Dornburg, where he became business manager of the workshop in 1924. With O.*Lindig, he designed cast components which could be assembled in different ways to form a variety of teapots for mass production. His wares were all very simple, relying for effect on monochrome glazes. Bogler took over artistic direction of the handwork section of the Velten-Vordamm stoneware and faience factory, 1925-26; there, his work became even more austere in form, but he introduced decoration that consisted of painted strips or contrasting glazes. In 1927, two years after his conversion to Roman Catholicism, he joined the Benedictine monastery of Maria Laach, becoming abbot, 1939-48. He took over direction of the monastery's artistic workshop, 1948-49, and again from 1951.
    Marks: TB (Bauhaus); TB on either side of a heraldic lily used by the Velten Vordamm factory.
Refs: Bock.

Bohemian porcelain. *See* Lessell, John.

Bohne, Ernst, Sohn. German porcelain manufacturers working in Rudolstadt, Thuringia, from 1854. The firm, producing luxury ornamental wares, was succeeded by Albert Stahl & Co. in 1945.
    Marks include a coronet over the initial N, or an anchor with B or EB.
Refs: Danckert; Weiss.

Boissimon, Charles de. *See* Langeais.

Boizot. *See* Sèvres.

Boleraz. Hungarian pottery established in the mid 18th century at Boleraz (Bélahàz) in Bratislava, initially producing wares similar to those of Holitsch. The works produced white earthenware with decoration influenced predominantly by painted Hungarian folk wares. Production ceased in the mid 19th century in the face of competition from mass-produced Czechoslovakian wares.
    Marks: B or from 1835 BOLERAS.
Ref: Csanyi.

Bollhagen, Hedwig (b 1907). German potter, born in Hannover. After training in *Höhr-Grenzhausen (1925), she worked at potteries including the *Karlsruhe factory, the Rosenthal factories and W.*Kagel's workshop, and in Berlin (1932). Bollhagen continued the tradition of linear decoration established by T.*Bogler and W.*Burri at Velten-Vordamm. At her own workshops, established in 1934 at the former Hael art pottery workshop in Marwitz, near Berlin, she made utilitarian ware alongside unique pieces which helped her to develop fresh designs for wares purchased in series. she initially adopted some shapes from the factory's former output, but quickly developed her own designs, employing a number of painters, some of whom had previously worked at Velten-Vordamm. She was joined at her workshops by the painter, Charles Crodel, who encouraged her to increase her technical range and introduce architectural ware, garden ornaments, etc. Burri also worked sporadically at the Bollhagen work-shop during the 1930s, making unique pieces with linear patterns, painted or incised. Although production was disrupted during World War II, her factory is still in operation.

Marks: HB painted, impressed or incised. At Velten-Vordamm, HB printed next to the factory's lily mark.
Ref: Bock.

Bondil, Joseph. *See* Moustiers.

bone china. A porcelain paste containing calcined bones, and made from a formula standardized by Josiah Spode in the late 18th century, although bone had been added to paste made at the Bow factory in the mid 18th century. Bone ash acts as a flux in porcelain paste, increasing the whiteness and translucency, and helping to reduce distortion in firing. Bone china has been used as the standard paste in the English porcelain industry since the early 19th century, and normally contains about two parts of bone ash to one each of china clay and Cornish stone.
Refs: D.A. Billington, *The Technique of Pottery* (Batsford, London, 1962); Fournier; M. Farr *Design in British Industry* (Cambridge University Press, 1955).

Bo'ness. Scottish pottery established in the late 18th century on the south shore of the Firth of Forth, West Lothian. The pottery, possibly engaged initially on the production of brown earthenware, made stoneware and, from 1784, creamware, becoming the largest pottery in the district by the mid 19th century. It passed into the hands of James Jameson or Jamieson (d 1854), and in 1826 traded as James Jameson & Co. In this period, the firm began to specialize in blue transfer-printed ware. Soon after Jameson's death, the pottery was owned by John Marshall (d 1870), at first under his own name and subsequently (until the late 19th century) as J. Marshall & Co. It closed in 1889. The output then included a series of patterns depicting Canadian sports, usually printed in black or occasionally a dark brown and sometimes painted over the glaze and gilded. The pottery continued use of the Bosphorus pattern, which was also produced by other firms. Bo'ness also specialized in decorative figures, brightly painted under the glaze, which included a variety of animals and birds.
Refs: Bo'ness Potteries: An Illustrated History (Falkirk Museum, 1977); Collard; Fleming; McVeigh.

Bonifas, Paul. Engraver, gilder and studio potter, working in France. Bonifas studied fine arts in Switzerland, where he went on to train in ceramic techniques. He established a workshop at Ferney-Voltaire (Ain) for his experiments with stoneware, porcelain and earthenware during World War I, but went to Paris in 1919 after the destruction of his workshop by fire. He worked in a porcelain factory before joining the staff of the review, *L'Esprit Nouveau.* He later returned to Ferney-Voltaire, where he reopened a small local pottery for the production of traditional earthenware and a small quantity of stone-ware, using mechanical methods for the production of series wares, but also making editions limited to 12, and throwing unique

pieces by hand. His work included mass-produced ware with a black, lustred finish, exhibited in the Salon d'Automne, 1927. He left teach ceramics in the United States in 1940. His ex-wife, Alice Sordet, and two daughters continued to run the pottery.

Marks: FERNEY VALOTAIRE above and below *Au Patriarche* and a figure of man with stick (1925); BOAS (1928).
Ref: Céramique française contemporaine.

Bonnet, Elzéar (d 1834). French potter. Working at *Apt, he made agate ware from the variable local clay. Display pieces, in-cluding vases, urns and covered cups, were in forms resembling those made in silver or gold. Bonnet also developed a white glaze of high quality. His successors made tureens, etc., in the styles of French faience, e.g. Strasbourg. The pottery was sold in 1860.

Mark: BONNET A APT impressed in a rectangle.
Refs: Ernould-Gandouet; Lesur (1971).

Bontjes van Beek, Jan (1899-1969). Studio potter of Dutch extraction, born in Vejle, Jutland, and brought up in Germany. He studied pottery under Valentin Frank in the Undenheim, Rhineland, in 1921 and estab-lished a workshop (1922) in Fischerhude, to the east of Bremen, with his sister-in-law Amelie Breling, producing earthenware with monochrome glazes or lustre. He studied at the Seger Institute in Berlin in the following year and went on study trips to Prague and Raudnitz, Elbe, in 1928, and to Sèvres and Paris in 1931-32. After his second marriage, he opened a workshop in Charlot-tenburg, Berlin, where he worked on the production of stoneware from 1933, with an interval in 1936, when he visited London for study. Bontjes van Beek was briefly im-prisoned in 1942 by the Gestapo, and his daughter was executed in the following year. His workshop was destroyed during bombing in 1943. He was engaged on mili-tary service, 1944-45, and worked as a

Jan Bontjes van Beek. Stoneware bottles made in Berlin, 1963-66.

lecturer in Weissensee, Berlin, 1946-50, before beginning the design of ceramics for mass production at the factory of Alfred Ungewiss in Dehme, near Hamburg. His de-signs were simple and included spherical vases. He was director of the Meisterschule für das gestaltende Handwerk in Charlotten-burg, 1953-60, and in 1960 succeeded O. *Lindig at the Hochschule für Bildende Künste in Hamburg, where he remained until his return to Berlin in 1966.

Bontjes van Beek had been inspired by the Chinese ceramics exhibited in Berlin, 1929, and subsequently worked with soft, rounded shapes until the 1950s, when he developed his interest in the geometry of form, often combining contrasting shapes to form a single piece. As a freelance, he pro-vided designs for vases produced at the *Rosenthal workshop in Selb, 1952-53. In the 1960s, he returned to the design of unique pieces. On his stoneware, which was light and refined in body, he used feldspathic matt or silk-textured glazes, in a range of colours that included bright blue, purple and rasp-berry pink. The glazes were used to produce such decorative effects as spots or splashes on the sides of the piece, or trickled on to give an incomplete covering.

Marks: fish with initials FKK (Fischerhude Kunstkeramik) 1925-30; subsequently *BvB* monogram incised, impressed or painted (at Dehme, with initial *U*).
Refs: Bock; B. Braumann *Jan Bontjes van Beek* (catalogue, Akademie der Künste, Berlin, 1977); A. Klein 'Jan Bontjes van Beek' in *Keramische Zeitschrift* 6 (1957).

Bon Ton. *See* Brush-McCoy Pottery.

Bookprinter, Anna Marie. *See* Valentien, Albert and Anna Marie.

Boote, T.& R., Ltd. Staffordshire pottery established in 1842 by Thomas L. Boote (retired 1879) and Richard Boote (d 1891), working in Burslem, at the Kiln Croft Works until 1864. The firm produced earthenware, often sets of jugs, with inlaid designs on a ground of a different colour, e.g. black on white or vice versa; the technique, described as mosaic and resembling relief decoration, although not raised, was patented in 1843 by R. Boote. In 1848, the Bootes registered a patent for a jug design produced in white stoneware with biblical scenes in low relief contained within relief arches. The firm acquired several factories and established the Waterloo works, also in Burslem, in 1850. Parian figures and groups, e.g. Peel, Shakespeare, Milton, Venus, introduced at this time, were shown in the International Exhibition, 1862. Jugs and tall vases were made in blue-tinted parian ware with white relief decoration of vines or flowers or foliage. From c.1850, ironstone china, decor-ated by hand for domestic use, was exported to America. The firm made large numbers of majolica tiles in the late 19th century and developed a method of moulding encaustic tiles from clay dust (patented by Boulton and Worthington in 1863). They produced plain white tiles (about 500,000) for the lining of the Blackwall Tunnel, which was completed in 1897. Decorated tiles included a series printed and hand-painted with Kate Greenway's Seasons (1881). After the closure of the Waterloo works in 1906, the firm's output was restricted to tiles.

Marks: T. & R.B. impressed; T. & R. BOOTE printed in black under the royal arms, or under a greyhound between laurel wreaths and surmounted by a crown or under a steamship.
Refs: Barnard; Blacker (1922a); Collard; Godden (1961); Jewitt (1964); Lockett (1979); Wedgwood & Ormsbee.

Booth, Richard. *See* Salt, Ralph.

Booths Ltd. Staffordshire earthenware manufacturers established in 1864 as Evans & Booth and working at Tunstall under the names of Thomas Booth and his son from c.1868, T.G. & F. Booth (1883-91), and Booths or Booths Ltd. from c.1898 until 1948. The firm took over the Church Bank Works in 1870, and also operated other potteries in the town in the 20th century. They were known for the production of ironstone china and semi-porcelain (Royal Semi-Porcelain and Silicon China) which they advertised in the late 1880s for use by hotels and shipping lines. The firm made imitations of 18th-century Worcester porcelain (some marked with a crescent monogram of CB or a Worcester seal mark) and other early porcelains, using an earthenware body. The firm combined with that of H.J.*Colclough in 1948 to become Booths & Colcloughs at Hanley and, from 1955, part of *Ridgway Potteries Ltd.

Printed marks incorporate TB & CO. (1860s); and TB & S (1870s); printed circular mark TGB in a belt surmounted by a crown, 1876-83; subsequently, printed marks incorporating the name BOOTHS and often a trade name describing the body, usually with a crown.
Refs: Bunt; Godden (1964); Jewitt.

Bopp, Harold F. *See* Kenton Hills Porcelain Inc.

Bordalo Pinheiro, Rafael. Portuguese potter and caricature artist, the founder of a factory at Caldas da Rainha in 1884. He produced in earthenware naturalistic figures of animals and birds, as well as plates decorated with satirical scenes of people engaged in work, religious activities, politics or current events. The factory was expanded and is still in operation.
Ref: D. Smith in *The Observer* (13th February 1977).

Bordeaux, Manufacture Royale de. *See* Johnston, D.

Bordollo, W.& B. *See* Grünstadt.

Bormann, Wilhelm (1885-1938). Ceramic modeller and designer, born in Brunswick and working in Vienna, where he studied from 1898. Bormann worked for the firm of L. Förstner from 1908. While teaching in the Technische Hochschule in Vienna, he provided models for production by the *Goldscheider firms.
Ref: Neuwirth (1974a).

T. & R. Boote Ltd. American Indian tiles, impressed with the greyhound mark of the Waterloo works, Burslem. 21.5 x 7 cm.

Borne, La. French pottery centre in the region of Berry (Cher), noted for the production of stoneware from the 18th century, but active from the 16th century. A beige body, touched with brown, and salt-glazed, with the addition of ash glazes, was traditionally used for fountains, religious pieces, writing sets, jugs, bottles and, notably, small figures, e.g. by the *Talbot family. H.-P.-A. *Beyer worked at La Borne from 1942, later joined in his revival of French stoneware by potters including V.*Ivanoff, E.*Joulia and J.*Lerat.
Refs: Céramique française contemporaine; Ernould-Gandouet; Lesur (1971).

Bosley Ware. In Australian ceramics, ornamental vases, mugs, candlesticks, figures, etc., made in earthenware with green, cream or, later, mixed green and blue glazes from the mid 1930s to 1940 by the firm of T.G.&

Thomas Bott. Decoration by Bott in white enamel on a deep blue ground. Detail of a tazza made by Kerr & Binns in Worcester and dated 1873 (a gilt border of palmettes was almost certainly executed three years after Bott's death in 1870).

*Walter Bosse. Grotesque figure, produced by *Augarten, c.1925. Marked with a crown and shield above* Wien. *19.7 cm high.*

A.G. Bosley in Mitcham, Adelaide. Plaques made to commemorate South Australia's centenary in 1930 have moulded decoration with green glaze, and sometimes a brown-glazed tree motif.

Marks: BOSLEYWARE MITCHAM S. AUS. impressed; T.G.& A.G. BOSLEY impressed; BOSLEY WARE ink stamp.
Ref: Graham; R. Phillips 'The Bosleyware Pottery' in *Australiana Society Newsletter* 4 (1980).

Bosse, Walter (b 1904). Austrian modeller and designer. Bosse trained at the Kunstgewerbeschule in Vienna as a modeller of figures and tableware, under F. Cizek and M.*Powolny, then studied 1921-22 in Munich under R.*Riemerschmid and A.*Niemeyer. While running his own workshop in Kufstein (1919-37), he modelled pieces for the Wiener Werkstätte (1921), very stylized figures for the Wiener Porzellanmanufaktur *Augarten (from 1924), and vases, animal figures, etc., for F.*Goldscheider (1926-36) and A. Fischer in *Ilmenau (from 1926). Bosse also worked for the firm of Goebel in *Oeslau (1938-57), but largely abandoned ceramics for metalwork after 1950, though he provided designs for the *Karlsruhe factory, 1950-72.
Ref: Neuwirth (1974a).

Bott, Thomas (1829-70). English portraitist, porcelain painter and designer, born near Kidderminster, Worcestershire. Training from 1846 at Richardson's glassworks at Wordsley, near Stourbridge, also in Worcestershire, Bott painted glass which was shown in the Great Exhibition, 1851. He worked as a portrait painter and in 1853 joined the *Worcester Royal Porcelain Co., where he worked on the Shakespeare service and subsequently specialized in white enamel designs featuring figure scenes, portrait

medallions, serpents, scrolled borders, etc., on darker coloured grounds, which achieved the effect of 16th-century Limoges enamelwork. His work included many plaques. Other Worcester artists working in the same style of Limoges enamels included his son, T.J.*Bott, and T.S.*Callowhill.
Signature, *T.Bott*, and date.
Refs: Binns (1897); Jewitt; Sandon (1978a).

Bott, Thomas D. English ceramic artist. Previously a painter at Worcester, where other members of his family were employed, Bott joined *Doulton & Co. in Burslem with Charles J.*Noke in 1889, remaining there until 1900. His work included plates shown in the World's Columbian Exposition at Chicago, 1893.
Refs: Atterbury & Irvine; Eyles (1980).

Bott, Thomas John (1854-1932). English porcelain decorator. Bott was apprenticed c.1866 at the *Worcester Royal Porcelain Works, where he trained under R.W.*Binns and succeeded his father, T.*Bott, as the factory's principal artist. He painted a number of plaques in the style of 16th century Limoges enamel ware, also working on dinner and dessert services. He joined the London studio of *Brown-Westhead, Moore & Co. c.1875, remaining in London as an independent decorator after the closure of the studio two years later. He carried out some freelance painting for the Worcester factory and returned to work there c.1883 until 1885 or 1886, when he went back to independent work, which he sold direct to London dealers, especially W.J.*Goode. Bott won a silver medal at the Paris exposition in 1889 for his mythological scenes executed in

Thomas John Bott. 'The Source', a porcelain plaque painted by T.J. Bott with a full-length portrait of a water nymph in white enamel against a deep blue ground. Reverse signed, Thos. J. Bott, Worcester, 1883. 25 x 14.5 cm.

white on a deep blue ground on vases and plates made at the Brown-Westhead, Moore factory in the same year. He was art director at *Coalport from 1890 until his death.
Signature and date.
Refs: Godden (1970); Jewitt; Sandon (1978a).

Bouché, Leclerq. *See* Sèvres.

Boulenger, Hippolyte and Louis. *See* Hautin, Boulenger.

Boullemier, Antonin (1840-1900). Ceramic painter, born in Metz (Moselle). Boullemier worked at the Sèvres factory until 1870, before moving to England, where he joined *Mintons Ltd in 1872, staying with the firm until his death. He exhibited portraits and miniatures at the Royal Academy in 1881. In ceramic decoration, Boullemier specialized in figure subjects, especially children and cupids, working on earthenware or porcelain in a delicate, sentimental style influenced by 18th-century French painting. His later work, still mainly for Mintons, was carried out independently, and Boullemier also worked for other firms, including *Brown-Westhead, Moore & Co.
His sons L.E.*Boullemier and H.P.*Boullemier followed their father's style and specialized in copies of Sèvres decorative work.
Antonin Boullemier's work was signed.
Refs: Aslin & Atterbury; Godden (1961); G. Godden in Atterbury (1980); Rhead.

Boullemier, Henri P. Ceramic decorator, working in a style resembling that of his father, A.*Boullemier. He carried out some painting of cherubs, female figures and portraits on services for *Doulton & Co. in Burslem, 1901-04, probably as a freelance artist, and succeeded his brother L.E.*Boullemier at the *Minton factory after 1911.
Refs: Aslin & Atterbury; Eyles (1980).

Boullemier, Lucien Emile (1876-1949). Ceramic painter. He worked in a style similar to that of his father, A.*Boullemier, for *Mintons Ltd c.1895-c.1911, also carrying out independent work c.1905 as an outside painter of figure subjects on plates, etc. for the porcelain factory in Osmaston Road, *Derby. He went on to work in America for W.S.*Lenox and from the early 1820s for C.T.*Maling. He worked in Hanley, Staffordshire from 1932.
Signature, *L. Boullemier*.
Refs: Aslin & Atterbury; Bell; Eyles (1980).

Boulogne-sur-Mer. A short-lived French porcelain firm operating in the late 1850s at Boulogne-sur-Mer (Pas-de-Calais) under Edouard and Firmin Haffringue and partners Clarté and Dunand. The partnership made elaborate pieces with relief decoration in highly translucent biscuit porcelain, including services made for painting in Paris, animal studies from life, and vases. Some pieces were modelled by P.*Comoléra. François Duval, formerly employed at the Verlingue faience factory (in operation 1773-c.1800 at Boulogne), returned to make coarse earthenware in Boulogne in 1801. His output included household ware, *jardinières*, inkpots,

tobacco jars, and pots in the form of animals. The pottery later made decorated tiles and house numbers until its closure in 1820. Other local potters continued to make heavy household earthenware, tobacco pipes, whistles and toys decorated in bright colours, as well as tiles and refractory ware.
Mark: anchor and initials of the firm inside a square.
Refs: A. Lefèbvre *La Céramique Boulonnaise* (Boulogne-sur-Mer, 1899); Lesur (1967); Litchfield; V.J. Vaillant *Les Céramistes Boulonnais* (Boulogne-sur-Mer, 1882); Weiss.

Boulter, Charles J. (d 1872). American potter employed by W.E.*Tucker and J.*Hemphill. He worked for A.*Miller as foreman and then superintendent of the firm's new factory between c.1835 and 1850, and established his own factory c.1850, remaining a proprietor until his death. The firm made furnaces (for assayers, dental engineers, etc.), tiles and firebricks. His daughters carried on the business after his death.
Mark: monogram of CB on work for Tucker & Hemphill.
Refs: Barber (1976); Myers.

Boulton, James (b c.1867). English ceramic artist, noted for his flower painting. His work included dessert sets shown in the World's Columbian Exposition, Chicago, 1893, by *Doulton & Co., for whom he worked in Burslem from his apprenticeship in 1880 until 1917. He is also thought to have provided patterns for the Blue Children series of underglaze printed ware.
Ref: Eyles (1980).

Bourg-la-Reine. *See* Chelsea Keramic Art Works.

Bourne, Joseph (1788-1860), and son John Harvey Bourne (c.1869). Derbyshire potters. In 1812, John Bourne took over a pottery established three years earlier on an estate at Denby, near Ripley, which held a deposit of clay already in use at his father's *Belper Pottery, and in the making of saggars at the Derby factory. He closed the Belper Pottery in 1834, moving the plant and employees to Denby. In the previous year he had reopened the *Codnor Park Pottery, which was transferred to Denby in 1861, and in 1845 he acquired the Shipley Pottery, which he moved to Denby in 1856. In 1836, Bourne patented an improved kiln for the firing of saltglaze, which constituted his main output. He produced a wide variety of heat-resistant domestic ware, as well as such items as hot water bottles for use at home and on journeys, medical, nursery and chemical ware, mortars and pestles, and a range of decorative bottles in the form of portrait figures, reform flasks, etc. The pottery's specialities include jugs decorated in low relief with hunting scenes (sometimes with handles in the form of greyhounds) and preserving jars. Terracotta, also a product of the pottery, was buff-coloured and included flowerpots and vases, water bottles, narrow-necked jugs with snake handles, cheese stands, butter and water coolers, scent jars and, after improvement of the clay body in c.1880, plaques.

Joseph Bourne. Salt-glazed Reform flask for spirits, c.1835. Impressed mark, J. Bourne & Sons. 19.5 cm high.

Joseph Harvey Bourne was a partner from c. 1850 before succeeding his father in the firm, which continued to trade as Joseph Bourne (Ltd), acquiring *Langley Mill Pottery in 1959. The output consists of table and kitchen wares.

Marks: much of Bourne's early output was unmarked, but impressed marks often incorporate BOURNES POTTERIES and the locations, e.g. DENBY & CODNOR PARK; later marks, impressed and printed, include DENBY, often with BOURNE.
Refs: Bradley; Bunt; Jewitt; Oswald.

Bourne, Samuel (c.1789-c.1865). Staffordshire ceramic painter, noted for views and romantic landscapes. Born in Norton, Bourne trained as an enamel painter under E.*Wood until 1818. He painted landscapes and figures on ware made by the firm of G.M. and C.J. *Mason and sold in 1818 and 1822. While working for *Mintons Ltd from 1828 until his retirement through ill health in 1863, he became chief designer. His son, also Samuel Bourne (b 1822) was a painter of flower subjects.
Refs: Aslin & Atterbury; Godden (1966a, 1968); Jewitt.

Bourne, Thomas. *See* Norfolk Street Works.

Bourne, William. *See* Belper Pottery.

Boutet, Claude. *See* Auxerre.

Bovey Tracey Pottery Co. English earthenware manufacturers, the partnership of Buller & Divett, successors in 1842 to John and Thomas Honeychurch at the Folley Pottery, Bovey Tracey in Devon. Buller & Divett enlarged the blue-printed domestic earthenware for local sale in south-west England or export to the Mediterranean area. The firm was succeeded by the Bovey Pottery Co. Ltd, c.1894-1957.
Printed or impressed marks incorporate B.T.P. Co; later marks include a shield bearing a cross with *Bovey Pottery*, printed or impressed.
Refs: Cushion (1980); Godden (1964); Jewitt; Litchfield.

Bown, Louis. *See* Buffalo Pottery.

Boyd, Arthur (b 1920). Australian potter and painter, son and pupil of M.*Boyd and brother of D.*Boyd. With Peter Herbst and fellow painter, John Perceval, he founded the AMB (Arthur Merric Boyd) Pottery at Murrumbeena, Victoria. Arthur Boyd and several friends, including C.*Cooper, produced utilitarian pots from 1944 but, after the lifting of wartime restrictions, introduced underglaze painting in a fresh style reminiscent of European folk wares. Later, he painted impressionistic landscapes, powerful figurative scenes and modelled sculptural pieces, while John Perceval specialized in angel sculptures. The AMB pottery broke up in 1958, though individuals went on producing work.
Refs: G. Edwards *The Painter as Potter* (Melbourne, 1982); F. Phillip *Arthur Boyd* (London, 1967).

Boyd, David (b 1924) and Hermia (b 1931). Australian potters. David Boyd learned pottery techniques as a child from his father M.*Boyd at Murrumbeena, outside Melbourne. He helped his brother Guy in the establishment of a commercial pottery called the Martin Boyd Pottery, in 1946. His wife Hermia Lloyd-Jones, who had trained as a painter, worked as an assistant. In 1949, they held their first exhibition of art pottery, thrown by David and decorated by Hermia. In 1950, the Boyds lived in London, where they worked as potters, sometimes reversing the roles of maker and decorator. They moved to France in the following year and have since made pottery in England, France, Italy and Australia.
Ref: J. Vader *The Pottery and Ceramics of David and Hermia Boyd* (Sydney, 1977).

Boyd, Merric (1889-1959). Australian artist potter, born in Melbourne and working from 1911 at Murrumbeena, Victoria, where he established a studio with Doris Boyd. He worked in an Australian commercial pottery (where he made Australia's first studio stonewares) before 1914 and studied ceramic techniques in Stoke-on-Trent, Staffordshire, 1917-20. Boyd explored the expressive potential of Art Nouveau, which he adapted in expressing his dark, mystical vision of the Australian landscape. His work includes a jug with painted decoration of trees, dated 1915, preserved in the National Gallery of Victoria. Later work continues the theme of trees, with jug handles in the form of twisted branches, or leaning trees carved in low relief on the sides of vases and jugs, and

many sculptural pieces inspired by natural forms. He also made large pieces decorated with animals and human figures.
Refs: Cooper; Graham.

Boyden, George Washington. *See* Belding, David.

Boyle, John (c.1845). Staffordshire potter. Boyle was the son of Zachariah Boyle, who made earthenware and porcelain 1823-50, working at Hanley until 1830 and subsequently operating the Anchor Works at Stoke-on-Trent (which was later occupied by *Minton, Hollins & Co.). John Boyle established his own pottery, making earthenware from 1826. Ten years later, he became a partner of H.*Minton. When the partnership dissolved in 1841, he joined his brothers in business and in 1843 acquired a share in the firm of Wedgwood.
Refs: Godden (1968); Jewitt.

Bracquemond, Félix (1833-1914). French designer, engraver, ceramic artist. Inspired by his discovery in 1856 of a volume of sketches (part of Manga) by Katsushika Hokusai, he designed a series of woodcuts of birds, butterflies and flowers, which were copied on an earthenware service produced in 1866 by F.E.*Rousseau, who was at that time a retailer of glass and ceramics in Paris. The Rousseau Service made at *Creil was edged with hatched lines in bright blue. Bracquemond became interested in ceramic decoration and designed large plates, which were produced in earthenware by T.*Deck in the early 1860s; he then worked briefly at the Sèvres factory. In 1872 he became art director of C.*Haviland's Auteuil design studio, where he worked from the following year until 1881 in association with artists including Eugène Delaplanche, Edouard Lindeneher, J-P.*Aubé, A.-L. and E.-A. *Dammouse and E.*Chaplet. His own designs were influenced by the techniques and

Merric Boyd. Earthenware jug modelled with a landscape of the Australian bush, handle in the form of a eucalyptus tree, in greys and greens, 1925. 24 cm high.

Félix Bracquemond. Plates from a service after designs by Bracquemond, made at Creil-Montereau (see Creil) by the firm of Lebeuf, Milliet & Cie for E. Rousseau, c.1867.

composition of Japanese art as well as Impressionism, and include plates in earthenware or porcelain with low relief decoration (moulded and brightly painted under the glaze in the case of some bold landscapes, or with detailed designs), impressed with a cast taken from an etching on metal and covered with glaze, sometimes a pale celadon. The parian service (1876) featured landscapes with waves, flights of birds, etc., derived from Japanese prints depicting the changing seasons. An animal series with ducks, cockerels, fish, galloping ponies, moulded or engraved under a celadon glaze, was made by Haviland in 1878 with underglaze colours, and eighteen of the subjects were reissued in 1941 in outline only. A series of plates decorated with a Bracquemond design of flowers and swirling ribbons on shapes by E.A. Dammouse, regarded as a precursor of Art Nouveau (and later known as the Art Nouveau service), was originally made at the Haviland factory in porcelain with slip decoration under the glaze; it was reproduced for Haviland in very white earthenware painted under an almost colourless glaze by Barluet & Cie for Creil in 1879. After leaving Auteuil, Bracquemond continued work as an engraver and collaborated with Alexandre Charpentier and Jules Cheret c.1900 on interior decoration, also designing vases for production by E.*Müller, as well as enamelled jewellery and bookbindings.
Refs: Brunhammer *et al* (1976); d'Albis *et al*; Hakenjos (1974); Heuser & Heuser; *Japonisme in Art* (Committee for the Year 2001 and Kodansha International Ltd, Tokyo, 1980); *Keramik* (catalogue, Kunstgewerbemuseum der Stadt Köln, 1975).

Braddon, Arthur. *See* Brannam, Charles Hubert.

Braden, Norah (b 1901). English studio potter. Norah Braden studied drawing at the Royal College of Art in London and became a pupil of B.*Leach at St Ives in 1925. While teaching ceramics, she also worked with K.*Pleydell Bouverie from

1928 until she abandoned pottery making in 1936. She made fine stoneware in simple thrown shapes, undecorated except for e.g. encircling lines, slightly raised and following the direction of throwing, which accentuate interesting and subtle glaze effects, or brush strokes, sparely and precisely painted.
    Marks: impressed or painted monogram of NB.
Refs: Godden (1964); Haslam (1977); Rose; Wingfield Digby.

Bradshaw Lane. *See* Soil Hill Pottery.

Bragdon, William Victor (d 1959). American potter. He trained as a ceramic engineer at the *New York City School of Clayworking and Ceramics until 1908, then taught ceramics at the University of Chicago (1909-12), *University City Pottery (1912-14), and the California School of Arts & Crafts in Berkeley, California, from 1915. He began to make art pottery in partnership with Chauncey R. Thomas in 1916, moving by 1922 to new premises, also in Berkeley, changing the firm's name then to The Tile Shop, and, in 1924, to *California Faience. Bragdon and Thomas left the pottery in the hands of their employees in the mid 1920s, and produced art porcelain which was made at the works of West Coast Porcelain Manufacturers, a sanitary ware company working in Millbrae, California, where Bragdon and Thomas

Norah Braden. Dish with decoration in red and black glaze against a grey-glazed ground, 1938. 29 cm in diameter.

developed high-temperature glazes and directed the making of moulds. Production was continued briefly at Millbrae after their return to Berkeley. Bragdon bought his partner's share in California Faience in the late 1930s and worked briefly for the new owners after selling the firm in 1950.
Refs: W.F. Dietrich *The Clay Resources and the Ceramic Industry of California* (California State Mining Bureau, Sacramento, 1928); Evans.

Brain, E., & Co. Staffordshire porcelain manufacturers; successors in 1903 to Robinson & Son at the Foley works, Longton, built in the 19th century. The owner, E. Brain (d 1910), in partnership briefly with G. Hawder and, later, his son, William Henry Brain, made mainly utilitarian porcelain, noted for its clean, simple design. E. Brain travelled widely to extend his export market. His son, who succeeded him, introduced decorative pieces before World War I and went into semi-retirement c.1924. In an attempt to improve commercial standards of design under the art director, Thomas Acland Fennemore, the firm entered an experimental association with the Royal Staffordshire Pottery (*see* Wilkinson, A.J., Ltd) and commissioned work by contemporary artists between 1932 and 1934. The resulting pieces made in earthenware by Wilkinsons, and in bone porcelain at the Foley works, were decorated to the artists' designs, often in a combination of printing and hand painting over the glaze in small editions. They bore the firm's marks and the signatures of artist and decorator. The original list of artists invited by Fennemore, the designer, Milner Grey, and the artist, Graham Sutherland, to provide designs included V.*Bell, John Armstrong, D.*Grant, Barbara Hepworth, Dod Procter, Ernest Procter, Paul Nash and Ben Nicholson; the selectors themselves were also to submit designs. The list was augmented by A.C.A.*Shorter and G.M. Frank Brangwyn, Laura Knight, Ann Riach, John Everett, Forsyth himself and his daughter, Moira Forsyth. London exhibitions were organized (British Industrial Art in Relation to the Home at Dorland Hall, Lower Regent Street, 1933, Modern Art for the Table at Harrods in the following year and the British Art in Industry exhibition at the Royal Academy in 1935) and the displays circulated in the provinces and Sydney, Australia, but the experiment was not commercially successful. W.H. Brain's son, Eustace, joined the pottery in 1931, later becoming a director. The firm, having specialized in bone porcelain tea and breakfast sets, extended its range to include services for hotels and shipping lines, exporting the majority of its output. It has since taken over the porcelain production of Cauldon Potteries Ltd, (formerly *Brown-Westhead, Moore & Co.), and acquired *Coalport China Ltd. The firm is now part of the Wedgwood group.
    Marks usually incorporate E.B.&CO and FOLEY.
Refs: Bunt; Godden (1964); Watkins *et al*; P. Wentworth-Shields & K. Johnson *Clarice Cliff* (L'Odeon, London, 1976).

Brambach. Short-lived German porcelain factory established by Alfred Aurnhammer in Brambach, Saxony, 1904. The firm made small, luxury items and exported ware to the Far East until its closure (by 1910).

Mark: two long-legged birds with MADE IN GERMANY.

Ref: Danckert.

Brameld, John (d 1819), and sons William (d 1813), Thomas (1781-1850), George Frederic (1792-1853) and John Wager (1797-1851). Yorkshire potters and porcelain manufacturers. John Brameld, with sons William and Thomas, took over the *Swinton Pottery in 1806, trading as Brameld & Co. After their bankruptcy in 1826, the family received further financial help from the landowner Earl Fitzwilliam and introduced the production of a porcelain paste developed by Thomas Brameld, who ran the factory in partnership with his brothers George Frederic, who acted as the firm's European agent, and John Wager, landscape, flower and figure painter, designer, and the firm's representative in the United Kingdom. After the closure of the factory following further financial difficulty in 1842, Thomas is thought to have run a flint mill, with permission granted by Earl Fitzwilliam in 1842, possibly in partnership with George F. Brameld, who was described as a manufacturer of ceramic materials in the census of 1851. John Wager Brameld subsequently continued work as a ceramic decorator, painting flowers from natural specimens. He was working independently in London by 1838 and showed several pieces in the Great Exhibition, including a brown-glazed cup and saucer with painted flowers and gilded rose, shamrock and thistle. He is also known to have painted the Rhinoceros vase now preserved in Rotherham museum.

Refs: A.& A. Cox *The Rockingham Works* (Sheffield, 1974); Eaglestone & Lockett; T.A. Lockett 'The Bramelds in London' in *The Connoisseur* 165 (June 1967).

Brangwyn, Frank. *See* Brain, E., & Co.; Doulton & Co.

Brannam, Charles Hubert. English potter. Brannam studied at the school of art in his

Charles H. Brannam. Left: Cat wearing a bow tie, its green body brushed with blue and white. Marks: C.H. Brannam Barnstaple *and* Royal Barum Ware, *impressed. 20 cm high. Right: Cat with blue glaze. Mark:* C.H. Brannam, *impressed. 27.5 cm high.*

home town, Barnstaple, North Devon, where his father, James Brannam, produced red earthenware at two potteries in the mid 19th century. After experiments in art pottery in the late 1870s, Charles Brannam took over his father's works in Litchdon Street, Barnstaple, in 1879, at first continuing the production of *sgraffito* ware in traditional local styles and, c.1882, introducing Barum ware, adopting the Roman name for the town. This line of art ware was initially marketed in London exclusively through *Howell & James and remained in production until c.1914. Early Barum ware of the 1880s included small jugs and vases with floral designs neatly incised through white slip to expose the dark red earthenware body; the colours of slip and body were sometimes reversed in the decoration of light earthenware. The outlines of *sgraffito* designs were sometimes filled in with coloured slips under clear or coloured glaze. After receiving the patronage of Queen Victoria in 1885, the ware was often referred to as Royal Barum. By the 1890s, carved and *sgraffito* ornament and painted slip were used together under coloured glazes (notably blue or green) developed by Brannam.

Details—flower petals, strands of seaweed, etc.—were often picked out in thick slip to achieve a raised effect. The line was increased to include hollow ware, normally thrown in simple shapes (except tea and coffee pots, which were moulded) and usually coated in colourless glaze. Artists included W.L.*Baron and Arthur Braddon. Motto ware was introduced in the 1890s, and commemorative pieces were produced to celebrate the Royal Jubilee in 1897. Green glaze, often used alone over simple relief decoration (e.g. by the artist J.*Dewdney) also appears on small modelled caricatures of contemporary politicians. (A similar range of ware by A.*Lauder was also marked Barum.)

Brannam's firm became a limited company in 1914 and abandoned many earlier styles for simpler wares with monochrome glazes (e.g. a matt orange). The company took over the works of W.L.*Baron in 1939, and continued the production of pitchers, flowerpots and terracotta garden vases as well as a variety of decorative ware. It remained in the hands of the Brannam family until 1979.

Marks: usually incised or impressed and incorporating the name *Brannam* and sometimes the name of ware, e.g. *Barnstaple Ware, Gwent Ware, Castle Ware, Royal Barum Ware.* C.H. BRANNAM/BARUM/ N.DEVON was impressed, c.1900-14. *Ltd* included in rubber-stamped or impressed marks after 1914.

Refs: Blacker (1922a); P. Brannam *A Family Business* (privately published, 1982); Coysh (1976); Forsyth; Lloyd Thomas (1974); Wakefield.

Brantjes, Wed. N.S.A. *See* Haga, Plateelbakkerij.

Brard, Léon (1830-1902). French potter, born in Caen (Calvados). He initially worked as a painter in Paris, exhibiting in 1849, and specializing in still-lifes, sea scenes and landscapes. Developing an interest in ceramics, he joined C-J.*Avisseau briefly at Tours (Indre-et-Loire), entered a workshop at nearby Saint-Radegonde for two years and returned to Tours after the death of Avisseau in 1861. In 1888, he established a workshop on behalf of Destreguil, who was rebuilding a pottery which had been destroyed by fire at Saint-Pierre-des-Corps (Indre-et-Loire). The production of earthenware in early styles was not profitable, and the business closed in 1895. After his return to Tours, Brard copied faience from the 18th century and executed original interpretations, e.g. still lifes of fish on bowls in shapes from Strasbourg or Rouen faience.

Marks: pieces in Tours signed *L. Brard.* sometimes with *Tours* and date.

Refs: Heuser & Heuser; Lesur (1971).

Brauckman, Cornelius (1864-1952). American potter. Brauckman established the Grand Feu Art Pottery at Los Angeles, California, c.1912, and produced vases, using a refined stoneware marketed as Gres-Cerame, thinly potted in simple, thrown shapes and relying for decorative effect on a wide range of high-temperature glazes, e.g. Sun Ray (shades of brown, beige, and green), Moss Agate (mottled green and brown with violet tints), Mission (mottled brown), Turquoise, Tiger Eye and other colours, crystalline, glossy or

E. Brain & Co. Pieces from a tea service designed by the artist, Graham Sutherland, for E. Brain & Co., c.1937.

matt. The work of the Grand Feu Pottery was exhibited until 1916.

Marks: BRAUCKMANN ART POTTERY; GRAND FEU POTTERY/L.A., CAL..

Refs: Evans; Kovel & Kovel.

Brayton, Kellogg & Doolittle. American firm, among early makers of stoneware at Utica, New York, from 1827. The pottery, beside the Erie Canal, changed hands in 1832 and was acquired, by 1839, by N. White, who then became the only stoneware potter in the area.

Refs: Stradling; Webster.

Breetvelt, Henri Leonardus August (1863-1923). Dutch artist and ceramic decorator, born in Delft. Breetvelt trained at the Tekenonderwijs Polytechnische School, Delft, and (1883-85) the Academie van Bildende Kunst in The Hague. He worked at the *Zuid-Holland pottery from 1900, for the Société Céramique (*see* Sphinx, De) from 1902 and as chief designer (1906-09) of a Noordwijk pottery, De Kroon, where underglaze and enamel-painted wares were produced 1906-10. He then opened a studio in The Hague, where he worked on many designs for unique pieces and series made at the Zuid-Holland Pottery from 1916 until his death.

Refs: R. Hageman 'H.L.A. Breetvelt' in *Biografisch Wordenboch van Nederland* 1 (1980); Scheen; Singelenberg-van der Meer; van Straaten.

Breeze, John. *See* Adams family.

Bremer & Schmidt. *See* Eisenberg.

Brentnall, Thomas. English porcelain painter working initially at the porcelain factory in Nottingham Road in his home town *Derby, where he specialized in flower subjects, including studies in the style of Dutch painter, Jan van Huysum, on porcelain plaques. On leaving Derby in 1821, Brentnall went with other artists who had been discharged at the same time in R.*Bloor's economy measures, to work at *Coalport. He moved to Yorkshire, working as a painter of fruit and flowers at the *Swinton Pottery, where he is recorded as one of the painters on the Royal dessert service. He worked for the firm of *Ridgway Potteries Ltd from the mid 1840s and was employed as a decorator in Hanley in 1861.

Refs: A.& A. Cox *The Rockingham Works* (Sheffield, 1974); Godden (1970, 1972); Jewitt; Rice.

Bretby Art Pottery. English art pottery established 1883 at Woodville, Derbyshire, by H.*Tooth in partnership with W.*Ault for the production of decorative earthenware, which included vases, bowls, jugs, *jardinières*, umbrella stands and figures. Some early vases were simple in form, but many pieces were moulded in irregular shapes with low relief decoration. The firm compounded a wide variety of coloured glazes, notably *sang de boeuf*, and some splashed or flowing effects resembling those of the *Linthorpe Pottery. New lines were developed after Ault's departure in 1887. There were some hand-modelled figures and busts were produced, but examples are now rare. The

modellers included Tooth's daughter, Florence. Larger rustic figures and statuettes, introduced c.1900, were moulded and hand-finished in limited editions. Tooth imitated other materials in such lines as vases, *jardinières*, and plaques with low-relief figures representing Japanese carved bamboo (early examples in the mid 1890s have ivory-coloured glaze picked out in brown or black); Ligna ware, moulded in red clay, unglazed, to represent sections of tree trunk, with enamelled flowers and fruit on the bark; Cloisonné ware, mainly vases, with semi-matt black glaze hand-painted in reserves with birds and flowers outlined in gold; Copperette ware (vases, *jardinières*, candlesticks, etc.), heavily potted in imitation of hammered copper with rivets at the seams); lustre-glazed or painted ware decorated with ceramic jewels inspired by Art Nouveau metalwork set with semi-precious stones. *Trompe l'oeil* novelty items included ashtrays and small dishes containing realistic nuts and a nutcracker, biscuits, a lighted cigar, reels of thread, a thimble and scissors, or a corkscrew in a cork, with a lemon. Clanta ware with black or metallic glazes was decorated with geometrical designs resembling *repoussé* work.

Tooth's son, who succeeded him at the time of World War I, continued operation until 1933. Since then, his successors have made moulded and slip-cast decorative wares, with a break in production during World War II. The factory, still standing on its original site, retains a photographic record of designs produced in the early 20th century and a collection of early wares.

Marks: rising sun over BRETBY, printed or impressed from 1884, with *England* from 1891 or *Made in England* in the 20th century. Tooth's monogram occurs until c.1900.

Refs: Blacker (1922a); Coysh (1976); Haslam (1975); Lloyd Thomas (1974).

Brewer, Henry, and sons, William and James. English potter and modeller, Henry Brewer worked for J. Wedgwood & Sons before moving from Staffordshire to work at the *Watcombe Pottery until its period of closure in 1883. He then established a pottery at St Marychurch, Torquay, where he made red earthenware vases, etc., with slip decoration of foliage similar to the scroll motifs used at the *Aller Vale Pottery, but with *sgraffito* inscriptions often on a band of cream slip on a dark green ground; flowers were painted on grounds of green or cream. Brewer, who probably retired in the 1890s, was assisted by his sons, William (also formerly employed at the Watcombe Pottery) and James (a pottery decorator) who subsequently took over the *Longpark Pottery in partnership with Ralph Willcott, making slip-painted tablewares, vases, mugs, jugs, beakers, tobacco jars, initially in a pale orange-pink body and from c.1900 a dark brown body with fine white speckling. After leaving Longpark in 1905, the brothers moved to Park Road, St Marychurch, where they made pottery at their home. William Brewer later returned to work at the Watcombe Pottery at the time of World War I.

While working at Longpark, William and James Brewer incised work with BREWER/*Longpark*/*Torquay* (c.1895-c.1905).

Ref: Lloyd Thomas (1978).

Brewer, John (1764-1816). English porcelain painter, born in Madeley, Shropshire, the son of ceramic decorators. After working as a painter in watercolours, specializing in studies of insects, John Brewer started work in 1793 at the porcelain factory in Nottingham Road, *Derby, where he was joined by his brother, R.*Brewer, four years later. The factory's pattern books make no distinction between the work of the two brothers, but accounts of John Brewer's wages mention landscapes, plant and flower studies (often labelled with a Latin name), birds, figure subjects, landscapes and nautical scenes, and border designs of roses among his work. He was probably responsible also for scenes of military encampments. After establishing himself as a drawing teacher in Derby, Brewer continued to carry out some porcelain decoration and painted plaques bought from the factory.

Ref: Twitchett (1980).

Brewer, John Hart (1844-1900). American potter and porcelain manufacturer. Having joined the firm of Bloor, Ott & Booth (*see* Ott & Brewer) in 1865, he bought out Bloor's interest with a partner in 1873, and took responsibility for the preparation of work for the Philadelphia Centennial Exhibition in 1876. He initiated the United States Potters' Assocation, becoming secretary and later president, and was elected to US congress in 1875. Brewer was subsequently a partner in the company operating the Trenton Pottery (*see* *Taylor & Speeler) until shortly before his death.

Refs: Barber (1976); Evans.

Brewer, Robert (1775-1857). English porcelain painter, born in Madeley, Shropshire. He worked as a landscape painter in London, exhibiting at the Royal Academy in the late 1790s, and joined his brother, J.*Brewer, as a painter at the porcelain factory in Nottingham Road, *Derby, 1797. Robert Brewer painted landscapes in a distinctive style, without preliminary washes of colour, often using chrome green, and bright touches of colour in the fore-ground; his trees often bear leaves in curving, upright groups of five. He succeeded his brother as an art teacher in Derby, 1816. His son, Francis Brewer, became a modeller for T.M.*Randall, afterwards working in Staffordshire c.1840-75.

Ref: Twitchett (1980).

Brianchon, Jules-Joseph-Henri. *See* Gilet & Brianchon.

Brick House Works. *See* Adams Family.

Bridge End or **Jericho Pottery.** English pottery established by 1844 at Monkwearmouth, Sunderland, by the owners of the *Wear Pottery, for the production of brownglazed earthenwares for domestic, garden and dairy use. Much of the output was sold in Denmark and southern England. The pottery underwent several changes of ownership before passing in 1881 to John Patterson, formerly manager of the Wear and Bridge End Potteries, and in 1896 to C.E. Snowden (d 1906), who in 1900 absorbed the nearby Sheepfolds Pottery established by T.*Rickaby and formed the company Snowden, Pollock & Snowden by 1904, with his son and a

partner. Pollock continued until the Bridge End Pottery's closure in 1941.
Ref: Shaw.

Brighton Pottery Co. *See* Arc-en-Ciel Pottery.

Brinton, Annie Haslam. *See* Bennet, Edwin.

Brisbane, H.L.,& Co. *See* Calyx Porcelain and Paint Co. Ltd.

Bristol Pottery. English earthenware works established at Water Lane, Bristol, in the 18th century, making the transition from delftware to cream-coloured earthenware when Joseph Ring (d 1788), formerly a cabinetmaker and partner in a distillery, succeeded his father-in-law as owner in 1784, naming his business the Bristol Pottery. Under his widow and partners Henry Carter (who became sole manager 1798-1815) and William Taylor, the firm began making pearlware, thinly potted and decorated with coloured glazes, a granite effect, or underglaze painting. Overglaze painting, introduced in 1798 on smooth, simple shapes, included botanical flowers, the freely brushed bouquets and flower sprays associated with W.*Fifield and, on a jug dating from 1814, harvest scenes and neat illustrations of the implements used.

John D. Pountney, manager from 1815 until his death in 1852, expanded the production of commemorative ware, started in 1801, for sale and as documentary records for the pottery. In his partnership with Edwin Allies (1816-35), Pountney produced fine, white earthenware with some transfer-printed decoration in underglaze blue (Willow pattern, views including the port of Bristol) or overglaze black (landscapes), as well as Fifield's brightly coloured flowers. Under the partnership, Pountney & Goldney (1836-49), the range of printed colours was extended to include green and brown, and, in the 1840s, unglazed figures, birds' nests, flowers, etc., were modelled by Samuel, the grandfather of E.J.*Raby. The pottery also

Bristol Pottery. Commemorative mug with transfer-printed decoration, c.1802.

produced a small quantity of Etruscan ware, which consisted of vases and bowls resembling those made at the *Cambrian Pottery. Under the direction of Pountney's widow from 1852, the pottery made stoneware jugs with relief decoration, e.g. ears of barley designed by C.*Toft, hops, etc.

The business was moved to Victoria Pottery on Temple Back, and in 1906 to new buildings in Fishponds, where domestic earthenware and semi-porcelain dinner services and toilet sets were made. The firm, still trading as Pountney & Co., under T.B. Johnston (d 1938), exported to Europe, North America, Australia and South Africa. Johnston was a pioneer in the use of litho-printing, but hand-painting remained an important part of the factory's work and in the 1920s included patterns derived from delftware decoration, particularly *chinoiseries* from the 18th century. Later designs were commissioned from contemporary ceramic artists. The Bristol Pottery, which was the last surviving works in the city by the 1950s, became part of the Cauldon Potteries group (*see* Brown-Westhead, Moore & Co.) and moved to Redruth, Cornwall, in 1969.

A variety of marks incorporate BRISTOL, or the names of Pountney and partners.
Refs: Bunt; Forsyth; Jewitt; Owen; Pountney; C. Witt 'Good Cream Colour Ware' in *The Connoisseur* (September 1979).

Bristol ware. Stoneware with pale body dipped in leadless glazes of ochreous brown on the upper part, yellowish-cream on the lower portion. It was evolved in 1835 by Anthony Amatt (1759-1851), manager of W.*Powell's pottery at Temple Gate, Bristol, and subsequently produced e.g. by J.*Stiff and H.*Doulton in Lambeth with glazes bought from Bristol. Doulton himself evolved a comparable glaze in the 1860s. Bristol glazes largely replaced saltglaze for domestic stoneware.

Bristol ware is also a generic term used for a large class of yellowish-brown wares, not always stoneware, often modelled with drinking scenes and made, for example, in Yorkshire.
Refs: Fishley Holland; Fournier; Oswald; Owen; Pountney.

Britannia Pottery. Glasgow pottery established in 1857 by Robert Cochran, owner of the *Verreville Pottery. The Britannia Pottery produced everyday earthenware for sale in South America and the United States, and transfer-printed ware with a series of views of Quebec (from c.1880 until the 20th century) for the Canadian market, as well as designs called Syria, Damascus and Oriental, printed in pale blue on pearlware. The firm also made decorative pieces for sale in Britain, which included relief-decorated jugs in white stoneware, smear-glazed over touches of bright blue on the relief and lined with lead glaze; puzzle jugs, also decorated in relief, were often brightly coloured (e.g. a pattern showing a robin perched on ivy growing by a wall). A tableware design, Ceres, with decoration of sheaves in relief and in underglaze colour, introduced c.1865, became very popular.

Alexander Cochran, who had inherited the pottery from his father in 1869, was in partnership with the manager, James Fleming, from the 1890s, and the firm then traded as

Cochran & Fleming. After Cochran's death, Fleming and his son J. Arnold Fleming worked the pottery together until 1911. It was subsequently operated by J.A. Fleming alone until acquired by the Britannia Pottery Co. Ltd (1920-35), who continued the production of utility earthenware and semi-porcelain.

Marks include a figure of Britannia accompanied by COCHRAN and/or FLEMING or BRITANNIA POTTERY CO. LTD. and usually the name of the pattern, printed; others normally incorporate COCHRAN with the body (*semi-porcelain, royal ironstone china*), printed. Impressed marks COCHRAN or C & F G. also occur.
Refs: Collard; Fleming; Godden (1964); Hughes (1961); Jewitt.

British Nankin. *See* Mason, Miles.

Britton, Richard. *See* Leeds Pottery.

Broad, John. English sculptor and modeller; worked at Doulton's Lambeth studio 1873-1919. His modelled figures, usually signed, and produced in editions of varying sizes, included a bust in 1906, and the Boer War Soldier. Broad worked chiefly in terracotta, but some figures, e.g. one of Queen Victoria to commemorate her Diamond Jubilee, were made in salt-glazed stoneware, and some in the hard porcelain paste which the firm had developed for laboratory ware. A pair of large vases (about 155 cm high) modelled by Broad and painted by J.*Eyre with scenes from the legends of Ariadne and Perseus and Andromeda were included in a large display by the Lambeth Studio at the World's Columbian Exposition in Chicago, 1893. As well as figures, Broad also modelled fountains, garden statuary and small pieces, such as portrait medallions in stoneware and terracotta.

Mark: monogram of JB.
Refs: Atterbury & Irvine; Dennis (1971); Eyles (1975).

Broadhurst, James, & Sons Ltd. Staffordshire earthenware manufacturers. The firm of Broadhurst & Sons, established c.1855 at the Crown Pottery in Longton, was under the control of James Broadhurst from 1864. The output included lustre ware. Broadhurst continued the production of high-quality earthenware after moving to the Portland Pottery, Fenton, in 1872; he was followed at the Crown Pottery by J.*Tams, c.1875. The firm operated under the title James Broadhurst & Sons Ltd from 1897.

Printed marks incorporate the initials JB, JB & S, or JB & S LTD, or *Broadhurst*, or JAS BROADHURST & SONS LTD.
Refs: Godden (1964); Jewitt.

Broad Street, Shelton. *See* Morley, Francis.

Broadway Pottery. *See* Goodwin, John.

brocade or **Imari pattern.** Decoration featuring flowers, birds and circular motifs painted in red, blue and gold and derived from patterns inspired by figured brocade that were painted on *Arita porcelains originally exported to Europe through the port of Imari. The Japanese patterns were adopted at Meissen in the 18th century and inspired decoration at other European factories, e.g.

in *Derby and *Worcester. (*See also* japan patterns.)

Bromley, William (d c.1890). Staffordshire potter. Bromley went from the factory of W.H.*Goss to help establish the successful manufacture of a similar porcelain paste at *Belleek and travelled to America in 1883, joining J.H.*Brewer and then *Willets Manufacturing Co. to supervise the development of Belleek ware.
Refs: Barber (1976); D. Rees & M.G. Crawley *A Pictorial Encyclopedia of Goss China* (The Ceramic Book Co., Newport, 1970); Rhead.

Brongniart, Alexandre (1770-1847). French ceramist, trained as a mineralogist and noted for his technical developments at the Sèvres factory during his period of administration, 1800-47. He was appointed to restore the output to technical perfection and solve the factory's financial problems by increasing productivity and sales. Brongniart made changes which included the replacement of the factory's output of soft porcelain paste with a hard paste and increasing the range of colours available for painting high-fired porcelain. He introduced the techniques of casting for chemical ware and large plaques, and transfer printing for borders and monograms. Fearing failure of the kaolin deposits at Saint-Yrieix, he instituted geological searches which revealed sources of kaolin in the Pyrenees, Normandy and Champagne and undertook a survey of the production of ceramic materials in France for the departmental prefectures. Brongniart also initiated a policy of information between Sèvres and the Parisian porcelain factories. He was instrumental in setting up the ceramics museum at Sèvres, and in 1844, wrote a *Traité des arts céramiques*. He also opened a workshop at the factory, which produced stained and painted glass, 1824-52. The artistic development which he achieved at Sèvres depended on the production of high-quality wares by ceramists on the factory's staff and the commissioning of designs from established independent artists.

In his own designs for vases made at the factory, Brongniart was inspired by Etruscan wares, describing his models as Etruscan or Olympian. His father Alexandre-Théodore Brongniart (1739-1813), an architect, also provided designs for vases.
Refs: Auscher; Burton (1906); Chavagnac & Grollier; Guillebon; *Sèvres Porcelain* (catalogue, Smithsonian Institution Press, Washington D.C., 1980).

Brookes, William (1805-1839). English ceramic decorator working in Hanley, Staffordshire. Brookes supplied the Wedgwood factory with engravings of the Ferrara pattern (an Italian harbour scene) in 1832 and continued other designs for transfer printing.
Refs: Batkin; Reilly & Savage.

Brooks, Hervey (1779-1873). American country potter making lead-glazed red earthenware at Goshen, Connecticut. Brooks worked for Jesse Wadhams (b 1773), a Goshen potter, 1795-1810, combining work for the pottery and the fulfilment of his own orders with trading and casual labouring jobs. Brooks's detailed account books (1802-73) list

domestic ware: jugs and pitchers of varying sizes, cream pots, bowls, jars, cooking pots, etc. The firm also carried out jobs, for several other local potters throwing, glazing, decorating, and digging clay. Decoration on Wadhams's and Brooks's own pottery consisted of designs or inscriptions trailed in white slip, or splashes of colour in the glaze. With the decline in demand for household ware in the mid 19th century, Brooks concentrated on the production of ornamental and commemorative ware, as well as flowerpots, drainpipes, and safes for stove pipes, which constituted his principal output by 1845. He wrote a history of the South End district of Goshen in 1858. Brooks ceased active potting in 1867.

Mark, when used, *H. Brooks* impressed with iron tool.
Refs: Stradling; Watkins (1959).

Broome, Isaac (1835-1922). Canadian-born painter, sculptor and ceramist, known for his work in America. During his artistic training, Broome studied Greek and Etruscan ceramics. In the mid 1860s, he made vases and architectural ware in terracotta at his own works, briefly established in Pittsburg, Pennsylvania. Broome worked on portraits, frescoes and sculpture, before opening a pottery in Brooklyn, New York, c.1871 for the production of architectural terracotta, but he had to cease operation because his kiln presented a hazard to nearby buildings. For *Ott & Brewer, he prepared designs for work shown at the Centennial Exhibition, Philadelphia (1876) and drew lithographic plates for printing in gold, black and other colours. In 1878, he became special commissioner on ceramics for the US government and the state of New Jersey at the Exposition Universelle in Paris and studied developments taking place in ceramics outside America.

*Isaac Broome. Parian ware bust of Ulysses S. Grant, modelled by Broome for the firm of *Ott & Brewer, 1875. 26 cm high.*

Broome built a small pottery in Miami City, a suburb of Dayton, Ohio, where he taught local amateur decorators and fired their work, in 1880 becoming instructor in decoration at a night school run (from 1877) by the Dayton education board. With M.S. *Morgan, he established the Dayton Porcelain Pottery in 1882 and began production of porcelain completed in one firing with decoration and glaze. The firm made a small group of small vases in simple, rounded shapes with rich, mottled glaze effects. After his return to Trenton, New Jersey, Broome worked as modeller for several tile factories, including the *Trent Tile Co. and the *Providential Tile Works.

Frequent themes include portraits, classical and contemporary figures, e.g. a head of Sappho in relief on a tile, and allegorical panels representing the Muses, for *Beaver Falls Art Tile Co., and a pair of baseball vases, and figures of players for Ott & Brewer. He also carried out detailed modelling of flowers, garlands, etc., in low relief.

Marks: B or BROOME, impressed, often on the face of tiles with relief decoration of his own design. Vases made at Dayton were marked with an adaptation of the sign of Jupiter scratched under the glaze.
Refs: Barber (1976); Evans; Lehner.

Broseley. *See* Maw & Co.

Brough, Charles. English ceramic decorator. Brough was a painter of flowers, birds, fish and figure subjects on wares made by the firm of W.T.*Copeland, before joining *Doulton & Co. in Burslem, 1903-11.
Refs: see Copeland, William Taylor; Doulton & Co.

Brougham, Henry and Isaac. *See* Chesapeake Pottery.

Broughton, Joseph (1805-75). English porcelain decorator. Broughton was apprenticed as a gilder and painter at the porcelain factory in Nottingham Road, *Derby, in 1816. He later specialized in *japan patterns and worked at the King Street factory, Derby, 1848-75.
Refs: Gilhespy; Twitchett (1980).

Brouwer, Theophilus A., Jr. (1864-1932). American artist potter, oil painter, and artist in metal, wood, plaster and concrete. After a year's experimentation with lustre glazes, Brouwer opened the Middle Lane Pottery at East Hampton, New York, in 1894. Taking entire responsibility for design and production, despite his lack of previous technical experience, he developed a unique range of rich, iridescent glazes with vivid textures and shadowy variations of colour resulting solely from the effect of fire in the kiln. By 1900 Brouwer had developed five classes of ware: Fire Painting, with a coloured glaze used on biscuit clay, rapidly fired in great heat to produce varied iridescent effects in a highly glossy surface; the similar Iridescent Fire Work, with a glaze containing metallic colours and resembling ancient glass with surface crystallization; Sea-Grass, with plain glaze containing radiating streaks of green, brown or grey; Kid Surface, a glaze roughly applied to the biscuit, resulting in a variety of solid colours with a smooth, matt surface; and Gold Leaf Under-

Theophilus A. Brouwer Jr. Vase with black and purple iridescent glaze over green, made by Brouwer in East Hampton, New York, c.1898-1902. 18.4 cm high.

glaze (the only class of ware to have any other decoration than the effects of the heat on the glaze), with butterflies, flowers, etc., or occasionally an entire coating of gold leaf embedded between layers of glaze.

After the sale of the pottery at East Hampton in 1902, he built the Brouwer Pottery at West Hampton, New York, and worked to achieve reliable success in Flame Ware, which had first been produced at East Hampton. This line consisted of bowls, vases, animal figures and occasionally vegetable shapes, made in a hard body and all unique, for the moulds were destroyed after use. Barber notes an early example, an oval bowl with iridescent green-gold glaze containing flame-shaped shading, the handles in the form of frogs with iridescent red glaze.

Brouwer had begun by 1911 to concentrate on other interests, including concrete sculpture, but formed the Ceramic Flame company in 1925 for the manufacture of art pottery. No work is known, though the company was not dissolved until 1946.

Marks: M (for Middle Lane) under jawbones of whale (which formed a gateway to the pottery) impressed and incised; signature, *Brouwer*; Flame Ware marked with *Flame* and/or drawing of a flame, incised.
Refs: Barber (1976); Evans; Kovel & Kovel.

Brouwer, Willem Coenraad (1877-1933). Dutch sculptor and potter, trained in his birthplace, Leiden. Brouwer worked, 1898-1901, for the *Goedewaagen factory in

Gouda, where he also had his own kiln, and moved to Leiderdorp, near Leiden, establishing his own workshop in 1901. His business became N.V. Fabriek van Brouwer's Aardewerk in 1905. His early ceramics included vases in simple, rounded shapes, with incised decoration, covered in yellow or green glazes which Brouwer developed. He experimented with combinations of *sgraffito* and applied decoration, inlaid patterns of contrasting clays, and a variety of glaze effects, with mottled or flowing colours. Decorative designs consisted of regular abstract or floral patterns as well as patterns based on animal farms. He also made architectural ware, fulfilling commissions for buildings in The Hague, Rotterdam and Utrecht. His later work included heavy pots covered in white or grey crackle glazes (developed in 1915); a Jubileumvaas of this type is preserved in Utrecht Central Museum. Brouwer's sons, Klaas and Coen, succeeded him, and the workshop continued until 1956.

Marks: monogram, incised, sometimes within the initials G or L, or impressed in a circular mark with *Brouwers Aardewerk Holland.*
Refs: E. Ebbinge in *Mededelingenblad Vrienden van de Nederlandse Ceramiek* 97/98 (1980); Singelenberg-van der Meer; van Straaten.

Brown, Asa. *See* Lamson Pottery.

Brown brothers. *See* Huntington Pottery.

Brown, Edith. *See* Paul Revere Pottery.

Willem Coenraad Brouwer. Vase with brown-grey metallic effect over a blue glaze. Marked Brouwers Aardewerk, 1909. 16.5 cm high.

Brown, John. *See* Daniel, Henry.

Brown, Reginald (1909-62). English ceramic artist. He was apprenticed in 1925 under H.*Betteley as a painter at the *Doulton & Co. factory in Burslem, and specialized in flowers and landscapes. He worked from c.1930 in the department responsible for the painting of figures and animal models, eventually becoming foreman and manager. From 1951, he was in charge of overglaze decoration.
Refs: Atterbury & Irvine; Eyles (1980).

Brown, Thomas. *See* Ferrybridge or Knottingley Pottery.

Brown, Wilmot (b c.1865). English ceramic artist. He was apprenticed to John *Slater at *Pinder, Bourne & Co. in Burslem from 1879 and trained at local schools of art, subsequently working for *Doulton & Co. until 1930. Brown was known for his painting of historic buildings and landscapes, and designed patterns for printing. He also painted animals, notably cattle and sheep, and flowers, sometimes on Spanish and Luscian wares. He was also concerned with the decoration of wares with high-temperature glazes.
Marks: signature or initials.
Refs: Atterbury & Irvine; Eyles (1980).

Brownfield, William (d 1873). Staffordshire potter and porcelain manufacturer. Brownfield was partner from 1836 in a firm, Wood & Brownfield, producing earthenware with sponged or blue-printed decoration at Cobridge and sole owner from 1850 until he was joined by his son William Etches Brownfield in 1871. The firm then traded as W. Brownfield & Son, producing moulded stoneware, noted for its high quality; a design wih relief basketware surface was registered in 1855. Jugs in stoneware and parian paste were a speciality. High-quality earthenware toilet sets, table ware, etc., often have underglazed transfer printing further decorated with enamels and gilding. A dinner service designed by Hablot Knight Browne ('Phiz') with transfer-printed classical scenes tinted by hand in pinkish-mauve was in production from 1862 until the 1870s. The firm was also known for ornamental and domestic ware made in majolica with brilliantly coloured glazes, and produced ironstone ware. Parian statuary and enamelled figures included work from models by A.E.*Carrier de Belleuse. Production of porcelain started 1871 in new, purpose-built workshops. Apart from ordinary domestic ware, elaborate services with modelled dessert dishes and centrepieces were made; figures representing the seasons were modelled by H.*Prôtat. Two vases with painted decoration in the manner of William Etty, were entitled Morning and Mid-Day. L.*Jahn was appointed art director in 1872. The number of workers employed increased from over 500 in the 1870s to more than 600 in the following decade; much work was exported to Europe and America. F.A.*Rhead, as art director succeeding Jahn, designed and decorated the Gladstone Testimonial Vase for presentation to the politician by the Burslem Liberal Club in 1888. The *pâte-sur-pâte* decoration of the vase depicted Liberty flanked by Homer and Dante and, on the reverse, St George with William Wallace at one side and Brian Boru at the other. A cooperative company, trading as Brownfields Guild Pottery Society Ltd, formed soon after the retirement of W.E. Brownfield in 1890, failed in 1898, and the factory was demolished in 1900.

Marks: early printed earthenwares were marked with the firm's initials; later earthenware and porcelain bear the printed mark of a double globe with the firm's name and COBRIDGE STAFFS on ribbon. A Staffordshire knot, impressed, with the initials WB was used on majolica; also BROWNFIELD impressed.
Refs: Blacker (1922a); Godden (1971); R.V.E. Hampson in *Northern Ceramic Society Journal* 4 (1980-81); Jewitt; Reilly & Savage; Rhead; Watkins *et al.*

brown gold. *See* gilding.

Brown-Westhead, Moore & Co. Staffordshire manufacturers operating the Cauldon Place works, Hanley, which had been established c.1802 by Job *Ridgway. The firm of Bates, Brown-Westhead & Co. succeeded J. Ridgway, Bates & Co. (headed by John *Ridgway) in 1858 and became T.C. Brown-Westhead, Moore & Co., 1862-1904. William Moore (d 1866), formerly employed by the Ridgways, was followed as potting manager by his brother, James Moore (d 1881), who was a partner from 1875. William Moore's son, Frederick T. Moore, became manager of the pottery workshop in 1881 and, from the death of T.C. Brown-Westhead in the following year, shared the management of the whole business with his brother, William B. Moore. The brothers enlarged the firm, afterwards employing more than 1,000 workers. The firm made a wide variety of table and toilet wares as well as ornamental pieces in earthenware and porcelain. Specialities included pieces decorated with flowers in relief, enamelled and touched with gold or silver, and services with ground colours and gilding of high quality, some carried out to commissions from Edward, Prince of Wales (1876-77), the Imperial Court of Russia, and other patrons. The firm also made eggshell porcelain, lined with pink enamel glaze, parian ware, and majolica (which was included in the display at the Exposition Universelle in Paris, 1878), and continued (until the 1860s) the production of full-colour printed pot lids started in 1855 by Ridgway, Bates & Co., briefly employing J.*Austin in 1859. Austin's work included two engravings for the Robert Burns Centenary, 1859. The pot lids were made in a fine, smooth body, initially with a glaze that was liable to craze. Except for Austin's prints, for which the key plate was brown, the firm used black key plates in printing patterns on the lids. J.*Rouse worked as a decorator at Cauldon Place in the 1870s. A. *Boullemier, also one of the firm's painters, carried out a pair of vases to commemorate the Queen's Jubilee in 1887. Work by T. J.*Bott was shown in Paris at the 1889 Exposition Universelle. A few tiles were produced, apparently for export. The firm became Cauldon Ltd in 1904, and later Cauldon Potteries Ltd in the 1920s and 1930s. Cauldon made colour-printed plates and other tableware in semi-porcelain with bubbly, honey-coloured glaze. The pro-

duction of porcelain later passed to E.*Brain & Co. and that of earthenware in 1962 to Pountney & Co. Ltd of the Bristol Pottery. The firm became Cauldon Bristol Potteries Ltd in 1969.

Marks incorporate initials or name of firm and/or CAULDON.
Refs: Godden (1966a, 1972); Jewitt; Lockett (1979); Williams-Wood.

Brubensul. *See* Bennett, Edwin.

Bruff, Charles Clarke. English potter. Bruff returned from service in the Indian army to manage the *Coalport factory, which had been bought in the 1880s by his father, Peter Schuyler Bruff (d 1900), an engineer. He revived the manufacture after a period of decline, re-issuing earlier designs and introducing new patterns. He also extended the works and reorganized production. Bruff became managing director of *Craven Dunnill & Co.
Ref: Godden (1970).

Bruges. Belgian faience factory making table services and everyday ware at Bruges from the mid 18th to the early 19th century.
Refs: A. Duclos *Bruges, Histoire et Souvenirs* (1910); Litchfield.

Bruning, Heinrich-Christian. German porcelain painter working at *Fürstenberg 1797-1855 and known for pastoral views and allegorical studies.

Brunnemann, Horst Carl. German ceramist, manager of the *Meissen factory 1895-1901. Brunnemann developed crystalline glaze effects, which were used in pieces in Art Nouveau style.

Brush, George S. (d 1934). American potter. He joined J.B.*Owens's pottery as editor of the company paper, *The Owens Monthly*, and in 1905 became sales manager for the pottery. He organized and acted as manager of the Brush Pottery Co. (1906-07) in the Zanesville works formerly used by C.B.*Upjohn and, in the interim, by the Union Pottery, whose moulds he acquired for the production of domestic ware. He also made a wide range of specialities in stoneware. After destruction of the works by fire in 1908, Brush became manager of the J.W.*McCoy Pottery, which traded as the *Brush-McCoy Pottery Co. from 1911 and the Brush Pottery from 1925 (the original Brush Pottery Co. had been legally dissolved in 1912). Brush became president of the firm in 1931.
Refs: Evans; Kovel & Kovel; Lehner.

Brush Guild. A group of pottery students, including the sculptor, Lucy F. Perkins (Ripley), her mother, Annie F. Perkins, and Mrs C.B. Doremus, who worked from c.1897 in New York City under the guidance and with the encouragement of George De Forest Brush, who was a follower of William Morris and avoided all use of machinery, even the potter's wheel. Unique pieces in terracotta with black finish were hand built; decoration copied from Etruscan originals was carved in damp clay. The group exhibited regularly in New York from 1903; Lucy Perkins was awarded a bronze medal in the exhibitions at

St Louis, 1904. Both Annie and Lucy Perkins moved in 1908 to Bridgeport, Connecticut.

Mark: a known example is marked with incised x and the signature, *Perkins*, in red crayon.
Refs: Evans; Kovel & Kovel.

Brush-McCoy Pottery. American pottery manufacturers, formerly the J.W.*McCoy Pottery in Roseville, Ohio, which was re-organized in 1911 under the management of G.S.*Brush. In the following year, the company purchased moulds, formulae, etc., from the pottery established by A.*Radford, and continued production of the Radford lines, Radura (matt green glaze), Ruko (resembling jasper ware) and Thera (matt glaze with slip decoration). The firm also took over former pottery of J.B.*Owens in Zanesville while maintaining the works at Roseville. Moulds from Owens's Henri II line formed the basis of a simpler matt green and white ware marketed as New Navarre. Already in production were Loy-Nel-Art, made by J.W. McCoy from 1906; matt green-glazed ware; a line with realistic decoration depicting corn, later adopted by the *Shawnee Pottery; marbled ware. Old Ivory, Basket Weave and Venetian lines were soon produced. Other introductions included Moss Green, Old Egypt, Sylvan (relief decoration of trees) in 1915; Bon Ton, Grecian, Vogue, and Woodland, advertised in 1916; Art Vellum, Stonecraft (decorated ware in grey body with fluted sides) in 1920; Egyptian, glossy glazed Green Woodland, Jetwood (tree design in black on shaded ground), Nuglaz, glossy glazed Onyx, Zuniart (decoration derived from Zuni Indian art, with glossy glaze) in 1923. Utilitarian ware, produced at Zanesville until the plant was destroyed by fire, included Nurock (brown-glazed cooking ware), Dandy-line (yellow-glazed kitchen ware), White Stone (cooking and toilet wares), made 1915-18; toilet sets decorated with pink roses and ribbon bows introduced 1916 and marketed as Lucila; kitchen ware, under the names Bristol (blue and white) and Yellow Dandy. A cheap line in brown and green, garlanded with flowers and marketed as Roman was introduced in 1930. The later art lines were mainly mass-produced and not generally marked. In 1913 the firm was the subject of a film by the Royal Photo Film Co. of Columbus, Ohio, which showed the pottery techniques used at the Zanesville plant and covered many of the lines produced.

The firm was renamed the Brush Pottery in 1925 and now makes jars, novelties and florists' ware.

Marks: THE BRUSH-MCCOY POTTERY CO./ *M-i-t-u-s-a* [stands for Made In The USA] TRADEMARK/ZANESVILLE. OHIO, 1915-25; BRUSH (letters interspersed with brushes standing in vase), WARE on belly of vase; seal shape containing BRUSH/STUDIOS above and below two-handled vase bearing ART, stamped, 1930-33.
Refs: Brush Pottery Co. catalogues (1927, 1930, 1962); Evans; Kovel & Kovel; Lehner.

Brussels. A centre of Belgian ceramic production from the establishment of faience manufacture in the 18th century. The works, opened by Corneille Munbaers in 1705, remained in operation until 1825. Brussels faience, in general resembling that made in Delft and northern France, included tureens in the shapes of vegetables, etc. Porcelain was made and decorated from the late 18th century. In 1818, F.T.*Faber opened a factory in rue de la Madeleine. His technical manager, Christophe Windisch, established his own factory at Etterbeck in 1832, and produced gilded porcelain with high-quality relief decoration, and pieces in the style of Medici porcelain. A successor, Théodore Vermeren-Coché, produced polychrome-painted pieces, 1852-69, but the factory then turned increasingly to mass production of wares in a high-quality paste. The firm operated under the title Demeuldre-Coché and then in the name of Henri Demeuldre as Etbs. Demeuldre S.P.R.L., Manufacture de Porcelain de Bruxelles. Damage during World War II permanently reduced the factory's operations.

Marks include *DC./Bruxelles* with a tree on hand-painted wares and normally the name *Demeuldre* with Bruxelles.
Refs: Danckert; Weiss.

Bryk, Rut (b 1916). Swedish-born designer and graphic artist. Rut Bryk studied at the Finnish school of Industrial Art and joined *Arabia as a designer in 1942. She specialized in plaques and ornamental tiles decorated in a naturalistic manner with painted or *sgraffito* patterns and coloured glazes, and sometimes assisted in the decoration of shapes by her husband, designer Tappio Wirkkala, whose work included wares for production by the *Rosenthal factory. In 1959, Rut Bryk herself designed a ceramic relief panel for Rosenthal. She also designed patterns for the firm's Studio Line.
Refs: Aro; Beard; Préaud & Gauthier; *Rosenthal Hundert Jahre Porzellan* (Kestner-Museum, Hannover, 1981).

Bucher, Hertha (b 1898). Ceramic modeller born near Cologne and trained at the Vienna Kunstgewerbeschule under C. Cizek from the age of 13, and later under M.*Powolny (1917-19). She established her own workshop in 1920 in Vienna, where she produced tableware, garden ornaments, vases, boxes, lamps, clock cases, figures and other decorative pieces, often using a red body, which in places showed through a white glaze, highlighted with metal oxides. Bucher also worked as a freelance porcelain modeller for the *Wiener Werkstätte in the early 1920s and for the *Augarten factory, designing clock cases, lamps and a wide range of figures.
Marks: signature or monogram, incised.
Ref: Neuwirth (1974a).

Buen Retiro. Spanish porcelain factory established in 1759 on the accession to the Spanish throne of Charles III, who transferred the Capodimonte factory from Naples, where it had opened in 1743, to the Buen Retiro palace in Madrid. Production changed from soft paste porcelain to a hard paste in 1804 under the direction of B. Sureda, who had visited Sèvres to study in 1802. The factory was known for rustic figures and groups, at first closely reproducing the work of Capodimonte and, towards the end of its operation, produced elaborate table decorations incorporating many figures and flowers, as well as pieces in neo-classical style. Operation ceased 1808-12, and stock and equipment were transferred to La *Moncloa by Ferdinand VII.

Under Sureda, the factory adopted an 18th-century mark, the initials sn in two triangles, or a crown over M^d in red.
Refs: Danckert; J.F. Riano *Industrial Arts in Spain* (London, 1879, 1890); Weiss.

Buffalo Pottery. American pottery, established 1901 in Buffalo, New York, as part of the Larkin Co. Group, a soap manufacturer, to supply premiums which were provided with purchases of soap or sold by mail order and in retail shops. With Louis Bown, formerly sales representative of the Crescent Pottery (one of the *Trenton Potteries Co. group) as general manager, the pottery was erected under the supervision of works-superintendent, W.J.*Rea, and started production in 1903. R.*Stuart joined the pottery in the same year. Semi-porcelain, moulded from thrown prototypes, was decorated with high-quality underglaze colours prepared at the pottery and sometimes also painted or printed over the glaze with enamel colours or gilding. A number of pieces were also made in bone china. Among the early products were services of semi-porcelain tableware given away with soap products. An underglaze blue willow pattern for tableware, introduced in 1905, was also issued with hand decoration in a wide range of underglaze and enamel colours (Gaudy Willow) and continued in use after 1915, when the semi-porcelain was largely superseded by a vitreous body.

Among the firm's art lines, Deldare Ware was a range of semi-porcelain produced 1908-10 and 1923-25. It was sold through normal retail outlets at a relatively high price and only briefly offered as a premium through the Larkin Co. in the winter of 1922-23. The line, consisting of tableware, trays, vases and toilet sets, was characterised by a delicate olive green body with decoration (originated by R.*Stuart) carried out by hand over transfer prints in bright colours and under a glossy, high-quality glaze. Designs include: the Fallowfield Hunt series (1908-09) from fox-hunting prints by English artist Cecil Charles Windsor Aldin (1870-1935), Ye Olden Days (1923-25), depicting scenes from village life (some inspired by 'The Vicar of Wakefield') and a series of tavern scenes, Ye Lion Inn, also appearing in both periods of production.

Emerald Deldare, made in 1911, is distinguished by the use of elaborate border designs, sometimes purely geometrical and sometimes incorporating natural forms, in contrast with Deldare Ware, which was rimmed with rows of houses, figures, jumping horses or landscapes appropriate to the main decorative theme, or simply with a dark line that echoes the lines along handles and knobs of teapots, etc. Green was a dominant colour in many Emerald Deldare designs; Dr Syntax was a subject frequently depicted, and some pieces have Art Nouveau patterns at the centre. Emerald Deldare was superseded by Abino ware in 1911. Both Deldare lines were marked with the title of the range, date and artist's name or initials.

Abino ware was a limited range produced until 1913; the majority of pieces date from 1912. The characteristic decoration of sailing scenes or an early 19th century windmill identifiably represents Abino Point, a boating resort not far from Buffalo on the Canadian shore of Lake Erie. These designs, as well as pastoral landscapes, which mainly appear on decorative plates, were transfer printed and then hand painted under the glaze by three artists, Stuart, Charles Harris and W.E. Simpson, in misty, subtle colours, mainly pale green and rust, sometimes highlighted in blue. Other subjects, rarely found and perhaps ordered individually, include a desert scene with a camel, signed by Stuart, and a lighthouse at Portland, Maine, by Harris. The shapes were those of the preceding Deldare range and the same semi-vitreous body was used. The title of the line and the year of manufacture are often accompanied by a three-digit series number, often starting with 2.

The pottery also produced lavishly decorated special items, advertising ware for other firms, sets of plates with designs of game, fish or fowl, and tableware which was sold commercially. The company had outlets in New York, Chicago and St Louis by 1908 and was exporting extensively by 1911. The works, enlarged in 1917, made wares for military use and accepted commissions for individually designed services from businesses and institutions e.g. the Chesapeake & Ohio Railroad. In 1923 the pottery ceased to provide premiums for the Larkin Company and concentrated on the production of hotel and institutional ware. Coloured bodies in blue, pink, yellow, ivory, brown, and an agate ware mixture known as Multifleure were introduced by 1928. Copies in limited edition of the Portland vase, first made in 1925, were reissued in 1946. The company was reorganized as the Buffalo Pottery Inc. in 1940 and traded as Buffalo China Inc. from 1956; manufacture of mass-produced ware for hotels and institutions continues.

Marks incorporate a buffalo and BUFFALO POTTERY or, after 1915, BUFFALO CHINA.
Refs: S.& V. Altman *The Book of Buffalo Pottery* (Crown, New York, 1969); Evans; Kovel & Kovel.

Bulgarian ceramics. Until the 19th century only earthenware was made in Bulgaria. The country's liberation from Ottoman rule in 1878 occurred in the period of peak production and artistic achievement, which lasted for about 50 years in the 19th century. Bulgarian potters made lead-glazed wares in clean, curving shapes with local red clays. Incised decoration was mainly geometrical in design leaving smooth, unbroken surfaces.

Bulgarian ceramics. Slip-trailed earthenware bowl, 20th century. 9.8 cm high.

Black and white slip painting was carried out on a brown ground of glaze coloured with manganese; green and yellow glazes were often used over white slip. Relief ornament featured flowers and animal figures (human figures were rare and restricted to silhouettes), as well as the traditional geometrical patterns. Wedding jugs, often with six handles, were lavishly decorated with flowers, animals and patterns formed by grooves and knobs of clay.

Bulgarian pottery centres include Gabrovo, Karlovo, Trŭn, Plovdiv, Vidin and Bansko.
Ref: G. Bakurdjiev *Bulgarian Ceramics* (Bulgarski Hudozhnik, Sofia, 1955).

Buller & Divett. *See* Bovey, Tracey Pottery Co.

Bullers Ltd. English porcelain manufacturers established 1842 in Bovey Tracey, Devon, by J. Buller and J. Devitt. The company moved to Staffordshire, working as W.W. Buller & Co. in Hanley by 1862, and became Bullers Ltd in 1890. A new factory built at Milton in 1912 was in full production by 1920. The main output consisted of electrical porcelain, but the firm also produced chemical porcelain, door furniture, etc.

G.M.*Forsyth, as Principal of the Burslem School of Art, obtained supplies of the firm's hard paste for experimental use by his students, and pieces were exhibited in 1933. In collaboration with Forsyth, the firm established a small studio which was opened in 1934 under the control of A.*Potts, with help from fellow students and the firm's employees, including glaze chemist R.G. Harris, for the production of figures and other ornamental wares, as well as tableware. The studio closed in 1939, but reopened the following year under the guidance of A.*Hoy, who designed the majority of subsequent work until the final closure of the studio in 1952. Bullers Ltd continued production of industrial porcelain.

The work of the studio, when marked, bears the name of the firm and marks of individual designers and decorators, including Forsyth (initials GMF), the artist James Rushton (JR), M. Leach (ML). Agnete Hoy's monogram was incorporated in the firm's mark, 1940-52.
Refs: M. Batkin & P. Atterbury *Art among*

*Bullers Ltd. Porcelain dish painted by J.*Rushton for Bullers Ltd, c.1945.*

the Insulators. The Bullers Studio 1932-52 (catalogue, Gladstone Pottery Museum, Stoke-on-Trent, 1977); Haggar (1947, 1950); Honey (1952); E. Rosenthal *Pottery & Ceramics* (Penguin, Harmondsworth, 1949); W. Ruscoe *Sculpture for the Potter* (Academy Editions, 1975).

Bunzlau. German ceramic centre active from the Middle Ages. The area's potters specialized in stoneware with shiny brown slip-glaze, which included jugs and tableware decorated with applied relief, often in white clay. From 1800 attempts were made by the state to encourage Bunzlau potters to vary their style. Johann Gottlieb Altmann moved to Bunzlau in 1810 and carried out work in classical style. He introduced a feldspathic glaze in 1829, giving his pottery the appearance of porcelain. Vessels which had a matt or slightly glossy white glaze combined with a slip glaze were copied by other Bunzlau potters; some were in neo-gothic style. The traditional folk decoration of flowers, animals and heraldic motifs survived, but was increasingly simplified in the late 19th century. A local pottery school (Töpferei-Fachschule) was established in 1897. That, and an increasing market for pieces inspired by folk pottery revived interest in the work of Bunzlau potters until they left for West Germany at the end of World War II.
Refs: Borrmann; B. Mundt *Historismus* (catalogue, Kunstgewerbemuseum, Berlin, 1973).

Burgau. German porcelain factory established 1902 at Burgau, near Jena, Thuringia, by Ferdinand Selle, for the production of kitchen ware as well as ornamental pieces in Art Nouveau styles. The factory was noted for the high quality of its modelled decoration. Some designs by A. Müller were produced in the early 20th century.

Printed mark: shield with PBM and fish.
Refs: Danckert; Haslam (1977); Scherf.

Bürgeler Kunstkeramische Werkstatten. German pottery workshop established by Carl Fischer at Bürgel, near Jena, c.1900, mainly for the production of ornamental wares.
Printed mark: the initials BKW in a triangle, over *Bürgel*.
Ref: Haslam (1977).

Burgess, Levi (d 1943). American pottery decorator. A nephew of S.A.*Weller, Burgess worked 1905-07 at Weller's studio, painting the Louwelsa line (notably with American Indian portraits) and early Dresden Ware. He subsequently opened an art shop (1909), and decorating business (1912), later working as an illustrator in Cincinnati.
Mark: initials or monogram.
Refs: Barber (1976); Kovel & Kovel.

Burgess & Campbell. *See* International Pottery.

Burgess & Leigh Ltd. Staffordshire earthenware manufacturers occupying the Central

Burmantofts. Vase painted with Isnik foliage design in blues, green, sepia and pink. 25.4 cm high.

Pottery, Burslem until 1870, a portion of the Hill Pottery premises 1867-c.1890 and subsequently the Middleport Pottery, also in Burslem, for the production of domestic and ornamental wares for the home and export markets. The firm's output included Art Deco wares. The Middleport factory buildings remain unmodernized.

Marks include monogram of BL, initials B & L or BURGESS & LEIGH, often with beehive or across globe; *Burleigh* occurs in printed marks from the 1930s.
Refs: Blacker (1922a); Godden (1964); Jewitt.

Burmantofts. Yorkshire pottery established 1858 in Leeds by the firm of Wilcock & Co. for the production of bricks, drainpipes and terracotta architectural ware from local clays. Burmantofts Faience, a hard, buff-coloured earthenware body fired to high temperature, with feldspathic glazes coloured by metallic compounds, was used in the making of tiles and, by 1881, art pottery (which was exhibited by *Howell & James in the middle of that year). The firm made tall vases, bowls, ashtrays, *jardinières*, pedestals and some tableware pieces modelled after oriental or middle-eastern forms were covered with *sang-de-boeuf*, orange-yellow, lime green or turquoise glazes and later in blended colours. Relief decoration of flowers or scrolls, geometrical patterns, lizards and other animals was carved, incised (sometimes with stippled effect) or moulded and applied. Designs in silver lustre were used on dark red or blue grounds. Glazed tiles were moulded with designs in low relief, or painted with foliage, flowers, birds, cherubs, etc., in slip.

By 1889 the firm was run by the Leeds Fireclay Co., which continued to produce and market ornamental wares under the description Burmantofts Pottery, which included vases with flowers painted in natural colours over a raised design, or in thick slip; imitations of W.*De Morgan's Persian-inspired pieces; terracotta was painted with sprays of flowers in the manner of *Watcombe and other Torquay potteries. The production of art pottery ceased in 1904, but the firm continued to manufacture glazed bricks and terracotta.

Marks include: BURMANTOFTS FAIENCE (impressed); monograms of BF, LFC, LEFICO, or *Leeds Fireclay Company*.
Refs: Coysh (1976); Grabham; Jewitt; Lawrence; Lloyd Thomas (1974).

Burnap, James. *See* Taft, James Scholly.

Burri, Werner (b 1898). Studio potter, born in Switzerland and working in Germany. Burri trained at the Bauhaus workshop in Dornburg 1921-25 and went on to succeed T.*Bogler as design director (1926-31) at the pottery in *Velten-Vordamm (1926-31), where he followed Bogler's principle of combining simple shapes to form pieces for production in series, using linear decoration or bands of hatching to emphasize shape or, on cylindrical pieces, coloured bands of differing length and thickness to produce an effect recalling the work of Mondrian. Between 1933 and 1940, Burri worked at intervals in Berlin and at the H.*Bollhagen workshop in nearby Marwitz. He taught ceramics 1941-63 at the school for art and industry in Berlin.

Mark: W incised or painted.
Ref: Bock.

Burroughs, William. *See* Edmands, Barnabas.

Burton, Joseph (1868-1934). English ceramic chemist, trained in Manchester and at the Royal College of Science in Dublin. He assisted his brother, W.*Burton, in the running of *Pilkington's Tile & Pottery Co. and acted as sole manager from 1915 until his death. Burton worked on the development of glazes with his assistant Abraham Lomax and, after the departure of G.M. *Forsyth, took control of the firm's artistic development, adopting a restrained style influenced by his love for Chinese art of the Ming and Sung periods. His later inventions include the minutely bubbled glaze which was to achieve the misty effect of Lapis ware. He was succeeded by his son, David, who had been assistant manager for several years and who worked as manager until he was forced to retire through ill health.
Refs: Cross; Godden (1966a); Lomax.

Burton, William (1863-1941). English ceramic chemist, historian and teacher. Born in Manchester, where he trained and worked as a schoolmaster, Burton won a scholarship (1885) to study chemistry at the Royal School of Mines, but cut short his studies to join the firm of J.*Wedgwood & Sons Ltd as chemist (1887-92), also lecturing on chemistry in ceramics. As head of *Pilkington's Tile & Pottery Co., 1892-1915, he initiated the production of decorated pots and developed glazed ornamental ware, which was marketed as Lancastrian Pottery, sharing with his brother, J.*Burton, and their assistant,

Abraham Lomax, the development of glazes, influenced by the work of his friend B. *Moore.

He was examiner in pottery and porcelain for the City & Guilds of London Institute, a member of the committee appointed to advise the Board of Trade on the question of lead poisoning in the ceramic industry and worked on the cataloguing of ceramics, including the Salting collection at the Victoria & Albert Museum.

Burton was extremely influential in the development of English ceramics in the early 20th century, combining exceptional technical skill with wide aesthetic appreciation. His books on ceramics include: *The Use of Lead Compounds in Pottery* (1899), *A History and Description of English Porcelain* (1902), *A History and Description of English Earthenware and Stoneware* (1904), *A General History of Porcelain* (1904) and *Josiah Wedgwood and his Pottery* (1922).
Refs: Cross (1980); Godden (1966a); Lomax.

Busbee, Jacques (d 1947) and Juliana (d 1962). American craft patrons, whose interest in the folk art of North Carolina led them to seek out surviving potters in the wooded region of the state, which had a tradition of making household wares and whiskey jugs dating back to the 1750s.

In 1917 they began to organize the training of potters and sought a market for the surviving potteries in the area. They opened a tearoom in Greenwich Village, New York, at which Juliana Busbee sold pottery, while her husband worked in North Carolina. Jacques Busbee, formerly a New York art teacher, made a collection of pottery for sale in his wife's shop and managed to locate farmer-potters who had abandoned the craft for farm work and other jobs. In 1921 he opened a workshop, the Jugtown Pottery, about 15 miles from Steeds in Moore County, for the production of red-bodied earthenware jugs, plates, dishes, cooking pots, preserving jars, teasets, candlesticks, etc., adapted from traditional domestic ware, without surface decoration, and yellow, orange or brown in colour through the interaction of body and glaze. After studying oriental shapes and glazes with his master potter, Ben Owen, Busbee began production of grey stoneware with blue, green and white decoration or glazed in black, white, blue, green or dark brown in shapes influenced by Korean, Chinese and Islamic wares, for the New York market. Simple relief decoration of flowers, incised or thumb-printed, also occurs on some pieces. The work, designed and glazed by Busbee, was thrown, from 1923, by Ben Owen, while several assistants worked on the preparation and firing of clay. Busbee concentrated on the achievement of beauty in form, which he believed to be the embodiment of art and the basic requirement for an interesting pot. The work of Jugtown pottery was frequently exhibited between 1925 and 1949. The tearoom moved to a more central position in New York City, and closed in 1926, when Juliana Busbee settled at the pottery. After Jacques Busbee's death, his wife ran the pottery with Ben Owen until she became ill in 1958. The pottery closed in the following year because of the financial and legal confusion resulting from her illness, and Ben Owen left

to establish his own pottery. Jugtown Pottery reopened in 1960 as a non-profitmaking concern, and is still in operation.
Mark: JUGTOWN WARE in a circle, impressed.
Refs: J. Crawford *Jugtown Pottery: History and Design* (John F. Blair, Winston-Salem, 1964); Donhauser; Kovel & Kovel.

Busch & Ludescher. *See* Förster, A., & Co.

Buthaud, René (b 1886). French painter, engraver and artist potter, born at Saintes (Charente-Inférieure). He trained at l'Ecole des Beaux-Arts in Bordeaux. Buthaud worked in ceramics from 1919. He used vivid enamel colours in the decoration of stoneware or hard earthenware vases in simple, massive shapes with stylized foliage, geometrical patterns or, notably, female nude figures, firmly outlined, that echo the sweep of a vase. His vases and bowls were exhibited at the Salon d'Automne, 1920-29. Buthaud was appointed director of a factory producing ceramics for the Atelier *Primavera, near Tours, in 1923. He exhibited faience and earthenware, 1928-65, at the Rouard Gallery. Vases painted with portraits, figures or floral designs on a variety of coloured ground, in some cases have lustre effects.
Refs: Bénézit; Faré; H.J. Heuser *Französische Keramik Künstler* (Museum für Kunst und Gewerbe, Hamburg, 1977); Lesur (1971).

Butler, Frank A. English designer and decorator of stoneware; he was deaf and dumb. Butler worked at Doulton's Lambeth studio 1872-1911, both making his own pieces and designing work for production by assistants. He used a wide range of techniques, including carved, perforated, impressed and folded decorative motifs to produce varied designs, but is known for his use of intricate strapwork and close arrangements of foliage and fruit, with the colour restricted to shades of brown with pale green or off-white, and using blue less freely than other Doulton artists. He adopted a bold use of Art Nouveau features in his designs from c.1895.
Incised mark: monogram of FAB.
Refs: see Doulton & Co.

René Buthaud. Earthenware bowl painted in brown and with crackled celadon-coloured glaze, 1920s. 20 cm in diameter.

Mary Butterton. Vase painted by Mary Butterton with Passiflora *against a lace-textured ground shaded in yellow and green. Impressed mark,* Doulton & Slater's Patent, *on the rim, 1887. 72.5 cm high.*

Butler, J. *See* Wilkinson, A.J. Ltd.

Butner, John (1778-1857). Potter of the *Moravian community in North Carolina. Butner was apprenticed in 1789 to R.*Christ, for whom he worked until 1802. He then took over the Moravian community's pottery in Bethabara, remaining there until at least 1819, and worked as a potter until his retirement, c.1850.
Ref: Bivins.

Butterley Iron Co. *See* Codnor Park Pottery.

Butterton, Mary. English ceramic designer and decorator, working for *Doulton & Co. in Lambeth c.1874-c.1894. She was noted for her firm, original treatment of natural forms in decoration, often stylized and combined with geometrical patterns. Her work was included in the firm's display at the Philadelphia Centennial Exhibition in 1876.
Monograms of MB.
Refs: see Doulton & Co.

Buttle, George Allen (1867-1925) English ceramic artist, noted for his figure painting. Buttle worked for J.*Wedgwood & Sons Ltd, the Hanley firm of Bishop & Stonier, and *Moore Bros, before joining *Doulton & Co. in Burslem, 1905-11. For Doulton, he painted classical figures, cupids, child portraits on vases, plates and dessert sets, miniatures and ceramic cameos. He returned to work as art director for Bishop & Stonier.
Refs: Atterbury & Irvine; Eyles (1980).

Button family. Yorkshire potters. Isaac Button (d 1905), owner of the Fountains Pottery, Liversedge (between Halifax and Dewsbury), which he established in 1866

and worked until his death, made horti-cultural ware from local clay. In 1897, he bought the *Soil Hill Pottery, where he was succeeded by his sons, Arthur (d 1943), George (d 1942), and David, who retired from Soil Hill in 1934. Arthur was followed by his sons, Isaac, who was the sole owner from 1947 until his retirement in 1965, and Arthur.
Refs: Brears (1971a, 1974); Lawrence.

Bux, J.B. *See* Schrezheim.

Byrdcliffe Pottery. American art pottery established in the early 20th century by Edith Penman and Elizabeth Hardenbergh at Woodstock, New York, with encourage-ment from Ralph Radcliffe Whitehead, a student of John Ruskin in England and founder of the Byrdcliffe arts and crafts colony. The first pieces, made c.1902, were entirely hand-built, and the work was fired at the pottery of C.*Volkmar. It was in simple shapes decorated only with coloured glazes, notably Byrdcliffe blue, apple green, and 'withered rose'. Penman and Hardenbergh first exhibited in 1907 at the New York Society of Keramic Arts, and their last exhi-bition took place there in 1925; their work continued until at least 1928.
Mark: a wing motif, with BYRDCLIFFE, usually impressed.
Refs: Evans; A. Evers *The Catskills: From Wilderness to Woodstock* (Doubleday & Co., Garden City, New York, 1972).

Cable, Margaret Kelly (d 1960). American potter and teacher. She trained at the Handi-craft Guild in Minneapolis, Minnesota, studied under C.F.*Binns and F.H.*Rhead, and subsequently worked at potteries in East Liverpool, Ohio, before teaching pot-tery techniques. She carried out experiments with a variety of American clays and worked as an artist at the *North Dakota School of Mines from 1910 until her retirement in 1949.
Ref: Kovel & Kovel.

Cadborough Pottery. Originally a brick-works operating at Cadborough on the outskirts of Rye, Sussex, in the early 19th century under the ownership of James Smith, who was succeeded by his son, Jeremiah Smith, sheep farmer, hop grower and several times mayor of Rye. The earliest identified specimen of Cadborough pottery is a jar made in 1808. The works was managed from c.1830 and purchased in 1840 by William Mitchell (d 1871), who was assisted by his sons Henry and F.*Mitchell. Trading as Wm Mitchell & Son from 1859, the firm advertised 'Brown Ware of every descrip-tion', producing domestic earthenware (often speckled with manganese under the glaze) and flowerpots, chimneypots and drainpipes, as well as money-boxes with simple relief decoration and glazes in green and brown, ale jugs in the shape of pigs, and plant pots painted under the glaze to simu-late the lines of bricks and mortar. Henry Mitchell retired after his brother's estab-lishment of the *Belleview Pottery in 1869.
Incised marks: OLD SUSSEX WARE/RYE and other marks incorporating the place name; MITCHELL or initial M.
Refs: Brears (1974); C. Dawson 'Sussex Pottery' in *Sussex Archaeological*

Cadogan pot. Pot made in stone china by the firm of Copeland & Garrett (see W.T. Copeland), c.1843.

Collections 46 (1903); Godden (1964); Jewitt; Lloyd Thomas (1974).

Cadell, William. *See* Prestonpans Pottery.

Cadet de Vaux, Benjamin. *See* Denuelle, Dominique.

Cadogan pots. Lidless earthenware pots filled through a tube running inwards from the base, made 1806-42 at the *Swinton pottery. The pots, inspired by Chinese wine containers, were probably intended to hold hot water and range from 9 cm to 19 cm in height. They are normally covered with a Rockingham glaze and decorated with trail-ing foliage in relief (sometimes picked out in gold). Similar vessels occur with Copeland or Minton factory marks.
Ref: Jewitt.

Caen. French factory making hard-paste por-celain, established c.1797 at Caen (Calvados). Under the direction of Michel Ducheval from 1802, the workshop produced heat-resistant ware for laboratory use and sold domestic porcelain for decoration in Paris. A firm directed by Fontaine took over the factory after its failure in 1806, making display vases, cabaret sets, tableware and accessories in Empire style, sometimes with relief beading recalling earlier neo-classical pieces. Painted decoration includes flowers, garlands knotted with ribbon, fruit, animals painted *en camaïeu* in brown, village scenes, and seascapes. The firm also made busts, plaques and portrait medallions in biscuit porcelain, before its failure in 1814.
Marks include the name of the town printed or stencilled over the glaze, sometimes in a cartouche or label.
Refs: Auscher; Burton (1972); Chavagnac & Grollier; Lesur (1967).

Caledonian Pottery. Scottish pottery estab-lished during the late 18th century as the Glasgow Pottery and thought initially to have produced porcelain following the styles of the Worcester porcelain factory. After its acquisition (1807) by Aitchison & Co., the pottery was retitled the Caledonian Pottery and produced table services in bone china and underglaze-decorated earthenware, using moulds, patterns and equipment pur-chased on the closure of the *Delftfield Pottery in 1810. At that time, the decoration of bone-china tableware included brightly coloured bouquets in white reserves with yellow enamel ground and lavish gilding.

The pottery was sold in 1840 to a Glasgow ceramic retailer, James Couper, who worked in the partnership Murray & Couper, makers of high-quality bone china, semi-porcelain and earthenware. In 1857 (because of difficulties in firing white ware) production was turned over to stoneware bottles, relief-decorated jugs, figures and such pieces as handles for canes. The pottery moved to Rutherglen in 1870. In 1891, black basalt was introduced by the firm, which had started trading as W.F. Murray & Co. Ltd by the 1870s.

Marks include a lion, impressed or printed, in the late 19th century.
Refs: Blacker (1922a); Fleming; Godden (1964); Hughes (1961).

Caiger-Smith, Alan (b 1930). English potter. After studying in London and at Cambridge, Caiger-Smith trained in pottery techniques at the Central School in London (1954) and established a pottery at Aldermaston, Berkshire, in 1955. With several assistants, he produces tin-glazed earthenware, painted freehand, which includes tableware and many unique pieces. Caiger-Smith has developed a range of colours wider than that traditionally used in painting on a tin glaze, including, for instance, shades of brown, which are fired under conditions of some reduction in a wood kiln. He has also carried out research on painted lustre, achieving distinctive glowing effects.

Marks: monogram of ACS in a square; the workshop mark; the initial A in a circle.
Refs: A. Caiger-Smith *Tin-Glaze Pottery in Europe and the Islamic World* (Faber, London, 1973), and in *Ceramic Review* 59 (1979); E. Cameron and P. Lewis *Potters on Pottery.* (Evans, London, 1976).

Caille, Pierre (b 1912). Belgian painter, designer and potter, born in Tournai and trained in Brussels. Encouraged by H.C.*van de Velde, Caille turned to ceramics in 1937, during the preparation of displays for the Exposition Internationale des Arts et Techniques in Paris. He worked in earthenware and later in stoneware, relying for effect on an original use of glazes and a wide range of decorative techniques. He became a lecturer at the school of architecture and applied art in Brussels in 1949. His subsequent work includes murals and sculptural pieces.
Refs: Bénézit; Hettes & Rada; Préaud & Gauthier.

Caire, Frederick J. *See* Huntington Pottery.

Caldas da Rainha. Portuguese ceramics centre active by the 15th century. Pottery production was a cottage industry in the early 19th century. The potters included Maria dos Cacos, producer of grotesque figures. The *Mafra factory was established in 1853, and R.*Bordalo Pinheiro started a factory in 1884. Others include the Secla factory, now a wide exporter of realistic earthenware figures representing crustaceans, molluscs, reptiles and birds. Pornographic wares are also made in the area.

Caldwell, James. *See* Wood, Enoch (1759-1840).

California Faience. American pottery in Berkeley, California, owned by W.V. *Bragdon and Chauncey R. Thomas, trading initially as Bragdon & Thomas, then The Tile Shop and, from 1924, as California Faience. The firm produced art pottery, mainly cast in red or (more rarely) buff-coloured earthenware, also tiles and small plaques which were hand-pressed in plaster moulds with an incised design. The decorative outlines on the finished tiles stood out unglazed, while the spaces between were filled with glazes, usually matt, in blue, turquoise, pink, yellow and white. This technique was occasionally applied to vases, etc., but the decoration of art pottery was normally restricted to matt or, less often, glossy monochrome glazes. The shapes were simple and many pieces were intended for flower arranging. Bragdon, who took responsibility for the technical procedures, and his partner, who worked on the development of glazes, generally shared the work with two or three assistants.

No art ware was made after 1930, and the production of tiles was suspended in the same year (but resumed c.1932 in preparation for the World's Fair in Chicago). The pottery made glaze materials and firing facilities available to local artists and amateur decorators. Dolls' heads were cast and fired for a local company, whose artists went to the pottery premises to apply the glazes.

Bragdon bought his partner's share in the late 1930s and continued the business as California Faience, working briefly for its new owners after selling out in 1950.

Mark: *California Faience,* incised on the pottery's own work; this name was already used when the firm traded as The Tile Shop.
Refs: W.F. Dietrich *The Clay Resources and Ceramic Industry of California* (State Mining Bureau, Sacramento, California, 1928); Evans.

California Pottery. *See* Trentvale Pottery.

*Lotte Calm-Wierink. Group produced at the *Wiener Werkstätte, with the Werkstätte mark and a monogram of* L.C. *21.9 cm high.*

Callowhill, James (1838-1913) and Thomas Scott (b 1843). English porcelain decorators. Both brothers worked for the *Worcester Royal Porcelain Co. from the mid nineteenth century, specializing in the painting of figure subjects and portraits; they also painted examples of Raphaelesque ware and designed rich decoration in Persian style (1878). James Callowhill had been a prize-winner at the government's school of design in Worcester, 1851, and became known for the execution of chased gilding, especially for Japanese-style designs of storks and grasses in raised gold. T. Scott Callowhill painted portraits on the jewelled *déjeuner* service made to celebrate the marriage of the Earl of Dudley, and with T.J.*Bott continued the painting of classical subjects in the manner of Limoges enamel work developed by Bott's father. He was also a gilder of vases with modelled panels depicting Japanese craft workers by J.*Hadley. Working together as Callowhill & Co., the brothers independently decorated wares, often tea sets, bought in the white from Staffordshire manufacturers in the 1870s and early 1880s. Both are listed as local residents in the Worcester Trades Directory of 1885, but left shortly before that year to work in America. James Callowhill carried out designs for a Baltimore tileworks, worked for Rogers Art Gallery and made lithographs for the Baltimore & Ohio Railway. T. Scott Callowhill worked briefly at a pottery in Phoenixville, Pennsylvania, and subsequently at the *Providential Tile Works. One of the brothers returned to England later in the century and carried out raised gold work for *Doulton & Co. in Burslem.

Marks: monograms of JC and TSC; *Callowhill & Co.* on independent work, 1870s and 1880s.
Refs: Binns (1865); Eyles (1980); Sandon (1978a).

Calm-Wierink, Lotte (b 1897). Ceramic modeller, born in Weinberge, near Prague. She studied at the Wiener Kunstgewerbe-schule, 1914-19, also working at the Wiener Werkstätte, 1918-25. After her marriage in 1927, she travelled to the Far East and India.

Her work included figures and groups as well as pieces decorated in relief with plant forms and small figures in relief.

Marks: signature *Calm* or *Lotte Calm*; initials LC.
Ref: Neuwirth (1974a).

Caln Pottery. *See* Vickers family.

Calvert & Lovatt. *See* Langley Mill Pottery.

Calvertine. *See* Chesapeake Pottery.

Calyx Porcelain and Paint Co. Ltd. Australian producers of semi-porcelain tableware and kitchen utensils at Subiaco, Western Australia, from 1919. After its purchase by the Australian Government, the works produced table and utilitarian wares for the armed forces under the control of *Wunderlich Ltd and the manufacturers H.L. Brisbane & Co. Ltd, users of the trademark BRISTILE since 1929. The firm of H.L. Brisbane & Wunderlich Ltd was producing architectural terracotta, including relief tiles, in the 1950s.
Ref: Graham.

Cambrian Pottery. Welsh pottery established on the site of a former copper works in Swansea, leased in 1764 and in production from c.1767, making drab stoneware and buff or cream-coloured earthenware, as well as its main output of redware utensils for farm and dairy.

After reorganization under the partnership of George Haynes (1745-1830) and John Coles (d 1799), son of the founder, the pottery produced coloured stonewares (black basalt, caneware, etc.) and creamware closely following the work of the Wedgwood factory. Experimental porcelain, of which little survives, was made c.1796. Transfer-printed decoration, initially in blue, black, brown or purple under the glaze of cream tableware, was also carried out over the glaze from c.1800. T.*Pardoe, who was employed as decorator from c.1785 until 1809, was instrumental in developing the pottery's varied style in painting. After his father's purchase of the lease in 1801, L.W.*Dillwyn ran the pottery with assistance from Haynes, who remained as manager until 1810. Haynes was succeeded in the partnership by T. and J.*Bevington. W.W.*Young, employed as decorator, 1803-06, painted birds and butterflies in the style of natural history illustration, and Pardoe's work became noted for accurate botanical detail. Painted studies of shells were also introduced as a decorative subject. The Bevington partnership increased the use of overglaze transfer printing, which included birds after woodcuts by Thomas Bewick. S.*Walker, who had joined the pottery with W.*Billingsley in 1814, was in charge of the search for a more profitable porcelain paste, and developed a formula containing bone ash, which resulted in porcelain with a duck-egg green translucency and, by 1817, a paste containing soaprock (resembling the early Worcester formula) which was characterized by a brownish translucency and slightly pitted glaze.

The output of porcelain, mainly tableware, also included small vases, candlesticks, inkstands and other decorative pieces. Billingsley took control of the painting work-shop; apart from flower painting done by him or under his direction, and his landscapes, the decoration consisted of sprays, small bouquets and sprigs of flowers (including wild species), *chinoiseries*, sometimes painted by hand over printed designs, and japan patterns. The firm's decorators included H.*Morris and W.*Pollard, and some of the ware (especially Walker's early bone-ash paste) was painted by T.*Baxter in 1816 and 1817 and by London workshops for the dealer J.*Mortlock & Co.

The manufacture of porcelain virtually ceased when L.W. Dillwyn left, succeeded 1817-24 by the Bevingtons, who decorated the remaining stock of porcelain, mainly with flowers. On regaining control of the pottery in 1824, Dillwyn, too, concentrated on the production of earthenware, with painting generally restricted to rapidly brushed landscapes with rustic cottages, a swan on water, or other simple scenes, often in pink lustre, with lavish flower painting reserved for rare presentation pieces.

Dillwyn's son, Lewis Llewellyn Dillwyn, joined the pottery in 1831 and took over from his father in 1836. Transfer printing, still of high quality, included friezes of figures in black outline on vases made 1847-50 in local red-firing clay and marketed as Dillwyn's Etruscan Ware, although based in form on Greek pottery; the black ground was laid in enamel colour.

The firm passed to a partnership, Evans & Glasson, in 1850. After the death of Glasson, his partner David Evans was joined by his son, who was in sole control after 1862, trading as D.J. Evans & Co. The pottery then made a limited range of earthenware until its closure in 1870.

Marks: SWANSEA (impressed) until 1811; CAMBRIAN or SWANSEA(written by Pardoe) 1795-1809; DILLWYN & CO (impressed) 1811-17; thereafter impressed or printed marks usually include surname of proprietor.
Refs: P. Hughes *Welsh China* (National Museum of Wales, Cardiff, 1972); W.J. Grant Davidson in *Transactions the English Ceramic Circle* Vol 7, Part 1 (1968); Jenkins; E. Jenkins 'William Weston Young' in *Glamorgan Historian* V (1968); John; W.D. John *Nantgarw Porcelain* (Newport, 1948); *William Billingsley* (Newport, 1968); Nance; Turner; Williams.

Cambridge Art Pottery. American art pottery established in 1900 in Cambridge, Ohio, with Charles L. Casey as president and manager. *Jardinières*, pedestals, umbrella stands, tankards, cuspidors, etc., were produced from early 1901 in local clays covered with glazes of high quality, notably in brown, deep purple, red and several blended shades. C.B.*Upjohn was employed as designer and modeller. A line with underglaze slip decoration, marketed as Terrhea and introduced in 1902, resembled wares with brown grounds from the *Rookwood Pottery, S.A.*Weller and J.B.*Owens potteries. Similar pottery without slip painting was sold as Oakwood. Red-brown earthenware lined with white for kitchen use was introduced in 1903 under the title Guernsey (Cambridge is in Guernsey County) and formed the pottery's main output from 1904 until the brief introduction (1907-08) of a line of artware with dull green matt glaze (resembling that of W.H.*Grueby) and entitled Otoe; shapes were from moulds used earlier.

The pottery became Guernsey Earthenware Co. in 1909 and was sold in 1925, subsequently working as The Globe China Co. and merging with the Atlas China Co. of Niles, Ohio. The resulting firm, Atlas Globe China Co., closed in 1933.

Marks include CAMBRIDGE, impressed, and an acorn containing a monogram of CAP with the name of the line, printed; O.T.O. with a pattern name.
Refs: H.& J. Bennett *The Cambridge Glass Book* (Wallace Homestead Book Co., Des Moines, Ohio, 1970); Evans; Kovel & Kovel; Lehner.

Cambridge Art Tile Works. American tile company established in 1887 at Covington, Kentucky, by the partners, A.W. Koch, F.W. Braunstein and Heinrich Binz, for the production of relief-decorated and enamelled tiles. The firm developed an extensive production of tiles in varying shapes and sizes for use in friezes, fireplaces and decorative panels, also specializing in imitation mosaics. *Intaglio* decoration was frequently used for the reproduction of photographs with shading achieved by varying depths of glaze. The principal designer and modeller, F.*Mersman, decorated panels and tiles with figures in relief, e.g. illustrations of the Seasons and Daughters of the Sea.

The firm became Cambridge Tile Manufacturing Co. in 1889 after merging with Mount Casino Tile Works. In 1927, it acquired the Wheatley Pottery Co. (*see* Wheatley, T.J.), which was operated as a separate unit, the Wheatley Tile & Pottery Co., until its closure in 1930. All production was then carried out at a new plant in Hartwell, Ohio, until 1936.

Mark: *Cambridge*, impressed.
Refs: Barber (1976); Barnard; Kovel & Kovel; K.M. McClinton *Collecting American Victorian Antiques* (Charles Scribner's Sons, New York, 1966).

Cameo China. *See* Wheeling Pottery Co.

Campbell, Colin Minton (1827-85). Staffordshire potter. Campbell went into partnership with his uncle, H.*Minton, and M.D.*Hollins in 1849. He succeeded Minton as managing director in 1858 and, from the following year, continued the production of earthenware and porcelain in the firm then trading as Herbert Minton & Co., while the manufacture of tiles passed to Hollins's part of the firm, *Minton, Hollins & Co. On the formal, complete division of the two branches of manufacture in 1868, Campbell took over the stock of moulds and equipment at a valuation of £30,000. He later went into partnership with R.M.*Taylor in establishing a rival tile firm, the *Campbell Brick & Tile Co., while remaining as head of Mintons. Campbell's efficient management contributed much to the Minton firm's success. He gathered information in the course of travelling widely and controlled the firm's displays in International Exhibitions. *Pâte-sur-pâte* was introduced in 1871, under his management. With W.J.*Goode, Campbell developed a technique of etching on porcelain decorative designs which were then filled with pigment before firing in the enamel kiln; the few known examples include a plaque dated 1865. Campbell was also a

local Justice of the Peace, Mayor of Stoke-on-Trent, Chairman of the North Stafford Railway, High Sheriff of Staffordshire (1869) and Conservative MP for North Staffordshire (1874-80).
Refs: Wedgwood & Ormsbee; *see also* Mintons Ltd.

Campbell, James, & Sons. Australian pottery manufacturers, successors to G.*Fischer at the Albion works in Brisbane in 1885, trading under the Campbell name from the 1890s. The firm made earthenware, including covered jugs, teapots and small animal figures (e.g. pairs of dogs), often moulded or slipcast, with brown glaze. Production continued until the 1950s.
Marks: firm's name and *Albion Pottery,* impressed.
Ref: Graham.

Campbell, Joan (b 1925). Australian potter, born in Geelong, Victoria, but living in Western Australia since 1940. She began her ceramic training in 1959 with a Dutch potter, Daniel de Blancken, and the Australian potter Eileen Keys. She has worked in raku from 1967, and held her first exhibition in 1969. She was a member of the Crafts Board of the Australia Council (1974-77). She now teaches ceramics, working with students in her own studio at Scarborough, Perth.
Ref: Lucielle Hanley (ed) *Joan Campbell - Potter* (Fremantle Arts Centre Press, 1984).

Campbell, John (1857-1927). New Zealand-born potter living in Australia from his childhood. Campbell began work at the *Bendigo Pottery when he was 12 years old and moved to Launceston, Tasmania, in the 1870s. He entered a partnership to form the Jorg-Campbell Steam-Brick Co., soon acquiring A.*Cornwell's pottery at Launceston. He extended its production to include domestic earthenware with coloured lead glazes. Products of the 1930s are usually slip-cast. The output of pottery ceased in 1960.
Marks include JOHN CAMPBELL/ MANUFACTURER/SANDHILL/LAUNCESTON and on slip-cast ware a signature, *John Campbell,* incised.
Ref: Graham.

Campbell, Justin. American potter, the earliest known maker of stoneware at Utica, New York, at a pottery built c.1825. However, a salt-glazed jar with decoration incised and filled with blue has the date 1823 as part of the design and bears the mark *J. Campbell/ Utica.* The pottery was bought in 1830 by Samuel H. Addington, who in turn sold out to an employee, N. White, by 1839.
Ref: Webster.

Campbell Brick & Tile Company. Staffordshire tile manufacturer established at Stoke-on-Trent in 1875 by C.M.*Campbell and R.M.*Taylor. They produced a wide range of tiles, including encaustic, with glazes in several colours, and majolica tiles. Geometrical tiles often have relief decoration of flowers and fruit. Surface designs were printed or hand-painted. Tiles were also made in varied geometrical shapes for tesselated pavements designed e.g. by the architect J.P. Seddon, C.*Dresser, and others. Studies of trees, birds and flowers by Taylor were used to decorate tiles for walls, ceilings,

Ulisse Cantagalli. Earthenware vase with enamel painting. Marked with a painted cockerel in underglaze blue.

flower containers, etc. The firm traded as the Campbell Tile Co. from 1882.
Marks, impressed or moulded, usually incorporate the points of the compass in a circle, or the name of the firm.
Refs: Barnard; Blacker (1922a); Lockett (1979).

Camrath, Johannes Ludwig (1779-1849). Porcelain painter, employed at the Royal *Copenhagen Porcelain Factory from 1794 until the year of his death. He was noted for his studies of flowers and fruit.
Ref: Danckert.

Candia. Firm working 1921-39 in Vienna on the sale and manufacture of ceramics (e.g. figures in a style resembling that of M.*Powolny) and other goods. Disabled servicemen were among those employed on the production of designs created exclusively by Austrian artists.
Marks include a helmet within C; CANDIA. impressed.
Ref: Neuwirth (1974a).

caneware. Cane-coloured stoneware developed from an earlier buff stoneware body in the late 18th century by Josiah Wedgwood for useful and ornamental wares, sometimes decorated with touches of bright blue, green and, from c.1800, red enamel. Other makers included S.*Hollins, and similarly coloured, fine stoneware was among the bodies used (normally with smear glaze) in the mid to late 19th century by makers of *relief-decorated jugs. Strong, heat-proof ironstone china was used in Derbyshire in the mid 19th century

for buff-coloured pie dishes and other cooking ware.

Canneto sull'Oglio. Italian factory established 1872 by the firm Ceramica Furga for the production of kitchen ware, table services, dolls, dolls' heads, etc., in hard-paste porcelain.
Marks include a castle; the initials CF below a crown; the name FURGA.
Refs: Cushion (1980); Danckert.

Cantagalli, Ulisse (d 1901). Italian potter working at Doccia, near Florence, in a factory established in the 15th century, which he inherited in 1878. Trading as Figli di Giuseppe Cantagalli, he produced copies of Middle Eastern and early Italian tin-glazed wares, and (c.1899) earthenware vases decorated with stylized animal and plant forms in the Art Nouveau manner. The firm later specialised in the production of tablewares, but continued production of earlier styles. In 1901, the factory produced vases and dishes from designs by W.*De Morgan. These were marked with DM over a C, with the anchor mark of the decorating workshop.
Marks also include a crowing cockerel painted in underglaze blue.
Refs: G. Liverani *Italienische Majolika* (Cologne, 1960); B. Mundt *Historismus* (catalogue, Kunstgewerbemuseum, Berlin, 1973); Préaud & Gauthier.

Canton china. See Steubenville Pottery Co.

Canton ware. Chinese porcelain decorated in Canton (Kuangtung province) and exported to Europe in the 18th and early 19th centuries. Porcelain was sent in the white from *Ching-tê-chên for painting in coloured enamels. Much of the ware was produced to commissions.

Canuck Pottery at Labelle, Quebec. *See* White, Joseph.

Capes, Mary. English designer and painter, working for *Doulton & Co. in Lambeth,

Canton ware. Two-handled cachepot painted with scenes of officials and ladies speaking together in panels on a gilt ground and decoration in relief of squirrels among leaves and berries, early 19th century. 23.5 cm high.

*Capodimonte. Beaker painted in soft
colours. Marked with a fleur-de-lis in
underglaze blue and n incised. 6.5 cm high.*

c.1876-c.1883. Mary Capes executed a variety
of decorative patterns, primarily on Lambeth
Faience. She also developed a technique of
painting in enamel colours on coloured saltglaze; this work often echoed Japanese
elements in style.
Mark: monogram of MC.
Refs: see Doulton & Co.

Capey, Reco. *See* Doulton & Co.

Capodimonte. Italian porcelain factory
established at Naples in 1743 under the
Bourbon king, Charles III. The output of
cream soft-paste porcelain, mainly intended
for the court, included snuff boxes, vases
decorated with mythological scenes in high
relief, and the figures for which the factory
is known: street traders, *contadini* and *commedia dell'arte* characters. The factory
transferred to *Buen Retiro in 1759. Some
moulds were subsequently sold to *Doccia.
They were copied in large numbers, some in
Thuringian factories, in the mid-late 19th century. Many are still in production at Doccia.
Factory mark (when used) is a *fleur-de-lis*
impressed or painted in underglaze blue.
Copies were sometimes marked with N and
a crown.
Refs: Danckert; Weiss.

Caranza, Amédée de. *See* Longwy.

Carbonnel, Guidette. French designer. From
the 1940s, she modelled pottery, often as
unique sculptural pieces and including tile
panels with decoration incised or in relief
for architectural use.
Refs: Faré; Forsyth.

Cardew, Michael (1901-82). English potter.
While still an undergraduate at Oxford (1919-
23), he learned to throw in the Devonshire
pottery of W. Fishley Holland (1921-22). He
joined the St Ives Pottery as a pupil of B.
*Leach in 1923; his work there included jugs
and mugs with inscriptions (often in Cornish)
scratched through pale slip under a yellow
or brown glaze.
After leaving St Ives in 1926, Cardew
rented a pottery, closed since 1915, at Greet
in Gloucestershire. He reopened it as the
*Winchcombe Pottery, aiming to produce

domestic earthenware for everyday use at
reasonable prices. Helped by between two
and four assistants, he worked in a style
based on the traditional *sgraffito* slipware of
North Devon.
Cardew left the Winchcombe Pottery
under the management of his partner, R.
*Finch, in 1939, and started a pottery at
Wenford Bridge, Cornwall, returning to
Winchcombe briefly in 1942-44, before replacing H.*Davis as pottery instructor at
Achimota College in the Gold Coast colony
(now Ghana) in a scheme to develop local
crafts into large-scale production. He continued the making of stoneware, bricks and
tiles established by Davis, using native
materials.
When the scheme was abandoned in 1945,
he went to Vumé-Dugamé, a traditional
pottery centre on the Lower Volta River
and spent two years in building a pottery
and experimenting with local clays and
glazes. He made stoneware with a dark
body, cutting *sgraffito* decoration through
even darker slip and obtaining touches of
rust or orange colour with iron oxide. Forced
through illness to return to England in 1948,
he rebuilt the Wenford Bridge kiln, changing
production to stoneware, which had pale
decoration in shades of grey and blue.
Cardew was appointed Pottery Officer in
the Nigerian Department of Commerce and
Industry (1950) and investigated pottery
resources in northern Nigeria, opening a
pottery training centre at Abuja in 1952.
There, his stoneware was generally dark in
colour, greyish-green, black or brown, with
vivid glazes. He also used a light-coloured,
opaque glaze with decoration painted in
iron or cobalt pigments, a glaze derived
from wood-ash, which is bright blue when
applied over dark clay rich in iron, and a
yellow-brown slip glaze, of which a variant
was later used at Wenford Bridge. The influence of traditional African pottery shows in
his development of high rims round the lids
of casseroles, teapots, etc., and in such
elements of decoration as vertical ridged
lines and sweeping leaf forms; seats supported by long, pulled handles were inspired
by ceremonial stools.
Cardew spent part of each year in Nigeria
and part in Cornwall, where he settled on
his retirement in 1965. He visited New
Zealand and Australia in 1968, assisting in

Michael Cardew. Earthenware dish with
sgraffito *decoration.*

the establishment of a pottery training centre
for Aborigines in the Northern Territory of
Australia. He was joined in the Wenford
Bridge Pottery by his son, Seth, in 1971.
Mark: impressed monogram of MC.
Refs: M.A. Cardew *Stoneware Pottery*
(pamphlet, Berkeley Galleries London,
1950, 1959, 1962), *Pioneer Pottery*
(Longman, London, 1969/St Martin's Press,
New York, 1971), 'Potters and amateur
potters' in *Pottery Quarterly* X, 38 (1971),
'What pots mean to me' in *Ceramic Review*
32 (March, April 1975); M. Casson *Pottery
in Britain Today* (Tiranti, London, 1967);
G. Clark *Michael Cardew* (Faber, London,
1978); S. Leith Ross *Nigerian Pottery*
(Ibadan University Press, 1970); E. Marsh
'Michael Cardew: a potter of Winchcombe,
Gloucestershire' in *Apollo* 37 (March
1943); *Michael Cardew* (Crafts Advisory
Committee, London, 1976); Rose.

Carlisle Works, Longton. *See* Plant, R.H.
& S.L., Ltd.

Carlton Ware. *See* Wiltshaw & Robinson.

Carmody, Ida Florence. Australian potter,
born in Gunnedah and educated in Armidale,
New South Wales. Mrs Carmody later became a student and associate of L.J.*Harvey
in Brisbane, exhibiting pottery and other
crafts with the Brisbane Arts & Crafts Society throughout the 1930s and 1940s. She was
instrumental in the formation of Red Cross
remedial handicraft teaching in Queensland
after World War I.

Carnelian. *See* Roseville Pottery Co.

Carpenter, Frederick (1771-1827). American potter, born in Lebanon, Connecticut.
Carpenter worked at a stoneware pottery in
Boston until 1796 and in New Haven shortly
before 1801, when he moved to Charlestown
and began the production of stoneware
butter pots, jugs, pickle jars, etc., which he
sold through the Boston merchant, William
Little, the owner of his pottery. Carpenter's
work is simple in shape, decorated with
tooled lines below the necks of bottles or the
rims of storage jars and sometimes a tas-
selled swag, impressed. Some examples are
stained a mahogany colour. The mark,
Boston, was used with the date 1804. By
1814, Carpenter was living near the pottery
established by B.*Edmands in Charleston,
Massachusetts in 1812, where he worked
until his death and continued to produce
domestic stoneware, including pitchers,
bottles, jar covers and plates, in a warm
grey clay body, sometimes dipped in ochre
stain at the rim and base, and decorated
only with small stamped designs of hearts,
eagles, crosses, etc.
Marks incorporate the place name,
Charlestown.
Refs: Stradling; Webster.

Carpentier, Jean Baptiste. *See* Waly.

Carr, James (1820-1904). Potter, born in
Hanley, Staffordshire and working from
an early age; he travelled to America in
1844 and immediately found work in the
American Pottery Co. at the *Jersey City
Pottery. He remained there until 1852, and
then went into partnership with Thomas

Locker at the Swan Hill Pottery in South Amboy, New Jersey, which had been established in 1849 for the production of yellow and Rockingham-glazed earthenware. He opened the New York City Pottery in 1853, trading as Morrison & Carr until his partner left in 1877, and continuing as sole owner until the pottery closed in 1888. At first making only commercial white wares, he also worked on the development of bodies and glazes, achieving high-quality results. He was among the early American makers of majolica, which formed part of the firm's displays in the Philadelphia Centennial Exhibition in 1876 (alongside parian ware, *pâte-sur-pâte*, granite ware and painted plaques) and the Paris exhibition in 1878. Carr's firm produced figures, groups and portraits in parian porcelain; W.H. Edge, principal modeller c.1876, made a number of busts, e.g. George Washington, General Grant and Carr himself. During a brief partnership with the English potter Edward Clark, Carr operated the pottery built by H.*Speeler at Trenton, New Jersey, trading as the Lincoln Pottery Co. and making cream-coloured and white granite wares.

Marks: *Morrison & Carr*, impressed; lion and unicorn with shield bearing the initials JC, often used on white granite ware.
Ref: Barber (1976).

Carr, John. *See* Northumberland Pottery.

Carr & Patton. *See* Phoenix Pottery.

Carrara. *See* Doulton & Co.; Wedgwood, Josiah, & Sons Ltd.

Carrier-Belleuse, Albert-Ernest (1824-87). French sculptor and ceramic modeller. He studied at l'Ecole des Beaux-Arts in Paris (1840) and established a studio for reproductions of 18th and early 19th century sculptures. His assistants included Auguste Rodin. He modelled a figure of Charity for production in parian ware by J.*Wedgwood & Sons Ltd, which was shown in the Great Exhibition in London, 1851, and he was among European artists employed at *Mintons Ltd, where he modelled parian ware, e.g. a bust of the Duke of Wellington, a figure of Prometheus, and the cupids at the base of a vase with *pâte-sur-pâte* decoration executed by L.-M.-E.*Solon. His pieces were also produced in majolica, including a sea-horse and shell (1858), and glazed porcelain. After his return to Paris c.1855, Carrier-Belleuse continued to fulfil occasional commissions for Mintons and other firms; a pair of candelabra modelled for production in gilt bronze by a Paris firm for the International Exhibition in London, 1862, were also produced in majolica by Mintons. He also provided designs produced in ceramics by W.*Brownfield, W.T.*Copeland and, in ironwork, at Coalbrookdale. Carrier-Belleuse worked as art director at the Sèvres factory from the 1870s, and was succeeded briefly on his death by his pupil and son-in-law, J.*Chéret. His son, L.-R.*Carrier-Belleuse, worked as an artist and designer.
Mark: A CARRIER.
Refs: Brunhammer *et al* (1976); Rhead.

Carrier-Belleuse, Louis-Robert (1848-1913). French painter, sculptor and designer; pupil of his father, A.-E.*Carrier-Belleuse. He first exhibited paintings in 1870 and sculptures in 1889. As art director of the *Hautin Boulenger & Co. factory, he modelled architectural ware, including fireplaces, fountains large vases and table centrepieces. He also modelled portrait busts and mythological subjects in terracotta at Choisy-le-Roi (Seine).
Refs: Bénézit; Ernould-Gandouet.

Carrière, Ernest 1858-1908. French painter and ceramic modeller, born in Strasbourg, brother of painter Eugène Carrière (1849-1906). Carrière worked at the studio of T.*Deck from 1890. He was noted for painted or relief decoration of animals, especially birds and fish, on plates, vases, etc., frequently working in glazes with firm outlines in the manner of *cloisonné* enamels. He was an exhibitor at the Salon Nationale des Beaux-Arts in 1892. Carrière became artistic director of the Sèvres factory shortly before his death.
Mark: incised signature.
Refs: Bénézit; Heuser & Heuser; Haslam (1977); Thieme & Becker.

Carriès, Jean (1855-94). French sculptor and ceramist, trained in sculpture at l'Ecole des Beaux-Arts in his native town, Lyons (Rhône), and working in Paris c.1874. Attracted by stoneware in the Japanese display at the Exposition Universelle in 1878, he moved in 1888 to *Saint-Amand-en-Puisaye to study stoneware techniques, and exhibited his first pieces in his own Paris studio early in 1889. He worked with Armand Lion (*see* Lion, E.) before building his own kiln at Saint-Amand-en-Puisaye, and also worked at the nearby Château Montriveau. Carriès

Jean Carriès. Stoneware vase with crackle glaze over gold, late 19th century. 19 cm high.

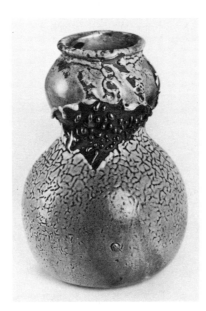

developed a wide range of glazes, including trickled effects, and achieved colour variations with the use of ashes or feldspar. He was commissioned by the Princesse de Scey-Montbéliard to make a doorway in glazed stoneware decorated with masks and animal figures from designs by his friend E.*Grasset. A wide variety of his stoneware shown at the Société Nationale des Beaux-Arts in 1892 included vases of oriental inspiration in the shape of gourds or other natural forms, large vases in simple shapes, pinched pots, rustic pieces and ceramic sculpture, which characteristically represent masks or monsters, half-human, half-beast in form, e.g. a human head on the body of a frog, or such creatures as frogs with rabbits' ears. After his death, Château Montriveau and the Saint-Amand workshop were sold to his pupil, G.*Hoentschel, and, later, N.I.J. Graf *Barck. A commemorative exhibition was held in Paris in 1900. Carriès's influence continued in the work of other pupils P. *Jeanneney, P.*Pacton, and J.*Pointu. P. *Nordstrom followed Carriès's procedures in his own development of stoneware.

Mark: incised signature.
Refs: Brunhammer *et al* (1976); Baschet; Camart *et al*; Céramique française contemporaine; Hakenjos (1974); Heuser & Heuser.

Carr's Hill at Gateshead. *See* Newcastle-upon-Tyne.

Carr's Hill Pottery. *See* Fell, Isaac.

Carstens, C.& E. German porcelain manufacturers working at Reichenbach, Thuringia, from 1900. The firm made domestic tableware of very high quality, opening branches for the production of similar wares at Zeven (Hannover) in the early 20th century and Sorau (Brandenburg) in 1918, and also making earthenware at Neuhaldensleben (Saxony) from 1904. The firm now operates nationalized porcelain workshops at Reichenbach, as part of the *Kahla combine.
Marks: at Reichenbach, the initial R, crowned, and enclosed in a wreath, sometimes with *Carstens/Porzellan*; at Sorau, C&E above a shield bearing C, two stars and an arrow, SORAU with crown and wreath or in a cartouche with a pattern name.
Refs: Cushion (1980); Weiss.

Carter, Henry. *See* Bristol Pottery.

Carter, Jesse (1830-1927). English pottery and tile manufacturer at Poole, Dorset. In 1873, Carter (formerly an ironmonger and builders' merchant in Surrey) bought and enlarged the pottery established by J.*Walker at East Quay, Poole, taking his sons, Ernest Blake (1856-83), Charles (b 1860) and O. *Carter into partnership by 1881. He sold tile blanks to W.*De Morgan for decoration in Chelsea during the 1870s and supplied De Morgan with undecorated bowls and dishes from the 1880s. His firm purchased the

*Architectural Pottery Co. in 1895, producing glazed earthenware and terracotta in Hamworthy and plain floor tiles at East Quay until c.1900, when the firing of majolica and terracotta garden ware was transferred to East Quay, and tile manufacture to the Architectural Pottery. Locally, both ventures were collectively referred to as the Poole Potteries, and the place name appears in marks used by *Carter & Co. and *Carter, Stabler & Adams, but the title, Poole Pottery Ltd. was not taken officially until applied to Carter, Stabler & Adams in 1962. Carter retired in November 1901. He owned deposits of red clay at Corfe Mullen and had also entered into an unsuccessful business venture, buying part of a tile and brick works in *Worcester.
Ref: Hawkins.

Carter, Owen (1862-1919). English painter, designer and ceramist. He joined the pottery operated by his father, J.*Carter, at Poole, Dorset, in 1881, and traded as *Carter & Co. in partnership with his brother Charles from 1901. In private research on lustre decoration, he made stoneware vases, bowls, *jardinières*, etc., in simple, thrown shapes (some with moulded relief decoration) glazed in a wide range of colours, including redgold, yellow, green, blue and purple. Later experiments resulted in the production of unglazed bricks intended for filling with perfumed oil, and lustred stoneware beads, for which he designed a miniature tunnel kiln.
Ref: Hawkins.

Carter or **Adams**, Truda (Gertrude) *née* Sharp (1890-1958). English designer, Truda Sharp studied at the Royal College of Art in London, where she met and married J.*Adams. She went with her husband to South Africa in 1914, teaching art classes at the Durban School of Art. After returning to England, she designed many decorative patterns for *Carter, Stabler & Adams. Her stylized flowers, some based on needlework designs, elaborate and highly coloured, decorated a large proportion of Carter, Stabler & Adams's production. Other patterns included foliate designs, arrangements of fruit, vegetables, and fish. She continued work at the pottery after her divorce from

Truda Carter. Dish made by Carter, Stabler & Adams c.1924 after a design by Truda Adams before her marriage to Cyril Carter. Marks include AC, painted. 31 cm in diameter.

Carter, Stabler & Adams. Vases made at Poole, c.1930. 27 cm and 24.8 cm high.

Adams in the late 1920s, and c.1931 married Cyril Carter, grandson of J.*Carter and co-founder of Carter, Stabler & Adams. She designed the Spring pattern, based on an earlier design of a leaping deer, and the new Leaf pattern after World War II. Some of her floral patterns remained in production on the Traditional Poole range after her retirement in 1950, following which she worked at home as a design consultant.
Ref: Hawkins.

Carter & Co. English pottery and tile manufacturers at Poole, Dorset, formed by the partnership of O.*Carter with his brother Charles after the retirement of their father, J.*Carter, in 1901, and operating as a limited company in 1908. From 1900, the firm produced majolica, lustre-glazed pieces and terracotta garden ware, including fountains, pergolas, balustrades and large pots, decorated with interlaced bands and knots in Celtic style (which were marketed by *Liberty & Co.) at the pottery on East Quay. The manufacture of tiles was transferred to the *Architectural Pottery Co. works and a nearby pottery in Hamworthy which the firm acquired in 1901 for the production of white and cream glazed tiles. The firm employed J.R.*Young as designer by 1904. Under the technical and artistic direction of Owen Carter, the pottery produced an increasing range of work, including grey or off-white stoneware and, probably by 1915, red earthenware dipped in pale slip, painted under the glaze after a first firing. The firm also produced pieces from prototypes thrown by R.*Fry (1914-c.1917) for sale at the Omega Workshops. After the death of Owen Carter in 1919, Charles and his son, Cyril Carter, invited H.*Stabler and J.*Adams to form a subsidiary company, *Carter, Stabler & Adams (established in 1921), which was to market its ware as Poole Pottery. Working in close association, Carter & Co. made glazed earthenware, stoneware, garden ornaments and tiling, and

Carter, Stabler & Adams produced an increasing range of domestic earthenware and stoneware.

Carter & Co. were among the main British producers of tiles and architectural decoration in the 1920s and 1930s. Their commissions include tiles for the Hoover Factory in West London, department stores, food shops, banks, railway and London Transport stations, swimming pools, public houses and restaurants (including Lyons Corner Houses). Some moulded tiles were made to designs by Harold Stabler.

The firm combined with Pilkington Tiles Ltd (*see* Pilkington's Tile & Pottery Co.) in 1964 and, with Carter, Stabler & Adams, became part of the Thomas Tilling Group in 1971; all three companies continued as autonomous units.
Marks: CARTER & CO.; CARTER POOLE.
Ref: Hawkins.

Carter, Stabler & Adams. English pottery manufacturers, formed as a subsidiary of *Carter & Co. by Charles Carter (1860-1934) and his son, Cyril Carter (1888-1969), who were joined by J.*Adams and H.*Stabler. Stabler's wife Phoebe modelled figures for production at the pottery. Their work included earthenware for table use and, notably, slip-coated stoneware painted with bold, colourful brushwork under a creamy matt glaze. Designs were also painted in enamel colours on a white glaze. The company employed external designers, e.g. artist Edward Bawden, who designed a booklet outlining the firm's work and including a map of Poole later used as tile decoration, and also provided tile designs for Carter & Co. Other designers included Minnie McLeish and D.M.*Batty, but John Adams designed most of the shapes, and his wife (*see* T. Carter) designed the majority of patterns, including bright floral patterns which were to become characteristic of the pottery's best-known work. The glazes introduced by John Adams include Chinese blues (e.g. a mottled greenish blue and a bright turquoise crackle glaze), powder and sapphire blues, tangerine, Zulu black, and some streaked and mottled glazes based on wood ash, etc. The orange-pink earthenware body was superseded by cream or white by 1930. Within the following ten years, production became fully standardized and consisted mainly of tableware made in sets. John Adams's Streamline shape, introduced c.1936, became a very popular line, and the firm sold a large quantity of undecorated Utility ware in World War II. Post-war developments included a heat-resistant body for cooking ware. The firm's name was changed to Poole Pottery Ltd in 1962, and in 1971 it became part of the Thomas Tilling Group.

Marks include POOLE/ENGLAND, impressed or printed, with a dolphin, printed from c.1950.
Ref: Hawkins.

Cartledge, Thomas. *See* Hunslet Hall Pottery.

Cartlidge, Charles (1800-60). Porcelain manufacturer, born in Burslem, Staffordshire, and working in England before going to America in the early 1830s as an agent for *Ridgway's. With Herbert Q. Ferguson, formerly a distributor for W.*Ridgway in New Orleans, he established a workshop and showroom at Greenpoint, Long Island, in 1848 trading as Charles Cartlidge & Co., producers of hard-paste porcelain door furniture, knobs for drawers and window-catches, bell pulls, etc., as well as buttons. The output later included tableware in bone china. Joined by his brother-in-law, J.*Jones, who contributed many designs and models, Cartlidge extended his production to include dinnerware, candlesticks, inkstands, paperweights, animal figures, snuff boxes, chessmen, draughtboards, cane handles, medallions, etc. Decorators included E. *Tatler and Frank Lockett. Jones modelled many portrait busts of American personalities (notably Daniel Webster, General Zachary Taylor, Chief Justice Marshall, Henry Clay), which were produced in biscuit porcelain or parian ware. Pitchers were made in squat, curving forms derived from 18th-century rococo shapes with relief decoration of oak leaves and twigs, patriotic symbols, such as the eagle, the American flag, etc., and a corn design by Jones. A wide variety of pieces was shown at the International Exhibition in New York, 1853. The works closed in 1856, re-opening only briefly the following year.
Refs: Barber (1976); J. Brown and D. Ment *Factories, Foundries and Refineries. A History of Five Brooklyn Industries* (Brooklyn Rediscovery, Brooklyn Educational & Cultural Alliance, New York); Clement (1947).

Cartlidge, George (b 1868). English painter, ceramic modeller and decorator. He was an apprentice at the *Sherwin & Cotton tile works in 1882 and signed or initialled tiles decorated with portraits or figure subjects in *émaux ombrants* from the 1890s. Cartlidge often worked from photographs, some of which are preserved in the Stoke-on-Trent City Museum with a collection of his tiles. As a decorator in Stoke-on-Trent from the 1890s to the early 20th century, he worked on designs of plants outlined in trailed slip for the firm's Morris ware. In America for a time after World War I, he continued to model portrait panels and designed tiles for a manufacturer in Newport, Kentucky, also sending designs for production in England.

Refs: Godden (1966b); Lockett (1979).

Casey, Charles L. *See* Cambridge Art Pottery.

Casseday, Samuel. *See* Indiana Pottery Co.

Casson, Michael (b 1925). English studio potter. He studied painting and worked as a teacher before establishing a workshop in London with his wife, Sheila. The Cassons moved in 1959 to Great Missenden, Buckinghamshire, where they developed an output of domestic stoneware and unique pieces in stoneware or porcelain. Michael Casson's individual work includes large bread crocks, jugs and storage jars with a variety of rich glaze effects. In the 1970s he experimented with patterns in white porcelain inlaid in a darker, hard earthenware or stoneware body. Casson is a noted teacher of ceramics. In 1963, with Victor Margrie, he started a vocational course for potters at Harrow School of Art.
Refs: E. Cameron & P. Lewis *Potters on Pottery* (Evans, London, 1976); M. Casson *Pottery in Britain Today* (Tiranti, London, 1967), *The Craft of the Potter* (BBC Publications, London, 1978); *Ceramic Review* 24 (1973), 43-47 (1977); Rose.

Castex, Joseph. *See* Auvillar.

Castleford. Yorkshire pottery on the River Calder, north-west of the town of Castleford, comprising brick and tile kilns built in the 1720s, a small coarseware pottery established c.1780 and a pottery making fine earthenware and stoneware, built in 1785 or 1786. The business was in the hands of D. *Dunderdale from 1790 to 1821.

Early cream-coloured earthenware, of which few marked examples are known, resembled the work of the *Leeds Pottery. The firm also made ornamental ware in black basalt. The fine, white feldspathic stoneware associated with the pottery, resembling basalt in texture, was used to make jugs, mugs, bowls and, notably, moulded teapots; marked examples are known. Decoration included a partial coating of brown glaze combined on jugs with moulded scenes, blue or red enamel outlining, relief moulding and hand-painted panels. The teapot designs which can be certainly attributed to the pottery were made in black basalt as well as white stoneware, and were adapted for other items of teaware.

Financial difficulties resulted in the dissolution of the firm in 1820, and the fine ware pottery was then divided; a part initially occupied by former employees of Dunderdale continued to make domestic earthenware (reabsorbing the remainder of the works in 1883) and then produced institutional ware until the pottery's closure in 1961. The coarse-ware works continued to make stoneware, utilitarian earthenware and, by the twentieth century, bricks.

Castleford has become a generic term for similar stoneware made by many English and Scottish potteries from the early 19th century. It was mainly well-potted, sometimes translucent. The decoration often took the form of reliefs on classical themes. Makers include the firms of W.T.*Copeland, Davenports, Hollins, Wedgwood, Wood, Walley of Cobridge, Stevenson of Cobridge.

Dunderdale's ware was marked D.D. & CO or CASTLEFORD (sometimes both marks) impressed on creamware and stoneware.
Refs: Bemrose; Grabham; Jewitt; Lawrence; D.E. Roussel *The Castleford Pottery 1790-1821* (Wakefield Historical Publications, Wakefield, 1982); *Stonewares and Stone China* (catalogue, City Museum and Art Gallery, Hanley, Stoke-on-Trent, 1982); Towner (1957).

Castle-Harris, John (1893-1967). Australian potter, born in New South Wales. He studied under U.*Deerbon in Melbourne, before moving to the Blue Mountains, outside Sydney, where he built a studio and worked until his death. Castle-Harris was a skilful modeller. Before moving to Sydney, he may have worked for a time at the *Premier Pottery, and a large vase from the pottery's Remued line in the Australian National Gallery has as part of its decoration a lizard in a style which links it to his known work, but he is better known for large, sinister dragons often engaged in fierce combat around the rims of urns or vases.
Ref: John McPhee *Australian Decorative Arts* (Australian National Gallery, Canberra, 1982).

Castle Hedingham. *See* Bingham, Edward.

Catherall, Samuel. *See* Denholme Pottery.

Catherall family. *See* Soil Hill Pottery.

Caughley. English porcelain factory established in the 18th century at Caughley, Shropshire. On the retirement of Thomas Turner, proprietor, the works and equipment were purchased by a former employee, J.*Rose, who continued the production of biscuit ware at the factory for decoration and glazing at the Coalport works. Rose demolished the factory and removed its effects to Coalport in 1814.
Refs: Barrett (1951); Godden (1969); R.L. Hobson in *Transactions of the English Porcelain Circle* III (1932); C.C. Roberts 'Salopian China' Parts I, II and III in *The Connoisseur* 54 (August 1919), 55 (December 1919), 57 (July 1920).

Cauldon Potteries Ltd. *See* Brown-Westhead, Moore & Co.

Caulkins, Horace James (1850-1923). American ceramist. Working as a dental supplier, he developed a kiln for firing dental enamel, which was also sold under the name Revelation for firing overglaze ceramic decoration. With M.C.*Perry, he developed a gas-fired pottery kiln, later used in a number of American art potteries. From 1903, they produced art ware which was initially sold under the Revelation name. Within a year, the Pewabic Pottery was established, with Caulkins acting as clay technician, while Mary Perry designed and glazed the ware.
Refs: Eidelberg; Evans; Kovel & Kovel.

Cazaux, Edouard (1889-1974). French potter. One of a family of potters in the Landes region, Cazaux was apprenticed in a pipe factory at Tarbes (Hautes-Pyrénées) from c.1903. He went to work in a small Paris factory in 1907, and subsequently studied design at Mont-de-Marsan (Landes). He

received a grant in 1912 enabling him to study sculpture and ceramics. He settled in Varenne, near Paris, after his marriage in 1918 and produced earthenware and stoneware, including many monumental pieces. Painted or modelled decoration was inspired by religious or mythical subjects (Creation, Annunciation, nymphs, musicians, etc.). Cazaux also used thick glazes scraped away to show the body beneath in patterns of plant forms or geometrical motifs.
Ref: Céramique française contemporaine; Faré; H.J. Heuser *Französische Keramik-künstler Um 1925* (catalogue, Museum für Kunst und Gewerbe, Hamburg, 1977).

Cazin, Jean-Charles (1841-1901). French painter, engraver and ceramist, born in Samer (Pas-de-Calais). He worked as a teacher from 1866 and became director of the Ecole des Beaux-Arts and curator of the museum at Tours (Indre-et-Loire) in 1869. While in Tours, he carried out experiments in earthenware techniques.
Cazin worked in London as an art teacher in Kensington (1871) and at the Lambeth School of Art (1872-73); his pupils included R.W. and W.F.*Martin. While working for C.J.C.*Bailey at the Fulham Pottery, he made stoneware jugs and mugs, incised or impressed with floral designs (often in the Japanese manner), heraldic emblems, etc. On his return to Paris, he worked as a painter from 1875, exhibiting from the following year, and also made stoneware with a grey body, sometimes coated with contrasting slip. Some work was decorated with modelled relief. Cazin used high-temperature colours in shades of black, brown and predominantly grey, with thin, shiny glaze.
Mark: incised signature.
Refs: Heuser & Heuser; Rose.

Cazin, J.-M. Michel (1869-1917). French potter, son of J.-C.*Cazin. He studied art under his parents and became a skilful sculptor and medallist, working at his own studio in Equihen (Pas-de-Calais). He first exhibited at the Salon of the Société Nationale des Beaux-Arts in 1897. From 1900, he made stoneware with relief decoration of fruit, flowers, etc. Some pieces were in the shape of leaves, fruits or textured like tree bark. In 1900, he established his own studio in Paris. Although he had used coloured glazes, his later work was no longer glazed. He used a coloured clay body in the making of some freely modelled pieces. Cazin was killed in an explosion in Dunkerque. His wife, Berthe, also worked as a potter.
Mark: name in capital letters, incised.
Refs: Bénézit; Heuser & Heuser; Lesur (1971).

Ceccaroni, Rodolfo (b 1888). Italian designer and ceramist. Ceccaroni trained as an artist, designer and restorer, and then studied ceramics while teaching in Grottaglia and Sesto Fiorentino. He built his own wood-fired kiln in 1917 and produced plates with coloured slip decoration often on religious themes under a clear glaze, trying to recapture early craft traditions.
Ref: Préaud & Gauthier.

celadon glazes. A range of oriental glazes varying in colour from greenish or blue-

grey when used on a pale stoneware or porcelain to olive green on a darker body, according to the amount of iron present in the glaze. Green-glazed wares were made in China during the Han dynasty (206 BC-AD 220) and reached a jade-like quality in the Lung-ch'üan ware made near Hangchou in Chekiang province in the Sung dynasty (AD 960-1260). The velvety appearance of celadon glazes is due to the presence of fine bubbles.

Central Pottery. *See* Wilkinson, A.J., Ltd.

Century Vase, The. *See* Müller, Karl.

Ceramica Industrial Montgalina. Spanish porcelain manufacturers, established at Montgat, Barcelona, in 1935, for the production of everyday tableware.
Mark: triangular monogram, c containing ɪ and ᴍ.
Refs: Danckert; Weiss.

Ceramic Art Co. *See* Lenox, Walter Scott.

Ceramic Club. *See* Fry, Laura Anne.

Ceramic marble. *See* Eason, Alfred.

Ceramicas Hispania. Spanish manufacturers of porcelain and earthenware established at Manises, Valencia, in 1941. The output includes domestic ware in porcelain, earthenware with coloured glazes, and ornamental pieces.

Mark: a monogram of cʜ with the verticals of the ʜ extended to represent smoking chimneys.
Refs: Cushion (1980); Danckert; Weiss.

Céramique, La, S.A. *See* Pouyat family.

Ceres. *See* Britannia Pottery.

Chair, Henry (1858-1920). Porcelain painter working for the *Worcester Royal Porcelain Co. for 42 years from the 1870s. He specialized in painting roses, and his work included garlands of flowers on perforated ware by G.*Owen.
Ref: Sandon (1978a).

Chalot, Jacques-Louis. *See* Chantilly.

Chamberlain, Robert. *See* Worcester.

Chambers, John. English ceramic designer. He worked as the first designer employed by *Pilkington's Tile & Pottery Co. from 1893, becoming head of the firm's architectural pottery department. Chambers worked with consultant designers, e.g. L.F.*Day, W. *Crane, C.F.A.*Voysey, in the supervision of tile making. He designed the shapes of some early pieces of Lancastrian ware; his patterns include a repeating design of peacock feathers for tiles. His son, Arthur Chambers, working for Pilkington's as a chemist (1927-38), developed a matt, mottled glaze (Cunian) for tiles and pottery.
Refs: Cross; Lomax.

Chambers, William. *See* South Wales Pottery.

Chameron, Marie-Louise. *See* Talbot family.

chamotte. A class of coarse stoneware bodies containing particles of ground, fired clay (grog) which is added for its effect on the throwing quality of the body, to aid drying, to reduce shrinkage and increase strength in firing, or for the appearance and texture of the unglazed body. The grog itself is also sometimes referred to as chamotte.

Chang. *See* Doulton & Co.

cha-no-yu. *See* tea ceremony.

Chantilly. The soft-paste porcelain factory started by Louis-Henri de Bourbon, Prince de Condé, at Chantilly (Oise) closed at the end of the 18th century.
In 1803 the town's mayor, Pigory, with a partner, Vallée, established a factory for the production of hard-paste porcelain and *faïence fine,* but without financial success. In 1812, their business passed into the hands of Jacques-Louis Chalot, who died in the late 1830s, and Pierre-Louis Toussaint-

Chantilly. Biscuit figure in 18th century costume, coloured and gilt, 1875-1900. 36.5 cm high.

Ernest Chaplet. Porcelain bottle, late 19th century.

Bougon, who made finely finished relief-decorated or perforated pieces, often oval or octagonal in shape. Bougon, by then sole owner, sold the business to M.*Aaron and Charles-Alphonse Chalot in 1845. Aaron was succeeded by his son Eugène-Edouard. The factory's output then included biscuit figures, sometimes decorated with enamels, as well as porcelain and earthenware for domestic and restaurant use, until its closure in 1870.

A new factory, opened in 1944, made imitations in hard paste of the 18th-century soft-paste porcelain, along with some modern styles.

Marks include P or MA/CHANTILLY with hunting horn; B & C [Bougon and Chalot]; *Manufacture de Porcelaine de Chantilly* from 1944.
Refs: Burton (1921); Chavagnac & Grollier; Ernould-Gandouet; Garnier.

Chapallaz, Edouard (b 1921). Swiss ceramist, trained at the Ecole Suisse de Céramique at Chavannes-Rennes. Chapallaz established a workshop in 1953 and taught ceramics in Geneva (1958-68). With his brother, André, he specialized in austere, glazed pieces. His output includes miniature wares exhibited in Japan, 1980, and architectural decoration. He taught ceramics in Geneva, 1958-68.
Refs: Hettes & Rada; Préaud & Gauthier.

Chaplet, Ernest (1835-1909). French ceramist, a pioneer in the artistic renewal which started in French ceramics during the 1870s. Chaplet worked at the factory in Sèvres, his

home town, from 1843, studying decoration, design and ceramic techniques. He worked for a time at Choisy-le-Roi (Seine) c.1855, before joining the *Laurin factory (1857-74), where he made painted earthenware. He also introduced *barbotine decoration on terracotta. He subsequently increased the range of colour and achieved subtler background shading with the more advanced technical facilities at C.*Haviland's studio in Auteuil, where he worked from 1875, assisted by F.*Bracquemond's policy of engaging designers who were already working in impressionistic and Japanese-inspired styles.

In 1881, Chaplet began to use unglazed brown stoneware of a type used by folk potters in Normandy, soon perfecting his technique at a studio put at his disposal by Haviland on rue Blomet, Vaugirard, where he was assisted from 1882 by A.-L.*Dammouse. He made simple forms ornamented with Japanese-inspired designs in low relief, or painted in coloured slips with outlines in gold. The decorators included J.-P.*Aubé, J.-D.*Ringel d'Illzach, A.-L. and E. Dammouse. The moulds were used for the production of porcelain, decorated under the glaze, at Haviland's Limoges factory in 1884.

Increasingly preoccupied with the interrelation of material, form and decoration, Chaplet began experiments to reproduce the Chinese *sang de boeuf* glaze, working initially in stoneware and then in porcelain, and achieving his first success early in 1885. He took full control of the rue Blomet studio on the withdrawal of the Haviland firm in 1886 and continued production of glazed stoneware, then beginning his collaboration with P.*Gauguin.

In 1887, Chaplet settled at Choisy-le-Roi, perfecting his *sang de boeuf* glaze and exploring other glaze effects based on copper. After 1891 he achieved colours ranging from purple to white and celadon. His vases became increasingly austere in form, and he moved away from oriental influences in style. He was forced by the loss of his sight to abandon ceramics in 1904 and gave up his studio in Choisy-le-Roi to his son-in-law, E.*Lenoble.

Marks: at rue Blomet, H & CO within a rosary (*un chapelet*), impressed; rosary alone, usually painted, when working independently.
Refs: Brunhammer *et al* (1976); Céramique française contemporaine; d'Albis *et al* (1976); Heuser & Heuser; Lesur (1967, 1971); Tilmans (1954).

Chappel, Stephen. *See* Leeds Pottery.

Chapus, Jean (1867-1933). French porcelain decorator and manufacturer working in Limoges. Chapus worked with W.*Guérin before becoming director of the Alary decorating workshop on rue Montmailler in 1890. With a partner, Denardon, he took over a factory on the site of an Augustinian convent on the road to Paris in 1900, producing decorated tableware, notably for use in restaurants. His three sons joined the

firm and, on the retirement of Denardon in 1928, bought the factory of M.*Raynaud in the Faubourg Montjovis, where they traded as Manufacture Porcelainière Limousine, producing tableware in clean, simple styles. In 1933, the firm became s.a.r.l. Porcelaines Chapus Frères, under the direction of the eldest son, Louis, who had worked with his father for 24 years. The brothers made ware in classical shapes after World War II and later restricted themselves to decoration, selling the name Chapus to André Raynaud in 1974.

Marks include M/L/LIMOGES/FRANCE; in green; *astral* in a rising sun, with LIMOGES. Chapus Frères marks: C.F. in a rectangle with LIMOGES/FRANCE; LIMOGES in a rising sun; CHAPUS & FILS/CHAPUS FRERES/LIMOGES/FRANCE. Recent mark: *Royal/Chapus Frères/Limoges/France* with a closed wreath.
Ref: d'Albis & Romanet.

Charité-sur-Loire, La (Nièvre). *See* Warburton, Peter and Francis.

Charles Dickens Ware. *See* Asbury, Edward.

Charpentier. *See* Magnac-Bourg.

Chastagnac, Alexandre. *See* Redon, Martial.

Chaumeil, Paul (b 1902). French studio potter. Chaumeil attended classes in design organized by the Gobelins factory and then studied ceramics at the Paris Conservatoire d'Arts et Métiers. He then concentrated on the making of earthenware at a pottery established by his grandfather. His work includes dishes and vases decorated only with a band of ribbing under pale, opaque glaze, with a dark earthenware body exposed at foot and rim. Chaumeil taught modelling in a Paris studio, 1959-74.
Ref: Céramique française contemporaine.

Chauvigné, Auguste (1829-1904). French potter. After training as a painter, specializing in studies of fruit and game, he studied pottery techniques under C.*Avisseau, later establishing his own pottery at his home town, Tours (Indre-et-Loire). Chauvigné made Palissy ware and other pieces, notably display plates decorated with the arms of Tours. He was succeeded by his son, also Auguste Chauvigné (1855-c.1929).

Mark: signature or painted monogram.
Refs: Bénézit; Heuser & Heuser; Lesur (1971); Thieme & Becker.

Cheavin, George and Winston. *See* Fulham Pottery Ltd.

Chekanov, Alexander. Russian earthenware maker. He was the founder of a factory which operated at Yekaterinburg (Smerdlovsk) from 1864 to the early 20th century. His output included tableware with painted or printed decoration, often floral designs.
Refs: Bubnova; Serebryannikov *Porcelain and Faience of the Urals* (Veka, Perm, 1926).

Chekhonin, Sergei Vasilievich (1878-1936). Russian painter, designer and ceramist. In 1896, Chekhonin entered the School of the Society for the Encouragement of the Arts, where his studies included ceramics. In the following year, he transferred to a St Petersburg studio, where he trained until 1900. He joined the *Abramtsevo workshop in 1904 and produced designs for mosaics used in the refurbishing of the Metropol Building in Moscow under P.K. Waulin, whose studio he entered in 1907 to continue work in ceramics. In St Petersburg, he carried out murals in majolica for the decoration of churches. After 1913, he became a specialist in the Ministry of Agriculture's art section and took control of the school of enamel painting in Rostov. In 1917, he became artistic director of the *St Petersburg porcelain factory, where he designed a Jubilee dish in 1918, and tableware with monograms, slogans and brightly painted decoration. He also produced designs for engraved gilding. His own painting included complex, detailed patterns of flowers, fruit and foliage, as well as portraits, e.g. of Lenin, Rosa Luxembourg and, on a large oval dish, the principal figures of the October Revolution. His allegorical studies include Hunger, Sadness and Horror. In 1923, he became artistic director of the Novogyb porcelain works on the Volkov (formerly owned by the *Kuznetsov family). *Ref:* Gollerbach.

Chelsea Keramic Art Works. American pottery company established in 1872 as James Robertson & Sons, when J. and G.W.*Robertson joined A. and H.C.*Robertson at Chelsea, Massachusetts, and trading as the Chelsea Keramic Art Works c.1875-89. In 1873, the partnership began production of art ware (marketed 1876-78) inspired by ancient Greek terracotta, and bronzes found at Pompeii. made in fine-textured red earthenware, pieces were polished with linseed oil before being engraved with minutely detailed decoration. The black ground of copies of Greek red-figure ware was painted on before the whole vase was polished. Artists included J.G.*Low (until 1878), sculptor Franz Xavier Dengler, Boston artist G.W. Fenety, as well as members of the Robertson family. Chelsea faience, introduced 1877, was made of buff or yellowish clay in simple forms, covered with the high quality glazes for which the works became noted. Floral decoration was either carved directly in the damp clay, impressed with natural flowers, grass, etc., or hand-modelled and applied on the clay surface, which was sometimes previously hammered in the manner of metalwork and inlaid with patterns of white clay underneath a semi-transparent glaze. Ware sold as Bourg-la-Reine of Chelsea from c.1877 was painted in coloured slips (like the barbotine ware revived by E.Chaplet at the *Laurin factory, Bourg-la-Reine), often against a blue or green ground, and covered with transparent glaze. After the death of James Robertson in 1880 and the departure of Alexander (1884), Hugh Robertson began production of a hard, pale stoneware body in simple, curving shapes without ornamentation except for a number of Chinese-inspired glazes which he developed. He continued production of wall plaques with high relief decoration, some resembling woodcarving in effect, others with incised designs. Raised ornament on a smooth ground was sometimes glazed to represent blue and white jasper ware.

The pottery closed after financial failure

in 1889 and was reopened on a more effective commercial basis as the *Chelsea Pottery US, with backing from Boston businessmen and under the management of H.C.*Robertson.

Marks: CHELSEA KERAMIC ART WORKS/ROBERTSON & SONS (until the death of James Robertson), impressed; CKAW in a lozenge shape, impressed; four-leaved clover with initials CPUS, one on each leaflet, impressed; paper label; decorator's mark incised.
Refs: Barber (1976); Evans; L.E. Hawes *The Dedham Pottery and the earlier Robertson's Chelsea Potteries* (Dedham Historical Society, 1968); Kovel & Kovel; J.J. Young *The Ceramic Art, a Compendium of the History and Manufacture of Pottery and Porcelain* (Harper & Brothers, New York, 1878).

Chelsea Pottery US. American pottery established in 1891 at Chelsea, Massachusetts, under the direction of H.C.*Robertson after the closure of the *Chelsea Keramic Art Works. The need for a profitable output resulted in the high-fired Cracqule Ware, which was characterized by a grey crackle glaze discovered earlier and perfected by Robertson with help from his son, William. The decoration in underglaze blue was restricted to the rims of bowls, plates, cups, saucers and other tableware. The first border was a simple pattern of rabbits in profile, which initially faced anti-clockwise around the rim, but by late 1891 faced in the opposite direction. Other borders of clover, horse chestnuts, pineapples were added as a result of a competition open to students of the Museum of Fine Arts School, Boston. The early decoration was carried out with the aid of raised outlines made by pressing the clay in engraved moulds, but decorators preferred to paint freehand and achieved livelier results without the lines, which were removed from the moulds before 1895. Occasional pieces survive with imperfectly smoothed lines in a different pattern from the one painted. In 1895, the pottery moved to new premises which had been in construction at Dedham, Massachusetts, from 1893, and began trading as the *Dedham Pottery.

Mark: four-leaved clover with initials CPUS on the leaflets, impressed.
Refs: Barber (1976); Eidelberg; Evans; Kovel & Kovel.

Chelsea Ware. *See* Low, John Gardner.

Chelsea Works, Burslem. *See* Cooper, Susie.

Chenavard, Aimé. French designer; painter and artistic consultant at the Sèvres factory from 1830. His *Nouveau recueil d'ornements*, published in 1833, contained designs combining motifs from a variety of sources, including Greek, Assyrian, Egyptian and Oriental art, as well as those associated with Gothic and Louis XV styles. His work included *guéridons*, vases and table ornaments for the Sèvres factory.
Refs: Bénézit; Lesur (1971).

Joseph Chéret. Decorative dish with matt glaze, 1894. Signature, Joseph Chéret, *incised.*

Chéret, Joseph (1838-94). French sculptor, ceramic designer and metal worker. He was the younger brother of the graphic artist, Jules Chéret, studied under his father-in-law, A.-E.*Carrier-Belleuse, and worked as a designer of furniture (1870), glass (1877) and pewter. Chéret joined the Sèvres factory as a modeller, briefly succeeding Carrier-Belleuse as artistic director in 1887. His work included the design of a porcelain vase (*Les Masques*) with relief decoration of figures and grotesque masks with glaze shading from blue at the base to yellow at the rim, signed.

Mark: incised signature.
Refs: Bénézit; Brunhammer *et al.*; Haslam (1977); Heuser & Heuser; Lesur (1971); Thieme & Becker; P. Vitry 'L'Orfèvrerie à l'Exposition' in *Art et Décoration* 8 (1900).

Chesapeake Pottery. American pottery established at Baltimore, Maryland, 1880-81 by the English potters, John Tunstall, Henry Brougham and Isaac Brougham, for the production of yellow and Rockingham-glazed earthenware. Bought in 1882 by D.F.*Haynes & Co., it traded as the Chesapeake Pottery from 1887, Haynes, Bennett & Co. from 1890, and D.F. Haynes & Son from 1895. Lines of utilitarian and ornamental articles included Clifton ware, a high-quality earthenware body with coloured majolica glazes; Avalon ware, a fine, ivory-tinted body with soft glaze, decorated with sprays of flowers in relief, coloured and with gilded highlights; Calvertine, similar to Avalon in body, but engine-turned and decorated with bands of relief ornament, delicate colours and dark gilding; Severn ware, a vitreous body which fired to a greyish-olive tint, introduced in 1885. The output also included relief portrait panels, medallions of the seasons by B.*Thorwaldsen, relief plaques (1885) depicting heads of cattle modelled by sculptor James Priestman (who also did work for E.*Bennett), and modelled flowers (1895), all in a parian paste noted for its richness of colour and translucency. The firm made a wide variety of toilet wares in an ivory body and, from 1886, in 'semi-porcelain', which was also used for dinner services in an extensive range of shapes. The firm's display in the World's Columbian Exposition (1893) included a large, wide-bodied vase in Renaissance style, with handles in the form of winged figures and finial in the form of flames, designed by Haynes and known as the Calvert vase; several copies were made with varying glazes and decorative treatments.

A variety of marks incorporate a monogram of Haynes's firm with BALT and the name of the ware, e.g. *Avalon* or *Clifton*. From c.1890, a device of three interlocking circles with the initials of Haynes and Bennett or the Chesapeake Pottery, and the titles of shape and pattern. From c.1900, HAYNES/BALT°.
Ref: Barber (1976).

Chester Pottery Co. *See* Phoenixville Pottery.

Chesterfield Pottery Company. Australian stoneware works in operation at Footscray, Melbourne, by 1866. The production of brown saltglaze, thought to have been inspired by Derbyshire stoneware was under the control of a Melbourne coal merchant from c.1870 until the closure of the works in 1872. Chesterfield Pottery Ware was made alongside brown-glazed Rockingham Pottery in 1875, at another site, by the Footscray Pottery. In 1880, the successors, *Yarraville Pottery, made breakfast sets, etc., in porcelain, as well as kitchen wares.
Ref: Graham.

Chevannes, Faïencerie de. French faience workshop established by the 17th century as a tileworks at Chevannes, near *Auxerre, and producing pottery with enamelled decoration in 1792. The tileworks absorbed a nearby faience workshop which had been in operation 1793-96. Production of tiles and faience became separate after the sale of the premises in 1811, when the faience workshop was let to a potter named Paitard from Toucy (Yonne). François Pommier (d 1827), from Auxerre, was an employee and then took over production in 1822, calling in as partners his brothers-in-law, Joseph Lachiche and the painter Jean-Baptiste Ergot (d 1823), who was succeeded by his son, Edmé-Nicolas. Pommier's widow briefly continued production with her nephew and gave up the lease in 1829. Using thickly potted orange, or later, yellow clay, the workshop produced wares with crackled, sometimes bluish or greenish tinged glaze, decorated *en camaïeu* with manganese, and sometimes with manganese splashed grounds. The Ergots introduced bands of colour with geometrical motifs. Patriotic decoration introduced in the Revolution was revived c.1830 on a porcelain body made with local kaolin. The later wares were made in simple

shapes resembling those of *Arthé and *Montigny. Decoration became restricted to patterns in manganese and copper green, with touches of blue or yellow. The factory closed c.1860.
Refs: Huillard; Lesur (1971).

Chicago Terra Cotta Works. American pottery, established 1866 in Chicago, Illinois, for the production of architectural terracotta, statuary and garden ornaments in classical styles. Under the direction of an English potter, James Taylor, who joined the firm in 1870, a line of vases was made, also in terracotta, 1876-79. The pottery closed c.1880.

Mark, when used, CHICAGO TERRA COTTA WORKS, with year.
Refs: Barber (1976); Evans; Watkins (1950).

Chikuzen. A line of Japanese porcelain makers and decorators working in Kyoto through four generations. Miura Chikuzen studied under *Dohachi II and made porcelain strongly influenced in style by Chinese wares; he was noted for copies of *Shonsui wares. Masakichi Watanabe (1853-1915), also using the name Miura Chikuzen, established his own kiln in 1883; he, too, made imitations of imported pieces after first becoming known for his celadon wares.
Refs: Jenyns (1965); Roberts; Uyeno.

Chilcote, Charles. American pottery designer, apprenticed to C.B.*Upjohn at the Weller Pottery in 1904. His signature is found on the work of J.B.*Owens's pottery company, and he took charge of design for the Zane Pottery Co. (successors in 1921 to Peters & Reed).

Mark: signature, *Chilcote*, or initials CC.
Refs: Evans; Kovel & Kovel; Lehner.

china painting. The decoration of pottery and porcelain with underglaze or enamel colours, a popular activity among amateurs in England in the 1870s and 1880s. Classes were held at *Minton's Art Pottery Studio by employees of the Minton factory, and *Howell & James held annual exhibitions of work by amateurs from 1876. Similar exhibitions were held elsewhere in England, and books of patterns and technical information

china painting. Tile made in Staffordshire by Minton, Hollins & Co., Stoke-on-Trent, and painted c.1875 in Cincinnati by Jane Porter Hart Dodd (1824-1911). 15.2 cm square.

were published. The painters normally signed and dated their work, which was carried out on blanks issued by Mintons and other firms, usually with a factory mark.

In America, china painting developed as a movement in the field of art wares during the 1870s. Facilities were provided by commercial potters, e.g. E.*Lycett, who taught decorative techniques at his New York workshop in the late 1860s before working as an instructor in St Louis, Missouri, in 1877 and Cincinnati, Ohio, from the following year. Specialist workshops established for the sale of paints, pottery or porcelain blanks and hand-painted tableware and providing lessons in decorating techniques were the Western Decorating Works of Grunewald & Schmidt in Chicago, where firing facilities were offered from 1878 to painters who had previously used small individual kilns.

In Cincinnati, K.*Langenbeck and M.L.*Nichols Storer began experiments in overglaze painting in 1873, and in the following summer Benn Pitman organized a class at the *Cincinnati School of Design. A committee formed by local women to prepare for the Centennial Exhibition in Philadelphia (1876) sponsored an exhibition in May 1875 of work by Nichols, M.L.*McLaughlin, C.C.*Newton and others to raise the funds needed to enter a display in the Exhibition and to promote china painting as a potential source of employment for women. McLaughlin was to become an authority, publishing several books on decoration, and in 1879 organized the *Cincinnati Pottery Club, with Newton as secretary and L.A.*Fry as an honorary member. The club worked at the *Coultry Pottery, where they experimented with underglaze painting and relief techniques as well as with enamel decoration. McLaughlin had in 1877 begun to seek ways of reproducing the slip-painted wares of C.*Haviland, which had been shown in Philadelphia, together with Chinese and Japanese wares, the other main source of inspiration for the decorators. Underglaze ware like McLaughlin's, which she called 'Limoges faience', became more widely known as Cincinnati faience as the city became associated with other decorators and potteries producing similar slip-painted wares. McLaughlin eventually made her own clay bodies, slips and glazes, developed skills in throwing, and began to work with porcelain. Nichols also saw a need for skill in a wide range of ceramic techniques and for less dependence on commercial producers for equipment and materials. After her early work in a studio at F.*Dallas's pottery, where her pieces were potted and fired, she established the *Rookwood Pottery, which produced blanks for decorators, notably the Cincinnati Pottery Club.

S.*Frackelton, working at her own pottery in Milwaukee from 1883, organized the *National League of Mineral Painters in 1892, with a membership that included A. Alsop-Robineau, Laura Fry, M.C.*Perry and C.*Volkmar. Further efforts in the development of ceramic decoration as a serious study combining artistic and technical training were made by F.H.*Rhead, P.E.*Cox and L.V.*Solon. The Newcomb College Pottery arose from the interest of a group of amateur decorators in New Orleans in the 1890s.
Refs: Barber (1976); Callen; S.S. Darling

Chicago Ceramics & Glass (Chicago Historical Society, Chicago, Illinois, 1979); Donhauser; Evans; S.G. Frackelton *Tried by Fire* (D. Appleton & Co., New York 1886); F.E. Lewis *China Painting* (Cassell, London, 1883); M.L. McLaughlin *Pottery Painting under the Glaze* (R. Clarke & Co., Cincinnati, 1880), *Suggestions for China Painters* (R. Clarke & Co., Cincinnati, 1884); T. McLennan 'The Art Industries of America: IV China Decorating' in *Brush & Pencil* 3 (June 1905); Peck.

Chinese Jade. *See* Doulton & Co.

Chiné ware *See* Doulton & Co.

Ching-tê chên. The site of the Chinese Imperial porcelain kilns, active as a ceramic centre by the 10th century in the northern Kiangsi province. In the Ch'ing dynasty (1644-1912) the number of kilns including Imperial kilns and those that were privately owned at Ching-tê chên reached about 3,000. Fire damage in the mid 19th century caused extensive rebuilding (1864). The centre is still active, and the output includes eggshell porcelain.
Ref: M. Carter *Crafts of China* (Aldus Books, London, 1977).

Chini, Galileo, Guido and Chino. Italian pottery manufacturers. In 1896-97, ceramic designer Galileo Chini established a factory, L'Arte della Ceramica, in Florence with a partner, Vittoria Giunti. Chini, who acted as art director, was joined by his cousins Guido and Chino. Galileo Chini was inspired by early tin-glazed wares and the work of oriental potters, as well as contemporary designers and painters, e.g. Gustav Klimt. He designed stoneware, specializing in vases with lustre decoration in rich, velvety colours, some with oriental-inspired decoration, Galileo and Chino Chini left two years after the factory's move to Fontebuoni, Florence, in 1902, and established a firm, Chini & Co., at Mugello. The Chini factory, Manufattura Fornaci San Lorenzo, was destroyed by bombing in 1944. Chini & Co. produced stoneware and revived the craft of tinglaze, using traditional majolica patterns and lustre glazes, and also producing Art Nouveau pieces.
Refs: Bossaglia; Préaud & Gauthier.

Chin Jukan (1835-1906). Japanese potter, descended from a Korean who had worked as a potter in Japan from the late 16th century. He was noted for his efforts to improve the quality of *Satsuma ware. Chin Jukan moved the last remaining kiln at Kagoshima to Naeshirogawa in 1874. He was active in expanding the overseas market for the ware. His own work includes pieces with delicately carved and perforated decoration, which was an innovation in Satsuma wares.
Refs: Roberts; Uyeno.

Chivers, Frederick H. (c.1881-1965). English porcelain painter, specializing in studies of fruit. After working in *Worcester, then at *Coalport, where he painted vases and display plates from c.1906 until World War I, and again in Worcester, Chivers was employed at the porcelain factory in King Street, *Derby, soon before its closure. He is thought to have gone on to work for *Paragon China

Cincinnati Art Pottery. Vases of the Hungarian faience line, made in the 1880s. 26.7 cm, 21 cm, 25.4 cm high.

Ltd. The characteristic speckling of his backgrounds was achieved by working the pigment with a frayed matchstick.
Mark: signature, *F.H. Chivers.*
Refs: Godden (1970); Sandon (1978a); Twitchett (1980).

Chokushi. *See* Shigaraki ware.

Choso Mikawa. *See* Kiyomizu.

Chowaken. *See* Yosabei II.

Choy, Katherine Pao Yu (1929-58). Artist potter, born in Hong Kong and working in America. She succeeded S.A.E.*Irvine as head of the ceramic department and teacher at the Newcomb Pottery in 1952, also making individual pieces of her own.
Ref: Kovel & Kovel.

Chozo Makuzu (1797-1851). Japanese potter born in Kyoto. Chozo established a workshop c.1830 at Makuzugahara, where he made pottery that became known as Makuzu ware, under the stylistic influence of Korean, Chinese and raku wares. His patterns frequently contained an ivy-leaf motif. He was also noted for his copies of *Ninsei ware.
Ref: Roberts.

Christ, Rudolf (1750-1833). German-born potter, working in America from 1766, when he was apprenticed to a fellow Moravian, Gottfried Aust (1722-88), a potter in Bethabara and Salem, North Carolina. Christ started his own pottery at Bethabara in 1786 and moved to Salem in 1789, taking over a pottery started for the local Moravian community by Aust. He produced slip-decorated earthenware and, by 1795, a small quantity of saltglaze. He made moulded plates with scalloped edges, leaf dishes, etc., and by 1800 bottles and flasks in the form of animals. Christ's output of hollow ware, which was thrown, includes mugs with horizontal ribbed lines, small bowls, covered storage jars and other pieces, some with mottled glaze. In the early 19th century, he made water pipes. Christ retired because of ill

health and failing eyesight in 1821 and was succeeded by his assistant, J.F.*Holland.
Ref: Bivins.

Christoffersen, Helge. Danish sculptor. Christoffersen worked at the Royal *Copenhagen Porcelain factory. His main work consists of small figures in stoneware, which express a preoccupation with Nature and Man's relationship with it, e.g. Apollo and Daphne, opaque white glaze (1949); Pan, with a reindeer, unglazed (1951); girl with an armadillo, Sung glaze (1952). A large relief commemorating the resistance movement of 1940-45, with *sang de boeuf* glaze, is in the Danish Parliament building.
Ref: Hiort.

Chromal. *See* Peters & Reed.

chromolithography. *See* lithography.

Church Gresley. *See* Ault, William.

Church Works, Hanley. *See* Ridgway, William; Ridgway Potteries Ltd; Wilson, David.

Cincinnati Art Pottery. American art pottery company formed 1879 in Cincinnati, Ohio, to finance continued research in Cincinnati faience by T.J.*Wheatley, who left the firm in 1882. By 1884, the firm produced Hungarian faience with delicate floral designs moulded in relief in white clay painted overglaze in pink, yellow, pale blue, dark blue and black, with gilded highlights. Portland blue faience was painted in gold on deep blue ground which imitated the deep blue ground colour of the Portland vase. Biscuit ware, mainly in shapes adapted from Greek and Roman forms, was produced for decoration outside the pottery. Kezonta ware was decorated with chrysanthemums, etc., in natural colours and scrollwork painted in gold against an ivory-coloured ground; shapes included pilgrim bottles and a fan-shaped wall pocket; production continued until the closure of the pottery in 1891. W.*Dell, the manager, obtained moulds, notably of Hungarian faience pieces, for production at his own pottery.
Marks: c.a.p. co., impressed; kezonta (an Indian name for a turtle); kezonta cincinnati and a turtle within a circle.

Refs: Barber (1976); Evans; Kovel & Kovel; Lehner; Peck.

Cincinnati faience. *See* china painting.

Cincinnati Pottery Club or **Women's Pottery Club.** A group of American ceramic decorators formed in 1879 in Cincinnati, Ohio, 'to uphold the standard of good craftsmanship of the best workers in the different branches of pottery', with organizer M.L.*McLaughlin as president, C.C.*Newton, secretary, and Alice Belle Holabird, treasurer, and a membership of eight others, including L.A.*Fry, increasing to about 20. The club worked in a room rented from the Cincinnati Women's Art Association, at first taking advantage of facilities available to amateur decorators (*see* china painting) at the *Coultry Pottery (where they met three times a week), and employing two throwers. From the autumn of 1879 work was sent for firing at the pottery owned by F.*Dallas, where they rented a room and carried out experiments in decorative techniques with the help of Dallas and J.*Bailey, but independently of the work of M.L.*Nichols Storer in another part of the works. The group's first Annual Reception and Exhibition was held at the Dallas Pottery in 1880, selling enough work to balance the budget for a whole year; at least 200 pieces were shown, many decorated with naturalistic floral and animal designs, inspired by oriental, Middle Eastern or classical examples. McLaughlin carried out slip decoration, and the group's other work included painting in blue and other colours on a biscuit ground, incised, carved or inlaid decoration, and designs etched by Fry on stoneware in a style resembling the work of *Doulton & Co. at Lambeth. Relief modelling was also carried out in parian ware. In 1881, the group moved to a rented studio at the *Rookwood Pottery; after their eviction in 1883, they returned to overglaze decoration.

When the club, which had served as a model for other pottery associations in Chicago, New York, etc., disbanded through lack of funds in 1890, some members formed a group, the Associated Artists of Cincinnati, again with McLaughlin as president and Newton as secretary. Ceramic decoration exhibited together with metalwork by club

Cincinnati Pottery Club. Porcelain plaque made in Limoges, painted by Amanda Merriam, 1879-90. 31 cm in diameter.

members in the World's Columbian Fair (1893) included porcelain vases with delicate enamel painting and gilded tracery.

The Porcelain League of Cincinnati was organized at the studio of Laura Fry, with Newton as secretary, by former members of the Pottery Club.

Mark: *Cin. Pottery Club*, incised with initials of artist and date.
Refs: Barber; Evans; Clark & Hughto; Kovel & Kovel; Lehner.

Cincinnati School of Design. Ohio college offering a class in ceramic decoration for women which was instituted in 1874 by Benn Pitman, an instructor in carving. He organized the class outside normal school hours and engaged a teacher, Maria Eggers, German born and trained in Dresden. The original students, including L.*Nichols, C.C.*Newton and M.L.*McLaughlin, painted with enamel colours on porcelain, and in 1875 auctioned their work at a meeting of the Women's Centennial Executive Committee of Cincinnati in aid of the Mount Vernon fund, all showing work in the Women's Pavilion at the Philadelphia Centennial Exhibition. From the outset, the class engaged in experimental work with colour-mixing, glazing and firing, though the output was mainly fired at commercial potteries.
Refs: Barber (1976); Kovel & Kovel; Peck; A. Perry 'Decorative Pottery of Cincinnati' in *Harpers Monthly* (23rd May 1881).

City Pottery, The. *See* Rhodes & Yates.

clan kilns or **fief kilns.** Japanese producers of ware made under the patronage and protection of local feudal chieftains in the Edo period (1615-1868), primarily to augment the estate's finances. In some areas, the kilns were available at certain times for the firing of pieces made by local potters. Many of them found it profitable to produce domestic pottery for local sale (as well as supplying the feudal lord) and continued working as *folk kilns after the fall of the Tokugawa regime in 1868.
Refs: Gorham; Mizuo; Okamura.

Clanta ware. *See* Bretby Art Pottery.

Clark, Decius W. (1815-87). American potter, born in Burlington, Vermont, and living from his boyhood at West Troy, New York, where he served a seven-year apprenticeship at a stoneware pottery. He worked at a stoneware pottery in Gardiner 1837-41 before joining the works run by J.*Norton at Bennington. As superintendent of the United States Pottery (*see* Fenton, C.W.), Clark became noted for his skill in ceramic chemistry. He investigated clay bodies and glazes, and promoted the use of native American materials. In 1857-58, Clark took charge of experimental work at the *Southern Porcelain Manufacturing Co. to solve technical difficulties encountered there in the use of local clay. He worked in close association with Fenton and, after the closure of the Bennington factory in 1858, joined him 1859-c.1862 in establishing an Illinois pottery (later the *Peoria Pottery Co.) for the production of yellow, Rockingham-glazed and white wares. Clark later worked at Croton, New York, where he settled in 1876.

Refs: Barber (1976); Spargo; Watkins (1950).

Clark, Edward. *See* Carr, James; International Pottery.

Clark, L.W. *See* New England Pottery Co.

Clark, Nathan. American potter making stoneware from 1805 at Athens, New York, in partnership with his brother-in-law Thomas Howe (d 1813), whom he succeeded as sole owner of the business. He also opened branches in Rochester, Lyons and Mount Morris, putting them in the care of potters whom he had trained. Ethan Fox, Clark's partner from 1829, bought the main works in 1838, selling it back in 1843 to Clark, who installed his son Nathan Jr (d 1891) as manager. In 1893, Thomas and Edward Ryan took over the works from Nathan Clark's successor, Nathan E. Clark, trading as the Athens Pottery until the closure of the works in 1900.

The pottery produced earthenware from local clay and saltglaze from a mixed-clay body which fired to colours ranging from grey to buff or red. The output included bottles, wine casks, water coolers, beer mugs and pharmaceutical ware, as well as stove pipes, and a large number of special and ornamental pieces. Albany slip was used to line many vessels, and decoration was painted in a deep, rich cobalt blue, sometimes with incised outlines. A Clark & Fox handbill of 1837 advertised a full range of domestic stoneware and red earthenware.

Clark's family retained the Lyons branch from its establishment in 1822 until 1852 when it passed to the manager, T.*Harrington. The output of salt-glazed domestic ware was distributed for sale along the Erie Canal. The pottery continued under Harrington's successor until 1902 and was run by a workers' cooperative until 1904 or 1905. At Mount Morris, Clark produced stoneware from 1835 until 1846, when the manager, G.G. Williams, became proprietor. The works probably closed by 1850. Clark purchased a working stoneware pottery at Rochester between 1836 and 1841, installing Harrington and a potter from Alsace, John Burger, as joint managers and transferring the business to them in 1852. Burger was sole proprietor after the withdrawal of Harrington in 1854, and moved to new premises in 1861.

Mark: names of firms impressed.
Refs: Ketchum (1970); J.R. Macfarlane 'Nathan Clark, Potter' in *Antiques* 60 No 1 (July 1951); Webster.

Clark, Richard. *See* Don Pottery.

Clarke, Thomas. *See* Derby.

Clauss family. Porcelain manufacturers working in France. Jean-Marc Clauss (c.1778-1846), born near Treves in Germany, settled in 1821 in Paris, where his brothers Louis-Daniel and Jean-Etienne were porcelain throwers. Jean-Marc Clauss established a factory c.1830 on rue Pierre-Levée and bought the premises in 1852. Work exhibited in 1834 included a tea service decorated with roses and floral scrolls. He was succeeded by his son Marc-Alphonse Clauss (d 1868) and subsequently his grandson Marc-Eugène, who continued to run the factory until he entered into a partnership, Clauss & Cie, with Léon Bourdois and Achille Bloch in 1887, retiring three years later. The firm became known for luxury wares: lavish table services and vases, as well as biscuit figures and groups. Decoration was inspired by the paintings of Boucher, Chardin and Watteau. Bloch, working alone after the retirement of Bourdois in 1900, was followed by his family, who continued operating the factory to the present day, working from 1948 as Porcelaine de Paris. The output now includes household and sanitary wares.

Marks include crossed swords with EC; a single trident, or two tridents, crossed (1868-87); others incorporate crossed arrows, a crown, or monogram of AB.
Refs: Danckert; Guillebon.

Claycraft Potteries Co. *See* Robertson, Frederick H.

Clement, Adolphe. Ceramic chemist. As technical manager at the Royal *Copenhagen Porcelain Factory, Clement began in 1886 to experiment with crystalline glazes on porcelain, very much influenced by the work of Sèvres: zinc silicates were used to form crystals, and colour effects were produced with metallic oxides. Clement based his own experiments on the account of research by Sèvres chemists Lauth and Dutailly, published 1888, and used copper, tin, cobalt and chromium as colouring agents in his own work on hard Copenhagen porcelain. His first crystalline glazes were successfully fired on vases c.1889. Clement left the Copenhagen factory in 1891 and was succeeded by V.*Engelhardt.
Ref: Bodelsen.

Clement, Lillemor, and **Larsen,** Inger Folmer. Danish potters working in Hareskovby by the late 1940s. Their earthenware includes tableware in simple shapes, often tin-glazed, with ribbed or painted lines and repeating geometrical patterns, occasionally in lustre.
Ref: Hiort.

Clementson, Joseph. Staffordshire earthenware manufacturer working at the Phoenix Works in Hanley from c.1832, initially in the partnership Reed & Clementson. In 1845 Clementson, by then working as sole proprietor, enlarged the pottery and in 1856 he bought the nearby Bell Works, formerly occupied by W.*Ridgway. His firm became known for high-quality printed decoration. Clementson retired in 1867, succeeded by his sons, who traded as Clementson Bros (Ltd) in Hanley until 1916. The firm produced granite ware, white, painted or printed, much of which was exported to North America, where Clementson established an effective Canadian retail outlet.

Printed marks incorporate the names *Clementson* or *Clementson Bros.*
Refs: Cushion (1980); Godden (1964); Jewitt.

Clevedon Court. *See* Elton, Edmund Harry.

Cleveland Fine Brick & Pottery Co. Ltd. *See* Commondale Pottery.

Clewell, Charles Walter (c.1876-1965). American metalworker, creator of a range

of ceramics coated with metal. (The technique was later used by L.C.*Tiffany.) After experiments starting in 1899, and working from 1906 at his own studio in Canton, Ohio, Clewell covered biscuit wares bought from other makers, e.g *Roseville Pottery Co., S.A.*Weller, *Cambridge Art Pottery, *Knowles, Taylor & Knowles, with a thin coating of metal. He was advertising copper, burnished copper and silver finishes by 1909. The metal coating of pitchers, vases, etc., was hammered, engraved, or sometimes decorated with raised marks simulating riveted joints. Inspired by a bronze wine jug in the J.P. Morgan Memorial Collection at Hartford, Connecticut, thought to be of Roman origin, c.200 BC, he managed to produce the effect of blue bronze-patina on ceramics after 1923. (His formula was destroyed after his death.) Clewell achieved other coatings by chemically induced oxidation and tarnishing; in later work, he concentrated on matt green or light bluish-green surfaces.

Marks: *Clewell/Canton O.*, several versions, usually incised; *Clewell/Metal Art/Canton O.*; the mark of the pottery that provided the blank sometimes appears on the base of the piece.
Refs: Evans; Kovel & Kovel.

Clews, James (1790-1861). Staffordshire producer of earthenware and stone china. Clews worked in partnership with his brother Ralph (b 1788) at rented potteries in Cobridge from c.1815 until their bankruptcy in 1834 (having survived an earlier bankruptcy in 1827). They also inherited their father's interest in a brewery business and owned flint mills and a colliery. Their firm made earthenware for table and domestic use, transfer-printed in deep blue with designs that included Thomas Rowlandson's scenes of Dr Syntax (1815-21), bordered with roses and other large flowers, and identified by a title in a rectangular cartouche; a number of small illustrations from the story of Don Quixote, again with flowered borders; several designs after domestic scenes by Sir David Wilkie; many English and American views, buildings and historical scenes. Designs such as the Landing of Lafayette, views of the Hudson River and named American states, exported to America, were sometimes marked with the blue-printed backstamp of a New York retailer, Greenfield's China Store. Other patterns included an Indian Sporting series (a subject attributed mainly to J.*Spode's factory).

After leaving the Cobridge factory, Ralph Clews stayed at Newcastle-under-Lyme, while James Clews went to America in 1836 and became a partner in a large pottery at Troy, Indiana, which was incorporated as the Indiana Pottery Co. and went into production by June 1837. The firm absorbed the *Lewis Pottery Co. and, after an unsuccessful attempt to make and market creamware, soon restricted the output to yellow and Rockingham-glazed ware. Clews sold his shares in the Indiana Pottery in 1842 and returned to Stoke-on-Trent between 1847 and 1849, having left the pottery under the management of J.*Vodrey (who stayed there until 1846). It was sold by the founding partner in 1859.

Impressed marks 1818-34 incorporate CLEWS WARRANTED STAFFORDSHIRE, some-

times in a circular mark enclosing a crown.
Refs: Barber (1976); Coysh (1972); Cushion (1980); Godden (1964); S. Laedecker *Anglo-American China* (Bristol, Pennsylvania, c.1951); Ramsay; F. Stefano Jr in Atterbury (1980).

Cliff, Clarice (1899-1972). Staffordshire pottery decorator and designer. In 1916, she started work for A.J.*Wilkinson Ltd, initially as a lithographer, and gained experience of design, modelling, gilding and firing before attending evening classes at the Burslem School of Art in 1924-25; in 1927 she briefly joined the Royal College of Art in London to study sculpture. She returned to set up a small design studio at Wilkinson's Newport showroom, where she painted stock shapes with stylized trees, abstract patterns, etc., in vivid colours, boldly brushed.

Her work was put on the market in winter 1928-29, under the name Bizarre. By late 1929, Wilkinson's Newport works was devoted to the production of ware designed by Clarice Cliff, who became the company's art director in 1930.

Encouraged by A.C.A.*Shorter, Clarice Cliff developed the range to include a variety of lines distinguished by shape and pattern. New shapes for lines of tableware, vases, bowls, etc., were introduced from 1929, with emphasis on cubes, cylinders, cones and other geometrical forms. Le Bon Dieu (teaware in contorted, knobby shapes, painted with soft green and brown that merged in splashes and streaks), My Garden (tall shapes with handles of modelled and brightly enamelled flowers), Raffia and Corncob combined texture or relief decoration with set painted patterns, but lines of particular shapes could be decorated with various patterns from the normal ranges, or with special designs to customers' suggestions.

As well as tableware, Clarice Cliff's designs included matching napkin rings (embroidery patterns for table linen were available with the same designs); centrepieces (e.g. a Viking ship, and holders made in sections for arrangements of flowers or candles); smokers' requisites (holders for cigarettes, matches, as well as sets of ashtrays). Age of Jazz figures (1930) consisted of clay silhouettes painted with the costumes and features of dancers and a band; Queer figures comprised model animals, human figures and grotesques. Among other relief pieces were flower

Clarice Cliff. Bowl in the form of a tree-trunk with turquoise and white glaze, with grain and knots painted in yellow and brown. On the base: Le Bon Dieu—I think I shall never see a form as lovely as a tree—Clarice Cliff.

Clarice Cliff. Jug, marked with Bizarre, *the name of the ware, and a facsimile signature. 17 cm high.*

holders, candlesticks and vases, bird book-ends, novelty cruet sets, inkstands, black-bird pie centres and, telephone covers. Masks representing the nations were modelled by M.M.*Davies, a student engaged from Burslem School of Art; masks and wall pockets were sometimes matt-glazed.

Patterns added to early geometrical motifs on tableware and vases include a range Fantasque (the first to be introduced with a name that was added to the backstamp), Crocus, and other patterns featuring flowers or foliage; Autumn, Alpine, Capri, Harvest, Latona, Secrets (featuring a cottage), in-spired by trees, foliage and landscape; Appliqué, with scenes made up in bright blocks of colour. Others include Blue Chintz and Delphinium, recalling fabric designs; Cries of London and Knight Errant, rep-resenting prints or illustrations; Dolphins (red dolphins at play); Love Birds (a pair in relief on vases and bowls); geometrical motifs, such as Ravel (stylized leaf sprigs) and simple banded patterns such as Gordon; Hello (black bands with green, ink or ochre spots); Newport (banding and a floral border used on Biarritz dinner services); Modern (platinum banding with customer's mono-gram); Rainbow. Ground colours include Goldstone (a glaze speckled brown with particles of metal) and, notably, Honeyglaze, a pale cream glaze used on much of the ware, and named in a printed mark.

Clarice Cliff was also engaged in the pro-duction of earthenware with decoration designed by contemporary artists in a joint experiment organized by E.*Brain & Co. and Wilkinson's, 1932-34. After her marriage to Shorter in 1940, and the imposition of wartime restrictions on the production of decorated ware, she was mainly concerned with administration, as decorating manager and later also a director of Wilkinson's (from 1950) and the Newport Works (from 1955). After the takeover of both companies by W.R.*Midwinter Ltd, she retired in 1965.

Signature printed or occasionally stamped in relief occurs on earthenware produced by Wilkinson's, 1925-63; Bizarre ware was marked '*Bizarre/by/Clarice Cliff*'; the earthenware limited editions made in conjunction with Brain's were marked with the designer's name and '*Produced in*

Bizarre by Clarice Cliff', accompanied by Wilkinson's mark.
Ref: P. Wentworth-Shields & K. Johnson *Clarice Cliff* (L'Odeon, London, 1976).

Cliff, John. English stoneware potter. From 1858, Cliff was owner of a works in Lambeth, where he introduced a number of technical advances in stoneware production, includ-ing a patent kiln for the making of Bristol ware (c.1862), improvements for the salt-glaze kiln, and his own patent wheel and lathe (c.1863); he also experimented with Siemens's gas furnace. After the closure of his Lambeth pottery, he moved in 1869 to Cheshire, where he made utilitarian stone-wares in a pottery at the Old Quay, Runcorn.
Refs: Blacker (1922b); Brears (1974); Jewitt.

Cliff Bank Pottery. *See* Davenport's.

Clifton Art Pottery. American art pottery established in 1905 at Clifton, Newark, New Jersey. The owners, Fred Tschirner and W.A.*Long, working with few assistants (seldom more than 12), were noted for the production of two main lines: Crystal Patina —vases, etc., made from 1905 in simple shapes in a white body resembling hard-paste porcelain covered at first with a crystalline glaze in the green colour of oxi-dized bronze and later a number of semi-matt glazes, including green, brown and yellow, and Clifton Indian Ware—vases, jugs, mugs and ornamental and souvenir ware made of red clay, with shapes and painted decoration inspired by American Indian pottery, usually coated on the inside with glossy black glaze, but with the exterior unglazed. Other lines include ware similar to Crystal Patina, using the same dense body, with matt glaze, notably in pale Robin's-egg Blue, a ware briefly produced with Art Nouveau decor-ation in low relief, and Tirrube painted with flowers in light-coloured slips against a matt ground. After the departure of Long in 1909, art pottery was discontinued c.1911 in favour of high-fired wall and floor tiles with a high quality leadless glaze in a variety of colours. The pottery became the Clifton Porcelain Tile Co. in 1914.

Marks: *Clifton*, usually incised on Crystal Patina, impressed and often accompanied by the source of the design on Indian Ware; various monograms of CPA.
Refs: Barber (1976); Evans.

Clyde Pottery. Willow-patterned soup plate, c.1880.

Clifton China. *See* Wildblood, Heath & Sons.

Clifton Indian Ware. *See* Clifton Art Pottery.

Clifton ware. *See* Chesapeake Pottery.

Cline, Robert. *See* New Hall.

Cloisonné Ware. *See* Bretby Art Pottery.

Clowes, William. *See* New Hall.

Clyde Pottery. Scottish earthenware pottery established in 1816 at Greenock, Renfrew-shire by a company headed by James and Andrew Muir, and continued by a number of successive owners who retained the title, Clyde Pottery Co. The initial output of creamware, plain or with sponged, painted or printed decoration, included large bowls for punch or toddy, and among the designs was a painted pattern of lilies of the valley, bordered with gold lustre. Some of the ware was made for export. Later proprietors continued the production of earthenware,

Clifton Art Pottery. Earthenware vases from the pottery's Indian Ware line, 1910-12. 22.2 cm, 31.8 cm and 17 cm high.

including pearlware, until the pottery's closure, c.1903.

Marks include CLYDE GREENOCK or C.P.CO.G., impressed or printed.

Refs: Blacker (1922a); Hughes (1961); Jewitt.

Coade's Artificial Stone Works. *See* Coffee, William.

Coalport or **Coalbrookdale.** English porcelain factory established by J.*Rose c.1796 at Coalport, near Broseley, Shropshire. The factory's early porcelain, mainly painted or printed in underglaze blue, is difficult to distinguish from the work of the *Caughley factory purchased by Rose in 1799, much of which was sold in bulk for decoration outside the factory on commission from retailers, such as J.*Mortlock & Co. In the early 19th century, Coalport porcelain became characterized by its soft, white colour, pure glaze and creamy translucency and, for a period starting in the 1820s, the factory produced a variation of the paste made at Nantgarw by W.*Billingsley and S.*Walker, who went to Coalport in 1819. Rose purchased stock and moulds from Nantgarw and Swansea in the early 1820s. Coalport won the award of the Society of Arts for a leadless glaze, introduced in 1820. The simple tableware which was the main product of this period was sparsely decorated, generally with flowers, for which the factory was noted, sometimes painted in outlines. Patterns introduced at this time include Green Dragon and Indian Tree. Moulded designs were also used. Gilding was usually light and brassy in colour. The ornamental ware of the 1820s was richly decorated in revived rococo style with relief flowers, painted predominantly in pink and green. The factory's artists included Jesse *Mountford. Pieces encrusted with flowers

Coalport. Jug commemorating election in Shropshire in 1835, with gilt inscription on a deep blue ground. 29 cm high.

were often referred to as Coalbrookdale and are occasionally marked with the name in blue.

The founder was succeeded by his partners, including his nephew, William Frederick Rose (d 1863), who began the production of copies of Sèvres, Meissen and Chelsea porcelains, sometimes to the extent of imitating the original mark. Coalport was the first English factory to achieve successful reproduction of the Sèvres *rose du Barry* ground, which was used on a prize-winning dessert service shown in the Great Exhibition, 1851. This service and one commissioned by Queen Victoria for presentation to Tsar Nicholas I, also shown in the Great Exhibition, won the firm other commissions for luxury services. Other ground colours include Chelsea claret, a sharp green, and the mazarine blue used at the Derby factory.

From the 1840s, the firm also produced a small quantity of high-quality parian ware and slabs of porcelain painted with flowers and fruit for use in trays or as wall plaques with gilt frames. A porcelain paste introduced in 1845 was very thinly potted in the production of eggshell pieces.

William Pugh, one of Rose's partners, became sole proprietor of the factory from William Rose's retirement in 1862 until 1885, during which time the production underwent a decline. The artists employed by the factory in the 1870s included R.F. *Abraham. J.*Aston, the elder J.*Birbeck, C.*Palmere, J.H.*Plant. Under the subsequent management of C.C.*Bruff from 1889, the firm's early designs were revived and new patterns were introduced. After its purchase by Cauldon Potteries Ltd (*see* Brown-Westhead, Moore & Co.) in 1925, the firm retained its autonomy despite removal to Staffordshire; it became part of the Wedgwood group in 1967.

Marks usually incorporate *Coalbrookdale* or *Coalport*. Others include the combined initials C, S (Coalport, Salopian), forming a mark resembling an ampersand, and enclosing the initials, C, S and N (Caughley, Swansea, Nantgarw) in three loops. Modern marks usually incorporate a crown.

Refs: Barrett (1951); Bemrose; Cushion (1974); Godden (1961, 1964, 1970); Jewitt.

Cobden Works. *See* Ridgway Potteries Ltd.

Cocker, George (1794-1868). English modeller. Cocker was an apprentice figure maker at the *Derby factory (Nottingham Road) from 1808 and modelled biscuit porcelain figures until c.1817. He executed flowers in relief at *Coalport, 1817-19, then briefly started a business of his own, which closed after a few months, in Jackfield. He worked at Worcester, 1819-21, before returning to Derby, 1821-25. In partnership for about a year with a gilder, John Whitaker, Cocker established a workshop in Friar Gate, Derby, c.1826, producing ornamental ware, including figures (biscuit or glazed), portrait busts, baskets of flowers and small animal groups, and tea and dessert services. Cocker continued alone after the dissolution of the partnership, going in 1840 to London, where he set up a workshop and separate showroom. He went to Stoke-on-Trent in 1851 and was employed as a modeller by Mintons c.1853-55, although the factory had earlier produced pieces either designed by him or

copied from his work. He subsequently worked for Staffordshire firms, including John Mountford, producer of parian figures, etc., in Stoke-on-Trent.

Biscuit figures, e.g. Roman Matron, Boy with a Hurdy-Gurdy, Dying Drunkard, sometimes bear Cocker's incised signature.

Refs: Godden (1968); Haslem; Hughes (1977); Twitchett (1980).

Cockpit Hill. *See* Derby.

Cockson & Harding. *See* New Hall.

Codnor Park Pottery. Derbyshire pottery making brown salt-glaze bottles, built in 1820 by the Butterley Iron Co. and managed by a foundry employee, William Burton. After closure in 1832, the pottery was taken over by J.*Bourne in the following year. Household ware, bottles, spirit flasks and dairy ware were made as well as fine, buff terracotta, which was used for vases, flower baskets, narrow-necked jugs, spill jars, etc., often with foliage in relief. Bourne closed the pottery in 1861, transferring the workers and equipment to his Denby Pottery.

Mark: DENBY & CODNOR PARK/BOURNES POTTERIES/DERBYSHIRE.

Ref: Bradley; Oswald.

Coffee, William (d 1846). English porcelain modeller, son of a worker at the Chelsea porcelain factory, and probably trained there. Coffee subsequently worked at Coade's Artificial Stone Works, a manufacturer of statues, vases and religious stonewares in Lambeth. He joined the porcelain factory at Nottingham Road, *Derby, c.1792 and left in 1795 to work at the pottery started in the previous year by Sir Nigel Gresley at Church Gresley. He returned to Derby, setting up his own workshop c.1798 for the production of figures, etc., to his own designs in terracotta and later biscuit porcelain. Coffee is best known for his modelling of animals. He is thought to have worked later in London and in America.

Mark: incised signature.

Refs: Blacker (1922b); Bradley; F. Brayshaw Gilhespy & D.M. Budd *Royal Crown Derby* (Skilton, London, 1964).

Colclough, Herbert J. Staffordshire porcelain manufacturer. After establishing the firm of Colclough in 1895, he took over the Osborne works at Longton in 1907, the Regent Works (founded 1850) in 1918, and was also owner of the Vale factory in Longton from 1897, using the trade name Vale China in marks. The firm made earthenware and bone china, merging with *Booths Limited in 1948.

Various printed marks incorporate the initials HJC or the name *Colclough*, which was retained in some marks by Booths & Colcloughs.

Refs: Bunt; Godden (1964, 1972).

Cole, George (d 1912). Porcelain painter working for *Grainger & Co. and by 1880 for the *Worcester Royal Porcelain Co. Cole specialized in flowers, notably roses.

Ref: Sandon (1978a).

Cole, Sir Henry, or Felix Summerly (1808-82). English designer and artistic reformer, born in Bath. He worked as a civil servant in

Rebecca Coleman. Earthenware wall plate made by *Mintons Ltd and painted by Rebecca Coleman, 1877. 43.3 cm in diameter.

the Public Records Office from 1838. Cole adopted the pseudonym Felix Summerly initially for literary work. He designed a set of terracotta bricks for children (produced by Mintons), and in 1846 an earthenware tea set, which was made at the Minton factory and submitted with two beer jugs to the Society of Arts competition of that year. Both entries gained silver medals.

Cole launched Summerly's Art Manufactures in 1847 with the aim of achieving the best possible standards in the design of objects in everyday use, without sacrificing function to decoration, and drawing ornamental themes as directly as possible from nature. His scheme encompassed glass, silver and other materials as well as ceramics, which were to be designed by contemporary artists for production by established manufacturers. The same designs were intended for production in a variety of media. The painters William Dyce, J.C. Horsley, Daniel Maclise, William Mulready and Richard Redgrave were among the artists included in the scheme, and manufacturers included the Coalbrookdale ironworks, the Sheffield metalworkers, James Dixon & Sons, and the firms of Copeland, Minton and Wedgwood. Cole also commissioned designs from sculptor John Bell (a figure, Dorothea, produced 1847 in parian ware by Minton) and H.J. *Townshend (a jug, The Hop Story, designed 1846 and produced by Minton from the following year). The jug and other pieces entered in the Society of Arts competition in 1847 won four out of the ten gold medals offered. Cole abandoned the scheme in 1849, although production of the designs continued into the 1860s. Cole was involved in preparation for the Great Exhibition from 1849, and became secretary of the South Kensington Department of Practical Art in 1852.

Mark: monogram of FS features in several printed or relief marks, used with the name of the artist and manufacturer's mark.
Refs: Aslin & Atterbury; S. Bury 'Felix Summerly's Art Manufactures' in *Apollo* 85 (January, 1967); *Dictionary of National Biography* Vol XI (Smith & Elder & Co., London, 1967); N. Pevsner *Studies in Art, Architecture & Design* Vol II (Thames & Hudson, London, 1968).

Cole, Solomon. Porcelain painter working for the *Worcester porcelain factory of Flight, Barr & Barr. Cole was a pupil of T.*Baxter 1814-16 and specialized in landscapes with figures. He and T.*Lowe succeeded Baxter as the firm's main figure painters in 1821; he remained until the factory's closure. He exhibited portraits at the Royal Academy.
Refs: Binns (1897); Chaffers; Sandon (1978b).

Cole & Trelease. *See* Exeter Art Pottery.

Coleman, Rebecca (d 1884) and Helen Cordelia. English ceramic decorators, sisters of W.S.*Coleman. One of the sisters was working as a flower painter at *Minton's Art Pottery Studio in 1872. Rebecca Coleman was noted for her studies of heads, e.g. Dora, a portrait on porcelain, shown in the ninth annual exhibition held by *Howell & James in 1884. Both sisters decorated pieces made at the Minton factory after the Art Pottery Studio's closure in 1875 and exhibited as professional decorators at the Howell & James galleries. They shared the freedom of style and fresh approach to colour that characterized their brother's ceramic decoration.
Refs: Aslin & Atterbury; Callen; *Magazine of Art* (review of annual show by Howell & James, 1874).

Coleman, William Stephen (1829-1904). English designer, illustrator and watercolourist. Coleman began experiments in pottery decoration in the 1860s and worked briefly at the factory of W.T.*Copeland. At *Mintons Ltd, where he worked from 1869, initially as a freelance decorator, Coleman painted bowls, plaques and slabs for fireplaces. His Naturalist service (1869) echoes the work of F.*Braquemond. Coleman became art director of *Minton's Art Pottery Studio, 1871-73. His designs for the studio included a plaque and a pair of pilgrim bottles painted with birds and foliage, and a bowl decorated with fish and underwater plants; he was also known for studies of nude children engaged in sports or other pastimes, often in the open air. Initially working in underglaze pigments (with glaze

William S. Coleman. Earthenware wall plate made by *Mintons Ltd, c.1875. Signed W.S. Coleman and bearing the printed mark of T. Goode & Co. and Minton, impressed, c.1875. 39.5 cm in diameter.

applied thickly over intense colours and brushed thinly over delicate shades), he later favoured bright enamels painted over the glaze with brown underglaze outlines. After his resignation from Minton's studio in 1873, Coleman continued to send work there for firing, then working mainly as an illustrator and painter.

Mark: name impressed on the reverse of tiles.
Refs: Aslin & Atterbury; Callen; Godden (1961); Rhead.

Colenbrander, Theodorus Christiaan Adriaan (1841-1930). Dutch textile and ceramic designer, born in Doesburgh. After training as an architect in Arnhem and studying art in Paris, 1869-70, Colenbrander made an unsuccessful attempt to establish his own pottery and subsequently became artistic director of the *Rozenburg Plateelfabriek, 1884-89. There he designed vases, plates and display pieces painted with floral forms in bright shades of blue, green, red, brown, yellow, purple and white on a white ground. His designs combine elements of European

Theodorus C.A. Colenbrander. Covered vase painted with stylized foliage in yellow and brown, made at the *Rozenburg factory in 1886. 38.5 cm high.

Eugène Collinot. Earthenware vase with enamel painting on a yellow crackle glaze, 1873. 12.3 cm high.

stylistic preoccupations (e.g. naturalism, symbolism, Art Nouveau) with the influence of Javan batik patterns.

Colenbrander worked as art director of a carpet factory in Amersfoort, 1895-1901, and returned to ceramics as decorator at the *Zuid-Holland factory in 1912. He became art director at the Plateelbakkerij *Ram in Arnhem, 1920. From 1912, his plates and other pieces were often large in size, with painted decoration in brown and matt blue. His patterns became increasingly realistic. Some of his later pieces were left unglazed.

Marks: at Zuid-Holland, painted monogram of TC (formed like a script H) with a flag; circular printed mark COLENBRANDER/'RAM'/ARNHEM.-HOLLAND enclosing a ram's head.
Refs: W.J. de Gruyter 'In Memoriam Th.A.C. Colenbrander (1841-1930)' in *Elsevier's Geillustreerd Maandschrift* 80 (1930); C. Doelman 'De Jugendstil en Colenbrander' in *Mededelingenblad Vrienden van de Nederlandse Ceramik* 17 (1959); D.J. Hulsbergen 'Th.A.C. Colenbrander en de Plateelbakkerij ''Ram'' te Arnhem' in *Bulletin* Vol VII, no 1 (Museum Boymans-van Beuningen, Rotterdam, 1956); C.A. Lion Cachet 'Th.A.C. Colenbrander' in *Elsevier's Geillustreerd Maandschrift* 54 (1917); Singelenberg van de Meer; van Straaten.

Coles, John. *See* Cambrian Pottery.

Collier, Charles. *See* Edmands, Barnabas.

Collinot, Eugène Victor (d 1882). French potter; a maker of earthenware at Boulogne-sur-Seine (Hauts-de-Seine). Collinot contributed illustrations of Islamic and Renaissance arts to the first *Recueil de Dessins pour l'Art et l'Industrie* in 1859, and his work in ceramics included copies of middle-eastern ceramics shown at the Exposition of 1867. His later work was characterized by decoration outlined with manganese in the manner of *cloisonné* enamel. The birds, foliage and other ornament were in low relief achieved by the application of several layers of slip. The pieces, although described as Persian, were often copied from 15th or 16th century Italian maiolica.
Refs: Y. Brunhammer in *Japonisme in Art* (Kodansha, Tokyo, 1980); Charleston; Ernould-Gandouet; Heuser & Heuser; Lesur (1971).

Collis, Charles. *See* Della Robbia Pottery.

Colonna, Edward (1862-1948). Designer and decorative artist, born in Cologne, Germany. Colonna trained as an architect in Brussels. In America from 1882, he worked briefly for L.C.*Tiffany's firm, Associated Artists, before settling in Dayton, Ohio, where he designed interiors for railroad cars, furniture, and wrote and illustrated his *Essay on Broom-Corn* (1887). He worked briefly as a furniture designer in Canada before going to live in Paris, 1898-1903. He executed designs for S.*Bing in a wide variety of media, including metal mounts for ceramics by A.*Bigot, and porcelain made by *G.D.A. He used decoration of flowing plant forms incised and in relief, e.g. under transparent straw-coloured glaze on a vase, or touched with underglaze colour on tableware. Colonna collaborated with G.*de Feure and Eugène Gaillard on Bing's pavilion at the Exposition Universelle, 1900. After the closure of Bing's shop, Colonna travelled in Europe and subsequently worked in New York, finally settling in the south of France.
Refs: Brunhammer *et al* (1976); d'Albis & Romanet.

Colonnata. *See* Richard-Ginori, Società Ceramica.

Columbia. *See* Allen, Thomas.

Columbian Art Pottery Company. American pottery, established at Trenton, New Jersey, in 1893, the year of the World's Columbian Exposition in Chicago. The founders, W.T.

Edward Colonna. Porcelain vase made in Limoges from a design by Colonna.

Morris, formerly at the *Belleek factory, and his partner, F.R. Willmore, had worked at *Worcester and for *Ott & Brewer. One of the early American manufacturers of Belleek ware, the firm made tea and table ware, toilet sets, and ornamental pieces including candlesticks, *jardinières*, umbrella holders, toby jugs and souvenirs.
Marks: name of the pottery surrounding *Trenton, N.J.*; printed initials M and W in a tulip-shaped outline, with *Trenton NJ* and *Belleek* or *Belleek ware*.
Ref: Barber (1976).

Columbian Pottery. American pottery established 1808 in Philadelphia by backers Archibald Binny and James Ronaldson in association with the English potter, Alexander Trotter. The firm advertised tea and coffee pots, pitchers, and kitchen and other household vessels in Queensware, which was considered to be of very high quality. The output included a jug and goblets used in the Republican Dinner on 4th July 1808. The pottery may have closed in 1814. By the following year, Trotter was making similar wares in Pittsburgh.
Refs: Barber (1976); S.H. Myers *Handcraft to Industry* (Smithsonian Institution Press, City of Washington, 1980).

Combaz, Gisbert (1869-1941). Belgian artist and collector, born in Antwerp. Combaz showed paintings at La Libre Esthétique, beginning in 1893 and as a regular exhibitor from 1897. In that year, he showed tiles and other ceramics made by E.*Muller and decorated with birds, salamanders and wave-forms.
Refs: Brunhammer *et al* (1976); Haslam (1977).

Comfort, Elijah (1860s-1945). English country potter, working as chief thrower for the Beckett family, owners of the *Winchcombe Pottery until 1916. Comfort was then employed as a farm worker before rejoining the Winchcombe Pottery in 1926, and until 1930 continued to throw large washing pans, which had been made earlier, under the Becketts. Afterwards, he made some large pieces of the standard production, including casseroles, lidded dishes, oval oven dishes, plates and serving platters. When M.*Cardew had left for West Africa in 1942 and R.*Finch had joined the National Fire Service in the following year, Comfort carried on the pottery.
Refs: Michael Cardew (Crafts Advisory Committee London, 1976); M. Coleman 'Ray Finch's Workshop' in *Crafts* (September, October 1970); R. Finch 'Workshop Organization: Winchcombe Pottery' in *Ceramic Review* 3 (May/June 1970).

comforter dog. *See* Staffordshire dogs.

commemorative ware. Ceramics decorated with scenes or inscriptions recording historical personalities or events. Commemorative tin-glazed wares had been made in the 17th century in England (portraits of monarchs) and in Revolutionary France (*faiences patronymiques*) but the large-scale sale of commemorative ware, which depended on mass-production techniques and good communications, reached a peak in England in the late 18th and 19th centuries after the development of cream-coloured earthenware

and, later, ironstone china, with transfer-printed decoration. Portrait bottles, and flasks commemorating the Reform Bill (1831) were mass-produced in saltglaze.
Ref: J.& J. May *Commemorative Pottery* (Heinemann, London, 1972).

Commondale Pottery. Yorkshire pottery near Commondale in the Cleveland Hills to the south-east of Middlesbrough. The works formerly occupied by the Cleveland Fire Brick & Pottery Co. Ltd (1861-76) were reopened in 1872 and operated under the name of the Commondale Brick Pipe & Pottery Co. Ltd. Workers brought in from Staffordshire and Wales made buff-toned terracotta architectural ware, garden figures, statuettes and ornamental pieces. The pottery closed c.1884, because of difficulties in maintaining the workforce in such an isolated situation.

Thomas Ness reopened it in 1893, succeeded on his death by the firm of Crossley, the former owners. The output then included a variety of teapots, sometimes with Rockingham glaze, jugs, bowls, jars, candlesticks, *jardinières*, vases, plaques, and tea and toilet sets.

Marks: COMMONDALE POTTERY, impressed in a circle, OR CROSSLEY/COMMONDALE.
Refs: Coysh (1976); Lawrence.

Comoléra, Paul (1818-97). French sculptor, born in Paris and a pupil of François Rude. Primarily working in bronze, Comoléra became a noted *animalier*, and specialized in studies of birds and game, first exhibiting at the Salon in 1847. He modelled pieces made in biscuit porcelain by the *Pouyat factory and shown in the Paris exposition, 1855. His work for the Pouyat factory, which extended over 20 years, included plates with unglazed fruit in relief at the centre, for dessert services; a soup tureen decorated with wheat, maize, vegetables; and table ornaments, e.g. a palm stem with three storks and a group of smaller birds, modelled with great accuracy of detail. Animal studies were produced at Boulogne-sur-Mer, 1857-59, in porcelain. His son, also Paul Comoléra, worked as an *animalier*, exhibiting 1870-87.

Mark: *C.2.* appears on Boulogne porcelain.
Refs: Aslin & Atterbury; Bénézit; Lesur (1967); J. Mackay *The Animaliers* (Ward Lock, London, 1973).

Compton Pottery. English earthenware and terracotta workshop established c.1902 at Compton, near Guildford, by Mary Seton Watts, wife of the painter G.F. Watts. The pottery made press-moulded garden ware, and unglazed figures, mainly religious in inspiration, painted in tempera, as well as a small quantity of tableware and mugs. Garden pots decorated with Celtic motifs and designed by Mary Watts were sold by *Liberty & Co. R.*Saywell, employed as a potter from 1920, began the production of large, thrown ware, including chimneypots. Despite fire damage in 1922, the pottery continued until the Depression of the 1930s. The Potters' Art Guild, in control from 1938, produced slip-moulded wares, still using unfired colours, until the closure of the works in 1956.

Marks: COMPTON/POTTERY, impressed;

COMPTON/GUILDFORD SURREY, printed or impressed in the outline of a bowl from c.1945.
Refs: Anscombe & Gere; *Ceramic Review* 64 (1980); Coysh (1976).

Connelly, William. *See* Trenton Potteries Co.

Conta & Böhme. *See* Pössneck.

Conty, Edmé. *See* Sèvres.

Cook, Albert. *See* New Hall.

Cook, Charles Howell. *See* Cook Pottery Co.

Cook, William (c.1800-76). Staffordshire porcelain painter, born in Burslem. Cook is thought to have worked for T.M.*Randall in London and moved to Madeley between 1841 and 1843. His flower painting in rich, glossy enamels was mainly carried out in reserve panels on vases, etc., and on the borders of plates and dishes, but some groups of flowers and fruit appear on the centre of plates, or on vases also bearing bird paintings by J.*Randall. His flower arrangements often contain a characteristic cluster of small fine-leaved flowers washed over in one colour.

Mark: his signature occasionally occurs on plaques.
Refs: Barrett (1951); Godden (1961, 1969); Jewitt; *see also* Randall, Thomas Martin.

Cook Pottery Co. American art pottery firm established at Trenton, New Jersey, in 1894. The firm, which was incorporated in 1897 with the Trenton potter, Charles Howell Cook, as president, produced white and cream-coloured earthenware and granite ware, as well as Belleek ware, at the Etruria works formerly occupied by *Ott & Brewer. The Belleek ware includes vases and ewers with high-relief cactus and lotus plants in natural colours highlighted with gilding. Much of the output was sold to amateur painters. In 1896, the firm introduced pottery inspired by Dutch Delft ware: *jardinières*, pedestals, plates, ewers and bowls were often hand-painted by decorator P. Paul Gasper with windmills, sailing boats, etc., and pastoral scenes. Creamware was transfer-printed, often with commemorative themes. Underglaze painting with six to eight colours, including pink and carmine, was introduced in 1898, mainly on *jardinières*. Small quantities of art pottery were produced by 1906: Nipur ware was matt-glazed over a textured surface in imitation of pottery excavated at the ancient Sumerian city of Nippur; Metalline ware was covered with smooth metallic glazes. The company soon concentrated on the production of hotel ware, and Cook retired in 1926.

Marks include c painted on the base in gold-coloured glaze.
Refs: Barber (1976); Evans.

Cookson & Jardine. *See* Portobello Pottery.

Coombes & Holland. *See* South Wales Pottery.

Cooper, Carl (d 1968). Australian potter, born in Melbourne. Cooper was a friend and associate of A.*Boyd. He took up pottery as therapy c.1940, while recovering

from poliomyelitis, which had left him confined to a wheelchair. He worked with Boyd at the AMB Pottery before setting up his own studio nearby in Murrumbeena, where he made a series of wares incorporating adaptations of Aboriginal bark paintings. Some of his work is in collections at the National Gallery of Victoria and the Shepparton Arts Centre, Victoria.

Cooper, Susie (b 1902). Staffordshire designer, trained in Burslem. Susan Vera Cooper joined A.E.*Gray & Co. Ltd as a decorator in 1922, and worked as a designer, 1924-29. She also designed textiles.

In partnership with her brother-in-law, she established a decorating firm, working in Tunstall and then Burslem, eventually at the Crown Works. Susie Cooper bought earthenware from local manufacturers for decoration with designs, simple patterns of animals, flowers, bright polka dots and bands of colour. She commissioned wares which included vases, table and nursery ware, lamp bases and wall plaques. Shapes in tableware include Curlew (a line with low-swept forms and dropped handles) and Kestrel (rounded forms with streamlined handles placed to the sides of lids rather than directly at the centre). The Dresden pattern, an arrangement of bright, stylized flowers printed on a wide range of tableware, was the first of many lithographs which she used in decoration; aerography and *sgraffito* work were also used, but hand painting continued on tableware and ornamental pieces.

In 1940, Susie Cooper became the first Royal Designer for Industry to have been selected solely for work in ceramics. Joined in the firm by her husband, architect Cecil Barker (married 1938), she resumed production after a fire at the Crown Works in 1942, re-establishing export outlets in America, South Africa and Australasia. New ceramic designs shown in the Britain Can Make It Exhibition in London, 1946, included fluted tableware printed with floral patterns. Susie Cooper acquired a factory in Longton for the production of bone china, of which examples were shown and used at the Festival of Britain, 1951; pieces commissioned for use in the Royal Pavilion were printed with lions and unicorns in white resist and black with blue or dark red grounds. Susie Cooper designs were also commissioned for use by the Royal Society of Arts, and others include a bicentennial plate presented

Susie Cooper. Earthenware jug with hand-painted decoration in enamel designed by Susie Cooper, 1930 or 1931.

to the Society by the Royal Designers for Industry in 1954. In patterns of flowers and animals, her style became increasingly naturalistic in comparison with her early stylized treatment of similar subjects.

The Susie Cooper Pottery merged with the firm of R.H. & S.L.*Plant in 1961. The firm subsequently concentrated on the output of bone china, as earthenware production was not resumed, but the Crown Works retained its autonomy after 1966, when Plants became part of the Wedgwood Group, for whom Susie Cooper was to produce designs for bone china tableware in the 1960s and 1970s.

Marks: signature *Susie Cooper* on her own designs at Gray's from 1922; at the Crown Works, a skipping deer with A/SUSIE COOPER/PRODUCTION./CROWN/WORKS/BURSLEM ENGLAND; on bone china, signature over BONE CHINA*/*England*.

Refs: Batkin; *Wedgwood of Etruria & Barlaston* (City Museum & Art Gallery, Stoke-on-Trent, 1980); A. Woodhouse *Elegance & Utility 1924-78: the work of Susie Cooper RDI* (catalogue of an exhibition, Josiah Wedgwood & Sons Ltd, Barlaston, 1978).

Copeland, William Taylor (1797-1868). English manufacturer of earthenware and porcelain. Copeland acted as a Member of Parliament for 25 years, contributed to the establishment of art schools throughout England, and became Lord Mayor of London, 1835-36. In 1824 he joined his father William Copeland (d 1826) in partnership in the London warehouse of J.*Spode, which had traded as Spode & Copeland from 1811. He succeeded his father in the partnership, buying the Spode family's shares in the London business, the Stoke-on-Trent factory, its equipment and stock in 1833. He took into partnership a former colleague Thomas Garrett, trading as Copeland & Garrett until Garrett's retirement in 1847.

He continued to produce dessert, tea and toilet sets, and table services in porcelain and earthenware, with decoration ranging from simple gilt or coloured bands to lavish painting and relief ornament. The work shown in the Great Exhibition (1851) included figures in parian ware (produced from the 1840s until 1914), porcelain slabs painted with flowers, and tableware with painted, gilt and jewelled decoration. The firm's jewelled decoration included mirrored glass set into the body, a technique attributed to W.H.*Goss, art director in the mid 19th century, and still in use on earthenware. The firm's painters included C.F. *Hurten, L.*Brooke, S.*Alcock, D.*Lucas (son), and W.*Birbeck. G.*Eyre, art director in the 1860s, was succeeded by R.F. *Abraham until 1895.

Styles in porcelain and earthenware table services were sometimes derived from Japanese art in the 1870s and 1880s. The decoration of ornamental ware was often very lavish. Porcelain vases, bottles and other pieces were painted or jewelled and gilded, sometimes with flowers or figures modelled in high relief. The firm achieved ground colours in an intense turquoise (Cerulean blue), Sardinian green, and a rich vermilion. The output included tiles, hand-painted (e.g. by R.J.*Abraham) or transfer-printed, sometimes with printed

W.T. Copeland & Sons. Tile transfer-printed and painted against a yellow ground, c.1878. Impressed marks: Copeland Faience and a monogram. 15.5 x 15 cm.

designs filled in by hand. Majolica tiles were also made.

Copeland took his four sons into partnership in 1867 and was succeeded by the youngest, Richard Pirie Copeland (d 1913), and later generations of his family. The firm traded as W.T. Copeland & Sons Ltd until the name reverted to Spode (as Spode Ltd) in 1970. The factory remains on its original site in Stoke-on-Trent, and holds an important museum collection of the firm's works.

Marks 1833-47 incorporate the names or initials of Copeland & Garrett. Marks from 1847 include various renderings of *Copeland, late Spode*; *Copeland*, sometimes enclosed in a wreath, crowned; crossed Cs over *Copeland*; a bee over the label *W.T. Copeland & Sons*; SPODE/COPELAND with C superimposed on a Chinese-type seal (c.1875-89); ship with sail bearing crossed Cs and *Copeland, late Spode* along the top (1894-1910). Subsequent marks incorporate the names *Copeland* and/or *Spode*, usually with *England*.

Refs: Godden (1970); A. Hayden *Spode & his Successors* (Cassell, London, 1925); L. Whiter *Spode, A History of the Family, Factory & Wares from 1733-1833* (Barrie & Jenkins, London 1970); S.B. Williams *Antique Blue & White Spode* (B.T. Batsford, London, 1943).

Copenhagen, Royal, Porcelain Factory. Danish porcelain factory operating as a private company supported by the Danish Royal family, 1775-1867. The factory was known for the high quality of its hard-paste porcelain and its extensive research, and its products were frequently bought by Russian aristocrats. The Flora Danica service was made 1790-1802 for Catherine the Great, who did not live to receive it, and subsequently remained the property of the Danish Royal House. In forms of neo-classical inspiration, it was painted with named plants from Oeder's *Flora Danica* and the border pattern includes an acanthus motif. A service made for King Frederik VI at Christianburg Palace was in Empire style, introduced c.1825 under the direction of G.F. Hetsch. C.W. Bergsøe was director from 1833.

Royal Copenhagen Porcelain Factory. Dish from a set painted with Centaurea nigra, from the Flora Danica, 20th century. It has a printed circular mark and the factory's wave mark in underglaze blue. About 30 cm in diameter.

A. Falck bought the factory from the state in 1867, obtaining the right to the name and mark. A period of artistic and technical decline that had started during Denmark's political upheaval in the early 19th century ended in 1884, when P.*Schou took over the factory, moved it from Köbmagargade to *Aluminia A.S. at Smallegade and, with his artist A.*Krog, revived underglaze painting for which the factory had become famous in the late 18th century, developing new decorative styles under the influence of Japanese art and French Impressionism, winning the Grand Prix in Paris at the Exposition Universelle of 1889. Painters and modellers in the late 19th century included the landscape artist and animal painter Gotfred Rode (b 1862), Anna Smidth (b 1861) painter of landscapes and flower studies, J.*Meyer, B.*Nathanielsen, E.*Nielsen, and C.*Thomsen and C.F.*Liisberg. The abstract style of slip-cast figures in the 1890s later gave way

Royal Copenhagen Porcelain Factory. Porcelain vase painted under the glaze. Crown and wave mark. Mounted in silver by Lucien Gaillard in Paris, 1900. 12.2 cm high.

to naturalism in the models of sculptor, Arno Malinowsky and others. Models made by the Danish sculptor Gerhard Henning from 1909 included a female nude with nodding head that sways. A range of Art Nouveau animals (dragonflies, crabs, amphibians, bears, etc.) modelled on small dishes, ashtrays and other small pieces were shown with a new line of glazes in the Paris Exposition of 1900. The chemists A.*Clement and his successor, V.*Engelhardt, inspired by new developments in glazes at Sèvres, developed crystalline effects (exhibited in Berlin). F.*Dalgas, succeeding Schou in 1902, maintained the improvement in artistic standards. The production of Aluminia faience and Royal Copenhagen porcelain was augmented in 1912 by P.*Nordström's introduction of stoneware (previously attempted c.1904 by Krog). The ware was mass-produced, with layered glazes also developed by Nordström. A new porcelain paste ('iron porcelain') developed at the factory in 1923 was a soft paste with lead glaze. Under C.*Joachim, artistic director 1916-30, a crackle glaze was developed for porcelain with decoration over or under the glaze. Dalgas was succeeded as director by Christian Christensen in 1931. Present-day products range from early 18th-century imitations to modern forms, including tableware with botanical patterns from the Flora Danica service. Tableware with decoration in underglaze blue comprises a large part of the output. Sculptors making figures included Helge Christofferson, and Johannes Hedgard (figures of maidens c.1950, unglazed or contrasting unglazed portions with bright glazes). An experimental workshop established in 1958 gave young Scandinavian women potters the chance to work out their designs; its output is known as Tenera Faience.

Royal Copenhagen Porcelain Factory. Group, The Kiss, made at the Royal Copenhagen factory, 1897. Marked, Royal Copenhagen Dansk. 47 cm high.

Hans Coper. Stoneware vase with thin, milky glaze over a granular surface, shading to a deep brown border, c.1960. 15.2 cm high.

Marks usually incorporate a crown and a motif of three waves, sometimes with *Denmark, Danmark* or *Royal Copenhagen*; year letters start at A in 1885.
Refs: Borrmann; V.P. Christiensen *Den Kgl. Danske Porselaine Fabrik* (Copenhagen, 1938); Hannover; Pelka; Porzellankunst.

Coper, Hans (1920-81). Studio potter, born in Germany, where he trained as an engineer. He left in 1939 for England, where he subsequently worked. After service in the Pioneer Corps, he joined L.*Rie's studio in 1946 as an assistant. There, he took part in the development of a range of domestic ware, which included cups, saucers, tea and coffee pots, jugs and bowls, all in brown and white. His own work included beakers, vases and jugs with scratched decoration showing a white body through a dark coating coloured with manganese. He established a workshop in Hertfordshire in 1958, while also working as a consultant to a development group concerned with the use of clay products in building. His pottery consisted of vases, all thrown, sometimes in more than one piece, in either a light clay body coated with white slip and coloured with oxides in shades of brown or light buff, or a dark body under black or dark brown metallic slip, with matt surface and fired at 1250°C. Coper worked from a limited range of forms, which he constantly and gradually developed, making subtle changes in shape, texture and colour. He moved in 1969 to a London workshop and later to Somerset.
Mark: initials HC.
Refs: Architectural Review 116 (September 1954), 124 (October 1958); T. Birks *Hans Coper* (Collins, London, 1983); Rose.

Coppens, Omer (1864-1926). Landscape painter, engraver and designer, born in Dunkerque, and working in Belgium. Coppens trained as a painter at the Ghent Academy, and was an exhibitor at the Salon de la Libre Esthétique (1895) and the Brussels Exhibition (1910). He was a founder and (in the 1890s) president of the group, *Pour*

l'Art. He is known for vases modelled in low relief and covered with monochrome glazes, produced c.1906, but an earthenware bottle painted in slip with sketchy floral motifs under a green glaze was attributed to Coppens and dated c.1895 when later exhibited in America.
Refs: Brunhammer *et al* (1976); Thieme & Becker.

Copperette ware. *See* Bretby Art Pottery.

Copson, Octar H. (b 1851). Painter of fruit, birds and other subjects for the *Worcester Royal Porcelain Co. c.1872-80.
Ref: Sandon (1978a).

Coquerel, Athenase-Marie-Martin. *See* Legros d'Anisy, François-Antoine.

Coral Ware. *See* Worcester.

Corden, William (1797-1867). English porcelain decorator, born in Ashbourne, Derbyshire. Corden was an apprentice at the porcelain factory in Nottingham Road, *Derby, in 1811, and was employed there until 1820, initially as a landscape painter, but soon became known for his painting of figure subjects and portraits. He continued to paint small scenes in the border decoration of plates. His work included copies of Thurston's illustrations of Shakespeare plays on a dessert service. Corden turned to enamelwork on metal, went to London and became a portrait painter, exhibiting at the Royal Academy from 1826. A painting of Jebediah Strutt dressed in a yellow coat, signed and dated 1822, executed on a plaque made at *Coalport was probably carried out independently. Corden was among the painters engaged on the dessert service commissioned by King William IV from the *Swinton Pottery in 1830.
Refs: Eaglestone & Lockett; Godden (1970); Rice; Twitchett (1980).

Cork & Edge. Staffordshire earthenware manufacturers working in the Newport Pottery, Burslem, 1846-60. The firm made low-priced table services, novelties and other earthenware, including lustred ornamental pieces, also developing a method of inlaying decorative patterns in an earthenware body; examples were shown in the Great Exhibition, 1851. The output also included black basalt. The firm's successors were Cork, Edge & Malkin (1860-79), and Edge, Malkin & Co., working until 1903.
Printed marks incorporate the firms' names or initials, and often a trade name for the body, e.g. *Staffordshire stoneware, Pearl White Ironstone.*
Refs: Godden (1964); Jewitt.

Cornes, Domaine des. French faience factory in operation 1825-70 on the large agricultural estate, Domaine des Cornes, at Chatel-Gérard (Yonne). A previous attempt to produce faience had been made c.1804. Using a pinkish body made from a mixture of local clays, Jean Philippot, owner of the estate, made faience decorated with colours that included a pure, intense blue, orange-red and later green and shades of yellow, with a clear, white glaze. Patterns consisted of slender-stemmed plants with bright green leaves, frequently with sunflowers in red

Coultry Pottery. Vase made at the Coultry Pottery, 1879, with modelled decoration attributed to Edwin Griffith. 35.3 cm high.

shading to yellow, touched with dark blue. Later floral decoration became more profuse and convoluted. Figures were produced in large numbers from c.1840. Some pieces, e.g. bottles in the form of female portrait busts, were copies of work produced at *Ancy-le-Franc. The output after c.1848 included straight-sided bowls for salad. After absorbing the nearby *Vausse factory in 1858, the workshop continued production of animal and human figures from the Vausse moulds until its closure in 1870.
Refs: Huillard; Lesur (1971).

Cornwall, Hugh & Arthur. *See* Portobello Pottery.

Cornwell, Alfred (c.1833-90). English engineer, born in Cambridge and working in Australia from 1853, when he undertook a contract in the brick industry in Victoria. In 1861, he established a pottery at Brunswick, Melbourne. Starting with four assistants, he made glazed earthenware, winning a prize in the Dublin Exhibition (1865), and stoneware, exhibited in Melbourne (1866). Cornwell later made Rockingham-glazed earthenware, as well as terracotta vases and architectural ware, and stoneware with Bristol glaze, for which he imported materials from England. In 1876 he established a branch at Sandhill, Launceston, in Tasmania, where he found a good deposit of white clay and made domestic wares, bottles, moulded vases, and drainage ware. Cornwell was proprietor of the Sandhill works (which he called the Victorian and Tasmanian Pottery) until 1880. John *Campbell afterwards took over the pottery. At Brunswick, Cornwell was succeeded by James Allard, who managed the works until Cornwell's sons were sufficiently experienced to take control, and

the works remained in operation under the Cornwell family until the 1950s. Later products include vases with coloured glazes.
Ref: Graham.

Corona. *See* Owens, John B.

Cory, Kate. *See* Volkmar, Charles.

Coulter, Dibb & Co. *See* Twigg, Joseph.

Coultry Pottery. American pottery, formerly the Dayton Street Pottery established 1859 in Cincinnati, Ohio, by Samuel Pollock (d 1870) for the production of earthenware with yellow or Rockingham glazes. Pollock was succeeded by his family and in 1874 by Patrick L. Coultry, who made yellow ware and cream-coloured pottery in Egyptian and classical shapes. After the success of early experiments by M.L.*McLaughlin in underglaze decoration at the pottery, using the yellow ware body in 1877, T.J.*Wheatley joined the firm briefly in 1879 as artist, and instructor of a class in china painting. He was followed in 1880 by pupils John Rettig and A.R.*Valentien, who taught underglaze decoration using blanks produced and fired at the Coultry Pottery. The pottery also provided ware and firing facilities for amateur painters, ceasing operation in 1883, when the fashion for ceramic decoration was regarded as over.
Marks: decorators' marks incised; R-V, incised for Valentien's class; one known piece bears *Coultry*, incised.
Refs: Barber (1976); Clark & Hughto; Evans; Kovel & Kovel; Lehner.

Couper, James. *See* Port Dundas Pottery Co.

Courtenay or **Cortney Bay Pottery.** *See* White, Frederick J.

Courtille or **Basse Courtille,** Manufacture de la. Paris porcelain factory on rue de la Fontaine-au-Roi, founded by Jean-Baptiste Locré and operated by Laurentius Russinger, manager from 1777, owner from 1787, and in partnership from 1800 with François Pouyat (*see* Pouyat family), who was sole proprietor 1808-10. The firm then became Pouyat Frères under his sons, who obtained the patronage of the duc de Berry in 1815. The initial production consisted of decorated table services with landscapes, printed views, flowers, fruit, costume studies, portraits or reproductions of paintings in reserves, on a wide range of coloured grounds, some matt in effect, with a biscuit porcelain of creamy tone used for figures and medallions. The Pouyat family concentrated on utility ware, while also making holy water stoups, writing sets, tobacco pipes, *veilleuses* and pharmacy display bottles, as well as ornamental biscuit porcelain in imitation of Wedgwood's blue jasperware. The Pouyat brothers sold the factory in 1823, and the business was later transferred to rue Trois Bornes.
Marks include crossed tridents or arrows.
Refs: Chavagnac & Grollier; Ernould-Gandouet; Lesur (1967); Guillebon; Fontaine.

courtyard kilns or **garden kilns.** Japanese producers of oniwayaki (honourable garden wares), which included tea wares and high-quality presentation pieces, for the lord of a

fief in the Edo period (1615-1868). Korean immigrants working in courtyard kilns were given Japanese nationality and raised to the status of samurai, the highest honour that could be given by feudal lords. Many of the kilns that began by making wares exclusively for the feudal lords later worked as *clan or *folk kilns. Examples include *Hirado, *Mikawachi, *Nabeshima, *Okawachi.
Refs: Gorham; Mizuo; Okamura.

Cowan, R.Guy (1884-1957). American potter, one of a family of potters established for several generations at East Liverpool, Ohio. He worked in his father's pottery, then, after studying under C.F.*Binns in New York (graduating in 1908), taught ceramics and design in Cleveland, Ohio. With help from the district Chamber of Commerce, he established the Cleveland Pottery & Tile Co. (later called the Cowan Pottery Studio) in 1912, making tiles, vases and other decorative pieces in red or buff earthenware covered with glazes in a variety of colours. After army service (1917-19) he briefly reopened the studio, moving in 1920 to new premises at Rocky River, a Cleveland suburb, where he made tiles in buff Ohio clay and a wide range of slip-cast porcelain, concentrating on the production of well-designed pieces in a way that would be comercially viable. His output included figures in limited editions, some modelled by the pottery's leading artist, W.*Gregory, many ornamental articles, such as lamps, bookends, pen holders, inkstands, ashtrays and doorknobs, plates with raised outlines of relief decoration exposed through a sprayed coating of coloured slip, and a range of table and domestic ware, which included containers for invalids' food. Figures of dancers with the base adapted to hold flowers were introduced in 1925, and porcelain decanters in the shape of characters from Lewis Carroll's *Alice through the Looking Glass* in 1929. A mass-produced line, largely for florists, marketed as Lakeware, was introduced in 1928. The pottery was known for its coloured glazes, which included an oriental red. A.E.*Baggs, who worked at the pottery, 1925-28, developed Persian green and Egyptian blue. Mottled effects were introduced in 1930, and lustre and crackle glazes were used in a wide range of colours. Cowan himself provided most of the designs until 1927, when limited editions were introduced. Other artists were Alexander Blazys, a sculptor teaching in the Cleveland School of Art, who modelled figures (e.g. a group of Russian Dancers in 1927, Moses, 1930), clay and glaze chemist Richard Hummel (who modelled a number of vases), Raoul Josset, French wood carver José Martin (who carried out intricate designs for moulding), and the sculptors F. Luis Mora and Walter Sinz. From 1928, Cowan ran an experimental workshop at the Cleveland School of Art, employing his students at his pottery and exhibiting their work through annual shows run by the Cleveland Museum. R.*Aitken, P.*Bogatay, E.*Eckhardt, Edward Winter and his wife Thelma Frazier were among his early pupils. He is regarded as a pioneer in promoting sculptural work in American ceramics.
The Cowan studio employed about 50 workers, producing an annual output of over 175,000 items, but was unable to withstand the Great Depression. After the closure

of the pottery in 1931, Cowan worked as consultant art director for the Onondaga Pottery. The Rocky River public library now has a collection of work, catalogues and letters comprising the Cowan Pottery Museum.

Marks: usually the name of the pottery; later examples bear a circular printed mark, COWAN, incorporating the initials RG. Early ware marked *Lakewood*, and the cheap, slip cast line LAKEWARE, usually without the pottery's name.

Refs: J. Brodbeck 'Cowan Pottery' in *Spinning Wheel* 29 (March 1973); D.H. Calkins 'Cowan Returns Home' in *American Art Pottery* (March 1978); Clark & Hughto; R.G. Cowan 'Fine Art of Ceramics' in *Design* 38 (November 1937); *Cowan Pottery Studio* (Cowan Pottery Museum, Rocky River, 1978); Lehner.

Cowper, Joan. English studio potter, working at the *Doulton & Co. studio in Lambeth, 1937-39. She was a thrower of individual pieces, specializing in containers for flowers, some in coarse stoneware, unglazed, others with salt or wood ash glazes.

Mark: full signature.
Ref: Eyles (1975).

Cox, F.E. (d 1965). Studio potter and fabric printer, born and trained in England and working in Australia. He began making pottery in Melbourne in the mid 1930s, inspired by the Kent Collection of Chinese ceramics in the National Gallery of Victoria. His wares are all hand-built and wood-fired, with Chinese-inspired forms and glazes, but often decorated with Australian floral designs. In 1946 he established the Jolliff Studio in Murrrumbeena, Victoria. Merric *Boyd, his son Arthur *Boyd, L.& H.*Beck, and H.R.*Hughan all worked at Cox's studio from time to time.

Mark: *Jolliff* with monogram of FEC, incised.
Refs: Cooper, Graham.

Cox, George. English artist potter. After training at the Royal College of Art in London, Cox established a pottery in Mortlake, Surrey, where from c.1910 until 1914

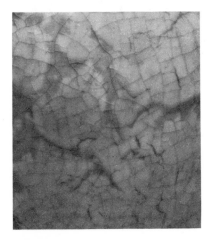

he experimented with high-temperature glazes for his ceramics, which were inspired by early Chinese wares. His book, *Pottery for Artists, Craftsmen and Teachers*, published in 1914, stresses the importance of artistic values (rather than scientific) for potters. Cox went in 1914 to America, where he taught at the Columbia University Teachers' College in New York.

Marks: MORTLAKE or monogram, both incised.
Ref: 'Potters' Parade' in *Pottery & Glass* (January 1950).

Cox, Paul E. American potter; trained under C.F.*Binns. As director of the *Newcomb Pottery, 1910-18, he was concerned with the technical problems of bodies and glazes; his developments include matt glazes in blue and green. He also improved the pottery's rate of production with revised methods and modern kilns. Cox established works in New Orleans, where he mass-produced pots for use in the local fruit-preserving industry, employing R.*Staffel part-time in the 1930s.
Refs: Clark & Hughto; Evans; Kovel & Kovel.

Coxon, Charles (1805-68). American potter and ceramic modeller. Coxon was chief modeller at the pottery of E.*Bennett, where he worked c.1850-61. His work included a Rebekah at the Well teapot (1852), pitchers depicting the hunting of wild boar or stag, a hound-handler pitcher with hanging game, others showing a stork or group of fish, and a pitcher portraying Daniel Boone. He established the firm Coxon & Co. in partnership with J.F. Thompson for the production of cream-coloured earthenware and white granite ware at Trenton, New Jersey, in 1863, and was succeeded by his widow and sons, all potters, John, Charles, Frank and Jonathan (later partner of W.S.*Lenox in the Ceramic Art Co.). In 1884, the works was sold to Alpaugh & Magowan, afterwards becoming known as the Empire Pottery and joining other potteries in the *Trenton Potteries Co., 1892.

Mark: a badge with the eagle of the United States at the centre and the firm's name on a ribbon, in black under the glaze.
Refs: Barber (1976); Clement (1947).

Cozzi, Geminiano. Manufacturer of soft-paste porcelain working in Venice, where with backing from the city he established a factory which was in operation 1765-1812. His porcelain, often grey-tinted and with very runny glaze, included copies of pieces from Meissen and other European factories, particularly those with Japanese-inspired decoration.

Marks: an anchor in red on *Venezia*, sometimes with *Geminiano Cozzi*.
Refs: Danckert; Weiss.

Crabtree, Jonas & Ellis. *See* Soil Hill Pottery.

crackle, cracquelure. A decorative effect achieved in high-fired wares (porcelain or stoneware) when a rate of contraction more rapid in the glaze than the body after firing results in a network of fine cracks (*see* crazing). The crackle may be stained with manganese or other pigments before the piece

Thomas Crafts. Red earthenware teapot made by Crafts in Whateley, Massachusetts, c.1825.

has fully cooled and is sometimes fixed by a further firing.

Craque Ware. *See* Chelsea Pottery US; Dedham Pottery.

Craddock, Charles. *See* Wheeling Pottery Co.

Craemer & Heron. German porcelain manufacturers working from 1909 at Mengersgereuth, near Sonneberg in Thuringia. The firm, producing cups and novelty items, is no longer in operation.
Refs: Danckert; Weiss.

Crafts family. A family of New England porcelain manufacturers producing mainly stoneware in the mid 19th century.

Thomas Crafts (b 1781) established a pottery in his home town, Whately, Massachusetts, in 1802 for the production of red ware. He made teapots in fine red earthenware with black (manganese) glaze from 1821, and stoneware from the enlargement of his works in 1833 until its closure in 1848. Most stoneware was marked *T. Crafts & Co/Whately*. He was joined in the pottery by sons Martin (b 1809), Elbridge G. and, in 1841, James M. Crafts (b 1817), the first manager (c.1838) of another pottery started by his father in Nashau, New Hampshire. Thomas Crafts's daughter Tryphena married stoneware maker D.*Belding six weeks before her death.

After training in his father's pottery at Whately, Martin Crafts worked, 1834-38, in Portland, Maine (Mark: *M. Crafts & Co/Portland*) and went to Nashua in 1839, buying the pottery c.1841. He produced salt-glazed jugs, jars, etc., some with blue decoration, but mainly plain. His marks were initially *T. Crafts & Co./Nashua*, and then variations with his own name until 1851, a year before the pottery's closure. His brother, James M. Crafts, returned from Whately to Nashua in 1849 and, with another brother, Thomas Spencer Crafts, took over management of the pottery when Martin Crafts left to run a wholesale agency selling stoneware in Boston, Massachusetts. When the Nashua pottery had closed, James became a farmer in Whately, 1852.

Thomas Craft's brother Caleb (b 1800) worked until 1837 in Troy, New York. He subsequently ran his nephew's pottery in Portland from 1837; marks include *C. Crafts & Co./Portland*. He followed Martin Crafts to the Nashua pottery by 1841 and returned to Whately 1845-54. Martin Crafts, too, worked in Whately, 1857-61.

Edward A. Crafts was in partnership at Whately with David D. and Isaac N. Wells, who were working in the area from the late 1840s until c.1855.
Refs: Stradling; Webster.

Crailsheim. German faience and porcelain works established in the early 18th century at Württemberg and still working c.1827. The founder, Georg Veit Weiss, succeeded by members of his family, made tankards painted with shields, figures, animals, etc., in a palette that featured an egg-yolk yellow. Ewers and jugs often have eye-like motifs on each side of the spout, handles with a flat thumb mark, and painted designs of carnations, etc. The shapes, in rococo style, are edged with shaded tones of bluish green and sometimes maroon.

Marks, when used, include *Crailsheim* and sometimes the initial w.
Ref: Hüseler.

Cranch, Edward Pope (1809-92). American artist and pottery decorator. While working as a lawyer in Cincinnati, Ohio, he was employed part-time at the *Rookwood Pottery, both as decorator (1880-90) and in the administration of the pottery. He was noted for humorous line drawings on pitchers, beer mugs, etc., with smear glaze, and on a series of tiles illustrating traditional rhymes and tales, e.g. Giles Scroggins's Ghost. A set of designs for mantelpiece tiles depicting the 18th-century New England ballad of Isaac Abbott was published 1886 in a book dedicated to the Cincinnati Literary Club.

Mark: signature, CRANCH, or initials EPC.
Refs: Barber (1976); Evans; Kovel & Kovel.

Crane, Walter (1845-1915). English artist and designer, born in Liverpool. After his apprenticeship to wood engraver, W.J. Linton, in 1859, he worked as a painter, exhibiting from 1862, and as an illustrator

*Walter Crane. Vase made by *Pilkington's Tile & Pottery Co., 1907, painted in lustre to a design by Crane, with* Bon Accorde *repeated twice at the rim. Impressed marks: monogram,* PL, *with bees, and* ENGLAND; *painted marks include Crane's monogram and laurel wreaths.*

Craven Dunnill & Co. Panel painted in red lustre, c.1897-1901. Moulded mark: Craven Dunnill, Shropshire, England. *90.8 x 45.1 cm.*

from 1863. His ceramic designs include occasional work for the Wedgwood factory from 1867 until a visit to Italy (in 1871-72), e.g. drawings for painting on creamware, usually classical figures in delicate outline; a jug with decoration entitled Imagination, 1868. He also executed some designs for the ornamentation of Minton's Henri II ware. Tiles produced by *Maw & Co. from 1874 included a series of nursery characters, seasons and the times of day. Crane designed and painted the prototypes of a series of seven vases produced in cream earthenware with red lustre decoration, resembling some work by W.*De Morgan. He was art superintendent of the London Decorating Co., which specialized in encaustic tiles. For *Pilkington's Tile & Pottery Co., he designed tiles in the early 20th century, e.g. a set of six depicting female figures with floral emblems—daffodil, harebell, poppy, cornflowers with wheat, and others entitled Flora's Train, and between 1904 and 1906 a number of bowls, vases, plaques, etc., which were in production until the closure of the firm.

Mark: a crane and v v inside a c.
Refs: Coysh (1976); Cross; Lockett (1979); Lomax; Reilly & Savage; I. Spencer *Walter Crane* (Studio Vista, London, 1975); *Studio Yearbook* (1906).

Cranz, Ferdinand. *See* Pirkenhammer.

Craven Art Pottery Co. American art pottery established 1904 at works formerly occupied by the *Oakwood Pottery Co. at East Liverpool, Ohio. W.P.*Jervis joined the pottery in 1905. Earthenware vases and utilitarian ware were made in yellow Ohio clay. The early work was decorated in a similar technique to that developed by F.H. *Rhead at the Avon Faience Co. Carved or incised patterns were also used, and a line of ware was produced with combinations (of shade or colour) of matt glazes which included blue, green, yellow, orange, pink, crimson and black. Jervis left in 1908, and the company was dissolved in the same year.

Mark: c incised on a single specimen now in the Smithsonian Institution.
Refs: Barber (1976); Evans; Kovel & Kovel; Lehner.

Craven Dunnill & Co. English manufacturers of inlaid, printed and majolica tiles, working in Jackfield, Shropshire, 1872-1951. The firm's output included floor tiles pressmoulded with grooved patterns that could be filled in with grouting to give the appearance of small mosaic pieces. Hand stencils and lithographic printing were among the decorative techniques used; styles were varied. The firm commissioned designs from contemporary architects, e.g. Alfred Waterhouse (1830-1905). A small quantity of gold-lustred art pottery was also made.

Marks include the name of the firm and/or the place name JACKFIELD.
Refs: Blacker (1922a); Coysh (1976); Lockett (1979).

Crawley, Minna L. English ceramic designer and painter, working for *Doulton & Co. in Lambeth, c.1878-c.1885. She was noted for her floral painting in the style of Islamic pottery, including Rhodian ware.
Refs: see Doulton & Co.

crazing. A mesh of fine cracks in a ceramic glaze resulting from more rapid cooling in the glaze than the body after firing, or from subsequent expansion of the body, e.g. during the heating of kitchen ware. Crazing usually refers to the effect on earthenware (*see* crackle).

creamware, cream-coloured earthenware, faïence fine, faïence anglaise, cailleloutage, terre de pipe anglaise, flintporslin, steingut, terraglia. Light-coloured earthenware developed in Staffordshire in the 18th century with the use of white Devonshire clay, made by many potters from the 1770s, and Britain's main ceramic product from then until c.1820. Makers in the early 19th century included J. *Mayer, E.*Wood (1759-1840) and *Davenport's in Staffordshire, *Herculaneum in Liverpool, potteries in the *Sunderland area, *Bristol, the *Cambrian Pottery and the *Leeds, *Swinton, *Don, *Castleford, *Belle Vue and other Yorkshire potteries. Early creamware, often simple in shape and decoration, also light in weight and relatively inexpensive to produce, was widely exported to Europe. It was made in France, e.g. by G.*Wood and at Creil-Montereau, Italy (at *Nove) Germany, Scandinavia and elsewhere in Europe as well as in America. Wedgwood marketed his cream-coloured ware as Queensware. Developments included pearlware and the white earthenware bodies which largely superseded cream-coloured ware in the 19th century.

Ref: D.C. Towner *Creamware* (Faber & Faber, London, 1978).

Creil. French manufacturer producing cream-coloured earthenware established at Creil (Oise) by Saint-Cricq-Cazaux (d 1840), who worked in partnership with an Englishman, Bagnall, from 1796 until the factory was joined with *Montereau in 1819. The output of table services and other domestic ware was covered with brittle glaze, tinged slightly green by traces of copper. The Creil-Montereau association also produced pieces in the white, some for decoration in black or red by Paris workshops, as well as fine black stoneware, which was used for such small pieces as fluted sugar bowls and teapots, and a small quantity of soft-paste porcelain. Early in the 19th century, styles followed earlier, Empire influences, and the shapes of ewers, soup tureens, and vegetable dishes, all carefully finished, often resemble those made in silver. Painted decoration includes garlands of small flowers, and a streaked, brown tree pattern (resembling the pattern of mocha ware and entitled Deuil de Reine), which was accompanied by an acid green rim. The Paris decorators, Stone, Coquerel and F.A.*Legros d'Anisy bought pieces for printing with views, mythological scenes or Napoleon's conquests in black or sepia, with a variety of border patterns—vines, oak leaves, swans. *Chinoiseries* depicting pagodas or weeping willows in blue, introduced at the factory c.1819, were copied c.1840 at Bordeaux. During the reign of Louis-Philippe, the success of white earthenware allowed an increase in production of coffee services, tableware, trays, display vases, etc. Coloured edges on grounds and rims included bright yellow or, more rarely,

Creil-Montereau. Clock with painted dial flanked by figures in a garden, c.1880. The stand, in the form of an easel, is made of metal. 46 cm overall.

deep green. Printed designs followed general stylistic concerns in France and included rustic scenes, scenes from current life, large bouquets (soon changing to one or two isolated flowers) with butterflies or other insects or birds. *Chinoiseries* remained popular. Painted decoration, already used only rarely, included blue garlands inspired by Tournai porcelain. The factory also made fine unglazed pottery, c.1830, with ochreous body painted in blue, white and black with large flowers.

The firm of Lebeuf, Milliet & Cie. bought Creil-Montereau in 1841, introducing a new, hard earthenware body which they called Pétrocérame. The output also included a light, hard earthenware with very glossy glaze, which the firm identified with English earthenware bodies, and a feldspathic body marked FELDSPATH PORCELAINE in green. Coloured bodies also occur. F.*Bracquemond's Art Nouveau service was reproduced in earthenware between 1879 and 1884 by Barluet & Cie, owners of Creil-Montereau, 1877-84. The firm afterwards became Société Anonyme des Faïenceries de Creil-Montereau.

The factory at Creil closed in 1895, and production was restricted to Montereau.

Marks usually incorporate the place names CREIL and MONTEREAU and *L.M.& Cie* or LMC, sometimes in a bowl shape.
Refs: M. Aries *La Manufacture de Creil, 1795-1894* (Paris, 1974); Baschet; d'Albis *et al*; Ernould-Gandouet; Lesur (1967, 1971).

Creke Pattern. *See* Ault, William.

Crescent Pottery. *See* Jones, George.

Crescent Pottery, Stoke on Trent. *See* Robinson, Harold Taylor.

Crescent Pottery Co. The. *See* Trenton Potteries Co.

Cresswell, William (d 1870). English porcelain painter. Cresswell was apprenticed as a flower painter at the porcelain factory in Nottingham Road, *Derby, and left in 1821 to work at *Coalport. He is thought to have left Coalport by 1841 to work in the south of France. He returned to England, working in Staffordshire from 1848 as painter and subsequently dancing teacher.
Refs: Godden (1970); *see also* Derby.

Crock Street Pottery. *See* Donyatt.

Crofts, Stella Rebecca (1898-1964). English sculptor and designer. Stella Crofts studied the form and movement of animals from life in the London zoo, while training at the Central School of Arts & Crafts. She went on to study sculpture and pottery at the Royal College of Art. She exhibited at the Royal Academy between 1925 and 1962. Working in her studio in Billericay, Essex, from 1925, she made animal and bird models in earthenware, using her own kiln and assisted by her father. Her work as a freelance modeller for the *Worcester Royal Porcelain Co. formed part of the firm's exhibition at the Beaux Arts Gallery in London, 1931.

Mark: signature, *Stella R. Crofts*, incised or painted.
Refs: Godden (1964); Sandon (1978a).

Crolius Pottery. Salt-glazed stoneware jug c.1794-1838, with the impressed mark, C.Crolius/Manufacturer/Manhattan-Wells/New York. 28.6 cm high.

Crolius Pottery. American stoneware pottery run by members of the Crolius family on Potter's Hill, New York City, from the mid 18th century, on land adjoining that of the *Remmey family, to whom they were related by marriage. Clarkson Crolius (b 1773), son of the founder, moved to Bayard Street, New York, in 1812 and was succeeded, 1838-50, by his son, also Clarkson Crolius. The firm made salt-glazed domestic ware with decoration incised, carved or, sometimes, impressed and touched with cobalt blue.
Refs: Stradling; Webster.

Cross, Peter. New England potter working in the early 19th century at Hartford, Connecticut, where he bought a pottery in 1805. He produced red ware and slip-decorated earthenware, unmarked, and stoneware with the mark *P.Cross/Hartford*, 1805-c.1815.
Ref: Stradling.

Stella R. Crofts. Earthenware figure with coloured glazes, 1925-35.

Crossley. *See* Commondale Pottery.

Crown Devon. *See* Fielding, S. & Co. Ltd.

Crown Ducal. *See* Richardson, A.G.,& Co. Ltd.

Crown Earthenware. *See* Derby.

Crown Filter Co. *See* Port Dundas Pottery Co.

Crown Lambretta. *See* Doulton & Co.

Crown Lynn Ceramics Ltd. *See* Jones, Alfred B.

Crown Point. *See* Volkmar, Charles.

Crown Porcelain Co. *See* Derby.

Crown Pottery Co. *See* Peoria Pottery Co.

Crown Pottery, Longton. *See* Broadhurst, James, & Sons Ltd.

Crown Staffordshire Porcelain Co. Ltd. English porcelain manufacturers, successors to T.A.& S. Green (*see* Green & Co.) at the Minerva Works, Fenton. Under the management of H. and C. Green, grandsons of Thomas Green, with a partner, Mellor, in the early 20th century, the company became known for painstaking research into the reproduction of Chinese colours, including powder blue, used on vases. Successful copies were made of 17th-century *famille verte* and 18th-century *famille rose* porcelains, and 18th or 19th-century English wares, notably the flower painting of W. *Billingsley. The firm's title became Crown Staffordshire China Co. Ltd in 1948.

Printed marks usually incorporate STAFFORDSHIRE and often a crown; later marks include FINE BONE CHINA/CROWN/EST/1801/STAFFORDSHIRE/ENGLAND arranged around a crown device.
Refs: Andrews; Blacker (1922a); Godden (1964); Jewitt.

Crown Works. *See* Cooper, Susie.

Croxall Brothers. Firm of American potters, Samuel, Jesse, Thomas and John Croxall, who made yellow and Rockingham-glazed wares at a factory previously belonging to Bennett Brothers at East Liverpool, Ohio, from 1844. John, the only brother still alive c.1890, was senior member of John W. Croxall & Sons (successors to the partnership Croxall & Cartwright) making Rockingham and yellow wares, still at East Liverpool, 1898-c.1912.
Refs: Barber (1976); Lehner; Ramsay.

Crute, Harry E. English potter working in Torquay, Devon. Crute is thought to have worked as a decorator at the *Watcombe Pottery before joining the *Torquay Terra-Cotta Co., where he was employed during World War I. He established a small workshop, the Daison Pottery (named after the nearby Daison estate), in the partnership Lemon & Crute, on Teignmouth Road, Torquay, c.1918. He produced a wide variety of decorative and table ware (much of it for sale to tourists) painted underglaze with flowers, butterflies and birds, including sea-

gulls in flight, peacocks, bluetits. Grounds were frequently pinkish mauve, with streaked effect, or later uniform shades of blue. Crute also made a range of vases, bowls and plant pots, combining glazes in different shades, usually blue or green, in the 1920s. After the partnership ended in 1928, the business became H.E. Crute & Co. Torquay Ltd. Crute continued the pottery until the early 1930s, then worked again for Watcombe as decorator and subsequently sales representative. He is thought to have been associated with a pottery in Dartmouth in 1960.
Ref: Lloyd Thomas (1978).

Crystalis. *See* Roseville Pottery Co.

crystalline glaze. Ceramic glaze containing crystals which result from the presence of mineral salts. The final result is difficult to control, but it is known that zinc, titania (titanium oxide, TiO_2) and rutile (iron bearing titanium ore) favour crystallization; a low content of alumina and slow cooling are also essential. Aventurine glazes, resembling aventurine quartz, with the crystals (often of hematite, Fe_2O_3) evenly spread, include the tiger-eye glaze, accidentally discovered at the *Rookwood Pottery in 1884, which is black/brown in colour, containing golden crystals. Crystals may also occur in clusters or, as in *matt glazes, on the surface.

In the late 19th and early 20th centuries, many factories carried out research in the control of crystalline glaze effects: the Royal *Copenhagen Porcelain Factory from 1886, Meissen (exhibiting in Paris, 1900), and in America the *University City Pottery (from 1909), under the direction of T.*Doat.

Crystal Patina. *See* Clifton Art Pottery.

Cumella, Antoni (b 1913). Catalan ceramist working at Granollers, near Barcelona.

crystalline glaze. Detail of a glaze developed by Albert Heinecke and used on a vase made at the Berlin factory, c.1900.

Charles E. Cundall. Vase made by Pilkington's Tile & Pottery Co. and painted in gold lustre by Cundall, 1906. Impressed with the factory mark of bees, the monogram of PL and a monogram of CEC. 19.5 cm high.

Cumella is known for panels, murals, vases and sculptural pieces made in stoneware. His shapes are simple and austere, with spots, streaks and trails of decoration applied in glaze or incised patterns.
Refs: Hettes & Rada; Préaud & Gauthier.

Cundall, Charles E. (b 1890). English painter and pottery decorator. Cundall joined Pilkington's Tile & Pottery Co. in 1907, studying under G.M.*Forsyth, and attended evening classes at the Manchester School of Art. After army service, 1914-17, he returned briefly to Pilkingtons, then left to work in London as a portrait painter. His work for Pilkingtons included painting of flowers and other plant forms, usually formal in treatment, and a pair of vases with lustre designs of heraldic beasts.

Mark: monogram of CEC.
Refs: Cross; Godden (1966a); Lomax.

Cunian. *See* Pilkington's Tile & Pottery Co.

Curlew. *See* Cooper, Susie.

Curnock, Percy Edwin (1872-1956). English porcelain decorator; born in Staffordshire. Curnock worked for *Doulton & Co. in Burslem from the start of his training under Charles J.*Noke in 1885 until his retirement in 1954. He was among the artists concerned in the development of the fresh style of flower painting, using flat, transparent washes of colour, initiated by J.*Slater, and first exhibited in the Paris Exposition, 1889. Curnock devised the floral pattern painted overglaze in mauve, with edging of gold and green, on Glamis Thistle bone porcelain tableware, in production 1937-61, and other

schemes for lithoprinted tableware (e.g. Passion Flower, Arcadia and Clovelly), but he was especially associated with fine painting of roses and other flowers taken from watercolour sketches which he made from countryside and garden plants. His landscapes include woodlands, Italian lake scenes and subjects after Corot.
Refs: see Doulton & Co.

Curtis, George. *See* Littlethorpe Pottery.

Cushman, Paul (1767-1832). American potter born in Charleston, New Hampshire and working at Albany, New York. He was a farmer and travelled in Canada, subsequently settling in Albany, where he worked as a building contractor, before he established a pottery in 1809, making lead-glazed earthenware with a red body, and then the salt-glazed stoneware with which he is associated: jugs, pitchers, a variety of jars, large pots for pickle, butter, etc., churns, inkstands, rather sketchily decorated with incised birds, fish and other designs, sometimes splashed with blue glaze; a jar glazed with Albany slip has handles and name stamp touched with blue. After Cushman's death, the pottery was sold to a firm trading as Charles Dillon and Co.
Marks: *Paul Cushman*; *Paul Cushman's Stoneware Factory, 1811*; *Paul Cushman's Stoneware Factory, half a mile west of the Albany goal, 1809.*
Refs: Barber (1976); Stradling; Webster.

Cuthbertson, J.D. *See* Vance Faience.

Cutts, John (1772-1851). English porcelain decorator. Cutts worked as a landscape painter at the *Pinxton porcelain factory, where his casually painted scenes were characterized by frequent use of pale red and yellowish brown. He became manager, partner and, for a short period before its closure, sole proprietor of the Pinxton works. After moving to Staffordshire in 1812, Cutts started the decoration of bone porcelain samples for the firm of Wedgwood, with flowers and, again, landscapes, which often feature cottages, great houses, bridges and other architectural pieces. After leaving the Wedgwood factory c.1816, Cutts established a decorating workshop in Hanley, where he carried out enamelling and gilding with his sons as partners by 1842, and employing about 50 decorators. His son, James Cutts (b c.1811) later worked as an independent engraver of patterns for use on ceramics.
Refs: S.W. Fisher *The Decoration of English Porcelain* (Derek Verschoyle, London, 1954); Godden (1972); Jewitt; Reilly & Savage.

Cybis Porcelains. American studio specializing in porcelain sculpture, established in 1941 by Polish-born artist Boleslaw Cybis and his wife Marja at Trenton, New Jersey. Their output comprises a wide range of finely modelled subjects, all unique, including birds, mammals, flowers, naturalistically modelled and coloured, and idealized figures drawn from literature, the theatre and ballet, or religious in theme.
Ref: Schwartz & Wolfe.

Cyfflé, Paul-Louis. *See* Niderviller.

Cyrano. *See* Owens, John B.

Jens Peter Dahl-Jensen. Porcelain hawk modelled by Dahl-Jensen and made by *Bing & Grøndahl, 1901. 38 cm high.*

Da Costa, Mendes. *See* Mendes da Costa, Joseph.

Dagoty, Pierre-Louis (1771-1840). French porcelain manufacturer. With his brother, Jean-Baptiste-Etienne Dagoty (d 1801), he trained in the firm of *Dihl et Guérhard and made porcelain at a workshop on Boulevard Poissonnière, Paris, with another brother, Isidore, who died before 1800. The brothers also occupied (from 1800) a workshop (Manufacture de l'Impératrice) on Boulevard du Montparnasse. Pierre-Louis Dagoty bought his brother's share in the premises on Boulevard Poissonnière and entered into a partnership, 1816-20, with Edouard, the son of F.-M.*Honoré, uniting the Dagoty works with Honoré's factories at La Seynie and in Paris. The Dagoty-Honoré partnership made dessert, tea and coffee services, known for their careful finish, and decorative items which included tulip-shaped cups in the natural colouring of the flowers. Knobs were modelled in the form of butterflies, etc., spouts as animals. Other decoration included flowers painted on grey or brown grounds in medallions against overall light grounds. Some patterns were brightly painted against matt black. The subjects included landscapes, figure scenes, and imitations of Chinese lacquer patterns painted in gold on a vermillion ground. Some pieces were lined with gilding. In 1819, the firm exhibited vases with relief decoration in the style of Wedgwood's *jasper ware, and biscuit statuary. Edouard Honoré took over Dagoty's share in the partnership, taking over the saleroom on Boulevard Poissonnière and

the Montparnasse factory; Dagoty retained the factory at La Seynie which he let to D. *Denuelle.
Marks incorporate *Dagoty*, sometimes with *Honoré*.
Ref: Guillebon.

Dahl-Jensen, Jens Peter (b 1874). Danish sculptor. Dahl-Jensen studied 1893-96 at the Copenhagen academy and then worked as designer and modeller for *Bing & Grøndahl, 1897-1917. He then became artistic director of the Norden factory (*see* Bing & Grøndahl) in Copenhagen from 1917 until the establishment of his own porcelain factory, also in Copenhagen, 1925. He is known for the design of individual pieces in Art Nouveau styles.
Printed marks include *DJ/Copenhagen* under a coronet.
Refs: Bénézit; Danckert; Porzellankunst; Weiss.

Dahlquist, Edward (1877-1927) and Elizabeth Burnap (1875-1963). American potters, trained at the Minneapolis School of Art and the Chicago Art Institute. Edward Dahlquist also studied at the Art Students' Institute in New York, and Elizabeth Dahlquist under Lucy Perkins of the *Brush Guild. They established the Shawsheen Pottery (named after a brook in the grounds of their home) at Billerica, Massachusetts, with Gertrude Singleton Mathews in 1906, first exhibiting work at Boston in the same year. They made hand-coiled pottery in dark clay from Gay Head, Massachusetts, achieving tones of copper and bronze on the black ground of vessels which resembled Etruscan bronzes and ceramic wares, incising or carving decoration with wooden tools. In 1907, the Dahlquists moved their pottery to Mason City, Iowa, teaching ceramics there and at their home in Clear Lake. They designed, potted and fired all their own work and added throwing to their repertoire soon after the move to Iowa; the pottery's output also included the work of students. Vases, *jardinières*, teasets and bowls were made, often with relief decoration of leaves, partly defined figures, etc. Edward Dahlquist taught at Memorial University, Mason City, and became an instructor in hand-building at *University City Pottery in 1910, returning to Iowa in the following year. Both Dahlquists subsequently moved to Chicago, where they continued to teach pottery. Elizabeth Dahlquist opened a shop in Chicago c.1915, selling *objets d'art*, and abandoned the making of pottery.
Marks: monograms of SP, incised or impressed, where used.
Refs: Evans; Kovel & Kovel.

Dainty White. *See* Foley Potteries.

Daisy Bank, Lane End. *See* Mason, George Miles and Charles James.

Dale Hall. *See* Mayer, T.J.& J.

Dalgas, Frederick (1866-1934). Danish potter and porcelain maker. In 1902, he succeeded his father-in-law, P.*Schou, as director of the amalgamated *Aluminia A.S. and Royal *Copenhagen Porcelain factories. Dalgas stressed the importance of good design for earthenware as a material in

its own right (rather than as a cheap replacement for porcelain). Under his direction, artists were encouraged to design for the material better suited to their artistic intentions. Dalgas retired in 1931, and was succeeded by Christian Christensen.
Refs: see Royal *Copenhagen Porcelain Factory.

Dallas, Frederick (d 1881). American potter. In 1865, Dallas bought a pottery which had made Rockingham and yellow-glazed ware, and brown-ware fruit jars at Hamilton Road, Cincinnati, Ohio, since 1856. In 1869, he turned production over to cream-coloured earthenware and granite ware. In 1879, the Dallas Pottery provided facilities for the firing of decorated ware, an underglaze kiln and a glaze kiln financed by M.L. *McLaughlin and M.L.*Nichols Storer. Dallas let a studio to the *Cincinnati Pottery Club and a smaller workroom to Mrs Nichols Storer for her early experiments with clay and glazes, providing unfired and biscuit ware for decoration by his tenants, and other outside decorators from as far afield as Washington and Chicago. He concentrated until 1879 on the manufacture of transfer-printed table and toilet wares of high quality, but in 1880 employed a decorator on his own staff and began to produce slip-painted ware, which was successfully exhibited in the same year, and opened a showroom. He was succeeded in 1881 by his widow, who abandoned underglaze decoration early in 1882. The superintendent of the pottery, J.*Bailey Sr., took charge of the Rookwood works in 1881, while continuing to work at the Dallas Pottery, which closed in July 1882.
Marks: (few marked pieces known) usually *Dallas*, sometimes with *Hamilton Road Pottery*.
Refs: Evans; Peck.

Dallwitz. Bohemian factory established in 1805 by Johann von Schönau (d 1821) on his estate at Dallwitz (Dalovice), for the production of creamware and porcelain. Under the direction of Benedikt Hasslacher, the factory produced tableware, tea and coffee sets, vases, flower pots and children's miniature teasets, etc., in creamware. The firm's display in the first exhibition of Bohemian industrial products in Prague, 1828, included a gilded crucifix, plates decorated with animals, coffee ware, and small pieces of tableware and writing sets painted to represent wood graining. At this time, the output also included candlesticks, fruit baskets and salt cellars supported by modelled dolphins.
Von Schönau's son, Wolfgang Julius, received permission to produce porcelain in 1830, although little was produced before the purchase of the factory in 1832 by Wenzel Lorenz, who concentrated on mass production. Lorenz submitted a display of dinner, dessert and coffee wares in creamware and porcelain at the international exhibition in Vienna in 1836. The decoration included transfer-printing from 1844, and the factory, then employing about 100 workers, became known for woven fruit baskets. Franz Fischer, owner from 1850, formed a partnership, Fischer, Lorenz & Urfuss, which remained the firm's title until its sale to Riedel von Riedelstein in 1872.

Frederick Dallas. Vase made by Dallas at his pottery in Hamilton Road, Cincinnati, 1880. Decorator unknown. 15.3 cm high.

The factory was subsequently owned by Baron von Springel 1889-91, Proeschold & Co., and, from 1918, EPIAG. The output c.1940 consisted of everyday wares produced in series.
Marks include the initals D or DF; DALLWITZ; DALLWITZER/FABRIK/FRANZ URFUS; DF with the EPIAG mark and *Germany* or *Czechoslovakia*.
Refs: Danckert; Meyer; Weiss.

Dalpayrat, Pierre-Adrien (1844-1910). French ceramist born in Limoges. Dalpayrat worked from 1867 in Bordeaux and subsequently in Toulouse before running a pottery in Monte Carlo (1876-88). In 1889, Dalpayrat established a stoneware workshop at Bourg-La-Reine (Hauts-de-Seine) with A. Voisin Delacroix, who modelled

Pierre-Adrien Dalpayrat. Stoneware vase with grey and green glaze over dark green flecked with yellow. 10 cm high.

some work until 1891. Dalpayrat also collaborated with Adèle Lesbros, with the aim of producing reasonably priced stoneware, and executed designs by such artists as M. *Dufrêne (for La *Maison Moderne), Ferdinand Faivre and Constantin Meunier. He perfected a copper red glaze, which he exhibited in 1892, and which he used in combination with yellow, green or blue to obtain marbled effects on pieces in the forms of gourds or other fruit, decorated with animals or figures in high relief, or in shapes derived from Japanese bottles. As well as stoneware, Dalpayrat worked with earthenware and porcelain, which became an increasing preoccupation after 1902.

Mark: bomb symbol; signature, *Dalpayrat*, incised or impressed.
Refs: Bénézit; Brunhammer *et al* (1976); Camart *et al*; Hakenjos (1974); Heuser & Heuser; Lesur (1967, 1971); Thieme & Becker.

Dalton, Burn & Co. *See* Stepney Bank Pottery.

Dalton, William B. English studio potter and teacher of ceramics. Dalton was Principal of the Camberwell School of Arts & Crafts and a member of the first council of the Design & Industries Association in 1915. He worked as a potter in London from 1900, and in Longfield, Kent, by the 1930s (frequently participating in crafts exhibitions). He emigrated to America in 1941.
Encouraging the recognition of ceramics as one of the fine arts, Dalton drew inspiration in his own work from a wide range of sources, e.g. Isnik and Italian tinglaze for earthenware vases and bowls (before 1920), and, later, oriental stoneware and porcelain for vases, covered jars, boxes (often footed or on a raised base), and candlesticks, with opalescent, crackled effect, dull grey-green glaze, etc. He also made 'appreciation pieces' decorated with an American eagle painted under the glaze, or in relief. Dalton developed a repertoire of clay bodies through his own experiments with English and American clays.

Mark: incised or painted monogram.
Refs: W.B. Dalton *Craftsmanship & Design in Pottery* (Pitman, London, 1957); Forsyth; Godden (1964).

Daly, Matthew Andrew (1860-1937). American ceramic decorator born in Cincinnati, Ohio. Daly studied under T.J.*Wheatley at the Coultry Pottery. He worked briefly for M.*Morgan and then at the *Rookwood Pottery, 1882-1903. Examples of his decoration include a jug painted with a spray of large chrysanthemum flowers (1887) and a wide-bodied vase with flowers painted under the glaze and scrolled leaves in silver. After leaving Rookwood, he took charge of the art department at the US Playing Card Co. until 1931.

Mark: initials or signature.

Refs: Clark & Hughto; Evans; Kovel & Kovel; Peck.

Damm. German faience factory established 1827 near Aschaffenberg by Anna Maria Muller, who was succeeded by her son, Daniel Ernst Muller. The factory produced wares resembling those of *Höchst, acquiring moulds for figures and groups formerly used at the Höchst factory in 1830. The Damm factory suffered financial failure in 1882.

Mark: six-spoked wheel, or initial D.

Ref: Hüseler.

Dammouse, Albert-Louis (1848-1926). French sculptor, ceramist and glass artist, son of a modeller and decorator at the Sèvres factory, Pierre-Adolphe Dammouse. He studied at the Ecole des Arts Décoratifs in his native Paris, and under the sculptor François Jouffroy at the Ecole des Beaux-Arts. Dammouse was an apprentice under L.-M.-E.*Solon and collaborated with him in the use of *pâte-sur-pâte* decoration. He exhibited first in 1869. Working at Sèvres (Hauts-de-Seine), where he established his own studio, Dammouse provided designs for factories in Limoges, including a service with pierced decoration filled in with translucent glaze, and two large vases, included in *Pouyat's display at the Exposition Universelle in Paris, 1878, and a service made by T.*Haviland for Queen Maria-Pia of Portugal, shown in 1900. He joined the C.

*Matthew A. Daly. Earthenware vase, painted by Daly with a yellow rose and a bird against a shaded amber, moss green and straw-coloured ground. Made at the *Rookwood Pottery, 1890. 42 cm high.*

Albert-Louis Dammouse. Stoneware vase, with brown, yellow, green and blue glazes, c.1900. Marked AD. 21 cm high.

*Haviland studio at Auteuil and worked there on the shapes for a service in porcelain with decoration of birds after F.*Bracquemond. He also assisted E.*Chaplet in his development of brown stoneware in 1882. With his brother, E.-A.*Dammouse, he established a studio at Sèvres, where he produced earthenware, stoneware and porcelain in shapes derived from Japanese and Chinese examples, at first decorated only with monochrome glazes and later painted with patterns of flowers, foliage and algae. From 1898, Dammouse worked in glass, notably *pâte de verre* and *pâte d'émail*.

Marks include D, crossed by a sweeping stroke, over A SEVRES; signature; AD over S.

Refs: Bénézit; Bloch-Dermant; Brunhammer *et al* (1976); Camart *et al;* Heuser & Heuser; Thieme & Becker.

Dammouse, Edouard-Alexandre. French painter and ceramic decorator; born in Belleville, Paris. Dammouse studied painting under F.*Bracquemond before working with E.*Chaplet at the *Laurin factory, and then joined the group of artists who included his brother, A.-L.*Dammouse, working under Bracquemond at the C.*Haviland studio at Auteuil. He stayed there until the studio's closure in 1881. He went with Chaplet to the workshop on rue Blomet, 1882-86. His work there was in naturalistic and oriental styles. With A.-L. Dammouse, he established a workshop at Sèvres (Hauts-de-Seine), producing stoneware and, later, glass.

Refs: Bénézit; Brunhammer *et al* (1976); d'Albis *et al*; Heuser & Heuser.

Damura. See Shigaraki ware.

d'André, George. *See* Batiz.

Dandy-Line. *See* Brush-McCoy Pottery.

Dangar, Anne (1887-1951). Australian-born painter and studio potter working in France. Anne Dangar studied and later taught at the Julian Ashton School in her native Sydney. With the modernist painter Grace Crowley, she went to France in 1926 and studied under André Lhote in the following year. She began to work in ceramics at Viroflay, near Paris. In 1930 she settled in France and joined the cultural centre opened by painter, Albert Gleizes, and his wife, Juliette Roche, at Moly-Sabata (Isère), where she worked as a potter until her death. She taught the making of small earthenware figures, slip-painted and lead-glazed, to children from neighbouring villages while producing utilitarian wares in the local tradition, and painted dishes, etc., strongly influenced by the religious/mystical ideology of Gleizes. She was also inspired by the traditional wares of Morocco, which she visited c.1939.

Refs: Céramique française contemporaine; M. Gauthier 'Moly-Sabata' in *Art et Décoration* (1938).

Daniel, Henry (1765-1841). Staffordshire potter and ceramic decorator. In partnership with John Brown, Henry Daniel ran a decorating business in Hanley and at a workshop which was in effect a decorating department for J.*Spode's factory, at Stoke-on-Trent. From 1806, Brown worked independently at Hanley, and Daniel continued to carry out decoration, including the training of painters and ground layers, in the preparation of colours, etc., for Spode until c.1820. While working for Daniel & Brown, John *Hancock (1757-1847) developed platinum lustre. Daniel also employed John *Hancock (1777-1840), and trained his own son Thomas Daniel (b 1798), who was his apprentice from 1812. By 1823, Henry Daniel established a factory at Stoke-on-Trent for the production of high-quality porcelain. He introduced an improved ground-laying technique in 1827, and his output included several

Henry Daniel. Vase with panels of flowers on a green ground, c.1828. Marked H.& R. Daniel. 21 cm high.

lavishly painted and gilded services commissioned by the Earl of Shrewsbury in 1827.

Although much of Daniel's work was unmarked, many pieces made for the Earl of Shrewsbury bear a printed mark of flowers with an urn and a harp, surrounding the name H & R DANIEL/*Stoke-upon-Trent*/STAFFORDSHIRE.

After working as his father's partner, Richard Daniel (b 1800) continued the Stoke-on-Trent factory until the early 1850s, and was subsequently employed at the Hill Pottery, Burslem. A branch worked under the title Henry Daniel & Co. at Shelton from 1843. Henry Daniel's third son, John Daniel (b 1802), worked for a Liverpool businessman before becoming a dealer in ceramics at Nottingham.

Rare marks include *H. & R. Daniel* (1820-41) and *H. Daniel & Sons* (1829-41).
Refs: M. Berthaud *H. & R. Daniel 1822-46* (Micawber Publications, 1980); Jewitt; Shaw; *Staffordshire Advertiser* (obituary, 17th April 1841); Whiter.

Daniel, John (1756-1821). Staffordshire potter, the son of Ralph Daniel of Cobridge. John Daniel became manager of *New Hall, and partner in the firm Hollins, Warburton, Daniel & Co., purchasers of New Hall in 1810.
Refs: Holgate; Jewitt; *Staffordshire Advertiser* (27th January 1821); Stringer.

Darlington, George William (1872-1927). English porcelain painter, born in Stoke-on-Trent. After serving an apprenticeship at *Minton's, Darlington moved to the porcelain factory in Osmaston Road, *Derby, where his style became influenced by the work of D. *Leroy, with whom he worked 1890-1907. He was a painter of brightly coloured, exotic birds, and flowers, which include roses. Darlington was also a skilful gilder; his work occurs on a plate dating from 1909.
Refs: see Derby.

Darmstadt. *See* Rosenthal.

Darte brothers. Porcelain manufacturers working in France. Louis-Joseph Darte (1765-1843), born in Namur (then in the Netherlands), was naturalized French by 1786. With his brothers Joseph and Jean-François, he bought a porcelain factory on rue de Charonne in Paris c.1795. The partnership split in the early 19th century, when Joseph Darte bought a porcelain factory which had been established on rue Popincourt in 1791. Louis-Joseph and Jean-François Darte bought a workshop at 90 rue de la Roquette and traded from 1808 as Darte Frères. They made decorated domestic ware, and large pieces which were decorated at independent workshops, including that of P.-L. *Dagoty, as well as in their own studios. Their own lavishly painted wares included dessert services, *veilleuses*, pastille burners, spill jars, clock cases and portrait cups. Louis-Joseph took his son into partnership briefly (1824-25) and continued production until 1833, despite his bankruptcy five years earlier.
Marks: *Darte aîné à Paris* [Joseph Darte]; *Darte Frères*, often with versions of the firm's depot address, *Palais Royale No 21* or *rue Vivienne*.

Refs: Chavagnac & Grollier; Danckert; Guillebon.

Davenport, Maud. American ceramic decorator. Maud Davenport joined the *Dedham Pottery as an artist in 1904 and stayed until 1929; her work included designs for borders of pond lilies, cats, dogs and chicks, and a Republican plate. Painting with fine brushwork, she had as her mark a small 'o' hidden in the design. Her brother, Charles, joined the pottery in 1914 and became head of the decorating department.
Refs: Evans; Kovel & Kovel.

Davenport's. Staffordshire firm making earthenware, flint glass (from 1801), hard-paste porcelain (or from c.1805 bone china), caneware, basalt, and later stone china. The founder, John Davenport (1765-1848), bought and enlarged the pottery at Unicorn Bank, Longport, in 1794, and the firm traded under his name until his retirement in the early 1830s. In 1804, Davenport was the owner of the Cliff Bank Pottery at Stoke-on-Trent, which he leased to William Adams (*see* Adams family). He bought the Newport works c.1810, opening a warehouse and saleroom in Liverpool by 1812. An extensive export trade was begun in c.1815. By the early 1830s, the firm employed about 1400 workers.

Davenport made white and cream-coloured ware with green-tinged glaze, often transfer-printed in blue, or sold for decoration (e.g. painting of flowers and landscapes in sepia and a pale, bluish green by the decorator, William Absolon, early in the firm's history). The usual decoration consisted of simple patterns at the rim; botanical paintings became popular after c.1815. The output also included ware in deep yellow or orange-buff, painted with landscapes in black or red.

White stoneware jugs and mugs were made in large quantities 1800-20, lined with glossy glaze and smear-glazed on the exterior, usually with the addition of a brown or, less frequently, blue enamel band on rim and handle. The firm also made high-quality stone china c.1805-c.1820, including dessert services, some pieces with simple perforated

Davenport's. Porcelain basket, c.1805-15.

decoration. A dessert service was made for King William IV in 1830. Ironstone bodies, advertised until the 1880s, were made in large quantities for export to America.

Davenport's porcelain was of high quality and included lavishly painted and gilded tea and dessert services. After John Davenport's retirement, the firm passed to his sons Henry (d 1835) and William (d 1864), who subsequently traded as W. Davenport & Co. His son, Henry Davenport, carried on until 1881, when the firm became a private company, Davenport & Co., which continued to specialize in decoration, which was predominantly in deep blue and red and richly gilded, closely resembling the Japan patterns used at the Derby factory. The company ceased operation in 1887. Among the artists who had been employed were R. *Ablott, James Cutts, E. *Lessore (independently); D. *Lucas, J.F. *Marsh, Jesse *Mountford, J. *Rouse, William *Slater Sr and Edwin *Steele.

Marks often incorporate DAVENPORT printed in blue, over an anchor; also a crown over DAVENPORT/LONGPORT/STAFFORDSHIRE, c.1870-87.
Refs: Blacker (1922a); Collard; Godden (1964); Jewitt; Lockett (1972); Rhead.

Davies, Margaret May. English ceramic modeller, specializing in figures. Born in Burslem, Peggy Davies won a scholarship to the Burslem School of Art at the age of twelve, and later trained under G.M. *Forsyth. In the 1930s, at the age of fifteen, she modelled a series of wall masks for production by A.J. *Wilkinson Ltd, and worked as an assistant to C. *Cliff. In 1939, she started work for *Doulton & Co. in Burslem under Cecil *Noke, specializing in the modelling of figures, including a series of historical personalities, ballet dancers, musicians, children and crinolined ladies. She worked independently after World War II, but entered into a contract with Doulton & Co. Her figures were detailed and often intricate, with careful treatment of costume. A group, The Marriage of Art & Industry, was included in the Doulton display at the international exhibition in Brussels, 1958.
Refs: P. Wentworth Shields & K. Johnson *Clarice Cliff* (L'Odeon, London, 1976); *see also* Doulton & Co.

Harry Davis. Covered vase in Royal Worcester porcelain painted with Highland sheep and gilded. Marks include shape no. 2330, the date mark for 1910-11, and the painter's signature, all in puce. 37 cm high.

Lewis F. Day. Earthenware vase decorated with gryphons and stylized leaves in crimson lustre against a salmon pink ground, made by *Maw & Co. Ltd, c.1890, after a design by Day. Marked Maw & Co. Ltd Jackfield.

Davies, Oscar (d 1950). English potter and designer. After returning from a career at sea in 1934, Davies established the *Roeginga Pottery with his wife, G.*Barnsley, taking responsibility for the firing and selling of the earthenware produced. He painted a combined milk and coffee pot (Duopour), for serving white coffee in a moving ship, which was produced at the Wedgwood factory c.1935. Davies returned to the navy in 1939, and sold the Roeginga Pottery after World War II, because of ill health.
Ref: Victorian & Edwardian Decorative Art (catalogue of the Handley-Read Collection, Royal Academy, London, 1972).

Davies, Richard, & Co. *See* Tyne Main Pottery.

Davies, Colonel Thomas J. Cotton planter, born in Georgia. Davies began the production of firebrick in 1862 near Bath, South Carolina, using labour from his own estate. His workers also made household articles in coarse earthenware, including water jugs covered in a purplish glaze, and decorated with human facial features, the eye-whites and teeth inlaid in pale clay. In 1863, he started the manufacture of jars and pitchers, for use in Confederate hospitals. Production ceased at the end of the Civil War (1865). Davies then turned his attention to the mining of clay for ceramics.

Refs: Barber (1976); Stradling.

Davies, Cookson & Wilson. *See* Stepney Bank Pottery.

Davis, Harry (1885-1970). English porcelain painter working for the *Worcester Royal Porcelain Co. He joined the factory in 1898 and was apprenticed under E.*Slater in the following year. Davis was foreman of painters, 1928-54, and continued to work in his own studio at the factory until the year before his death. He was known for paintings of sheep in pastoral or mountain settings, but also painted landscapes in the styles of Claude or Corot, woodland scenes, cottages, and gardens and urban scenes. He painted the two services made for Prince Ranjitsinji with views of the Prince's English and Indian homes. Davis also carried out etchings of cathedrals, other buildings, and, later, gamebirds, fish and coaching scenes to provide a printed outline for the training of painters, which he signed H. SIVAD. After World War II, he worked on the colouring of some bird models by D.*Doughty.
Ref: Sandon (1978a).

Davis, Harry and May. English potters. Harry Davis trained as a thrower at *Carter, Stabler & Adams and worked for B.*Leach at the St Ives Pottery, 1934. He later ran the pottery at Achimota College, Gold Coast,

until 1942 and travelled widely. With his wife, May, he established the Crowan Pottery at Praze in Cornwall for the production of stoneware pieces, all thrown, for table and household use. In 1962, the couple moved to New Zealand, where they continued production of domestic ware.
Refs: Rose; Wingfield Digby.

Davis, Louisa J. English ceramic designer and decorator, who worked for *Doulton & Co. in Lambeth c.1873-c.1895. She decorated stoneware with stylized flower and plant motifs, notably reeds, sedges and grasses.
Refs: see Doulton & Co.

Dawson, John (c.1760-1848). English potter, trained under the *Maling family at Hylton Pot Works. Dawson was the owner of the Low Ford Pottery, making fine earthenware and semi-porcelain at South Hylton, to the west of Sunderland, by 1799; his sons Thomas (1796-1839) and John (1798-1832) both entered the firm. The varied output included dinner services, jugs, platters, tea sets, etc., with transfer-printed or hand-painted patterns, and frequent use of pink, copper or silver lustre; some jugs have views of the Wearmouth Bridge painted in black against a bright yellow ground. Transfer printing was sometimes overpainted in enamel. Ornamental tiles depict landscapes, architectural features (often ruins), battle scenes, etc., and table tops intended for mounting in wooden frames portray Napoleonic battles and other scenes. Money boxes, inkwells in the form of birds' nests, marbles, eggs for presentation on birthdays or at Easter, and animal figures were also made. New buildings and machinery came into use in 1836. John Dawson was succeeded by his grandsons John and, briefly, Charles Frederick, who started his own pottery making brownware at Bank Top, South Hylton. In 1838, a group of workmen from the Low Ford Pottery took over the Seaham Harbour Pottery (established two years earlier as a brownware works), intending to produce white and printed earthenware, but their venture failed in 1841. John carried on production of white earthenware, but moulds, printing plates and other equipment were sold at auction in 1864.

Marks: *Dawson*, impressed; printed patterns sometimes incorporate the name of the firm, and sometimes *Ford, Low Ford*, or *Ford Pottery, South Hylton*.
Refs: Shaw; Towner (1957).

Day, Alfred. *See* Lonhuda Pottery.

Day, Josephine. *See* Robertson, Hugh Cornwall.

Day, Lewis Foreman (1845-1910). English designer, author and lecturer, born in Peckham, London. After working (1865) as clerk in a firm of glass painters, Day produced designs for a wide variety of media, including stained glass, textiles, furnishings and book binding. He designed tiles for the manufacturers *Maw & Co., and *Pilkington's Tile & Pottery Co., and the Welsh firm of J.C. Edwards at Ruabon. Day was a founder member (1884) and later master of the Art & Crafts Exhibition Society. He worked within the stylistic idiom of the Arts & Crafts

Movement, but abstract elements in his treatment of natural forms anticipated the preoccupations of Art Nouveau.
Refs: Anscombe & Gere; E. Aslin *The Aesthetic Movement* (Elek, London, 1969); Cross; Lockett (1979); Naylor.

Daysh, Barbra. *See* Harris family.

Dayton Porcelain Pottery. *See* Broome, Isaac.

Dayton Street Pottery. *See* Coultry Pottery.

Deakin, H.H. English porcelain painter working at the porcelain factory in Osmaston Road, *Derby, during the late 19th century. His work, listed in the factory's pattern books of 1878, included a wide variety of subjects: birds, many flower studies, fruit, butterflies, fish, seaweed and water scenes.
Refs: see Derby.

Dean, J.E. (d 1935). English porcelain decorator working at *Mintons Ltd c.1882–c.1925, and specializing in naturalistic studies of animals, fish and game, normally signed.
Refs: see Mintons Ltd.

Dean, William Edward James (d 1956). English porcelain painter. Dean worked at the porcelain factory in Osmaston Road, *Derby from his apprenticeship in the late 1890s until shortly before his death. He was noted for seascapes and nautical scenes, with sails, rigging and other details accurately portrayed, using as source material sketches and photographs which he made during trips on trawlers. Dean also painted views and landscapes in Lakeland and the Derbyshire Dales, e.g. scenes of Bakewell and Ullswater in 1913, and High Tor, Matlock, c.1946, as well as floral studies, especially small bouquets.
    Much of his work was carried out on large plates and signed.
Refs: see Derby.

de Blanken, Gerrit (1895–1961). Dutch potter, born in Leiderdorp. He worked 1910–23 in a number of potteries before establishing his own workshop (1923) in Zoeterwoude. He worked with P.*Groeneveld in 1924 and produced designs by the artist Chris Lebeau c.1926. The work included series of vases and plates, as well as individual pieces.
    Mark: full name, with HOLLAND.
Refs: E. Berkovich 'De pottenbakker Gerrit

Théodore Deck. Earthenware jar painted in Rhodian style, 1862–67. Initialled THD. *35 cm high.*

de Blanken', in *De Vrouw en haar Huis* 31 (June 1936); *International Exhibition of Ceramic Art* (catalogue, Metropolitan Museum, New York, 1928); Scheen; Singelenberg-van der Meer; van Straaten.

de Bonneval, Hippolyte. *See* Dupré, François and Jules.

de Bruin, Cornelis (1870–1940). Dutch painter, draughtsman and ceramic decorator, born in Utrecht and trained at the Amsterdam Rijksacademie. He was a designer at De *Distel (c.1900–03) before starting his own studio in Utrecht.
Refs: Scheen; Singelenberg-van der Meer.

Decaen, Frères. *See* Arboras-Grigny.

de Camarsac, Lafon (1821–1905). French porcelain manufacturer. He invented a technique for the reproduction of photographs on porcelain in 1854, showing examples of this work in the International Exhibition, London, 1862.

de Caranza, Amédée. *See* Vieillard, Jules.

Deck, Théodore (1823–91). French ceramist, born at Guebwiller (Haut-Rhin). Deck worked as a stovemaker in France, Germany and Austria before settling in Paris where he became foreman of a factory producing ceramic stoves. He worked as a modeller of terracotta and again (1851–55) as a stovemaker. He established a workshop in Paris, producing pottery inspired by Middle Eastern ceramics, primarily Isnik ware, with floral decoration in turquoise and blue with touches

of red and green; subsequently some of his work derived from Chinese stoneware and porcelain. Having achieved the first *flambé* glazes of this period in France (exhibited 1884), he also developed a celadon glaze, which was used over incised designs, and after visiting Venice developed an underglaze gold, which he used as a ground colour. His work was decorated at the studio by noted painters. Wall plates were shown at the exhibition of industrial arts in Paris in 1861 and, with designs by F.*Bracquemond and other artists, in the Exposition Universelle, 1878. Within the next two years, Deck's work clearly showed the inspiration he had derived from Japanese ceramics in the same exhibition. His book *La Faïence* was published in 1887, the year in which he also became art director of the Sèvres factory. There, he improved the soft-paste porcelain, increasing the possible size of pieces that could be achieved without sacrificing the beauty of soft paste and its glazes. He developed a stoneware body (*grosse porcelaine*) with hard-wearing transparent glazes for the production of vases, sculptures and garden ornaments.

Marks: impressed, name in capitals with initials TH combined; from c.1880, profile portrait in circular impression, with THEODORE DECK CERAMISTE.
Refs: Brunhammer *et al* (1976); A. Girodie 'Biographies Alsaciennes XIII: Théodore Deck' in *Revue Alsacienne Illustrée* (1903); Hakenjos (1974); Heuser & Heuser.

Decoeur, Emile (1876–1953). French ceramist. Decoeur was apprenticed in 1890 to

Théodore Deck. Egg basket in the form of a cockerel, with black and pale yellow plumage, tomato red wattle, and interior glazed pale blue, late 19th century. 39 cm high.

Théodore Deck. Ornamental jar with hard, grey body and green glaze, early 1870s. Impressed mark TH DECK. *5.4 cm high.*

E.*Lachenal, learning faience techniques, glazes and firing. Exhibiting independently from 1901, he continued his collaboration with Lachenal, subsequently worked with F.*Rumèbe briefly in 1903, and developed an interest in stoneware. He experimented with flown and *flambé* glazes (c.1905) and a variety of ornamental techniques: incising, painting (1910-20) and the decorative use of glazes. Relief ware included vases in vegetable forms (c.1905) and a green and yellow-glazed match holder in the form of a frog, signed by designer Marie Gautier and executed by Decoeur for exhibition in Paris in 1907 (Salon of the Société Nationale des Beaux-Arts).

He established his own studio (1907) in Fontenay-aux-Roses (Seine) where he made porcelain as well as stoneware, using the same glazes and decoration for both materials. In Paris after World War I, he concentrated on simplicity in style, using only limited geometrical decoration, carefully related to form, and relying for effect on glazes, often matt or satin. Adding kaolin to the stoneware body from c.1927, he made bowls, vases and goblets in pure, simple shapes with thick, matt glazes in yellow, green, blue, violet, pink or white. He worked at the Sèvres factory 1939-42, and was among the firm's artistic consultants until 1948.

Marks: incised or painted signature; painted monogram of DE.
Refs: Années 25; Bénézit; Brunhammer *et al* (1976); Céramique française contemporaine; Hakenjos (1974); Heuser & Heuser; G. Janneau *Emile Decoeur* (Paris, 1923); Valotaire.

Décorchemont, François-Emile (1880-1971). French painter, glass artist and ceramist. Décorchemont studied in Paris 1893-97, exhibited stoneware in 1901, and a year later established a kiln at his home town of Conches (Eure). His work included vases with foliage in relief at the rim and acting as

Emile Decoeur. Stoneware vases. Left, c.1910, right, c.1920. 17 cm high.

handles. From 1903, he worked primarily as a glass artist.
Mark: monogram of FD; circular signature, impressed.
Refs: Brunhammer *et al* (1976); F. Duret-Robert 'François Décorchemont' in *Encyclopédie Connaissance des Arts* (June 1973); Hakenjos (1974).

Dedham Pottery, formerly the *Chelsea Keramic Art Works, which began operation in 1895 at new premises built in Dedham, Massachusetts, changing its name with the move. The director, H.C.*Robertson, continued the production of Cracqule ware developed at Chelsea, and hand-thrown vases decorated with high-temperature glazes, including *flambé*, and 'volcanic' effects achieved by the blending and running of two or more heavy glazes.

The Cracqule ware for which the pottery was noted was decorated with over 50 stock patterns of animals and plant forms, and some others—elephant, swan, dolphin, lion,

François-Emile Décorchemont. Covered dish in stoneware decorated with foliage and fruits in relief and bearing the monogram, FD. 6 cm high.

owl, chicken, crab, lobster, turtle, and birds in an orange tree—were available to order. All designs were painted freehand, after the first few, which were raised in outline on the rims of plates pressed in incised moulds. The crackle effect was accentuated with lamp black rubbed into cracks which resulted from rapid cooling of the glaze after firing. The glaze was grey, sometimes with a tinge of green, brown or pink.

W.*Robertson succeeded his father as manager in 1908, and production continued until 1943.
Marks: various marks showing a rabbit, impressed or printed in blue; *Dedham Pottery*, incised.
Refs: Barber (1976); Eidelberg; Evans; L. Hawes *The Dedham Pottery and the Earlier Robertson's Chelsea Potteries* (Dedham Historical Society, 1968); Kovel & Kovel.

De Distel. *See* Distel, De.

Deerbon, Una (1882-1972). Australian potter, born in Melbourne. She studied at the Slade School of Fine Art in London and the Michigan Art School, Chicago. Una Deerbon exhibited pottery in both Sydney and Melbourne in the 1930s and operated a handcraft shop in Melbourne. She taught pottery to J.*Castle-Harris. Her work, including large decorative urns made for the State Theatre in Sydney, is characterized by a bold cheerful style and often features modelled fruit, glazed in a profusion of bright colours.

Dedham Pottery. Stoneware plates, with stock border patterns of ducks, 'snowtrees' and rabbits. Plate with rabbits 15.5 cm in diameter.

Una Deerbon. Earthenware jug with sgraffito *decoration, c.1933. 22 cm high.*

de Feure, Georges (1868-1928). Illustrator, artist and designer, born in Paris of a Dutch family. He studied under the artist Jules Chéret in Paris from 1890. With Eugène Gaillard and E.*Colonna, he created S.*Bing's pavilion for the Exposition Universelle in 1900. De Feure created designs in a wide variety of media, including porcelain tableware, for sale in Bing's shop. His designs for pieces with Art Nouveau decoration painted, and sometimes in relief, under the glaze, e.g. a snow scene with a female figure (entitled 'La Neige') and scrolled plant forms at the base and spout of a chocolate pot (exhibited in the 1902 Salon of the Société Nationale des Beaux-Arts in Paris) were made by Limoges firms. One of them, *G.D.A., also produced porcelain tableware to de Feure's design with green or pink decoration on a white ground, exhibited at the S.N.B.A. Salon in 1901 and in Turin the following year. Vases, ashtrays, boxes and

Auguste Delaherche. Stoneware vase with thick glaze. Signed and dated 1893. 8.5 cm high.

match holders designed by de Feure for production by G.D.A. were sold exclusively by Bing.

Mark: signature, *de Feure*, painted or impressed.

Refs: L'Art Décoratif 3 (1901), 4 (1902); Brunhammer *et al* (1976); d'Albis & Romanet; J. Lacambre 'Nouvelles acquisitions des musées de province...' in *Revue du Louvre* 6 (1972); Madsen (1956, 1967); R. Puaux 'Georges de Feure' in *Deutsche Kunst und Dekoration* 12 (1903); G.P. Weisberg 'Georges de Feure's Mysterious Women...' in *Gazette des Beaux-Arts* (Paris, 1974).

De Forest Brush, George. *See* Brush Guild.

de Geiger, Baron Alexandre. French potter who succeeded his father-in-law F.-P. *Utzschneider as administrator of the factory at *Sarreguemines in 1836 until his son, Paul Geiger, took over 1871-1913. He employed Victor Jullien and, from 1860, Auguste Jaunez.

Refs: Ernould-Gandouet; Lesur (1971).

Degenring, Theodor. *See* Gehren.

Degotschon, Johann. *See* Tillowitz.

Delacroix factory. *See* Apt (Vaucluse).

Delaherche, Auguste (1857-1940). French artist potter, born at Beauvais (Oise). After receiving his *baccalauréat* in 1877, he studied until 1882 at the Ecole des Arts Décoratifs (with a break 1878-79 for military service), and took courses at studios making stained glass or precious metalwork. His first pottery, made 1883-86 at the L'Italienne factory established in the 1790s near Goincourt (Oise), included stoneware goblets, tobacco jars and pitchers decorated with thumb prints or fluting, or in slip, inspired by traditional tiles of the Beauvais district. Delaherche aimed to make popular art that was cheap and easily available. He took part in the restoration of stained glass windows at Ecouen, north of Paris, and worked on glass for the Chapelle de Chantilly. He subsequently became director of a metal plating workshop for the Paris firm of Christofle in 1886. In the following year, he bought the studio on rue Blomet from E.*Chaplet and began experiments in ceramics, concentrating on the thick drip glazes inspired by Japanese work. He evolved a technique which allowed gradations of colour and explored the effects of oxydising and reducing atmospheres. He took part in the 1887 exhibition at the Union Centrale des Arts Décoratifs and won a gold medal at the Exposition Universelle of 1889, where his display included vases with naturalistic relief decoration under blue, purple and yellow drip glazes, vases in the shape of gourds, and pear-shaped cups. Decoration of stylized flowers, clematis, iris, carnations and poppies, either singly or in garlands occurs on vases as well as architectural pieces (as friezes or on chimneys and ventilators).

Flower and vegetable forms (e.g. melons and courgettes) also inspired the modelling of vases and dishes; some were modelled in the form of flower heads. Delaherche achieved crystalline, iridescent or opaque drip glazes in shades of yellow, blue and reddish purple, using the glaze effects to accentuate the

Auguste Delaherche. Stoneware pot with five roundels stamped at the shoulder and crackle glaze over grey slip, painted in blue, 1910 or later. Signed Aug. Delaherche. *17.7 cm high.*

form of his pieces. After holiday visits to Héricourt (Haute-Saône), where he made stoneware with decoration restricted to fluting or vertical ribs in 1891 and 1892, under the influence of local wares, he designed in very simple shapes.

Delaherche left Paris in 1894, built a kiln and workshops at Armentières near Beauvais, and concentrated increasingly on the effects of glazes, gradually abandoning relief ornament. He used drip glazes, often dark on a cream or beige ground, or in light colour on dark ground; monochrome glazes varied from crackled celadon to pink, mauve, pale green or grey, resembling those used later by E.*Decoeur.

Delaherche produced porcelain increasingly c.1900, and from 1904 threw his own pots (until then his designs had usually been executed by other potters). His pieces were unique, generally small, and in white with carefully placed aventurine or golden-brown drip glazes. He also made stoneware with glazes in grey, brown, beige, reddish brown or green.

From 1910, Delaherche made delicate, white porcelain, often very translucent and carved or pierced with floral motifs in the manner of Chinese Fukien ware, with the apertures filled with transparent glaze. He was the subject of a film made in 1932 as part of a series on French craftsmen, and held a ceramics conference in his home in the same year.

Marks: name incised on circular band, or monogram of AD; small objects marked with initials A.D.L.H. in a lozenge with a number at the centre. Date of each piece noted in code on the base.

Refs: Brunhammer *et al* (1976); Camart *et al*; Céramique française contemporaine; Eidelberg; Hakenjos; Heuser & Heuser.

Delaney, Anna. *See* Stuart, Ralph.

Delaware Pottery, The. *See* Trenton Potteries Co.

Deldare Ware. *See* Buffalo Pottery.

Delft. *See* Owens, John B.

Delftfield Pottery. Scottish earthenware pottery established by the firm of Dinwoodie & Co. in Glasgow, 1748, for the production of delftware. White stoneware, black basalt, creamware and bone china were also in production by the early 19th century. The firm was known for bone china teaware, glazed in soft brown, or painted with brightly coloured flowers and foliage against a matt, black enamel ground. The firm gained the appointment 'potters to H.R.H. the Prince of Wales' in 1805, but the pottery closed five years later. Moulds, patterns and other equipment were sold to the *Caledonian Pottery.
Refs: Fleming; Hughes (1961).

Dell, William (1856-92). American potter. Foreman at *Cincinnati Art Pottery from 1879, he became manager by 1887, and after the pottery's closure continued production of Hungarian faience, using the pottery's moulds and glaze formulae and trading as William Dell & Co.
Mark: *Wm Dell/& Co/CinO*, incised.
Ref: Evans.

Della Robbia Pottery. English pottery established in December 1893 at Birkenhead, Cheshire, by H.B.*Rathbone and sculptor Conrad Dressler, with encouragement from Frederick Leighton, W.*Morris and W.*Crane and, on the foundation council, painters G.F. Watts and W. Holman Hunt. Despite severe technical problems with flaking and cracking of slip or coloured glazes, the firm produced vases, bottles, jars, jugs, plates, dishes and clock-cases, using a red-brown body thinly coated with cream or white slip, with *sgraffito*, or painted designs and sometimes elaborately modelled relief decoration, inspired by Italian maiolica. The output also included relief plaques and

Della Robbia Pottery. Wall plate decorated by Liza Wilkins in yellow and green with the terracotta body exposed. Marked with a galleon, incised, and the decorator's initials, and dated 1900. 34.5 cm in diameter.

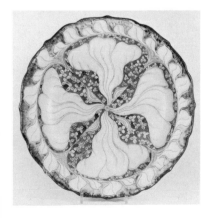

architectural earthenware, e.g. a fountain (1897-99) for the Savoy Hotel in London, designed by T.E. Collcut, and wall panels for the Liverpool Domestic Museum at Toxteth. The Italian sculptor Carlo Manzoni, who had managed a small pottery in Hanley, Staffordshire, joined the staff after 1895, when production expanded. Designs were provided by Ford Madox Brown, Robert Anning Bell (Director of the Liverpool School of Art Architecture) and Dressler, and a number of artists recently out of art school who took part in the production of their own designs. Decorators, who initialled their work on the base, included modeller Ruth Bane (RB), Charles Collis (C), painter James Hughes (HJ), Manzoni (M), Casandia Ann Walker (CAW), E.M. Wood (EMW), Liza Wilkins (LW) and Violet Woodhouse; the initial R is thought to be Rathbone's own mark. After merging with a firm of ecclesiastical sculptors in 1900, the pottery traded as Della Robbia Pottery & Marble Co. Ltd; it went into liquidation in 1906.
Marks: a ship between the initials DR, incised, usually with the initials of modeller and, often, a date (also incised) and the painter's initials (painted).
Refs: Blacker (1922a); J. Cooper *Birkenhead Della Robbia Pottery 1893-1906* (catalogue, 1980); Coysh (1976); Haslam (1975); B. Tattersall 'The Birkenhead Della Robbia Pottery' in *Apollo* 97 (February 1973).

Delotte & H. Tarnaud. *See* Aaron, Michel, and Valin, Jean-Baptiste.

del Pierre, Francine (1913-68). French potter, apprenticed in Vallauris, 1946. She opened a studio in Paris, 1948, and became inspired in the early 1950s by the work of H.*Coper, L.*Rie and B.*Leach. Using earthenware, she coiled vases, bottles and other decorative pieces to careful designs, some flattened or otherwise shaped after completion of coiling. Francine del Pierre used a wide range of glazes, including shades of brown, red, blue, white, and a celadon colour, over geometrical designs or plant forms modelled or carved in relief. Her work was exhibited alongside that of Leach and S.*Hamada at the Museo de Bellas Artes in Caracas (1966) and the Museum für Kunst und Gewerbe in Hamburg (1967).
Ref: Céramique française contemporaine.

de Madron, Durrio (1878-1940). Spanish-born potter. De Madron went to Paris as a young man and became associated with an artistic and literary circle that included P.*Picasso. Working at his own kiln in Montmartre, he exhibited stoneware vases and *jardinières* with restrained enamelled decoration.
Ref: Préaud & Gauthier.

Demartial & Tallandier. French porcelain decorators working in partnership from 1867 in Limoges. In their first year of production, the firm exhibited two allegorical vases representing Ireland and Scotland, and two pails painted with garlands of roses. In 1878, they showed plates with painted and perforated decoration, cups with foliage in *pâte d'or* with enamelled and jewelled decoration, vases, *jardinières*, baskets, etc.

In 1883, Gustave Demartial was the sole proprietor of a factory in the rue des Pénitents-Blancs. His firm won a silver medal in the Exposition Universelle, 1889. In 1893, Demartial set up a decorating workshop and agency in rue Ventenat, with partners Lagarde & Cox; the firm closed c.1909.
Marks: D &T over L, 1867-83; GD&CO/LIMOGES used by Demartial & Tallandier.
Ref: d'Albis & Romanet.

Demeuldre, Henri. *See* Brussels.

De Morgan, William (1839-1917). English artist associated with the Arts & Crafts Movement. De Morgan attended art classes while studying at University College, London, and entered the Royal Academy schools, 1859-61. He subsequently designed stained glass, tiles and furniture panels for Morris. He set up a kiln at his parents' home in Fitzroy Square in 1869 for his own work in tiles and, especially, stained glass. During the early 1870s he attempted to reproduce the lustre decoration of Islamic and Hispano-Moresque earthenware of the 14th and 15th centuries, and developed a range of lustre colours, based mainly on copper and silver, which included a deep red, pink, yellow and grey. He also achieved a palette, consisting mainly of blue, turquoise, green and clear red, which he described as Persian colours. Initially using tile blanks bought from commercial makers (e.g. the *Architectural Pottery Co., J.*Wedgwood & Sons), De Morgan carried out designs which were transferred to tiles as outlines of powdered pigment shaken through holes pricked in a paper pattern to serve as a guide for lustre painting. In the case of Persian colours, patterns were painted within traced outlines on a sheet of thin paper which was laid between a coating of wet slip and the glaze, burning away in the firing. After moving to Chelsea in 1872, he employed several decorators to work to his designs, also engaging Frank Iles to carry out the firing and, later in the 1870s, decorators C. and F.*Passenger.

De Morgan's early tile designs included flowers, birds or animals, often painted in Persian colours or other non-lustre colours on a cream or white ground. Ship designs occurred increasingly from the mid 1870s

William De Morgan. Earthenware dish painted with a fish against waves and a border of sea-horses, c.1882-88.

William De Morgan. Earthenware tile, 1888-97. Impressed mark, William De Morgan, Sands End, Fulham.

De Morgan began to produce his own tiles, but continued to buy hollow ware in the white, until in 1882 he moved to new workshops at Merton Abbey, where he employed a thrower. Vases were usually in simple shapes, often inspired by Middle Eastern wares. Decorative subjects included ships, fish, or birds and animals against a background of leafy trees. Lustre, especially red, was more frequently used.

In 1888, De Morgan entered into a partnership with architect Halsey Ricardo to build a factory near his home (which was by then in The Vale, Chelsea) and started work at Sands End, Fulham, in 1889. De Morgan spent winters in Florence for about 15 years from 1892, sending back to England paper designs copied and prepared for him by local painters with pigments sent from his workshop. He introduced the use of two or more layers of lustre in designs and occasionally combined lustre with Persian colours. He also used a greyish iridescent effect and added dark blue to his repertoire of ground colours, using it with gold, silver or copper effects, sometimes all three in combination, e.g. in the Moonlight and Sunlight suite. The De Morgan workshop fulfilled a contract from the P&O Line for tile panels in the mid 1890s and carried out relief designs for moulded tiles and plates by Ricardo. In 1897, Reginald Blunt was appointed as general manager, but the partnership failed in 1898. A new attempt made by De Morgan in partnership with the Passengers and probably Frank Iles continued until 1907, although De Morgan had stopped designing some time earlier. The Passengers and Iles continued to work as decorators in south west London, using De Morgan's designs with his permission. Fred Passenger then worked as decorator in Bushey Heath, 1921-33. De Morgan settled in Chelsea and worked as a novelist from 1906 until his death.

Initially tiles were unmarked. Later, marks included DM over a tulip with two leaves; WILLIAM DE MORGAN & CO/SANDS END POTTERY FULHAM, surrounding a tudor rose; DM over two figures denoting the year (e.g. 98) in a circle; *WdeMerton Abbey* in a rectangle, with A forming the steeple in a sketch of the abbey.
Refs: Catalogue of works by William De Morgan (Victoria & Albert Museum, H.M.

Stationery Office, London, 1921); W. Gaunt & M.D.E. Clayton-Stamm *William De Morgan* (Studio Vista, London, 1971); N. Prouting 'William de Morgan' in *Apollo* 57 (January 1953).

Denaby Pottery. Yorkshire pottery near Mexborough, initially making firebricks. From 1864, under the ownership of John Wardle, a Staffordshire potter, formerly working in Burslem, and partners, Wilkinson (until 1866), and subsequently John Blyth, the pottery produced earthenware for domestic, use, including creamware and pearlware with sponged and printed decoration in enamel or lustre colours and sometimes gilded. The output also included yellow-glazed ware, buff-coloured stoneware and tiles. Clay was obtained from Conisbrough, to the south-east of Mexborough, where the firm established a branch.

Marks (rarely used) incorporate a Staffordshire knot with DENABY POTTERY/ NEAR ROTHERHAM and sometimes the initials of Wardle & Wilkinson. Later, *John Wardle &Co.* or *Wardle*.
Refs: Godden (1964); Jewitt; Lawrence.

Denaura. *See* Denver China & Pottery Co; Long, William A.

Dengg, Gertrude (b 1885). Designer and modeller born in Vienna, and trained at the Kunstgewerbeschule in Vienna. In ceramics, she modelled animals and children, sometimes in low relief on decorative pieces, e.g. *jardinières*. She also worked in bronze.
Ref: Neuwirth (1974a).

Dengler, Franz Xavier. Sculptor working in America. At *Chelsea Keramic Art Works in 1870s, he modelled vases with decoration of children, foliage, birds, etc., in high relief on unglazed red earthenware body. He died at the age of 25.
Mark: monogram of FD, incised.
Refs: Barber (1976); Evans; Kovel & Kovel.

Denholme Pottery. Yorkshire pottery established near the village of Denholme in 1784 by Samuel Catherall, who was succeeded in the mid 19th century by his widow and his son, John Catherall (d 1893). The works were then let to an employee, N.*Taylor, until 1907. Using local clay, the pottery produced earthenware with deep red body and black or dark brown lead glaze: teasets, mugs, containers for salt, tobacco, bread, knife boxes and other pieces for domestic use. Nicholas Taylor made a range of ware with slip-trailed decoration, including plates, large dishes, mugs and puzzle jugs.
Marks used only by Taylor: his name, incised, sometimes with *Denholme*.
Refs: Brears (1971a); Lawrence.

Denuelle, Dominique. French porcelain manufacturer, working by 1819 at a factory on rue de Crussol, Paris (established 1789); until 1820, in partnership with Benjamin Cadet de Vaux. The producer of mainly tea and coffee services, tableware and decorative items, Denuelle was noted for lavishly gilded pieces with tortoiseshell ground, and obtained the patronage of the duchesse de Berry. The firm moved to La Seynie, 1823-47, renting the P.-L*Dagoty works, but retained a decorating studio on Boulevard

Saint-Denis, Paris, which produced romantic Spanish views and figure scenes. Denuelle was working c.1849-52 as a maker of porcelain pastes and enamel colours in Paris.
Marks incorporate *Denuelle*.
Refs: Chavagnac & Grollier; d'Albis & Romanet; Ernould-Gandouet; Guillebon.

Denver Art Pottery. *See* White, Frederick J.

Denver China & Pottery Co. American pottery established 1901 in Denver, Colorado, by W.A.*Long, who used predominantly local materials to produce domestic ware with flint blue glaze, *jardinières*, umbrella stands, pitchers, etc., with coloured glazes, and a range of art ware. Long continued production of the line made at his *Lonhuda Pottery, using a light-coloured ground as well as dark brown, and introduced Denaura in 1903, with native Colorado flowers modelled in low relief under various glazes, iridescent or, most frequently, a distinctive matt green with fine, satiny finish. Artists included Eugene Roberts, noted for his painting of fruit on Lonhuda pieces, and Claude Leffler, flower and animal painter, who had both worked for Long in Ohio. The choicest ware was slip cast, but other techniques, such as press moulding, were used. The pottery merged with the Western Pottery Manufacturing Co. in 1905.
Marks (printed): *Denver*, sometimes with a shield bearing a monogram of LF [Lonhuda Faience], both impressed; *Denaura/Denver* with arrow.
Refs: Barber (1976); Evans; Kovel & Kovel.

Denver Gray Ware. *See* White, Frederick J.

Deptford Pottery. English earthenware pottery established in 1857 at Deptford, Sunderland, for the production of flower-pots by William Ball (1817-84), the son of a Staffordshire potter who had left Burslem for the north-east of England. Ball was succeeded by his sons William Richard (1842-1918) and Thomas Lees, trading as Ball Brothers. The output of horticultural and coarse domestic ware, made from local clay, increased in 1863 to include brown ware vessels with white interior lining. The firm also bought white earthenware and porcelain, which they printed with patterns in black, blue, green, or brown, from transfer plates bought at the closure of other local potteries: *Garrison, *Wear, *Scott Brothers,

*Derby. Porcelain plaque painted in the manner of T.*Steel with bunches of fruit on a shaded brown ground. Made by Robert Bloor & Co., c.1825. 23 x 35 cm.*

T.*Snowball. The firm's later lustre decoration differs from earlier pink lustre in showing strong orange tints. Some jugs, breakfast sets, dessert services, etc., were painted with patterns commissioned by purchasers. Other hand-painted work included black-glazed earthenware door or drawer knobs with flower patterns.

The printed mark, *Copyright Ball Bros, Sunderland*, occurs, with a pattern commemorating the bravery of a local hero, Jack Crawford, at the Battle of Camperdown; some printed patterns bear the marks of their original users.
Ref: Shaw.

Derby. A porcelain factory built on the Nottingham Road, Derby, by the partnership formed in 1756 by painter and enameller William Duesbury, John Heath, a banker and owner of a porcelain factory which operated at Cockpit Hill, Derby, 1752-59 and, briefly, porcelain maker Andrew Planché. The factory continued traditions set up in the period of Duesbury's joint ownership of the Derby and Chelsea porcelain factories, with an output which included figures modelled after Meissen and Sèvres, and coffee cans in a Sèvres shape, without foot rings. Original figures were also produced, and many models were copied by other English porcelain factories. Patch marks, resulting from the use of balls of clay for support during firing, persisted on figures made until 1811. The figures were slip cast. Decorative patterns for tableware included naval victories and other sea scenes painted, notably, by G. *Robertson (1777-1833). Landscapes until c.1820 were mainly executed by Robertson, J.*Brewer, or R.*Brewer, and flowers by W. 'Quaker' *Pegg, W.*Pegg and L.*Lead.

After the death of William Duesbury, son of the founder, in 1797, M.*Kean became manager of the factory and married Duesbury's widow. He left when the marriage broke up in 1811, and the works passed into the hands of R.*Bloor, who started by selling the existing stock, which included imperfect pieces, but continued the production of high-quality wares, e.g. large vases and other ornamental pieces, as well as many services brightly decorated with Japan patterns, some based on Meissen examples. A green ground often accompanied painting in reserves. Bloor engaged the painters T.*Steel, R.*Dodson, M.*Webster and D.*Lucas, and persuaded W. 'Quaker' *Pegg to return to the factory.

However, in 1821 he was obliged to discharge a number of artists, including T. *Brentnall, Jesse *Mountford, W.*Hall and W.*Cresswell, in the interests of economy. Among the firm's other painters were R. *Ablott, W.*Corden and H.L.*Pratt, who were noted for landscapes, J.*Barlow, W.*Dixon, J.*Haslem (figure subjects and portraits). Mercury gilding, which replaced honey gilding c.1800, was used on bell-shaped vases with ring handles, and urn shapes with scrolled handles, decorated with fruit, flowers or landscapes, usually in reserves with elaborate gilding; the gilding of services was also lavish.

The figures produced in Bloor's time were made in dry, chalky porcelain paste, and painting, where used, was carried out in bright colours, with blue and chrome green predominant. Modellers included J. Keys

and E.*Keys, S.*Keys Jr, R.*Blore, G. *Cocker and J.*Whitaker.

Bloor died after a long illness, during which the factory had been under the management of James Thompson. Alderman Thomas Clarke, Bloor's representative and the husband of his grand-daughter, decided on the sale of the works and stock, which was eventually carried out in 1848.

Marks incorporate a crown, with *Bloor* (c.1820-c.1840) and *Derby* or the initial D.

King Street factory.
After the closure of the factory on Nottingham Road, W.*Locker, with S.*Hancock, J. Hill, Samuel Fearn, Samuel Sharp and John Henson, all former employees, established a porcelain works in King Street, Derby, where they resumed production, trading as 'Locker & Co. Late Bloor' from 1848 until 1859, when Locker was succeeded in the partnership by a draper George Stevenson (d 1866), and the firm traded as Stevenson, Sharp & Co. The subsequent titles were Stevenson & Co., Stevenson & Hancock, and finally Sampson Hancock, until the firm was taken over by Royal Crown Derby in 1935. The works had been purchased from Hancock's successor J.*Robinson by W. Larcombe in 1916. F. Howard Paget, Larcombe's partner from 1917, took control for the last years before the merger.

The quality of production was high, and from the start the main output consisted of dinner, dessert and tea services, and decorative ware in designs formerly used at the Nottingham Road factory, especially with Japan patterns, sprays of flowers, and flowers painted by Hancock and Hill. All enamelled decoration was carried out by hand, and no printing was used. F.H.*Chivers painted studies of fruit, G.*Jessop, A.*Machin and W.E.*Mosley painted flowers, and E.*Prince landscapes.

The employees never numbered more than 35, and while most of the output was made at the factory, the firm bought ware for decoration from other makers, including J.*Aynsley & Sons, *Mintons Ltd, the *Worcester Royal Porcelain Co., J.*Wedgwood & Sons Ltd, and *Coalport. Some ware was sold to dealers for decoration outside the factory.

The factory's 'jewelled ware' was decorated with raised enamel resembling precious stones. Other decorative pieces included sprays of modelled flowers and baskets, mirror frames and other pieces, e.g. figures, with flowers modelled in high relief by the artists Shufflebotham, W.B.*Stephan and James Barnet; production of modelled flowers continued throughout the working life of the King Street factory.

Many designs for figures came from the output of the earlier factory. These include sets of Seasons and the Elements, gardeners, shepherds and shepherdesses, Tythe groups, dwarfs, and models by Whitaker and E. Keys, as well as a series of Dr Syntax.

The firm made matching pieces and replacements for services which had been made in Nottingham Road (e.g. the Queen's Service of 1842, with green borders and panels painted with flowers, insects and birds), and continued production of such patterns as Witches, Old Crown Derby Bramble, Peacock, Butterflies, Duesbury Sprig, Sprig and Star, Bloor Rose, Rose

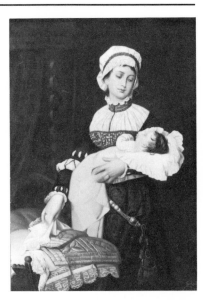

Derby Crown Porcelain Co. Plaque painted by G. Landgraf, c.1884. Signed, Landgraf Derby. *54.6 cm high.*

Barbeau, and a number of patterns with roses and other flowers. The firm was noted for high-quality yellow grounds.

Larcombe and Paget opened a London showroom in Mayfair, and in 1924 entered a display in the British Empire Exhibition at Wembley.

Marks: *Locker & Co.* or *Stevenson, Sharp & Co.* on a buckled belt; the mark of Stevenson & Hancock incorporates a crown, crossed swords and the initial D.

Derby Crown Porcelain Co. (Royal Crown Derby, from the granting of the title by Queen Victoria in 1890). This factory was established in 1876 by a limited company. The original directors were William Litherland, Liverpool dealer in ceramics and glass, Henry and John Litherland, Edward Phillips (a Staffordshire potter), John McInnes, Henry and Walter Evans, H.W. and W. Bemrose, F. Robinson, and C.E. Newton). The firm was in production at Osmaston Road from 1877. The output maintained the traditions of the earlier Derby factories. Such figures as Dr Syntax and the Mansion House Dwarfs continued. Original models include representations of Tribulation, Supplication, Force, Persuasion, etc., and a small quantity of parian ware, e.g. Little Dorrit, and a medallion showing the head of Christ.

Under the art direction of R.*Lunn, the factory became known for lavish decoration, with an output that included vases in a number of new shapes, and services painted with game subjects, sea and river scenes, birds, etc., in detailed, naturalistic style, accompanied by jewelled effects and raised gilding. The porcelain included an eggshell paste, used for delicate cups and saucers with gilded patterns, an ivory paste, and tinted paste in mauves or greens. Perforated baskets were noted for their delicacy and fine finish.

Printed decoration was carried out in a purpose-built wing added to the factory in

1891. The technique was mainly restricted to additional patterns on porcelain, which was generally decorated by hand, but frequently occurs on the borders of services in Crown Earthenware, produced from the outset of the factory until 1914, mainly for dinner ware, and a small number of large plaques.

The firm increased the use of Japan patterns on dinner, dessert and tea ware, as well as useful and ornamental pieces, adding to the patterns first produced at Nottingham Road. Some late 19th-century designs are still in production and Japan patterns were often used on the line of miniature decorative pieces from shapes in the firm's normal production, made from 1904 to the 1940s.

In the early 20th century, ornamental pieces were strongly influenced in style by French wares. The artist D.*Leroy worked for the firm 1890-1908, with assistance from G.W.*Darlington; P.*Taillandier followed Leroy in style. The firm's painters included R.*Barratt and A.*Gregory who specialized in floral subjects; D.*Birbeck, C. Gresley, C.*Harris, painters of birds, flowers, etc.; W.E.J.*Dean, ships and landscapes; R.E. Hague, figure subjects. Jessop and Mosley were among painters who had formerly worked at King Street, and J.*Rouse had earlier worked at all three Derby factories. Dean, Gregory and Gresley were responsible for much of the firm's hand-painted ware in the 1930s, and their work was then usually signed. The production of figures increased in this period, and included re-issues of models of the 1880s, e.g. Dickens characters, Don Quixote, characters from Shakespeare, Robin Hood. Production was mainly restricted to utilitarian wares during the period of World War II, but quickly returned to normal. Later wares included services for export to the Middle East, and models of birds and animals by the modeller Arnold Mikelson.

Under the control of H.T.*Robinson and his successors from 1929, the company acquired the King Street factory in 1935, itself became part of Allied English Potteries Ltd (*see* Pearson, S. & Sons Ltd) in 1964 and continues in production, but is now part of the Doulton group.

Marks: versions of a crown, sometimes with crossed Ds and, from c.1890, ROYAL CROWN DERBY. The year of production is indicated by a cypher from 1882 and later by Roman numerals, starting with I in 1938.
Refs: Gilhespy; F.B. Gilhespy & D.M. Budd *Royal Crown Derby China* (Skilton, London, 1964); Godden (1964, 1966a); Haslem; F. Hurlbutt *Old Derby Porcelain and its Artist-Workmen* (Laurie, London, 1925); Twitchett (1976, 1980).

Derbyshire Ironstone. *See* Sharpe, Thomas.

Derbyshire stoneware. English salt-glazed stoneware ranging in colour from buff to dark brown according to the minerals contained in the local clay, made in those areas of Derbyshire which centred on Belper, Chesterfield, Codnor Park, Denby and Ilkeston. Small local potteries, increasing in number in the 18th century, made useful ware for household and farm, footwarmers, and such ornamental items as puzzle jugs, toby jugs, and money boxes. Spirit flasks were made in the form of portrait figures,

pistols, books, etc., and items for domestic use, such as teapots, toast-racks, jugs and dishes, were often elaborately decorated in relief with sporting scenes, animals, oak trees and foliage, buildings, portraits, etc. The handles of mugs were sometimes made in the form of greyhounds. The producers included J.*Bourne, G.*Evans and Pearson & Co.

In the early 19th century, Derbyshire, especially Denby, dominated the English market in the production of bottles for ginger beer, polish, etc., but this trade declined with competition from containers in other materials until, by 1940, pots for jam and preserves were the only salt-glazed containers produced for commercial packaging. The salt-glazing of drainage ware ceased c.1970, because of pollution and health risks. Pearson & Co. continued the production of casseroles and other household ware until 1979.

Except spirit flasks, few pieces were marked before the late 19th century.
Refs: Bradley; Oswald.

de Rudder, Isidore (1855-1943). Belgian ceramist, trained as a sculptor. De Rudder worked at his own kiln in Brussels, also providing many designs for *Vermeren-Coché in collaboration with the firm's potter who developed matt glazes for porcelain and stoneware made by de Rudder. As well as domestic ware, he made masks in porcelain and stoneware, either individually or in editions of up to 50, representing theatrical personalities, figures from Belgian history, etc.; he also made Art Nouveau portrait plaques in a technique which achieved the effect of *pâte-sur-pâte.* He was a teacher at the Académie Royale, 1911-27.
Refs: Brunhammer *et al* (1976); Dr E. Thovez 'The Turin Exhibition: The Belgian Section' in *The Studio* 27 (1903).

Derval, Jean (b 1925). French potter and sculptor, trained in Paris and, after working in *Saint-Amand-en-Puisaye 1945-47, studied under S.*Ramié in Vallauris (1948). He opened his own Vallauris studio in 1952. Using earthenware, stoneware or porcelain, he made small painted figures, vessels with carved decoration, etc., later going on to make large sculptural works. His pieces were wood-fired and often matt in surface texture, with colour effects achieved with ash or copper salts. Derval also used a tin glaze.
Refs: Céramique française contemporaine; Lesur (1971).

de Saint-Amans, Pierre-Honoré Boudon (1774-1858). French ceramic chemist and technician. After spending time studying in factories in France and, from 1793, in England, he experimented c.1816-22 at Sèvres on the production of white earthenware and other types of pottery and porcelain with particular reference to the techniques of slip-casting and transfer-printing then used in England. He took out several patents in 1822 for the manufacture of faience and other kinds of earthenware using French materials. De Saint-Amans also discovered the formula of ironstone china in 1825, but was unable to adapt his results to industrial use and, after unsuccessful efforts to finance research, made his patents public in 1829,

continuing to experiment at Sèvres, 1829-36. His results were used at Creil from the 1830s. De Saint-Amans was associated with the firms of *Lahens & Rateau and later D.*Johnston in starting the production of white earthenware at Bordeaux. From c.1836 until his death, he produced porcelain at Lanarque near his home town, Agen (Lot-et-Garonne).
Refs: Chavagnac & Grollier; Garnier; Lesur (1971).

de Saint Marceaux, René (1845-1915). French sculptor and modeller born in Reims (Marne). He exhibited from 1868 and became a member of the Société des Artistes Français in 1885. He modelled figures for production in porcelain at the Sèvres factory. His other work included sculptural details for monumental pieces by A.*Bigot.
Mark: MARCEAUX.
Refs: Bénézit; Haslam (1977).

Deschamps-Avisseau, Edouard-Léon (1844-1910). French sculptor potter, born in Tours (Indre-et-Loire). He worked with his father C.*Avisseau for 15 years, then with his uncle from 1861, as a skilled modeller. He exhibited work in London, 1871, and showed a portrait medallion at the Société des Artistes Français in 1875. In Paris 1882-92, he made medallions, busts, and statuettes in terracotta after 18th-century styles.
Marks: DESCHAMPS-AVISSEAU or a version of his grandfather's cypher.
Refs: Bénézit; Ernould-Gandouet; Heuser & Heuser; Lesur (1971).

Desmant, Louis. French ceramist; exhibited faience and stoneware from 1892. After 1913, working at Subles (Calvados), he concentrated on lustre glazes. He painted a series of lustre pieces with scenes from the Bayeux tapertry.
Incised marks, *Desmant* and *Subles.*
Refs: Haslam (1977); Lesur (1971).

de Sorra, Olivier. *See* Pierrefonds.

Despréz. A firm of French porcelain makers. Berthélémy Despréz, a modeller (1773-83) and paste chemist (1786-92) at the Sèvres factory, was working in Paris by 1796. He was succeeded by his son, who worked in Faubourg Saint-Martin from c.1825 until after 1834. As well as making cameos in biscuit porcelain for the decoration of furniture, the firm sold glassware and medals.
Marks: the name DESPREZ and sometimes a Paris address.
Ref: Guillebon.

d'Estampes, Abel. French porcelain manufacturer from Vierzon (Cher), working in American from c.1870. He made porcelain on a small scale in New Orleans, then formed the New Orleans Porcelain factory with the French engineer, Eugène Surge, who also lived in New Orleans. In 1883, he formed his own firm, the French Porcelain Co. which was apparently short-lived.
Ref: Evans.

De Stijl. *See* Stijl, De.

Destreguil. *see* Brard, Léon.

Deusch & Co., Metallporzellanfabrik. German porcelain manufacturers working from 1898 at Lorch, Württemberg, on the production of everyday and luxury wares. The master engraver Friedrich Deusch developed in 1898 a technique of electroplating porcelain with a coating of metal which could be polished to a brilliant finish.

Marks: an ewer with *Deusch* and METALLPORZELLAN.
Refs: Danckert; Weiss.

Deutscher Werkbund. Association of manufacturers, artists, architects and writers established 1907 in Munich by the architect Hermann Muthesius (1861-1927), who became influenced by Arts & Crafts work while working in London, 1896-1903. The group aimed to bring together art, craft and industry in the production of functional designs. They held exhibitions, e.g. in Cologne (1941) and built an exhibition ground in Stuttgart in 1927, also publishing yearbooks. After closure by the Nazis, the group resumed activity in 1947. The Werkbund served as a model for groups in Austria (1910), and Switzerland (1913).
Refs: H. Eckstein *50 Jahre Deutscher Werkbund* (Frankfurt-am-Main, 1958).

Deutsche Werkstätten. German workshops established with the aim of creating a national art that was not imitative in style and was based on cooperation between designer and producer. In 1897, R.*Riemerschmid was among the founders of the Münchener Vereinigte Werkstätten für Kunst im Handwerk; the Dresdener Werkstätten für Handwerkkunst began under the management of furniture maker Karl Schmidt in the following year.

Devers, Joseph or Giuseppe (1823-82). Painter, ceramist and sculptor, born in Turin. From 1853, Devers worked in Paris. He made faience in the style of the Della Robbia family in 15th-century Florence, reviving the tradition of painting directly on unfired glaze with high-temperature colours. His designs for tile panels made at the factory of J.*Loebnitz included copies of Della Robbia ware with blue or gold grounds and underglaze painted decoration (examples shown in Turin, 1884). Devers often used motifs associated with Renaissance styles, e.g. salamanders.

Marks include painted monogram of JD or initials JD, incised.
Refs: Bénézit; Ernould-Gandouet; Lesur (1971).

Devon Art Pottery (Hart & Moist). English pottery established 1894 in Exeter by a partnership, formed by William Hart and the potter Alfred Moist (d 1910). They were joined by Moist's younger brother Joseph (1872-1954), also a potter, who became sole proprietor on Hart's retirement in 1921. Using a brown or rust-coloured body, the pottery produced everyday domestic wares decorated with painted designs in coloured slips and *sgraffito* inscriptions on a white

*engobe under an amber glaze. A blue slip used for decoration, which often appears green through amber glaze, was sometimes used as ground colour under a colourless semi-matt glaze. After the first few years of production, the pottery concentrated on imitating the work of the *Aller Vale Pottery, especially their motto wares, for sale to local tourists as well as for sale in other parts of Britain and for export. It closed in the 1930s.

A.*Lauder also used the name Devon Art Pottery for his ware.
Ref: Lloyd Thomas (1978).

Devon Art Pottery or **Devon Art Ware.** *See* Lauder, Alexander.

Devon Pottery in Stoke-on-Trent. *See* Fielding, S., & Co.

Dewdney, John. English designer and potter working for the firm of C.H.*Brannam as designer and decorator of Barum ware, 1882-c.1910.
Marks: initials or monogram, incised.
Refs: see Brannam, Charles Hubert.

Dewsberry, David (c.1852-1929). English ceramic designer, trained in the firm of S.*Alcock & Co. in Burslem. Dewsberry was working at the *Doulton & Co. factory in Burslem by 1884, when a vase painted by him in purple with raised gold outlines was exhibited in London. He stayed in Burslem until 1919. He signed some pieces of Spanish, Luscian and Lactolian wares, and was among the artists, led by J.*Slater, who developed a style of flower painting using flat washes of transparent colour, firing each layer before painting on another. He was engaged especially on the painting of vases and display plates, notably with orchids, but examples painted with other flowers, foliage, hummingbirds and landscapes (including Scottish views) occur.
Marks: painted monogram or signature.
Ref: Eyles (1980).

Dexter, William (1818-c.1860). English painter and decorator, known for his studies of birds, fruit and flowers, influenced by oriental styles. He was apprenticed at the factory in Nottingham Road, *Derby, but probably left soon afterwards. He visited Paris in 1839 and again some years later, working as a painter of porcelain. He also worked at a decorating studio opened by the son of G.*Mellor in London, went to live in Nottingham by 1847, and returned to work in London as a watercolour painter. His drawings were published in the book *Birds and Nests* (Paul Jarrard, London, c.1851). Dexter travelled to Australia in 1852, and died in Melbourne.
Refs: see Derby.

diamond mark or **registry mark.** A mark used on British products (ceramics, glass, metal, textiles, etc.) after the registration of a form or decoration, at the Patent Office in London, to prevent imitation for an initial period of three years. Porcelain and earthenware fell into the category indicated by the Roman numerals IV enclosed in part of a circle outside the top corner of a diamond outline, which contained coded information: in the top corner, the letters SX, H, C, A, I,

F, U, S, V, P, D, Y, J, E, L, K, B, M, Z, R, O, G, N, W, Q, T, denoted the year of first registration (1842-67 respectively); digits in the right hand and bottom corners referred to the day of the month and the parcel number, and a letter in the left hand corner gave the month (from January, C or O, G, W, H, E, M, I, R, D, B, K, A, except 1st-19th September 1857 and 1st-8th December 1860, lettered K and R respectively). From 1868, the day of the month was given in the top corner, the letters X, H, C, A, I, F, U, S, V, P, D, Y, J, E, L, K, B, M, Z, R, O, G, N, W, Q, or T in the right hand corner indicated the years 1868-83, the bottom corner showed the month, coded as before, and the left hand corner the parcel number. The letters RD appear at the centre. The diamond mark was replaced in 1884 by a numerical system which is still in operation. *See* J.P. Cushion *Handbook of Pottery & Porcelain Marks* (Faber & Faber, London, 1980) for a list of those who registered designs with the British Patent Office, 1842-83.

Dickens ware. *See* Weller, Samuel A.

Dickinson & Jackson. *See* Holmes Pottery.

Diederich, Hunt (1884-1953). Hungarian-born sculptor and designer. Diederich studied in Paris, Rome and Philadelphia. Although working mainly in bronze, he produced individual painted pieces (plates, etc.) in earthenware in New York in the 1920s, displaying work in the International Exhibition of Ceramics at the Metropolitan Museum of Art in 1928. Diederich exploited the translucency of glazes to give depth to his designs of animals, etc. He also created designs for industrial production.
Refs: Clark & Hughto; *Critical Comments on the International Exhibition of Ceramic Art* (American Federation of Arts, New York, 1928).

Diehl, George. Pennsylvania potter making earthenware near Rock Hill in Bucks County in the 19th century. He established a pottery in 1832 for the production of utilitarian ware for domestic use; no decorated ware has so far been identified. Diehl was succeeded by his son, William, who continued production until the destruction of the pottery by fire in 1894.
Refs: Barber (1976); Spargo.

Dieterlé, J.-P.-M. *see* Sèvres.

Diffloth, Emile (1856-1933). French ceramist, born at Couleuvres (Allier); trained at the Ecole des Arts Décoratifs in Paris. Diffloth learned modelling techniques from his father, a porcelain modeller, then worked at Sèvres. While employed in Belgium as art director for *Boch Frères, c.1899 until c.1910, he developed crystalline glazes for use on stoneware and porcelain. Diffloth travelled to America, joining the *University City Pottery, where he taught ceramic techniques under the direction of T.*Doat. His work there included vases in porcelain with crystalline glazes. An example dating from 1910 is simple in form, embellished only with a constriction at the base of the neck and a ring of shallow beading at the shoulder; the off-white glaze contains splashes of blue and white with a crystalline effect. After returning to France, Diffloth exhibited at the Musée

Galliera and won a gold medal in 1929 as a member of the Société des Artistes Français.

Marks: initials ED intertwined, printed in green (at University City Pottery), with American Women's League mark.
Refs: Bénézit; Evans.

Diglis Road, Worcester. *See* Hadley, James.

Digoin. *See* Sarreguemines.

Dihl & Guérhard. Paris manufacturers of hard-paste porcelain at a factory formally established on rue de Bondy by Christophe Dihl (1753-1830) in 1780, under the protection of the duc d'Angoulême, which was moved to the rue du Temple in 1795, and Boulevard Saint-Martin in 1825. Dihl, born in Neustadt and working in France from 1778, was a modeller, ceramist, and technical director, while Antoine Guérhard (d 1793) administered the factory, succeeded by his widow. The partnership was known for lively, accomplished underglaze painting, especially portraits, but also produced biscuit figures of children, allegorical groups for the decoration of clock cases, etc. Production ceased several years before the factory's final closure in 1829.

Marks include DIHL ET/GUERHARD/A PARIS printed in red; *MANUFRr/du MM/Guerhard et/Dihl a Paris*; *MANUF/Mcr le DUC/ Angoulême/Paris* impressed in biscuit.
Refs: Chavagnac & Grollier; Ernould-Gandouet; Fontaine; Guillebon.

Dillon, Charles, and Co. *See* Cushman, Paul.

Dillwyn, Lewis Weston (b 1778). Naturalist and potter, working in Swansea, South Wales and proprietor of the *Cambrian Pottery from the purchase of the lease by his father, American-born Quaker businessman William Dillwyn.

L.W. Dillwyn learned ceramic techniques from G.*Haynes, who remained as the pottery's manager until 1810. He engaged W.W. *Young as a painter of butterflies and birds, and encouraged T.*Pardoe to adopt a botanical approach in his flower painting. Later, he introduced transfer-printed overglaze patterns of shell studies, as well as birds from woodcuts by Thomas Bewick.

After visiting *Nantgarw, Dillwyn arranged for W.*Billingsley and S.*Walker to begin the manufacture of porcelain in Swansea in 1814. He leased the Cambrian Pottery to his partners, T.& J.Bevington, three years later, but took over again in 1824, afterwards concentrating on the production of earthenware. His son, Lewis Llewellyn Dillwyn (b c.1814), joined the pottery in 1831 and took over as proprietor 1836-50.
Refs: Blacker (1922a); Charles; P. Hughes *Welsh China* (National Museum of Wales, Cardiff, 1972); Jenkins; John; Nance.

Dinham family. *See* Donyatt.

Dinmore Pottery. Australian pottery established in Queensland at Ipswich, Brisbane, in the mid 1890s by James Gibson and James Rumble, who was sole proprietor in the early 20th century. Under Rumble, the pottery produced tableware, storage jars, toilet sets and such items as candlesticks and spittoons, in majolica, Rockingham-glazed or

cream-coloured earthenware. The works were taken over by the *Reliance Pottery before 1917.
Ref: Graham.

Dinwoodie & Co. *See* Delftfield Pottery.

Disabled Soldiers' Pottery. Australian pottery started under the auspices of the Red Cross in York Street, Sydney, New South Wales, for the employment of injured soldiers returning from World War I. The output, initially fired and glazed by *Bakewell Brothers, was later made at improved premises after a move to Redfern. With private backing, the pottery was marketed from c.1923 in New South Wales, Melbourne and Brisbane, and sent in small quantities to England. The output included jugs, vases, and the Jenolan line of small, decorative items (so named because of their likeness in colour to the Jenolan caves in New South Wales), with glazes in blues and purples or orange-browns. The colours were usually dark in tone; a shiny, uniform black occasionally occurs. The pottery's operation continued until 1925 or 1926.

Mark, from 1921, *D/Pottery/S* in a cross, impressed.
Ref: Graham.

Discry. French porcelain manufacturer. In 1823 he purchased a Paris porcelain factory founded in the rue de Charonne c.1795. Discry moved to the rue Popincourt in 1834, three years later taking as partner Talmours, who became sole owner in 1841. The firm was noted for high-temperature ground colours, developed by 1839 and including chrome green, brown and flesh pink, applied by a dipping technique leaving reserves often painted with *chinoiseries*. The firm went on to produce a range of Chinese-inspired wares, including vases with celadon glaze. Discry was working as a colour maker in 1844.
Refs: Chavagnac & Grollier; Danckert; Ernould-Gandouet; Guillebon.

Distel, De. Dutch ceramics factory established 1895 in Amsterdam by J.M. Lob for the production of painted earthenware and tile panels. The factory's initial output was similiar in style to the work of *Amstelhoek. In 1901 or 1902 the firm took over the Lotus tile factory, established at Watergrafsmeer in 1896 by L.*Nienhuis, who had been painter and designer at De Distel in 1896-97 and took charge of the decorating department. Under his direction, there was a change in style towards matt glazes with geometrical decoration on simple shapes in white clay. Tiles, also designed by Nienhuis, formed an important part of production. The firm's other designers and painters include J.*Eisenloeffel, C.*de Bruin, W.G.F.*Jansen and C.A.*Lion Cachet. T.W.*Nieuwenhuis was responsible for the Carduus line of earthenware with incised patterns filled with bright colour. The business merged with Amstelhoek in 1910 and transferred to Gouda after a further amalgamation with *Goedewaagen in 1923.

Mark (printed): a crown over DISTEL and

a triangle containing three crosses.
Refs: R.W.P. de Vries jr 'Aardewerk De Distel' in *De Vrouw en haar Huis* 5 (1910/11); Hakenjos (1974); *Kunsthandwerk um 1900, Jugendstil—art nouveau—modern style—nieuwe kunst* (catalogue, Hessisches Landesmuseum, Darmstadt, 1973); E. Thorn Prikker *Nederlandsche kunstnijverheid* (catalogue, Rotterdam, 1905); van Straaten.

Dixon, William. English artist and ceramic decorator, working in the early 1820s at the porcelain factory in Nottingham Road, *Derby. He was known for his painting of figure subjects, and his work for the Derby factory included the decoration of large mugs with grotesque figures from engravings in *Human Passions Delineated* (1773) by John Collier, illustrating e.g. a dental extraction and the effects of drinking spirits.

A William Smith is also recorded as a decorator of some porcelain made at the *Herculaneum works.
Refs: see Derby.

Dixon, Austin & Co. Sunderland potters. Robert Dixon (1779-1844) and William Austin (b 1778), formerly employees at the North Hylton Pottey, also called the Hylton Pot Works, established by the *Maling family, went into partnership c.1820 and succeeded John Phillips there and at the *Garrison Pottery. Dixon was followed by two of his sons, Thomas (1810-72) and Robert (1816-56). Austin's son, William (1806-62), worked as a ceramic printer at the Hylton works and later as printing foreman in the Garrison Pottery. His grandson, William S. Austin (b 1833), was a painter at the Garrison Pottery in 1851. Alexander Phillips (1793-1871) joined the partnership in the 1820s, and in 1827 the firm became Dixon, Austin, Phillips & Co. until the 1830s, subsequently Dixon, Phillips & Co. until the closure of the Garrison Pottery in 1865. The firms made earthenware, including creamware, Pratt wares, and lines with yellow glaze or lustre decoration. Transfer-printed views of the Tyne Bridge are recorded.

Marks of the North Hylton Pottery:
Hylton Pot Works on very early work, and a number of marks including *John Phillips* and *Hylton Pottery*.
Refs: Jewitt; Shaw.

Doat, Taxile (1851-c.1938). French painter and ceramist, born in Albi (Tarn). Doat studied design while working in the telegraphic industry and then attended the Ecole des Beaux-Arts in Paris under the sculptor Dumont. After joining the Sèvres factory in 1877, he specialized in *pâte-sur-pâte* decoration and installed a kiln at his home (c.1892) to facilitate his research in clay and porcelain glazes, developing *flambé*, crystalline and metallic glazes. He built a wood-burning kiln at Sèvres in 1898 and entered a notable display in the Exposition Universelle, 1900. With growing interest in stoneware, Doat attempted a combination of stoneware body and porcelain paste in the same pieces. Vases, in many cases gourd-shaped, made in France and later in America, often feature crystalline glazes in a wide variety of colours, including cream with green crystalline effect highlighted in red, or drip glazes in orange, pink and green. Doat continued the use of

Taxile Doat. Gourd-shaped porcelain vase. Signed T DOAT *Sèvres and dated* 1900. *18 cm high.*

pâte-sur-pâte decoration, often in the form of a cameo portrait medallion on vases and bottles or at the centre of plates, or allegorical paperweights.

Doat's study 'Grand Feu Ceramics' was translated and published by Samuel Robineau (*see* Robineau, A.A.). He was called to America as Director of the School of Ceramic Art at University City, Missouri (*see* University City Pottery) and visited America to advise the American Women's League on the design and equipment of the pottery in 1909. Production started in the following year. Doat remained at the pottery after the League foundered in 1911. His work included the execution of plaques modelled by Mabel G. Lewis to commemorate her husband's foundation of the Californian colony of the American Women's Republic in 1912.

Doat returned to France in 1915. Working in Sèvres (Hauts-de-Seine), he continued to make porcelain, the last pieces dating from the late 1930s.

Marks: monograms of TD *or signature. Refs:* L. Bélot *Taxile Doat, Céramiste* (Sèvres, 1909); Clark & Hughto; Eidelberg; Evans; Jervis; L.H. Kohlenberger 'Ceramics at the People's University' in *Ceramics Monthly* 24; I. Sargent 'Taxile Doat' in *Keramic Studies* (8th December 1906); M.D. Verneuil 'Taxile Doat' in *Art et Décoration* (September 1904).

Doccia. Italian porcelain factory established by the 1730s by the Marquis Carlo Ginori (d 1757) and under the control of the Ginori family until it merged with the Giulio Richard faience factory in Milan to form the Società Ceramica *Richard-Ginori in 1896-97. Figures, both white and enamelled, sometimes tin-glazed, included mythological, pastoral and religious groups, and *commedia dell'arte* characters. Some moulds were acquired after the closure of *Capodimonte. After the Richard-Ginori merger, the firm was strongly influenced by Art Nouveau (e.g. in architectural ware) and later by the neoclassical style adopted by G.*Ponti, who provided some designs. Decoration included acanthus scroll handles. Porcelain bottles were made with spiral ribbing under pale glazes; vertically ribbed jars had matt black glaze or red alternating with greyish blue. Portrait plaques were printed in gold from photographs. Vases were lavishly gilded, with patterns combining matt and polished surfaces, or gold and underglaze blue. Tableware was printed with landscapes and other patterns in purple. Art Deco earthenware and porcelain have patterns of dancing nudes or sea scenes with yachts and dolphins, and earthenware vases dating from the 1930 have sharply angled shapes or bands of contrasting colour.

The factory was badly damaged during World War II. It continues to make industrial porcelain but no longer produces art wares.

Marks include *Richard Ginori* with three stars, N under a coronet, or a coronet with *Richard Ginori*.
Refs: Danckert; Préaud & Gauthier; Weiss.

Dodge, Jabesh. *See* Lamson Pottery.

Dodson, Richard. English porcelain painter, working in *Derby, the son of William Dodson (d c.1820), also a painter. He was apprenticed at the factory in Nottingham Road, Derby, c.1813 and continued to work there until c.1820. His work included dessert services, small vases and other ornamental ware, painted with brightly coloured birds (generally several birds to each design) in natural landscape settings, often with a river. After leaving the Derby factory, Dodson established an enamelling workshop nearby, in the Nottingham Road.
Refs: see Derby.

Doe, William. English painter of birds, feathers and insects for the *Worcester porcelain manufacturers, Flight, Barr & Barr. Doe's work also included landscapes and figures; he was a pupil of T.*Baxter. Before the 1850s, he worked as a freelance decorator in a partnership Doe & Rogers in Worcester, working on porcelain made locally (e.g. at Chamberlain's) or by the *Swinton Pottery and other factories.

Doe usually signed work carried out in partnership with Rogers.
Ref: Sandon (1978b).

Dohachi II or **Takahashi** Mitsotuke (1783-1855). Japanese potter, Takahashi Mitsotuke working under the artistic name of Dohachi, who also took the priestly name of Nin'ami. He was successor to the 18th-century Kyoto craftsman Dohachi, or Takahashi Shuhei (d 1793). Dohachi II is thought to have been apprenticed, with his brother *Shuhei to the *Hozan line of potters in Awata, and to have studied porcelain techniques under O.*Eisen. His work included raku ware of high quality, copies of Iga and Shigaraki wares, Chinese and Korean pieces, and the work of *Kenzan. He also revived interest in painted enamels in the style of *Ninsei. Dohachi's porcelain included blue-painted ware, and a number of bowls bearing the unkin (cloud and brocade) pattern, with which he is most associated: cherry blossom, representing cloud, and maple (brocade) painted in white, red, brown and green, outlined in gold. He also made shrine figures and incense burners in human and animal forms. As a teacher in Kyoto and provincial kilns, Dohachi was among the artists who strengthened the influence of Kyoto on the ceramics of the Edo period (1615-1868). He worked in Gojazake from 1811, and later in Satsuma province, at Mushiake, Takamatsu in Shikoku, Kairakuen (Wakayama prefecture), and Saga, near Kyoto. He founded the Sanyo kiln in Sani (Kagawa prefecture) and in 1842 or 1843 a kiln at Momoyama in Fushimi, a suburb of Kyoto. His pupils included Yohei I (Taizan).

He was succeeded by Dohachi III (1810-79), who worked at the Momoyama kiln and from 1848 at Satsuma. Noted for the production of blue and white porcelain, this Dohachi was invited by the prince of Hizen to visit Arita in 1869 to teach the Kyoto styles of decoration.

Dohachi IV (d 1897) worked in Kyoto,

Dohachi II. Vase, one of a pair in white porcelain embossed with prunus blossom, made in Kiyomizu.

followed by Dohachi V (d 1915), who became president of the association of Kyoto potters, and Dohachi VI. The family's work is characterized by a lively and realistic treatment of subjects drawn from nature.
Refs: Brinkley; Cort; Fujioka Ryoichi *Tea Ceremony Utensils* (Weatherhill, New York/Shibundo, Tokyo, 1973); Hannover; Hayashiya Seizo *Artistic Development of Japanese Ceramics* (Kawade Shobo, Tokyo, 1960); Jenyns (1965, 1971); Mikami; Miller; Minamoto; Munsterberg; Okuda; Roberts; Sato.

Dohei or **Etsubei** (c.1782-1854). Japanese potter thought to have been born in Nagoya, working at the *Inuyama kiln from the mid 1830s until the time of his death. He made pieces painted with landscapes, mainly depicting the neighbourhood of Inuyama, in underglaze blue. Early pieces were also decorated with poems, some by Dohei himself. He was noted for his calligraphy, as well as for accurate detail in his painting, coupled with a lively, spontaneous approach. Some specimens of his work, including a water jar, cake dish and square box with cover, were painted in blue, under the glaze, with red and green (*see* *gosu aka-e*).
Ref: Jenyns (1971).

Dohei Imai (b 1823). Japanese potter working in his birthplace, Nagano. Dohei studied glazing techniques in Kyoto; his work included a large water basin with turquoise glaze, dating from 1867, in the Tarao family temple at Tarao, Shigaraki. He is noted for the production of teapots and teabowls painted in underglaze blue over a coating of white slip to give the appearance of porcelain, a style which became widely used in Shigaraki. Dohei reired to Kyoto, succeeded by his son Kinsaku, Dohei II (1864-1902), a maker of ceramic charcoal-stoves (hibachi), which were to become the staple output of the Shigaraki, workshops in the 20th century. After leaving Shigaraki, Dohei II established the Yunotsu kilns in Shimane prefecture, later working in Iwami.
Ref: Cort.

Doll brothers. *See* Altenburg.

Donatello. *See* Rosenthal; Roseville Pottery Co.

Don Pottery. Yorkshire pottery situated by the Don Canal at Swinton. Established on a small scale c.1790 and in production again in 1801 after considerable enlargement which took place over about a year, it was owned by John Green (*see* Green family) in partnership with Richard Clark, a Leeds rope manufacturer, and John and William *Brameld. With four additional partners from 1803, the firm traded as Greens, Clark & Co. William Green succeeded his father as a partner in 1805 and ran the pottery with his brother, also called John, producing table, toilet and ornamental ware in high-quality creamware and fine, white earthenware, many pieces closely resembling the products of the Leeds Pottery, e.g. open basketwork tureens and twig baskets. The standard of flower painting on dessert services, etc., was high. Many of the creamware shapes were also covered with a green glaze transfer-printed in black, mainly with rustic scenes bordered only with

a black line. Blue transfer-printed Italian views on dinner ware and other articles (two footbaths are known) have floral borders incorporating cherubs and an urn; other designs included a landscape series bordered with floral panels, pastoral scenes, views of buildings, Willow and Broseley patterns. Some lidded jugs in creamware, white or drab-coloured earthenware decorated all over with daisies are distinguished from similar jugs made at other potteries by a line incised between the flowers. A small amount of porcelain was made experimentally c.1810-c.1812. Orange Jumper jugs in pearlware with a transfer-printed and hand-painted design of a figure in colourful clothes, holding aloft an orange hat bearing the words 'Milton for ever', were made in support of Lord Milton, heir to Earl Fitzwilliam, for an election held in 1807; these jugs are marked *Don Pottery* in red.

In addition, the pottery made caneware and black basalt with relief decoration, figures, trophies and decorative borders applied in black on the buff body of teapots, sugar boxes, jugs. Scent jars, etc., were made in red-bodied stoneware.

The pottery was advertised for sale after the Greens' bankruptcy in 1834 and acquired by Samuel Barker and his three sons, who succeeded him. Plates were thickly potted and transfer-printed; toilet sets and tableware were enamelled, gilt and sometimes lustred. A brief closure followed the retirement of Edward Barker in 1882, but operation was resumed in the same year by a new partnership and finally ceased in 1893. Part of the site was then rented by a firm of ceramic importers, decorators and wholesalers, specializing in gilt and lustred ware.

Marks, where found, usually incorporate the name of the pottery painted in red or impressed with the name GREEN and include a lion with a flag marked *Don* and the word, POTTERY, impressed by Greens or printed with *Barker*; briefly after c.1850, a crest with an eagle rising from a ducal coronet. Pattern names were printed on a garter.
Refs: Bemrose; Coysh (1974); Eaglestone & Lockett; Jewitt; Lawrence; Towner (1957).

Donyatt, Somerset. English pottery centre with an established production by the 17th century. The three potteries in operation in the late 18th century continued to concentrate on puzzle jugs and domestic wares, using *sgraffito* decoration of scrolls, rosettes, tulips or cockerel motifs outlined freehand in a ground of white slip, or designs scratched with a comb into the slip. The glaze was often stained green by copper impurities.

Three generations of potters called James Rogers operated the Crock Street Pottery until its closure in 1900. Excavations of the site in the mid 20th century revealed examples of slipware, including plates, mugs, jugs, and jars, with combed and rouletted *sgraffito* decoration, and trailed slip, dating from the mid 18th century. The Pit Pottery closed in 1910.

The old Donyatt pottery at nearby Horton, where pottery is thought to have been made in Roman times, was making slipware in the 17th century. It was operated by the Dinham family by the late 18th century and sold by a Mr Dinham to a potter called Arledge, whose sons Caleb and Gus Arledge were working there in the 1930s. Using local clay, the

pottery produced flowerpots in large quantities, as well as vases, and small jars. Doug Back, who learned pottery techniques from the Arledge brothers in the 1930s and later took over the workshop single-handed, continued production on traditional pieces until the pottery's closure in the early 1970s, also making casseroles, lamp bases, birds' nesting boxes, etc. He developed slim puzzle jugs with *sgraffito* inscriptions in red on a cream background in place of the earlier rounded shapes with brown glaze and dark lettering. Dome-shaped money-boxes and modelled birds and a nest in a 17th-century design continued in production.
Refs: Brears (1971a, 1974); *Ceramic Review* 16 (July, August 1972), 51 (May, June 1978).

Dorchester Pottery. American stoneware pottery established in 1895 at Dorchester, Massachusetts, by George Henderson (d 1928), formerly a partner in a firm making stoneware in New Haven, Connecticut, who was succeeded by his son, Charles Henderson (d 1967). The firm extended the range of domestic stoneware in 1940, introducing a line of white tableware decorated with cobalt blue, painted or used as a ground which was then carved or incised to show the body of white New Jersey clay. Decorative themes included natural forms such as blueberries, pussy willow, pine cones, flowers and fish, stripes, scrollwork and lace designs. Green or gold decoration was available to order.
Refs: 'The Dorchester Pottery' in *National Antiques Review* (October 1969); F. Evans 'Stoneware and the Dorchester Pottery' in *Western Collector* 6 (May 1968); Kovel & Kovel.

Dordtsche Kunstpotterij. Dutch pottery in operation at Dordrecht, 1903-08. C.*de Bruin was a designer and decorator until 1906 and J.*van der Vet was associated in the business 1905-07. The workshop's output included decorative earthenware, especially vases with raised decoration, figures and relief tiles. Tiles and dishes were unglazed. The decoration consisted of geometrical patterns, or designs which followed *Rozenburg in style. Everyday earthenware sometimes bore a painted text or verse.
Mark: the pottery's name or initials DKP, with HOLLAND.
Refs: J.M. de Groot 'De Dordtsche Kunstpotterij 1903-1908' in *Antiek* 8 (1971); Singelenberg-van der Meer; 'Uit Dordrecht "Kunstpotterij" ' in *Onze Kunst* III (1904); van Straaten.

Dornheim, Koch & Fischer. *See* Gräfenroda.

Dose, Frederic. *See* Vogt, John, Charles and Gustave.

Doughty, Susan Dorothy (1892-1962). English naturalist, watercolour painter and porcelain modeller, the daughter of the poet and traveller, Charles Doughty. Dorothy Doughty is associated with full-size, accurately detailed bone china figures of birds produced in limited editions by the *Worcester Royal Porcelain Co. from 1935. The first model was American Redstarts on Hemlock, after Audubon's *Birds of America*; later pieces were modelled from life, and Doughty was sent by the firm on study visits

to America in 1953 and 1956. She also executed Alpine flower models from named botanical specimens. She continued working in World War II and went to live in Cornwall after an illness in 1943. She had been introduced to the firm by her sister, Freda Doughty (d 1972), who had designed models for the Worcester company from 1931. Freda Doughty's work includes figures of small children, each representing a month or day of the week; others illustrate nursery rhymes, different nationalities; individual titles include Grandmother's Dress, and Boy with Parakeet.
Refs: Cushion (1974); *see also* Worcester.

Douglas, Mollie. Australian potter. During a course in design and crafts lasting until 1942 at the East Sydney Technical College (where she taught, part-time from 1944 and full time 1954-68), Mollie Douglas trained in the techniques of earthenware with slip decoration or matt glazes. After experimenting with local materials, she developed a heat-proof body for domestic ware (often with dark, rich iron glazes), which she makes alongside porcelain bowls and other pieces thrown in cool, single shapes with white or celadon glazes. Her style in porcelain is influenced by the work of L.*Rie. Decorative effects are restricted to simple geometrical motifs or bands carved in relief, dipped glazes or paper resist patterns in the glaze for contrasts in texture or colour, and sparse, crisp brushwork in iron or cobalt oxides. Mollie Douglas produces her own small output at a studio in Turramurra, New South Wales, while teaching (from 1968) at St George Technical College. She writes articles for *Pottery in Australia* and *The New Zealand Potter* and was a founder member of the Potters' Society of Australia.
Ref: Hood.

Douglas-Hill, Otto Douglas (1897-1972). German studio potter born in Beerberg, Silesia and trained 1913-16 as a sculptor. After war service 1916-18, during which he was seriously wounded, he studied at the Akademie für Bildende Künste in Berlin from 1920 and opened a pottery in 1922. He took over workshops in Oranienburg in Berlin later in the same year, and in 1926 a stoneware factory at Westheim, which then traded as Keramische Werkstätten Douglas-Hill. He was concerned with form rather than decoration, and the pieces, including small vases, mainly thrown, were glazed in pastel colours (or a Persian blue inspired by Islamic pieces exhibited 1919 in Munich), with matt surface and muted, smoky effects. He also made small figures and designed monumental pieces, which were made under his supervision by assistants. Douglas-Hill joined the Vereinigte Staatsschule für freie und angewandte Kunst as head of the experimental ceramics department in 1929 and taught at the Hochschule für Bildende Künste in Berlin from 1939. His workshop was destroyed by bombing in 1943 and he was conscripted in the following year. He worked in Santiago, Chile, from 1948 until his return to Germany in 1955. During the next seven years, he worked on commissions for ceramic sculptures in Berlin and doors for the cathedral at Minden. From 1962 until his death, he lived in Malaga, Spain, where he established a workshop.

Marks include family crest of heart and crown, c.1926; crest with *Douglas-Hill*, 1927-29; highly stylized version of crest with heart as triangle, sometimes with *Douglas-Hill,* used from 1930.
Ref: Bock.

Doulton, Sir Henry (1820-97). English ceramics manufacturer. The son of J.*Doulton, he joined the firm of *Doulton & Watts in 1835 and trained there in ceramic techniques, meanwhile studying both artistic and scientific subjects in the evenings. Like his father, Doulton became known for the throwing of large pieces (e.g. a 300-gallon chemical jar which was exhibited at the Lambeth Pottery).

After careful research, he developed a light-coloured stoneware with smooth glaze, and devised methods and equipment for the production of special items, including airtight storage jars and, later, threaded stoppers for bottles. His other innovations included a water filter using blocks of carbon, which was shown in the International Exhibition in London, 1862. He was also concerned with marketing, and travelled intermittently as the firm's representative in the 1840s.

Doulton rented a factory near the Lambeth Pottery, making stoneware drainage pipes and conduits 1846-53 under the title Henry Doulton & Co., backed by his father and assisted by his brother Frederick (b c.1822), who became a partner. Henry Doulton also set up other works near Dudley (1848) and at Smethwick (1850 until closure, in 1919). He became head of the new firm, *Doulton & Co., formed in 1854, in partnership with his father and brothers. Having achieved financial stability for the company through the production of architectural terracotta and, particularly, sanitary wares, Doulton agreed to collaboration with the Lambeth School of Art, where students, taught by John Sparkes, produced decorative ware at the Lambeth Pottery. Doulton was a member of the school's management committee from 1863.

He acquired an interest in the factory of *Pinder, Bourne & Co. in 1877, continuing the production of domestic and ornamental earthenware, and in 1884 extended the factory for the manufacture of bone porcelain. He was succeeded by his son (and from 1881 partner) Henry Lewis Doulton, who had joined the firm in 1873 and formed it into a limited company in 1899. Two years later, the company was permitted to use the title Royal Doulton. Lewis J. Hooper, grandson of Henry Doulton, became the firm's Chairman, 1925-55. Henry Doulton published his *Random Recollections of a Life* in 1896.
Ref: D. Eyles (ed) *Sir Henry Doulton* (Hutchinson, London, 1970).

Doulton, John (1793-1873). English potter. Having served his apprenticeship and subsequently worked at the *Fulham Pottery, Doulton invested in a pottery producing utilitarian saltglaze in Vauxhall Walk, Lambeth, in 1815, after working there for three years as a thrower. From the withdrawal of the third partner, widow of the founder, in 1820,

until the retirement of J.*Watts late in 1853, the firm traded as *Doulton & Watts, expanding in 1826 to a pottery in Lambeth High Street and later to premises nearby. In the 1820s, he extended the output to include terracotta garden ware, chimneypots and other architectural pieces, Doulton, working with a moulder and other throwers, who made the smaller items, threw much of the larger ware, including huge jars for special orders.

His eldest son, John (1818-62), joined the accounts department of Doulton & Watts in 1832, subsequently working as a dealer in Staffordshire earthenware, and established a factory making stoneware pipes (1847-53) in St Helens, Lancashire, under the title John Doulton & Co.
Refs: see Doulton & Co.

Doulton & Co. English ceramics manufacturers. The company was established 1st January 1854, following the dissolution of *Doulton & Watts and the firms owned by H.*Doulton and his brother John. The production of utilitarian stoneware continued at the Lambeth Pottery, but work shown in the International Exhibition (1861) also included a copy of a 16th-century Rhenish salt cellar, which had been made in 1859 at the request of a friend of Henry Doulton. In 1864, Henry Doulton produced a set of large terracotta portrait plaques designed by John Sparkes, art master of the Lambeth School of Art from 1856 (and later principal of the National Art School at Kensington), who was instrumental in the formation of a creative partnership between the pottery and the school in Lambeth. Subsequently, Sparkes's students collaborated with the Doulton workshop in the production of stoneware jugs and vases encircled with lines of impressed patterning and some plaques with scenes of classical figures incised and outlined with colour, shown in the Paris Exposition Universelle, 1867.

Doulton then employed G.*Tinworth, whose work had been shown in Paris, and commissioned further designs from Lambeth students in preparation for the International Exhibition at South Kensington in 1871. H.B. and A.B.*Barlow provided freelance designs in 1870 and joined the firm full time in the following year. By the end of 1873, the artists working at the studio included 13 women, of whom E.J.*Edwards had been among the first to join. Tinworth, Arthur Barlow and F.B.*Butler were among those inspired by 16th- and 17th-century German stoneware, Hannah Barlow and M.*Mitchell by 18th-century Staffordshire scratch blue. E.*Banks, F.E.*Barlow and E.*Simmance worked in coloured slips built up to achieve low-relief decoration in experiments 1876-77; this ware was made in very small quantities, and production at Lambeth lasted no longer than ten years. The carved, incised and modelled ware, which made up a range of c.1600 shapes by 1882, included vases, bowls, jugs, spirit barrels for hotels and public houses, decanters, bottles, clock-cases, sporting cups and trophies, loving cups, candelabra, lamps, chessmen, religious pieces, plaques, house and street nameplates, and commemorative pieces with inscriptions to order.

The success of Doulton's ware resulted in an expansion of the studios to additional buildings, and by 1881 the firm employed 36

Doulton & Co. Left to right: 1) Electroplate mounted jug decorated by Louisa J. Edwards, glazed in sea-green and blue against a buff ground, trailed with white slip, 1878. 27 cm high. 2) Jug designed by Frank B.*Butler, glazed in shades of blue, brown and mauve, 1875. 37 cm high. 3) Silver and pewter mounted jug incised by Louisa J.*Davis, glazed in shades of blue, pale olive and ochre on a buff ground, 1880. 24.2 cm high.

artist decorators and modellers, with a large number of assistants. The artists included J.*Broad, L.J.*Davis, F.E.*Lee, F.M. *Linnell, E.D.*Lupton, F.*Pope, L.*Watt, M.V.*Marshall, his assistant H.*Barnard, and later H.*Simeon and A.L.*Harradine. Henry Doulton encouraged his artists to develop their individual creative ideas, giving them the chance to work alone, or share small studios with one or two other artists. The leading artists continued to design shapes and decoration, but some pieces were made by assistants, and usually sold with a cross in place of the artist's signature accompanying the firm's mark on individual work. Slip-cast ware was introduced in the 1880s in editions of about 1000.

The simplicity of early pieces, with finely incised patterns against light-coloured, semi-matt ground surfaces, gave way to buff grounds, with decoration often including a coloured border extending over much of the surface. In the late 1880s and 1890s, the main designs were less extensive, leaving large portions of the surface plain or textured with small impressed circles or stars, and less formal flowers or foliage remained frequent subjects, with incised outlines sometimes replaced by tube-lining. An increased amount of modelled work in the late 1880s and 1890s included humorous groups of mice or frogs by Tinworth, reptiles by Marshall, figures by Harradine and Broad.

Silicon ware, in production from 1880, was a smooth, light reddish-brown or occasionally off-white stoneware body, fired at

very high temperature, with fine texture and smear glaze. Decoration was incised, carved, perforated, applied in relief or, occasionally, painted in matt slip. Pieces were further ornamented with touches of gilding or copper lustre. Many were made by the studio's leading artists, but some simple designs were produced in series by their assistants. Production ended in 1912, but was revived (1923) for limited editions of jugs, etc., to commemorate the discovery of Tutankhamen's tomb hoard.

A white stoneware, made c.1887-c.1896, resembling marble in appearance and sold as Carrara, was usually covered with translucent matt glaze, then painted with coloured enamels or lustre decoration and gilded; it could also be modelled in relief, pierced, or decorated with foliage designs or strapwork in dull red or sage green. Matt-glazed architectural ware, made 1885-1939 and very popular in the early 20th century, also went under the trade name Carrara. Its uses included relief panels by Broad depicting oriental figures at the doorway of Asia House in London (c.1885), decorations on the Savoy Hotel in London (1904), and the facing of a number of early 20th-century shopping arcades, as well as large murals, pavilions, fountains, etc.

Chiné ware, normally made in stoneware (1885 or 1886-1914), but also in earthenware (until c.1908), was characterized by a netted surface texture obtained by pressing moistened fabrics, often lace, on the surface of unfired clay. The resulting pattern was further decorated with moulded floral motifs, scrolls and borders, which were applied and then glazed in several colours. The process was developed and patented by John *Slater, and pieces (jugs, vases, tankards, etc.) normally bear a version of the impressed mark 'Doulton Slater's Patent'. The effect of Autumn Foliage, Natural Foliage or Repoussé ware was achieved with the impressions made by leaves on moist clay. Vases, *jardinières*, umbrella stands, etc., decorated in the technique were then painted with rich autumn tints. Production started in 1883 and

continued until the 1950s, although in smaller quantities after World War I.

Earthenware had been made from 1872, and production continued in a separate department at the Lambeth studio until World War I. Vases, bottles, plant pots, pedestals, tiled panels and architectural ware were made in a fine-textured body marketed as Lambeth Faience, which contained kaolin, china-stone and calcined flint. After biscuit firing and decoration, the ware was given separate firings to fix the colours for glazing and, if necessary, for gilding. Designs of flowers, birds, landscapes, portraits, etc., were painted directly on the biscuit clay before the application of a yellow-tinged glaze or, from 1900 a colourless, leadless glaze. Some decoration was inspired by earlier types of maiolica, although original designs were produced, notably among those painted in monochrome. The technique allowed the use of bright, clear colours. Specialist painters included F.E.*Lewis, M.L.*Crawley, M.*Butterton.

A class known as Impasto ware, developed in the 1870s and mainly produced 1879-1906 (but continued in smaller quantities until World War I), was thickly painted in coloured slips, sometimes against the textured ground of Chiné ware. The technique resembled fresco painting in effect, and was used for architectural decoration c.1890-1914.

A fine-bodied ivory earthenware, known as Crown Lambeth, was made c.1892-1900 and first exhibited in Chicago in 1893. The body made possible delicate colour effects in underglaze painting, but the repeated glazings necessary for richness and translucency made production very expensive.

Marqueterie ware was characterized by a chequered body that was built up in contrasting colours of clay, sliced thinly and then moulded to make vases and dishes as well as tea sets, very light in weight. Pieces were glazed and sometimes gilded; some contained panels of Lambeth Faience body. The technique was patented under the names of Henry Doulton and W.P.*Rix in 1887, and production continued in limited quantities until 1906. The name was also applied to pieces with the coloured clays forming a marbled pattern resembling 18th-century English agate ware.

Studio work represented only a small proportion of the firm's output at Lambeth. Much stoneware was produced from stock designs. As well as quantities of tableware, relief decorated hunting jugs, and teapots with similar decoration (made well into the 20th century), the pottery produced advertising ware with trade-names and slogans of brewers and distillers and intended for use or display in public houses, for which the firm also made architectural decoration and pieces such as ashtrays, tankards, bottles, pump handles and ornamental ware, e.g. pieces representing copper or leather vessels, and in the 1920s Toby jugs (some designed by Simeon), which were cast in layers, with coloured slip for decoration applied to each section of the mould before it was assembled and used for casting the piece. Other output included invalid and nursery ware, feeders, hot-water bottles, water filters, toys, such as miniature ware for dolls' houses, money boxes, whistles, and decorated tiles.

Production continued on a reduced scale after World War I. J.H.*Mott led experiments with oriental glaze effects and increased the range of colours that could be used with salt glaze. W.E.*Rowe and Simeon designed a series of Persian ware with coarse biscuit body coated in white slip and painted in turquoise, green and rust before glazing and firing. Later artists at Lambeth included V.*Huggins and J.*Cowper, who designed hand-thrown ware much influenced in style by contemporary English studio pottery. Marshall and Simeon were among the designers of garden ware (bird baths, figures of animals and gnomes); the sculptor Gilbert Bayes provided designs 1923-39.

Restrictions on the production of decorated wares in World War II again reduced the activity of the studio. After the war, the pottery continued its output of commemorative plaques and panels (including the plaques erected by the London County Council on buildings associated with famous people), and the studio was built up in the early 1950s under the direction of the Danish potter and designer A.*Hoy, but closed in 1956.

Henry Doulton had bought the major shareholding in the Nile Street Pottery of *Pinder, Bourne & Co. at Burslem in 1877, appointed J.C.*Bailey as general manager, and bought out the previous firm completely in 1882. Doulton & Co., trading as Royal Doulton from 1901, continued to produce tableware which remained an important part of the output, in fine earthenware until the 1960s, stone china in the late 19th and 20th centuries, porcelain after the enlargement of the premises in 1884, and bone china (which was perfected by John Slater) in a new building acquired in 1907. Hotel and institutional ware were first introduced in the 1890s. From c.1885 to the early 1900s the firm also made stained glass, some designed by Slater.

Under Slater's art direction and with Charles *Noke as modeller and designer from 1889, the Burslem factory made a wide range of decorative ware, including ornately modelled vases, richly painted with birds, fish, cherubs, landscapes, etc., and finely gilded. Artists whose work was shown in the Chicago World's Columbian Exposition, 1893, included R.*Allen, H.*Betteley, L.*Bilton, T.D.*Bott, J.*Boulton, W.G.*Hodkinson, the French figure painter Charles Labarre, who spent about a year in Burslem painting large vases for the Doulton display, T.*Phillips, H.*Piper, G.*White, and S.*Wilson.

A group of ware, delicately decorated in a style known as Hyperion, with poppies, lilies, vines and other, mainly floral, subjects in subtle shades (sometimes with lightly brushed, freehand outlines) against white or coloured grounds, was made in bone china and introduced in the 1890s. Artists included A.C.*Eaton.

A new bone china paste and velvety glaze, both devised by John Slater, were used in Luscian ware, introduced c.1896 and produced until 1914. These pieces were painted with flowers, birds, hill and woodland scenes, figures, etc., in softly coloured enamels which sank into the surface of the glaze. The main artists who collaborated with Charles Noke on the design of Luscian ware were D.*Dewsberry, noted for his studies of orchids, Wilson, with paintings of cattle and birds; also Robert Allen, Bilton, Joseph

*Hancock, L.*Langley, H.*Mitchell, W.*Nunn, Piper, E.J.*Raby, Walter Slater, and White.

In the late 1890s John Slater, helped by Hodkinson, developed the *pâte-sur-pâte* decoration that characterized Lactolian ware, using bone china and a version of the body containing feldspar that had been used for pieces, including figures, shown in the Chicago Exposition. Many designs were provided by Robert Allen, and the artists included Dewsberry, J. Hindley, Hodkinson, White and Walter Slater. John Slater had developed the Spanish ware decoration combining raised gold outlines of flowers, foliage and tracery with patterns (flower studies, etc.) in enamel and raised slip, often on vellum or ivory grounds. The painters included L.*Bentley, Bilton, W.*Brown and Dewsberry. This decoration was often combined with modelled ornament, e.g. dragons as handles or in relief on the surface, and was especially popular in the 1890s.

Slip-painted decorative pieces, sold as Barbotine ware, made c.1890-1915 and, in smaller quantities c.1920-39, were patterned with birds, trees, trailing plants, seascapes, etc., against light grounds; blue, green, orange and cream were frequently prominent in the colour scheme.

Holbein ware, also slip-decorated, was produced 1895-1914, in a porcelain body developed by Slater, and comprised vases, candlesticks, plaques, bowls, loving cups, etc., with inlaid or relief decoration in contrasting coloured clays, usually combining painted patterns with one or more portraits resembling 16th-century originals in style and general colour effects. The principal artists were Eaton, Hodkinson, H.*Tittensor and Nunn. The very hard earthenware body, containing high proportions of kaolin and feldspar, was covered with a translucent, liquid-looking and slightly uneven ivory glaze. In c.1898, Charles Noke introduced Rembrandt ware, which resembled Holbein ware in the sombre range of colours. The pieces, all hand-thrown in coarse-textured earthenware made from local clays, were decorated in layers of slip, usually brown, green, ochre or black, with portraits after Rembrandt accompanied by borders of stylized foliage, etc., and often an inscription. Eaton and Nunn were among the main artists. Many pieces, which included a variety of vase shapes, were equipped with metal lids and stands. Production ceased in 1914. Kingswares, also introduced c.1898, but produced until 1939, had decoration in coloured slip (red, light brown, yellow, green) with low-relief effect, which was moulded together with the dark brown body for a wide range of shapes: tea and coffee ware, mugs, shaving mugs, loving cups, clock cases, candlesticks, bottles, flagons, smokers' requisites, vases, plaques and, notably, whisky containers, some carrying advertisements. The ware was coated with transparent, sometimes yellow-tinged, glaze.

Successful research in lustre ware by John Slater resulted in the production of many pieces, especially vases and bowls, with lustre decoration from the 1890s to 1930s. An interruption in the war years was followed by a small output until the 1950s. The colours included shades of yellow, silver and grey, green, brown, pink, purple, orange, ruby, blue and mother-of-pearl; decorative designs,

sometimes in resist, ranging from geometrical patterns, stylized foliage, arabesques, accompany the use of Titanian and *flambé* glazes, and a new range of lustred and opaline effects coincided with the introduction of a thinner, lighter porcelain paste c.1915.

Experiments begun by Charles Noke and John Slater in the late 1890s with high-temperature glazes increased on the arrival of C.*Bailey, who collaborated with B.*Moore, consultant to the Burslem studio. *Flambé*-glazed ware shown at the St Louis World's Fair (1904) and at Brussels (1910) was inspired by Chinese pieces; the glazes were shortly afterwards used over painted landscapes (mainly by Brown and C.*Yeomans) or on animal figures (e.g. elephants modelled by Charles Noke in the early 20th century—some still in production) as well as oriental figures, 'spooks' or grotesques designed by Tittensor, and later models of fish.

A group of transmutation glazes with additional colour obtained by the use of metallic oxides were initially included in the Flambé range but carried the name Sung from 1919; they were first exhibited as such at the British Industries Fair at Crystal Palace in 1920. A wide range of colour effects was achieved, notably a streaked blue. Variations of the line included Veined Sung, with a marbled effect.

Like the Flambé wares, Sung pieces often have painted underglaze decoration in black.

Doulton & Co. Salt-glazed figure of a dog, The Guardian, with brown, blue and green glazes, modelled by Gilbert Bayes. Paper label, dated 1936. 49.3 cm high.

Doulton & Co. Group, The Marriage of Art and Industry, modelled by M.M.*Davies and shown at the Brussels Exhibition, 1958. One of a limited edition of 25.

The patterns include peacocks, birds of paradise, and other animals, as well as landscapes, and scenes featuring pixies. Decorative designs in white enamel outlined with gold were often oriental in inspiration, e.g. cranes, sprays of prunus. Designers included H.*Nixon, the chief artist working with Charles Noke on the development of designs to exploit high-temperature glaze effects, as well as F.*Moore, Eaton, and Hodkinson.

Reco Capey (1895-1961), Professor of Design at the Royal College of Art, designed some *flambé* pieces between 1916 and the early 1930s. (He also produced some oven ware and other stoneware pieces at the firm's Lambeth Pottery. Except for early pieces, which were sold through Doulton & Co., this stoneware does not bear the firm's mark.)

Although *flambé* effects continue in production to the present day, tableware with these glazes was produced in sets for only a short time in the early 20th century because of difficulty in ensuring the consistency in the colour of the glaze for matching pieces. Examples normally have plain red colour and are mounted in silver. Individual pieces were produced in large numbers.

Crystalline glazes date from the period between 1907 and 1914. Similarly, Chinese Jade wares, featuring a thick, creamy glaze, streaked and shaded with green and turquoise, that resulted from experiments starting in 1913, were made only in small quantities from their introduction on the market in 1920 until 1936, and production ceased in the early 1940s. The pieces include vases, sometimes in forms inspired by Chinese bronze and pottery, and animal models, e.g. leaping fish, elephants. Chang porcelain, developed in the 1920s by Charles Noke (in association with Cecil Noke and Nixon) and named after a legendary Sung Chinese potter, was characterized by thick opalescent or brightly coloured glazes, often used in three or more layers, with the outermost glaze crackled and trickling down the surface of vases, cups, jars, or such moulded

pieces as the rocky base supporting a dragon figure, c.1930. Chang pieces normally bear the signatures of Charles or Cecil Noke, or Nixon; production ceased in the early 1940s.

Titanian ware, introduced 1915 after four to five years of research, remained in production until 1929. Tall vases, flasks, etc., some influenced in shape by the work of *Rozenburg, and made in a strong, thin, translucent porcelain were decorated with pastel-coloured, lustrous enamel in clouded effects covering the whole surface. The designs ranged from abstract sheets of colour to paintings of peacocks, butterflies, flowers, rabbits, polar bears, crows or human figures, often in landscape settings. The characteristic smoky blue reminiscent of *Copenhagen porcelain decoration was achieved by the use of titanium oxide in the glaze, which gave the ware its name. Principal artists who collaborated with Charles Noke on the design of this decoration were H.*Allen, Raby, Tittensor; many early pieces were decorated by P.E.*Curnock. Although some tablewares were transfer printed, e.g. with a bird of paradise, or an Egyptian pattern, pieces were mainly individual. Titanian glazes were also used on figures of a series of Australian, English and Canadian servicemen: Digger, Blighty, Canadian Mountie.

Figures were made in Burslem after experimental production in the early 1890s, and Charles Noke exhibited examples in Chicago, 1893, designing several more in the following ten years. Artists at the Lambeth studio, notably Broad, Marshall, Harradine, Simeon and Tinworth included figures in their modelled work. Charles Noke commissioned a selection of models from sculptors and modellers including P.*Stabler, C.*Vyse, and himself contributed several designs. After exhibition of the figures in 1913, other modellers, including Hanley sculptor Ernest Light, as well as Harradine and Tittensor, extended the range of figures made in Burslem, which were painted by such artists as H. and C. Nixon, H.*Allen, N.*Woodings, W.E.*Grace; later also R.*Holdcroft and E.A.*Webster. Jugs and jars modelled in the forms of figures and portrait busts were produced at Lambeth until 1939 (principal designers include Simeon). Charles Noke introduced a related series at Burslem in the early 1930s; his main collaborators were Harradine and H.*Fenton.

The company's large-scale production of domestic and tableware included many series of patterns that remained in production over long periods of time, e.g. a range of Dickens characters (one of a variety of decorative lines based on the work of Dickens), introduced in 1908 and last produced as the pattern of a display plate in 1967; a printed scene with a windmill, entitled Norfolk (1906-61); scenes of Blue Children, printed and hand-painted (late 1880s-1928); services with patterns in raised gilding (c.1890-1950s); Blue Persian earthenware (1917-42); Bird of Paradise (1922-35). Many other patterns were printed, lithographed, or painted for briefer periods, and the firm was noted for its wide range of styles. Elements of Art Nouveau appeared in the decoration of tableware and in some decorative schemes for Titanian ware, finally ending at the beginning of World War I. The slip-cast Morrisian ware, introduced c.1900 and produced in limited quantities until c.1924,

included vases, teapots, jugs, bowls, covered jars and washstand sets in earthenware, printed in black with designs that included a range derived from illustrations to Beauty and the Beast by the American artist Will Bradely (published 1896), as well as scenes of country dancers and musicians, under yellow or red glazes.

Patterns were also adapted from the work of illustrators, e.g. female portraits by Charles Dana Gibson, nursery rhymes by William Savage Cooper, Ralph Caldecott's cartoons, cartoons of cats by artist David Souter (also produced as figures), hunting scenes and dogs by Cecil Aldin, and cartoons by H.M. Bateman. Other designs were inspired by historical, literary and sporting subjects, as well as floral and animal studies.

The firm produced earthenware designed by the artist Frank Brangwyn in the 1930s. Table services, tea and coffee sets, vases, storage jars, candlesticks, lamps, ashtrays, trays and plaques were made in a buff-coloured body, moulded or incised with outlines of the pattern, which was then splashed or painted with coloured slips, frequently in blue, pink, pale yellow, cream, shades of green, olive and tan. Artists included the Nokes, Nixon, and Fenton. The ware was intended for sale at low prices, but failed to become a commercial success.

Series of patterns intended for nursery use, produced at Burslem from the beginning of the 20th century, included scenes from traditional rhymes, Alice in Wonderland, and many animal designs; nursery patterns commonly associated with the company are the Bunnykins range, introduced in 1934, and initially designed by Barbara Vernon, daughter of Cuthbert Bailey. This series superseded all the earlier nursery ranges within a few years of its introduction, and pieces were marked with the Vernon signature until the 1950s, although other designers had extended the range of patterns from the late 1940s.

The principal artists in collaboration with Charles Noke on the design of tableware included his son, with A.C.*Eaton, Grace, Holdcroft, L. Langley, Nunn and S. Woodnam. Series frequently included display plates, starting from a group (Isthmian Games) decorated with Greek sports and mythological subjects, which had been introduced by Pinder, Bourne & Co. in the late 1870s, and continued until the 1970s.

The company underwent a number of mergers with other firms, finally combining with the Allied English Potteries group (*see* Pearson, S., & Sons Ltd) in 1968. Among the companies in the group, Doulton & Co. now make glass, and wares for the building, engineering and sanitary industries; the section concerned with table and domestic wares trades as Royal Doulton Tablewares Ltd.

Marks usually include DOULTON and LAMBETH (from 1858) or BURSLEM (from 1882); ROYAL DOULTON, ENGLAND around four interlaced Ds, often under a lion, usually on a coronet, from 1902. Pieces may also carry the name of the ware (e.g.

Marqueterie, Silicon, Carrara) and the artist's mark.
Refs: Atterbury & Irvine; Blacker (1922a, 1922b); Dennis (1971, 1975); Eyles (1975, 1980); Eyles & Dennis (1978); E. Lloyd Thomas 'Forgotten Artists of Lambeth Ware' in *Country Life* (July 1969); K.M. McClinton in *Spinning Wheel* (October 1977).

Doulton & Watts. London manufacturers of salt-glazed stoneware, J.*Doulton and J. *Watts, working at Vauxhall Walk, Lambeth. The partners expanded their business in 1826 to premises in Lambeth High Street, which became known as the Lambeth Pottery, but continued the Vauxhall Walk works for some years.

Besides maintaining the previous firm's main output of bottles, jugs and domestic ware, Doulton & Watts made jugs and mugs with portraits of Nelson, Wellington, Napoleon, and other relief designs, spirit flasks in the form of fish, pistols, etc., and gunpowder containers, whistles and money-boxes. They added the production of stone-ware pipes (c.1827), and bottles with relief decoration commemorating the Reform Bill (passed 1832); similar bottles depict the Irish patriot, Daniel O'Connell. Architect-ural terracotta was made at additional premises in Lambeth High Street acquired in 1840; early examples include a coat of arms made for a nearby school, and a statue of Sir John Crosby for Crosby Hall in Bishopsgate. The firm introduced a light-coloured glazed stoneware (in response to the Bristol ware of W.*Powell) developed by H.*Doulton, who had joined the business in 1835. The Doulton & Watts display in the Great Exhi-bition (1851) included stoneware bottles, relief jugs, jars, chemical ware and, in terra-cotta, garden ware and a figure personifying time.

Doulton & Watts. Salt-glazed tankard, modelled as a bust of Admiral Lord Nelson, c.1821-30. 19 cm high.

When the partnership ended with the retirement of Watts, the firms of Henry Doulton and his eldest brother, John, were dissolved, and a new company *Doulton & Co. was formed on 1st January 1854.

Marks, impressed, moulded or incised, give the firm's name and *Lambeth Pottery* with *London* or *High Street/Lambeth*.
Refs: Blacker (1922b); Jewitt; Wakefield.

Dragon Lustre. *See* Makeig-Jones, 'Daisy'.

Dresden. *See* Cooper, Susie.

Dresler, Paul (1879-1950). German studio potter, born in Siegen. Dresler studied medicine and trained as a painter under H. Obrist before joining the ceramics school at Landshut in 1912. In 1913 he established the Grootenburg pottery in Krefeld, employing between six and eight assistants. His early work included richly painted earthenware recalling Middle Eastern and Renaissance Italian ceramics, he also adapted patterns from Sung Chinese relief decoration. A few pieces were decorated only with a plain Persian blue alkaline glaze. Inspired by the exhibition of Chinese art in Berlin (1929), Dresler began experimenting with the pro-duction of stoneware with the help of potters in the Westerwald region. He first exhibited work in stoneware in 1931, and from 1936 it became his main output. Dresler became known for the variety in colour and texture of the glazes he developed for high tem-perature firing. The shapes were simple, frequently spherical or ovoid. A year before his death he started as manager of the cer-amics workshop in a Wiesbaden art school and taught in Krefeld. His pottery is still in operation.

Mark: PD incised or painted; *Grootenburg* impressed; castle in shield, sometimes with initials PD.
Ref: Bock.

Dressel, Kister & Co. German porcelain manufacturers working at Passau, Bavaria, from 1840, under the Lenck family in the late 19th century, and taken over by Philipp Dietrich in 1937 until closure in 1942. The firm made art porcelain and used *Höchst moulds obtained from the Mehlem firm in Bonn. They also made good imitations of models from other earlier porcelain manu-facturers, copying the original marks.
Refs: Danckert; Weiss.

Dresser, Christopher (1834-1904). British architect, designer and author, born in Glasgow. He trained in design at Somerset House, London, from 1847, then studied botany, in which he gained a doctorate, and lectured in 1860 at the Department of Science and Art. He wrote articles for the *Art Journal*, 1857-58, examining the relation-ship of structure to function in plants and its significance in design. His own designs, in a variety of media including silver, metal-work, textiles and glass, as well as ceramics, were intended to achieve a close alliance of function and form.

*Christopher Dresser. Coffee pot designed by Dresser and produced at the *Linthorpe Pottery.*

In the 1860s and 1870s Dresser worked extensively as a freelance designer of shapes and patterns produced by *Mintons Ltd and J.*Wedgwood & Sons, in some cases on a large scale. His work for Mintons included pieces made at the Art Pottery Studio from 1867, and others inspired by oriental *cloi-sonné* wares made from the 1870s until c.1900. The firm used Dresser's patterns, or adaptations of them until the 1880s, on shapes created by him or other designers. His designs for Wedgwood included a cyl-indrical, four-footed vase with ring handles, made in caneware and decorated with stylized flowers (1867).

After a government-sponsored visit to Japan in 1876-77, Dresser became a collector of Japanese art and in 1878 established a shop, which was short-lived, selling oriental goods. He adapted elements of Japanese design for use in his own work.

In 1879, Dresser initiated the establish-ment of the *Linthorpe Pottery, taking the post of Art Superintendent, and called in H.*Tooth as manager. Until his withdrawal from the pottery in 1882, he designed shapes which were distinctively simple and grace-ful, drawing inspiration from a wide range of ancient cultures, including Egyptian, Moorish, Indian, pre-Columbian, Greek, Roman and Celtic, as well as Chinese and Japanese. His designs (1892-96) for vases made by W.*Ault at Swadlincote contain a greater element of fantasy, for instance in a double gourd shape with four handles in the shape of a goat's head, with the beard ex-tended to end in a clawed foot.

Dresser established a studio for designs in all media, working from 1882 in Sutton, Surrey, and subsequently (from 1889) in Barnes, London. He expounded stylistic opinions in books, e.g. *The Art of Decorative Design* (1862), *The Principles of Decorative*

Design (1872-73), *Studies in Design* (1875-76), *Japan, its Architecture, Art and Art Manufactures* (1882), *Modern Ornamentation* (1886), and *The Chromolithograph* (1868).

Designs for Linthorpe and Ault potteries were marked with an impressed facsimile signature.
Refs: Anscombe & Gere; *Christopher Dresser 1834-1904* (catalogue, Fine Arts Society, London, 1972); *Christopher Dresser 1834-1904* (catalogue, Camden Arts Centre/Dorman Museum, London and Middlesbrough, 1979-80); Haslam (1975); J. Levine *Linthorpe Pottery, an Interim Report* (Teesside Museums & Art Galleries, 1970); N. Pevsner *Pioneers of Modern Design* (Penguin Books, Harmondsworth, 1960); Wakefield.

Dressler, Conrad. *See* Della Robbia Pottery.

Dryander, Louis-Guillaume. *See* Niderviller.

Dryden, John & Co. *See* Phoenix Pottery.

Dryden, Cookson & Basket. *See* Stepney Bank Pottery.

Dubois, Léopold. French porcelain manufacturer working in Limoges. Formerly a pupil of the sculptor Lemaire, Dubois worked 1841-43 for J.-B.*Raud. He entered into a partnership with H.*Jouhanneaud in 1843 at a small Limoges factory, moving in 1846 to larger premises, where the firm employed over 150 workers. The output in the 1850s was notable for high-temperature colours developed by the chemist Halot which ranged from ultramarine, azure, turquoise and aquamarine to greyish, yellowish and pure bright greens. By 1855, the firm produced vases with bands of high-relief decoration by the sculptor Constant Sevin, and figures by Schoenwerk. Dubois continued alone after 1866. In 1868, he formed a new company with Utschneider & Co. of *Sarreguemines. At the end of the association in 1876, he sold the factory to W.*Guérin.
Refs: Burton (1906); d'Albis & Romanet; Ernould-Gandouet.

Dubois et Jamet. *See* Vierzon.

Duché, Jean. *See* Nivet, Michel.

Ducheval, Michel. *See* Caen.

Ducluzeau, Madame. *See* Sèvres.

Dudson, James (d 1882). Staffordshire potter working at the Hope Street works, Hanley, from 1838, and succeeded by his son. The firm produced figures, vases and decorative tableware in porcelain or fine stoneware, and exhibited a number of ornamental figures, including comforter dogs, in the international exhibitions of 1851 and 1862 in London. Dudson and his successor, who ran the firm under the title J.T. Dudson, 1888-98, became known for jasper ware in drab, blue or sage-green bodies with relief decoration. Many designs for jugs registered at the Patent Office were based on natural forms: ferns, wheat, barley, pineapple. Tea and coffee pots, sugar bowls, jugs, etc., were made in a mosaic technique from 1856, with patterns inlaid in differently coloured clays.

The firm continued as Dudson Bros from 1898 until the present day.
Impressed or printed marks incorporate *Dudson* and sometimes *Hanley*.
Refs: Godden (1964, 1966a); Jewitt.

Duesbury, William. *See* Derby.

Dufraisseix, Jean-Baptiste. *See* G.D.A.

Dufrêne, Maurice (1876-1955). French designer. While still a student at the Ecole des Arts Décoratifs, Dufrêne started work for La *Maison Moderne in 1899, regarding the experience he gained in relating objects to clients' needs as his true training in decorative art. He worked in a wide variety of media: metal, leather, textiles and wood as well as ceramics, and was in 1901 a founder member of the Société des Artistes Décorateurs. His designs in stoneware, executed for La Maison Moderne by A.*Dalpayrat, include a vase, hand-thrown, with relief decoration of foliage under a *flambé* glaze, which was mounted in silver after purchase in 1899 and exhibited in Paris, 1900, and St Louis, 1904. His work also included a chocolate pot made c.1901 in porcelain with relief decoration of heart-shaped leaves at the rim as an extension of the handle, which sweeps up from the base. After 1906, Dufrêne abandoned Art Nouveau characteristics in his style. While teaching design in Paris from 1913, he continued his own work in furniture, metalwork and ceramics, supporting the use of industrial techniques in 1921, and established the design studio La Maîtrise at Galéries Lafayette.
Mark: printed signature.
Refs: Années 25; Bénézit; Brunhammer *et al* (1976); Hakenjos.

Dufy, Jean (1888-1964). French painter, watercolourist and porcelain decorator. After studying at the Ecole des Beaux-Arts in his home town, Le Havre (Seine-Maritime), he joined his brother, the painter Raoul Dufy, in Paris. He exhibited paintings as a member of the Salon d'Automne from 1920, and designed silks, porcelain, etc. During work as a designer and decorator for the firm established by T.*Haviland, starting in 1915, Dufy designed relief borders including Syringa, Feuille de Chêne, Serpent, patterns including Salonique, a series of Châteaux (1924), Pivoines (Peonies) and other painted flowers; vases painted with horsemen, *châteaux*, birds, services with ears of wheat painted and in relief. He moved to Bussière-Potevine in 1921 and continued in collaboration with William Haviland until c.1925. His work was characterized by an exuberant style with bold brush strokes in clear, bright colours and free use of flowers and foliage to add richness to his designs. He retired to paint at his home in the Loire region.
Refs: Années 25; Bénézit; d'Albis & Romanet; McClinton.

Duinvoet. *See* Muijen, Cornelius Jacobus.

Duke, Sir James, & Nephews. *See* Alcock, Samuel, & Co.

Dumas, Johann Christoph. *See* Durlach.

Dumortier, Joseph-Adrien. *See* Ancy-le-

Franc; Vausse, Faïencerie de.

Dunashora, Tatyana. *See* Artistic Ceramics Cooperative.

Duncan, George. *See* Port Dundas Pottery Co.

Dunderdale, David (1772-1824). Yorkshire potter, thought to have been an apprentice at the *Leeds Pottery. Dunderdale took over the *Castleford Pottery at the age of 18, in partnership until 1803 with the Leeds merchant, John Plowes (d 1812), and trading as D. Dunderdale & Co. He left the pottery in 1821.
Refs: Jewitt; Lawrence.

Dunmore Pottery. Scottish pottery established beside the River Forth, about a mile from the village of Dunmore in Stirlingshire, in the early 19th century. The works produced domestic ware, often with brown glaze over a coating of white slip, and in 1855 advertised tea and dessert services, leaf-shaped dishes, chimney ornaments, flower pots, garden seats, etc. In 1861, the business was taken over by Peter Gardner, who introduced a range of ornamental Dunmore Ware with glazes in red, brown, orange, blue, green, etc., sometimes in combination to produce a mottled effect. The pieces included vases in classical shapes, (e.g. with a stand in the form of a dolphin), baskets with handles twisted from thin strands of clay, figures, animal models and large pieces, such as walking stick holders. Through the interest of the Countess of Dunmore, the ware was sold by London retailers and became popular for a short time c.1900. Gardner retired in 1903, succeeded by the Dunmore Pottery Co. until the closure of the works in 1911.
Impressed marks incorporate *Dunmore* and often *Peter Gardner*.
Refs: Coysh (1976); Fleming; Godden (1966a); Hughes (1961); Jewitt; McVeigh.

Dunn, Constance. English artist potter. Constance Dunn studied at the Cambridge School of Art and from 1924 at the Royal College of Art in London under D.M. *Billington and W.S.*Murray. She taught ceramics in Middlesbrough, Yorkshire, for two years and from c.1933 worked at Billingham, Durham. Her experimentation in stoneware, carried out with her husband, a chemist, was interrupted by World War II, but she was able to build a new oil kiln to her own design in 1946. Constance Dunn's work includes bowls and vases, thinly potted in smooth, round forms, with simple brushed ornament.

Marks include w inside a triangle, incised. She worked initially as Constance Wade, her name until her marriage in 1928.
Refs: Godden (1964); Wingfield Digby.

Duntze, Ursula. *See* Scheid, Karl.

Dupré, François and Jules (1811-89). French porcelain decorators. After gaining technical experience in porcelain production at Nante (Loire-Atlantique) and then at l'Isle-Adam, where he made porcelain for sale in his Paris showroom, in 1825 François Dupré became director of a porcelain factory established by the military general, Marquis Hippolyte de Bonneval, at Coussac-Bonneval (Haute-

Vienne) and in operation 1819-55. His wares resembled Paris porcelains and were unmarked.

His son, Jules Dupré, born in Nantes, was apprenticed as a porcelain painter. He exhibited landscapes of the Limoges area in Paris in 1831 and was a member of the Barbizon school.
Refs: d'Albis & Romanet; Danckert.

Dupré. *See* Islettes, Les.

Dupuy, André & Emile. *see* Sauviat-sur-Vige.

Durandeau, Léon. *See* Angoulême.

Durant Kilns. *See* Rice, Jean Durant.

Durlach. German factory making faience and later cream-coloured earthenware in Baden, 1723-1847. A variety of faience included small, pear-shaped jugs and coffee pots, chiefly painted with figures of people at work and made as gifts. The jugs are usually dated and bear rhymes, or dedications and the owner's initials, normally in black lettering, and borders, often of vine leaves. Painting was careful. In general the factory used a smooth, white or creamy glaze on faience. Inscriptions were often used; other decoration included reliefs in rococo style, and dragon heads (on tea and coffee sets). The palette included pale blue, manganese purple, yellow, green, brick red and greyish black. The painters Johann Jacob Keim, Friedrich Gottlieb Keim (1788-1836), Carl Wetlach (1801-1877) and Johann Christoph Dumas were among artists who signed their work.

Creamware was in production before 1900, with yellowish or yellow-brown tinged glaze, and decorated with borders of vine leaves painted in brown or in relief. Other patterns included cupids (on plates).

Durlach. Decorative jug made in earthenware at Durlach, 1830.

Duxer Porzellanmanufaktur. Royal Dux group, the male dancer with red tunic and white and gold turban, the girl in a red skirt. Marked with a pink triangle. 31 cm high.

Refs: Ducret (1940); Haggar (1960); Hannover; Honey (1949-52); Hüseler; Towner (1957).

Dürrbeck & Ruckdäschel. German porcelain manufacturers making everyday porcelain and gift ware at Weissenstadt (Oberfranken) from 1920.

Mark: a crown over *Bavaria* and *Weissenstadt* around a triangle containing D & R/W.
Refs: Danckert; Weiss.

du Tremblay, Alexis. French potter. Owner of the château at Rubelles (Seine-et-Marne). Du Tremblay went into partnership with Baron P.-C.*Amable and built a factory, where they experimented on the production of glazed earthenware *lithophanes, expanding the factory in 1842 and taking out a second patent on Amable's process in the same year. They started full production of their *Nouvelle Porcelaine Anglaise* at that time, employing about 40 workers. Using clays from Arcueil and Montereau, they made table and toilet ware, a wide variety of vases, some in the form of cabbages, melons, etc., paperweights, candle-holders, clock cases, jewel boxes, perfume containers, inkwells, as well as plaques, medallions and panels for walls and fire-places. Hollow ware was thrown before decoration with detailed landscapes, seascapes, hunting scenes, incidents in the conquest of Africa, still lifes, portraits, copies of paintings or floral designs, especially vine leaves, moulded from engraved copper or, later, plaster. After undercutting and a first firing, the decorated pieces were dipped in coloured glaze, for designs *en camaïeu*, or painted with colour (e.g. yellow or violet with contrasting edge in blue or green, or vice versa), so that the glaze filled crevices in the design, leaving higher portions of the relief more lightly glazed (*émaux ombrants*). Finished

pieces retain traces of the pegs on which they stood during the firing of the glaze. Attempts to cut costs in production after 1852 were reflected in the quality of the glaze, which became dry, brittle and easily scratched. The factory's other output included earthenware for decorative or domestic use and, c.1836, items of *Palissy ware. Du Tremblay was succeeded in 1850 by his son-in-law, J. Hocédé, until the closure of the factory in 1867, when the stock was auctioned to local dealers. The moulds were sold to Choisy-le-Roi, Vallauris and Golfe-Juan, and to J.*Wedgwood & Sons Ltd in England.

Marks: BREVET D'INVENTION surrounding the initials ADT in a circle; other marks incorporate *Rubelles* and often ADT.
Refs: Ernould-Gandouet; Lesur (1967).

Duval, François. *See* Boulogne-sur-Mer.

Duval, Pierre. *See* Rochechouart.

Duxer Porzellanmanufaktur. Bohemian porcelain manufacturers established 1860 at Dux by E. Eichler, owner of the *Blankenhain factory, and still in production in the mid 20th century. The firm produced a wide range of ornamental wares under the name Royal Dux.

Marks include a raised triangle incorporating the initial E on a stylized acorn and ROYAL DUX BOHEMIA; others usually incorporate an acorn.
Refs: Danckert; Haslam (1977); Weiss.

Dymkovo or **Vyatka toys.** Russian low-fired earthenware toys, traditionally female figures in bell-shaped skirts, or a three-headed horse, associated with the Dymkovo district of Kirov (which was called Vyatka, 1780-1934). Similar figures, originally pagan symbols of the goddess of the home, and the three horses drawing the chariot of the sun god, were made in the 11th century, originally to celebrate the spring festival of the sun god (23rd May); 59 families of toymakers were still working in the Dymkovo district of Vyatka in 1856. Using red loam and fine sand from the riverside, mixed with sand and kneaded by hand, potters' families made figures in batches of separate units (skirts, heads, torsos, etc.), which were then assembled. After several days' drying, the figures were baked in domestic ovens and dipped in a mixture of chalk and milk to provide a base for painting in traditional bright colours, which were fixed with egg-white.

Though the craft died out in the late 19th century, the author A.A. Denshin published a celebration of the figures, later persuading makers to renew the craft. Successful displays were sent to the USSR Agricultural Exhibition, 1936, and World's Fairs in Paris, 1937, and New York, 1939. Figures made by traditional methods are now sold in the USSR and abroad. Similar toys made at Tula village in Filimonovo and Kargopol in Karelia, less brightly painted, relate to pre-historic pieces excavated at Kiev-Rus and Novgorod.
Ref: Ovsyannikov.

Dyson Perrins, Charles William. *See* Worcester.

Eagle Pottery. Yorkshire pottery established 1853 at Castleford by three partners in a company which had taken over a portion of the *Castleford Pottery premises after the dissolution of D.*Dunderdale's firm. Their production of printed and painted earthenware, some pieces with moulded flowers, and blue and white banded kitchen ware was continued by successive owners, Pratt & Abson (1855-56) and Hugh McDowall. The pottery had become a glassworks by 1878.
Refs: Jewitt; Lawrence.

Eagle Works, Hanley. *See* Meakin, J. & G., Ltd.

earthenware. Pottery with a porous body fired below a temperature of about 1200°C. When a glaze is used, glaze and body remain as distinct layers. The term covers industrially produced white earthenware, fine-grained and fired at the top of the temperature range and all lower-fired bodies down to soft, unglazed wares. Few studio potters fire earthenware above 1150°C.

Eason, Alfred (1854-1921). English ceramist. After working for the firms of J.*Spode and *Mintons Ltd, Eason spent time in America, engaged in the production of encaustic and moulded tiles. After returning to England, he worked for *Carter & Co. from 1888, throughout World War I and until shortly before his death, as glaze chemist and eventually works manager. He was responsible for the development (c.1909) of Carter's Ceramic Marble, weatherproof architectural ware which was produced in white, cream (slightly speckled) and shades of green. (Ceramic Marble was a rival of Doulton's Carrara ware.) His son William Eason (b 1894) worked in Carter's design department at East Quay from 1909 and continued work for Carter & Co. (Tiles) until 1960.
Ref: Hawkins.

East Liverpool Potteries Co. A group of American potteries operating at East Liverpool, Ohio, in the late 19th and early 20th centuries. The company was formed under

Eberly Pottery. Red earthenware group, one of two commemorating the Battle of Fisher's Hill (1864), made in 1894 from clay collected at the battleground. 40.6 x 38.1 x 38.1 cm.

the general management of Silas M. Ferguson in an attempt to compete with larger local manufacturers, particularly H.*Laughlin and *Knowles, Taylor & Knowles, by six East Liverpool potteries: the Globe Pottery Co., part of the group from 1888, owned by N.A. Frederick and J.H. Schenkle, makers of white granite ware; Wallace & Chetwynd, makers of fine tablewares 1881-1903 (member of the group from 1900); the East Liverpool Pottery Co., operating c.1884-1903 as manufacturers of white granite tablewares, including a line marked *Waco China*; the George C. Murphy Pottery Co. making hotel wares, etc., in semi-porcelain 1900-03; the East End Pottery Co., (under Gus Trenle from 1909); the United States Pottery Co. of Wellsville, makers of high-quality semi-porcelain 1899-1903. All the companies except the Globe Pottery and the United States Pottery left the group in 1903, and the company was finally closed by the two remaining potteries in 1907, although the United States Pottery continued to use the title East Liverpool Potteries Co.

The firms marked their output of semi-vitreous wares with a shield bearing USA and SEMI-VITREOUS PORCELAIN above EAST LIVERPOOL POTTERIES CO.
Refs: Barber (1976); Gates & Ormerod 'East Liverpool Potteries Company' in *Historical Archaeology* Vol 16, 1-2 (Society for Historical Archaeology, 1982).

Eastwood. *See* Baddeley family.

Eastwood Pottery, Hanley. *See* Meakin, J. & G., Ltd.

Eaton, Arthur Charles (b c.1875). English ceramic artist, trained as a painter under John *Slater and R.*Allen from 1889 at the *Doulton & Co. factory in Burslem, where he worked until 1932. He also studied at Burslem School of Art, later teaching there and in Tunstall. He executed landscapes and rural scenes, animals, flowers, figures and portraits over or under the glaze and, notably, in coloured slips. He assisted Charles *Noke in the artistic development of Holbein and Rembrandt wares. He also painted Hyperion ware and carried out exotic patterns, e.g. dragons and birds of paradise, for the decoration of *flambé* and Sung wares.
Refs: see Doulton & Co.

Ebelmen, Jacques-Joseph. *See* Sèvres.

Eberly Pottery. Red ware pottery operating in the Shenandoah Valley in the late 19th and early 20th centuries. The pottery was established in 1880 at Strasburg, Virginia, by Jacob Jeremiah Eberly, farmer and businessman, with the help of journeyman potters, who taught his son, Letcher Eberly, and Theodore Fleet, son of an employee of the *Bell family. As well as utilitarian red ware and, for a time, stoneware, the output included some ornamental pieces with applied decoration, which was noted for its originality: shells, lizards, fish, human hands

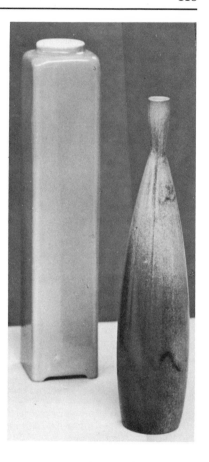

Otto Eckert. Glazed vases, 20th century.

and faces (often moulded in profile on circular pads of clay), birds or wings, lions and flowers of various kinds. Lead glazes were often splashed with green (copper oxide) or brown (manganese) and used over a coating of white slip. Large flowerpots, etc., were often moulded, usually in sections. Two known cabin groups were produced in 1894 to commemorate the Battle of Fisher's Hill thirty years earlier; each consists of a log cabin with a family outside the door. The pottery closed in 1906.
Marks: *J. Eberly & Co/Strasburg, Va., J. Eberly & Bro./Strasburg, Va., From/J. Eberly & Bro/Strasburg, Va., Eberly & Son, Strasburg, Va.*, in that order, all stamped.
Refs: Rice & Stoudt; Wiltshire.

Echizen ware. Japanese stoneware made at a number of kilns that operated in Fukui prefecture from the 12th century. Echizen, although it had a relatively small output, was among the 'Six Old Kilns' working in Japan in the Kamakura and early Muromachi periods (12th-16th centuries). The workshops made funeral wares, storage jars and other pieces for domestic use, and developed as folk kilns supplying the surrounding rural area with vessels for storing grain, water and preserves that strongly resembled the wares of *Tokoname. The forms were simple and decoration restricted to drip glazes.
Only the Taira kiln has been working from the Muromachi period to the present day; kilns of later origin belonging to the

Kuruba, Omoya and Sakon families also continue to supply the surrounding district of Hokuriku. A ceramic arts community has been established as part of a project for the renewed development of Echizen ware.
Refs: Jenyns (1971); Koyama; Mizuno; Mizuno 'Echizen' in *Sekai Toji Zenshu II* [Collection of World Ceramics] eds Koyama *et al* (Zanho Press, Tokyo, 1955-58).

Eckert, Otto (b 1910). Czech ceramist, one of a family of potters. Eckert studied in Prague, 1926-33, and worked independently before taking charge of the ceramics department in the main Prague art college in 1946. He became very influential in the development of studio ceramics in Czechoslovakia and was named a National Artist in 1970. His individual work includes tall vases and bottles in angular shapes with brightly coloured glazes.
Refs: Hettes & Rada; M. Ruzicka & T. Vlcek *Keramik der Gegenwart* (Odeon, Prague, 1979); D. Sindelar *Otto Eckert* (Odeon, Prague, n.d.).

Eckhard, Christian Jakob. *See* Kahla.

Eckhardt, Edris (b 1907 or 1910). American studio potter and teacher of ceramics and glass, born in Cleveland, Ohio. She graduated from the Cleveland Institute of Art in 1932, having studied ceramic sculpture under R.G.*Cowan in her last year. She established a studio, where she carried out experiments in glazes. In 1933, she took part in the Welfare Art Program, the government's attempt to overcome the effects of the depression on the arts by commissioning work from individual artists. Under her direction, a ceramic sculpture division established through the Welfare Art Program at Cleveland in 1935 produced earthenware figures from children's stories, e.g. *Mother Goose, Alice's Adventures in Wonderland* and *Green Mansions* for display in libraries, as well as garden ornaments and murals for public places. When the project ceased in 1941, Edris Eckhardt continued to make ceramic sculptures, including Huckleberry Finn (commissioned by Eleanor Roosevelt in 1939) and a painted mask, which was shown in the exhibition of work by Cleveland Artists & Craftsmen in 1947. She worked in glass from 1953.
Refs: D. Barrie 'Edris Eckhardt Interviewed' in *Link*, Cleveland Institute of Art Newsletter 12, No 3 (Spring 1978); Clark & Hughto; Kovel & Kovel; K.A. Marling *Federal Art in Cleveland 1933-43* (Cleveland Public Library, 1976).

Eda. *See* Shigaraki ware.

Edelstein, S.A. German porcelain manufacturers established 1932 at Küps, Bavaria, for the production of everyday porcelain and gift ware.
    Mark: *Edelstein*/BAVARIA, sometimes with a crown.
Refs: Danckert; Weiss.

Edge & Grocott. Impressed mark used on figures with a background of leaves and branches produced c.1830 in Tunstall, Staffordshire, and resembling those made by J.*Walton. Details of the firm are not clear, but Samuel Grocott, possibly a partner in the company, was a manufacturer of earthen-

ware, including figures, in Liverpool Road, Tunstall, in the 1820s.
Refs: Godden (1964); Haggar (1955); Rhead.

Edge, Malkin & Co. *See* Cork & Edge.

Edge, W.H. *See* Carr, James.

Edgerton Art Clay Works. *See* American Art Clay Works.

Edgerton Pottery. American pottery firm organized by several shareholders of the Pauline Pottery of P.*Jacobus to take over the works at Edgerton, Wisconsin, after the original pottery's failure in 1894. The firm manufactured utilitarian ware, including water filters, and continued production of art ware under the title, Rock Pottery, which may have been an independent enterprise, but used moulds acquired from the Pauline Pottery. Marked examples show similarities in form, decoration and such details as a C-scroll handle to pieces made at the Pauline Pottery or *Norse Pottery. The firm failed in 1901, and some of its effects were sold to Mrs Jacobus.
    Mark: *Rock Pottery with Edgerton, Wis.* (incised).
Ref: Evans.

Edmands, Barnabas. American pottery owner. While running a brass foundry in Charlestown, Massachusetts, he bought land in partnership with his brother-in-law William Burroughs for the establishment in 1812 of a stoneware pottery, which was operated by F.*Carpenter. In 1850, Edmands was succeeded by Edward T. Edmands, Thomas R.B. Edmands and Charles Collier, operating as Edmands & Co. until c.1865. The firm became Powers & Edmands in 1868 and Edmands & Hooper until 1905.
    Marks: until c.1820 *Charlestown*; *Barnabas Edmands/Charlestown; Barnabas Edmands/& Co/Charlestown; Edmands & Co/Charlestown.*
Refs: Stradling; Webster.

Edwards, Emily J. (d 1879). English pottery decorator working at Doulton's Lambeth studio c.1872-c.1876. Emily Edwards specialized in foliate patterns (e.g. acanthus leaf, freely drawn foliage), carved, incised and coloured. She was among the first female artists at the studio to design and decorate her own pieces and trained other artists in the decoration of stoneware. Her stamped patterns combined natural forms with elaborate, diapered grounds, using colour to emphasize the relief effect.
    Mark: monogram of EJE.
Refs: see Doulton & Co.

Edwards, James (d 1867). English potter working in Staffordshire. James Edwards, formerly working as a thrower for J. and G. *Rogers, and a pottery manager in Longport and Cobridge, worked in partnership with his brother. In c.1825 James and Thomas Edwards succeeded the firm of J.& T. Hanley, c.1825, at the Kiln Croft Works in Burslem as makers of transfer-printed earthenware and ironstone china, much of which was exported to Canada and the United States. In 1841, the firm registered a pattern for plates and dishes which depicted the four Cunard

steamships *Britannia, Acadia, Caledonia* and *Columbia* on panels in a border surrounding one of four views of ships' cabins and saloon. The series, described on a backstamp as Boston Mails (the ships travelled from Liverpool to Boston via Halifax 1840-c.1850), was transfer printed in light blue or, more rarely, black, lavender or brown. In 1842, James Edwards acquired the pottery in Dale Hall, Burslem, operated by J.& G. Rogers, where he worked until his retirement c.1861, succeeded by his son Richard, who had been his partner since 1851. James Edwards was known for the production of high-quality ironstone china and won a medal for the design and technical merit of work shown in the Great Exhibition, 1851. A Tunstall company, Knapper & Blackhurst, took over the firm in 1883.
    Marks incorporate *Edwards* or the makers' initials. Working with his son, James Edwards used printed or impressed marks, J.E. & S. or JAMES EDWARDS/& SON. DALE HALL.
Refs: Collard; Godden (1964); Jewitt; Ormsbee.

'Effeco'. *See* Florentine Pottery Co.

Eger, Hermann. *See* Phillips, Moro.

Eggers, Marie. *See* Cincinnati School of Design.

eggshell. Very thin porcelain. In China during the Ming and Ch'ing dynasties the ware was pared, scraped or smoothed when partly dry until it was so thin as to be described as 'bodiless' (t'o t'ai). In America *Belleek ware is sometimes referred to as 'eggshell china'. The *Rozenburg factory became known for a line of very thinly potted earthenware produced in the late 19th and early 20th centuries.

Egypto. *See* Roseville Pottery Co.

Ehrmann, François-Emile (1833-1910). French painter, born in Strasbourg. While working for T.*Deck, Ehrman painted plates, often large in size. He also designed two tile panels entitled Commerce and Navigation for Deck's display in the French pavilion at the exhibition of 1883 in Amsterdam.
    Mark: F. EHRMANN.
Refs: Bénézit; Heuser & Heuser; Thieme & Becker.

Eichhorn, H.K. *See* Schney.

Eichler, E. *See* Blankenhain.

Eichwald. *See* Bloch, Bernard.

Eiraku. *See* Hozen; Wazen.

Eisen Okuda (1753-1811). Japanese potter. After an early retirement from his pawnbroking business, Eisen became an amateur potter in his native city, Kyoto. He attempted to reproduce celadon glazes and Chinese ware decorated only in underglaze blue. His main output imitated Chinese *gosu aka-e porcelain, mainly decorated with flowers, birds and scrollwork; these pieces provided inspiration for *Shuhei, *Hozen and a number of Kyoto potters. Eisen also made pieces in the style of *Kochi ware. Working

primarily in porcelain, he is credited with the introduction of porcelain production to the Kyoto area. His pupils included *Dohachi II and *Mokubei.
Refs: Gorham; Jenyns (1965); Koyama; Mikami; Miller; Munsterberg; Roberts.

Eisenberg. German faience and porcelain factory established 1796 at Eisenberg, Thuringia, by H.E.*Muhlberg, who was succeeded by his widow and son. The firm produced everyday wares decorated in underglaze blue with patterns that included the Meissen onion pattern (*Zwiebelmuster*). The porcelain was similar to that of *Gera, and the faience to that of Altenberg, a factory also owned by Muhlberg. In the early 19th century, decoration also included brightly painted flowers, a pattern of small blue flowers, or views of ruins painted in black. After the owner's bankruptcy, the factory passed to Hermann Schulz and closed for a time in 1856. Production was resumed by 1864. Under the ownership of porcelain industrialist, Friedrich August Reinecke, and his successors from the following year, it merged in 1960 with the Wilhelm Jäger factory, established 1867 in Eisenberg for the production of tea, coffee and luncheon services for hotel use. The firms operated jointly as V.E.B. Vereinigte Porzellanwerke Eisenberg, now part of the Kahla group.
The manufacturers Bremer & Schmidt, established a factory at Eisenberg in 1895 for the production of household wares, table services and cups, some exported to the Balkan countries and the Far East.
Marks include a shield bearing three turrets and topped with a crown; several incorporating Jäger's name and *Eisenberg*, or a lion holding the initial WJ in its forepaws with *Eisenberg*; crossed lines containing the initials RPME over REINECKE/GEGRÜNDET/1796; a crown over crossed lines containing the initials BSE [Bremer & Schmidt, Eisenberg].
Refs: Danckert; Scherf; Weiss.

Eisenloeffel, Johannes or Jan (1896-1957). Draughtsman, designer and manufacturer of utilitarian and decorative metal, glass and ceramics, who worked mainly as leader of the metalwork section of *Amstelhoek. He was involved, 1900-03, in the formation of 't *Binnenhuis and then De Woning, both in Amsterdam. In 1910, he opened a workshop in Laren. From c.1904, he provided designs for earthenware services and other wares (vases) that were produced by De *Distel, De *Sphinx and *Zuid-Holland.
Mark: monogram of *je*.
Refs: Scheen; van Straaten.

Ekberg, Josef (1877-1945). Painter and designer, working in Sweden for the *Gustavsberg factory, 1898-1945.
Mark: painted signature.
Refs: Danckert; Haslam (1977).

Elanware. *See* Adams & Co.

Elbogen. A centre of Bohemian porcelain manufacture, now Loket. The brothers Haidinger established a factory in 1815, initially for the production of a hard, greytinged paste sold for decoration outside the factory. However, the firm began to participate in exhibitions by the 1830s and

A.*Brongniart acquired some pieces which are preserved in the museum at Sèvres. The Haidingers' heirs sold the factory to the firm Springer & Oppenheimer which operated 1873-85 as Erste Elbogener Porzellan und Kohlen Industrie KG. Oppenheimer withdrew from the firm in 1885. Springer & Co. became part of ÖPIAG (*see* EPIAG) in 1918
Marks include a mailed fist holding a sword; a circle containing GEBRUDER HAIDINGER ELBOGEN with the date 1868; and others incorporate *Haidinger*. Modern marks incorporate EPIAG.
Winter & Co. became established as producers of everyday wares in 1880. Another factory started by them in 1887 made stoneware and porcelain from the following year and was, from 1891, under the control of H. Kretschmann (in the partnership Kretschmann & Wurda until 1899), who built up a large export trade in simple everyday wares. The works finally closed in 1945.
Marks include HK on a shield with GESCHUTZT.
In 1890, the partnership Winter, Lochschmied & Co. established a works (making blue-printed everyday wares), which passed to Karl Speck & Co. in 1896 and closed in 1937.
Marks usually incorporate AUSTRIA and include a monogram of HPA (Hegewald & Persch were owners from 1902) enclosed in a circle bearing MADE IN CZECHOSLOVAKIA.
Persch was succeeded by the firm Porag in 1937 and the factory closed after World War II.
Refs: Danckert; Meyer; Weiss.

Elgee Pottery. *See* Gonder, Lawton.

Elgersburg. German faience and porcelain factory established at Elgersburg, near Ilmenau, in 1806, by Christian Ludwig Droesse or Drässe (d 1814), who had formerly worked at Henneberg, in partnership with Gotha businessmen Ernst Friedrich Arnoldi and Wilhelm Madelung. In 1812, the firm began producing water pipes with a high content of porphyry (a rock rich in the feldspar orthoclase), which is also thought to have been an ingredient of the firm's porcelain, when it was first introduced in 1829. As well as blue and white tableware, the firm supplied chemical and pharmaceutical wares. The production of household ware continued until the factory turned over

completely to technical porcelain after World War II. The firm is now nationally owned.
Marks: E in underglaze blue in the early 19th century; FABRIK ARNOLDI/ELGERSBURG in a circle; E on a shield at the centre of a sunburst; A placed like an arrowhead with the Arnoldi initials E, F and C twined round the shaft.
Refs: Danckert; Scherf; Weiss.

Elite. *See* Guérin, William.

Elkin, Knight & Co. *See* Foley Potteries.

Elliott, Liddle. *See* Mayer, T.J.& J.

Eloury, François. *See* Loc Maria.

Elton, Sir Edmund Harry (1846-1920). English studio potter. During his early experiments with pottery, Elton built a series of kilns at his home in Clevedon, Somerset, at first employing a flowerpot maker to throw pieces under his supervision, and teaching himself to throw c.1881. At his workshop, which he called the Sunflower Pottery, he developed a decorative process by 1882, in which he applied a ground of slip over a pattern (often flowers, shells or reptiles) deeply incised in the clay body, and later filled in the outlines with thick, brightly coloured slips, which he modelled in low relief to represent plant or animal forms, after a period of drying. The pieces were covered with a colourless lead glaze. Occasionally decoration such as medallions on tankards was moulded. Elton made his earthenware in local clay, which required heavy potting in rounded shapes, and concentrated on ornamental pieces, some very large, but he also produced commemorative mugs, teapots and small bottles. The shapes, often complicated, included onion vases with several handles, vases with twisted necks,

Sir Edmund H. Elton. Glazed earthenware c.1890. The double-mouthed vase with mulberries has a marbled ground in bright blue and purple; the ewer is decorated with a flowering twig and berries in brown and green on a moss green and brown ground; the trumpet-shaped vase is ribbed and has incised decoration and green, slate and buff glaze with trailed patterns in brown and green. All marked Elton. 26 cm, 19 cm, 24 cm.

émaux ombrants. Earthenware plate with impressed decoration covered by translucent glaze. Made by A.*du Tremblay at Rubelles.

pierced ware, sometimes with double walls, and a variety of gourd forms. The decoration, always designed to complement the form, was often executed in bright reds and browns against dark grounds of streaked blue and green slip with other colours: (red, buffs, brown) added. A marbled ivory body also occurs.

Elton experimented with metallic effects c.1902, using gold, silver and bronze in a tar oil medium over a deeply crackled glaze fired at a low temperature. These effects, which Elton called platinum crackle, blue platinum crackle, bright platinum crackle or copper crackle, provided the sole decoration of small pieces and covered only parts of larger items, e.g. patches of copper on a light blue ground. Occasionally the colour of the glaze showed through at the cracks (e.g. green under gold). Elton made small batches of some pieces, but his work mainly consisted of items that were unique or developed in series, e.g. a bird motif used on a bottle eventually developing into combined handle and spout. Sources of his shapes included Mycenean pottery, which was being excavated at the time, and he made his own adaptations of Chinese forms, for which he developed a *sang-de-boeuf* glaze.

The pottery continued after 1920 under George Masters, who died the following year, and Elton's son, Sir Ambrose Elton, until 1930.

Marks: *Elton*, painted or incised; a small cross was added after Elton's death.
Refs: Blacker (1922a); Coysh (1976); Haslam (1975); Lloyd Thomas (1974); P. Ruck 'A Victorian Squire and his Eccentric Pottery' in *Art & Antiques* (27th March 1976); Wakefield.

Emaux de Longwy. *See* Longwy.

émaux ombrants. Ceramic decoration consisting of a design carved, moulded or impressed in unfired clay and flooded with coloured, transparent glaze; the intensity of colour varies with the contours of the relief. The technique was introduced commercially by A.*du Tremblay, in France and later used at the *Wedgwood factory in England in the 1860s and by G.*Cartlidge in America in the 1890s. *Majolica makes comparable use of coloured glazes over relief decoration.

Bruno Emmel. Vase, made at the Wiener Kunstgewerbeschule, c.1903. Initialled B.E. *14.3 cm high.*

Emery, Henry. Australian potter working in Victoria. In 1866, he established the Fitzroy Pottery Pipe & Tile Works, where he made domestic ware, vases, flowerpots, etc., in brown-glazed earthenware or terracotta. He also worked in partnership with his brother at Collingwood. The Fitzroy works remained in the hands of the Emery family until the 1890s. Other potters of the same name working in Victoria include Michael Emery, maker of drainage ware and domestic pottery at Preston, near Melbourne from 1861. *Ref:* Graham.

Emmel, Bruno (b 1877). Austrian ceramist, trained at the Wiener Kunstgewerbeschule. His work included stoneware vases in irregular shapes with running glazes, as well as vases, flower holders, covered jars, etc., in earthenware. He designed pieces for production at the Wiener Kunstkeramischen Werkstätte, Alexandrinenthal porcelain factory (*see* Recknagel, T.) and at a stoneware factory in Znaim, where he taught at the school of ceramics from 1912.

Mark: initials B.E. (with the B resembling a D in outline).
Ref: Neuwirth (1974a).

Empire Pottery. *See* Coxon, Charles.

Empire Pottery, The. *See* Trenton Potteries Co.

Empire style. A decorative style which developed in France in the early 19th century, and was in effect a phase of the neo-classical style that included exact imitation, primarily of ancient Greek and Roman forms and motifs, but also of elements from Etruscan and Egyptian decoration. Designs for the refurbishment of Malmaison for Napoleon Bonaparte established the elegance and grandeur of the style which persisted for some years after the fall of Napoleon's Empire. Typical motifs include acanthus leaves,

wreaths, palm leaves, torches, trophies, musical instruments, eagles, swans, lions, mythical beasts and draped figures. Porcelain in the Empire style, produced notably at Sèvres, Vienna and St Petersburg, was richly painted, often in the manner of oil painting, and gilded.

enamel. Pigments with a wide colour range which fuse at low temperatures. The colours are applied over the glaze and fired at about 800°C in a muffle kiln, where they are protected from fierce heat. The term is also sometimes used to denote opaque, coloured earthenware glazes.

encaustic tiles. Decorative floor tiles patterned with inlaid clay slip or dust in colours which contrast with that of the body.

Endo Heikichi. *See* Shigaraki Ware.

Enfield Pottery & Tile Works. American pottery established c.1906 in Laverock, Pennsylvania. The firm produced art pottery covered with heavy enamels or transparent, coloured glazes, e.g. a puzzle jug made in red clay with hollow twig-like handles and a design in relief representing a bicycle rider under a blue-green glaze, with the interior glazed in white. Handmade tiles were decorated from medieval or Californian mission designs, etc., for fireplaces and other architectural decoration.

Mark: *Enfield*, incised, and paper labels.
Refs: Evans; Kovel & Kovel.

Engelhardt, Valdemar (1860-1915). Danish ceramic chemist employed at the Royal *Copenhagen factory from 1891, and successor to A.*Clement from the following year until his death. He developed crystalline and *flambé* glazes, as well as effects similar to semi-precious stones, and worked with K.*Kyhn on the development of stoneware c.1903-04.

Mark: painted initials VE.
Refs: Bodelsen; Danckert; Préaud & Gauthier.

Englefontaine (Nord). French pottery centre with a tradition dating back to the 15th century. The area is known for earthenware with bright red body decorated with either simple geometrical designs of dot and lines, or flowers and foliage, in light yellow slip, sometimes highlighted with red or green under the glaze. The pieces include dishes, match holders, spittoons and large containers for cooking potatoes, as well as tiles and panels, which continued in quantity until the mid 19th century. The number of potteries dwindled from about 30 at the beginning of the century to just over 10 in 1850.
Refs: Ernould-Gandouet; Lesur (1971).

English Porcelain. *See* Mason, George Miles and Charles James.

Englund, Ivan. Australian sculptor, painter and potter. After studying art in Sydney, Englund served in the Royal Australian Air Force and returned to art training in 1949. He experimented with clays and glazes while teaching in Victoria from 1952 and subsequently established studios in Appin, New South Wales (1955) and Mount Kembla (1956), where he worked with his wife,

Patricia Englund, while both taught at Wollongong. He became a Fellow of Sydney Technical College after writing a thesis (unpublished) on the use of igneous rocks from Illawarra in glazes for studio stoneware, and was appointed head teacher of painting at the National Art School in Sydney. Englund makes domestic ware as well as wall panels and sculptural pieces. He was initially much influenced by the work of B.*Leach and *Hamada. With his smooth-textured pots, such as bottles, bowls and decanters, he uses brushed oxides which streak and swirl with the glaze on firing. Using stoneware, thrown and built up with coils, he sometimes cuts, beats, models or adds clay in swirls and lumps before using a heavy glaze, often matt white, to give his work the appearance of eroded or encrusted rock formations. He also works in porcelain. He is noted for his technical control in the achievement of natural, spontaneous effects. Patricia Englund makes thrown porcelain and stoneware, including large bowls and globular bottles with brushed decoration. She is also known for the successful use of copper glazes.
Ref: Hood.

engobe. A layer of slip applied over a clay body to provide a smooth surface for glaze or decoration. The term usually implies the covering of a wide area of the piece with slip by dipping or brushing.

Ens, Johann Karl (1756-1823) and his son, Karl. Porcelain painters working in Germany. J.K. Ens trained at Bruckberg (Ansbach). He married into the *Greiner family in 1790 and was working at Limbach in the following year. His son, Karl, was also a porcelain painter, and a partner in a decorating workshop run by Ens & Greiner in Lauscha. He became proprietor of the Triebner factory of *Volkstedt-Rudolstadt in 1898.
Ref: Scherf.

Enterprise Pottery, The. *See* Trenton Potteries Co.

Eocean or **Eosian ware.** *See* Weller, Samuel A.

EPIAG. A group of porcelain manufacturers operating from Karlsbad and established in 1918, when the firms of Proeschold & Co. at Dallwitz, Springer & Co. (*Elbogen), O.& E. Gutherz (*Altrohlau), Fischer & Mieg (*Pirkenhammer), joined to form Österreicher Porzellan Industrie A.G. (ÖPIAG). The name became Erste Porzellan Industrie AG in 1920. Later, the group included individual factories and small groups at Meierhöfen, Lubau and Lickwitz (closed 1939), Klösterle and Thurn (closed 1934) and Metzling.
    Marks incorporate EPIAG.
Refs: Danckert; Weiss.

Epsom Pottery. *See* Bendigo Pottery.

Equitable Pottery, The. *See* Trenton Potteries Co.

Erdös, Stephan (1906-56) and Ida (b 1897). Studio potters who worked in Austria and Germany. Stephan Erdös, born in Znaim, Mähren, trained at the Staatliche Porzellanfachschule in Karlsbad and in

Ida Erdös-Meisinger. Stylized figure in hard earthenware painted under the glaze in black, brown and shades of green over white slip, c.1955. 31.5 cm high.

Vienna (1925-29) before becoming assistant to M. *Powolny, 1929-32. His wife, Ida Erdös-Meisinger, studied in her native Prague before training under Powolny and subsequently working (1928-33) in Vienna. The couple established a studio in Znaim, where they worked together, with Ida Erdos specializing in figures and decoration, while her husband became known for the development of crackled glazes, which he fired in a reducing atmosphere. His range of delicate, translucent colours included matt grey, leaf green, mottled black-brown, and clouded effects in ivory, pale blue and pink. His pieces were simple, smooth and rounded in shape. The couple moved to Tittmoning in Upper Bavaria in 1946, and at that time Stephan Erdös became influenced by the work of M.*Laeuger, adopting his style, but using a wide range of colour in decoration. He became director of the Staatliche Glasfachschule, Zweisel, in 1953, and was appointed to the Akademie der Bildenden Künst in Stuttgart in 1956. Ida Erdös continued the workshop after her husband's death.
    Marks: the initials SE flanking a monogram of IM.
Refs: Bock; Neuwirth (1974a).

Ergot, Jean-Baptiste. *See* Chevannes, Faïencerie de.

Eriksen, Gutte (b 1918). Danish ceramic artist, trained (1936-39) in Copenhagen. She established her own studio in 1941, working in both earthenware and stoneware. Gutte

Eriksen's work includes household jugs, bowls, etc., with simple decoration stamped or painted primarily in dark blue or rust and, often, light-coloured glazes. She travelled to Japan and, in 1948, worked briefly with B.*Leach at St Ives.
Refs: W. Hall *Danish Ceramic Design* (catalogue, Museum of Art, Pennsylvania State University, 1981); Hettes & Rada; Hiort.

Erikson, Algot (b 1868). Swedish ceramist and sculptor. Erikson studied at technical school in Stockholm from 1882 and worked 1886-1920, as modeller and designer of vases and tableware at the Rörstrand porcelain factory, where he introduced a decorative combination of underglaze painting and relief modelling. He was also known for slip-painted patterns.
    Marks: painted initials AE.
Refs: Danckert; Haslam (1977); Porzellankunst.

Escallier-Légérot, Eleanore (1827-88). French ceramic decorator, born in Poligny, Jura. She learned painting under J.-C.*Ziegler, specializing in studies of flowers and fruit, and exhibited in Paris, 1857-80. She also worked for the firm of T.*Deck. Her style was influenced by Japanese art; plates dated 1867 are painted with asymmetrical designs of birds with flowing plumage, perched on branches over flowers or large-leaved plants. At the Sèvres factory, they took part in the development of *pâte-sur-pâte* decoration and, as a painter, 1874-88, continued to specialize in fruit, flowers, and birds.
    Mark: signature, or initials EE with first E reversed.
Refs: Bénézit; Heuser & Heuser; Lesur (1967); Thieme & Becker.

E.S.K.A.F. N.V. (Eerste Steenwijksche Kunstaardewerkfabriek). Dutch pottery established at Steenwijk in 1919 for the production of art pottery, tableware, tiles and architectural ware. The earthenware, in distinctive shapes, is often matt-glazed in cream or black. Stylized figures and pieces with painted decoration were also made. After liquidation in 1927, production was set up in Huizen, where H.J. Fokke Hamming (son of one of the owners, H. Hamming)

*Eleanore Escallier-Légérot. Earthenware dish painted by Eleanore Escallier. Made and signed on the reverse by T.*Deck, 1867.*

began to make decorative earthenware. The painter, W. Evers, who had also worked in Steenwijk, developed decorative wares flecked in dark green or brown. In 1932, H. Hamming left the business, and his son went to undergo further training in France. The business failed c.1934.

Marks usually incorporate ESKAF and *Steenwijk* or *Huizen*.
Refs: Singelenberg-van der Meer; M.C. Spruit-Ledeboer *Nederlandse Keramiek 1900-1975* (Assen/Amsterdam, 1977); van Straaten.

Esser, Max (1885-1945). German sculptor and *animalier*. Esser trained part-time at the Berlin museum of decorative arts and was the only pupil of the sculptor August Gaul (1904-05). He worked at the Schwarzburger Werkstätten für Porzellankunst and provided several animal models for the Meissen factory in the 1920s and 1930s. His Meissen pieces included a table service with characters from the fable Reynard the Fox (1922), chessmen and boards with decorative edging, a seagull, and an otter (1937) which appeared in the firm's prizewinning display at the Paris exhibition in the same year.
Refs: Danckert; Forsyth; Ware.

Essex Art Pottery Co. *See* Bingham, Edward.

Estié, E. *See* Haga, Plateelbakkerij.

Etchu-Seto. Japanese pottery centre established in the town of Tateyama (Toyama prefecture) in the late 16th century as a clan kiln, firing domestic ware for the feudal lord's own use. A number of kilns were in production on a large scale until the Meiji period (1868-1912). Production ceased

Max Esser. Figure of an otter, designed by Esser and produced at *Meissen, c.1914.

George Eyre. Earthenware dish painted by Eyre c.1850.

temporarily, but was revived in the Showa period (from 1926) and continues today. Many potters were trained in Seto and maintained the local techniques. The area produced bowls, often green-glazed, intended to hold a gruel of tea and rice.
Ref: Mizuo.

Etsubei. *See* Dohei.

Evans, David. Ceramic decorator, working at the *Cambrian Pottery between 1811 and 1824. In writing about the pottery, Turner and Jewitt mention a local painter, David Evans, noted for his studies of wild flowers. Jewitt also mentions a flower artist named David Evans who worked at Grainger's *Worcester factory in the first half of the 19th century.
Refs: Jewitt; John; Nance; Turner.

Evans, D.J., & Co. *See* Cambrian Pottery.

Evans, George (d 1832). English potter making stoneware at Ilkeston, Derbyshire, from 1807. Evans was succeeded by his son, Richard, who enlarged the pottery and extended its output of bottles to include barrels, water filters, a range of hot-water bottles, and pharmaceutical ware, as well as drainage pipes. The pottery also produced terracotta. Richard worked with another George Evans in 1841, and he was still in business in 1876.
Refs: Bradley; Jewitt; Oswald.

Evans, George (1899-1958). English porcelain painter, working for the *Worcester Royal Porcelain Co. until the 1930s. Evans was known for landscapes, and was the factory's first painter to work in the style of Corot. He later worked on the colouring of Mediterranean scenes printed in outline from designs by W.*Sedgley (using the signature H. George). Evans worked for *Doulton & Co. in the 1930s, but returned to Worcester as one of the first painters of D.*Doughty's bird models.
Refs: Sandon (1978a); *see also* Doulton & Co.

Evans, Henry and Walter. *See* Derby.

Evans & Booth. *See* Booths Ltd.

Evans & Co. *See* Watcombe Pottery.

Evans & Glasson. *See* Cambrian Pottery.

Excelsior Pottery Works. *See* Young, William, & Sons.

Exeter Art Pottery. Small pottery established by Cole & Trelease, and working in Exeter, Devon, 1892-96. The firm's known work mainly consists of mugs and jugs in brown body, dipped in white slip, with *sgraffito* inscription and finished with amber-coloured glaze. Some pieces are decorated with sprays of leaves brushed in white slip on a blue ground. False dates from the late 17th or early 19th centuries sometimes occur.

Impressed marks incorporate *Exeter Art Pottery* with ENGLAND.
Ref: Lloyd Thomas (1978).

Exeter Pottery Works. *See* Lamson Pottery.

Eyck, Charles Hubert (b. 1897). Dutch architect, painter, sculptor and designer, born in Meerssen. Eyck designed religious figures, reliefs and tiles for production mainly by De*Sphinx, the Westraven faience and tile workshop (in operation under the firm Gebr. Ravesteyn from 1907), and Russell-Tiglia, a tile factory in operation 1936-1955 at Tegelen.

Marks: E or CE.
Refs: Scheen; Singelenberg-van der Meer.

Eyre, George (1816-87). English ceramic decorator and designer, noted for his painting of figures on earthenware. Eyre trained in Stoke-on-Trent and at the Government School of Design at Somerset House in London, c.1845-47. He was engaged in the production of tiles at *Mintons Ltd from 1847 and provided designs for floors made with encaustic tiles. By 1854, he worked for S.*Alcock & Co. and their successors at the Hill Pottery, Sir James Duke & Nephews. His design for a dessert service made in parian ware and glazed porcelain was included in a prizewinning display at the International Exhibition, 1862. Eyre succeeded T.*Battam as art director at the factory of W.T.*Copeland, 1864-65.
Refs: Godden (1961, 1968); Rhead.

Eyre, John (1847-1927). English painter and ceramic decorator. After training in South Kensington, Eyre worked at *Minton's Art Pottery Studio from 1872 or 1873, where his studies ranged from decoration and design to superintendent of firing. He joined the factory of W.T.*Copeland as designer, c.1874-80. At the *Doulton & Co. workshop in Lambeth (from c.1885), he completed designs which included eight panels illustrating Agriculture, Commerce, Columbus's Life, etc., for the World's Columbian Exposition in Chicago, 1893.
Refs: J. Barnard *Victorian Ceramic Tiles* (Studio Vista, London, and New York Graphic Society, Greenwich, Conn., 1972); Godden (1961); Rhead.

Eyre, Vi (1870-1956). Australian potter, born in Sydney. After a short period of art

Vi Eyre. Earthenware vase with inlaid decoration, made at Vi Eyre's workshop in 1947. 25 cm high.

teaching, she took up pottery full-time, joining the Arts & Crafts Society of New South Wales in 1918. By the mid 1920s, she had established her own studio with a large output, which she fired in a gas kiln. She pioneered the use of inlaid clay decoration in Australia and carried out research into the properties of Australian clays. Her pottery was all glazed earthenware, generally decorated with naturalistic flowers or spirited designs of birds and animals, either modelled or inlaid.

Faber, Frédéric Théodor (d 1844). Porcelain manufacturer of German descent working in Brussels. Faber, an engraver and miniature painter, was appointed director of a porcelain factory established in Brussels in 1818 under the patronage of King William of Holland. The output resembled that of other European factories, especially Sèvres, in shape and decoration, and included tall vases painted with flowers or figures, cups and other pieces painted with views of Brussels, and a service painted with birds after Buffon commissioned for the Dutch royal house. Other decorative subjects included Italian landscapes, monuments, mythical scenes, garlands, bouquets and, later, named botinical specimens of flowers, figures in national dress, copies of paintings or engravings. Faber's firm was noted for the lavish use of gilding. He was succeeded by his sons Henri and Edouard until 1849 and subsequently by the firm of Capellmann.
Painted marks include *Faber, 13 rue de la Madeleine à Bruxelles.*
Refs: Danckert; H. Nicouse *La Porcelaine de Bruxelles* (1936); Weiss.

faience. Tin-glazed earthenware inspired by Chinese porcelain, including 17th-century Dutch Delft and later styles that were developed especially in France, Germany and Scandinavian countries. The term is also applied to dark-bodied earthenware which is coated with pale slip before painting and glazing, as in *Haban Fayence.

Faience Manufacturing Co. American pottery and porcelain manufacturers at Greenpoint, New York. The company was established in 1880 for the production of earthenware decorated with flowers modelled by hand and applied to the surface before painting under the glaze, and subsequently without decoration, other than coloured glazes which were sometimes combined in streaked or marbled effects. E.*Lycett joined the firm in 1884, becoming director until 1890; his son Joseph was also employed as a decorator and designer. The firm became the American agent of a French factory in 1890 and closed in 1892.
Marks: initials FMCo incised on early pottery, painted monogram 1886-92; a double circle enclosing R and topped with a crown, briefly, when the name *Royal Crown* was used to designate bodies finer than the initial faience.
Refs: Barber (1976); Evans; Kovel & Kovel.

Faience Pottery. American firm producing a wide variety of domestic and ornamental ware in Zanesville, Ohio, from its incorporation in 1902 until its dissolution in 1906.
Refs: Evans; Kovel & Kovel; Lehner.

Faïencerie de Longwy et Senelle. *See* Longwy.

Faïencerie du Port, La. *See* Auvillar (Tarn et Garonne).

fairings. Porcelain figure groups made in Germany c.1850-90, after English models for sale as souvenirs at country fairs. The forms were simple, about 10 cm high, in heavy paste, and were decorated in high-temperature colours with light gilding. The subjects were often humorous or *risqué* comments on marriage, e.g. Last in Bed Puts Out the Light, or were inspired by popular songs. Enormous quantities were sold cheaply in Britain, but fairings were not popular in France or Germany.

fairing. Inscribed Cancan. *Late 19th century. 9 cm high.*

Fairyland Lustre. *See* Makeig-Jones, 'Daisy'.

Falcon works, Stoke-on-Trent. *See* Goss, William Henry.

Falise, August (1875-1936). Dutch sculptor and medallist born in Wageningen. Falise designed models for production at *Hagen (Purmerend).
Mark: full name in relief.
Refs: Scheen; Singelenberg-van der Meer; van Straaten.

Faraday, Samuel Bayliss. *See* Mason, George Miles and Charles James.

Farkashazy, Jeno (1863-1926). Hungarian ceramist, grandson of M.*Fischer, born in Tata. He was a writer on ceramics, and his work included a book on Bernard Palissy (1887) and a history of the Della Robbia family (1896). Farkashazy bought the *Herend factory in 1896, restoring his grandfather's high standards of manufacture. Because of financial problems, he transformed the firm into a company in 1923, remaining director until his death.
Refs: see Herend.

Farnham, Surrey. Until the mid 19th century, a centre where many small potteries in Farnham and the surrounding district made domestic earthenware for sale in London which was within easy reach by water or, later, by road. Most of the potteries closed by 1870 and the only one to survive into the 20th century is that of the *Harris family at Wrecclesham. The Harris pottery maintained a close relationship (1889-1943) with the Farnham School of Art, where the pottery department was later under the direction of H. F.*Hammond in association with P.*Baron.
Ref: Brears (1971b).

Farrar, William. *See* Southern Porcelain Manufacturing Co.

Fasold & Staunch. German porcelain manufacturers producing decorative wares at Bock-Wallendorf, Thuringia from 1903.
Marks include a monogram of FS or the initials F & S; a crown on a six-spoked wheel.
Refs: Danckert; Weiss.

Favrile Pottery. *See* Tiffany, Louis Comfort.

Fearn, Samuel. *See* Derby.

Fedyashin, Iosif. Russian potter, founder of a workshop operating 1866-1918 in the *Gzhel region. He developed an agate ware body, used for tea and dinner services, inkwells, figures, floor tiles, etc. Fedyashin's factory made porcelain and a hard white earthenware from the 1870s, and in the 1880s developed a range of ware with black glaze on the exterior of vessels made in a fine, dark red body and lined with white glaze. After the late 19th century, the workshop restricted production to earthenware in a coarse white or greyish body.
Mark: Fedyashin in Cyrillic characters, 1866-1918.
Anna Fedyashin, a descendant, became chief painter at the *Artistic Ceramics Cooperative factory in Gzhel.
Ref: Ovsyannikov.

Fell, Isaac. English earthenware manufacturer. His firm, Isaac Fell & Co., produced brown-glazed or pink-lustred ware at several works in north-east England, including Carr's Hill Pottery, Gateshead (1867-71), South Hylton or Ford Pottery, Sunderland, and 1871-78 the Tyne or South Shields Pottery. Much of the output was exported to Europe.
Refs: Bell; Jewitt.

Fell, Thomas, & Co. English earthenware manufacturers working at St Peter's Pottery, Newcastle-upon-Tyne, which was built in 1817 by Thomas Fell and Thomas Bell. The company produced white earthenware or ironstone china for domestic use, with printed, sponged or enamelled decoration, and a small output of figures, also in earthenware. Printing was frequently carried out under the glaze. The output also included pearlware plates with birds or landscapes (often with sponged foliage) and borders feathered in green. The display at the International Exhibition (1862) included dinner ware, a vase, a table top, lamps and washstand ware. The firm became a limited company in 1869 and ceased work c.1890.
Marks: *Fell* or F with an anchor until c.1830; later FELL & CO with an anchor, impressed. Printed marks often incorporate the name of the pattern: *Wild Rose, Corinth, Berry, Lasso, Bosphorus*, etc., or the body used (e.g. *stone china, ironstone*) as well as the firm's name or the initials F. & CO or TF & CO.
Refs: Bell; Coysh (1974); Jewitt; Towner (1957).

Fell & Thropp. *See* Taylor & Speeler.

Fennemore, Thomas Acland. *See* Brain, E., & Co.

Fensom, David (b 1845). English-born potter working in Australia from 1862, trained under G.*Fischer. In 1877, Fensom bought the Queensland Works established three years earlier in South Brisbane, where he worked until 1899. Apart from a staple output of drainage ware, he made garden pottery shown in the International Exhibition in Melbourne, 1880, and probably domestic ware.

Fenton China Arms Ware. *See* Hughes, Edward, & Co.

Fenton, Christopher Webber (1806-65). American potter. He initially worked with his father, Jonathan Fenton, as a maker of earthenware and stoneware at East Dorset, Vermont, and entered a partnership with his brother-in-law Julius *Norton at Bennington, Vermont, 1843-47. He subsequently established a pottery (1847) making white tableware and yellow and Rockingham-glazed wares for domestic use, working independently for some months in part of the Norton premises. Fenton continued experimental production of porcelain, which had briefly been undertaken by Julius Norton. He worked in partnership, principally with businessman and lawyer A.P. Lyman (1806-83), until 1852, building a new factory in Bennington, 1850, which produced table services, toilet sets and domestic ware in white earthenware; yellow-ware kitchen utensils; toilet ware, mugs, basin, pitchers and articles such as cow creamers, caskets and boxes inscribed

for presentation with the owner's name in granite ware; decorative fruit stands and other pieces for the table in semi-porcelain (sold as stone china). The wide range of Rockingham-glazed ware included Toby mugs, jugs, bottles, pitchers, cow creamers, inkstands, soap dishes and door furniture; most of the output of jelly moulds, baking dishes, figures of poodles, hound-handled pitchers and cow creamers were Rockingham-glazed (as distinct from the more brilliant *flint enamel ware). A solid agate body was used in the production of some toilet sets, spittoons and, occasionally, decorative items such as tulip vases. The pottery also made red earthenware for domestic use, hard-paste porcelain with glossy or smear glaze, soft-paste porcelain and, after the discovery of a source of kaolin near the pottery, parian ware. Jugs were made in porcelain with relief decoration (usually floral, sometimes with figures) in white against a coloured ground (green, blue, tan, etc.) with a hammered texture.
The firm, briefly under the full control of O.A.*Gager 1952-53, adopted the title United States Pottery Co. and showed work at the New York Exhibition in 1853. After its failure in 1858, Fenton went briefly with D.W.*Clark and D.*Greatbach to the factory in Kaolin, S. Carolina, which became the *Southern Porcelain Manufacturing Co. and then to Peoria, Illinois, where Clark joined him in establishing a factory which was intended to produce on a large scale a variety of wares, including Rockingham, white and stonewares, as well as glazed brick and architectural decoration, in separate units. The first parts of Fenton's project were in operation in 1860 and 1861, making Rockingham ware and stoneware, but the company failed two years before Fenton's death in an accident.
Marks (not commonly used) included *Norton & Fenton, Bennington, Vt; Fenton's Enamel Patented 1849; Lyman Fenton & Co, Bennington, Vt*; various marks incorporating *United States Pottery Co.*
Refs: Barber (1976); Clement (1947); M.J. Nelson 'Art Nouveau in American Ceramics' in *Art Quarterly* 26 No 4 (1963); Osgood; Spargo; Watkins (1950).

Fenton, Harry. Ceramic modeller, working in England and America. At the *Doulton & Co. factory in Burslem, 1903-11, Fenton modelled table and other domestic ware. He then went to America, working at potteries mainly in Trenton, New Jersey, and became an American citizen. In 1928, he returned to Doulton's Burslem factory where he modelled Toby jugs and other jugs portraying rustic characters, as well as loving cups and presentation jugs for production in limited editions. He was also associated with Charles *Noke and L.*Harradine in the modelling of some figures.
Refs: see Doulton & Co.

Fenton Potteries. *See* Pratt, F. & R., & Co.

Fenton Stone Works. *See* Mason, George Miles and Charles James.

Ferguson, Herbert Q. *See* Cartlidge, Charles.

Fermanagh Pottery. *See* Belleek.

Feroza. *See* Owens, John B.

Ferrell or **Ferrel,** Frank L. American ceramic designer and decorator, working on the Louwelsa line for S.A.*Weller until 1905. Ferrell was a modeller, decorator and designer of industrial art ware made by J.B. *Owens for whom he became art director in 1907. He designed for *Peters & Reed after leaving Weller's firm and later worked for them as a salesman and a designer until 1917. His work included the Moss Aztec line. As art director at the *Roseville Pottery Co., 1918-54, Ferrell developed Pine Cone, Ferrella, Sylvan and many other lines which often feature floral patterns.
Marks: initials, monogram or signature, *Ferrell*.
Refs: Evans; Kovel & Kovel.

Ferrella. *See* Roseville Pottery Co.

Ferrybridge or **Knottingley Pottery.** Yorkshire pottery established near Pontefract in the early 1790s as the Knottingley Pottery, by a partnership which c.1800 included Ralph Wedgwood, nephew of Josiah Wedgwood, and the founder William Tomlinson (c.1746-1833). The works, operating as the Ferrybridge Pottery from 1804, produced creamware, printed pearlware, in imitation of Wedgwood's Queensware, marbled ware, and a variety of stoneware bodies including buff, black, and jasper ware in two shades of blue. A pattern book and other documents dating from this period have recently come to light in the Wedgwood archives at the University of North Staffordshire, Keele. After Tomlinson's retirement in 1832, Reed & Taylor of the Mexborough Reed Pottery (*see* Mexborough) took over a part of the works which was subsequently run by Benjamin Taylor and his son after the partnership with Reed split up in 1842. Transfer-printed ware then became the main product, usually in a white earthenware body, but stone china, ironstone and opaque china were also marketed. Lewis Woolf, a London retailer, leased the premises from 1851 until he became the owner in 1856. His sons built the adjoining *Australian Pottery. The Ferrybridge Pottery was leased in 1883 to Thomas Poulson (d 1893) and his brother Edward Llewellyn Poulson, owners of the West Riding Pottery nearby, succeeded in 1895 by Thomas Brown and Charles Sefton, a farmer, who purchased it in 1902. The owners traded as Sefton & Brown until the pottery became the sole property of the Brown family, and continued as Thomas Brown & Sons Ltd. The output consisted of domestic earthenware.
Marks: WEDGWOOD & CO., impressed c.1796-1801; FERRYBRIDGE impressed from c.1804; R & T c.1843-56; L.W. in many printed marks c.1856-70, sometimes with *Ferrybridge* and *Australian Potteries*; later marks also incorporate proprietors' initials.
Refs: Coysh (1972); Godden (1964); Jewitt; Lawrence; Towner (1957).

Fetisov brothers. Russian makers of earthenware and porcelain. They were the founders in 1822 of a factory at Shradinsk, possibly the first to be established in the Urals. Their output included tableware shown in the first exhibition of Russian manufacturers at St Petersburg in 1829.
Refs: Bubnova; N.N. Serebryannikov

Porcelain and Faience of the Urals (in Russian, Velca, Perm, 1926).

Ficquenet, Charles. *See* Sèvres.

fief kilns. *See* clan kilns.

Field, Thomas (c.1814-1880). Australian potter, born and trained in England. Field established a pottery in 1843, not long after settling in Sydney, where he became one of the largest producers of domestic stoneware, earthenware, chimneypots and pipes.

Fielding, S., & Co. Ltd. Staffordshire earthenware manufacturers. In 1870 the firm established the Railway Pottery in Sutherland Street, Stoke-on-Trent, for the production of majolica and black, green or brown-glazed ware. In the early 1880s, the firm introduced a line, Majolica Argenta tableware, with white body and glaze, relief decoration and painting in majolica colours; the patterns, e.g. shell and net, ribbon and leaf, daisy and fan, were used on a variety of pieces, including ice dishes, trays, cups, saucers. Some pieces of majolica were decorated with flowers and foliage modelled in full relief, naturalistically coloured, and twined around the belly of vases, etc. The firm's white-bodied earthenware, which went into production c.1880, was used for tableware and toilet sets with a variety of floral patterns and relief designs, e.g. horseshoes held by a ribbon on jugs with the handle in the form of a whip. From 1911, the firm operated the Devon Pottery in Stoke-on-Trent, using the trade name Crown Devon, among others. The firm continued to produce hand-painted decoration on vases, etc., in the 20th century.

Marks include the firm's name or initials, impressed or printed.
Refs: Andrews; Godden (1964); Jewitt.

Fife Pottery. Scottish pottery at Kirkcaldy, established as the Gallatoun Pottery in the late 18th century, and making creamware by 1805. The works, controlled by Robert Paterson and Andrew Gray from 1810, produced a distinctive, creamy white earthenware body with clear, blue-tinged glaze c.1825. Decoration included transfer-printed plant motifs, and painting in a free, vigorous style. Sprigs of flowers were often executed in magenta, black and green. J.*Methven bought the pottery after the firm's bankruptcy in 1827 and it subsequently traded as the Fife Pottery. He was succeeded in 1837 by Robert Heron, his son-in-law, who introduced Wemyss ware, a line of earthenware brightly painted by artists including K. *Nekola, and named in honour of Lady Grosvenor of Wemyss Castle. Until c.1900, the line consisted of large pieces painted against a white ground with flowers (e.g. Canterbury bells, irises, carnations, violets, sweet peas, roses, shamrock) or fruit, such as apples, citrus fruit, cherries, plums, strawberries, red currants. Flowers were depicted in a sketchy, vigorous style, which was already characteristic of the area. The ware included tall, cylindrical mugs painted with chickens, and often rimmed with painted red or green lines, and models of pigs, cats, etc. Some vases were painted with *chinoiseries*. The ware was sold through T. Goode & Co. (*see* Goode, W.J.). Later Wemyss ware, in general rather smaller, included

special commissions and pieces commemorating Queen Victoria's Diamond Jubilee, and the coronations of Edward VII and George V. Under the management of the Staffordshire potter Eric Sandland (d 1928) from 1916, the pottery evolved a more impressionistic style, sometimes using underglaze colours. Backgrounds were often black, or brushed in dark colours.

The firm Robert Heron & Sons continued until the pottery's closure in 1930, and the *Bovey Tracey Pottery Co. bought the rights to Wemyss ware designs.
Refs: Coysh (1976); McVeigh.

Fifield, William (1777-1857). English pottery painter, born in Bath and apprenticed to a glass stainer. Fifield decorated wares at the *Bristol Pottery from the early 19th century (possibly earlier than the date 1807 usually given) until 1855, becoming the factory's principal decorator. His painting of bright sprays of flowers became an important feature of the pottery's style. His work also included a tile panel depicting the pottery in 1820 and a series of plaques showing the houses of Blaise Hamlet built from 1811 for workers on the estate of Blaise Castle, Bristol. Fifield was involved in the decoration of the pottery's Mansion House service, although some pieces are printed over the glaze in black before hand painting. Sketch books used by Fifield are preserved in the Victoria & Albert Museum, London. His son John also worked at the pottery until 1849, when he emigrated to New Zealand.

Marks: signature or initials.
Refs: Owen; Pountney; C. Witt 'Good Cream Color Ware. The Bristol Pottery 1786-1968' in *The Connoisseur* 202 (September 1979).

Filey, Yorkshire. *See* Morton, John Thomas.

Finch, Alfred William (1854-1930). Painter and ceramic artist of English extraction born in Brussels, and noted for his influence on the ceramics of Finland which resulted from his teaching there. Finch studied at the Brussels academy (1878-80) and worked as a landscape painter, soon adopting elements of Impressionism in his style. He was among the founder members of the Groupe des Vingt, in the early 1880s. On a visit to England in 1886, he became associated with the Arts & Crafts Movement. He later became interested

Alfred W. Finch. Earthenware dish and mug, made at the Iris workshop, c.1900.

in Pointillism and after 1888 executed some paintings in the style of Georges Seurat. At the invitation of A.*Boch, a fellow member of Les Vingt, Finch worked as a decorator for her family in La Louvière, 1890-93. He visited England again in 1891. His early earthenware, made for the *Boch Frères workshop, was simple in style, influenced by Art Nouveau, and included vases, goblets, jugs, dishes, plates and candlesticks in a rough, red body covered with slip and glazed in ochre, fawn, dark green or blue, with spots of lighter colour and incised linear decoration. He subsequently continued to work as a painter while experimenting with ceramics (mainly glazed earthenware). He opened his own studio at Forges-Chimay in 1896. With encouragement from H.*van de Velde, he sold ceramics through La *Maison Moderne. Invited to Finland by designer Louis Sparre, who had seen ceramics signed by Finch while visiting Brussels in 1897, he established kilns at Borgå (Porvoo), east of Helsinki, where Sparre had set up his Iris workshops for the production of furniture, woodcuts, glass, and other handicrafts, as well as paintings. Finch's work was mainly utilitarian. He carried out decoration in a range of coloured slip glazes in floral or sweeping patterns, e.g. on jars with wavy rims echoed in flowing patterns in dark brown against a mottled green glaze, or with paired handles and a marine design in brown, blue and white on a green ground. Some designs were incised. From the closure of the Iris workshops in 1902, Finch was head of ceramics at a school of industrial arts in Helsinki, experimenting with complex high-temperature glaze effects on stoneware. His pupils included T.*Muona and E. Elenius. Finch taught until 1930, and abandoned ceramics to return to painting, in which he became associated with the Finnish painter Magnus Enckell.

Mark: initials, incised.
Refs: Brunnhammer *et al* (1976); *De Art Nouveau* (catalogue, Museum voor Sierkunst, Ghent, 1979); *Retrospective A.W. Finch* (catalogue, Palais voor Schoone Kunsten, Brussels, 1967); Rheims.

Finch, Raymond (b 1914). English potter. Finch studied under D.*Billington briefly at the Central School of Arts & Crafts in London and joined M.*Cardew in 1936 at the *Winchcombe Pottery, of which he became manager in 1939 and later owner. He continued production of lead-glazed earthenware, but eventually abandoned it in favour of an increasing output of stoneware. Finch concentrated on the production of domestic ware of high quality, known for its generous, sweeping shapes, mainly with pale dolomite, greenish or temmoku glazes in combination with a grey stoneware body that often develops a rich brown surface gloss in wood firing. Winchcombe pottery mark.
Refs: Cooper; Rose; Wingfield Digby.

Finlay, Ernest. Australian potter, born in Victoria. He first worked with his brother Alan as an underglaze decorator at the Epsom Pottery (*see* Bendigo Pottery), before moving to Melbourne, where the brothers built a kiln and produced thrown or moulded pots. Ernest Finlay exhibited with the Arts & Crafts Society of Victoria from 1908 until about 1913. He then moved to Sydney,

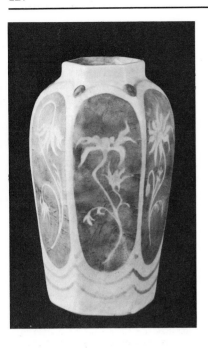

Ernest Finlay. Soft-paste porcelain vase stencilled with Australian flannel flowers against a blue ground, 1926. 20 cm high.

where he exhibited regularly with the Arts & Crafts Society of New South Wales. As early as 1921 he was experimenting with stonewares and with Chinese transmutation glazes with the colour variations controlled in such a way that they depicted Australian native flora and fauna. Finlay was a keen experimenter in ceramic techniques and produced a varied output.

fireclay. Sedimentary clays often found in association with coal measures, which may be fired at high temperatures without fusion, producing a dark-coloured ceramic body. The term is also applied to coarse refractory clays which withstand high temperatures and are therefore used in making firebricks, saggars, etc.

*Adams & Co. produced wares in a fire-clay body. Large vases, jugs, wine coolers, garden ornaments, etc. in Greek or Etruscan shapes, enamelled black in imitation of black basalt and produced at the *Caledonian Pottery, were known as fireclay ware, although they were low-fired and porous; patterns were either in relief or painted in white enamel.

Firth, John Thomas. English potter working at Mill Brow, Kirkby Lonsdale, Westmorland, from c.1890 to 1904, after training as a painter and modeller. At his own small studio, Firth initially used red clay obtained from nearby Burton, where he sent work for firing until he built his own kiln. He produced unglazed black ware, developed as the accidental result of other research, and, late in the life of his pottery, a creamy white earthenware body. He was sometimes assisted by his daughter Ellen, who carried out *sgraffito* decoration, and by his son Sydney. Firth provided pots for decoration by *Pilkington's Tile & Pottery Co.
Refs: Coysh (1976); Godden (1964); Lomax.

Fischer, Arno. *See* Ilmenau.

Fischer, Carl. *See* Bürgeler Kunstkeramische Werkstatten.

Fischer, Christian (b c.1810). Bohemian chemist and porcelain manufacturer, the son of Johann Martin Fischer, partner in the *Pirkenhammer factory. Fischer succeeded his widowed mother in the partnership in 1831, after studies in the natural sciences. Sole owner of the factory 1846-53, he bought a porcelain factory at Zwickau, Saxony, in the mid 19th century. He was a member of the Central Court Commission for the Vienna exhibition, 1873.
Ref: Meyer.

Fischer, George (b 1825). Bavarian-born potter, trained in Germany and working in Australia from 1857. He joined a pottery making terracotta and salt-glazed drainage ware in Brisbane before briefly establishing a pottery in Sydney and working in Newcastle, New South Wales. He subsequently established a pottery at Breakfast Creek, Brisbane, in the 1860s, and the Albion Pottery nearby in 1873 or 1874. His work included drainage ware, flowerpots, utilitarian domestic ware and some vases, mainly in terracotta. On his retirement in 1885, Fischer sold the Albion works to James Campbell & Sons.
Ref: Graham.

Fischer, Ignaz and Emil. Hungarian potters. After working at the *Herend factory owned by his father-in-law, M.F.*Fischer, Ignaz Fischer established a workshop (1866) in Budapest, where he made tableware, vases, sweet dishes, etc., in cream-coloured earthenware, in styles used at Herend. The ware has a yellowish-tinged, soft lead glaze. He was succeeded in 1890 by his son, Emil Fischer, who had trained in England. Emil Fischer closed his father's workshop in 1908 and briefly opened a new factory. His later wares were influenced by those of V. Zsolnay in style. Eventually, his factory turned to the production of building materials.

A variety of marks usually incorporate *Fischer* and *Budapest*; Emil Fischer's monogram occurs under a crown.
Ref: Csanyi.

Fischer, Johann Martin. *See* Pirkenhammer.

Fischer, Moritz Farkashazy (1800-80). Hungarian ceramist born in *Tata. After running a pottery in Prague, he took part in the establishment of the *Herend porcelain factory in 1838 in the hope of developing a national style that might compete with mass-produced imports on the Hungarian market. Sole owner from 1839, he was responsible for research into the materials and techniques used in copying early porcelain from the Sèvres and Meissen factories and from the Far East, developing from them lines which went into Herend's regular production. Fischer insisted on maintaining high standards at the expense of the factory's profitability, despite success in several international exhibitions which resulted in many export orders. He was ennobled by the Emperor Franz Josef in 1865 and took the name Farkashazy. He was appointed supplier to the Emperor's court in 1872. Two years

later, he left Herend to establish a small factory in Tata, where he worked until his death.
Refs: see Herend.

Fischer, Vilhelm Theodor (b 1857). Danish painter and porcelain decorator, born in Holbaeck, and trained in Copenhagen. Fischer was known for his animal studies, especially those depicting birds in landscapes. He worked as a painter for the Royal Copenhagen Porcelain Factory c.1890, and his work was shown in the Exposition Universelle in Paris, 1900.
Refs: Bénézit; Danckert; Weiss.

Fisher, Alexander. *See* Torquay Terra-Cotta Co.

Fishley family. Devonshire potters. George Fishley (1771-1865) established a workshop at Fremington, near Barnstaple, on the site of medieval and Tudor potteries. Apart from ovens and ordinary domestic earthenware, his work included animal groups, portraits, busts and figures, freely modelled and often drawn from his own experience. He also made harvest wares, but few have survived. In later years, Fishley concentrated on decorative pieces, including wall pockets and flowerpots in the local gold-brown clay, with applied decoration in white clay.

His son, Edmund Fishley (d 1861), was known for harvest jugs, made from the 1820s; most have linear *sgraffito* designs showing red clay. The use of a heart-shaped cartouche containing an inscription is a characteristic feature; these are normally below the handle, but sometimes placed across the front of pots, just above the widest part of the belly. He made puzzle jugs and also two-handled wassail cups with nearly cylindrical bodies, low-domed lids and a spout at the front for sucking out the contents. Modelled and applied decoration includes merry-making figures, a finial in the form of a fiddler, with a model of a cat.

Incised mark: *Edmund Fishley Maker* and a date.

Robert Fishley carried out similar work to that of his brother, Edmund. His *sgraffito* designs were varied, and included birds, fish, flowers and foliage, portraits, and flags. Many have inscriptions such as 'Long Life' and 'Success to the Farmer' (this occurs in a heart-shaped cartouche at the base of the handle, as in Edmund Fishley's work). Robert Fishley also made use of the stamped designs used by his father: rosettes and acorns, masks and small leaves (sometimes used to form resist patterns in a white slip ground).

Edwin Beer Fishley (d 1911), the son of Edmund, took over the pottery on his grandfather's death in 1865, and remained there until his own death. He made a wide range of wares, adopting new styles, materials and methods, but continued the production of harvest wares with red *sgraffito* patterns, and retained the family's characteristic use of inscriptions, sometimes with the recipient's name surrounded by a *sgraffito* wreath. His introductions included an iridescent glaze in several colours, usually mottled green. Like J.*Phillips (at Aller Vale), he was influenced by examples of Mycenean, Etruscan, Wrotham and early Staffordshire wares, sometimes using inscriptions and dates that suggest 17th-century manufacture, e.g. on tygs (large vessels with three or more handles) with yellow glaze mottled with green and paintings of birds and tulips.

Mark: 1860s-1906, E.B. FISHLEY/ FREMINGTON/N DEVON, incised.

William Fishley Holland (1889-1970) joined the pottery in 1902 and succeeded his grandfather Edwin Beer Fishley as manager. He sold out to a Staffordshire firm in 1912, and established a pottery in Braunton, Devon, moving to Clevedon, Somerset in 1921. His harvest jugs are carefully finished, with glossy glaze. Pulled handles have a single scroll at the base and a pad of clay at the top to act as a grip. His sons, George and William Fishley Holland both worked with him at the Clevedon pottery.

Marks: incised initials or signature.
Refs: Blacker (1922a); Brears (1971a); Coysh (1976).

Fitzroy Pottery, Pipe & Tile Works. *See* Emery, Henry.

Fix-Masseau, Pierre-Félix (1869-1937). French sculptor, modeller; born in Lyons. His ceramic designs included figures and decorative pieces for production in stoneware by A.*Bigot. E.*Lachenal exhibited sculptural pieces after Fix-Masseau's designs in 1895. Fix-Masseau became director of the Ecole Nationale d'Art Décoratif at Limoges.

Marks: incised signatures.
Refs: Bénézit; Brunhammer *et al* (1976); Haslam (1977).

flambé glazes. Ceramic glazes, usually on porcelain, which are splashed or streaked with copper reds and purples. They are among the oriental glazes which European potters sought to reproduce in the late 19th century. Research at Sèvres resulted in experimental pieces in 1848, and regular production from 1882. *Hautin, Boulenger & Co. achieved a red glaze on an earthenware body in 1877. T.*Deck exhibited porcelain with *flambé* glazes in 1880, and E.*Chaplet perfected the glaze for C.*Haviland in 1883. H.*Seger carried out research in Berlin, and experiments by B.*Moore in England with C.*Bailey led to commercial production by *Doulton & Co. in Burslem. Other producers included G.*Cox, W.*Moorcroft, W.H. *Taylor and *Pilkington's Tile & Pottery Co. in England. In America, the *Rookwood Pottery revived *flambé* glazes in the 1920s.

Refs: A.G. Bleininger (ed) *The Collected Writings of Hermann August Seger* (Easton, Pennsylvania, 1902); A. Dawson *Bernard Moore Master Potter 1850-1935* (Richard Dennis, London, 1982); C. Lauth & G. Dutailly 'Sur les Rouges de Cuivre, Les Flammés et les Céladons' in *La Manufacture Nationale de Sèvres 1879-1887* (Paris, 1889); J. Mellor in *Staffordshire Weekly Sentinel* (1st July 1905).

Flamen-Fleury. Paris porcelain manufacturers working in the rue de Faubourg Saint-Denis from the establishment of a firm by Jacques-René Fleury, who worked there from 1803. Fleury was succeeded by his widow and, in 1816, by his son-in-law, Placide-Félicien Flamen, who traded as Flamen-Fleury (noted for high-quality workmanship) until 1831. The firm's products included a tea service

flatback. Prodigal's Return. The left-hand figure has a pink cloak, the right-hand one an orange cloak and blue sash, made 1850-1900.

imitating wood marquetry; pieces in the shape of flowers, fruits or leaves (bought by the Chinese Emperor for a Peking temple); dessert services with each piece in the form of a different shell. Flamen produced tea and dessert wares, lampshades, vases, match holders and other novelty items, mainly for export.

His work was marked with his full name, often stencilled in red and surrounded by a square.
Refs: Chavagnac & Grollier; Ernould-Gandouet; Guillebon.

Flamminian ware. *See* Moorcroft, William.

flatbacks. Earthenware figures and groups made in England (especially in Staffordshire) and Scotland from the mid 19th century. Peak production occurred from the 1850s to the 1870s. The figures, intended for display on mantelpieces, etc., where they would be seen from only one side, were press-moulded in simple shapes, painted in underglaze colours or enamels, and gilded. They generally portrayed events or personalities of immediate contemporary interest, and were produced at low cost. S.*Smith was among many makers.
Refs: Oliver; Pugh.

Fleet, Theodore. *See* Eberly Pottery.

Fleming, James. *See* Britannia Pottery.

Fleury, Jacques-René. *See* Flamen-Fleury.

Flight, Joseph (d 1838). English porcelain manufacturer. With his younger brother John Flight (d 1791), Joseph Flight managed the *Worcester Porcelain Co. purchased by his father in 1783. He took into partnership M.*Barr, one of his brother's executors.

Flight's share in the factory and showroom passed to Barr's sons equally in 1840. Flight was also a painter; he had worked on porcelain and exhibited miniatures at the Royal Academy in 1801-06.
Ref: Sandon (1978b).

Flight, Barr & Barr. *See* Worcester.

flint enamel ware. In America, ware with a variation of the brown glaze developed at the *Swinton Pottery and used on *Rockingham ware. Flint enamel ware is coloured with streaks and splashes of green, orange, yellow and blue oxides sprinkled on the brown glaze before firing. The glaze was developed at the United States Pottery (*see* Fenton, C.W.) and patented in 1849.

Flögl, Mathilde. Austrian porcelain modeller and designer. Flögl studied at the Wiener Kunstgewerbeschule from 1909 until she joined the Wiener Werkstätte in 1916. She designed tableware for the *Augarten factory, e.g. a tureen in stepped, spherical shape, boldly painted with flowers (1927), but is known for the lively modelling of figures and groups in simple, stylized forms. She established her own studio in Vienna, 1931-35, before working as a teacher in Czechoslovakia, and from 1941 in Vienna. She subsequently continued work with J. *Hoffmann, and taught drawing in Salzburg, where she died.

Her work was initialled, F, or marked *Flögl*.
Ref: Neuwirth (1974a).

Florence Pottery Co. *See* Gonder, Lawton.

Florentine Mosaic. *See* Mosaic Tile Co.

Florentine Pottery Co. American pottery established 1900 at Chillicothe, Ohio, and operating from 1901 under the supervision of George J. Bradshaw (d 1902), an English potter formerly employed in America by J.B.*Owens and H.*Laughlin. The firm produced art pottery—vases, *jardinières*, umbrella stands, etc. Bradshaw's assistant, F.J.A. Arbenz, superintendent from 1902, discovered and developed a unique bronze glaze, almost identical in appearance to the metal, which was used on a line of art ware sold under the name Effeco, and exhibited at St Louis in 1904. The firm discontinued the production of art pottery, which was unprofitable, and turned over to the manufacture of sanitary ware. After reorganisation by its secretary and treasurer, F.C. Arbenz, with W.E. Eberts, in 1907, the operation moved in 1919 to a modern factory in Cambridge, Ohio.

Mark: a plant in a flowerpot with FLORENTINE/CHILLICOTHE.
Refs: Barber (1976); Evans; Kovel & Kovel; Lehner.

Florian ware. *See* Moorcroft, William.

Florsheim. German faience factory established 1765 at Florsheim. The output included decorative jugs and useful wares in peasant style, and ornamental wares such as table centrepieces. Decoration was carried out in blue and other high-temperature colours, also overglaze colours in the style of Strasbourg.

*barbotine decoration. Earthenware vase
decorated with stylized trees, made by
Doulton & Co., c.1910. 22.6 cm high.

Below:
*Arita. Plate with underglaze blue and
overglaze enamel decoration of rice plants
by Yoshinori Imaizumi, 1971. 31.5 cm in
diameter.*

Above:
*Amphora (Teplitz). Vase with Amphora
mark and Manufactured Austria, c.1900.
22 cm high.*

Below:
Awaji ware. Incense box, c.1830.

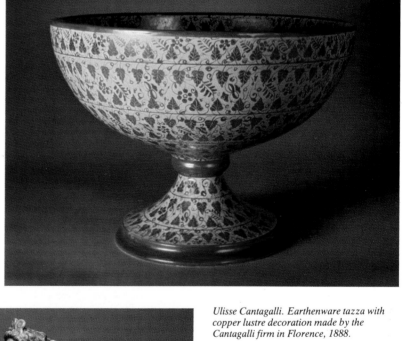

*Hannah Barlow. Salt-glazed vase made by
*Doulton & Co., with incised scenes of lions
by Hannah Barlow. Surrounding and incised
decoration by Frank Butler, c.1877.
73.7 cm high.*

Top right:
*Dora Billington. Earthenware cup, saucer
and plate designed by Dora Billington for
J. & G. *Meakin, c.1930.*

*Ulisse Cantagalli. Earthenware tazza with
copper lustre decoration made by the
Cantagalli firm in Florence, 1888.*

*René Buthaud. Femme à l'unicorne.
47 cm wide.*

Nathan Clark. Stoneware cooler with incised
and cobalt decoration made by Nathan Clark
and Ethan Fox, Athens, New York.

Below:
Susie Cooper. Earthenware plate, soup dish
and stand made at the Crown Works,
Burslem, 1937.

George Cox. Earthenware vase with mutton-
fat glaze and streaks of red and blue glazes
potted by Cox at Mortlake Pottery, 1912.

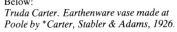

Incised marks: Mortlake, cross and crescent
device and Cox's monogram.
21.7 cm high.

Below:
Truda Carter. Earthenware vase made at
Poole by *Carter, Stabler & Adams, 1926.

*Kaj Franck. Northern Lights cup and saucer designed for *Arabia, made c.1956.*

Below:
Clément Massier. Vase, c.1900. Signed Clément Massier, Golfe-Juan. 51 cm high.

Heubach family. Magpie, porcelain, modelled by Paul Zeiller and made at the Lichte factory of Gebr. Heubach, early 20th century.

Gustavsberg. Earthenware jar, c.1933.

Below:
Joseph Meyer. Vase with incised oak tree motif and underglaze colour, thrown by Joseph Meyer and decorated by Leona Nicholson. 21 cm high.

Kawai Kanjiro. Stoneware dish, 1930s.

Left:
*Emile Gallé. Plate moulded in high relief
with six Chinamen and a fish. Signed
E. Gallé, Nancy. 58 cm in diameter.*

Below:
*Pietro Krohn. Pieces from the Heron service
designed by Krohn and made by Bing and
Grøndahl.*

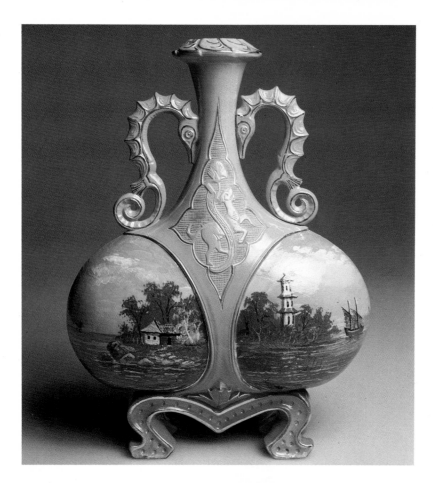

Gio Ponti. Italian porcelain vase designed by Ponti, 1927.

Below:
Charles J. Noke. Table centrepiece of mermaids modelled by Noke with raised gilding by W. Hodkinson, made by Royal Doulton for the Chicago Exhibition of 1893.

Matt Morgan. Vase made in Cincinnati by the Matt Morgan Art Pottery Co., 1882-84. 41.3 cm high.

Below:
Alfred Powell. Covered jar decorated by Powell in gold lustre for Wedgwood, 1930.

Léon Solon. Vase with girl juggling in a landscape, made by *Mintons Ltd, c.1900. Signed Léon V. Solon. 24 cm high.

Right:
Rozenburg. Octagonal eggshell vase decorated by W.P.*Hartgring and pair of octagonal eggshell cups and saucers decorated by S.*Schellink, all with year mark for 1904. Vase 16.5 cm high; cups 8 cm high.

A.G. Richardson. Vase designed by Charlotte Rhead and made by A.G. Richardson, c.1930.

Right:
Ram. Vases, the top row a set of five meant to be put on a cupboard top, with stamped marks Colenbrander RAM, Arnhem.

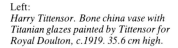

Camille Tharaud. Vase made in Limoges and signed C. Tharaud. *15 cm high.*

Left:
Harry Tittensor. Bone china vase with Titanian glazes painted by Tittensor for Royal Doulton, c.1919. 35.6 cm high.

Charles Vyse. Figure, Darling, designed by Vyse for Royal Doulton and introduced into their range in 1913. 19 cm high.

Right:
Zsolnay. Vase with light blue crystalline glaze on a white ground and with the firm's medallion mark in relief. 28.5 cm high. Lustre vase pierced and modelled in high relief with roses and other flowers and leaves, and stamped Zsolnay Pecs. 31 cm high.

Cream-coloured earthenware included allegorical and portrait figures from the late 18th century. The factory had ceased operation by 1922, when the kilns were taken down.
Refs: Honey (1952); Hüseler.

flow or **flown blue.** Transfer-printed ware with underglaze blue decoration blurred during the fusion of the glaze. The effect is a technical fault occurring in certain firing conditions, but was deliberately produced by the addition of a flux to the colour and has been much sought by collectors.

Foley, James. *See* White, Joseph.

Foley China Works. *See* Wileman, Henry.

Foley Potteries. Staffordshire potteries built by John Smith at Fenton in the 1820s and named after a local family of landowners. The premises were occupied by Elkin, Knight & Co., manufacturers of blue transfer-printed earthenware. John King Knight, the sole proprietor by 1853, took into partnership H.*Wileman, who continued the firm after Knight's retirement in 1856, making cream-coloured and granite wares, printed and sometimes lustred, and built the adjoining Foley China Works for the production of plain white or gilt-banded porcelain in 1860. He was succeeded in 1864 by his sons James and Charles, who operated the business together for two years before taking control of the earthenware and porcelain works respectively. James Wileman, sole owner after his brother's retirement in 1868, took J.B.*Shelley as a partner in the production of porcelain in 1872, and concentrated on the earthenware works from 1884 until its closure, when he retired in 1892.

Shelley and his family continued to operate the china works under the title Wileman & Co. until 1925, when they renamed the firm Shelley; the trade name Foley (also used by E.*Brain & Co.) was replaced on the firm's backstamp by a Shelley mark in 1910. Succeeding his father, who died after an illness in 1896, P.*Shelley commissioned designs from R.*Morris, notably the fluted and scalloped Dainty White range of tea ware, which was in production 1896-1966. The Dainty White shapes were among lines later decorated with coats of arms, and were also issued with a painted flower in high relief on the handles under the name Floral Dainty from 1932.

The works were extended to accommodate earthenware production in 1898, and F.A.*Rhead, art director c.1896-1905, created a number of hand-painted decorative lines, including Intarsio, which was marketed in large quantities. Earthenware display plates, vases, etc., in a variety of styles outside the named lines were marketed as 'Faience' and identified with individual artists.

The firm made pieces to commemorate events in Britain and abroad (from Queen Victoria's Golden Jubilee in 1887, and including the Battle of Waterloo) as well as a small number of model buildings, monuments, etc. in delicate porcelain and (by 1906) carefully painted models of hats, footwear, animals and war machinery, and miniature editions of the normal lines of table or ornamental ware. In World War I, commemorative pieces briefly included parian busts of military leaders, Lord Kitchener, Sir John French and Maréchal Joffre. The firm's output had earlier included glazed *sgraffito* pieces made in parian paste.

Under Rhead's successor, Walter *Slater, the firm produced Roself ornamental earthenware (introduced 1915), with a rose motif stencilled and hand finished on green, blue, grey, pink, mauve, brown or, most commonly, black. Variations included patterns of violets (introduced 1916) and carnations (1917). A more limited range of vases was brightly hand-painted with birds, (parrots, kingfishers, bluebirds), also against a black ground. Moiré Antique, a watered-silk effect printed in fine lines, was used on earthenware and porcelain from 1914, mainly in pink, blue or green.

In 1920 the firm introduced a mother-of-pearl glaze, based on bismuth, for which Walter Slater developed decorative schemes to exploit grounds of crimson, shades of blue, sea-green, purple, orange, with oriental-style patterns, especially Japanese scenes, fish, butterflies, water lilies, or Celtic geometrical patterns, and a series featuring vines and a bird on an off-white ground (Vinta). A series sold as Spano-Lustra used metallic lustres.

A staple output consisting of earthenware dinner services, utilitarian household items in earthenware or porcelain, invalid ware, and jugs, ashtrays, etc., advertising brands of whisky, accompanied the bone porcelain tea and dessert sets for which the firm became noted. Toilet sets were sold in large quantities, some in simple shapes designed by Walter Slater. Nursery ware had been introduced in 1902 with a range of nursery rhyme designs, increased to include other series, e.g. Peter Pan, and from 1925 simple patterns showing children at play by illustrator Hilda Cowham. Teasets by Mabel Lucie Attwell included pieces modelled in the shape of animals, toadstools, etc.; in 1937 a series of Mabel Lucie Attwell figures was introduced.

Queen Anne shapes, octagonal hollow ware and square plates, registered in 1926, were among the range of delicate porcelain tea ware especially associated with Shelley's in the 1920s and 1930s, when over 40 ranges of shapes were available. Some of the decorative patterns were also used on matching earthenware dinner services, and from 1937 the firm made lamp bases in earthenware or bone porcelain, with bone porcelain shades, to match table or decorative wares. E.*Slater,

Foley Potteries. Mushroom teapot from a nursery tea set designed by Mabel Lucie Attwell, 1926, and made by Shelley Potteries.

who took over from his father as art director, created further new designs for bone porcelain tea and coffee wares, which were modernistic in style. He also supervised the development of Harmony Art Ware, a hard earthenware body hand-decorated over the glaze with simple bands in graduated shades of one or more running colours (introduced 1932). The same decoration was also used on bone porcelain teasets and earthenware in ordinary production.

The firm withstood wartime restrictions, helped by the extensive export trade that Shelley and his brothers had built up for traditionally, and sometimes elaborately, styled tableware. Immediately after World War II the whole works was devoted to the production of porcelain, and the earthenware output ceased. Lithographic and photo-lithographic techniques gradually supplanted the high-quality printing and hand finishing for which Shelley's tea wares had been noted in the 1920s and 1930s. Porcelain dinner services had been introduced when, in 1939, the factory combined in production with the adjacent porcelain works of Jackson & Gosling (a branch of *Copelands), in compliance with Board of Trade restrictions, and the output continued after the war.

Having limited their participation in exhibitions to displays in the British Industrial Fairs, 1920, 1921, 1933, and the British Industrial Art Exhibition in 1920, the firm took part in the 'Britain Can Make It' Exhibition in 1946, and followed displays in four pavilions at the Festival of Britain (1951) by exhibiting in international trade fairs for gifts and fancy goods held at Harrogate and Blackpool. They responded to the fashion for streamlined shapes and swirling, chequered or dotted patterns, but continued the production of traditional styles.

Percy Shelley's nephews joined the firm, Alan Shelley in 1946 as sales director, and Donald Shelley in 1948 as technical director. Donald Shelley's developments in electrical kilns resulted in the formation of a subsidiary company, Shelley Electrical Furnaces Ltd (1956), for the manufacture of kilns on the adjoining Jackson & Gosling site (bought in 1953). Both Shelley China Ltd (the name was changed from Shelley Potteries Ltd in 1965) and the subsidiary kiln company were acquired by Allied English Potteries (*see* Pearson, S., & Sons Ltd) after the death of Norman Shelley in 1966. The Foley Works was renamed Montrose Works and turned over to producing Royal Albert bone china.
Refs: Andrews; Bunt; Watkins *et al.*

Foley works, Longton. *See* Brain, E., & Co.

folk art ware. *See* mingei ware.

folk kilns. In Japanese ceramics, the makers of utility wares to supply the everyday needs of people in provincial towns and villages. Some were in existence from the start of the Edo period (1615-1868), but production by folk kilns reached a peak in the 19th century. The potters were craftsmen of humble status and some of them worked part of their time at other occupations, such as farming. Their work was recognized in the 20th century by members of the Japanese folk art movement (*see* mingei ware).
Refs: Mizuo; Munsterberg; Okamura; Sanders.

Fomin factory. Russian factory established by 1830 at the village of Kusiaevo in the former district of Bogorodsk, probably by T. Fomin. The owner, succeeded by his sons, produced enamelled and gilded earthenware and porcelain tableware, except for a short period during the late 1850s, until the factory's closure in 1883.

Marks include Cyrillic F; *Petra Fomina* in Cyrillic characters.
Refs: Ross; Saltykov.

Fontaine. *See* Caen.

Fontana, Lucio (1899-1968). Argentinian sculptor. Fontana made some sculptural pieces in ceramics, working mainly in Italy, where he studied 1914-15 and again from 1928 in Milan. Ceramic work, carried out in the Mazzotti factory at Albissola, 1936-38, included modelled still-lifes, e.g. Pear and Bananas (1938), in earthenware. Fontana also made plaques, coated with slip and sometimes decorated in the manner of paintings with scratched lines or slits. He used terracotta for the series, Nature (1959) and Small Theatres (1964). He was among artists mainly known for work in other media who contributed to the revival of ceramic art in Italy. He provided three designs for the *Rosenthal Studio Line in 1967-68.
Refs: Hettes & Rada; Préaud & Gauthier; *Rosenthal Hundert Jahre Porzellan* (Kestner-Museum, Hanover, 1981).

Fontanille & Marraud. French porcelain decorators working in Limoges. In 1936, the decorator Martial Fontanille, who had run a workshop from 1928 in rue de l'Hermitage, engaged as director his son-in-law, Maurice Marraud. The firm specialized in luxury wares painted in coloured slip or underglaze blue, which included a range of miniature pieces. In 1942, the partners bought a small factory in rue de l'Université, where they became known for pieces decorated with reliefs in white on a blue ground. In 1947, Marraud retired, succeeded by his sons Michel and Bernard.

Marks: PORCELAINE ARTISTIQUE/FM/ LIMOGES/FRANCE; MADE IN/LIMOGES/FRANCE, between the initials and M.
Ref: d'Albis & Romanet.

Fontebasso, Fratelli. Italian ceramics manufacturers in Treviso. The firm was a family concern working under Giuseppe and Andrea Fontebasso in the late 18th and 19th centuries. The output mainly consisted of everyday, mass-produced earthenwares for sale in Italy, Greece and Turkey, but also included porcelain with greyish-tinged paste, and decorative earthenwares.

Marks include FF or G.A.F.F., sometimes with *Treviso*; a two-headed eagle; a crown over *Fontebasso/Treviso*.
Refs: Brosio; Danckert; Weiss.

Ford, Thomas and Charles. Staffordshire porcelain manufacturers working in Cannon Street, Hanley. Under the titles, Thomas & Charles Ford (1854-74), Thomas Ford (1871-74) and Charles Ford (from 1874), the firm specialized in porcelain tableware, tea, dessert and breakfast sets. Purchased by J.A. Robinson & Sons Ltd (*see* Robinson, H.T.) in 1904, the pottery operated as a branch of Robinson's firms from 1907, and

Lucio Fontana. Earthenware group entitled Fight, made in Milan, c.1951.

production later moved to the premises of *Arkinstall & Son Ltd).

Impressed or printed marks incorporate the initials TF or CF; a monogram of CF within the outline of the swan was used for about four years before purchase by Robinson.
Refs: Andrews; Godden (1964); Jewitt.

Ford City China Co. *See* Lessell, John.

Ford Potteries. *See* Maling, Christopher Thompson.

Ford & Pointon. *See* Norfolk Street works.

Ford Pottery. *See* Fell, Isaac.

Forges-les-Eaux. Several small factories were producing cream-coloured earthenware at Forges-les-Eaux (Seine-Maritime) until the late 19th century. Among the best known was that established by G. Wood. In general, the factories produced domestic ware, including bowls with sponged decoration, tobacco jars decorated with acorns, and printed ware on commemorative and patriotic themes.
Refs: Ernould-Gandouet; Lesur (1971).

Förster, A., & Co. Austrian firm established 1899 for the production of porcelain and work in other materials by the sculptor Alexander Förster, who commissioned wares from Bohemian factories to designs by himself and other artists. The work included vases, *jardinières*, etc., but Förster specialized in figures and groups, either biscuit or glazed. He developed crystalline glazes, which he exhibited in 1900. After going into liquidation in 1908, his workshop produced similar work under the firm of Busch & Ludescher. R. Busch was sole owner from 1909. The firm ended in 1940.

Mark: an insect in a circle, with FÖRSTER.
Refs: Danckert; Neuwirth (1974a).

Forster, Ellis Sidney. English potter. Forster moved from Staffordshire to work at the *Watcombe Pottery, and became a partner

in the firm of H.F. Jackson & Co. (established 1922 for the production of pottery at Barton Road, Torquay), becoming manager and later managing director (by 1926). He produced a wide variety of small pieces for the tourist trade, varying from early work decorated with roses on a trellis against a white ground, or a pale ground with thin splashes of pigment, to later pieces with decoration on a bright blue ground. The pottery's decorative designs included seagulls painted in slip standing on a brown rock, and moonlight scenes of buildings and trees or boats. The business was reorganized in 1934, but closed down in the following year.
Ref: Lloyd Thomas (1978).

Forster, J.J. *See* Prestonpans Pottery.

Forsyth, Gordon Mitchell (1879-1952). Ceramic designer, decorator and teacher, born at Fraserburgh, Aberdeenshire. Forsyth was also a watercolour painter; he trained in Aberdeen and at the Royal College of Art in London, travelling on a scholarship to study art and design in Italy. He worked as art director for *Minton, Hollins & Co., 1903-05. In 1906 Forsyth took charge of the art department at *Pilkington's Tile & Pottery Co. His designs, carried out in a vigorous, confident style, included five large vases in the firm's display at the Franco-British Exhibition, an example with a silver lustre design showing the Ride of the Valkyries against a cobalt blue ground, and others with Orpheus and the Beasts on a blue ground, a scene with the Eumenides in gold lustre against a scarlet ground, a relief design of Saint George and the Dragon on a pale blue ground, a dark green vase with a ship design and the quotation 'They that go down to the sea in ships, that do business in great waters, These see the works of the Lord/And his wonders in the deep', and another in the same colour with ribs of lustre and floral

A. Förster & Co. Porcelain vase with perforated lid, c.1900. 20 cm high.

Gordon Forsyth. Vase painted in silver and ruby lustres, made by *Pilkington's Tile & Pottery Co., 1909, with the firm's mark of bees impressed and Forsyth's mark.

scrolls. Forsyth frequently made prominent use of lettering, in mottoes or a title. Inspired by the destruction of the British section of the Brussels Exhibition in 1910 by fire, Forsyth completed a vase, painted in lustre with flames playing on twisted girders. His other work included tile panels for Liverpool Museum. As art director, he encouraged throwers to produce individual decorative designs and to sign and date their own work.

Forsyth served as a designer in the Royal Air Force, 1916-19, and returned briefly to Pilkington's before his appointment as superintendent of art instruction at the Stoke-on-Trent School of Art, where he remained until his retirement in 1945. His influence on English ceramic design was extensive and he taught many pupils, including Reco Capey, C.*Cliff, S.*Cooper, A.*Machin, Cecil J.*Noke, Eric Owen, Eric Slater, V. *Skellern, W.*Ruscoe and M.*Taplin.

He was noted for his breadth of approach in artistic education, including the social aspects of design, and a consciousness of the demands of industry. Forsyth was the prime mover in the establishment of a pottery studio at *Bullers Ltd, under the control of another of his students, A.*Potts. He also designed pottery, as a freelance, e.g. for E.*Brain & Co.; other design work included stained glass. Forsyth was art advisor to the British Pottery Manufacturer's Federation and wrote *The Art and Craft of the Potter* and *20th Century Ceramics*. His daughter Moira Forsyth worked as a potter, making earthenware figures and groups in London from 1930.

Forsyth's work for Pilkington's was marked with a painted rebus of four scythes crossed in a square.
Refs: see Pilkington's Tile & Pottery Co.

Forsyth, John, & Co. *See* Johnston, William; Port Dundas Pottery Co.

Forth Banks Pottery. *See* Newcastle Pottery.

Fosdick, Marion Lawrence (1888-1973). American sculptor, painter and ceramist. She studied at the Museum of Fine Arts school in Boston, 1900-12, and subsequently for a year in Berlin, returning to work in Boston (1914-15). At Alfred University, New York, she became professor of drawing and designs in 1915 and professor of sculpture and pottery from 1920. Exhibiting ceramics widely from the late 1930s, she won first prize in the Ceramic National Exhibition of 1941 with a stoneware bowl painted with dashes and wavy lines over concentric circles cut in the clay.
Refs: Clark & Hughto; M.L. Fosdick 'Modelled Treatment of Pottery' in *American Ceramic Society Journal* 9 (1926); J.N. Norwood *Fifty Years of Ceramics at the State College of Ceramics* (Alfred, New York, 1950).

Foster, Herbert Wilson (1848-1929). English painter and porcelain decorator, trained at the school of art in Hanley, Staffordshire, and in South Kensington, London. Foster exhibited at the Royal Academy and in Europe. He worked on both earthenware and porcelain while employed at *Mintons Ltd, 1872-93, and was among the artists concerned in Minton's Art Pottery Studio. Foster's style was influenced by the work of T.*Deck. He specialized in portraits of contemporary personalities, including members of the English royal family, actors and actresses, but also executed paintings of animals and birds. He taught at the Nottingham School of Art from 1893.

His work was normally signed.
Ref: Aslin & Atterbury.

Foucard-Jourdan. French pottery manufacturers working at *Vallauris from 1892. The family firm employed about 300 workers in the production of lead-glazed earthenware. Now with a workforce numbering seven or eight, the pottery produces kitchen and tablewares, still in local styles, using clay from nearby Claussonne, hand-thrown and fired with pine wood, under the direction of Françoise Foucard (b 1926). Some of the work is decorated with red or white slip, and the lead glaze is sometimes green in colour.
Ref: Céramique française contemporaine.

Fougeray. *See* Loc Maria.

Foulnier, Charles-Bernard-Bonaventure. *See* Ancy-le-Franc; Vausse, Faïencerie de.

Fountains Pottery, Liversedge. *See* Button family.

Fouque-Arnoux. French pottery firm founded c.1800 by Joseph-Jacques Fouque (1761-1829) working with his brother-in-law Antoine Arnoux at Toulouse (Haute-Garonne). The firm made urns, vases and utilitarian ware in faience and other glazed earthenwares, including marbled pieces, and experimented with hard-paste porcelain. Decorated ware was painted with simple designs or rimmed in yellow or blue. The output included house

numbers in 1815. The partnership was succeeded by Fouque's sons François and Henri, and his nephew (Arnoux's son), also called Antoine, who traded as Fouque, Arnoux et Cie, and moved the Toulouse production by 1832 to a branch at La Valentine, near Saint-Gaudens, which they had established in 1820 and continued until liquidation c.1860. Printed decoration, introduced c.1825, included views of the district surrounding Toulouse. Hard-paste porcelain, richly decorated and gilded, was among the work produced at La Valentine.

Fouque, followed by his sister Claire Arnoux, had made earthenwares at *Apt. Their grandson J.-F.-L.*Arnoux, son of Antoine Arnoux (*fils*), and Fouque's daughter Miette worked in England at *Mintons.
Refs: Ernould-Gandouet; E. Fouque *Moustiers et ses Faïences* (Aix-en-Provence, 1889); Lesur (1967); M. Provence 'Fouque' in *Faïence des Moustiers* (Marseilles, 1952); P.S. Wadsworth 'Fouque-Arnoux. A family of potters in England' Parts I and II in *Apollo* 63 (February, March 1956).

Fowler family. Australian potters working in or near Sydney from the establishment in 1837 by Enoch Fowler (1807-79) of a brick and tile works in Sydney, with an additional output of bottles, chemical and other industrial wares. In 1913, they took over a pottery at Longueville, near Sydney, producing an output that included, from the 1920s, Toby jugs, vases supported by a figure of a kangaroo in white clay body with transparent glaze, and free-standing animal figures, as well as a range of blue-glazed tea sets and decorative pieces, probably introduced by the Scottish potter Robert Leiper, who had gone to Sydney in 1884, and worked at the pottery first as proprietor and subsequently as Fowler's employee. Bristol-glazed furniture lifters to protect carpets from wear, chicken feeders, etc., were produced from 1910 to the 1920s.

Fowler was succeeded by his son Robert Fowler (1839-1906) and the firm remained in the control of his family (trading as R. Fowler Ltd from 1919. The Fowlers established a branch at Thomastown, Victoria in 1927, making vases with coloured glazes. The Sydney works produced household pottery including sturdy hotel wares and brown-glazed, rough-textured Langley ware. Straight-sided coffee or cocoa pots, teapots, pudding basins and storage jars in vitrified china from c.1933 had white ridged bands and handles accompanied by a coating of deep Saxe blue slip under the glaze. Lettuce green domestic ware increased the range in 1936. Jugs with relief decoration depicting hunting scenes, scrolls and dolphins, etc., were glazed in brown or blue and green.

Marks include *Fowler* impressed and stamped with the symbol of an archer, and *Australia*.
Ref: Graham; S. Mills *Fowler's Pottery* (Sydney, 1908).

Fox, Ethan. *See* Clark, Nathan.

Foxton family. *See* Littlethorpe Pottery.

Frackelton, Susan Stuart Goodrich (1848-1932). American potter and ceramic decorator, a noted pioneer in the artistic production of a refined salt-glazed stoneware.

She studied under the German painter Heinrich Vianden in her home town of Milwaukee, Wisconsin. Working as a ceramic decorator, she was a prizewinner at the International Cotton Exposition in Atlanta, Georgia, 1881, and in 1883 established the Frackelton China & Decorating Works in Milwaukee. She organized the *National League of Mineral Painters in 1892. Her own research resulted in the design of a new gas kiln described in her book *Tried by Fire* (1885) and marketed by a New York company, as well as the Frackelton Dry Colours (shades of gold and bronze) for which she won medals at a competition in Antwerp, 1894. Her salt-glazed art stoneware, made to explore the qualities of local clay and exhibited at the World's Columbian Exposition in Chicago in 1893, ranged from vases to hanging bowls decorated in a variety of styles, and included a Luck Jug with four-leaved clover and Romany inscription, modelled 1881 in a Milwaukee pottery, but not fired until shortly before the exhibition, and an olive jar about 60 cm high, with lid and stand, decorated with a fruiting olive branch in relief. Using the same stoneware body, she developed a line of ware painted under the glaze with flowers, inscriptions, etc., in cobalt blue, shown in the Paris Exposition of 1900; tiles were decorated in the same way with cherubs, windmills, ships, etc., in the manner of Delft ware. Lacking her own facilities, Frackelton sent work to potteries, e.g. in Minnesota and Ohio, for firing; she apparently abandoned pottery on moving to Chicago by 1904.

Mark: signature or monogram incised; signature often accompanied by date.
Refs: Barber (1976); Clark & Hughto; Evans; S. Frackelton *Tried by Fire: A Work on China Painting* (Appleton, New York, third edition 1905); Henzke; Jervis; Kovel & Kovel.

Franck, Kaj Gabriel (b 1911). Finnish designer of glass and ceramics. Franck studied at a Finnish school of industrial art and in 1945 joined the *Arabia factory, where he became head of a department designing household wares. His pieces for everyday use, in porcelain, earthenware or chamotte,

*Kaj G. Franck. Stoneware, the jug in the middle made from a body with a high content of chamotte, by Franck at the *Arabia factory, 1955. 6 cm, 28 cm, 25.6 cm.*

rely for decorative effect on coloured glazes and include a square serving dish composed of four inverted pyramid shapes. Franck became art director at the Notsjö glassworks in 1951.
Refs: Aro; Beard; H. Newman *An Illustrated Dictionary of Glass* (Thames & Hudson, London, 1977).

Frank & Friedheim. German porcelain manufacturers making utilitarian wares from 1924 at Freienorla, near Orlamünde (Thuringia). The firm is no longer in operation.
Marks include the initials FF; a star with monogram of PMF at the centre.
Refs: Danckert; Weiss.

Franzheim, Charles W. *See* Vance Faience; Wheeling Pottery Co.

Fraureuth, Porzellanfabrik. German porcelain manufacturers working at Fraureuth, Saxony, from 1866. The firm produced mainly utilitarian wares, but extended the output to include decorative pieces in the 1920s and 1930s, having worked as a branch of *Wallendorf, 1919-26. The factory closed in 1935.
The firm of Römer & Födisch made delicate porcelain at Fraureuth in the 1880s.
Marks include F or a monogram of PF in a circle topped by a crown, sometimes with SAXONY or FRAUREUTH, or DIE MARKE FRAUREUTH IST EINE GARANTIE on a banner.
Refs: Danckert; Weiss.

French, Myrtle. American potter who trained under C.F.*Binns, receiving her BA in 1913 and going on to further study at Alfred University. While teaching in Chicago, 1930-50, she encouraged students, who included G.*Lukens, to experiment with unfamiliar techniques and materials, while recognising the need for basic skills in craftsmanship in searching for artistic expression. She is regarded as influential in American ceramics of the 1930s and 1940s through the value she placed on artistic interchange between ceramics and other media.
Refs: Clark & Hughto; Donhauser.

French Porcelain Co. *See* d'Estampes, Abel.

Frey, Théophile. French ceramic decorator, who worked at the Sèvres factory for twelve years before joining the pottery of C.W. *Fenton in America in 1849. His work included the decoration of a granite ware jewel box with floral patterns and inscription in gold, a betrothal gift, and a number of ornamental pitchers. He was among those United States Pottery employees who attempted to start the manufacture of similar wares in West Troy, New York in 1859.
Ref: Spargo.

Freytag, Daniel. American potter working in Philadelphia 1806-24. He was working at a pottery owned by Michael Freytag, probably his father, by 1808, and remained in control until 1824. He also ran a retail outlet for earthenwares from 1818. Freytag's output included fine earthenware by 1811, when he was mentioned in a city directory as a maker of painted and gilded wares.
Refs: Barber (1976); S.H. Myers *Handcraft to Industry* (Smithsonian Institution Press, Washington D.C., 1980).

Porzellanfabrik Fraureuth. Porcelain lamp, the girl wears a yellow dress, and holds white and purple flowers. Mark: Fraureuth Kunstableitung. 51 cm high.

Freytag, Moritz. *See* Grossbreitenbach.

Friberg, Berndt. Swedish ceramic modeller. Friberg joined the *Gustavsberg factory c.1935 as assistant to W.*Kåge. His individual pieces in stoneware are decorated with glazes in subdued colours, including hare's fur.
Refs: Danckert; Lagercrantz.

Friedlander, Margarete or **Wildenhain,** Marguerite (b 1898). Artist potter, born to German and English parents in Lyons, France. After studying sculpture in Berlin, she worked as a designer in a Thuringian porcelain factory. During training in ceramics under G.*Marcks at the Bauhaus from 1919, she made functional earthenware, including moulded mugs covered with monochrome glazes. From 1925, she taught ceramics in Halle-Giebichenstein, near Leipzig, also providing designs for the Royal Berlin Porcelain Factory. After leaving Germany for Holland in 1933, the year of her marriage, she established a workshop in Putten with her husband, F.*Wildenhain. Working in stoneware, she made table services in shallow, wide forms, covered with pastel glazes and sometimes with simple decoration of concentric circles, etc., either painted or in low ribbing; kitchen ware included storage jars with white glaze and narrow bands painted in dark grey. She also designed pieces for mass production in porcelain at P.*Regout's factory. In America (where she works as Marguerite Wildenhain) from 1940, she taught in Oakland, California, running a summer school. She established her own workshops in California, at Guerneville in 1942 and Pond Farm in 1948. While her work remained functional, Marguerite Wildenhain ceased to design for mass production, stressing instead the value of a craftsman's way of life. Her pieces include urns decorated with human figures or plant motifs, which accentuate the curves of the pots. After

1955 the emphasis shifted from surface decoration and textured glazes to texture in the body achieved by incising or the inclusion of coarse sand or grog.
Refs: Bock; 'Ceramics' double issue of *Design Quarterly* 42-43 (1958); Clark & Hughto; M. Duberman *Black Mountain: an Exploration in Community* (E.P. Dutton, New York, 1972); M. Wildenhain 'Pottery as a Creative Craft' in *Craft Horizons* 10 No 2 (November 1950), *Pottery: Form & Expression* (American Crafts Council and Reinhold Corporation, 1959), *The Invisible Core: a Potter's Life & Thoughts* (Pacific Books, Palo Alto, California, 1973).

Fritsch, Andrew (1808-96) and his son, Augustus. German-born potters working in Australia from c.1851. By 1853, at their workshop at Richmond on the outskirts of Melbourne, they made red earthenware in simple shapes for domestic use. Andrew Fritsch was still working as a potter in the 1870s. His son became a brickmaker.
Ref: Graham.

Fritsch, Waldemar (b 1909). Ceramist and porcelain modeller, born in Altrohlau, Bohemia, the son of a farmer. He was apprenticed in a porcelain factory in 1924, and studied porcelain techniques in Karlsbad (1926-29) and in Prague (1929-34). In 1931, he won a grant to study porcelain modelling in Germany, where he was inspired by the 18th-century models of F.A. Bustelli at Nymphenburg, and the work of P.*Scheurich. He taught in Teplitz-Schönau, Sudetenland, and from 1939 in Karlsbad. Fritsch went to Württemberg during World War II, and in 1947 to Ansbach, where he acted as technical consultant in faience. He modelled figures as a freelance designer for the *Rosenthal workshop in Selb 1948-54. He remained as a lecturer at the art school in Ansbach until 1952, subsequently working independently as a maker of ceramic sculptures, still inspired by 18th-century German figure modelling.
Ref: Meyer.

Fritts, C.E. *See* Kiss, Charles.

frog mugs. English earthenware mugs containing realistically modelled frogs, which become visible as the liquid is drunk. Examples were made in Staffordshire and, often with a copper-lustred frog, in the north-east (e.g. at the *Newcastle Pottery), mainly in the 18th and 19th centuries.

Frugier, René. French porcelain manufacturer. After training at Sèvres, Frugier rented the Limoges factory, des Tanneries, in 1899 and became owner in 1907. He developed a heat-resistant porcelain using a high proportion of clay to fluxes, which he fired to 1430° C and made in rounded shapes, with or without decoration, for use in cooking. The ware, covered in hard glaze and resistant to sudden changes in temperature, was marketed as Aluminite; it won exhibition prizes in Paris, 1900 and 1901, and London, 1902. In 1910, Frugier enlarged his business, which he then called L'Aluminite, S.A. During World War II, he made laboratory ware to replace supplies formerly imported mainly from Berlin. He subsequently made refractory glass, but resumed production of tableware after World War II. In 1964,

Laura Anne Fry. Smear-glazed jug in a grey body with sgraffito *decoration by Laura Fry. Made at the* *Rookwood Pottery, 1881. 22 cm high.*

L'Aluminite merged with La Porcelaine Haviland in Limoges.
Marks: ALUMINITE/FRUGIER/LIMOGES FRANCE.
Ref: d'Albis & Romanet.

Fry, Laura Anne (1857-1943). American pottery decorator and designer, born in Indiana. She trained in painting, drawing, modelling and woodcarving at the *Cincinnati School of Design, 1872-76, then studied ceramic techniques in Trenton, New Jersey, and subsequently in France and England. She was among the original members of the *Cincinnati Pottery Club; her work with the club included a glazed earthenware plaque (1881) painted with birds in flight. While a decorator at the *Rookwood Pottery from 1881, she used incised decoration in a style reminiscent of H.*Barlow's, e.g. on a pitcher with a design of ducks and water lilies with cobalt blue rubbed in incised outlines, made at Rookwood and bearing the Pottery Club mark as well as the artist's initials. Laura Fry was also an instructor in the Rookwood School for Pottery Decoration, and designed some of the pottery's early forms.
In 1884, she introduced a technique of slip decoration using an atomizer, which allowed more delicate, even blending of colours than the previous method of application with a brush, and was extensively used in the laying of ground colours on Rookwood's Standard ware. Although she was granted a patent for the method in 1889, she was unable to prevent its use at Rookwood despite a court case heard in 1898. After leaving the pottery in 1887, she worked as a freelance (still occasionally for Rookwood) and as Professor of Industrial Art at Purdue University, Indiana, 1891-92. At *Lonhuda Pottery (1892-94), she continued use of her decorative technique, frequently for floral designs. She was founder of the Lafayette (Indiana) Ceramic Club, and in 1894 the Porcelain

League of Cincinnati (*see* Cincinnati Pottery Club). She continued work at her own Cincinnati studio while again teaching at Purdue University until her retirement in 1922.
Mark: monogram, LAF.
Refs: Barber (1976); Callen; Clark & Hughto; Eidelberg; Evans; Henzke; Jervis; Keen; Kovel & Kovel; Peck; H. Peck 'Amateur Antecedents of Rookwood Pottery' in *Cincinnati Historical Society Bulletin* 26 (October 1968); K.E. Smith 'Laura Anne Fry...' in *The Bulletin of the American Ceramic Society* 17 (1938).

Fry, Roger (1866-1934). English painter, art critic and founder in 1913 of the *Omega Workshop, with the aim of providing employment for artists in the production of decorative work. Fry's first experience of ceramics was gained in Mitcham, Surrey, where a maker of flowerpots threw pieces to Fry's design in 1913. He trained at the Camberwell School of Arts & Crafts in London, where the ceramics department was noted for its production of painted earthenware. Fry subsequently made tinglaze, including pieces for table and domestic use, and ornamental plates, concentrating on simplicity in shape, using a tin glaze in white, turquoise or deep blue, often without further decoration, and selling his work through the Omega Workshop. Fry experimented to improve the quality of his earthenware body, carrying out his research 1914-c.1917 at the *Carter & Co. pottery in Poole, for whom he also threw basic shapes to be produced at the pottery.
Refs: M. Haslam 'Some Vorticist Pottery' in *The Connoisseur* (October 1975); Hawkins;

Fudji or **Fujiyama** Gazo. Japanese artist working in America, who designed decoration in oriental styles at the *Roseville Pottery Co. in the early 20th century. He was the creator of the pottery's Rozane Woodland ware and variations of this line. By 1906, he was designer at the pottery of S.A.*Weller, who marketed a line, Fudzi, that was indistinguishable from the Fudji line made at Roseville, unless bearing a factory mark.
Mark: G.
Ref: Kovel & Kovel.

Fujina. Japanese pottery centre near Matsue in the Shaimane prefecture. A kiln opened at Fujina in 1764 under the patronage of the feudal lord, Narusato. Using a close-textured, greyish-white earthenware body resembling that of *Awata, the *Funaki family made both elegant pieces for the local clan, and utility wares, but specialized in tea bowls of Korean inspiration. Their output, in strong, simple shapes resembling *Hagi ware, was glazed with rich brown, resembling a glaze used in the Seto area, bluish green glaze, aventurine glazes like those of the nearby *Rakuzan workshop, or a waxy yellow with decoration in gold, red and green (which became associated with other kilns in the area). Some pieces were lavishly and delicately painted in enamel colours. Production of Fujina wares was carried on mainly by the Funaki, *Tsuchiya and Sawa families until operation ceased in 1865, after five years of decline. The workshop, revived as a folk kiln after 1925, produced tableware in Western styles under the influence of B.*Leach and developed a tradition of slip decoration and lead glazing, rare in Japan.

Other potteries in the area include Sodeshi, established in 1894 and later noted as a folk kiln, and Yumachi, opened in 1923 and making tablewares similar to the output of the Fujina kiln.
Refs: Brinkley; Mizuo; Munsterberg; Roberts; Sanders.

Fujiwara Kei (b 1899). Japanese potter and poet working in his native district of Bizen, where he established a kiln in 1937. With his teacher, *Kanashige, from whose techniques he developed a new style in decorative and tea wares, Fujiwara was outstanding among modern makers of *Bizen ware. His work, based on an intensive study of Bizen traditions and made from the local clay, includes hidasuki pieces (wrapped in brine-soaked straw rope to produce streaks of red on an underglaze surface during firing). He was designated Holder of the Technique for Bizen Ware in 1970, and in 1974 his work was exhibited in France and Belgium.
Refs: Living National Treasures; Masterpieces; Munsterberg; Roberts; Sanders.

Fukagawa Eizaiemon. Japanese potter and porcelain maker, the eighth generation of a line of potters working from the mid 17th century in Hizen. In 1856 Fukagawa inherited the family workshop, where he concentrated on the production of domestic wares until his loss of patronage in 1868. In the following year, he opened a warehouse at Deshima in Nagasaki for the sale of *Arita porcelains. He established the *Koran-sha group at Arita in 1879.
Ref: Brinkley.

Fulham Pottery Ltd. English manufacturers operating the Fulham Pottery (which was established in the 17th century by John Dwight), after its sale (completed 1891) by C.J.C.*Bailey to George Cheavin, a producer of stoneware filters. Cheavin's company made jugs, bottles, sanitary and laboratory wares, and from the 1920s a range of moulded vases and other decorative pieces alongside the output of filters; the wares were mainly

Fukagawa Eizaiemon. Dish painted in underglaze blue and enamel colours with a peony and other flowers on a bitter chocolate ground, 1879. Mark, Fuka-gawa sei. 42 cm in diameter.

Fulper Pottery. Earthenware centrepiece raised on three crouching figures with powder blue matt glaze, the bowl with streaked glaze in cornflower and midnight blue, c.1910-1912. It bears the firm's mark, printed. 19.5 cm high.

Bristol glazed. A new company formed in the 1920s included Winston Cheavin, who retired in 1969. From 1956 the firm operated mainly as suppliers of ceramic materials and studio equipment, but has continued the production of pottery to order.

Marks incorporate the name FULHAM POTTERY and LONDON or ENGLAND, impressed.
Refs: Fulham Pottery Ltd (firm's catalogue, 1983); Godden (1964); Oswald.

Fulper Pottery. American pottery operating at Flemington, New Jersey, from 1814, though late 19th and early 20th-century advertisements and a trademark registered in 1913 give the founding date as 1805. An employee, Abraham Fulper (d 1881), rented and in 1860 purchased the pottery from the executors of its founder, Samuel Hill (1793-1858), at first continuing his production of drain tiles and then making domestic articles, e.g. butter churns, preserving jars, bottles, mugs and jugs in earthenware and stoneware.

Fulper was succeeded by his sons, George W. (retired c.1911), William H. (1872-1928), Charles and Edward B. Fulper, and the firm was incorporated (1899) as the Fulper Pottery Co. Extensive experimentation resulted in the production of a line of art stoneware marketed by late 1909 as Vasekraft. In this range, the heavy New Jersey clay in normal use at the pottery was made into a wide variety of decorative ware, vases, *jardinières*, flowerholders in the form of animals, etc., candleholders, lamps, desk-sets and clock cases which were fired alongside the commercial domestic wares. Matt, crystalline, lustre or high-gloss glazes were marketed under such titles as Mirror Glaze (brownblack, tinged with green), Verte Antique (green), Alice Blue (pale blue), Elephant's Breath (grey), Violet Wisteria, Café-au-lait, Mulberry, Cat's Eye, Leopard Skin (crystals with light centres on grey or mauve ground). A group of glazes termed *famille rose*, developed by W.H. Fulper Jr and regarded as the rediscovery of an ancient Chinese secret, were used on traditional Chinese forms, sold at prices as high as $100 for one piece; peach bloom, shades of rose, apple blossom and a deep, matt rose pink ware included in the line. Some examples of the firm's art

Fulper Pottery. Lamp. 48.3 cm high.

ware were made in weighty forms, regarded as 'sometimes too odd' by an American critic in 1916.

Under the technical supervision of J.M. *Stangl c.1911-c.1915, the Fulper company further expanded the range of glazes and won an award at the San Francisco Exposition in 1915. During World War I, the pottery introduced unglazed dolls' heads and bodies which were produced until 1921; life-sized heads were also made for retailers' use in display.

A new factory in Trenton, New Jersey, working from 1928, and a second factory in Flemington increased production to compensate for the loss of the original Flemington plant and a large quantity of stock in a fire in 1929. After its purchase by Stangl in 1930, the firm produced a limited amount of art ware until 1935, when the remaining Flemington works closed. The company continued to produce lamps, vases, flowerpots, ash trays and other gift ware at Trenton, as well as oven-proof domestic ware, and changed its title in 1955 to the Stangl Pottery Co.

Marks: versions of *Fulper* moulded, impressed or printed.
Refs: Clark & Hughto; Evans; Kovel & Kovel; *Stangl: A Portrait of Progress in Pottery* (privately printed, New Jersey, 1965).

Funaki family. Japanese potters working at *Fujina. Yajibei Funaki (d 1773) and his descendants Shinzo (d 1803), Kakusaburo (d 1825) and Kenemon (d 1856) worked under the patronage of the feudal lords. Despite the decline of the kiln and the downfall of the clan system in 1868, Funaki V (also named Kenemon) was still active at Fujina in the early 20th century, and the kiln became the most prominent at Fujina after 1925. Michitada Funaki was among the potters of the *mingei movement. Inspiration for his work came from Korean wares and, under the influence of B.*Leach (who worked briefly at Michitada's pottery), slipdecorated English earthenware, e.g. large, oval dishes with combed slip decoration and items for table use in both Japanese and European traditions. He frequently used yellow or cream lead glazes. His son Kenji

Funaki (b 1927) also continues to work the Fujiyana Pottery at Fujina. Kenji's work includes plates, dishes and tiles with designs of animals, e.g. horses, poultry, fish, and octopus, painted in slip. He, too, uses lead glazes and traditional techniques. Other branches of the Funaki family worked at other factories in the neighbourhood.
Refs: Brinkley; *Contemporary Japanese Ceramics* (Kodansha, Tokyo, 1975-77); Mizuo; Munsterberg; Sanders.

Furada. *See* Weller, Samuel A.

Furman, Noah. American stoneware maker. Owner and shipper of clay deposits from Cheesequake, Madison, New Jersey (then South Amboy) near a pottery which he operated from c.1840 until its destruction by fire in 1856.
A piece of stoneware marked N FURMAN 39 PECK SLIP NY (probably a sales address) is decorated with a spray of leaves in black on a light brown ground. Another mark, on a cylindrical jug, gives the place name SOUTH AMBOY.
Refs: Stradling; Webster.

Furnival, T., & Sons. Staffordshire earthenware manufacturers working from 1851, and the owners of two Cobridge factories, where they produced utilitarian, printed granite ware and ironstone china, and decorated toilet sets, for export to Europe and North America. The company also made ironstone tableware, decorated for the home market, and dinner services in plain shapes with delicate *intaglio* moulded decoration filled with glaze to provide a smooth surface. The firm's Swan and Nautilus services were gilded and enamelled. Some unglazed ware was sold for decoration by amateur artists. The firm traded as Furnivals Ltd, 1913-1960s. The factory closed in 1968, but the name and some patterns were purchased by Enoch Wedgwood Ltd (*see* Wedgwood & Co.).
A variety of marks incorporate *Furnivals*.
Refs: Blacker (1922a); Jewitt.

Furoken Kamefu. *See* Yosabei II.

Fürstenberg. German porcelain factory established 1747 under Duke Charles I of Brunswick. The factory was noted for the

Funaki family. Tile decorated in treacle-brown and cream slips under an amber glaze, mid 1950s. 13.5 cm square.

Fürstenberg. Porcelain mocha jug designed by W.*Wagenfeld for Fürstenberg, 1934.

quality of its painting, which included landscapes and allegorical subjects by the painter Heinrich Christian Brüning, who worked at Fürstenberg, 1797-1855. Modelling in rococo style was developed under the direction of L.-V.*Gerverot. The firm was in private ownership from 1876 and modernized in the late 1880s. The later output included everyday tableware and services to designs e.g. by W.*Wagenfeld, as well as copies of the factory's earlier productions.
Marks: the initial F, sometimes with a crown; export wares from c.1915 have F and a crown inside an oval band bearing BRUNSWICK/GERMANY.
Refs: Danckert; Ducret (1965); *Fürstenberg Porzellan aus 3 Jahrhunderts* (catalogue, Kestner Museum, Hanover, 1956); C. Scherer *Das Fürstenberger Porzellan* (Brunswick, 1965); Weiss.

Futagawa. Japanese folk pottery in Fukuoka prefecture, Kyushu, established in the late 19th century as a branch of the Yumino kiln (*see* Osotoyama) and now maintaining the traditions of takeo *Karatsu ware. The output includes water pots, storage jars, large mixing bowls and other domestic articles with white and dripped brown or amber glazes. Many pieces are decorated at the base with finger-wiped wavy lines. The pottery is also associated with large bowls used in wax making, with pine trees brushed in green and brown on white slip.
Ref: Okamura.

Gádor, Istvan (b 1891). Hungarian artist and potter who studied in Vienna (1910), and initially worked as a sculptor, exhibiting regularly in Budapest, 1912-18. He was making pottery by 1914. He left Hungary in 1919, after the overthrow of the republic, and became a member of the *Wiener Werkstätte. On his return to Hungary, he continued to experiment in ceramics, concentrating on glaze techniques, and held one-man shows in Budapest (1921 and 1922). His work, mainly animal figures, influenced both by expressionism and by primitive art, stressed the characteristic features of subjects to the point of caricature.
From the late 1920s, Gádor was increasingly influenced by the traditional shapes and decoration of Hungarian peasant pottery;

he made vases and dishes painted with birds, flowers etc., and later with human figures. Simply modelled figures and groups were taken from village life or fairy tales.
In 1934 he joined a group of artists aiming to express socialist principles and produced a series of figures representing workers, and a large low-relief panel entitled Labourer with Wheelbarrow. He decorated his pottery with geometrical designs trailed in slip over the whole vessel, and later with bands of birds or animal motifs. Other ornament included stylized or realistically depicted birds, fish or flowers, and scenes of village life.
Gádor was a professor at the Hungarian academy of applied arts from 1945. Later work, in various styles, included a series of animal figures painted with flowers, realistically modelled figures and groups, and brightly coloured pottery after traditional peasant ware. Asymmetrical vases, either hand-modelled or thrown, often based on the female form, were covered with glossy, matt or crackle glazes, sometimes with painted decoration. Other vases were made in elongated shapes, covered with bright monochrome glazes. Large dishes and plates have simple line paintings of still life, buildings, fish, or birds, with careful employment of coloured glazes.
Refs: Az I. Magyar Iparmuveszeti Kiallitas Katalogusa (catalogue of first exhibition of applied arts in Hungary, Budapest, 1952); A. Dobrovits *Gador Istvan muveszete* (Budapest, 1955); I. Pataky-Brestyánszky *Modern Hungarian Ceramics* (Corvina, Budapest, 1961).

Gager, Oliver A. (c.1825-89). American ceramic retailer in New York. Gager invested in the firm established by C.W.*Fenton c.1851, and the business traded under the name O.A. Gager & Co. for a short time from late 1852 until the formation of the United States Pottery, a continuation of Gager's firm, in which he participated in 1853. Gager was also a member of the firm A.A. Gilbert & Co. which resumed operation for a year in the premises of the United States Pottery three months after that company's closure. Gager took over the retail business of C.F.*Haviland in the early 1870s.
Ref: Spargo.

Gallatoun Pottery. *See* Fife Pottery.

Gallé, Emile (1846-1904). French designer, glass artist and potter; the son of Charles Gallé Reinemer, a producer and retailer of decorative glass and earthenware at Nancy (Meurthe-et-Moselle). Gallé learned pottery techniques and worked as a decorator at a faience workshop acquired by his father c.1850 near Saint-Clément. He also studied in the glassworks of Burgun, Schverer & Co. at Meisenthal (Alsace-Lorraine). After brief infantry service in the Franco-Prussian War (1870-71), he travelled in Europe, visiting London and Paris before returning to head the family glass and faience business on his father's retirement in 1847. He established a small studio at his home in the same year, initially making earthenware later experimenting with stoneware and porcelain.
Gallé's tin-glazed earthenware included *jardinières*, vases, candlesticks and tableware,

which were painted with heraldic emblems, sprays of flowers, game, landscapes with figures, etc. There were other motifs which in general recalled the decoration of 18th-century French faience, and some of Japanese inspiration, e.g. fans, blossoms, seals. His pieces were often large in size. Gallé also continued the production, started by his father, of figures of heraldic animals, notably lions, holding candlesticks or inkstands, and made from 18th-century moulds. Other animal figures included smiling, glass-eyed cats, their bodies painted with spots, hearts, small flowers, or other repeating patterns, on yellow, brown or green grounds; dogs and birds (owls, parrots) also occur. Gallé exhibited experimental pieces with *sgraffito* decoration in 1884 and at the Exposition Universelle, 1889. He sometimes used a thin coating of gold, silver or platinum under a coloured glaze with moulded decoration, or achieved an iridescent effect using metal in the form of powder or small filings. This appears as decoration which features the insects and plant forms also used on Gallé's glass and other ceramics, e.g. dragonflies with trefoil plants painted against a scale-patterned ground on a rounded vase, or insects in relief on the sides and top of an open-sided *jardinière*.

As the leader of a group of artists (Ecole de Nancy) working in the 1890s, who drew inspiration from his techniques and style, Gallé became a figure of importance in glassmaking, for which he is chiefly known, also producing furniture from 1884. After his death from leukaemia, Gallé was succeeded by his wife and daughters until his son-in-law took over the firm in 1905.
Refs: J. Bedel 'Emile Gallé, cet inconnu' in *Guide des Antiquités* 40 (1968); Brunhammer *et al* (1976); L. de Fourcaud *Emile Gallé* (Paris, 1903); H. Demoriane 'Le cas etrange de Monsieur Gallé' in *Connaissance des Arts* (August 1960); E. Gallé *Ecrits pour l'Art* (Henri Laurens, Librairie Renouard/Berger et Levrault, Paris/Nancy, 1908); P. Garner *Emile Gallé* (Academy Editions, London, 1976); B. Hakenjos 'Arbeiten von Emile Gallé in Kunstgewerbemuseum Köln' in *Wallraf-Richartz-Jahrbuch* 31 (1969); Hakenjos (1974); Heuser & Heuser; Lesur (1971).

Gallen-Kallela, Axel. *See* Arabia.

Gallimore, William Wood. English-born ceramic modeller and designer, the son of an engraver and colour maker. Gallimore worked for a solicitor in Burslem, Staffordshire, while studying in the evenings at Stoke-on-Trent art school. He subsequently learned modelling and design in a Burslem studio and then under a French artist, Louis Kremer. He became noted for his studies of children and cupids, usually depicted in a pastoral setting. He worked at the Belleek factory and continued modelling despite the loss of his right arm in a shooting accident. He was among the employees of the W.H. *Goss who left with W.*Bromley (1863) to assist in developing the products of the Belleek factory. After his return he modelled portrait busts (including one of the ceramic historian Llewelyn Jewitt) for production in parian ware by Goss. He settled in Trenton, New Jersey, and succeeded I.*Broome as designer and modeller at the

Emile Gallé. Falcon made in faience, with plumage painted in yellow, blue and brown, signed Emile Gallé, Nancy, with a shield monogram. 32 cm high.

*Trent Tile Co., 1886-c.1893. While there, he modelled the coat of arms of the state of New Jersey for architectural use, and a large tile panel with figures in relief. He also designed vases, etc., for the Ceramic Art Co. of W.S.*Lenox. Gallimore supervised his sons William and Jesse in their establishment of a design and modelling workshop. His daughters Flora and Marian worked as modellers of floral relief decoration.
Refs: Barber (1976); Kovel & Kovel.

Galloway & Atkinson. *See* Ouseburn Bridge Pottery.

Galluba & Hoffmann. German porcelain manufacturers at Ilmenau, Thuringia, from 1888. The firm, no longer in operation, made luxury wares, figures, etc.

Marks include a cross with divided foot and often incorporate the initials G & H; GALLUBA, vertically in a rectangle, or a shield bearing initials also occur.
Refs: Danckert; Weiss.

Gambone, Guido (1909-65). Italian ceramic artist born in Avellino. Gambone worked in a studio at Vietri sul Mare from 1925 and taught himself pottery techniques. He was in Florence from 1950. His work included stoneware in unusual forms, e.g. a bottle flattened between sheets of white-glazed clay with sparse decoration in blue, and bowls with distorted rims, or sculptural pieces, such as a mother and child fashioned from flattened strips of earthenware (1954).
Mark: GAMBONE/ITALY.
Refs: Hettes & Rada; *Keramik* (catalogue, Kunstgewerbemuseum, Cologne, 1975); Préaud & Gauthier.

Gambut, Emil. *See* Palissy ware.

Garde, Fannie. *See* Bing & Grøndahl.

garden kilns. *See* courtyard kilns.

Gardner factory. Russian hard-paste porcelain factory established at Verbilki, to the north of Moscow, by the English businessman Francis Gardner (d 1796), who had worked in the timber trade since settling in Russia in 1746. Gardner established retail outlets for his own porcelain in Moscow and Tver. Firing with wood from the forests surrounding Verbilki and using clays from nearby Dmitrov, the factory initially employed foreign artists and technical experts, including the painter I. *Kestner from the *Meissen factory and the Swiss chemist Franz Gartenberg (who went on to the Imperial factory at St Petersburg in 1803), but gradually replaced them with Russian workers, mainly serfs. The 18th-century production included figures of Russian peasants and artisans, sometimes taken from costume prints (e.g. the popular city and provincial characters in Zelentov's engravings for the magazine *Magic Lantern*, published 1817-18) and in the 1860s a series devoted to Gogol's *Dead Souls*. Figures of the early 19th century were brilliantly glazed and stood on circular or rectangular bases banded in gold. The bases of later examples (c.1830-c.1860) were scrolled, or represent earth. Both underglaze and overglaze colours were often used on the same piece. Neoclassical shapes persisted in tableware, tea and coffee sets, and painted decoration was mainly restricted to portraits (war heroes, etc.), rustic scenes, views of St Petersburg, a

Guido Gambone. Tall earthenware bottle with patterns painted in coloured glazes, c.1954.

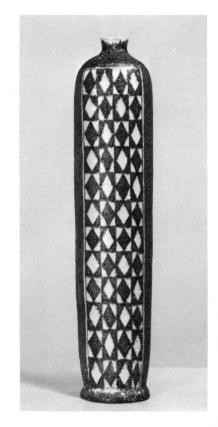

Gardner factory. Biscuit porcelain figure of a cobbler, mid 19th century. Marked with an eagle and medallion in red with the factory mark impressed. 12.5 cm high.

series of military cartoons, floral designs, etc. Mass-produced teaware, with red roses in white reserves on grounds of blue or green, was much exported after c.1850.

Francis Gardner was succeeded by his son and then his grandson, Alexander, as head of the factory. Alexander Gardner's successors sold their interests in the firm to their uncle, Peter, who formed a corporation in 1857 with his own sons, Vladimir, Alexander and Pavel (d 1869), subsequently trading as the Gardner Porcelain and Faience Co. Experiments started in 1829 had resulted in the commercial production of white earthenware by 1833, and semi-porcelain, for a large range of dinner services and tea sets with painted or printed decoration and, less often, relief ornament. In the period between 1847 and 1853, the factory's production of white-bodied earthenware was greater than the output of porcelain. The firm's semi-porcelain was praised in the report of the ninth exhibition of Russian manufacturers in 1849, and won the firm the right to incorporate the state emblem in its mark after the tenth exhibition in 1853. Some of the pieces were made in intricate forms with curved rims, moulded relief ornament and curled handles, lavishly painted with floral designs, e.g. a teapot now in the Russian state museum of history. Designs became more restrained in the 1870s and 1880s.

Under Pavel Gardner who had succeeded his father as head of the factory in 1862, the firm provided training for its own porcelain painters in the 1870s, sending the talented children of workers to study in Moscow. After becoming part of the *Kuznetsov combine in 1891, the factory continued under the Gardner name, mass-producing porcelain for the home and foreign markets, with decoration mainly restricted to mechanical processes such as transfer printing.

The factory was nationalized after the October revolution in 1917 and traded as the Dmitrov porcelain plant, at first continuing pre-revolutionary forms decorated with flower patterns. In 1938, a research studio was formed to improve the firm's artistic achievement. Designers included S. Orlov. The production of sculptural and artistic pieces ceased during World War II, and the firm now specializes in tea and coffee sets.

Marks: the Roman or Cyrillic initial G; various marks incorporating the name Gardner in Cyrillic characters.
Refs: B. Alekseev *Porcelain* (in Russian, Kuskovo guidebook, Moscow, 1958); Cherny; R. Hare 'Porcelain of the Russian Empire' in *The Connoisseur* (October 1958); G. Lumkomskij *Russischer Porzellan* (Berlin, 1924); A. Popoff 'The Francis Gardner & Other Russian Porcelain Factories' in *The Connoisseur* 96 (August 1935); D. Roche and I. Issaievitch *Exposition de céramiques russes anciennes* (catalogue, Sèvres Museum, 1929); Ross; Saltykov.

Gardner, Peter. *See* Dunmore Pottery.

Gareis, Kühnl & Co. German porcelain manufacturers making household porcelain, vases, and mass-produced ornamental pieces at Waldsassen (High Palatinate) from 1899.
Various marks incorporate the initials GKC or GKCO.
Refs: Danckert; Weiss.

Garibaldi, G. *See* Richard-Ginori, Società Ceramica.

Garrison Pottery. English pottery established near the barracks at Sunderland in the early 19th century, rented, and by 1813 owned, by John Phillips, who in 1815 took over the works established by the *Maling family in North Hylton. The two potteries worked in amalgamation until the closure of the North Hylton Pot Works in the 1840s under Phillips's successors (*see* Dixon, Austin & Co.). The last owners, Dixon, Phillips & Co., dissolved their partnership in 1865, and the pottery closed. Printing plates and moulds were purchased by the *Deptford Pottery.

The Garrison Pottery produced a large variety of sponged, printed, painted and lustred earthenware for the home and export markets. Orders for brown ware were passed on in the pottery's later years to the works established by T.*Rickaby. In addition to commemorative queensware, the firm produced figures of the child Samuel, Joan of Arc, Napoleon, the Duke of Wellington, the Seasons, Shepherds, Highlanders, etc., busts of Lord Nelson, John Wesley, models of lions with large teeth, greyhounds and comforter dogs of the type made in Staffordshire, and such items as cockle plates, pin boxes, eggs, carpet bowls, rolling pins, stands for clocks and watches. They also made ranges of lustre ware jugs, plates, etc., painted with houses, as well as yellow ware with transfer-printed patterns. Some pieces were decorated with views of the Wear Bridge.
Marks incorporate the names of the firms, *J.Phillips, Sunderland*; *Dixon Phillips & Co.* (enclosing an anchor); DP & Co. impressed square mark.
Refs: Jewitt; Shaw.

Garrive, Jean and Henri. *See* Angoulême.

Gartenberg, Franz. *See* Gardner Factory.

Gärtner, Hanna (b 1899). Austrian sculptor and ceramic modeller trained at the Vienna Academy and under F.*Barwig at the Wiener Kunstgewerbeschule from 1916. She modelled a Girl with Cat in terracotta in 1927, and provided a number of models for the *Augarten factory.
Ref: Neuwirth (1974a).

Gasper, P. Paul. *See* Cook Pottery Co.

Gates Potteries. *See* American Terra Cotta & Ceramic Co.

Gates, William Day (1852-1935). American potter, trained as a lawyer, called to the bar in 1879, and practising in Chicago. He established the *American Terra Cotta & Ceramic Co. at Terra Cotta, Illinois, for the manufacture of drain tiles, brick and terracotta for architectural use. Gates designed many early shapes for the artware which was made experimentally from 1895 and produced commercially from 1901. His sons, William Paul and Ellis Day Gates, with Elmer Gorton, all graduates in ceramics from Ohio State University, carried out most of the research leading to the introduction in 1901, on a commercial basis, of art ware which had been made experimentally under the name Teco from 1895. W.D. Gates devised many of the early shapes, mainly flower vases, and employed a number of artists and architects as designers, building up a repertoire of over 500 forms by 1910. He was also a contributor to F.H.*Rhead's periodical *The Potter* on such subjects as clay, glazes and firing. He sold his pottery c.1930.
Refs: Donhauser; Evans; Kovel & Kovel.

gaudy ware. Brightly painted English wares produced for export to America. White earthenware plates and tea ware made in Staffordshire c.1810-c.1830 were sold in large quantities to the Pennsylvania German market and termed Gaudy Dutch. Flower-patterned transluscent tea ware made in Wales, particularly the Swansea area, c.1830-c.1845, became known as Gaudy Welsh.

Gauguin, Jean (d 1961). French ceramic modeller, the son of P.*Gauguin; he became a naturalized Dane in 1909. Gauguin worked at the *Bing & Grøndahl factory, becoming chief designer and modeller. He created many sculptural pieces, noted for their animation and vigour and often representing animals; he also made vases, covered jars, etc., sometimes with finials modelled in the shape of animals. Gauguin frequently worked in a fireclay body, which he called *roche céramique*, leaving the surface unglazed, or using brilliant and varied glaze effects.
Refs: J. Bing *Bing & Grøndahl/Copenhagen Porcelain* (Bing & Grøndahl Porcelain Ltd, Copenhagen, c.1978); Cox; Forsyth; Hiort.

Gauguin, Paul (1848-1903). French painter, sculptor and graphic artist, who worked in ceramics briefly in the late 19th century. In collaboration with E.*Chaplet at the rue Blomet studio between May or June 1886 and April the following year, he decorated stoneware, often cylindrical vases and mugs from Chaplet's normal output, with Breton scenes featuring figures, sheep or geese and trees, painted in distinctive coloured glazes, contained within greasy resist that fired to a

Jean Gauguin. Stoneware group, 20th century. 65 cm high.

firm, dark outline, a standard technique at Chaplet's workshop. Gauguin also made freely, and sometimes rather clumsily modelled vases, mugs, etc., in the workshop's dark stoneware body, often with long rolls of clay looped and attached as handles or linking separate vessels to form one piece. Again at the rue Blomet workshop on his return from Martinique in November 1887, Gauguin made portrait vases with incised designs and painted slip, and bowls and dishes with modelled figures (e.g. female nude stepping down to bathe). As the quality of Gauguin's modelling improved and his technical skill with clays and glazes increased, his work became more sculptural. Self portraits with trickles of red colour in the glaze, and figures including Eve and Black Venus were made 1888-89; apart from some figures in stoneware made on a brief visit to Paris in 1893-95, these were Gauguin's last ceramics.

Marks: signature, P.GO or P. Gauguin, sometimes with mark of Chaplet and, in the case of the earliest pieces, a Haviland factory mark.
Refs: M. Bodelsen Gauguin's Ceramics in Danish Collections (Munksgaard, Copenhagen, 1960); Brunhammer et al (1976); Camart et al; J.& L. d'Albis & C. Romanet Ernest Chaplet, 1835-1909 (Presses de la Connaissance, Paris, 1976); C. Gray Sculpture & Ceramics of Paul Gauguin (John Hopkins Press, Baltimore, 1963).

Gaul, August. (1869-1921) German animal sculptor. In 1922, fifteen pieces by Gaul were bought for production in red stoneware and white porcelain at *Meissen. The figures, including lions, bears, a dog, a seagull and game animals, though monumental in style, convey an impression of vitality. The firm of *Rosenthal bought twelve of his models in

1928 and 1929 for production in porcelain and stoneware.
Refs: see Meissen; Thieme-Becker.

Gauldrée-Boilleau, Charles-Théodore. See Magnac-Bourg.

Gauthier, S. See Sèvres.

Gautier, Marie. See Decoeur, Emile.

Gävle. See Upsala-Ekeby.

Gay Head Pottery. American souvenir ware produced by W.F. Willard with several assistants at Martha's Vineyard, Massachusetts, from c.1879. Vases were thrown in mixtures of the differently coloured clays (red, blue, grey and buff) found on the western end of the island, scraped to reveal the marbled streaks of clay, and then allowed to dry naturally in the sun. Other articles made in the red clay were fired, but lost their colour in the kiln.
Mark: Gay Head impressed on the side of the piece.
Refs: Barber (1976); Evans; Kovel & Kovel; Watkins (1950).

Gazzard, Marea (b 1928). Australian artist potter, born in Sydney. She studied ceramics at the National Art School in Sydney, and then at the Central School of Arts & Crafts, London (1955-58). She lived (1959-60) in Montreal, Canada, where she had her first exhibition, then established a workshop in Australia and has exhibited regularly since 1963. In 1973, Marea Gazzard was appointed first Chairman of the Crafts Board of the Australia Council. She also served as Vice President of the World Crafts Council, Asian Region, and was later the Council's President. She makes large, coil-built sculptural forms which are intended, when grouped together, to evoke particular environments. Some evolve from geographical locations, e.g. her Uluru series, introduced 1973, which is based on the area around Ayers Rock and the Olgas in central Australia.
Refs: Recent Ceramics, An Exhibition for Australia (travelling exhibition in Europe, Crafts Board for the Australia Council/ Department of Foreign Affairs of the Australian Government, 1980); P. Thompson Twelve Australian Craftsmen (Sydney, 1973).

G.D.A. (Gérard-Dufraisseix-Abbot). French porcelain manufacturers at Limoges, successors to C.F.*Haviland in the firm established in the late 18th century by F. *Alluaud. The partnership of Emile Gérard, Jean-Baptiste Dufraisseix (decorator), and a colour technician, Morel, took over Alluaud's company with Gérard as director and Dufraisseix remaining as partner after the withdrawal of Morel in 1890. The firm's American agent, Edgar Abbot, became a director in 1900. From 1884, the partners steadily improved the firm's efficiency and output. Morel, who specialized in high-temperature colours, enlarged the palette of grey, brown and mauve, to include bright clear colours including blue, yellow, pink and green, which were used on a table centre-piece by A.*Dammouse with modelling by E.*Hexamer in 1892. From 1901, the firm produced ceramics for sale by S.*Bing, including designs by E.*Colonna, and G.

*de Feure, and opened a Paris branch by 1902. After the financial crisis of 1929, G.D.A. purchased *Haviland & Co., but the firm's rights to models and marks were returned to the Haviland family in 1941. G.D.A. continued to operate in the Alluaud factory, the oldest remaining works in Limoges, under the direction of Raymond Clappier, a descendant of Gérard, from 1950.

Marks include LEUCONOË printed on work produced for Bing, but usually incorporate the initials G.D.A.
Refs: Brunhammer et al (1976); d'Albis & Romanet.

Gebauer, Walter (b 1907). German studio potter born in Thalbürgel, near Bürgel, Thuringia. Gebauer trained under his father in the workshop of his uncle, Carl Gebauer, before studying (1925-27) in Bunzlau, at a stoneware factory in Bonn, at the state factory in Karlsruhe, and in Lanzburg, Switzerland. He worked for the Munich Werkstätten, 1930-31, and established his own workshop in Bürgel in 1934. His output consisted of traditional slip-painted earthenware fired in a wood-burning kiln and, later, simple, unglazed ware with incised and applied decoration. After extensive research in bodies and glazes, he produced wares from a variety of clays, fired at about 1200°C, with glossy, matt or silk-textured glazes in muted pastel shades of beige, yellow, light blue and green. From 1946, when he resumed work after World War II, Gebauer worked with textured glazes, in an increasing range of colours, including a luminous blue. His work is mainly thrown, but also includes architectural wares.
Mark: WG over Bürgel, impressed with circular stamp; unique pieces initialled WG.
Refs: Bock; Hettes & Rada.

Gebleux, Léonard. See Sèvres.

Geddes, John; Geddes, Kidson & Co. See Verreville Pottery.

Gehren. Porcelain factory established near Ilmenau in the early 1880s by Theodor Degenring, formerly at Eisenach. Until World War I, the firm produced mainly bottle tops, egg cups, large kitchen spoons, whisks, etc. After 1920, under a new director, Preissler, the factory turned to the production of utilitarian ware, children's sets, bowls, book-ends and figures of dancers, animals, etc., with an increasing production of stoneware in the 1930s. The firm now operates as the Thuringian porcelain workshop at Gehren, formerly Günthersfeld.
Marks: a circular stamp with crossed swords and the initial G; later, a circle with PG crossed by a sword, with a crown and Günthersfeld.
Refs: Danckert; Scherf.

Geiger, Paul. See de Geiger, Baron Alexandre.

Gekka. See Bizan.

Gelria. Dutch art pottery established in 1926 at Arnhem by H.C. Oud, N. Koerse and K.*Vet (who was director until 1931) for the production of simple ornamental ware after types already made in Arnhem and Gouda. The factory closed in 1932.

Marks incorporate ARNHEM/HOLLAND and sometimes GELRIA.
Ref: Singelenberg-van der Meer.

Gen Asao. *See* Sozen II.

Gen'emon, Aoya or Awaya (1791-1863). Japanese potter and porcelain maker, born in Komatsu, Ishikawa prefecture, and noted for his contribution to the revival of *Kutani ware. He trained in Kyoto and after studying under *Honda, assisted in the development of the *Yoshidaya and *Ono kilns, and helped with the establishment of the *Rendaiji kiln in 1847. Gen'emon's work at his own kiln included porcelain bottles, incense burners, etc., resembling the wares of the Yoshidaya kiln. He also made earthenware with a coarse, soft body resembling raku ware, painted in enamel glazes over a coating of white slip, which he used to make tiered boxes, ink slabs, sets of shelves and other intricate pieces, as well as some objects of scientific interest, e.g. a water-clock and an automatic fountain. His pupils included *Shoza.
Refs: Jenyns (1965); Nakagawa; Okuda.

Geoffroy, Guérin & Co. *See* Gien.

Georgii, Ernst Wilhelm and Ferdinand. *See* Rauenstein.

Gera. Thuringian porcelain factory established c.1750 at Gera, Thuringia, initially producing faience. In 1800, the factory passed to heirs of Georg Greiner (*see* Greiner family), who sold it nine years later to Tobias Albert (d 1826), a porcelain painter and manufacturer formerly working at Pössneck. The factory remained the property of Albert's family until 1852. The output included porcelain, initially with a grey-blue or grey-green tinge, later pure white and of fine quality, painted with flowers, landscapes, mythological scenes, often in dark cobalt blue. Cups and cabaret sets are delicately painted. Some figures, including costume studies, musicians, shepherds, gardeners and other workers stand on naturalistically modelled bases, others have rococo scrolled stands. The firm became Eduard Lieber in 1855, and subsequently Lieber & Hoffmann, but changed hands again in the 1880s. The factory closed in World War I.

Mark: *Gera* or the initial G, usually in underglaze blue.
Refs: Danckert; Scherf.

Gérard, Emile. *See* G.D.A.

Gerold & Co. *See* Tettau.

Gertner, Frederick Martin (1886-1960). English porcelain modeller. Born in Worcester, Gertner worked for his father as a woodcarver, attending night school in the city's Victoria Institute. He was an art teacher in Llanelli, Dyfed, c.1913. He joined the *Worcester Royal Porcelain Co. in 1915 and was responsible for much of the firm's modelled work until 1960. His many figures

included naval and military subjects, early historical figures, the first two models of the Papal Guards series and English birds; he assisted D.*Lindner with the firm's first limited edition equestrian figure.
Ref: Sandon (1978a).

Gerverot, Louis-Victor (1747-1829). Ceramic painter, colour chemist and potter, born in Lunéville and working at many factories. Gerverot was a painter at Sèvres (1764-65), Niderviller, Fulda, Ludwigsburg, Ansbach, Höchst, Frankenthal, Offenbach, Weesp (c.1771), Schrezheim (1770s), Oude Loosdrecht (c.1777-78). He worked with John Turner at Lane End, then at a creamware factory in Cologne (1788-92), and managed the Fürstenberg factory (1795-1814). Under his control the works made imitations of jasper ware and other wares. Gerverot was at *Wrisbergholzen in 1816.
Refs: Haggar (1960); Hannover; Honey (1952); Riesebieter.

Gerz, Simon Peter. *See* Höhr-Grenzhausen.

Gesso. *See* Barnard, Harry.

Gibson, W.C., & Co. Ltd. *See* Adams & Co.

Gibus, Pierre-Justin (1821-97). French porcelain manufacturer, working in his home town of Limoges. With Alpinien Margaine (c.1826-78), formerly a partner of P.-L. *Sazerat, and M.*Redon in the firm Gibus & Cie, he established a factory in rented premises in the rue des Trois-Châtains in 1853. Gibus took charge of the technical side of production, while Margaine, who had been trained in fine arts, was responsible for pieces which were noted for their elegance of form, until his withdrawal from the business in the early 1870s. Porcelain exhibited by the firm in Paris in 1855 won praise for the whiteness of the porcelain paste and the beauty of its design. C.*Haviland, impressed with the quality of the output, in 1865 obtained the right to sell the firm's ware in the USA. In Paris, 1867, the firm exhibited pieces which included lamp bases with marbled grounds of high-temperature blue, and others decorated with painted

Gien. Earthenware wall plate painted and signed by E. Petit with a tit perched on a branch with pink, white and yellow flowers, dragonflies in flight, executed in thick slip, 1877. Marked Gien. 85.7 cm in diameter.

designs or relief motifs in white or tinted (green and gray) biscuit paste, low-relief figures were applied in biscuit, glazed or slip-coated porcelain on reserves in coloured grounds. A new factory built in Faubourg des Casseaux to handle the increased production, and in operation 1872, employed about 2000 workers and supplied direct to America. The firm became Gibus & Redon in the early 1870s. High-temperature decoration became a speciality, and in the Exposition Universelle, 1878, the firm showed large vases with medallions painted in slip, as well as pieces painted in blue and other underglaze colours. The factory was among the first to employ steam-driven machinery in the calibration of plates, and won praise in the report of the Exhibition for its general contribution to the development of industrial methods. Gibus retired in 1881, becoming a deputy administator of the Bank of France, and left Redon as owner of the firm to pursue commercial interests.

Mark: *G et Cie* in grey occurs.
Ref: d'Albis & Romanet.

Gien. French factory established at a former convent in Gien (Loiret) in 1822 for the production of cream-coloured earthenware. The factory used an opaque, white clay body to make pieces edged with acid yellow. The printed decoration included local views and currently fashionable subjects, such as the *Contes de Perrault*, the return of Napoleon's ashes, and jokes concerning Parisian life. The firm, de Boulen & Co., were the proprietors 1834-40. Geoffroy de Boulen & Co. sold earthenware marked *porcelaine opaque*, with which they won a medal at the Paris Exposition of 1844. Until the factory came under the ownership of Geoffroy, Guérin & Co. in 1856, only everyday tableware was made, often undecorated or marbled, sponged, or ornamented simply with a turned line. After 1860, some of the output was devoted to copies of faience from Moustiers, Niderviller, Marseille, or Delft. Some pieces were decorated with heraldic emblems. The *Gilet & Brianchon technique was adopted to produce an iridescent effect. Printed designs at this period included hunting scenes and classical scenes *en camaïeu*. Ornamental pieces included imitations of jasper, mother-of-pearl or agate. The firm also added lustred or watered and *flambé* effects to the range of glazes, which were criticized in 1888 for imitating all effects, including wood, but not ceramics. Soon afterwards, the firm became noted for the size of its vases (sometimes 3 metres in height and 1.2 metres in diameter).

Most marks incorporate the name, *Gien*, and sometimes the body (e.g. *porcelaine opaque, terre de fer ivoire*).
Refs: Ernould-Gandouet; M. Hayot 'La faïence de Gien' in *L'Oeil* 293 (December 1979); Lesur (1971); Tilmans (1954).

Giesshübel. Bohemian factory established in 1803 at Giesshübel, near Buchau, by Christian Nonne (d 1813) for the production of porcelain and creamware, both made from local kaolin. The output of porcelain, in grey, brown or yellow-tinged paste with flawed glaze, included wares with painted patterns of birds and rocks in underglaze blue, designs of chrysanthemums, patterns of wild flowers and geometrical arrangements of sprigs of flowers or lines and dots in purple or iron-red over the glaze. The factory's technical achievements improved under new ownership from 1810. The painter Joseph Müller carried out decoration featuring mythological scenes for the factory in the 1820s, using delicate foliage and gilt borders. Pastoral scenes and views of Karslbad, etc., also occur. Benedikte Knaute, leaseholder from 1815 or 1817, worked from 1835 in partnership with the factory's former manager Franz Lehnert, who succeeded him on his retirement in 1840. The factory, employing 55 workers in 1842, produced a variety of utilitarian and luxury wares in a fine, white porcelain paste, which were noted for their freshness and elegance of form; many were exported to Poland, Russia and Turkey. Later patterns were often taken from book illustrations and included hunting scenes and landscapes with figures.

The factory reverted in 1846 to the owner, Wilhelm Anton Ritter von Neuberg, who was succeeded in 1855 by his son Johann. The firm later underwent several changes and traded as Priviligierte Gräfliche Czerninsche Porzellan-Fabrik from 1892. In the early 20th century, the output consisted of tableware, figures and vases, produced for an extensive export market. The factory was still in operation in 1941 under the name of Johann Schuldes, owner from 1904.

Marks: the initials G pierced by an arrow, either painted or impressed and with the initials BK after 1815; the place name in a circle, impressed; initials of the Neuberg factory with a G in several versions, written as N.G.F.
Refs: Danckert; Meyer; E. Poche *Böhmisches Porzellan* (Prague, 1956); Weiss.

Gilbert, A.A., & Co. See Gager, Oliver A.

Gildea & Walker. See Mayer, T.J.& J.

gilding. The application of gold decoration. From the mid 19th century, gilding was sometimes raised, that is, applied over relief patterns. Brown gold, made with a thin paste containing gold chloride, bismuth oxide and borax which, when fired, produced a dull surface for polishing, was developed in 1853, but little used before the 1860s. Gold leaf could be applied to a prepared surface before transfer printing with a pattern (often delicate and intricate) in a protective ink consisting of asphalt, oil and gold size; the unprotected gold was washed off to leave the pattern, which was then cleaned before firing. Liquid gold, rarely used before the mid 19th century, and depending on the ability of some oils containing sulphur to hold in suspension or dissolve gold, produces brilliant, but not durable, gilding. The development in the late 18th century of mercury gilding, using an amalgam of powdered gold, proved suitable for mass production, because of its ease of application and fixing, with a brighter, more brassy result than some earlier methods. Once applied, gold was sometimes tooled or etched with further decoration.
Refs: L. Ginori-Lisci *La porcellana di Doccia* (Milan, 1963); A. Lane *Italian Porcelain* (Faber, London, 1954).

Gilet et Brianchon. French porcelain manufacturers, Jules-Joseph-Henri Brianchon (d 1880) in partnership with his brother-in-law, Gilet, who worked at several Paris addresses, 1855-80. The firm was noted for porcelain patented by Brianchon in 1857, with iridescent glazes resembling mother-of-pearl and based on bismuth, the paste sometimes tinted with coloured oxides. Among their specialities were large, pink shells, very like real shells in appearance.

Marks incorporate G.B. or *Brianchon* BREVETE or *Céramiques brevetees* [sic], and, often, *Paris*.
Ref: Lesur (1967).

Gilham, Lily (1897-1968) and Gertrude (1902-74). English potters working for *Carter & Co. and *Carter, Stabler & Adams, at Poole, Dorset. Lily Gilham joined the firm in 1914, as a modeller specializing in insects and reptiles for the decoration of vases, etc. She later carried out tile decoration, trailing the outlines of designs in slip, and joined the pottery studio headed by J.R.*Young, becoming a skilled thrower of thin, fine pieces. She left the pottery in 1923. Her sister Gertrude Gilham was employed by the firm from 1916. She became chief thrower for Carter, Stabler & Adams, and was also a teacher at the local art school. She was among the employees who left Poole to join the pottery of E.*Baggaley.
Ref: Hawkins.

Gill, William (d 1883). Yorkshire potter working in Castleford. In 1859, Gill took over a stoneware pottery at Allerton Bywater, where he probably made white earthenware, remaining until at least 1869. In 1863 he bought the Providence Pottery, Castleford, built in 1858 by George Gill, who made household white and printed earthenware there until the mid 1870s. William Gill took over the works, joined and finally succeeded by his son Thomas Gill (d 1928). The pottery closed in 1929.
Refs: Jewitt; Lawrence.

Gille (d 1868). Paris porcelain maker, formerly a gem-setter. Gille established a porcelain factory on rue Paradis-Poissonnière in 1837 and employed the modeller Charles Baury. Promoting the use of porcelain as a medium for interior decoration, he produced monumental pieces, including tables, mantelpieces and, especially, a wide range of biscuit figures, up to two metres in height, which included religious statuettes, portraits of notable people (e.g. Bernard Palissy), caryatids, and animals. The figures were sometimes coloured and gilded. Gille's plaques and figures won a bronze medal when exhibited in 1849, and he displayed biscuit figures and groups in the Great Exhibition in London, 1851. His successors, Désiré Vion and Baury, moved the firm to Choisy-le-Roi in 1875.

Marks include *Gille à Paris*, impressed; an anchor in green, *Gille Jne Fcant à Paris*, impressed; a seal with monogram of G.L. impressed or marked in blue.
Refs: Danckert; Ernould-Gandouet; Guillebon.

Ginori family. Italian manufacturers of porcelain and earthenware, owners of the *Doccia factory since its formation by Marchese Carlo Ginori in the 1730s. (*See also* Richard-Ginori, Società Ceramica.)

Refs: Danckert; Préaud & Gauthier; Weiss.

Girard, Abel (d 1878). Owner of a pottery at *Aprey (Haute-Marne), 1853-78. From 1860, he made finely decorated faience, using 18th-century shapes. His firm's output included imitations of Rouen wares decorated *en camaïeu* in blue, and pieces decorated with seascapes in pink after Niderviller, or reproductions of paintings by Jarry.
Mark: monogram of AG.
Refs: Chavagnac & Grollier; J. Chompret *Les Faïences d'Aprey* (Chaumont, Paris, 1933); P. Deveaux *Les Faïences d'Aprey* (Paris, 1908); Garnier; Hannover; Lane; Lesur (1971); Tilmans (1954).

Giraud & Bronsseau. *See* Sauviat-sur-Vige.

Gladstone China. *See* Poole, Thomas.

Glamorgan Pottery. Welsh pottery in operation in Swansea from 1813 until its purchase by the nearby *Cambrian Pottery in 1838. The founder manager William Baker and his partners William Bevan and Thomas Irwin produced earthenwares, mainly transfer-printed in black. The firm's work, similar in style to that of the Cambrian Pottery, included milk jugs in the shape of cows and printed with rustic scenes in black or, occasionally, decorated in pink lustre, and many jugs commemorating the Parliamentary Reform Bill (1832); some hand-painted wares were also produced. The plant, moulds and copper plates were transferred to the *South Wales Pottery on closure of the pottery.

Various marks incorporate *Baker, Bevan & Irwin*, or their initials.
Refs: R. Charles 'Swansea and Nantgarw' in *English Porcelain* (ed. R.G. Charleston, Ernest Benn, London, 1965); P. Hughes *Welsh China* (National Museum of Wales, Cardiff, 1972); John; Nance.

Glasgow Pottery. *See* Caledonian Pottery; Moses, John.

Glatigny, Atelier de. Ceramics studio established at Versailles in the late 1890s by a group of anonymous artists, potters and glaze chemists with the aim of producing pieces comparable with the work of studio potters but at lower prices. Some stoneware was made (including a bowl decorated with peacocks in white and gold, c.1915-18), while the company specialized in porcelain with *flambé* glazes and crystalline effects. Decoration, inspired by natural forms, included glazes figured with patterns resembling plant tissues. Glaze materials were imported from Africa, the South Pacific, etc. Vases, inkwells, etc., in the studio's output were frequently made in limited numbers. The work was sometimes mounted in silver by the Paris jeweller and silversmith Lucien Gaillard.
Refs: Années 25; Lesur (1971); Rheims.

glaze. A vitreous coating fused to pottery or porcelain, providing an impervious surface for a porous body as well as decorative effect. Silica (silicon dioxide), the glass-forming material in glazes and most ceramic bodies, fuses alone at 1713°C, but will melt at lower temperatures in the presence of a flux (another oxide which lowers its melting point). Oxides of lead, lithium and strontium are suitable for low-temperature firings. Boron oxide, a glass-former operative at low temperatures, is a non-toxic alternative to lead. Sodium, potassium and calcium oxides will fire at higher temperatures. The main flux of *Bristol glaze is zinc oxide.

Glazes are generally applied as a mixture of minerals, oxides and water, and in studio pottery are often used as raw materials, sometimes fired in the same operation as the body. Industrially, they are used in the form of frit.

Lead oxide can be used alone as a flux or combined with small quantities of potassium or calcium. Lead glaze, known probably since the third century BC in China, is fired at temperatures between about 750° and 1150°C. Though transparent, it may be stained in the clay body, green (copper), blue (cobalt) and purple/brown (manganese). The addition of tin oxide produces an opaque, white tin glaze on which high-temperature pigments may be applied before firing.

Stoneware glazes, fired at 1200-1350°C, are generally based on feldspar (alumino-silicates of potassium, sodium, calcium or, rarely, barium) or wood ash, which may be applied directly by dusting the ash on the surface of the pot, before firing, as a mixture, or by accidental contact with the clay body in a wood-firing kiln. The glaze ashes contain metal oxides, silica and other inorganic material from the soil in quantities which vary according to the type or even the part of the plant used and the soil in which it grew: grass stems have a high silica content, wood from a tree trunk may contain much stored lime, and young, sappy wood may be high in alkalis. The addition of feldspar, clay and such minerals as dolomite ($CaCO_3$.$MgCO_3$, 184) may also be needed to produce a satisfactory ash glaze. The carbon content of partially burnt wood provides some reduction in firing.

Slip glazes, based on highly fusible clay, which melts at stoneware temperatures, e.g. Albany slip, provide colours ranging from dark brown to black, occasionally with reddish tinge. They are normally fired in an oxidizing atmosphere. Saltglaze is achieved by the introduction of common salt in the kiln at temperatures at or above 1200°C, and a smear glaze may occur at any time when glaze material is present in the firing of unglazed wares.

The control of colour and effect in glazes has been a preoccupation among many studio potters and manufacturers in the production of *majolica and other wares in which form is designed to show glazes to advantage, e.g. when a rim or relief pattern is left sharp, to encourage a break in the glaze colour. Deliberately simple shapes are generally used when glazes are trickled on in a partial covering over another of contrasting colour, when glazes are used in layers (sometimes with patterns in resist), when differently coloured glazes are allowed to flow and intermingle, or when the glaze is bubbled or cratered in texture, or has a shimmering aventurine effect.

Oriental glazes were the subject of much research from the mid 19th century, and efforts to reproduce them intensified after the display of Japanese ceramics at the 1878 Exposition Universelle in Paris. The artist potters E.*Chaplet and J.*Carriès carried out glaze research, followed by A.*Bigot, G.*Hoentschel, P.-A.*Dalpayrat and A.*Delaherche, and European factories, including *Berlin and the Royal *Copenhagen factory. Experiments at *Sèvres had resulted in red glazes in imitation of the Chinese *sang-de-boeuf on porcelain by the middle of the 19th century. H.A.*Seger in Berlin and Georges Vogt at Sèvres both succeeded in formulating porcelain paste, fired at about 1280°C. with *flambé* glazes derived from copper. *Kähler Ceramics and *Hautin, Boulenger & Co. reproduced the same range of colour on earthenware. T.*Deck achieved *flambé* glazes on porcelain c.1880.

In America, H.C.*Robertson began research into *sang-de-boeuf* after seeing Japanese ceramics on display in the Philadelphia Centennial Exposition (1876), achieving success in the 1880s; he used crackle glazes from the 1890s. In her own research at the *Rookwood Pottery, M.L.*Nichols Storer produced red glazes using copper salts. Rookwood produced an *aventurine glaze sold as 'tiger eye' in the 1880s, and celadon glazes, which had been achieved earlier in Copenhagen.

English makers of *flambé* glazes included W.H.*Taylor and B.*Moore, who was engaged in experiments with C.*Bailey. 'Chang', 'Sung' and *flambé* glazes went into production at the *Doulton & Co. factory in Burslem. Other pioneer producers of high-temperature glazes in England included R.*Wells and G.*Cox.

Smooth, matt surfaces shown in a display of work by Chaplet, Delaherche and other French potters at the World's Columbian Exposition in Chicago (1893) inspired W.H.*Grueby, who produced an opaque enamel glaze with matt surface about five years later. At the same time, A.*Van Briggle began the reproduction of Chinese matt glazes; he later increased his range of colours. Matt glazes were in production from 1901 at

Rookwood, followed by many other potteries. They were popular among European makers in the 1920s, e.g. *Carter, Stabler & Adams, *Pilkington's Tile & Pottery Co., and J.*Wedgwood & Sons Ltd (Moonstone glaze) in England, and E.*Decoeur in France.

Temmoku glazes made in the 20th century by many Japanese potters including *Hamada and others at *Mashiko, have become a frequent feature of studio pottery.

Glebe Street works. *See* Robinson & Leadbeater.

Glinitz. Faience manufacture established in 1752 under the ownership of Countess Anna Barbara von Gaschin, who took over a factory founded in the previous year at Zborowski and moved it to Glinitz, Silesia, in 1767. Glazed, white or cream-coloured earthenware was introduced in the early 19th century. From 1830 to 1870, the factory was in the hands of the Mittelstadt family.
Marks: *Glinitz*; G, impressed.
Refs: Haggar; Honey (1952); Hüseler; Pazaurek; Riesebieter; Stoehr.

Globe China Co. *See* Cambridge Art Pottery.

Gloriana faience. *See* Amphora (Teplitz).

Gloucester China Co. *See* American Porcelain Manufacturing Co.

Gmundner Keramik. *See* Schleiss, Franz and Emilie.

Gobert, A.T. *See* Sèvres.

Godéchal brothers. *See* Islettes, Les.

Godwin, Thomas (1752-1809) and Benjamin (1754-1814). Successive owners (from 1783 and 1809 respectively) of a number of Burslem factories, which were continued by their descendants until c.1865. In the late 18th century, Thomas and Benjamin Godwin were described as makers of queensware and china-glazed earthenware (pearlware). Their firm passed to another Thomas Godwin in 1834, owner of the Canal Works, pottery at Burslem Wharf, where he produced for export transfer-printed earthenware with American views and designs related to incidents in American history (e.g. a view of Boston). Dinner services printed in blue, brown, green or red were bordered with nasturtiums and convolvulus, interspersed with sprays of tiny flowers and foliage.
Marks include, initials of Thomas and Benjamin Godwin printed or T.& B. GODWIN/NEW WHARF, impressed; later, several marks, e.g. OPAQUE CHINA/T GODWIN/ WHARF, printed.
Refs: Coysh (1972); Coysh & Henrywood; Godden (1971); Moore.

Goedewaagen, Koninkliche Hollandsche Pijpen- en Aardewerkfabriek. Dutch pipe factory in operation at Gouda. The workshop began producing domestic and ornamental earthenware in 1919. Four years later, Goedewaagen took over De *Distel, which continued as an autonomous branch of the firm. Under the direction of W.H. van

Friedrich Goldscheider. Bust by the sculptor, Montenave, with opal glass cabochons in the head-dress. Marked with Montenave, *and Goldscheider's mark. 35.5 cm high.*

Norden, who was with L.*Nienhuis among the firm's designers.

Marks: ROYAL GOEDEWAAGEN/GOUDA/ IN HOLLAND; GOEDEWAAGEN added to the Distel mark, with GOUDA HOLLAND.
Refs: Singelenberg-van der Meer; van Straaten.

Goldscheider, Friedrich, Wiener Manufaktur. Austrian manufacturers of ceramics and, later, metalwork. The businessman Friedrich Goldscheider (1845-97) established a factory in Vienna, 1885, for the production of earthenware and porcelain. He also owned potteries in Pilsen and Vienna and opened decorating studios in Vienna and Karlsbad. His output included painted terracotta busts, figures, plaques and other decorative pieces. The Viennese artist Hermann Klotz co-operated with Goldscheider's firm on the production of sculptures depicting wool and cloth merchants, etc. In Karlsbad, the firm produced tableware, dessert, tea, coffee and mocha sets, toilet wares, cooking vessels, vases, *jardinières* and plant pots. The output also included many colourful figures, e.g. traders, national types, satirical fashion studies.

In 1891, Goldscheider patented a bronze-plating process for terracotta, porcelain, earthenware, plaster and cement, which he used on reproductions of classical or medieval sculptures. In the following year, he started a bronze factory in Paris. He was succeeded by his widow, Regina Lewit-Goldscheider (d 1918), and sons Alois and (until 1916) Walter. In the early 20th century, the firm owned the Vienna factory, studios in Florence and Leipzig, the bronze workshop and a branch in Paris, and trade outlets in Berlin.

Glazed earthenware became a more important part of the output than terracotta after 1900, but the emphasis remained on figure production. Animal models were increasingly made, together with bowls, vases, *jardinières*, lamp stands, clock cases, etc. The output of figures was glazed with a glossy finish on costume and a matt finish on faces and hands. Bright, strong colours replaced the earlier light green, grey and beige tones. Designers included I.*Schwetz-Lehmann and I.*Erdös-Meisinger. The firm cooperated closely with the Austrian museum for art and industry on the production of classical and Renaissance sculptures after originals in the museum collection, which were sometimes bought or exhibited by the museum. Its products included work in marble, pewter, alabaster and artificial stone. Architectural decoration was carried out in majolica mosaics.

After the death of Regina Goldscheider, Walter returned to run the firm with M. *Goldscheider and continued production of a wide range of decorative wares. He moved in 1938 to America, where he established a firm in Trenton, New Jersey. He returned to Vienna in 1950, but was unable to revive production, and the firm went into liquidation in 1954. C.& E. *Carstens bought the rights to some models and the firm's name.

Marks incorporate *Goldscheider* and sometimes *Vienna* or *Wien*; under *Walter and Marcel Goldscheider*, the firm's name with monogram of WM.
Refs: Danckert; Neuwirth (1974a).

Goldscheider, Marcell. Austrian ceramics manufacturer, trained in chemistry and ceramic techniques at the Vienna Kunstgewerbeschule. He worked with Walter Goldscheider from 1920 before establishing the Vereinigte Atelier für Kunst und Keramik, also in Vienna, 1926. Goldscheider commissioned work from independent artists, e.g. H.*Bucher (who had worked for the firm of Friedrich *Goldschieder), L.*Rie, and S.*Singer. While producing the major part of his output, he also ordered pieces to his specifications from other producers ad operated as a dealer. His firm closed c.1938.
Mark: a face formed from the letter M with GOLDSCHEIDER/KERAMIK.
Ref: Neuwirth (1974a).

Goldsmith, Mary. *See* Scheier, Edwin.

Marcell Goldscheider. Figure of Harlequin, 1928-30. 28.5 cm high.

Gonder, Lawton. American potter. After working at the Ohio Pottery Co. (in operation 1900-23), the *American Encaustic Tiling Co. and the Cherry Art Tile Co. at Orlando, Florida, Gonder became manager of the Florence Pottery Co. at Mount Gilead, Ohio, in 1938. There he produced art ware for the *Rum Rill Pottery Co. After the destruction of the Florence Pottery by fire in 1941, Gonder acted as consultant to other ceramic firms, and bought the *Zane Pottery Co., formerly operated by H.S.*McClelland, where he traded as Gonder Ceramic Arts, Inc. He employed artists to design art pottery, which was made with *flambé* and crackle glazes (one golden in colour) and included reproductions of Chinese styles. In 1946, he opened a factory for the production of lamp bases, which traded as the Elgee Pottery and was destroyed by fire in 1954. His firm ceased operation in 1957.
Refs: Evans; Kovel & Kovel; Lehner; N.F. Schneider 'Lawton Gonder' in *Zanesville Times Signal* (11th November 1956).

Gonic Pottery. An American pottery operated in Gonic, New Hampshire, from c.1839 by Elijah Osborne, followed by his sons, James and John, who worked in partnership until c.1875, when John Osborne left. James Osborne then carried on the pottery assisted by his son William A. Osborne (b 1856). Using local, red-firing clay, the pottery produced thrown domestic ware (jars, cups, jugs, etc.) with clear lead glaze, sometimes only on the interior, or coloured with cobalt (blue), copper (green), iron (yellow or brown), or manganese shades of brown). Body and glaze were fired in one operation (in a wood-firing kiln) to keep prices down. The ware was sold at the pottery or through general stores in nearby towns.
Refs: Stradling; Watkins.

Goodale, Daniel, Jr. American potter. Goodale made stoneware in Massachusetts from 1815, then in Hartford, Connecticut, from 1818, and working alone, 1825-30. He made jugs with banded necks, resembling earlier German and English designs, and also presentation pieces, usually with incised decoration.
Marks: name, sometimes with *Hartford*.
Refs: Stradling; Watkins (1950); Webster.

Goodchild, Doreen (b 1900). Etcher and potter born in South Australia. She studied at the South Australian School of Arts and Crafts, privately (under Dattilo Rubbio) in Sydney and at the Central School of Arts & Crafts in London. On her return to Australia in 1927, she established a kiln in Aadelaide with her husband and, from 1929, produced domestic earthenwares and small figure sculptures. She also produced a small number of porcelains, some of the first made in Australia.

Goode, Thomas, & Co. *See* Goode, William James.

Goode, William James (1831-1892). English designer and painter. Goode worked in his father's firm, Thomas Goode & Co., retailers of ceramics from 1827 in London, in which he was a partner from 1857, and took over the firm on his father's retirement in 1867. His ceramic designs, all produced by *Mintons

Ltd., included plates, influenced in style by the work of W.S.*Coleman, several services for British diplomatic residences, and a Golden Wedding plaque presented by Queen Victoria to the Emperor and Empress of Germany in 1879. With C.M.*Campbell, Goode developed a method of etching decorative designs on porcelain; examples were exhibited at the Paris Exposition Universelle in 1878. The family firm sold work from Mintons and in 1878 bought the factory's entire display in Paris for exhibition in the London showroom, later exhibiting Minton wares in its display in Paris at the Exposition Universelle of 1889. Goode commissioned from Mintons copies of his own extensive collection of Sèvres porcelain, which was dispersed after his death.
Ref: Aslin & Atterbury.

Goodwin, John. English potter. After working in Longton, Staffordshire, from 1846, Goodwin established a pottery at Seacombe, Cheshire, in 1851 for the production of earthenware, ironstone china (mainly transfer-printed in blue under the glaze) and parian ware. His pottery closed by autumn 1871.
Marks include *J. Goodwin* or *Goodwin & Co*, with *Seacombe Pottery, Liverpool*.
Refs: G. Godden *Handbook of British Pottery & Porcelain Marks* (Barrie & Jenkins, London, 1968); Jewitt; H. William in *Journal of Ceramic History* No 10 (Stoke-on-Trent City Museum, 1978).

Goodwin, John (d c.1875). English-born potter. Goodwin worked in Staffordshire before travelling to America in 1842. He subsequently worked for J.*Bennett, and in 1844 established his own small pottery in East Liverpool, Ohio, for the manufacture of yellow and Rockingham-glazed earthenware. Suffering from ill health, he sold the works to Samuel & William Baggott in 1853 and retired for 10 years. He established the Novelty Pottery Works in 1863, and held an interest (1870-72) in the *Trenton Pottery Co., which then traded as Taylor, Goodwin & Co., making ironstone china, cream-coloured earthenware and sanitary ware. Goodwin returned to East Liverpool and bought the Broadway Pottery, which was operated after his death by his sons, trading as Goodwin Brothers, who enlarged the works and increased the range of products to include cream-coloured earthenware, semi-porcelain and ironstone china. The firm was incorporated as Goodwin Pottery Co. in 1893.
Marks incorporate the names *Goodwin's* or *Goodwin Bros* and sometimes the ware, e.g. HOTEL CHINA.
Refs: Barber (1976); Lehner.

Gorbunov. Russian porcelain factory established in 1806 at Gorbunov near Moscow by Karl Melli, a former steward at the *Gardner factory, and acquired five years later by A.G.*Popov.
Refs: Hare; Nikiforova; A. Popoff 'The Francis Gardner & Other Russian Porcelain Factories' in *The Connoisseur* 96 (August 1935); Ross; Rozembergh; Weiss.

Gordon, Robert and George. *See* Bankfoot Pottery.

Gordon, William. English sculptor, designer and potter. Gordon was a designer and metalworker before beginning his output of salt-glazed stoneware at Chesterfield, Derbyshire, in 1939. He resumed production at the Walton Pottery near Chesterfield, 1946-56. The work, mainly moulded from models by Gordon, included vases, dishes, figures and lamp bases.
Marks: circle crossed by vertical or diagonal line, incised or impressed.
Refs: H. Wakefield 'William Gordon's Saltglaze' in *The Studio* 141 (April 1951); Wingfield Digby.

Görgény. Hungarian pottery established in the early 19th century, probably at Görgény-szentimre (Maros-Torda). The initial output consisted of pieces with a yellow finish achieved by dipping biscuit ware in a glaze containing salt before refiring. The later white earthenware was generally painted over the glaze. The factory was still in operation in 1889.
Mark: GÖRGENY, impressed.
Ref: Csanyi.

Gorka, (Géza) (b 1894). Artist potter working in Hungary. Gorka was born in Topolcany, Czechoslovakia, and spent time during his childhood in Mezőtur. He began an artistic training in Trencin, Czechoslovakia, in 1917, but returned to Mezőtur in 1918 to study pottery under B.*Badar. He left Hungary after the fall of the republic to work in Germany, and studied glaze techniques under M.*Laeuger at Karlsruhe, returning to work for Badar in 1922, and moved to Nograd-veröce, near Vac in 1923.
Gorka became art director and one of the founders of the firm, Keramos, at first producing pottery which combined peasant traditions with modern concepts and techniques. He left to start his own workshop, also in Nogradveröce, in 1927, employing a number of craftsmen. He exhibited pottery in Venice, 1928. He concentrated on the production of domestic and ornamental ware, initially inspired by peasant pottery, especially 18th-century Haban Fayence, and forms of prehistoric vessels, but came increasingly to rely on simple, elegant forms, finally abandoning the Haban style of decoration. He developed glazes in rich, subtle colours, often using combinations of tone and, sometimes, crackle or bubbled effects.
In the 1940s, Gorka carried out research in glazing techniques at the *Zsolnay factory, achieving high-quality figured, running and layered glazes suited to the factory's new high-temperature kilns, and on some pieces returning to Haban ornamental motifs in combinations of green with white or red and blue. He returned to Nogradveröce in 1948.
Ref: I. Pataky-Brestyánszky *Modern Hungarian Ceramics* (Corvina Verlag, Budapest, 1961).

Goroemon. *See* Mori family.

Gorton, Elmer. *See* Gates, William Day.

Goss, William Henry (1833-1906). English potter and porcelain manufacturer. After artistic training in London, Goss joined the firm of W.T. *Copeland in 1857, working mainly on the design of parian figures and statuettes. He started a factory in partnership (1858), subsequently establishing his own

W.H. Goss Ltd. Parian bust, c.1880.

works in Stoke-on-Trent and moving to the larger Falcon Works in the same town in 1870. From 1858, he made parian ware, notably portrait busts, also producing terracotta household ware with bands of painted decoration, e.g. in blue, green, yellow or black and white, usually unmarked. By 1873, Goss had patented a method of inserting jewels in clay before firing which was used in making trinkets and costume jewellery. He also made small brooches, ear-rings, and openwork porcelain baskets decorated with flowers, in white biscuit porcelain (sometimes in the case of flowers tinted in natural colours) or in the patent ivory paste associated with his firm. W. Bromley, foreman until 1863, was succeeded by Joseph Astley, who was responsible for modelling Goss's designs, including busts of Queen Alexandra as Princess of Wales, and Georgiana Jewitt. The firm made small souvenirs with heraldic decoration from the 1880s until World War I, starting with shields of schools and universities and increasing the range to include simple shapes with the arms of English towns and seaside resorts. Later shapes included accurate copies of architectural details and whole buildings (lighthouses, chapels and the homes of famous people). Small vases, bowls and jugs were transfer-printed with landscapes. Goss was succeeded by his sons Victor Henry (d 1913) and William Huntley. The firm, trading as W.H. Goss Ltd, was absorbed into Cauldon Potteries Ltd (*see* Brown-Westhead Moore & Sons Ltd) and the works ceased production in 1940. There is a collectors' club devoted to Goss's wares.
Printed marks include W.H. GOSS, with goshawk, wings outstretched.
Refs: Andrews; Blacker (1922a); J. Galpin *Goss China* (privately published, 1972); J. Jarvis *Goss Record* (8th ed., Milestone, 1973; originally published 1914); Hughes (1977); Jewitt; N. Pine *The Price Guide to Goss China* (Milestone, 1978), *Goss China: Arms Decorations and their Values* (Milestone, 1979); D. Rees & M.G. Cawley

A Pictorial Encyclopaedia of Goss China (The Ceramic Book Co., Newport, 1970).

Gosse, François. *See* Bayeux.

gosu aka-e. In Japanese porcelain, decorative patterns of birds, flowers, scrolls, etc., painted in blue, red and green. A mixture of cobalt blue (gosu), unrefined and usually containing a quantity of manganese and iron compounds, was painted under the glaze.The red and green were in enamel. At the low temperature of enamel firing, the manganese produces a purple tone, but high-temperature firing drives off the manganese, giving the indigo *sometsuke*. The patterns are characteristic of Swatow ware produced in the Fukien and Kwantung provinces of Southern China from the late Ming (1368-c.1644) to early Ch'ing periods (c.1644-1912) and reproduced by the Japanese artists *Eisen, *Mimpei, *Dohei, *Mokubei, *Dohachi, and *Rokubei, and in *Banko ware.
Refs: Gorham; Jenyns (1965); Munsterberg.

Gotha. German porcelain factory established c.1757 at Gotha in Thuringia for the production of small sets of tableware, vases, figures, etc. The founder's widow sold the factory in 1802 to Prince August von Sachsen-Gotha-Altenburg, who let it to the court chamberlain, Friedrich Egidius Henneburg (d 1834), initially in partnership with the former managers, Schulz & Co., and sole proprietor by 1814. The firm had moved to new premises in 1804. After lengthy financial problems caused by competition from Bavarian wares, Henneberg's grandson sold the factory in 1883 to the Simson brothers, owners of a munitions works in Suhl, who restricted production to everyday tableware. The firm moved again in 1912 and ceased operation in 1934.
Other firms working nearby, *Morgenroth & Co., their successors Friedrich Schwab & Co., and F. Pfeller, established 1892, are no longer in operation.
Marks: from 1802 or 1805, G or *Gotha* in underglaze blue, or various colours over the glaze. From 1834, a hen and PORZELLAN MANUFAKTUR GOTHA in sepia or purple. Oval stamp, GOTHA, 1860-83.
Refs: Danckert; R. Graul & A. Kurzwelly *Altthüringer Porzellan* (Leipzig, 1909); Scherf; Weiss.

Gotomaki. *See* Shino ware.

Gottbrecht, F. *See* Reichmannsdorf.

Gotha. Cup and saucer in white porcelain, made at Gotha, 1851.

Goumot-Labesse, Albert. *See* Tharaud, Camille.

Goupy, Marcel. French artist and designer of glass and ceramics in the 1920s. His ceramic designs included earthenware services (notably decorated in ochre and blue) with flowers, animals and butterflies, produced by *Boch Frères for the Paris retailer Géo Rouard, and porcelain services for the T. *Haviland and C.*Tharaud factories. Work usually signed.
Refs: Années 25; Baschet; d'Albis & Romanet; Lesieutre.

Gousse. *See* Angoulême.

Grace, William E. (b 1889). English painter and ceramic artist, who was apprenticed at the *Doulton & Co. factory in Burslem in 1902. He was taught by H.*Piper in the department producing choice ornamental ware under R.*Allen, and attended classes at Burslem School of Art. Initially a designer of patterns for engraving and lithoprinting, he then assisted Charles *Noke in the development of underglaze patterns for ranges of printed tableware. He also painted jugs and loving cups in limited editions, and a number of earthenware figures. He worked for Doulton until 1959.
Refs: see Doulton & Co.

Gradl, Hermann. *See* Nymphenburg.

Graf, Fritz. *See* Grossbreitenbach.

Gräfenroda. Thuringian procelain centre. The factory of modeller, Heinrich Dornheim, in the partnership Dornheim, Koch & Fischer, produced porcelain from 1880 until the late 1930s. The output included utilitarian ware as well as decorative pieces and dolls' heads.
A later factory, established 1895 and owned from the following year by Wilhelm Heene, produced a wide range of goods, initially egg cups, salt cellars, etc., and later clock cases, lamps, mocha cups and figures. Production ceased in 1916. The factory established in 1910 by Reinhold Voigt produced decorative and utilitarian wares.
Decorating studios established in the area included that of August Heisnner, in operation c.1930.

DKF

Marks: Dornheim, Koch & Fischer used various arrangements of crossed lines, some resembling the Meissen mark, sometimes with initials DKF; Voigt used a crown with initials RV and G.
Refs: Danckert; Scherf; Weiss.

Gräfenthal. Thuringian porcelain centre. A factory established 1861, with a ducal concession, by the partnership of Carl Unger, a modeller from Schmedefeld, Carl Schneider (d 1885), a Wallendorf merchant, and Hermann Hutschenreuther, also from Wallendorf, produced children's sets, kitchen utensils and other utilitarian ware, often decorated under the glaze in blue, e.g. with the Meissen onion pattern (*Zwiebelmuster*)

or Immortals patterns, or simply gilded. After the retirement of Unger in 1885 and Hutschenreuther the following year, the factory passed to Schneider's heir, Paul Schneider (d 1912), in partnership with Wilhelm Wedel, who had been works chemist from 1889. By this time, the output included figures in rococo or Biedermeier styles, animal models (sometimes life-size), religious statuary, memorial wares and dolls' heads. The factory traded under the name of Carl Schneider's successors until 1973.
Other local factories included those of Carl Scheidig, established 1906 for the production of utilitarian and decorative wares (including figures) and electrical porcelain, the firm's staple product in the 1920s; Weiss, Kuhnert & Co., founded in 1891; A.H. Pröschold and Theodor Wagner (both 1897), and Heinz & Co. (1900). The two firms still in operation, Carl Scheidig and Heinz & Co. are now part of VEB Vereinigte Zierporzellanwerke Lichte.
Marks: versions of the initial G pierced by an arrow (Unger, Schneider & Hutschenreuther); WKC in a circle with a cross and Graefenthal (Weiss, Kühnert & Co.); monogram of H & CO G inside a hexagon (Heinz & Co.); an eagle with CS pierced by an arrow, or a very stylized eagle and KUNSTPORZELLAN (Scheidig).
Refs: Danckert; Scherf; Weiss.

Grafton China Works. *See* Jones, Alfred B.

Graham Pottery. American pottery established at Brooklyn, New York, in 1880 for the production of stoneware for the chemical industry. After experimenting with the production of decorative ware, the owner, Charles Graham, in 1885 patented a method of etching designs through the dark, saltglazed surface to expose a light-coloured body. The factory also produced the work of Charles C. Benham, who had begun experiments in decorating salt-glazed stoneware before 1876 and continued until the turn of the century. His designs were carved or incised through a coating of dark (usually blue) slip before the stoneware was fired. On some vases, carved decoration of figures, foliage, stylized wave motifs, etc., stands out pale in relief against a more deeply carved coloured ground. Decoration acid-etched by Graham's technique included portraits and animal scenes, e.g. stag hunting, and birds wading among water plants. In the early 20th century, the output of art ware ceased, though the factory continued to produce chemical stoneware.
Marks: CHAS. GRAHAM with *Pat'd April 7th 1885* in a rectangular outline, or with BROOKLYN/N. Y. in an oval outline.
Refs: Barber (1976); Evans.

Grainger & Co. Porcelain makers working in *Worcester from 1801, when Thomas Grainger (d 1893), a relation by marriage of Robert Chamberlain, established a factory in St Martin's Street in the east of the city. He worked in the partnership Grainger & Wood before going into partnership with his brother-in-law in 1812 as Grainger & Lee, at new, larger works built across the road from the original factory after its destruction by fire. Grainger, who was subsequently sole proprietor until his death, was succeeded by his son, who traded as George Grainger &

Grainger & Co. Moon flask with pâte-sur-pâte decoration on an olive green ground, lavishly gilded, late 19th century. Impressed shield mark. 20.5 cm high.

Duncan Grant. Earthenware vase painted by Grant, c.1937. 25.8 cm high.

A.E. Gray & Co. Ltd. Earthenware toucan in buff body. Squirrel designed by Nancy Catford, 1934-37. 28 cm and 17.7 cm high.

Co. The firm made vases, figures and ornamental ware in parian paste. Perforated ware, a speciality, included vases held by eagles or dolphins, vases in the form of flowers, wall pockets in the form of orchids, pilgrim bottles and spill jars. The firm also made chemical and photographic ware in a semi-porcelain which was characterized by strength and resistance to heat. The firm's other output included high-quality *pâte-sur-pâte* reproductions of wares by Dr Wall with paintings of fabulous birds against a blue-scale ground, as well as wall tiles and door furniture. The principal artists included members of the *Stinton family, G.*Cole and E.*Locke. Grainger & Co. merged with the Royal Worcester Porcelain Co. in 1889 and ceased production in 1902.

Marks incorporate the name or initials of the company and, often, *Worcester*; printed or impressed shield mark with initials G. & Co/w used from c.1870 was surrounded c.1889-1902 by ROYAL CHINA WORKS/WORCESTER/ENGLAND, accompanied by year letters A (1891) to L (1902).
Refs: see Worcester.

Grand Feu Art Pottery. *See* Brauckman, Cornelius.

Grande Maison, Manufacture de la. *See* Loc Maria.

granite ware. *See* semi-porcelain.

Granlund, Svea (b 1901). Ceramic decorator, trained at the Finnish school of industrial art and working at the *Arabia factory from 1923. Granlund painted a variety of designs, e.g. monograms, leaves, fruit, in underglaze colours, often to supply commissions.
Ref: Aro.

Grant, Duncan (1885-1978). English painter who was also engaged in ceramic decoration. His earliest surviving patterns on pottery, abstract designs, human figures, etc., were carried out on holiday in Tunisia in 1911. Grant painted pieces (mainly plates and

bowls) made at the *Omega Workshops 1913-18, working in a style that was influenced by R.*Fry's interest in ancient and oriental ceramics, and often incorporated calligraphic designs (especially on fireplaces or table tops).

Grant seldom took part in the production of pieces that he painted. He usually worked independently, and much of his work was for private use rather than sale, but some of his patterns were commercially produced on tableware, e.g. by E.*Brain & Co.
Refs: Ceramic Review 52, 53 (September, October 1978).

Grasset, Eugène (1845-1917). Designer, sculptor and illustrator, born in Lausanne. Grasset worked in France from 1871, becoming naturalized c.1890. As well as furniture, stained glass, jewellery and complete interior schemes, his design work included ceramics, executed by his friend, J.*Carriès, and E. *Muller. A prominent exponent of French Art Nouveau, he took charge of the course in decorative composition at the Ecole Normale d'Enseignements in Paris, publishing *La plante et ses applications ornamentales* (1897) and *La méthode de composition ornamentale* (1905).

Mark: initials, with E inside G.
Refs: Brunhammer *et al* (1976); J. Mayor 'Eugène Grasset (1845-1917)' in *Gazette des Beaux-Arts* (July 1918).

Graves, William. *See* Grueby, William Henry.

Gray, A.E., & Co. Ltd. Staffordshire ceramic decorators established as a wholesale business at Stoke-on-Trent in 1907 by the former glass and pottery salesman Albert Edward Gray (1871-1959) and in operation as a decorating workshop at the Glebe Works in Mayer St, Hanley, by 1912, when the name A.E. Gray & Co Ltd was registered. Early pieces included miniature souvenir bottles, mugs and jugs with printed and hand-painted decoration commemorating Football Association teams. The company came to specialize in decoration, either done solely by hand or hand-finished, of wares bought from the

manufacturers, sometimes in shapes commissioned from Gray & Co's own designs. The designers of patterns included G.M. *Forsyth (for the Gloria Lustra line, from its introduction in 1923) and S.*Cooper, who was on the staff 1922-29 and designed a number of patterns for the large output of lustre ware. The range of decoration was very wide. Freehand floral painting was carried out on plaques, jugs, etc., in bright colours in response to imports of Czechoslovakian peasant ware in the mid 1920s. Transfer-printed designs used in the late 1920s included patterns of hazel catkins and almond blossom by Susie Cooper, but few were used until World War II. A number of dotted or banded patterns in the 1930s were available with a range of several ground colours. Stoneware cooking pots, jugs, ashtrays, etc. were sold from the early 1930s, with bands and thin stripes in a variety of colours. The firm also decorated copies of early Staffordshire groups, animal models and a series of masks, but in general Gray's did not produce many figures.

After moving to larger premises in Stoke-on-Trent, in 1933, A.E. Gray bought an interest (1936) in the Kirklands Pottery, primarily manufacturers of hospital ware, at Etruria. He and his son R.E. Gray (who had joined him in 1920 and become a director of A.E. Gray Ltd in 1923) became directors of Kirklands where shapes were produced for decoration by Gray's until World War II. A.E. Gray retired in 1947, succeeded by his son and the firm's art director, S.C. Talbot, as joint managing directors. The firm was purchased in 1959 by the designer Susan Williams-Ellis and merged in 1961 with the firm of W.*Kirkham to form Portmeirion Potteries Ltd, in operation from January 1962.

Marks incorporate the name of the firm

A.E. Gray & Co. or, from 1933, *Gray's Pottery* and include a circular mark centering on a football with GRAYS/ SPORTS/CHINA; an oak leaf (1914); a square mark with Sunburst in gold and black and GLORIA LUSTRE; a variety of marks featuring a galleon; PORTMEIRION WARE, sometimes with *'designed by Susan Williams-Ellis'*.
Refs: Andrews; Bunt; Forsyth; G.M. Forsyth *The Art and Craft of the Potter* (Chapman & Hall, London, 1934); Godden (1964); A.E. Gray 'The Encouragement of Art in the Potteries' in *Transactions of the Ceramics Society* 22 (1917-18); *Gray's Pottery* (catalogue, Stoke-on-Trent City Museum, 1982); *Pottery & Glass* (August 1959); *Pottery & Glass Record* (June 1924, December 1932, March 1934, March, April and October 1935); *The Studio Year Book* (1920).

Gray, Robert Bix. *See* Randall, Thomas Martin.

Gray, Thomas. *See* New England Pottery.

Greatbach, Daniel (d after 1866). English-born ceramic modeller and designer, employed by the *Ridgway family before settling in America c.1839. As a modeller at the American Pottery Manufacturing Co. (*see* Jersey City Pottery), from 1838 or 1839 to c.1848, he made hound-handled pitchers, Toby Jugs, an Apostle jug and a tea set made in cream-coloured earthenware with floral decoration in relief. He probably worked independently as a ceramic modeller, 1849-57, before becoming chief designer and modeller for C.W.*Fenton, 1852-58. His work included series of Toby jugs and bottles, often derived from English designs made in Staffordshire, and he possibly originated the cow creamers and models of lions made in Bennington from traditional English designs. Other animal figures include a stag, a doe and a cow. Greatbach went with Fenton and D.W.*Clark to Kaolin, South Carolina, and then Peoria, Illinois, afterwards working in East Liverpool, Ohio, and by 1865 in Trenton, New Jersey, where he died.

Daniel Greatbach. Hound-handled pitcher produced by the American Pottery Manufacturing Co. 24.8 cm high.

Refs: Barber (1976); Clement (1947); Spargo.

Greaves, Jervis. *See* Holmes Pottery.

Grecian. *See* Brush-McCoy Pottery.

Green & Co. Staffordshire porcelain manufacturers operating the Minerva works, Fenton, formerly occupied by G.M. and C.J.*Mason. The works passed to Richard Hassall, who was joined as a partner by Thomas Green (d 1859) in 1833. The firm then specialized in miniature wares, including tea and dinner services, mugs, jugs, basins, ewers and ornamental pieces. After Hassall's retirement, Green worked in the partnership Green & Richards until 1847, and subsequently James *Leeds continued the firm as M. Green & Co. In the mid 19th century, production turned to high-quality domestic porcelain, including table services, toilet sets, invalid and nursery ware, etc., often reproducing earlier styles. In copies of Chinese porcelain, the firm achieved a pink enamel colour (which had not been successfully reproduced after 1800), and a powder blue. The title became T.A. & S. Green 1876-89, and subsequently *Crown Staffordshire Porcelain Co. Ltd in 1948.
Marks include T. GREEN/FENTON POTTERIES or a Staffordshire knot topped by a crown and containing FENTON/T.G.(1847-59) or T.A. & S.G. (1876-89).
Refs: Blacker (1922a); Hughes (1977); Jewitt.

Green family. Yorkshire family from the Swinton area; some members were concerned in the operation of the *Leeds Pottery. Joshua Green (b c.1720) was one of the firm's original partners; his successor, and probably son, Ebenezer Green (d 1827), worked at the pottery until his bankruptcy in 1820.
Savile Green (b c.1743), Joshua's cousin, was a book-keeper and one of the original partners in the Leeds Pottery. His son, also Savile Green, worked as the pottery's agent in Rio de Janeiro until his death there in 1820.
John Green (1743-1805), nephew of Joshua, born in London, was a founder partner and probably responsible for running the pottery. He sold his shares soon before his bankruptcy in 1800, then settled at Newhill near the *Swinton Pottery, in which he shared a controlling interest with other partners of the Leeds firm. In 1801 he established the *Don Pottery, where he was joined by sons John, a partner from 1803, and William Green (1776-1841), who started as clerk and succeeded his father in the partnership, 1805. The brothers ran the pottery, backed by a number of partners, including their mother and other members of the Green family, until its sale following their bankruptcy in 1834.
Refs: Eaglestone & Lockett; Jewitt; Lawrence; Rice.

green-glazed ware. Earthenware with glaze coloured green with oxides, usually copper or chrome. Green was among the glaze colours developed by Josiah Wedgwood (1730-93) in the mid 18th century for dessert and other wares, and green glazes were used on majolica by many makers in the mid 19th century. They were also a feature of rustic

wares, e.g. those made at the *Cadborough and *Belle Vue potteries.

Green, James. *See* Littlethorpe Pottery.

Green, Stephen. *See* Imperial Pottery.

Green Woodland. *See* Brush-McCoy Pottery.

Greenfields works. *See* Adams family.

Greengates Pottery. *See* Adams family.

Greenpoint, Long Island. *See* Cartlidge, Charles.

Greens, Bingley & Co. *See* Leeds Pottery.

Greens, Clark & Co. *See* Don Pottery.

Greenwood Pottery Co. American pottery established in 1861 by Staffordshire potter, James Tams, with James P. Stephens at Trenton, New Jersey, and trading from 1868 as the Greenwood Pottery Co. The firm made granite ware or ironstone china until the introduction (1876) of vitrified, translucent ware for use by hotels and transport companies, also producing porcelain hardware, door furniture, etc., as well as insulators and other electrical ware. Very thin art porcelain made from 1883 included unique vases, plaques, etc., decorated in the style of the Royal Worcester factory, often with raised gold, silver or bronze decoration against an ivory ground. Other decorative techniques included *pâte-sur-pâte* decoration. The factory developed a rich, blue ground colour.
Marks include the arms of New Jersey (white wares) or G.P./Co. (stamped on early porcelain) until c.1875; GREENWOOD CHINA/TRENTON, N.J. (impressed) from 1886; a printed mark resembling that of the Royal *Worcester Porcelain Co., topped by a curved banner bearing GREENWOOD.
Ref: Barber (1976).

Gregory, Albert. English porcelain painter. After his apprenticeship at Mintons Ltd, Gregory joined the porcelain factory at Osmaston Road, *Derby, in the 1890s. He was a skilled painter of flowers in a naturalistic style. His luxuriant bands of full-blown flowers contain cabbage roses in pink or yellow, anemones, streaked tulips, etc. Gregory became associated with a large rose, which often featured in his paintings of grouped flowers. He left Derby in 1908, possibly to visit America, but returned later. His work is found on services and vases.
Marks: signature or initials.
Refs: see Derby.

Gregory, Waylande De Santis (1905-71). American ceramist and designer, born in Baxter Springs, Kansas. Gregory studied in Kansas, Chicago and Italy. In 1928, he left the Chicago studio where he had initially worked, mainly in bronze, to become R.G. *Cowan's principal artist for the modelling of figures, which included Diana and the Two Fawns (a limited edition of 100), Marguerite at her Lessons, and a Torso (1929), Burlesque Dancer (1932), Pan Sitting on a Toadstool, Swan, Salome, Alice in Wonderland, and stoneware vases decorated in low relief with animals, e.g. a dog, a squirrel among foliage, in 1930. Gregory left the

Cowan studio in 1932 and worked as an artist in residence at the Cranbrook Academy of Art, a colony of artists and teachers founded by the newspaper publisher George C. Booth, where he was succeeded as director in 1938 by M.*Grotell. While there, he designed a porcelain dinner service, and accessories (lamp, ashtrays, etc.) decorated with designs of polo players carved through coloured slip to show the light paste below.

He subsequently established his own workshop in Bound Brook, New Jersey. His sculptural work was often very stylized and included humorous figures representing octaves in a Musical Fountain, a child's head exhibited at the Syracuse Museum of Fine Arts in New York, and a Fountain of the Atoms (1938), shown in the World's Fair, New York, the following year and including twelve figures, each weighing over a ton, built up in a honeycomb fashion which Gregory developed himself and called 'inner modelling'.
Refs: 'The Art with the Inferiority Complex' in *Fortune* 16, No 6 (1937); Clark & Hughto; Cox; Forsyth; M. Hughto *New Works in Clay by Contemporary Painters and Sculptors* (Everson Museum of Art, Syracuse, New York, 1976).

Greiner family. German potters and ceramic decorators, working in Thuringia. Gotthelf Greiner (1797) was the founder of porcelain factories at *Wallendorf and *Limbach, and purchaser of factories at *Grossbreitenbach (1782) and *Ilmenau (1786). Gotthelf's son, Ernst Friedrich Ferdinand (1768-1821), was director of the *Kloster Veilsdorf factory, which he owned in partnership with his four brothers, Johann Georg Daniel, Johann Friedmann (director of *Grossbreitenbach), Johann Jakob Florentin, and Johann Michael Gotthelf Greiner (d 1849). Also partners were Johann Friedrich (d 1820) and Christian Daniel Sigmund Greiner (1761-1808), owners of the *Rauenstein factory, in which J.M.G. Greiner was a shareholder through his marriage. He and J.J.F. Greiner both remained at Limbach.

Johann Georg Wilhelm and Johann-Andreas Greiner, decorators from Volkstedt, were owners of the *Gera factory from 1780; Wilhelm Heinrich Greiner held an interest in Volkstedt in 1799.

Eugen Georg Friedrich Theodor (d 1821), son of C.D.S. Greiner, married a granddaughter of Gotthelf Greiner who retained a share in the Rauenstein factory until 1858, when she sold her interest to G.H. Wirth.
Refs: Danckert; Scherf.

Grenzhausen. *See* Höhr-Grenzhausen.

Gresley, Cuthbert (c.1876-early 1960s). English porcelain painter; one of a family of watercolour artists. Gresley was apprenticed at the porcelain factory in Osmaston Road, *Derby, in 1893 as a painter of flowers and landscapes. His work (painted on table services) included meadowland with sheep or cows, and views of great houses seen across water; a signed view of Chatsworth House dates from c.1920. Gresley was skilled at portraying depth in his bouquets of flowers, which often included hollow-centred roses. He also painted fish on a service produced for Princess May of Cambridge on her marriage; pigeons, pheasants and other birds on rare services, and lakeland scenes on decorative plaques.
Mark: signature.
Refs: see Derby.

Greta Bank Pottery. *See* Bateson family.

Grey-Edge. *See* Kåge, Wilhelm.

Grey-Smith, Guy (1916-81). Painter, printmaker, potter and teacher, born in Western Australia, In England, Grey-Smith studied pottery at the Woolwich Polytechnic under H.*Mathews in 1945-47. On his return to Australia, he set up his own pottery at the end of 1948, making pieces in the style of English slipware until c.1950, when he turned to painted decoration in oxides on domestic wares, including platters and vases, made with local clay. The forms derive from the Western Australian landscape, but Grey-Smith was also influenced by the work of W.S.*Murray. Although he was better known as a painter, he devoted a considerable part of his working life to pottery and exhibited his wares frequently throughout Australia

Griemert, Hubert (b 1905). German potter born in Keula, Thuringia, and trained, 1921-25, at the Kunstgewerbeschule in Hildesheim. He continued his training at Frohburg, Saxony, where he studied painting and the modelling of ceramics for architectural decoration (1925-27), Bunzlau Staatliche Keramische Fachschule (1927-29), and in Halle-Giebichenstein, near Leipzig, where he was an apprentice with M.*Friedlander, G.*Marcks, and F.*Wildenhain (1930-33). Griemert worked as a teacher, 1934-46, operated his own workshop in Schötmar, Lippe, 1947-54 (while also teaching at the Werkkunstschule at Krefeld from 1950), and conducted the master class at the Staatliche Werkschule für Keramik in Höhr-Grenzhausen, 1954-70.

Griemert's simple, uncluttered shapes stem from his adoption of the stylistic principles of the *Bauhaus. He used matt glazes, sometimes with crystalline effects (based on zinc silicate with barium and nickel) in a wide range of rather sober colours. His thorough technical knowledge enabled him to follow up accidental glaze effects arising in his experiments with detailed investigation to repeat the results in a controlled way. His concern for form led to a design collaboration with the *Berlin factory, producers of his Crocus set of tableware (1952-57) and a service combining circular and oval shapes (1965), as well as a range of vases. His shapes range from cylinders and other geometrical forms to natural, cupped flower buds and crocus blooms.

Marks: HG impressed or painted on pieces with glazes devised by Griemert in Halle; HG with Giebichenstein Castle, over the bridge across the Saale (impressed); in Höhr-Grenzhausen, HG with a stamped mark depicting the ceramic school.
Refs: Bock; *Deutsche Wertarbeit* (catalogue,

Kunstgewerbemuseum, Zurich, 1943); W. Dexel *Keramik—Stoff und Form* (Brunswick/Berlin, 1958); E. Klinge in *Deutsche Keramik* I (Düsseldorf, 1975); E. Köllmann in *Keramos* 5 (1959); R. Smeets 'Hubert Griemert' in *Kunst und Handwerk* (1971).

Griffen, Smith & Hill. American firm operating the *Phoenixville Pottery as Beerbower & Griffen from 1877; producers of white granite ware. The firm became Griffen, Smith & Hill in 1879 and began manufacturing Etruscan majolica in the following year. Tableware was often made in leaf forms moulded from natural objects; coral, seaweed and shells were closely copied, and English green-glazed pieces representing cauliflowers, etc., were imitated. Some decorative pieces, e.g. table comports supported by three dolphins, flower shells and jewel cups, very thinly potted and covered with mother-of-pearl glaze, resemble Belleek ware. Production of majolica ceased in 1890 after extensive damage to the pottery by fire. Examples of experimental hard-paste porcelain shown in the New Orleans Exhibition (1904) included a pitcher with flattened circular body, decorated in relief with American emblems in pinkish buff against a gold ground, the spout in the form of a tricorned soldier's head. This design was also produced in white earthenware, glazed and gilded. The company became Griffen, Smith & Co., then Griffen, Love & Co. and, finally in 1891, the Griffen China Co., producers of plain white table services in translucent porcelain, until the closure of the works in 1892.
Marks: monogram of GSH, sometimes impressed in a circular mark and surrounded by the name of the ware; ETRUSCAN or ETRUSCAN MAJOLICA.
Ref: Barber (1976).

Griffiths, John Howard (1826-98). Ceramic decorator. Griffiths was born in Staffordshire, where he worked before settling in London, Canada. His brother James Griffiths (d 1897), was also a decorator in Staffordshire, and both brothers served apprenticeships at the Minton factory, with a younger brother, who was a trainee presser of hollow ware.

On reaching Canada, John Griffiths started a farm, which was eventually worked by his son, and worked as a tin-painter before opening a photographic studio (c.1865). He was among the founders and later principal of the Western School of Art in London, Ontario, and taught china painting. In 1887, he painted a porcelain *tête-à-tête* service for presentation to Queen Victoria on her Golden Jubilee, with pieces circled with wreaths of maple leaves and decorated with a crown and VR in foliage and small roses. While specializing in the painting of roses, Griffiths also painted figures, birds and studies of other flowers. Often using Wedgwood blanks, he decorated everyday tableware.

Work sometimes signed, usually on reverse.
Ref: Collard.

Grindley Hotel Ware Co. *See* Robinson, Harold Taylor.

Grittel, Emile (1870-1953). French painter, sculptor, medallist and potter. Through

G.*Hoentschel, he met J.*Carriès, under whom he studied. He established a studio in Clichy, Paris, where he also fired stoneware made by Hoentschel, meanwhile working in association with E.*Lion at Saint-Amand-en-Puisaye (Nièvre). Grittel's work, often of Japanese inspiration, included pieces in the shape of apples, pears, etc., with monochrome glazes in muted colours, highlighted with gold, and vases with relief decoration of natural forms.

Marks: incised or painted signature.
Refs: Brunhammer *et al* (1976); Camart *et al*; Hakenjos (1974); Heuser & Heuser.

Grocott, Samuel. *See* Edge & Grocott.

Groeneveld, Pieter (b. 1889). Dutch artist and potter, born in Batavia. He studied painting and drawing at the Rijksacademie in Amsterdam and started training as a potter in 1923 near the *Amphora factory, where his work was fired. He established a workshop in Wassenaar for the production of flower vases in 1925, and founded the Groeneveld Aardewerkfabriek Voorschoten.

Marks include a vase with a pedestal formed by the initials PG, and the initials over three crescents.
Refs: Scheen; Singelenberg-van der Meer; M.G. Spruit-Ledeboer *Nederlandse Keramiek 1900-1975* (Amsterdam, 1977); van Straaten.

Groff, John. *See* Leidy, John.

Grootenburg pottery. *See* Dresler, Paul.

Grossbreitenbach. German porcelain factory established 1778 in Grossbreitenbach, Thuringia, and operated 1782-1869 by the *Greiner family. The output consisted mainly of everyday tableware and figures, which in the early 19th century included beggars, saints and portrait figures of Napoleon, Martin Luther, etc. After its sale in 1869, the factory produced figures, vases, clockcases, boxes, cane handles, tobacco pipes, etc., under H. Bühl & Sons, for three generations. The firm purchased part of the former Moritz Freytag business, afterwards trading under Freytag's name until nationalization in 1873. The factory now produces tableware.

Other factories operating in Grossbreitenbach from the mid 19th century included those of Fritz Graf (making low-priced gift wares); Adolph Harras (1861) and Julius Harras (1886), mass producers of gifts and everyday tableware.
Refs: Danckert; Scherf; Weiss.

grosse porcelaine. A porcellaneous stoneware body introduced at the Sèvres factory, under the direction of T.*Deck, for architectural use. The body, which remained plastic for sufficiently long when unfired to allow modelling (rather than the speedier processes of casting and moulding) was used to make vases, garden ornaments and sculptural pieces, with hard-wearing transparent glaze.

W.H. Grueby. Ochre-glazed pottery vase, 1910. 19 cm high.

Grosvenor, Frederick. Potter working in Scotland. Grosvenor established the Bridgeton Pottery in Glasgow in 1869 for the production of salt-glazed and Bristol-glazed stoneware, including spirit jars, bottles and chemical ware, as well as brown-glazed earthenware teapots. In 1870 he took out a patent for the machine production of bottles and jars. He was joined in business by his son in 1899 and operated the Eagle Pottery from 1906. The firm continued unitl 1926.

Printed marks include the name of the firm and an eagle.
Refs: Godden (1964); Hughes (1977); Jewitt.

Grotell, Maija (1899-1973). Studio potter, born in Finland, where she studied painting, sculpture and design at the school of industrial arts. Grotell was a postgraduate pupil of A.W.*Finch. She settled in America in 1927, subsequently working for a ceramic studio in New York City, and taught ceramics at a settlement house and then at Rutgers University, New Brunswick, New Jersey, 1936-38. Her early work in simple, ovoid, spherical or cylindrical forms, painted with Art Deco patterns of harbour scenes, etc., won prizes at exhibitions in Barcelona (1929) and Paris (1937). In a New York gallery, she exhibited thrown dishes decorated with stylized human figures. She later experimented with geometrical relief designs on matt-glazed stoneware, also using ash glazes over painted slip, and crackle glazes with colour rubbed into the network of lines.

Maija Grotell joined Cranbrook Academy of Art at Bloomfield Hills, Michigan, where she succeeded W.D.*Gregory as head of the ceramics department, 1938-66. Her own work there in earthenware and stoneware ranges from shallow bowls to large, thrown vases, still in simple, forceful shapes. Using deep turquoise blues, rust and shades of red, she painted strong designs carefully related to form and size. Continually experimenting, Maija Grotell became noted for rough-textured glazes, including a cratered glaze achieved by using a clear stoneware glaze over Albany slip. In her

teaching, she encouraged self-reliance and independent thought in her students, while insisting that they gained a thorough grounding in technical skills.
Refs: 'Ceramics' in *Design Quarterly* 42-43 (1958); Clark & Hughto; Donhauser; E. Levin 'Maija Grotell, Herbert Sanders' in *Ceramics Monthly* 24 (November 1976); J. Schlanger 'Maija Grotell' in *Craft Horizons* 29 (November, December 1969).

Gruber, Jacques (1870-1933). French painter, designer and craftsman, born in Sundhouse (Bas-Rhin). Gruber studied, on a scholarship from the city of Nancy, under Gustave Moreau at the Ecole des Beaux-Arts in Paris. Returning to Nancy, he worked at the Daum glassworks from 1894-97. He also taught at the Ecole des Beaux-Arts, persuading local industrialists to finance his students' projects. His pupils included the painter and designer, J.*Lurçat. He designed glass, furniture, bookbindings, etc., as well as ceramics, which were produced by J. *Mougin.

From 1900, Gruber designed and made furniture. Ten years later, he opened a stained glass studio, where he was succeeded by his son.

Mark: painted signature.
Refs: Bénézit; Bloch-Dermant; Brunhammer *et al* (1976).

Grueby, William Henry (1867-1925). American potter. Grueby trained in ceramics at the tileworks of J.G.*Low c.1880-90, then started a pottery making architectural earthenware, including wall panels, wainscoting, etc., at Revere, Massachusetts, and in 1891 entered a brief partnership with Eugene R. Atwood, trading from the office of agents of the Boston Fire Brick Works as Atwood & Grueby. He acted as representative for the brickworks at the World's Columbian Exposition in Chicago (1893). Still based in the same Boston premises, he formed the Grueby-Faience Co. in 1894, making glazed bricks, tiles and terracotta and initially following historical styles, e.g. Moorish and Chinese tiles, or plaques after the Della Robbia family. He developed the company in 1897, with G.P.*Kendrick among the principals, first exhibiting vases and lamp bases designed by Kendrick in the same year. Grueby's art ware was thrown in the heavy clay from New Jersey and Martha's Vineyard that was used for tiles, in shapes at first inspired by the work of A.*Delaherche, which had been displayed in the World's Columbian Exposition in Chicago (1893). Decoration was restricted to natural forms, either austere in treatment or botanically specific—flowers of the daffodil or narcissus, leaves of the mullein, plantain, lotus, magnolia, or grasses – all modelled by hand on the forms, which were initially thrown. After biscuit firing, pieces were glazed with matt enamels in blue, yellow, brown, shades of grey, an ivory crackle glaze and, notably, in the green matt with delicate veining and mottling resembling the rind of cucumber or watermelon that became associated with Grueby and was widely copied by 1906, e.g. by A.*Van Briggle, T.J.*Wheatley and the *Denver Art Pottery, Hampshire, *Merrimac, Pewabic, *Rookwood and Teco Potteries, and in *Zanesville. On some later pieces, two or three colours were used in combination, and raised parts of the decoration were sometimes accentuated with touches of glaze. Grueby also used his green glaze on architectural ware, but the decoration of tiles was much wider in inspiration than the art ware and included illustrations from Lewis Carroll and Rudyard Kipling, as well as floral or geometrical designs. The *cloisonné* technique was often used for tiles, but only rarely on vases. Glazed paperweights in the form of scarabs were made from 1904. In 1899, the title Grueby Pottery (company incorporated in 1907) was used to designate art ware, with Grueby Faience reserved for architectural faience. The division between the firms is not clear; vases were glazed and fired by Grueby Faience and the Pottery provided designs for architectural ware. After the bankruptcy of Grueby Faience in 1909, Grueby organized the Grueby Faience & Tile Co. for the production of architectural ware using his own glazes and techniques. The Grueby Pottery continued, at first under the management of former business manager William H. Graves, with K.*Langenbeck as superintendent and technician, but the production of art ware ceased in 1911. The Grueby Faience & Tile Co. was rebuilt after damage by fire in 1913, and was moved to New Jersey in 1921 after purchase by the C. Pardee Works of Perth Amboy in 1919. Grueby died in New York.

Marks: impressed mark featuring a lotus flower (Grueby Faience Co.), GRUEBY POTTERY, also impressed, after 1905.
Refs: Barber (1976); R.W. Blasberg 'Grueby Art Pottery' in *Antiques* 100 (August 1971); Eidelberg; Evans; Henzke; Jervis; Keen; Kovel & Kovel; Watkins (1950).

Grünstadt. German earthenware factory operating from 1801 at Grünstadt, Rhineland. The founder, Johann Nepomuk van Recum (d 1805), began production of white earthenware using moulds and materials dating from his ownership of the Frankenthal porcelain factory from 1797 until its closure in 1800. Van Recum's heirs sold the Grünstadt factory to Wilhelm and Bernard Bordollo, whose family were owners until the 1880s. The output of decorative earthenware was characterized by a strong yellow tinge; the firm also made stoneware.

W.H. Grueby. Earthenware tile painted in brown, coffee and pale yellow, with green leaves. 15.5 cm square.

Marks: FB, GB or GBG (Gebrüder Bordollo Grünstadt), a double circle containing GB at the centre surrounded by FABRIK GRUNSTADT and surmounted by a crown.
Refs: Danckert; Haggar (1960); Honey (1952).

Guéden, Colette. Painter, sculptor and designer, born in Cochin-China, working in France. She studied at the Ecole des Beaux-arts at Saint-Etienne (Loire) before going to Paris, where she worked in textiles, wood and metal as well as ceramics, and from 1927 provided designs (including earthenware figures) for the Atelier *Primavera, later becoming manager of the studio. Her pottery was primarily decorative (e.g. large vases decorated with figures, or relief plaques of still-lifes, which she made in collaboration with Claudette Vignon), but included stoneware for the table in low, wide, flanged shapes, also sold through Primavera.
Refs: Faré; Forsyth.

Guérin, Louis. *See* Neppel, Pierre.

Guérin, William (1838-1912). French porcelain manufacturer, born in Mas de l'Ange, Couzeix, near Limoges. After training in porcelain techniques and the completion of his military service, Guérin rented a decorating workshop in the Faubourg Montjovis, Limoges in 1836, carrying on an export trade. In 1872, he took over a porcelain workshop at the same site, and in 1877 he bought the factory in rue du Petit-Tour established by H.*Jouhanneaud and L.*Dubois. Guérin produced everyday tableware, architectural pieces such as friezes and fountains decorated with high-temperature colours, and laboratory ware. A catalogue of c.1888 lists openwork baskets and some rather elaborate pieces, such as lamp bases.

Guérin produced a service, Vague, with waves and scrollwork in white on pale pink, blue and green under the glaze. His Athénien service in classical forms was designed by P.*Comoléra. Large pieces included bowls, vases and *jardinières* decorated in high-temperature colours. Guérin's sons, William and André, joined him in 1903 and their firm, W. Guérin & Cie bought the neighbouring *Pouyat factory in 1911. The combined firms traded as Guérin & Cie, with the Guérin family owning three-quarters of the business. After Guérin's death and the departure of his sons to war in 1914, a new company, Guérin Pouyat Elite, was formed in 1921, following the purchase of Guérin & Cie in the previous year by the Montreal trading firm Bawo & Dotter Ltd, owners of the mark, Elite. Carl Bawo (b 1871), an American citizen born in Germany, was technical director of Guérin Pouyat Elite in 1923. The factory was demolished in 1933 after its closure in the previous year.

Marks: *W.G. & Cie* between two LS with LIMOGES/FRANCE after 1890. GUERIN & CIE (1912-20); GUERIN POUYAT ELITE; or *Pouyat* or earlier Guérin marks and ELITE, with arms of Limoges.
Ref: d'Albis et Romanet.

Guernsey Earthenware Co. *See* Cambridge Art Pottery.

Guest & Dewsbury. *See* South Wales Pottery.

Guignet. A porcelain factory established c.1808 by François Guignet in a former cotton-printing works at Giey-sur-Anjou (Haute-Marne). The factory's output included decorative baskets, and tableware, with the feet of baskets and *jardinières* often ending in lions' claws. Gilding was of high quality. Painted decoration, which included lavish flower patterns, was abandoned in 1837; the work was afterwards sent to Paris workshops for decoration. The firm also made jugs and laboratory ware in a coarse, greyish porcelain paste containing flint. At its peak, the factory employed about 400 workers, with another 400 or so employed at a branch in Beauvoisin near Langres. The firm failed in 1844.

Marks: in green or gold, *E. Guignet, Giey.*
Ref: Lesur (1967).

Guimard, Hector (1867-1942). French architect and designer, born in Lyons (Rhône). He studied at the Ecole des Arts Décoratifs and then at the Ecole des Beaux-Arts, 1882-85. Guimard conceived his buildings as a whole with furnishings and decoration, and the Castel Béranger (completed in 1898) was his first full expression of the Art Nouveau style with which he became associated. He used stoneware in the decoration of buildings and designed three shapes for production in soft paste porcelain at Sèvres (1903-04) with crystalline glazes.
Refs: Brunhammer *et al*; Préaud & Gauthier; Rheims.

Gulbrandsen, Nora. Norwegian potter. She became art director of the *Porsgrund porcelain factory in the mid 1920s and helped in the formation of an individual design for the output, based firmly on the development of style from function. Her aim of improving craft and industrial design arose in part from a reaction against the romantic idealization of folk art.

Gulin factory. Russian porcelain factory established in the village of Friazevo in the 1830s by the peasant Vasilii Gulin succeeded by his sons, who made tableware, tea services and figures. The factory was let to the Chernov brothers in 1856, closing in the following year.

Marks: originally VG; impressed '*Of the factory of the Gulin Brothers*'; an underglaze capital G.
Refs: Ross; Saltykov.

Gunmetal ware. *See* Owens, John B.

Gunther factory. Russian earthenware and porcelain factory working 1818-70 at St Petersburg. The firm's main output comprised coloured, glazed cream jugs, vases, etc., with applied relief decoration of flower sprigs, classical figures, key-fret patterns, acanthus leaves, etc. White earthenware table services were also made.

Mark: *E. Gunther & S/SPB* (1850-63).
Ref: Bubnova.

Guryshev factory. Russian pottery in the village of Minino, Bronnitsy, in the *Gzhel area, working 1850-70. The production included white earthenware, often with printed scenes containing figures surrounded by a floral border.
Ref: Bubnova.

Gustavsberg. Earthenware bowl painted in enamel on a tin glaze, designed by Stig Lindberg for the Gustavsberg factory, 1952.

Gustavsberg. Swedish factory established near Stockholm in the 18th century for the production of faience, and later creamware, transfer-printed in imitation of English wares. Porcelain, introduced in 1822, followed English styles until the late 19th century. The output included majolica, bone porcelain and parian ware from the 1860s, although the production of parian ware ceased in the late 19th century. Under the art direction of G. Wennerberg, c.1900, the firm made pottery with simple *sgraffito* floral patterns. W.*Kåge joined the firm in 1917, later becoming art director. The firm then produced domestic earthenware and porcelain, and individual pieces in stoneware. Kåge's own work included stoneware with green glaze decorated in silver and gold. Other lines introduced at the same time included Cintra (an exceptionally translucent porcelain paste), Farsta (copper-glazed ware) and Farstarust (pieces with geometric patterns in iron oxide). B.*Friberg, who joined the firm in the 1930s as Kåge's assistant, made individual pieces in stoneware. The firm's output was further expanded after reorganization in 1937 under the Swedish Cooperative Union and Wholesale Society, and Kåge's successor, the designer Stig Lindberg, produced ornamental wares, including slab-built figures with monochrome glazes, as well as a full range of functional tableware. He also headed an experimental studio which was set up in 1942 for the creation of individual designs and the development of new forms for the factory's main production. The designers included Karen Björnquist, whose Vardag service dates from c.1950. Glaze research was carried out by B. Friberg.

Marks usually incorporate GUSTAVSBERG GUSTAFSBERG and often an anchor device; names of body or pattern also appear in a variety of marks. The initials SSF printed within a circle appear from 1930.

The firm AB Gustavsbergs Fabriks Interessenter was founded in 1827 for the production of household wares.
Refs: Beard; Danckert; Forsyth; Pelka; Porzellankunst; Préaud & Gauthier; Weiss.

Guthrie, George. *See* Bendigo Pottery.

Guzhev factory. Russian workshop making porcelain and white earthenware in the village of Cherniatka near Tver from 1860. Under the founder, N.A. Guzhev, the works made household and garden ware as well as figures (modelled under the supervision of

sculptor N.V. Annenski) and vases. The workshop was sold to S.I. Maslennikov in 1879.
Mark: *Guzhev* in Cyrillic characters.
Refs: Ross; Saltykov.

Guzul wares. Ceramics produced by Guzul Ukrainian potters in the East Carpathian mountains. Production flourished from c.1825 to c.1875. A widely varied output included utilitarian ware and a range of decorated pieces: bowls, jugs, mugs, ring or disc-shaped wine bottles, flowerpots, candlesticks, model animals, whistles, etc., as well as stoves. Simple decoration was incised through white slip, and painted in red-brown slip or green and yellow pigments coloured with metallic oxides. Traditional Ukrainian patterns included flowers and foliage, geometrical motifs, working scenes, fairy tales, dancers, religious and military subjects. Much of the work was anonymous, but known artists included Petro Baranyuk (1816-80), who was noted for bold designs in bright colours painted over red slip. His pupil, Olexa Bakhmetynk or Bakminsky (1820-82), developed the theme of labour in painted decoration. Later 19th-century Kosov potters followed the immediate local tradition of working in a naturalistic style. Potters at the village of Pistyn also relied on natural forms, but mainly as a basis for more stylized designs. The work of Dmitro Zwitynk in the 1840s-60s made use of contrasting forms in bold patterns. His son and grandsons adapted his style, placing more stress on colour than form in design. Petro Koshak (1864-1940), also working in Pistyn, interpreted subjects in the folk tradition; Pavlina Tsvilyk (1891-1963), whose pieces included flasks painted with animals, shepherd, children at play, etc., also created warm, spontaneous decorative images.

The local tradition is preserved by folk art schools, where many of the potters learn their craft. Production now centres on the village of Kosov.

Gyngell, Albert (d 1894). Painter of landscapes and studies of grasses for the *Worcester Royal Porcelain Co. from his start as an apprentice in the 1870s.
Ref: Sandon (1978a).

Gzhel. Russian ceramic centre comprising the villages in the Bronnitsky and Bogorodskoye districts of Moscow province, which was rich in high-quality clay and noted for its pottery. After producing clay toys in the 15th and 16th centuries, potters in the region made tableware from local clay in the 17th century and, by the late 18th century, their flowerpots, jugs, mugs, jars, dishes and small figures in coarse earthenware with opaque white glaze were sold over a wide area, giving way in the early 19th century to a finer white or greyish-bodied earthenware and porcelain for domestic use by the middle classes and wealthier peasants.

Local peasant potters, who owned most of the smaller workshops, used greyish-white clay from a source discovered nearby in 1802, to make pitchers, jugs, bottles, etc., in forms already current in the 18th century, but replaced their earlier polychrome decoration with blue or, occasionally, brown and green in the 1820s. Their ware was often heavily potted in the rather coarse body, but

the decoration, well-suited to the shapes, was spontaneous and original. Painted subjects, often with a date prominently placed, were predominantly floral, but also included animals (notably cockerels) and features of the countryside (cottages, fences, etc.). Many of the pieces, especially jugs, bottles, vases, salt cellars, etc., were also decorated with small, stylized figures in relief on the rims, the shoulders of bottles and as finials. The figures, also produced freely as individuals or groups, included peasant musicians, workers, children at play, girls carrying out domestic tasks or dancing, etc., and animals, e.g. lion, horse, cockerel. All were painted with sketchy details (facial features, costume, harness of horses, etc.) in occasional dabs of bright colour. A.L.*Kiselev's yellowish-gold 'bronze' ware was widely copied locally until c.1840, and similar ware (jugs, candlesticks, salt cellars, ink pots, etc., as well as large pitchers, flagons and toilet sets) was painted with designs in pink lustre in the mid 19th century.

Pavel Kulikov, one of the Gzhel potters employed at the *Otto factory at Perovo, near Moscow, left after one year's work for Karl Otto, to open his own workshop, where he made porcelain. Within about 20 years of the theft of his formula by G.*Khrapunov and Kulikov's neighbour Ivan Kopeikin, the Gzhel district became an important centre for the production of Russian porcelain, with many workshops making display pieces, as well as simpler tablewares and figures of dandies, court ladies, Chinese men and women, negroes, shepherds and shepherdesses in costumes with gilded embroidery, street hawkers, servants and beggars.

Potteries working in the 19th century included those of the *Barmin Brothers and the Khrapunov family in the Bogorodskoye district and, in the Bronnitsy region, I.*Fedyashin, the *Guryshevs, the *Samsonov Brothers, the *Zhadin family and the Terekhov brothers, whose factory was taken over by Kiselev. Many of these workshops produced printed ware in large quantities in patterns similar to those used e.g. at the *Gardner factory.

Nationalization of some factories in 1919 was followed by the closure of small workshops in the 1920s. Craftsmen united to form the *Artistic Ceramics Cooperative and founded a factory at Turygino in 1934, and the area remains noted for the production of household wares with sketchy decoration of flowers, etc., in underglaze blue, and very stylized figures, which include animals covered with floral patterns and geometrical designs by Ludmila Azarova.
Refs: Bubnova; Ivanova; Ovsyannikov; Rozembergh; Saltykov.

Haag, Johann Jakob Heinrich and Johann Friedrich. Ceramic painters working independently in Thuringia in the second half of the 19th century. They were among many outside decorators of *Nymphenburg porcelain. J.F. Haag also worked at Regensburg, where he painted porcelain made at Ansbach and Nymphenburg for export to the Middle East. J.J. Haag also worked as an independent painter of silhouettes at Wallendorf.
Refs: Danckert; Scherf; Weiss.

Haas & Czjsek. *See* Schlaggenwald.

Haban Fayence or **Hafner ware.** Lead-glazed earthenware, originally mainly tiles, made by Hafner (stove makers) from the Middle Ages in Germany, Switzerland, Austria and Central Europe. Despite the development of tin-glazed ware in the 17th century, Haban Fayence, which was decorated in slip (from the late 16th century, generally with *sgraffito* designs) survived as folk art, especially associated with the Lower Rhine area. Decoration includes biblical scenes, equestrian figures, workers and costume studies.

Habertitzel, Josef Andreas Raphael. *See* Klösterle.

hachiro-de or **akaji-kinga.** Japanese porcelain decoration, often representing classical Chinese subjects, carried out in gold or silver on a red ground, and associated with the artist *Hachiroemon (and subsequently *Wazen). As decorator of the *Miyamotoya kiln at Kutani, Hachiroemon evolved a style which contained elements of both the *aka-e technique developed at the *Minzan kiln, using fine lines drawn in red enamel, highlighted with gold, and the more lavish patterns used in the *Ono workshop, which featured enamels in red and other colours, also with gold. For his patterns, he also drew inspiration from late 16th-century Chinese ink drawings of pavilions, birds, mythical subjects, children at play, etc., against geometrically patterned grounds. *See also* kinrande.
Refs: Gorham; Munsterberg; Nakagawa.

Hachiroemon Iidaya (1805-52). Japanese porcelain decorator associated with patterns in *hachiro-de style on *Kutani ware. Hachiroemon was born in Kanazawa (Ishikawa prefecture). Formerly a fabric designer, he was employed from the mid 1830s as decorator by *Miyamotoya, whose kiln was later also known as the Iidaya kiln. His style of decoration was widely imitated and, with the related *kinrande decoration, became identified with Kutani ware and sold in large quantities in Japan and overseas.
Refs: Jenyns (1951); Nakagawa; Roberts.

Hackefors. Swedish porcelain factory, making tea and coffee sets, gift ware, etc., from 1929, under the management of J.O. Nilson.
    Mark: HACKEFORS, under two crossed arrows with lightning-flash shafts and a line ending in an asterisk.
Refs: Cushion (1980); Danckert; Weiss.

Hackwood, William (c.1757-1839). Ceramic modeller. Hackwood worked for the firm of J.*Wedgwood & Sons Ltd, 1769-1832, as chief modeller of decorative pieces. His work included busts, portrait medallions and relief patterns of mythical subjects.
Refs: Batkin; Reilly & Savage.

Hackwood & Son. *See* New Hall.

Haddock, Albert (c.1888-1971). English ceramic gilder, apprenticed at the porcelain factory in King Street, *Derby, in 1902. He was employed at *Mintons from 1912 until he joined the army in 1914. He returned to King Street, and continued to work for Royal Crown Derby when the two firms merged. Haddock carried out the gilding of

James Hadley. Figure of a cricketer modelled by Hadley in blue-coloured clay, shaded ivory and gold. Hadley's signature, with impressed and printed marks. 20 cm high.

high-quality figures and services, including some made for Near Eastern rulers, and took responsibility for the training of apprentices in his later years, before retiring in the late 1960s.
Refs: see Derby.

Hadley, James (1837-1903). English ceramic modeller and designer. Hadley was working at the Royal *Worcester Porcelain Factory from the mid 1860s until he left to work as a freelance modeller in 1875. He executed many of the firm's vases and figures, including some reticulated ware and, notably, pieces in ivory porcelain imitating the Japanese shibayama technique on ivory. His Japanese figures and vases with relief decoration portraying Japanese lacquer workers, silk-weavers and potters were included in the firm's exhibition displays from the early 1870s. The decoration of a pair of ivory porcelain vases in Renaissance style after Cipriano Picolpasso, shown at the Paris Exposition Universelle in 1878, portrayed 16th-century Italian pottery techniques. Until 1894, much of the freelance work carried out in Hadley's studio in Worcester High Street (mainly figures and groups) was bought by the Royal Worcester factory, and issued with his individual mark. His work at this time included a series of figures after Kate Greenaway, gilded in a variety of shades and often carrying baskets. He also produced terracotta, often plaques, at the High Street workshop.
    Assisted by his sons, Howard, Louis and Frank, Hadley established a small factory (1896) in Diglis Road, Worcester. Early experimental work included thinly glazed earthenware, used in the production of candlesticks and vases with coloured clay mounts. Sinuous, stylized relief decoration

gave way to a more naturalistic style, often using coloured clays from c.1900. From 1896, Hadley produced porcelain, sold as Hadley Ware, resembling the work of the Royal Worcester company and often using an ivory-coloured paste. These vases, *jardinières*, etc., were characterized by scrolls and other moulded decoration in tinted clay, often a bluish green, combined with painting of full-blown flowers, often brightly coloured, with highlights wiped out.
    Hadley's sons sold his works to the Royal Worcester company in 1905. Work in the style of Hadley Ware continued in production for many years, with painting carried out in a special department at the factory.
    Marks include *Hadley*, incised or impressed on work modelled for the W.R.P. Co. until 1894; printed or impressed monogram of JH & S, 1896-97; printed (with ribbon labelled FAIENCE from 1900) until 1902; FINE ART/HADLEY'S/TERRA-COTTA, impressed c.1897-1902; *Hadleys* over a ribbon labelled *Worcester England*, printed 1902-05.
Refs: Godden (1961); Jewitt; Sandon (1978a).

Haeger Potteries. *See* Stangl, J. Martin.

Haeger Potteries Inc. American pottery established by David Haeger as the Haeger Brick & Tile Co. at Dundee, Illinois, in 1871. The founder's son, Edmund Haeger, started to produce industrial art ware in 1914, also making a line of florists' ware. The firm later operated as Haeger Potteries Inc.
Refs: 1871-1971: Haeger—the Craftsmen for a Century (Haeger Potteries Inc., Dundee, Illinois, 1971); J. Rogers 'Haeger Potteries 100 years old' in *Collector's Weekly* (November 1971).

Hafner ware. *See* Haban Fayence.

Haga, Plateelbakkerij. Dutch ceramics factory evolved from the Brantjes factory, which had made tiles and earthenware 1895-1904, at Purmerend, in styles inspired by De

Haga. Earthenware vase, painted with deep green, olive, yellow and grey. Marked Faience de Purmerend, Holland. *38 cm high.*

*Porceleyne Fles and *Rozenburg. From 1904 the works produced pottery designed by artists who included C.J.*Lanooij (art director, 1906-07), R.*Sterken, C.J.*van der Hoef, C.J.*van Muijen and J.H.*Teixeira de Mattos. Lanooij and the designer G.J.D. Offermans experimented with lustre glazes for vases. The firm merged with *Amstelhoek in 1907.

Marks include a monogram of HG with PLATEELBAKKERY/HAGA/*Purmerend*/HOLLAND; the monogram with HAGA; HAGA/PURMEREND; a wooden shoe, with *Faience de Purmerend*.
Refs: Hakenjos (1974); *Jugendstil uit Purmerend* (catalogue, Museum Waterland, Purmerend, 1978); van Straaten.

Hagi ware. Japanese pottery, mainly tea vessels, associated with the town of Hagi in Yamaguchi prefecture, Honshu Island, from c.1600. The ware was made initially by a Korean potter, Rikei, who took the name Koraizaemon. Eleven generations of his descendants included the 7th generation Sukehachi (d 1824), his successor Shimbe (d 1878) and the 9th generation Dosuke, who was working in the early 20th century.

The kilns are known for the tea bowls of Ido Korean inspiration, in a thick, fine-grained body, with crackle glazes resembling eggshell in texture and ranging in colour from light yellow to red. The 17th-century potter Miwa Kyusetsu, working at the branch kiln at *Matsumoto, introduced very thick pale green and blue or mauve-tinged glazes. A distinctive feature of Hagi ware is the cutting of the body with a spatula to interrupt the regular outlines of wheel-thrown bowls and vases; the shapes are simple and elegant. Pots made after the Momoyama period (1568-1614), when work was carried out for the ruling family, have notches cut in the foot to show that they were not produced for the aristocracy.

A branch at *Matsumoto and related kilns at *Fujina make wares derived from Hagi, and the *Rakuzan kiln was founded by Hagi potters.
Refs: Brinkley; Jenyns (1971); Koyama; Munsterberg.

Hague, Reuben E. English watercolourist and porcelain painter, apprenticed at the porcelain factory in Osmaston Road, in *Derby, in 1893. In 1906, Hague moved to Stoke-on-Trent, Staffordshire, where he worked independently as a ceramic painter. He painted tiles and panels with mermaids and other fabulous subjects, frequently for the export market, later also working as a designer of patterns for transfer printing. His later painting as a freelance for the Derby factory included portraits and reproductions of well-known paintings, often on plaques. As a watercolour artist, he was known for his landscapes.
Mark: signature.
Refs: see Derby.

Haidinger brothers. *See* Elbogen.

Haig Pottery. American pottery established 1810 in Philadelphia by Scottish-born potter, Thomas Haig (d 1831) for the production of red earthenware, sometimes black-glazed. Working in new premises from 1814, the pottery made plates and meat dishes with wavy or zig-zag lines trailed in slip. Haig moved his pottery again by 1819. He was succeeded by his sons James (d 1878) and Thomas, who expanded the business, adding stoneware (including chemical and domestic ware) to the output by 1843. The Haig brothers, working from 1844 on Second Street, Philadelphia, continued to produce tiles and firebrick as well as yellow and Rockingham-glazed wares and, briefly, vases and plaques with relief decoration. Thomas made and signed money boxes in the form of log cabins. In the late 19th century, the pottery's output included terracotta flower pots and such decorative ware as hanging baskets, pitchers and vases. Miniature thrown jugs, mugs, vases, etc., were a speciality of John S. Jennings, and another employee was noted for puzzle mugs after 18th-century models.
Refs: Barber (1976); S.M. Myers *Handcraft to Industry* (Smithsonian Institution Press, Washington, 1980).

Haile, Thomas Samuel (1909-48). English artist potter and painter. Sam Haile studied under W.S.*Murray at the Royal College of Art in London (1931-34). He taught ceramics from 1935 in Leicester, then at the Kingston and Hammersmith schools of art in London, where he shared a studio (1936) in Raynes Park. Although he was influenced by Surrealism in the paintings of his pots, his approach to ceramics arose from an awareness of the medium's special requirements. With his wife, the potter Marianne de Trey, he went to America in the late 1930s. Haile taught at Alfred University (*see* New York State College of Ceramics) and in 1942-43 at the University of Michigan at Ann Arbor. His work in America sometimes shows inspiration from Pre-Columbian sculptures, and, in the brushed decoration, Pueblo Indian pottery. In England after his enlistment (1943-45) in the army, he made slip-decorated earthenware with his wife at Bulmer Brickyard, Sudbury, Suffolk, and then established a pottery at Shinner's Bridge, Dartington, Devon in 1947. He was killed in a motoring accident. Haile favoured simple techniques, as in glazes with few ingredients which depended on the effects of firing for variation in colour. He is known for pots with decoration that made constructive use of the form, either by emphasizing its lines or by breaking down its limitations

Sam Haile. Bowl, Roman Baths, with figures in white against a grey ground, 1936. 33.3 cm in diameter.

(e.g. at rims) to make the pot and its decoration inseparable.
Mark: monogram of SH in a rectangle, impressed.
Refs: Clark & Hughto; G. Clark 'Sam Haile' in *Studio Potter* 1 (1978); Rose; A.C. Sewter 'T.S. Haile 'English and American Design Problems' in *The Bulletin of the American Ceramic Society* 21 (1942); Rose; A.C. Sewter 'T.S. Haile, Potter and Painter' in *Apollo* 44 (December 1946), *The Surrealist Paintings and Drawings of Sam Haile* (catalogue, Manchester City Art Gallery, 1967); Wingfield Digby.

Halcyon Art Pottery. American art pottery established 1909 at Halcyon, a Theosophist settlement near Pismo Beach, California, with Leon Awerdick as manager and A.W. *Robertson as teacher and pottery director. The output included vases, often angular in shape, bowls, pitchers, paperweights, match holders, incense burners, etc., in coarse, red clay, chiefly unglazed and with modelled decoration of natural forms, notably lizards; many pieces by Robertson were decorated with a single lizard in full relief. The pottery closed c.1913 in the re-organization of the colony, until G.R.*Wall ran summer courses in pottery-making there in 1931 and 1932 for the University of California, making white earthenware covered with glazes developed at the *Walrich Pottery. The pottery was dismantled in 1940.
Marks: HALCYON/CAL. surrounding a triangle; HALCYON/CALIF., both impressed on early work. In the 1930s, when marked, work bears an incised monogram of HP.
Ref: Evans.

Hall, Agnes. *See* Harris family.

Hall, Sidney (b 1877). English ceramic artist working at the *Doulton & Co. factory in Burslem from his apprenticeship under John *Slater in 1891 until 1952. Hall painted dessert services, plates, vases and other pieces with landscapes, studies of game and fish and, notably, flowers. He eventually became head of a department producing hand-painted wares in series, and took charge of training a group of junior painters.
Refs: see Doulton & Co.

Hall, William (1800-61). English porcelain decorator, born in Staffordshire. Hall worked as a flower painter at the porcelain factory in Nottingham Road, *Derby, leaving in 1821 with Jesse *Mountford to join the *Coalport factory until 1830. He was working in Staffordshire by 1831, for firms including those of S.*Alcock & Co., and W.T. *Copeland.

Work initialled by him includes a plate made at Coalport in 1822, painted with a basket of flowers in a landscape setting.
Refs: see Derby.

Hall, William (d late 1920s). Porcelain decorator working for the *Worcester Royal Porcelain Co. from 1874. Initially trained under J.*Hopewell, Hall painted subjects including fruit, flowers and birds; he carried out *cloisonné*-type decoration, gilding and the laying of ground colours. His flower paintings included fern, heather and old English flowers.
Ref: Sandon (1978a).

Halliday family. Potters working in York-shire, where they are thought to have moved originally from Scotland. Members of the family operated potteries near Halifax from the mid 17th century. George and Abraham Halliday left their brother Isaac to continue the family's pottery at Bate Hayne, which closed on his death in the 1780s. They est-ablished another earthenware works at Howcans in 1775. Abraham and his son, John (d 1850s), were listed as proprietors in the 1830s, when John took over management. The output of domestic ware from red-brown local clay was augmented in the mid 1840s with firebrick and chimney pots, which eventually became the sole product by 1900. The pottery closed on the death of John's son, William Halliday, in 1916.
Refs: Brears (1971a); Lawrence.

Hallstadt Keramik. *See* Baudisch, Gudrun.

Halot, F. French porcelain maker and decor-ator. Halot had a workshop in rue d'Angou-lême, Paris, where he specialized in painted porcelain by 1823. He also owned a factory in Montreuil-sous-Bois, and by 1844 started production in Mehun-sur-Yèvre (Cher), while continuing the Paris workshop until 1846. He patented a technique for the improvement of high-temperature ground colours, winning an exhibition award in 1839. He entered into partnership (c.1845) with his son Eugène, a porcelain enameller, who left him in 1855 to join Charles Pillivuyt (*see* Pillivuyt, L.).
Ref: Guillebon.

Halpern, Lea Henie (b 1899). Potter, born in Mikuliczyn, Poland, and living in Germany until 1917, when she moved to Holland. She trained in Berlin, under M.*Powolny in Vienna and 1928-32 at the Rijkschool voor Klei- en Aardewerkindustrie in Gouda. She subsequently taught at the Nieuwe Kunst-school and ran her own workshop (1930-40) in Amsterdam. Her work includes small modelled pieces, and she is especially known for her varied glazes. In 1940, she moved to New York.
Marks: signature, or initials with AMSTERDAM.
Refs: W.J. de Gruyter 'De pottenbakkerswereld en Lea H. Halpern' in *Elsevier's Geillustreerd Maandschrift* 49 (1940); *Lea Halpern* (Frans Hals Museum, Haarlem, 1974); J. Romijn 'Lea Halpern' in *Mededelingenblad Vrienden van de Nederlandse Ceramiek* 72 (1973-74).

Halpern, Stanislav (1919-69). Polish-born painter, sculptor and potter, trained at the School of Fine Arts, Lvov. Halpern moved to Australia in 1939 and settled in Melbourne, where he studied sculpture and painting. He began making pottery in the mid 1940s, and in 1946 set out to establish himself as a full-time potter, first exhibiting in 1950. He re-turned to Europe in 1951, from time to time working in France, and in 1964 established a pottery at Bouzigues. He returned to Mel-bourne in 1966. Shortly after his death, the National Gallery of Victoria held a retro-spective of his painting and pottery. Influ-enced by traditional Polish pottery, he worked with coarse, heavy, terracotta or earthenware clay. The decoration, painted in earthy colours, is abstract expressionist in style.

Hamada Shoji. Stoneware jug with temmoku glaze and rust-coloured patches. Made by Hamada at St Ives, 1920-23. 14 cm high.

Hamada Shoji (1894-1978). Japanese potter, noted for his contribution to the develop-ment of *mingei ware; born at Mizonokuchi (Kanagawa prefecture). Hamada trained in the ceramics department of Tokyo's technical high school, graduating in 1916. He also studied with the potters of *Tamba. Ham-ada's early work was influenced in style by Korean ceramics of the Yi dynasty, and he studied the glazes of early Chinese wares. Working primarily in stoneware and using ash or iron glazes, he produced vases and utilitarian wares in strong, simple shapes with muted colouring (olive, grey, brown and black), brushed with abstract designs, or patterns inspired by natural forms.
In 1920, Hamada visited England with B.*Leach and took part in experiments with lead-glazed slipware, a further influence on his style. After his return to Japan in 1924, he joined a rural pottery community in Okinawa. He later lived in *Mashiko, mak-ing domestic ware for sale in Tokyo, and carrying out research in the local clay. With Kawai and the critic and scholar Muneyoshi (Soetsu) Yanagi, he formed the Nihon Mingei-kan in Tokyo, 1929, and Japanese folk pottery provided another important influence in his work. He sometimes adopted the use of drip glazes, as well as the colour and textural effects of salt glazing. After a visit to England (1929-30), he built his own kiln in Mashiko. He perfected the persimmon glaze for which Mashiko ware is noted. His use of angular moulded or slab-built forms in the late 1950s and 1960s inspired other Japanese potters. His later work also includes raku-style ware. In 1955, Hamada was de-signated Holder of an Intangible Cultural Property of the Nation by the Japanese government for his mingei ware. His work is characterized by a direct approach to ma-terials and techniques, and a confident but unassuming treatment of form. He succeeded Yanagi as Director of the Folk Art Museum in 1962 and received the Order of Cultural Merit in 1963.
Mark: none, on principle, except for the brief use of a seal, impressed in a rectangle, at St Ives in the early 1920s.
Refs: Koyama; Masterpieces; Miller; Munsterberg; Okada; Roberts.

Hamann, Johann Wolfgang. *See* Wallendorf.

Hamilton, Cuthbert Fraser (1884-1959). English Vorticist painter. Hamilton worked at R.*Fry's Omega Workshop, where he designed carpets, rugs, lamp-shades and interior schemes, but left in 1913, dissatisfied with the Workshop's artistic values. By 1915 he was working as an artist potter in Yeo-man's Row, Kensington, in collaboration with W.S.*Murray. Pottery initialled by Hamilton has strictly formalized decoration, well-related to the thrown shapes and painted on a coating of white slip. Examples were shown at the Group X exhibition in London (1920).
Ref: M. Haslam 'Some Vorticist Pottery' in *The Connoisseur* 190 (October 1975).

Hammersley, Freeman & Co. *See* Asbury, Edward.

Hammersley, Titus. *See* Adams, Harvey.

Hammond, Henry Fauchon (b 1914). English artist potter and painter who trained at the Royal College of Art, London, under W.S. *Murray. Hammond initially worked mainly in stoneware with brushed decoration of natural subjects such as fish or ducks, and, celadon glazes in blue-green or grey. He taught at Farnham School of Art from 1939, with an interruption in World War II for army service. Again in Farnham from 1946, he made earthenware painted in slip with foliage, fish, etc., and returned to stoneware (c.1951), which he brushed with patterns in cobalt or iron of grasses, bamboo, etc., some-times using wax resist to control coloured glazes.
Marks: monogram of HH, impressed, in a rectangle.
Refs: Rose; Wingfield Digby.

Henry Hammond. Stoneware vase painted in dark brown on lighter glazes, c.1938. 37 cm high.

Hampshire Pottery Co. *See* Taft, James Scholly.

Hancock, Frederick (b 1817). English-born potter, in America from 1829. He trained in the stoneware pottery of I. Seymour in Troy, and from 1839 at the Norton & Fenton works in Bennington, Vermont, he started producing stoneware in Louisville, Kentucky, with his father, John *Hancock (d 1842) in 1840, and went back to Bennington in the following year. He established a pottery in partnership at Worcester, Massachusetts, 1858, and returned again to Bennington after selling out in 1877.
Refs: Barber (1976); Watkins.

Hancock, Frederick (d 1931). English ceramic artist. After brief employment as a clerk, Hancock worked as a painter for *Pinder, Bourne & Co. and subsequently for *Doulton & Co. in Burslem, 1879-1913, initially training under John *Slater. He was noted for the variety of his subjects, which included birds, cattle, game, wild animals and fish in their natural settings, flowers (e.g. roses, carnations, chrysanthemums and marshland plants), studies of fruit, Oriental and Middle Eastern scenes, and British landscapes. He decorated table services, plaques and other ornamental pieces, including large vases. He carried out several commissions for Doulton & Co. after leaving full employment with the firm in 1913.
Refs: see Doulton & Co.

Hancock, George (d c.1850). English ceramist and porcelain decorator; a noted painter of flowers. Hancock was the second son of John *Hancock (1757-1847) and brother of John *Hancock (1777-1840). After working c.1801-02 at the decorating studio established by W.*Billingsley at Mansfield, and then in Staffordshire, e.g. for the firm of Job *Ridgway at Cauldon Place, Hancock established himself as an independent decorator in London, but returned to work in Staffordshire. During subsequent employment (1819-35) at the porcelain factory in Nottingham Road, *Derby, he carried out floral painting in a bold style, often on large pieces. He taught other artists, including J.*Haslem, and, as a layer of ground colours, supervised the use of a new technique in which powdered colours were laid through stencils. Hancock went on to oversee the making of porcelain at Burton-on-Trent, but again returned to the Potteries by 1836. He was briefly employed at a French factory near Lyons in 1839, and finally as a decorator of glass at Wordsley, near Stourbridge. Hancock also painted in watercolours; studies of flowers, insects and shells are preserved in Derby museum.
Refs: Godden (1972); Jewitt; L. Whiter *Spode* (Barrie & Jenkins, London, 1976).

Hancock, James (d 1865). English ceramic decorator, son of John *Hancock (1757-1847). He worked as a colour maker and ground layer at Worcester. His son, S.*Hancock, became proprietor of the porcelain factory in King Street, *Derby, and his nephew, also James Hancock, became manager of the Royal *Worcester Porcelain Co. in 1862.
Refs: see Derby.

Hancock, John (1757-1847). English ceramic decorator, born in Nottingham. After completing his apprenticeship at the porcelain factory in Nottingham Road, *Derby, 1769-76, Hancock specialized in flower painting, working briefly at the *Cambrian Pottery in Swansea and subsequently in Staffordshire, c.1785, where he worked for the firm of Turner at Lane End (closed 1806). Hancock is credited with the development of new techniques of gilding and with the introduction of silver lustres, based on platinum, used by H.*Daniel at the *Spode factory, where he was indentured 1805-07 as an enameller and ground layer. He worked as a colour maker and manager of the enamelling department at the Wedgwood factory from 1816, and died at Etruria.
Hancock was the father of G.*Hancock, John *Hancock (1777-1840) and James Hancock; he also had a grandson named John Hancock (1804-39) and a great-grandson (son of S.*Hancock) called John Hancock (1839-1911).
Refs: U. des Fontaines *Wedgwood Fairyland Lustre* (Sotheby Park Bernet, London, 1975); S. Shaw *History of the Staffordshire Potteries* (1829); W.D. John in Atterbury (1980); letter from John Hancock in *Staffordshire Mercury* (1846).

Hancock, John (1777-1840). English porcelain decorator; son of John *Hancock (1757-1847). Hancock was a colour maker and ground layer employed 1805 at the workshop of H.*Daniel in Stoke-on-Trent, and later working at the porcelain factory in Nottingham Road, *Derby, under his brother, G.*Hancock, from c.1820, and remaining in the same department until his death. He painted birds, often imitating the style of Sèvres. His son, John Hancock (1804-39), is thought to have worked at the Derby factory 1823-36 as a painter of birds, flowers, fruit and figure subjects, as well as heraldic crests.
Refs: see Derby.

Hancock, John (d 1842). English potter. Hancock was manager and colour chemist at the pottery of J.& R.*Clews, and later employed by L.W.*Dillwyn. He went to America in 1828, and started a pottery at South Amboy, New Jersey, for the production of stoneware and yellow-glazed earthenware. He established a stoneware pottery with his son, Frederick *Hancock (b 1817), at Louisville, Kentucky, in 1840, and the following year was among the partners in *Salt, Mear, Ogden & Hancock.
Refs: Barber (1976); Watkins.

Hancock, Joseph (b c.1876). English ceramic artist, apprenticed from 1890 at the *Doulton & Co. factory in Burslem and trained under H.*Piper and Charles *Noke. Hancock is noted for his painting of game birds, fish and other animals, e.g. cattle. He also painted landscapes after Corot, genre subjects featuring country people at work, and Egyptian scenes (e.g. Under Great Pyramid, on a vase c.1895). He remained at the Doulton factory until 1926 and returned there 1942-45.
Refs: see Doulton & Co.

Hancock, Sampson (1817-98). English porcelain manufacturer and decorator. The grandson of John *Hancock (1757-1847), and son of James *Hancock, he worked as a flower painter at the porcelain factory in Nottingham Road, *Derby, and was joint-founder (1848) of the factory in King Street, Derby, of which he was eventually sole proprietor. He taught his grandsons Henry Sampson Hancock (d 1834), who specialized as a painter in flowers and landscapes, and J.J. Robinson. Hancock and Robinson lived at Sampson Hancock's home while training at the factory.
Refs: see Derby.

Hancock, W.S., and Cook, C.H. *See* Trenton Potteries Co.

Hanke, August (1875-1928). German potter, the son of Reinhold Hanke and owner of the Kunsttöpferei Reinhold Hanke, making traditional salt-glazed stoneware at *Höhr-Grenzhausen. In 1893, August Hanke began a study of chemistry, and attended the Munich Kunstgewerbeschule. In 1901, with his brother, Carl Hanke (d c.1910), as business manager, he succeeded his mother, who had been director of the family's workshop since c.1886. He followed R.*Mutz in developing a wide range of glaze colours, including red, violet and a crystalline blue, and at the Industrial Exhibition in Düsseldorf (1902), the brothers showed work designed by H.*van de Velde, and a 'China red' copper reduction glaze developed by August Hanke. P. Behrens was among other designers employed by Hanke, sole owner of the factory after his brother's death, who collaborated with established artists on the design of his stoneware. Figures designed by Hans Wewerka were covered with a green glaze c.1910. The workshop's output also included large garden vases (over two metres high). Hanke carried out glaze research and design work at his own small studio, where he continued to make unique thrown pieces

*August Hanke. Stoneware vase designed by H.*van de Velde and produced by Hanke in Höhr-Grenzhausen, 1902.*

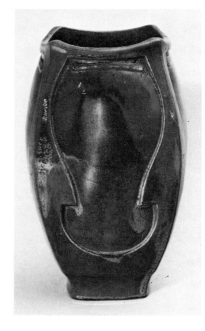

when the workshop ceased production in the 1930s. He was also concerned with maintaining traditional wares, winning the master's competition in Cologne (1937) with a jug which has a pattern of a stag and other game among foliage incised and painted in blue and manganese.

Marks: from c.1901, HANKE, impressed, sometimes impressed mark of van de Velde or logo of Deutscher Werkbund, of which Hanke was a member from c.1910. Incised signature, *A. Hanke*.
Refs: Bock; G. Reineking von Bock *Meister der deutschen Keramik 1900-1950* (catalogue, Cologne, 1978).

Hanley, J.& T. *See* Edwards, James.

Hansen-Jacobsen, Niels (1861-1941). Danish sculptor and ceramist. He studied in Copenhagen, 1884-89, afterwards touring Germany and Italy. He exhibited sculpture in French galleries in 1892 and 1893, returning to Denmark in 1894. He made earthenware and stoneware at his own workshop. His work included sculptural pieces and vases, strongly influenced in style by Japanese stoneware.
Ref: Bodelsen.

Hansen-Reistrup, Karl Frederik Christian (b 1863). Danish painter, sculptor and ceramic decorator. He studied in Copenhagen, 1881-82, and trained as a ceramic decorator, painting porcelain at the Royal *Copenhagen factory. In Paris 1885-87, he was a painter of battles and studied sculpture. On returning to Denmark, he began a collaboration with H.A. Kähler (*see* Kähler Ceramics).
Painted initials.
Refs: Beard, Bénézit; Haslam (1977).

Hansuke. A line of Japanese potters working at *Seto in the 19th century. Shentoen Hansuke, nephew of *Jihei, was noted for his copies of *Shonsui wares.
Refs: Jenyns (1965); Roberts.

Hansuke Kawamoto and Masukichi. Japanese potters working at Yokkaichi in Mie prefecture in the late 19th century. Kawamoto Hansuke was noted for his reproductions of 18th-century *Banko ware. Masukichi was among the potters exhibiting in the international exhibition in Vienna (1873); his work included the decoration of large plaques with landscapes, birds and other subjects. He also made porcelain tableware, vases and slabs with paintings of flowers, insects, fish, human figures, etc., in underglaze blue.
Refs: Jenyns (1971); Morse.

Hardenbergh, Elizabeth. *See* Byrdcliffe Pottery.

Harder, Charles (1889-1959). American ceramist and teacher, born in Birmingham, Alabama. He attended university in Texas and studied in the US Army training corps until 1919 and then at the Chicago Art Institute (where he later taught) until 1925. After teaching at Peabody High School in Pittsburgh, Pennsylvania, he became an instructor in 1927, and assistant professor in 1931, at the New York College of Ceramics, Alfred, continuing his own study under C.F.*Binns. After a year spent on research in Chicago, he returned to Alfred in 1936

and, as professor of ceramic art, re-organized the ceramics courses to comply with state requirements. Harder was head of the design department from 1944, after acting as deputy for four years. His own work, including salt-glazed domestic stoneware, depended more for effect on surface texture than on decoration, which was kept to a minimum. When he did use ornament, Harder tried to 'ram it into the wet clay while the pot is still fresh and tie it up with the glaze treatment in such a way that it can't get away from the form.' He won a gold medal at the International Exhibition in Paris (1937) and in the following year the Binns Medal of the American Ceramic Society, which he had joined in 1928, becoming a Fellow in 1947.
Refs: Clark & Hughto; C.M. Harder 'Functional Design' in *The Bulletin of the American Ceramic Society* 21, No 8 (August 1942), 'A Message to Ceramic Designers' in *Ceramic Industry* (June 1945); J.N. Norwood *Fifty Years of Ceramic Education at State College of Ceramics, Alfred* (Alfred, New York, 1950).

Harding, W.& J. *See* New Hall.

hard-paste or **true porcelain.** Fine, white clay body containing kaolin and silica and fired to vitrification at a temperature in the region of 1350°C. Chinese true porcelain is a mixture of white china clay (kaolin) and petuntse or china stone (a fusible rock of granite origin) glazed with powdered feldspathic rock and flux in a single firing. The secret of its manufacture was discovered by the German alchemist Johann Friedrich Böttger c.1708 and used at Meissen.

Haring or **Herring,** David (1801-71). Pennsylvania potter, born of German parents in Haycock, Bucks County. He trained with his elder brother, John Haring, who had established a pottery (c.1820) in Nockamixon, also in Bucks County, before himself starting a pottery in the same township, 1828. Haring made useful and ornamental earthenware with *sgraffito* or trailed slip decoration. His work included a *sgraffito* dish decorated with impressions of leaves, a tobacco jar with openwork sides, and a simple goblet with brownish red glaze over the red clay; also crocks for preserves made from the local apple harvest. Small earthenware toys were made as samples in trials of new clays. Haring retired in the mid 1860s. His son, Jared R. Haring, established a pottery c.1861, making useful and decorative wares, including toys and whistles, about a mile from his father's pottery.
Ref: Barber (1976).

Hariu kiln. *See* Tsutsumi ware.

Harker Pottery. American pottery established 1840 at East Liverpool, Ohio, by the English emigré, Benjamin Harker (d 1844), for the production of yellow wares and Rockingham-glazed wares. Harker let the works to experienced potters, one of whom he hired to train his sons Benjamin and George S. Harker (d 1864). In 1846, the Harker Sons were joined by a partner, James Taylor (*see* Taylor & Speeler). Harker, Taylor & Co. made Rockingham-glazed ware (including hound-handled pitchers), as well as door knobs, toys and tiles. Benjamin

Harker Jr left in 1853 to form a company with G. Smith and made Rockingham and yellow-glazed wares. He returned to the family pottery after 1855. With his sons, he established the Wedgwood Pottery, East Liverpool, in 1877, making cream-coloured earthenware until its sale in 1881.

The partnership George S. Harker & Co. continued the Etruria pottery built in 1846 by Harker, Taylor & Co. From 1877, the firm was under the management of W.W. Harker, son of George S. The production of Rockingham and yellow-glazed wares was replaced by ironstone in 1879, and the output consisted of tea and toilet sets, dinner ware and cooking utensils in 1880. The firm was incorporated in 1890 as the Harker Pottery Co. and soon began production of semi-porcelain. The firm moved to Chester, West Virginia, in 1931. The production of wares in white granite and semi-porcelain continued, with the addition of novelty items for advertising purposes. The firm's output included ware decorated in low relief, blue on white, with the mark Cameo ware; other lines were White Rose, Bakerite and Hot Oven. Operation ceased after purchase of the firm by the Jeanette Glass corporation in 1972.

A variety of marks include HARKER/THE OLDEST/POTTERY IN/AMERICA and several incorporate the founding date, *1840*. Marks featuring a bow and arrow device were in use from the late 19th century.
Refs: Barber (1976); Gates & Ormerod 'The East Liverpool Pottery District' in *Historical Archaeology* Vol 16 (Society for Historical Archaeology, 1982); Lehner; Ramsay.

Harkink, Daniel (1862-1953). Dutch artist and ceramic painter. He worked for De *Porceleyne Fles until 1883 while studying at the art academy in The Hague, and then joined the *Rozenburg factory as a technician concerned in the development of colours. In 1901, he was engaged on the analysis of clay, pigments and glazes at *Zuid-Holland, where he also worked as a designer and decorator. After his retirement in 1924, he worked as a painter.
Mark: initials DH.
Refs: Scheen; Singelenberg-van der Meer; van Straaten.

Harkort, Hermann. *See* Velten-Vordamm.

Harmand, François. *See* Montgarny.

Harmony Art Ware. *See* Foley Potteries.

Harper, Helen M. *See* Lonhuda Pottery.

Harradine, Arthur Leslie (d 1965). English ceramic modeller. Harradine started as an apprentice with *Doulton & Co., working at the Lambeth studio, 1902-12, and on a freelance basis in Burslem, c.1920-60. His designs produced at Lambeth included a series of characters from Charles Dickens, slip-cast in cream stoneware; a set of spirit flasks depicting such politicians as A.J. Balfour, R.B. Haldane, Neville Chamberlain, Lloyd George, H.H. Asquith, as well as Samuel Johnson, each in limited editions of 250 in brown saltglaze, and in the same period, a Roosevelt mug in white saltglaze. He also modelled figures of birds in stoneware with

*Arthur Leslie Harradine. Figure of a North African warrior modelled by Harradine for *Doulton & Co. With monogram of LH. 24.5 cm high.*

decoration in coloured slips. His commemorative pieces included busts of King George V and Queen Mary, and in 1920 Charles Dickens. Harradine also modelled a number of figures in a hard porcelain paste originally developed for laboratory ware.

Having moved to Canada in 1912, Harradine joined a Canadian regiment, fought in France during World War I and, on his return to England, worked as an independent artist. He designed hundreds of figures for production at Doulton's Burslem factory, including Top o' the Hill, Autumn Breezes, Fruit Gathering, the Old Balloon Seller and the Goose Girl. The series of characters from Dickens and *The Beggar's Opera*, previously made in stoneware at Lambeth, were reissued in porcelain. His modelling is noted for its liveliness and portrayal of movement.

Mark: monogram of LH.
Ref: Eyles (1975, 1980).

Harras, Adolf and Julius. *See* Grossbreitenbach.

Harrington, Thompson. American stoneware potter trained in Massachusetts and at Hartford, Connecticut. Harrington moved in 1826 to Lyons, New York, where he managed and, from 1852, owned the pottery established by N.*Clark. The pottery's work, noted for its high quality, included a jar with a sunburst design that centred on a face sketched in slightly raised dashes of coloured glaze, and a water fountain with twisted handles, decorated with a bird perched on a sprouting tree stump, with lines of shading applied in glaze from a quill. Harrington was also joint manager of Clark's Rochester

branch by 1841, and a partner in the pottery 1852-54. He was succeeded at Lyons by Jacob Fisher, who managed the pottery from 1872 and purchased it in 1878.
Refs: Ketchum (1970); Stradling; Watkins; Webster.

Harris, Charles. English porcelain painter, apprenticed at the factory in Osmaston Road, *Derby, in the 1890s. Harris painted delicate sprays of flowers, and brightly coloured birds in the Chelsea tradition, and worked with C.*Gresley on a marriage service for Princess May of Cambridge. After leaving the Derby factory c.1911, he is thought to have emigrated to America.
Refs: see Derby.

Harris, Charles. *See* Buffalo Pottery.

Harris family. English potters making mainly domestic earthenware in the area to the south of Farnham, Surrey, and in Hampshire.

Absalom Harris (b 1837) learned pottery techniques while working for relatives who ran potteries in the area surrounding Bishop's Waltham, Hampshire. In 1860, he rented a disused pottery at Elstead, near Farnham, where he made flowerpots, chimneypots and tiles for sale locally, while also working as a farmer. Six years later, he built a new pottery, The Holt, south of Farnham in the Alice Holt forest, and made plant pots, garden equipment, drainpipes, storage containers, and a small quantity of decorative ware. Suffering kiln losses due to a high content of lime in his local clay, he moved to Wrecclesham, where he built a pottery on land bought in 1873 for the production of horticultural and domestic pottery and a few pieces with yellow or brown glazes. After fulfilling a commission to copy a French green-glazed garden pot for watercolourist and illustrator Birket Foster, he began to reproduce other pieces on request, including a collection of green-glazed ware made from Farnham clay in the 16th century. Using

Thompson Harrington. Salt-glazed stoneware jar made by Thompson Harrington in Lyons, New York, 1852-72.

white clay from the same area and a glossy, iridescent glaze of even dark green containing copper oxide, Harris developed a line of Farnham Green-ware, with some designs copied from Tudor originals and many other pieces (including moulded birds, animals and architectural ornament) designed by W.H. Allen, art master at Farnham School of Art. Allen was associated with the pottery 1890-1943, encouraging his students to design and decorate pots which were made and fired at Harris's pottery, and making available at the art school courses in art and design for potters. Decorators of *sgraffito* ware included Ada K. Hazell in the 1890s and later Barbra Daysh, who executed geometrical patterns or copies of earlier designs (e.g. Hispano-Moresque) in the 1920s. Agnes Hall, who executed Art Deco *sgraffito* designs in the 1920s, was a teacher at Farnham Art School.

By 1905, the pottery made a variety of horticultural ware, garden ornaments, vases, hearth and mantel tiles, table and toilet ware and *sgraffito* art ware. Harris was assisted and succeeded by his sons William F. Harris, who took over the running of the pottery, and Ernest Harris, manager of business affairs, and daughters Gertrude and Nellie, modellers, decorators and designers. The pottery expanded steadily until 1914, and after World War I produced art wares with lead glazes in bright, blue, green and yellow. Still in the hands of Harris's descendants, it continues to produce horticultural ware.
Refs: Brears (1971a, 1971b).

Harris Manufacturing Co. *See* Trent Tile Co.

Harrison, John. English ceramic modeller, who worked at the *Copeland factory before going to America (c.1843-45) at the request of J.*Norton to assist in experimentation with the manufacture of porcelain at Bennington using local materials. His work included the modelling of a small basket holding a sleeping baby, surrounded by flowers and fruit, in unglazed grey porcelain, thought to be the first piece of porcelain produced at Bennington.
Refs: Spargo; Watkins.

Harrison, John. *See* Linthorpe Pottery.

Hart, Charles H. (b c.1867). English ceramic artist, born in Burslem, Staffordshire. Apprenticed under John *Slater at the factory of *Pinder, Bourne & Co. in 1880, Hart also studied at Burslem School of Art, and continued to work for *Doulton & Co. until 1927. He specialized initially in flower painting, but became known for his studies of fish and game. He also painted lakeside scenes and castles. His son, also Charles Hart (b c.1908), joined Doulton's as his apprentice in 1922. He followed his father as a painter of fish and game, but later helped in the development of the underglaze painting of figures.
Ref: Eyles (1980).

Hart, William. *See* Devon Art Pottery.

Hartgring, W.P. (b c.1874) and Johannes Hendricus (1876-1951). Dutch ceramic decorators, born in The Hague. W.P. Hartgring worked at *Rozenburg (1888-1907) and the

*Zuid-Holland factory (1908-17) before joining the firm of K. and J.*Vet in Arnhem as a designer and decorator. J.H.*Hartgring worked mainly at Rozenburg between 1892 and 1898 and subsequently at Zuid-Holland until 1928.

Marks: the signature *W.P. Hartgring*, or a heart; Johannes Hartgring used the initial J., a heart and GO.
Refs: Scheen; Singelenberg-van der Meer; van Straaten.

Hartley, Greens & Co. *See* Leeds Pottery.

Harvey, Isaac. *See* Knowles, Taylor, & Knowles.

Harvey, Lewis J. (1871-1949). English-born modeller, woodcarver and teacher, who lived in Australia from 1874. Harvey became a teacher, primarily of wood-carving, at Brisbane's Central Technical College, at first part-time, 1908-10, and then full-time, c.1913-c.1940. His work, with the exception of a few moulded or slip-cast pieces, is hand-built, with incised or *sgraffito* patterns resembling the decoration of wood, metal or leather; he occasionally painted under the glaze. Harvey was a gifted teacher and it was through his efforts that, during the 1920s and 1930s, the Brisbane Arts and Crafts Society (of which he was a founding member) exhibited more pottery and wood-carving than any similar society in other states. Student works closely follow the shapes, designs and glazes defined by Harvey.
Refs: G. Cooke *L.J. Harvey and His School* (Brisbane, 1983); Graham; W. Moore *The Story of Australian Art* (1934).

Hasami. Japanese kilns in Nagasaki prefecture, primarily making porcelain that closely resembled Old *Imari ware in paste and decoration. Established at Hatanohara, the kilns moved to several sites along the banks of the Toishi river, including Sannomata Hongama, Nakao Honnobori and Nagao Hongama, and on the Kawatana river, Uchinomi. All the kilns made utilitarian ware including plates, often with impressed patterns of flowers, saké bottles,

Lewis J. Harvey. Earthenware jar with pierced and sgraffito *decoration, painted and glazed, 1938. 10 cm high.*

Hasami. Vase painted in underglaze blue with a daikon and two butterflies, c.1900. 26.5 cm high.

rice bowls of varying shapes and sizes, cups for noodle sauce and tea. Wares were exported through Imari.
Ref: Okamura.

Haslem, John (1808-84). English writer, painter and porcelain decorator. Haslem was born in Carrington, Cheshire, and lived with his uncle, James Thomason, in Derby. He was apprenticed under R.*Bloor at the porcelain factory in Nottingham Road in 1822 and remained in Derby until 1835, when he left to work as a painter in London. Afterwards, he returned intermittently to carry out commissions for the factory, specializing in portraits and figure subjects, and eventually settled in Derby in 1857. He wrote for a local paper, compiled catalogues, and wrote from first-hand experience *The Old Derby China Factory* (1876), which became a standard work, and *A Catalogue of China* (1879). He served on the corporation's art gallery committee in the year before his death.
Refs: see Derby.

Hassall, Richard. *See* Green & Co.

Hasslacher, Benedikt. *See* Dallwitz.

Hastings & Belding. *See* Belding, David.

Hatanohara. *See* Hasami.

Haubrich, Albert (1875-1931). German-born ceramic artist. He moved with his family to Steubenville, Ohio, and worked as decorator (1897-1903) on the Louwelsa and Eocean lines for S.A.*Weller, and later for J.B.*Owens. He became manager of the decorating department at the pottery of A.*Radford (1903-04). In 1920, he moved to Columbus, Ohio, and established his own interior decorating business.
Refs: Barber (1976); Evans; Kovel & Kovel.

Hautin, Boulenger & Co. French earthenware factory established 1804 at Choisy-le-Roi (Seine) by the Paillart brothers, of whom one was replaced by Hautin, 1824. Hautin subsequently worked alone and was then in partnership with Louis Boulenger until 1864. He was succeeded by Hippolyte Boulenger, who formed a company in 1878.

The early tableware, with slightly yellow-tinged white glaze, included pieces with relief beading or perforated basketwork borders. Printed decoration was at first executed in deep red, then in black, often on a ground of roses. Later, elegant, simple scenes from Roman history, provincial views, royal portraits, etc., were surrounded by a garland of stylized flowers or simple black lines. Relief borders of gadroons or arabesques appeared in the 1830s surrounding scenes depicting working life. Other subjects included Paul et Virginie. The initial wood firing was replaced by coal in 1840, and the lead glazes were superseded by a harder glaze containing borax, used on a white body. Relief and printed decoration were further developed and included fantasy subjects printed in white on a pale blue ground, although most printing was carried out in black with hasty dabs of colour added. Some black-printed plates were given blue borders. the firm also produced *émaux ombrants* and *trompe l'oeil* plates for asparagus or oysters, and pots in the form of a duck or pig. H. Boulenger also produced Palissy ware and imitations of Henri II ware, afterwards experimenting with such decorative techniques as *pâte-sur-pâte* and crystalline and, later, *flambé* glazes. Applied crabs and other animals in relief were glazed with a blue crystalline effect on a cream ground.

L.-R.*Carrier-Belleuse was art director and designer. H. Boulenger also produced work carried out by E.*Chaplet while he was working for C.*Haviland at the rue Blomet studios.

In 1934, the Faïencerie H. Boulenger & Cie formed a group with Creil-Montereau and a workshop making rustic ware in Alençon, closing the Choisy-le-Roi factory in the same year.

Marks include a monogram of HB & Co. and the firm's initials, and often incorporate *Choisy-le-Roi* or *Choisy le Roy*.
Refs: Bodelsen; Ernould-Gandouet; Lesur (1971).

Haviland, Charles (1839-1921). Limoges porcelain manufacturer, born in New York. With his father, D.*Haviland, and brother, T.*Haviland, he established Haviland & Cie (1864), of which he was director from 1866. Until 1872, the firm's decoration consisted mainly of lines or bands, with some small bouquets of lilies-of-the-valley, moss roses, etc., but display services included one shown in the Exposition Universelle (1867) with a blue ground, reserves painted *en camaïeu*, and biscuit figures incorporated in the design. Haviland went to Paris in the 1870s, opening in 1873 an experimental studio in the suburb of Auteuil, which he put under the direction of F.*Bracquemond (subject to Haviland's own approval of samples for commercial production), intending to use the designs developed there to bring the firm's output up to date both artistically and technically. In 1875, E.*Chaplet introduced barbotine decoration, which was carried out on vases, etc., both by artists employed at the studio and by freelance decorators, but Haviland discontinued this work when it proved unprofitable. The studio, however, went on creating decoration for porcelain made at Limoges until 1914.

In 1881, Haviland took over direction of the Auteuil workshop and made available a studio on rue Blomet, Vaugirard (nearer to the centre of Paris), where Chaplet worked on the development of his brown stoneware. Artists at the rue Blomet studio, including A.-L. and E.-A.*Dammouse, J.-P.*Aubé, D.*Ringel d'Illzach, used coloured slips to decorate vases, bottles, etc., with naturalistic or Japanese-inspired motifs, either in low relief or painted within outlines of resist to give a *cloisonné* effect when fired. The studio supplied moulds to Limoges for production in porcelain with underglaze decoration. The high-fired body was otherwise unglazed in this early work, but by 1885 wholly or partially unglazed pieces were being produced, with decoration of animals or floral designs outlined in black or gold. Chaplet also carried out research in copper red glazes on stoneware. In early 1886, Haviland withdrew from the studio, leaving Chaplet in full control. He dissolved Haviland & Cie in 1891, forming a new firm, Haviland & Co., with his eldest son G.*Haviland. He remained a director until his death.

Mark: H & Co., underlined and sometimes over the initial L from 1876 and with the addition of FRANCE. The mark *Haviland/France* was used 1893-1930 and sold to Haviland S.A. (*see* Haviland, W.) in 1941.
Refs: Brunhammer *et al* (1976); Chavagnac & Grollier; d'Albis *et al*; d'Albis & Romanet; Heuser & Heuser.

Haviland, Charles Field (b 1842). Limoges porcelain manufacturer, born in New York. He worked for his uncle D.*Haviland in Limoges from 1852 until 1859, when he left to form a company on rue de la Mauvandière with his uncle, Richard Haviland, setting up a small workshop (employing eighteen workers) for the decoration of Alluaud porcelain (*see* Alluaud, F.) for export to New York, where he started the firm Ch. Field Haviland in 1870. Working in partnership with his father, Robert Barclay Haviland, and brother Frederick from 1865, he also rented a factory in Limoges, producing white ware, wood-fired, of high quality and in styles which appealed to American taste. In 1876, he took control of the Alluaud factory, having married Louise Malevergne, grand-daughter of the elder François Alluaud, in 1858. He retired in 1881, and the firm then passed to Gérard-Dufraisseix-Morel (*see* G.D.A.).
Mark: double circle containing CH FIELD HAVILAND/LIMOGES.
Refs: Chavagnac & Grollier; d'Albis & Romanet.

Haviland, David (1814-79). American-born porcelain manufacturer working in France. In 1829, David Haviland joined the business of his brother Edmond, selling English creamware in New York. With another brother, Daniel, he set up an import company D.G.& D. Haviland in 1838, later trading with their brother Robert as Haviland Brothers & Co., New York. The New York house failed in 1865. As retailers, the Havi-

*Charles Haviland. Porcelain vase produced by Haviland in Limoges to a design by E.*Chaplet and F.*Bracquemond, 1884.*

lands sold the work of Limoges firms, e.g. F.*Alluaud, and the *Pouyat and *Baignol families. In 1841, David Haviland went to Foécy (Berry) with his wife, Mary, and son, C.*Haviland. His second son, T.*Haviland, was born in Limoges, where the family settled in 1842. David Haviland acted as agent to the New York retail business and started a decorating workshop in 1847. He produced porcelain from 1855, also retaining exclusive rights to shapes commissioned from Alluaud, P.-J.*Gibus, Pouyat, etc. His firm made a wide range of everyday porcelain designed to appeal to American taste, often moulded in oval shapes with naturalistic floral decoration. Industrial methods were adopted as well as traditional techniques; the firm introduced chromolithography c.1875. Haviland was succeeded by his sons Charles (who was director of the firm from 1866) and Théodore in 1871.
Refs: Auscher; Chavagnac & Grollier; d'Albis & Romanet.

Haviland, Frank (1886-1971). French artist and designer, the youngest son of C.*Haviland and his second wife, Madeleine Burty. Frank Haviland acted as administrator of his father's firm after 1921, and was associated with a decorating studio in Limoges.

From 1908, a mark incorporating Frank Haviland's name appeared on high-quality decoration carried out for Haviland & Co. His paintings were signed *Frank Burty*.
Ref: d'Albis & Romanet.

Haviland, Georges (b 1870). French porcelain manufacturer, born in Limoges, the son of C.*Haviland and his first wife, Marie Guillet, who was the great grand-daughter of Etienne Baignol (*see* Baignol factory). Haviland worked in New York, and then

took charge of his father's Limoges factory. In 1895, he decided to build a new factory, which was opened at Mas-Loubier in 1904.

The firm continued to make display services for royal and diplomatic customers, but during the early 20th century effected a gradual return to simple shapes in normal production ware.

In 1925, Georges Haviland formed a new company in Limoges, with the Mirabeau bank as main shareholder, and an agency, Haviland China Co., in New York. After a financial failure in 1930, Haviland joined *G.D.A. in 1931; his factory site was sold to a Limoges businessman.
Ref: d'Albis & Romanet.

Haviland, Johann. German porcelain manufacturer working at Waldershof from 1907, on the production of everyday ware. The factory worked under Haviland's name until 1924, when it became Porzellanfabrik Walder-As Porzellangeschirrfabrik Waldershof it was acquired by the *Rosenthal firm in 1937.

Marks usually incorporate Haviland's or initials and *Waldershof* or *Bavaria*.
Refs: Danckert; Weiss.

Haviland, Robert (b 1897). Limoges porcelain manufacturer, the grandson of C.F.*Haviland. In 1924, Haviland established his own factory, Robert Haviland & Co.; he worked in partnership with his brother-in-law, Pierre Le Tanneur, from 1926 until Le Tanneur's retirement in 1949. The firm won prizes at the Exposition Internationale des Arts Décoratifs in Paris, 1925, with work decorated by E.*Alluaud and the Parisian artist Mme de Glehn, in Cairo and Barcelona, 1929, and again in Paris, 1937. In 1938, Haviland's company took over L'Union Céramique (established 1909); the proprietor, Camille Parlon, joined Haviland and Le Tanneur in that year, becoming Haviland's partner in 1949. The firm underwent great expansion from the late 1950s and specialized in reproductions made for the Museum of Modern Art in New York, as well as decorative plates designed by artists who included Jean Cocteau, Yves Brayer, Leonor Fini, Labisse and Touchaque. The output was noted for its careful finish; a large quantity of work was continued by hand, especially the pieces which depended for effect on the interplay of light and shade in relief decoration. Tableware and toilet sets, the main products, were decorated in enamel or underglaze colours, notably a pinkish-brown, by a number of painters.

Marks incorporate Haviland's initials or name, and the names of his partners, with *Limoges*; the trademark of Charles Field Haviland, after purchase of the mark in 1942 (this mark later used by G.D.A.).
Ref: d'Albis & Romanet.

Haviland S.A. See Haviland, William.

Haviland, Théodore (1842-1919). Limoges porcelain manufacturer. He worked for his father D.*Haviland and brother, C.*Haviland, until 1892. After establishing the promise of a sales outlet in New York through the Haviland agent, he made temporary arrangements for the production of samples with R.*Jouhanneaud, and in 1893 established a factory which became one of the largest in Limoges, with modern equipment, employing 800 workers in 1906. Haviland made progress in the technique of firing, and produced *flambé* grounds as well as underglaze decorated ware. He produced a paste, *porcelaine mousseline*, and developed biscuit pastes which could be lightly glazed for architectural use; examples shown in the Exposition Universelle of 1900 were modelled by Antoine Bourdelle, a pupil of Auguste Rodin. In the same exhibition, the firm also displayed a service painted by Léonce Ribière, *flambé* vases by Jouhanneaud, and a service designed by A.-L.*Dammouse for Queen Maria-Pia of Portugal. The low relief scrolls and floral decoration of this service stand out in white against a ground lightly tinted under the glaze with chrome oxide; plates with wavy rims have gilded edges and a monogram and crown in gold on the rim.

W.*Haviland opened a branch of the firm in America and succeeded his father in 1919.

Marks include the initials TH, either alone or with MONT-MERY; *Théo Haviland/ LIMOGES/FRANCE*; *Porcelaine mousseline/ Limoges/FRANCE*.
Ref: d'Albis & Romanet.

Haviland, William. Limoges porcelain manufacturer. He joined his father T.*Haviland in 1903, becoming the firm's administrator in the following year and proprietor in 1919. Work which he commissioned from J.*Dufy, S.*Lalique, and E.*Sandoz became influential in the development of modern styles after being shown in the Exposition Internationale des Arts Décoratifs in Paris, 1925.

Théodore Haviland. Flask and cover in puce and white designed by Edmond-Marcel Sandoz. Mark: Théodore Haviland, Limoges, Deposé Sandoz. *22 cm high.*

Subsequently, the firm's decoration was restricted to simple motifs in gold, red or silver near the rim, against a background of fine, ivory paste, or a newly developed silvery-green.

In 1941, the company bought the rights to models and marks used by D.*Haviland, and began trading as Haviland S.A. William Haviland retired in 1957, succeeded by his sons Harold and Théodore until the early 1970s. The firm is still in operation.

Marks: HAVILAND/FRANCE; HAVILAND LIMOGES/FRANCE.
Refs: Années 25; Baschet; d'Albis & Romanet.

Haviland China Co. *See* Haviland, Georges.

Haviland & Co. *See* Haviland, Charles.

Hawker, G. *See* Brain, E., & Co.

Hawkins, William A. (1858-1930). Porcelain painter working for the *Worcester Royal Porcelain Co., 1874-1928. Hawkins painted portraits, scenes with figures and still-life subjects on the centres of plates or in panels on vases, eventually becoming the painters' foreman. Outside the factory, he was a painter of miniatures.

Mark: W.A.H.
Ref: Sandon (1978a).

Hawley family. English potters working in Yorkshire. William Hawley (d 1818) established the *Top Pottery, Rawmarsh, in 1790, trading as Harley & Co., succeeded by his wife, Elizabeth (d 1844), and subsequently sons, Abraham (the pottery's manager) and George (c.1795-1863), who took over the *Low Pottery, which he bought in 1859. George Hawley was also owner from 1855 of the *Northfield Pottery, which operated under the management of his son, Charles and, from 1864, sons William (d 1868) and George Jr, who ran both potteries as W.& G. Hawley. William was succeeded in the partnership by his three sons, Matthew (c.1840-88), Arthur George (c.1850-97) and Walter, until a split after which George operated the Low Pottery alone from 1873 until his financial failure; however his nephews bought back the works from his successors in 1884. Sidney and John, sons of Matthew Hawley, became partners of their uncle, George, until his death, subsequently trading as Hawley Bros Ltd until 1903, with John running the Low Pottery and Sidney taking Northfield.

The initial output consisted of simple, enamelled wares, some decorated in colours resemblng Pratt ware. Late wares were printed.

Marks, when used, incorporate *W.& G. Hanley* and often a pattern name.
Refs: Jewitt; Lawrence.

Hawley, Philip and Thomas. *See* Kilnhurst Old Pottery.

Haynes, David Francis (b 1835). American potter. Haynes worked at a shop selling pottery at Lowell in his native state of Massachusetts from 1851. After travelling in Europe on behalf of his employers, he returned to America in 1856 and worked for a firm of plate iron manufacturers in Baltimore, Maryland, taking charge of the works in 1861.

Haynes was employed in the iron industry in Virginia from the end of the Civil War until his return to Baltimore in 1871 to take up an offer of a share in a pottery warehouse. He bought the *Chesapeake Pottery, and began to design pottery in response to the demand which he had noted during his selling experience. He aimed to improve the design of ware for everyday use.
Ref: Barber (1976).

Haynes, George. *See* Cambrian Pottery.

Hazell, Ada K. *See* Harris family.

Head & Dalton. *See* Stepney Bank Pottery.

Headman, Andrew, Charles, John and Peter. Pennsylvania potters. Andrew Headman made slip-decorated earthenware in Rock Hill, Bucks County, in the early 19th century, and was followed in the pottery by his son, Charles Headman, until late in the century. Two pie plates with *sgraffito* designs of tulip flowers surrounding, in one case, a parrot-like bird and Headman's initials, are dated 1808. Charles Headman's work included branched flower holders in coarse red earthenware with coloured slip decoration in low relief, of which examples are dated 1849.

A nearby pottery was worked by John Headman, who died at the age of 100 late in the 19th century. He was succeeded by his son, Peter, and subsequently a potter named Watson, making in the later years only flowerpots, drain, tile and basic domestic ware.
Ref: Barber (1976).

Heath, Lewis. *See* Adams family.

Heber & Co. German porcelain manufacturers working at Neustadt (Gotha) from 1900, on the production of everyday ware, figures, etc.

Mark: the initials HC on a shield, topped by a crown.
Refs: Danckert, Weiss.

Hedingham Art Pottery. *See* Bingham, Edward.

Heene, Wilhelm. *See* Gräfenroda.

Hegermann-Lindencrone, E. *See* Bing & Grøndahl.

Heidland pottery. *See* Amphora (Teplitz)

Heinecke, Albert. *See* Seger, Hermann August.

Heinrich, Franz. German porcelain decorator. Franz opened a decorating workshop, Heinrich & Co. at his home in Selb, Bavaria, where he employed several decorators for the painting of wares bought e.g. from Lorenz Hutschenreuther (*see* Hutschenreuther family). Heinrich & Co. started the production of porcelain, which was on sale from 1902, and the firm continued, with a break during World War II.

Marks incorporate H & Co with *Selb* or *Bavaria* sometimes with a crown.
Refs: Danckert; Haggar (1960); Weiss.

Heinz & Co. *See* Gräfenthal.

Heissner, August. *See* Gräfenroda.

Hemphill, Judge Joseph (1770-1842). A judge, and representative of the city of Philadelphia in the American Congress, Hemphill invested in W.E.*Tucker's American China Manufactory in 1831 and took over the administration of the factory in 1833, after Tucker's death, with his son Robert Coleman Hemphill as a nominal partner. His backing made it possible for the factory to be moved to a larger site, and there was a subsequent increase in production. Decoration consisted of sprigged patterns, flower studies, borders of roses, forget-me-nots and tulips, landscapes in sepia or charcoal, monograms and emblems, and a variety of gilt borders, including a spider pattern. The firm produced a wide variety of pieces—the pattern books presented to Pennsylvania Museum of Art list over 140 standard designs in tableware and vases alone. Others include *veilleuses*, frames for miniatures and larger pictures, scent bottles, inkstands, etc. The firm was incorporated as the American Porcelain Co. in 1835. After personal financial difficulties, Hemphill retired in 1937 and sold his interest in the factory, which was then leased to T.*Tucker.

Mark: *Manufactured/by Jos. Hemphill/Philad.*
Refs: Barber (1976); Clement; P.H. Curtis in *Ceramics in America* ed. M.G. Quimby (University Press of Virginia, Charlottesville, 1972); James; Ramsay.

Henderson, D.& J. *See* Jersey City Pottery.

Henderson, George and Charles. *See* Dorchester Pottery.

Henk, Christian (1821-1905). German-born painter, working as a ceramic decorator in England. He was employed by *Mintons Ltd from the 1840s and specialized in landscapes with figures, after Jean-Antoine Watteau, but also painted scenes with cupids.

His work was seldom signed.
Refs: Aslin & Atterbury; Godden (1968).

Henk, John (1846-1914). Ceramic modeller, son of C.*Henk. He was an apprentice at *Mintons Ltd in 1859 or 1860. As the firm's chief modeller, he specialized in animal figures, notably in majolica.
Refs: Aslin & Atterbury; Godden (1968); G. Godden in Atterbury (1980).

Henneburg, Friedrich Egidius. *See* Gotha.

Henning, Gerhard. *See* Copenhagen, Royal, Porcelain Factory.

Henri II ware. Earthenware made in the mid 19th century, following the designs of French 16th-century lead-glazed earthenware with inlaid decoration associated with Oiron (Deux-Sèvres) and Saint-Porchaire, near Poitou (Charente-Maritime) and sometimes known as Faïence d'Oiron or de Saint-Porchaire. The ware was copied at *Mintons Ltd by J.-F.-L.*Arnoux c.1858; elaborate Renaissance designs of clay varying in tone from reddish brown to black were inlaid in the cream-coloured or buff earthenware body of ewers, jugs, *tazze*, covered vases, plaques, etc. The work of C.*Toft, noted

Henri II ware. Vase and cover inlaid with blue, brown and olive green. Marked with a monogram, AP, *inlaid, and a paper label of the retailer,* Amirauld à Parthenay. *Made in France, mid-late 19th century. 50 cm high.*

artist in this style at the Minton factory, included a case for barometer and thermometer dating from the early 1870s, and a series inspired by the book *Recueil de toutes les pièces de faïences française dite Henri II* published in 1861 by C. Delange, which illustrated all known 16th-century examples. Imitations or adaptations were also made by potters at Parthenay, including P.*Jouneau, by U.*Besnard, E.*Lenoble, and by C.-J.*Avisseau, who showed Henri II ware at the International Exhibition in London in 1862. English makers included J.*Wedgwood & Sons; some firms, e.g. Kerr & Binns in *Worcester, copied the designs purely as surface decoration without using the inlay technique. In America, a line of pottery introduced late in 1900 by the J.B.*Owens Pottery Co. featured designs of Art Nouveau inspiration excised and filled in with coloured clay. Moulds for the line were acquired by the *Brush-McCoy Pottery and issued 1912 with white designs on a matt green ground in the company's New Navarre line.
Refs: Aslin & Atterbury; Evans; Ernould-Gandouet; Haslam (1975); Kovel & Kovel; Lesur (1971); Tilmans (1954).

Henson, John. *See* Derby.

Hentschel, Julius Konrad (1872-1907). German sculptor and modeller, trained at the Meissen school (1890-95) and at the Munich academy (1891-93). Hentschel worked as repairer and modeller, 1884-97, and his work included *déjeuner* services and a naturalistically modelled Crocus service in 1896. He later devised a wing pattern (1901).
Ref: Danckert.

Hentschel, Karl (1884-1959). German painter and potter, born in Dessau. Hentschel studied painting in Dresden, 1903-07, lived and

worked in Holland from 1907, and visited Italy and France on study trips. In 1929, he began the design of furniture, working in Oberlausitz. He moved to Großschonau in 1933. He was forced by the Nazi regime to abandon painting at the age of 50, and turned to ceramics. From 1936 he collaborated with Erna Leitner, who fired her work at her pottery in Bischofswerda. On his return from war service which lasted from c.1940-45, Hentschel rejoined the Leitner workshop, which had been moved in 1943 to the craft colony at Tittmoning. His early glazes were mainly blood-red or brown and based on iron. In Tittmoning, he increased his range of glaze colours to include pastel shades, mainly with a silky matt surface. He also developed a pearl glaze resembling dewdrops in appearance. From c.1950 he worked in porcelain.

Marks: GW monogram, painted or incised (1934-36); H painted or impressed (1938-56). *Refs:* Bock; Klein.

Hentschel, William and Alza Stratton. *See* Kenton Hills Porcelains Inc.

Hepworth & Heald. *See* Kilnhurst Old Pottery.

Herb, Hugo. *See* Owens, John B.

Herculaneum. Liverpool pottery established near the Herculaneum dock in the south of the city, c.1793. Worthington, Humble & Holland, proprietors from 1796, employed a staff of about 40 workers from Staffordshire on the production of blue-printed dinner, tea, coffee services and toilet sets, punch bowls, mugs and jugs in white or cream-coloured earthenware. The firm was particularly noted for creamware jugs with decoration in black on the glaze. Many wares were made for export to America, e.g. figures of George Washington. The output also included terracotta ware, relief-decorated stoneware jugs and porcelain. The company, formed by the proprietors in 1806, dissolved in 1833, and the premises were leased to Thomas Case and James Mort, followed c.1836 by a partnership, Mort & Simpson, until the closure of the works in 1841.

Herculaneum. Sugar box made in stoneware with smear glaze at the Herculaneum pottery in Liverpool, 1800-05.

Marks incorporate the name *Herculaneum* impressed or occasionally printed in blue. Under Mort & Case, a liver bird, impressed or painted.
Refs: Hughes (1977); Jewitt; H.B. Lancaster *Liverpool and her Potters* (W.B. Jones & Co. Ltd, Liverpool, 1936); S. Smith *Illustrated Guide to Liverpool Herculaneum Pottery* (Barrie & Jenkins, London, 1970); Towner.

Herend. Porcelain factory founded in 1838 near Lake Balaton, western Hungary and in operation from 1839 under the ownership of M. Farkashazy *Fischer. The management at first attempted to evolve a national style in porcelain, using patriotic motifs and Hungarian colours in decoration but, unable to compete with imported Czech porcelain, began making imitations of earlier Meissen, Sèvres and Chinese wares, providing replacement pieces for table services and using research into the original materials and techniques in the development of new lines for the factory's own production: a service initially ordered by Queen Victoria, with decoration of butterflies and flowers, is still made, and replacements commissioned for a Chinese service belonging to the King of Sardinia inspired the Ming range. On the closure of the Imperial porcelain factory in *Vienna, Herend obtained the right to use a number of its moulds and designs.

On his retirement in 1874, Fischer was succeeded by his sons, but the firm was declared bankrupt in the same year. Production was resumed in 1876, but failed to match the earliest work in quality or quantity. After several changes in management and temporary closure in 1896, the factory was reopened later the same year by Fischer's grandson, J.*Farkashazy, who revived production according to his grandfather's ideals, and began to manufacture figures (only a few had been made before). In 1923, a company was formed, remaining under the direction of Farkashazy until his death in 1926; the state took control in 1948, rebuilding and modernizing the factory while retaining its workshop traditions.

A variety of printed marks include HEREND or a shield.
Refs: C. Boncz & K. Gink *Herend China* (Pannonia Press, Budapest, 1962); J. Ruziska *Herender Porzellan* (Budapest, 1950); Weiss.

Hering, Julius, & Son. German porcelain manufacturers working in Koppelsdorf, Thuringia, from 1893, on the production of tea and coffee services, figures, etc. From 1945, the firm traded as VEB Hochvolt-Porzellan, or under Hering's name.

A variety of marks incorporating JHS

include the outline of a fish, a triangular outline and a tricolour flag.
Refs: Danckert; Weiss.

Herold, John J. (1871-1923). Dutch-born ceramic chemist and designer, working in America. Herold was among artists connected with J.B.*Owens's pottery. He joined the *Roseville Pottery in 1900, working as designer and art director, and developed the Rozane Mara and Mongol lines. He founded the Herold China Co. at Golden, Colorado, in 1908.
Mark: initials, JH.
Refs: Evans; Kovel & Kovel; F.H. Rhead in *The Potter* I (January 1917).

Herold, Otto. Potter, working in America. With his brother, Paul, Herold assisted their uncle, D.*Schmidt, at *Zanesville Art Pottery for some years in the early 20th century. He moved to the *Roseville Pottery (1914-18), the *American Encaustic Tiling Co. and subsequently the *Zane Pottery. Paul Herold, meanwhile, worked as an artist in Chicago before he joined his brother (1936) in establishing a firm, LePere Pottery, which operated until 1962.
Refs: Kovel & Kovel; L.& E. Purviance & N.F. Schneider *Roseville Art Pottery in Color* (Wallace-Homestead, Des Moines, Iowa, 1970), *Zanesville Art Pottery in Color* (Mid-America, Leon, Iowa, 1968); 'Zanesville Art Pottery' in *Zanesville Times Signal* (11th November 1956).

Heron, Robert. *See* Fife Pottery.

Herrsching Ceramic Workshops. German pottery in operation at Munich in the early 20th century and ending in the 1920s. The output in 1912 consisted of slip-painted wares, but by the following year, the workshop produced fine stoneware with a variety of glazes over the upper portion of the pot, and a smooth, luminous glaze from the belly to the base. Some of the glazes were aventurine, with the effect of gold dust.
Mark: *Herrsching,* stamped in relief.
Ref: Bock.

Herstine Pottery. American pottery operated by Cornelius, Daniel and David Herstine, three generations of Pennsylvania German potters making slip-decorated earthenware at Nockamixon, Bucks County, c.1785-c.1875.
Ref: Barber (1976).

Hertel, Jakob, & Co. German porcelain manufacturers, working at Rehau, Bavaria, from 1906, on the production of gift ware, vases, boxes, as well as coffee sets and tableware.
Marks, incorporating the firm's name or initials, include versions with a crown or a running deer.
Refs: Danckert; Weiss.

Hertz. *See* Annecy.

Heubach family. German porcelain manufacturers descended from Gabriel Heubach, who, with his eleven children, established a porcelain factory in 1764.
Christoph and Philipp Heubach bought the *Lichte factory in 1843, after working at Lauscha (Saxe-Meiningen). Philipp's son, Louis Heubach (d 1887), became sole owner

Heubach family. Figure of a motorist, made at the Heubach porcelain factory in Lichte, Thuringia, after 1906.

of the factory in 1876, succeeded by his sons, who formed a joint stock company, Gebr. Heubach A.C. Lichte in 1904. Edward Albert Heubach (1836-1904), a member of the branch of the family who were shareholders of the *Wallendorf factory, moved to *Kloster-Veilsdorf, where in 1863 he turned production to such wares as bottle tops, industrial components, sanitary ware and dolls' heads.

The firm Heubach, Kämpfe & Sonntag made porcelain at Altwasser, Silesia c.1870, and the *Wallendorf factory was under the joint ownership of Gabriel Heubach and Friedrich Kämpfe in 1883. Other members of the family included Ernst Heubach, working at Koppelsdorf, Thuringia, from 1887, whose firm made industrial porcelain and, from 1919, dolls' heads, and was still in operation in 1950; Gustave Heubach, working at Steinbach, Thuringia, in the twentieth century; Hugo Heubach, at Sonneberg from 1894 into the 20th century; Rainer Heubach, whose family left East Germany in 1945, now working in Goslau. The Heubach firms were mainly known for production of industrial wares, and components for dolls.
Refs: Danckert; Scherf; C.A. Stanton *Heubach's Little Characters: Dolls and Figurines 1850-1930* (Living Dolls Publications Ltd, Enfield, Middlesex, 1978).

Hewitt, Matthew. *See* Hunslet Hall Pottery.

Hewitt & Leadbeater. Staffordshire manufacturers of porcelain and earthenware at the Willow Potteries, Longton. The partnership between Edwin Leadbeater, son of the senior partner of *Robinson & Leadbeater, and his brother-in-law, Arthur Hewitt, was formed in 1905. The firm made a wide variety of ware, including flower holders, vases and other ornamental ware, ecclesiastical statuary, and models of crosses, churches and other buildings, cars, aeroplanes, etc., decorated with crests and sometimes local views, and commemorative figures of soldiers, sailors and nurses in World War I. Vases in the shape of open flowers (e.g. an arum lily with green leaves) and vases or jugs decorated with moulded bunches of hops on dark green grounds, or vines and grapes on cream ground, were marked with the trade name Willow Art.

When Leadbeater left the partnership in 1919, Hewitt Bros continued to produce heraldic items and novelty pieces, sometimes in an ivory-coloured body. The firm was bought by H.T.*Robinson in 1925, afterwards trading as Willow Potteries Ltd, with the trade name Willow Crest; it then became part of the Cauldon group (see Brown-Westhead, Moore & Co.). By 1927, Willow China was produced at the Arcadian works (see Arkinstall & Sons Ltd). The firm's moulds were used after 1930 by the Goss China Co. (see Goss, W.H., Ltd).

Marks include WILLOW ART, with a weeping willow tree, and CHINA/LONGTON/STAFFORDSHIRE, printed.
Refs: Andrews; Godden (1964).

Hexamer, Frédéric. French ceramist decorator working under E.*Chaplet and A.*Dammouse at the Haviland studio in Auteuil on the painting of pottery with coloured slips.
Refs: Brunhammer et al (1976); Préaud & Gauthier.

Hexter, Humpherson & Co. See Phillips, John; Watcombe Pottery.

Heytze, Jan Carel (1873-1943). Dutch painter, designer and ceramic decorator, working 1887-96 at the *Rozenburg factory. he was a designer for the *Holland factory, 1896-1913. As art director for *St Lukas, 1913-c.1930, he worked with lustre effects and experimented with the surface texture of the earthenware.

Mark resembles the mathematical sign meaning approximately equals.
Refs: W. Schipper 'De N.V. Kunstaardewerkfabriek St Lukas te Utrecht' in *Antiek* 11 (1976); Singelenberg-van der Meer.

Hicks, Richard. Staffordshire potter. After serving an apprenticeship at *Caughley, Hicks worked in partnership 1805-08 with John and Edward Baddeley in Shelton, took over from that firm, and worked in partnership with J.*Meigh. Working as Hicks & Meigh and then Hicks, Meigh & Johnson until 1835, his company made blue printed earthenware and a similar body to Mason's Ironstone (which they marketed as stone china), as well as some porcelain. The firm was followed by W.*Ridgway and his son-in-law, F.*Morley, in a partnership trading as Ridgway & Co., later F. Morley & Co.
Refs: Bunt; Godden (1964); Jewitt.

Hicks & Meigh. See Hicks, Richard.

Hicks, Meigh & Johnson. See Hicks, Richard.

Higayashima kiln. See Nishishinmachi.

High Pottery. See Scott Brothers.

high temperature or **underglaze colours.** Metallic oxides applied to unfired or biscuit clay before glazing or, in some cases (e.g. tin-glazed ware), painted on the raw glaze. The range of colours is limited to those pigments which will withstand the temperature of firing.

Hildebrand, Friedrich. Pennsylvania potter working near Tyler's Port, Montgomery County, c.1825-40. He produced earthenware with decoration scratched or pricked through pale slip to show a red body beneath. Surviving examples are characterized by a grotesque element in design: heraldic lion, or animal with antlered head and fish-tail, each surrounded by an inscription in German, meaning 'I like fine things/Even when they are not mine/And cannot become mine/I still enjoy them'. The surface is smear-glazed.

Mark: on one plate, signature of a workman, *Johannes Leman.*
Refs: Barber (1976); Stradling.

Hill, Albert (b 1840). Porcelain decorator for the Royal *Worcester Porcelain Co. from his start as an apprentice in 1859 until the 1870s. Initially engaged in the colouring of figures and decoration in turquoise and gold, Hill later carried out neat freehand painting, often of birds. He worked as a freelance decorator, e.g. for E.*Locke, using his own muffle kiln. A teacher of china painting, he exhibited his own work at the gallery of *Howell & James.
Ref: Sandon (1978a).

Hill, Asa. See Wheeler, L.D.

Hill, James (1791-1854). English porcelain decorator. After his apprenticeship at the porcelain factory in Nottingham Road, *Derby, he worked there as a gilder and flower painter until the factory's closure. A pattern comprising a large rose with scattered sprigs of different colours became known as Hill's Flowers. He is also thought to have modelled small animal figures. Hill was one of the workers who joined W.*Locker in founding the porcelain factory in King Street, Derby.
Refs: see Derby.

Hill, Samuel. See Fulper Pottery.

Hillardt, Johann. See Klösterle.

Hinchco, Benjamin. See Indiana Pottery Co.

Hirado ware. See Mikawachi.

Hirasa. Japanese porcelain kiln established in the early 18th century by craftsmen from *Arita in Kagoshima prefecture. The initial output of everyday ware, either white or sparingly painted with underglaze blue, was extended to include choice blue and white or enamelled porcelain.

Refs: Jenyns (1971); Mitsuoka; Munsterberg.

Hirashimizu. Japanese folk kiln established c.1800 in Yamagata prefecture. The workshop produced stoneware resembling *Soma wares, porcelain similar to *Arita wares, domestic vessels for local sale, and a range of pieces with relief decoration. Amber (ame) and purplish black (kuro gusuri) glazes are used; some pieces are coated in white slip. The kiln is still in production. The other kiln now active in Yamagata prefecture is at *Shinjo.
Ref: Mizuo.

Hirschfield, N.J. American pottery decorator. His work for M.S.*Morgan, c.1882-83, included a pair of gilded vases painted with white flowers on a turquoise ground, and a gourd-shaped vase painted with rushes and a dragonfly. He was also employed at the *Rookwood Pottery from c.1882, leaving by 1885.

Mark: initials NJH with or without full stops.
Refs: Barber (1976); Evans; Kovel & Kovel; Lehner; Peck.

Hirstwood, Haigh (1778-1854). Yorkshire porcelain decorator, born near Huddersfield. Hirstwood trained in the making and decoration of porcelain at the *Swinton Pottery, where he worked as a flower and insect painter for about 40 years. With his sons, Joseph and William Hirstwood, also painters at the works, he was among the artists engaged on the dessert service commissioned by King William IV in 1830. He established a decorating workshop (York China Manufactory) in The Groves, York, in 1839, painting and finishing porcelain services, vases and figures bought in the white from Staffordshire potteries, in a style developed from his painting at Swinton. Hirstwood's son-in-law, William Leyland (d 1853), a painter and gilder, acted as his assistant and eventually partner until the closure of the workshop c.1850, and afterwards worked briefly in London.
Refs: A.& A. Cox *The Rockingham Works* (Sheffield City Museums, 1974); Grabham; Jewitt.

Hisaka. Japanese folk kiln established in Takefu (Fukui prefecture) in the Meiji period (1868-1912). The output of everyday wares included storage vats and jars. The kiln was known for fine temmoku and white drip glazes.
Refs: Mizuo; Munsterberg.

Hizen. Japanese province, the centre of ceramic production on Kyushu, noted for the early development of Japanese porcelain in the 17th century. It covered the area of the present day Saga prefecture and part of Nagasaki. The province had a long tradition of ceramics, with pottery making at *Karatsu, and porcelain at *Arita, which with *Nabeshima and *Kakiemon wares was shipped from *Imari to Nagasaki for distribution to other parts of Japan and export to the West. Kilns in Nagasaki included *Nagayo, *Hasami and *Kameyama. The porcelain of *Mikawachi was exported from Hirado.
Refs: Audsley & Bowes; Brinkley; Jenyns (1965, 1971); Mikami; Mitsuoka; Munsterberg.

Hjorth family. Danish potters, making stoneware and some porcelain in Rønne on the island of Bornholm at a factory established by Lauritz Adolph Hjorth in 1859. The factory's output includes covered cylindrical jars, thinly potted in a heavy stoneware body, with dull, dark brown glaze, and vases with high-temperature glazes. Vases, covered jars, etc., in smooth, hard stoneware were decorated with bands of stylized foliage, or groups of fruit in shades of buff, brown, dark blue and olive green. Production also includes figures. Hollow ware is still hand thrown.

L. Hjorth (1859-1931) was owner from 1905 after several years spent working in other Danish potteries. His successor, Erik Hjorth (b 1906), was apprenticed at the factory and trained in Höhr-Grenzhausen (1927-28). He took over as director of the factory in 1959. His daughters Marie (b 1941) and Ulla (b 1945) now work as the firm's art directors. Their work was shown in an exhibition of work by three generations of the Hjorth family at Bornholm museum in 1977. L.*Munch Petersen and G.*Vasegaard are relatives of the Hjorth family.

Marks: *Hjorth*; a stag.
Refs: Bodelsen; Cox; *De Art Nouveau* (catalogue, Museum voor Sierkunst, Ghent, 1979); W. Hull *Danish Ceramic Design* (catalogue, Museum of Art, Pennsylvania State University, 1981); Préaud & Gauthier.

Hobbel, Paulus Jacob (1879-1966) and Maria (1881-1946). Dutch potters, trained under C.J.*Lanooij in Gouda. The Hobbels established their own workshop in 1918 at Laren for the production of thrown domestic wares. Paulus Hobbel also made decorative earthenware, while his wife concentrated on everyday wares. The couple frequently fired the work of other artists.
Marks: *Hobbel/Laren*, or P.J.H. Maria Hobbel signed her work, *Maria*, or the initial M with a line through.
Refs: Scheen; Singelenberg-van der Meer; van Straaten.

Hobson, P., & Sons. *See* Swinton Pottery.

Hocédé, J. *See* du Tremblay, Alexis.

Höchst. German porcelain and faience works in operation 1746-96. The factory was known for figures and luxury tablewares. Its moulds were owned by the *Damm factory from 1830 until its closure in 1882, and subsequently the factory of F.A.*Mehlem, until their sale to Dressel, Kister & Co. at Passau in 1904.
Ref: Penkala.

Hodgkiss, James (fl 1900-25). English artist and designer employed at the Wedgwood factory. As chief designer, he was associated with D.*Makeig-Jones in the production of lustre decoration. Hodgkiss worked with art director J. Goodwin and chemist George Adams on the development of powder colours, and designed a number of patterns for bone china bowls and vases with printed designs in gold over a powder-blue ground.

He also painted a series of bone china dessert sets with scenes of birds in landscapes.
Work often signed.
Refs: Batkin; Reilly & Savage.

Hodkinson, William G. (b c.1860). English ceramic artist, born in Derby. Hodkinson trained at Hanley and Stoke-on-Trent schools of art and as an apprentice at *Mintons Ltd. Working for *Doulton & Co. in Burslem, 1880-1920, he became known for the wide range of his techniques. His painting included flower subjects, varying widely in style, and landscapes that often featured sheep or cattle, and he collaborated with Charles J. *Noke on panels decorated with enamel, moulded effects and raised gilding. He was also concerned in the development of Holbein ware, and designed several shapes for tableware, influenced by Art Nouveau, in the early 1900s. He worked with Noke on the artistic exploitation of *flambé* effects, gilding delicate patterns of birds, swimming fish and other water creatures on a red *flambé* ground.
Refs: see Doulton & Co.

Hódmezővásárhely. Hungarian pottery centre in Czongrad County on the Great Plain. At least 400 potters were working in Hódmezővásárhely in the 19th century. The town's craftsmen produced earthenware with painted patterns in blue on a white ground and, especially wares in the traditional honey-coloured glaze, splashed with yellow, brown and additional green pigments. Dishes were sometimes moulded, rather than thrown, and decorated with openwork patterns. Special pieces, including wine jugs made to order for family occasions, were often decorated in relief and inscribed with a date. Trailed slip decoration also occurs.

Before World War I, local craftsmen united to establish a workshop using traditional methods. Some of their early styles were inspired by Art Nouveau. The workshop continues to maintain traditional styles and methods.
Refs: E. Fel, T. Hofer & K.K. Csilléry *Hungarian Peasant Art* (Corvina, Budapest, 1958); M. Kresz 'Hungarian Slipware and Unglazed Pottery' in *Ceramic Review* 63 (May, June 1980).

Hoentschel, Georges (1855-1915). French designer and ceramist, formerly an architect. He collaborated in the 1890s with J.*Carriès in experiments in stoneware at the colony of artist potters at Saint-Amand-en-Puisaye (Nièvre), and was at the start strongly influenced by Japanese ceramics. His work was noted for gold glaze effects, and the frequent use of metal mounts. Much of his inspiration was drawn from floral forms. Some years after the death of Carriès, he acquired Château Montriveau, where he continued work with E.*Grittel until he moved to Paris, working at Grittel's studio shortly before his death.
Impressed monogram.
Refs: Baschet; Brunhammer *et al* (1976); Camart *et al*; E. Gallé 'Le Pavillon de l'Union Centrale des Arts Décoratifs à l'Exposition Universelle' in *Revue des Arts Décoratifs* 29 (1900).

Hoetger, B. *See* Kandern Tonwerke.

Hoffman Brick Co. Australian pottery established 1870 at Brunswick, Victoria, for the production of bricks, tiles and sanitary ware. The output also included stoneware for domestic use from c.1912 and, by c.1930, glazed kitchen ware. After acquiring a small branch works, the firm produced Melrose art pottery consisting of vases, bowls, jugs, etc., moulded with gum leaves, opossums and other Australian flora and fauna in low relief, often under matt glazes in blues, greens or greyish brown, and marketed under the trade name Mel-Rose. The firm also made jugs for the advertisement of spirits sold by Milne's, an Adelaide merchant, and in 1934 moulded jugs to commemorate the Melbourne centenary. Manufacture is now under the control of the Clifton Brick Co.
Marks include MELROSE/AUSTRALIAN/WARE stamped in ink.
Ref: Graham.

Hofman, Vlatislav. *See* Artĕl.

Hoffmann, Josef (1870-1956). Austrian architect and designer, trained in Munich and Vienna. Hoffmann was among the founders of the Vienna Secession in 1897, taught at the Wiener Kunstgewerbeschule (1899-1941), and with K.*Moser established the *Wiener Werkstätte in 1903. He also founded the Österreichischer Werkbund in 1912. Hoffmann and Moser designed ceramics for the Wiener Porzellan-Manufaktur Jos.*Böck in 1899 (as well as glass, metalwork and furniture). His designs for the Werkstätte included dishes, vases, bowls and coffee services, with graceful, flowing shapes, e.g. a coffee pot and

Georges Hoentschel. Vase made in the 19th century.

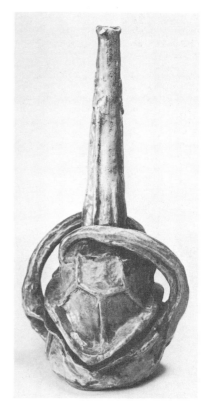

sugar bowl in almost cylindrical shapes, but with gently curving sides (1910), and a stemmed cup with the handle shaped in the outline of a leaf (1920). Other ceramic designs by Hoffmann included pieces with geometrical patterns in black on white for production by the *Wiener Keramik workshop. He also designed table services for the *Augarten factory (c.1928) which include ribbed shapes with vertical bands of colour, and a coffee service with gourd-shaped pot, jug, covered bowl, and lobed saucers.

Marks: initials and monograms.
Refs: Neuwirth (1974a, 1974b); Préaud & Gauthier.

Hofmanstahl, Emanuel. *See* Prague.

Hohlt, Otto (1889-1960). Potter born in St Domingo, West Indies, who worked in Germany, where he grew up. Hohlt studied at the Debschitz Kunstgewerbeschule in Munich, trained as a painter, and went on study trips to Italy, France, England and Hungary. With his sons, Albrecht Hohlt (1928-60) and Görge Hohlt (b 1930), he established a workshop in Katsbach in 1946, with the aim of applying controlled ceramic techniques in the production of pottery in spontaneous traditional styles. His work consisted mainly of sculptural pieces, architectural reliefs and freely built vessels.

The workshop's limited experimentation with glazes was initiated by Hohlt's sons. Albrecht Hohlt had been inspired by Chinese ceramics exhibited in Cologne, 1948, and went on to study at the Akademie der bildenden Künste in Munich under the sculptor Toni Stadler in 1951, and visited Italy, Milan, Venice and Ischia in the following year. He died in Freiburg. Görge Hohlt trained at the Munich academy (1952) and then at the state engineering school for ceramics at Höhr-Grenzhausen, 1956-59. He worked as a technician in the Steatite-Magnesia company, Lauf, 1959-64, and took over the family workshop in 1965. He had collaborated closely with his brother until 1959, and continued work in the same style when working alone. His range of glazes included blue and blood red, often with splashes of buff. He introduced aventurine effects in 1965, and worked with ash glazes in the 1970s. His work, mainly thrown, is sometimes distorted by beating or modelling of the clay.

The Hohlt workshop mark is a cat over wavy lines, incised (1946-53) or impressed. Individual marks: signature O. HOHLT,

Otto Hohlt. Relief plaque depicting a bareback rider, 1956.

Höhr-Grenzhausen. Stoneware flagon with grey body highlighted in blue, made by the firm of Simon Peter Gerz. 22.5 cm high.

incised; HOHLT, stamped (1957-60 on porcelain by Albrecht Hohlt). Görge Hohlt used the workshop mark, impressed.

Refs: Bock; Eckstein; *Albrecht Hohlt* (catalogue, Neue Sammlung, Munich, 1961); H. Spielmann *Otto Hohlt und Albrecht Hohlt* (catalogue, Hetjens museum, Düsseldorf, 1962).

Höhr-Grenzhausen. German centre of stoneware production in the Westerwald, one of many local towns active from the 16th century in the production of stoneware, notably jugs and tankards with decoration incised and stamped in the grey body. Manufacture lapsed in the 18th century, but was gradually revived in the 19th and 20th centuries, often in contemporary rather than traditional styles. The workshop of Reinhold Hanke was making traditional saltglaze in the 19th century, and his son A.*Hanke returned to continue the workshop after study in Munich, producing designs by H.*van de Velde, P. Behrens, H.*Wewerka and other artists. Simon Peter Gerz, working at Höhr in the early 20th century, made wares with modern designs and decoration, e.g. by R.*Riemerschmid. However, traditional styles inspired E.*Balzar-Kopp and W.*Mühlendyck, who were both working in Höhr-Grenzhausen in the late 1920s, initially together.

Among potters who trained at the Werkschule für Keramik in Höhr-Grenzhausen were W.G.*Albouts, H.*Bollhagen, G. *Schmidt-Reuther, W.*Schmidt-Tummeley, H. Storr-Britz, and the son of W.*Kagel. H.*Griemert was a teacher at the school, 1954-70.
Refs: Bock; Haggar (1960); Honey (1952).

Hokusai. *See* Amphora.

Holbein ware. *See* Doulton & Co.

Holdcroft, Rowland. English ceramic artist apprenticed at the *Doulton & Co. factory in Burslem under H.*Tittensor in 1925, and employed by the firm until 1973. He was noted for paintings of landscapes and rural scenes on large vases, and designed series patterns for tableware and display plates. He was also a skilled painter of facial features and other detailed work on the firm's output of figures.
Refs: see Doulton & Co.

Holford, William (1841-1914). Potter trained in Staffordshire and, in Australia, at the *Lithgow Pottery from 1882. At his own pottery near Sydney, his output included Rockingham teapots, jugs and other domestic ware. He left New South Wales for Adelaide in the 1880s, and in 1889 established (in partnership) the London Pottery Works at Maylands, trading as the Adelaide Pottery Co. Ltd, c.1895. In 1901, when Holford was in partnership with his son, Thomas Henry Holford, the pottery reverted to his family name.
Refs: I. Evans *The Lithgow Pottery* (Flannel Flower Press, Sydney, 1980); Graham.

Holitsch. Hungarian faience factory established by Franz von Lothringen in 1743 on an estate formerly owned by the Czobir family, and drawing a large proportion of the labour force from Haban potters already working in the area. From the 1780s until its closure in 1827, the factory produced creamware with openwork borders or painted over the glaze in patterns that were heavily influenced by other European faience factories as well as Meissen blue painted ware and Chinese porcelain.

Marks: HOLICS, HOLITSCH or HOLITSH, OR H impressed.
Ref: Csanyi.

Holland, Fayence- en Tegelfabriek. Dutch pottery making tiles and earthenware at Utrecht from 1893. The works passed to J.W. Mijnlief in 1894 and the decorators, J.C.*Heytze and Johannes Karl Leurs joined from *Rozenburg in 1896. The tableware, vases, etc., resemble the work of the Rozenburg, *Haga and *Zuid-Holland factories. Services designed in simple forms by H.P. *Berlage were produced for 't Binnenhuis, 1900-06. The factory closed in 1920.

Marks incorporate HOLLAND, UTRECHT and sometimes the designer's initials or monogram. Pieces produced for 't Binnenhuis were marked with B in a circle.
Refs: W. Schipper 'De Faience - en Tegelfabriek "Holland" te Utrecht' in *Antiek* II (1977); Singelenberg-van der Meer; van Straaten.

Holland, John Frederic (1781-1843). American potter. Holland, the son of an Englishman, was born in Salem, North Carolina, where he worked among other *Moravian potters. After serving his apprenticeship under R.*Christ, 1796-1802, and working as a journeyman potter from c.1803, Holland succeeded Christ on his retirement from the pottery at Salem, retaining the business when it passed out of the hands of the Moravian community in 1829.
Ref: Bivins.

Holland, William Fishley. *See* Fishley family.

Hollins, Michael Daintry (1815-98). English potter and tile manufacturer, the grandson of S.*Hollins and a nephew of H.*Minton. Formerly a surgeon, Hollins joined Mintons Ltd by 1838, and entered a partnership with his uncle in the early 1840s. In 1859, he took over the firm's tile manufacture in the newly formed *Minton, Hollins & Co., while his cousin C.M.*Campbell, as managing director of Mintons, maintained production of the firm's other wares. On the formal separation of the two companies in 1868, Hollins gained £30,000 from the sale of Mintons' equipment to Campbell, and built a new factory. He retained the use of the name Minton for his production and sale of tiles, winning court cases in 1871 and 1875 to control competition in tile manufacture from Campbell and R.M.*Taylor.
Refs: Lockett (1979); Wedgwood & Ormsbee; *see also* Mintons Ltd.

Hollins, Samuel (1748-1820). Staffordshire potter. Hollins worked in the 18th century as a maker of fine stoneware at Shelton, where he was succeeded by his sons T.& J. Hollins, earthenware manufacturers c.1795-1820. Hollins was a founding partner in the original *New Hall company and the joint stock company which bought the New Hall estate in 1810.
Refs: Jewitt; *Stoneware & Stone China* (catalogue, Northern Ceramic Society, 1982); Wedgwood & Ormsbee.

Hollóháza1. Hungarian creamware factory established in 1830. The lease was held by Franz Istvanyi in the 1930s, and the factory was purchased by a firm called Szakmarys in 1939. Painted porcelain has since been produced at Hollóháza.
Marks: HOLLOHAZA until 1939.
Ref: Csanyi.

Holmes Pottery. Yorkshire earthenware pottery established c.1850 in Rotherham. The first proprietors, Jervis Greaves (d c.1867) and the Rotherham potter, William Earnshaw, exhibited porcelain lettering at the Great Exhibition (1851). The pottery was operated from 1854 by Dickinson & Jackson and from 1860 by a company headed by John Jackson (d c.1881), succeeded by his partner, George Shaw (d 1892). Thomas and Charles Shaw continued the firm, trading from 1909 as George Shaw & Sons. The pottery produced kitchen wares and transfer-printed tableware until c.1931.
Marks: JJ & Co; GS & S.
Refs: Jewitt; Lawrence.

Holtzendorf, Count G. Porcelain painter, working in England at the porcelain factory in Osmaston Road, *Derby, 1878-c.1888. He was a painter of cupids and other figure subjects, and landscapes, which included the views of Derbyshire on dishes and plates of the Gladstone service designed by R.*Lunn.
Mark: initials, G.H.
Refs: see Derby.

Honda Teikichi or Sadakichi (1766-1819). Japanese potter, born in Hizen. After working in Arita and Kyoto, Honda joined *Mokubei in making *Kutani ware at *Kasugayama in 1807. He subsequently discovered a source of clay at Hanazaka, and in 1811, with tile maker and local official Hayashi Hachibei, established the *Wakasugi kiln nearby. As chief potter there, he is regarded as responsible for the style of the output, which was strongly influenced by *Arita wares. His own work included fine decoration in underglaze blue. Honda's pupils included *Gen'emon.
Refs: Jenyns (1971); Nakagawa; Roberts.

Honeychurch, John & Thomas. *See* Bovey Tracey Pottery Co.

Honoré, François-Maurice (d 1855). Paris porcelain manufacturer. Honoré owned a factory on the Petite Rue Saint-Gilles until c.1811 and subsequently another factory (established 1808) at La Seynie, near Saint-Yrieix (Haute-Vienne). He backed his son, Edouard Honoré (d 1855), in a partnership with P.-L.*Dagoty at La Manufacture de L'Impératrice on Boulevard Poissonnière in 1816, later trading under the name Manufacture de la duchesse d'Angoulême. They were noted for biscuit reproductions of sculptural pieces and provided ware for the palaces of Versailles and Compiègne. The partnership was dissolved in 1822, when Dagoty retained, and quickly let, the factory at La Seynie to D.*Denuelle. Edouard Honoré kept the Paris factory as a studio, moving his porcelain production to Champroux (Allier). He took out patents for the application of high-temperature coloured grounds and for the development of lithographic techniques in ceramics. Using Limoges clay with the addition of local kaolin, Honoré made utilitarian and decorative ware, including octagonal or oval moulded pieces, perforated baskets, which were painted or transfer printed in the Paris workshop. After 1840, relief-decorated ware was inspired by Greek, Byzantine or Chinese themes. Edouard Honoré's son, Oscar, sold the factory in 1865.
Marks incorporate the names of the factory owners.
Refs: Chavagnac & Grollier; Ernould-Gandouet; Guillebon.

Hood, George. *See* Walton, John.

Hoop, De. *See* Vet, Klaas and Jacob.

Hooper, Lewis J. *See* Doulton, Sir Henry.

Hope St. Works, Hanley. *See* Dudson, James.

Hopewell, John (1834-94). Porcelain painter working for the *Worcester Royal Porcelain Co. c.1855-90. After painting grasses and other plants and flowers in the late 1850s, Hopewell became known for his naturalistic treatment of birds.
Ref: Sandon (1978a).

Hop ware. *See* Belleview or Bellevue Pottery.

Horecj, Jaroslav. *See* Artĕl.

Horn Brothers. *See* Australian Pottery.

Hornsea Pottery. Yorkshire pottery established in 1949 by Desmond and Colin Rawson at their home in Hornsea. Initially producing miniature Toby jugs, the brothers moved in 1957 to larger premises, where they made vases, small dishes, ashtrays and cruets with bands of black glaze. They subsequently developed a method of screen printing tableware (in a decorative technique that became associated with the pottery) with resist patterns fired matt against a ground of thick, glossy glaze. The pottery at Hornsea, and a second established as part of an industrial development scheme jointly run by the University and the City Corporation in Lancaster, are still in operation as a family concern.
Marks incorporate HORNSEA POTTERY and a hunting horn. The trade mark of a curved horn was introduced in the early 1960s.
Ref: Godden (1964).

Horova, Julie (b 1906). Studio potter, born in Czechoslovakia and trained in Prague. Horova also studied in France under R. *Lachenal. She taught in Bratislava. Her work was inspired by a study of folk wares, and later pieces include figures (e.g. a stylized llama, two metres high, unglazed) and other ornamental pieces (e.g. a spherical bottle decorated only with a narrow band of vertical ribbing, scraped surface texture and splashes of turquoise glaze).
Ref: Hettes & Rada.

Horti, Paltol. Hungarian potter. Horti travelled around Hungary in the 1890s, teaching modern methods of glazing and decoration, and introduced new decorative motifs, which the local potters used on traditional shapes. His own stoneware and porcelain, made in the factory of I. Gröhe, were decorated with patterns of stylized flowers. He sent a display to the exhibition in Turin, 1902.

Hosowara. *See* Shigaraki ware.

hotel china. *See* semi-porcelain.

Houghton, George (b 1855). Porcelain painter working for the *Worcester Royal Porcelain Co. 1868-84. His work included views and, in the 1880s, figure subjects.
Ref: Sandon (1978a).

Hoult, Frederick. *See* Maling, Christopher Thomas.

Howarth, Guido. *See* Owens, John B.

Howe, Thomas. *See* Clark, Nathan.

Howell & James. English pottery and porcelain retailers established in Regent Street, London, c.1820. From the opening of their new gallery in Regent Street in 1876, until the mid 1880s, the firm held annual exhibitions of painted pottery and porcelain with separate sections, one for professional ceramic artists and one for the work of amateur decorators on vases, plaques, etc., bought undecorated from such manufacturers as *Mintons Ltd and W.T.*Copeland Ltd. The work of Doulton artists including F.E. *Lewis, L.*Watt and H.B.*Barlow was shown, as well as that of R. and H.*Coleman, C.*Moreau-Nélaton and L.F.*Day. Howell & James published a decorators' handbook by John Sparkes (*see* Doulton & Co.) and J.*Haslem, and also prompted the fashion for commercial art ware. In 1880, the firm

Howell & James. Plaque, The Young Gardener – Winter, painted by Mrs Anne Sealy, and exhibited in 1884. 51.5 x 28 cm.

advertised daily classes in art pottery decoration. The following year they exhibited over 2,000 pieces at the gallery, but the numbers subsequently diminished with a rise in the standards of selection. As exclusive London retailers of early Barum ware (until the expiry of the original contract with C.H.*Brannam), the firm contributed to Brannam's commercial success, and to his achievement of royal recognition in 1885; Howell & James also exhibited and sold *Burmantofts Faience.

Paper label: HOWELL & JAMES'/ ART-POTTERY EXHIBITION with date, exhibitor's name, and the title of the decoration.

*Agnete Hoy. Plate painted in shades of brown on an oatmeal glaze, made in the *Bullers Ltd workshop, c.1950. 28 cm in diameter.*

Refs: Callen; Coysh (1976); Haslam (1975); Lloyd Thomas (1974).

Hoy, Agnete. Danish-born designer and potter. Agnete Hoy trained in Copenhagen, subsequently working as a designer at Holbeck and with N.*Krebs. In England from 1939, she studied under G.M.*Forsyth and joined *Bullers Ltd, reopening the firm's pottery studio in 1940. She designed most of the shapes (which included vases, bowls, dishes, cups and other table or display ware) and some of the decoration. She continued part-time work at the studio from 1948 until its closure. She designed stoneware for Doulton & Co. in Lambeth, 1952-56, later working as a studio potter, mainly using porcelain.

Marks: monogram of AH, incised; signature, incised, impressed or painted.
Refs: Art Among the Insulators (catalogue, Gladstone Pottery Museum, Stoke-on-Trent, 1977); Godden (1964).

Hozan. A line of Japanese potters making Awata ware in Kyoto from the 7th generation of the Unrin'in family, who moved from Omi to Awataguchi, where he established a workshop. The 9th generation head of the family named Yasubei Bunzo (d 1723) earned the artistic name Hozan, which was continued in use by the family. Until Hozan XI (d 1769), who also made porcelain, the family worked mainly in earthenware painted in underglaze blue with landscapes and other designs resembling the decoration of delftware. Hozan XV, Kumanosuke (d 1842), who succeeded his younger brother as head of the family, was a porcelain maker and teacher of *Hozen. His successor, Unrin'in Bunzo (1820-89), specialized in tea ceremony ware, and served the cloistered Imperial prince Shoren'in, who gave him the additional artistic name, Taihei (peace), in 1857.

The family produced a widely varied output, including faience with raised decoration in thick slip (copied on wine bottles, flowerpots and, rarely, vases by *Tanzan) or enamels, e.g. tendrils and leaves built up into high or low relief in slip surrounding a central blossom, and designs of arabesques and scrolls in thick, blue enamel against white, yellow or unglazed ground, as well as blue and white porcelain. The arabesques and floral scrolls in high relief (warabi-de, or fern scroll style) were followed by Tanzan c.1900. The family was also known for the briefly fashionable Tsuishu-de (carved red lacquer style) ware, faience painted in reserves against a ground of red lacquer with incised diaper patterns.
Refs: Jenyns (1965, 1971); Hannover; Morse; Roberts.

Hozen Eiraku (1795-c.1854). Japanese potter, the adopted son of *Ryozen and his successor as head of the Zengoro family, 1841. He took part in his family's production of stoves for the tea ceremony before embarking on a study of ceramic techniques in Awata in the early 19th century. His teachers included Kumanosuke, fifteenth in the *Hozan line and Ichiemon. In Kishu from 1827, Hozen worked at the Kirakuen kiln on the Wakayama estate of the clan lord of Kishu (*see* Kishu wares); there he made official pieces for the chieftain and other wares often in imitation of Kochi earth-

enware. He made celadon-glazed wares, and was inspired by Chinese blue and white porcelain of the Yung-lo reign, receiving the gold seal Yeiraku or Eiraku (the Japanese reading of the Chinese characters Yung-lo) and the silver seal Kahei Shiriu. Hozen also achieved a fine aubergine glaze, used on porcelain, and rich combinations of turquoise, purple and yellow on faience, but is noted for his *kinrande porcelains derived from Chinese Yung-lo wares, and used a coral enamel glaze of high quality.

He established a workshop at Kaseyama (Nara district), where he made a variety of wares, and briefly visited Setsu in 1840 to teach. Leaving his adopted son, Nishimura Sozaburo (1834-76), in charge of the Nara pottery, he opened a new kiln in Narikatamachi, near Omuro in Kyoto, where he found good earthenware clay and specialized in imitating the tea bowls and gilded porcelains of Ninsei, using lavish decorative designs of animals and plants in gold and red on finely crackled ivory glaze. His output of porcelain at Omuro (Omuro-yaki) has a glossy, grainy glaze decorated in gold, red, silver, white and black. In 1850, Hozen moved to Otsu on the shores of Lake Biwa, where he made kinrande or blue and white porcelain. He was succeeded by *Wazen, Zengoro XII.

Marks: imitations of Kochi ware stamped *Kairaku-en*; kinrande wares stamped *Eiraku.*
Refs: Brinkley; Hannover; Jenyns (1965); Koyama; Mikami; Miller; Morse; Munsterberg; Okuda, Koyama & Hayashija *Nihon No Tozi* [Japanese ceramics] (Toto Bunka Co., Tokyo, 1954); Roberts.

Hubandière, Antoine de la. *See* Loc Maria.

Hübel, Joseph Emanuel. *See* Prague.

Hudson, Frank. *See* Lamson Pottery.

Huggins, Vera. English ceramic designer and decorator. Initially joining the *Doulton & Co. Lambeth studio in 1923, she remained as one of the last designers employed on the small output of decorative stoneware produced at the Lambeth workshop for export during World War II. Vera Huggins was known for a very simple style, with decoration, when used, incised or painted in slip. She used delicate colours and designed some shapes which relied for effect on monochrome, mottled or crystalline glazes.
Refs: see Doulton & Co.

Hughan, Harold R. (b 1893). Australian potter, born in Mildura, Victoria. Initially an engineer, Hughan became interested in pottery in the 1930s and worked briefly with F.E.*Cox. His early work included simple, coiled shapes. Hughan built his own woodfired kiln for the production of earthenware, often with elaborate decoration. Later, inspired by B.*Leach's *A Potter's Book*, by Chinese Sung and T'ang wares in the National Gallery of Victoria and by modern British stonewares, he began to experiment with high firing temperatures, and built a new kiln, still firing with wood until 1952. He is the first Australian potter to specialize in stonewares. Other influences in his work came from English medieval wares and from the colours of the Australian landscape. Using a limited range of shapes, mainly

functional domestic pieces, thrown on a home-made kick wheel, Hughan glazes his work by introducing ash from garden leaves into the kiln, as well as using celadon, temmoku or dolomite glazes. Decoration includes glaze splashes, brushed patterns of leaves, etc., flowers trailed in slip containing titanium and iron oxides, impressed bands under white slip, or regular fine vertical lines incised in the sides of faceted jars. His first one-man exhibition was held in 1950, and the National Gallery of Victoria showed a retrospective exhibition of his work in 1968. He works at Glen Iris, Melbourne, concentrating on the functional aspect of ceramics. The National Gallery of Victoria held a second retrospective of his work (in honour of his 90th birthday in 1983).
Refs: G. Edwards *H.R. Hughan* (Melbourne, 1983); K. Hood 'The Pottery of Harold Hughan' in *Craft Australia* 2 (1983).

Hughes, Edward, & Co. Staffordshire earthenware manufacturers of earthenware and bone china, established 1889 at the Opal Works, Fenton, by Edward Hughes (d 1908), for the production of tea sets, jugs and tableware. Some of the pieces were decorated with coats of arms, as well as local views. White or green glazes were used. In 1907, the firm advertised mugs, beakers, vases and dishes with the trade name Fenton China Arms Ware. From the founder's death until its closure in 1953, the firm concentrated on the production of tea and breakfast services.
Marks: impressed H (1890s); the initials HF in a diamond, impressed or printed 1895-1905; later printed marks usually incorporate the name or initials of the firm and the name of the body, e.g. *Royal China*, *Paladin China*, 'Eusancos' *China*.
Refs: Andrews; Jewitt.

Hughes, James. *See* Della Robbia Pottery.

Hull Pottery. American pottery established as the Acme Pottery Co. (manufacturers of tableware) at Crooksville, Ohio, in 1903, and trading as the A.E. Hull Pottery Co. after purchase by Addis E. Hull in 1905. In 1917, the firm began production of industrial artware, sold to florists and gift shops throughout the US. They also produced tiles, 1927-29, and imported pottery until 1929 from France, Germany and England. The output included candlesticks and lamp bases, novelties (slippers, poodle figures, etc.), flowerpots in the shape of ducks, smokers' accessories, table decorations, decorated earthenware for domestic use (Blue Bird and Zane Grey lines of kitchen ware), and stoneware, as well as art pottery. The factory was destroyed by fire in 1950, but the firm resumed production two years later, trading as the Hull Pottery Co. under J. Brandon Hull, and is still in operation, though the production of art ware ceased in the early 1950s.
Marks: *Hull Art US*; *Hull USA*; after 1952, *Hull*.
Refs: Evans; Kovel & Kovel; Lehner.

Hulme, Thomas. *See* Macintyre, James.

Hulse & Adderley; Hulse, Nixon & Adderley. *See* Adderleys Ltd.

Hummel, Richard. *See* Cowan, R. Guy.

Hundley, George (b 1841). Porcelain painter working for the *Worcester Royal Porcelain Co. from the 1850s until 1897. Hundley specialized in flowers and plant designs, sometimes working in raised enamels on floral patterns featuring birds.
His brother, W. Henry (Harry) Hundley, painted flowers, often in raised enamel thickened with dry white, marked with the initials H.H. Harry Hundley was also a market gardener and independent flower painter.
Several painters with the surname Hundley working at the Worcester factory in the 1880s included Walter Hundley (b 1866), who had started work there in 1880, and remained until 1894.
Ref: Sandon (1978a).

Hungarian Faience. *See* Cincinnati Art Pottery.

Hunsletesque Co. *See* Senior, James Wraith.

Hunslet Hall Pottery or **Petty's and Victoria Potteries.** Yorkshire pottery established at Holbeck, Leeds, in 1800 by Samuel Rainforth (1764-1817), a local potter formerly employed at the *Swillington Bridge Pottery, who made creamware or pearlware painted under and over the glaze, or transfer-printed in blue or black. Rainforth's successors, Samuel Petty and Matthew Hewitt, made blue-printed household earthenware under the titles Petty & Hewitt or Petty & Co. (c.1814-24), until joined by Petty's son, Samuel, when the firm became Samuel Petty & Son (1825-45). The works was then split, part becoming known as the Victoria Pottery. John Mills, owner from 1827 of a small workshop where he had made yellow-glazed ware and probably black earthenware, succeeded the Petty family in 1846, and ran both parts of the works 1853-61, making brown-glazed earthenware. He subsequently retained the Victoria Pottery, which he continued with his son, while Petty's portion of the pottery was let to J.W.*Taylor from 1861 until its closure in 1881. Mills's successors left the works in the early 1870s.
Another pottery, later named Hunslet Hall, was established nearby at the end of the 18th century by Thomas Cartledge, son of a potter at Middleton, working with his own son, William, by 1813. Cartledge's output consisted of black earthenware, and stoneware bottles. Later owners, working under the name of Hunslet Hall Pottery, made white earthenware for domestic use. The works closed in 1896.
Several other potteries worked in the Hunslet and adjacent Holbeck areas, making coarseware, terracotta, horticultural goods, etc.
Refs: Hurst; Lawrence; Towner (1957).

Hunslet New Pottery or **Taylor's Pottery.** Yorkshire pottery built by 1823 near to the *Leeds Pottery, and run by a family called Taylor. George and Samuel Taylor, sons of the founder, were succeeded by J.W.*Taylor and his brothers. The staple product is thought to have been white earthenware, transfer-printed in blue or black, or sketchily painted, predominantly in red and dull green.

Allison's Pottery, occupied in 1803 by Robert and Joseph Allison, soon followed by John Allison (until the 1820s), and subsequently called the Jack Lane Pottery, made brown and black earthenware and, in later years, stoneware. After its purchase by George and Samuel Taylor in 1854, it was run as one unit with the Hunslet New Pottery, which closed in 1887.
The mark ROBINSON/*Jack Lane Pottery*/LEEDS, impressed in an oval, has been found on stoneware made 1848-66 by William Robinson (d 1884) at a pottery established 1840 as Cooper, Hardy & Robinson between Taylor's and the Leeds Pottery in Jack Lane, Hunslet.
From 1866, Robinson worked with his sons, who succeeded him until the 1890s. The pottery continued until the 20th century.
Refs: Grabham; Jewitt; Lawrence.

Hunter, W.H. *See* Long, William A.; Lonhuda Pottery.

Huntington Pottery. American pottery established in the mid 18th century near the harbour of Huntington, Long Island, in a district where pottery vessels had earlier been made from local clay by American Indians. It was operated from 1805 by Samuel Wetmore & Co. and subsequently by Moses Scudder, a partner in the earlier firm, until 1825, followed by Benjamin Keeler (1825-27), Henry Lewis and Nathan H. Gardner (as Lewis & Gardner) and their successors until 1854, Frederick J. Caire (1854-63), and finally Brown Brothers until its closure in 1904. The earliest wares, thrown or press-moulded for domestic use from local brick clay, were smudged with brown or black; later work was dipped in slip glaze, usually containing red lead, which fired to a rich red-brown. Grey salt-glazed stoneware, often with incised and blue painted decoration, which was introduced in the late 19th century, was used to make preserving jars, narrow-necked jugs, and other articles for domestic use. Later earthenware was made in clay from New Jersey, Albany, etc., and glazed with varying shades of brown dependent on firing conditions; some work by Brown Brothers shows a reddish tinge. Decorative designs were sometimes trailed in pale slip. Production in the last years of the pottery was restricted to flowerpots.
Earliest mark: *Lewis & Gardner*, stamped on stoneware.
Refs: Barber (1976); Clement (1944); Stradling; Webster.

Hürten, Charles Ferdinand (1818-1901). Ceramic decorator, born in Germany and working mainly in France and England. Hürten became one of Europe's foremost flower painters, working independently for several French porcelain decorating workshops after arriving in Paris, 1836; he fulfilled several commissions for the Sèvres factory. His work was shown in the Paris Exposition of 1858, and he was invited to join the firm of W.T.*Copeland, where he remained from 1859 until his retirement in 1897; his work featured in all the firm's displays in major exhibitions during his period of employment. Hürten's realistic studies of flowers, taken from natural specimens or his own gouache sketches from growing plants, and noted for their delicacy in texture and colour, included

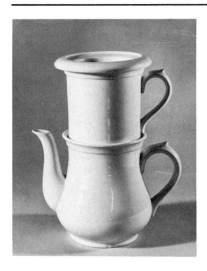

Hutschenreuther family. Coffee maker designed before 1890. Produced by Lorenz Hutschenreuther at Selb, 1915-30.

earthenware plaques and panels of porcelain vases, often signed. Hürten's other subjects included studies of birds and fruit.
Refs: G. Godden in Atterbury (1980); Jewitt; Rhead.

Huth, Louis. *See* Pössneck.

Hutschenreuther family. German porcelain makers, among the earliest founders of the large German joint stock ceramic manufacturing companies. Karl Magnus Hutschenreuther, porcelain painter from Wallendorf, established a factory at Hohenberg, Bavaria, in 1814. He was succeeded by his widow and sons, Christian and Lorenz (d 1886). By 1939, his factory employed 2,300 workers.

Lorenz Hutschenreuther founded a factory at Selb, Bavaria, which grew to employ 3,000 workers by the mid 20th century. It was managed from 1860 by Christian Hutschenreuther (in partnership), followed by his son Albert, a painter in underglaze blue. This firm absorbed factories in Selb (1917) *Tirschenreuth (1927), and the *Bauscher Brothers factory in Weiden (Oberfalz), the separate branches of the firm were united in 1969. The Hutschenreuther family also acquired factories at Altrohlau (1918) and Arzberg, as well as decorating workshops in Radeberg, near Dresden. H. Hutschenreuther worked a factory in Probstella. Most of the family's output consisted of high-quality tableware, figures, etc.
Refs: Danckert; Haggar (1960); Weiss.

Hüttensteinach. German porcelain factory established 1817 at Hüttensteinach, Thuringia, by a partnership, Greiner & Künzel, for the production of everyday domestic ware. The factory was under the control of Edward and Gustav Greiner and the lease-holder Carl Müller from 1835, Müller's stepson, Emil Fichtner, with Gustav Greiner from 1847, and Robert Swaine, an Ohrdruf merchant, in the early 1850s. William Swaine (d 1914) joined his brother in 1856, becoming owner of part of the business in 1869. He was joined by his son-in-law, Georg von Conta, in 1907. The other half of the factory

Hutschenreuther family. Model of a snowy owl on faceted base with gilt foliate medallions and green borders, made in Selb, 1930s. 24 cm high.

was bought in 1859 by the brothers Carl and Edouard Schoenau, who let it to Swaine & Co. until 1863, taking over operations in the following year under the name of Gebr. Schoenau. A successor, Albert Schoenau, took over the Swaine firm in 1917. His two sons, Adolf Günther and Horst Schoenau, became partners in Swaine & Co. in 1920. The factory then made electrical components until its closure in 1955.

Marks: a cross, a triangle, or the initial s with H; *Hüttensteinach* below a shield bearing the initial s.
Refs: Danckert; Scherf; Weiss.

Hüttl, Theodor (d 1910). Hungarian porcelain decorator and producer. Hüttl established a decorating workshop in Budapest in 1852, later producing porcelain, mainly to supply commissions, which included tableware for the Hungarian royal household. The factory also made toilet sets, decorative pieces, and tableware for cafés and restaurants. Hüttl was succeeded by his son-in-law and his son, Arthur, sole proprietor from 1927.

A variety of marks incorporate *Hüttl* and *Budapest.*
Refs: Danckert; Weiss.

Hylton Pot Works. *See* Dixon, Austin & Co.

Hyperion. *See* Doulton & Co.

Hyten, Charles Dean 'Bullet' (1887-1944). American potter. Hyten succeeded his parents at the Eagle Pottery in Benton, Arkansas, which he ran, with two brothers, trading as Hyten Bros Pottery. He developed a method of combining differently coloured clays, which mingled in swirling streaks when thrown, and in 1909 formed the *Niloak Pottery Co. for their production at the Eagle Works, acting as superintendent and making most of the variegated ware. He bought full control of the firm in 1918. He worked with native Arkansas clays, naturally coloured blue, red, white, grey, brown and beige, or occasionally tinted with metallic oxides, adding whiting and ground flint before working the clay, and firing the pottery for one-and-a-half to two days at a temperature

slowly rising to about 1150°C. His technique was granted a US patent in 1928. He continued the stoneware production inherited from his father, making jugs, jars, churns, flowerpots, etc., eventually at a separate works about three kilometres from Benton. He lost control of the firm in the mid 1930s, remaining for a time as a sales representative, and subsequently joined a pottery in Camden, Arkansas, where he worked as a salesman until his death.
Refs: Evans; Kovel & Kovel.

Ichimo or **Ichigo** Asai (1836-1916). Japanese potter. Like his elder brother *Takeuchi and their teacher, *Hachiroemon, he was noted for the decoration of *Kutani ware predominantly in red and gold.
Refs: Roberts; Uyeno.

Ichinokura ware. Japanese porcelain made at Ichinokura village in Mino province (Gifu prefecture) in the early 19th century, consisting primarily of small bowls of eggshell delicacy for tea or wine, glazed white on the exterior and painted inside with clouds and cranes, prunus blossom, or a small house with pine foliage. Decoration was often carried out in Tokyo workshops, where the pieces were furnished with protective coverings of basketwork or split bamboo.
Ref: Brinkley.

Ideal Pottery. *See* Trenton Potteries Co.

Iga ware. Japanese pottery of ancient origin made in the former province of Iga (now in Mie prefecture). Production is thought to have begun in the 14th century, and Iga was among the wares selected in the 17th century by tea master Kobori Enshu as worthy of tea-ceremony use. Utility ware was produced for local rural households. Coiled in heavy clay, with a coarse, sandy surface when fired, it results from similar technical traditions to those followed in nearby *Shigaraki. The original kiln closed by the 18th century, but production was revived briefly in the early 19th century and again in the Tempo era (1830-44) at Marubashira, the present centre for Iga folk-kiln production. *Ogawa Tokusai worked in Iga for five years in the 1830s.

In the 1920s, the area produced large quantities of kisha dobin, the small green-glazed containers for tea sold at railway stations, were manufactured in the area. After extensive study of early Iga ware in the late 1930s, the potter Toneo Kikuyama established production of stoneware which resembled the original Iga ware. It is characterized by a coarse body containing large sandy particles which come to the surface during intense and repeated firing with pine wood. The ash glaze produces a greenish coloration against the red, unglazed areas of the body; the portions subjected to most smoke appear scorched. The forms of water containers and flower vases, with which the area is associated, are frequently distorted by the length and intensity of firing.
Refs: Cort; Jenyns (1971); Mizuo; Munsterberg; Sanders.

Ikonnikov, Ivan Alekseivich. Russian potter and porcelain maker. In 1865 he leased the factory of N. and V.*Sipiagin, making white earthenware and porcelain until 1879. The factory was noted for the quality of figures produced, which were painted with enamel colours over a biscuit porcelain surface. In 1875 the firm bought moulds for figures and plates from the successors to A.G.*Popov.

Marks usually incorporate the name *I.A. Ikonnikov* over the glaze, sometimes with flowers, or a medal.
Refs: Ross; Saltykov.

Iles, Frank. *See* De Morgan, William.

Illingworth, Nelson (1862-1926). Sculptor and potter, working in Australia. Illingworth was born in Plymouth, Devon, and trained at the Lambeth School of Art and the *Doulton & Co. workshop. He arrived in Sydney with his family in 1892 and joined the staff of the newly-founded Sydney Technical College as an instructor in modelling. In the next year, he set up his own studio, where he carried out commissions for sculptural pieces, produced finely modelled ceramic brackets, plaques and figures, and made a range of moulded flowerpots, probably his staple product. He later concentrated on portrait sculpture.

Ilmenau. German porcelain factory established 1777 by Christian Zacharias Gräbner at Ilmenau, Thuringia. The factory produced everyday domestic ware, figures, tobacco pipes, cane handles, etc., in a low-quality paste until the 1790s. In 1792, the factory lease passed to Christian Nonne (d c.1813) from Volkstedt, who was joined by his son-in-law, Ernst Karl Roesch. Nonne and Roesch improved the quality of the output using Bohemian kaolin. Their work included vases and plaques in the style of Wedgwood

Nelson Illingworth. Terracotta statuette of Sir Henry Parkes, 'Father' of Australian federation, c.1899. 45 cm high.

jasper ware c.1800, as well as tea, coffee and chocolate sets, and individual pieces for table use. The design was influenced by Louis XVI and Empire styles, with painting of views, etc., in light brown, and gold borders. Landscapes were sometimes edged with delicate leaves and garlands. The firm suffered financial difficulties in the mid 19th century and became a joint stock company in 1871, with the main creditor, Herman Stürke, an Erfurt banker, and local mill owner Franz Wenzel as trustees. The firm's former accountant, Hering, became director in 1874, followed by Theodor Albrecht, who also joined as an accountant in 1898 and became director in 1902. A branch opened in Stadtilm, in 1896, remained in operation until 1915 and was sold two years later. After a brief closure in the 1930s, the Ilmenau factory reopened in 1934 under the direction of Emil Lentner, who introduced a line of ware with decoration in bright cobalt blue, richly gilded. From 1945, the factory traded under the name of the Count of Henneberg. After nationalization in 1947, the works underwent modernization. The ware, now of very high quality, is known as Henneberg porcelain.

19th-century marks include J,N&R (from 1808), various marks incorporating the initials J or IPM and sometimes the date of establishment.

Other porcelain manufacturers at Ilmenau include the Galluba & Hofmann factory, established 1888 for the production of figures and luxury articles; Kuchler & Co. (c.1900); Metzler Bros & Ortloff (1875), makers of art and utilitarian wares; Arno Fischer (decorative wares from 1907). Schumann & Klett and August Schmidt opened decorating studios in 1920 and 1930 respectively.
Refs: Danckert; Scherf; Weiss.

Imaizumi Imaemon (1897-1975). Japanese potter born in Arita, the 12th in sucession of a line of decorators of *Nabeshima and other wares working under the protection of the local clan from the 18th century. The family took the additional name of Imaemon in the Meiji period, and after the collapse of the feudal system started to compound their own porcelain paste, which they fired in a cooperative kiln from 1871 until they built their own kiln c.1890. After financial failure in 1897, followed by difficulties with firing, the 12th Imaemon studied ceramics at the technical high school in Arita, building his own kiln on graduation. He continued to decorate wares after Nabeshima and *Arita styles, following traditional designs and techniques. With his predecessor he had worked to revive the tradition of enamelled (Iro) Nabeshima and to adapt the output to modern requirements. He also created new patterns based on earlier Nabeshima designs evolved from fabric designs. His workshop formed the institute for the preservation of Iro Nabeshima Imaemon Porcelain in 1970 with Imaemon XII as President, and the group was designated as Holder of the Important Intangible Cultural Property Iro Nabeshima in 1971. His successor Imaemon XII (b 1926) continued the work of reviving Nabeshima ware. After studying at the Tokyo fine arts school, he developed a distinctive style in decoration noted for the dynamic effects achieved in composition.

Imari. Double-gourd vase, the body decorated in underglaze blue, red and gold with chrysanthemum and prunus, late 19th century. Seal mark in underglaze blue. 23.5 cm high.

Refs: Jenyns (1965); Masterpieces; Mitsuoka; Munsterberg; Roberts.

Imari. Japanese port in the former province of *Hizen on the island of Kyushu, which is associated with wares shipped from there to Nagasaki for distribution elsewhere in Japan or to Europe in the late 17th and early 18th centuries. In Japan, the term Imari ware encompasses all the wares made in and around *Arita (except *Kakiemon and *Nabeshima wares and the blue and white Hirado wares of *Mikawachi), and Ko (Old) Imari refers to Arita porcelain developed in the mid 17th to mid 18th centuries, the most flamboyant period of polychrome enamelled porcelains in Arita. Old Imari, widely imitated since its first production, includes a variety of pieces ranging from jars, bottles, plates, bowls and other tableware to incense burners, statuettes and ornamental ware, some directly copied from 17th-century Chinese pieces, e.g. large lidded jars originally imported as holders for luxury and pharmaceutical goods. The characteristically lavish nishikide (brocade) enamelled decoration normally covering the pieces includes figure subjects (sometimes Dutch traders, European ships, etc.), landscapes, animals, birds, flowers, in Chinese or Korean styles, as well as themes from Japanese paintings or prints, surrounded by diaper designs, many of which were inspired by textiles or pattern books. The enamel colours, black, yellow, purple, clear blue, and a distinctive orange-red, accompanied painting in underglaze blue and lavish gilding. Simpler designs, many of flowers, in the same colours but showing more white ground, were referred to as five-colour Old Imari.

In Europe, the name Imari ware is generally applied to three-colour Arita ware combining underglaze blue with iron-red enamel and gold in *japan patterns derived from Chinese provincial ware of the late

Ming dynasty, which was produced for export and in turn imitated at *Ching-tê-chên. This ware sometimes has green, yellow or aubergine enamel decoration in addition to the three usual colours.
Refs: Hannover; Jenyns (1971); Mikami; Munsterberg.

Imbe. *See* Bizen ware.

Impasto ware. *See* Doulton & Co.

Impératrice, La Manufacture de l'. *See* Honoré, François-Maurice.

Imperial Pottery. English pottery established in Lambeth c.1820 by Stephen Green for the production of coarse red earthenware and later salt-glazed stoneware. Subsequently, Green's main output consisted of glazed stoneware bottles for blacking, spirits, etc., including barrels, flasks in the shape of pistols, an example dated 1837 in the form of a figure of Queen Victoria, and other portrait flasks, as well as drainage and chemical wares.

The pottery was sold in 1858 to J.*Cliff, who continued the production of stoneware until its closure in 1869.
Refs: Atterbury (1980); Blacker (1922b); Jewitt.

incised decoration. Patterns scratched or cut in a clay body before firing.

Indiana Pottery Co. American pottery firm established in 1837 near the village of Troy, down river from Louisville, Kentucky, by a local potter, Jacob Lewis (*see* Lewis Pottery Co.), earthenware importer Samuel Casseday, and J.*Clews for the production of table services in white earthenware with transfer-printed decoration, in which they were among American pioneers. James *Bennett was an employee before going to East Liverpool, Ohio. Clews was with the firm until 1842, when he sold his shares, and J.*Vodrey managed the works from 1839; he left by 1847. Samuel Casseday then remained as owner of the property, which he let to other producers until he sold out in 1859. John Sanders (d 1863) and Samuel Wilson leased the premises from 1851, making yellow and Rockingham-glazed wares until damage to the pottery by fire in 1854. After rebuilding, Sanders carried on alone until his death, succeeded by Benjamin Hinchco, until demolition of the works in the early 1870s.
Refs: Barber (1976); F. Stefano Jr in Atterbury (1980) and in *Antiques* (March 1974).

Inoue Yoshitaka or Ryosai (b 1828). Japanese potter, born in Seto and initially working at nearby *Inuyama. Inoue moved for a while to Tokyo and in 1866 established a kiln at Asakusa, where he took the name Togyokuen Ryosai. He was joined by Inoue Ryosai II (b 1888), who was born in Tokyo and studied there under H.*Itaya. He moved to Yokohama c.1913 and produced white-glazed porcelain that was traditional in design; his decorative patterns were influenced by Western work. He took part in the annual exhibitions organized by the ministry of education and other government-sponsored bodies in Japan.

Ref: Roberts.

Intarsio. *See* Foley Potteries; Rhead, Frederick Alfred.

International Pottery. American pottery built by H.*Speeler in 1860 at Trenton, New Jersey, and trading from 1868 as Henry Speeler & Sons. The firm was bought in 1878 by Edward Clark and James *Carr, and soon traded as the International Pottery Co. producing cream-coloured and white granite wares. It was sold in 1879 to William Burgess and John Campbell. Porcelain was made with varying degrees of success before the introduction of a high-quality paste in 1888. The firm specialized in toilet and dinner sets of elegant form in semi-porcelain, decorated under the glaze in grey, rich, dark blue or lighter blue, sometimes with flown effect. Porcelain was decorated with enamel painting, raised gilding and sometimes a vellum finish. The firm traded as Burgess & Co. after the withdrawal of Campbell in the early 20th century.

Marks normally incorporate the name of the pottery or *Burgess & Campbell*; some give a trade name e.g. *Royal Blue*.
Ref: Barber (1976).

Inuyama kiln. Japanese pottery in the *Seto area. Established at Bishu, near Inuyama castle, in the mid 18th century, and moved in the early 19th century to nearby Maruyama, the workshop produced stoneware or semi-porcelain with coarse, grey body and colourless glaze. The output included blue and white ware and *gosu aka-e (Inuyama gosu) painted from c.1835 by *Dohei. The kiln was associated with bright floral patterns or designs of maple leaves lightly sketched in black and enamelled in emerald green and reds that range from rust to a dark reddish brown, with the addition of white slip, like a glaze in appearance. The Lord of Inuyama is thought to have initiated (c.1836) the use of unkin (cloud and brocade) designs and patterns of cherry blossom and maple leaves also associated with *Dohachi.
Refs: Feddersen; Gorham; Honey (1945); Jenyns (1971); Munsterberg.

Inuyama kiln. Five-sided cake bowl painted with red flowers and green leaves, 1860. 14.6 cm.

*Sadie A.E. Irvine. Covered jar made by Sadie Irvine at the *Newcomb College Pottery, 1925-34. 22 cm high, overall.*

Ipson, Louis. Danish potter working in America from 1891 in association with T.P. A.*Samson. Ipson was a moulder at the pottery of P.*Jacobus for one year before establishing *American Art Clay Works with Samson in 1892. He returned to Denmark in 1896, but rejoined Samson in Illinois, remaining briefly at the Art Clay Works before establishing the *Norse Pottery in 1902. He probably left by 1907.
Refs: Evans; Kovel & Kovel.

Irelan, Linna. *See* Roblin Art Pottery.

Iris workshops. *See* Finch, Alfred William.

ironstone. In English ceramics, a hard, white earthenware body primarily associated with C.J.*Mason, who took out a patent in 1813. Other makers include *Davenport's, G.L., T.& J.*Ashworth, F.*Morley, Job *Ridgway and his sons and, briefly, J.*Wedgwood & Sons Ltd. J.*Spode marketed a similar body as 'stone china', and the wares were marketed under various trade names: Patent Stone China, Pearl Stone China, White Stone, Royal Ironstone, Imperial Ironstone, Genuine Ironstone. In the mid 19th century, the range of patterns, many of which had been oriental in inspiration, was extended to compete with inexpensive French porcelain, which was becoming widely exported, and some British ironstone bodies were trademarked Porcelaine Opaque, Parisian Porcelain, etc. Similar bodies made in America were sometimes sold as Graniteware or White Granite. (*See also* semi-porcelain).
Refs: Godden (1980); Haggar & Adams.

Irvine, Sadie Agnes Estelle (1887-1970). American pottery decorator working at the *Newcomb College Pottery, as a student

1903-06, then artist and teacher until 1952. She was mentioned by P.E.*Cox as the best decorator to have emerged from Newcomb's course of training. In the early 20th century she created the Bayou scene which features an oak draped with moss against a moonlit sky, a popular design on the pottery's work in the 1920s; however she is quoted as wishing that this had not been noticed to the exclusion of other work. She later became an artist in watercolours and block prints.
Refs: Barber (1976); Callen; Clark & Hughto; Eidelberg; Evans; Henzke; Keen; Kovel & Kovel; S. Ormond & M.E. Irvine *Louisiana's Art Nouveau: The Crafts of Newcomb Style* (Pelican Publishing, Gretna, La., 1976).

Irving, Hugh. *See* Paragon China Ltd.

Isabey, Jean-Baptiste (1767-1855). French court painter and miniaturist, born in Nancy and working for David in Paris. As painter of porcelain at the Sèvres factory c.1807-10 and briefly in 1816, he executed a number of his royal portraits, e.g. one of the Empress, which was used on cups. He also painted portraits of Napoleon and his generals on the *table des Maréchaux de l'Empire* in celebration of their victories.
    Mark: full signature on painting from Isabey's own designs.
Refs: Bénézit; Lesur (1967).

Isaburo Okeya or Saida (1796-1868). Japanese porcelain decorator working in the *Kutani area. A farmer from Sano village in Nomi county, Isaburo trained in the techniques of *aka-e enamelling under *Yujiro at the *Wakasugi kiln, and painting in underglaze blue at the *Yoshidaya kiln, before making study visits to Kyoto, Arita, Seto and other centres. He then opened a school of porcelain painting at Sano in 1835. At his workshop (the Sano kiln) in Terai, using porcelain bought in the white from a number of kilns, he made several innovations in the decoration of Kutani ware: his work included patterns in gold on a darker gold ground, with the piece sometimes fired a second time to impart a cool gloss to the gold, and the introduction of black in the red and gold Kutani palette. His subjects, including such Chinese themes as the Hundred Ancients and the Seven Sages, were widely imitated by his students and occur in local export ware.
Ref: Nakagawa.

Ishiguro Munemaro (1893-1968). Japanese potter, born at Niihama, Toyama prefecture; a collector of Chinese wares of the Han (206BC-AD220) and Sung (960-1279) dynasties. After experiments in raku ware starting in 1917, he studied alone in Tokyo, Saitama, Kanazawa and Kyoto. From the establishment of his own kiln (1935) at Yase, near Kyoto, he devoted himself to the study of T'ang and Sung wares, making high-quality reproductions of the three-colour wares of the T'ang dynasty, and Sung glaze techniques including Black Ting, the red brown kaki, temmoku, and konoha (leaf) temmoku, adding original features of style. He was designated Holder of the Technique for Iron-glazed Pottery in 1955.
Refs: Koyama; Living National Treasures;

Masterpieces; Mitsuoka; Munsterberg; Okada; Roberts; Sugimura.

ishi-haze (stone explosion). In Japanese ceramics, the peaked effect caused by the pressure of large particles of feldspar which explode on the surface of a pot during firing. This effect, traditionally a feature of *Shigaraki and *Karatsu wares, has been intentionally achieved by modern potters.
Refs: Cort; Sanders.

Iskra, Franz Xaver (b 1897). Austrian ceramist, born in Wien-Döbling. Iskra learned ceramic techniques and worked as an assistant at his family's pottery in Ober-Döbling. He subsequently studied at the Technische Hochschule and the Akademie der bildenden Künste, Vienna. He was co-founder and a contributor to the interior-design journal *Klima und Raum.* He is known for his development of a coral or tomato-red glaze, *Iskrarot,* in 1928. He ran his own school from 1930 until 1945, when he moved to Vorarlberg, where he ran a small workshop. He later settled in Mariazell. His work includes animal figures, bowls, lamps, containers and stove-tiles.
    Mark: a circle containing the outline of a vase on a pedestal.
Ref: Neuwirth (1974a).

Islettes, Les. French faience factory established by 1737 across the River Biesme from Les Islettes (Meuse)—actually at Bois d'Epanse (Marne). The proprietor, François Bernard (d 1800), was succeeded by his widow and son, Jacques-Henri Bernard, who was in turn followed in 1823 by his widow Marie Parfaite (d 1836). The family, employing 300 workers at the height of production, was noted for tableware, including large dishes bordered with three sprays of flowers or, more rarely, garlands of roses; the factory also produced statuettes, inkstands, Bacchus jugs, etc. Painting, generally overglaze in intense red, purple, green, bright yellow, and often outlined in black, included a wide range of subjects: military scenes, *chinoiseries,* flower baskets, bouquets tied with red ribbon, local animals and birds, and landscapes, often with large boulders in the foreground. Artists included landscape painters Jules Dupré (until 1825), who was noted for his *chinoiseries,* figure groups, and cupids, Antoine (d 1823), who often carried out his work *en camaïeu* in underglaze blue or grey, and G.*Michel. The decoration of rustic pieces was often confined to sketchy flowers or such patriotic emblems as a crowned eagle, wreathed *fleur-de-lis,* cockerel or tricolour flag. After purchase by the Godéchal brothers in 1840, the pottery closed in 1848.
    Marks include: *Bernard au Bois d'Epanse,* sometimes inscriptions.
Refs: Ernould-Gandouet; Fontaine; Garnier; Hannover; Lane; Lesur (1971); Riff; Tilmans (1954).

Islington Pottery, Liverpool. *See* Mason, Miles.

Isolde. *See* Rosenthal.

Itaya Hazan (1872-1963). Japanese artist potter. Born in Shimodate, Ibarake prefecture. Itaya completed his studies in

sculpture at Tokyo's school of fine arts in 1889 and subsequently learned the techniques of *Kutani ware while teaching sculpture at the Institute of Technology in Kanazawa until 1903. He established a workshop at Tabata, Tokyo, first exhibiting in 1906. Working only in porcelain, he always produced a small output (about 1000 pieces are now known), initially influenced by European styles; his later work was Chinese-inspired. Itaya became known for the high quality of his white and celadon-glazed porcelains, often decorated with floral patterns in low relief, as well as temmoku-glazed bowls. He also produced enamel-painted pieces, sometimes using patterns inspired by Indian and Dutch textiles. His work was in general characterized by careful treatment of the relationship of decoration, glaze and form and his effort to incorporate oriental and European elements, in a new style. A pioneer among Japanese studio potters, he was the first ceramic artist to be awarded the Order of Cultural Merit and served as a member of the Japanese Art Academy and the Art Committee of the Imperial Household. He was a professor at the technological high school in Tokyo.
Refs: Masterpieces; Mitsuoka; Munsterberg; Okada; Roberts; Uyeno.

Ito Tozan (1846-1920). Japanese potter born in *Awata and working in Kyoto. After studying painting, he became a potter in 1863 and established his own workshop in 1867. He made white earthenware in the Awata tradition decorated with a palette of underglaze colours that included blue, green, red, yellow, black, and purple. Some work was inspired by *Asahi ware. Among the leading potters of Kyoto, he was a member of the Art Committee of the Imperial Household. He was succeeded by two generations bearing the name Ito Tozan, of whom the second is regarded as the last master of traditional Awata wares.
Refs: Brinkley; Roberts; Sanders; Uyeno.

Ivanoff, Vassi (1897-1973). French artist, photographer and studio potter. He worked for one year at *Saint-Amand-en-Puisaye in the mid 1940s, moving to La*Borne. His early output, immediately after World War II, included reddish brown stoneware, and a porcellaneous body used for smooth vases, sometimes in the shape of human figures. His work became very varied, ranging from rough stoneware with a high content of chamotte to smooth, glazed pieces of abstract sculpture.
Refs: Céramique française contemporaine; Faré.

Ivory China. *See* Macintyre, James.

ivory porcelain. Ivory-coloured porcelain paste developed by the partnership of Kerr & Binns at *Worcester c.1856, and used in the making of figures, groups, busts and other ornamental pieces, sometimes with a soft, velvety glaze. The decoration of ivory porcelain included a celadon glaze and from the mid 1860s a film of silver, bronze, etc. From 1873, shapes and ornament of Japanese inspiration were designed, notably by J. *Hadley. The paste could be very thinly potted, but was expensive to produce because of high kiln losses. It provided the basis for the paste developed by the company for Raphaelesque porcelain c.1860.

Ivory-toned pastes were also used by W. H.*Goss and *Wedgwood & Co. of Tunstall.

Jack Lane Pottery. *See* Hunslet New Pottery.

Jackfield, Shropshire. *See* Craven, Dunnill & Co.

Jackson, Cicely H. *See* Moore, Bernard.

Jackson, H.F., & Co. Ltd. *See* Forster, Ellis Sidney.

Jackson, John. *See* Holmes Pottery.

Jacobin, E. *See* Aprey (Haute-Marne).

Jacobson. *See* Porceleyne Fles, De.

Jacobus, Pauline (1840-1930). American artist potter. Pauline Jacobus taught ceramic decoration at her home in Chicago before going to study pottery techniques under M.L.*Nichols Storer in Cincinnati. She established one workshop in Chicago in 1883 and a second three years later, selling her output, which included earthenware (monochrome, glazed or painted under the glaze with flowers and other patterns), red ware with incised and gilded decoration, and stoneware, through stores in New York, Boston and Chicago. She moved to Edgerton, Wisconsin, in 1888 and, with backing from local businessmen, established the Pauline Pottery which was incorporated in the same year. Sharing a site with a works manufacturing battery components, run by her husband, Oscar I. Jacobus (d 1893), she produced tiles, teapots, flowerpots, vases, ewers, candlesticks and lamp bases, often in complicated shapes with slender necks, wavy rims, scrolled or curling handles, etc. Her decoration included floral patterns painted freehand in muted colours and outlined in black on a white earthenware body under cream-tinged lead glaze. Raised decoration of leaves, etc., in full relief also occured, sometimes in buff stoneware. Gilding was often sponged or brushed on rims or around decoration. Some pieces were reminiscent of Italian maiolica. The pottery employed several women as decorators; other workers included, in 1891, T.P.A.*Samson, designer and modeller, and L.*Ipson, moulder (much of the Pauline pottery was moulded at that time).

Following the death of her husband, and the failure of his business, Pauline Jacobus lost control of the pottery and a new company, the *Edgerton Pottery, was organized to continue production. With a kiln and clay bought on the bankruptcy of the Edgerton Pottery, she established a workshop again operating as the Pauline Pottery, at her home in Edgerton (1902-09), employing student assistants and running a pottery summer school. In the winter, she worked on pottery made there. At that time Pauline Jacobus concentrated on the development of low-fired crackle glazes used on a white body, and blended glazes, notably a 'peacock' combination of deep blue and green, and also brown shading to yellow, yellow to dull green, green to pink, or dark blue to pink. She left Edgerton after the destruction of

her house by fire in 1911, subsequently living in Texas and Wisconsin.

Mark: *Pauline Pottery*, incised or PP forming the sides of a crown.
Refs: Barber (1976); Callen; Evans; Kovel & Kovel.

Jacquemin, E. *See* Petit, Jacob.

Jacquet, P. *See* Annecy.

Jacquotot, Marie. *See* Sèvres.

Jäger, Wilhelm. German porcelain manufacturer working from 1867 at Eisenberg, Thuringia. Jäger made blue-patterned tea and coffee sets, *déjeuner* services, and cups for export to the Balkan countries and the Far East. His firm now forms part of a collective with the former Reinecke factory at Eisenberg.

Marks, which incorporate Jäger's name or initials, or *Eisenberg*, include a lion holding w and j in its forepaws.
Refs: Danckert; Weiss.

Jahn, Louis (d 1911). Porcelain painter, born in Thuringia. After working in Vienna, Jahn travelled to England in 1862. At the *Minton factory, c.1862-72, he specialized in decorative porcelain in the Sèvres manner; vases painted with figure scenes after Watteau were exhibited at the International Exhibitions in London in 1862 and 1871. Jahn

*Louis Jahn. Bottle in parian ware designed by Jahn and made by the firm of W.*Brownfield, c.1880. 29 cm high.*

worked as art director and decorator for the firm of W.*Brownfield (1872-95) and after his return to the Minton factory (1895-1900). Jahn was subsequently museum curator in Hanley, Staffordshire, until his death.
Refs: Aslin & Atterbury; Godden (1961); G. Godden in Atterbury (1980).

Jaksch, Mathilde (b 1899). Ceramic modeller trained in Vienna. Jaksch made a wide range of graceful, rather whimsical figures and groups, some incorporating animals, for the *Augarten factory in the 1930s, portraying actors, dancers, young lovers, children, and a number of costume studies.
Ref: Neuwirth (1974a).

James, Philippa. Melbourne potter, a student of M.*Boyd. She joined the Arts & Crafts Society of Victoria in 1925 and exhibited there regularly throughout the 1920s and 1930s, also holding solo exhibitions in Melbourne galleries. She had her own kiln and prepared her own clays and glazes. Her work, typically small domestic earthenwares decorated with Australian flora, recalls that of Boyd.

Jameson, James, & Co. *See* Bo'ness.

Jameson, William. *See* Portobello Pottery.

Jammet, Georges. *See* Saint-Brice.

Janak, Pavel. *See* Artěl.

Japanese ceramics. The making of pottery in Japan is of ancient origin. Earthenware, stoneware and porcelain were all in production from the introduction of porcelain by Korean potters in the district of *Arita in the early 17th century. A rise in living standards and, in particular, the demand for *tea ceremony wares caused an increase in ceramic production by the mid 17th century. New kilns arose in the established centres of *Seto and *Mino, *Kyoto and the island of *Kyushu, as well as in other areas. The stylistic influence of Korean potters, originally brought to Japan after the invasions of Korea in the late 16th century, spread eastward through the country and continued to influence many kilns, which produced large quantities of utility ware with wood or straw ash glazes and, in smaller quantities, ware for the cult of tea.

In Japan, a distinction is sometimes drawn between dark or 'black' wares—dark-glazed stoneware (sometimes with brightly coloured glazes also applied) often associated with kilns in western Japan, e.g. *Koishibara, *Ryumonji, *Shodai and Tsuboya—and light or 'white' wares, generally made in dark stoneware with a coating of white slip. A wider production of white wares coincided with the spread of porcelain techniques, mainly at kilns which were commercially successful, e.g. *Osotoyama. They were usually painted under the glaze with iron or cobalt. The makers also used brushed slip (hakebiki), brush-tapped slip (uchibake), lines or patterns of small, incised markings and patterns made with the fingers through a layer of slip.

Porcelain production spread slowly, initially delayed by secrecy over techniques to protect the monopoly of e.g. *Nabeshima, although the manufacture of porcelain increased in the province of *Hizen. However, porcelain was also produced at *Kutani (Haga province) in the mid 17th century. The wide spread of porcelain techniques occurred mainly in the mid-late 19th century.

The great variety of wares produced in a cumulative fashion, with new developments flourishing alongside older traditions rather than superseding them, is characteristic of Japanese ceramic production. Equally, the special wares of *courtyard and *clan kilns differed from the main body of popular utilitarian wares, made in *folk kilns which were founded in rural traditions. The Old Imari porcelain of Arita, and Kutani wares, contrast with the unglazed stonewares made in *Bizen, at *Tamba, and in *Tokoname (Teppo kiln), which were often made by part-time potters who were also farmers. Overglaze enamels and porcelains found a market among a growing urban bourgeoisie. Helped by official shogunate policies of encouragement for local industries, a great expansion occurred c.1800, when many new potteries and porcelain kilns opened, with improved techniques of firing. The sharp regional divisions in style continued, with new kilns preserving the technical and stylistic influence of the older kilns from which they developed.

Large kilns were constructed at Seto and Arita in the mid 19th century, and later at Kyoto, *Shigaraki, etc., with increased efficiency, which lowered production costs, and brought porcelain within the reach of more people. Despite disturbances which resulted in the Meiji restoration in 1868, modern European methods were introduced, e.g. at Arita by the ceramist Gottfried Wagner (1831-92). The Japan Pottery (Nihon Toki) Co. and the Nagoya Pottery Manufacturing Co. were established in Nagoya, a centre of the modern porcelain industry.

The opening of Japan to the West in 1854 was followed in Europe by japonisme, and Japanese art had a wide and lasting influence on European decorative arts.
Refs: H. Garner Oriental Blue and White (Faber, London, third edition 1970); Gorham; Jenyns (1965, 1971); Koyama; Miller; Sanders.

japan patterns. Ceramic decoration painted in underglaze blue with red enamel and gilding on Japanese porcelain exported to Europe from the port of Imari (Arita) in the 18th and early 19th centuries. The patterns, often derived from brocade designs, were imitated from the late 18th century by most British manufacturers, notably J.*Spode (1803), *Mintons Ltd (1805), Chamberlain's of *Worcester (1811), the Derby factories (which became particularly associated with the production of japan patterns) and, on ironstone china, G.M.& C.J.*Mason. After a decline in popularity in the 1830s, the patterns were later revived; Davenport's became an important producer in the 1880s.

Jap Birdimal ware. See Avon Faience Co.; Weller, Samuel A.

japonisme. The adoption of styles derived from Japanese design in European applied arts from the mid 19th century. Japanese ceramics were first represented in the West by Satsuma ware shown in the Exposition

*japonisme. Earthenware vase made at the *Rookwood Pottery, painted by A.R. *Valentien, smear-glazed, with a peach and powder-blue ground. The banding at the neck is hammered gilt metal. Marks include* ROOKWOOD *1886, impressed. 22 cm high.*

Universelle in Paris (1867) and the work of studio potters in the International Exposition, Vienna (1873). All types of ware were shown in the Exposition Universelle (1878) and a group of ceramics sent by the Tokyo Ministry of Public Instruction at the Exposition Universelle in 1889. Japanese ware was shown in America at the Philadelphia Centennial Exhibition (1876), and subsequent exhibitions. Examples of Japanese workmanship showed a strong contrast with classical traditions of design and were quickly adopted in

japan pattern. Mason's Ironstone baluster vase, painted in red, blue, pink, green and gold. 37 cm high.

England and France. In ceramics, decorative elements such as roundel motifs, prunus blossom, pine branches, calligraphic and other patterns appeared, sometimes on traditional European shapes. There developed a freedom from symmetry in the composition of painted patterns, in which large areas were often left undecorated, and a tendency to avoid the confinement of decoration within borders. Also important were the accompanying ideals of fine craftsmanship and imaginative design evident in Japanese applied arts.

Jarman, William. Porcelain painter working for the *Worcester Royal Porcelain Co. in the early 20th century. Jarman specialized in paintings of peacocks, often using a wash of colour over patterns printed in brown. He also painted roses in the style developed by J.*Hadley, for whom he had worked before joining the Royal factory. He ceased porcelain painting on leaving the factory for service in World War I.
Ref: Sandon (1978a).

Jaschinski, Kuno (1897-1954). German potter, born in Bartenstein, East Prussia, one of a family manufacturing tiled stoves. Jaschinski trained in Höhr-Grenzhausen and after military service in World War I took over a pottery, established 1811, in Goslar. Working with his wife, Hilde, and a number of assistants, Jaschinski made mainly utilitarian ware, undecorated, all of which he himself threw. His workshop also supplied commissions for figures.
Mark: outstretched hand over Goslar, stylized flowers and J.
Ref: Bock.

jasper ware. Unglazed stoneware, stained with metal oxides, perfected c.1774 by Josiah Wedgwood and associated with his firm, although widely copied in Europe and America. The white body, fired at 1100°C, was coloured throughout (solid jasper) or coated with a wash of coloured jasper slip (jasper dip). The production of solid jasper was interrupted, but revived in 1856. The decoration was usually moulded in the unstained jasper body and applied to the surface. The designs are normally classical in style, although all-over patterns of plants were used in the 1850s.

Jean, Auguste. French ceramist, working in Paris, c.1855-c.1885. Jean made decorative earthenware, painted in the manner of porcelain, with colours that combined with the glaze on firing. His pieces included copies of 16th-century maiolica.
Mark: monogram or signature, painted.
Ref: Lesur (1971).

Jeanneney, Paul (1861-1920). French ceramist, sculptor, and noted collector of oriental ceramics. Jeanneney learned stoneware techniques after the death of his friend, J.*Carriès, moving to Saint-Amand-en-Puisaye in 1902. He bought the Château de Montriveau and worked there until the time of his death. Influenced by Chinese flambé ware and Japanese trompe-l'oeil stoneware (e.g. pieces representing a section of bamboo, or a double gourd), he produced vases, rounded or gourd-shaped bottles, cups and bowls inspired by Korean tea bowls and

Paul Jeanneney. Stoneware bowl with lid of turned ivory. Shown at the Exposition Universelle, Paris, 1900. 14.6 cm high.

other vessels that closely resembled oriental originals, while also making his own sculptural pieces. His glazes were often in muted brown, fawn, or grey, with matt effect. A vase with bracket fungus in high relief on the sides dates from before 1897 and was followed by other pieces with jutting decoration. He also produced stoneware casts of various Rodin bronzes including a head of Balzac (1903), and heads entitled Burghers of Calais. Jeanneney also worked in collaboration with P.-F.*Fix-Masseau.

Mark: signature incised.

Refs: Brunhammer *et al* (1976); Camart *et al*; Hakenjos (1974); Heuser & Heuser; Préaud & Gauthier.

Jeannest, Pierre-Emile (1813-57). French designer of ceramics and silver; son of sculptor Louis-François Jeannest. He worked for some time in England, where he was employed by *Mintons Ltd from the mid 1840s until 1852 and taught modelling c.1848-52 at the Potteries School of Design. His work included allegorical figures, The Rose of England and The Lily of France, produced in parian ware (1849), porcelain table services and a number of majolica pieces. After joining the Birmingham silversmiths, Elkington & Co., Jeannest continued occasional design work for Mintons.

Refs: see Mintons Ltd.

Jeffords, J.E., & Co. American pottery company established 1868 in Philadelphia as the Port Richmond Pottery Co. by J.E. Jeffords, formerly employed by Morrison & Carr in New York. By the late 19th century, Jeffords's firm operated two distinct factories at the Philadelphia City Pottery, one making high-quality yellow and Rockingham-glazed ware, often in early English styles, e.g. Toby ale-jugs, cow creamers, and kitchenware glazed in blue and white. The adjoining works produced white and decorated ware for table and toilet use. Overglaze-painted decoration was introduced only briefly because of its high cost; much transfer-printed ware was made. The firm also produced *jardinières* and teapots with coloured glazes, and stoneware bottles for travellers and sportsmen.

Mark: a diamond containing the initials J/E/J CO and the date of establishment, 68,

with WARRANTED FIREPROOF.

Ref: Barber (1976).

Jersey City Porcelain & Earthenware Co. American manufacturers established 1825 in Jersey City, New Jersey, by a financial partnership which included George Dummer, who was also concerned in the closely associated Jersey City Glass Co., former occupiers of the works. The firm specialized in a hard-paste porcelain, usually decorated with bands of gilding, which won the silver medal of the Franklin Institute exhibition in 1826 for 'the best china from American materials' and pioneered the commercial production of porcelain in America. The porcelain and earthenware company failed, and the works, as well as some glass-company land, were sold to David Henderson of the American Pottery Manufacturing Co. (later *Jersey City Pottery) in 1828-30.

Refs: L.W. Watkins 'Henderson of Jersey City and his Pitchers' in *Antiques* (December 1946).

Jersey City Pottery. American pottery established in 1828 on premises belonging to the *Jersey City Porcelain and Earthenware Co. by David Henderson (d 1845) in the partnership D.& J. Henderson, probably with his brother. The firm was incorporated as The American Pottery Manufacturing Co. in 1833. In 1830, the Hendersons had exhibited a fine body, Flint Stoneware, which they made alongside yellow and Rockingham-glazed ware (which included Toby jugs). Buff stoneware, produced in large quantities, included pitchers with applied relief decoration and Rockingham or smear glazes. A price list of 1830 mentions coffee pots, mugs, covered jars and other household ware, lamps, water coolers, ink stands, and toys. White earthenware introduced in the same year was used for relief-decorated jugs. Several of the firm's relief designs have been attributed to D.*Greatbach, an employee from 1839.

The company introduced transfer printing c.1839, taking a pattern (Casanova) from a dinner service made by the firm of J. *Ridgway. American emblems and portraits of W.H. Harrison 'The Ohio Farmer' were printed under the glaze in black on mugs and octagonal pitchers in earthenware issued in the presidential campaign of 1840. The output also included cream earthenware with sponged decoration.

The firm worked under Oliver S. Strong, president, and Thomas McGurran, secretary and superintendent in 1849, and became known as the Jersey City Pottery in the early 1850s, producing only white earthenware until it was dissolved in 1854. The succeeding company, formed by English potters, Owen Rouse and Nathaniel Lucett (briefly in a partnership, Rouse, Turner, Duncan & Henry), chiefly made high-quality ornamental ware sold for outside decoration (e.g. by the firm of E.*Lycett) marked with the British coat of arms and the initials R.& T. Huge quantities of porous pots were made for telegraph companies. After the death of Turner in 1884, Rouse continued alone until 1892, when the factory was sold and demolished.

Marks include D.& J./HENDERSON/JERSEY/CITY, in a double circle, and transfer-printed ware was marked *AM Pottery Manuf Co* from 1833. In the 1840s, work was marked

AMERICAN POTTERY Co, the name used at that time.

Refs: Barber (1976); Clement (1947); L.W. Watkins 'Henderson of Jersey City and his Pitchers' in *Antiques* (December 1946); Weiss.

Jervis, William Percival (1849-1925). Ceramist and author, born in Stoke-on-Trent, Staffordshire, working in America by 1896. Jervis became manager of the *Avon Faience Co. in 1902. He opened a studio in a stoneware pottery at Corona, New York, in the following year, but ceased work there within a few months, after a fire at the works. In 1904, he ran a pottery in Pennsylvania as part of the Rose Valley Association's plan to open workshops producing items for interior decoration, and continued experiments in the development of coloured glazes: matt finishes in shades of blue, green, yellow, or orange, and mottled colours are among those he achieved. Jervis exhibited vases with metallic and textured glazes in the New York Society of Keramic Arts, 1905. At the *Craven Art Pottery Co. from 1905, he carried out decoration of earthenware using the tube lining technique introduced at the Avon Pottery. He extended his range of colours in matt glazes, which were produced at the pottery from 1906, often combining several colours in a shaded effect on the same pot. In 1908, with F.H.*Rhead, he established a small pottery at Oyster Bay, New York, of 'Designed to function' vases. Outlines of ornament were incised through a covering of white slip which was then removed, leaving a white design standing out against the red clay body used for vases, jugs, flowerpots, etc., under an opaque or matt glaze; modelled leaves or flowers were occasionally applied; incised mottoes were frequently incorporated in the decoration of mugs. Metallic glazes, notably copper-coloured, and glaze with iridescent effects also occur. In general, Jervis expressed his intention to subordinate ornament to function, preferring to rely on the impact of glazes.

Marks: signature at Rose Valley; name, with large initial J, vertically inside the outline of a jar, sometimes with initials O.B, incised.

Refs: Evans; P. Hain *et al A History of Rose Valley* (privately published, 1973); W.P. Jervis *A Pottery Primer* (O'Gorman Publishing, New York, 1911), *Rough Notes on Pottery* (privately published, Newark, N.J., 1896); Kovel & Kovel.

Jessop, George (1882-1944). English porcelain decorator. Jessop specialised in the painting of flowers in loose bunches, often including a rose. He was apprenticed c.1896 as a painter at the porcelain factory in Osmaston Road, *Derby, where he worked until he joined a munitions works at Coventry in World War I. He returned to the Osmaston Road factory after the war, leaving in 1927 to work for three years as a railway signwriter, and afterwards joined the factory in King Street, Derby until 1935. Jessop's wife Annie Saville was a gilder at Osmaston Road.

Mark: signature, *G. Jessop.*

Refs: see Derby.

jigger and jolley. A machine used in the production of series wares to form clay into flat or hollow shapes. A die, which is brought down on a pivoted arm, presses the clay against a spinning mould, controlling the thickness of the clay and shaping the back of a plate or the interior of a hollow vessel. The shapes which can be reproduced by this method are restricted to those that can be lifted without distortion from the mould—cylindrical, flat, or flared at the rim.

Jihei, Sosendo (d 1865). Japanese potter. A pupil of *Tamikichi, Jihei worked at Seto. He was noted for his skill in making exact reproductions of the T'ien Ch'i Chinese blue and white ware exported to Japan through the port of Nanking, and fine imitations of *Shonsui porcelain, also a speciality of his nephew Shentoen Hansuke. Jihei was followed by many pupils, who continued the painting of landscapes and birds in a bright blue.
Refs: Jenyns (1965); Roberts.

Joachim, Christian Hans (b 1870). Danish artist and ceramic decorator. He studied painting at the academy in Copenhagen and exhibited portraits from 1893. As art director at *Aluminia and the Royal *Copenhagen (1916-30) porcelain factories, he painted porcelain in a lively, naturalistic style distinguished by the use of rich underglaze colours, e.g. an earthenware plate decorated with a pair of birds. He also produced a series of enamelled figures.
Refs: Bénézit; Weiss.

Jobs, Lisbeth and Gocken. Swedish potters. The Jobs sisters established a workshop outside Leksand, where they made pottery painted under the glaze with flowers, figures and other motifs drawn from Swedish folk art.
Ref: Lagercrantz.

Johnova, Helena (1884-1962). Czechoslovakian ceramist born in Sobieslau and trained, at first in needlework and painting, at the Prague school of arts and crafts (1899-1907), briefly at Waldenburg (Schlesien) and Bechyn in 1907 and 1908, and subsequently at the Wiener Kunstgewerbeschule (1909-1911), where she was later to teach ceramics. Johnova joined R.*Neuwirth and I.*Schwetz-Lehmann in the *Keramische Werkgenossenschaft in 1911 and in the same year exhibited tableware, figures and animal models in earthenware and stoneware. Her sculptural pieces were vigorous and often brightly coloured, her vessels large, in sweeping shapes.
Ref: Neuwirth (1974a).

Johnson, George (1859-1931). Porcelain painter working for the *Worcester Royal Porcelain Co. from 1875. Johnson specialized in painting birds, particularly game. He also painted many exotic birds on reproductions of the firm's 18th-century pieces; storks and flamingoes in lake or river settings; simpler studies, e.g. geese on a plate dating from 1901, and muted landscapes in the style of Chamberlain's factory. Johnson worked direct from nature when possible.
Ref: Sandon (1978a).

Johnston, David (1789-1854). Irish-born earthenware manufacturer working in Bordeaux (Gironde), where he became

mayor. With the encouragement of P.-H. Boudon *de Saint-Amans, Johnston established a factory in the early 1830s on the Quai de Bacalan, trading under the title Manufacture Royale de Bordeaux. His firm produced well-finished earthenware with white body and soft glaze, and some decorative pieces (especially in stoneware), but the main output consisted of table and toilet ware. Decoration of flowers, figure scenes and wind-blown trees was carried out in applied relief, often in white on blue, or the reverse. Other ornament included rice-grain perforations, fluting and basketwork. Mosaic motifs, often in coloured clay and picked out in enamel colours, were used on teapots, etc. Johnston made a speciality of printed decoration in brown, green, pink and, especially, blue for *chinoiseries*, romantic scenes, flowers, etc., and fabric or carpet patterns covering the whole piece. Johnston formed a company trading under his name in an effort to raise capital in 1840, with J.*Vieillard as partner, but the company went into liquidation and he retired in 1844.
Mark: *David Johnston, Bordeaux.*
Refs: Ernould-Gandouet; Lesur (1967, 1971); Meaudre de Lapouyade *Essai d'histoire des faïenceries de Bordeaux du XVIIIe siècle à nos jours* (Bordeaux, 1926).

Johnston, T.B. *See* Bristol Pottery.

Johnston, William. Scottish industrialist and pottery manufacturer. Johnston, owner of a large chemical works at Dobbies Loan, to the north of Glasgow, was also a partner in the firm of John Forsyth & Co., makers of domestic saltglaze, established 1815. The Forsyth firm moved to new works in 1821, and the title was changed to the *Port Dundas Pottery Co. The output then consisted of chemical ware and soon afterwards firebrick, as well as domestic ware. After the sale of the pottery in 1826, Johnston, Forsyth and a third partner, John McCall, reopened a nearby firebrick works and traded as W. Johnston & Co. 'potters, firebrick makers and dyestuff grinders'. By 1828, Johnston had built a new pottery at East Dundas Pottery Co. in partnership with William Richardson. He sold the company in 1835 and retired from business three years later, when he disposed of his interest in the firebrick works.
Ref: Craftwork 43 (Scottish Development Agency, 1981).

Jolliff Studio. *See* Cox, F.E.

Jones, A.G. Harley. English earthenware manufacturer, working from c.1905 in Fenton, Staffordshire, at factories including the Wilton Pottery and the Royal Vienna Art Pottery. Jones is known for ornamental pieces, frequently with lustre decoration, but from c.1920 he also made earthenware for domestic use. His decorative range included crested souvenir ware, which he advertised as 'Wilton heraldic china' in 1923, registering the mark four years later. Jones's firm concentrated on glazed fireplace tiles by 1933 and went bankrupt in 1934.
Printed marks usually incorporate the initials HJ or AGHJ, and several trade names including *Wilton Ware* and *Fentonia Ware.*
Refs: Andrews; Godden (1964).

Jones, Alfred B. English earthenware manufacturer working in partnership with his sons N.B. and A.B. Jones from 1900 at the Grafton China Works and other potteries in Longton, Staffordshire. The firm made tea and breakfast sets for export and the home market, as well as pieces decorated with crests or local views. By 1906, the range of souvenir ware included jugs, cups, vases, and trays, as well as figures, models of buildings, etc., in an ivory body, decorated with the coats of arms of cities or boroughs. Production of souvenirs continued until the 1920s. Commemorative figures made during World War I depicted soldiers in action; other pieces included grotesque or comical characters and animal models with coloured glass eyes. Jones's firm was followed by Crown Lynn Ceramics Ltd, using the trade name Royal Grafton.
Printed marks incorporate Jones's initials and the trade name *Grafton China* until the 1930s, *Royal Grafton Bone China*, often with a crown, from c.1949, and Jones's initials in a triangular monogram at the centre of a circular mark in the 1960s.
Refs: Andrews; Godden (1964).

Jones, George (d 1893). Staffordshire potter. In 1861, Jones established the Trent works in Stoke-on-Trent, in a firm trading as George Jones & Sons, for the production of a wide range of earthenware, stoneware and ironstone bodies, often for export. The output included vases, serving dishes, candelabra, etc., in majolica and Palissy ware. Porcelain, introduced in 1876, was of high quality and used for the production of baskets, etc., in modelled relief. The firm also produced pieces with relief and painted decoration in a fine earthenware body, delicately tinted. *Pâte-sur-pâte* decoration was executed by the modeller F.*Schenk. Jones's son, Horace, after training at South Kensington, worked as a designer. The Trent works was renamed the Crescent Pottery in 1907. (*See also* Robinson, H.T.)
Marks include the monogram G.J.; later examples incorporate a crescent.
Refs: Godden (1964); Jewitt.

Jones, Josiah (1801-87). Potter and porcelain modeller, born in England; he went to America in 1847. Working as a designer and modeller for his brother-in-law, C. *Cartlidge, he modelled portrait busts of eminent Americans, some from engravings or sculptures, others from life. Jones became manager of the *Southern Porcelain Manufacturing Co. at Kaolin, South Carolina, in 1856, and continued production of some models from the Cartlidge works. He was subsequently a modeller for several years in Trenton, New Jersey, where his work included a pitcher with relief decoration illustrating the shooting of Colonel E.E. Ellsworth at Alexandria, Virginia, produced by Millington, Astbury & Poulson (working in Trenton from 1860) and sent to the decorating workshop of E.*Lycett for painting of the relief designs. Among his last pieces of work was a copy of the Portland vase.
Ref: Barber (1976).

Jouhanneaud, Hippolyte (b 1820). French porcelain manufacturer. Hippolyte Jouhanneaud went into partnership with L.*Dubois at a small factory in the route d'Angoulême,

Limoges, in 1843, moving to larger premises in 1846. In 1866, Jouhanneaud left to establish his own firm in rue du Bas-Chinchivaud, where he worked from the following year. He specialized in fine tableware and biscuit porcelain, building up an export market in America after 1868. After a gradual retirement, he was succeeded at the factory by the firm of Aragon & Vultury in 1880. His heirs continued to let the factory until it was sold in 1907.
Refs: d'Albis & Romanet; Danckert; Ernould-Gandouet.

Jouhanneaud, Paul. Limoges porcelain manufacturer. Jouhanneaud ran a factory, La Pépinière, from 1868 in partnership with his brother and, until 1875, his brother-in-law, Paul Andrieux; the brothers continued to work together until 1891. In the following year, T.*Haviland used the factory briefly to make samples for his commercial production. He was joined for a short time at his new factory by Jouhanneaud and his son Charles before they moved to Faubourg des Casseaux, where they went into partnership with M.*Redon in 1906. Redon's firm then became La Porcelaine Limousine and passed to Paul Jouhanneaud's nephew (and partner from 1912), Georges Magne, from 1918 until the factory's closure in 1938.
Ref: d'Albis & Romanet.

Joulia, Elisabeth (b 1925). French artist potter, influenced by H.-P.-A.*Beyer and J.*Lerat. Joulia studied in Clermont-Ferrand, Paris and Bruges before settling at La *Borne where she made stoneware from 1949. Her early output, immediately after World War II, included salt-glazed pitchers textured to resemble tree bark, and plates imitating snail shells. She also made purely sculptural pieces, and used porcelain for small vases, bowls, etc. Her work was normally coated in slip and warm in tone; colours ranged from pinkish brown to rust and orange.
Refs: Céramique française contemporaine; Faré.

Jouneau, Prosper. French painter and ceramic decorator. Working 1882-1900 at a factory established c.1850 in Parthenay (Deux-Sèvres), Jouneau decorated earthenware bowls, vases, ewers, and candlesticks with translucent enamel colours (including reddish-brown and a dark blue) or inlaid clay in the style of *Henri II ware. In 1889, he exhibited a Renaissance-style vase with inlaid and applied decoration. In partnership with Paul Amirault from 1900, he worked on architectural decoration, including an earthenware ceiling.
Marks include monograms or signature.
Ref: Lesur (1971).

Jourdain, Francis (1876-1958). French painter, engraver and designer; born in Paris, the son of architect and designer Frantz Jourdain (1847-1937). After working as a painter, he became interested in a variety of decorative arts: furniture, wallpaper, textiles, stained glass. Jourdain founded Les Ateliers Modernes in 1912, expanding his business into a factory by the end of World War I, and selling through a Paris shop, Chez Francis Jourdain. His output included services in faience and slipware, some of which he designed. In interior design, Jourdain paid particular attention to the furnishing of increasingly small units of accommodation, and produced popular items at low cost, developing new designs in several media. He was a partner of Robert Mallet-Stevens, Pierre Chareau and René Herbst in a movement which resulted in the Union des Artistes Modernes (first salon opened 1930). His own ceramics included a thrown earthenware bottle decorated in slip with lines and squares in white, ochre and blue on a black ground, with yellowish glaze, signed F.J. in blue slip on the base, and dating from the early 1920s; a large dish in ochre earthenware, covered with red slip, with circles in blue slip, under a yellowish glaze, also initialled and dating from the same period.
Refs: Années 25; Baschet; Bénézit.

Jouve, Georges (1910-64). French decorator and artist potter, born near Paris. Jouve studied until 1929 at l'Ecole Boulle and then at a number of art schools. He escaped in 1941 from Germany to Nyons in the free zone, and at Dieulefit (Drôme) produced small crib figures in lead-glazed earthenware, which were fired in local kilns. He continued to make pottery on his return to Paris in 1945, making sculptural pieces with silky black or white glazes, large dishes, etc., and moved to Aix-en-Provence in 1954. There the range of his output extended to include earthenware vases and other pots, as well as sculptural pieces, fireplaces, enamelled fountains, sundials and religious ware. His work also included an altarpiece for a church in the Manche region. A variety of bright glazes, including lime green, red, yellow, dark green and white was used. Jouve worked with his wife, Jacqueline.
Refs: Céramique française contemporaine; Faré; Lesur (1971).

Joyce, Richard (1873-1931). English modeller and ceramic decorator, born in Derbyshire. Joyce studied at Swadlincote School of Art and taught at Burton-on-Trent School of Art. He worked briefly at the *Bretby Art Pottery as painter and designer, and for *Moore Bros, before joining *Pilkington's Tile & Pottery Co. in 1905. He executed work designed by other artists, including the painting of figures on vases designed by W.*Crane and exhibited in 1908, and the modelling of G.M.*Forsyth's panel depicting Saint George, but became known for his own modelling and painting (mainly in lustre) of many animals (including lions, leopards, cattle, deer, birds and fish), often from life sketches carried out in the zoological gardens at Belle Vue, Manchester.
Marks include signature, *R. Joyce*; monogram of RJ, with two dots, in the standard mark used by Pilkington's for designers and decorators.
Refs: Cross; Godden (1964); Lomax.

Juchtzer, Christoph Gottfried (1752-1812). German porcelain modeller. Gottfried Juchtzer joined Meissen as an apprentice in 1769, eventually becoming artistic director.
Ref: Danckert.

Jugendstil. *See* Art Nouveau.

Jugtown. Originally any community where jugs were made for the whisky industry in North Carolina. Production of the jugs reached a peak from the 1880s to c.1900, at between 50 and 60 workshops in North Carolina which specialized in making them until Prohibition in 1908. J. and J.*Busbee took an interest in the surviving pottery industry in North Carolina and started a workshop, which they called the Jugtown Pottery.
Refs: J. Busbee 'Jugtown Pottery: a new way for Old Jugs' in *Bulletin* of the American Ceramic Society XVI 10 (October 1937); Donhauser; Kovel & Kovel.

Kaestner, Friedrich. German porcelain manufacturer working near Zwickau, Saxony, from 1883, on the production of tea and coffee sets, table services and everyday ware.
A variety of marks incorporate crossed axes or, more rarely, crossed swords and the name *Kaestner* or initials FK.
Refs: Danckert; Weiss.

Kaga Kanazawa or **Maeda fief.** Japanese feudal domain of the Maeda family throughout the Edo period, extending into the provinces of Kaga, Noto and Etchu (Ishikawa and Toyama prefectures). Drawing great wealth from agriculture and shipping, it imported costly Chinese and, to a lesser extent, Dutch goods. Among Chinese imports, enamelled porcelain of the late Ming and early Ch'ing periods (early 17th century) prepared the market for local production of enamelled wares in the 17th and early 18th centuries, and the 19th-century revival of *Kutani wares.
Refs: Mikami; Nakagawa.

Kåge, Wilhelm (1889-1960). Swedish painter and ceramist. Kåge studied painting in Sweden, Denmark and Germany, and was a pupil of Henri Matisse. He joined the *Gustavsberg factory in 1917 and became artistic director until he left in 1949. He

*Richard Joyce. Vase with a moulded frieze and streaked lustre glazes in blue, café-au-lait and green, made at *Pilkington's Tile & Pottery Co. Impressed factory marks with R. Joyce, incised. 26 cm high.*

Wilhelm Kåge. Stoneware bowl from the Farsta range designed by Kåge at the *Gustavsberg factory, 1952.

produced stoneware, which was initially heavy, then lighter and more refined under the influence of ancient Chinese stonewares, with opaque figured and crystalline glaze effects. He both produced unique pieces and worked to raise the standards of designs for utilitarian ware. His porcelain tableware includes a Grey-Edge service, and Farstarust plates, etc. (*see* Gustavsberg). The shapes in both earthenware and porcelain were functional and intended for easy storage.
Refs: René Huyghe (ed) *Larousse Encyclopedia of Modern Art* (Larousse, Paris, 1961; Hamlyn, 1965); *see also* Gustavsberg.

Kagel, Wilhelm (1867-1935). German artist and potter. Kagel trained at the Munich Kunstgewerbeschule c.1887 and worked as decorator and fresco painter at Garmisch-Partenkirchen from 1890. He built his own kiln in 1904 and established a workshop for the large-scale production, by hand, of wares which combined artistic and technical excellence at a low cost. Kagel's workshop, in full production from 1906, initially produced hard earthenware (fired with coal at 125°C) painted, usually with flowers, in underglaze or enamel colours. Many patterns of garlands and stylized blooms were inspired by folk art from South Germany. Kagel was joined by his son, also Wilhelm Kagel (b 1906), as apprentice (1919-23) and as technical manager of the workshop from 1935, after training in Höhr-Grenzhausen. His other son, Eugen Kagel, worked as business manager from 1935. Wilhelm Kagel Jr added stoneware and faience to the workshop's output, retaining the folk-art influences in decoration. Production methods underwent modernization in 1930 and the workshop employed about twenty-five assistants. Decoration was generally stamped or incised; some trails or splashes of slip were used. The range of silky glazes included dark brown, golden brown, dark green and blue. Most of the wares were mass-produced by hand, but unique pieces were also made.

Heart-shaped mark, topped by a cross and containing wkp, impressed, printed or on a paper label 1906-30. For W. Kagel Jr, a monogram of wk, impressed or incised.
Refs: Bock; Klinge.

Kagiya. *See* Kinkozan.

Kahla. German porcelain factory established at Kahla by Christian Jakob Eckhard in 1843 for the production of tablewares. After bankruptcy in 1856, the firm passed to Friedrich August Koch, succeeded in 1872 by his son, Herman Koch; it became a joint stock company in 1888 and developed into one of the largest Thuringian porcelain factories by 1900. Nationalized in 1945, the firm merged with *Könitz in 1964 to form VEB Vereinigte Porzellanwerke Kahla-Könitz, and now has branches which include *Eisenberg and Reichenbach (*see* Carstens, C.& E.). The output consists of everyday tableware and hotel ware, much of which is exported. Patterns including Andante (1972), Capriccio (1973), Libretto (1974), Altthuringen (1976), and Serenade (1977) often comprise traditional motifs adapted to suit modern techniques.
Marks incorporate the name *Kahla* and, often, a crown.
Refs: Danckert; Scherf.

Kähler Ceramics. Danish pottery established by Joachim Christian Herman Kähler in 1839 at Naestved, Seeland, for the production of earthenware, initially stoves (made until 1888). Herman August Kähler (1846-1917) inherited his father's business in 1872, after working in Berlin (1866) and at the family pottery (from 1867). He introduced red metallic glazes, which were exhibited by the late 1880s. His work included vases, in simple forms, characterized by designs of flowers, stylized leaves, and other natural forms

Kähler Ceramics. Lustre-painted earthenware vase by Herman A. Kähler, with iridescent glaze and dark grey-green foliage and dark red flowers in a white ground, 1897. 32 cm high.

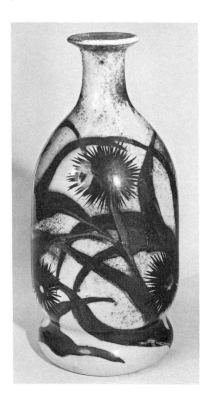

painted in lustre. Herman Kähler also used lustrous glazes, shaded in a single colour or in combinations of brown and blue, green and black, etc., patterned in slightly raised slip, again with plant forms. He was succeeded by his son, Herman H.C. Kähler.

Later, Herman J. Kähler (b 1904) glazed and fired stoneware, including bowls and jars with brushed decoration of sketchy figures, landscapes, etc., designed by his brother, Nils A. Kähler (b 1906). In the 1920s, their output included dishes designed by Jens Thiirsland; one example is triangular in shape and decorated with a stag. Work by designers including Thiirsland and K.F.C.*Hansen-Reistrup, and exhibited in New York, 1939, was light in weight, with crackled, greyish glaze, applied thinly to show patches of body colour. Shapes were sometimes distorted. The pottery's recent work includes architectural stoneware.
Marks include Herman A. Kähler's monogram, incised.
Refs: Beard; Cox; Haslam (1977); Hakenjos; *De Art Nouveau* (catalogue, Stad Gent Museum voor Sierkunst, Ghent, 1979).

Kahn, Isaac. *See* Wheatley, Thomas Jerome.

Kaipiainen, Birger (b 1915). Finnish ceramic artist, trained in Helsinki and working at *Arabia 1937-54 and again from 1958. He is known for ornamental pieces and wall panels in earthenware with painted and engraved decoration. Favourite early motifs include swans and other birds, and flowers, e.g. pansies. He worked as a guest artist at the *Rörstrand factory in the 1950s.
Marks include the name KAIPIAINEN impressed.
Refs: Aro; *Three Centuries of Swedish Pottery: Rörstrand 1726-1959 and Marieburg 1758-88* (catalogue, Victoria & Albert Museum, London, 1969).

Kakiemon family. A line of Japanese potters descended from Kakiemon Sakaida (1596-1666), makers of enamelled porcelain at Arita (*see* Kakiemon ware). In the 19th century, Kakiemon IX (1776-1836) and Kakiemon X (1805-60) are said to have concentrated on porcelain painted in underglaze blue, but later generations have continued the family's tradition. Kakiemon XI (1845-1917) trained his son Kakiemon Sakaida XII (1878-1963), who was responsible for restoring the quality of kaki (persimmon red) used in decoration and succeeded to the title in 1917. Kakiemon XII had studied at the ceramic training school in Arita and, assisted by his successor Kakiemon Sakaida XIII (1906-82), managed to restore the nigoshi-de (milk-white base) lost to Kakiemon ware in the late Edo period and designated an Intangible Cultural Property in 1955. The Institute for the Preservation and Improvement of Kakiemon nigoshi-de, formed in 1971 by experts in the Kakiemon studio, operates a system of divided labour in the stages of production from preparation of the paste to firing of the ware. The thirteenth generation continues work.
Refs: Jenyns (1965); *Living National Treasures*; Munsterberg; Roberts; Sanders.

Kakiemon ware. Japanese porcelain, delicately painted with enamel colours, made

Kameyama. Porcelain bowl painted in under-glaze blue with a landscape pattern, 1840s.

at the Nangawara kiln in Arita from the 1670s by the *Kakiemon family. The pieces, many of which were exported, were usually small in size and made with pure white porcelain paste from clays obtained in the Arita district. Painting was carried out in bright, clear colours: blue, green, yellow, black, gold and occasionally silver, as well as kaki (persimmon red) derived from iron oxide. The sparing, elegant patterns were inspired by designs on *famille verte* Chinese porcelains of the K'ang-hsi period and include figures in landscapes, birds, flowers and plants, e.g. the Three Friends, pine, bamboo and prunus, and symbolic animals, (tiger, dragon, or phoenix). The Kakiemon family also drew on western elements in their design, and their work was in turn copied at Ching-tê chên and many European factories. High-quality copies of early work have been made by later generations of the Kakiemon family. Some industrial copies are also made, notably in the region surrounding Arita.
Refs: Brinkley; Jenyns (1965); Koyama; Munsterberg; Okuda; Roberts; Sanders.

Kakuji. *See* Mori family.

Kalk. German porcelain manufacturer working from 1900 at Eisenberg, Thuringia, on the production of coffee sets, table services, etc. decorated in blue with traditional patterns. The firm passed to Geyer, Koerbitz & Co. and later joined the *Kahla group as VEB Porzellan-Fabrik Eisenberg.
Printed marks include crossed arrows either alone or with the name *Kalk*, sometimes in versions of a circular device topped with a crown. A shield bearing three towers also occurs.
Refs: Danckert; Weiss.

Kamashita. *See* Shino ware.

Kamaya. *See* Tamba ware.

Kameya family. A line of Japanese potters descended from Kameya Uyema, who had made ware in the style of *Dohachi II in the mid 18th century at Gojozaka, Kyoto. Subsequent generations made blue and white and enamelled porcelains at the family's Kyoto workshop, using the methods of hand building and fine painting developed in

Arita. Kameya III, using the artistic name Waka Kitei, is thought to have worked with the second *Rokubei in the mid 19th century. The family extended to seven generations until the mid 20th century.
Refs: Jenyns (1965, 1971); Morse; Roberts.

Kameyama. Japanese porcelain workshop established c.1803 on the outskirts of Nagasaki by a merchant of the city, Okami Jingobei, for the production of porcelain with underglaze blue decoration in the style of Chinese wares of the Ch'ien Lung reign (1736-95), and wares with celadon glazes. The blue and white ware, rather thickly potted in greyish-tinged porcelain paste and decorated by painters from Nagasaki in dull-toned blue, was exported in some quantity by Dutch ships. After the factory's bankruptcy in 1867, two brief attempts were made to revive production, the second in 1872.
Kameyama was also the source of a type of pottery made from the covers of earthenware wine jars imported from Szechuan, with the mark 'Made at Kameyama with clay from Soshu in China'. The fifth in line of the *Kenzan family established a kiln at Kameyama, where he was assisted by *Kenya.
Refs: Brinkley; Jenyns (1965); Hannover; Mitsuoka.

Kami-no-hara. *See* Koishibara.

Kamijo kiln. *See* Seba ware.

Kämmer, Rudolf. *See* Volkstedt-Rudolstadt.

Kämpfe & Heubach. *See* Wallendorf.

Kanashige Toyo (1896-1967). Japanese potter, born in Bizen-machi and 78th in line of the Kanashige family, traditionally makers of *Bizen ware. He is noted for restoring vitality to the ware with a return to the simplest of early styles. Until c.1925, he made chiefly sculptural pieces, e.g. lions, but he later concentrated on thrown wares. His work included vases, bowls and jars made from reddish clay, which were fired for long periods in intense heat and consequently suffered from slumping. His clay contained particles of rock which resulted in the ishihaze effect, showing as small peaks on the surface with radiating cracks.
Kanashige visited Europe and America, and was a member of the folk art movement (*see* mingei ware). He was Holder of the Designated Technique for Bizen Ware in 1956 in recognition of his efforts to stimulate production of the ware. His pupils included *Fujiwara Kei.
Refs: Jenyns (1971); Koyama; Masterpieces; Munsterberg; Sanders; Sugimura.

Kanazawa fief. *See* Kaga.

Kandern Tonwerke. Ceramic manufacturers at Kandern, Baden. The firm's production included figures after models by the sculptor Bernhard Hoetger, M. *Laeuger was artistic director 1895-1913.
Impressed mark incorporating Laeuger's monogram; incised monogram mark.
Ref: Haslam (1977).

Kano Mitsuo. Japanese potter working from the 1920s. He made vases and other pieces

in angular shapes, decorated with spiral or vertical lines of ribbing.

Kantor, Sandor (b c.1900). Hungarian potter, working at Karcaj, near Mezötur. He revived the then lost tradition of Tiszafured pottery in the 1930s, encouraged by Istvan Gyorffy, a professor of ethnography, also living in Karcaj. His pupils now work in the area.
Refs: E. Fel, T. Hofer & K.K.-Csilléry *Hungarian Peasant Art* (Corvina, Budapest, 1958); M. Kresz 'Hungarian Slipware and Unglazed Pottery' in *Ceramic Review* 63 (May, June 1980).

Karatsu wares. Japanese pottery made at about 200 kilns started by Korean potters in the 16th century in the area of North West Hizen (now Saga and part of Nagasaki prefectures) centred on the town of Karatsu. Coiled or thrown from greyish, sandy earthenware clay with high iron content, in simple shapes, Karatsu wares resemble Korean Yi dynasty wares for everyday use. Apart from domestic utensils, the kilns produced tea wares which were highly regarded by tea-masters. Japanese writers classified the ware into many categories dependent on form, decoration or use, but all groups share the same coarse body and feature wood ash, white feldspar or temmoku glazes. Decorative variations which developed among the kilns' output include Muji Karatsu, without decoration; e-garatsu (decorated Karatsu), painted in iron under the glaze with floral patterns or designs with birds, trees, etc. (a type of e-garatsu with abstract brushed designs has continued in the town of Karatsu to the present day); spotted or mottled Madaragaratsu with white glazes on feldspar clay ground; Seto Karatsu with opaque white (feldspathic) or yellow-green (wood ash) glazes, resembling Seto wares in style; Chosen or Korai Karatsu, glazed in white

Kandern Tonwerke. Lion cub after a model by Bernhard Hoetger, produced at Kandern, c.1911.

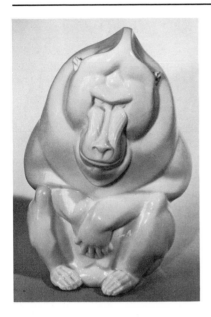

Karlsruhe. Seated mandrill in porcelain, modelled by Franz Blazek, 1910. Impressed mark: lozenge-shaped shield. 22 cm high.

and amber; Takeo Karatsu ware with iron decoration over a brushed slip ground, still made at *Osotoyama in the mid 19th century. Production diminished with the increase in competition from porcelain, and some potteries turned over to porcelain production. In the 1850s the feudal lord ordered the production of presentation pieces in fine, yellowish or brownish clay with crackle glaze and patterns of cranes flying among clouds (unkaku) inlaid in white. Makers of *Banko ware produced imitations of Karatsu wares in the 19th century. Karatsu kilns still in operation include Kuromuta in Takeo and *Tataro.
Refs: Brinkley; Gorham; Jenyns (1971); Mikami; Munsterberg; Sanders.

Karau, Werkstätten. Austrian workshop established in Vienna by the architect Georg Karau for the production of pottery and other crafts from 1919 until its closure in 1925.
Mark: square outline containing a snail shell, impressed.
Refs: Haslam (1977); Neuwirth (1974a).

Karlskröna. *See* Upsala-Ekeby.

Karlsruhe, Majolika-Manufaktur. German pottery established at Karlsruhe in 1901. The venture resulted from the combination of a ceramic studio set up by the painter Wilhelm Süs at Kronberg in 1898 for the production of majolica in Italian Renaissance style, and the larger workshop established in Oberursel by Hans Thoma, also a painter, who had in 1895 started production of a range of pieces inspired by *Haban Fayence. Karlsruhe production began in October 1901 at a pottery built by Grand Duke Friedrich I of Baden, with eleven employees making pieces designed by a number of artists, including Süs, Thoma and the sculptor Karl Maximilian Württemberger. August Fricke, business manager from 1908, initiated the artistic and technical reorganization of the

firm, developing characteristic lines of ware, which included a range painted in blue, often with *putti*, from designs by Süs, peasant-style domestic ware and individual pieces by artists, Hans Meid, Konrad Taucher, Georg Schreyögg, Emil Rudolf Weiss and others. Architectural ware became a staple product, which necessitated a move to larger premises in Hartwald, 1909. The output extended to include ornamental ware for parks, gardens and cemeteries in 1913, when court administration of the factory ceased. From 1914 to 1920 the firm of *Villeroy & Boch leased the factory, which was owned by the state of Baden from 1919 and subsequently administered by a private company. Branches opened in 1921 at Buchenweg and Ettlingen, and the firm was further enlarged as a joint-stock company in 1922. Designers in the 1920s, working in a masters' studio, included M.*Laeuger, Ludwig König, modeller of animal figures, Paul Speck, designer of utilitarian ware in simple, sometimes cuboid forms, and in the late 1920s P.*Scheurich. Architectural ware was designed by E.J. *Margold, A.*Niemeyer, K.*Riemerschmid, J.*Wackerle and others, mainly on a freelance basis. The firm was threatened by financial collapse and came under state ownership in 1927 as Staatliche Majolika-Manufaktur Karlsruhe AG, afterwards becoming profitable through a series of state commissions. The factory suffered bomb damage in 1944, and the output was restricted to utilitarian ware until 1951, when the production of decorative pieces was resumed. The firm continues to produce essentially hand-crafted ware designed by full-time and independent artists; the Katz Werke AG in Gernsbach has been a major shareholder since 1978.
Mark: a shield topped by a crown over the initials мм.
Ref: Karlsruher Majolika (catalogue, Badisches Landesmuseum, Karlsruhe, 1979).

Kasama. Japanese pottery centre in Iburaki prefecture. The production of unglazed wares in the early Edo period was extended in the late 18th century by a potter from Shigaraki under the patronage of the feudal lord Makino. From the mid 19th century, the kilns made utilitarian ware for the local farming population, and received a further influx of potters from Shigaraki. A folk kiln established near Karasuyama in the mid 19th century produced Koisago ware, strongly influenced by the output of Kasama, and makers of Kasama ware assisted in the development of pottery production at *Mashiko in the early 1850s.
Refs: Cort; Mizuo.

Kasaoka. Japanese pottery centre in Okayama prefecture. A kiln established in 1907 produces vases, plates, tea ware, etc., in traditional local styles.
Ref: Munsterberg.

Kaschau. Hungarian factory making creamware, c.1804-1845. The output was of a quality that rivalled wares made at *Holitsch.
Marks include *Kaschau,* impressed.
Ref: Csanyi.

Kasugayama kiln. Japanese porcelain workshop established at Kanazawa in Ishikana prefecture (which contains the old province

of *Kaga) by *Mokubei with the town's official backing in an attempt to revive the ceramics of the district surrounding *Kutani. After visiting Kanazawa in 1806, Mokubei returned in 1807 to build a kiln, with the assistance of *Honda, and went into production late in the same year. Mokubei was succeeded on his return to Kyoto in 1808 by the merchant Matsuda Heishiro (1760-1834), who worked under the artistic name Baso, with Honda among his assistants. Their output included celadon wares, and imitations of Chinese blue and white porcelain, red-enamelled ware (*see* aka-e), *Kochi ware, and Korean pieces with patterns brushed in iron pigment, continuing the styles introduced by Mokubei from Kyoto. The kiln ceased operation by c.1818. Soon afterwards, Takeda Shuhei revived production at Kasugayama with the establishment of a kiln operating under his art name, *Minzan.
Marks: stamped, incised or painted, incorporate the place names *Kimpu* or *Kinjo* (both names for Kanazawa), *Kanazawa,* or *Kasugayama.*
Refs: Jenyns (1965); Mitsuoka; Nakagawa.

Katayeva factory. Russian earthenware factory in the industrial district of Nizhne-Isetsk working 1850-80 on the production of low-priced tableware with floral printed designs and sometimes with lines of beading.
Mark: name and initials of the owner, G. Katayeva, in Cyrillic characters.
Refs: Bubnova; N.N. Serebryannikov *Porcelain and Faience of the Urals* (in Russian, Veka, Perm, 1926).

Kato family. Japanese potters noted as the first producers at Seto of porcelain, which became the main output of the area in the 19th century, predominantly with decoration in underglaze blue. They included *Kato Tamikichi, Kato Soshiro (Shuntai), the last of a line of potters, all related, but in some cases contemporaries, whose artistic names begin with the character shun, *Kato Hajime, and Kato Tokuro. The family claimed direct descent from the early Seto potter Toshiro (Kato Shirozaemon).
Refs: Brinkley; Jenyns (1965); Morse; Munsterberg.

Kato Hajime (1900-68). Japanese potter and ceramic historian, born in Seto City, Aichi prefecture. Kato was employed in 1926 at the Gifu Prefectural Institute of Ceramic Industry, and carried out extensive research. Kato established his own kiln at Hujoshi, near Yokohama in 1939. He made porcelain and stoneware, and became noted for enamel decoration and the use of gold. He also made a speciality of designs in gold on a pale green ground, but was skilled in a wide variety of decorative techniques, including incised patterns and applied or moulded relief. Kato studied the sites of Karatsu kilns at Motoyashi. He also revived Ming Chinese enamel techniques, e.g. oji kosai (red on yellow) and *kinrande, as well as ch'ing pai (shadowy blue), and underglaze red and gold. He became Professor of Fine Arts at Tokyo University in 1955. In 1961, he was designated Holder of the Technique for Enamelled Porcelain.
Refs: Fujioka; *Toki Zenshu* [collection of Ceramics] ed. Koyama Fujio (32 vols, Herbonsha, Tokyo, 1958-66); Koyama;

Masterpieces; Mitsuoka; Munsterberg; Roberts; Sanders; Sugimura.

Kato Tamikichi (1772-1824). Japanese potter, the founder of porcelain kilns at Owari, *Seto. Tamikichi went on a study visit to the Arita area on the instructions of the Governor of Asuta (the port of Nagoya) and the Lord of Owari, in an effort to revive production in Seto, which had suffered in the late 18th century from the rapidly increasing demand for porcelain. He learned the techniques of blue and white ware at a workshop on Hirado island in 1804, later working at the Ichinose kiln and in Sasamura, Hizen. In Seto from 1807, he established a kiln at Gozo and worked with his brothers Kichiemon and Toziaemon on the production of porcelain painted in underglaze blue with a greenish tinge; the paste is chalky and slightly coarse, and the glaze brilliant. He became noted for imitations of *Shonsui ware with very delicate decoration. Tamikichi achieved distribution of his output throughout Japan, and by the time of his death his workshop employed over 100 workers. He was succeeded by his nephew, Tamikichi II.
Refs: Jenyns (1965); Koyama; Munsterberg; Roberts.

Kato Tokuro (b 1898) and Mineo. Japanese potters. Tokuro, cousin of *Kato Hajime, was born in *Seto and made pottery in the styles of *Shino and *Oribe wares. He was a skilled restorer of early Seto pieces and made archaeological studies of the area's ancient kilns. He also compiled a dictionary of ceramic terms.

Tokuro's son, Mineo, worked with his father in Seto, mainly following the traditional styles of Seto, Shino and Oribe. He later began to experiment with the technique of coiling pots, which he then beat into angular shapes with a paddle bound in rope, which resulted in a rough, striped texture.
Refs: Koyama; Masterpieces; Munsterberg; Roberts; Sanders.

Kato Tomotaro (1851-1916). Japanese potter, born in Aichi prefecture into a family of *Seto potters. He studied from the early 1870s under *Inoue and later learned techniques which made possible the production of blue and white porcelain at low cost. At his own kiln, Yugyokuen, established in 1882, he developed purple, yellow and vermilion (tojuko) glazes. In 1900, Tomotaro became a member of the Art Committee of the Imperial Household. His wares are decorated in underglaze blue and enamels, with designs resembling in style the work of Japanese bird and flower painters who were his contemporaries.
Refs: Roberts; Uyeno.

Katzhütte. German porcelain factory working from 1864 under Christoph Hertwig, who was in partnership for the first five years with Benjamin Beyermann from Grossbreitenbach. Hertwig was succeeded as sole owner by his two sons, Karl and Friedrich, who started a production of luxury wares including trinkets, toys and religious pieces, as well as vases, figures, etc., with Art Nouveau stylistic elements persisting until the early 1930s. The firm now operates as V.E.B. Zierkeramik Katzhütte.

Katzhütte. Porcelain group, with factory marks and Thuringia. 22.5 cm high.

Marks include versions of a cat in a hut with the initial H, and sometimes the name *Hertwig*; the present-day mark is K with a cat's head.
Ref: Scherf.

Kawai Kanjiro (1890-1966). Japanese potter, born in Shimane prefecture. Kawai studied with his friend *Hamada at the technological institute in Tokyo, afterwards working at the municipal ceramics research centre in Kyoto in and established his own workshop in Kyoto in 1917. Kawai's work in the 1930s was inspired in form by Yi dynasty Korean wares and included jars and vases in brown, soft grey or blue, boldly painted or decorated in relief. His later work was decorated with abstract patterns in relief. He was noted for the high quality and variety of both the shapes and the glazes (including celadons, temmoku and dripped effects) in his work. His stoneware was often moulded or hand built, rather than thrown. Kawai was closely associated with the Japanese folk art movement (*see* mingei ware). An exhibition of his work was shown by the Kyoto National Museum of Modern Art in 1968.
Refs: Koyama; Leach (1966); Masterpieces; Mitsuoka; Munsterberg; Noma *The Arts of Japan* Vol 2 (Kodansha International, Tokyo and Palo Alto, California, 1967).

Kawakita Handeishi (1878-1963). Japanese potter, born in Mie prefecture. Kawakita worked in a bank, and started ceramics as a hobby c.1920 at his home in Chitiseyama in Tsu, where he built his own kiln and specialized in tea-ceremony utensils, including bowls inspired by *Shino wares.
Refs: Masterpieces; Roberts.

Kawamoto Goro (b 1919). Japanese ceramist, the son of a Seto potter. Kawamoto's work in earthenware includes dried flower holders– hollow cubes with the top perforated by a square hole. He submitted displays that won prizes in exhibitions of Japanese ceramics from the early 1950s, including, in 1962, the

Nitten Exhibition. He subsequently produced vessels in shapes clearly influenced by European wares, with abstract painting in overglaze enamels.
Ref: Japanese Ceramics Today (catalogue of an exhibition at the Smithsonian Institution, Washington D.C. and the Victoria & Albert Museum, London, 1983).

Kean, Michael (d 1823). Dublin-born porcelain manufacturer, working in *Derby. Formerly a miniature painter, Kean joined the porcelain factory in Nottingham Road in 1795 as partner to the founder's son, William Duesbury II, who died in the following year. He continued the production of ware with high-quality decoration, although the standard of the paste was less successfully maintained. Kean is credited with the introduction of a smear glaze for biscuit ware, and he was responsible for engaging the artists G.*Robertson, R.*Brewer and W. 'Quaker' *Pegg. After family quarrels, Kean left his wife, Duesbury's widow, whom he had married in 1798, sold his interest in the factory to his clerk, R.*Bloor, and went to London.
Refs: see Derby.

Keates, Norman W. (b c.1893). English ceramic artist, apprenticed under D.*Dewsberry at the *Doulton & Co. factory in Burslem from 1907, and trained as an art teacher at the Burslem School of Art. His painting included landscapes, scenes with figures, and notably flowers, particularly orchids and roses. Apart from an interruption 1917-19, Keates worked for Doulton's until 1960; he afterwards worked at *Coalport.
   Mark: signature.
Refs: see Doulton & Co.

Keeler, Benjamin. *See* Huntington Pottery.

Keeling & Co. Ltd. *See* Mayer, T.J.& J.

Keinyu Tanaka. *See* Raku family.

Kawai Kanjiro. Rectangular bottle moulded in stoneware and brushed with copper, iron and cobalt foliate decoration. Made in Kyoto, 1935. 22 cm high.

Keiser, Herman. *See* Wallendorf.

Keiundo. *See* Minzan.

Keller & Guérin. French pottery manufac-
turers making decorated earthenware at
Lunéville (Meurthe-et-Moselle) as Keller &
Cie by 1800. Later trading as Keller &
Guérin, the firm commissioned designs by
artists such as E.*Lachenal and the sculptor
Ernest Bussière.
  Marks, painted or printed, incorporate
the initials KG and sometimes a crown or the
arms of Lunéville.
Refs: Fontaine; Lesur (1971); Tilmans (1954).

Kelsterbach. German ceramics factory established in 1758 and operating from the
following year in Kelsterbach. Initially
making faience, the factory also produced
porcelain in the 1760s and 1790s, turning
production over to creamware in 1802. The
factory continued in operation until the 1820s.
Refs: Haggar (1960); Honey (1952); Hüseler.

Kendall family. American potters. Uriah
Kendall and his sons operated a pottery,
among the earliest in the area, at Cincinnati,
Ohio, under the titles Uriah Kendall (1834-
46) and Kendall & Sons (1846-50), before
leaving to work further west. The firm made
domestic stoneware, or earthenware with
yellow or Rockingham glazes of high quality.
Refs: Barber (1976); Lehner; Ramsay;
Webster.

Kendrick, George Prentiss. American designer and craftsman, principally known for
work in brass and silver. He was among
directors of the company incorporated by
W.H.*Grueby in 1897 for the production of
architectural and art ware, and until 1901
designer of the firm's early art pottery,
matt-glazed vases, bowls, lamps, etc., with
modelled ornament of conventionalized
plant forms.
Refs: Barber (1976); Eidelberg; Evans; Kovel
& Kovel; Watkins (1950).

Kennemerland Potterie. *See* Mertens,
Konrad.

Kent & Parr. Staffordshire potters. John
Parr, manufacturer of earthenware figures
in Burslem from c.1870, took a partner,
Kent, in 1880. Parr and Kent acquired moulds
from a variety of sources and produced a
series of figures (some based on engravings
of Shakespearean characters by Tallis in
1852-53, and others depicting political
personalities) collectively referred to as
Tallis figures. They were moulded in a heavy,
hard body and enamel painted, with titles
transfer-printed or impressed, and the bases
coloured brown and green in long, thin
strokes. The output also included models
such as dogs, hens on nests and cottages, as
well as carpet balls, watchstands, etc. The
company traded under the name of William
Kent from 1894, and the factory was then
renamed the Novelty Works. Production of
many models derived from 18th and early
19th-century figures continued for many
years. The firm traded as William Kent
(Porcelains) Ltd from 1944, and the output
was restricted to electrical ware from the
early 1960s, when production of decorative
earthenware ceased.

*Keller & Guérin. Fabergé silver-mounted
vase made in porcelain by Keller & Guérin
with a cover in the shape of a flower head.
The finial contains a wick for perfume-
burning. 13 cm high.*

Marks include a Staffordshire knot, with
KENT, printed from 1944.
Refs: T. Balston *Staffordshire Portrait
Figures of the Victorian Age*(Faber, London,
1958), *Supplement to Staffordshire Portrait
Figures of the Victorian Age* (John Hall,
London, 1963), 'Victorian Staffordshire
Portraits' in *Country Life Annual* (1951);
Godden (1964); Jewitt; P.D. Gordon Pugh
Staffordshire Portrait Figures (Barrie &
Jenkins, London, 1970).

Kenton Hills Porcelains Inc. American firm
established 1939 at Erlanger, Kentucky, by
Harold F. Bopp, chemist and superintendent
of the *Rookwood Pottery from 1929. Incorporated in 1940 by Bopp and ceramic
sculptor David Seyler, the company made
soft-paste porcelain from native clays with
colourful hand-painted decoration, or
brown slip under the glaze. As art director,
Seyler decorated vases, etc., and made
small figures of a bird, a lamb, and other
animals. The pottery closed soon after the
departure of Bopp in 1942. All the moulds
were destroyed.
  Marks: lotus flower enclosing the initials
HB, impressed (on experimental ware), or
tulip flower enclosing the initials KH,
impressed; mould numbers (impressed),
designer's or modeller's initials (impressed)
or decorator's initials (printed under the
glaze). Artists' marks: HB (Harold Bopp);
(Davis Seyler); WH (William Hentschel); AS
(Alza Stratton Hentschel).
Refs: Cox; Evans; Kovel & Kovel.

Kenya Miura (1820-99). Japanese potter.
Nephew of the fifth in line from the first
*Kenzan, he allowed the title Kenzan VI to
pass to Ogata Shigekichi, although his work

included earthenware painted in the Kenzan
tradition. Kenya Miura, producer in 1869 of
the first bricks made in Japan, also made
beads, hair ornaments and small decorative
pieces in the form of flowers, grasses, insects,
etc., in close imitation of originals by the
lacquer artist Ritsuo (1663-1747). He worked
at Fukagawa before settling in Mukojima,
Tokyo, and worked briefly in Kameyama,
1854. His basins, water jars, etc., were
boldly painted with natural forms, including
flowering twigs.
Refs: K. Herberts *Das Buch der
ostasiatischen Lackkunst* (Econ-Verlag,
Düsseldorf, 1959); M.& B. Jahss *Inro and
Other Miniature Forms of Japanese Lacquer
Art* (Tuttle, Rutland, Vermont, and Tokyo,
1971); Jenyns (1971); Leach (1966);
Munsterberg; Roberts; Uyeno.

Kenzan. A line of Japanese potters descended from Ogata Kenzan (1663-1743), a
pupil of Ninsei (*see* Ninsei ware), who
developed a style of enamel painting on soft
earthenware coated with white slip, which
was influenced by the work of his brother,
the painter Ogata Korin, with whom he
worked (1699-1712) near Kyoto. Kenzan's
work is characterized by a free, sensitive
treatment of plant forms; other subjects
include rivers, waterfalls and snowy landscapes.
  Later followers, none of whom was directly
descended from Kenzan, assumed the title:
Kenzan III was Tominosuke Miyazaki (d
1820), who lived in Tokyo (although a
Kyoto potter Gosuke also claimed the title
Kenzan III); Kenzan IV was the painter Sakai
Hoitsu (d 1828), who gained permission to
assume the title from Tominosuke's widow;
Kenzan V was Myakuen Nishimura (d 1853),
a maker of red-enamelled porcelain at
Kameyama. *Kenya Miura, nephew of
Kenzan, is thought to have refused the
title, which passed to Shigekichi Urano, an
adopted member of the Ogata family, and
teacher of B.*Leach, who shared the title
Kenzan VII with *Tomimoto Kenkichi.
Refs: Feddersen; Jenyns (1971); Koyama;
Leach (1966); Mikami; Miller; Mizuo; A.
Morrison *The Painters of Japan* (T.C.&

*Kenton Hills Porcelains Inc. Vase designed
by David Seyler (b 1917) and decorated by
Rosemary Dickman (b 1916), made 1942.
12.6 cm high.*

Kenzan. Porcelain inro in three sections painted over the glaze with an elephant, early 19th century. Signed Kenzan. 8 cm high.

E.C. Jack, London and Edinburgh, 1911); Munsterberg; Okuda; J. Rosenfield & S. Shimada *Traditions of Japanese Art* (Fogg Art Museum, Harvard University Cambridge, Mass., 1970).

Keramic studio. *See* Robineau, Adelaide Alsop.

Keramis. *See* Boch Frères.

Keramische Werkgenossenschaft. Austrian company established in 1911 by H.*Johnova, R.*Neuwirth, and I.*Schwetz-Lehmann. Work by these artists, exhibited from the following year, included figures, animal models, table decorations and other pieces in glazed earthenware, terracotta and bronze. The firm went into liquidation in 1920, but Schwetz-Lehmann was mentioned as a partner in 1932.
Mark: a square formed from the initials KW over WIEN.
Ref: Neuwirth (1974a).

Keramische Werkstätten Roth-Neusiedl. Austrian producers of art ceramics, in operation 1922-26. Under the architects Georg Karau and Ludwig Steiner, and manager Benjamin Karpf, the firm was a distributor for wares made in its own workshop and by the Werkstätten *Karau.
Ref: Neuwirth (1974a).

Keramos. Ceramic workshop established in 1923 at Nogradveröce, Hungary, under the artistic direction of F.*Gorka, who was also one of the founders. The pottery aimed to enliven traditional wares by the introduction of new techniques and design, and particularly of glazes. Gorka left when the company policy concentrated on low cost at the expense of aesthetic value.
Ref: I. Pataky-Brestyánsky *Modern Hungarian Ceramics* (Corvina, Budapest, 1961).

Keramos Vase, The. *See* Müller, Karl.

'Keramos' Wiener Kunstkeramik und Porzellanmanufaktur A.G. Viennese pottery established in 1920 for the production of useful and ornamental wares. In 1924 the workshop exhibited designs by artists including O. *Prutscher. Artists whose work was exhibited in the 1930s included H.*Bucher, E.*Klablena and I.*Schwetz-Lehmann.
The 'Keramos' workshop for the disabled, founded in 1922, produced lamps, figures, vases, etc., and was absorbed in 1924.
Marks: KWK in a triangle, over KERAMOS; a shield with a banner bearing KERAMIS, and WIEN.
Ref: Neuwirth (1974a).

Kerr, B.A. *See* Barker, Ernest.

Kerr, W.H. (d 1879). Porcelain manufacturer, born in Ireland. After working in Dublin, Kerr moved to *Worcester. He married the grand-daughter of Robert Chamberlain, whose firm he joined in 1850. He traded in the partnership Kerr & Binns (with R.W.*Binns) from the following year until his retirement in 1862.
Refs: Binns (1897); Sandon (1978a).

Kestrel. *See* Cooper, Susie.

Kettle, Edgar. English pottery decorator. His work for the firm of C.J.C.*Bailey at the Fulham Pottery in the 1870s included incised relief decoration on stoneware vases and jugs.
Mark: monogram of EK with the Fulham Pottery mark.
Refs: Godden (1964); Haslam (1977); Jewitt.

Keyakada Zengoro. *See* Awaji wares.

Keyes, Phyllis. English potter. She worked with R.*Fry as a decorator and made tin-glazed pottery in London in the 1930s with painted decoration by V.*Bell, D.*Grant and other artists.
Mark: crossed keys over P, incised or painted.
Refs: Cooper; Haslam (1977); Godden (1964).

Keys, Edward (b 1798). English ceramic modeller. Keys trained at the porcelain factory in Nottingham Road, *Derby, where he modelled domestic and farm animals, mice, a lion and lioness, as well as figures, which included a Dr Syntax series. He became foreman of the figure-making department in 1821, and then left in 1826 to work in Stoke-on-Trent, joining the Minton factory by 1831. While at *Mintons Ltd specializing in figure modelling, he also made modelled flowers and headed a team of modellers who are listed separately under his name in the firm's wages record of October 1831. In 1842, Keys attempted to start his own porcelain factory without success. He worked in 1845 for the firm of Wedgwood, and is thought to have modelled figures for production in Carrara ware.
Refs: Batkin; Reilly & Savage; Shinn; *see also* Derby.

Keys, Samuel, Jr. English porcelain modeller, son of a gilder at the porcelain factory in Nottingham Road, *Derby, during the 1820s. Keys modelled figures, including such theatrical characters as Paul Pry, and became foreman of figure production until he went to work as a figure modeller at *Mintons, where his brother E.*Keys was employed by the following year. In partnership with John *Mountford c.1849-57, Samuel Keys produced parian figures and groups, which received honourable mention when shown at the Great Exhibition in London, 1851. He produced earthenware in a partnership, Keys & Briggs, again in Stoke-on-Trent, in the early 1860s. He later went to work at Peterinck's factory in Tournai at the age of 72 or 73.
Marks: K. & M.; S.KEYS/& MOUNTFORD, impressed.
Refs: Godden (1964); Jewitt; Shinn; *see also* Derby.

Kezonta. *See* Cincinnati Art Pottery.

Khrapunov, Nikita S. Russian porcelain manufacturer. Khrapunov established a workshop by late 1812 at Kusiaevo, near Moscow, with a partner, F.M. Gusiatnikov, using a porcelain formula stolen from Pavel Kulikov, a porcelain maker in the *Gzhel area. The work of his factory included a figure of a monk carrying a girl in a sheaf of wheat, made in 1821 (and now preserved in the state museum of ceramics at Kuskovo), for which the maker was punished by Alexander I, and a teapot in the form of a seated monk holding a vodka bottle. Khrapunov's sons separately owned six factories at Mysa (Muzo) in the region of Gzhel; his grandson, Iakov, worked for him before inheriting, through his marriage to Agafya Novaya, the *Novyi Brothers' factory.
Refs: Ovsyannikov; Ross; Saltykov.

Kichiemon family. Japanese potters descended from a maker of unglazed tea ware working in Kyoto during the 16th century. The family is associated with *Minato ware, introduced by Kichibei, who is thought to have been the brother of Ichinyu, fourth generation of the *Raku family, and was the first in line to use the name Minato. His successor, Yahei, worked in Kyoto in the mid 18th century and was in turn followed by five generations of potters, all using the name Kichiemon, the last of whom died in 1852.
Marks: the Japanese characters *Minato* and later *Minato-yaki*, impressed.
Refs: Jenyns (1971); Koyama; Morse; Roberts.

Kichiemon Yabu. *See* Ono.

Kichizaemon. *See* Raku family.

Kidston, Alexander. *See* Verreville Pottery.

Kiev-Mezhegorye State Faience Factory.
Russian earthenware factory established in
1798 after the discovery of good clay on the
estate of the former Mezhegorye monastery.
The factory was in operation from 1801
under the management of the Kiev duma
(official assembly), then in 1804 under the
Governor of Kiev; it was eventually administered in conjunction with the state porcelain
factory at *St Petersburg by the Imperial
cabinet from 1822. By that time, it was the
largest producer of white earthenware in
Russia, employing well over 300 workers.
The factory sold its output at a shop in Kiev
and, later, in retail outlets throughout Russia,
as well as supplying private orders; however,
it never became commercially successful.

The fine, thinly potted earthenware, which
was noted for its high quality, included services, large display vases (especially in the
1820s and 1830s), tea and coffee sets, plates,
bowls, bread dishes, ash trays, cutlery rests,
mugs, inkpots, frames for mirrors and portraits, Easter eggs, candlesticks, icons and
lamps, *jardinières*, barrel-shaped garden
seats, and other individual pieces, as well as
pharmaceutical ware. In style, the factory was
responsive to western European developments, notably the Empire style, in satisfying
the demands of wealthy, sophisticated customers, who bought a large proportion of
the decorative ware produced. Simplicity in
form and decoration accentuated the high
technical quality. Printed decoration, introduced early in 1812, was very precisely
executed in monochrome, sometimes with
additional gilding. The engravers included
D.*Stepanov. Tableware printed to order
included a service for the Arakcheyev family
in the late 1820s, decorated with scenes of
their village, Gruzino, from engravings by a
local artist, Ivan Semyonov, which were
drawn in 1821-26, and also used in decoration
by the imperial porcelain factory (1825) and
Prince *Yusupov (1827). In general, printed
decoration consisted of landscapes, views,
scenes from village life, and fables (e.g. the
Fox and the Grapes). Folk themes appeared
in the 1840s, when the views became more
specifically Russian, and scenes included the
country's people, who were nevertheless
depicted in western European dress. Styles
developed for sale at lower prices from the
1840s included wavy-edged plates, sparingly
printed with arabesques and cupids or geometrical designs in light blue, and a small
floral diaper pattern.

Throughout its operation, the factory
made coloured ware, either in coloured
body with transparent glaze, or in the white
body with coloured glazes normally used
over relief decoration in the manner of majolica. The red, black or agate ware bodies
of the first few years were used in decorative
vases and dinner and tea services, e.g. a
service in simple, classical forms ordered for
the Babolovsky palace at Tsarskoy Selo in
orange-red body and rimmed with vine
patterns printed under the glaze in black. In
the 1840s, the range of body colours increased
to include blue, green, shades of brown,
orange-ochre and yellow for individual pieces

A range of green-glazed ware, made in
large quantities until the factory's closure,
included butter containers in the form of a
melon on a leaf, and plates decorated with
large vine leaves and other plant forms
(normally covering the whole plate, but
occasionally restricted to the rim). Relief
decoration, moulded or modelled, was in
general careful, well-finished and restricted
in theme to scale and leaf patterns, classical
motifs, or a naturalistic treatment of plant
forms. Decorative handles took the form of
snarling dogs' heads, mythical creatures, or
masks. A Guipure service, inspired by
English models, was decorated overall with
small flowers and leaves in relief. Similar
decoration occurs on services with greyish
blue, green or ochre glazes. Figures and
groups were elaborate and costly.

In 1844, one director, based in St Petersburg, was appointed for both factories.
Attempts to improve sales from Mezhegorye
in the 1850s included the introduction of
small biscuit figures and a range of ware
with painted relief decoration. Souvenir
plates were produced with portraits of topical
personalities in *émaux ombrants*. Unable to
compete with imported European wares
after the relaxation of protective tariffs in
1857, the cabinet leased Kiev-Mezhegorye
to the Barsky brothers, Kiev merchants, in
1858, but the factory reverted to Imperial
ownership in 1864. Between then and its
closure in 1875, it mainly produced pharmaceutical and sanitary wares, and household
items with simple patterns representing
wood-grain, etc., or overall printing of
flowers or rosettes.

Marks incorporate *Kiev*, with the date of
production after 1830, and from 1850 an
oval coat of arms supported by two lions.
From 1858, the shield was accompanied by
the name *N. Barsky*.
Refs: Bubnova; Ivanova; A. Popoff 'The
Francis Gardner & Other Russian Porcelain
Factories' in *The Connoisseur* 96 (August
1935); Rozembergh.

Kikoichiro Mori. *See* Mori family.

Kikusaburo Matsuya (1819-89). Japanese
maker of *Kutani ware in or near Komatsu.
Kikusaburo worked at the *Ono kiln in the
1830s and then joined his former teacher
*Gen'emon in establishing the *Rendaiji kiln
in 1847. After extensive research (1850-67)
into the pigments used in Old Kutani ware
(17th century), Kikusaburo began (in 1863)
the production of Ao Kutani ware in porcellaneous stoneware decorated with a palette
of bright, clear glazes, in which the yellow,
green and purple associated with *Kochi
wares predominated.
Refs: Jenyns (1965); Nakagawa.

Kiln Croft Works. *See* Boote, T.& R., Ltd;
Edwards, James.

Kilnhurst Old Pottery. Yorkshire pottery
established at Kilnhurst, near Rotherham,
in the mid 18th century. It was run by Philip

Hawley, who succeeded his father Thomas
as tenant from c.1808 until his own death in
1830. J.*Brameld and his sons worked the
pottery from 1832 until 1839, when it was
taken over by Benjamin, Joseph and John,
the sons of J.*Twigg, followed by their
successors until 1884. The early output,
probably consisting mainly of coarse earthenware made from local clay, included busts
of John Wesley coloured with metallic oxides
or painted only in underglaze blue. The
Twigg family produced a range of printed
earthenware, including nursery plates with
patterns representing the seasons or the
months of the year, and moulded octagonal
jugs with peacocks and flowers printed in
brown and hand-finished in enamel. They
also produced sponged, banded and painted
earthenware in red and blue, and used
*Swinton Pottery moulds and patterns after
the closure of that factory.

The firm of Hepworth & Heald, holders
of the lease from the retirement of Daniel
Twigg until the pottery ceased operation in
1929, made stoneware jugs and mugs with a
light buff body and a wide band of deep
brown glaze at the rim; moulded decoration
included old people drinking. According to
the last owner, the pottery closed when
earthenware mugs, the staple product, were
replaced by glass for use in public houses.
Hepworth & Heald exported to North and
West Africa, Australia and the West Indies.

Marks include TWIGG'S, impressed,
probably used at both Kilnhurst and Newhill
potteries.
Refs: Coysh & Henrywood; Jewitt;
Lawrence.

King, James (1796-1857). Scottish-born
businessman and entrepreneur, working in
New South Wales, Australia. He was the
proprietor of the Irrawang Pottery near
Raymond Terrace from 1833 to c.1855.
Excavation of the pottery site since 1967 has
shown that earthenware and stoneware
were produced for domestic use; some decorated jugs were made from moulds thought
to have been imported from Staffordshire.
King was also a pioneer of wine production
in the Hunter Valley, and some stoneware
wine jars from the pottery survive.

Mark: IRRAWANG/AUSTRALIA impressed.
Refs: A. Bickford in *Journal of the Royal
Australian Historical Society* (1971);
J. Birmingham *Industrial Archaeology in
Australia* (Melbourne, 1983); Cooper; R.I.
Jack & C.A. Liston in *Journal of the Royal
Australian Historical Society* (1982).

King, Wallace, L. *See* Taft, James Scholly.

King Street factory. *See* Derby.

Kinkozan. Japanese potters, the Kobayashi
family working in *Awata under the studio
name of Kagiya and the artistic name of
Kinkozan, which was awarded to the third
generation in the 1750s by the Tokugawa
shogunate. Kinkozan II made copies of
Delftware in the late 18th century, and he
and his successor made pieces inspired by
early *Ninsei ware. Kinkozan IV, Sobei
Kobayashi, working in the mid 19th century,
started the production of porcelain and,
from 1877, his successor, also named Sobei
Kobayashi (1867-1927), made large quantities
of lavishly enamelled ware for export, using

Kinkozan. Large faceted vase with a scroll of figures, a basket of flowers, and a pheasant perched on a rock overlooking a rice paddy with a view of Fujiyama, all reserved on a deep blue enamel ground with gilt florets, late 19th century. Impressed and gilt mark, Kinkozan tsuruku. 46.1 cm high.

the mark Kinkozan painted in red. This ware has a warm, creamy glaze, sometimes crackled, and is thickly painted with scrolled flower patterns in bright blue and green enamels embellished with gold and silver. Pieces made to Kinkozan's own taste were enamelled in a more restrained style. The family extended to eight generations by the mid 20th century.
Refs: Jenyns (1971); Roberts; Uyeno.

Kinose. *See* Shigaraki ware.

kinrande. In Japanese ceramics, gold decoration applied over a glazed or *aka-e enamelled ground. The method of application, using gold leaf with lacquer, fired at a low temperature, contrasts with the technique of kinsai (gold painting), in which gold is painted on a biscuit or glazed surface and fired before burnishing.

Kinrande often follows styles associated with Chinese ware of the Ming dynasty, which was reproduced in Kyoto in the 19th century, e.g. by *Hozen. *Mokubei and *Wazen, also in Kyoto, were instrumental in the development of kinrande, *aka-e and *hachirode as characteristic decoration of many *Kutani kilns. Later developments in the styles were made by *Shoza and *Isaburo.

The predominantly gold-on-red palette of kinrande also includes limited amounts of yellow, turquoise, underglaze blue and black. Gold patterns on a red or green glazed ground may be used to cover the entire piece or to surround paintings of birds, flowers, etc., in reserves. Red and green kinrande porcelain, made by the *Mikawachi kiln for the Imperial court by 1865,

appeared on exhibition in Paris, 1875.
Refs: Jenyns (1965, 1971); M. Medley *The Chinese Potter* (Phaidon, Oxford, 1976); Nakagawa; Roberts.

kinsai. *See* kinrande.

Kinsaku. *See* Dohei Imai.

Kintner, Jacob. Pennsylvania potter making slip-decorated earthenware at a pottery established c.1780 at Nockamixon, Bucks County, and active until c.1840.
Ref: Barber (1976).

Kirchner, Robert Stübchen. *See* Teplitz, Fachschule.

Kirk, William Boynton (1824-1900). Porcelain modeller, the son of a Dublin sculptor. Kirk was employed in *Worcester by the firm of Kerr & Binns and the subsequent Royal Porcelain Co. from the early 1850s. He modelled many early figures in parian ware and, notably, the Shakespeare service, a dessert service illustrating *A Midsummer Night's Dream*, with figures and groups as free-standing table decorations or incorporated in other pieces, e.g. as supports for dishes, for the Dublin International Exhibition in 1853.
Refs: Binns (1897); Sandon (1978a).

Kirkby, Thomas (1821-90). Staffordshire ceramic decorator, born at Trentham, near Stoke-on-Trent. Kirkby possibly worked for the firm of W.T.*Copeland before joining *Mintons c.1845, where he remained until his retirement in 1887, and was initially known for his painting of figures after the style of Jean-Antoine Watteau. He painted landscapes (rare) from c.1847, floral panels, scenes featuring cupids (e.g. on the elaborate Victoria dessert service shown in the Great Exhibition, London, 1851), figure subjects and portraits (e.g. a plaque portraying Queen Victoria, surrounded by grotesques in Renaissance style, exhibited in Paris, 1855). He also decorated tablewares modelled by P.-E.*Jeannest and from c.1851 carried out copies of Italian majolica. He was one of twelve British workmen sent to review the Exposition Universelle in Paris (1867). His work was last mentioned in factory records in 1882.
Refs: Atterbury; Godden (1968); G. Godden 'Thomas Kirkby: Victorian Ceramic Artist' in *Apollo* 72 (September 1960).

Kirkham, Joseph. American tile maker, connected with the *Providential Tile Works. He subsequently established Kirkham Art Tiles (closed 1895) at Barberton, Ohio, and, in 1898, the Kirkham Tile & Pottery Co. in California.
Ref: Kovel & Kovel.

Kirkham, William. Staffordshire manufacturer of earthenware and terracotta, working 1862-92. Kirkham bought and enlarged a tileworks in London Road, Stoke-on-Trent, where he began production of domestic ware, fittings for water taps, etc. His ornamental ware in terracotta was decorated with Etruscan figures, ferns, flowers, foliage and other patterns in relief, sometimes picked out or bordered with enamel and gilding. Kirkham was succeeded by his sons,

H.G. & D. Kirkham. In 1890, H.G. Kirkham bought the copper printing plates used by T.J.& J. Mayer and Bates, Elliot & Co. for re-issue in the decoration of pot lids; some of these plates had originally been made for use on tableware, etc. The prints were re-issued in the 1920s. The 19th-century versions typically appear on thickly moulded lids with crazed, greyish-tinged glaze extending over the insides of the rims. The later issues are on flat-topped lids with thick, creamy glaze. Kirkham's amalgamated with A.E.*Gray & Co. Ltd in 1961 to form Portmeirion Potteries Ltd.

Marks include w. KIRKHAM, impressed, and later printed marks, *Old Staffordshire/Porcelain*/KIRKHAM *1858/* ENGLAND; KIRKHAM/POTTERY/MADE IN ENGLAND from c.1946.
Refs: Godden (1964); Jewitt; Williams-Wood.

Kirsch, Hugo F. (1873-1961). Sculptor and designer, born in Hainsdorf bei Friedland, Bohemia and working mainly in Vienna. Kirsch trained in Teplitz-Schönau, at the Munich Kunstgewerbeschule, and from 1898 in the Vienna Kunstgewerbeschule. He worked independently from 1903 and established an art pottery in Vienna, 1906. His work consisted of unique pieces in porcelain, white earthenware, stoneware and bronze, as well as architectural ware. Figures, painted under or over the glaze, were a speciality. Vases were painted with bold, repeating designs in black; the subjects included Viennese townsfolk, the bourgeoisie, and various animals.

Marks include variations of the signature, *Kirsch* or H.F. KIRSCH; WIENER/PORZELLAN arranged in a circle containing H. KIRSCH; various monograms.
Ref: Neuwirth (1974a).

Kiselev, Afanasy Leontovich. Russian ceramist, born in Rechitsa in the *Gzhel area, and working from the early 1820s until the late 1850s. Kiselev made earthenware vases, and jugs painted with flowers (and often a date) in golden-brown over yellowish glaze, to resemble pieces in bronze. He joined the brothers Fyodor and Peter Nikolaevich Terekhov c.1832 at a factory newly established in Rechitsa, and produced tableware, dinner and tea services, small individual pieces, large vases and figures in porcelain and white earthenware. The forms were intricate and lavishly decorated with relief and painted ornament. Figures in classical decorative scenes, *chinoiseries*, etc., treated in a lively manner, were influenced by Russian folk art. Some figures were caricatures of topical personalities. Large tureens and dishes etc., were normally decorated with printed designs, often of mythological subjects in silhouette.

Kiselev was a noted inventor, responsible for improvements in the preparation of porcelain paste, as well as in throwing and firing. He raised the quality of tableware and figures produced, and enlarged the factory, which employed 500 workers at the peak of production.

In the early 1850s, Kiselev established his own factory not far from Rechitsa, where he made very thin, translucent porcelain and some white earthenware. His production of figures and tableware, which was painted with patterns derived from local peasant art, in the traditional bright colours, continued throughout the 1850s.

The marks of Kiselev's own factory usually incorporate his name or initials AK in underglaze blue. Terekhov-Kiselev wares (1833-50) were marked with the makers' names, sometimes on a mark depicting a basket with sprigs of foliage.
Refs: B. Alekseev *Porcelain* (in Russian, Kuskovo, Moscow, 1958); Bubnova; N.V. Bulochkin 'Porcelain and Faience Sculpture' in *Russian Decorative Art* III (Moscow, 1965); Ovsyannikov; Ross; Rozembergh; Saltykov.

Kishere, Joseph. English stoneware maker working in the early 19th century. Formerly apprenticed at a pottery making delftware and other earthenwares in the 18th century at Mortlake, Surrey, Kishere built a factory nearby in 1810 for the production of white stoneware. His output included spirit flasks, jugs and mugs with low relief decoration showing sporting and drinking scenes, as well as utilitarian, drab brown stoneware. He was succeeded by his son William, who was still working at the Mortlake Pottery in 1831. The pottery was in the hands of John Abbot in 1845, and he was succeeded for two years by a son, Thomas. It was demolished before 1868.
Marks include *Kishere Mortlake*, sometimes with *Surrey*.
Refs: Bemrose; Blacker (1922b); Honey (1952); Hughes (1977); Jewitt.

Kishu wares. Japanese stoneware or porcelain made from the early 19th century in Kii province (now Wakayama and Mie prefectures) and decorated mainly with floral patterns in low relief with coloured glazes in purple, yellow and turquoise, inspired by Chinese san-ts'ai ware of the Ming dynasty; white or green glazes were also used, and one group of the ware has green glaze veined with purple, decorated with medallions in contrasting colours. A private kiln opened on the estate of the lord of Kishu at Wakayama produced Kishu wares from c.1810 and closed in 1844; *Hozan was invited to work there in 1827. The lord of Kishu presented Tannyu (*see* Raku family) with the seal, Kairakuen, in 1826 for wares he made while teaching glazing techniques at Wakayama. Later, the kiln's output included raku wares. Other workshops opened at nearby Otokayama and, c.1860, at Ota, near Yokohama, where members of the *Miyakawa family later worked.
Refs: Jenyns (1971); Woodhouse.

Kiss, Charles. American potter. Kiss developed a 'secret process' enabling him to fire body, decoration and glaze in one operation and established the Kiss Art Pottery in 1910 at Sag Harbor, Suffolk county, for the manufacture of art pottery by this method. He remained as superintendent, assisted by his two brothers, after reorganization of the firm in larger premises as the Peconic Pottery

Co. with C.E. Fritts as its head (1912). The output, including *jardinières*, was thrown or moulded in local clay. Kiss moved to Meriden, Connecticut, by 1921, making decorated ware in partnership with his brothers until 1925.
Ref: Evans.

Kisuke or **Kawasuke** Toki. Japanese porcelain maker. After training as a puppet maker near Kyoto, Kisuke studied ceramic techniques under *Eisen. He specialized in small celadon-glazed pieces, e.g. incense burners, animal figures known as Mitaseiji. Kisuke worked by invitation at Sanda and in *Seto.
Refs: Jenyns (1965); Roberts.

Kitade Tojiro (1898-1969). Japanese potter born in Hyogo prefecture. After studying at Kansai University and Osaka Art School, he became a pupil of *Itaya and *Tomimoto carrying out research into traditional techniques. He was subsequently a teacher at an art school in Kanazawa. In his own work, he used the traditional methods of *Kutani but added his own variations in design.
Refs: Penkala; Roberts.

Kitson, Albert. *See* Littlethorpe Pottery.

Kitson, John. *See* Soil Hill Pottery.

Kiyomizu. Japanese ceramics centre, a district of Kyoto specializing in enamelled porcelain during the 19th and early 20th centuries. The area is associated with wares made mainly in Kiyomizuzaku and Gojozaka, but the term 'Kiyomizu wares' includes all types made in Kyoto after 1868 (except those made in *Awata, Iwakura and Mizoro) as distinct from the Kyo yaki made before the Meiji Restoration.
Kiyomizu became prominent among Kyoto districts with the growth of a new porcelain industry in the early 19th century, and after a decree in the Bunsei era (1818-29) only porcelain was made there. Like the potters of Gojo, Kiyomizu artists were associated with translucent glazes in green, purple, brown, and iron red, used to surround medallions of floral painting or as grounds for designs in gold, but the area also gave rise to various coloured wares: buff-coloured from c.1800, a yellowish type from the 1820s or 1830s. In the early 19th century, the potters copied old Arita ware, using a rich underglaze blue. Enamel decoration over greyish, crackled glaze, another speciality, was inspired by a group of Arita wares.
The output of earthenware as well as porcelain in Kiyomizu was the work of individual makers (rather than workshops) who included *Rokubei; *Mokubei; *Dohachi II (in Gojo-zaka); *Seifu (whose kiln was at Goyabashi); Mokubei's assistant, Okuda Kyuta; Choso Mikawa, a student of Mokubei; Waka Kitei (*see* Kameya family) and Kiyu, who was based at Kinkodo.
Refs: Brinkley; Hannover; Jenyns (1965, 1971); Munsterberg; Woodhouse.

Kiyu (1765-1837). Japanese porcelain maker living in Kinkodo and specializing in underglaze blue decoration. Kiyu taught ceramics in Sanda (1801) and later in *Tamba. His adopted son Kosaku, a pupil of *Eisen and

*Hozen, was noted as a maker of unglazed teapots, also producing imitations of Delftware and Kochi ware.
Ref: Jenyns (1965).

Kjaeregaard, Richard. Danish potter, born on the island of Fyn. He trained at the Kunsthaandvaerkeskolen in Copenhagen 1940-44, taught there from 1955 and became head of the ceramics department in 1970. Kjaeregaard was a designer for *Bing & Grøndahl after World War II, and established his own workshop in Kastrup in 1945. His work in earthenware and stoneware includes burnished tea and coffee wares, and decorative pieces with patterns painted in slip. A repeating pattern of parallelograms is a frequent decoration.
Mark: monogram of RK.
Refs: Hettes & Rada; Hiort; W. Hull *Danish Ceramic Design* (catalogue, Museum of Art, Pennsylvania State University, 1981).

Kjellberg, Friedl (b 1905). Austrian-born ceramist, working in Finland. At the *Arabia factory from 1924, she specialized in delicate porcelain, making bowls (sometimes with perforated patterns) and undecorated tableware. Some of her pieces in stoneware or porcelain depend for decorative effect on peacock-blue, *sang-de-boeuf*, celadon or other coloured glazes.
Refs: Aro; Hettes & Rada.

Klablena, Eduard (1881-1933). Artist and ceramic modeller, working in Austria. Klablena's family moved to Langenzersdorf in 1883, and he studied at the Vienna Kunstgewerbeschule. He designed figures for production in porcelain at the Berlin factory, 1909-10, and the *Keramos workshop in Vienna. In 1911, he established his own workshop in Langenzersdorf, where he produced humorous and whimsical figures, groups and animal studies, sometimes with crackled

Kiyomizu type stoneware bottle, painted in enamel over a brown glaze. Late 18th, early 19th century.

glazes, and some vases with painted decoration on a white ground striped in black.
Marks: versions of his monogram, EK.
Ref: Neuwirth (1974a).

Klaus, Ferdinand. *See* Tettau.

Klaus, Karl (b 1889). Austrian architect and designer working in Vienna. He was a woodworker in O.*Prutscher's workshop, and studied at the Vienna Kunstgewerbeschule from 1907 (under J.*Hoffmann, 1908-11). In his last year, he exhibited tea and coffee ware and vases with bold, intricate patterns made to his designs by the firm of E.*Wahliss. In 1911, he joined the Wiener Werkstätte. His designs for vases, figures and groups, boxes, sweet dishes and other pieces made by Wahliss were also exhibited in 1913-14 at the Österreichisches Museum.
Ref: Neuwirth (1974a).

Klieber, Anton. Sculptor, born in Pirkenhammer, Bohemia, and trained in Teplitz until 1905 and at the Vienna Kunstgewerbeschule, 1905-09. He designed ceramic figures and groups, which included children and animals, from 1909 and joined *Wiener Keramik as a modeller in 1912. Some of his work was done in collaboration with B.*Löffler. Klieber designed ceramics for the Vereinigte Wiener and Gmundner Werkstätte from 1913 and the *Candia workshop 1920-21.
Mark: monogram, AK.
Ref: Neuwirth (1974a).

Klopfer, Ludwig. *See* Lipp-Keramik.

Kloster Veilsdorf. German porcelain factory established 1760 in Thuringia by Friedrich Wilhelm Eugen (1730-95), youngest brother of the duke of Sachsen-Hildburghausen. In 1797, the founder's heir sold the factory to two companies, Gotthelf Greiners Söhne of Limbach, and Friedrich Christian Greiner of Rauenstein (replaced in 1799 by Johann

*Anton Klieber. Figure of a child with a garland of flowers, produced at the *Candia workshop, c.1921. Marks include CANDIA and AK.*

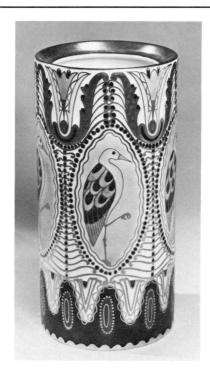

*Karl Klaus. Vase designed by Klaus and produced by E.*Wahliss. Stamped SERAPIS and indistinctly signed, WAHLISS; exhibited in Turin, 1911. 18.4 cm high.*

Adam Hofmann). The Greiner family made everyday wares at low cost until 1862, when the factory was sold. Fine, pure white paste was used to make tablewares, tea and coffee sets, thimbles, knife handles, and figures. The decoration, following Meissen in style, included *chinoiseries*, subjects from Boucher and Watteau, paintings *en camaïeu* and, in the 19th century, various stylistic revivals.

Under the ownership of Eduard Albert Heubach (*see* Heubach family) from 1863, the factory made dolls' heads, bottle tops and industrial components. Heubach's sons, Max and Hans Heubach, began the manufacture of electrical, chemical and other technological wares. The firm merged with the Strupp Bank of Meiningen in 1884, becoming a joint stock company. Specializing in technical and sanitary ware from the early 20th century, it was later nationalized.
Marks include the initials CV.
Refs: Danckert; Ducret (1962); Haggar (1960); Hannover; Honey (1952); Scherf; Ware.

Klösterle. Bohemian factory established at Klösterle in 1793 (after the discovery of clay deposits at nearby Tschernitz) for the production of earthenware on land at Klösterle belonging to Count Franz Josef von Thun (d 1810). Josef Andreas Raphael Habertitzel (born 1774) rented the works from 1798, and made improvements to buildings and equipment in 1814. From 1819, the output included porcelain tableware, coffee sets and tobacco pipes. Decoration, of battle scenes, mythological and allegorical figure scenes, portraits, plant studies or geometrical patterns, was painted in blue, sepia, rust or full colour. The count's successor, Mathias

Thun, took control of the works in 1820, appointing Habertitzel as a director until his retirement ten years later. After several years of financial difficulty and a number of changes in management, the factory came under the direction of a former treasurer, the chemist Johann Hillardt, who installed a third kiln and improved the quality of the ware, winning prizes at exhibitions in Prague in 1836 and Vienna in 1842 and 1845. The factory (then employing about 100 workers) made figures, vases, picture plaques and other pieces, some fired in a peat-burning kiln. Gold relief decoration was introduced in the 1830s, followed by transfer printing in 1843. A breakfast set made for the Empress Elizabeth was sparsely decorated in gold. Tablewares in general production were printed with traditional patterns, often in blue. The porcelain paste was noted for its pure white colour. The factory's output included figures and groups from c.1836, unglazed and painted in oil colours, and in the 1950s lithophanes. Production continues to the present day.

Marks usually incorporate the initial K, often with T (Thun) and, in the 20th century, a coronet and *Czechoslovakia* or *Thun*.
Refs: A. Bergmann *Egerländer Porzellan* (Amberg, 1975); Meyer.

Klotz, Hermann. *See* Goldscheider, Friedrich, Wiener Manufaktur.

Knapper & Blackhurst. *See* Edwards, J.

Knauf, Werner (1895-1959). German artist potter, born in Heidelberg. Knauf was an apprentice potter, 1912-15, and worked in a Mannheim factory, 1915-18. In 1926 he took over the factory in Saxony of which he had been manager since 1920, and traded as Knauf-Keramik, working with between two and four employees. He made earthenware fired at 960-980°C with a variety of glazes. From 1934, he concentrated on reduction

Werner Knauf. Display plate, made in earthenware, 1931-38. 20.5 cm in diameter.

firing, which he had first mastered in 1928; he became known for lustrous oxblood glazes produced by reduction in a cooling kiln, in which he carried out patterns of fish and waterweed, scrolled plant forms, etc.. After the destruction of his workshop by bombing in the early 1940s, he moved to Ittersbach, where he worked with his son, Horst Knauf, from 1950.

Marks: *Knauf* or WK impressed.
Ref: Bock.

Knight, John King. *See* Wileman, Henry.

Knight, Laura. *See* Brain, E., & Co.

Knörlein, Rudolf (b 1902). Viennese ceramic modeller, trained at the Vienna Kunstgewerbeschule, 1918-20 and 1927-29. He exhibited ceramics from 1922 and provided designs for production by the firms of F. and M.*Goldscheider, the *Wiener Werkstätte and C.& E.*Carstens. He was also a designer for a pottery in Gmunden, of which he became director in 1937. He was known for work in an increasingly simplified, naturalistic version of the style associated with other Viennese artists who were his contemporaries, restricting scrolled and spiral decoration to such details as hair on his portrait pieces. Heads of girls have details painted in colour.
Refs: W. Born 'Figürliche Keramik von Rudolf Knörlein' in *Deutsche Kunst und Dekoration* (1931-32); Neuwirth (1974a).

Knottingley Pottery. *See* Ferrybridge Pottery.

Knowles, Taylor & Knowles. American pottery and porcelain manufacturers established in East Liverpool, Ohio, in 1854 by Isaac Knowles, a cabinetmaker and carpenter, and Isaac Harvey, who opened a small pottery for the production of preserving jars. They made yellow queensware and also used a Rockingham glaze. Isaac Knowles continued alone from the mid 1860s until he brought his son, Homer S. Knowles (d 1892), and son-in-law, John N. Taylor, into the firm in 1870, trading as Knowles, Taylor & Knowles and becoming organized as a company in 1891. From 1872, the partners made ironstone china, introducing semi-porcelain c.1890 and rapidly enlarging the works to supply a wide home market. A brief production of Belleek ware was not resumed after fire damage to a newly built workshop in the late 1880s, but the similar Lotus ware, a very white, translucent bone porcelain used for thin shell forms or pieces decorated with leaves, flowers and lacework applied by hand, was marketed in the 1890s (ceasing c.1897), and replaced by semi-porcelain. Vases with mazarine blue ground under a soft, velvety glaze, and decoration of cupids and butterflies built up in white enamel, lavishly gilded, were shown in the World's Columbian Exposition in Chicago (1893); the same blue ground was also used on a larger vase in semi-porcelain (almost one metre high) painted with petunia flowers in tinted gold. Isaac Knowles had retired in the early 1890s, and his younger sons Willis and Edwin joined the firm. Homer Taylor joined in place of his father in 1914. In 1929, Knowles, Taylor & Knowles was among a group of companies forming the American Chinaware Corporation in an effort to revive falling profits, but the corporation went

into receivership after two years and as a result Knowles, Taylor & Knowles ceased operating.

Marks include a bison with KT& K and a lion and unicorn over the same initials.
Refs: Barber (1976); Donhauser; *Antiques* (October 1964); Lehner.

Kobayashi family. *See* Kinkozan.

Koch, A.W. *See* Cambridge Art Tile Works.

Koch & Fischer. *See* Gräfenroda.

Kochi ware. In Japanese ceramic history, a class of wares decorated in low relief with thick glazes, coloured in yellow, purple and green (in the manner later adopted in European majolica), which had been imported to Japan, possibly from Fukien, in the 17th century and were referred to as Kochi ware (from the Japanese name for Cochin China). Chinese specimens, in bodies that ranged from soft, light earthenware to stoneware and a coarse porcelain paste, were covered in lead silicate glazes; colours prevented from mingling by the use of impressed outlines and ridges of slip. The pieces most prized were small round boxes (kogo) with lids moulded in the form of animals, birds, fruit or flowers, which were used as incense holders in the tea ceremony. The ware was among the Ming Chinese ceramics most widely copied in the 19th century by Japanese studio potters, notably *Eisen, *Mokubei, and *Hozen. The same glaze colours occur in the work of *Kikusaburo and the stoneware of the *Yoshidaya kiln, as well as in *Minato and *Awaji wares.
Refs: Jenyns (1965, 1971); Matsumoto; Nakagawa.

Koisago ware. *See* Kasama.

Koishibara or **Koishiwara.** Japanese pottery centre at Koishiwara Sarayama in Fukuoka prefecture, which contains Nakano, where *Takatori potters established a clan kiln in the 17th century for the production of official pieces for use by the Kuroda clan, and everyday wares. A number of other kilns opened subsequently at Nakano and Kami-no-hara. Nine families of potters were still active at the village of Koishibara in the 1960s. Using fine-textured local clay, the kilns produced water containers, large, lidded preserving jars in bold shapes with dripped glazes, bowls, plates, saké bottles, tea jars and ritual wares, often glazed in three colours over white slip. Some pieces have chatter marks (a pattern of small cuts in a white slip coating) with splashes of coloured glaze. Thick glazes are sometimes trailed, e.g. in wave patterns, or poured in large uneven patches of rust, yellow, white or green against a dark brown glaze which sometimes blisters during firing.
Refs: Brinkley; Jenyns (1971); Kozuru *Agano & Takatori* (Kodansha International, Tokyo/New York/San Francisco, 1981); Munsterberg; Okamura; Sanders.

Kok, Jurriaan (1861-1919). Dutch architect and ceramist, born in Rotterdam and trained in Delft. In 1893, Kok was a consultant at the *Rozenburg factory. He became artistic director in 1895 and also took charge of technical direction in 1897. He introduced the eggshell-thin earthenware body with which the pottery became associated, designing shapes for decoration by skilled painters. In 1913, he left Rozenburg to work for the municipality of The Hague.
Ref: Singelenberg-van der Meer.

Kondo Yuzo (b 1902). Japanese potter born in Kyoto city. Kondo studied at the Kyoto Municipal Institute of Ceramic Industry (graduating in 1917) and became apprenticed to *Tomimoto, 1921-23. He exhibited porcelain painted in underglaze blue or copper red after 1928 and became a member of the Japan Crafts Association in 1955. His patterns in blue included pomegranates, plum blossom, landscapes, and he also painted calligraphic designs, verse or prose, with bold brushwork. He was professor at Kyoto Municipal Art College from 1958, and principal of the college, 1965-71. He was designated Holder of the Technique for Sometsuke (blue and white porcelain, *see* sometsuke) in 1977.
Ref: Living National Treasures.

König, Ludwig. *See* Karlsruhe.

Königsburg. German faience factory established c.1772 and making mostly cream-coloured earthenware from 1780 until 1811.
Refs: Haggar (1960); Hannover; Hüseler; Pazaurek; Riesebieter; Stoehr.

Könitz. German porcelain factory established by the Metzel brothers in 1909 at Könitz, Thuringia. The output of household ware includes services printed in blue, e.g. with onion pattern (*Zwiebelmuster*), introduced c.1930. The factory came under the control of a firm in Hermsdorf in 1950 and joined the Kahla combine in 1964 as VEB Vereinigte Porzellanwerke Kahla-Könitz.

Marks incorporate a monogram of GM and a coronet.
Ref: Danckert.

Konyu. *See* Raku family.

Kopriva, Ena. Viennese ceramic artist and designer, trained at the Vienna Kunstgewerbeschule from 1913, when she started as a part-time student. She modelled many figures, vases, etc., for the *Wiener Werkstätte and worked (1928-37) as assistant to J.*Hoffmann. She was appointed as teacher at the Vienna Kunstgewerbeschule in 1938 and conducted a master class in fabric printing in 1945.

Mark: initials EK, or signature.
Ref: Neuwirth (1974a).

Koran-sha (The Company of the Fragrant Orchid). Japanese porcelain factory in Arita, at which the Tsuji family made wares initially for official use and then for export, as well as for the home market. Koran-sha was also the title of an association founded in 1876 by *Fukagawa, to improve the technical standards of Arita porcelain. As head of the Koran-sha factory, Katsuzo Tsuji joined the society, leaving in 1880 to participate in the

formation of *Seiji-sha. Employing 450 workers by 1878, the Koran-sha group won prizes in the 1876 Philadelphia Centennial Exhibition, and in the 1878 and 1900 Expositions Universelles in Paris. As suppliers of porcelain to the Japanese Imperial household, the company became one of the country's most prestigious producers. Many of its styles are derived from those of Old *Imari and *Nabeshima porcelains.
Refs: Brinkley; Burton (1921); Jenyns (1965).

Körmöczbánya. Hungarian factory established in 1800 by pharmacist Mathias Wacholt and engraver Heinrich Karl, for the production of cream-coloured earthenware for domestic use, initially blue-printed and later decorated with moulded reliefs, or painted, e.g. by Béla Antal. From 1868, the factory was owned by the firm of Kossuch.
Marks: until 1884, KR, or *Kremnitz*; later, KÖRMÖTZ or KÖRMÖCZBÁNYA; the town crest also occurs.
Ref: Csanyi.

Kornilov factory. Russian porcelain factory established at St Petersburg in 1835 by Mikhail Savinovich Kornilov, its director until his death in 1885, and trading under the title of the Brothers Kornilov from 1893 until its closure in 1918. Employing workers from other established factories (St Petersburg, Gardner, Popov), Kornilov soon achieved a high reputation for artistic achievement, and won a gold medal in the Moscow ceramic exhibition, 1839. He commissioned designs from well-known artists, including A. Darte (*see* Darte brothers), who carried out work for Kornilov while mainly employed by A.*Miklashewski from 1844. Kornilov's porcelain, noted for its translucency and milky-white glaze, was painted with bright enamel colours and lavishly gilded.
In order to increase production in the mid 19th century, the firm rented other factories and installed equipment that was more advanced than most used in Russia at the time; chromolithography was introduced in 1881, and an electromagnetic system for cleaning clay in 1885. A kiln constructed in 1896 was

Kornilov factory. Pieces from a tea set painted with flower sprigs below a blue-ground border, mid 19th century. The saucer is 14.6 cm in diameter.

claimed to be the biggest in Russia. In the late 19th century, the firm began mass production of cheap porcelain for export and at the time of the World's Columbian Exposition in Chicago (1893) established a large export trade with America.
Marks in Russian include *'of the Brothers Kornilov in St Petersburg'* over the glaze; BRK or BK impressed; from 1884, shield with a coat of arms and ribbons with the inscription *'In St Petersburg/Of the Brothers Kornilov'*; English inscription: *'Made by the Kornilov Brothers'*, with a bear, for export ware.
Refs: I. Arbat *The Porcelain Village* (in Russian, Moscow, 1957); Emme; Hare; A. Popoff 'The Francis Gardner & Other Russian Porcelain Factories' in *The Connoisseur* 96 (August 1935); Ross; Rozembergh; Saltykov.

Kosobe wares. A range of Japanese pottery made in Settsu province (now Osaka and Hyogo prefectures) with fine, hard body, glazed in white or grey and sparingly decorated with sketchy patterns in brown. The Kyoto potter Igarashi Shimpei, maker of raku and *Ninsei wares, is thought to have established production in the late 18th century, followed by several generations of potters working under the name Shimpei, of whom the fourth was still active in the late 1870s. A former antique dealer, Tasuke Dainen, also made Kosobe wares between 1840 and 1870; his work is thought to have been inspired by earlier wares and is of high quality.
Refs: Brinkley; Jenyns (1965); Morse.

Koster's Premier Pottery. Australian pottery established in 1890 at North Norwood, Adelaide, by the brickmaker J.C. Koster (1855-1912) for the production of household earthenwares, such as brown-glazed barrels and water filters. Art pottery introduced in the 1930s included a wide range of vases, jugs, flower-holders and urns, often with mottled brown/purple glazes. Electrical insulators were the pottery's staple product from about 1932 until closure in 1980.
Marks: *Koster*, sometimes with *North Norwood*.
Ref: R. Phillips 'The Passing of a Pottery' in *Australiana Society Newsletter* No 1 (1981).

Kosugi. Japanese pottery at the town of Kosugi in Toyama prefecture, thought to have been established in the late 16th century and working as a folk kiln in the 1860s.

The output of domestic and ritual pieces included spirit bottles, writing accessories and vessels for religious ceremonies. While specializing in celadon glazes, the workshop also produced tea vessels with white or amber (ame) glazes.
Ref: Mizuo.

Kotaro. *See* Mori family.

Koto yaki. Japanese ceramics produced at kilns established in 1829 beside Lake Biwa. Between 1840 and 1860, production came under the control of Naosuke II, Lord of Hikone, who brought in a number of potters as teachers, e.g. *Hozen, who was skilled in *aka-e and *kinrande decoration. The Koto painters executed Chinese landscapes featuring distant figures of sages in the aka-e palette. The kiln's output also included copies of Chinese swaton ware (*see* gosu aka-e) with designs in blue under the glaze and flowers and birds in red and green. The kilns were most productive 1844-53 and closed in 1896.
Ref: Gorham.

Kovács, Margit. Hungarian artist potter, born in Györ. Kovács studied art from 1924, and then pottery in Budapest, before leaving Hungary in 1926. Working with H.*Bucher in Vienna, she studied a variety of techniques, with emphasis on glazes. In Munich, 1928-29, she studied modelling under the sculptor, Karl Killer, and ceramics under A.*Niemeyer.
After her return to Hungary in 1929, and a successful exhibition in Budapest (1930), Kovács worked under J.F.*Willumsen in Copenhagen (1932) and then as an apprentice for 18 months at the Sèvres factory, also fulfilling commissions in Paris. Work exhibited in Budapest (1935) included earthenware vessels, relief panels, and figures, modelled or thrown. These and subsequent figures depend for effect on the interplay of light, and the use of compact, often stylized shapes, with careful representation of certain details, e.g. hands, decorative elements of dress (although facial features may be merely suggested by sketchy incised lines). The subjects may be religious, or taken from everyday life. Kovács's later work includes a series of figures entitled Mourning Women (late 1950s); murals, often large and depicting many figures in scenes from country life or folklore, demonstrating a variety of techniques—relief-modelled (e.g. terracotta Girls Singing, 1953), glazed relief (Grape Harvest, 1955), or tiles painted in coloured glazes (e.g. Fruit Harvest, 1952); vessels, varied in shape and often decorated with animals, or plant forms, with surfaces painted, modelled or incised. Kovács was inspired by Hungarian folk art in her use of heraldic motifs in painted decoration, and her use of folk songs as themes for the decoration of some bowls and dishes.
A museum has been established at Szentendre, near Budapest, in recognition of Margit Kovács work as a ceramic sculptor.
Refs: I. Bobrovszky *Die Keramikerin Margit Kovács* (Corvina Verlag, Budapest, 1961); I. Pataky-Brestyánszky *Modern Hungarian Ceramics* (Corvina Verlag, Budapest, 1961).

Kowarcz, Eva (b 1904). Polish ceramic modeller, born in Przemyś. She studied in

the Vienna Kunstgewerbeschule from 1921 under J.*Hoffmann (until 1922) and M. *Powolny (1923-26). Subsequent work for the Wiener Werkstätte included covered vessels, vases, plates and table decorations.
Ref: Neuwirth (1974a).

Koyama. *See* Shigaraki ware.

Kozan. *See* Miyakawa family.

Kozlov factory. Russian porcelain factory operating near Moscow in the mid 19th century. As well as household wares, the firm produced figures, including costume studies of dandies and provincial ladies, coloured in warm tones.
 Marks: full name of maker or, more frequently, impressed monogram.
Ref: Rozembergh.

Kranichfeld. German porcelain factory established at Kranichfeld (Saxe-Meiningen) by Reinhard Rothe in 1903. The firm concentrated on decorative ware, e.g. vases, *jardinières*, a crucifix after B.*Thorwaldsen, figures in the styles of other sculptors.
 Mark: KPM below a torch.
Refs: Danckert; Weiss.

Krause, Daniel (d 1903). Potter working in Salem, North Carolina. He served an apprenticeship under H.*Schaffner in 1846 and became Schaffner's chief potter before succeeding him as owner of the pottery in 1877. He was the last potter making the traditional wares of the *Moravian community in Salem, and concentrated chiefly on the production of tobacco pipes during his last years of work.
Ref: Bivins.

Krautheim. German porcelain factory founded by Christoph Krautheim in 1884 at Selb, Bavaria, originally as a decorating workshop, but producing porcelain from 1912. Krautheim and the firm's successors, Krautheim & Adelberg, produced table services, tea and coffee sets, some for hotel use, as well as gift items and decorative wares.
 Various marks incorporate the initials K&A *Krautheim* and sometimes *Selb, Bavaria.*
Refs: Danckert; Weiss.

Krebs, Nathalie (1895-1978). Danish potter and ceramic chemist. After working for *Bing & Grøndahl (1919-29), Krebs shared a studio briefly with G.*Nylund before establishing her own workshop, Saxbo, at Herlev in 1930. She produced individual stoneware pieces in simple shapes, with a wide range of glazes, including temmoku, hare's fur, grey, black, reddish brown, buff, olive, blue or white or grey which was tinged with yellow and decorated with ribbed lines or incised patterns of small motifs, e.g. leaves, semicircles, diamond shapes. Japanese wares provided an important inspiration for both shapes and glazes, but the workshop also produced original forms, e.g. a pear-shaped jug with the neck split and extended to form the handle and spout, exhibited in New York, 1938. As an individual artist, Krebs was known for her sensitive treatment of variations in the body-texture and glaze-colour of her stoneware. She collaborated with a number of designers, notably E.

Nathalie Krebs. Large stoneware dish, decorated with a duck in low relief, grey and white with red and black at rim, c.1935. Impressed mark: two fish, a crown, and Saxbo. 41.6 cm in diameter.

*Staehr-Nielsen and the sculptors Hugo Liisberg and Olaf Staehr-Nielsen.
Refs: Beard; Cox; Hiort.

Krenn, Rosa or Rose (b 1884). Ceramic designer, born in Steiermark and trained at the Prague Kunstgewerbeschule. She joined the Vienna Kunstgewerbeschule, 1909-12, working under J.*Hoffmann for her last year. Her work included bird figures, plates and, subsequently, designs for production in porcelain by the firm of Jos. *Böck.
 Mark: initials.
Ref: Neuwirth (1974a).

Kretschmann & Wurda. *See* Elbogen.

Krister, Carl Franz (1802-67). German porcelain decorator and manufacturer. After working in Thuringia as a painter (known mainly for his work in underglaze blue) Krister went in 1823 to join the small porcelain factory run by the firm of Rausch, a former weaver, in Waldenburg, Schlesien. He went into partnership to establish his own factory in 1829, buying the Rausch works soon afterwards. The output of blue and white ware was taken for sale in Leipzig. Krister's successors merged with *Rosenthal in 1921.
 A wide range of marks incorporate the initials KPM, WPM, CK, or KPF, and sometimes the name of the ware, e.g. *Royal Ivory.*
Refs: Danckert; Weiss.

Krog, Arnold Emil (1856-1931). Designer, architect, painter, graphic artist and ceramist from a Norwegian family working in Denmark. Krog trained in architecture at the Copenhagen Academy, 1874-80, working on the measurement of Kronborg Castle and decorating the interior of the Palace of Fredericksburg when it was rebuilt after fire damage which had occurred in 1859. In 1882 Krog spent one year in Italy, where he studied Renaissance architecture and the maiolica techniques of northern Italy. On his return to Denmark, he worked on the buildings of the Panopticon in Copenhagen, and joined the Royal *Copenhagen Porcelain Factory as art director in 1885, following the

closure of the drawing office in which he had been employed. He travelled with P.*Schou to London and Antwerp in the same year and soon afterwards visited Paris, where in 1889 he was to exhibit porcelain painted in muted, bluish underglaze colours with patterns inspired by Japanese stencils, and simple animal sculptures painted in similar colours. As decorator (and effectively art director) of the porcelain factory, 1891-1916, Krog was responsible for reviving the underglaze painting, mainly in soft shades of blue, for which Copenhagen porcelain had been renowned in the late 18th century. With the aim of integrating decoration fully with material, he painted dishes, plaques and vases with misty Danish scenes featuring birds or distant figures, and seascapes (notably a wave painted on the side of a vase in 1888). The underglaze colours were also used on low-relief plaques in the late 1880s, and slip-cast figures in smooth, compact shapes, e.g. a pair of owls perched on gnarled twigs. Assisted technically by V.*Engelhardt and artistically by K.*Kyhn, Krog experimented with stoneware, but was unable to bring it into commercial production. His later work made use of relief effects in thickly painted slip. He created about 200 models for the factory.

Painted mark.
Refs: Bodelsen; Danckert; Haslam (1977); B. Rackham *A Key to Pottery & Glass* (London, 1940); Weiss.

Krohn, Pietro (1840-1905). Danish painter, designer and ceramist, trained at Marstrand and Skovgaard. He painted landscapes and

*Arnold Krog. Covered vase made at the Royal *Copenhagen Porcelain Factory and painted in pale colours by Krog. Marks: a crown and Royal Copenhagen in green. 18.5 cm high.*

*Pietro Krohn. Decorative cups made at the
Bing & Grøndahl factory, 1884.

genre scenes, 1872-78, and worked as a designer and decorator for *Bing and Grøndahl
(as art director, 1885-95). His work for the
factory included the Heron service, and he
introduced decoration in the style evolved at
the Royal *Copenhagen factory by A.E.
*Krog. He became director of the museum
of applied arts in Copenhagen in 1890.
Refs: Bénézit; Danckert.

Kroon, De. Dutch porcelain factory established in 1906 at Noordwijk by Egbert
Estié. H.L.A.*Breetvelt was one of the
shareholders and provided designs for production at the factory. The output included
tableware and decorative pieces. Patterns of
butterflies, leaves and stylized flowers were
painted in underglaze and enamel colours,
often on splashed green or black grounds.
The factory was sold in 1907 and closed
three years later.
   Marks incorporate a crown on *Noordwijk/
Holland* or 1908-10 *Amsterdam.*
Refs: Singelenberg-van der Meer; van
Straaten.

Kronester, J., & Co. German porcelain
decorators and manufacturers producing
domestic wares at Schwarzenbach on the
Saale from 1904.
   Marks incorporate name or initials of J.
Kronester, sometimes *Bavaria*, and a crown.
Refs: Danckert; Weiss.

Krop, Hildebrand Lucien (1884-1970).
Dutch sculptor and ceramic modeller. Krop
modelled pieces for *E.S.K.A.F. in 1919 and
established his own workshop in Amsterdam
in the following year, where he made jars
and dishes decorated with figures in relief
under thick, coloured glazes.
   Mark: signature or initial.
Refs: C. Doelman 'De avontuurlijke kant
van Hildo Krop' in *Mededelingenblad
Vrienden van de Nederlandse Ceramiek* 4
(1956); Singelenberg-van der Meer.

Kruprinszky, Ladislaus (1888-1945). Hungarian painter and ceramist. Kruprinszky
worked for a long time at the *Hódmezővásárhely artists' colony, where he experimented with porcelain, before becoming art
director at the *Herend factory, 1931-32.
His later work included imitations of faience,
particularly wares made at *Holitsch.
Ref: Csanyi.

Kujiri. *See* Ofuke wares; Shino ware.

Kumagai Koyo (b 1912). Japanese potter,
born in *Agano. After studying ceramic
techniques in north-eastern China as part of
his military service in World War II, he
studied tea-ceremony wares, particularly tea
caddies. Examples of his own ceramics include caddies in a simple globular ('apple')
form with an incised groove encircling the
widest part and blotched brown glaze. He
excavated the 17th-century Agano kiln at
Kamanokuchi on Mount Fukuchi.
   His eldest son, Yasuoki Kumagai (b 1940),
studied at the art college in Kanazawa until
the early 1960s, afterwards working at Agano,
where he specialized in large dishes with
incised decoration of plant forms, etc.,
coloured with copper glaze.
Ref: Kozuru *Agano and Takatori Wares*
(Kodansha, Tokyo/New York, 1982).

Kumakichi. *See* Yosabei II.

Kumpf, Johann Georg (1769-1835). German
potter and porcelain maker. Kumpf worked
as a thrower or figure maker at Nymphenburg from 1787 and in Vienna from 1802,
returning to Nymphenburg as chief repairer
in 1810. He took over management of the
Regensburg stoneware factory in 1823 and
ten years later bought a small porcelain
factory at Passau (Bavaria).
Refs: Danckert; Weiss.

Kudinov. Russian porcelain factory established 1818 at Lystsovo in the Kolomna
district, near Moscow, by modeller and
carver N.S. Kudinov, with the help of a
local landowner, who later granted Kudinov
his freedom from serfdom. In 1823, Kudinov
was joined by his brother, Semen, who later
operated his own factory in the same village
until 1861. Their porcelain, decorated with
brightly coloured flowers in traditional
Russian styles, was exported to countries
which included Persia. The original factory
operated under the name of the Kudinov
family, managers until the 1880s.
   Mark: usually a monogram of NK in
flamboyant Cyrillic characters. Semen
Kudinov used a similar mark.
Refs: Hare; Ross; Saltykov.

Kuhn, Beate (b 1927). German studio potter,
born in Düsseldorf. Kuhn studied in Freiburg
(1947-49), trained in ceramics under P.
*Dresler in Wiesbaden (1949-51), and at the
Werkkunstschule in Darmstadt under M.
Schott (1951-53). She took over a workshop

in Lottstetten/Waldshut with K.*Scheid
(1953-56), meanwhile working as a designer
of shapes and patterns for the firm of *Rosenthal in Selb. In 1957 she established her own
workshop in Düdelsheim bei Bündigen. Her
work with Karl Scheid included household
wares, bowls, vases, etc., many with surface
decoration representing abstract or cubist
figures. She later developed the sculptural
elements of her work, becoming one of the
first ceramic sculptors in Germany. Her
stoneware pieces, consisting of thrown
elements with clay applied in relief, were
decorated with glazes which were initially in
dark colours, with details incised or painted
in brighter glazes. Primarily realistic portrayals of female figures, etc., in the early
1960s later gave way to groups of shells, etc.
   Marks include a spiral, incised or
impressed, and the initial K.
Refs: Bock; R. Flöhl in *Deutsche
Keramische Kunst der Gegenwart* (Cremer,
Frechen, 1968); Klein; E. Klinge *Deutsche
Keramik des 20 Jahrhunderts* (catalogue,
Hetjensmuseum, Düsseldorf, 1975).

Kuhn, Bernhardine. *See* Bimini Werkstätten.

Kühn, Heinrich Gottlieb. *See* Meissen.

Kuji. Japanese pottery established at Osanai
village, Kuji (Iwate prefecture), as a *clan
kiln, and operating from 1822 as a *folk kiln
under Kumagi Jin'emon, a potter trained at
*Soma. The output of undecorated domestic
ware in simple shapes included plates, dishes,
jars and bottles, with amber (ame) glaze
over dark brown clay, cups to hold sauce for
buckwheat noodles and other small pieces
known as Ko (little) Kuji ware, and, notably,
pouring bowls in compressed forms with
greyish-white glaze.
Refs: Mizuo; Munsterberg.

Kurlbaum & Schwartz. American porcelain
manufacturers, established at Philadelphia
after experiments starting in 1851, which
resulted in a small display of gilded hard-
paste tea ware, highly praised at the 1853
exhibition of the Franklin Institute in the
State of Pennsylvania. The firm built a small
factory in Kensington, Philadelphia, making
high-quality porcelain with kaolin from
Chester County, Pennsylvania, under the
management of W.*Reiss, until its closure
in 1855. The firm employed painters and
gilders from Germany.
   Mark: K&S.
Refs: Barber (1976); Myers.

Kuruba family. *See* Echizen ware.

Kusube Yaichi (b 1897). Japanese potter
working in his home town, Kyoto. After
making a particular study of Chinese blue-
amd-white porcelains, he produced wares
with a wide range of painted decoration,
including underglaze blue, polychrome
enamels and patterns on a gold ground, as
well as relief moulding.
Refs: Masterpieces; Roberts.

Kutani. Japanese ceramic centre, a village
in the former province of Kaga (now part of
the present Ishikawa prefecture) which has
given its name to wares made and decorated
in the area extending north-eastwards from

the Daishoji river to Kanazawa. Kilns established across the river from Kutani village in the mid 17th century produced wares for the Daishoji clan chieftains, the Maeda family. Initially making earthenware tea vessels, Kutani grew to rival *Arita as the leading porcelain centre in Japan, making a variable, but generally coarse-grained, greyish paste, with bold enamel decoration, until the late 17th or early 18th century. Porcelain production at Kutani village was revived in the early 19th century with the establishment of the *Yoshidaya kiln, but ceased with the transfer of the kiln to Yamashiro in the 1820s. Production continued at kilns elsewhere in Kaga province from the late Edo period to the present day.

The term Kutani ware, describing lavishly enamelled porcelain made or decorated in Ishikawa prefecture, was introduced in the early 19th century; the 17th-century wares were then called Ko (old) Kutani to differentiate them from revivals.

After the initial brief revival of Kaga's porcelain production at the *Kasugayama kiln with help from *Mokubei, *Honda established the *Wakasugi kiln in 1811, his pupil Rokuemon started the *Ono kiln in 1819, and *Minzan founded his own kiln at Kasugayama in the 1820s. The Yoshidaya workshop passed to the manager, *Miyamotoya, who reopened it and employed *Hachiroemon. *Gen'emon founded his own workshop and helped in the establishment of the *Rendaiji kiln.

The red enamelled ware (see aka-e) produced in hard, white porcelain paste at Kutani in the 17th century, embellished with gold and silver, was echoed in the work of the Minzan and Ono kilns and provided a basis for the lavish *kinrande and *hachirode styles of decoration now associated with Kutani ware. The output of the Wakasugi kiln included aka-e ware painted in a free, sketchy style by *Yujiro, normally without gilding. *Wazen, who worked at a clan kiln in Yamashiro for five years c.1860, perfected the combination of patterns in gold on a red ground on the exterior of a piece and red enamel on white inside (akaji kinga). *Shoza combined the elements from the style of other Kutani kilns to form his own style,

Shoza-fu or saishiki kinran (coloured kinran), again an echo of Chinese wares. The decorator, *Isaburo, who opened a school of porcelain painting in 1835, brought several innovations to the ware.

Painting in underglaze blue, while it had been mainly restricted in Old Kutani wares to the reverse of plates etc., became a feature of everyday wares from the Wakasugi kiln in the form of simplified versions of Ming and Ch'ing Chinese patterns, and was used on wares made at Kasugayama. The rich enamel colours, predominantly green, yellow and blue or purple (as in *Kochi wares) but also including chocolate and red, which had been used on Old Kutani ware in bold designs of landscapes, birds, lions, tigers, human figures or simply geometrical patterns, were to inspire work at the Yoshidaya and Wakasugi kilns. Later, they were developed by *Kikusaburo for the decoration of a class of porcelain painted in green glaze with the addition of black, purple and yellow, which became known as ao-Kutani (green Kutani).

Despite a decline in production in the late 1860s, a kiln for decorated ware was established in 1869. Porcelain making and decorating workshops arose in the area, adopting materials and industrial techniques already in use in western countries; about ten kilns were operating in Terai and Kanazawa by the end of the 19th century. Despite an interruption in production at the time of the Meiji restoration, business revived by 1885, when about 2,700 workers were employed. At this time, the lavish saishiki kinran ware evolved by Shoza was among Japan's most exported ceramics, and local techniques were studied by potters from other parts of Japan. In the late 1890s, the ceramist Morishita Hachizoemon and a Kaga teacher and president of the Kaga products Joint Stock Co., called Shida Yasukyo made porcelain with decoration in red with underglaze blue, or blue-grey monochrome glazes inspired by the Chinese u-kwo-tien-tsing (blue of the sky after rain) and yueh-peh (clair de lune) glazes.

Marks: Kaga potters began to sign their wares c.1850.
Refs: Gorham; Jenyns (1965); Mikami; Nakagawa.

Kuznetsov family. Russian porcelain and faience makers. The smith and timber merchant, Iakov Vasil'evich, who later adopted the name Kuznetsov, established a factory in 1810 at Novo-Kharitonovo. His firm traded as the Brothers Kuznetsov under the name of his sons, who were directors of the factory until the 1870s. One of the brothers, Terentii Kuznetsov, established a further factory in the Pokrovski district in 1832, also, by 1851, renting the *Safronov factory which he later bought. His son, Sidor Kuznetsov (d 1864), inheritor of the former Safronov factory in 1853 or 1854, moved it from Korotkaia to Dulevo. The peak of earthenware production occurred c.1876.

The M.S. Kuznetsov Co. for the Manufacture of Porcelain & Faience Ware was founded in 1889 by Matvei Sidorovich Kuznetsov, who inherited and owned the Dulevo factory until 1917. The firm had already bought and reorganized the *Auerbach factory before taking over others, including the *Gardner factory in 1891. The firm produced porcelain and earthenware tea and

dinner services, decorative pieces in earthenware with coloured glazes (or sometimes in terra-cotta), as well as stoves, fireplaces, electrical porcelain and sanitary ware. Kuznetsov achieved high technical quality by the adoption of new techniques and models from abroad, and exported work to Persia, Turkey and the Balkan countries. He also supplied to the Russian court, and made an estimated two-thirds of the country's ceramics, but developed a reputation for concentrating on profit at the expense of the welfare of his workers and the artistic quality of the product. The wares were frequently decorated with floral patterns in bright, clear colours, notably blue and purple, with lavish gilding. Some vases, toilet sets, powder boxes and other pieces in pale pink, or pale or dark blue, were decorated with painted and gilded designs.

Marks usually incorporate *MS Kuznetsov* and the place of production. The Gardner mark was retained for the work of that factory.
Refs: Bubnova; Hare; W. Raeburn 'Pottery and Propaganda' in *Apollo* 83 (January 1966); Ross; Saltykov.

Kwiatkowski, J. See Pilkington's Tile & Pottery Co.

Knud Kyhn. A camel with a monkey, glazed predominantly in grey and blue, modelled by Kyhn and produced in porcelain at Copenhagen, c.1930. 31 cm high and 32 cm in length.

Kyhn, Knud (1880-1969). Danish ceramist born in Copenhagen, who specialized in the modelling of animals in both stoneware and porcelain, which he carried out while working as designer for *Kahler ceramics, *Bing & Grøndahl and, 1903-68, the Royal *Copenhagen Porcelain Factory. Many of his pieces were covered with Sung or celadon glazes varying in tone from brown to dark bluish green, but others, e.g. a doe in stoneware (1924), were painted under the glaze, or enamelled.
Refs: Cushion (1974); Hiort.

Kyokuzan. See Todaya Tokuji.

Kyoto. The seat of the Japanese Imperial court, which emerged as a ceramic centre in the Edo period (1615-1868) and was noted for the work of artist potters who operated individually and signed their output. The *Raku family has continued production in the Kyoto area from the 16th/17th centuries until the present day, but the city is associated with the development of vivid colours

Kutani. Earthenware dish painted by Jobu with five grey carp on a diapered ground, the underside painted with a scrolling pattern of lotus, mid 19th century. Painted mark: Kutani Han-za-ka sei Jo-bu ga. 46.2 cm in diameter.

Kyoto. Earthenware figure of a kylin with crackled glaze, enamelled and gilt, mid 19th century. 16.5 cm high.

in slips and glazes in response to the cultural influences which had been introduced to Kyoto (as the country's political centre) from overseas. Enamel decoration became associated with the area through *Ninsei and *Kenzan wares; later potters of enamelled earthenwares in the district of *Awata include the *Kinkozan, *Tanzan, *Hozan, *Taizan and *Bizan families, all makers of large quantities of ware for export. Individual artists, including *Eisen, *Rokubei II, *Dohachi II, *Hozen and *Mokubei, often worked in both earthenware and porcelain. The area of *Kiyomizu specialized in enamelled porcelain from the late 19th century.
Refs: Jenyns (1965, 1971); Munsterberg.

Kyushu wares. Japanese ceramics made on Kyushu, the most south-westerly of the country's main islands. Pottery production largely originated from the immigration of Korean potters in the 16th and 17th centuries, whose output, known as *Karatsu ware, was made in the area covered by Saga prefecture and part of Nagasaki prefecture. Pottery centres arose at *Osotoyama and *Tataro. *Shiraishi, now a folk kiln, was started for the production of porcelain. The wares of *Imari, *Kakiemon, *Nabeshima and *Mikawachi come from the district surrounding *Arita, the main centre of production on Kyushu. Workmen from Arita established the Hirasa porcelain kiln in Kagoshima prefecture, which also contains the kilns of *Naeshirogawa and *Ryumonji. Work at *Shodai (Kumamoto) was begun by potters from *Agano. Also in Fukuoka prefecture are *Koishibara and *Futagawa.
Refs: Mikami; Munsterberg; Okamura.

Labarre, Charles. *See* Doulton & Co.

La Belle Pottery Co. American pottery company established in 1887 by the managers of the *Wheeling Pottery Co. As part of the Wheeling company from 1889, the firm made semi-porcelains marketed between 1888 and 1893 as Adamantine China and from 1893 as La Belle China. The firm ceased operation in 1907.
Refs: Barber (1976); Evans; Kovel & Kovel.

Labouchère, A. *See* Thooft, Joost.

La-Charité-sur-Loire (Nièvre). *See* Warburton, Peter.

Lachenal, Edmond (1855-c.1930). French sculptor and ceramist, born in Paris. He joined T.*Deck's workshop at the age of fifteen, later becoming its director. He established his own workshop at Malakoff, south-west of Paris, in 1880, moving by 1887 to Châtillon-sous-Bagneux (Seine). Lachenal initially made earthenware in a Persian style, decorated in relief with figures, landscapes, flowers and foliage, later changing to stoneware and porcelain. He exhibited annually in a Paris gallery from 1884. In 1890, he perfected a means of achieving a velvety texture in glazed surfaces with the use of hydrofluoric acid. He experimented with metallic glazes in collaboration with *Keller & Guérin, meeting with success in 1895, when he also exhibited a group of sculptures after Auguste Rodin, P.-F.*Fix-Masseau and other artists. He worked in enamelled glass at the Daum glassworks, Nancy. Gradually Lachenal began to specialize in the production of ceramic vases in shapes derived from plant forms and covered with velvety glazes in ocean blue, rock brown, plum, pear, etc.; he also made small decorative objects such as small figures and models of farm animals. At the Exposition Universelle in Paris (1900), he displayed furniture in stoneware, the culmination of his efforts to use stoneware decoration. He was succeeded in his studio by his wife and son, R.*Lachenal.
Mark: painted signature.
Refs: Baschet; Bénézit; Brunhammer *et al* (1976); Camart *et al*; Hakenjos (1974); Heuser & Heuser.

Lachenal, Raoul (1885-1956). French ceramist, trained under his father, E.*Lachenal, whom he succeeded in his studio at Châtillon-sous-Bagneux (Seine) before moving to Boulogne-sur-Seine. From 1904, he exhibited stoneware with geometrical designs incised in relief, or in coloured glazes enclosed in the *cloisonné* manner with a deep orange outline; he also used matt or *flambé* glaze effects. His later output included porcelain decorated with a wide range of colours, notably a velvety black, and a salmon pink

Raoul Lachenal. Glazed earthenware vase with decoration in gold lustre and blue on yellow, 1920s. 35.5 cm high.

used as a ground under the white decoration.
Mark: painted signature.
Refs: Années 25; Lesur (1971); Haslam (1977).

Lachiche, Joseph. *See* Chevannes, Faïencerie de.

Lacombe, Paul. *See* Alluaud, François.

Lactolian ware. *See* Doulton & Co.

Laeuger, Max (1864-1952). German potter, painter, sculptor, architect and designer, born in Lörrach. In Karlsruhe, Laeuger studied painting and interior design (1880-84) and taught at the Kunstgewerbeschule (1885-90), while also working at potteries in Kandern during vacations. He studied at the Académie Julian in Paris (1892-93). In 1893, he started to make lead-glazed slipware, which he subsequently produced at the workshop of J. Armbruster in Kandern. His vases were decorated with low-relief designs and painted in bright colours. Laeuger was founder and director of a craft pottery in Kandern and in 1898 took up an appointment as professor at Karlsruhe university. His workshop produced plates painted with metal oxides over a coating of white slip, and covered with a crackled and slightly bubbled transparent glaze. Some blurred and smoky effects result from experimentation with reduction firing. Laeuger was co-founder of the Deutscher Werkbund in 1907. He established a studio at the Karlsruhe Majolikamanufaktur in 1916 and worked there until its destruction by bombs in 1944; meanwhile he continued teaching, taking up an appointment at Baden state art school, 1920-22. During the 1920s, Laeuger abandoned painted decoration in his own work, producing pieces that relied for effect on slips and glazes, which he fired in several stages to achieve subtle changes in tone. He also made decorative use of such technical faults as bubbles and fine cracks, and developed a turquoise glaze that became known as Laeuger blue. Laeuger's work chiefly consisted of bowls, vases and wall plaques, but he also experimented with ceramic sculptures depicting female figures, animals (notably elephants), etc. In 1944, he moved to Lörrach, where he died.

Marks: monogram of MLK in square outline, at Kandern; PROF LÄUGER stamped with the mark of the Karlsruhe Majolikamanufaktur; monogram of ML or initials incised, painted or impressed.
Refs: R. Bampi in *Keramos* 26 (1964); Bock; E. Brinckmann 'Neue Laeuger Keramik' in *Deutsche Kunst und Dekoration* (1970); E. Kessler 'Max Laeuger und die Manufaktur (1921-1929)' in *Karlsruher Majolika* (catalogue, Badisches Landesmuseum, Karlsruhe, 1979); A. Klein 'Max Laeuger. Der Plastiker und Keramiker von europäischem Format' in *Keramische Zeitschrift* 3 (1951); M. Laeuger 'Vom Wesen der Keramik' in *Deutsche Kunst und Dekoration* LXII (1928); F.R.W. Rauschenberg 'Prof. M. Laeuger,

Max Laeuger. Display plate made in Karlsruhe, 1930.

Karlsruhe' in *Deutsche Kunst und Dekoration* VII (1900-01).

Lafayette (Indiana) Ceramic Club. *See* Fry, Laura Anne.

Lagarde & Cox. *See* Demartial & Tallandier.

Lagrenée. *See* Sèvres.

Lahens & Rateau. French pottery manufacturers established c.1829 at Bordeaux and in production 1831-34. The factory was built on land belonging to Rateau, which held rich deposits of suitable clay. The firm's few surviving pieces, made in fine stoneware or cream and white earthenware, include powder boxes, tea services, etc. The stoneware was decorated with relief patterns (often in the body colour of white, pink, grey, blue, brown or yellow, rather than in contrast) which were moulded with the piece or applied to unfired clay in the manner of jasper ware. Creamware was sparsely painted or lustred; black-printed landscapes also occur.
Marks, impressed, include LAHENS ET RATEAU, or L containing a small R.
Refs: Ernould-Gandouet; Lesur (1971).

Lalique, Suzanne (b 1899). French painter and designer, born in Paris, the daughter of glass artist René Lalique (1860-1945). Suzanne Lalique designed many patterns for the decoration of porcelain made by her husband's cousin, W.*Haviland, during a collaboration which lasted from 1925 until 1931. Her work, always extremely careful in execution, included a design of grapes in black and silver, and notably Paquerettes (closely packed daisy-heads), which conveyed an impression of delicacy and freshness.
Mark: signature and Haviland's mark.
Refs: Années 25; Baschet; Bénézit; Brunhammer *et al* (1976); d'Albis & Romanet; Y. Rambosson 'La porcelaine limousine à l'exposition des arts décoratifs' in *La Vie Limousine* (August 1925).

Lamar. *See* Weller, Samuel A.

Lambert. *See* Archangelskoye; Yusupov, Prince Nikolai Borisovich.

Lambert, Guillaume, & Cie. *See* Sphinx, De.

Lambeth Faience. *See* Doulton & Co.

Lambeth Pottery. *See* Doulton & Co.; Doulton & Watts.

Lampl, Fritz. *See* Bimini Werkstätten.

Lamson Pottery. American red ware pottery established, probably in the late 18th century, at Exeter, New Hampshire, by Jabesh Dodge (c.1746-1806) and in operation from 1819 at the Exeter Pottery Works on Main Street under Dodge's sons Samuel (b 1783), who was still working at Exeter in 1849, and John (b 1791), and a grandson, Samuel J. Dodge (b 1814). Asa Brown Lamson (b 1818), an Exeter potter and probably Samuel Dodge's partner, worked with his son, Frank Hudson Lamson (b 1859), who took over the pottery until it ceased operation c.1895.
The pottery produced a wide variety of household ware, mainly thrown in simple shapes from local red-firing clay, covered with yellowish-tinged lead glaze, in some cases splashed with green (copper) and brown (manganese). In later years, the pottery's main output consisted of flowerpots.
Another pottery established in Portland, Maine, by Jabesh Dodge's grandson, Benjamin, who worked there 1847-68, was later owned by Rufus Lamson (b 1844), son of Asa Lamson and formerly a potter in Peabody, Massachusetts. Rufus Lamson operated the works in the partnership Lamson & Swasey in the 1870s. Longfellow's poem 'Keramos' was written there c.1875.
Ref: F.H. Norton 'The Exeter Pottery Works' in D.& J.G. Stradling *The Art of the Potter* (Main Street/Universe Books, New York, 1977).

Lancastrian ware. *See* Pilkington's Tile & Pottery Co.

Landais, Joseph (1800-83). French potter and ceramic modeller. After acting as assistant to C.-J.*Avisseau, whose sister he married in 1822, he established his own workshop in Langeais (Indre-et-Loire) and continued to produce *Palissy ware, as well as cups, ewers and other vessels decorated in Renaissance style. He was succeeded by his son, Alexandre Landais (1868-1912), who later worked in Paris, attempting to adapt the style of his uncle's Palissy ware to more varied uses, e.g. in mirror frames.
Both signed their work.
Refs: Ernould-Gandouet; Haslam (1977); Heuser & Heuser; Lesur (1971).

Landells, Flora (1888-1981). Australian artist potter and china painter, born in Adelaide and working in western Australia from 1896. Flora Landells joined the Western Australian Society of Arts in 1904 and first exhibited in its annual shows. She studied painting at Perth Technical College and taught art, before taking up pottery in the 1930s, when, with her husband Reginald Landells, a chemist and engineer (whom she married in 1913), she produced tableware to satisfy wartime demand caused by the lack of imported wares, using equipment bought from the *Calyx Porcelain and Paint Co. Ltd and beginning with a wood-fired kiln, which was later converted to oil. Flora Landells taught classes in art and pottery at her studio. She continued china painting

(started c.1900) throughout her life. Her pottery was all earthenware, apart from some stoneware made c.1960; her patterns were often based on wild flowers of Western Australia. She abandoned pottery-making soon after her husband's death in 1960.
Ref: Graham.

Landgraf, G. Porcelain painter. After working as the principal artist at the Königliche Porzellan-Manufaktur *Berlin, 1872-78, Landgraf was employed at the porcelain factory in Osmaston road, *Derby, 1880-85; his work there included romantic portraits painted on plaques. He is thought also to have worked for *Brown-Westhead, Moore & Co.
Refs: see Derby.

Landry, Abel. French architect and designer. Landry studied in his native Limoges and later at the Ecole des Beaux-Arts in Paris. First working as a painter and architect, he turned to interior design after study with William Morris in London. Landry subsequently became associated with La *Maison Moderne, where the majority of his designs, chiefly in metal and porcelain, were produced. In architectural designs, he made use of ceramic exterior decoration.
Refs: Brunhammer *et al* (1976); T. Leclère 'Abel Landry, architecte et décorateur' in *L'Art Décoratif* 9 (1907).

Landshut, Staatliche Keramische Fachschule. Professional school established by the Bavarian government in 1873, the first for potters in Germany. From c.1910, its output included porcelain figures.

Impressed mark.
Refs: Danckert; Haslam (1977).

Landsun. *See* Peters & Reed.

Lanfrey, François. *See* Niderviller.

Langeais (Indre-et-Loire). The site of a French earthenware factory which started with the introduction of fine earthenware by Charles de Boissimon at a former tile works, which he joined in 1839. Using a creamy-white body, the firm made a variety of enamel-painted ware, soon introducing oval, square, octagonal or lozenge-shaped pieces with yellow or black glaze. The addition of local kaolin to the body made it sufficiently plastic for the production of baskets (c.1850) in woven strips of clay. Relief decoration consisted chiefly of foliage, flowers or fruit, especially vine branches. Leaves were used in relief to decorate yellow or black glazed pieces, such as *jardinières*, baskets, ring stands, toilet sets, candle-holders, butter pots; some tobacco jars were in the form of logs or tree stumps, others combined ashtrays with holders for pipe and cigars. The lavish enamel decoration soon became replaced with lines, highlights or simple patterns in platinum lustre, or occasional gilding. Light touches of red or other colours were also used, and some pieces sold as '*bleu de Tours*' were decorated only in blue in the style of the Sèvres factory. Work was also sold in the white to Paris decorators. De Boissimon's family retained the factory until its sale c.1900. After further changes in ownership, the output was restricted to refractory wares.

Marks, not always used, include cb impressed in an oval, or *C. de Boissimon et Cⁱᵉ/Langeais/Indre-et-Loire* impressed in a rectangle.
Refs: Ernould-Gandouet; Lesur (1971).

Langenbeck, Karl (1861-1938). American potter and ceramic chemist. In 1873, he received a set of colours for ceramic decoration as a gift from a relative in Germany and was joined in experimentation by M.L. *Nichols Storer, his neighbour in Cincinnati, Ohio. After graduating from the Cincinnati College of Pharmacy in 1882, he studied in Zurich and Berlin. As chemist at the *Rookwood Pottery briefly in 1885, he worked to improve production and reduce kiln losses. After leaving Rookwood, he operated his own *Avon Pottery, 1886-88. He wrote *The Chemistry of Pottery* in 1884 and, as president of the American Ceramic Society (1900, 1901), contributed many articles to the society's bulletins. Langenbeck worked as chemist at the *American Encaustic Tiling Co. from 1890 to 1893, also acting as chemical adviser to J.B.*Owens from 1891. With H.T.*Mueller, he organized the *Mosaic Tile Co. in 1893, remaining there until 1903. He became superintendent of the Grueby Faience Co. in 1908, and in the following year replaced W.H.*Grueby as superintendent and technician of the Grueby Pottery. In 1922, he became chief chemist at the US Tariff Commission. He also served as consultant at the National Bureau of Standards.
Refs: Barber (1976); Evans; Kovel & Kovel; K. Langenbeck *The Chemistry of Pottery* (Chemical Publishing Co., Easton, Pennsylvania, 1895); Peck.

C.J. Lanooij. Vase with lustre decoration. 25 cm high.

Langley, Leonard. English ceramic designer, trained as John *Slater's first apprentice at *Pinder, Bourne & Co. from c.1868 and subsequently working for *Doulton & Co. until 1916. He designed a number of early patterns for series production and became head of a department for the design of cheaper lines of ware, printed from engravings, lithographs and blocks.

Langley initialled work produced under his supervision.
Refs: see Doulton & Co.

Langley Mill Pottery. Derbyshire pottery established 1865 by James Calvert at Langley Mill, near Heanor, for the production of brown salt-glazed stoneware. The firm, trading as Calvert & Lovatt and from 1895 as Lovatt & Lovatt, made bottles for ginger beer, blacking and furniture polish, as well as mugs, jugs and decorative terracotta, using local clays. It was acquired by the Denby Pottery (*see* *Bourne, J.) in 1931 and the title became Langley Potteries Ltd in 1967.

Marks: north shipley pottery/langley mills (Calvert); langley ware, impressed, from 1895; later marks usually incorporate the name langley.
Refs: Bradley; Godden (1964); Jewitt; Oswald.

Langley Ware. *See* Bendigo Pottery; Fowler family.

Langlois, Joachim (c.1769-1830). French porcelain manufacturer and ceramic chemist. He was the owner of a factory established 1793 at Valognes (Manches) from 1802 and moved the works to *Bayeux in 1810.
Refs: Chavagnac & Grollier; Cushion (1980); Lesur (1967).

Lanooij, Christian Johannes (1881-1948). Dutch painter, ceramist and designer of glass, textiles and wallpaper; born in Sint Annaland. Lanooij trained as a ceramic painter at *Rozenburg 1896-97, then worked as a decorator in the Hague and in Germany. He was in Gouda from 1900, worked at the *Zuid-Holland factory and, after military service, at other potteries. He joined *Haga as designer and art director in 1906, and in the following year established his own workshop near Gouda, where he continued glaze research which he had started several years earlier and largely abandoned decoration in his ceramics after c.1909. He moved to Epe in 1920, and continued his work in ceramics while providing many designs for the Leerdam glass factory (1919-c.1980)

Mark: signature, *C.J.Lanooij, Lanooye* or *Lanooy*.
Refs: C.J. Lanooy, kunstpottenbakker (catalogue, Het Princessehof, Leeuwarden, 1977); *Lanooij's ceramiek* (catalogue, Stedelijk Museum, Amsterdam, 1914); Scheen; Singelenberg-van der Meer; van Straaten.

Lanternier, Frédéric and Alfred (c.1859-1932). French porcelain manufacturers working in Limoges. Frédéric Lanternier worked as a porcelain decorator and exporter from rue Neuve des Carmélites in 1857 and from Champ de Foire in 1863. He entered into a partnership, Lanternier & Breuil (1885-87), for the production of white ware, reopening

a disused factory in rue de la Fonderie. His son, Alfred Lanternier, worked in England 1877-81 and was European representative for the firm of Wedgwood from 1881, before he joined his father in 1887. The firm moved three years later to the factory formerly used by H.*Ardant and R.*Laporte. Alfred Lanternier subsequently went into partnership with his brother-in-law, trading as A. Lanternier & Cie. Making utility tableware, tea and coffee services, etc., the firm built up an export market in the Low Countries, Germany, Italy, Great Britain, and America. During World War I, output was restricted to dolls' heads, but the production of tableware was soon resumed. Pieces made in the 1920s included octagonal forms with stylized flowers in shades of blue; stemmed teacups and saucers with festoons, garlands and bouquets in green, black and gold. The firm, after moving in 1960 to part of the *G.D.A. works, was still in the hands of the Lanternier family in 1978.

Marks: an anchor with a l and france (1890-1914); a shield, laurel wreath, france, with a. lanternier & co/limoges.
Refs: Années 25; d'Albis & Romanet.

Lapipe, Jacques-Philibert. *See* Vausse, Faïencerie de.

Lapis Ware. *See* Pilkington's Tile & Pottery Co.

Laporte, Raymond (c.1848-98). Limoges porcelain manufacturer working from 1872. He went into partnership with his father-in-law, H.*Ardant, 1873-83, and then established a factory on a nearby site. His work included reproductions (made with permission) of some Sèvres pieces and a display of 77 sculptural pieces and 13 cabaret sets made for exhibition in Limoges, in 1886. Laporte also made *jardinières*, and handles for umbrellas and brushes. He retired a year before his death.

Marks: *RL Limoges France* or rl/l with a dragonfly.
Ref: d'Albis & Romanet.

Larcombe. *See* Derby.

LaSa. *See* Weller, Samuel A.

Lesbros, Adèle. *See* Dalpayrat, Pierre-Adrien.

Lassell, J. *See* Lessell, John.

Lauder, Alexander. English architect and potter. As headmaster of the Barnstaple School of Art, he taught C.H.*Brannam. In 1876, he established Lauder & Smith's pottery at Pottington, near Barnstaple, where he leased clay deposits. Lauder manufactured bricks, tiles and architectural ornaments, turning to the production of art ware c.1880, when he became sole proprietor. His output was similar in style to Brannam's Barum ware, with incised, *sgraffito* and painted slip decoration on thrown vases bowls, etc., though he favoured rather more complex shapes, with flared rims and swirling handles, and decorative designs that expressed his desire to 'follow nature'. The ware, known as Devon Art Pottery or Devon Art Ware, was often less carefully finished than Brannam's. The pottery closed in 1914.

Laurin. Vase with ochre-coloured glaze and a pattern of birds painted in slip, probably exhibited in Vienna in 1873. 29.5 cm high.

Marks, impressed or incised, incorporate the name *Lauder*, *Barum* or *Barnstaple*, and sometimes, from c.1880-1914, the date.
Refs: Blacker (1922a); Coysh (1976); Lloyd Thomas (1974).

Laughlin, Homer. American potter. With his brother, Shakespeare Laughlin, he established a pottery wholesale business c.1868 and built a white ware pottery at East Liverpool, Ohio, in 1873-74. Homer Laughlin was sole owner from 1877 until 1897, when the firm became Homer Laughlin China Co. The firm mainly made white granite and produced cups and saucers, decorated under the glaze by E.*Lycett in 1879, which constituted an early attempt to make well-designed commercial ware in East Liverpool. Toilet sets shown in the World's Columbian Exposition in Chicago (1893) were decorated with raised designs in gold and dark colours on tinted grounds. C.*Nielson was briefly associated with the pottery in the early 1890s. Laughlin retired in 1898. Under a management headed by W.E. Wells and Marcus Aaron, the firm expanded rapidly and owned three factories by 1905. The company's output then consisted of semi-porcelain dinner services, hotel ware and toilet sets, as well as granite ware for kitchen use. A huge factory opened in 1905 at Newell, West Virginia, across the river from East Liverpool, was in production in 1907, and from 1929, production was centred on Newell. The tableware of the 1920s and 1930s included simple shapes with plain glazes in yellow, green, orange or blue, to allow a selection of colours to be picked for table setting. Lines in production 1930-60 included Fiesta, Harlequin and Eggshell. The Laughlin company now operates five factories in all, employing about 1300 workers, and specializing in dinner wares.

Marks: device incorporating *Laughlin* with an American eagle dominating a lion

(Britain) on white granite; a circular version of the same device on semi-porcelain toilet and table services, with the pattern name printed below; HL monogram or circular mark incorporating *Homer Laughlin* with HOTEL CHINA on hotel ware.

There has been a coding system on production ware since 1900, indicating month and year of manufacture as well as the factory which made it. From 1960, a backstamp on best china indicates year, A 1960, B 1961, to Z which is 1985, and months A (January) to L (December).
Refs: Barber (1976); Cox; Evans; W.C. Gates & D.E. Ormerod *Historical Archaeology* Vol 16, 1-2 (Society for Historical Archaeology, 1982); Lehner; Ramsay.

Laurent-Desrousseaux, Henri-Alphonse-Louis (1825-1906). French painter and illustrator, born at Joinville-le-Pont (Seine). He collaborated with H.-L.-C.*Robalbhen on stoneware in Art Nouveau styles from 1898.
Mark: incised signature.
Refs: Bénézit; Haslam (1977); Heuser & Heuser.

Laurin. French manufacturers of everyday earthenware at Bourg-la-Reine (Hauts-de-Seine). As well as painted ware and majolica, the firm made a quantity of ware for painting by outside artists and amateur decorators. The firm employed E.*Chaplet, from 1857, and later, E.-A.*Dammouse, until their move to the Haviland studio at Auteuil. Production ceased in 1910.
Marks: LAURIN; Chaplet's incised signature.
Refs: Brunhammer *et al* (1976); Lesur (1971).

Lauth, Charles. *See* Sèvres.

Leach, Bernard Howell (1887-1979). English artist potter. Leach, born in Hong Kong, was sent to school in England in 1897, and studied painting at the Slade School of Fine Art 1903, and etching at the London School of Art under Frank Brangwyn. In 1909, he went to Tokyo, initially to teach etching. He became interested in ceramics and began to study the production of decorated ware under Kenzan VI, who later gave Leach and *Tomimoto jointly the right to inherit the Kenzan title.

Leach built a kiln at his home in Tokyo and travelled throughout Japan to study the work of other potters, as well as studying the sources of their work in Peking (1916-19) and Korea. He rebuilt the stoneware kiln of Kenzan on a new site near Tokyo in 1919, returning to England with S.*Hamada in the following year. By 1920, he had produced a wide range of work, including porcelain painted in blue with oriental scenes; raku vases; dishes and jars with painted slip and incised decoration; tea utensils in stoneware, decorated with slip or incised patterns, and coffee ware with celadon glaze.

Leach established a pottery at St Ives, Cornwall, and with Hamada produced stoneware and raku, using local materials. He also returned to the 17th-century art of English slipware, including moulded dishes with marbled slip decoration. One of his aims was to 'provide sound hand-made pots sufficiently inexpensive for people of moderate means to take into daily use'. He was joined (1922-24) by Tsuranoske Matsubayashi, who designed a climbing kiln that is still in

use, though since modified, at St Ives. He started at this time to accept student apprentices, including M.*Cardew, (1923), K.*Pleydell-Bouverie (1924), N.*Braden (1925), and suggested in his pamphlet *A Potter's Outlook* (1928) that work by a team of potters who still retained individual responsibility for their work might present a solution to the difficulty of reconciling economic and artistic needs. He was convinced that 'pots must be made to answer to outward as well as inward need' and determined 'to counter-balance the exhibition of expensive personal pottery by a basic production of what we called domestic ware.' As productivity at the St Ives workshop increased, Leach continued to develop his own work, which included stoneware vases and bowls, compact in shape, sometimes with faceted sides, and generally restrained in decoration, and large slipware dishes with bold decoration of birds, fish, trees and other plant forms. He continued to produce slipware until the late 1930s, but recognized that the domestic needs of his customers were better met with durable, practical stonewares in which he hoped to match some of the qualities of Chinese Sung wares.

In 1933 Leach established a small pottery at Shinner's Bridge, South Devon, while teaching pottery at nearby Dartington Hall, and left his son, D.*Leach in charge of the St Ives workshop. In Devon, he used an updraught kiln, after Japanese models, to fire his slipware, which included dishes with combed decoration, to 1200°C, providing increased strength in the body. He returned to Japan in 1934 to continue work with Hamada, also visiting Korea to study. He expressed what he had learned technically and artistically in *A Potter's Book*, which was published in 1940 as a practical guide for other potters. His writing, teaching and work proved to be among the main influences on studio potters in Britain and overseas. In Japan, he had assisted Muneyoshi (Soetsu)

Bernard Leach. Grey stoneware vase shading to deep brown on one side. 30.5 cm high.

Yanagi in the development of the folk art movement (*see* mingei ware). In his work, Leach felt it 'reasonable to expect that beauty will emerge from a fusion of the individual character and culture of the potter with the nature of his materials – clay, pigment, glaze – and his management of the fire, and that consequently we may hope to find in good pots those innate qualities which we most admire in people.' Further, he regarded his pottery as an expression of his own philosophy. His individual work, though remaining functional in purpose, became more experimental, drawing on a wide range of influences, including Minoan, pre-Columbian and medieval English, as well as oriental wares. From the 1940s, he worked only in porcelain and stoneware, making freer use of carved and fluted decoration, or patterns of applied clay. Glazes range from dark temmoku to golden ash glazes. He used a wide range of decorative techniques, e.g. brushwork, stencils, wax resist, slip patterns, inlaid clay, stamped relief and occasionally modelling to develop motifs, some of which recurred over many years in his work.

Marks: stamped or painted initials.
Refs: Burlington Magazine 100 (April 1958), 103 (February 1961); M. Cardew 'The Pottery of Bernard Leach' in *Studio* 90 (1925); *Ceramic Review* 50 (1978), 58 (1979); J.P.Cushion 'Bernard Leach' in *Studio* 161 (May 1961); M. Fieldhouse 'The Leach Pottery' in *Pottery Quarterly* I (1954), 'B. Leach and Hamada' in *Pottery Quarterly* V (1958); C. Hogben (ed) *The Art of Bernard Leach* (Faber, London, 1978); B. Leach *A Potter's Book* (Faber, London, 1940), 'Craftsmanship, the Contemporary artist Potter' in *Royal Society of Art Journal* 96 (May 1948), *A Potter's Work* (Evelyn, Adams & Mackay, London, 1967), *Kenzan and His Tradition* (Faber, London, 1966); E. Marsh 'Bernard Howell Leach, Potter' in *Apollo* 37 (January 1943); M.C. Richards 'Leach, East and West' in *Craft Horizons* 20 (July 1961); Rose; G. Whiting 'Leach, Fifty Years a Potter' in *Pottery Quarterly* VII (1961-62); G. Wingfield Digby 'The Art of Bernard Leach' in *The Connoisseur Year Book* (1958).

Leach, David (b 1910). English potter. He joined the St Ives Pottery in 1930 as an apprentice to his father, B.*Leach. He taught at Dartington Hall School, where he started a pottery 1933-34, and studied at the North Staffordshire Technical College 1934-37. He subsequently returned to manage the pottery at St Ives, initiated the training of local apprentices and in 1938 introduced the making of stoneware in series (in addition to the unique pieces produced at the pottery). After his war service (1941-45), Leach returned to form a partnership with his father and ran the St Ives pottery until the establishment of his own workshop, the Lowerdown Pottery, at Bovey Tracey, Devon, in 1956, for the production of functional ware, some with brushed decoration, together with individual pieces in stoneware

David Leach. Stoneware teapot with off-white matt titanium glaze, 1970s.

and porcelain. Leach's own work includes porcelain bowls and boxes with fluting or small, stylized flowers sprays incised, often under a celadon glaze, with brushed decoration and sometimes spots of bright red glaze against a blue-washed ground, or with a white crackle glaze, its network of lines accentuated with pink or grey. A group of large stoneware dishes have white dolomite glaze applied to dark temmoku over wax resist patterns. Leach also uses ash glazes on vases and other pieces.

His work as a teacher includes the establishment of pottery classes at the Penzance School of Art; he has been a visiting lecturer at a number of art schools, an external assessor for the Harrow College of Technology and Art, and a member of the Scottish Education Department's Board of Assessors.

Marks: rectangular or circular outline enclosing the initial L with a D (or, for the

Janet Leach. Large stoneware dish decorated with trails and splashes of brown and buff slip on a matt brown ground. Marks include JL.

Lowerdown Pottery, a cross) in its angle.
Refs: E. Cameron & P. Lewis *Potters on Pottery* (Evans, London/Scribners, New York, 1976); R. Fournier (ed) *David Leach* (Fournier Pottery, Lacock, Wilts., 1977).

Leach, Janet (b 1918). Potter, born in Texas, working mainly in England. After training as a sculptor, Janet Leach (*née* Darnell) turned to ceramics in 1947 and studied at Alfred University (*see* New York State College of Ceramics) and began organizing a workshop in New York State, 1949. She became interested in Japanese ceramics on meeting B.*Leach and *Hamada in America, 1952, and went to Japan in 1954, working with Hamada and other potters, and in Tamba. She married Leach in 1956 and has since run the Leach Pottery at St Ives. Her own work has been in porcelain and stoneware bodies, which she mixes herself, and includes small pieces, but she is known for the making of large, often massive pots. The body colour is often darkened with the addition of bauxite or chrome ore and the decoration is restricted to small, paired handles, markings pushed or cut in the damp clay, or similarly shaped dashes of light or glossy glaze, and variations in glaze effect achieved in firing. Her work is mainly thrown, often with rims afterwards squeezed to elliptical form or the whole vessel flattened to a bisymmetrical form but some pieces are slab-built with edges and surface rawly finished.

Marks include the initials JL in triangular form, impressed.
Refs: T. Birks *Art of the Modern Potter* (Country Life, London, 1967); *Ceramic Review* 33 (1975), 51 (1978); J.P. Hodin 'Janet Darnell Leach' in *Pottery Quarterly* 9 (1967); Rose.

Lead, Leonard (1787-1869). English porcelain painter. Lead was apprenticed at the factory in Nottingham Road, *Derby, in the early 19th century and remained there until the 1830s. He was known for flower painting in a bright palette which included yellow, magenta and shades of red; his flowers were in bouquets and small sprigs, with, sometimes, a scattering of small sprays of flowers in addition to a central bouquet.
Refs: Haslam (1977); Honey (1952); Jewitt.

Leadbeater Art China. Staffordshire manufacturers of crested souvenir ware and ivory porcelain, working 1919-24 at Drury or Drewery Place, Longton, and established by Edwin Leadbeater (*see* Hewitt & Leadbeater). The firm made very small, hand-painted pieces, including models of monuments, until bankruptcy in 1924.
Ref: Andrews.

Leadbeater, Edward James. *See* Robinson & Leadbeater.

Leathley Lane Pottery, Leeds Union Pottery, Hunslet New Pottery, Stafford Pottery or Leeds Art Pottery. Yorkshire pottery established in Leathley Lane, Hunslet, Leeds, in

1824, known in 1830 as the Leeds Union Pottery and after its sale in 1832 as the Hunslet New Pottery. The works produced a varied output, including enamelled and underglaze printed earthenware, stoneware bottles, saltglaze and tiles. The pottery continued, through several changes in ownership during the 1840s and 1860s, to produce printed and painted earthenware, banded ware, and pieces with blue glaze and applied decoration in white. Joseph Wilson Taylor, proprietor from 1867, bought the works in 1871, changing the name to the Stafford Pottery. In 1890, the premises were taken over by J.W.*Senior's Leeds Art Pottery Co. The output of decorative tiles, hand-painted slipware and majolica then resembled the wares of the *Linthorpe and *Burmantofts potteries. The Leeds Art Pottery went into liquidation in 1900.

Mark: name or initials of the Leeds Art Pottery, printed.
Refs: Jewitt; Lawrence.

Lebeuf, Milliet & Cie. *See* Creil.

Le Comte, Adolf (1850-1921). Dutch designer, born in Geestbrug bij Rijswijk and trained at the Hoofdleraar Polytechnische School in Delft. His designs for De Porceleyne Fles, 1877-1919, included, notably, wall panels and small tile-pictures. He also provided designs for table services and developed new shapes and decoration for vases in the pottery's Berbas and Jacoba lines of earthenware.

Mark: initials, A.L.C.
Refs: 'Adolf Le Comte 1850-1921' in *Elsevier's Geillustreerd Maandschrift* 61 (1921); Scheen; Singelenberg-van der Meer; van Straaten.

Ledoux, Pierre-Nicolas. *See* Wood, George.

Lee, Frances E. English ceramic designer and decorator, working for *Doulton & Co. in Lambeth, c.1875-c.1890. She was known for finely incised and carved flowers and foliage, sometimes combined with thickly painted slip. She also introduced a decorative technique combining stamped decoration with other types of relief.
Refs: see Doulton & Co.

Lee, Joseph. *See* Northfield Pottery.

Leeds Art Pottery. *See* Leathley Lane Pottery; Senior, James Wraith.

Leeds Fireclay Co. *See* Burmantofts.

Leeds Pottery. Yorkshire earthenware pottery operating at Jack Lane, Hunslet, a mile to the south of the city of Leeds, from 1770. Members of the *Green family, partners in the firm Hartley, Greens & Co., running the Leeds Pottery, also worked the *Swinton Pottery under the title Greens, Bingley & Co., 1785-1806. Creamware, which became the main output of the Leeds Pottery from 1780, was used to make skilfully pierced decorative pieces with light body and strong glaze from the late 1770s, plates with edges of interwoven strips of clay, dishes with handles formed from strips twisted together, and centrepieces incorporating figures. Small, free-standing figures were made from the 1790s in creamware,

some painted under the glaze, but the main production of figures was in pearlware, introduced in the late 18th century. Later reproductions of figures and the firm's underglaze-decorated Pratt ware were marketed in large quantities. *Slee's Leeds and the work of J.W.*Senior included large quantities of creamware, often mistaken for the 18th-century product, as well as these copies. Black basalt tableware, introduced c.1800, was in some cases moulded, e.g. teapots encircled with a pattern of strawberries or other relief designs. Finials were made in the form of a swan, lion, small dog, or human figure, as at other potteries. The firm also produced small quantities of white stoneware with relief decoration.

The pottery closed for a time after John Green's bankruptcy in 1800, but reopened by 1813 under the management of the potter Justus Christian Ruperti (later a partner, who remained until 1830) and book-keeper Robert Nicholson. After further financial problems, William Hartley (d 1820), Ruperti and S.*Wainwright Jr, remaining partners of Hartley, Greens & Co., sold the pottery, which was then run until 1834 by Wainwright, who was succeeded by Stephen Chappel, manager and (from January 1842) owner, until his death in 1848. Joined by his brother James, he worked under the title S. Chappel & Co.

In the 19th century, the pottery produced Batavian Ware, pearlware dipped in a *café-au-lait* glaze with white reserve panels printed or painted in underglaze blue or enamel colours; agate ware; pieces encrusted with particles of clay, usually in a band encircling jugs, bulb pots, etc.; lustre ware, sometimes with the decoration on a biscuit-coloured or, occasionally yellow glaze; mocha ware.

Richard Britton, formerly Chappel's clerk and owner of the pottery from 1849, made domestic earthenware, including pearlware as well as brown-glazed ware, in partnership with Samuel Warburton (d 1863), then alone until 1872, when his sons John B. and Alfred Britton joined, and the firm became Richard Britton & Sons. His sons also operated as J.B. & A. Britton at the same works. Both firms went bankrupt in 1878. The pottery was then empty until taken over by Taylor brothers in 1881 and run briefly by J.W.*Taylor before it closed permanently.
Refs: Honey (1962); Hurst; Lawrence; Towner (1957, 1963) and 'The Leeds Pottery and its wares' in *Apollo* 65 (May 1957).

Leeds Union Pottery. *See* Leathley Lane Pottery.

Lees, Thomas. *See* Deptford Pottery.

Lefèvre, Jérôme. *See* Monnerie factory.

Leffler, Claude. *See* Denver China & Pottery Co.

Legros d' Anisy, François-Antoine (1772-1849). French porcelain decorator, born in Anisy-le-Château (Aisne). Legros d'Anisy, formerly employed at Sèvres, invented a ceramic printing process, using coated filter paper pressed on the piece and fired at a low temperature. He entered into partnership

with John Hurford Stone and his brother-in-law, Athénase-Marie-Martin Cocquerel, formerly partners in the Creil factory, and with them took out a patent in 1808 for transfer printing on ceramics and other materials by Legros d'Anisy's method. The partners worked at rue du Cadran in Paris. Legros d'Anisy continued alone from 1818, moving his workshops several times by 1834. His delicate, detailed decoration included illustrations of La Fontaine's fables, portraits, architectural subjects and views and historical and military scenes.

Marks: on Creil ware, STONE/COQUEREL/ET LE GROS/PARIS in a circular mark that incorporates *Manufre de Décors aux Porcelaine Faïence* .
Ref: Lesur (1971).

Leidy, John (1780-1838). Pennsylvania German potter, son of a tanner, making slip-decorated earthenware in Franconia, near Souderton, in Montgomery County, using both *sgraffito* and trailed slip decoration; known examples of his work, plates decorated with tulips surrounded by inscriptions at the rim, date from the late 18th to early 19th centuries. Leidy was succeeded on his retirement from the pottery (to work as a tanner) c.1815 by John Groff, who carried on the business, probably until c.1832.
Ref: Barber (1970).

Emile Lenoble. Stoneware vase with incised decoration, 1911-13.

Lenoble, Emile (1876-1939). French artist potter. After he had studied the techniques of faience, Lenoble worked from 1904 at Choisy-le-Roi with E.*Chaplet, whose daughter he married. Lenoble made stonework sometimes thrown in a very light, even body containing kaolin, and decorated with arabesques, flowers, or incised in body or slip, modelled in low relief or painted in enamel or underglaze colours, perfectly adapted to the form and showing great freedom of line. From c.1907, influenced by Sung Chinese and Korean ceramics, in the collection of his friend, Henri Rivière, he made high-fired bowls, cylindrical vases, painted in black, beige or white on a slip engobe, or over the glaze. In 1913, he used a

Jacques Lenoble. Terracotta coloured stoneware vase with white enamel decoration. Marks include L, incised.

turquoise copper glaze, a darker blue, and a light green used with decoration in black; some glazes had a crackle effect. Lenoble became known especially for geometrical designs in relief, carved or modelled, and occasionally inlaid.

Mark: monogram of EL impressed in a circle.

Refs: Années 25; Baschet; Cox; Faré; Haslam (1977); Lesur (1971).

Lenoble, Jacques (1902-67) French artist potter; son of E.*Lenoble. He studied the techniques of country potters in the region surrounding Cannes and Vallauris, and joined a factory making kitchen ware. His own work consisted of painted tiles and panels, and vases, etc., modelled or carved with geometrical designs and richly enamelled or covered with clear or coloured glazes. Some pieces were fired at high temperatures and relied for decorative effect on the colour and texture of the glaze.

Refs: Céramique française contemporaine; Faré.

Lenox, Walter Scott (d 1920). American porcelain manufacturer. Lenox was an apprentice at the *Ott & Brewer factory and *Willets Manufacturing Co., and later head of Ott & Brewer's decorating department. In partnership with Jonathan Coxon, formerly superintendent of the Ott & Brewer works, he established the Ceramic Art Co. (1889) in Trenton, New Jersey. Lenox was in sole control from 1894 or 1896, and the firm was renamed the Lenox China Co. in 1906. Lenox China made Belleek ware in ivory-toned paste, less glossy than the original Irish Belleek, but highly translucent. Until 1906 the emphasis was on gift ware, but table services then became an increasingly important part of the firm's output. Dinner ware in simple, graceful shapes was sometimes transfer printed, or etched and acid gilt. A white porcelain marketed as Indian China was sold for decoration by outside decorators. As well as tableware and vases, the company produced menu slabs, candelabra, inkstands, parasol handles and trinkets such as thimbles. Belleek ware with relief decoration carved by decorator

Kate B. Sears, e.g. a spherical vase, glazed only on the interior, with relief design of children and lilies, was shown at the World's Columbian Exposition in Chicago (1893). A dish designed c.1890 in the form of a swan with raised wings remained for a long time in production.

The firm, noted for its restraint in design, concentrated on the purity of the porcelain paste, using rigid quality control in the inspection of ware for sale. An account of production in the late 1930s describes the careful filtering and cleansing of clay, feldspar and water before slip-casting and firing; sand-blasting and cleaning with compressed air followed firing. Decoration was carried out over the glaze by acid etching, hand-colouring on etched or printed designs, and gilding.

During World War II, the firm produced insulating material and laboratory ware, using steatite, and components for instruments, using the standard porcelain paste. The Lenox name now covers a group of companies manufacturing bone china, glass, ovenproof wares, and a variety of other products. Porcelain is made at Pomona, New Jersey.

Marks include a wreath enclosing THE CERAMIC ART Co/TRENTON N.J. or, later, the initials of Lenox China Co. over LENOX; a painter's palette with the company's initials; the head of a brave with the words *Indian China* and, again, initials.

Refs: Barber (1976); Clement (1944); Cox; D. Robinson & B. Feeny *The Official Price Guide to American Pottery & Porcelain* (House of Collectibles, Orlando, Florida.).

Lenz family. *See* Zell.

Léonard, Agathon (b 1841). Léonard Agathon van Weydeveldt, sculptor and ceramic modeller, born of Belgian parents and naturalized French. Léonard studied in Lille (Nord), before working in Paris. He became a member of the Société des Artistes Françaises in 1887 and the Société Nationale

Walter Scott Lenox. Silver-mounted tankard in porcelain made by the Ceramic Art Co., 1894-96. 15.7 cm high.

des Beaux-Arts in 1897. He modelled a table centrepiece of fifteen dancing figures, Le Jeu de l'Echarpe, for production in biscuit porcelain at the Sèvres factory, c.1900. The figures, inspired by the American dancer, Loïe Fuller, were exhibited in the Exposition Universelle of 1900 in Paris, and later reproduced in bronze.

Mark: signature, *A. Léonard.*

Refs: Bénézit; Brunhammer *et al* (1976); Camart *et al*; A. Fay-Hallé 'Première Période, 1800-1847' in *Porcelaines de Sèvres au XIXe Siècle* (Musées Nationaux, Paris, 1975).

Leonardi, Leoncillo (1915-68). Italian ceramic sculptor. Leoncillo studied in Perugia and Rome, and exhibited at the Seventh Triennale in Milan (1940) and the first Venice Biennale (1948). His work consisted of figures, at first realistic, but increasingly abstract in the course of his career, in brightly glazed earthenware. He also made monumental and architectural pieces.

Ref: Préaud & Gauthier.

Leopard skin. *See* Pope, Frank.

Lepeltier, Odette (b 1914). French sculptor and ceramist. Lepeltier studied painting at L'Ecole des Beaux-Arts and, in 1937, under C.*Guéden at the Atelier Primavera. From 1944, she concentrated on sculptural ceramics: mirror frames, figures, etc., in terracotta or glazed earthenware. La Coquette, a monumental figure, was acquired by the Musée d'Art Moderne in Paris. Many decorative pieces by Odette Lepeltier were religious or allegorical in inspiration.

Refs: Céramique française contemporaine; Faré.

Le Pere Pottery. *See* Herold, Otto.

Lerat, Jean (b 1913) and Jacqueline (b 1920). French studio potters. Jean Lerat studied wood-carving at l'Ecole des Beaux-Arts in his home town, Bourges (Cher), from 1926. He later began making salt-glazed stoneware figures, tobacco jars and other pieces influenced by H.-P.-A.*Beyer, in whose studio he worked at La *Borne from 1941, with his wife Jacqueline Lerat, who had studied in Paris. Their output of vases, sculptural pieces, etc., was modelled, or thrown and subsequently shaped by hand, into free forms, almost always coated in slip. In 1955 the Lerats moved to Bourges, where Jean Lerat became a teacher in the ceramics department of l'Ecole Nationale des Beaux-Arts et des Arts Appliqués a l'Industrie; several of his students went on to make stoneware at La Borne.

Refs: Céramique française contemporaine; Faré; Lesur (1971); Préaud & Gauthier.

Leroy, Désiré (1840-1908). French-born porcelain decorator, born at Les Loges (Eure-et-Loir). Leroy is thought to have trained at the Sèvres factory from the age of eleven. Working in England from the 1870s, and at the *Minton factory c.1874-90, he painted many of Mintons important services. Leroy specialized in exotic birds and flowers, and also carried out painting in white on blue or turquoise grounds in the style of Limoges enamel. At the *Derby Crown Porcelain Co. from 1890 until his

*Agathon Léonard. Figures from Le Jeu de l'Echarpe modelled by *Léonard and exhibited in Paris, 1900. These pieces range from 46 cm to 53.5 cm high; base 28.5 cm high.*

death, he became art director, working in his own studio at the factory, and, with two assistants, continued painting in white enamel on grounds of dark blue, turquoise or rose. His designs, varied and usually elaborate, included birds in a landscape setting, fruit and flowers, musical trophies, and figure subjects. Leroy painted a dessert service for Princess May of Teck.
Refs: Aslin & Atterbury; Twitchett (1976).

Lesme, Jules. French ceramist making decorative porcelain at Limoges from 1852. Lesme was unusual in not specializing in useful ware, as did the majority of Limoges porcelain makers. His work included imitations of *Palissy ware in lead-glazed porcelain c.1860-70, and copies of Chinese wares from Canton. He also carried out the development of new ground colours, for which he took out patents in 1853. The Lesme family had earlier established a decorating studio at Limoges in 1839, employing 38 workers by 1844.
Marks: several signatures and monograms *J. Lesme*, J.L.; pseudo-Chinese marks; a version of the English *diamond mark.
Refs: Brongniart; d'Albis & Romanet; Ernould-Gandouet; Lesur (1971).

Lessell or **Lassell,** John (c.1871-1925). Potter and designer born in Mettlach (Rhineland). Working in America, Lessell became head of the decorating department of a Pennsylvania tableware manufacturer, Ford City China Co., until 1899 and later moved to Jersey City, New Jersey. In 1903 he was employed by the Bohemian Pottery, producers of domestic ware at Zanesville, Ohio, and helped to establish the *Arc-en-Ciel Pottery. As foreman of J.B.*Owens pottery, in 1905 he developed lines decorated with iridescent glazes. He formed his own firm, the Lessell Art Ware Co., at Parkersburg, West Virginia, in 1911 and exhibited art pottery, in forms which appeared to be made of riveted sheets of copper and bronze, in the New York showroom of W.H. Dunn & Co. within a few months, but his firm was dissolved in 1912. While working as designer

for S.A.*Weller in the early 1920s, he created lines which included Chengtu, Lamar, LaSa and Marengo. In 1924, he became head pottery expert of the newly-formed Art China Co., manufacturing decorated tableware in porcelain and semi-porcelain at Zanesville, moving with the firm to West Newark, Ohio, shortly before his death.
Mark: signature, *Lessell JH*, on work for Owens and Weller.
Refs: Evans; Kovel & Kovel.

Lessore, Emile (1805-76). French-born painter and ceramic decorator. Instead of following his father's profession as a lawyer, Lessore entered the studio of Ingres briefly and worked as an artist in oils and watercolour from the time of his first exhibition in Paris in 1831 until 1850. His first paintings on porcelain were carried out for the Sèvres factory, where he worked from 1851 until a visit to England in 1858. Lessore worked briefly at Mintons before joining the Wedgwood factory, where he was employed until his return to France in 1863. While at Mintons, he specialized in the decoration of majolica plaques, vases, etc., often basing designs on the work of Old Masters (e.g. copies of Raphael). At Wedgwood, his work included mythological scenes featuring cupids, and religious themes, e.g. The Last Supper and The Crowning of Christ. He was soon to change to a more relaxed style, using muted, delicate colours and free brushwork in his painting, often of figure subjects. With the development of his mature style, Lessore began to concentrate on scenes of contemporary life, children with their pets, family groups in outdoor settings, etc. Living near Fontainebleau after his return to France, he continued to send work for firing at the Wedgwood factory until the time of his death. Pieces, often signed, were included in Wedgwood displays at the International Exhibition in London (1862), the Exposition Universelle in Paris (1867) and in Vienna (1873). He also decorated blanks from the Davenport factory.
Lessore's grand-daughters were L.*Powell, and Thérèse Lessore (1884-1945) also a decorator, working independently for Wedgwood and painting in a style resembling that of Toulouse-Lautrec; she married Walter Sickert in 1926.
Mark: signature, *E. Lessore.*
Refs: Aslin & Atterbury; Atterbury (1980);

Batkin; H. Buten *Wedgwood & Artists* (Philadelphia, 1960); Godden (1964); Jewitt.

Le Tanneur, Pierre. *See* Haviland, Robert.

Letts, Joshua. *See* Warne & Letts.

Leube, Hermann. *See* Reichmannsdorf.

Leuchovius, Sylvia (b 1915). Artist potter working on an exclusive contract for the *Rörstrand factory and known for the making of wall-plaques, and slabs, often in stoneware containing a high proportion of chamotte, but delicate in effect. Her work also included dishes and vases in simple shapes with sparse decoration.
Refs: Beard; *Three Centuries of Swedish Pottery: Rörstrand and Marieberg* (catalogue, Victoria & Albert Museum, London, 1959).

Leuconoë. *See* G.D.A.

Leurs, Johannes Karel (1865-1936). Dutch artist trained in his home city, The Hague. He worked in the 1890s as a decorator at *Rozenburg and at the *Holland factory, where he designed and decorated vases.
Mark: initials JL, underlined.
Refs: Scheen; Singelenberg-van der Meer.

Levy, Col (b 1933). Australian potter, born in Sydney and trained 1951-52 at the East Sydney Technical College. Levy worked with I.*McMeekin at the Sturt Crafts Centre workshop in Mittagong, before opening his own pottery at Bowen Mountain, west of Sydney, in 1963. His preoccupation with the effects of firing have led him to explore the traditions of *Bizen ware.

Lévy-Dhurmer, Lucien (1865-1953). French Symbolist painter and ceramist, born in Algiers. Lévy-Dhurmer studied lithography, porcelain decoration, ceramics and design in Paris (1879) before becoming artistic director at the factory of C.*Massier in 1887. A collector of Middle-Eastern ceramics, he worked with Massier on the rediscovery of lustre glazes. His own ceramics were generally either in pale earthenware highlighted with gold, or in stoneware with muted glazes. Simple forms, usually inspired by Islamic styles, were sometimes decorated with ornamental handles or designs in relief. Painted or modelled motifs included plant forms, peacock feathers, landscapes, and female figures; Arabic characters also occur. Lévy-Dhurmer ended his collaboration with Massier in 1859, when he left for Italy, subsequently working as an artist, notably in pastels.
The painted signature *L. Lévy* is found with Massier's mark on certain pieces, probably from the last three years of collaboration.
Refs: Autour de Lévy (catalogue, Galéries du Grand-Palais, Paris, 1973); Battersby (1969a); Bénézit; Brunhammer *et al* (1976); Camart *et al*; Heuser & Heuser.

Lewis, Arthur. Porcelain painter working in *Worcester. After painting subjects, such as storks in landscapes, and iris flowers, for J.*Hadley, he joined the Royal Porcelain

Co. but left c.1930, soon before his death in his early fifties.
Ref: Sandon (1978a).

Lewis, Florence E. (d 1917) and Esther. English ceramic designers and decorators. Florence Lewis worked for *Doulton & Co. at Lambeth in 1875, after studying at the Lambeth School of Art. She was noted for paintings of flowers, foliage and birds on a wide range of wares, especially Lambeth Faience. Her work included a tea service decorated with primroses and purchased by Queen Victoria in 1887. After 1897, when she received a legacy, Florence Lewis ceased full-time work for the firm, travelled widely and exhibited watercolours and oil paintings regularly at the Royal Academy. She was responsible for the training of a number of decorators for Doulton & Co., and her book, *China Painting*, was published by Cassell & Co. in 1883.

Her sister, Isabel Lewis, worked at the Doulton studio until 1897. Esther Lewis, possibly a sister of Florence and Isabel, was employed by Doulton & Co. as a painter, specializing in landscapes, from 1877 to 1897. She was a prolific painter of tile panels. Esther Lewis also participated in exhibitions held by *Howell & James, and painted in watercolour. John Sparkes, in his account of Lambeth artists, described her work on Lambeth Faience as '…entirely satisfactory as broad, breezy representations of nature in quiet grey and warm tones.'

Marks: monogram of FL on Faience c.1875-c.1898; monogram of IL on Faience c.1876-c.1898; monogram of EL or signature on faience, impasto and Carrara wares c.1880-c.1895.
Refs: Callen; Dennis (1971); Eyles (1975).

Lewis, James Henry (b 1858). English porcelain painter and designer. After working at the *Coalport factory, Lewis joined the *Worcester Royal Porcelain Co. 1873-90 as a landscape painter, also carrying out gilding, including raised work. He was a watercolour artist and published a book of pencil drawings, *Designs and Adaptations*, in 1896. His son Percy worked as a gilder at the Worcester factory until his retirement in 1969.
Mark: signature, *J.H. Lewis*.
Refs: see Coalport; Worcester.

Lewis, Mabel G. *See* Doat, Taxile.

Lewis & Gardner. *See* Huntington Pottery.

Lewis Pottery Co. American pottery established by Jacob Lewis in 1829 near Louisville, Kentucky, for the production of high-quality cream-coloured earthenware from local clays. J.*Vodrey joined the company until 1939 when he moved to Troy, Indiana. The firm disbanded after failing to produce an output of consistently good quality. Lewis was subsequently a partner in the *Indiana Pottery Co.
Ref: Barber (1976).

Leyland, William. *See* Hirstwood, Haigh.

Liberty & Co. London retailers founded in 1875 by Arthur Lasenby Liberty (1843-1917), who sold Japanese blue and white porcelain, Indian silk, oriental *objets d'art* and, later,

items of interior decoration and costume in Regent Street. Selling English metalwork from the 1890s, as well as other European decorative items, Liberty's became associated with design in Art Nouveau style (also known as *stile Liberty*). The firm sold art pottery, often hand-thrown and featuring experimental or distinctive glaze effects, lustre decoration, *sgraffito* patterns, or other hand-executed techniques, by makers who included H.*Tooth, W.*Ault, the *Burmantofts Pottery, the *Foley Potteries, C.H.*Brannam, the *Aller Vale Pottery, *Pilkington's Tile & Pottery Co., Liberty's friend W.*Moorcroft, the *Della Robbia Pottery, the *Harris family and the *Compton Pottery. Later, they sold work by *Doulton & Co., *Wedgwood, and the Poole Potteries of *Carter & Co. and *Carter, Stabler & Adams.
Ref: Anscombe & Gere.

Liberty Cup, The. *See* Müller, Karl.

Lichte. German pottery established in 1804 at Lichte, near Wallendorf in Thuringia, by Johann Heinrich Leder. The firm produced stoneware as well as blue and white porcelain (mainly cups) and white-glazed tobacco pipes. After its purchase by Wilhelm Liebmann in 1830, the factory produced pipes and, after the removal of the monopoly of nearby Volkstedt in 1832, tableware in a porcellaneous body which Liebmann had developed. In 1843, the factory was sold to Christoph and Philipp Heubach (*see* Heubach family). Production of utilitarian tableware was extended c.1850 to include toys, small ornamental items and decorative pieces with painted decoration. During reorganization of the factory in 1898, the firm set up an art department, commissioning designs by established artists. Animal figures were modelled by H. Krebs, Christian Metzger, William Neuheuser and Paul Zeiller, and the production of figures lasted until after World War I. The decorators Louis and Albert Scherf became known c.1900 for portraits painted on decorative porcelain.

Limbach. Mirror frame with flowers and cupids in relief and birds painted in cartouches, late 19th century. Mark: crossed swords and star. 54 cm high.

The factory, nationalized in 1945, makes dolls' bodies and heads, as well as electrical wares, and operates as part of the national art porcelain manufacture, based in Lichte.
Marks include H and a candle symbol (*Licht* is German for light), sometimes with HEU/BACH, printed.
Refs: Danckert; Scherf.

Lidköping. *See* Rörstrand.

Lieber & Hoffmann. *See* Gera.

Liebmann, William. *See* Sitzendorf.

Ligna ware. *See* Bretby Art Pottery.

Liisberg, Carl Frederik (1860-1909). Danish sculptor and painter, working 1885-1909 at the Royal *Copenhagen Porcelain Factory, both as a modeller of figures and as a painter. He introduced a technique of painting in coloured porcelain slips in the late 1880s, and in 1892 gave details of his methods to the *St Petersburg factory.

Mark: monogram of CFL.
Ref: Danckert.

Liisberg, Hugo. *See* Krebs, Nathalie.

Limbach. German porcelain factory established 1772 by Gotthelf Greiner (*see* Greiner family) in Limbach, Thuringia, for the production of tea and coffee wares, figures, etc., By 1800, the factory was in the hands of Greiner's sons Johann Jakob Florentin Greiner and Michael Gotthelf Greiner, who continued the large output of blue and white ware. The factory also produced faience from 1813. Porcelain of the early 19th century was lavishly gilded, and some decoration (e.g. landscapes), was carried out in gold. Decorative subjects also included portraits. Later work increasingly consisted of mass-produced utilitarian ware, but the making of figures (mainly animals) was resumed in the late 19th century. The Limbach factory S.A. was regarded as successor to the Greiner factory. It ceased operation in 1944.

Marks include a single initial L (or sometimes two, crossed), and open imitations of Meissen marks in the late 18th and early 19th centuries; a clover leaf after 1788. The later factory used various clover-leaf marks, often incorporating a crown and the place name.
Refs: Danckert; Ducret (1962); R. Graul and A. Kurzwelly *Altthüringer Porzellan* (Leipzig, 1909); Haggar (1960); Hannover; Honey (1952); Scherf; Ware.

Limoges (Haute-Vienne). French centre of porcelain production which developed after the discovery of kaolin deposits at Saint-Yrieix, about 40 kilometres to the south in 1769. Factories in operation by the early 19th century included the business managed by F.*Alluaud from 1788 and bought by him ten years later. Early Limoges porcelain was rarely marked and followed the styles prevailing in Paris. After the Revolution some factories (e.g. *Pouyat) moved from Paris to Limoges, retaining studios in the capital, and at the time of Napoleon III, half the French porcelain manufacturers were working in the Limoges area. Those operating by the 1860s included: P.*Tharaud (1817), D.*Haviland (1855), F.& A.*Lanternier (1855), L.*Bernardaud & Cie (1863), M.*Aaron, and a branch of *Utzschneider. Design and decoration were carried out by skilled artists, such as P.*Comoléra for Pouyat, often in Paris. The products, in general utilitarian, were little exhibited before 1863, when a large display was shown in New York, and large quantities were exported to other European countries and, especially, America.

Few owners were able to continue work during the Franco-Prussian War (1870-71); Alluaud, P.-J.*Gibus and C.F.*Haviland were among those who could. However, the industry started artistic and technical development again after the war. Tableware was still the primary output but makers began to include luxury wares in their production c.1890. They adopted the newly fashionable Japanese elements, particularly the use of an isolated natural motif—seaweed, fish, a single flower—as a focus in decorative designs.
Refs: d'Albis & Romanet; Chavagnac & Grollier; Ernould-Gandouet; Grellier & Leroux.

Limoges China Co. *See* Sterling China Co.

Limoges faience. *See* McLaughlin, Mary Louise.

Lincoln Pottery Co. *See* Carr, James.

Lindberg, Stig. Swedish designer and ceramic decorator. Lindberg was a designer (1937-49) at the *Gustavsberg factory before succeeding W.*Kåge as artistic director. His designs included utilitarian ware, vases, etc., and sculptural pieces in a wide range of materials, e.g. stoneware, chamotte, earthenware and bone china. His decorative techniques included glazing in light, bright colours (sometimes over bands of incised hatching), and colourful painting of naive or surrealistic figures, abstract patterns, etc., as well as the use of small impressed motifs and abstract low-relief designs; some later pieces are in the form of bottles with outstretched or uplifted arms and stoppers in the shape of heads. Lindberg also made slab-built figures, and slip-cast pieces in unglazed porcelain. He became a teacher of arts and crafts in Stockholm.
Refs: Danckert; Lagercrantz; Lane.

Lindeman, Henry John (1872-1948). Australian potter, born in Sydney. Lindeman worked first as a book illustrator, turning to china painting and then to potting, in which he was largely self-taught, although he had some training at Sydney Technical College and, later, at East Sydney Technical College in the 1930s. Some of his painted decoration echoed earlier drawings (e.g. of butterflies) for book illustrations. He also made pieces in simple shapes derived from the Chinese (or from European versions of them, such as the Sung ware of *Doulton & Co.) with blue or red monochrome glazes. He sent all his

Henry John Lindeman. Earthenware vase painted with yellow roses on a blue ground, c.1920. 21 cm high.

work for firing outside his workshop, initially at the East Sydney Technical College.

Lindig, Otto (1895-1966). German sculptor and artist potter, born in Pössneck, Thuringia. Lindig trained as an artist and modeller (1912-13) and then studied sculpture (1913-15) at the Staatliche Kunstgewerbeschule in Weimar, under H.C.*van de Velde and Richard Engelmann. After his military service, he joined the Bauhaus, training (1920-22) in the ceramic department at Dornburg under G.*Marcks, and became technical director of the Bauhaus pottery, 1922-25. He taught in Dornburg from 1925-30, becoming head of the ceramics department.

Lindig was instrumental in developing the Bauhaus ideals of respect for material. He

Otto Lindig. Pieces made in stoneware at the Bauhaus workshop in Dornburg, c.1935.

was inspired by the need to provide practical, well-designed vessels for general domestic use, relying on simple shapes in the Thuringian tradition of form without ornamentation ('*Form ohne Ornament*'), and concentrated on the production of hard earthenware or stoneware, allowing as his only decoration simple glaze effects and the marks left by throwing (although some of his later pieces had horizontal lines painted under the glaze at the shoulder). He valued moulded forms as highly as unique hand-thrown pieces, and his shapes are characterized by sharp, convex rims, made possible by his use of a hard-fired body. His designs included large coffee pots, vases, jugs, pitchers, etc., characterized by a rounded form and flared neck. He also designed tall, graceful shapes, e.g. a tall, covered pitcher in earthenware with purple-flecked glaze and silver mount, dating from 1922-23. He leased the Bauhaus pottery for his own use, 1930-47, then becoming head of a ceramics class at the Hochschule für bildende Künste in Hamburg until 1960.

Mark: various monograms of OL.
Refs: Bock; Forsyth; Hettes & Rada.

Lindley Moor Potteries. Yorkshire pottery established at Salendine Nook, Lindley-cum-Quarmby, Huddersfield, and operated probably from the 17th century by a family named Morton, also owners of a pottery at Halifax. In the mid 19th century, a family quarrel resulted in the splitting of the pottery into two units; one was run by Joseph Morton and his sons, and known as the Lindley Moor Potteries until its closure in 1945, and the other was taken over by Enos Morton & Sons for the production of stoneware, and run in the early 1970s by Harold Morton. Both the potteries made traditional country pottery from local clay, specializing in domestic and horticultural ware, with some decorative pieces. The later output of Enos Morton's pottery consisted mainly of plant pots, bulb bowls, milk coolers and bread containers.
Refs: Brears (1971a); Lawrence.

Lindner, Doris. British sculptor, born in Llanyre, Radnorshire. Doris Lindner studied

sculpture in London and Rome, with particular emphasis on the modelling of animal studies. She worked on figures in porcelain for the *Worcester Royal Porcelain Co., starting with a range of dogs in 1931, and a series of animals at play in the 1940s. Her figures, which include racehorses, circus horses and a Santa Gertrudis Bull (modelled from life), are known for accuracy in detail, and the impression of movement they convey. Doris Lindner also works in bronze and stone.
Ref: Sandon (1978a).

Lindop, Hilda. *See* Moore, Bernard.

Lindstrand, Vicke (b 1904). Swedish glass and ceramics designer. His designs for pottery include simple forms which rely for decorative effect on glazes, and heavily textured pieces in the shape of fruits or vegetables.
Refs: Lagercrantz; H. Newman *An Illustrated Dictionary of Glass* (Thames & Hudson, London, 1977).

Lindstrom, Karl (1878-1933). Swedish porcelain modeller and decorator employed by the Rörstrand porcelain factory.
Mark: painted initials, KL.
Ref: Haslam (1977).

Links Pottery. Scottish pottery at Linktown, near Kirkcaldy, Fife. Founded in 1714 for the production of bricks and tiles, the works was under the control of the *Methven family from 1767 when the business was acquired by David Methven. The pottery was enlarged by his sons George and John in the 1830s to produce brown earthenware. John Methven's share passed to his nephew David Methven, who eventually took over the brick and tile business as well as the pottery, and produced creamware in large quantities from the 1850s. The ware, which was heavily potted, included pieces decorated by hand with simple floral designs in enamel colours, mainly dark red, shades of green and yellow, and marked with a sprig of heather and AULD HEATHER WARE, printed.
Other printed marks incorporate *Methven* or *David Methven*.
The pottery continued operation until the 1930s.
Refs: Fleming; McVeigh.

Linnell, Florence M. English ceramic designer and painter, working at the *Doulton & Co. workshop in Lambeth c.1880-85. She was known for the decoration of Lambeth Faience, including Impasto ware.
Refs: see Doulton & Co.

Linthorpe Pottery. English art pottery established on the site of the Sun Brick Works at Linthorpe village, Middlesbrough, by John Harrison, owner of the land, and by C.*Dresser, whose aims were to provide work in an area of low employment, and produce pottery that was functional, decorative and reasonably priced, as well as being consistent with his own ideas on design.
The success of a trial firing encouraged Harrison to build the factory, which became the first in Europe to use gas-fired kilns. H. *Tooth was appointed manager (1879-82); he was succeeded by Richard W. Patey, who had been in charge of modelling and design.

By 1885, Linthorpe employed 80-100 workers, some of whom went for further tuition to the Mechanics' Institute in Middlesbrough. Several workers had been engaged from Staffordshire potteries, and 14 from *Minton's Art Pottery Studio. The ware was at first made with brown brick-making clay, but white Cornish clay was in use from the mid 1880s for utilitarian ware and some of the later decorative lines. With the exception of early thrown pieces and one known slab-built box, the pottery was slip cast. Incised, impressed or slip decoration, or underglaze painting, were carried out when the clay was leather-hard, before the first firing at 1100-1200°C. Some of the pieces were left unglazed; transparent glazes were used over slip or painted patterns; other glazes were opaque, sometimes with mottled or running colours, or providing a matt surface on which enamels could be built up into a raised pattern. Some effects needed more than one glaze firing (at 1050-1120°C). The wide range of colours included violet, blue, orange and green. Some of the glazes were the result of experimentation by Tooth; early glazes had been brought from Staffordshire. Linthorpe was among the first potteries in 19th-century Europe to use glazes successfully as decoration in their own right. After Dresser's departure in 1882 or 1883, increasing emphasis was placed on decorated pottery, predominantly vases, but also including bowls, jugs, trays, tiles and plaques. Some vases had lizards or dragons entwined in pierced ornament, and other elaborate pieces included wall pockets in the form of butterflies with opened wings. A number of bowls and beakers were fitted with silver mounts, and ceramic handles were made for silver cutlery. Table and toilet wares were simple and restrained in design.
The factory, already suffering from rising costs, increasing competition and internal policy disagreements, closed after the owner's bankruptcy in 1889. An attempt to re-open in 1890 failed, and the factory's effect were sold in 1891.
The ware normally had several marks, showing the name of the pottery, the mould number, Dresser's signature (impressed, but not appearing on moulds numbered above 1700), Tooth's monogram (until 1882), the signature, monogram or initials of the artist, and a letter or symbol indicating the glaze used.
Refs: Blacker (1922a); *Christopher Dresser 1834-1904* (catalogue, Fine Art Society, London, 1972); *Christopher Dresser 1834-1904* (catalogue, Camden Arts Centre, London, and Dorman Museum, Middlesbrough, 1979); Coysh (1976); Grabham; Haslam (1975); Jewitt; Lawrence; J.R.A. Le Vine *Linthorpe Pottery: an Interim Report* (Teeside Museum & Art Galleries Service, 1970); Lloyd Thomas (1974).

Lion, Eugène (1867-1945). French ceramist. One of a family of potters making utilitarian stoneware at *St Amand-en-Puisaye. Eugène Lion was the last of the local potters to concentrate on throwing traditional utilitarian pieces. He continued the oriental inspiration in style introduced by his father Armand Lion, who studied under J.*Carriès. Eugene Lion's pupils included J.*Pierlot. His son, Pierre, is listed as having worked at St

Amand-en-Puisaye and at La *Borne.
Mark: incised signature.
Refs: Baschet; *Céramique française contemporaine*; Hakenjos; Haslam (1977); Lesur (1971).

Lion-Cachet, Carel Adolphe (1864-1945). Dutch designer and craftsman born in Amsterdam. He was among leading artists who provided designs for De *Distel factory in the late 19th and early 20th centuries and designed commemorative plates for De *Sphinx (1898). His work also included relief plaques and vases fired at De *Porceleyne Fles, De *Distel and *Goedewaagen. He was a member of 't*Binnenhuis and among pioneers in the use of patterns from Javanese batik fabrics in textiles (1880s), furniture (c.1900) and other media.
Mark: monogram of LC.
Refs: R.W.P. de Vries 'C.A. Lion Cachet' in *Elsevier's Geillustreerd Maandschrift* 43 (1912); Singlenberg-van der Meer; A. van der Boom *C.A. Lion Cachet 1864-1945* (Bussum, 1952).

Lippelsdorf. German porcelain factory established in 1877 at Lippelsdorf near Gräfenthal. Under the control of Kuch & Co. and a later firm, Wagner & Apel, the factory made figures of lace-clad dancers, children, animals, etc., boxes, vases with applied flowers (often roses and forget-me-nots) as well as smokers' requisites, everyday domestic ware and technical porcelain. The firm is now part of the VEB Gräftenthaler Porzellanfigurenwerke, which is associated with VEB Zierporzellanwerke Lichte.
Marks include W & A under a crown.
Refs: Danckert; Scherf; Weiss.

Lipp-Keramik. German pottery firm established by the Lipp family, of whom five generations operated the Meringer Kunsttöpferei, at one time also producing flowerpots. The founder of Lipp-Keramik, Georg Lipp (1832-93), was succeeded by his son Johann Lipp (1867-1948), who produced painted wares, thickly potted in simple shapes, resembling the output of the *Herrsching workshop. Lipp's painted designs included flowers, figures and patterns composed of geometrical motifs. In the 1920s, he was noted for coloured glazes which included orange and dark red. Ludwig Klopfer (1924-77), grandson of Johann Lipp, became owner of the workshop. He made many unique pieces and continued the use of coloured glazes, some flecked or shaded. The shapes remained simple.

Marks include a shield containing the monogram CFOM over MERING (C.F.O. Müller was Lipp's backer), impressed; initials J.L.M. impressed in script.
Ref: Bock.

Lipscombe, F., & Co. *See* Pearson & Co.

Litherland, William. *See* Derby; Worcester.

Lithgow Pottery. Australian pottery established 140 kilometres west of Sydney by the

Lithgow Pottery. Earthenware jardinière
with majolica glaze, c.1890. 131 cm high.

Lithgow Valley Colliery Co. with assistance
from Derbyshire emigrant J.*Silcock from
1879. The pottery developed as a department
of the company's brick production (established 1876) and by c.1882 developed under
a succession of managers a wide range of
bread plates, teapots, water containers,
fluted jugs, vases, cheese stands, jelly
moulds and other household ware with
mottled brown, ochre and blue glaze (sold
as 'majolica'), green or brown glazes. The
pottery also produced pieces in the white
with transparent glaze, and Bristol-glazed
ware. Decoration was moulded in low relief
and included inscriptions, such as 'Give us
this day our daily bread', ivy leaves, flowers,
and frequently fern leaves as all or part
of the design. The pottery failed to make a
profit and ceased in 1896, when the duty on
imported ceramics was removed, but was
briefly revived 1905-07 by Edward Arthur
Brownfield, an industrial chemist from
Cobridge in Staffordshire, who finished
existing stock and restarted production. The
colliery company's output of pipes, etc.,
continued, with figures of dogs intended as
garden ornaments or door stops as a sideline.
The figures, which resembled English comforter dogs (*see* Staffordshire dogs), were
made in pale clay with a black finish, or in a
reddish body with saltglaze. The company's
stock of tableware was cleared in 1946;
many of these pieces were decorated after
sale with a crazed, dull finish. Production
continued until 1973.

Marks: LITHGOW impressed; a variety of
circular marks with a kangaroo and the
name.
Refs: J. Birmingham (ed) *Lithgow Pottery*
(Sydney, 1974); I. Evans *The Lithgow
Pottery* (Flannel Flower Press, Sydney,
1980) and in *Craft Australia* I (1981).

lithography. A method of printing on ceramics using dilute nitric acid to remove
portions of a lithographic stone not protected
by a pattern drawn in resistant wax. The
design then left in relief on the stone is
printed in size or gluten on papers for transfer to ceramic surfaces, where it is dusted
with pigment for re-firing. The printing of
colours (chromolithography) is carried out
on separate sheets, normally in a progression
from dark to light shades, with time allowed
for drying between applications. The technique was first used on earthenware in
France under a patent, issued in 1839. F.-
M.*Honoré patented developments to the
process.

lithophanes. Panels of porcelain moulded
with patterns in *intaglio*, which became
clearly visible when held against the light.
    The technique was patented in Paris in
1827, and rights of manufacture in Germany
were purchased by Meissen. Both Meissen
and the Berlin factory produced lithophanes
from 1828. Berlin became the principal
producer, making 136,730 lithophanes during the following 30 years, and initiating
research to improve translucency. The
factory's designs included architectural
studies of Berlin, portraits (mainly of the
German royal family), copies of Teniers,
Rembrandt, Rubens, Ruisdael and modern
painters. English producers include *Belleek,
W.T.*Copeland, Grainger's *Worcester factory, and *Mintons Ltd. The largest examples of plaques, which were often mounted
in lead for hanging in front of windows,
measured about 15 x 20 cm. Lithophanes
were also used in lightshades and in plates
or at the base of cups, e.g. views of Karlsbad,
made by Bohemian factories.

Little, William. *See* Carpenter, Frederick.

Littlethorpe Pottery. Yorkshire pottery built
for the production of brick and tiles in the
early 1820s. The works remained in the hands
of its founders, the Foxton family, who
made brown earthenware (by 1834) and continued the production of bricks until 1904.
After its sale the pottery was leased to James
Green and then sold to a Mr Richardson.
The employees included four throwers,
chiefly making large garden pots, bread
crocks, huge conical bowls and drain pipes.
Throwers were N.*Taylor and Albert Kitson,
who was known for large pieces (bigware),
e.g. garden pots almost a metre high and a
metre in diameter. George Curtis, also
noted for throwing bigware, worked his way
up from clayboy to manager and was eventually owner of the pottery (1922-1970s); he
specialized in horticultural ware, plant pots
and garden urns in later years.
Refs: Brears (1971a); Lawrence.

Llanelli. *See* South Wales Pottery.

Lob, J.M. *See* Distel, De.

Locke, Edward (1829-1909). English porcelain painter, apprenticed at *Grainger &
Co., *Worcester, in 1845. His work included
pâte-sur-pâte treatment of floral subjects.
With his sons, he established works at Shrub
Hill, Worcester in 1895. The firm's work,
normally small in size, closely followed the
style of the *Worcester Royal Porcelain Co.

in flower painting, and the bird painting and
landscapes with animals carried out at
Grainger's works. The Royal Porcelain
Factory obtained a High Court injunction
preventing Locke from using the Royal
Worcester name and marks in 1902. His
firm ceased operation in 1904.
    Marks: signature on the base of Grainger
vases; *Locke & Co.* in a globe device.
Ref: Sandon (1978a).

Locker, William (d 1859). English porcelain
manufacturer. Locker was apprenticed at
the porcelain factory in Nottingham Road,
*Derby, in the time of M.*Kean and later
worked as clerk and warehouseman at the
factory. He led a group of workmen who
continued production of porcelain in King
Street, Derby from 1848, under the title
Locker & Co.
Refs: see Derby.

Locker, Thomas. *See* Carr, James.

Lockett, Frank. *See* Cartlidge, Charles.

Lockhart, David, & Co. *See* Victoria Pottery.

Lockyer, Thomas Greville (d 1935). Porcelain
painter working for the *Worcester Royal
Porcelain Factory from soon before World
War I until his death, with a break when he
was wounded in the war. Lockyer specialized
in paintings of fruit arranged against a
mossy background. He was also a watercolour painter and woodworker.
Ref: Sandon (1978a).

Loc Maria. French faience factory established in the late 17th century at Loc Maria,
Quimper (Finistère), was taken over in
1782 by Antoine de la Hubaudière (d 1794),
and continued by his family. The pottery reopened after a break in operation during the
Revolution and in 1807 produced stoneware
and a range of earthenware, including lead-
glazed pieces, tinglaze resembling Rouen
faience in style, figures of saints and dishes
decorated with religious symbols. Fougeray,
director in 1872, resumed production of the
factory's 18th-century wares, using the
original perforated paper patterns for the
application of pigment for armorial designs.
After prolonged financial difficulty, the
factory was taken over by another Loc
Maria faience workshop, Manufacture de la
Grande Maison, which was advertised as
founded in the 17th century. The flooding of
the Breton market with faience decorated
with regional heraldic emblems caused local
makers to identify their work with Quimper
by incorporating the place name in their
marks. Production ceased at the original
factory in 1914-15, but La Grande Maison
continued to make table and utility ware,
fountains, holy water stoups, religious
figures and a range of tobacco pipes, as well
as plates after Rouen faience. The firm now
makes glazed stoneware and a range of
earthenware, including faience.
    Marks usually incorporate the HB
monogram of the de la Hubaudière family.
    Other local factories using the rustic
decoration of stylized sprays of flowers,
spotted grounds and wide painted lines
characteristic of the household ware of the
Quimper area were founded e.g. by François
Eloury in the late 18th century. Beau &

Porquer, working in the late 19th century at a factory founded c.1705, decorated their work with scenes from Breton life.
Refs: Ernould-Gandouet; Lesur (1971).

Loebnitz, Jules. French potter. Proprietor from c.1857 of a Paris firm established by his grandfather, Pichenot Vogt (d 1849), for the production of stoves and tiles. From 1844, the firm had also made earthenware plaques, decorated with salamanders and other motifs in Renaissance style, or with copies of work by the Della Robbia family on blue or gold grounds, and Loebnitz extended its output of architectural wares. The decoration of tiles included adaptations of designs used on *Henri II and other earlier wares, as well as portraits. The firm fulfilled a commission to restore the tiles of the *château* at Blois. In 1881, Loebnitz established a branch at Charonne.

Marks include *Maison Pichenot, J. Loebnitz successeur,* and the firm's address; from c.1878 a variety of marks incorporating *Loebnitz.*
Refs: Ernould-Gandouet; Lesur (1971).

Löffler, Berthold (1874-1960). Painter, designer and graphic artist, born in Bohemia,and working in Vienna. After studying in Reichenberg, Löffler trained for nine years at the Vienna Kunstgewerbeschule. He was a co-founder of Wiener Keramik with M.*Powolny in 1905 and decorated many of the workshop's figures, including some modelled by Powolny. His work included vases and jars with geometrical patterns painted, sometimes over relief, in black, and also tiles.

Marks: initials BL; *BLö* or *Lö.*
Ref: Neuwirth (1974a).

Loket. *See* Elbogen.

London Decorating Co. *See* Crane, Walter.

London Pottery. *See* Stiff, James, & Sons.

Long, William A. (1844-1918). American art potter, chemist and painter; born in Ohio. Long worked as a druggist in Steubenville, and began experimenting with clay and glazes after seeing pottery in the Philadelphia Centennial Exhibition in 1876. He was joined after his first success by W.H. Hunter and the Steubenville potter Alfred Day, co-founders with him of the *Lonhuda Pottery. He entered into a partnership with S.A. *Weller early in 1895, for the large-scale production of Lonhuda Faience at Zanesville, but left Weller in the following year. He subsequently worked for J.B.*Owens (as art director in 1899) until c.1900, when he left to form the *Denver China & Pottery Co. (1901). Long moved to Newark, New Jersey, for the formation of the *Clifton Art Pottery, where he worked until his return to Ohio in 1909, then rejoining Weller as an employee. He was working at the *Roseville Pottery Co. by 1912, and for the *American Encaustic Tiling Co. in 1914. He died in Cincinnati.

Mark: monogram of WAL on Lonhuda ware.

Berthold Löffler. Earthenware putto *modelled by Löffler for the Wiener Keramik workshop, c.1912. 47.5 cm high.*

Refs: Barber (1976); Evans; Kovel & Kovel; Lehner; L. & E. Purviance & N.F. Schneider *Weller Art Pottery in Color* (Wallace-Homestead Book Co., Des Moines, Ohio, 1971).

Longpark Pottery. Devonshire pottery established in Longpark, Torquay, by 1883, for the production of terracotta. From the late 1890s, William and James Brewer, in partnership with Ralph Willott, made slip-painted table and decorative ware with a clear smooth glaze. The pottery was taken over by a new company of six local potters by 1906, and subsequently produced small, glazed domestic and ornamental pieces, continuing patterns introduced by the Brewers, as well as following those developed at the *Aller Vale and *Watcombe potteries, and generally using cream or dark green grounds. The company also used naturalistic studies of flowers, and originated its own slip designs, e.g. a riverside scene of ruined buildings silhouetted against a darkening sky. Among the details characteristic of Longpark ware are borders of repeating drops of blue and green or, occasionally, red and orange slip, and acanthus leaf stamps at the base of handles.

A company established as Royal Longpark Pottery Co. Ltd (Art) soon before World War I made art ware with coloured slip painting or relief decoration under translucent, coloured glazes in the manner of earlier work by C.H.*Brannam and was in operation until c.1923. After World War I, the pottery continued with the earlier patterns of a cockerel, a kingfisher and many flower subjects. The pottery closed during World War II and was afterwards acquired by the owners of the Watcombe Pottery, who produced patterns which had previously proved popular, e.g. Scandy (from Aller Vale), a black cockerel (a Brewer pattern),

studies of daffodils and cottages with mottoes. It closed in 1957.
Mark: LONGPARK/TORQUAY.
Refs: Godden (1964); Lloyd Thomas (1978).

Longwy (Meurthe-et-Moselle). French pottery started at the end of the 18th century in a Carmelite convent belonging to the family Huart de Nothomb. At first, firing was carried out at Senelle. The initial production included figures and decorative reliefs, and popular ware with revolutionary inscriptions. Napoleon commissioned a Legion of Honour service, decorated with bees, eagles and Imperial crowns, in 1808. In 1865, Fernand and Hippolyte d'Huart, whose family had inherited the pottery 25 years before, took over as managers. Both engineers, they opened new workshops and in 1875 started decorating earthenware with thick enamel in the *cloisonné* manner. The new branch of their production (Emaux de Longwy) was established by Amédée de Caranza, who left in the same year to work in Bordeaux. As well as the Emaux de Longwy with oriental or Middle Eastern motifs normally associated with the workshop, Longwy made tiles and majolica panels, and decorative pieces, e.g. Manon Lescaut and L'enfant aux pigeons (which was decorated and signed by the painter Eugène Carrière, brother of E.*Carrière). Soon before World War I, the *cloisonné* enamels were restyled in keeping with contemporary taste, but production ceased from 1914 until after the end of the war because of German bombardment. The pottery produced octagonal flasks, pilgrim bottles, boxes (round or triangular), many in Art Deco style with female nudes, sunset landscapes, stylized flowers, etc., and in the

Longwy. Earthenware beaker enamelled and gilt over glaze and white slip, made at Longwy before 1875. 14.5 cm high.

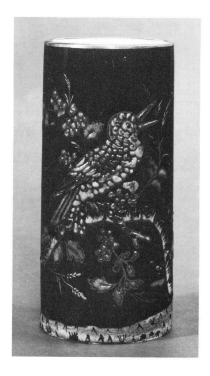

*Lonhuda Pottery. Ewer with decoration of
pansies painted in slip. 16.8 cm high.*

1920s, some for the Atelier *Primavera. The
name, Longwy, was used for brilliantly
enamelled ware sold at Le Bon Marché in
the 1920s. The factory ceased work from
1940 until the Liberation and now makes
fine earthenware, individual pieces and
publicity ware, as well as continuing the
production of Emaux, trading as Société des
Faïenceries de Longwy et Senelle.
    Marks incorporate *Longwy* and
sometimes the title of a line, e.g. *Henri II*.
Refs: Ernould-Gandouet; Lesieutre; Lesur
(1971); McClinton.

Lonhuda Pottery. American art pottery
established at Steubenville, Ohio, as a result
of successful experimentation in clays and
glazes carried out by W.A.*Long with W.H.
Hunter, editor of a local newspaper, and a
potter, Alfred Day, at Long's pharmacy.
The pottery began regular production of art
ware in 1892. The principal line was painted
under the glaze in slip under licence by the
technique developed by L.A.*Fry, who was
among the artists employed (1892-94). Decoration was also carried out by Sara R.
McLaughlin, Helen M. Harper, Jessie R.
Spaulding, and Long himself, in reds, browns,
yellows and greys on a yellow clay body.
The ware was made in simple, graceful
forms often derived from American Indian
pottery with the intention of developing a
characteristically American style. The
painted designs depicted Indians, famous
personalities, sea or landscapes, fish, birds
or other animals, and flowers. Clear or matt
glazes were used as well as the glossy brown
ground for which the pottery was noted. In
1895, production of the ware was transferred
to the Zanesville (Ohio) factory of S.A.
*Weller, who had been attracted to the
work shown in Chicago in 1893 and had
acquired an interest in the pottery in the
following year, and a new partnership, the
Lonhuda Faience Co. was briefly formed

before Long joined J.B.*Owens, leaving
Weller to continue the line as Louwelsa.
    Marks: monogram of LP CO below
LONHUDA, impressed; American Indian head
impressed from 1893, often with monogram
mark; LONHUDA over LF in a shield
outline used during Long-Weller partnership
(1895-96).
Refs: Barber (1976); Callen; Evans; Kovel
& Kovel; Lehner.

Losanti. *See* McLaughlin, Mary Louise.

Lotus. *See* Owens, John B.

Lotus ware. *See* Knowles, Taylor &
Knowles.

Louwelsa ware. *See* Weller, Samuel A.

Lovatt's Potteries Ltd. *See* Langley Mill
Pottery.

Low, John Gardner (1835-1907). American
tile maker, born in Chelsea, Massachusetts.
Low studied as a landscape painter and
spent the years 1858-61 in Paris. He joined
the *Chelsea Keramic Art Works c.1873 to
learn ceramic techniques while carrying out
his own experimentation. He designed red
ware, which included a large two-handled
urn in Grecian style now preserved in the
Museum of Fine Arts at Boston. In 1878,
financed by his father, John, he established
the J.& J.G. Low Art Tile Works in Chelsea,
with G.W.*Robertson as glaze technician
and A.*Osborne (from 1879) as artist and
designer; W.H.*Grueby was employed for
some years from c.1880. Tiles, first fired

*John G. Low. Two tiles with relief
decoration of flowers under deep green
glaze, c.1885. Each 19 cm square.*

successfully in 1879, were machine-pressed
by the dust process, or press-moulded in
plastic clay; hand-modelled tiles were undercut by hand after moulding to bring the
decoration into high relief.
    J.G. Low developed a method of manu-
facture, which he termed the 'natural'
process, moulding pairs of tiles, one with
intaglio impression of leaves, grasses,
lacework, etc., and another with the same
decoration in relief. Plastic sketches, a
speciality of the factory, were low-relief
plaques, up to 45 cm long, depicting animals, birds, portraits or groups of figures,
farm scenes on natural, mythological or
imaginary themes, nearly all designed and
made by Osborne. Ornamental tiles were
sometimes enclosed in ornate metal frames
made by the firm. Portrait panels included a
series of American presidents. The designs
were accentuated by coloured glazes developed by Robertson in yellow, white, red,
pink, blue and grey as well as the favoured
browns and greens, which collected in the
crevices.
    By 1882, the firm produced art pottery
jugs and vases with modelled decoration,
some by Osborne, and in the early 20th
century a regular line of Chelsea Ware vases,
recalling Japanese pottery in shapes and
glazes. Surfaces were generally undecorated
except by glazes in shades of brown or red,
or occasionally browns, greys, blues, greens
or yellows, which are combined two or more
on one piece. In 1889, J.G. Low patented a
design for a tiled soda fountain; an elaborate example was included in the firm's
work shown at the World's Columbian Exposition in Chicago (1893). At the retirement of John Low in 1883, his grandson
John Farnsworth Low, a ceramic chemist,
had joined the firm, which then traded as
J.G.& J.F. Low Art Tile Works. The company went into liquidation in 1907, but
operations are thought to have ceased some
time before.
Refs: Barber (1976); Evans; Kovel & Kovel;
Watkins (1950).

Lowe, Allan (b 1907). Australian potter,
born in Melbourne, where he set up a workshop in 1929. Ten years later he moved to a
studio at Mt Miller in Ferntree Gully. Though
Lowe attended classes in art schools and
technical colleges, his technique is essentially
self-taught, and he works exclusively in
earthenware. His early work was slip-glazed
and incised or carved in a manner inspired
by Aboriginal images and compositions. In
the 1930s, he experimented with modelled
forms, such as leaves and lizards, then produced by commercial potteries in Australia,
and with pierced decoration. Since the 1950s,
he has concentrated on simple shapes, primarily with monochrome glazes based on
those of Chinese wares, and specifically on
examples in the Kent collection in the
National Gallery of Victoria, where a retrospective of his work was held in 1979.
Refs: Craft Australia No 1 (1980);
G.Edwards *Allan Lowe – Pottery 1929-1979*
(Melbourne, 1979).

Lowe, Thomas. Painter of portraits and
figures for the *Worcester porcelain firm of
Flight, Barr & Barr. Lowe was a pupil of
T.*Baxter and succeeded him jointly with
S.*Cole as the factory's main figure painter

in 1821. He exhibited a portrait at the Royal
Academy in 1845.
Refs: Chaffers; Sandon (1978b).

Low Ford Pottery. *See* Dawson, John.

Low Pottery. Yorkshire pottery at Rawmarsh, making garden pots in the early 18th
century, and leased in the 1790s to John
Wainwright (d c.1830) and Peter Barker,
makers of white earthenware for domestic
use, who traded as Barker & Co. Wainwright
bought the pottery in 1810 and continued to
run it alone after 1812. The pottery was let
c.1833 by Wainwright's executors to a
company headed by Thomas Taylor, who
continued the production of white ware,
trading, in 1836, with his son, Elisha, and
partner, Robert Ask, as Taylor, Ask & Co.,
also proprietors of the Meadow Pottery,
Rawmarsh, where they made firebrick. Ask
operated the Meadow Pottery alone briefly
after the partnership was dissolved in 1838.
George Hawley (*see* Hawley family) took
over the Low Pottery, in 1840, buying it
nineteen years later. His son, also George
Hawley, ran the pottery alone from 1873
until his financial failure. His nephews,
Matthew and Arthur George Hawley,
bought back the works in 1884, changing the
name to the Rawmarsh Pottery, and produced sponged, printed or underglaze
painted ware, including tea services, toilet
sets, earthenware toys and miniature tea
and toilet wares. Matthew's sons Sidney and
John, who had succeeded their father in the
partnership, traded as Hawley Bros Ltd
from 1897, with John Hawley running the
former Low Pottery. The output consisted
of a range of domestic earthenware and
garden pots. The pottery passed to a syndicate under the title of Northfield Hawley
Pottery Co. in 1903, but was sold in the
following year and demolished in 1905.
Refs: Jewitt; Lawrence.

Loy-Nel Art. *See* McCoy, J.W., Pottery.

Lucas, Daniel (1788-1867). English porcelain
painter. After working at *Davenport's,
Lucas joined the porcelain factory in Nottingham Road, *Derby, by 1820, and became
the principal landscape painter until 1848.
His work, in a range of sombre, opaque
colours, resembled oil painting, and Lucas
was noted for his portrayal of light and
shade. He moved to Birmingham, where he
worked as a painter until his death. His sons
were apprenticed at the Derby factory: the
eldest John Lucas (d 1833) learned painting
under his father and went on c.1832 to the
*Swinton Pottery, where his work included
views of Waterloo, Chatsworth House, etc;
William, a gilder, later worked at *Mintons
before his early death; Daniel Lucas II
(b c.1818) was also a landscape painter,
working at *Coalport until 1860 and for
W.T.*Copeland, before establishing an
independent workshop in Longton, assisted
by his sons.
Refs: Godden (1970); Rice; *see also* Derby.

Luce, Jean. French designer and decorator;
retailer of ceramics and glass. From 1911,
Luce concentrated on the relation of ornament to form, using hand-painted or stencilled designs, sometimes naturalistic and on
other occasions stylized in Art Deco taste.
In completing designs commissioned by W.
*Haviland in the 1920s, Luce used gold and
platinum for stylized patterns of clouds
crossed by sun rays, and a geometrical arrangement of a hexagon extending to triangles
on the edge of a plate. His work is characterized by the combination of angular and
often asymmetrical motifs with curved
forms, e.g. flowers, clouds. His lines are
finely drawn, and the designs are often
enriched by the use of gilding. Luce sold
earthenware and porcelain tableware from
his own designs in his Paris shop.
Mark: two interlaced *Ls* in a rectangle,
painted.
Refs: Années 25; Baschet; d'Albis &
Romanet; Lesieutre.

Lucerni, Ugo (b 1900). Italian sculptor and
ceramist born in Parma and trained in Mod-
ena. He worked as a teacher from 1925 and
became director of the Italian Art School in
Tunis. He returned to work in Abruzzi and
subsequently Florence. He was commissioned
to provide decorations for buildings in Lausanne and the Liceo Italiano in Paris, and
his work includes coloured relief panels in
earthenware (portraits, etc.). Lucerni
settled to live and work in Florence.
Mark: LUCERNI.
Refs: E. Cerruti *Ceramiche di Ugo Lucerni
sculptore* (catalogue, Florence, n.d.);
Hettes & Rada; *Keramik* (catalogue,
Kunstgewerbemuseum der Stadt, Cologne,
1975).

Lüdicke, Karl Friedrich. *See* Rheinsberg.

Lukens, Glen (1887-1967). American ceramist and teacher. Lukens was born in Cow-
gill, Missouri, into a family of farmers, and
trained in agriculture in Oregon from 1921,
but began to study ceramics under M.
*French at the Chicago Art Institute, later
running a pottery course for the rehabil-
itation of servicemen wounded in World
War I. After moving to California c.1924,
he taught crafts to school children and became professor of ceramics at the University
of California architectural school in Los
Angeles in the mid 1930s until the 1960s,
apart from some years, starting in 1945,
during which he was involved in pottery
training in Haiti.
Lukens derived inspiration from the pottery of ancient cultures, e.g. that of New
Mexico. In his teaching, he advocated both
sensitivity to material and respect for traditions. He was inspired by Egyptian ceramic
jewellery, and experimented on the production of similiar low-fired pieces, using
alkaline minerals from the Death Valley
desert, which he exhibited, e.g. in San Francisco (1939). On simple forms, he used thick,
very glossy glazes, sometimes alkaline, in
turquoise, green or a strong yellow. The
names of a number of his own developments
in glazes were inspired by American deserts
from which some of his minerals were obtained, e.g. Mojave Golden Amber, Death
Valley Yellow, Mesa Blue. On some pieces,
Lukens glazed only the interior. A bowl
(1936) won the first prize for pottery at the
Fifth Ceramic National exhibition at Syracuse
Museum of Fine Arts in the year of its production. He was active in the promotion of
ceramics made in the western states of

*Edith Lupton. Jug with incised foliage and
applied studs in blue-green and brown on a
stippled buff ground, made at the *Doulton
& Co. Lambeth workshop, 1880. Marks,
incised artist's monogram and impressed circle
mark. With hinged metal cover, 26 cm high.*

America and shown in the first All-Cali-
fornia Ceramic Art Exhibition in 1938.
Refs: 'California Ceramics' in *Art Digest* 12
(March 1938); Clark & Hughto; Donhauser;
E. Lenin 'Arthur Baggs, Glen Lukens' in
Ceramics Monthly 24 (January 1976); G.
Lukens 'Ceramic Art at the University of
Southern California' in *Design* 38 (May
1937) and 'The New Craftsman' in *Design*
38 (November 1937); S. Peterson 'Glen
Lukens 1887-1967' in *Craft Horizons*
(March, April 1968).

Lundgren, Tyre. Swedish ceramic sculptor
and designer, active from the 1920s. She
worked at various times as a designer for the
*Rörstrand, *Arabia and Sèvres factories.
Her stoneware includes very thinly-potted
leaf-shaped vases and bowls, and stylized,
but lively, models of animals which include
feeding doves, birds among branches and
fish. Lundgren was a pioneer in the design
of relief panels for schools and public buildings in Sweden.
Refs: Cushion (1974); Hettes & Rada;
Lagercrantz.

Lunn, Dora. English studio potter working
in London, at Ravenscourt Park from c.1916,
and, later, Shepherd's Bush (1943-55).
Initially using earthenware, Dora Lunn
experimented with matt glazes on stoneware. Her work, in simple, graceful shapes,
includes tall vases with glossy monochrome
glazes, a stoppered ewer with ivory glaze,
and vases with speckled, matt effect.
Marks: RAVENSCOURT, printed, impressed
or incised (until 1928); DORA LUNN/POTTERY,
painted.
Refs: Forsyth; *Studio Year Book* (1919);
Wingfield Digby.

Lunn, Richard. English porcelain decorator and designer, working as art director at the porcelain factory in Osmaston Road, *Derby, 1882-89. Lunn was noted for his design of elaborate, costly pieces, which included dessert plates with raised gilding, vases made for presentation by the women of Derby to Queen Victoria on the occasion of her Jubilee in 1887 and the Gladstone service (1883), consisting of 26 pieces painted with Derbyshire views by G.*Holtzendorf and oval panels of flowers by J.*Rouse. Richard Lunn taught ceramics at the Royal College of Art in London from 1903.
Refs: see Derby.

Lupton, Edith D. (d 1896). English designer and decorator of stoneware at the Doulton & Co. workshop in Lambeth from c.1875. Her early work included vases and jugs incised with stylized floral designs, often extending over most of the surface. In the 1880s, Edith Lupton carried out *pâte-sur-pâte* decoration in a naturalistic style, and executed vases with fine perforated decoration. She is thought to have retired c.1890, but continued freelance work until her death.
    Marks: initials, EDL; a vase with painted flowers and incised borders, dated 1878, is signed with her full name and *Lambeth School of Art.*
Refs: see Doulton & Co.

Lurçat, Jean (1892-1966). French artist and designer, born in Brujères (Vosges). Lurçat studied under Victor Prouvé and worked as a painter, 1919-36. He was a leading designer in the French tapestry revival of the 1930s and 1940s. In the 1950s, he worked on ceramics made at the Saint-Vicens studios, near Perpignan. His designs included many dishes, jugs, etc. as unique pieces or in limited editions. He also produced murals, which included the Four Elements for a radio and television studio in Strasbourg (1959), another for the Saint-Vicens workshop (1961) and two in the year before his death for the Seine prefecture. His ceramic designs resemble those of his tapestries with

Jean Lurçat. Red earthenware plate with slip decoration in white on a brown ground, the base unglazed. Marks include Dessin J. Lurçat. *It was given by the Municipality of Perpignan to the City of Lancaster, c.1962.*

large areas of colour within sharp outlines and the themes are often based on animal symbolism.
    Mark: signature.
Refs: Lesur (1971); Préaud & Gauthier.

Luscian ware. *See* Doulton & Co.

lustre. A thin metallic film, often iridescent, applied as decoration on the surface of pottery or porcelain. The lustre technique was used on Islamic pottery in the Middle Ages and on Italian maiolica in the early 16th century. It was revived in Europe in the late 19th century. W.*De Morgan carried out experiments in an effort to reproduce the red lustres of Gubbio. He achieved success in the 1870s followed by other English manufacturers, such as *Maw & Co., *Craven Dunhill, and *Pilkington's Tile & Pottery Co. C.*Massier was producing lustre ware, also in the 1870s, in France, H.A. Kähler (*see* Kähler Ceramics) slightly later in Denmark and V.*Zsolnay in Hungary. Iridescent surfaces became a feature of decorative ware in Art Nouveau style, softer in effect than later Art Deco uses of lustre which sought a bright, metallic appearance.
    Lustre ware with simple patterns, quickly painted, sometimes in resist or transfer-printed, was produced in large quantities in England in the early 19th century and continued, particularly in Staffordshire and north-east England, where it became associated with Sunderland.
    Later industrial ware includes tableware painted by A. and L.*Powell for J. Wedgwood & Sons Ltd and by S.*Cooper for A.E. Gray & Co.

Lycett, Edward (1833-1909). English-born painter, potter and ceramic decorator who worked in America, after training in England while he was employed as a decorator at the factory of Copeland & Garrett, and at the *Battam workshop in London. Lycett painted facsimiles of Greek vases and prizes for distribution by the *Art Unions. His work was shown in the Great Exhibition (1851).
    He worked in New York from 1861, opening a decorating workshop, Warren & Lycett, where he employed 30-40 artists to paint and gild porcelain and furniture plaques, at first working on Greek patterns similar to the ones he designed in London, and soon developing his style of gilding from heavy bands and solid grounds to the delicate tracery with which his work is associated. Lycett's workshop also decorated tableware with monograms for clubs, hotels and individual buyers. After 1865, he provided facilities and instruction for amateur decorators and, leaving the decorating company under the supervision of his son William, he went to teach ceramic decoration at the School of Design in St Louis, Missouri, in 1877 and in Cincinnati the following year. He opened a decorating studio in East Liverpool, Ohio, working on blanks made by American potteries, including stoneware cups and saucers by H.*Laughlin, which were decorated under the glaze, also carrying out research into decorating techniques.
    In 1884, Lycett joined the Faience Manufacturing Co. and took over direction of the factory where he worked to improve bodies, glazes, forms and decoration. His designs included large vases in porcelain or granite

lustre. Two-handled jardinière *entirely covered in brilliant copper lustre. Made in Staffordshire, c.1810. 18.5 cm high.*

ware, resembling Persian or Moorish forms in style, with lavishly painted, modelled and gilded decoration. He developed a porcelain paste with high quality glaze and metallic lustre effects (*reflets métalliques* or *nacrés*) which captured the qualities of ancient Persian lustre glazes. After his retirement from the Faience Manufacturing Co. in 1890, he joined William Lycett's decorating studio in Atlanta, Georgia, and continued his research, notably into the use of metallic lustres on tiles, etc. During his career, he also decorated for the Jersey City Pottery and the Union Porcelain Works. He was regarded as an important figure in American ceramic decoration, having been directly concerned in the art there from 1861 until his death almost 50 years later.
    As well as William, his other sons, F. Lycett and Joseph Lycett, were decorators and teachers.
    Mark: signature, painted in red or gold.
Refs: Barber (1976); Evans; Kovel & Kovel.

Lynn, Jacob. *See* Baecher, Anthony W.

McBirney, D., & Co. *See* Belleek.

McCall, John. *See* Johnston, William; Port Dundas Pottery.

McClelland, Harry S. (d 1931). American potter. Employed at the *Peters & Reed Pottery from 1903, he was company secretary from 1909 and sole owner of the succeeding *Zane Pottery Co. after Adam Reed's retirement and death in 1922. On his own death, McClelland was succeeded as company president by his wife, who sold the pottery to L.*Gonder in 1941.
Refs: Evans; Kovel & Kovel.

McCoy, J.W., Pottery. American pottery established at Roseville, Ohio, by James W. McCoy in 1899. In production from the following year, the firm initially made only domestic ware, but soon introduced ornamental ware and employed about 100 workers by 1902. Mont Pelée, an art line introduced late in that year, with white body and black, slightly iridescent finish, was inspired by the discovery of an ancient treasure hoard on Martinique; much of the stock was destroyed in a fire in 1903. In 1906, McCoy introduced a line of *jardinières*, fern pots, umbrella stands, cuspidors, etc., with a matt green glaze resembling the one developed by W.H. *Grueby. Loy-Nel-Art ware, named after McCoy's sons, Lloyd, Nelson (N.*McCoy) and Arthur, was decorated by hand with embossed and incised designs and covered with glossy brown or matt green glazes. G.S.*Brush joined the firm in 1908. He took part in its reorganization in 1911, purchased the J.B.*Owens factory in Zanesville and traded at the Roseville factory under the title *Brush-McCoy Pottery Co. from the same year.

Mark: LOY-NEL-ART/McCOY impressed.
Refs: Evans; Kovel & Kovel; Lehner.

McCoy, Nelson (d 1945). American potter. In 1910, at Roseville, Ohio, he established the Nelson McCoy Sanitary & Stoneware Company, which operated at the same time as his father's J.W.*McCoy Company. The firm made kitchen utensils, churns, butter pots, etc., in stoneware (becoming a leader in that market) and from 1926 mass produced art ware. McCoy traded under the name of Nelson McCoy Pottery from 1933 and was

*William P. McDonald. Earthenware plaque of an American Indian Chief, painted by McDonald and produced by the *Rookwood Pottery, 1886. 28.5 x 59 cm.*

succeeded as company president by his nephew, Nelson McCoy Melich, in 1945. The firm was taken over by Mount Clemens Pottery Co. in 1967, and continued production of industrial art ware as late as 1972, when it became the Nelson McCoy Division of D.T. Chase Enterprises of Hartford, Connecticut. The output includes domestic ware, e.g. serving dishes, plantpots, ashtrays and cookie jars.

Marks: monogram of MC in 1930s, with USA or *Made in USA* from the early 1940s; *Mc Coy*, impressed in early 1940s, or embossed, 1940s-1960s; *McCoy/USA*, impressed 1940s.
Refs: Evans; Kovel & Kovel; Lehner.

McCredie, Nell (d 1968). Australian potter. After training in Brisbane, she established a studio in Sydney c.1930, where she taught a number of pupils. She went into partnership with her brother Robert in 1933 or 1934, and their joint venture was in full production by 1936. The studio's output, which included domestic ware and small animal figures, was fired at a workshop set up by Nell McCredie in Epping, sold at her Sydney studio, and shown in exhibitions held by the Society of Arts and Crafts and the Industrial Art Society. It was also sold at the Pylon Gift Shop in the Southern Pylon of Sydney Harbour Bridge. After Nell McCredie's death, her brother continued production until 1974.

Mark: name, *New South Wales* and monogram, sometimes with *Epping*.
Ref: Graham.

MacDonald, Edward C. *See* St John Stoneware Co.

MacDonald, James. *See* Avon Pottery.

McDonald, William Purcell (1865-1931). American ceramic designer and decorator. Born in Cincinnati, Ohio, he studied in the Graduate School of Design at the University of Cincinnati and worked at the *Rookwood Pottery from 1882 until his retirement in 1931. McDonald took charge of a workshop in 1894 and three years later led attempts to improve the quality of work among junior decorators. He succeeded A.R.*Valentien as head of the entire decorating department 1899-1902, subsequently becoming supervisor of the newly formed architectural department.

His work included a vase painted with a portrait of the chief of the Nez Percé Indians (1898); some pieces in Art Nouveau style, including a moulded vase (1900) with a female figure at the rim, matt-glazed, and a bookend in the form of an eagle (1931).

Marks: initials in capitals or script, W.P.McD. or monogram.
Refs: Clark & Hughto; Kovel & Kovel; Peck.

McDowall, Hugh. *See* Eagle Pottery.

Mace, Violet. *See* Poynter, Maude.

McGregor, D. *See* Tyne Main Pottery.

Macheleid, G.H.; **Macheleid, Triebner & Co.** *See* Volkstedt-Rudolstadt.

Machin, Arnold (b 1911). English sculptor, modeller and designer, trained at schools of

art in his home town, Stoke-on-Trent, and in Derby. He was apprenticed at *Mintons, and went on to paint figure subjects and flowers on porcelain. He studied on a scholarship at the Royal College of Art in London (1937-40), and first exhibited at the Royal Academy in 1940, becoming a member in 1956. He was the first figure modeller to be employed by J.*Wedgwood & Sons Ltd, and worked in a studio at the Barlaston factory from 1940. His work included large pieces in terracotta, and figures, groups and animal models, often humorous or whimsical in style, such as Bridal Group, Country Lovers, Ferdinand the Bull, Taurus the Bull, Cupid with Violin, as well as mythological subjects, portrayals of Roosevelt and Churchill, and a Madonna group. His other designs include relief panels, portrait medallions, and the decoration of jasper ware. He modelled cameo portraits for Coronation Ware (1953) and designed other commemorative pieces. In the 1950s, Machin taught in Stoke-on-Trent and London. He was engaged in the 1960s on the design of coins, for which he was awarded an O.B.E.
Refs: Batkin; Reilly & Savage.

McHugh, John (d 1892). Scottish-born potter working in Launceston, Tasmania, where he established a works c.1873 for the production of flowerpots, etc. He was succeeded by his sons, trading as McHugh Brothers, who made saltglaze and majolica alongside a staple output of drainage pipes, which was maintained after modernization of the works in 1918. A large output of ornamental ware made in the 1930s, and advertised as Autographed Art Pottery, included large figures of dogs, portrait jugs, plates with leaves in relief, and vases in simple shapes, all with variegated or mottled glazes. The production of art ware was not resumed after a temporary closure of the firm c.1940. McHugh Brothers Pty continued the manufacture of drainage ware as part of Humes Ltd from 1962.

Marks include *McHugh* incised in script.
Ref: Graham.

McInnes, John. *See* Derby.

Macintyre, James (d 1868). English potter working in Burslem, Staffordshire. In 1852, Macintyre went into partnership with his brother-in-law, William Sadler Kennedy, maker of artists' equipment from 1838, and house numbers, door furniture, etc., after a move to the Washington Works c.1847. Macintyre became sole proprietor soon after joining, and in 1863 took out patents for methods of turning non-circular shapes (oval, fluted, octagonal) on a lathe. He produced a cream-coloured body (which was marketed as Ivory China) and is thought to have been among the first producers of a black ware, which was made with brownish-red body under a dark cobalt glaze, and used for door furniture, ornamental inkstands, etc., sometimes gilded and enamelled. The firm continued as James Macintyre & Co. (Ltd), under a partnership formed by Macintyre's son-in-law William Woodall and the former manager Thomas Hulme (until Hulme's retirement in 1880), with an art pottery department headed 1897-1913 by W.*Moorcroft. The firm later specialized in the production of porcelain electrical fittings.

Mark: name or initials of the company, printed or impressed.
Refs: R. Dennis *William and Walter Moorcroft, 1897-1905* (Fine Art Society, London, 1973); Jewitt; Rhead.

McLaughlin, Mary Louise (1847-1939). American ceramic decorator, artist potter and porcelain maker, born in Cincinnati, Ohio. Her early work included underglaze painting in blue on white porcelain plates, which were made and subsequently fired at the *Union Porcelain Works, in 1875. After seeing the display of C.*Haviland's 'Limoges Faience' in the Centennial Exhibition at Philadelphia (1876), she experimented with

*James Macintyre. Vase designed by W.*Moorcroft in the manner of his Florian ware. Mark of the factory and Moorcroft's initials. 21.5 cm high.*

slip painting using Ohio clays and colours acquired from Paris, and having her work fired at the *Coultry Pottery. By January 1878, she developed a technique of painting in a slip of unfired clay mixed with mineral colours on a damp earthenware body, in contrast to the work of Haviland in which a slip of ground, fired clay was painted on a thoroughly dried body. She first exhibited her slip-painted ware, which she called Limoges faience, but which became more widely known as Cincinnati faience, in 1878. She received an honourable mention at the Exposition Universelle in Paris later in the same year. McLaughlin organized the *Cincinnati Pottery Club and worked at the pottery of F.*Dallas, where she contributed the cost of a kiln for firing underglaze decorated ware, later moving with the club to the *Rookwood Pottery, 1881-82. She ceased making Cincinnati faience in 1885, working until 1895 as an enamel painter, and carried out some designs for a tile company in Newport, Kentucky, while also doing ornamental metalwork. She patented a method of inlaid decoration in 1894, painting in light-coloured slip on the interior of a plaster mould, in which the piece was cast in contrasting clay to emerge with the design inlaid in the body surface. Pieces decorated by her process, which she termed 'American faience', were fired briefly at a Cincinnati pottery. She began the production of hard-paste porcelain at her home in Cincinnati, at first experimenting widely with pastes and glazes and achieving a successful paste in 1900, having shown the results of early research at a Cincinnati Art Museum exhibition in 1899. At the Pan American Exposition in Buffalo (1901), she showed a creamy-coloured translucent porcelain, with paste and glaze fired in a single operation at temperatures in excess of 1300°C, made with native materials and named Losanti (Cincinnati had been called Losantiville). She decorated early Losanti ware with trailing plant forms carved or applied in relief, also using perforated designs, filled in with glaze in the manner of rice grain decoration. She developed a range of glazes that included pastel blues and a peach shot with pale green. McLaughlin abandoned ceramics in 1906, in favour of wood carving, metalwork, painting, weaving, lacemaking and embroidery. A mention of

Mary Louise McLaughlin. Porcelain cups and saucers, all made in Limoges and decorated by McLaughlin, 1889 or 1900. Cups 4.4 cm (left), and 3.5 cm high.

McLaughlin (in connection with the work of the *Cincinnati Pottery Club) in the catalogue of the World's Columbian Exposition in Chicago (1893), crediting her with the invention of the underglaze technique used at Rookwood and other Cincinnati art potteries, was removed from subsequent editions of the catalogue at the request of W.W.*Taylor and later M.L.*Nichols Storer, and it was not until 1938 that McLaughlin received honorary membership of the American Ceramics Society in recognition of her achievements in underglaze decorative techniques.

Painted marks include *Losanti*, sometimes with the letters arranged vertically; initials *LMcL*.
Refs: Barker; Clark & Hughto; Eidelberg; Evans; Henzke; Jervis; Keen; Kovel & Kovel; M.L. McLaughlin *Pottery Decoration under the Glaze* (Clarke, Cincinnati, 1880), *Suggestions to China Painters* (Clarke, Cincinnati, 1883), *China Painting...* (Clarke, Cincinnati, 1897), 'Losanti ware' in *Craftsman* 3 (December 1902), *The China Painters' Handbook* (Vol 1 of The Practical Series, Cincinnati, 1917); 'Mary Louise McLaughlin...' in *The Bulletin of the American Ceramic Society* 17 (May 1938); *Overglaze Imagery* (collection of essays, California State University Art Gallery, Fullerton, California, 1977); Peck.

McLaughlin, Sara R. *See* Lonhuda Pottery.

McLeish, Minnie. *See* Carter, Stabler & Adams; Stabler, Phoebe.

McMeekin, Ivan. Australian potter. McMeekin started potting in Cornwall, where he worked with M.*Cardew at Wenford Bridge, 1949-50, and returned in the early 1950s to Australia. He established the Sturt Craft Centre at Mittagong and produced an output which included porcelain and fine stoneware inspired by Sung Chinese wares and the work of B.*Leach, and a range of standard domestic wares. McMeekin taught

at the University of New South Wales, and L.*Blakeborough and G.*Pigott were among students taught by him at Mittagong. His teaching and his book *Notes for Potters in Australia* (1967) have encouraged other Australian studio potters to follow him in searching out, investigating and using native materials for both bodies and glazes. From 1965, he helped to introduce pottery making to Aborigines in the Northern Territory.
Refs: G. Clark *Michael Cardew* (Faber, London, 1978); Cooper; Hood.

McQuate, Henry (1826-99). American potter, born of Irish and Scottish parents in Lancaster County, Pennsylvania. McQuate established a small pottery near Myerstown in Lebanon County, c.1845-c.1859. Working with no more than four assistants, he made thrown domestic earthenware with reddish brown glaze and, often, green slip brushed or stippled on the surface. Decoration was sometimes trailed or dotted in slip or, more rarely, incised. Jugs for milk, cider or vinegar constituted the main output, but special items and miniature pieces were also made. After the closure of his pottery, McQuate turned to farming and settled, in 1871, in Ohio with other members of the Dunkard sect of German Baptists, which he had joined in 1847.
Ref: Stradling.

Maddock, Thomas, & Sons. American pottery firm established as Millington & Astbury in 1853 at Trenton, New Jersey, operating as Millington, Astbury & Poulson from 1859. The company produced white earthenware and ironstone china, which included a pitcher with relief decoration modelled by J.*Jones depicting the shooting of Colonel Ellsworth at Alexandria, Virginia, at the outbreak of the Civil War. The output was sometimes decorated at the workshop of E.*Lycett, Trenton. Trading as Thomas Maddock & Sons in 1869 and Astbury & Maddock by 1876, the firm produced sanitary earthenware, and domestic pottery which was shown in the Philadelphia Centennial Exhibition (1876). Thomas Maddock & Sons also established the Maddock Pottery, producing table and toilet wares in semi-porcelain from 1893 at the Lamberton Works, Trenton.
Marks: MAP/TRENTON in oval impressed [Millington Astbury & Poulson] from 1859; TM & S in a circular ribbon, with the date 1859 printed on dinner ware; a similar mark with an anchor on sanitary ware; MADDOCKS/LAMBERTON/WORKS in a circle topped by an M; M on a shield with LAMBERTON/CHINA, or M/CHINA/L (Maddock Pottery Co.).
Ref: Barber (1976).

Madeley, Shropshire. *See* Randall, Thomas Martin.

Madoura. *See* Ramié, Suzanne.

Madsen, Theodor Christian (1880-1965). Danish ceramic modeller, noted for animal figures. After serving an apprenticeship at the Royal *Copenhagen Porcelain Factory in the mid 1890s, he returned in 1907 and worked for the factory until 1935 (with breaks, 1919-26 and 1932-33).
Mark: signature.
Ref: Porzellankunst.

*Walter Magnussen. Stoneware vase produced by J.J.*Scharvogel in Munich, c.1900, to a design by Magnussen. 27.8 cm high.*

Maeda fief. *See* Kaga.

Mafra & Son. Portuguese pottery established in 1853 by Manuel Cypriano Gomez Mafra at Caldas da Rainha. The firm's earthenware was usually splashed with metal oxides in the glaze. Mafra's son, Eduardo, produced Toby jugs, vessels modelled in the shape of animals, and Palissy ware. The firm continued production under Cipriano Gomez Mafra from 1897.
Marks include M. MAFRA/CALDAS/PORTUGAL with an anchor, impressed.
Ref: J. Queiroz *Ceramica Portuguesa* (Lisbon, 1948).

Magdeburg. German factory established in Hanover, 1754, initially for the production of faience, and making creamware from 1786, following English styles. Guischard, the founder, became one of the largest manufacturers of creamware in Germany and worked until 1839, using the impressed marks M or *Guischard*.
Similar wares were made 1806-65 by Georg Schuchard, in a factory established 1799 at Magdeburg for the production of earthenware.
Marks include *Schuchard Mg* and M/HS.
Refs: Cushion (1980); Haggar (1960).

Magnac-Bourg. French porcelain factory in operation 1819-60 at Magnac-Bourg (Haute-Vienne), to the south of Limoges, initially under a partnership of Charpentier, the owner of a source of kaolin at Coussac-Bonneval, and his brother-in-law Charles-Théodore Gauldrée Boilleau. Employing 250 workers, they produced high-quality ware, including figures, busts, *veilleuses*, etc. Some pieces were made in eggshell porcelain. Charpentier retired in 1829 and his

brother-in-law carried on alone until his bankruptcy in 1831. After a period of financial failure under several subsequent owners and damage by fire, the business passed in 1845 to Pierre Mousnier, who produced portrait busts and pieces by the sculptor Lefèvre, his partner, until the closure of the factory in 1860.
A smaller factory nearby made porcelain for everyday use.
Refs: d'Albis & Romanet; Danckert.

Magnussen, Walter (b 1869). German modeller and ceramist, born in Hamburg. Magnussen worked c.1900 in Munich, where he modelled complex shapes which were produced by his teacher J.J.*Scharvogel in stoneware with sombre brown glazes. Magnussen taught at an art school in Bremen c.1907. His work, fired at the Witteburg factory in Bremen, rapidly became much more austere in shape with linear patterns of figures, animals and stylized foliage painted in glazes. He went on to decorate his pieces with flowing glazes, *flambé* and crystalline effects. He used a hard, fine porcellaneous stoneware body.

Mark: impressed monograms.
Refs: Bock; Borrmann; Haslam (1977).

Mahood, Marguerite (b 1901). Australian potter, illustrator and sculptor, born in Melbourne. She studied drawing and painting (1916-18) at the National Gallery School in Melbourne and applied art at the Working Men's College (later Melbourne Technical College), 1929-30, but soon abandoned formal training. She produced her first pottery in 1931, firing it in a coke-fired kiln built by her husband. She exhibited annually in Melbourne from 1932 and held a solo exhibition in Sydney, in 1947. Much of her work features one or two colourful, comic dragons or grotesqueries in the decoration, as a result of her fascination with the creatures of European mythology, especially dragons. During the 1930s, Mahood wrote

Marguerite Mahood. Earthenware mask with clear glaze, 1936. 10 cm high.

*majolica. Earthenware vase made by
*Mintons Ltd, after a triton vase made at
Vincennes in 1754, decorated with majolica
glazes, c.1870. 41.5 cm high.*

many articles for magazines and regularly
lectured on design and interior decoration
on Melbourne radio.

Marks: all pieces are signed and dated
with a letter of the alphabet; A represents
1931, her first year of production.

maiolica. Tin-glazed earthenware made in
the Italian manner, with tin-glaze solution
applied to biscuit-fired earthenware, dried
and painted in high-temperature colours.
Although it was largely superseded by mass-
produced cream-coloured earthenware,
maiolica is still produced in Italy.

Maison Moderne, La. Paris retail shop established in 1898 by critic and art historian
Julius Meier-Graefe, who sold items in a
variety of decorative media, undertaking
the production of utilitarian objects in quantity, and exploiting the interest in craft
techniques that had arisen among artists in
the 1880s. Among ceramics sold were pieces
designed by M.*Dufrêne and executed by
P.-A.*Dalpayrat. Other ceramic artists
selling work through the shop included
A.W.*Finch. A.*Landry provided designs
for porcelain and metalwork.

Mark: monogram of LMM, LA MAISON
MODERNE and address, *82 rue des Petits
Champs,* printed.
Refs: Brunhammer *et al* (1976); M. Dufrêne
in *Art et Décoration* 39 (1921); Haslam
(1977).

majolica. Earthenware with relief decoration
and a range of coloured glazes initially developed by J.-F.-L.*Arnoux, art director of
Mintons Ltd in the late 1840s. Majolica was
inspired by Italian Renaissance maiolica,

but became totally separated from its source.
Makers including Mintons, G.*Jones and
J.*Wedgwood & Sons Ltd used shapes and
decoration drawn from a wide variety of
references: English silver, medieval art, the
work of the 16th-century French potter
Bernard Palissy, German stoneware, and
other historical sources, reflecting Victorian
preoccupations with architecture and design
in general. The qualities of moulded relief
under the rich glazes attracted many artists
and designers who developed a range of
stylistic expression with very wide appeal.
The output of majolica comprises domestic
ware and ornamental pieces from vases,
jardinières and garden ornaments to large-
scale architectural decoration. In addition,
the technical properties of earthenware and
the majolica glazes allowed the production
of decorated ware in larger quantities and
at lower cost than had ever been possible
before.

Manufacture in Britain was followed in
Europe, e.g. at *Rörstrand and *Gustavs-
berg in the 1860s, in America, e.g. by E.
*Bennett and *Griffen, Smith & Hill, and in
Australia, e.g. at the *Lithgow Pottery.

Majolica argenta. *See* Fielding, S., & Co. Ltd.

Makeig-Jones, 'Daisy' (1881-1945). An
English ceramic artist and designer, Susannah
Margaretta Makeig-Jones was born in Wath-
upon Dearne. Yorkshire. After studying at

*'Daisy' Makeig-Jones. Large Fairyland
Lustre vase with elves, fairies and dragons in
a chinoiserie waterside setting, on a blue
ground. Produced by J.*Wedgwood & Sons
Ltd to a design by Makeig-Jones.*

the Torquay School of Art, and in London,
she became an apprentice decorator for J.
*Wedgwood & Sons Ltd, 1909-11, and sub-
sequently worked as a designer in the firm's
art department. Her early work included
nursery ware and toy tea sets, dessert plates
and bowls patterned with soldiers, animal
subjects, or illustrations of Hans Andersen's
tales and, from c.1913, pieces decorated
with dragons and oriental figures. Working
with colours stippled in powdered effects
under lustres, she evolved a style of decoration which featured dragons, birds, butterflies, fish, small animals and exotic fruits,
and developed the range of Fairyland Lustre
with which she is mainly associated. This
line was produced to her designs from late
1915 and included bone china plates, vases,
bowls, etc., and plaques made in Queensware. The decoration of fantastic, dream-
like and sometimes grotesque landscapes
with figures (often fairies) and scenes with
dragons (Dragon Lustre) was painted in
bright underglaze colours (black, brown,
violet, crimson, shades of orange with green
and blue), mother-of-pearl lustre, and, from
1923, enamel (reds, blues, greens, mauve,
turquoise, beige), and printing in gold. The
subjects were grouped in colour schemes
appropriate to Day, Sunset or Flames, Night
or Moonlight; there were also Willow (bluish
in tone), and a coral-bronze range. The
Fairyland designs, initially incorporating
characters from the earlier nursery ware,
often emphasize the grotesque aspects of
fairies.

Daisy Makeig-Jones also decorated tableware, tea and coffee sets in Queensware and
bone china, and ornamental pieces
with Celtic, Middle Eastern or, less often,
Grecian ornament, and designed themes for
the firm's range of lustre wares. She retired
in 1931.

Marks: backstamp *'Designed by S.M.
Makeig-Jones'* occurs (exceptionally for a
Wedgwood artist) after 1916; printed initials
or signature in gold.
Refs: Batkin; U. des Fontaines *Wedgwood
Fairyland Lustre,* (Sotheby Parke Bernet,
London, 1975); *Pottery Gazette* (April 1916,
April 1917); Reilly & Savage.

Maki. *See* Shigaraki ware.

Makuzu ware. *See* Chozo Makuzu.

Malevich, Kasimir (1878-1935). Russian
painter, born in the Ukraine of Polish parents. Malevich first exhibited Suprematist
work in Petrograd in 1915 and gathered his
followers into an Institute for Artistic Culture. Working with students N.*Suetin and
Ilya Chashnik, he designed ceramics for the
*St Petersburg porcelain factory with decor-
ation closely related to Suprematist painting.
In the late 1920s, Malevich re-introduced
figurative elements into his work, which
included representations of peasants achieved
with wide, flat blocks of sombre colour. Ten
cups and saucers in the Museum of Modern
Art in New York bear the mark of the St
Petersburg factory, the word Suprematism, and the name of Malevich. Other
pieces by Malevich and his pupils, shown in
the Badisches Landesmuseum at Karlsruhe,
bear similar marks and Suprematism.
Refs: T. Andersen *Malevich* (Amsterdam,
1970); S. Compton 'Malevich and the 4th

Kasimir Malevich. Half cup, 1918. 6 cm high.

Dimension' in *The Studio* 187 (1974); K. Malevich *Essays on Art 1915-33*, (edited by T. Andersen Wittenborn, New York, 1971) and *The Non-Objective World* (Chicago, 1927).

Maling, Christopher Thompson (1824-1901). English potter. He succeeded his father at *Ouseburn Bridge Pottery in 1853 (*see* Maling family). Two years after his marriage to Mary Ford in 1857, Maling built the Ford (A) Pottery, also in Ouseburn, where he carried out production of pots, jars and bottles for meat and dairy products, preserves and ink in great quantities (more than 800,000 articles per year). Maling built a huge, second factory, Ford (B) Factory, occupying a fourteen-acre site half a mile away at Walker, in 1878. There he produced jars for marmalade and other preserved foods. Both the factories also produced table and toilet wares, as well as household articles. The firm was self-sufficient in the treatment and use of raw materials.

Maling took his sons into partnership in 1889 and retired in 1899. John Ford Maling, manager of Ford (A), and his two brothers who managed Ford (B), traded as C.T. Maling & Sons Ltd, a title which was retained until the firm ceased operation in 1963. They continued the output of jars for proprietary products, also increasing the range of table, toilet and household wares with lavishly decorated dinner, tea, dessert and toilet sets and flowerpots, as well as sanitary, electrical, laboratory and photographic wares. L.*Boullemier was art director from the early 1920s until c.1932. The firm built up a large export trade, especially in lustre ware, but closed the Ford (A) pottery after suffering losses in the General Strike (1926) and the American Depression, and more specifically from the competition of Staffordshire ware on the home market and the gradual replacement of commercial pottery by containers made from other materials. The firm was sold to Hoult's Estates in 1947, and underwent a brief period of renewed development under Frederick Hoult, but finally ceased ceramic production in 1963.

Marks include MALING, C.T. and MALING, C.T.M.

Refs: Bell; Bunt; Shaw.

Maling family. Pottery manufacturers of Huguenot extraction working in the north east of England from the establishment by William Maling (d 1765) of the Hylton Pot Works at North Hylton on the River Wear in 1762. His son, Christopher Maling (1741-1810), a lawyer and academic, and his brother John (1746-1823), a banker, were

succeeded as proprietors of the factory by John's son, Robert Maling (1781-1863), who entered the firm c.1797 and transferred production to *Ouseburn Bridge Pottery in 1817, having sold off the pottery at North Hylton to the owners of the *Garrison Pottery. His son, C.T.*Maling, took over the pottery in 1853, and moved to new works in Ouseburn in 1859, building a second factory at Walker in 1878. His sons, John Ford Maling (1858-1924), Christopher Thompson Maling (1863-1934) and Frederick Theodore Maling (1866-1937), joined him in partnership in 1889, and began trading as C.T. Maling & Sons on his retirement ten years later. Frederick Maling's son, the fourth member of the family to be named Christopher Thompson Maling, entered the firm in 1929 and remained there, apart from an absence in World War II, until its sale to Hoult's Estates in 1947. He later entered the glass industry.

Refs: Bell; Bunt; C.T. Maling *The Industrial Resources of the District of Three Northern Rivers, the Tyne, Wear and Tees* (1864); *Pottery Gazette and Glass Trade Review* (1952); Shaw.

Malinowsky, Arno. *See* Copenhagen, Royal, Porcelain Factory.

Mangin-Brichard. *See* Waly.

Mann & Porzelius. *See* Pfeiffer, Max Adolf.

Manners, Erna. English studio potter and designer. She studied at the Royal College of Art in London and in the early 20th century at a workshop in Ealing, where she made plates and vases decorated in enamel with stylized flowers, etc., as well as figures, until the 1930s. She also worked as a freelance designer, e.g. for *Carter, Stabler & Adams, for whom she created patterns called Grape and Fuchsia.

Marks: painted monogram; incised or painted signature.

Refs: Godden (1964); Haslam (1977); Hawkins.

Manor House Pottery. Yorkshire pottery built in 1837 at Eccleshill, Bradford, by William Woodhead, who took two partners in the 1850s, trading as Woodhead, Davison & Cooper. The output of earthenware and glossy brown saltglaze with very granular texture included garden vases, statuettes and busts of personalities, such as the Duke of Wellington, Robert Burns, Lord Byron, and Sir Walter Scott, and household ware, including decorative jugs, salt kits, knife boxes, and puzzle jugs with relief figures round the belly. When he died in the early 1860s, Woodhead was succeeded by his widow Hannah and his son-in-law William Marshall, who concentrated on the production of bricks, chimney pots, etc., and continued to work at the pottery after its sale in 1879, remaining there until the 1890s. The works were bought by Leathers Chemical Co. Ltd in 1920.

Mark: *Woodhead, Davison & Cooper.*
Ref: Lawrence.

Mansard. *See* Ziegler, Jules-Claude.

Manufattura Fornaci San Lorenzo. *See* Chini, G.G.& C.

Manzel, Ludwig (1858-1936). German sculptor, working in Berlin from 1889. His designs included low-relief plaques for the Cadinen workshop.

Mark: incised initials.
Ref: Haslam (1977).

Manzoni, Carlo. *See* Della Robbia Pottery.

Marblehead Pottery. American art pottery, initially (in 1904) part of a scheme to establish a group of craft industries, Handcraft Shops, offering activities, such as wood-carving, weaving and metalwork as therapy for patients suffering from nervous exhaustion in a sanitorium at Marblehead, Massachusetts. The workshop became independent of the medical project in 1905 and, under the technical and artistic supervision of A.E.*Baggs, reached an output of about 200 pots per week by 1908. The work included heavy earthenware vases, *jardinières* and lampstands in simple shapes with restrained decoration, restricted at first to geometrical designs or severely stylized motifs of fruit, flowers, animals or seaweed, ships and other themes drawn from the New England coast. The patterns were mainly coloured with metallic oxides in three or four shades, often within incised outlines. There was a growing output of ware decorated only with matt glazes in a wide range of colours: deep turquoise (known as Marblehead blue), grey, yellow, brown, green, rose and wisteria (mauve); the interiors of bowls were frequently enamelled in a contrasting colour. All the pottery's products were thrown or hand-built, except for tiles, bookends, etc., which were moulded. Individual items, such as sculptures, garden ornaments and decorative jars or pieces with a specific glaze were supplied to order. A range of tin-glazed tableware decorated in soft colours on a light background was introduced commercially in 1912, after the development of a light-coloured body which could be potted thinly. Other experiments resulted in lustre decoration and bright glazes coloured red (selenium), or blue (copper in an alkaline base).

Marblehead Pottery. Vase glazed in a finely speckled dark mustard colour with decoration in muted brown, green, orange and blue; the interior is glossy blue-green, c.1910. Mark: sailing ship and MP. 9.5 cm high.

Marks: a ship with initials MP in a circle; items with experimental glaze or decorative effects, appearing especially in later years, marked with Bagg's initials.
Refs: Eidelberg; Evans; Kovel & Kovel.

Marcks, Gerhard (b 1889). German sculptor, designer and potter, born in Berlin. Marcks was a member of the expressionist Novembergruppe. He modelled figures, mainly of animals, for ceramics firms, starting with a Pacing Lionness (1910) for the Schwarzburger Werkstätten Vordamm, Meissen (*see* Pfeiffer, M.A.), and later models for *Velten Vordamm, and other manufacturers. He also made decorative plaques for the restaurant at the Deutscher Werkbund exhibit in Cologne (1914). Marcks made woodcuts and taught ceramics at the *Bauhaus, 1919-24, while also teaching modelling in Berlin 1918-20. With the Thuringian master potter Max Krehan, he established the Bauhaus pottery in Dornburg in 1920; the workshop moved to Dessau four years later. Marcks painted many of the pieces made by T.*Bogler and O.*Lindig, and produced designs (for plates, etc.) which were developed by M.*Friedlander and H.*Griemert, but he was mainly concerned with teaching artists through the production of unique pieces. In 1925, he moved to Halle-Giebichenstein, near Leipzig, where he worked on his own sculpture, leaving the running of the Bauhaus pottery to M. Friedlander. He later experimented with porcelain, using a kiln lent by the *Berlin factory, and designed a tea service for production at the factory. Marcks moved to Niehagen in 1943, became professor at the Landeskunstschule in Hamburg, 1946-49, and eventually settled in Cologne where he worked independently as a sculptor.

Marks: incised, impressed or painted cyphers.
Refs: Bock; Forsyth.

Marcolini, Camillo. *See* Meissen.

Mardochée, Jacob. *See* Petit, Jacob.

Margaine, André-Emile (1841-1928). French porcelain modeller, born in Limoges, and a distant relation of Alpinien Margaine (*see* Gibus, P.-J.). He made many plaques with *pâte-sur-pâte* decoration, often allegorical in theme, or with such subjects as flower fairies.
Ref: d'Albis & Romanet.

Margold, Emanuel Josef (b 1889). Graphic artist and designer born in Vienna, where he also studied. Margold worked in Darmstadt before settling in Berlin (1929). His ceramic designs included biscuit containers for the manufacturer, H. Bahlsen.
Mark: printed signature on pieces of his design.
Ref: Haslam (1977).

Marieburg. *See* Rörstrand.

Markham, Herman C. (d 1922). American potter, watercolourist and wood engraver

*Gerhard Marcks. Two-spouted pot designed by Marcks and made at the Staatliche Majolika-Manufaktur*Karlsruhe, c.1921.*

employed in the archaeology department of the University of Michigan. At his home in Ann Arbor, Markham began the experimental production of flower vases, aiming at a container that would hold water at an even, cool temperature, to discourage wilting of the flowers, initially calling the ware Utile. After experimenting with decorative finishes, he produced two matt-glazed lines: Reseau with fine, veined tracery, slightly raised, and Arabesque with a maze of raised, irregular lines, slightly rough to the touch. The colours ranged from ochre and rust to earth-brown, shot with green and often metallic in appearance, and recall the ancient pottery vessels that inspired the effect. The vases were moulded in soft earthenware body from thrown shapes adapted from classical models. Markham was joined in the pottery by his son Kenneth in 1905. They moved to National City, California in 1913, working in space provided at a tileworks, and extended the range of products to include teasets, pitchers, steins and a limited amount of architectural ware as well as vases. Production ceased in 1921.
Marks: early Utile ware marked with monogram UP; incised name *Markham*.
Refs: Evans; L.G. Jarvie *The Markham Pottery Book* (leaflet published by the pottery, a reprint of an article in *Sketch Book* V, 1905); Kovel & Kovel.

Markus, Lili. Studio potter, born in Hungary, where she worked from 1932 on the production of tableware, vases, relief panels and modelled figures. In England, Lili Markus worked for a time in the design studio of Grimwade's at Stoke-on-Trent.
Refs: Forsyth; G.M. Forsyth 'Lili Markus; Artist Potter' in *Pottery & Glass* (January 1946).

Marqueterie ware. *See* Doulton & Co.

Marraud, Maurice. *See* Fontanille & Marraud.

Marsh, James F. English ceramic modeller working at *Davenport's in the mid 19th century. Marsh exhibited a terracotta wine cooler in revived Renaissance style at the Great Exhibition (1851) and assisted R. *Morris on the making of sculptures for the Wedgwood Institute, 1865-69. At the Industrial Exhibition in Hanley, 1865, he showed terracotta and an adaptation of a medieval jug.
Ref: Mankowitz & Haggar.

Marshall, John. *See* Adams, Harvey; Bo'ness.

Marshall, Mark Villars (d 1912). English ceramic designer, modeller and sculptor. Marshall worked c.1874 as an assistant to the *Martin Brothers, and was mainly concerned with the modelling of architectural decoration. He was employed at the *Doulton & Co. Lambeth studio from the late 1870s until the year of his death. Marshall is known for his models of lizards, and other reptiles, salamanders, frogs and dragons, which he made as decoration for vases, e.g. a leaf form with reptiles and frogs, c.1905, or as free-standing models, sometimes intended as doorstops or paperweights, e.g. a seahorse in Carrara ware, or a cowled head with scowling face in saltglaze. His other work included pieces in saltglaze with ornate, foliate patterns, scrolls and masks, carved or modelled, and sometimes gilded. The handles of some slender vases and ewers decorated in this style bear elaborate leaf scrolls in high relief. One example in buff-bodied stoneware with portrait masks and trailing foliage bears the mark of the Art Union of London. Marshall's well-known Borrogrove Vase, modelled in the form of an animal, half-hedgehog, half-fish, and issued in several colour combinations, was inspired by Lewis Carroll's *Jabberwocky* verses. Marshall also modelled chess pieces and portrait jugs in stoneware, as well as plaques, and was among the resident artists mainly responsible for making the firm's architectural terracotta. His figures included portrayals of Queen Victoria (to commemorate her jubilee in 1897), his own wife, and a soldier of the Boer War. Some of his work was carried out in mottled brown (Leopardskin) stoneware. In the early 20th century, Marshall made a group of vases in stoneware decorated with designs of poppies, stylized foliage, rabbits seated at the foot of trees, etc., influenced in style by Art Nouveau, and executed in bright, flowing colours, not always completely contained by incised outlines.
Marks: although some of the smallest animal models were not signed, they were generally unique pieces, bearing Marshall's incised initials. Much of his other work was produced in large editions; these pieces are unsigned.
Refs: see Doulton & Co.

Martin Brothers. English potters, Robert Wallace, Edwin and Walter Frazer *Martin, who worked in partnership on the production of stoneware, often individual pieces. The brothers opened a studio at Pomona House in Fulham (1873), and their early work was fired at nearby workshops that included the *Fulham Pottery. They employed as assistant M.V.*Marshall, who worked as a modeller

Martin Brothers. Martinware bird, c.1900. 34.3 cm high.

before going to work at *Doulton's Lambeth Studio. The brothers subsequently established a workshop at Southall, Middlesex (1877), where they made and fired saltglaze. The brothers shared the work of production between them: Robert Wallace Martin was mainly responsible for modelling, Walter for throwing, and Edwin for decoration and the making of a number of miniature pieces. The management and administration of the pottery was undertaken by their brother Charles Martin (1846-1910), who also ran a retail department in Holborn, London. From the mid 1880s to the mid 1890s, they were assisted by Walter Wiley, who designed and decorated some hollow ware.

With the exception of a small amount of terracotta made at Southall, and a brief attempt at the production of painted earthenware, 1896-98, the majority of Martinware was produced in saltglaze stoneware. By the early 1880s, R.W. Martin had begun the making of modelled animals, especially reptiles, amphibians and birds, in a variety of shapes and sizes; the larger bird models had detachable heads. From c.1885, he made jugs with distorted faces in relief, usually on each side of a flattened circular form, but occasionally below the lips of cylindrical jugs. Other relief-modelled pieces included plaques and architectural decoration, garden ornaments, figures and chessmen.

Thrown ware, especially vases and jugs, the workshop's main output, also included punch bowls, tobacco jars, lamp bases,

puzzle jugs, double-walled vases, and a little tea and coffee ware. Early shapes (until the early 1880s) were often angular and heavy, with thick handles. Decoration, incised, carved or moulded, was influenced in style by Doulton ware. Simpler, more rounded shapes followed in the 1880s to 1890s, with incised decoration, often scrolls of foliage, and natural flower sprays, and an increasing range of colour, brown predominating instead of the earlier blue. Motifs included dragons and lizards coiled around the pot, birds (ducks, a kingfisher), water plants (reeds, iris), insects, fish or tadpoles in *sgraffito* or low relief. In the early 20th century, the brothers made pots in the form of gourds and squashes, with natural colour and texture. Other motifs (on conventional vase forms) included grasses, wild flowers, and aquatic creatures modelled in low relief with suggestions of swirling water. The many miniature pieces made at this time by Edwin Martin were tiny versions of the normal ware.

The workshop ceased production of Martinware in 1914, except for the firing of some work by R.W. Martin, although his son, Clement Wallace Martin, who had worked in the studio, subsequently made simpler wares until the 1930s. The buildings were destroyed in 1942.

Marks: *R W Martin/Fulham*, (1873-74), *London* (mainly 1874-78), or *Southall* (c.1878-79), incised; MARTIN/SOUTHALL/ POTTERY, impressed in oval (c.1878-79); *R W Martin/London and Southall* (c.1879-82), with *Bros* or *Brothers*, 1882-1914.
Ref: Haslam (1978).

Martin, Edwin. (1860-1915) English artist potter. Martin studied at the Lambeth School of Art and succeeded his brother W.F. *Martin at *Doulton's Lambeth workshop in 1872. In partnership with his brothers (*see* Martin Brothers), he made saltglaze in Fulham and, working as *Martin Bros, in Southall, Middlesex. Edwin Martin was responsible for much of the decoration of hollow ware and is particularly associated with the use of underwater themes. He also made a number of small pieces.

Work occasionally marked with initials EBM.
Ref: Haslam (1978).

Martin Brothers. Miniature vase made by the Martins with decoration of flowering branches in dark brown on a buff ground. 4 cm high.

Martin, José. *See* Cowan, R. Guy.

Martin, Pierre and Charles. *See* Nivet, Michel.

Martin, Robert Wallace. (1843-1923). English artist potter. Martin worked as a sculptor's assistant and then as a stone carver engaged on the building of the Palace of Westminster. He studied modelling at the Lambeth School of Art from 1860 and sculpture at the Royal Academy Schools (1864). Modelled terracotta, which Martin exhibited in the Royal Academy from 1867 (e.g. Girl at a spring, 1869), was fired at the Doulton workshop. After working briefly as a modeller at the *Watcombe Pottery in 1870, he carried out independent work, which was fired at the *Fulham Pottery, where he worked in 1872 as a decorator, with J.-C.*Cazin. Martin opened a studio in Fulham (1873) with his brothers (*see* Martin, E. and Martin, W.F.), and organized the partnership *Martin Brothers at Southall, Middlesex, in 1877. He worked on architectural commissions, which were an important part of the Martin Brothers' early output, and is known for the modelling of animal figures and a group of grotesques, including pieces intended to serve as spoon-warmers, toast racks, etc.(made from 1879), containers for tobacco in the form of birds (from c.1880) and jugs decorated in relief with grimacing faces (from c.1885). He continued to work on a small number of pieces after the closure of the Martin Brothers studio in 1914.

His work was occasionally marked with the initials RWM.
Ref: Haslam (1978); Lloyd Thomas (1974).

Martin, Walter Frazer (1859-1912). English artist potter. Like his brothers R.W.*Martin and E.*Martin, he studied at the Lambeth School of Art and worked at the *Doulton studio in Lambeth. In partnership with his brothers, he made salt-glazed stoneware in Fulham and subsequently in Southall, Middlesex. Walter Martin, who had learned throwing at the *Fulham Pottery, was responsible for the preparation of clay, throwing of vases and firing; he also carried out incised decoration and, in the course of experiments with saltglaze, developed a range of decorative colours that included shades of green, grey and yellow as well as blue and brown.
Ref: Haslam (1978).

Martinez, Maria (1884-1980). American Pueblo potter, born in San Ildefonso, New Mexico. From 1897 she made pottery painted with red clay slip and a black pigment derived from wild spinach. With her husband Julian Martinez (d 1943), she worked on the reproduction of burnished silver-black pottery excavated from the Frijoles Canyon, while also making polychrome pottery, notably jars. After her husband's death, Maria Martinez concentrated on the production of burnished black pottery, followed by several members of the Martinez family.

Marks incorporate *Marie* and the name of a partner, e.g. *Marie & Julian* (until 1943).
Refs: Clark & Hughto; *Contemporary American Ceramics* (Syracuse Museum of Fine Arts, Syracuse, New York, 1937); M. Hughto *New Works in Clay by Contemporary Painters & Sculptors* (Everson Museum of

Robert W. Martin. Terracotta grotesque,
1898. Signed R.W. Martin & Bros Southall
London. 32 cm across.

Art, Syracuse, New York, 1976); S. Peterson
Maria Martinez (Kodansha International,
Tokyo, 1977).

Marubashira. *See* Iga ware.

Marusen kiln. *See* Takato ware.

Masakichi Watanabe. *See* Chikuzen.

Mascarin, Mario (1901-66). Italian accountant, journalist and potter. Working as a
correspondent for an Italian newspaper in
Bergen, he experimented with pottery in
workshops making traditional Norwegian
wares in 1927 and studied ceramics at *Nove
in 1929. He moved to Switzerland in 1930,
establishing his own studio near Zurich in
1935. Initially he worked in earthenware
with the sculptor Arnold d'Altri. He then
went on to work in collaboration with manufacturers, and taught ceramics. His own
work included simple bowls in stoneware.
Ref: Préaud & Gauthier.

Mashiko. Japanese ceramic centre in Tochigi
prefecture, in production from the establishment of a kiln in 1853 by Otsuka Keisaburo
with the assistance of potters from *Kasama.
Under the patronage of the Kurowa fief
lord, Oseki, Mashiko became the largest
centre of pottery production in the Kanto
district, sending kitchen wares 80 kilometres
to Tokyo for sale. The output included
water jars and salt pots glazed in brown and
persimmon, and teapots made in the manner
of *Shigaraki with landscapes, prunus
branches, etc., painted in reserves, and
hollowed-out bases to withstand direct heat.
Techniques were also drawn from *Soma,
*Aizu, and Kyoto, and the decoration in-
cluded relief motifs applied with a coating of
white slip. The pots are sturdy and simple in
shape. A spotted effect (goma, which means
sesame seed) occurs naturally in glaze used
over the local, iron-rich clay.
   *Hamada settled in Mashiko on his return
from England in 1924, and the village subsequently developed as a focus of the folk
art movement (*see* mingei ware), with about
30 potters in the vicinity making mainly stoneware for sale in Japan and overseas. Sakuma
Totaro mass-produces pieces, often with
rouletted decoration; his pupil, Shimaoka
Tatsuzo, noted for strong, simple shapes

with fine glazes in olive, pale grey-blue and
other colours, throws or moulds his ware,
sometimes beating or pressing bottles into
an oval shape.
   In general, the area maintains a high
quality of production, made anonymously
and simply labelled *Mashiko ware.*
Refs: B. Adachi *Living Treasures of Japan*
(Kodansha International, Tokyo/New
York, 1973); Cort; Koyama; Masterpieces;
Miller; Mizuo; Noma *Seiroku* [The Arts of
Japan] (2 vols, Kodansha International,
Tokyo/Palo Alto, California, 1966-67);
Okuda, Koyama & Hayashuja Senzo (eds)
Nihon no Toji [Japanese Ceramics] (Toto
Bunka Co., Tokyo, 1954); Roberts; Sanders.

Mashimizu Zoroku (1822-77). Japanese
potter born near Kyoto and working under
the artistic names Hyakuju, Sokan, Tahei
and later Zoroku. The son of a potter,
Shimizu Gen'emon, he learned pottery
techniques from his uncle, Waka Kitei (*see*
Kameya family). Also studying the tea
ceremony, he eventually established his own
kiln, where he made tea-ceremony wares.
After 1868, he continued experiments in
early techniques with the government's
backing and made close copies of *Asahi,
*Ninsei and other early wares.
   His successor Mashimizu Zoroku II
(1861-1942), worked in Kyoto from 1912
until c.1940 under the artistic name Deizo,
making reproductions of Ninsei ware.
Refs: Jenyns (1971); Roberts.

Mason, George Miles (1789-1859) and
Charles James (1791-1856). English potters
working in Staffordshire. The brothers
George and Charles Mason took over the
firm of their father M.*Mason, and occupied
the Minerva Works, Lane Delph until c.1816,
as well as the nearby works (Bagnall's)
which had previously been leased in the

Mashiko. Stoneware bottle with rust-coloured
and temmoku glaze, c.1965. 27 cm high.

name of their brother W.*Mason and was
eventually owned by George and Charles
Mason briefly in 1825-26. The early output
at the Minerva Works (which had been
established in 1801) consisted of transfer-
printed domestic ware and other simple
wares with gilding or lustre decoration.
Charles Mason made porcelain, which included biscuit figures of Queen Victoria and
the Prince Consort and tea sets and dessert
services in revived rococo style. He was
granted a patent in 1813 for the manufacture
of 'English Porcelain', in fact a durable earthenware, which they marketed as patent
*ironstone china. Produced initially at the
Minerva Works and also at the Fenton
Stone Works, which the brothers had bought
just before the issue of the patent, Mason's
patent ironstone soon constituted the greatest
part of their output. The remainder, blue-
printed earthenware and moulded relief,
formed only a small fraction. The Mason
brothers produced table services, sets of
octagonal or hexagonal jugs with handles in
the form of snakes or dragons, vases, and a
variety of useful and decorative pieces, as
well as footbaths and barrel-shaped garden
seats. Decoration was carried out in bright
underglaze colours and enamels, often over
transfer-printed outlines. Much of the printing was carried out in underglaze cobalt
blue, but black, sepia or pink enamel were
also used. Thick washes of enamel were
applied in iron red, yellow, blue-green,
yellow-green, pale orange, royal blue,
crimson and pink. A deep mazarine blue
glaze was used primarily as a ground for
lavish gilding, but sometimes delicately
painted in enamel. Japan patterns in underglaze blue with red and green enamel and
gilding were the firm's staple decoration,
and *chinoiserie* designs were often transfer-
printed in blue. The many subjects quickly
brushed in polychrome enamel included
prunus sprays, daisies and other flowers,
birds of paradise, waterfowl in flight, and
insects. Rare painted landscapes have been
attributed to S.*Bourne. The firm also
supplied decorations to special order.
   George Mason retired from his active part
in the administration of the firm in 1826,
subsequently living in Stoke-on-Trent, where
he unsuccessfully contested an election in
1832 for the newly formed borough; he then
moved to live in Small Heath, Birmingham.
   After his brother's retirement, C.J. Mason
continued the firm, entering into a brief
partnership with Samuel Bayliss Faraday
(1797-1844) in the early 1840s. He made
porcelain, which included biscuit figures
(e.g. statuettes of Queen Victoria and
Albert, Prince Consort) and dessert and tea
wares in revived rococo style. Mason also
extended the range of ironstone china to
include large pieces – fireplaces, over-
mantels, bed-posts – selling quantities of his
ware at auctions throughout England. However, he failed to dispose of all his enormous
output and was declared bankrupt early in
1848; nevertheless he showed a large display
that included garden seats, fish tanks, jars,
jugs and a variety of table and toilet wares at
the Great Exhibition (1851). He was working
at Daisy Bank, Lane End, in the same year,
but ceased to operate there in 1853.
   F.*Morley, who acquired many of Mason's
moulds and printing plates in the bankruptcy sale in 1848, passed them through his

partnership with Taylor Ashworth to the later firm of G.L.*Ashworth & Bros Ltd, producers of Mason's original shapes and patterns to the present day, and trading from 1968 as Mason's Ironstone China Ltd.

A variety of marks incorporate the initials G.& C.J.M., or *G.M.& C.J. Mason*; *Patent Ironstone China*, often with a crown. Much ware was unmarked. After 1826: several printed marks incorporating the name or initials of Charles James Mason. The name *Mason* also appears in the marks used by G.L., T. and J.*Ashworth & Bros Ltd, from the late 19th century.
Refs: Atterbury (1980); Blacker (1922a); S. Fisher; Godden (1971, 1980); Haggar (1952); Haggar & Adams; Jewitt.

Mason, Miles. (1752-1822). English porcelain retailer and manufacturer. While working as a porcelain dealer in London from the early 1780s, Mason became a partner of porcelain manufacturer George Wolfe at the Islington Pottery, Liverpool, in 1796, and in Lane Delph, Staffordshire. Their business association ended in 1800. Mason had ceased to work in London by 1804, when he advertised porcelain printed underglaze with Chinese scenes and landscapes (marketed as British Nankin), or decorated with patterns in enamel. He used bone china from c.1806 until at least 1813. He moved by 1807 to the Minerva Works at Fenton, which operated under the name of his son, George Mason, by 1815. Mason or another of his sons W. *Mason were in addition listed from 1811 as occupants of the factory established by Sampson Bagnall in Fenton, although Miles Mason is thought to have ceased to take an active part in manufacture in 1813, and is recorded as living in Liverpool in 1816 and 1818. His sons G.M. and C.J.*Mason continued the firm. The early products, thickly potted in hard-paste porcelain with a greyish tinge, included tea sets, dinner and dessert services, and ornamental pieces, e.g. vases, bulb pots, mainly following the styles of Chinese export wares. The firm also made punchbowls, matches and replacements for oriental armorial services, and white earthenware for table and domestic use. Decoration in underglaze blue was often directly derived from Chinese originals and included a version of the Broseley Willow pattern as well as other scenes with Chinese figures (which were in many cases in the repertoire of other factories) and a *chinoiserie* pattern featuring sheep, which was exclusive to Mason's. A large number of high-quality patterns were bat printed. Enamelled decoration often took the form of delicate floral sprays resembling the decorative schemes of New Hall porcelain.
Marks include M. MASON impressed.
Refs: Godden (1971, 1980); Haggar & Adams; A. Smith in *Transactions* of English Ceramic Circle, Vol 8, Part II (1972).

Mason, William (b 1785). English potter and ceramic retailer. He worked with his father M.*Mason from 1806, becoming his partner by 1811 in the factory leased from Sampson Bagnall at Fenton, Staffordshire. At a retail shop in Manchester, William Mason sold pottery, including in 1815 creamware made at the *Wedgwood factory. He made blue-printed earthenware at a pottery at Fenton Culvert briefly from 1822, but had

Miles Mason. Porcelain teapot, c.1810-15.

ceased operation there by May 1824, and subsequently worked in London.
Mark: W. MASON, printed (possibly his retail mark).
Refs: Coysh (1972); Godden (1971, 1980); Haggar (1952).

Massanetz, Karl. *See* Böck, Jos., Wiener Porzellan-Manufaktur.

Massarelos, Fabrica de. Portuguese pottery founded 1738 at Sobre-o-Douro, Oporto. Manuel Duarte Silva, the owner from 1788 until his death in 1845, let the factory to Francisco de Rocha Soares, owner of the factory of *Miragaia, from 1824 or 1829 until 1844. The subsequent owners, João da Rocha e Sousa, his nephew Antonio Rodrigues de Sa Lima and successive members of de Sa Lima's family, ran the factory until 1892. After closure in 1895, the works were rebuilt, closed again in 1898 and re-opened 1900 under William Maclaren. Chambers & Wall were the owners when the factory was finally destroyed by fire in 1920.

The output, which included tiles (*azulejos*) and household ware, was painted in blue and other colours. Some pieces were dipped in blue glaze. A cylindrical mug, painted in blue, green, yellow and maroon on an opaque white glaze, with a medallion containing S. Bento and Santa Escolastica, is marked with DA PRIMEIRA FABRICA EM MASSARELOS-PORTO.

Other marks include FRP or FABRICA REAL PORTO; *Massarelos, Porto*, impressed; *Massarelos, Porto*, C&W, above crown between laurel branches.
Refs: J. Queiros *Ceramica Portuguesa* (Lisbon, 1948); P. Vitorino *Ceramica Portuense* (Ediçoes Apolina, Gaia, 1930).

Massié. *See* Angoulême.

Massier, Clément (1845-1917). French ceramist, one of a family of potters working from the late 19th century at Vallauris (Alpes-Maritimes). The family firm was separated, by 1899, into branches run by Jérôme, Clément and Delphin Massier. Jérôme Massier et Cie made lead-glazed decorative ware, wood-fired, in a soft, coarse earthenware body, with grey-green, blue and brown enamel. In 1872, the firm set up a studio (on the site next to an established factory making domestic ware) producing luxury pieces, which was run by Clément Massier, with the aim of improving the technical and artistic quality of ceramics in Vallauris. In the 1880s, he established his own workshop in nearby Golfe-Juan. He

Clément Massier. Jardinière and stand, with deep red glaze lightly streaked, c.1890. Impressed mark. 104 cm overall.

perfected a technique of lustre decoration, painting metal-bearing, ochreous slip over a fired copper glaze and firing the piece in a reducing atmosphere. J.*Sicard, who worked closely with Massier, introduced the technique at the *Weller pottery in America in the early 20th century. L.*Lévy-Dhurmer became artistic director of the Golfe-Juan studio in 1887 and collaborated with Massier until 1896 on the production of lustre-glazed ware. Massier was also associated with the Swiss sculptor James Vibert. He exhibited the earliest known example of his lustre decoration in 1888, but sent a large display to Paris in the following year.

Massier produced earthenware plaques and vases in shapes adapted from Greek and Roman originals, using his iridescent glazes, often in peacock blue or emerald green, in stylized plant designs, including rose, cactus, *Eryngium* flowers and foliage. Both Jérôme and Delphin Massier also produced marked pieces of lustre ware. In 1900, Clément Massier opened a Paris shop, where he sold the work of artists including O.*Milet. The sale of Massier's lustre ware, which was expensive to produce and suffered high kiln losses, began to diminish in the early 20th century.

Marks incorporate the names or initials of Clément or Jérôme Massier.
Refs: M. Battersby *Art Nouveau* (Hamlyn, Feltham, Middlesex, 1965); Céramique française contemporaine; *China, Glass & Pottery Review* (October 1903); Evans; B. Grissom 'Clément Massier – Master Potter' in *Spinning Wheel* (September 1971); Heuser & Heuser; F. Pelka 'Exposition Lévy-Dhurmer' in *L'Art et la Mode* (February 1896).

Félix Massoul. Stoneware vase made by Massoul and painted with stylized leaves under a matt glaze, 1920-25. Mark: CMassoul [Céramique Massoul]. 16.3 cm high.

Massoul, Félix (1872-1938). French artist potter, working with his wife Madeleine at Maisons-Alfort (Seine). Originally a painter, Massoul started potting in 1900, having studied a wide range of processes from those used in Gallo-Roman pottery to soft-paste porcelain techniques of the 18th century. Using a highly siliceous clay body resembling that of ancient Egyptian pottery, he made dishes and vases, either with geometrical patterns enamelled in dark blues, greens, black or gold, or relying for effect on form alone. He achieved shades of dark blue that were noted as outstanding. At Sèvres in 1930, he exhibited vases with polychrome decoration on a light blue ground, trickled with yellowish matt glazes, or in Greek and Roman styles, as well as dishes with drops of blue glaze on a white ground, and red lustre ware inspired by Hispano-Moresque pottery.
Refs: Baschet; Lesur (1971).

Mathews, Heber (1905-59). English artist potter. After studying painting and design at the Royal College of Art in London, Mathews spent the years 1927-31 as a pupil of W.S. *Murray. From 1931 until the year before his death, he worked at Lee, near Woolwich in Kent, on the individual production of large jars, vases, etc., brushed with swirling patterns, in stoneware and porcelain. He was also a teacher, concerned himself in the Arts & Crafts Society and the Crafts Centre, and acted from 1932 as pottery advisor to the Rural Industries Bureau.
Mark: incised initials HM.
Refs: Godden (1964); Rose; A.C. Sewter 'Heber Mathews – Potter in *Apollo* 46 (August 1947); Wingfield Digby.

Matsumoto ware. Japanese pottery initially made in the 17th century by the potter Miwa Kyusetsu, who made tea ware with a thick, bluish-white glaze, (using the same materials as those used in *Hagi wares, also made at

Matsumoto, in Yamaguchi prefecture) and in production until the 19th century. A class of earthenware now made at Matsumoto has a body of raku type and slip decoration either brushed or inlaid in the Korean manner.
Refs: Jenyns (1971); Koyama; Munsterberg.

Matsushiro. Japanese pottery centre in Nagano prefecture, most active from c.1816 until c.1930. Many folk and clan kilns produced domestic ware, including a wide variety of large and small storage vessels, mixing and serving bowls, plates, saké cups and bottles, cooking pots, stoves, etc., in quantities that were sufficient to supply most of the needs of the surrounding district (noted for the growing and consumption of buckwheat). Their production declined as improvements in transport increased the distribution of wares mass-produced industrially in other parts of Japan. Matsushiro ware, in heavy clay with coarse texture, which shows reddish brown at rims where the glaze is thin, was made in strong, simple shapes with glazes including amber (ame) glaze derived from iron, copper and feldspathic glazes, and effects, derived from the ash of straw or mixed hardwoods, that exploit the speckled appearance of the coarse body. Decoration is restricted to horizontal ribbing, or trickled glazes in white or a deep, lustrous green.
Ref: Mizuo.

Matsuyama. Japanese kiln making *Kutani ware in Matsuyama village, near Kaga. It was founded in the late 1840s by order of the Daishoji clan for the production of presentation ware and declined after the withdrawal of clan patronage in the 1860s. Using local clays, the potter Yamamoto Hikoemon made porcelain decorated in the manner of the nearby *Yoshidaya kiln, with designs, primarily in yellow, green and blue, extending over the whole piece.
Ref: Nakagawa.

Mattson, Julia (d 1967). American ceramist and teacher, trained at the University of North Dakota, Art Institute of Chicago, Taos School of Art, and the University of New Mexico. Mattson taught ceramics at the *North Dakota School of Mines, 1924-63, also designing and decorating pottery.
Mark: initials, JM.
Ref: Kovel & Kovel.

Mattyasovszky-Zsolnay, Laszlo. *See* Zsolnay.

Mauresque ware. *See* Ault, William.

Mauksch, Johann Karl (d 1821). A painter at Meissen specializing in landscapes and battle scenes.
Mark: signature.
Refs: Danckert; Porzellankunst; Weiss.

Maw & Co. English tile manufacturers, established in 1850 by the brothers George and Arthur Maw who bought the premises and equipment of a tileworks on the site of the Flight, Barr & Barr *Worcester porcelain factory, then moved in 1852 to the Benthall works near Broseley, Shropshire. After experiments starting in 1851 with local and other clays, the firm began full production of plain and mosaic tiles in 1857, becoming the world's largest single tile manufacturer

in the late 19th century. Tesserae for use in decorative mosaics were brought into production in 1861. Encaustic tiles were often decorated with Roman or medieval designs, and majolica tiles with relief patterns and rich glazes in Hispano-Moresque or Italian styles; a full range of majolica colours was developed. Examples of a transparent turquoise glaze were displayed in the Exposition Universelle in Paris, 1867. The firm's wide range of decorative techniques included *sgraffito* designs carved through layers of clay to reveal a contrasting colour below, enamel colours painted over patterns in slip, moulded relief ornament applied to a ground of contrasting colour, and repeating designs that were transfer printed. The tiles, despite mass production, were noted for their high quality. A steam press was introduced in 1873. In the 1870s, designs were commissioned from J.P. Seddon, L.F.*Day, M. Digby Wyatt, George Street and other artists. The firm also produced art pottery, vases, dishes, etc., in majolica with relief decoration. A series of vases designed by W.*Crane and painted in ruby lustre were produced c.1889. Tiles with lustre designs after Isnik styles were marketed as Persian Ware in the 1890s, under the influence of W.*De Morgan.

After transferring to new premises in Jackfield, Shropshire in 1883, the firm operated under the Maw family until 1888 and then as a limited liability company. Several changes occurred in the firm after World War II, and operation ceased in 1967.

Marks include MAW, *Maw & Co./Benthall Works/Broseley/Salop* or *Jackfield/Salop*; the name MAW sometimes occurs enclosed in a circular label FLOREAT SALOPIA.
Refs: Barnard; C. Eastlake *Hints on Household Taste* (third edition, 1872); Godden (1966a); Lockett (1979); M. Messenger *Ceramics & Tiles of the Severn Valley* (Remploy, Newcastle-under-Lyne, 1980); T. Herbert *The Jackfield Decorative Tile Industry* (booklet No 20.01, Ironbridge Gorge Museum Trust, 1978); Wakefield.

Max, Ella (b 1897). Viennese ceramic modeller, trained under M.*Powolny at the Wiener Kunstgewerbeschule, 1916-18, and again in the 1920s. Her work included relief patterns of a lemon, fish, etc., for vessels

Maw & Co. Charger painted in ruby lustre against a white ground, 1886. Marks include Maw & Co.'s monogram with Benthall Jackfield 1886, painted. 34 cm in diameter.

and tiles. Between 1917 and 1920 she modelled figures and a flowerpot for the Wiener Werkstätte.
Ref: Neuwirth (1974a).

Maximov, Ivan. Russian potter, descendant of a family making traditional pottery at *Skopin, and a member of the cooperative of craftsmen responsible for reviving the local pottery craft in the 1930s. Maximov copied early specimens of Skopin ware and also introduced new forms, e.g. a kvass jar with a five-pointed star in the wheel-shaped body, and remodelled the shape of a flower vase into a desk lamp.
Ref: Ovsyannikov.

Mayer Bros & Elliott. *See* Mayer, T.J.& J.

Mayer, Elijah, & Son. Staffordshire pottery manufacturers working at Hanley in the late 18th century; enameller Elijah Mayer (d 1809) took his son Joseph Mayer (d 1860) into partnership in 1804. Their firm made creamware of good quality, light in weight and with an apple-green tinge to the glaze, which included baskets with openwork sides for cake or fruit, and a wide variety of tablewares. Among other products were black, cane-coloured or drab stoneware, used to make teapots, jugs, bowls, etc., with relief decoration that was crisp and well finished. The firm's black basalt was noted for its fine texture and included many commemorative pieces; jugs bearing a portrait of the Prince of Wales were issued on his appointment as Regent in 1811. Some pieces without relief decoration rely for effect on a smooth elegance of shape. Bamboo wares were decorated with lines of foliage in blue and green enamel.

Some creamware was edged with a brown enamel band. Tea sets were often in fluted forms decorated with vertical stripes in blue enamel, and teapots were made in simple shapes, often straight-sided with a rounded top and spherical finial.

Joseph Mayer ran the pottery alone from his father's death until 1835, letting part of the works to his cousin W.*Ridgway in 1832 when he retired from full-time potting. Joseph Mayer's firm merged in 1836 with that of his brothers, T.J. & J. Mayer.
Marks: E. MAYER impressed, or E. MAYER & SON impressed or printed.
Refs: Godden (1974); Jewitt; Rhead; Williams-Wood.

Mayer, Eugen (1890-1961). German designer, sculptor and ceramic modeller, born in Altenburg. Mayer studied at the Wiener Kunstgewerbeschule (1909-14) under teachers who included F.*Barwig. After service in World War I, he worked as a sculptor in Tetschen then, in Vienna, made metal sculptures, enamel work and woodcuts. His ceramics included figures, model animals, and garden ornaments. He taught at the Wiener Kunstgewerbeschule from 1922 and was appointed professor in 1955.
Ref: Neuwirth (1974a).

Mayer, T.J.& J. Staffordshire potters. Thomas Mayer (working until 1858) established a pottery at Cliff Bank, Stoke-on-Trent, in 1826, moving to a works in Longport briefly in 1835. His brother John Mayer (working until 1862) started a small pottery

at Foley, near Fenton, in 1833. Three years later, the brothers entered into partnership at the Dale Hall Works, Longport, merging with the firm of their elder brother Joseph Mayer (*see* Mayer, E., & Son). After Joseph Mayer's death, his brothers took into partnership Liddle Elliott and traded as Mayer Bros & Elliott from 1855, which was succeeded by a series of firms with Liddle Elliott as a partner. Colour printing was introduced on the firm's earthenware (e.g. for pot lids). Highly vitreous stoneware was used for the introduction of tea urns normally made in metal. The firms at the Dale Hall Works specialized in relief modelling, generally of plant designs, including lavish arrangments of modelled flowers on vases. Gildea & Walker, owners 1881-86, produced a variety of dinner and tea services and toilet sets, plain, printed, or enamelled, painted and gilded, as well as jugs and spirit flasks in earthenware. They continued the colour printing introduced by the Mayers on services, pot lids and ornamental pieces, and developed techniques in the printing of gold. In the 1870s Bates Elliott & Co., followed (1875-78) by Bates Walker & Co., made reproductions of 18th-century jasper ware, using an earthenware body coated with coloured slip and marketing the pieces as Turner's Jasper Ware, from the moulds of Stoke-on-Trent stoneware potter John Turner (1738-87). The pottery also made crisply modelled terracotta figures (some portraying classical subjects), and sanitary, pharmaceutical and garden wares. The firm of Keeling & Co. (Ltd) succeeded Gildea & Walker in 1886, and worked the pottery until 1936.

Various printed marks include T.J.& J. MAYER (and sometimes DALE HALL POTTERY/LONGPORT), MAYER BROS; BATES, WALKER & CO. PATENTEES; B.W. & CO.; B.G. &W or G.&W, LATE MAYERS; K.& CO. B.
Refs: Blacker (1922a); Godden (1964, 1971); Jewitt; Rhead; Williams-Wood.

Mayer Pottery Co. Ltd. American factory established at Beaver Falls, Pennsylvania, in 1881. The firm produced table and toilet wares in white granite with coloured glazes or underglaze decoration, before specializing in semi-porcelain, plain or decorated, in the early 20th century.

A wide variety of printed marks incorporate the firm's name, *J. & E. Mayer* or the initials J.& E.M.
Ref: Barber (1976).

Mayer Pottery Manufacturing Co. Ltd. *See* Arsenal Pottery.

Mayodon, Jean (1893-1967). French artist potter. After working as a painter, Mayodon began work in ceramics, establishing a kiln at Sèvres (Hauts-de-Seine) c.1918. He later acted as artistic consultant to the Sèvres factory (1934-39) and then as artistic director (1941-42). Using stoneware or an earthenware body made more refractory by the addition of fired, pulverized clay, and

Jean Mayodon. Stoneware dish, c.1925.

influenced in style by Middle Eastern pottery, Mayodon made vases, bottles, bowls, plates, etc., decorated with historical scenes, figures or stylized animals (notably deer), modelled in low relief or painted in oxides of iron, copper, chromium, manganese, and sometimes touched with gold. Some pieces resemble the work of A.*Metthey, although the body is lighter in weight. A noted tile maker, Mayodon produced work for use on the steamship *Normandie*.
Refs: Baschet; Faré; Lesieutre; Lesur (1967, 1971).

Mead, Henry. American physician working in New York, and owner of a factory that was among experimental producers of porcelain in the 1810s. A vase in Empire style with soft-paste body and very white glaze is thought to have been made in 1816. Records conflict over the date and location of Mead's factory: J. Leander Bishop suggests in his *History of American Manufacturers* that the factory started in 1819 in New York, while an obituary of Mead places his factory in Jersey City. Work is thought to have continued for several years.
Ref: Barber (1976).

Meade, Laura (d 1959). American potter, formerly a student of ceramics at the University of North Dakota. With Robert Hughes, whom she married in 1943, she established the Rosemeade Pottery at Wahperton, North Dakota, in 1940, making brightly coloured vases, condiment sets, cream jugs, sugar bowls, etc., with matt glazes. The pottery continued to work until 1961.
Mark: *Rosemeade* in black or blue.
Refs: Kovel & Kovel; Grace M. Weiss 'A Native of North Dakota: Rosemeade Pottery' in *The Antique Trader* (27th February 1973).

Meadow Pottery, Rawmarsh. *See* Low Pottery.

Meakin, Alfred. Staffordshire pottery manufacturers established at the Royal Albert Works, Tunstall, in the early 1870s. The firm produced a wide range of ironstone china and other earthenware bodies for domestic use, much exported to America and other countries, trading from c.1913 as Alfred Meakin (Tunstall) Ltd, and after

Gudrun Meedun Baech. Stoneware vase and bowl with light grey glaze, made at the *Bing & Grøndahl factory, 1952. The vase is 20 cm high, the bowl 10 cm in diameter.

purchase by Myott & Son Co. (Ltd), as Myott-Meakin Ltd.

Marks include ALFRED MEAKIN and the name of the body, e.g. *Royal Ironstone China*.
Refs: Godden (1964); Jewitt.

Meakin, J.& G. Staffordshire pottery manufacturers. James Meakin, founder of the firm in 1845, moved from Longton to Hanley in 1848. He was succeeded on his retirement in 1851 or 1852 by his sons James and George (d 1891), who concentrated on the mass production of domestic earthenware, especially white granite imitating French porcelain in style. The demand for their work, much of which was exported to America, was so great that the firm needed to commission other manufacturers to fill orders, and the Eagle Works, Hanley, built by the firm in 1859, was enlarged in 1868. The firm operated branches in Cobridge and Burslem, and in 1887 took over the business established in 1883 at the Eastwood Pottery, Hanley, by their brother Charles, who had been working c.1876-82 in Burslem. George Meakin was succeeded from 1891 to 1927 by his son George Elliott Meakin, formerly an apprentice at the Eagle Pottery and assisted by his brother James and cousin Kenneth Meakin. The firm subsequently produced semi-porcelain with transfer-printed and later hand-painted decoration. Lithographic printing afterwards became the main method of decoration. The firm remained under the control of the founder's family, who enlarged the Eagle Pottery after selling the Eastwood Works in 1958, and became part of the Wedgwood group in 1970.

Marks: *J. & G. Meakin*; *ironstone china*; a trade name SOL, with a rising sun used from 1912; Charles Meakin marked wares with his name, the Royal Arms and, sometimes from 1883, *Hanley* or *England*.
Refs: Bunt; Jewitt; B. Hollowood *The Story of Meakins* (1951).

Measham ware. *See* barge ware.

Medinger, Jacob (d 1932). American potter making red ware at Neiffer in Montgomery County, Pennsylvania, in the 1920s. He was the son of a potter, William Medinger. Work-

ing with his wife and William McAllister, a woodcarver, who carried out the more elaborate decoration, he produced pie plates with *sgraffito* patterns often inspired by the work of earlier Pennsylvania slipware makers, e.g. S.*Troxel (a design incorporating three birds), and the 18th-century potters, Georg Hübener (peacock plates) and Joseph Smith (bird and heart pattern), or with his own decoration of animals, e.g. horse, rabbit, cow. Medinger also made plates with wavy lines of trailed slip, and a variety of red ware, including pitchers, jars, bowls, milk pans, cups and saucers, flowerpots and hanging baskets, candlesticks, and some animal figures (including a bird with raised wings).
Ref: C. Weygandt 'A Maker of Pennsylvania Redware' in Stradling.

Meedun Baech, Gudrun (b 1915). Danish potter, trained in Copenhagen. Gudrun Meedun Baech worked for N.*Krebs, 1945-46, then joined the firm of *Bing & Grøndahl, where she worked as an artist until she established her own studio in 1953. She married the painter Johannes Baech and lives in Viborg, Jutland, where she makes sculptural pieces in red earthenware, usually with ash glazes, and wares with decoration painted in blue, applied in slip, inlaid or *sgraffito*.

Mark: signature, *G. Mee*.
Ref: W. Hull *Danish Ceramic Designs* (catalogue, Museum of Art, Pennsylvania State University, 1981).

Mehlem, Franz Anton. German pottery manufacturers producing useful and ornamental wares near Bonn from 1836. From 1884 until 1903, the firm re-issued models that had initially been made in porcelain at *Höchst and then in creamware at *Damm from moulds acquired on the closure of the Höchst factory.

Monogram of FAM incorporated in a variety of printed marks.
Refs: Danckert; Haslam (1977); Pazaurek.

Mehwaldt, Charles August (b 1808). Potter working mainly in Germany and America. Mehwaldt was born near Berlin, into a family of potters. He spent several years as a journeyman potter, working in Russia, Palestine, and in Germany. In 1851, he emigrated with other families from his home area, joining a German community formed in the 1840s at Bergholtz, New York State, where he established a pottery in the following year making large quantities of domestic red ware, often with mottled lead glaze. Special work included animal whistles, miniature ware for children, a chandelier for his local church and two memorial wreaths of flowers finely modelled in earthenware. Mehwaldt also made tiled stoves, chimney crocks and milk pans. He ceased work late in the 1880s.
Ref: Stradling.

Meier, Emil (b 1877). Austrian sculptor and modeller. Meier trained as a goldsmith in Turnau before attending the Vienna Kunstgewerbeschule, where he trained in metal and sculpture, 1901-03. He subsequently worked for a Vienna silversmith. Ceramic designs carried out for *Wiener Keramik c.1910 included figures, paperweights and vases issued in earthenware and porcelain.

He collaborated with Johanna Meier Michel, who was herself a metal sculptor, and designer of figures in earthenware and porcelain for the Wiener Werkstätte and the firm of F.*Goldscheider.

Marks: *Meier* or EM; the signature of *Johanna Meier Michel.*
Ref: Neuwirth (1974a).

Meier, Otto (b 1903). German sculptor and potter. Meier studied sculpture and architecture at the Kunstgewerbeschule in his native Dortmund. In 1925, he went to Worpswede, where he studied ceramic techniques and began work as a potter. He made individual pieces, including vases, bowls, cups, candleholders, with abstract designs, slip-painted or *sgraffito* until 1930. Meier used clay from Lesum, fired in an open peat kiln. After taking over the two potteries attached to an artists' cooperative in Bremen, in 1928, he went over to coal firing. His work after 1930 was made with the grey or red-brown clays of Westerwald. Meier studied at the technical school for ceramics in Bunzlau, 1929-30, later developing his wide range of glazes, which included a copper reduction glaze. After military service in World War II, during which his Bremen workshop was destroyed, Meier established a new workshop in Worpswede for the production of stoneware. He installed an electric kiln in 1958, but until 1964 continued to use a coal kiln for reduction firings at 1100°C. He continued to make vessels as well as sculptural pieces composed mainly from thrown components.

Marks incised or impressed.
Ref: Bock.

Emil Meier. Figure of a girl portraying Winter, made by the Wiener kunstkeramische Werkstätte, c.1910. Signed, Meier. 28 cm high.

Meier-Graefe, Julius F. *See* Maison Moderne, La.

Meigh, Job, his son, Charles, and his grandson, also Charles. Staffordshire pottery manufacturers. Job Meigh (d 1817) built the Old Hall works, Hanley, c.1770, for the production of red and cream-coloured earthenware. The firm traded as Job Meigh & Son 1812-35, under the control of his second son, Charles Meigh (formerly works manager) after his father's death, and subsequently as Charles Meigh until 1847. The output of earthenware included a variety of durable table and toilet wares with hard, clear glaze and high-quality printed decoration by the early 19th century. Some pieces were painted by hand over printed outlines. A convolvulus pattern in natural colours was registered in the early 1840s, but afterwards widely copied. Dessert services were enamelled, and sometimes jewelled and gilded. The firm also made fine, hard stoneware with elaborate relief decoration cast with the body (rather than applied) on vases and, especially, jugs, of which large quantities were produced in the 1840s and 1850s. The decoration of jugs included architectural detail in Gothic style with panels of figures (e.g. a design registered 1842, and the York Minster Jug, registered in 1846), or vines and Bacchanalian scenes (e.g. a shape registered in 1844). The firm's display in the Great Exhibition (1851) included large vases. Charles Meigh, in a partnership, Charles Meigh, Son & Pankhurst, 1849-51, subsequently traded with his son and in 1861 transferred the business to the Old Hall Earthenware Co. Ltd, of which T.*Ashworth, Charles Meigh's son-in-law, became a shareholder. The production of earthenware (sold as Opaque Porcelain) and ironstone wares continued; much was exported to the United States, France and Germany. The firm's title became the Old Hall Porcelain Co. from 1886 until its closure in 1902. The works were later demolished.

Marks include MEIGH, impressed, from the early 19th century until 1834; OLD HALL, impressed or printed from 1805; J.M. & S.; impressed marks with *Charles Meigh* and the date of design, 1835-49; printed or

*Meissen. Coffee service designed by H.*van de Velde and made at the Meissen factory, 1903.*

impressed marks of imitation Chinese seals (used by Job Meigh and later); name or initials of Charles Meigh & Son.
Refs: Blacker (1922a); Jewitt, Rhead; Shinn; Wakefield.

Meissen. Porcelain factory established at Meissen, near Dresden, in the early 18th century. The factory worked under the directorship of Camillo Marcolini from 1774 until his death in 1814. Financial difficulties forced it to close temporarily in 1813.

Decorative work of the early 19th century and before the rococo revival included *chinoiseries*, relief patterns painted white on pastel grounds, painted portraits and printed patterns (1814-c.1870). Copper green was frequently used from 1817, e.g. as the predominant colour in a range called Weinlaubdekor, which is still in production. Artists included the painters, D. Schubert and J.K. Mauksch, and the modellers Schönheit, Juchtzer, Matthai and A.F.*Wegner. Shapes became simpler.

Heinrich Gottlieb Kühn (d 1870), the factory's director from 1849, discovered the technique of brilliant gilding in 1827, and introduced a relief decoration, Greek in inspiration, which was intended to display gilding and painting to the best effect, he also developed iridescent colours, which were commercially produced from 1852. A revival of 18th-century models, including figures made from the factory's original rococo-style moulds, was followed by newly modelled child musicians, mythological groups, etc. (1860-90), and figures in contemporary costume, e.g. soldiers and sportswomen (from 1870). Underglaze blue was revived for the decoration of tableware. In the late 19th century, the management enlarged the buildings and extended the programme of technical research. Export to America began in 1878 and quickly expanded. A very fine porcelain paste (muslin porcelain), additions to the range of high-temperature colours and, in 1878, slip-painted decoration were among the technical innovations.

Under the direction of Brunnemann (1895-1901), the factory developed a range of crystalline glazes and began to produce wares painted under the glaze in the style of exhibits shown by the Royal *Copenhagen factory in Paris (1900). Decoration (including relief ornament) in Art Nouveau styles was often used on shapes evolved from earlier

Meissen. Clock with Zwiebelmuster (onion pattern) in blue highlighted with gold. 39 cm.

designs, e.g. a tall octagonal bottle painted with *Dianthus* buds and flowers. Subsequently, artists including H.*van de Velde and R.*Riemerschmid were commissioned to produce new designs for tableware.

With M.A.*Pfeiffer as director from 1918, the factory largely reverted to 18th-century designs for tableware, but new models for figures were provided e.g. by M.*Esser, A.*Gaul, J.K. Hentschel and P.*Scheurich.

Variations of the factory's crossed swords mark include curved guards (1860-24), the addition of dates 1710 and 1910 in the bicentenary year, and a dot between the sword blades (1924-34).
Refs: K. Berling *Das Meissner Porzellan und Seine Geschichte* (Leipzig, 1900); W. Doenges *Meissner Porzellan* (Dresden, 1921); Ducret (1968); E. Kollmann *Meissner Porzellan* (Brunswick, 1960); L. Nékan *Meissen Porcelain in the Budapest Museum of Applied Arts* (Corvina Kiado, Budapest, 1980); R. Rückert *Meissner Porzellan 1710-1810* (Bayerisches Nationalmuseum,

Meissen. Böttger stoneware candlestick with removable sconce, c.1930. Marks include crossed swords, incised. 25.5 cm high.

Thomas Mellor. Vase with pâte-sur-pâte decoration and deep turquoise ground. Decorated by Mellor at *Mintons Ltd. Mark: monogram with the factory mark. 27 cm high.

Munich, 1966); O. Walcha *Meissner Porzellan* (Dresden, 1973).

Melandri, Pietro. Italian painter and ceramist. His influence in 20th century Italian ceramics is regarded as comparable with that of M.*Laeuger in Germany. Melandri trained as a stage designer in Milan and subsequently worked as a portraitist and landscape painter. He made his first ceramics while in Vienna as a prisoner in World War I. In 1918, he established a workshop in his birthplace, Faenza. He has exhibited in Faenza, in the Venice Biennale, and in the Milan Triennale. His work in earthenware and stoneware included vases with painted lustre and sometimes modelled relief in a wide variety of styles, some inspired by early maiolica pieces. He also makes sculptural portraits, masks, figures and wall panels.
Mark: MELANDRI.
Refs: Keramik (catalogue, Kunstgewerbemesse der Stadt, Cologne, 1975); A. Totti 'Pietro Melandri' in *Keramische Zeitschrift* 10 (1958).

Melchior, Johann Peter (1742-1825). German sculptor and porcelain modeller. After working as *Modellmeister* at Höchst (1767-79), he joined the porcelain factory at Frankenthal and, after its closure, modelled many pieces for production at *Nymphenburg (1797-1822). In the 19th century, he was known for portrait plaques and busts in biscuit porcelain.
Mark (at Frankenthal): signature: JOAN PETR/MELCHIOR (18th century).
Refs: see Nymphenburg.

Meli, Giovanni. Sculptor and ceramic modeller, born in Sicily and working from the early 1840s in Staffordshire. He worked as an independent modeller for W.T.*Copeland, 1840-50, and for Sir James Duke &

Nephews and other firms, c.1840. Meli established his own Glebe Street works in Stoke-on-Trent c.1858 for the production of parian figures and groups, selling the business and equipment to *Robinson & Leadbeater in 1865. Work shown in the International Exhibition (1862) included religious and literary figures, butter tubs, decorative jugs, dessert ware and vases. On his return to Italy, he attempted to start a terracotta works, but left for America, where he started terracotta production in Chicago.
Refs: Batkin; Jewitt; Reilly & Savage; Shinn.

Mellor, George (c.1776-1861). English porcelain decorator. After serving an apprenticeship at the porcelain factory in Nottingham Road, *Derby, and working with W.*Billingsley, he was employed at *Coalport from c.1800 until 1811, and subsequently in Staffordshire until his death. Mellor specialized in studies of flowers and insects, executed in a delicate style. His son, also George Mellor, worked as a gilder and painter of Japan patterns at the Derby factory until 1828, when he left to work as an independent decorator in London.
Refs: see Coalport; Derby.

Mellor, Joshua. *See* Plant, R.H.& S.L., Ltd.

Mellor, Thomas. English ceramic decorator. Working at *Minton's c.1872-85, Mellor trained under L.-M.-E.*Solon in the technique of *pâte-sur-pâte*, and specialized in classical-style ornament, using several colours. Some work under Mellor's name closely imitated the work of Solon. He worked in the 1880s for J.*Wedgwood & Sons Ltd, carrying out inlaid decoration. His work included vases, dressing-table ware and a tea set shown at the World's Columbian Exposition in Chicago (1893). He subsequently worked as a decorator of jasper ware.
Refs: Aslin & Atterbury; Batkin; Reilly & Savage.

Mendes da Costa, Joseph (1863-1939). Dutch sculptor and ceramic artist. Mendes da Costa trained in his father's stonemasonry workshop in Amsterdam, and under the sculptor P.J.H. Cuypers at the Rijksschool voor Kunstnijverheid. He carried out designs for production in earthenware, 1891-98, and was a fellow member (with the sculptor L. Zijl, his collaborator 1885-88), of the Labor et Ars group, which was formed in 1885 as a reaction against academic attitudes to the applied arts. In 1898, Mendes da Costa established his own pottery, where he made coarse, brown, domestic earthenware. His work has a mystical quality expressed in later jugs, vases, etc., through medieval elements in design. He also made small figures, groups and model animals in similar clay with grey glaze flecked with blue and brown. He experimented with *sgraffito* decoration and carried out some work in stoneware. From c.1900, he worked in association with H.P.*Berlage and other members of 't*Binnenhuis. He was also a teacher at the Industriesschool in Amsterdam.
Mark: a cypher formed of the initials JM and a circle, with a date.
Refs: 'Kunstniverheid te Kopenhagen, 1904' in *Joseph Mendes da Costa 1863-1939,*

beeldhouwer (catalogue, Synagogecomplex, Amsterdam, 1976); Singelenberg-van der Meer.

Mercer, Henry Chapman (1856-1930). American potter and tile maker, born in Doylestown, Pennsylvania. He graduated from Harvard University in 1879 and practised law for several years. A founder member of Bucks County Historical Society in the 1880s, Mercer worked as an archaeologist and anthropologist throughout the late 1880s and early 1890s. In 1893, he was a member of the US Archaeological Commission for the World's Columbian Exposition in Chicago. He began to write about Colonial America, and in 1897 published an article on pioneer implements; in the course of study, he examined the tools used in a number of handcraft trades, including pottery. He started experiments relating to the manufacture of tiles at Doylestown in 1897, and went to Germany to study pottery techniques, establishing the Moravian Pottery & Tile Works on his return home in 1898. With a number of assistants, Mercer made tiles from local red clay covered with a heavy glaze in various colours, or white clay from New Jersey, usually with a blue or green glaze. Later tiles were often left unglazed to exploit the colour and texture of the clay. Mercer drew decorative inspiration initially from Moravian stove plates collected from the Pennsylvania region and later introduced designs from varied sources—German, Spanish and medieval English tiles, tapestries, archaeological discoveries, flowers, animals—as well as decorative motifs used by American Indians. Mosaic designs were made from coloured clay cut into small pieces, often set in concrete; the shapes, many of them irregular, sometimes followed the outlines of the pattern. Mercer used a wide range of decorative techniques, e.g. modelled, *sgraffito* or slip-painted designs or smear glazes; some floor tiles were glazed only in the recesses of the pattern. He always sought the effect of production by hand. The colours were often unrealistic—orange sky, yellow tree, etc. Plain geometrical tiles were produced in brown, black, green, blue, buff or red, and special designs made to order, as well as other articles, e.g. inkwells, cups, penholders, sconces, vases, bowls. Mercer bequeathed his estate to the Bucks County Historical Society, who continued to operate the tileworks as a living museum.
Marks: HCM monogram and MORAVIAN in semicircular outline, impressed, or

Henry C. Mercer. Mosaic tile, set in concrete, portraying Adam and Eve, with green, red, yellow and black glazes. Early 20th century.

MORAVIAN, stamped in large type.
Refs: Barber (1976); B.H. Barnes *The Moravian Pottery: Memories of Forty-Six Years* (Bucks County Historical Society, 1970); Eidelberg; C. Fox 'Henry Chapman Mercer: Tilemaker, Collector, and Builder Extraordinary' in *Antiques* 104 (October 1973); Keen; Kovel & Kovel; C.G. Reed *The Arts and Crafts Ideal* (Institute for the Development of Evolutionary Architecture, Syracuse, 1978); F.K. Swain 'Moravian Pottery and Tile Works Founded by H.C. Mercer, Doylestown Pa' in *Antiques* 24 (November 1933).

Mercer Pottery Co. American pottery established 1868 at Trenton, New Jersey, and making dinner services and toilet sets (plain or decorated) in semi-porcelain 'Parisian Granite' ware, which was claimed by James Moses, the proprietor, to be the first produced in the United States.

A variety of marks incorporate the company's name or monogram, or MERCER CHINA.
Refs: Antiques (July 1976); Barber (1976).

Mérillon, Jean. French potter; owner, from 1918, of the former Poterie Caffin, which had produced majolica 1882-1913 at Cauderan, Bordeaux. Mérillon made tea and coffee sets, garden ornaments and toys in high-fired earthenware. His workshop, in operation to the present day, also produced pottery with a buttercup-yellow finish, tin-glazed ware and high-fired pieces with red, crackled glaze.
Mark: a leopard, three crescents and the initials C.A.B.
Ref: Lesur (1971).

Merkelbach & Wicke. German stoneware manufacturers working at Grenzhausen, near Coblenz. In the early 20th century, Reinhold Merkelbach produced jugs, bowls, etc., designed by artists who included R. *Riemerschmid, Paul Wynand, Charlotte Krause, and figures by Hans Wewerka (1888-1917). Merkelbach's successors joined with other stoneware manufacturers to form Merkelbach & Wicke, who employed the artist Peter Behrens as designer.
Refs: Bock; Haslam (1977).

Merrimac Pottery. American pottery organized 1897 as the Merrimac Ceramic Co. at Newburyport, Massachusetts, for the production of glazed tiles and florists' ware,

enlarged c.1898, and trading as the Merrimac Pottery Co. from 1902. The founder and proprietor T.S. Nickerson, an American who had studied in England, introduced art ware, mainly small vases and flower containers, using white or red earthenware bodies. Seeking simplicity in form and colour, he restricted decoration to soft-coloured glazes, at first mainly in matt greens or yellows, and increasing the range to include, by 1903, matt pink, black, orange and shades of purple, iridescent dark blue and purple; some glazes were finely crackled. Garden ornaments were often styled after Etruscan models, and generally without decoration, although larger pieces were occasionally ornamented with garlands, rosettes, satyrs' heads. A line of ware introduced before 1903 reproduced Arretine Roman red ware, moulded with low-relief designs. The works and much stock were destroyed by fire in 1908, soon after Nickerson's sale of the pottery.

Mark: a sturgeon (merrimac is an American Indian name for the fish), with *Merrimac Ceramic Company* on a paper label, 1900-01; afterwards impressed or incised with name MERRIMAC.
Refs: Barber (1976); Evans; Kovel & Kovel.

Mersman, Ferdinand. Pottery designer. Mersman studied at the academy of fine arts in Munich before going to America. In 1881, he executed some work at the *Rookwood Pottery, including vases with figures hand-modelled in high relief, and a pitcher (sold in two sizes) in a grey body with smear glaze, in memory of President Garfield, whose portrait appeared in relief on the piece. He became principal designer at the *Cambridge Art Tile Works, and modelled tile panels with figures in low relief.
Refs: Barber (1976); Kovel & Kovel; Peck.

Mertens, Konrad (1889-1953). Designer, born in Bonn, but working in Holland. Mertens designed pieces for De Vier Paddenstoelen (1920) and for the Potterie Kennemerland, which he established at Velsen in 1920 in partnership with E. Snel, also an associate of De *Vier Paddenstoelen. Mertens and Snel left in 1923 or 1924. Mertens established a pottery, De Swing, in Noordwijk 1927-c.1931, producing hard earthenware, mainly grey, striped in blue, orange or green. In 1932 he started the Potterie Mertens, again in Noordwijk.

André Metthey. Earthenware vase decorated with deer and foliage against a red and gilt speckled ground. Mark: monogram of AM impressed in a circle on the base. 26 cm high.

The mark used at Kennemerland under Mertens incorporated VELSEN HOLLAND.
Ref: Singelenberg-van der Meer.

Merton Abbey. *See* De Morgan, William.

Metalline ware. *See* Cook Pottery Co.

Methven family. Scottish potters working at Kirkcaldy and Cupar, Fife. David Methven (d 1827) acquired the brick and tile works which became the *Links Pottery, leaving the business to two of his sons, George Methven (d 1847) and John Methven (d 1837). John Methven was succeeded at the *Fife Pottery by his son-in-law Robert Heron and at the Links Pottery by his nephew David Methven, formerly a maker of coarse earthenware at Cupar.
Refs: Jewitt; McVeigh.

Metthey, André (1871-1921). French ceramist. At 14, Metthey worked with a stonemason in his home town of Laignes (Côte-d'Or). The following year he settled with his family in Paris, beginning study with a plaster modeller, but having to maintain his family after the father's death. As a soldier in Auxerre, he studied drawing and became interested in ceramics after reading Garnier's *Traité de Céramique*; he was self taught as a potter. The ten years after his release from the army were marked by financial difficulties and a search for technical expertise (mainly directed towards the production of stoneware in Japanese and Korean styles, using *flambé* glazes) while working full time. He first exhibited ceramics in 1901. Attracted by traditional French faience, Metthey opened a studio in Asnières (Hauts-de-Seine), where he prepared his own clay and glazes, and built himself a kiln. He began the production of tin-glazed ware, rather heavily potted, and called on a number of painters of the Paris school to decorate his work: Odilon Redon, Georges Rouault, Henri Matisse, Pierre Bonnard, Edouard Vuillard, Othon Friesz, André Derain and Maurice de

Merkelbach & Wicke. Plant pot probably designed by Paul Wynand for Merkelbach and produced in Höhr-Grenzhausen, 1910.

Merrimac Pottery. Earthenware lamp base. Decorated with dark green dripping over brown/green glaze. Mark: paper label with firm's name and a sturgeon. 52.7 cm high.

Vlaminck. The palette was limited by the high firing temperature and Metthey ended this project after two years, later abandoning the use of tin glaze. He began in 1908 to paint white earthenware under clear alkaline glazes in the Persian manner, returning to the production of stoneware in 1912 and, towards the end of his career, experimented with *pâte de verre*. He retired through illness in 1920.

Marks: signature or initials incised.
Refs: Années 25; Baschet; Bénézit; Brunhammer *et al* (1976); Camart *et al*;

Heuser & Heuser; M. Rheims *L'Art 1900* (Arts et Métiers Graphiques, Paris, 1965); M. Valotaire in *Connaissance des Arts* (September 1962).

Mettlach. *See* Villeroy & Boch.

Metzler Bros & Ortloff. German porcelain manufacturers at Ilmenau, Thuringia from 1875. The firm made decorative wares, gifts and small pieces for everyday use.

Marks include the initials MO, under a crown; a monogram of MO with a crown in a circular outline; MO with I and crossed hammers.
Refs: Danckert; Weiss.

Mexborough. Yorkshire town, near Swinton. The Mexborough Pottery was established in 1800 by a firm which was trading in 1804 as Robert Sowter & Co., and possibly made stoneware teapots. Jesse Barker leased the pottery in 1811 and ran it with his brother Peter from the following year until his son Samuel Barker (d 1856) took over in the late 1820s, buying out his uncle, Peter, in 1838. Barker purchased the *Don Pottery in the following year and worked both businesses together until at least 1848. The Barkers' output included transfer-printed earthenware, black basalt, mocha ware banded in brown and with the tree-like designs in black against brown or grey grounds, and white earthenware splashed with underglaze colours in the manner associated with F.& R.*Pratt. Samuel Barker's son, also named Samuel, converted the premises for use as an iron foundry.

The Mexborough Rock Pottery, built in the late 18th century against a sandstone outcrop, made earthenware from the early 19th century under the partnership of James Reed and Benjamin Taylor (also of the *Ferrybridge and *Swillington Bridge potteries), remaining in the hands of Reed's family from the break-up of the partnership in the early 1840s until its sale to Sydney Woolf of the *Ferrybridge Pottery in 1873. The Reed family replaced the previous output of brown household earthenware and cane ware (of which no known pieces survive) with white earthenware, transfer-printed or green-glazed, and terracotta. They used the mark REED impressed or printed on a small proportion of transfer-printed ware. The firm used moulds and engraving plates bought during the sale of *Swinton Pottery stock in 1843. The Mexborough Rock Pottery closed in 1883.

Emery's Pottery was built for the production of brown earthenware by James Emery (d 1874), who worked there after selling the business in 1841 to Peter Emery, and continued, despite Peter's death, in the late 1850s. He was later joined by Alfred Emery and another Peter Emery, retailer of pottery in Mexborough and listed as a potter until 1886. An incised mark—*J Emery, Mexbro*—has been recorded with the date 1838.

Alfred, the son of I.*Baguley, moved in 1865 from Swinton to Mexborough, where he continued to operate as a decorator.
Refs: Grabham; Hurst; Jewitt; Lawrence; *White's Directory of the West Riding* (1822).

Meyer, Jenny (1866-1927. Danish porcelain decorator specializing in flower studies. She worked for the Royal *Copenhagen Porcelain Factory, 1892-1927.
Mark: signature, *Jenny Meyer*.
Ref: Porzellankunst.

Meyer, Joseph Fortune (1848-1931). American potter, born in France. Meyer moved to Biloxi, Mississippi, with his father, a potter, by the 1860s. He worked in New Orleans, at first making simple pots thrown in local clay at his own workshop. From 1886, he was employed by the *New Orleans Art Pottery. He joined the *Newcomb College Pottery in 1896, staying as designer and chief potter until 1925, throwing almost every piece decorated at the pottery until failing eyesight forced his retirement in 1925.
Refs: Barber (1976); Clark & Hughto; Eidelberg; Evans; Henzke; Jervis; Keen; Kovel & Kovel; S. Ormond & M.E. Irvine *Louisiana's Art Nouveau: The Crafts of the Newcomb Style* (Pelican Publishing, Gretna, Louisiana, 1976).

Meyer, Siegmund Paul. German porcelain manufacturer, working at Bayreuth in 1900. His firm made household and hotel wares.
Marks: shields, topped by a crown and bearing the initials SPM, sometimes with WALKÜRE.BAYREUTH/BAVARIA.
Refs: Danckert; Weiss.

Mezhegorye. *See* Kiev-Mezhegorye State Faience Factory.

Miami Pottery. American art pottery briefly in operation between 1902 and 1905 at Dayton, Ohio. Students in handicraft classes run by the Dayton Society of Arts and Crafts (formed in 1902) produced vases, bowls, etc., hand-built in yellow clay from the Miami river valley. They made simple shapes, sometimes with modelled ornamentation in low relief, covered in a characteristic matt dark bronze glaze noted for its rich, luminous quality.
Refs: Evans; Kovel & Kovel.

Michel, François. *See* Michel, Gabriel.

Michel, Gabriel. French decorator of faience and porcelain, working in the early 19th century at Les *Islettes. He specialized in baskets or bouquets of mixed flowers and painted birds, e.g. cockerels or a pheasant and, occasionally, animals. In 1827, at Les Islettes, he painted a porcelain tea service with garlands and gilded foliage alternating

with pansies, forget-me-nots, and medallions containing doves. His work also included a faience luncheon set, decorated with garlands of cornflowers tied with purple ribbons and small golden rosettes. Michel's uncle, François Michel, was also a flower painter at Les Islettes.
Refs: Ernould-Gandouet; Lesur (1971).

Michelaud Frères. *See* Saint-Brice.

Middle Lane Pottery. *See* Brouwer, Theophilus A.

Middlesbrough Pottery. Yorkshire pottery established 1834 by a partnership trading as the Middlesbrough Pottery Co. for the production of a variety of household wares. Among the output were transfer-printed table and toilet sets, enamelled or lustred creamware and black or brown-glazed kitchen articles, as well as horticultural ware and chimneypots. The company became Middlesborough Earthenware Co. 1844-52, and subsequently Isaac Wilson & Co. until the pottery's closure in 1887. Transfer-printed ware remained the main product; other decorative techniques included sponged enamel colours, gilding and pink lustre.

Printed marks incorporate MPCO, or later IW & CO, and the pattern name.
Refs: Grabham; Hurst; Jewitt; Lawrence.

Midwinter, W.R., Ltd. Staffordshire earthenware manufacturer. After working for fourteen years at the *Doulton & Co. factory in Burslem, W.R. Midwinter established a small factory at Bourne's Bank c.1910. He produced tea sets, toilet ware and brown-glazed teapots. Midwinter served in the Royal Navy during World War I, leaving the business under the management of his wife. He extended the works by 1918, then buying the Albion Pottery and adjoining business producing tea and toilet wares, and another Burslem factory. By the outbreak of World War II, his firm employed about 700 workers. He was succeeded by his son, W. Roy Midwinter, who returned from war service in 1946.

Marks incorporate MIDWINTER or W.R. MIDWINTER LTD, and sometimes the name of the body.
Refs: Bunt; Godden (1964).

Mikawachi or **Mikochi.** Japanese ceramic centre in Nagasaki prefecture, to the south of *Arita. Kilns established in the 17th century as offshoots of a kiln on Hirado Island operated there under the patronage of the princes of Hirado from 1751 to 1843. Their output of pure white porcelain was fine textured, with a lustrous, velvety glaze and neat, delicate painting in pale blue, mainly landscapes, figures, trees and flowers, of Chinese inspiration, with a deeper blue used as ground colour or, occasionally, combined with dark brown glaze. Relief modelling often occurs, either as decoration or in the form of free-standing statuettes or animal figures. By 1840, porcelain workshops at Mikawachi numbered 37. Export trade was carried on through the port of Hirado. Known as Hirado ware, the kilns' output by 1865 included white eggshell porcelain and ware enamelled in red and green; both classes of ware were supplied to the Imperial court, and displayed in Paris in the 1870s.

Porcelain with polychrome enamelled decoration was sold on the general market in Japan from 1878.
Refs: Honey (1945); Jenyns (1965); Munsterberg.

Mikelson, Arnold. *See* Derby.

Miklashewski, Andrei. Russian porcelain maker. He established a factory in 1839 after the discovery of high-quality kaolin on his estate at Volodino (or Volokitin) in the Ukraine; he employed A. Darte as manager (1844-51), and made porcelain for sale in southern Russia and the Ukraine with restrained, painted decoration of flowers, often arranged singly or in small bouquets and, occasionally, with inscriptions in French. Later display pieces, including vases, were lavishly decorated with flowers modelled in high relief. Figures made under Darte show a French influence in style, but examples subsequently made by local workers trained at the factory are derived from Ukrainian embroideries and other specimens of folk art. The factory also made a huge screen and chandelier for the village church at Volodino. The freeing of the serfs, who had supplied the main work force, made the factory unprofitable, and it closed soon after their liberation in 1861.
Marks: MA monogram, usually in overglaze blue or green; AM in red under the glaze, sometimes *Volokitin*.
Refs: Hare; Ivanova; A. Popoff 'The Francis Gardner & Other Russian Porcelain Factories' in *The Connoisseur* 96 (August 1935); Ross; Rozembergh.

Milburn, Benedict. *See* Alexandria Pottery.

Milet, Optat. French ceramic modeller and decorator. Like his father and brother, Milet was employed at the Sèvres factory (1862-79). He established his own studio nearby in 1875 or 1877, and exhibited a series of *flambé*-glazed stonewares in 1884.
Milet was associated with C.*Massier in Golfe-Juan, but had exhibited work fired in Vallauris as early as 1878. As well as stoneware with glazes in a variety of colours and effects, including celadon, blues, titanium yellow and crystalline, Milet made fine earthenware with *cloisonné* glazes, sometimes on a gold ground, and barbotine ware. His son Paul took over the workshop in 1890.
Father and son both marked work with their initials.
Refs: Lesur (1971); Heuser & Heuser.

Miller, Abraham (d 1858). American potter. Miller worked a pottery established by his father, Andrew Miller (d 1826), in the late 18th century in Philadelphia, for the production of domestic earthenware. Miller worked in partnership with his brother, also Andrew (d 1821), at the pottery from 1809 until Andrew Miller's death, and became owner of the works on the death of their father. He won an award for an example of porcelain shown in the Franklin Institute exhibition in 1824, but Miller is not thought to have produced a commercial output of porcelain throughout his career. He made decorated cream-coloured earthenware and Rockingham-glazed ware, and produced silver lustre decoration by 1824. He also made earthenware cooking stoves. His own

work as a modeller included the originals of Rockingham-glazed Tam O'Shanter mugs which were sold in great quantities in the 1840s. At that time he expanded his business, moving to larger premises and retaining his father's works as a warehouse. He eventually settled at a new pottery in Callowhill Street, and worked there until his death, when the business closed. The next known occupants of the site, a firm making fire-brick and crucibles, were listed there in 1867. Miller became a senator for his state.
Refs: Barber (1976); Clement (1947); S. Myers *Handcraft to Industry* (Smithsonian Institution Press, Washington, 1980).

Miller, James (d 1905). Scottish potter. Manager of *Port Dundas Pottery from 1849 and owner in 1856, he had a branch of the firm at Garngad Hill, Glasgow, producing Rockingham-glazed earthenware and cane-coloured stoneware. He also owned the *North British Pottery, 1867-74, trading as James Miller & Co. with a partner, William Grant, and producing painted and printed earthenwares. Miller built an extension to the Port Dundas works across the road from the main works by 1885. There he began producing electrical insulators until the demolition of that part of the works in 1905 to allow for further construction work on the Caledonian Railway. Miller was succeeded by his son James W. Miller, in partnership with Stanley Miller.
Ref: Craftwork 44.

Millington & Astbury; Millington, Astbury & Poulson. *See* Maddock, Thomas, & Sons.

Mills, John. *See* Hunslet Hall Pottery.

Milton Pottery. Yorkshire pottery established 1902 at Skiers Spring, Hoyland, for the production of traditional domestic earthenware, which included breadpans and cooking utensils, and such pieces as chests of drawers and money boxes. Using local clay, the workshop employed eight potters; it closed in 1937.
Ref: Lawrence.

Mimpei Kashu or Kaju (1796-1871). Japanese potter, author and teamaster, born in Inadamura, Awaji. He studied ceramics from c.1819 and was a pupil of *Shuhei in Kyoto. He produced pottery of raku type at Inadamura before 1829 and started to make *Awaji wares in 1831. At that time, he was developing the technique of reproducing the smooth, waxy, deep apple green and Imperial yellow glazes of Chinese porcelain, which he used on a hard, pale grey stoneware body. Joined by Shuhei from 1834 until 1836, he continued his glaze research, subsequently developing greyish white (1838) and mirror black (1839) glazes, followed by a range that included tortoiseshell and the combination of green, yellow and aubergine characteristic of *Kochi ware. Mimpei also made enamelled dishes, plates, cake boxes and other small pieces resembling *Awata wares, with a finely crackled creamy glaze and embellished with gold and silver. His relief decoration is carefully modelled.
In 1842, he became superintendent of an official factory newly opened in Awaji, leaving his younger brother Tsunezaemon (d 1856) in charge of his kiln. Mimpei became

ill in 1862 and retired, succeeded at his own kiln in 1870 by his nephew Sampei.
Refs: Fujioka; Jenyns (1965, 1971); Munsterberg; Roberts.

Minato ware. Japanese pottery made at the town of Sakai in Izumi province (now Osaka prefecture). The coarse, buff earthenware body was decorated with green, yellow and aubergine lead glazes in designs of figures outlined with ridges of clay or applied in broad areas without containing lines, in the manner of *Kochi wares. Small incense boxes for the tea ceremony were often in the form of birds, etc., or topped with an animal figure, and small dishes were leaf-shaped.
Refs: Audsley & Bowes; Brinkley; Jenyns (1971); Koyama; Roberts.

Minerva works, Lane Delph. *See* Mason, George Miles and Charles James.

mingei or **folk art ware.** In Japanese ceramics, the mingei movement was initiated by the critic and scholar Muneyoshi (Soetsu) Yanagi (1889-1961) and so named as an alternative to getemono (inferior goods), the term normally used in Japan to refer to the utilitarian wares of ordinary people. With Kanjiro Kawai and Shoji Hamada, Yanagi encouraged the revival of a number of existing folk kilns and the establishment of others in the 1920s and 1930s, forming the nucleus of what was to become the folk craft movement, in a time of growing awareness of the aesthetic value of utilitarian objects. The Mingei Association, formed for the encouragement of craft-workers and the education of people in appreciating hand-crafted products, received official recognition in 1929, and initiated lectures, exhibitions and publications, also establishing museums of folk art in Tokyo and Kurashiki.
Yanagi and his associates looked to domestic and other useful wares, for beauty of various kinds (e.g. 'healthy', 'artless', 'frugal', 'unobstructed') arising from the inter-relation between materials, production techniques, form and function, on which the vitality and natural dignity of everyday wares depend. They echoed the tea masters' emphasis on humility and the appreciation of immediate experience, which they found in the utilitarian wares of *Seto, *Shigaraki, *Bizen, *Kutani and other sources formerly noted mainly for tea-ceremony wares or fine porcelain, as well as the output of the exclusively folk kilns.
All the wares which qualified for their approval were made in natural materials, often used in a relatively unrefined state, by methods founded on long experience and tradition; many were glazed before the first firing, and the kiln atmosphere was often neutral, without notable oxidizing or reducing effects. The decoration ranges from the extreme simplicity of dripped glazes and white slip to the lavish, but traditional, overglaze painting of *Osotoyama, *Tsuboya or *Imari wares, for example.
Folk pottery had been made in Japan from the 17th century by anonymous craftsmen (sometimes farmers who worked only part-time as potters). Many small kilns were administered by local clan authorities and initially supplied the feudal lord, increasing production to furnish the needs of nearby towns and villages; local people provided

Minton, Hollins & Co. Two tiles, late 19th century. Each 15.2 cm square.

their only market after the Meiji Restoration in 1868. The folk kilns reached the peak of their production in the 19th century, but declined late in the century with the development of industrial production, until the intervention of the folk art movement.
Refs: Cort; Mizuo; Munsterberg; Okamura; Sanders.

Mino. Japanese region of ceramic production, formerly the province of Mino, now the southern part of Gifu prefecture, containing kilns which were noted for *Shino and *Oribe wares in the area extending from Kukuri near the town of Tajimi to the town of Toki. Ancient kiln sites date from the Heian period, which ended in 1184. Mino's output is closely associated with that of neighbouring *Seto, and the eastern part of the region supplanted Seto as the production centre of tea-ceremony wares in the 17th century.

The Mino potters made Yellow Seto tea bowls, plates, flower vases and other decorated wares in fine, white, local clay with yellow iron and ash glaze, greenish-tinged when high-fired, or a dull yellow resulting from a lower temperature in firing, and Black Seto, with a rich, pure black iron glaze fired in an oxidizing atmosphere and quickly cooled. As well as tea wares, Mino produced storage jars, bowls, plates, saké bottles, water droppers and other domestic wares with yellow or dark Seto glazes. From the late 19th century, the folk kilns were gradually ousted by industrial manufacture and the work of individual artist potters.

Porcelain, introduced to the area in the early 19th century, included some blue and white ware, the eggshell porcelain made by 1830 at *Ichinokura, and the later flowers modelled from natural specimens of wisteria, prunus blossom, etc., at Tajimi and shown in the first Japanese exhibition of native manufactures in 1877. By the late 19th century, eggshell porcelain became the staple product of potters near Tajimi, who made and exported the ware in large quantities, employing Tokyo workshops to carry out decoration of landscapes and human figures.
Refs: Brinkley; Burton (1906); Fujioka; Jenyns (1965, 1971); Mikami; Mizuo; Munsterberg.

Minton, Herbert (1793-1858). English potter, born in Stoke-on-Trent, the son of T.*Minton. In 1817, he became a partner in the Minton firm with his elder brother Thomas, at first working as sales representative and after his father's death as head of the company. With successive partners, J.*Boyle, and his nephews M.D.*Hollins and C.M.*Campbell, he embarked on the company's expansion. He varied the production, increasing the output of ornamental ware. Having bought the rights to Samuel Wright's method of producing encaustic tiles (whereupon he abandoned his own experiments), he was able to put tiles into commercial production by c.1835. In 1840, Minton acquired a share in Richard Prosser's technique, by which tiles were moulded in tightly packed clay dust, and he used this process from the same year. In 1848 he bought an interest in the process of lithography on ceramics, which he used in the production of tiles designed by A.W.N. *Pugin for the Palace of Westminster. The firm's output, which until c.1830 had consisted mainly of earthenware and bone china, increased to include parian, majolica and *Palissy wares. Under Herbert Minton's control, the firm gained spectacular successes in international exhibitions, starting with the Great Exhibition in 1851 and the Paris Exposition Universelle in 1855. After his death in Torquay, Minton was buried at Hartshill, Stoke-on-Trent, his home for many years, where he endowed schools and a church.
Refs: Aslin & Atterbury; Barnard; Godden (1968).

Minton, Thomas (1765-1836). Staffordshire potter and ceramic decorator, born at Wyle Cop, Shrewsbury, and trained as an engraver at the *Caughley factory. After working in London, he moved in 1789 to Staffordshire, where he became established as an engraver of designs for transfer printing, including a pattern, Buffalo, which was produced by the Spode factory. In partnership with Joseph Poulson and William Pownall, he founded the firm which traded initially as Minton & Poulson and eventually as *Mintons Ltd (from 1873).

Minton was also the main partner in the Hendra Co. at St Denis in Cornwall, which operated until the 1850s, supplying china clay and china stone to Staffordshire manufacturers. He developed a formula for bone porcelain, which he produced together with creamware and stoneware. In 1817, he took his sons into partnership. H.*Minton became head of the firm in 1836.
Refs: see Mintons Ltd.

Minton, Hollins & Co. Tile manufacturers established at Stoke-on-Trent in the early 1840s as a branch of Mintons working under M.D.*Hollins. In 1855, the firm took out a fresh patent for the production of encaustic tiles. Imitations of Hispano-Moresque and Italian tiles were made possible by the development of improved glazing techniques by J.-F.-L.*Arnoux, and majolica tiles were introduced in 1850. Early examples of printed tiles, designed by A.W.N.*Pugin, were used to cover walls and floors in the Houses of Parliament, completed 1852.

The firm became a distinct part of the parent company in 1859 and separated completely in 1868, for a time becoming England's leading tile manufacturer. The output of tiles included unglazed geometrical pieces for pavements and glazed or unglazed tiles with encaustic decoration for flooring or hearth decoration; other ornamental tiles included majolica with relief designs, painted or printed tiles, and tile pictures. The firm operated as a limited company from 1928 and ceased operation in 1962.

Marks: initials or name of the firm and *Stoke-on-Trent*; *Minton & Co.* used on floor tiles.
Refs: Barnard; Blacker (1922a); Lockett (1979).

Minton's Art Pottery Studio. English ceramic decorating workshop started by *Mintons Ltd in 1871 at Kensington Gore, London. Its establishment followed a collaboration between Mintons and students of china painting at the National Art Training School in the production of tiles designed by Edward Poynter for the Grill Room at the South Kensington Museum (1868-70), and was part of a scheme initiated by the South

Minton's Art Pottery Studio. Vase marked Minton AP Studio Kensington Gore, *and date code for 1871. 36 cm high.*

Kensington authorities to provide employment for artists, especially women. A site for the building was leased by the Commissioners of the Great Exhibition.

Under W.S.*Coleman as manager and art director and with the help of professional decorators from Stoke-on-Trent, who included J.*Eyre, H.W.*Foster and A.*Boullemier, students from the training school and Lambeth School of Art decorated biscuit pottery and, more rarely, porcelain made at the Minton factory, with underglaze or enamel colours, which were then fired at the studio or, occasionally, returned for firing to the factory at Stoke-on-Trent. Artists including H.B.*Barlow (briefly in 1871), E.G.*Reuter and one of Coleman's sisters (*see* Coleman, R. and H.C.) decorated plaques, tiles and ornamental pieces to designs by other artists (often Coleman himself). On his retirement in 1873, Coleman was succeeded by other studio managers. The studio did not re-open after fire damage in 1875, but the freshness of designs used there influenced earthenware produced at the main factory in Stoke-on-Trent.

Circular printed mark: *Minton's Art Pottery Studio Kensington Gore*, with impressed mark of Minton and date cypher. *Refs:* Aslin & Atterbury; Callen; Rhead.

Mintons Ltd. Staffordshire pottery established at Stoke-on-Trent in 1793 by T. *Minton in partnership with the ceramist Joseph Poulson, (d 1808), and backed by Liverpool businessman William Pownall. The company, in production from 1796 traded as Minton & Poulson (until 1806), Minton & Boyle (from 1836), Herbert Minton & Co. (from 1841), Minton & Co. (from 1845) and took the title Mintons Ltd in 1873. The initial output consisted mainly of transfer-printed tableware in earthenware and, from 1797, porcelain. By 1811, the range of patterns included neo-classical scenes and landscapes, *chinoiseries*, wide-bordered Imari designs and flower arrangements. Overglaze enamels were used, sometimes over outlines transfer-printed under the glaze, and often with lavish gilding, although black border patterns became

Mintons Ltd. Majolica cabaret set in a style inspired by Japanese taste. Marks include date codes for 1867 and 1868. Tray, 33 cm.

popular in the mid 1820s. The firm also made stoneware and black basalt. There was a break in the production of porcelain from 1816 to 1824.

Chimney ornaments had been mentioned in stock books c.1810, and figures in a list of moulds in 1817. After the resumption of porcelain production, the firm made flatback figures c.1826 and figures modelled in the round from c.1828. Portrait pieces made from c.1830 were followed by sculptural work based on European 18th-century subjects, sculptures by Claude-Michel Clodion and Antonio Canova, and political personalities, as well as a variety of religious, mythical, literary and historical themes. The firm also commissioned designs from established artists for production in terracotta. Figures in parian ware, which Mintons developed under that name in 1846, were produced in association with H.*Cole for issue through Summerly's Art Manufactures, and from the earlier moulds for biscuit porcelain. A.-E.*Carrier-Belleuse was a modeller of new designs from the early 1850s. Production of parian figures continued until the end of the 19th century. An elaborate dessert service included in the firm's display at the Great Exhibition in 1851, and bought by Queen Victoria, was made with figures and other modelled ornament in parian, and baskets or dishes in richly-decorated glazed porcelain. In the 1850s, the firm developed a tinted parian paste for decorative pieces and tableware, often used in combination with glazed bone porcelain in the same piece.

After Herbert Minton's purchase of the patent taken out by Samuel Wright in 1830 for the production of encaustic tiles, the firm produced copies of medieval tiles for the floor of Westminster Chapter House in the early 1840s, issuing a catalogue of Old English Tiles in 1842. Some designs were the work of A.W.N.*Pugin and others were based more directly on medieval originals. The firm took out a fresh patent covering encaustic tile production in 1856.

Colin Minton Campbell succeeded Herbert Minton as head of the firm, and the following year, M.D.*Hollins took over tile production in the branch of the company, *Minton, Hollins & Co. After complete separation of the branches in 1868, Mintons continued to produce glazed ornamental tiles and R.M.*Taylor established a tileworks

Mintons Ltd. Caisse à fleurs and stand, painted with roundels of putti and allegories of music against a ground of bleu-céleste, c.1860. 29 cm high.

in Fenton. The rivalry in use of the Minton name resulted in litigation which was decided in Hollins's favour in 1871 and 1875. Nevertheless, Campbell and Taylor went on to form the *Campbell Brick & Tile Co. in 1875.

The main firm of Mintons first used the litho printing process for the reproduction of flat-coloured patterns to designs by A.W.N. Pugin on tiles in the Palace of Westminster, and produced a wide variety of patterns by the 1860s. Press-moulded tiles with relief ornament painted in bright majolica glazes were made c.1860-1910 as components of entire decorative schemes. The patterns frequently featured Renaissance or medieval motifs, but naturalistic designs also occur. Tube lining, an alternative method of producing raised patterns, was introduced c.1900 for Art Nouveau designs.

The firm's tableware, eventually produced in various semi-porcelain bodies as well as in ironstone china, white earthenware and bone porcelain, was produced in large quantities, transfer-printed with oriental, Renaissance and Gothic patterns, some of which dated from the early 19th century and remained in use until the end of the century. Painted decoration was carried out by artists including T.*Kirkby, E.*Rischgitz, A. and L.-E.*Boullemier and A.*Birks to designs by P.-E.*Jeannest, W.S.*Coleman, W. *Crane and others. The technique of acid-etched gilding was introduced in 1863, when C.M.*Campbell bought the patent rights for Mintons.

Although tableware was to remain the main output, H.*Minton, head of the firm from 1836 until 1858, increased the range of ornamental porcelain, much influenced by the contemporary work of other firms and the earlier work of Chelsea. The painters included T.*Steel, J.*Bancroft and J.*Simpson, who joined the firm from the *Derby factory, and S.*Bourne.

J.-L.-F.*Arnoux became art director in 1849, a year after joining the firm, and remained in the post until 1892. His many innovations included majolica, initially

inspired by Italian Renaissance tinglaze (which provided the basis for work by Kirkby and, c.1860, the painter and sculptor Alfred Stevens, as well as Arnoux); later, the name referred mainly to brightly glazed earthenware, which was produced throughout the rest of the 19th century. His designers included Carrier-Belleuse and Jeannest, who were responsible for modelling relief ornament, and painters Kirkby, Rischgitz and E.*Lessore. The subjects included many figures and other decorative pieces designed originally for production in porcelain and parian ware. Other stylistic inspiration came from the work of 16th-century potter Bernard Palissy, already reproduced by C.-J.*Avisseau in France, and Limoges enamels, which inspired pieces painted by Stephen Lawton and Benjamin Lockett, who worked for the firm in the 1850s, specializing in these wares, and by Kirkby.

The firm's St Porchaire ware, then known as Henri II, was introduced by Arnoux, who carried out the first examples in 1858, combining painted and inlaid decoration, but became particularly associated with C. *Toft. After the publication of C. Delange's *Recueil de toutes les pièces de la faïence française dite Henri II* (Paris, 1861), which was also used as a source by Avisseau, Toft based a series of pieces in limited editions on Delange's illustrations.

Many decorative pieces from the mid-1850s to the 1880s, although made in bone porcelain, closely imitated 18th-century Sèvres wares, and were in some cases cast from originals. They were technically very accomplished, and Arnoux successfully reproduced ground colours in turquoise, dark blue, pink, apple green and yellow. Some close copies were made to fulfil commissions; freer interpretations of Sèvres ware were sometimes combined with other (e.g. oriental) stylistic elements. Painters included T.*Allen, C.*Henk, D.*Leroy, L.*Jahn and modellers Carrier-Belleuse and later J.E.*Dean and L.E.*Boullemier.

The production of *pâte-sur-pâte* porcelain started after the arrival of L.-M.-E.*Solon at the Minton factory in 1870. Using the parian paste developed for the tinted pieces, Solon carried out original designs stylistically influenced by French and Italian paintings and engravings, helped from c.1872 by a department that included F.H.*Rhead, T. Miller, A. and L. Birks, and H. Sanders, who was later to work for *Moore Brothers. These assistants completed basic stages of the technique, while Solon was responsible for painting the figures.

A Middle-Eastern influence in design over the latter half of the century derived in part from the interest of Colin Minton Campbell, managing director from 1858, who bought Persian tiles in that period. Further inspiration was drawn from the pottery and metalwork of Islamic countries. The distinctive rusty red of Rhodian ware was reproduced in time for inclusion in the firm's display in the International Exhibition in London 1871.

However, the use of oriental motifs (derived from Japanese prints and illustrations which were first available in Europe c.1860), as well as lacquers, ivories, jade, bronze, *cloisonné* enamels, and Chinese monochrome-glazed ceramics, provided possibly the greatest influence on the firm's cheaper wares from the mid 1870s. Arnoux, with his interest in Chinese ceramics, made early developments in their reproduction, as seen in a bottle in hard-paste porcelain with crackle glaze, dating from c.1862. Charles Toft and J.*Henk notably produced designs of oriental inspiration.

In 1902, the firm introduced Secessionist ware, designed by L.V.*Solon and J.W. *Wadsworth, influenced by the Vienna Secession movement: ornamental pieces, tableware and toilet sets in Art Nouveau forms were painted with majolica glazes that ran together unless contained in trailed or moulded outlines, generally in abstract floral patterns echoing the decoration on Minton tube-lined tiles.

In the 20th century, the firm continued as a leading producer of high-quality tablewares. Colin Minton Campbell was succeeded by John F. Campbell until 1918, and then by Colin H. Campbell. In 1968, the firm became part of the Doulton group.

Marks: except for the name of the sculptor John Bell in relief on parian ware produced for Cole, marks normally incorporate *Minton*. The firm's standard marks also featured a globe from the 1860s until the adoption of a wreath in 1951. Year cyphers were impressed from 1842.
Refs: Aslin & Atterbury; Blacker (1922a); Godden (1968); Jewitt.

Minzan (1772-1844). Japanese potter Takeda Shuhei, working under the artistic name of Minzan. The son of a samurai, Minzan went to Kanazawa from his native Harima, Sanuki prefecture, in 1814, and entered the service of the Maeda clan. In an effort to revive production of *Kutani ware at *Kasugayama, he established his own kiln for the production of porcelain, with the help of *Todaya, and built an enamelling kiln at his home, inviting the decorator Nabeya Kichibei (d c.1854) to paint his work. Minzan's wares, pink-tinged and fired at a lower temperature than true porcelain, though made from porcelain clay, were decorated with red enamel applied in fine lines and highlighted with gold, the colour combinations of *kinrande and *hachiro-de. Rare pieces occur with a decorative palette of yellow, purple and green as well as red.

Minzan was also a sculptor (under the name of Yugetsu), a teamaster, an artist in ink and, under the name Keiundo, the founder of miniature landscape arrangements. His kiln closed at the time of his death.
Mark: two characters denoting Minzan.
Refs: Jenyns (1965); Nakagawa; Roberts.

Miragaia, Fabrica de. Portuguese pottery established 1775 in rua de Esperansa, Oporto (near the church of S. Pedro de Miragaia). The owner, Francisco da Rocha Soares (d 1829), nephew and successor of the founder, left the pottery under the direction of his cousin José Bento da Rocha for 20 years until his return from South America in 1799, afterwards introducing a large and varied production. His son, also F. da Rocha Soares, took over the pottery in 1830. The pottery's cream-coloured earthenware was moulded in high-quality imitations of English and other foreign wares, including oriental porcelains, decorated mainly in blue, yellow, green, and orange, under a fine, milky glaze. The factory closed in 1852, and the moulds passed to the Santo Antonio de Val-de-Piedade factory.

Marks: R (owner's initial); after 1832 M, MP or *Miragaia-Porto*. Pieces marked SP may also come from this factory.
Ref: P. Vitorino *Ceramica Portuense* (Ediçoes Apolina, Gaia, 1930).

Miraku Kamei (b 1931). Japanese potter working in his native Takatori, Fukuoka prefecture, and 14th in succession of the Miraku line in 1963. He trained under his grandfather and followed the traditions of *Takatori wares, making a particular study of pieces made in the early 17th century. He is noted for the production of tea caddies of Chinese inspiration, and has exhibited widely in Japan and overseas since the mid 1950s.
Ref: Kozuru *Agano & Takatori* (Kodansha International, Tokyo, New York, San Francisco, 1981).

Mission. *See* Owens, John B.

Mission ware. *See* Niloak Pottery Co.

Mitchell, Frederick (d 1875). English potter. Son of William Mitchell, owner of the *Cadborough Pottery, Sussex, until his death in 1871. As his father's assistant and, from 1859, his partner, he began the production of decorative wares at the pottery, starting c.1850 with experimental pieces decorated with flowers and foliage applied in light clay on a darker body. He also added metallic oxides or powdered metal to clay bodies, in order to stain the lead glaze during firing. The green effect achieved with powdered brass was frequently used on moulded plates and as a ground for bands of applied ornament, doves, sprays of oak leaves and buttercups, chrysanthemums or other flowers, on decorative tableware in pale clay. After winning first prize for his ornamental pieces, which were described as Sussex ware, in a local industries' exhibition at Hastings, 1867, Frederick Mitchell built a new home between Cadborough and Rye, where he established a showroom and the small *Belleview Pottery, which was in production from 1869. He continued the production of decorative ware, specializing in flowerpots and *jardinières*.
Refs: Brears (1974); Jewitt; Lloyd Thomas (1974).

Mitchell, Henry. English ceramic painter, primarily depicting animals, birds, fish, human figures, mermaids, seaweeds, shells and landscapes in a style that was noted for its delicacy. He was employed by *Mintons Ltd from c.1860, continued working in Staffordshire after 1871, and joined *Doulton & Co. in Burslem 1891-1908. His landscapes are characterized by the use of silver-grey tints in the distance, and his careful animal studies are often set against delicately drawn wooded or moorland backgrounds. Mitchell's work won medals in exhibitions in Paris (1867) and Vienna (1873).

Work often signed.

Refs: Eyles (1980); Godden (1961, 1972); Jewitt.

Mitchell, Mary. English ceramic designer and decorator, working for *Doulton & Co. in Lambeth c.1874-c.1887. She was known for her portrayal of rustic figures, e.g. on a stoneware vase dated 1880, with incised decoration (in the manner of scratch blue) of flowers surrounding country scenes of children in reserves.

Mark: monogram of MM.

Refs: see Doulton & Co.

Mitchell, William, & Son. *See* Cadborough Pottery.

Mitsutoki Takahatsu. *See* Dohachi II.

Mittenhoff & Mourot. *See* Val-sous-Meudon.

Mitterteich. German porcelain factory established in 1886 at Mitterteich, Bavaria. It produced domestic ware and decorated tea and coffee sets, mainly under the firm of Josef Rieber, also the owners of a branch at Thiersheim.

The Mitterteich porcelain factory, established 1917, made household and gift wares, marked MITTERTEICH/BAVARIA. Marks of the Rieber factory often incorporate *Rieber*, or initials R or JR, a crown and BAVARIA.

Refs: Danckert; Weiss.

Miwa Kyusetsu or **Kyuwa** (1895-1981). Japanese potter, born in Hagi, Yamaguchi prefecture, and son of the keeper of the Miwa kiln, which was officially patronized by the Mori clan. In 1927, he took the name Miwa Kyusetsu as head of the tenth generation. He became known for a style combining Japanese and Yi-dynasty Korean elements in his output of tea bowls. He frequently used white glazes. He assumed the name Kyuwa on his retirement in 1967. He was made Holder of the Designated Technique for Hagi Ware in 1970.

Ref: Living National Treasures.

Miyakawa family. A line of Japanese potters working in Kyoto and at Ota, near Yokohama, who adopted Miyakawa as the family name c.1800. Shozan (also known as Makuzu or Yukansai) worked from 1879 at Ota, where he made copies of early *Satsuma wares and other pieces in faience with relief decoration of birds, reptiles, crustacea, flowers, etc. He later specialized in glaze effects, notably red, inspired by Chinese wares, also producing porcelain painted under the glaze in red and blue after Chinese examples from the Kang-hsi period.

Choso Miyakawa was a pupil of *Mokubei and specialized in copies of *Ninsei ware. His son, Toronosuke Miyakawa (1842-1916), worked under the artistic name Kozan, at first in Kyoto, where he studied the techniques of painting in underglaze blue and the use of *flambé* glazes. He was noted for his imitations of Satsuma ware. Kozan was called with his son to work as designer and maker of export wares at a kiln newly established at Minami Otamachi by two Yokohama merchants. There he produced a widely

Miyakawa. Porcelain vase, modelled in the form of an icy cavern with two polar bears, early 20th century. Seal mark of Makuzu impressed. 21.6 cm high.

varied output (known as Ota ware) with which he achieved renown overseas as well as in Japan, partly through his displays at various international exhibitions. In 1896, he became a member of the Committee of the Imperial Household and an official of the Imperial Household Museum.

Refs: Brinkley; Gorham; Hannover; Jenyns (1971); Roberts; Uyeno.

Miyamotoya Uemon. Japanese potter, a maker of *Kutani ware. Miyamotoya, manager of the *Yoshidaya kiln until its closure in 1831, took over the works and resumed production in 1835, operating as the Miyamotoya kiln. He was joined by *Hachiroemon, who took responsibility for decoration, specializing in Chinese subjects in red enamel and gold in *hachiro-de style. Miyamotoya's son, Riemon succeeded his father in 1840, and the kiln eventually became known as Iidaya, after Hachiroemon. It was abandoned by the 1840s.

Refs: Jenyns (1965); Nakagawa.

Mobach family. Dutch potters working at Utrecht. Klaas Mobach (1855-1928), formerly a modeller at the *Holland workshop, established an art pottery at Utrecht in 1895, where he produced pieces with decoration initially inspired by Friesian carving and later influenced in style by contemporary artistic developments. Geometrical patterns were incised and painted in coloured slips. Matt glazes, mainly in blue or green, were also used. The founder was succeeded on his retirement in 1925 by his four sons, Bouke (1884-1953), Ale (1888-1965), Johannes Dirk (1890-1968) and Klaas (1893-1976), and his grandson, also named Klaas, who changed the workshop's output to rough-textured stoneware made with clay from Westerwald and decorated with glazes, some matt, resulting from their own research. The factory resumed work after a break

(1940-45) and remains under the control of the Mobach family.

Refs: J. Romijn '80 jaar Mobach' in *Mededelingenblad Vrienden van de Nederlandse Ceramiek* 81 (1976); Singelenberg-van der Meer; van Straaten.

mocha ware. Pottery characterized by branching decoration which resembles the markings of mocha stone (moss agate). The pattern is achieved by dropping on damp slip an acid infusion of tobacco juice in, traditionally, urine or hop extract (to which is added metallic oxide pigment, usually brown, sometimes blue, green, black or, after c.1880, pink). The mixture spreads to form feathery motifs, aided by capillary action, tilting or the use of a blowpipe. In England, the technique was used in the 18th and 19th centuries, mainly on measuring mugs for ale, shrimps or dry goods, occasionally on vases, pot-pourris and household ware. The work was initially in creamware, with the decoration applied on horizontal bands of chestnut, blue, yellow, white or grey slip, and later also made in pearlware (from c.1820), white earthenware or cane-coloured ware (from c.1830). Mugs and jugs were frequently intended for use in taverns; those dated later than 1824 normally bear a government stamp issued after tests for measure by the Local Government Inspector. After the introduction of mocha ware in Staffordshire, where makers included the *Adams family at Greengates Pottery, Tunstall, the firms of James *Broadhurst & Sons Ltd, J.*Tams, *Cork & Edge, *Pinder, Bourne & Co., and J.*Macintyre, large quantities were produced in the north east of England c.1810-c.1890 (e.g. by the firm of C.T.*Maling), as well as in Scotland and at the *Cambrian Pottery in Wales. T.G.*Green was among other known English makers, and studio potters who have since experimented with the technique in the mid 20th century.

Refs: Atterbury (1980); Bell; Collard; Nance; S. Shaw *Chemistry of Pottery* (1837); N. Teulon *Porter Collection of Mocha Pottery* (City Museum & Art Gallery, Stoke-on-Trent, n.d.); W. Turner *William Adams, an Old English Potter* (1904).

mocha ware. Buff-coloured earthenware jug, decorated with bands of white and brown slip with mocha decoration in brown and pink, mid 19th century. 21.5 cm high.

Modern Movement. A general term used to describe the evolution in design in the applied arts in Europe and America which started in the 1860s with a reaction against lavish decoration and culminated in the form-oriented design of the 20th century. It covers such stylistic developments as the Aesthetic Movement, Art Nouveau, the Arts and Crafts Movement, the Bauhaus and Art Deco, and arose from social, political and technical changes as well as aesthetic considerations.
Ref: Haslam (1977).

Moehling, M. Johann. Porcelain manufacturer working at Aich, in Bohemia, from 1849, and mainly known for his output of figures and other modelled ornamental pieces. He extended the range of his production to include utilitarian ware and eventually sold his factory to A.C. Auger in 1862. Menzel & Co. were co-owners from 1918 until the factory merged with EPIAG in 1923. It closed ten years later.
Marks include *Aich* and a cypher combining A and X.
Refs: Danckert; Weiss.

Moiré Antique. *See* Foley Potteries.

Moist, Alfred and Joseph. *See* Devon Art Pottery.

Mokubei Aoki (1761-1833). Japanese scholar, poet, landscape painter, metalworker and ceramist, Gensa Aoki, working under several artistic names, mainly Mokubei. He was born in Kyoto and a pupil of *Eisen. Inspired by a Ch'ing Chinese description and the country's ceramics (T'ao-shuo) he concentrated on the re-creation and development of many Chinese wares, notably blue and white porcelains, including *Shonsui ware and such enamelled wares as *gosu aka-e, *kinrande and K'ang-hsi *famille noire*, as well as celadons and *Kochi ware. He also became known for his production of small, long-handled teapots moulded in pottery, unglazed, and derived from Yi-hsing examples, though differing from them in shape, and made stoneware of various types. Much of his work was produced for use in the sencha (leaf tea) ceremony. His painting was accomplished and in general he worked with a fresh, inventive approach. The quality of materials and workmanship in his copies are regarded as equalling the finest originals. Mokubei was well established as a Kyoto potter when he was invited to start the *Kasugayama kiln in 1806 for the production of *Kutani ware, after the town's decision to revive the local porcelain industry and make use of local clay. He returned to Kyoto in 1808, founding a kiln at Awata. From 1824 he was more active as a Nanga painter. His daughter Rai worked as a potter, noted for her imitations of ancient pieces.
Refs: Brinkley; Fujioka; Hannover; Jenyns (1965, 1971); Koyama; Masterpieces; Morse; Munsterberg.

Mokuhaku or **Kashiwaya** Buhei (1799-1870). Japanese potter born in Nara and working under the artistic name of Mokuhaku at Akahada, c.1830-44. His work included imitations of *Ninsei ware, decorative figures in porcelain, tea bowls patterned with scenes from the Land of the Immortals, and water jars with figure scenes, stork designs, etc. His seal of two characters appears on red raku tea bowls made at Akahada.
Refs: Gorham; Jenyns (1971); Morse; Roberts.

Möller, Siegfried (1896-1970). German potter, born in Hamburg, where he trained as a sculptor until 1920. Möller established a stoneware pottery in the Upper Palatimate where he worked 1923-26, before becoming artistic director for several stoneware factories and undergoing further training in Hamburg (1933-34). He was later to work briefly at *Karlsruhe (1937). He founded his own workshop in 1934, and became known for the making of unglazed earthenware with careful, detailed painting, often in cobalt blue, also developing his own technique for transfer printing and the moulding of low relief decoration on plates and jugs. His patterns, which include hunting scenes, and generally feature animals and plants, e.g. a crowing cockerel set among flowers, a hound eating a duck at the foot of a tree, appear on display plates (c.1940). Möller also designed domestic ware for industrial production, and taught ceramics in Bremen, Hamburg and Kiel. From 1954 until his death, he had a workshop in Plön, also acting as consultant to the *Fürstenberg porcelain factory.
Painted or impressed marks, M with BK or KK (workshop monogram).
Ref: Bock.

Möller, Tom and Grete. Swedish studio potters, working in the mid 20th century on the production of pottery with black body and tin glaze, in a style founded in Scandinavian folk traditions.
Refs: Hettes & Rada; Lagercrantz.

Möller & Dippe. German manufacturers producing pottery and some porcelain at Unterköditz, Thuringia, from 1846. The firm's output included figures.
Marks include an anchor with the initials MD./U.
Refs: Danckert; Weiss.

Moncloa, La. Porcelain factory established in 1817 near Madrid, with stock and equipment transferred by Ferdinand VII from the Buen Retiro factory, which closed in 1812. Under the management of Bartholomeo Sureda, the factory made porcelain in styles resembling those of French wares in the same period. It closed in 1850.
Marks: crown with the initials REM or MD, or with the place name, MONCLOA.
Refs: Danckert; Weiss.

Monnerie factory. Limoges porcelain workshop established in part of a former Augustinian convent after its purchase in 1793 by a local businessman, Léonard Monnerie, who worked until 1796 with Jean Joubert, a trained thrower. The factory's output included a small tea service exhibited in Limoges in 1802, a large pharmacy jar with handles modelled in the form of masks, and a dish by Monnerie's son, Laurent. Medallions and lithophanes were also produced. Monnerie worked there until he let the works to F.*Alluaud, 1813-17. The factory then closed until Laurent Monnerie started work there with his son-in-law, Jérôme Lefèvre, in 1819. The firm exhibited work at an exhibition of industrial products in Paris, 1819, and moved in 1825 to new premises in Saint-Léonard (Haute-Vienne). The factory was let until c.1840, when it was sold to J.-B.*Ruaud.
Ref: d'Albis & Romanet.

Montene. *See* Peters & Reed.

Montenot, Edmé-François. *See* Auxerre.

Montereau. French faience factory established in the late 18th century for the production of fine creamware, using English techniques. In the early 19th century, the firm specialized in lustre ware. It was united with *Creil in 1819 under the direction of Saint-Cricq-Cazaux & Co., later in partnership with Louis Lebeuf. Printed decoration, mainly restricted to scenes from classical mythology printed in black, became a more important part of production in the reign of Louis-Philippe. Montereau excelled in sentimental scenes, e.g. Fête de Bonne Maman and Soeurs de Lait, and records of such current events as the return of the Emperor's ashes, or the African campaign of 1839.
The factory also made imitations of Wedgwood jasper ware in an earthenware body coated with coloured slip and with white relief patterns on classical themes. Some pieces were entirely covered with relief ornament and coloured in shades of green or mauve-blue before coating with a very brilliant glaze. Blue or green-coloured bodies were also used.
Printed decorations came to include scenes based on word-play, songs, cries of Paris and, increasingly, circuses, as well as commemorating political events. *Chinoiseries* persisted until the late 19th century. The children's designs that became a speciality of Montereau were then printed in sepia and enlivened with touches of colour.
Lebeuf and his partners bought Creil-Montereau in 1841. Their successors, Lebeuf, Milliet & Cie, sold out to Barluet & Cie in 1877. The Society controlling the factories by 1884 took the title S.A. des Faïenceries de Creil et Montereau in that year and was taken over in 1920 by La Société Hte Boulanger de Choisy-le-Roi. The Creil factory had closed in 1895, but its name was retained in the firm's title until the closure of Montereau in 1955.
Marks incorporate the firms' names or initials.
Refs: Baschet; d'Albis *et al*; Ernould-Gandouet; Lesur (1971).

Montgarny. French pottery established at Montgarny (Meuse) by François Harmand, and in operation from 1796. Harmand let the works, 1802-21, then resumed direction until 1828. The output resembled the faience of other factories, particularly Les *Islettes, with decoration of flowers, including roses, predominantly in red, blue and green; also birds and figure subjects.
Refs: Lesur (1971); Tilmans (1954).

Montigny. French pottery, originally a brick and tile works in operation at the Château de Montigny-sous-Perreux (Yonne) from the construction of the *château* c.1600.

Faience was produced from the 1730s until c.1836, with a break in production during the Revolution. In the early 19th century, decorative designs were devoted to military or floral themes, with outlines drawn in manganese. Decorated tiles had polychrome designs of birds, etc., or copies of Delft patterns in blue. Only bricks were produced after the pottery changed hands in 1836.
Refs: Huillard; Lesur (1971).

Mont Pelée. *See* McCoy, J.W., Pottery.

Montrose Works. *See* Foley Potteries.

Moon, Milton (b 1926). Australian artist potter, trained (1950-53) in Brisbane, where he was later Senior Pottery Instructor at the Central Technical College. Moon makes large reduction-fired pieces, often with a white, speckled iron glaze. Many pieces have decoration, notably landscapes, painted in cobalt, iron or copper, derived both in subject and treatment from Japanese traditions. He left Queensland in 1969 for a senior lectureship in ceramics at the South Australian School of Arts and has since worked at the Summertown Pottery in the Adelaide Hills, South Australia.
Refs: Craft Australia No 2 (1980); Dennis Pryor *Focus on Milton Moon* (St Lucia, 1967); P. Thompson *Twelve Australian Craftsmen* (Sydney, 1973).

Moonstone glaze. *See* Wedgwood, Josiah, & Sons Ltd.

Moorcroft, William (1872-1945). Staffordshire potter. After training in his home town, Burslem, Moorcroft qualified as an art teacher in 1897, but then became a designer for J.*Macintyre. His early work included vases, bowls, biscuit barrels, teaware, etc., transfer-printed with floral designs and scale-pattern borders or panels, predominantly in iron red, gold and underglaze blue (Aurelian ware). In 1898, Moorcroft took charge of the firm's art pottery department, which had been formed in the

William Moorcroft. Claremont bowl painted in reds, deep blues and pale green against an olive green ground. Marks include Made for Liberty & Co. *and signature,* W. Moorcroft.

previous year, and developed a line of art pottery under the trade name Florian Ware, in a close-textured white porcellaneous body with patterns of flowers, foliage, peacock feathers, etc., outlined in trailed slip and painted with metallic oxides under a clear glaze. The ware was sold through Tiffany's in New York, Liberty's in London, and in Paris, as well as at Macintyre's London showroom.

Moorcroft designed most of his shapes for throwing, rather than moulding, and devised decoration that would emphasize the form—many patterns swirl in the direction of throwing, or curve with the outlines of the pot. Landscape patterns with trees were introduced in 1902, designs based on toadstools in 1903, and on pomegranates, in 1911. Moorcroft also designed commemorative mugs, vases, etc., sometimes with heraldic devices.

After the closure of Macintyre's art pottery department in 1913, Moorcroft established a workshop in Cobridge with assistants trained by him at Macintyre's, and continued the development of his earlier work. He introduced a Powder Blue range of tableware, which was produced 1913-63, and enriched his range of colours, often making use of deep grounds (e.g. bluish purple), but returned to pale ground colours for salt-glazed ware with simple, abstract patterns in the 1930s. Moorcroft created Flamminian Ware, a lustre range with small medallions or other simple decoration and monochrome glaze introduced at Macintyre's in 1905, followed by an increased variety of glazes in red, yellow, orange, copper blue or green with lustre effects, and *flambé* wares, which he produced from 1919. As well as the pieces thrown to his designs, he produced a variety of other shapes, such as toast racks, clock cases, smokers' and writers' accessories, buttons and brilliantly coloured brooches. Miniatures, started at Macintyre's, remained part of Moorcroft's output. Throughout World War II, the firm concentrated on the production of ware for export. Moorcroft continued to experiment, e.g. with matt-glazed wares.

Under his son, Walter Moorcroft (b 1917), who worked for the firm 1936-40 and succeeded his father in 1945, the company continued to develop on the traditions established by William Moorcroft with the

Bernard Moore. Vase of albarello form with flambé glaze and panels of flowers in ruby against a mushroom-coloured ground. Initialled BM. *36 cm high.*

introduction of new designs and glaze colours. Despite the increasing use of slip-casting, hand-painting and finishing continued.

Marks: Moorcroft's signature with the name of the ware and, initially, Macintyre's mark, printed; MOORCROFT/BURSLEM, impressed, 1913-c.1921; MOORCROFT/MADE IN ENGLAND, impressed, c.1921-1930; an impressed signature, *W. Moorcroft*, with POTTER TO HM THE QUEEN, c.1930-1946. Later marks incorporate Walter Moorcroft's signature, impressed or painted, and MOORCROFT impressed.
Refs: R. Dennis *William and Walter Moorcroft 1897-1905* (Fine Art Society, London, 1973), *William Moorcroft and Walter Moorcroft 1897-1973* (Fine Art Society, London 1973).

Moore, Bernard (1850-1935). Staffordshire ceramist. He succeeded his father, Samuel Moore (d 1867) at St Mary's Works, Longton, where he traded with his brother, Samuel Vincent, as *Moore Bros until the sale of the business in 1905. Bernard Moore was President of the Ceramic Society, 1902-03, and used knowledge gained in his own extensive research in his work as consultant to many firms in Britain, other European countries and America, on technical problems in production; in the same way, he collaborated with Cuthbert *Bailey in 1901. Health risks to pottery workers became a preoccupation. Moore was to work on a

Government Committee on Lead and Dust Regulations in the Pottery Industry in 1926, and delivered an influential paper to the British Ceramic Society in 1932, suggesting changes in production that would reduce lung disease among the makers of bone porcelain. Glaze research which he had begun in the 1880s resulted in the successful reproduction of Chinese *flambé* on porcelain by 1902.

In 1905, Moore established a workshop at Wolfe Street, Stoke-on-Trent, where he decorated and glazed stock from Moore Bros, and blanks made by other Staffordshire manufacturers. He was joined in 1906 by his son, Joseph Moore. His continued research into oriental and Middle Eastern glazes resulted in successful reproductions of Persian blue, aventurine and crystalline glazes as well as a range of *flambé* and *sang-de-boeuf* effects. These glazes were often used over decoration of birds, flowers, etc. Moore also mastered the firing of lustres, often using patterns inspired by Islamic or Japanese designs. Until 1914, he employed artists including J.*Adams, E.H.*Beardmore, D.M.*Billington, G.A. *Buttle, Cicely H. Jackson, R.*Joyce, Hilda Lindop, Annie Ollier, Reginald Tomlinson, Edward R. Wilkes, to make signed exhibition pieces at his workshop.

Marks: BM painted; BERNARD MOORE painted or printed, sometimes with date.
Refs: J. Adams 'Potters' Parade' in *Pottery & Glass* (November, 1949); A. Dawson *Bernard Moore, Master Potter 1850-1935* (Richard Dennis, London, 1982); obituary in *Pottery Gazette* (May 1935).

Moore, Frederick. English ceramic artist working 1927-57 for *Doulton & Co. in Burslem. Moore is noted for his design of *flambé* and Sung wares. His son Warwick Moore also designed *flambé* ware for the company.
Refs: see Doulton & Co.

Moore, George Storey. *See* Wear Pottery.

Moore, Samuel, & Co. *See* Wear Pottery.

Moore, William. *See* Brown-Westhead, Moore & Co.

Moore Bros, Staffordshire manufacturers of bone china and earthenware, B.*Moore and his brother Samuel Vincent were owners from 1870 of St Mary's Works, Longton (which had been established in 1830 and rebuilt by their father in 1862). The brothers made high-quality tableware and ornamental pieces, which included lamps, baskets, table decorations and large frames for looking glasses. The firm was noted for modelled work, e.g. a teapot in the shape of a kneeling camel, with the head and neck forming a spout, and the handle formed by a driver tugging at the load (1874), table centrepieces decorated with modelled cupids, animals (often dogs), or plants (e.g. a cactus). R.J.*Morris was among designers of decorative modelled ware. The firm's output also included imitations of Chinese *cloisonné* enamel, heavily gilded, and reproductions in porcelain or earthenware of Japanese pottery. A clear, turquoise glaze was a speciality. Table services were painted e.g. with roses or cornflowers. Lamp bases,

vases, etc., were often decorated with modelled cupids. In the Sydney International Exhibition, 1879, Moore Bros won a gold medal for a display that included ornamental wares with *pâte-sur-pâte* decoration (which had been introduced c.1878), modelled flowers, and enamelled patterns. The firm also participated in the Melbourne International Exhibition, 1880, and the World's Columbian Exposition in Chicago, 1893. R.*Pilsbury, art director and designer 1892-97, supervised the execution of high-quality painted decoration. The factory was acquired in 1905 by Thos C. Wild & Co.

Marks: MOORE or, from 1880, *Moore Bros.*, impressed or incised; name printed with globe device also occurs from c.1880.
Refs: J. Adams 'Potters' Parade' in *Pottery & Glass* (November 1949); Bernard Moore's obituary in *Pottery Gazette* (May 1935); A. Dawson *Bernard Moore, Master Potter 1850-1935* (Richard Dennis, London, 1982); Godden (1966a); Jewitt; G. Phillips Bevan (ed) *British Manufacturing Industries* (London, 1876).

Moorhead Clay Works. American pottery established 1866 at Spring Mills, Montgomery County, Pennsylvania, by A.S. Moorhead and William L. Wilson for the production of architectural ware, plant containers, statuary and garden ornaments in terracotta, as well as drain-tiles, pipes, firebrick, etc.
Ref: Barber (1976).

Moravian Pottery & Tile Works. *See* Mercer, Henry Chapman.

Moravian pottery. Ceramics, mainly earthenware, or (after 1800) stoneware, made by members of the Moravian community of protestants, originally from Poland and Czechoslovakia, who settled in America at centres including Bethlehem, Pennsylvania and Wachovia, North Carolina, by the mid 18th century.

Pottery, made at Salem and Bethabara, was one of their main early industries. Excavations in the 1960s showed that the potters made jugs, bottles, mugs, plates, lamps, flowerpots and cooking utensils out of earthenware, with a body made from local clay and varying in tone from light red (Bethabara) to buff (Salem), usually lined with pale slip under a clear glaze and decorated in brown slip. Most of the ware was thrown, although some items, e.g. tobacco pipes, stove tiles and plates, were press-moulded. Slip decoration was frequently trailed in abstract or geometrical patterns (cross hatching, circles, dots and arched fish-scale or comb motifs) and coloured with copper, iron or manganese oxides, or carried out in red clay. Trailing in red and light-coloured slip was often carried out against a dark brown ground.

The makers included R.*Christ, his assistant and successor J.F.*Holland, H. *Schaffner, D.*Krause and J.*Butner.
Ref: Bivins.

Moreau-Nélaton, Adolphe-Etienne (1859-1927). French landscape painter, author and ceramist, born in Paris. He studied under the painter Henri-Joseph Harpignies from 1871, joined a group of artists which was to become the society L'Art dans Tout, and first exhibited his ceramics in the society's

third exhibition, 1898. He had learned ceramic techniques from his mother, C. *Moreau-Nélaton, and from traditional potters living on his estate, La Tournelle, near Fère-en-Tardenois (Aisne), where he carried out his work: earthenware painted in richly coloured slip with plant motifs, lush flowers and fruiting branches, in a style resembling that formerly used by his mother; animal figures; utilitarian ware in a strong, peasant style. His stoneware, delicately decorated in few colours, appeared soon after 1900.

Mark: incised monogram.
Refs: Bénézit; F. Henriet 'E. Moreau-Nélaton, Paris 1907' in *L'Art Décoratif* XXI; Heuser & Heuser; Lesur (1971); F. Monod 'Les Poteries de M. Moreau-Nélaton' in *Revue des Arts Décoratifs* 19 (1899); Thieme & Becker; Valotaire.

Moreau-Nélaton, Camille (1840-97). French painter and ceramist, born in Paris. She studied painting at her uncle's studio, where she met the painter and graphic artist, Adolphe Moreau (1827-82), whom she married in 1858. Her first experience in ceramics (1867) was gained in overglaze painting of naturalistic motifs—eels and other fish, seaweed, plants and flowers—which recalls F.*Bracquemond's treatment of Japanese motifs. In the same year, she first exhibited her work and joined the studio of T.*Deck, where she painted vases and flasks with designs of birds, notably parrots, and flowers in overglaze enamels. While the composition of her designs remained oriental in feeling, the subjects were usually of European species. She started painting in slip in 1873, using a style resembling E.*Chaplet's. Her work was fired at the *Laurin factory until interruption caused by serious illness. She resumed work in 1891, afterwards sending pieces to be

Adolphe-Etienne Moreau-Nélaton. Stoneware vase with beige glaze speckled brown, 20th century. 26 cm high.

*Matt Morgan. Earthenware vase made by the
Morgan Art Pottery Co. The painting,
apparently in oils over the glaze, is in white.
The decorator's initials, NJH, are incised at
the bottom of the design. The firm's mark,
impressed, 1882-84. 48.6 cm high.*

fired in the workshop of E.-A.*Dammouse.
She died in a fire.
Mark: painted signature, *Clle Moreau.*
Refs: Bénézit; Heuser & Heuser; E.
Moreau-Nélaton *Camille Moreau, peintre et
céramiste 1840-97* (Paris, 1899); Thieme &
Becker; Valotaire.

Morel. *See* G.D.A.

Moreton, John and Anson. Potters working
in Australia. Staffordshire potter John
Moreton, transported to New South Wales
in 1819, and his son Anson Moreton (b 1811)
made pottery figures and busts resembling
those of E.*Wood at the Surry Hills Pottery,
Sydney, from the early 1820s until 1844.
Anson Moreton was still active in 1847.
Ref: Graham.

Morgan, James, Jr (d 1822). American stoneware potter. Morgan made salt-glazed domestic ware at Cheesequake, Madison, New
Jersey (then part of South Amboy) at a
pottery inherited from his father, also James
Morgan (d 1784). He worked in a partnership
that also included his brother-in-law, Jacob
Van Wickle, at Old Bridge, Middlesex
County, by 1805, and may have had shares
in both potteries at the same time. Fragments
of jars, jugs and cylindrical mugs excavated
at the Old Bridge site have brown-tinged or
slip-coated interiors and decoration (notably
scale patterns or spirals) trailed in blue slip
or incised designs e.g. of flowers, animals,
birds, human figures or geometrical patterns,
often filled with blue; the clay body is variable in colour.
Refs: Clement (1947); *New Jersey Pottery to
1840* (catalogue, New Jersey State Museum,
Trenton, 1972); Stradling; Webster.

Morgan, Matthew Somerville (c.1839-90).
English-born artist and designer working in
America from 1873. Morgan worked as
lithographer for a Cincinnati firm, Strobridge
& Co., from 1878. He formed the Dayton
Porcelain Co. in 1882 with I.*Broome and,
on his return to Cincinnati in the same year,
he established the Matt Morgan Pottery Co.
(1883-85). There he began the production
of vases and plaques decorated after the
Hispano-Moresque style, with the benefit of
research into clays and glazes carried out for
him by George Ligowsky. He also made
Cincinnati faience with underglaze slip
painting, notably by N.J.*Hirschfeld and
M.A.*Daly, gilded ware with a ground of
glossy deep blue glaze, and terracotta (introduced 1884) with low-relief decoration
and ground colour developed in one firing.
He collaborated on the design of shapes
with modeller H.T.*Mueller. After the
company's failure and subsequent reorganization of the pottery, briefly under
Ligowsky as manager, 1884-85, Morgan
worked mainly as a lithographer in Cincinnati
and, later, New York.
Mark: MATT MORGAN/ART POTTERY Co
arranged in an oval shape, often
surrounding -CIN.O-, impressed; a paper
label was often used without any other
mark.
Refs: Barber (1976); Evans; Kovel & Kovel;
Lehner.

Morgenroth & Co. German porcelain manufacturers working at Gotha from 1866 on the
production of luxury wares, figures, etc. Their
successors, Friedrich Schwab & Co., made
everyday tableware and decorative pieces
including imitations of Royal *Copenhagen
and *Meissen wares, as well as contemporary
designs.
Marks include the initial M and *Gotha* at
the base of a semicircle of radiating lines.
Refs: Cushion (1980); Danckert; Weiss.

Mori family. A line of Japanese potters,
makers of *Bizen ware in the 16th century
and active until the 20th century. The later
members of the line included Yoseimon
Mori (d c.1775), who was succeeded by his
son Goroemon (d c.1810) and grandsons
Kakuji (d c.1853) and Moemon (d c.1860).
Kotaro (d 1882), son of Kakuji Mori, was
succeeded by his own son, who was working
in the early 20th century. Kikoichiro Mori,
member of another branch of the family,
joined Kozan Makuzu (*see* Miyakawa
family) near Yokohama before working at
*Mushiake.
Refs: Brinkley; Jenyns (1971); Orange.

Morley, Francis (retired 1862). English
potter, born in Nottinghamshire. Morley
joined his father-in-law W.*Ridgway in the
firm of Ridgway, Morley, Wear & Co.
c.1835-c.1842. After the break-up of the
partnership, Ridgway and Morley continued
at the same works in Broad Street, Shelton,
until 1845. Their output of blue-printed
wares included a series with a pattern entitled Agricultural Vase, marked with the
initials R & M. Working alone from 1845,
Morley purchased the assets of Hicks, Meigh
& Johnson (*see* Hicks, R.), and continued
their manufacture of stone china and a variety
of earthenware bodies. He also bought many
of the moulds and copper plates auctioned

after the bankruptcy of C.J.*Mason, and
continued production of Mason wares at the
Broad Street Works, winning a first-class
medal at the Exposition Universelle in Paris
(1855) with samples of ironstone from the
ordinary output. He went into partnership
with T.*Ashworth in 1858, and retired to
Breadsall, Derbyshire in 1862.
Refs: Collard; Godden (1964, 1971); Jewitt;
Rhead.

Moroney, Martin. Australian artist in stained
glass, leadlight manufacturer, glass em-
bosser, glass bender and china decorator,
according to his own advertisement in 1909,
Moroney commissioned earthenwares to his
own design from a Brisbane commercial
pottery. His painted decoration on these
pieces usually represented Australian flora
and fauna. He regularly exhibited with both
the Brisbane and Victorian Arts & Crafts
Societies of which he was a member. A very
large group of his characteristic blue and
white wares was shown at the Panamanian
Exhibition in San Francisco in 1912. He
seems not to have decorated pottery after
World War I.

Morris, Henry (1799-1880). Ceramic decorator, working for many years in Swansea,
South Wales. Morris joined the *Cambrian
Pottery as an apprentice in 1813. He became
known for his painting of brightly coloured
garden flowers, often arranged in dense
bouquets, and was influenced in style by
W.*Billingsley. His work at the pottery
included the Lysaght service. Morris worked
in London and in Staffordshire before
returning to Swansea, where he worked
independently on porcelain bought in the
white from Staffordshire manufacturers;
he was also among the painters who acquired for decoration examples of the last
pieces made at the Cambrian Pottery by
T.*Bevington and his son before Billingsley
introduced the manufacture of porcelain. He
claimed to have painted these pieces as
late as 1825.
Marks: signature and date on some
pieces.
Refs: Fisher; Honey (1948a); Jenkins; W.D.
John in *Collector's Guide* (July 1969); K.S.
Meager *The Swansea and Nantgarw
Potteries* (Swansea, 1949).

Morris, Rowland James (1847-1909). English
ceramic modeller and designer. After training
under H.*Protât at the Hanley Art School,
Morris worked in Staffordshire, e.g. for
*Mintons Ltd, and then studied at the
National Art Training School in South
Kensington, London, from 1863. He worked
as a modeller on terracotta panels made
between 1865 and 1873 for the Wedgwood
Institute in Burslem, which included a series,
Labour of the Months, for the façade, and
another, Processes of the Pottery Industry.
Other models made for J.*Wedgwood &
Sons at this time were mainly produced in
majolica. He modelled parian busts in the
late 1860s for *Robinson & Leadbeater, for
whom he became chief designer, and designed ornamental ware for *Moore Bros
(c.1885-90). His later work included the
design of Dainty White porcelain for P.
*Shelley at the *Foley Potteries. Many of
his designs were carried out on a freelance
basis.

William Morris. Tile panel decorated after Edward Burne-Jones, 1870s.

Marks include incised signature.
Refs: The Artist (November 1898); Batkin; Haggar (1953); Watkins *et al.*

Morris, William (1834-96). English painter, writer, designer, printer and craftsman, originator of a handcraft revival which inspired the *Arts & Crafts Movement. In 1861, he founded a furnishing and decorating firm, Morris, Marshall, Faulkner & Co., which was reorganized in 1875 as Morris & Co., with Morris as proprietor. In ceramics, he was mainly concerned with tile design, first using handmade tiles imported from Holland for his own home, The Red House, in 1862, and later producing designs by artists Edward Burne-Jones, D.G. Rossetti, Ford Madox Brown and Philip Webb, carried out on tile blanks by his firm. Designs by Morris himself included conventional floral patterns and border decoration; he collaborated on the design of tile panels fired by W.*De Morgan, whose lustred earthenware and Persian-style pieces were sold at the Morris & Co. showrooms in Oxford Street, London. Morris's ideas as expressed through the Arts & Crafts Movement influenced the work of his friend and associate De Morgan, and such firms as the *Della Robbia Pottery initiated by H.B.*Rathbone and the sculptor Conrad Dressler. His ideal of one craftsman managing all stages of production was later adopted as a principle by many studio potters.
Refs: Barnard; Lockett (1979); Naylor.

Morris, W.T. *See* Columbian Art Pottery Co.

Morrisian ware. *See* Doulton & Co.

Morrison & Carr. *See* Carr, James.

Morrison, George. *See* Portobello Pottery.

Mort & Case; Mort & Simpson. *See* Herculaneum.

Mörtl, Michael. German ceramic modeller. During his training at the Wiener Kunstgewerberschule (from 1899) he exhibited a vase entitled Adam und Eva, with handles in the form of kneeling figures, at Klagenfurt in 1903. For A.*Förster & Co., he produced models for ewers *jardinières* and a *tazza*, made in stoneware or porcelain, and exhibited by the firm in 1906. He also modelled animal figures, both for Förster and for the Wiener Kunstkeramische Werkstätte. Mörtl headed the modelling department of the Fachschule für Tonindustrie in Znaim from 1910. He was a director of sculptural work for a firm of furniture makers in 1920 but soon returned to the Znaim ceramic school.
Mark: signature, *Mörtl.*
Ref: Neuwirth (1974a).

Mortlake Pottery. *See* Cox, George; Kishere, Joseph.

Mortlock, John, & Co. London porcelain dealers, established 1746. The firm purchased white wares, which they commissioned independent painters to decorate. They were agents for the sale of wares from such firms as the *Coalport, *Worcester, and *Derby, factories, *Mintons Ltd, and the *Swinton Pottery, also selling a large part of the output of the *Cambrian Pottery, which was painted to their order after Sèvres styles.
In 1877, John Mortlock opened a shop in Orchard Street, London, selling ware marked MORTLOCK'S STUDIO LONDON; from the 1880s, his mark incorporated the maker's name, surrounded by a ribbon.
The firm, trading from 1899 as Mortlock's Ltd, lasted until c.1930.
Refs: Godden (1970); Hughes (1977).

Morton family. *See* Lindley Moor Potteries.

Morton, George M. *See* Taft, James Scholly.

Morton, John Thomas (b 1875). English potter. After working for J.W.*Senior at the Leeds Art Pottery from 1888, and briefly at Hunslet in 1907, Morton established a workshop at Harehills, Leeds, where he continued to make similar wares. He worked with his son until c.1914, when he closed the pottery. In 1933, he built a workshop at Filey, Yorkshire, where he made copies of earlier creamware and agate ware. His pottery closed during World War II and reopened briefly afterwards. In 1947, Morton moved to Burniston, north of Scarborough, where he worked until the 1950s.
Mark: *J.T.Morton/Filey*, incised in script, c.1920-48.
Refs: Godden (1964); Lawrence.

Mosa factory. Dutch porcelain works established in 1883 by Louis Regout & Son for the production of domestic ware and tiles. The output was painted or printed with patterns in blue, often inspired by Chinese or Delft Wares. Later, the factory produced commemorative ware and modelled pieces,

such as teapots in the form of animals. New designs for services were used in the 1950s and the factory ceased operation in 1958.
Marks: the outline of a triple arch over MOSA; a triangular mark containing the initials PMM over PORSELEINFABRIEK/MOSA/MAASTRICHT.
Refs: Singelenberg-van der Meer; C. Thewissen (ed.) *N.V. Porselein—en Tegelfabriek MOSA 1883-1958* (Maastricht, 1958); van Straaten.

Mosaic Tile Co. American pottery established in 1894 by H.T.*Mueller and K. *Langenbeck, with a group of backers, at Zanesville, Ohio. The firm's production of floor tiles in local buff clay, decorated with designs applied through perforated patterns, was soon augmented by a line called Florentine Mosaic, heavy tiles for floors and walls, with designs of coloured clay inlaid under pressure by a method patented by Mueller, and finished with a dull glaze. Some tiles were inlaid with many small blocks imitating *tesserae*. Decorations were inspired by Inca tapestries and the pottery decoration of Zuni, Pueblo and Moqui Indians. After the departure of Langenbeck and Mueller in 1903, William M. Shinnick, general manager from 1907, enlarged the range of tiles made. Faience wall tiles in pastel shades, introduced in 1918, were made under the supervision of H.*Rhead, c.1920-23. Other introductions included ceramic mosaic, art mosaic, and plain or decorated tiles for walls and mantelpieces. Special issues of portrait tiles representing e.g. Simon Bolivar, Abraham Lincoln, William McKinley, General Pershing, Woodrow Wilson, were often produced in white basalt relief against a blue ground.
With the decrease in building during the years of the Great Depression, the output began to include other articles, such as bookends, badges, souvenirs, boxes and hotplates. In 1954, the firm bought the Roseville Pottery Co. works. Production of faience tiles ceased in 1959; the firm closed in 1967.

Marks: monogram of MTC in circle, moulded in relief, or firm's name and *Zanesville, Ohio.*
Refs: Barber (1976); Barnard; T.P. Bruhn *American Decorative Tiles* (catalogue, University of Connecticut, Storrs, 1979); Kovel & Kovel; Lehner.

Mosbach. German faience factory established 1770 at Mosbach, Baden. Production changed over to lead-glazed earthenware in the early 19th century. The firm of Roemer & Co., the owner 1787-1828, was followed until 1836 by Heinrich Stadler, formerly its manager.
A variety of marks include T (Tännich), MT (Mosbach-Tännich) or, for cream-coloured wares after 1818, MOSBACH, impressed.
Refs: Haggar (1960); Honey (1952); Hüseler.

Moseley, George (d 1973). Porcelain painter working for the *Worcester Royal Porcelain factory from his apprenticeship c.1919 until c.1939. Moseley painted fruit and birds, especially English garden birds, bullfinches etc.

Mark: monogram of GM on small mugs.
Ref: Sandon (1978a).

Moser, Kolo (1868-1918). Austrian painter, designer and decorative artist. Moser studied at the Akademie in Vienna until 1892, and at the Kunstgewerbeschule (1892-95), where he returned to teach painting (1900-18). He designed ceramics for production at the Kunstgewerbeschule and by the firm of J. *Böck. His work included vases and covered jars with restrained relief decoration, e.g. low-relief scales or petals, horizontal ribbing, and carved perforations.

Mark: incised or painted monogram of KM.
Ref: Neuwirth (1974a).

Moses, James. *See* Mercer Pottery Co.

Moses, John (b 1832). Irish-born potter working in America from the early 1850s. After his apprenticeship in a dry goods business in Philadelphia, he rented a pottery (1863) where yellow and Rockingham-glazed wares had been made. Trading as the Glasgow Pottery, his firm started production of cream-coloured earthenware and, soon afterwards, white granite and ironstone ware. Tea and toilet sets and tableware were painted by a freelance decorator, at first with bands of colour or lines of gilding and gradually with more elaborate decoration. The output also included ware for hotel and ship use, and souvenir cups and saucers used at Centennial Tea Parties (1876). Among institutional ware was the pottery for use at the National Home for Disabled Volunteer Soldiers, printed with the institution's seal (1899), and ware printed U.S.M.C. for the Marine Corps, and with appropriate initials for other Government departments.

Marks include GLASGOW POTTERY/Co./ TRENTON/N.J. printed in black; an eagle over a shield bearing stars and stripes, with J.M. & Co.; a wreath surrounding a date and S.P. (semi-porcelain), and various other marks incorporating the name of the ware.
Ref: Barber (1976).

Mosley, William Edwin (d 1954). English ceramic decorator. Mosley was apprenticed at the porcelain factory in Osmaston Road, *Derby, c.1893 as a painter, mainly of flowers, leaving in 1912 to work at the King Street factory. After travelling to Australia with R.*Barratt in the early 1930s, he rejoined the factory in Osmaston Road, and remained in Derby until his death. He was noted for his miniature portraits, bird paintings and landscapes, as well as delicate arrangements of flowers, which often included roses and forget-me-nots.
Refs: Barrett & Thorpe; Twitchett (1980).

Moss Aztec. *See* Peters & Reed.

Moss Green. *See* Brush-McCoy Pottery.

Mostique. *See* Roseville Pottery Co.

Mott, J.H. English ceramic artist, working at the *Doulton & Co. Lambeth workshop 1880-1950. Mott succeeded W.P.*Rix as art director, 1897-1935, afterwards acting as consultant. He had a wide knowledge of ceramic bodies, glazes and colours, and assisted in the development of refractory porcelain for laboratory use. He designed simple shapes for decoration with matt and semi-matt glazes, crystalline or *flambé* effects, and lustre decoration, in response to changes in stylistic demands in the early 20th century. Mott himself made a number of experimental pieces with oriental glaze effects that were unusual on stoneware. Under his direction, the range of colours for the decoration of saltglaze was extended to facilitate the development of new designs, e.g. by W.E.*Rowe and H.*Simeon.

Mark: initials, JHM.
Refs: see Doulton & Co.

Mougin, Joseph (1876-1961) and Pierre (1879-1955). French potters, makers of industrial stoneware; sons of a glassmaker. Joseph Mougin studied sculpture in his native town, Nancy, and at the Ecole des Beaux-Arts in Paris. Impressed by an exhibition of the work of J.*Carriès c.1895, he built a studio and kiln at Montrouge (Hauts-de-Seine) with help from a sculptor, Lemarquier, and possibly his brother, Pierre Mougin. After two years' unsuccessful experimentation, Joseph Mougin went to study ceramics at Sèvres. The brothers then established a workshop in Vaugirard (Seine)

Joseph Mougin. Stoneware vase of ribbed double-gourd form in a shaded blue, partially crystalline, glaze. Incised mark: GRES MOUGIN NANCY. 23.5 cm high.

and started production of pale-bodied stoneware, despite continuing technical problems, particularly with glazes. Their work included peasant figures cast after models by Ernest Wittman, and a Mother and Child cast from a model by another native of Nancy, artist Victor Prouvé, at whose instigation they began exhibiting in Paris. They subsequently returned to Nancy c.1900, where they began production in 1905 and, in collaboration with other members of the Ecole de Nancy including Prouvé, Alfred Finot and Ernest Bussière, exhibited stoneware in Art Nouveau styles in Paris and Nancy until World War I. They opened a studio at the faience works in *Lunéville for the production of art pottery. After winning the Grand Prix de la Céramique at the Exposition des Arts Décoratifs in Paris 1925, Joseph Mougin left Lunéville in the early 1930s and returned to the Nancy studio, where he resumed production in 1936, helped by his daughter Odile and son François until his retirement in 1960.

Mark: *Mougin,* incised or painted.
Refs: Brunhammer *et al* (1976); Hakenjos (1974); Heuser & Heuser.

Moulin père et fils. *See* Sinceny.

Mount Casino Tile Works. *See* Cambridge Art Tile Works.

Mount Clemens Pottery Co. *See* McCoy, Nelson.

Mountford, Jesse (c.1799-1861). English porcelain painter, specializing in landscapes. Born in Hanley, Staffordshire, Mountford was apprenticed, like his brother, John *Mountford, at the factory in Nottingham Road, *Derby, and remained there as a painter of decorative pieces until he was discharged by R.*Bloor in 1821. He subsequently designed patterns for tableware at *Coalport and, from the mid 1830s until 1861, for *Davenport's. His son, also Jesse (b 1835), was listed as a 'china painter' in the census of 1851.
Refs: Barrett (1951); Barrett & Thorpe; Godden (1970); Lockett (1972); *see also* Derby.

Mountford, John (b 1816). English ceramic modeller; brother of Jesse *Mountford. After his apprenticeship as a figure maker at the porcelain factory in Nottingham Road, *Derby, Mountford worked for the firm of W.T.*Copeland, where he claimed to have discovered the fine-textured paste which was later marketed as *parian ware, in the early 1840s. Mountford went into partnership with S.*Keys Jr., trading (1850-57) as Keys & Mountford, makers of parian ware. In the Great Exhibition (1951), the partnership exhibited figures, e.g. Flora, Prometheus tormented by the Vulture, two Circassian slaves, animal models (game dogs, greyhounds), a table centrepiece consisting of boys with baskets, and a ewer. Mountford was working alone at Stoke-on-Trent in 1864.

Marks: KEYS & MOUNTFORD; incised signature *J. Mountford, Stoke,* recorded, but very rare.
Refs: Godden (1964); Haslem; Jewitt; Shinn; *Staffordshire Advertiser* (20th September 1851).

Mousnier, Pierre. *See* Magnac-Bourg.

Mousseux, Emile. *See* Bézard, Aristide.

moustache cup. In English ceramics, a cup with a guard at the rim to protect the user's moustache from the contents of the cup. Moustache cups were produced, mainly in porcelain, in the latter half of the 19th century by English manufacturers, e.g. Mintons Ltd, the Worcester Royal Porcelain factory and in Derby. Examples were imported from Germany for sale as gifts and souvenirs.

Moustiers. A French faience centre since the 17th century. In the late 17th and early 18th centuries, local styles followed those established at a factory established by Pierre Clérissy c.1679. The decoration featured historical or mythological scenes and, especially, hunting subjects after work by the Florentine painter Antonio Tempesta (1555-1630). Borders grew increasingly light and lacy, in keeping with patterns used c.1710-c.1748 from the works of Jean Berain (c.1639-1711), French draughtsman, and court designer to Louis XIV from 1674. Berain's work is characterized by arabesques, fantastic creatures, birds, scrollwork, festoons and foliate ornament. The style associated with Joseph Olérys, who returned to Moustiers after travelling to *Alcora, features scenes of grotesque figures covering the whole area inside a rim of garlands, sometimes interrupted by medallions painted in high-temperature colours: green, blue, violet, yellow, orange, black. Later work at Moustiers, often carried out in enamel colours, included *chinoiseries*, landscapes *en camaïeu*, and sprigs of flowers, in the style of Marseilles faience and floral decoration imitating that of Strasbourg. In the 19th century, fine decoration was still carried out, although many pieces were only sparingly painted and much work was left in the white. Clerissy's factory continued under the partnership J.F. Pelloquin & J. Fouque (from c.1749) and Fouque's successors until 1852. Jean-François Thion worked from 1788; his factory closed in 1874. Works established in 1759 by J.B. Jauffret passed to the Bondil family, successors to his partner, Joseph Bondil, and lasted until 1836. There was a works, the Feraud factory, in operation 1779-1841, and Joseph-Pierre-Toussaint Feraud (d 1901) worked in Moustiers 1852-74. Modern imitations of Moustiers ware have been made at *Gien and in Malicorne (Sarthe).

A variety of marks painted in underglaze blue mentioned the factory and the place name, *Moustiers*. Decorators' signatures occur.
Refs: E. Fouque *Moustiers et ses faïences* (Aix-en-Provence, 1889); Hannover; H. Requin *Histoire de la faïence artistique de Moustiers* (Paris, 1903) and *Généalogie des Clérissy fabricants de faïence à Moustiers* (Paris, 1905); P.S. Wadsworth 'Fouque-Arnoux' in *Apollo* 63 (1956).

Moyr Smith, J. English painter and designer, retained by *Mintons Ltd in the 1870s and 1880s as a designer of tiles transfer-printed in a wide range of colours, e.g. with humorous rustic scenes, illustrations of folk tales, Tennyson's 'Idylls of the King', Scott's Waverley novels, 24 scenes from Shakespeare

Emile Müller. Stoneware jug made at Müller's workshop in Ivry-sur-Seine by James Vibert. 16 cm high.

(c.1880), and a series of Seasons (c.1885). He employed a clear, linear style, reminiscent of W.*Crane.
Refs: Barnard; *Christopher Dresser 1834-1904* (catalogue, Camden Arts Centre, London, and the Dorman Museum, Middlesbrough, 1979); Lockett (1979).

Mueller, Herman T. (d 1941). German tile manufacturer. Mueller had an artistic training in Nuremberg and Munich before working as a modeller of porcelain figures in Thuringia. In America from 1875, he designed many relief tiles for the *American Encaustic Tiling Co. and worked for the same firm as modeller from 1886. He produced plaques and tile panels with classical figures representing the seasons, women with children, doves, etc. He established the *Mosaic Tile Co. with K.*Langenbeck in 1894, and received a medal from the Franklin Institute in Philadelphia in 1898 for his invention of the process used in making the firm's Florentine Mosaic tiles. He worked for G.W. *Robertson from 1903 and subsequently formed his own tileworks, Mueller Mosaic Tile Co., in 1908, to make mosaic tiles for walls and floors, decorative panels and signs. A small water spout in the shape of a turtle, moulded on a tile base and matt-glazed in green and brown, dates from 1910. The firm closed in 1938.

Marks: designs and modelled work, initialled. On pieces made by the Mueller Mosaic Tile Company, three shields bearing M M Co, below ribbon bearing FAIENCE.
Refs: Barber (1976); Eidelberg; Evans; Kovel & Kovel.

Mühlberg, Heinrich Ernst (d 1826). German manufacturer of earthenware and porcelain. After training in Volkstedt and Gera, Mühlberg established a porcelain decorating workshop in Roschütz (1789) and a factory at Gisenberg (1796) which was until 1809 under the management of his brother, Johann

Anton Mühlberg, subsequently the founder of a decorating workshop at Friedrichstanneck. Mühlberg's wife, Emilie von Schütz (d 1845), continued production after his death, succeeded by their son Karl Mühlberg until his bankruptcy c.1850.
Ref: Scherf.

Mühlendyck, Wim (b 1905). German potter, born near Cologne, where she was an apprentice-potter 1925-27, before attending the ceramics school in Höhr-Grenzhausen. She established a workshop at Grenzhausen in 1931 for the production of pottery following the traditional styles and techniques of the Kannenbäckerland in the region of Cologne. With E.*Balzar-Kopp, she pioneered a revival of traditional Westerwald stonewares. Her incised or engraved plant motifs were symbolic in intent (e.g. the tree of life, flower/sun, twigs arranged in the shape of a cross). The work was also painted in grey, blue or brown slip.

Marks include Mühlendyck's full signature, incised.
Ref: Bock.

Mulhauser, Jean-Pierre. Porcelain decorator. Mulhauser ran a painting studio at Nyon, Geneva, 1805-18, marking his work with the initials PM, and *Genève or *Manufacture J. Mulhauser/Genève*.
Refs: Danckert; Weiss.

Müller, Albin. *See* Hanke, August.

Müller, Emile (d 1889). French potter, formerly an engineer, and the maker of architectural stoneware and editions of stoneware sculpture. In 1854, he established a tileworks, the Grande Tuilerie d'Ivry at Ivry (Eure), selling through a Paris showroom. Müller experimented to perfect a stoneware body and high-temperature glaze that would withstand sudden changes in temperature when used on tiles. After Müller's death, his son Louis took over the firm, which then traded as Emile Müller & Cie. As well as glazed brick and wall tiles, the firm made architectural terracotta and produced stoneware with *flambé* glazes from designs by contemporary sculptors, including E.*Grasset, H.*Stoltenberg-Lerche, J.-D.*Ringel d'Illzach, and J. Vibert. The firm supplied glazed panels and roof tiles designed by H.*Guimard in 1893, and executed La Frise du Travail depicting industrial workers and craftsmen in high relief modelled by Anatole Guillot for decoration of the main entrance to the Exposition Universelle, 1900, and a frieze, Les Salamandres, by the Belgian painter, sculptor and designer, Gisbert Combaz (1869-1941). Other designs by Combaz for Müller & Cie included tiles modelled with birds or foaming waves (resembling the Hokusai prints), exhibited in 1897. Stoneware plaques included a portrait of the *diseuse* Yvette Guilbert by Toulouse-Lautrec and a series 'Les Heures' after designs by Grasset. The firm also produced a series of vases and *jardinières* decorated with orchids in green and pink glazed stoneware, c.1897, after the bronze by Philippe Wolfers.

Mark: *Müller/Emile* within circle or oval, with IVRY/PARIS.
Ref: Brunhammer *et al.*

Müller, Joseph. Ceramic decorator born in Gitschin. He became known for paintings of mythological subjects which he carried out at Schlaggenwald in 1810, and later at Giesshübel, where he started work early in 1811. He was also responsible for delicate gilt edgings of arabesques and foliage on vases.
Ref: Meyer.

Müller, Karl. German-born sculptor and artist. Müller studied in Paris before going to America, where he worked as chief designer and modeller for the *Union Porcelain Works from 1874. Models by him were shown in the firm's display in the Philadelphia Centennial Exhibition (1876): the Century Vase, with six relief panels in biscuit representing events in American history, as well as paintings relating to technology and engineering; a relief portrait of George Washington; a gilded eagle; heads of American animals, and handles in the form of bison heads; a tea set with human heads as finials, a goat's head on the handle of the cream jug and rabbits as legs (the pieces were elaborately painted); the Keramos Vase with raised decoration illustrating the history of ceramics as depicted in Longfellow's poem 'Kéramos'; the Liberty Cup with figures modelled in white clay against a lavender ground, and the handle a figure of Liberty standing on an eagle; busts made in buff body of Edwin Forrest as William Tell and Charlotte Cushman as Meg Merrilees were modelled from photographs. Müller also designed and modelled a series of statuettes, pitchers and busts in biscuit porcelain, notably a Poet's Pitcher decorated with relief portraits of Homer and other poets (1877).
Ref: Barber (1976).

Muller, Leenerdt Johan (1879-1969). Dutch painter and designer. Muller trained in Amsterdam and worked at the *Zuid-Holland factory from 1898, eventually becoming head of design. He was known for his designs for undecorated tea sets in plain, modern shapes, produced 1924-25.
    Mark: initials LJM.
Refs: Scheen; Singelenberg-van der Meer; van Straaten.

Mullowny, John. *See* Washington Pottery.

Munakata. *See* Aizu.

Münchener Vereinigte Werkstätten. German craft workshops established in Munich by the designers Hermann Obrist, Bruno Paul, Bernhard Pankok and R.*Riemerschmid in 1897; a forerunner of the *Deutsche Werkstätten.

Münch-Khe, Willy (b c.1884). Painter, sculptor and graphic designer, who worked as a ceramic modeller for Meissen. Münch-Khe joined the factory's staff early in 1912 as a designer of decoration, mainly for vases, jars and dishes, and remained there until the end of the following year. He began to concentrate on the modelling of animal figures, notably foals, donkeys and deer, which he carried out freelance after World War I, initially in porcelain but, in the 1930s, in red stoneware, which became his preferred material.
Ref: Walcha (1973).

*Lisbeth Munch Petersen. Pierced porcelain filled with glaze in the manner of rice-grain decoration. Made at the *Bing & Grøndahl factory, c.1960.*

Munch Petersen, Lisbeth (b 1909). Danish potter, born in Ronne; a relative of the *Hjorth family. She shared a workshop with her sister, G.*Vasegaard, 1933-35, and subsequently worked as a designer, 1961-66. Her work includes decorative pieces in a coarse body, often with portions left unglazed to form a contrast with patterns in glossy glaze. Some pieces have monochrome glazes, or a combination of glazes in brown, dark blue and cream. She also used painted designs and sharply textured relief decoration.
Refs: Hettes & Rada; Hiort; W. Hull *Danish Ceramic Design* (catalogue, Museum of Art, Pennsylvania State University, 1981).

Muncie Pottery. American pottery established 1922 in Muncie, Indiana, by Charles Benham, making vases and other pieces for flower-arranging, with a variety of glazes, for sale through florists and department stores, until closure of the works in 1939.
    Mark: MUNCIE, incised.
Ref: Kovel & Kovel.

Muona, Toini. Finnish ceramic artist. After studying under A.W.*Finch, she joined *Arabia in 1931 and designed stoneware dishes, vases, etc., in simple and sometimes angular shapes, with monochrome glazes. The pieces were often large. She also produced wall panels decorated with plant forms, e.g. pressed leaves.
Refs: Aro; Beard.

Murray, James, & Co. *See* Port Dundas Pottery Co.

Murray, Keith (b 1892). Architect and designer, born in Auckland, New Zealand. Murray travelled to England in 1906 and studied architecture after war service (1915-18). He began designing glass in the early 1930s, ceramics for J.*Wedgwood & Sons from 1933, and silver from the following year. His ceramic designs share the functional simplicity of his work in other media. Clean, crisp shapes for bowls, vases, mugs, coffee sets, etc., influenced by oriental forms and relying for decorative effect mainly on turned grooves and plain, stepped surfaces, were made in black basalt or earthenware with semi-matt Moonstone glaze or matt cream, green or straw-coloured glazes; glaze of celadon colour was sometimes cut in turning to expose cream slip beneath. The

forms for most designs were thrown, but a jug featuring six convex panels, rectangular ashtrays, bookends, etc., were moulded. Ceramics designed by Murray continued in production until the late 1950s, although the last designs date from c.1939.
    Murray designed the new Wedgwood factory (for which the foundation stone was laid in 1938) with his partner, C.S. White, and concentrated on architectural design after World War II.
    Designs for Wedgwood were often printed with the signature or initials of Keith Murray as well as Wedgwood marks.
Refs: Batkin; Coysh (1976); Haslam (1977); Reilly & Savage.

Murray, W.F., & Co. Ltd. *See* Caledonian Pottery.

Murray, William Staite (1881-1962). English artist and ceramist. After living in Holland (where he collected Delft and Chinese export ware), training as a painter in Paris c.1900, and working as an engineer, Murray began his own experiments in pottery c.1912 in Kensington, London. Studying until 1913 at Camberwell School of Art, he made earthenware with brushed decoration (for which Camberwell was noted). Murray later stated that he had looked upon potting as fundamental among the abstract arts.

*Keith Murray. Vase made by J.*Wedgwood & Sons Ltd to a design by Keith Murray, c.1930. 19.8 cm high.*

During World War I, he collaborated with the artist C. Fraser *Hamilton on the production of painted earthenware at 18 Yeomans Row, London (*see* Yeoman Pottery), and built a low-temperature gas kiln. Murray was working by 1820 at his brother's engineering works in Rotherhithe, where he made stoneware which included tall, wide vases, jars, etc., in a white body with flinty texture, glazed and usually undecorated except for occasional splashes and streaks of colour. Subsequently, in Brockley Heath, Kent, he built and patented a high-temperature kiln fuelled with crude oil. He had formed a collection of Chinese pottery and maintained his interest in oriental art, including the work of the 17th-century Japanese artist and potter Koetsu. From the early 1920s, his work showed the influence of other oriental artists including *Hamada. Using a yellowish or red firing stoneware body, he made pieces, sometimes with painted or incised decoration, often only partially glazed. With the aim of gaining acceptance of pottery as an art form, Murray gave titles to his work, unique pieces which he exhibited in art galleries, setting his prices relatively high. While at the Royal College of Art, London, from 1925, he taught pupils including T.S.*Haile, H. *Mathews and H.F.*Hammond.

Using (from c.1936) shapes inspired by English medieval earthenware, sometimes very tall and narrow, Murray developed a variety of fine glazes, often in muted shades. His later pieces often stand on conspicuously modelled feet. Murray ceased production of stoneware after settling in Southern Rhodesia (now Zimbabwe) in 1939.

Marks: at Rotherhithe, scratched signature; later, M in a pentagon, impressed.
Refs: Beard; Coysh (1976); Haslam (1977); Rose; 'Some Vorticist Pottery' in *The Connoisseur* (October 1975); Wingfield Digby.

William Staite Murray. Vase with thick, crimson flambé *glaze and touches of blue-green, an example of Murray's experimental work with glazes. Incised mark: W.S. Murray L.D. London 1923. 21.2 cm high.*

Murray & Couper. *See* Caledonian Pottery.

Mushiake. Japanese pottery centre in Oku county, Okayama. A local clan kiln began to make domestic wares for general sale in the neighbourhood for some years in the early 1860s, producing ware which was glazed (in contrast to the *Bizen ware of nearby Imbe). The output included saké bottles with overlapping glazes in different colours leaving a patch with transparent glaze and decoration of plum blossom, orchid, bamboo or chrysanthemum brushed in iron oxide. Mushiake ware also included the output of Kakatori Mori.
Refs: Jenyns (1971); Mizuo.

Musselburgh Pottery. Scottish pottery established 1800 at Newbigging, Musselburgh, by W.*Reid for the production of stoneware with brown or white body as well as a hard, greyish-white earthenware with flinty texture, which included commemorative jugs (painted, printed or decorated in relief), Toby jugs and puzzle jugs. The wares were mainly for local sale. Reid's firm became Wm Reid & Son, 1837-43, and the pottery was purchased in the 1840s by the brothers Robert and Thomas Tough, afterwards producing mainly stoneware water filters, jars for preserves, and other utilitarian items. It continued in operation until after 1910.

Marks: Reid's crown mark; *Muss.* or *Musselburgh*, scratched with a pointed tool, and sometimes a date.

William Mussill. Vase made in Paris and painted by Mussill with a landscape of river or lake and trails of wild flowers and a bird's nest, c.1865. Signed by Mussill. 42.7 cm high.

Refs: H.J.S. Banks in *Apollo* 66 (December 1957); Fleming; Jewitt; McVeigh.

Mussill, William (d 1906). Ceramic decorator, born in Bohemia. Mussill worked at the *Sèvres factory after studying in Paris. In England, he worked for Mintons Ltd from 1872 until his death. Mussill was a noted painter of flowers, birds and fish (studies frequently taken from nature) in rich, vividly coloured slip, mainly on earthenware (sometimes with coloured body) but also painted on porcelain. His work is found on plaques, vases, etc. Paintings signed by Mussill on Wedgwood wares exist but are unlikely to have been commissioned by the factory.
Mark: signature, *W. Mussill.*
Refs: see Mintons Ltd.

Mutabara. *See* Shino ware.

Mutz, Hermann (1845-1913). German ceramist working at a pottery established in Altona, 1854, by his father for the manufacture of tiled stoves. Hermann Mutz took his son, R.*Mutz, as a partner 1896-1904. The production of stoneware developed by Richard Mutz was continued after 1904 by a craftsman in the Hermann Mutz workshop, Ernst Leinweber. Hermann Mutz was succeeded by his widow until the workshop passed to Paul Hadel in 1921. It closed in 1929. Ernst Leinweber continued the production of wares in the style of Richard Mutz for a short time at his own workshop in Hamburg (c.1930).

Marks include MUTZ-KERAMIK impressed.
Refs: Bock; W. Schölermann 'Die Töpferfabrik von Hermann Mutz in Altona', in *Kunst und Handwerk* 51 (1900-01).

Mutz, Richard (1872-1931). German ceramist. He went into partnership with his father, H.*Mutz, in 1896 and concentrated on the making of vases and bowls, marked *Mutz/Altona* to distinguish them from the workshop's normal output. His work was first exhibited in the Hamburg Museum für

*Hermann Mutz. Covered jar produced at his workshop in Altona, designed by his son, R.*Mutz, c.1900.*

Kunst und Gewerbe, 1898. Mutz collaborated on the production of a plaque modelled in low relief by E.*Barlach and cast in stoneware to commemorate the museum's 25th anniversary in 1902. He and Barlach also produced wall fountains and vases. After establishing his own workshop in Berlin (1904), Mutz continued his association with Barlach and made vases, bowls, ashtrays and figures in a pale body with drip glazes mainly in dark green and blue, with a wide range of other colours including red, brown, yellow and white. He formed the Keramische Werkstätten Mutz & Rother in 1906 in Liegnitz for the production of architectural ware, and later worked at the *Karlsruhe factory. He also established a workshop making wall tiles and stoves after moving to the Gildenhall artists' colony at Neuruppiner See, but ceased work in ceramics two years before his death at Gildenhall.

Marks: MUTZ-ALTONA incised or impressed; RICHARD MUTZ WILMERSDORF impressed on a circle.
Refs: Bock; K. Reutti *Mutz-Keramik* (catalogue, Ernst-Barlach-Hauses, Hamburg, 1966).

Myakuen Nishimura. *See* Kenzan.

Mycock, William Salter (1872-1950). English pottery decorator, working for the *Pilkington's Tile & Pottery Co. from 1894. Mycock was at first engaged in the painting of tiles, but began working on vases, etc., at the introduction of lustre painting, and retired when it was discontinued c.1930. Mycock was noted for his bold, simple execution of stylized plants and geometrical patterns in lustre. He also carried out (on lapis ware) incised and *sgraffito* linework of ships, seagulls, etc., and carved plaques, winning a gold medal in the Paris Exposition Internationale des Arts Décoratifs et Industriels Modernes (1925). He was a local magistrate from 1929, councillor and, in 1937, Mayor of the Borough of Swinton and Pendelbury; he received the Freedom of the Borough in 1949.

Mark: monogram of WSM within rectangular outline.

*William S. Mycock. Lapis Ware wall plate made at *Pilkington's Tile & Pottery Co. and decorated by Mycock with a design of a goose in pale blue and green against grey. Impressed factory marks and Mycock's monogram; date code for 1936. 29 cm in diameter.*

Refs: A Catalogue of the Lancastrian Pottery at Manchester City Art Galleries (Manchester City Art Gallery, 1981); Coysh (1976); Cross; G. Godden 'Pilkington's Royal Lancastrian Pottery' in *Apollo* 75 (October 1961); Godden (1966a); Lomax.

Myott, C., & Son Ltd. *See* Meakin, Alfred.

Nabeshima ware. Japanese porcelain initially made for the exclusive use of lords of the Nabeshima clan or for presentation to other officials. The kiln produced simple white or blue-painted wares and celadons in the 17th century at Iwakayakawachi, and delicate enamelled porcelains, after a move to Okawachi (or Okochi), near *Arita. Specializing in sets of dishes for table use, the kiln continued to produce bowls, bottles, brush boxes, etc., as well as elaborately modelled vases, using a milk-white paste with slight bluish tinge. The pieces, many with deep foot rims, were generally small, and all were neatly potted and well finished. The enamel painting of landscapes, and a wide range of plant designs, including reeds, cherry blossom, hollyhocks, camellia, persimmon, hibiscus, and gourds, with arabesques, scrolls and brocade patterns, in many cases echoed textile design or paintings by the Kano and Tosa schools. Pieces are often patterned on the exterior with vines and interlaced circles. The enamel palette consists of iron red, green, yellow and sometimes black and purple, with underglaze blue that is more sparingly used than is the case with *Imari ware. The glaze has an orange-peel texture resulting from its content of wood ash.

The ware became generally available after the Meiji restoration in 1868, and production continues to the present day. *Imaizumi Imaemon succeeded as 12th in line of the traditional makers of Nabeshima ware.
Refs: Brinkley; Jenyns (1965); Munsterberg; Penkala; Sanders.

Nabeya Kichibei. *See* Minzan.

Nadelman, Elie (1882-1946). Polish-born sculptor and ceramist. After service in the Russian army, Nadelman worked in Paris from 1905 and America from 1915. He began experimenting with clay in the 1930s, setting up a New York kiln, where he produced figures in earthenware with glazes which he developed 1933-35. Some plaster figures made by Nadelman from the late 1930s were produced in terracotta by an assistant after his death.
Refs: D. Bourdon 'The Sleek, Witty and Elegant Art of Elie Nadelman' in *Smithsonian* (February 1975); *Ceramics Monthly* 23 (May 1975); Clark & Hughto; L. Kirstein *Elie Nadelman* (Eakins Press, New York, 1973); *New York Times* (17th March 1974); J. Silver 'Elie Nadelman: a Simple Notion of Style' in *ARTnews* (November 1975).

Naeshirogawa. Japanese ceramic centre producing *Satsuma ware, and active since the production of tea-ceremony wares for Lord Shimazu of Satsuma. The making of dark-coloured wares extends as far back as the end of the 16th century. Kilns were opened by Korean potters at Mikawa, where two remain. Throughout their period of operation, the Naeshirogawa kilns have

used iron glazes giving a range of colours from pale grey and blue to ochre, brown and red. Applied relief motifs and combed patterns were used. The output included spirit flasks, some intended for use by workers in the fields; sweet-saké containers with relief decoration depicting the god of wealth; flower-bowls with applied motifs of flowers, pine and rope; footed cooking pots usually with temmoku glazes. The wares are noted for fine workmanship and finish. In style they retain the Korean influence to the present day.

Earthenware made out of local white clay from the mid 18th century was used for incense burners, wine bottles, small figures, etc., sparingly enamelled with flowers, keyfret and diaper patterns in red, green, purple, blue, black, yellow and gold on a soft, finely crackled ground.

Production at Naeshirogawa, which was on a large scale at a factory employing several hundred workers, resumed soon after an interruption caused by political changes in 1868. White earthenware with brocade designs was exported in large quantities c.1870, and imitations were made in Kyoto, Awata and Mie prefecture; imitations sometimes have a pale glaze over a dark body, which results in a greyish tone.
Refs: Audsley & Bowes; Jenyns (1971); Koyama; Munsterberg; Okamura.

Nagano. *See* Shigaraki ware.

Nagao Hongama. *See* Hasami.

Nagayo. Japanese kiln established in the 17th century by the Omura clan about twelve kilometres from Nagasaki. Its output includes blue and white porcelain, celadon wares and pieces laid with mottled glazes in green, yellow, and aubergine in the manner of Chinese 'tiger skin' pieces made in the reign of K'ang Hsi (1662-1722).
Refs: Jenyns (1965); Mitsuoka; Munsterberg.

Nagoya. Traditional Japanese ceramic centre, capital of the *Seto region. The products of the area include enamelled earthenware with crackled glaze, and grey stoneware coated with opaque white glaze. Modern firms making porcelain tableware in western styles for export include the *Narumi China Co. and *Noritake.
Refs: Brinkley; Jenyns (1971).

Nagymarton. Hungarian pottery making yellowish-tinged creamware from its establishment at Mattersdorf in 1818 by the Ziegler family until the 1860s. Styles followed those of earlier wares, including Viennese porcelain.
Mark: *Mattersdorf*, impressed.
Ref: Csanyi.

Naka. *See* Shino ware.

Nakano. *See* Koishibara.

Nakao Honnobori. *See* Hasami.

Nakazato Muan or Taroemon (b 1895). Japanese potter, one of a family making *Karatsu wares. Nakazato carried out intensive research into the origins and methods of Karatsu pottery production, adapting traditional styles and techniques in his own

work, and specialized in jars and pitchers which were shaped by beating with a paddle. He succeeded to the name Taroemon XII in 1927 and assumed the name Muan in 1969, when he gave the title Taroemon XIII to his eldest son, Tadao. He was designated Holder of the Technique for Karatsu Ware in 1976.
Refs: Jenyns (1971); *Living National Treasures; Masterpieces;* Roberts.

namako glaze. *See* Aizu.

Nangawara kiln. *See* Kakiemon ware.

Nantgarw China Works. Welsh pottery established in 1813 at the village of Nantgarw, to the north of Cardiff, by W.*Billingsley and S.*Walker. The partners built a pottery, saleroom and two small kilns, and within a year succeeded (with financial backing from W.W.*Young) in making a fine, translucent, soft-paste porcelain. The pottery closed in the autumn of 1814, when Billingsley and Walker moved to work for L.W.*Dillwyn at the Cambrian Pottery. In 1817 Billingsley and Walker returned to Nantgarw, reopened the pottery and made high-quality soft-paste porcelain resembling that used at Sèvres and influenced by French porcelain in style— both 18th-century (e.g. plates with wavy edges and rim) and contemporary work with feet in the form of lions' paws, and other elements of the Empire style. Little of the porcelain, which was mainly tableware, was painted at Nantgarw, as the work was generally sent for decoration in London, where J.*Mortlock & Co. acted as the principal dealers. High losses in firing resulted in financial failure, and Young took over the pottery early in 1820. He engaged T.*Pardoe, with his son as assistant, to paint and gild the stock that remained, selling it at auction in South Wales in 1821 and 1822, after which the equipment was sold to J.*Rose.

The pottery remained closed until William H. Pardoe reopened it in 1833 for the manufacture of earthenware and stoneware. His work included large quantities of bottles for spirits, beer, ink, etc., in salt-glazed stoneware; lead-glazed tiles inlaid with slip; teapots, butter jars, etc., with rich Rockingham glaze in red earthenware or pipeclay body, often made from local clay; and bowls, dishes and jugs in cream-coloured earthenware with stripes of blue, brown and red. The Pardoe family also made Toby jugs and decorated water filters, as well as tobacco pipes, one of the staple products. The pottery closed in 1920 after difficulties in obtaining local labour and a decline in the demand for clay pipes. Plans for the restoration and preservation of the site, and the establishment of a museum, are under discussion.
Mark: NANT-GARW, impressed, generally over CW (china works)
Refs: W.D. John *Nantgarw Porcelain* (1948); Nance; Williams (1932).

Naokota. *See* Tanii Rijuro.

Naples. Italian porcelain factory established in 1771 by King Ferdinand IV and operating in the royal palace from 1773 until 1806. The output included reproductions in biscuit porcelain of bronze and marble statuary. French occupation interrupted production in 1806, but the factory was reopened by a

Naples. Cream-coloured earthenware plate printed with a view of the Temple of Neptune at Paestum. Made at the del Vecchio factory, early 19th century. Mark: FDV *over* N *impressed. 24 cm in diameter.*

French firm in 1807 and continued under several changes of ownership until its final closure in 1834. The later work included busts, figures and tableware in Empire style.
Mark: N with a crown.
Refs: Danckert; A. Lane *Italian Porcelain* (Faber, London, 1954); Weiss.

Naraoka. Japanese *folk kiln working in Akita prefecture until the mid 20th century. The kiln was established in 1863 by a potter from Shiraiwa, also in Akita, where a similar kiln was in operation c.1770-c.1897. Both kilns were noted for their use of the streaked blue-white iron glaze (namako) characteristic of the Tohoku region, in which Akita is situated. Naraoka produced covered jars, bowls and other domestic ware for local use, with namako glaze over brown or green ground glazes.
Refs: Mizuo; Munsterberg.

Narumi. Japanese porcelain factory established in the 20th century at Nagoya for the production of tableware, etc., for export.
Marks include the head of a classical column below NARUMI/CHINA on a printed rectangle.
Ref: Jenyns (1965).

Nase, John. Pennsylvania potter, working, probably from the late 1820s, at the pottery in Tyler's Port, Montgomery County, established by his father, J.*Neesz. Nase continued some of his father's slip-trailed or *sgraffito* decoration, the majority of designs featuring tulips or fuchsia flowers. His work is distinguished by the use on some pieces of a smear glaze instead of the usual glossy lead glaze, or a dull, black surface achieved with a covering containing manganese through which designs of flowers, leaves, etc., were scratched to show the red body. Trailed slip, used less frequently than the *sgraffito* decoration, featured birds, flowers and verse inscriptions. His modelled work included a cream pitcher and sugar bowl, dotted and trailed with yellow slip, and brown-glazed. The squat, rounded shape of the sugar bowl, which is surmounted by thin strips of clay modelled in a crown shape, is reminiscent of some forms occurring in the

folk pottery of Switzerland, where the Neesz family is thought to have originated.
Ref: Barber (1976).

Nashville Art Pottery. American art pottery established in Nashville, Tennessee, in 1883, originally as a clay-working and decorating studio at the Nashville School of Art by the school's founder and principal, Elizabeth J. Scovel. The first work was fired in 1884, and after expansion in the following year, the pottery operated until 1889. At first producing red ware with a brown glaze, Scovel modelled the forms of pitchers, vases, etc., and made her own moulds with assistance in the firing and heavy work. A vase in the shape of a broken egg, now preserved in the art museum of Princeton University, is painted with green leaves, edged with gold, against a tracery of gold lines. In 1888, she introduced two distinct wares: Goldstone, red earthenware with a dark brown glaze that took on a sparkling gold effect when fired at a high temperature, and Pomegranate, a fine, white body, with a mottled pink and blue-grey glaze, veined with red also as a result of high firing.
Mark: *Nashville/Art Pottery*, incised in script.
Refs: Barber (1976); Callen; Evans; Kovel & Kovel.

Nast, Jean-Népomucène-Herman (1754-1817). Porcelain manufacturer, born in Austria and living in Paris from 1780 after working at the Vincennes porcelain factory. He established a factory on rue Popincourt (1782), where he made large vases (1.5 metres high) and porcelain columns, as well as clock cases, biscuit figures, and tableware in hard-paste porcelain. With his chemist, Vauquelin, he developed new colours, including a high-temperature green derived from chromium, and fine blue grounds. Vases with chrome green used in the decoration were exhibited in Paris in 1806. Nast was succeeded by his sons Henri (b 1790) and François (b 1792), working as Nast Frères until 1831, under royal patronage from 1819. Henri Nast continued alone until the firm's closure in 1835. The firm made large quantities of biscuit ware, which included clock cases modelled with mythological or allegorical scenes, as well as tea and coffee wares, serving dishes, lamps and items for interior decoration.
Mark: NAST/À/PARIS stencilled in red.
Refs: Chavagnac & Grollier; Ernould-Gandouet; Guillebon.

Nathanielsen, Bertha (1869-1914). Porcelain decorator, born in Stavanger, Norway. She worked 1893-1906 for the Royal *Copenhagen Porcelain Factory, specializing in flower studies and landscapes.
Mark: signature, *Bertha Nathanielsen*, painted in blue.
Refs: Porzellankunst; Weiss.

National League of Mineral Painters. An association of ceramic clubs and professional china decorators formed in America in 1892 to foster closer relationships between ceramic artists throughout the country and to raise the decorative standards of American artwares through coordinated work and study. Annual exhibitions were intended to give an indication of progress and suggest the course

Camille Naudot et Cie. Porcelain dish with a perforated pattern of mimosa filled with coloured glaze, c.1900. Monogram of CN *in blue. 12.3 cm in diameter.*

of further research, and members' work was shown in the Paris Exposition Universelle in 1900. S.S.G.*Frackelton was founder and vice-president; other active members included A. Alsop-Robineau, L.A.*Fry, M.C.*Perry Stratton and C.*Volkmar.
Refs: Barber (1976); Evans; S.S.G. Frackelton *Tried by Fire* (1886).

Natural Foliage. *See* Doulton & Co.

Natzler, Gertrud (1908-71) and Otto (b 1908). Artist potters, born in Vienna. In 1933 they met and opened a workshop, where they collaborated on the production of pottery. Simple, refined forms, often bowls which ranged from very shallow to deep and narrow, were thrown by Gertrud Natzler, who had studied at the Wiener Kunstgewerbeschule; her husband developed the glazes. The Natzlers moved to America in 1938, settling in Los Angeles the following year. Working in earthenware, they became known for their control of glazes, especially rough-textured and cratered types. After his wife's death, Otto Natzler became involved with forms as well as glazes and exhibited slab-built pots in 1977.
Refs: The Ceramic Work of Gertrud & Otto Natzler (Los Angeles County Museum of Art, 1966); Clark & Hughto; Donhauser; O. Natzler 'The Natzler Glazes' in *Craft Horizons* 24 (July/August 1964) and *Gertrud & Otto Natzler Ceramics* (catalogue of a private collection, Los Angeles County Museum of Art, 1968); 'Natzler Retrospective Exhibition' in *Ceramics Monthly* (19th October 1979).

Naudot, Camille, et Cie. French porcelain workshop established in Paris by Camille-Victor Naudot in the 1890s and working until after 1919. The firm made very translucent porcelain stylistically resembling the soft paste produced at the Sèvres factory in the 18th century and specialized in perforated decoration filled with translucent enamel glaze (*émaux à jour*). Bowls, enamelled and gilded with sprays of flowers, were included in the firm's display at the Exposition Universelle in Paris (1900).

Marks: monogram of CN, printed; insect, with initials in 20th century.
Refs: Lesur (1967); Haslam (1977).

Nautilus Porcelain Co. or **Possil Pottery Co.** Scottish manufacturers of porcelain and earthenware, established 1896 in Glasgow as the Nautilus Porcelain Co. and working as the Possil Pottery Co. (in Possil Park) 1898-1901, while continuing to use Nautilus Porcelain as a trademark. The firm specialized in ornamental porcelain, including tea, dessert and dressing table sets and figures. Small souvenir pieces decorated with views or coats of arms, introduced in 1903, were produced in large quantities by 1907; some were made in eggshell porcelain.
Marks include NAUTILUS PORCELAIN, POSSIL POTTERY and a winged snake motif.
Refs: Andrews; Godden (1964).

Neale & Co. *See* Wilson, David.

Neatby, W.J. (1860-1910). English ceramist and designer. Neatby worked for an architect before joining the *Burmantofts Pottery as a decorator c.1880-90. He assumed control of the architectural department at *Doulton & Co., 1890-1907, and modelled Carrara ware friezes, masks, caryatids and other architectural details in a style influenced by Art Nouveau. He also designed tile panels in terracotta, including a set painted with life-sized female figures for the Winter Gardens, Blackpool (1896), the façade for a Bristol printing works depicting Johannes Gutenberg, W.*Morris, etc. (1901), and twenty circular pastoral or hunting scenes for Harrods, London. Technical advances made at Doultons under Neatby's supervision included an eggshell finish for earthenware (similar in effect to Carrara stoneware), which he used with raised relief or *intaglio* ornament in many schemes for interiors, and salt-glazed stoneware with painted decoration over white slip, in a bright range of colours (inspired by the palette of the Della Robbia family in 15th-century Italy) frequently used in the 1920s. Neatby worked as a freelance designer after leaving the Doulton factory, but continued to carry out occasional projects with the architectural department. He made stained glass, furniture and metalwork in a style influenced by C.F.A.*Voysey and others associated with the Arts & Crafts Movement.
Marks: initials.

Refs: Atterbury & Irvine; Barnard; Eyles (1975); Lockett (1979).

Neesz or **Nesz,** Johannes (1775-1867). Pennsylvania potter working his own pottery at Tyler's Port in Montgomery County by 1800. He made plates, teasets, preserving jars, measuring jugs, barber's bowls, children's toys, etc., with *sgraffito* decoration showing red body through pale slip. Some designs show similarities (especially in the drawing of figures and horses) with the work of D.*Spinner, at whose pottery Neesz may have learned his trade. Pie plates often bear a design of a mounted soldier, supposed to have originally represented George Washington. Neesz was succeeded by his son J.*Nase, probably by 1830.
Ref: Barber (1970).

Johannes Neesz. Pie plate in red earthenware with sgraffito *pattern and an inscription in Pennsylvania 'Dutch' dialect meaning: 'I have been riding over hill and dale/and everywhere have found pretty girls', 1810-20.*

Nekola, Karel (d 1915). Ceramic decorator, working in Scotland. Nekola moved from Bohemia to work for R.*Heron on the decoration of Wemyss ware at the *Fife Pottery in 1883 and remained until his semi-retirement, through illness, in 1910. Subsequently, he continued to paint the ware in a workshop at his home. While at the Fife Pottery, Nekola was reponsible for the training of other artists, including his sons Joseph and Carl. Joseph Nekola moved to Devon to continue decoration when the *Bovey Tracey Pottery Co. bought the rights to Wemyss ware designs.
Refs: Coysh (1976); McVeigh.

neo-classical style. A style of ornament derived from ancient Greek and Roman art, adopted in France during the mid 18th century after the excavation of Pompeii and Herculaneum (which started in 1738) and in the rest of Europe and America during the 18th and early 19th centuries. The style was associated with the revolutionary painter Jacques Louis David in France, the sculptors Canova and B.*Thorwaldsen in Italy, and with work by the sculptor Flaxman for Josiah Wedgwood in Britain. Decoration in this style displays a restrained, formal treatment of themes and motifs from classical antiquity, e.g. mythological scenes, cherubs, urns, tripods, lyres, ram and lion masks, satyrs, cloven hooves, dolphins, acanthus leaves, draperies, guilloches and fluting. The phase of the classical revival roughly coincided with the reign of Louis XVI, and gave way to the *Empire style in the early 19th century.

Neppel, Pierre. French porcelain maker working at Nevers (Nièvre). Neppel owned a factory in rue de Crussol, Paris, c.1805-16, and then bought a former bottle factory. Having taken out a patent in 1809 for under-glaze printing from paintings, he produced porcelain by 1818, specializing in the under-glaze printing of a variety of subjects. From 1843, he worked with a partner, Bonnot. He was assisted by his son Louis Neppel and his son-in-law Louis Guérin until the factory was taken over by Charles Pillivuyt et Cie at Mehun.

Mark: signature.
Refs: Lesur (1967); Guillebon.

Ness, Thomas. *See* Commondale Pottery.

Neuhaus. German porcelain factory est-ablished 1833 at Neuhaus, Thuringia, by Gabriel Heubach (*see* Heubach family), in partnership with Johann Georg Kämpfe (d 1889), Paul Valentin Kessler and Peter Greiner. The firm produced ornamental pieces in styles derived from Copenhagen, Sèvres, the Worcester factory, Delft ware and contemporary porcelain. The factory later worked under the name of Rudolph Heinz & Co. until its closure.

Marks under Heinz incorporate R H & Co.
Refs: Danckert; Scherf.

Neuhäuser, Wilhelm. *See* Pfeiffer, Max Adolf.

Neuheuser, William. *See* Lichte.

Neuwalder-Breuer, Grete (b 1898). German ceramic modeller, born in Berlin. She studied at the Wiener Kunstgewerbeschule, 1914-19, and subsequently modelled figures and portrait busts for the firm of Goldscheider and for the Wiener Werkstätte. She died in a concentration camp.
Ref: Neuwirth (1974a).

Neuwirth, Rosa. Ceramic modeller, born near Prague and working in Vienna, where she studied at K.*Moser's technical school, 1903-04 and at the Kunstgewerbeschule, 1899-1905 and 1906-11. With fellow students, H.*Johnova and I.*Schwetz-Lehmann, she was a member of the Keramische Werk-genossenschaft, in Vienna in 1911. She worked independently after the closure of the workshop in 1920. She used earthenware, stoneware or porcelain in modelling plates, vases, etc., but is known for her animal figures.

Mark: signature, NEUWIRTH.
Refs: Neuwirth (1974a); *Studio Year Book* (1909).

Newcastle Pottery or **Forth Banks Pottery.** English pottery established c.1800 off Forth Banks, a road in Newcastle-upon-Tyne, by the firm of Addison, Falconer & Co. for the production of earthenware, which included frog mugs and commemorative pieces (e.g. mugs showing the death of Nelson, and

political events of the early 19th century). James Wallace & Co. occupied the pottery from c.1838 until 1857, making earthenware with lustre decoration, e.g. death mugs. The company's successors continued in oper-ation until 1893.

Marks include NEWCASTLE POTTERY.
Refs: Bell; Godden (1966); Jewitt.

Newcastle-upon-Tyne. A centre of earth-enware production in north-eastern England from the late 18th century. Among early potteries were Carr's Hill at Gateshead, which came under the control of I.*Fell in 1867, and the *Sheriff Hill Pottery, near Gateshead, established before 1773. *St Anthony's and *Stepney Bank potteries were among a group established at Ouseburn, Newcastle, between 1780 and 1790. The *Northumberland Pottery started at North Shields on the mouth of the Tyne in 1814, and St Peter's Pottery (*see* Fell, T., & Co.) was established in 1817, the year in which the *Maling family's production was moved from North Hylton on the River Wear to *Ouseburn Bridge Pottery. The *Phoenix Pottery opened ten years later at Ouseburn, and the *Tyne Main Pottery operated in the 1830s and 1840s. In 1863, C.T.*Maling mentioned six Tyneside firms making white and printed earthenware, three producers of brown ware and four making both white and brown earthenware; the trend in the late 19th century was towards fewer and larger firms. The *Newcastle Pottery was one which lasted throughout the century.

Ware was made locally for sale at relatively low prices both to supply the needs of the immediate area and for export to Denmark, Norway, Germany, the Mediterranean countries, India, North America and the British Colonies. In general, raw materials were obtained from outside the area (e.g. as ballast in returning coal ships), which did not encourage the development of a charact-eristic local body. Most of the early fine earthenwares were cream coloured. In some cases, the pieces resembled the lattice and perforated ware associated with the Leeds Pottery (e.g. work made at St Anthony's Pottery). Other adopted styles included Gaudy Welsh (Tyne Main); Sunderland lustre (Ouseburn Bridge, Northumberland). Transfer printing was introduced in the north-east of England by the Maling family at the Hylton Works. The Willow pattern was among designs produced by Maling, T. Fell, and the Sheriff Hill, Stepney Bank, St Anthony's and Railway Bridge (Ouseburn) potteries.
Refs: S.W. Fisher *British Pottery and Porcelain* (Arco, London, 1962); Haggar (1950); G.B. Hodgson *Borough of South Shields from the earliest period to the close of the nineteenth century* (Andrew Reid & Co., Newcastle-upon-Tyne, 1903); Jewitt; G. Lewis *An Introduction to English Pottery* (Art & Technics Ltd., London, 1950); C.T. Maling *The Industrial Resources of the District of the 3 Northern Rivers, the Tyne, Wear and Tees* (second edition, 1864); Shaw; Towner (1957).

Newcomb College Pottery. American pottery started in 1895 under the direction of artist Ellsworth Woodward and his brother W.*Woodward at The Sophie Newcomb Mem-orial College, New Orleans (established

1886), part of Tulane University, Louisiana. The project was intended to provide prac-tical vocational training related to advanced courses in art and design. Professional potters were engaged to carry out throwing, glazing and firing. M.G.*Sheerer, who joined the pottery to teach slip-painting and enamel decoration as well as the artistic appreciation of pottery, acted as supervisor. The decorators, initially undergraduates working at home, and later including several graduates (e.g. M.T.*Ryan, A.F.*Simpson) working permanently at the pottery, were encouraged to be spontaneous and original in their decoration of forms—bowls, vases, lamps, candlesticks, mugs, tea and coffee ware—from a selection determined by Mary Sheerer and, later S.A.E.*Irvine. The ware was thrown by J.F.*Meyer, in buff-coloured or, from c.1900, white clays from Mississippi and Louisiana; a red clay was used for undec-orated terracotta. Early decoration, imi-tating the *Rookwood Pottery's standard ware, in slip and underglaze colours carried out on unfired body, was soon superseded by underglaze painting on low-fired biscuit. In a new style which emerged c.1897, designs were incised on unfired clay, which had been sponged after throwing to provide a suit-able surface. After the first firing, underglaze colours were painted on, predominantly in a blue/green range, as well as yellow and a black which was occasionally used in the more deeply incised lines. The wares were then coated with glossy, transparent glaze. The misty effect of Newcomb ware resulted from the presence of silica in the clay surface. Early geometrical designs gave way to sub-jects which were said to reflect the area's natural environment, but were in fact in-ternationally used—wisteria, conifers, palm trees, maple, orange blossom and syringa and simple floral designs, often representing the whole plant; themes were generally conventionalized in treatment. A design, credited to S. Irvine c.1910 and produced in quantities in the 1920s, shows a tree hung with Spanish moss against a moonlit sky.

P.E.*Cox, engaged as ceramist 1910-18, developed a matt glaze which could be successfully applied over the colours already in use, notably blue and grey-green, and superseded the earlier glossy glaze. Cox was succeeded for two years by F.E.*Walrath in

*Newcomb College Pottery. Glazed earthen-ware vase made by J.F.*Meyer, and painted by Maria Hoe-LeBlanc, 1900-10. 14 cm high.*

1918, and the pottery transferred to premises in the college's new campus, where the emphasis became more experimental and less commercial, and students were able to participate more fully in the production processes and to make more varied use of decorative techniques. After Woodward's retirement in 1931, only limited quantities of art ware were made (until 1940s) under the name of the Newcomb Guild, and the main production concentrated on a plain ware.

Marks: every piece was marked until at least the 1920s. NC for the pottery; artist's initials, potter's initials, code numbers for the clay body and glaze, and an inventory number were incised by hand and sometimes filled in with colour.
Refs: F. Adams *Two Decades of Newcomb Pottery Pieces from 1897-1917* (exhibition catalogue, Newcomb College, New Orleans, February 1963); Barber (1976); Callen; Donhauser; Eidelberg; Evans; Kovel & Kovel.

New Delftware. *See* Porceleyne Fles, De.

New England Pottery Co. American pottery established 1854 in East Boston, Massachusetts, by Frederick Meagher, for the production of Rockingham and yellow-glazed ware. The pottery was taken over in 1875 by Thomas Gray and L.W. Clark, who produced cream-coloured earthenware and white granite for domestic use. Trading as the New England Pottery, 1886-95, the firm made decorative ware with coloured bodies in semi-porcelain, marketed as Rieti ware. Porcelain tableware and other pieces in graceful shapes were sparingly decorated with printed designs, and good glazes, notably mazarine blue and an 'old ivory' shade. Ornamental ware in semi-porcelain or ironstone china was lavishly painted and gilded. The firm continued as the New England Pottery Co. until 1914.

A wide variety of marks include the initials or monogram of the New England Pottery Co. and often incorporate the name of the body (e.g. *stone china*) or the line (RIETI, PARIS WHITE, etc.).
Refs: Barber (1976); Watkins (1950).

New Hall. English factory opened in 1782 at Shelton, Staffordshire, for the production of porcelain by a company led by S.*Hollins and J.*Warburton, purchasers in the previous year of the patent for the manufacture of hard paste taken out by R. Champion of Bristol. Under the management of J.*Daniel, tableware was made in shapes derived from contemporary silver, often decorated with sprig designs (e.g. a pattern resembling sprigged muslin) and formal borders, or *chinoiseries* (e.g. a scene with a boy flying a kite). In 1810, the New Hall estate was purchased by a joint stock company: Hollins,

Daniel, P.*Warburton, and William Clowes, a sleeping partner in the previous firm. By this time, the output included a porcelain containing bone ash, glassy in appearance when fired, which was to replace the hard paste c.1812; many earlier patterns continued. The company used a delicate paste in the production of tea sets with patterns of flowers, fruit, etc., in enamels. The manufacture of porcelain ceased in 1835, and remaining stock was sold off.

After a brief closure, the works were re-opened for the production of white and printed earthenware; porcelain was made for a short time by W. Ratcliff, whose work has only recently been identified. Under the firm of Hackwood & Son from 1842, production was mainly for export to Europe. Cockson & Harding, proprietors from 1856, and the brothers W.& J. Harding, owners 1862-69, made printed creamware, Rockingham-glazed ware, black basalt and other coloured stoneware bodies, and pharmaceutical ware. The works were then split, one part being let to a metalworker, and the rear portion to Thomas Booth & Son (*see* Booths Ltd) for the manufacture of printed earthenware, services with painted and gilded decoration, jugs, teapots, etc., in stoneware, and decorative jasper ware. Booths were succeeded by Ambrose Bevington & Co. c.1870-c.1890.

The New Hall Pottery Co., established in 1900, took over the factory from the firm of Plant & Gilmore, tenants from 1892. Robert Audley (b c.1860) increased production, which included low-priced toilet and household wares, and extended the works. He took into partnership his sons-in-law Albert Cook and Robert Clive. At Clive's instigation, the output of jugs and toilet wares was replaced by institutional wares and dinner services. In the 1930s, the firm also produced pottery premiums (free gifts promoting the sale of other goods) acquiring another factory to increase output in 1936. New Hall was a supplier to the armed forces in World War II, and afterwards built up an increased export trade.

Marks: *New Hall* printed in red, enclosed in a double circle on bone porcelain c.1812-35. The New Hall Pottery Co. used NEWHALL/HANLEY/STAFFS in marks incorporating a castle.
Refs: Atterbury (1980); *The Connoisseur* (April 1956); Godden (1964); Holgate;

New Hall. Pieces from a dessert service with pale blue ground, and moulded borders depicting exotic birds and foliage, c.1815.

Jewitt; G.E. Stringer *New Hall Porcelain* (Art Trade Press, London, 1949).

Newhill Works. *See* Twigg, Joseph.

New Milford Pottery Co. *See* Wannopee Pottery Co.

New Navarre. *See* Brush-McCoy Pottery.

New Orleans Art Pottery. American pottery organized in 1888 at Baronne Street, New Orleans, with assistance from W.*Woodward and his brother, failing financially in the following year. The workshop produced earthenware for painting by outside decorators and provided firing facilities for the local art league. G.E.*Ohr and J.F.*Meyer were associated with the pottery and remained with the Art League Pottery Club of advanced students at the Sophie Newcomb and Tulane colleges. The group met at Tulane under William Woodward and used facilities at Baronne Street for about five years.

Mark: *N.O. Art Pottery*, incised.
Refs: Barber (1976); Evans;

New Orleans Porcelain Factory. American porcelain works established in 1880 in New Orleans by the civil engineer, Eugene Surgi, and A.*d'Estampes, using kaolin from Texas. Despite the large quantity of their output (6,000 pieces within the first few months) the factory ceased operation in 1883 because of the difficulty in finding skilled labour. It then passed to other owners, eventually the Louisiana Porcelain Manufacturing Co., making biscuit ware with imported kaolin. An employee, Jules Gabry, became the first potter associated with the *Newcomb College Pottery. The factory closed in the mid 1880s.
Refs: Barber (1976); Evans.

Newport Pottery. *See* Shorter, Arthur Colley Austin; Wilkinson, A.J., Ltd.

Newport Pottery, Burslem. *See* Cork & Edge.

Newport works. *See* Davenports.

New Pottery. *See* Stepney Bank Pottery.

Newsome, T.H., Co. Ltd. *See* Australian Pottery.

Newton, Clara Chipman (1848-1936). American ceramic decorator, born in Delphos, Ohio. She moved in 1852 to Cincinnati where she was a schoolmate of M.L.*Nichols Storer

Clara Chipman Newton. White porcelain plate manufactured 1858, painted by C.C. Newton in 1875 and shown in the Women's Pavilion in the Philadelphia Centennial Exhibition in 1876. 24.3 cm in diameter.

and studied at the *Cincinnati School of Design 1873-74. After decorating ceramics for the Centennial Exposition and the Cincinnati Loan Exhibition (1878) she became secretary of the *Cincinnati Pottery Club in 1879. She decorated a large vase (over 52 cm) with arabesque foliage design painted in cobalt blue, and a network of gilt lines and gold bands at the base and the rim, made at the Hamilton Road Pottery (1880). As secretary at the *Rookwood Pottery, 1881-84, she took charge of office administration while continuing her own decorative work, which was often Japanese in inspiration and reminiscent of the faience of E.*Gallé in treatment, e.g. a 'horn' pitcher. For a while, she continued painting with cobalt blue on a white body, e.g. a stein, painted with a fishing scene, made in 1881. After the disbanding of the Pottery Club, she continued freelance overglaze decoration. She established a studio in Cincinnati and taught at the Thane Miller School.

Mark: initials or monogram.
Refs: Barber (1976); Clark & Hughto; Evans; Kovel & Kovel; C.C. Newton 'The Cincinnati Pottery Club' in *The Bulletin of the American Ceramic Society* 19 (September 1940); Peck.

Newtone. *See* Bakewell Brothers.

New York City Pottery. *See* Carr, James.

New York City School of Clay Working and Ceramics. *See* New York State College of Ceramics.

New York State College of Ceramics. School of ceramics at the Alfred University, New York, established in 1900 as the New York City School of Clayworking and Ceramics under C.F.*Binns as director until his retirement in 1931, with the first classes held in Spring 1901. A wide variety of experimental work was done. Binns insisted that his students should be trained in all the techniques, including firing, and demanded high standards in both design and workmanship with particular regard to the material. Early pupils included P.E.*Cox, F.E.*Walrath, E.G. Overbeck, and M.C.*Perry Stratton.

It was not the first American school of ceramics, as one had been started at Ohio State University in 1894 (and operated under A.E. *Baggs, professor of ceramics, 1928-47). They were soon followed by the New Jersey School of Clay Working and Ceramics at Rutgers University, New Brunswick, in 1902 and another at the University of Illinois in 1905. (*See also* North Dakota School of Mines.)
Refs: Cox; Donhauser; Evans; N.J. Norwood *50 Years of Ceramic Education at State College of Ceramics, Alfred* (New York State College of Ceramics, Alfred, 1950).

Nichols & Alford. American pottery firm, producing stoneware and Rockingham-glazed earthenware 1854-56 at Burlington, Vermont. The output included hound-handled pitchers from designs reputedly modelled by D.*Greatbach. Stoneware was made for domestic use, with brushed decoration in cobalt blue. The firm underwent several changes in ownership, trading as Nichols & Boynton from 1856 to c.1859, O.L. & A.K. Ballard from c.1859, then A.K. Ballard from 1868, then Ballard & Brookes, F. Woodworth from 1872, H.E. Sulls until 1895.

Marks: name and address of firm, sometimes with date.
Refs: Barber (1976); Stradling; Watkins (1950); Webster.

Nichols Storer, Maria Longworth (1849-1932). American art potter. After experiments in ceramic decoration with a neighbour, K.*Langenbeck, starting in 1873, she joined a decorating class in her home town of Cincinnati, 1874. Inspired by books of Japanese designs received as a gift in 1875, and the French and Japanese pottery shown in the Philadelphia Centennial Exhibition the following year, she began research into clay. bodies and glazes in 1879. She worked at the pottery of F.*Dallas, like M.L.*McLaughlin, in an individual studio, had a kiln built there for the firing of her overglaze decoration (some had been fired at the New York workshop of E.*Lycett), and developed a palette of cobalt blue, light blue, dark and light green, brown and black. Her work at this time included vases with relief decoration of aquatic subjects (fish, nets) and underglaze colouring. In 1880, with financial backing from her father, she established the *Rookwood Pottery, where she continued to make art pottery alongside the pottery's main initial output of domestic and tableware. Her own work combined motifs of Japanese inspiration, such as spiders, dragonflies and crabs, with European shapes, e.g. a basket with feet in the form of lions' heads, painted underglaze in fawn, black and white, and gilded (1882). She continued to use relief decoration, e.g. on a vase with seahorses under a dark red glaze with slight iridescence.

She handed over management of the pottery to W.W.*Taylor in 1883 and after the death (1885) of her first husband, George Ward Nichols, and her subsequent remarriage to lawyer and diplomat Bellamy Storer in 1886, she travelled to Europe. She moved to Washington D.C. in 1889, transferring her interest in the Rookwood Pottery to W.W.*Taylor in the following year, but retained a studio at the pottery for her own use. She achieved lustrous copper red glazes

in later research, still using designs of oriental origin, carved on the body of vases or in the decoration of metal mounts, with increasing efforts to inter-relate form, colour and texture. Eventually, she settled with her husband in Europe, where she died.

Mark: the initials MLN occur on early Rookwood Pottery.
Refs: Barber (1976); Eidelberg; Evans; Kovel & Kovel; Henzke; Jervis; Keen; Peck; K.R. Trapp 'Japanese Influence in Early Rookwood Pottery' in *Antiques* 103 (January 1973).

Nickerson, T.S. *See* Merrimac Pottery.

Nicol family. *See* Old Cumnock Pottery.

Nicollet. *See* Angoulême.

Niderviller. French factory founded at Niderviller (Meurthe-et-Moselle) in the mid 18th century by Baron Jean-Louis de Beyerlé, a counsellor to the King and director of the mint at Strasbourg, for the production of faience and, by 1768, hard-paste porcelain. The firm's chemist François Lanfrey (d 1827), director from 1780, introduced earthenware resembling the English creamware made at Leeds or in Staffordshire and purchased the factory in 1801, specializing in the production of figures and groups, glazed and enamelled, or unglazed. The figures, often made in a red body, coated in slip and a thin tin glaze, included pieces from moulds by the modeller Paul-Louis Cyfflé (1724-1806). Other pieces included decorative plaques and pieces with

M.L. Nichols Storer. Vase made at the Dallas Pottery in Hamilton Road, Cincinnati, and painted by Nichols Storer in 1879. 31.3 cm high.

polychrome decoration of flowers, figures and *trompe-l'oeil* subjects. Lanfrey continued to include porcelain in the factory's output until 1827, when the works were sold to Louis-Guillaume Dryander, who made only earthenware, including services, table ornaments, figures and groups; much of the ware was moulded, and earlier styles often revived.

Dryander's mark incorporates the arms of Niderviller.

Refs: Auscher; Baschet; Brunhammer *et al* (1976); Burton (1976); Ernould-Gandouet; Fontaine; Hüseler; Lesur (1971); Tilmans (1953, 1954).

Nielsen, Erik (1857-1947). Danish sculptor, trained at the Copenhagen Academy. Nielsen modelled animal figures for the Royal *Copenhagen porcelain factory, 1887-1926.

Marks: signature or monogram.
Refs: Porzellankunst; Weiss.

Nielsen, Jais (1885-1961). Danish sculptor, painter and ceramic artist. With K.*Kyhn, he was one of the pioneers of Danish stoneware, working on sculptural pieces. Nielsen worked as a designer for the Royal *Copenhagen Porcelain Factory from 1921. His sculptures were simple in form and often portrayed religious subjects, e.g. Pontius Pilate, the Good Samaritan (1923), David & Goliath, all in dark-coloured glazes. Bowls, vases, etc., were often celadon glazed.
Refs: Cox; Hiort.

Nielsen, Kai or Kay (1884-1924). Danish sculptor, painter and ceramic artist; modeller of mythological and allegorical subjects for figures and groups produced by *Bing & Grøndahl. His work included a lifesize Venus and a series of dolphins, tritons and human groups representing the sea.
Refs: Bénézit; Cox.

Jais Nielsen. Porcelain group depicting St Paul slaying the lion in thick sang-de-boeuf *glaze flecked with turquoise. Made at the Royal* *Copenhagen Porcelain Factory, c.1925. 62 cm high.*

Nielson, Christian (1870-1955). Danish-born potter, working in America from 1891, at the C.*Pardee Works and, briefly, at the pottery of H.*Laughlin. He joined the *American Encaustic Tiling Co. as designer, 1894-1902, and subsequently became the superintendent of the *Roseville Pottery. He took over a small stoneware pottery previously making filters in Zanesville, Ohio, where he formed the Nielson Pottery Co., incorporated 1905, making stoneware and art pottery with coloured glazes for a short time before closure of the works within a year.
Refs: Evans; Lehner; L.& E. Purviance and N.F. Schneider *Zanesville Art Pottery in Color* (Mid America Book Co., Wallace Homestead, Des Moines, Iowa, 1968).

Niemeyer, Adalbert (b 1867). German painter, designer and ceramic sculptor, co-founder of branches of the Deutsche Werkstätten and Professor at the state school for applied art in Munich. Niemeyer's pupils included M.*Kovács. He designed earthenware for the firm of *Villeroy & Boch, and porcelain tableware for production at the Meissen factory.
Refs: Haslam (1977); Hettes & Rada.

Nienhuis, Lambertus (1873-1960). Dutch designer and artist potter trained in his native Groningen and at the Rijksschool voor Kunstnijverheid in Amsterdam. As a painter and designer at the De*Distel factory from 1895, he devised simple shapes, painted under the glaze with motifs or stylized natural forms, generally on a white ground. Regarded as an influential figure in Dutch applied arts, he taught at several art schools in Holland and (1912-17) in the ceramics department of the Kunstgewerbeschule in Hagen (Westphalia). On his return to Holland, he worked independently as an artist potter, producing simple shapes covered with elaborate, often vari-coloured glazes, also taking charge of a pottery department established at the Quellinus school, Amsterdam, in 1917. Some of his designs were produced at *Goedewaagen in 1935.

Mark: signature, *Bert Nienhuis.*
Refs: Bulletin XVII, 2-3 (Museum Boymansvan Beuningen, 1966); L. Nienhuis in *Jaarboek Nederlandsche Ambachts & Nijverheidkunst* (1921, 1927); Scheen; Singelenberg-van der Meer; van Straaten.

Nieuwenhuis, Theodorus Wilhelmus (1866-1951). Dutch architect, draughtsman and designer, trained at the Kunstnijverheidsschool and under P.J.H. Cuypers in Amsterdam. From 1895, he provided designs for manufacture by De*Distel. He opened his own studio for the applied arts in 1908.

Mark: monogram of TN.
Refs: R.W.P. de Vries Jr 'T. Nieuwenhuis' in *Elsevier's Geïllustreerd Maandschift* XLVII (1914); Singelenberg-van der Meer; van Straaten.

Nile Street Pottery. *See* Doulton & Co.

Niloak Pottery Co. American firm established in 1909 to exploit the method developed (and later patented) by C.D.*Hyten of treating coloured clays so that they would combine to form streaked agate ware when thrown, without shrinking apart during drying and

firing. Hyten's pottery (which was enlarged during the repairs after damage by fire) continued the production of stoneware inherited from Hyten's father who had worked under the title, Eagle Pottery. The variegated vases, pitchers, bowls, mugs, match holders, tobacco jars, *jardinières*, fern dishes, clock cases, umbrella stands, novelties, and other pieces, originally marketed as Mission ware, were produced under the Niloak name. The combination of colours (including deep browns, buff, grey, red, pink, white, blue and light greens, streaked in the action of throwing) was unique to each piece; white is only rarely predominant, and early pieces are thought to have been rather subdued in colour. The pots were generally lined with an impermeable glaze and left with a soft, dull finish, unglazed, on the exterior. During the Depression of the 1930s, a less costly line of ware marketed as Hywood, and cast in solid-coloured or variegated clay, finished with gloss or matt glazes, superseded the Mission ware, which was not produced after c.1942. After a change in ownership in the mid 1930s, the pottery continued until 1946.

Marks: NILOAK impressed from 1910, with US patent number (1,657,997) after 1928; *Hywood by Niloak* appears on early cast pieces, which were later marked simply *Niloak*, sometimes with raised, moulded letters.
Refs: Evans; Kovel & Kovel.

Ninsei ware. Japanese earthenware with decoration painted in enamels by the 17th-century potter Ninsei (Nonamura Seibei) and his followers. Ninsei was a pioneer among Japanese potters in overglaze painting, which he executed in a classical Japanese manner, retaining much of the feeling of traditional court art and avoiding in his patterns the then important influence of Chinese wares, although some jars strongly resembled South Chinese pieces in shape. Working in the west of Kyoto from c.1647, he made a wide range of tableware, tea vessels and ornamental pieces, but especially storage jars, water jars, tea bowls and four-handled jars for the storage of leaf tea, all carefully and thinly potted in a light, close-textured body, mainly of Seto clay, with evenly crackled glaze. Ninsei painted pines and camellias, plum blossoms and a moon, the cherry trees of Mount Yoshino, wisteria, landscapes containing a pavilion, carp climbing a waterfall, poppies, rustic temples and other designs in a varied palette of gold, silver, red, blue, purple, yellow, green and black, achieving strength, precision and complexity in a composition that often echoes painting of the Kano school. He was also inspired by designs from the Yamato-e tradition and illustrations from pattern books of the time.

Ninsei's work directly influenced his pupil *Kenzan and, later, *Mokubei, *Dohachi II, *Hozen, *Wazen, and many makers of *Kiyomizu ware; it affected *Banko, *Akahada, *Kutani, and *Hirasa wares.
Refs: Brinkley; Honey (1945); Jenyns (1971); Leach (1966); Mitsuoka; K. Tomimoto 'Pottery Technique of Ninsei & Kenzan' in *Sekai Toji Zenshu* [Collection of World Ceramics] Vol 5 (Zanho Press/Kawade/Shobo, Tokyo, 1955-58).

Nipur ware. *See* Cook Pottery Co.

Harry Nixon. Bowl with cream-coloured crackle glaze, painted in grey. Made by *Doulton & Co. in Burslem, c.1920. Marked Chang, England, Noke, HN. 31 cm in diameter.

Nishimura Sozaburo. *See* Hozen.

Nishimura Sozaburo. *See* Hozen.

Nishishinmachi. Japanese pottery centre in Fukuoka prefecture, active until the early 20th century; the site of the Higayashima kiln established in the early 18th century under the control and patronage of the Kuroda clan. The kiln produced tea ware and decorative pieces in the tradition of *Takatori wares for the clan until the Meiji restoration in 1868. Potters who had moved to Nishishinmachi from *Koishibara also made domestic wares from the clay used for tea wares in styles which were characterized by the same simplicity and elegance, applying a green glaze trickled with brown, yellow or white. By 1720, the *Nishiyama kiln opened nearby.
Refs: Jenyns (1971); Kozuru *Agano and Takatori* (Kodansha International, Tokyo/ New York/San Francisco, 1981); Munsterberg; Okamura.

Nishiyama kiln. Japanese pottery established by 1720 near *Nishishinmachi for the production of domestic ware by a potter from *Koishibara under the patronage of the Kuroda clan. Using a dark, fine-textured clay, the pottery produces ware resembling the output of *Agano, with thick, three-coloured glazes. Pieces for everyday use, as well as shrines, are also decorated with purple-white (namako) and black (kameguro) glazes.
Refs: Jenyns (1971); Kozuru *Agano and Takatori* (Kodansha International, Tokyo/ New York/San Francisco, 1981); Okamura.

Nivet, Michel (d 1859). French porcelain manufacturer. Nivet established a factory 1826 in Limoges for the production of table services, coffee and tea sets, vases and decorative items. He worked in partnership until 1834 and subsequently alone until he took into partnership G. Thomas, to whom he let the works on his retirement in 1858. After Thomas's retirement c.1866, the factory passed to Léon Pailler, 1867-82. Nivet's family, still owners of the factory, let it in 1882 to Pierre Martin, who worked from 1886 with his brother Charles Martin, purchaser of the buildings in 1905. Charles Martin was working alone by 1897, when he won a gold medal in the Brussels exhibition with a display which included vases in blue, turquoise and gold. In 1919, Martin was

joined by his son-in-law Jean Duché (partner c.1923). The factory closed soon after 1929.
Marks under the Martin firm include C.M. in a circle with a crown; CM/FRANCE DEPOSE; CM in a triangle *Limoges*/FRANCE/ DEPOSE.
Ref: d'Albis & Romanet.

Nixon, Harry (b 1886). English ceramic artist and draughtsman. Nixon was apprenticed to *Doulton & Co. in Burslem from 1900 and studied at the Burslem School of Art, where he later taught part-time. He was known for paintings of flowers on table services and ornamental ware, and collaborated with Charles *Noke on the decorative schemes for Titanian and *flambé*, Sung, Chang and Chinese Jade wares. His own work included a covered vase with red glaze, which he designed for Lichfield Cathedral in 1946. He also assisted in the development of figure modelling, under Noke.
   Mark: initials HN.
Refs: see Doulton & Co.

Noke, Cecil J. or Jack (d 1954). English ceramic artist, son of Charles J.*Noke. After architectural apprenticeship and service in World War I, Noke joined *Doulton & Co in Burslem, initially learning painting techniques under L. Bentley and R.*Allen; he also studied at the Stoke-on-Trent and Burslem Schools of Art. Noke collaborated with his father and H.*Nixon on the production of *flambé*, Sung and Chang wares, and took charge of the factory's engraving department before succeeding his father as art director in 1936. He provided designs for tableware and assisted in the production of pieces by designer Frank Brangwyn, also introducing figures of championship dogs, and animal models by Raoh Schor.
Refs: see Doulton & Co.

Charles J. Noke. Lamp base in the form of a potter at work under a canopy of trees, with Chang glaze over multicoloured high-temperature glazes. Made by *Doulton & Co. in Burslem, with the marks of Charles Noke and Harry Nixon. 30 cm high.

Charles J. Noke. The Dante Vase, modelled by Noke with decoration by C. Labarre and G. White, and shown at the World's Columbian Exposition in Chicago, 1893.

Noke, Charles John (1858-1941). English ceramic chemist, modeller and designer, born in Worcester, the son of a collector and retailer of ceramics. Noke was apprenticed as a modeller and designer at the Worcester porcelain factory at the age of 15, and studied at the local school of design. He left Worcester in 1889 to join *Doulton & Co. as chief modeller. His work included large vases with relief and painted ornament, table services and centrepieces. He also modelled parian and ivory-glazed figures, including, by 1894, Henry Irving and Ellen Terry in theatrical costume, and later The Jester, The Moorish Minstrel, Columbus, etc. His later modelled work included small figures for production in bone china with other designs commissioned from established artists to form a range which was first exhibited in 1913 and marked the beginning of his revival of figure-making on an extensive scale at Doulton's.
   In the early 20th century, assisted especially by W.G.*Hodkinson, Noke made tiles, plaques and large plates in a feldspathic body resembling parian ware, decorated with literary or mythological scenes modelled and filled in with transparent enamel used not as paint but built up in the manner of enamelling on metal (and then sometimes lavishly gilded). The technique required repeated firings. Few pieces are now known.

Noke had helped to extend the firm's production with the introduction of Holbein and Rembrandt wares, and after the departure of C.*Bailey took responsibility for the technical and artistic development of high-temperature glazes. He was assistant head of Doulton's art department in Burslem from c.1912 with John *Slater, whom he succeeded in 1914. As art director, he introduced Titanian, Sung, Chinese Jade and Chang wares, assisted by H.*Nixon and, from 1920, by his son C.J.*Noke, who succeeded him as art director in 1936. Although he retired officially at that time, Charles Noke continued to work at the factory until the time of his death.

Refs: Atterbury & Irvine; Eyles (1980); Sandon (1978a).

Nolan, Luke (c.1837-1901). British-born potter working in Australia from the late 1850s. In 1871, he established the Gillbrook pottery at Brunswick, Victoria, where he made domestic and ornamental earthenware and possibly stoneware, as well as fireclay ware and drainpipes. His output included majolica vases, bread plates, etc., in the 1880s. Nolan was also a director of the *Hoffman Brick Co. His pottery ceased operation in 1909.

Ref: Graham.

Nonconnah Pottery. *See* Stephen, Walter Benjamin.

Norden. *See* Dahl-Jensen, Jens Peter.

Nordstrom, Patrick (1870-1929). Swedish-born sculptor and ceramist, working mainly in Denmark. Nordstrom served his apprenticeship as a wood carver before making earthenware with bright, alkaline glazes at his own workshop in Copenhagen, 1902-07. In Vanløse, 1907-10, Nordstrom made porcelain with prepared paste and glazes imported from Germany. He studied reports of stoneware techniques employed by J. *Carriès and at the Sèvres factory, in 1911 achieving matt glazes. On joining the Royal *Copenhagen porcelain factory in 1912, he introduced stoneware production, as A.E. *Krog had earlier tried to do. His range of glazes included brown with ochre or green tinges; a pale grey ash glaze; yellowish brown, grey-blue or grey-green glazes spotted with rutile and characterized by the varied play of light in them, and a roughness of surface; glazes striated with ochreous yellow, and crystalline effects of high quality. Evolving his own variations of the French techniques, Nordstrom applied glazes in layers, covering a colourless glaze of clay and ash with one containing rutile, and sometimes a third clay glaze, often using Scandinavian materials, including clay from his native Höganäs, stone from the island of Öland, and ash acquired from a Copenhagen baker. After his return to Sweden in 1922 to establish his own studio, some of his developments remained in production at the Copenhagen factory, notably a mottled glaze, the greyish white and iron brown inspired by Sung glazes, and *sang-de-boeuf*. His glaze developments influenced subsequent studio pottery in Denmark and Sweden.

Mark: painted monogram.

Refs: Bodelsen; Cushion (1974); Haslam (1977); Weiss.

Norfolk Street works. Staffordshire factory established 1870 at Cauldon Place, between Stoke-on-Trent and Hanley, by R.G. Scrivener and Thomas Bourne, who traded as R.G. Scrivener & Co. The output of porcelain services, tea, breakfast and dessert sets, and fancy articles, as well as earthenware toilet sets, etc., was in general well finished and decorated.

Pointon & Co., owners from 1883 until the sale of the works in 1917, and a newly-formed company Ford & Pointon, subsequent proprietors, made decorative items and tableware, as well as crested ware, by World War I. Ford & Pointon became a branch of J.A. Robinson (*see* Robinson, H.T.) in 1919, and the firm ended in the amalgamation of Cauldon and Coalport potteries.

Marks include versions of the initials R.G.S. &CO., impressed; *Coronet Ware*, trademark used by Ford & Pointon.

Refs: Andrews; Godden (1964); Jewitt.

Noritake. Japanese porcelain factory established in 1904 at Nagoya. The firm produces large quantities of tableware in western styles for export.

Printed marks incorporate the name of the firm.

Ref: Jenyns (1965).

Norse Pottery. American art pottery established 1903 at Edgerton, Wisconsin, by T.P.A.*Samson and L.*Ipson, for the production of red earthenware reproductions of ancient bronze excavated in Scandinavia, and covered with dull, metallic glazes with green highlights resembling verdigris. Samson and Ipson adapted early Egyptian and Greek designs. Oil paints were used in some decoration. The output included tankards, jars, bowls, *jardinières*, candlesticks, ashtrays, each accompanied on sale by an outline of the history of its original. The firm was bought in 1904 by Arthur Washburn Wheelock, owner of a wholesale pottery business in Rockford, Illinois, and began operation in new buildings at Rockford late in that year; apparently ceased production in 1913.

Mark: *Norse* (the rest of the word enclosed in large N), impressed.

Refs: Evans; Kovel & Kovel.

North British Pottery. Scottish pottery established 1810 (initially as the Osley Pottery)

Norse Pottery. Earthenware with dark matt finish and incised decoration resembling traditional Scandinavian patterns, before 1906. 6.7 cm, 10.3 cm and 19.7 cm. high.

in Glasgow for the production of bone china. However, by 1820 the manufacture was turned over to stoneware and earthenware made by a succession of proprietors (ending with J.*Miller from 1867) until the pottery passed 1874-1904 to Alexander Balfour, who specialized in granite ware with bright, sometimes sponged, decoration for export and on occasions with inscriptions in African languages. Balfour also made cream jugs in the form of a cow lying on an oval base painted with green under the glaze; egg cups in the form of thistle heads, transfer-printed with Scottish scenes; and, briefly, white stoneware jugs with relief decoration, lined and thinly glazed on the exterior with lead glaze.

Marks: James Miller & Co., earthenware manufacturers, used the initials I.M. & Co. or J.M. & Co. in printed marks between 1869 and 1875.

Refs: Fleming; Jewitt; *Craftwork* 44.

North Dakota School of Mines. Section of the University of North Dakota established in 1892 for the study of mineral resources. After showing an item of pottery made from local clays at the St Louis World's Fair (1904), the department provided tuition in the use of clays and glazes and ceramic techniques, employing an experienced potter to work in the department. M.K.*Cable, J.*Mattson and M.*Pachl were artists; Flora Huckfield worked 1923-49 as a decorator. The work, moulded or thrown, varied in style, but was always made from North Dakota clays and often featured local flora or fauna in decoration. A range of matt glazes was built up to include green, brown, orange, pink, mauve and blue, often used without other ornament. Relief ware included *intaglio* borders or overall designs.

Marks: *University of North Dakota, Grand Forks, N.D. Made at School of Mines N.D. Clay*, all in a circular mark (cobalt blue under glaze); more rarely, *U.N.D. Grand Forks, N.D.* After 1963: students' signatures.

Refs: M.K. Cable 'The Development of Ceramic Work at the University of Dakota' in *Journal of the American Ceramic Society* Vol 5, No 3 (March 1922); D. Dommel 'University of North Dakota Pottery' in *Spinning Wheel* (June 1973); Kovel & Kovel.

Northfield Pottery. Yorkshire pottery established at Northfield, Rotherham, in 1852 by Joseph Lee, who made simple, enamelled earthenware, as well as bottles for proprietary products, and lettered signs in

fireclay with white enamel. Sold in 1855 to George Hawley, and subsequently under the management of the *Hawley family, the pottery produced an increased range of table and toilet wares, usually transfer-printed in blue, or colour printed, as well as black or brown-glazed ware, garden pots, and glass. In the 1880s, some earthenware and experimental pieces of porcelain were decorated with Japan patterns and lavish gilding (e.g. gilt-lined cups). Green-glazed plates were decorated in relief, e.g. with a thistle pattern.

A syndicate of workers from the *Castleford and *Ferrybridge potteries, who took over in 1903, trading as Northfield Hawley Pottery Co., advertised, in 1913, souvenirs and commemorative pieces, and a variety of earthenwares, dipped, sponged or printed, as well as pots for preserves. The company also produced ornamental ware painted in slip, and used lithographic reproduction in decorating dinner and tea ware. The pottery ceased operation by 1916, but reopened after modernization by the Co-operative Wholesale Society Ltd.

Marks include a lion resting a front paw on a globe, impressed – used by the Hawley family and Northfield Hawley Pottery Co. Ltd.

Refs: Grabham; Jewitt; Lawrence.

Northfield Hawley Pottery Co. *See* Low Pottery; Northfield Pottery.

North Hylton Pottery. *See* Dixon, Austin & Co.; Maling family.

Northrup, Harry M. American ceramic decorator. Northrup worked at *Zanesville Art Pottery and subsequently the *Mosaic Tile Co. until 1917. After war service, he became head of casting, decorating and glazing at the *American Encaustic Tiling Co. He worked at the *Roseville Pottery from 1935, and then for the US Air Force.

Ref: Kovel & Kovel.

North Staffordshire Pottery Co. Ltd. *See* Ridgway Potteries Ltd.

Northumberland or **Low Light Pottery.** English earthenware pottery established 1814 in North Shields, initially producing brown and black wares and ordinary earthenware. From 1856 under the proprietors, John Carr (b 1806), his first son, who joined him in 1858, and their successors, the works produced creamware, blue-printed, painted and lustred, much of it for export via the Mediterranean ports. The manufacture of pottery ceased in 1900, but the works continued to make firebricks.

Marks: impressed stag's head over JOHN CARR & SONS on a buckled belt surrounding an anchor (rare); a lion, over JC & S, printed; the initials J.C. & Co. with *Warranted Staffordshire.*

Refs: R.C. Bell *Tyneside Pottery* (Studio Vista, London, 1971); G.B. Hodgson *Borough of South Shields from the earliest*

period to the close of the nineteenth century (Andrew Reid & Co, Newcastle-upon-Tyne, 1903); Jewitt; C.T. Maling *The Industrial Resources of the District of the 3 Northern Rivers, the Tyne, Wear and Tees* (second edition, 1864); Towner (1957).

Northwestern Terra Cotta Co. American pottery making architectural terracotta from 1887 to mid 1950s in Chicago, Illinois. The company produced vases in simple shapes with crystalline glazes briefly after 1904. Architectural ware of the 1920s and 1930s included plaques and doorways with relief borders and leaf scrolls resembling contemporary French decorative ironwork.

Mark: *North-Western Terra-Cotta Company;* some specimens of glazed ware marked NORWETA in addition.

Refs: Cox; Evans; Kovel & Kovel.

Norton, Edward (1815-85). American pottery manufacturer, the cousin of Julius *Norton. He joined the pottery at Bennington, Vermont, in 1850, initially taking charge of sales. After Julius Norton's death, he went into partnership with C.W. Thatcher, who bought the half-interest that had been owned by L.P.*Norton.

Refs: Osgood; Spargo; Stradling; Watkins (1950); Webster.

Norton, Edward Lincoln (c.1865-1894). American potter. Norton inherited the half-interest of his father E.*Norton in the pottery at Bennington, Vermont, after about three years' work as salesman for the firm. While continuing the production of stoneware, he began wholesale dealing in glassware, porcelain and earthenware, both American and imported.

Refs: Barber (1976); Osgood; Spargo; Stradling; Watkins (1950); Webster.

Norton, John (1758-1828). American potter, owner of the first pottery known to have been established in Vermont (before the state's admission to the union). After serving in the Revolutionary Army 1776-81, he bought a farm at Bennington, Vermont, which he worked for seven years, and in 1793 established a kiln for the production of red ware and, by 1800, stoneware. Much of the red ware was lead-glazed, though slip glazes were also used. Stoneware was salt-glazed Norton took his sons John and L. *Norton into the business by 1815, trading as John Norton & Sons. The sons owned and operated the pottery from 1823, though it remained closely associated with the family's other interests (farm, distillery, smithy and shop).

Refs: Barber (1976); Osgood; Spargo; Stradling; Watkins (1950); Webster.

Norton, Julius (1809-61). American potter at Bennington, Vermont. He worked with his father L.*Norton before taking over operation of the family pottery c.1835 and formal ownership in 1841. The manufacture of firebrick was introduced in 1837. An advertisement of 1841 lists firebrick with products for domestic use, including inkstands and ornamental pitchers, as well as churns, kitchen utensils and storage jars in stoneware, and milk pans, flowerpots, etc., in earthenware. D.W.*Clark was employed

from 1840. J.*Harrison was invited to Bennington (arriving probably in late 1843) to assist in the experimental production of porcelain, which was apparently not resumed after a fire at the pottery in 1845. By that time, Norton had entered a partnership with his brother-in-law C.W.*Fenton, which ended in 1847.

As well as stoneware, the pottery's commercial output under the Norton & Fenton management included white tableware, domestic yellow ware (milk pans, mixing bowls and other cooking utensils) and Rockingham-glazed ware using the same yellow earthenware body. After separation from Fenton, Norton concentrated on his production of stoneware and, in 1850, took into partnership his cousin Edward Norton (1815-85), who initially took charge of sales and had earned half-ownership of the pottery by 1865. In 1859, Julius Norton's son L.P.*Norton entered the firm, which then traded as J.& E. Norton & Co. until Julius Norton's death.

Refs: Barber (1976); Clement (1947); Osgood; Spargo; Stradling; Watkins (1950); Webster.

Norton, Luman (1785-1858). American potter; son of John *Norton. He worked on his father's farm at Bennington, Vermont, before entering the family pottery, going into partnership with his father c.1812 and brother (also John) by 1815. He was sole proprietor from the departure of his brother in 1827, until he was joined by his son Julius *Norton as partner. He moved the pottery to larger premises in the following year and retired in 1840.

Refs: Barber (1976); Spargo; Stradling; Watkins (1950); Webster.

Norton, Luman Preston (b 1837). The son of Julius *Norton, he inherited his father's interest in the family pottery at Bennington, Vermont, and worked as business manager in the partnership E.& L.P. Norton from 1861 with his father's cousin Edward, to whom he sold his share on retirement in 1881.

Refs: Barber (1976); Osgood; Spargo; Stradling; Webster.

Norton, Wilfred and Lilly. English sculptors and studio potters. The couple worked in London from the 1920s on the production of earthenware figures (until the 1930s) and other pieces, both individually and in collaboration.

Incised or painted mark, with initials LNW, 1920-56.

Refs: Godden (1964); Haslam (1977).

Norwich Pottery. American stoneware works established before 1845 in Norwich, Connecticut, by Sidney Risley (c.1814-75), who was succeeded as owner by his son, George L. Risley (d 1881). The pottery was reopened as the Norwich Pottery Works about a year after George Risley's death in an explosion and finally closed in 1895. The pottery produced stoneware pitchers, jugs, bottles, storage jars, etc., generally simple in style, although a water cooler with applied decoration of an American eagle, and the stems of vine leaves forming handles, survives with the mark NORWICH POTTERY WORKS/ NORWICH/CONN.

Other marks include the Risleys' names and addresses, impressed.
Refs: Stradling; Webster.

Nosoyama. Japanese pottery established in the 1820s at Kamobe Nosoyama in Kochi prefecture by potters who moved there from a kiln at Ozu Odo after the discovery of porcelain clay in large quantities. Using a soft paste and a cloudy white glaze, the kiln produced pieces resembling *Tobe ware, as well as blue and white porcelain. From the late 19th century, the output included domestic pottery – lidded jars, bowls for kneading and grinding, rice bowls (goroshichi) in rounded shapes with white slip decoration, and teapots with green or brown glaze, made in light, hard stoneware.
Refs: Mitsuoka; Okamura.

Nosworthy, Daisy. Australian potter, trained under L.J.*Harvey in Brisbane in the 1920s. She quickly developed her own style and produced a wide range of delicately painted earthenwares which she fired in her own kiln (from the early 1930s). She exhibited regularly with the Brisbane Arts & Crafts Society from the early 1920s until the 1940s, as well as showing work in Sydney and Melbourne.

Nottingham Road, Derby. *See* Derby.

Nove. Italian faience and porcelain factory established near Venice in 1728 by Giovanni Battista Antonibon. Giovanni Baroni and his son Paolo rented the factory 1802-24, but it was otherwise under the Antonibon family's

Daisy Nosworthy. Earthenware vase with sgraffito decoration in pale brown slip, 1927. 20 cm high.

Nove. Porcelain dish in a form derived from silverware, painted with bright flowers, made at Nove, c.1820. 59 cm in diameter.

control until c.1832.

Since the 19th century, Nove has developed as one of the main Italian centres for ceramic production, with several factories.

The original factory's wares were marked with a star, the place name, *Nove,* monogram of GBA, or the names or initials of G. Baroni.
Refs: Danckert; Honey (1952); G. Lorenzetti *Maioliche Venete del Settecento* (Venice, 1936).

Novelty Pottery Works. *See* Goodwin, John (d 1875).

Novyi Brothers. Russian porcelain and faience manufacturers; founders of a factory at Kusiaevo in the Bogorodskoye district of *Gzhel in the early 19th century. Ivan Novyi was nominal head of the firm until 1832, followed by his brothers Tikhon and (from 1845) Semen Novyi, who was succeeded by his wife Avdotia. Iakov Gerasimovich Khrapunov (*see* Khrapunov, N.S.), their son-in-law, took over in the 1850s; he and his family were owners of the factory until 1918. Tableware, generally of high quality, was decorated with printed flowers, landscapes, views and, in the case of cups, painted portraits of the Tsar Nicholas I and contemporary figures, achieving a specifically Russian provincial style, free from other European influences. The firm also made figures, more variable in quality.

Marks until 1820s, usually Cyrillic N, underglaze blue or impressed; variations of 'From the factory of the Novyi Brothers'; *FKA Novia* [factory of the merchant-woman A. Novyi], c.1852; initials of Iakov Khrapunov-Novyi.
Refs: Emme; Ross; Rozembergh; Saltykov.

Nowotny, August. *See* Altrohlau.

Nuglaz. *See* Brush-McCoy Pottery.

Numata Kazumasu (1873-1954). Japanese potter, born in Fukui prefecture. After training under the sculptor Takeuchi Kyuichi (1857-1916), Numata went to study the techniques of ceramic sculpture at the *Sèvres factory and returned to introduce European methods of modelling in Japan. He was a teacher at the Tokyo School of

Fine Arts and served as juror for the Japanese Imperial art academy's annual exhibitions.
Ref: Roberts.

Nunn, Walter. English ceramic artist. After studying at the South Kensington Schools of Art, London, Nunn joined *Doulton & Co. in Burslem in the 1890s, working there until 1910. He is noted for his painting of scenes and characters from Shakespeare, with careful historical detail. His work also included a portrait of a cavalier set against a landscape on a Luscian ware vase c.1895.
Refs: see Doulton & Co.

Nuremberg. German faience factory working 1712-1840 and known for its 18th-century production of bottles, dishes and other tableware painted with ferns, foliage, birds, landscapes, biblical illustrations and heraldic devices on forms that moved away from oriental and Dutch influences towards traditional German shapes. In the 19th century, under the last owner, Johann Heinrich Strütz, the output consisted mainly of everyday tableware and imitations of new designs by other factories.
Refs: Ducret (1940); Hannover; Hüseler; Pazaurek.

Nurock. *See* Brush-McCoy Pottery.

Nylund, Gunnar (b 1904). Swedish ceramic designer, trained as an architect. Nylund worked (1929-30) with N.*Krebs on the production of unique pieces in stoneware at reasonable prices. He became chief designer for the *Rörstrand factory at Lidköping from 1931 until 1958 or 1959. His work includes animal figures in stoneware (especially apes, monkeys, elephants and the cat family), vases painted e.g. with fish, and white porcelain tableware with simple impressed motifs forming a highly translucent repeating pattern under a matt glaze. He also exploited the contrast of very coarse stoneware body and glossy glaze in decorative pieces.
Ref: Three Centuries of Swedish pottery: Rörstrand 1726-1954 and Marieberg 1758-88 (catalogue, Victoria & Albert Museum, London, 1959).

Nymphenburg. German porcelain factory in production from 1753 in Neudeck-ob-der-Au, near Munich, established under the

Nymphenburg. A pair of Kinderkopfen. The boy has a yellow jacket, the girl a rose in her hair, c.1900. Printed and impressed shield marks. 24.8 cm and 25.4 cm high.

Nymphenburg. Dish, painted and gilt, 19th century. Marked with the arms of Bavaria on a shield with M & B impressed. 30.2 cm.

patronage of Maximilian Joseph, Elector of Bavaria, and under state control until 1862, when it was let to a private company, Arendts & Scotzniovsky. Production moved to a new factory which is still in operation at Nymphenburg Palace. The output of porcelain was of high quality, white and almost flawless, with a grey or greenish tinge in the glaze. In the 18th century, the factory became known for the production of figures, tableware and ornamental pieces in rococo style; original figures were re-issued in the white by Albert Bäuml, who took over the factory from Scotzniovsky in 1888. Production remains in the hands of Bäuml's family.

Artists in the 19th century included C. *Adler, A.*Auer, J.J.H. and J.F.*Haag, and J.G.*Kumpf. In the 20th century, the factory has continued to produce work in rococo style as well as new designs commissioned from contemporary artists. The Moderna service, wavy-edged forms painted with fish and seaweed, designed by Hermann Gradl before 1900, is an example of German Art Nouveau. Other work included pieces with linear decoration by A.*Niemeyer (1905), crinoline figures by J.*Wackerle, and models of stylized animals by Theodor Karner.

Marks: a shield, often impressed. Modern work has the shield, topped with a crown, over the name, *Nymphenburg*. Reproductions of models from the 18th-century Frankenthal factory are marked with a lion in blue, or a monogram of CT and a crown (from the Frankenthal mark) with a date and the Nymphenburg mark, impressed. Höchst models were reproduced after the acquisition of moulds from *Damm.
Refs: Danckert; Weiss.

Nyon. Swiss factory established in 1781 for the production of porcelain, which ceased in 1813. From then until the factory closed in 1860, the output consisted of earthenware, mainly white or cream-coloured, in neoclassical styles, and imitations of jasper ware.
Mark: a fish in underglaze blue.
Refs: Danckert; Honey (1952); Weiss.

Nyudo. Japanese pottery established in the Koshinetsu district in 1859 by Tanaka Gozaemon, initially as a clan kiln and operating as a folk kiln after 1868. Production of ware

including water storage jars, mortars, teapots, saké bottles, oil lamp dishes and, notably, pots referred to as fishermen's helmets, for catching shrimps, continued until 1918. Gozaemon's younger brother Shigeba went to manage the Yamazaki kiln (*see* Seba ware).
Ref: Mizuo.

Oakland Art Pottery. American pottery making decorative ware, architectural terracotta, water coolers, drainpipes, flowerpots, etc., at Oakland, California, in the early 20th century, having started production by 1901. No examples of the pottery's large output have been documented.
Ref: Evans.

Oakwood Pottery. American pottery established c.1877 at Dayton, Ohio, and in operation until 1926. A wide variety of earthenware and stoneware, both utilitarian and ornamental, was made from local clay. Decorative ware included vases with flowers modelled in full relief (known examples date from c.1880) and a display of matt green-glazed ware shown in the St Louis World Fair in 1904.
Mark: *Oakwood Pottery/Dayton, Ohio*, incised.
An Oakwood Pottery Company established in 1900 at East Liverpool, Ohio, was reported to have made art pottery until the following year, when production was turned over to white ware for table use. The works were occupied by the *Craven Art Pottery Co. by 1904.
No marks are known.
A factory established in 1882 by John Patterson & Sons in Wellsville, Ohio, for the manufacture of yellow and Rockinghamglazed ware made art ware decorated underglaze, from 1911, which was advertised as Oakwood Art Pottery. The factory was sold to the *Sterling China Co. in 1917.
No known mark.
Oakwood was also the name of a line of art ware made at the *Cambridge Art Pottery. The mark OAKWOOD was impressed on the base of vases, etc., with the firm's monogram, a C containing AP.
Refs: Evans; Kovel & Kovel; Lehner; Ramsay.

Oberg, Thure. *See* Arabia.

Obsieger, Robert (1884-1958). Ceramist, born in Moravia and trained at the Fachschule für Tonindustrie in Znaim. During postgraduate study at the Kunstgewerbeschule in Vienna (1909-14) he carried out life-size pottery figures. During this time he also worked at the Wiener Kunstkeramische Werkstätte and in Steyr. Obsieger's work included vases, figures, tile stoves and other pieces, decorated in a wide range of techniques: relief, slip painting, etc. He was known for his influence as a teacher of ceramics in Vienna and succeeded M.*Powolny as head of the pottery department at the Kunstgewerbeschule (1932-38).
Mark: signature, incised.
Ref: Neuwirth (1974a).

Odell & Booth Brothers. American pottery producing majolica and underglaze-decorated ware from c.1878 at Tarrytown, New York. The firm made vases, umbrella stands, lampstands, chandeliers and tiles, as well as

plaques painted with landscapes, animals, birds, etc. After its closure in the late 1880s, the factory was occupied by a manufacturer of decorative tiles.
Refs: Barber (1976); Evans.

Oeslau. Thuringian porcelain factory in operation from its establishment by Franz Detlew Goebel in 1871 to the present day. The firm remained in the hands of the Goebel family mass-producing tableware in porcelain, white earthenware and other bodies. A patent soft-paste porcelain is marketed as Goebelit. Figures of children modelled by Sister M.J. Hummel were produced in stoneware from 1934.
Other Oeslau manufacturers include the firms of J. Walther, makers of decorative ware and dolls' heads; Wilhelm Isberner, figures and tableware, established 1946; and Fischer & Co., makers and decorators of gift ware from 1950.
Refs: Danckert; Weiss.

Offermans, Gerrit J.D. (1857-1914). Dutch painter and designer of table and ornamental earthenware. Working at De *Porceleyne Fles from the mid 1880s, he developed the Berberas line of earthenware with A.*Le Comte and H.W. Mauser. He worked at *Haga on glaze research with C.J.*Lanooij, c.1906, and at *St Lukas in 1909, taking charge of the art department in 1913. Offermans was noted for lustre decoration, and his work included many vases sparingly painted in a Japanese-inspired manner with natural subjects, such as plants, insects and fish under a gold glaze.
Ref: Singelenberg-van der Meer.

Ofuke wares. Japanese pottery made at Akazu, near Nagoya castle and two miles from Seto, in the early 17th century for Mitsumoto Tokugawa, Prince of Owari. The output, originally tea jars in the Seto tradition, with light, close-textured body, included blue and white wares with ash glaze and, in the early to mid 19th century, imitations of Korean pots, with greyish white body and creamy, crackled glaze, which were inscribed Sobokai. Another group of wares had a soft, opaque glaze in brown shading to blue-green and red, splashed with white. The kiln is also associated with a decoration of broad bands of ochre with aventurine effect over a semi-transparent crackle glaze streaked with violet and green. After a break in operation the workshop was revived in the 1830s under *Shuntai and abandoned soon afterwards.
Similar wares were made at Kujiri and Ohira.
Refs: Brinkley; Gorham; Jenyns (1971); Morse.

Ogata family. *See* Kenzan.

Ogawa Tokusai (1785-1865). Japanese potter. Ogawa travelled throughout Japan to study ceramic techniques before settling in Nagano, *Shigaraki. In the early 1830s, he went to work in *Iga for five years; his work included copies of early Iga wares (made to satisfy an urban demand for such pieces) and of *Kenzan ware. He also made sensha (green tea) utensils and pieces painted in cobalt blue over white slip. After his return to Nagano, Ogawa made delicate teapots

and other wares using local clay with a thin ash glaze.
Ref: Cort.

Ogaya. *See* Shino ware.

O'Hara, Dorothea Warren (1875-1963). American potter, born in Missouri. O'Hara studied in Munich, Paris and London, exhibiting ceramics at the Royal College of Art in London. On her return to America, she started a workshop in New York, where she taught pottery and produced her own work, also writing for magazines, including A.A.*Robineau's *Keramic Studio.* In Darien, Connecticut, from 1920, she established her own Apple Tree Lane Pottery, producing red-bodied earthenware, for which she developed a strong tin glaze and, after extensive research, an Egyptian blue glaze. Her work included bowls and other vessels decorated with birds, stylized plant forms, etc., modelled in relief.
Refs: Clark & Hughto; *Critical Comments on the International Exhibition of Ceramic Art* (American Federation of Arts, New York, 1928).

Ohi family. Japanese potters working in Ohi, near Kanazawa, and descended from a member of the *Raku family (the founder, Haji Chozaemon, was a son of Raku III). The Ohi kiln was established in 1666 for the production of yellowish-brown tea ware in the Raku tradition for the Maeda family. The fifth and sixth generations also made wares in the style of *Ninsei and *Kenzan; the seventh generation, who was the first to make wares for public sale, made tea bowls in helmet shapes designed by the teamaster Senso. The ninth in line was working in the late 1950s.
Refs: Jenyns (1971); Morse; Munsterberg.

Ohira. *See* Ofuke wares.

Ohr, George E. (1857-1918). American studio potter. Ohr worked at a variety of trades before studying ceramics with his friend, J.F.*Meyer; he established a pottery at his home town, Biloxi, Mississippi, in the early 1880s. He exhibited work in the New Orleans Cotton Centennial Exposition (1884-86) and worked with Meyer in New Orleans in the 1880s. After returning to

George E. Ohr. Earthenware teapot divided into two sections by an inner wall, with two lids. One half of the pot has iridescent glaze, mottled green and yellow, the other a mottled blue-grey lustre, late 19th-early 20th century. Mark: G.E. Ohr Biloxi, Miss., *impressed*

Biloxi, he worked with the assistance of his eldest son, Leo, who helped to prepare the bodies: white or red clays from Florida or Mississippi, and experimental bodies from other areas. Ohr made unique pieces, varying greatly in size from miniature vases to objects the height of a man. The work, mainly thrown, was characterized by extremely thin potting, and pinching, twisting or pleating of the clay walls into grotesque and often graceful shapes, before firing at a low temperature in a wood-burning kiln. Among modelled designs noted by Barber are crabs, shells, the head of a wildcat, and pieces with handles in the form of lizards, serpents or dragons. Ohr made inkwells in many shapes—ass's head, artist's palette, log cabin, etc.—and a range of puzzle jugs and spouted jugs. Some pieces bear incised inscriptions or floral decoration. He used a wide variety of glazes: yellow, green, brown, red, purple, blue, a bright pink with contrasting drip glazes, many mottled effects and some metallic lustres. Flowerpots, water coolers and flues are also said to have been made. Noted for his eccentricity, Ohr placed much of his work in storage because it was not appreciated by the public. He closed the Biloxi Pottery c.1909. The pottery, rebuilt in 1894 after a fire, was depicted on souvenir plates made in Europe for Biloxi.
Marks: (impressed or incised) Ohr's name, with BILOXI or BILOXI, MISS; sometimes his signature.
Refs: Barber (1976); R.W. Blasbeg *George E. Ohr and his Biloxi Pottery* (Carpenter, Port Jervis, New York, 1972); Clark & Hughto; Eidelberg; Evans; Henzke; Jervis; Keen; Kovel & Kovel; G.E. Ohr 'Some Facts in the History of a Unique Personality' in *Crockery and Glass Journal* 54 (December 1901).

Ohrdruf. In German ceramics, a centre of Thuringian porcelain production from the mid 19th century to the 1930s. A factory established in 1834 by Christian Friedrich Kling and trading as Kling & Co. made everyday tableware, later producing dolls and figures of children. Production ceased in 1939.
Mark: a bell with initial K. The factory of Adolf Kästner, established 1860 for the production of luxury ware, miniature services and dolls' heads, used the mark K & CO.
The partnership Bähr & Röschild, established 1872 by George Bähr (d 1894), made luxury pieces and dolls, ceasing production in 1936.
Refs: Danckert; Scherf.

Okawachi or **Okochi.** *See* Nabeshima Ware.

Okuda Bunshiro. *See* Rakusui.

Okuda Kyuta. *See* Kiyomizu.

Okuda Mijokichi. *See* Shigaraki ware.

Okuro Seishichi. *See* Wazen.

Old Cumnock Pottery. Scottish pottery established in 1786 in Ayrshire for the manufacture of coarse earthenware. After the death of the founder, James Taylor, in 1825, the pottery was bought by the Nicol family, who retained it until its closure in 1919. The firm became associated with *sgraffito* ware

in local red clays under a pale slip, decorated with sketches and such inscriptions as 'I'm no greedy, but I like a lot'; 'The proof o' the puddin is i' the preein' o't' or, for cream jugs, 'Straught frae the coo'.
Refs: Fleming; Hughes (1961).

Oldfield & Co. Derbyshire manufacturers of salt-glazed stoneware, working from 1810 at The Pottery, Brampton, near Chesterfield, initially under the title Oldfield, Nadin, Wright & Hewitt. Using a fine-textured brown stoneware body, sometimes dipped in coloured slip before saltglazing, the firm made a variety of household and dairy utensils, storage jars and bottles, carriage warmers and animals' drinking dishes, as well as relief-decorated jugs and mugs, Toby jugs, puzzle jugs, cheese stands, fruit bowls, trays, tea and coffee pots, watch stands, candlesticks, tobacco jars and other items. The pottery was owned from 1838 by John Oldfield, nephew of one of the original partners; it was taken over c.1888 by a member of *Pearson & Co. and later merged with Pearson's Whittington Moor Pottery.
Marks include: *Oldfield Manufactory/Chesterfield* (impressed); OLDFIELD.
Refs: Bradley; Jewitt; Oswald.

Oldfield, Nadin, Wright & Hewitt. *See* Oldfield & Co.

Old Hall Porcelain Co. Ltd. *See* Meigh, Job, Charles and Charles.

Old Ivory. *See* Brush-McCoy Pottery.

Old Pottery, Swinton. *See* Twigg, Joseph.

Old Sussex ware. *See* Cadborough Pottery.

Ollier, Annie. *See* Moore, Bernard.

Ollivier family. *See* Aprey (Haute-Marne).

*Thorkild Olsen. White porcelain bowl, made by *Aluminia A.S., 20th century.*

Olsen, Thorkild. Danish ceramic artist. Olsen was noted for his bowls, vases and other pieces in *blanc de chine* with carved designs of lines, small ovals, etc,. all over the surface of simple shapes. Made at the Royal *Copenhagen Porcelain Factory in the 1940s. He also designed tableware.
Ref: Hiort.

Omega Workshops. London studios established in 1913 by R.*Fry for the production and sale of applied art. The decorative work

Omega Workshops. Earthenware dish painted in blue, black and red, probably by D.*Grant, 1913-18. Mark: Greek character, Omega, impressed. 23 cm in diameter.

was influenced by Post Impressionism in style. Specializing in schemes for the whole interior environment, the workshop produced furniture, carpets, printed textiles, etc., as well as earthenware, initially tin-glazed, and inspired by 17th-century English delftware, though painted with bright, fluid designs that resembled the work of Derain and Matisse. In general, the output was produced by amateur artist-craftsmen with little technical training. The ceramics sold at the workshop included Fry's own work, produced in association with *Carter & Co., pieces decorated by V.*Bell and D.*Grant, and examples of North African peasant pottery, which strongly influenced the style of Fry and his decorators. The advertised range of pottery comprised ashtrays, inkstands, paperweights, jam pots, cruet stands, salad bowls, fireplace tiles, handpainted teasets, vases and bowls, large jars, jugs, etc.

Mark: Greek character, omega, within a square.
Refs: Anscombe & Gere; M.Haslam 'Some Vorticist Pottery'in *The Connoisseur* (October 1975); Hawkins; T. Hennell *British Craftsmen* (Collins, London, 1943); Rose.

Omoya family. *See* Echizen ware.

Omuro. *See* Hozen.

Onada. *See* Shino ware.

Onda. Japanese pottery centre, Onda Sarayama, seventeen kilometres from Hida (Oita prefecture). Production started with the establishment of a kiln by a potter from *Koishibara in the early 18th century and was developed by local families who were part-time potters. The present kiln at Onda is worked by several families of potter-farmers. Traditionally the kilns have produced a wide variety of domestic pottery, including large containers for water or preserves, lidded jars with trickled glazes in white, green, brown or yellow, cooking and serving bowls, dishes, pitchers, saké bottles and small pots for salted fish. A teapot in rounded shape with greenish blue glaze is preserved in the Museum of Modern Art,

New York. The decorative techniques include applied relief, *sgraffito* and brushed slip patterns, variations of texture achieved by comb or fingers, and chattermarks (patterns of small nicks cut in the body or in a coating of slip), as well as combinations of black, brown and green glaze.
Refs: Jenyns (1971); Munsterberg; Okamura.

Ono. Japanese kiln making *Kutani ware at Ono Village, Nomi county, from 1819 when it was established by a local farmer Rokuemon Yabu (1790-1868), who had previously studied under *Honda. Soon after the improvement of the porcelain paste with high-quality local clay, the kiln was taken under the protection of the district administrator and engaged the potters *Gen'emon, *Kikusaburo and *Shoza, mainly for the production of elaborately decorated porcelain with enamel hatched in red in the manner of *Minzan, as well as polychrome enamel patterns and lavish gilding. In the hands of the founder's son Kichiemon Yabu, the kiln concentrated on the production of porcelain in the white for decoration at other workshops in the Kutani area.
Refs: Jenyns (1965); Nakagawa.

Onondaga Pottery Co. American pottery established 1871 at Syracuse, New York. The works produced dinner and toilet services in white granite (until 1893) and cream-coloured earthenware, plain and decorated, and introduced porcelain c.1890. Examples of porcelain hotelware decorated underglaze and initialled by A.A.*Robineau date from the early 20th century. R.G.*Cowan became art director after the closure of his pottery in 1931. The company later became the Syracuse China Corporation.

Marks include the New York coat of arms on white granite ware, 1874-93; a globe with SYRACUSE CHINA O.P. Co; various marks incorporating O.P.Co.
Refs: Barber (1976); Evans; Kovel & Kovel.

Onyx. *See* Brush-McCoy Pottery.

Opalesce. *See* Owens, John B.

Opaque Porcelain. *See* Meigh, Job, Charles and Charles.

Orcutt, Walter. *See* Belding, David.

Oribe ware. Japanese pottery made from c.1600 in *Mino, initially for tea-ceremony use and later consisting of a wide variety of pieces—candleholders, inkstones, water droppers, bowls, plates, serving dishes, covered jars, saké bottles and other tablewares—as well as tea bowls, jars for tea or water, incense burners, boxes. The ware, often made in a pale buff clay body, characterized by the predominance of deeply lustrous green glazes and free, often abstract, patterns in iron black, comprises several stylistic groups.

Green Oribe includes square plates and dishes with green glaze poured across the corners, leaving a diagonal patch of white usually decorated boldly and freely with iron oxide in a manner derived from the tie-dying of cloth, with lattice patterns, cross hatching or fish scales. The green glaze also

appears as an entire coating of pieces with designs incised or impressed under it.

Narumi Oribe is characterized by green glazes on a white body with areas of red clay painted with white slip and iron pigments. The related Red Oribe is in similar clay with iron decoration and touches of white slip.

Black Oribe, with black glazes poured or trailed to leave parts of the body bare, includes tea caddies, plates and shoe-shaped bowls. Shino-style Oribe has a white glaze and patterns similar to those of Shino ware, but is crisper and sharper in effect.

The kilns also produced wares in shapes derived from *Iga (vases and water jars) and *Karatsu wares. The centres of production were located at Kujiri, Tajimi, Ohira and Okaya, with scattered kilns in surrounding areas. The ware derives its name from Furuta Oribe-no-sho Shigenari (1544-1615), a military general and pupil of teamaster Sen-no-Rikyu, who brought about fresh and original developments in the wabi tea ceremony practised by Rikyu. The square or distorted shapes which frequently occur are regarded as representing a deliberate break with convention.
Refs: Fujioka; Jenyns (1971); Mikami; Munsterberg.

oriental glazes. *See* glaze.

Osborne, Arthur. American tile designer. Chief modeller for J.G.*Low by 1879, he designed the majority of Low's tiles produced by the firm. He trained as a sculptor in England, and his work included portraits, a variety of animal, bird and floral studies. His decorative panels, marketed as 'plastic sketches', and depicting pastoral or allegorical subjects, landscapes, *japonaiseries*, etc., were modelled in relief and varied in size up to about 45 cm long. Osborne also modelled relief decoration for jugs and vases.

Mark: monogram of AO on tiles and plaques.
Ref: Barber (1976).

Osborne family. *See* Gonic Pottery.

Osley Pottery. *See* North British Pottery.

Osmaston Road. *See* Derby.

Osotoyama. Japanese pottery centre extending southwards from Kawayo to Uchinoyama, and bordering mountainous regions in the west of Saga prefecture, where a number of kilns produced Takeo *Karatsu ware from the early 17th to the late 19th century. Few of the kilns are thought to have specialized in pieces for tea-ceremony use, and the main output consisted of domestic ware for local people, notably large dishes and kneading bowls, very thinly potted in stoneware and edged with patterns cut, or made with, fingers, and glazed in green and brown. Some decoration was brushed in iron oxide and green glaze, usually representing such plant forms as pine or growing millet. Large slip-coated bowls and jars, made by a series of kilns at Yumino from iron-rich clay and often painted with scenes of wooded mountains, pine branches, temple gateways, cranes, etc., were sold throughout Japan and on mainland Asia. Ware made at the Titani kiln included slip-coated pieces with combed or wiped

patterns under two contrasting glazes, and some wares vigorously painted with patterns in iron oxide or cobalt blue. A kiln at Kurunda made plain Karatsu ware as well as pieces with combed decoration under a dripped amber glaze and is still in production.
Refs: Jenyns (1971); Okamura.

Ota. *See* Miyakawa.

Otani. Japanese kiln established near Tokushima on the island of Shikoku in the 1770s, initially for the production of porcelain. It is now noted for the making of such large pieces as garden bowls, storage jars and pots for the growing of trees, some marketed in Kansai. The larger pots are formed by a combined method of coiling the base, beating the walls thin and high with paddle, and finally throwing. Impressed patterns at the rim serve to compress and strengthen the clay; other techniques include incised and applied relief decoration. Patterns include lotus, chrysanthemum and a lightning design. Smaller pieces, e.g. candleholders, vases, and chicken feeders, are glazed with a brown iron-rich clay and bamboo ash glaze, or a black glaze containing manganese, or occasionally left unglazed. Saké bottles often have household marks trailed in white slip.
Ref: Okamura.

Ott & Brewer. American company operating the Etruria Pottery, Trenton, New Jersey, which had been established in 1863 by Bloor, Ott & Booth. J.H.*Brewer joined the firm in 1865, and the company traded as Ott & Brewer from 1873. Until 1876, the main output consisted of cream-coloured earthenware and granite ware. I.*Broome designed and modelled a series of work in parian porcelain for the firm's display in the Philadelphia Centennial Exhibition (1876), which included a grey-tinted teaset with relief decoration of flowers and profile portraits of George and Martha Washington, vases with figures in low relief illustrating fashions of the 18th and 19th centuries, a pair of vases with baseball players in low relief on the sides and in full relief at the base, a pastoral vase with rustic decoration supported on a bracket in the form of a faun's head, and a portrait bust of Cleopatra. Elaborate decorative pieces, with

Ott & Brewer. Belleek ware dish painted in green and gold, 1885. 21 cm square.

high-quality glaze, were eclectic in inspiration and freely combined stylistic idioms from varied sources. In 1876, the firm introduced an 'Ivory Porcelain' paste with gold or black lithographic patterns. Belleek ware, made from 1882, was introduced with the help of W.*Bromley, his brother John and his son, William Bromley Jr., and subsequently developed to very high quality, in a wide variety of forms, both ornamental and useful. Larger vases, usually simple in outline, were often ornamented with pierced decoration, enamel colours, gilded relief and chased gilding. A *bonbonnière* in the form of an ostrich egg was decorated with honeycomb perforations over the entire surface. As well as porcelains, the firm produced granite and opaque china tea and dinner services, and toilet sets, printed or hand painted. The firm suffered as a result of a potters' strike in Trenton and the Depression in 1892, and closed in 1893.

Marks include versions of the British coat of arms on white granite ware; a Maltese cross with ETRURIA POTTERY CO. OPAQUE CHINA; a crown and a sword with BELLEEK; various marks incorporating the name or initials of the company.
Ref: Barber (1976).

Öttingen-Schrattenhofen. German faience factory which was established in Öttingen in 1735 by potters from Ansbach and moved to Schrattenhofen in 1737. August Friedrich Köhler (d 1802) arrived in 1749, taking over as one of the partners in 1756. In 1757, he opened a new factory still in Schrattenhofen. He was succeeded by his son-in-law (owner of another Schrattenhofen factory from 1792), and his son-in-law's son. The company ceased operation in 1830.
Ref: Hüseler.

Otto, Karl. The founder of a short-lived Russian earthenware and porcelain factory in operation 1801-c.1812 at Perovo, on the *Gzhel road out of Moscow. Otto produced earthenware with either reddish ochre or white body and fine glaze, or in porcelain, painted with bouquets of flowers, or printed in the style of a service made at the *Kiev-Mezhegorye factory for the Babolovsky palace. He sold the works to Ivan Krause in 1812.
Mark: L:Otto:
Ref: Bubnova.

Ouseburn Bridge Pottery. Tyneside pottery established by Robert Maling (*see* Maling family), who transferred his family's earthenware manufacture to the newly built works at Ouseburn Bridge, Newcastle-upon-Tyne, in 1815. In production from 1817, the pottery made white, sponged and lustre-decorated earthenware. Maling continued production of underglaze-printed ware, which had been introduced to north-eastern England by his family at the Hylton works on the River Wear; among the patterns were views of the Monkwearmouth Bridge, and the High Level road and railway bridge constructed

in 1849 across the River Tyne. He was succeeded in 1853 by his son C.T.*Maling, who moved to the first Ford works in 1859. The Ouseburn Bridge works were reopened under the name Albion Pottery by the brothers Isaac and Thomas Bell, followed c.1864 by Galloway & Atkinson, who continued the production of printed ware. The last proprietor, W. Morris, succeeded William Atkinson by 1871 and the pottery closed c.1875.
Ref: Bell.

Overbeck Pottery. American pottery established 1911 by the sisters Margaret (1863-1911), Hannah B. (1870-1931), Elizabeth G. (1875-1936 or 1937) and Mary F. Overbeck (1878-1955) at their family home in Cambridge City, Indiana.

Margaret Overbeck, who had studied at the Art Academy in Cincinnati, Ohio, and at Columbia University, worked at a pottery in Zanesville, Ohio, and taught in the faculty of art at De Pauw University, Greencastle, Indiana. An experienced ceramic decorator, she won several competitions in ceramic design held by A.A.*Robinson's journal, *Keramic Studio*, and was regarded as the prime mover in founding the family pottery, but died soon after its opening.

Hannah also studied with her sisters Margaret and Mary at the Art Academy in Cincinnati. Although an invalid, she carried out decoration at the Overbeck Pottery and was its principal designer until her death.

Elizabeth studied 1909-10 under C.F.*Binns in New York and took charge of the technical aspects of the pottery, experimenting with clay and glazes, and throwing or hand-building the pieces. Mary, an art teacher, studied at Columbia University and, like her sisters Hannah and Margaret, provided designs for *Keramic Studio*. Specializing at the outset of the pottery in designing and the application of glazes, she continued production on a diminished scale after the death of her sisters. All the sisters had experience of a wide range of the tasks necessary for the operation of a pottery.

Apart from some moulded cups and saucers and some small figures, the pieces made at the pottery were thrown or hand built, and unique, and the work was noted for its originality. At first using a mixture of Pennsylvania feldspar, kaolin from Delaware, and Tennessee ball clay, or on some occasions red-firing clay from their orchard, and later a white earthenware body, the Overbeck sisters made vases, bowls, flower holders, candlesticks and tiles, as well as the ceramic sculpture which was later introduced. The decoration was mainly carved or carried out in inlaid glazes. The range of glazes increased from muted matt colours to a brighter palette which included shades of pink, mauve, blue, green, dark grey and, notably, turquoise and a creamy yellow. After the death of her sisters, Mary carried out all the aspects of the work, gradually restricting her output to small figures, often moulded, dressed in the fashions of earlier years, animals, birds or humans treated humorously and, to special order, portrait figures of people or pets. Ceramic brooches made after 1942 often represent women or birds.

Marks: monogram of OBK, with letters below to indicate making by Elizabeth (E on the left) and decoration by Hannah or Mary

(H or F respectively on the right), after 1937, the monogram with joined initials, MF; monogram of EO, often with date, '10, used by Elizabeth on work made during study in New York.
Refs: Evans; Kovel & Kovel.

Ovodov, Fyodor. Russian potter working at *Skopin in the early 20th century. Apart from the usual household ware, his workshop was noted for the production of figures and display pieces. An apprentice, Grishanin, produced a jug in the shape of a two-headed Imperial eagle, and another apprentice, Cheberyashkin, was associated with decorative Kvass jugs. Fyodor Ovodov made a decorative samovar with glistening glaze.
Ref: Ovsyannikov.

Owen, Ben. *See* Busbee, Jacques and Juliana.

Owen, Eric (1903-75). English potter, born in Staffordshire. Owen was an apprentice in a tileworks before entering the firm of *Mintons Ltd, where he worked as a modeller for 25 years. He became chief modeller at the *Wedgwood factory in 1946-47 and worked as a freelance modeller at the factory from 1967 until his death. His work for Wedgwood included tableware and heat-resistant ware, as well as portrait medallions.
Refs: Batkin; Reilly & Savage.

Owen, George (1845-1917). English porcelain decorator working for the *Worcester Royal Porcelain Co. in the late 19th century. Owen was known for his finely perforated Reticulated ware, for which he perfected his own technique, preserving great secrecy. Using vases, etc., which were made by his son, a skilful caster, he painstakingly carved network patterns in the unfired porcelain which, when it became too dry, was softened in the

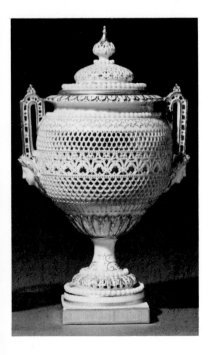

*George Owen. Reticulated vase made at the Royal *Worcester Porcelain Factory and signed by Owen. 20.5 cm high.*

John B. Owens. Earthenware vase with the head of a horse in burnt sienna and lemon yellow on a shaded mustard, burnt sienna and chocolate ground, c.1900. Mark: UTOPIAN J.B. OWENS, *impressed, and the painted signature of the artist, Mae Timberlake.*

moist atmosphere of a metal-lined box containing damp cloths. He also modelled flowers for application to vases or trinkets, mainly privately, for family or friends.

Mark: incised signature, *G. Owen.*
Ref: Sandon (1978a).

Owens, John B. (1859-1934). American potter and tile manufacturer. After working as a travelling salesman in stoneware, he established his own pottery at his home town, Roseville, Ohio, in 1885, for the manufacture of flowerpots. The firm J.B. Owens Pottery Co. (incorporated 1891) moved to Zanesville, Ohio, where it was in production from 1892. K.*Langenbeck was head chemist from 1891. The firm made *jardinières* and teapots with glaze of a Rockingham type from 1895. After the introduction of underglaze slip-painting and new glazes by W.A. *Long, who was associated with the pottery from 1896, art ware marketed as Utopian was produced. Similar to Long's art ware made at the Lonhuda Pottery, Utopian was painted with flowers, animals or portraits, notably of American Indians, in slip, usually against a dark background under a high-gloss glaze. However, blue, pink and a lighter brown also occur as ground colours, and a matt-glazed version in light colours was introduced in 1905. Variations included Utopian Opalesce, slip-painted under glaze with similar subjects and characterized by the use of metallic effects.

A staff engaged by Owens as designers, decorators, and glaze chemists included J.*Herold, A.*Radford and, later J.*Lessell, who was foreman in 1905. Long's Utopian range was quickly followed by other named lines: Alpine, with shaded grounds in soft grey, blue, green or brown and matt decoration, usually flowers and fruit, painted

freehand; Lotus, painted with natural subjects against a light, shaded background; Cyrano, introduced 1898, with blue, red, dark brown or black background and raised filigree decoration in white, buff or brown; Henri II introduced 1900, with intricate inlaid designs in Art Nouveau style; Poster, with designs portraying Greek actors or musicians against a brown background; Corona, coloured to simulate the varied shades of bronze; Mission, with matt glaze and splashed landscapes featuring the mission buildings of Central America, introduced in 1903; Wedgwood Jasper, probably introduced by Radford; Delft, simple forms with Dutch scenes painted in blue on white also introduced in 1904; Rustic, *jardinières* and window boxes, matt-glazed and modelled in imitation of tree stumps and trunks introduced 1904. A group of lines featuring metallic effects included Feroza, introduced 1901, with a surface resembling hammered bronze, the later Venetian (1904) with the iridescent effect of the glaze accentuated by the irregular surface of the clay beneath, and Gunmetal ware, unglazed earthenware, often with decoration engraved in the metallic finish. Art Vellum was decorated under the glaze in earthy, autumnal colours and characterized by a soft, smooth finish.

A printing department under the supervision of G.*Brush published advertising material and a journal, *The Owens Monthly.* The firm eventually acquired a second plant in New York City and the Zanesville factory, rebuilt after a fire in 1902, was enlarged in 1905 to house a tileworks, which operated as The Zanesville Tile Co. until it was taken over by a syndicate of local tile makers and closed in 1907. The mass production of *jardinières*, vases, etc., was discontinued and the pottery concentrated on the production of high-quality art ware, which was marketed from 1906 as Owensart. Austro-Hungarian Guido Howarth, and F.*Ferrell were employed to design new lines of art ware, and the German wax worker, Hugo Herb, joined the firm as modeller. Lines introduced in this period included: Opalesce, with decoration of wavy, haphazard lines in olive green or a light colour on a metallic ground (an inlaid version has floral designs outlined in black); Red Flame (1905), with embossed floral decoration under a red glaze; Sunburst (1906), a development of Utopian, with glossy glaze; Aborigine (1907), matt-glazed ware inspired by American Indian pottery; Soudanese (1907), with designs of flowers, animals, birds in lavender or pearly tints on ebony-glazed ground; Aqua Verdi, an iridescent green-glazed line often with relief designs in Art Nouveau style; a matt-glazed version of the Lotus line, with Lotus Parchment and Brushmodel Lotus, all characterized by a waxy appearance. Corona Animals, introduced 1905, in unglazed earthenware ranged widely in size from small pieces to large garden ornaments.

Production of art pottery apparently ceased before the closure of the Zanesville Tile Co. In 1909, Owens established a new firm, J.B. Owens Floor & Wall Tile Co. (incorporated 1923 as the Empire Floor & Wall Tile Co.), which absorbed other firms and opened new factories at Metuchen, New Jersey (closed 1929), and Greenburg, Pennsylvania (closed 1927). The main Empire factory was rebuilt after a fire in 1928, but Owens retired to

Florida when his firm failed financially in 1929. His former factory in Zanesville was occupied by the *Brush-McCoy Pottery Co. from 1911.

Marks: *Owens* or monogram of JBO, names of wares; marks incorporating OWENSART.

Refs: Evans; Jervis; Kovel & Kovel; Lehner; N.F. Schneider *Zanesville Art Pottery* (privately published, Zanesville, Ohio, 1963).

Owensart. *See* Owens, John B.

oxidizing atmosphere. Kiln conditions in which the air intake is plentiful so that elements oxidize freely and oxides remain unchanged. Earthenware (except copper reds, lustres and some raku) is normally fixed in an oxidizing atmosphere.

Oxshott Pottery. *See* Wren, Denise K.

Pachl, Margaret. American ceramist and teacher. Born in Lincoln, Nebraska, she studied at Kansas Art Institute, North Texas Agricultural College and at New York State College of Ceramics, Alfred. She taught at Alfred, and, in 1948, at the Kalamazoo Institute of Arts before joining *North Dakota School of Mines, 1948-70, as teacher and artist.

Ref: Kovel & Kovel.

Pacton, Abbé Pierre (1856-1938). French ceramist. Pacton was a follower of J.*Carriès and made stoneware in collaboration with the carpenter André Minil. He was the parish priest at Arquian, near St Amand-en-Puisaye (Nièvre).

Mark: monogram of Pacton's initials combined with those of Minil.

Refs: Haslam (1977); Lesur (1971).

Paget, F. Howard. *See* Derby.

Paillart brothers. *See* Hautin, Boulenger & Co.

Pailler, Léon. *See* Nivet, Michel.

Paitard. *See* Chevannes, Faïencerie de.

Paladin China. *See* Hughes, Edward, & Co.

Palissy ware. Earthenware made in the 19th century in imitation of the work of Bernard Palissy (1510-90): both his *'rustiques figulines'*, with realistic high-relief decoration in the form of small reptiles, frogs, molluscs and aquatic plants (often cast from natural specimens) and his allegorical scenes with figures in low relief, surrounded by masks, grotesques, and other Renaissance ornament.

Interest had already arisen in Palissy's writing in the 18th and 19th centuries, but although the information he gave about his work was full, his formulae and exact techniques had to be rediscovered. After over ten years of research, C.-J.*Avisseau of Tours (Indre-et-Loire) finally achieved reliable methods with predictable results in the early 1840s. He was followed by members of his family, and pupils L.*Brard and A.*Chauvigné, all working at Tours. Other makers of Palissy ware included: T.-V.*Sergent, V.*Barbizet, G.*Pull in Paris; J.*Lesme in Limoges; Louis Tinier in Tours;

Paragon China Ltd. Bone china tea service, printed in green and painted by hand, c.1931. Marks include Hand painted China by Paragon England *and* Tulip.

Emile Gambut (1870s) in Chalon-sur-Saône (Saône-et-Loire).

In England, close copies of Renaissance-style (rather than rustic) pieces were made by *Mintons Ltd in the 1850s. Later, in the 1860s and 1870s, Mintons used the same techniques on work in other 16th-century styles, modelled by a number of French artists, e.g. A.-E.*Carrier-Belleuse. Other English makers included J.*Wedgwood & Sons Ltd c.1860, and E.*Bingham made a plaque in tribute to Palissy, c.1890.

Pieces influenced by Palissy ware were produced by Sèvres, *Bichweiler of Hamburg, and *Mafra & Son at Caldas da Rainha, Portugal.

Refs: M. Haslam 'Bernard Palissy' in *The Connoisseur* (September 1975); Heuser & Heuser; Lesur (1971); J. Morley 'Palissy and the English' in *Apollo* 76 (1962); Thieme & Becker.

Pallandre, Henri-Léon. Porcelain decorator, working as a flower painter at Sèvres, 1853-70. Pallandre designed a series of plates for production in porcelain with *Plantes Maritimes* painted in colour by the firm of O.*Haviland by 1876, the year in which the series was included in the Haviland displays in exhibitions in Paris and Philadelphia. In 1879, he was working for a firm in Versailles.

Refs: Brunhammer *et al* (1976); A. Dubouché 'La Céramique Contemporaine à l'Exposition de l'Union Centrale des Beaux-Arts' in *L'Art* (October 1976); Lesur (1967); J. Young *The Ceramic Art* (Harper & Bros, New York, 1878).

Palmere, Charles. English painter of figure subjects, often in the style of David Tenniers II, for the *Worcester Royal Porcelain Co., c.1867-80, and the *Coalport factory in the 1870s.

Refs: Sandon (1978a); *see also* Coalport.

Papa. Hungarian creamware factory established in the early 18th century at Papa by the firm of Schneller & Postbichel. Mathias Winter (d 1832), owner from c.1810, reorganized the factory, installing fifteen English kilns. The output included finely moulded jasper ware and other relief decoration. Winter's family leased the factory to J. Farkashazy *Fischer in 1838, but sold it a year later to Georg Johann Mayer, who introduced the production of porcelain. The factory closed in 1866.

Marks include the place name with monogram or name of owners.

Ref: Csanyi.

Papendieck, Auguste (1873-1950). German studio potter, trained as a painter, 1900-05. After studying chemistry 1905-06, she worked at potteries in Bunzlau, Zeven and Lesum and established her own workshop in Bremen-Achterdieck. Initially producing moulded tableware painted with flowers in blue with white glaze and fired at a high temperature, she abandoned decoration in the 1920s, turning to thrown vases, bowls and small boxes. Her bowls were often bell-shaped, and all the ware was very thinly potted, relying for effect on shaded glazes, in soft grey-beige, green or blue/purple.

Marks: monograms of AP; a monogram with two horses' heads in an oval outline.

Refs: Bock; H.W. Haase *Keramik von Auguste Papendieck* (catalogue, Focke-Museum, Bremen, 1973).

Paragon China Ltd. Staffordshire manufacturers of bone porcelain working at Longton. The firm was established as the Star China Co. in 1897 under the direction of H.J. Aynsley and Hugh Irving. The title became Paragon China Ltd in 1919, with Irving then the sole proprietor. He was later joined by his sons Leslie (in 1928) and Guy (in 1933). The output, tea and breakfast wares, mainly for export to Australia, New Zealand and South Africa, expanded in the early 1930s to include dinner services for export to North and South America. The firm merged with T.C.*Wild & Sons Ltd in

1960, but continued production under the Paragon name, and became part of Allied English Potteries (*see* Pearson, S., & Son, Ltd).

Printed marks include a crown with s.c. co and a star from c.1900. Other marks from c.1904 incorporate a star and PARAGON CHINA. From the firm's appointment as China Manufacturers to Queen Mary in 1933 (and to subsequent members of the Royal Family), the marks incorporate the Royal Arms.

Refs: Bunt; Cushion (1980); Godden (1964).

Pardee, C., Works. American tile manufacturer established before 1893 at Perth Amboy, New Jersey, making paving stones, drainpipes and glazed tiles for floors and walls. Art tiles (produced by 1893) included *intaglio* modelled portraits of Kaiser Wilhelm, American presidents, Benjamin Harrison and Grover Cleveland, etc., and tiles with painted or printed designs either under or over the glaze. C.*Nielson was employed soon after his arrival in the United States. The firm acquired W.H.*Grueby's Faience & Tile Co. and subsequently moved that operation to Perth Amboy.

Refs: Barber (1976); Evans; Kovel & Kovel.

Pardoe, Thomas (1770-1823). English ceramic painter, born in Derby, and trained at the Derby porcelain factory. While chief painter at the *Cambrian Pottery in Swansea, he carried out much of the pottery's early decoration. Pardoe is noted for his freshness of style and his versatility. He painted animals, figures, views and romantic landscapes as well as flowers and patterns of Oriental inspiration. His detailed, careful paintings of flowers and plants, many of them copied from botanical illustrations, which contrast with his normal fluent style, probably reflect the scientific interests of his employer, L.W. *Dillwyn. A skilled gilder, he favoured border patterns formed of ellipses and often added small gilt insects to his work; his gilded ground patterns included the Sèvres *fond caillouté*. Pardoe occasionally painted borders in dark blue (under the glaze) or pink; some

Thomas Pardoe. Dish painted with a specimen of Persian cyclamen, before 1809. Impressed mark, Swansea. 25 cm in diameter.

plates with sparse decoration have border patterns in brown or green.

After leaving the Cambrian Pottery, Pardoe worked as an independent decorator in Bristol, from 1809, engaged by W.W.*Young to decorate the stock of porcelain remaining at Nantgarw after the departure of W.*Billingsley and S.*Walker in 1820, and executed work similar to his painting at the Cambrian Pottery, including patterns of Japanese inspiration and lavish flower bouquets, sometimes with birds, but fewer named botanical specimens.

His son, William Henry Pardoe (d 1867), began production of utilitarian ware and tobacco pipes at the Nantgarw works in 1833; he was succeeded by his family until the closure of the pottery in 1920.

Mark: Thomas Pardoe's signature on his decoration.

Refs: Barrett (1951); Charles; Peter Hughes *Welsh China* (National Museum of Wales, Cardiff, 1972); Williams (1932).

Parfaite, Marie. *See* Islettes, Les.

parian ware. A matt, white porcelain body, slightly translucent and often smear glazed. parian ware is generally marble-like, ivory-tinged and silky in texture, in contrast with the slightly gritty, pure white appearance of biscuit porcelain. The ware was first produced commercially by the firm of W.T.*Copeland as 'statuary porcelain' in 1846. T.& R. *Boote Ltd marketed parian ware from 1850, claiming its development in 1841. Pieces were manufactured by J.*Wedgwood & Sons Ltd under the trade name Carrara,

parian ware. Group, The Wounded Scout, after a model by the American figure maker John Rogers. One of several American Civil War subjects reproduced in parian ware by European manufacturers. The copperhead snake represents a threat from Confederate sympathizers in the North. 48 cm high.

but *Mintons Ltd, who claimed production from 1845, were the first to use the name parian ware. Production of the ware was encouraged by the commissioning of parian figures as prizes by the *Art Unions, and the patronage of H.*Cole, who included examples by Mintons, *Coalport and Wedgwood in his Felix Summerly catalogue.

The parian paste, initially used to make sculptural figures and groups, was often used in combination with glazed porcelain for centrepieces, etc. By the late 1860s, a wide variety of pieces in production included jugs, vases, tea sets and trinkets. Later developments included a tinted parian ground, used with relief ornament in white, e.g. for jugs. Mintons Ltd produced tableware, often lavishly gilded, in large quantities, and parian slip provided the basis of *pâte-sur-pâte* decoration by L.-M.-E.*Solon. A version of parian ware using hard-paste porcelain was developed in the late 1840s and produced alongside the original soft paste. The *Belleek factory, initially manufacturers of both soft-paste and hard-paste parian, eventually produced a similar paste with iridescent glaze. *Robinson & Leadbeater were among manufacturers who produced parian ware well into the 20th century, although production in Britain diminished after the 1890s.

Other European makers included the *Rörstrand and *Gustavsburg factories. In America, the styles of parian ware were imitated in biscuit porcelain from the 1850s by many manufacturers. *Ott & Brewer, E.*Bennet and the Chesapeake Pottery were among makers of parian ware.

Ref: Shinn.

Paris porcelain. Of the factories started in Paris before the French Revolution, in many cases under aristocratic patronage, those of *Dihl et Guérhard, F.-M.*Honoré and M.*Schoelcher and the Manufacture de la *Courtille survived into the 19th century. Much porcelain associated with Paris until this time was not identified with the maker by a mark, but this also occurred outside Paris, making attribution of unmarked pieces uncertain. However, as early as the Empire period, the choicest pieces began to be carefully marked. After the Restoration, the emphasis in Paris began to shift from porcelain production to the decoration of pieces sent from provincial manufacturers to Paris workshops, many of which claimed by the middle of the century to rival the decorative standards of Sèvres. However, the output of such firms as J.*Petit, Talmours (*see* Discry), *Flamen-Fleury and D.*Denuelle earned a high reputation for production as well as for decoration, and Parisian makers were generally known for the production of ornamental ware, rather than of useful items. Among the makers who remained in Paris until the late 19th century were *Gilet et Brianchon, *Gille and E.*Samson et Cie.

Parlon, Camille. *See* Haviland, Robert.

Parnell, Gwendoline. English potter working (c.1916-35) in Chelsea, London, where she produced earthenware figures. She subsequently worked for the *Worcester Royal Porcelain Co.; her work included models of the London Cries series, *chinoiserie* figures, and the firm's first limited edition figures,

King George V and Queen Mary for the Silver Jubilee of 1935.

Marks: CHELSEA CHEYNE incised, sometimes with date; initials with a rabbit mark, c.1916-c.1935; G.M.P. painted under Worcester figures.

Ref: Sandon (1978a).

Parr, John. *See* Kent & Parr.

Parthenay. *See* Jouneau, Prosper.

Parvillé, Léon (d 1885). French architect and ceramist. Parvillé was a student of Isnik pottery and began his collection while working in 1863 on the restoration of historic Turkish buildings; he published *Architecture et décoration turques en XVième siècle* in 1874.

In decorating pottery, in which he was assisted by his sons, Achille and Louis, he took designs mainly from Persian sources and used the technique developed by E.V. *Collinot, with very thick enamel glazes. His work was exhibited from early in the 1870s. Later he also painted some work with Japanese motifs and adopted modern styles.

Mark: painted monogram.
Refs: Heuser & Heuser; Lesur (1971); Thieme & Becker.

Passenger, Frederick and Charles. English pottery decorators. The brothers assisted W.*De Morgan (Charles from c.1877 and Frederick from c.1879) and became his partners from 1898 until 1907, although De Morgan ceased active participation in 1905. After the firm's closure, they continued to decorate pottery in the Brompton Road, London until 1911, using De Morgan designs, with his permission. Fred Passenger worked at a pottery in Bushey Heath, Hertfordshire, 1923-33, still using designs inspired by De Morgan's work, particularly the ones that were Isnik in inspiration.

Charles Passenger's initials are sometimes found on Queensware from the Wedgwood

*Fred and Charles Passenger. Painted dish with a design of swans, signed by W.*De Morgan and initialled CP. 24 cm in diameter.*

factory decorated while he was working for De Morgan.

Refs: Apollo (January 1953); W. Gaunt & M.D.E. Clayton Stamm *William De Morgan* (Studio Vista, London, 1971); M. Haslam *English Art Pottery 1865-1915* (Antique Collectors' Club, 1975); Lockett (1979); R. Pinkham (ed.) *Catalogue of the Pottery of William De Morgan in the Victoria & Albert Museum* (London, 1973); Reilly & Savage.

Pastello. *See* Rhead, Frederick Alfred.

Pate, Klytie *née* Sclater (b 1912). Australian potter born in Melbourne. She studied drawing at the National Gallery School, and modelling and sculpture at the Melbourne Technical College, encouraged by her aunt Christian Waller and her uncle, the sculptor Napier Waller. She married William Pate in 1937. She was appointed to a lectureship in pottery in Melbourne, 1938-45 and subsequently worked full time as a potter making earthenware, often with carved or incised decoration of animals, or themes from Classical and Egyptian mythology. Her treatment contains clear references to Art Deco. Her extant works, which range in date from 1932 to 1982 are characterised by her experimental use of glaze effects, including a brilliant, glassy finish.

Ref: Klytie Pate Ceramics (National Gallery of Victoria, Melbourne, 1983).

pâte-sur-pâte. Decorative technique in which designs, usually in white on a darker ground, are built up in low relief with layers of porcelain slip, so that the varying thicknesses give the effect of shading (as in a cameo) in the design. The method was developed at the Sèvres factory in the mid 19th century and examples were exhibited in Paris, 1855. The technique was further developed by L.-M.-E.*Solon and executed e.g. by E.*Escallier-Légérot and T.*Doat. Apart from the painstaking design and execution of the decoration (with each layer of slip taking time to dry thoroughly before the application of the next layer and the final glazing), the method represents a considerable technical achievement in developing porcelain slips that were suitable for detailed painting, but did not flake or crack after firing. The method was very costly and, although *Mintons Ltd and Solon himself continued its use into the 20th century, it was not widely used after c.1890. *Knowles, Taylor & Knowles showed in the World's Columbian Exposition, Chicago (1893) examples of a similar technique with designs built up in enamel over the glaze.

English makers included W.*Brownfield, G.*Jones, *Moore Brothers, and the *Worcester factories.

Refs: Godden (1961); Lesur (1967).

Paterson, Robert. *See* Fife Pottery.

Patey, Richard W. *See* Linthorpe Pottery.

Patterson, John. *See* Bridge End.

Patterson, John, & Sons. *See* Oakwood Pottery.

Pauleo. *See* Roseville Pottery Co.

Paul Revere Pottery. Vase with incised and painted decoration is glazed in blue, green and tan, bearing the initials SEG (Saturday Evening Girls), 1916. 11.5 cm high.

Pauline Pottery. *See* Edgerton Pottery; Jacobus, Pauline.

Paul Revere Pottery. American pottery established in 1906 as part of a programme of artistic training for girls from immigrant families in Boston, Massachusetts, who studied crafts as members of the Saturday Evening Girls' Club. In regular production from 1908 at a pottery in their new club house, with the assistance of a professional potter, the girls made children's breakfast sets comprising jug, bowl and plate, decorated with nursery motifs—domestic animals or birds, rabbits, boats, flowers, nursery-rhyme scenes, etc.—and a variety of table and toilet ware, as well as vases, lamp bases, candlesticks, desk sets, paperweights and tiles. Decoration was painted in flat colours outlined in black (sometimes the outline was first incised). The patterns on vases usually feature large flowers, iris, narcissus, rose or, notably, chrysanthemum; a vase showing a lakeside scene with pine trees was illustrated in 1914. Matt glazes were normally used in soft shades of white, yellow, green, blue, grey and brown, but the range also included glossy glazes. Tile designs included Boston scenes, Paul Revere's ride, the ships of Christopher Columbus, incised, coloured and matt glazed. Unglazed dolls' heads were made briefly in World War I, but not marketed.

Edith Brown (d 1932), director, principal designer and one of the founders of the pottery, designed a new building (opened 1915) in Brighton, Massachusetts, taking particular pride in the clean, attractive working conditions it provided. The pottery's operation, always heavily substantial despite the popularity and high quality of the ware ended in 1942.

Marks include impressed or printed circular scenes of Paul Revere; painted initials PRP or SEG [Saturday Evening Girls].

Refs: Callen; Eidelberg; Evans; Kovel & Kovel.

Paulus, Carl (1792-1822). German porcelain porcelain painter, son of Johann Georg

Paulus, founder of the *Schlaggenwald factory in 1793, where Carl Paulus was employed from 1809 and trained under J.*Müller. He is thought to have specialized in the painting of rustic scenes.
Refs: Danckert; Weiss.

Peach Bloom. *See* Plant, R.H.& S.L., Ltd.

Pearce, Arthur. English engraver and water-colour artist, trained at the South Kensington School of Art in London, and in Paris. Working for *Doulton & Co. in Lambeth, 1873-1930, Pearce specialized in designs for tiles and architectural ornament, but also carried out etched patterns for the decoration of advertising ware, especially spirit flasks. Noted for his wide knowledge of design history, he was among the artists whom John *Slater consulted in the early artistic development of the company's Burslem factory. Pearce was responsible for the design of several exhibition stands for Doulton's displays.
    Work occasionally signed.
Refs: see Doulton & Co.

Pearson, Edward Meakin (b 1848). Potter and porcelain manufacturer. Born in Staffordshire, son of a Cobridge manufacturer of pottery for export. Pearson learned pottery in his father's firm, and became a partner in 1868, trading as Edward Pearson & Son. After settling in America, 1873, he carried out research directed towards the production of white ware in East Liverpool, Ohio, at the factory of Knowles, Taylor & Knowles. In partnership with H. and S.*Laughlin, he set up (1874) and managed a plant later operated by Homer Laughlin. He then became associated with five later factories in East Liverpool. Pearson moved to Wheeling, West Virginia, becoming manager of the Wheeling Pottery Co. and president (in 1890) of the company formed by amalgamation of the Wheeling and La Belle potteries.
Ref: Barber (1976).

Pearson, S., & Sons Ltd. A large holding company which provided financial assistance for *Booths Ltd during the 1930s, and began its serious expansion in the ceramics industry with the purchase of H.J.*Colclough in 1944 and the Lawley retail group in 1952. In 1964, the company bought T.C.*Wild & Sons, the Royal Crown *Derby Porcelain Co., and grouped its ceramic interests under the title Allied English Potteries. Shelley China Ltd and a subsidiary concerned with electrical ware (*see* Shelley, P.) were taken into the group in 1966. The Derby factory was later merged with Royal Doulton Tableware Ltd, also part of Allied English Potteries.
Refs: Twitchett (1976); Watkins *et al.*

Pearson & Co. Derbyshire stoneware manufacturers, working the Whittington Pottery, near Chesterfield, with a staple output of bottles. The pottery was acquired in 1810 by Catherine Johnson (*née* Pearson) and remained in the hands of her family. Under James Pearson (d 1905), the firm took over the Oldfield Pottery (established 1810 in Chesterfield) in 1884, and amalgamated it with the London Pottery of F. Lipscombe & Co., patentees of a type of stoneware water filter. The firm became Pearson & Co.

(Chesterfield) Ltd in the 1920s and later worked as the Whittington Moor Potteries.
    Marks: a heart-shaped iron-stand marked *Pearson & Co Whittington, Chesterfield* dates from 1846; other known pieces include a mug marked *Pearson Potter 1906*. The mark P.&Co also occurs.
Refs: Bradley; Oswald.

Peche, Dagobert (1887-1923). Austrian artist and designer, trained (1906-10) in Vienna at the Akademie der bildenden Künste and Wiener Technik. From 1913, he designed shapes and decoration for tableware produced in porcelain by the firm of Jos.*Böck, collaborating with J.*Hoffmann on a mocha service, for which Hoffmann designed the forms. He also modelled pieces for Vereinigte Wiener und Gmundner Keramik and the Wiener Werkstätte. He was a leading artist of the Werkstätte from 1915 until his death, leaving Vienna 1917-18 to run a branch in Zurich. Peche was also a designer in other media, including glass, metalwork and wallpaper.
    Marks incorporate the initials DP or P and sometimes a four-pointed star.
Ref: Neuwirth (1974a).

Pecht, J.A. *See* Schmidt-Pecht, Elisabeth.

Peconic Pottery Co. *See* Kiss, Charles.

Peel Works, Longton. *See* Wildblood, Heath & Sons.

Pegg, William (1795-1867). English porcelain decorator. Pegg was apprenticed at the factory at Nottingham Road, *Derby, c.1810 and worked there as a flower painter until c.1819. He afterwards worked with W.*Billingsley, a family friend, before entering the Lancashire textile industry as a designer, establishing his own business at Heaton Norris, Stockport.
Refs: see Derby.

Pegg, William 'Quaker' (1775-1851). English ceramic painter, born in Whitmore, near Newcastle-under-Lyme, Staffordshire, the son of a gardener at Etwall Hall, near Derby. At ten years old, Pegg started work in an earthenware factory; he began his training as a painter in 1788, and became an apprentice decorator two years later. He entered into a five-year agreement to work at the porcelain factory in Nottingham Road, *Derby, where he painted dishes, plates, other items of tableware, and panels on vases with studies of flowers, normally almost life-size and taken direct from nature, which are notable for a lightness and freedom of treatment, achieved without any sacrifice of botanical accuracy. His style is careful and detailed, especially in the portrayal of foliage (often carried out in opaque chrome green), and the flowers, or a single bloom, generally occupy the entire surface of the painting without further decoration apart from, usually, a band of gilding at the rim. Pegg normally labelled the subjects in red enamel on the reverse. He joined the Society of Friends in 1800, leaving the factory in the following year, and subsequently worked as a stocking maker until 1813, when he was persuaded to return to work for R.*Bloor. During the last years of his painting career, Pegg adopted a rather more flamboyant

style, placing as many as four species of showy flowers in free arrangements on each piece. Religious scruples on the subject of adornment led him to abandon painting in 1820, when he opened a general store in Derby with his wife Ann, whom he had married in 1814.
Refs: A.M. George *'Quaker' Pegg* (exhibition catalogue, A. Amor Ltd, London, 1977); *see also* Derby.

Peigney, Pierre. *See* Ancy-le-Franc.

Peltner, George (b 1921) and Steffi (b 1922). German potters. The Peltners worked together from 1946 in workshops at Oberfranken, Stuttgart (1946-49) and Höhr-Grenzhausen, where George Peltner trained as a ceramic technician, 1949-52. In 1953, they started their own workshop in Höhr-Grenzhausen, where they made stoneware, fired at 114°C, with sponged decoration in the tradition of Bunzlau potters, and painted patterns on white Westerwald clay, under a clear feldspar glaze.
    Mark: painted monogram of GSP.
Ref: Bock.

Penman, Edith. *See* Byrdcliffe Pottery.

Penn China Co. *See* Phoenixville Pottery.

Pennington, John (c.1765-1842). Porcelain painter, probably born in Liverpool. Pennington was an apprentice at the *Wedgwood factory and became the chief artist at the *Worcester factory of Flight & Barr.
    His early work included monochromes (e.g. on the Duke of Clarence's 'Hope' service) but he later painted in colour.
Ref: Sandon (1978b).

Pensée service. *See* Schmuz-Baudiss, Theodor Hermann.

Peoria Pottery Co. American pottery operating in Peoria, Illinois, from 1873 in buildings erected (1859) by C.W.*Fenton and D.W.*Clark for the manufacture of a wide variety of wares, including white ware, Rockingham-glazed ware, stoneware and enamelled architectural ware. Rockingham and yellow-glazed ware and stoneware were made at the factory after the failure of the Fenton & Clark venture in 1863. The Peoria Pottery Co. continued the manufacture of stoneware until its replacement in 1889 by white granite, cream-coloured earthenware (discontinued in 1899) and decorated tableware. The company exhibited services tinted in delicate green, pink and other light colours at the World's Columbian Exposition in Chicago, 1893. The firm combined with the Crown Pottery Co. of Evansville, Indiana, makers of white granite and ironstone china in the early 1890s to form the Crown Potteries Co.

Marks include versions of the English coat of arms, the firm's monogram and PEORIA/ILLINOIS (an early mark).
Ref: Barber (1976).

Pépinière, La. *See* Jouhanneaud, Paul.

Peppin, Mylie. *See* Poynter, Maud.

Perceval, John. *See* Boyd, Arthur.

Percier, Charles. *See* Sèvres.

Percy, Arthur (b 1886). Swedish painter and ceramist. Percy studied under Henri Matisse and painted figures, interiors, landscapes, etc. His designs for ceramics were based on traditional forms and include wares painted with flowers in a style reminiscent of floral decoration on faience in the 18th century, as well as plain white porcelain in austere, refined shapes. Percy also made functional and decorative wares in white earthenware, and after World War II produced gently rounded designs in stoneware.
Refs: Bénézit; Hettes & Rada; Lagercrantz.

Pereco. *See* Peters & Reed.

Perkins, Lucy F. and Annie F. *See* Brush Guild.

Perry or **Stratton,** Mary Chase (1868-1961). American porcelain painter and artist potter, born in Hancock, Michigan, and trained in clay sculpture and ceramic painting at art schools in Cincinnati and New York. She studied briefly under C.F.*Binns and was a member of the *National League of Mineral Painters. Working in partnership with her neighbour in Detroit, H.J.*Caulkins, she made pottery under the name, Revelation, used by Caulkins in marketing his kilns, and in 1903 she established the Pewabic Pottery, named after a Michigan river. (Pewabic is a Chippewa Indian word referring to clay of a

Mary Chase Perry. Earthenware vase made at the Pewabic Pottery, 20th century. 26.7 cm high.

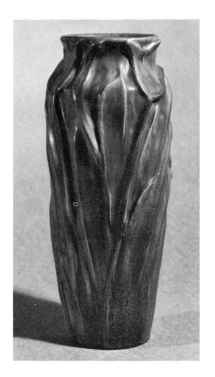

copper colour.) Caulkins acted as clay technician, while Mary Perry designed forms, which were then thrown for her by a trained potter, and carried out research into glazes. A dark green matt glaze was followed by yellow, brown, buff, and, by 1911, a range including yellow and orange streaked with brown; blue, purple and white; a spotted crystalline effect; deep blues resembling ancient Egyptian and Islamic glazes. A new pottery, built in 1906, was designed by the firm of William Buck Stratton, whom Mary Perry married in 1918; it was enlarged in 1910. The relief decoration of Mary Perry's early work was influenced by European Art Nouveau and particularly the styles of W.H. *Grueby and L.C.*Tiffany, but the shapes became simpler as her interest in glaze effects increased. Using a high-fired white clay body, she applied flowing glazes over a contrasting colour, and in the last phase of her work explored iridescent and lustre glazes, often exploiting subtle interplays of colour. Some of her choicest vases were acquired by the Detroit millionaire and collector of Oriental ceramics, Charles L. Freer, and passed into the collections of American museums and art institutes. Mary Perry also designed architectural ware, for which her pottery became noted, after fulfilling a commission to make tiles for St Paul's Cathedral, Detroit, in 1908. She designed fountains and alcoves as well as tiles, carrying out much of the relief decoration herself, and always emphasizing the direct involvement of her small staff in the creative and artistic side of production. In 1968, four years after her death, the Pewabic Pottery was reopened by the University of Michigan to teach ceramics and provide studio facilities for Detroit potters.

Marks: triangular device containing lighted candle with initials MCP and *Revelation Pottery Detroit*; PEWABIC with five maple leaves; circular marks containing PP/*Detroit*. Usually impressed.
Refs: Barber (1976); F. Bleicher *et al. Pewabic Pottery: an Official History* (Ars Ceramica, Ann Arbor, Michigan, 1977); Clark & Hughto; Eidelberg; Evans; Henzke; Keen; Kovel & Kovel; A. Robineau 'Mary Chase Perry – the Potter' in *Keramik Studio* VI No 10 (1905); M.C.P. Stratton in *The Bulletin* of the American Ceramic Society 25 (15th October 1946).

Persian. *See* Peters & Reed.

Persian colours. *See* De Morgan, William.

Persian ware. *See* Simeon, Harry.

Peters & Reed. American pottery firm established in 1898 by John D. Peters and Adam Reed (d 1922), both former employees of S.A.*Weller. The partners rented a stoneware pottery built c.1892 in Zanesville, Ohio, but were unable to exercise a purchase option in the same year, when the works was bought by the *Roseville Pottery Co. At new premises in South Zanesville, Peters & Reed produced flowerpots and *jardinières* in red earthenware and (c.1903-1906) kitchen ware lined with white slip. After the enlargement of the pottery in 1907, they continued production of plant containers and spittoons, and introduced *jardinières* with painted decoration over glazes in red, green

and blended shades. Art ware designed and modelled by Adam Reed had been made occasionally from 1901, but the first regular line, Moss Aztec, was not introduced until 1912. Created by F.*Ferrell, also a Weller employee, who provided designs for Peters & Reed before joining their firm full-time, Moss Aztec pieces were moulded in local red clay and coated in a finish which was then wiped off the raised portions of relief decoration, leaving a mossy effect in the recesses; interiors were clear-glazed. Later art lines included: Landsun, with blended effects of different colours; the similar Chromal, with scenic effects suggested by the variations in colour; Montene with iridescent copper-bronze or semi-matt shaded green finish; Pereco and Persian, both with plain coloured semi-matt effects. After the retirement of Peters in 1920, Reed took over as company president (changing the firm's title to the *Zane Pottery Co. in 1921) and himself retired in 1922, succeeded as owner by H.S.*McClelland.
Refs: E.M. Clark *Ohio Art & Artists* (Garrett & Massie, Richmond, Ohio, 1932); Evans; Kovel & Kovel; Lehner.

Petit or **Mardochée,** Jacob (1796-1868). French ceramist, Jacob Mardochée, working under the surname of his wife, Ann Petit. He studied painting under Antoine Gros, then travelled round Europe and became interested in decorative design while visiting England. After his return to France c.1830, Petit brought out a *Recueil de Décoration intérieure comprenant tout ce qui a rapport à l'ameublement.* Regarding porcelain as an important medium for the expression of taste, he established a short-lived workshop at Sèvres (Seine-et-Oise). Petit founded a business at Belleville soon afterwards, and by 1834 bought a factory making hard-paste porcelain at Fontainebleau, quickly trebling the number of its workers. Using a fine, very white porcelain, Petit concentrated from 1838 on decorative ware, initially simple in style with flowers meticulously painted or modelled, but soon drawn from a wide range of sources; he was described as combining the nostalgic feelings for the East expressed in Victor Hugo's songs with those evoked by Alfred de Musset for the Middle Ages. He developed a version of the revived rococo style (first exhibited in 1834) for skilful ornamental pieces decorated with colourful, full-blown flowers in a palette which included black, bright green or garnet grounds and a new range of pinks, greens and mauves. Petit's factories became noted for fashionable toys: vases in the form of tree trunks, cornucopiae or flowers, *veilleuses*, perfume bottles, tobacco jars or beer mugs in the form of figures, inkwells representing boats, reclining figures or animals from fables. Dogs, nesting birds and reptiles emerged as favourite themes. His biscuit ware included delicate figures draped in lace.

Petit was a keen inventor and took out patents for *veilleuses* which told the hour, and porcelain dolls' heads, also experimenting with new techniques in moulding and gilding. He located both his factories in Basses-Loges-sur-Avon, 1850, but settled in rue Paradis-Poissonnière, Paris, in 1862, selling his business to an employee, Jacquemin, who bought moulds, models and marks. Petit then made vases with garlands of

Jacob Petit. Stoppered perfume flask painted with flowers in panels on a turquoise ground and decorated in relief with portraits, lion masks and scrollwork, c.1840. Initialled J.P. in underglaze blue. 27 cm high.

flowers, as well as many pieces in the white for decoration by professional and amateur artists.

Marks usually incorporate initials, JP.
Refs: Baschet; Ernould-Gandouet; Guillebon; Lesur (1967).

Petit, Nicholas Edmé. *See* Vausse, Faïencerie de.

Petri-Raben, Trude (1906-68). German designer. Trude Petri was known for tableware in smooth, simple forms commissioned for machine production in porcelain by the Berlin factory. Her designs included the Urbino service, described by Köllmann as 'the classic service of modern times', produced without decoration, 1930-32, together with a coffee set in celadon, black and white; the Arcadian service (1938), shapes designed by Trude Petri, with biscuit medallions on a glazed ground, relief patterns by Siegmund Schütz; a mocha set (1948). She emigrated to America.
Refs: E. Köllmann *Berliner Porzellan 1751-1954* (Kunstgewerbemuseum der Stadt, Cologne, 1954), *Berliner Porzellan* (Brunswick, 1960).

Pétrocérame. *See* Creil.

Pétry & Ronsse. French porcelain manufacturers. Pierre-Romain-Joseph Pétry and Jean-Joseph Ronsse, initially bankers, formed a new partnership in 1829 for the sale and manufacture of porcelain, working from rue Vendôme, Paris, where they had their office, and a factory established 1815 in Vierzon, which they purchased in 1829. A further partnership formed in 1842 with Adolphe Hache Pétry was dissolved in 1845. By 1844, the firm employed 500 workers at Vierzon, and 100 decorators in Paris in the production of cabaret sets, vases, holy water stoups, sconces, etc.
Ref: Guillebon.

Petty, Samuel; **Petty's Pottery.** *See* Hunslet Hall.

Pewabic Pottery. *See* Caulkins, Horace James; Perry, Mary Chase.

Peyre, Nicolle. *See* Sèvres.

Pfeiffer, Max Adolf (1875-1957). German porcelain maker. In 1908, he took over the factory previously occupied by the manufacturers Mann & Porzelius at *Unterweissbach, which he operated as the Schwarzburger Werkstätten, making art porcelain until 1913. With A.*Niemeyer, he designed everyday wares, and he called upon such artists as E.*Barlach, Adolf Brütt, M.*Esser, G. *Marcks, Wilhelm Neuhäuser, Otto Pilz, Anton Puchegger, Richard Scheibe, P. *Scheurich, and Otto Thiem to design figures. He joined the Meissen factory in 1918. As director of the factory, he commissioned figures by Esser and Scheurich. Pfeiffer then worked 1938-46 at the Berlin factory, again employing Esser and Scheurich. He took control of the Staatlichen Glas-Manufaktur, Karlsbad in 1941, and joined the firm of *Rosenthal 1947-50, working as head of the Selb factory. He designed figures in relief for the firm's art workshop in Selb.

*Max Adolf Pfeiffer. Porcelain group of guinea fowl modelled by M.*Esser and made at the Schwarzburger Werkstätten, c.1911. Marked with the workshop's name and a fox. 39.5 cm high.*

His Schwarzburg workshop was under the control of Ernst Schaubach from the 1920s, and he became its owner in 1940. From the end of World War II the workshop made decorative porcelain, operating under state control. It became part of the Lichte group. The output of carefully hand-made art porcelain continued.
Refs: Danckert; Pelka; Ware.

Pfeller, F. *See* Gotha.

Philippot, Jean. *See* Cornes, Domaine des; Vausse, Faïencerie de.

Phillips, Edward. *See* Derby; Worcester.

Phillips, Ernest John (d 1932). English porcelain painter working for the *Worcester Royal Porcelain Co. from 1890. Phillips was noted for his polished, accurate studies of flowers in the neat style of early Worcester flower painting at the centre of plates. He was a keen gardener and watercolour painter of flowers.
Ref: Sandon (1978a).

Phillips, John (d 1897). Devonshire potter, antiquarian and educationalist. In 1868, Phillips bought a pottery established three years earlier for the production of domestic earthenware, and added architectural terracotta and firebricks to the output. A lecturer in arts and crafts, Phillips was also among the patrons of Kings Kerswell Art School and employed students under the guidance of an experienced potter to produce art wares from 1881, when the pottery was rebuilt after fire damage. Phillip's firm operated as the *Aller Vale Pottery from 1887 and took the title Royal Aller Vale Pottery after receiving the patronage of Princess Louise two years later. After his death, the company was bought by the firm of Hexter, Humpherson & Co., clay merchants and manufacturers of sanitary ware at Kingsteignton, who combined Aller Vale with the *Watcombe Pottery in 1901.

Incised marks *Phillips/Aller* or *Phillips/Newton Abbot* used c.1881-c.1887.
Ref: Lloyd Thomas (1978).

Phillips, John. *See* Dixon, Austin & Carr; Garrison Pottery.

Phillips, Moro. American stoneware maker. Phillips established a pottery in 1850 at a site rich in suitable clay near Wilson's Landing, Virginia. He moved the works to Philadelphia by 1855, producing chemical ware and, later, household vessels decorated underglaze in blue by the German potter, Hermann Eger (d 1891). He also ran a chemical works in Philadelphia. His pottery operated at Camden, New Jersey, from 1870 to 1897.
Refs: Barber (1976); S. Myers *Handcraft to Industry* (Smithsonian Institution Press, Washington, 1980); Webster.

Phillips, Thomas. English ceramic artist, working, after his apprenticeship at the *Worcester Royal Porcelain Factory, for *Doulton & Co. in Burslem, 1888-1930. He decorated examples of Spanish ware, and his work was included in many of the company's exhibition displays. He was later in charge of a department concerned with underglaze decoration.

Phoenix Pottery. Tyneside Pottery established at Ouseburn in 1827 by John Dryden & Co. for the production of brown earthenware, and later making white ware, some with printed decoration. Dryden's firm was succeeded by Isaac Bell (by 1844), Carr & Patton (1847), followed by John Patton alone, and finally the Phoenix Pottery Co. from c.1856 until the conversion of the buildings into a chemical works in 1860.
Refs: Bell; Jewitt.

Phoenixville Pottery. American pottery, operated by the Phoenix Pottery, Kaolin & Fire Brick Co., organized 1867 in Phoenixville, Pennsylvania, for the manufacture of firebrick and yellow or Rockingham-glazed wares. The works was leased in 1870s by a firm, Schreiber & Betz, producers of terracotta animal heads (hounds, stags, antelopes, boars) for decorating the walls of taverns. The output included majolica from 1882. The pottery was subsequently in the hands of *Griffen, Smith & Hill and taken over after closure (1892-94) by a firm trading as the Chester Pottery Co. of Pennsylvania and, from 1899, the Penn China Co., makers of semi-porcelain, which they printed underglaze in black. In 1902, the pottery was briefly rented by the Tuxedo Pottery Co., makers of semi-porcelain with underglaze decoration in flown blue or coloured glazes.

Marks: the arms of Pennsylvania within a circle bearing the partners' initials B. & G.
Refs: Barber (1976); James.

Picasso, Pablo (1881-1973). From 1947, the painter Picasso decorated ceramics made in the Madoura Pottery of S. and G.*Ramié at Vallauris. His early work included a tinglazed dinner plate finger-painted with a pigeon design in pale buff-coloured slip on a black ground (1947), and a fireclay panel painted in slip and coloured glazes with a still life entitled 'Nature Morte à la Cafetière' (1948). Picasso's interests progressed from painted or relief decoration carried on out on flat surfaces to the painting of vases which were eventually made to his own plan. In all these cases, his preoccupation was with the development of ornamentation from form, even when he had not designed the shape of the pot, and the function of vessels was frequently subordinated to this artistic intention. His designs on plates include scenes of bullfighting, or centaurs and other mythical figures, painted in bold brush strokes.

Picasso's later ceramic work was very varied. An exhibition mounted by the Arts Council of Great Britain in London (1957) showed 72 pieces selected by the artist, including a pitcher in the form of a mallard duck supported by two hands; a tureen decorated with spots in blue on a white tin glaze and entitled 'Taches et Pois'; a jug 'Soleils et Taches' and an urn 'Quatre Visages', both unglazed and decorated in pastels, dated 1953; 'Pigeon sur son nid', modelled in crumpled clay and painted in blue and black; two jugs with resist decoration of painters and models.
Refs: Céramique francaise contemporaine; D.H. Kahnweiler *Picasso-Keramik* (Fackelträger-Verlag/Schmidt-Küsler GmbH Hannover); Klein; *Pablo Picasso* (exhibition catalogue, Ingelheim am Rhein, 1981); S.& G. Ramié *Céramique de Picasso* (Paris, 1951); Wykes-Joyce.

Pablo Picasso. Figure of an owl, painted red and white, 1953.

Piccardt family. See Porceleyne Fles, De.

Pierlot, Jeanne (b 1917) and Norbert (1919-79). French potters. Jeanne Pierlot was apprenticed to E.*Lion at Saint-Amand-en-Puisaye in 1938 and later worked in Paris. With her husband, the actor Norbert Pierlot, she left Paris in 1951 to work at the Château de Ratilly at Treigny, where the couple developed a cultural centre and school for potters. In 1962, they organized an important exhibition of contemporary stoneware. Developing her style on a basis of local traditions, Jeanne Pierlot produced utilitarian pieces, including boxes, bottles and tableware, in simple forms with plain glazes. Her husband worked with her at Ratilly after abandoning acting.
Ref: Céramique française contemporaine.

Pierrefonds. In the late 19th century, the Count Hallez (Olivier de Sorra) produced fine stoneware at Pierrefonds (Oise), achieving crystalline glazes, which he used on vases, etc., in simple shapes c.1885. He also made earthenware decorated with heraldic

Pierrefonds. Stoneware vase with blue crystals in a green/beige glaze. Marks include H/PIERREFONDS. *20 cm high.*

emblems. His firm became La Société faïencière héraldique in 1904 under the direction of Eugène Santerre.

Marks include a knight's helmet, with initals *Fh* [Faïencerie héraldique] or surrounded by CERAMIQUE HERALDIQUE/ OLIVIER de SORRA within a circle; FAIENCERIE HERALDIQUE DE PIERREFONDS in a circular mark.
Refs: Haslam (1977); A. Klein *Keramik aus 5000 Jahren* (Schwann, Düsseldorf, 1969); Lesur (1971).

Pigott, Gwyn (b 1935). Australian studio potter, born in Ballarat. She studied under I.*McMeekin and later worked in England with R.*Finch, B.*Leach and, 1964-65, M.*Cardew. She established a workshop in London in 1960, making tablewares fired to stoneware temperatures in an electric kiln. She established a pottery in France in 1967 and produced wood-fired stoneware and porcelain. With John Piggot, she started a pottery in Tasmania in 1975 making wood-fired domestic wares. She moved to Adelaide in 1980 and continued to make elegant porcelain pots for everyday use, glazed with celadon inside and pink/grey outside.
Ref: Janet Mansfield (ed) *The Potter's Art* (Cassell, Sydney, 1981).

Pilkington's Tile & Pottery Co. Lancashire pottery established in 1891 for the manufacture of wall, floor and fireplace tiles and architectural ware at Clifton Junction, near Manchester, by four Pilkington brothers after the discovery of suitable clay in the course of a search for coal seams. W.*Burton took technical and artistic control from the opening of the factory in 1893 until his retirement in 1915, when he was succeeded by his brother and associate in glaze research, J.*Burton. J.*Chambers was engaged as designer, and J. Kwiatkowski modelled tiles, panels and plaques to his own and others' designs. The firm also made a variety of small articles (heads for hatpins, buttons), decorated pieces made by J.T.*Firth, and moulded vases from 1897, when they engaged a potter, Robert Tunnicliffe, who had formerly been employed at *Mintons Ltd on the making of pots for decoration by L.-M.-E. *Solon; E.T.*Radford joined the firm as thrower in 1903 for the start of full production.

In the Exposition Universelle in Paris (1900), the firm's display included architectural earthenware, tiles, several pots, and a pair of lion figures (from moulds by Alfred Stevens for the railings of the British Museum) covered with brown crystalline glaze discovered in 1893 and called Sunstone. This glaze was followed by eggshell effects in 1896. Lancastrian Ware, with a variety of glazes, was developed after the chance discovery of an opalescent effect in experiments late in 1903. The first examples, exhibited in June 1904, consisted of simple thrown shapes derived from Greek, Persian and Chinese originals. The many colours in glazes range from pale pink and blue to dark purple, green and tan, and the textures from vellum (allied to eggshell), developed during the ten years up to 1904, to fruit skin, with a surface resembling the skins of melon, pear, apricot or orange accompanying shades of yellow, green olive, deep russet. A glaze containing tin oxide was used in conjunction

Pilkington's Tile and Pottery Co. Royal Lancastrian vase designed by G.M.*Forsyth. 27.2 cm high.

with transparent glazes on shapes that stressed the colour effects as the glaze settled in crevices. Other glazes featured shaded, mottled, speckled, clouded effects; opalescent glazes were developed in shades of vivid ultramarine (1903), and variations in effect (striations, patches of opalescence, feathered or cloudy areas) were achieved by the addition of mineral compounds; orange glazes differed in shade according to the content of uranium; *flambé* glazes in pink or red, occasionally had a lustrous sheen. From 1913, the firm's pottery was sold as Royal Lancastrian, with the permission of King George V.

The development of iridescent lustre by William Burton resulted in painted lustre pottery, produced in quantity from the construction of a special muffle kiln in 1906. From that year, until he left the firm in 1920, G.M.*Forsyth took charge of the decorating department, which included W.*Mycock, R.*Joyce, G.M.*Rodgers and, from 1907, C.E.*Cundall, developing a distinctive style of decoration featuring mythological subjects, heraldic beasts and calligraphy. The artists were encouraged to follow their own, original, designs in lustre, and lustre ware became the firm's main output apart from tiles. Moulded, modelled and carved pieces were also produced; among them were animals and birds modelled by Joyce.

Mottled, matt glazes, marketed as Cunian, and developed by Arthur Chambers, works chemist 1927-38, were used on both pottery and tiles. The firm's tile commissions had included panels designed and painted by Forsyth for staircases to the ceramic gallery of Liverpool museum, and tiles, also by Forsyth, for bathrooms on the liner *Titanic*. Tiles continued to form the main output; freelance designers included W.*Crane, L.F.*Day and C.F.A.*Voysey.

In 1928, lustre painting ceased, and an ornamental line, Lapis ware, was introduced, with patterns painted on the biscuit pottery in colours developed by Joseph Burton (predominantly green, on tinted grounds), which reacted with the matt, opaque glaze used over them to produce a misty, slightly raised effect (caused by air bubbles and particles suspended in the glaze). The production of ornamental ware ceased in 1937, although decoration of existing stocks continued until the following year. Tile manufacture continued, and the pottery department re-opened in 1948-57 under the direction of William Barnes. The factory still stands on its original site.

Marks: P, incised, c.1897-1904; monogram of P and L, with bees, printed 1904-05, impressed until 1914; Tudor rose, sometimes with ROYAL LANCASTRIAN, impressed c.1914-c.1920; line drawing of Tudor rose device, enclosing P, 1948-57. *Refs:* Anscombe & Gere; Coysh; Cross; Godden (1966a); G.Godden 'Pilkington's Royal Lancastrian Pottery' in *Apollo* (October 1961); Lomax; L. Thornton 'Pilkington's "Royal Lancastrian" Lustre Pottery' in *The Connoisseur* (May 1970).

Pillivuyt, Louis (d 1840). French porcelain maker who established a factory at Foëcy (Cher) in 1802, with partners Klein and Deville. The business, while not owned by Pillivuyt, was associated with him and his successors throughout the 19th century; he was a partner from 1818 and the firm traded as L. Pillivuyt & Cie until 1822, subsequently working under his name. The factory's output was at first mainly undecorated, although some pieces were garlanded with flowers, touched with gold. Later decorative wares produced under Napoleon III were influenced by Greek wares or Louis XIV style. Charles Pillivuyt, who succeeded his father in 1840, opened branches at Mehun-sur-Yèvre (Cher) in 1840, Ainay-le-Château (Allier) in 1860 and took over existing factories at Noirlac (Cher) 1840 and Nevers (*see* Neppel, P.) in 1866. His firm exhibited in London in 1862 and in Paris in 1867. The output included some pieces with *pâte-sur-pâte* decoration.

Marks include the firm's name; the initials AP or AP & Co over FOECY or FRANCE; a shield, topped by a castle, with MANUFACTURE DE FOECY (CHER). *Refs:* Ernould-Gandouet; Guillebon; Lesur (1967).

Pilsbury, Richard (1830-97). Staffordshire ceramic painter. Pilsbury studied at the school of design in his home town of Burslem. At *Mintons Ltd, 1866-92, and as art director of *Moore Bros from 1892, he executed naturalistic studies of flowers, in later years notably orchids, from sketches he had made in *gouache* from growing specimens. *Refs:* Godden (1961); Jewitt.

Pilz, Otto. *See* Pfeiffer, Max Adolf.

Pineau & Patrus. *See* Angoulême.

Pinder, Bourne & Co. Staffordshire pottery manufacturers, operating the Nile Street Works, Burslem, from c.1860 in the partnership Pinder, Bourne & Hope, also working

the factory at Fountain Place formerly occupied by E.*Wood (1759-1840), and the possessors of some of Wood's moulds for figures and Toby jugs. The firm traded as Pinder, Bourne & Co. from 1862. The output included cream-coloured earthenware for table use, plain, printed under the glaze in blue, sepia or other colours with landscapes, etc., or occasionally hand-painted over printed outlines; gilded tea ware, with printed patterns; vases painted with flowers and cupids and stippled in gold against deep blue grounds; vases, jugs, bowls and *jardinières* in terracotta or earthenware, often painted with sprays of flowers, birds, butterflies, shells, against gilded grounds, or scenes from Greek or Egyptian mythology, predominantly in orange on deep red grounds. Decoration in general featured a wide variety of stylistic influence; a stoneware jug produced in 1877 was decorated with sprigs of Japanese prunus blossom, moulded in low relief and blue glazed, and a handle representing a gnarled stick in form. The firm maintained the use of Enoch Wood's figures and jugs, also producing toilet ware, terracotta garden furniture, electrical and sanitary wares. Thomas Shadford Pinder, great nephew of one of the original partners, became sole proprietor in 1877, entering partnership with H.*Doulton and his brother, James Duneau Doulton in the same year. In 1882, the firm became part of *Doulton & Co., and J.C.*Bailey was appointed general manager.

Marks incorporate the firm's name or initials. *Refs:* Eyles (1980); Godden (1964); Jewitt.

Pine Cone. *See* Roseville Pottery Co.

Pinxton China Factory. English porcelain factory established at Pinxton, Derbyshire, in 1795, and in production from the following year, initially using a paste developed by W.*Billingsley, who remained at the factory until 1799. The output comprised tableware decorated with flowers and landscapes. After decoration of the remaining stock, Billingsley's paste was replaced by a less translucent porcelain, under the management of J.*Cutts, who became a partner in the firm and rented the factory from 1806 until its closure in 1813.

Marks: sometimes *Pinxton* written in full, occasionally the pattern number; also, the crescent and star from the family crest of the founder, John Coke; arrow mark. *Refs: The Connoisseur* (January, February 1963); H.G. Bradley *Ceramics of Derbyshire 1750-1975* (privately published, 1978); C.L. Exley *The Pinxton China Factory* (privately published, 1963); Godden (1966a); Jewitt.

Piper, Enoch (b c.1842) and son, Harry (c.1865-1912). English ceramic artists. Enoch Piper was known as a painter of arms and crests, working with his son Harry at *Coalport until 1892, when both men joined *Doulton & Co. in Burslem. Enoch Piper worked there as a heraldic artist, painting flowers, landscapes and game birds, and decorated some pieces of Luscian ware. Harry Piper was a noted flower painter, specializing in roses, and his work included dessert ware and vases shown in the World's Columbian Exposition in Chicago, 1913. He

also painted birds and studies of fruit, and was responsible for the artistic training of apprentices. He remained with Doulton & Co. until the year of his death.
Refs: Eyles (1980); Godden (1970).

Pisgah Forest Pottery. *See* Stephen, Walter Benjamin.

Pit Pottery. *See* Donyatt.

Pittsburgh Encaustic Tile Co. *See* Star Encaustic Tile Co.

Pirkenhammer. Bohemian porcelain factory established in the village of Hammer by the merchant and landowner Friedrich Hoecke for the production of tableware, tobacco pipes, etc. The works, operated by a small labour force of potters from Thuringia, had two kilns. Hoecke let the factory briefly c.1806 to Ferdinand Cranz (d 1807) in partnership with the Thuringian businessman Friedrich Brothausser. After some years of financial difficulty, Hoecke sold the business in 1811 to Johann Martin Fischer and the scientist Christof Reichenbach. Fischer was succeeded by his widow and, in 1831, his son C.*Fischer, sole owner after Reichenbach's retirement in 1846. Under the Fischer family, the factory produced porcelain that was regarded by contemporary writers as among the best in Bohemia, approaching French wares in the quality and translucency of the paste. Painted vases and tableware were shown in the first exhibition of industrial products at Prague, 1828. In the exhibition of the following year, the jury praised the forms, painting and gilding of the firm's display. The work shown in 1831 included a delicately painted copy of a Chinese porcelain bowl and won the silver medal. By this time, the factory employed over 130 workers. Transfer printing had been introduced in 1829. Decorations in the 1830s included Bohemian landscapes and copies of contemporary engravings; flowers, e.g. pansies, roses, auricula, forget-me-nots, in naturalistic style (on large plates); portraits of Napoleon Bonaparte; cupids and, in useful wares, a form of decoration known as the Viennese grass pattern. Some pieces shown in the Vienna Exhibition, 1835, were decorated with gilded reliefs; the factory won the gold medal at Vienna in 1839. It remained in the hands of Fischer's family after his departure for Zwickau c.1853 and traded under the name of Fischer and his

Pirkenhammer. Cup and saucer made at the Pirkenhammer factory, 20th century. 5.3 cm high.

son-in-law Ludwig van Mieg. In the early 20th century, the output included lithophanes made by J.A.*Wolff.

Marks often incorporate the proprietors' initials or name, and some versions include crossed hammers.
Ref: Danckert; Meyer; Weiss.

Plankenhammer. German porcelain factory established at Plankenhammer in 1908 for the production of household, hotel and gift wares.
Marks often incorporate P and a hammer in a triangle, sometimes with *Plankenhammer* or *Bavaria*.
Refs: Danckert; Weiss.

Plant, John Hugh. English ceramic painter, known for landscapes and animal studies. Plant was apprenticed to *Brown-Westhead, Moore & Co. in the 1870s and studied at the Hanley School of Art. He worked as a landscape painter at *Coalport in the 1880s and then for J.*Wedgwood & Sons Ltd, before joining *Doulton & Co. in Burslem 1902-c.1920. His work included views of Venice, Rome and other Italian cities, a variety of architectural subjects and rustic scenes, as well as nautical subjects (with a wide range of vessels), animals, game birds, fish and feathers.
Signed work includes a view of Exeter Cathedral.
Refs: Godden (1972); M. Messenger *Caughley & Coalport Porcelain* (catalogue of a collection in Clive House Museum, Shrewsbury, 1976); *Collectors' Guide* (August 1974); *see also* Doulton.

Plant, R.H.& S.L., Ltd. Staffordshire porcelain manufacturers. A member of a family who had been potters at Lane End in the 18th century, Richard Hammersley Plant (1847-1904) began work as a child apprentice for Hulse, Nixon & Adderley (*see* Adderleys Ltd.), eventually becoming the firm's manager about c.1880. In 1881, he established the firm R.H. Plant & Co. working with his brother at the Carlisle Works, Longton, where they produced tea and breakfast wares and trinket sets, some for export as well as souvenirs and gifts, advertised in 1885. Plant and his brother moved to the Tuscan China Works, also at Longton, in 1898, working under their joint names. In c.1900, they opened a branch, Plant Bros, at the Stanley Works, Longton, initially producing household ware and later under R.H. Plant's son Harold, with artist Joshua Mellor as art director and designer from c.1912, developing lines of tea, coffee and morning sets in fine bone porcelain.
R.H. Plant was succeeded at the Tuscan Works by his two sons H.J. and A.E. Plant, who, after a limited company was formed in 1915, took responsibility for production. R.H. Plant's brother S.L. Plant was joined by his own son F.S. Plant in managing the sales. The chemist and art director, J.B. Clarke, developed a fine body for hotel and

*John Hugh Plant. Porcelain vase painted with a view of Bodiam Castle by Plant and manufactured by *Doulton & Co. in Burslem, early 20th century. 16 cm high.*

institutional ware which was marketed as Metallised Hotel China; other developments included a pale, tinted porcelain paste, Peach Bloom. Decorative pieces in a fine ivory paste, bearing the arms of the UK and dependencies were introduced by 1906. The firm advertised heraldic ware from 1908 until the mid 1920s, and made a speciality of miniature pieces in World War I. The output in the 1930s included models of animals and crinolined figures. The firm remained under the control of the founder's family, and continues in operation.
Marks: (printed) incorporate RHP & Co (1881-98) or the name *R.H. & S.L. Plant*, often with the trade name *Tuscan China* and sometimes a Staffordshire knot.
Refs: Andrews; Bunt; Godden (1964); Jewitt.

Plant & Gilmore. *See* New Hall.

Pleydell Bouverie, Katherine (1895-1985). English studio potter. After studying at the Central School of Arts & Crafts in London, 1921-23, and under B.*Leach at St Ives, Cornwall, in 1924, she established a pottery at Coleshill, Wiltshire, where she worked with N.*Braden from 1928. Using a wood-fired kiln designed by the Japanese potter, Matsubayashi, she produced domestic wares and vases, often in fluted forms, carrying out the first systematic study in England of the use of wood and plant ash in glazes. She developed a fine range of matt glazes, e.g. white or light grey, using clean, sieved ash from reeds or grasses, greens and browns (various types of wood), blue (lauristinus) in combination with clay and feldspar. Plant pots and bowls were sometimes left unglazed in grey-white or pink stoneware body. Katherine Pleydell Bouverie worked alone from Norah Braden's retirement in 1936. In 1946, she established an oil-fired kiln at Kilmington, Wiltshire.
Her later work comprised unique, functional pieces, generally small in size, that were sometimes decorated with vertical ribbing,

and glazed in muted greys or greens. She used only an electric kiln from c.1960.

Marks: initials or monogram incised or impressed.

Refs: Ceramic Review 28, 30 (1974), 66 (1980), 92 (1985); Rose; Wingfield Digby.

Pløen Erik (b 1925). Norwegian ceramic artist working in the mid 20th century. He experimented with clay and glazes at his own workshop, where he produced stoneware in simple and often angular shapes. Some large vases and bottles were decorated with ribbing and other repeating patterns in relief under streaked or spotted glazes.
Ref: Hettes & Rada; World Ceramics.

Plympton & Robertson. *See* Robertson, James.

Podmore, Walker & Co. Staffordshire earthenware manufacturers, working in Tunstall from c.1825. Thomas Podmore, Thomas Walker and their partner, Enoch Wedgwood, made earthenware of high quality and a variety of bodies marketed as Pearl Stone Ware, Imperial Ironstone China, etc., at potteries in Well Street (c.1834-53), Amicable Street, and Swan Bank in the 1850s. The wares, printed or brightly painted, included dinner and toilet sets, frequently exported. The firm was succeeded by Wedgwood & Co. in 1859, operating at Amicable Street.

Printed marks incorporate P.W & CO. or P.W. & W.
Refs: Collard; Godden (1964); Jewitt.

Poillon Pottery. American pottery established c.1901 in Jersey City by Clara Louise Poillon (c.1936) and Mrs Howard A. Poillon, both experienced ceramic painters. Operating soon afterwards in Woodbridge, New Jersey, they made earthenware with glossy glazes, notably in blue, green or yellow, lustres in orange or gold, and a number of matt glazes. The initial art ware was widely exhibited in New York from 1901. By 1904, the pottery also made tableware, including

Katherine Pleydell Bouverie. Stoneware vase with fluted decoration under a celadon glaze, 1940s. Impressed with a monogram of KPB. 20 cm high.

Léon Pointu. Stoneware vase of gourd form with layered green glazes. 20th century. Mark: POINTU FEC. *30.5 cm.*

tea and coffee pots, breakfast and luncheon sets, lamps and tiles. Terracotta garden pots were carved with relief designs. Clara Poillon retired in 1928.

Marks: *POILLON/Woodbridge/NJ* incised; monogram of CLP, often enclosed within a circle.
Refs: Barber (1976); Callen; Evans; Kovel & Kovel.

Pointon & Co. *See* Norfolk Street Works.

Pointu, Jean (1843-1925) and son Léon (1879-1942). French ceramists, probably descended from a family of potters, who made stoneware at St-Amand-en-Puisaye (Nièvre), in a style resembling that of J. *Carriès.

Marks: J. Pointu, incised rebus or monogram; L. Pointu, incised signature, *Pointu.*
Refs: Baschet; Heuser & Heuser.

Pollard, William (1803-54). English ceramic decorator, working at the *Cambrian Pottery from 1815. Pollard was known for his painting of wild flowers, fruit and landscapes. His flowers, which included wild species, often a group of three dog roses, were arranged in loose bunches, with spaces between the blooms painted in a shadowy, dark purple. After leaving Swansea, Pollard worked as a freelance decorator in Wales and Staffordshire.
Refs: Bemrose; S.W. Fisher *The Decoration of English Porcelain* (Derek Verschoyle, London, 1954); Honey (1948a); Jenkins.

Pollock, Samuel. *See* Coultry Pottery.

Pommier, François. *See* Chevannes, Faïencerie de.

Pommier, Léon. *See* Pouyat family.

Poncet, Pierre. *See* Ardant, Henri.

Ponti, Gio (b 1891). Italian painter and designer. In 1923, he entered into a collaboration with *Richard-Ginori, in which he provided designs for porcelain decoration, giving the firm the right to adapt the patterns by changes in colouring, the addition of other motifs, etc. His work included geometrical *trompe l'oeil* patterns and the figurative series, Le Mie Donne.
Ref: Préaud & Gauthier.

Poole, Thomas. Staffordshire manufacturer of porcelain and earthenwares. Originally a potter's printer, Thomas Poole established his own pottery in 1845, working initially at the High Street, Longton, and then at the Cobden Works, also in Longton. For a while, he worked in the partnership Johnson & Poole. He specialized in domestic ware for sale in England and abroad.

Under Poole's son, also named Thomas, who took over c.1865, the firm pioneered such technical developments as steam-heated driers for flatware, adopted oil firing in the 1920s, and introduced teasets with 21 pieces, instead of the 40 or so pieces formerly expected. Horace Poole (b c.1886), who had joined the firm in 1902 and trained at the factory, acquired the Longton company, Gladstone China, in 1937. In the early 1950s, the two companies united under the title Royal Staffordshire China, which the Poole firm had used as a trade name for bone porcelain since the early 19th century, with the Gladstone works run by Peter Poole and the Cobden works remaining under the control of Raymond Poole, son of Horace. The output comprised tea and dinner services, often with litho-printed decoration.

A variety of marks, printed, often incorporate *Royal Stafford China*, and sometimes the name of style or body.
Refs: Bunt; Godden (1964); Jewitt.

Poole Pottery Ltd. *See* Carter & Co.; Carter Stabler & Adams.

*William Pollard. Dish painted with rose, erica, strawberries and other plants, made at the *Cambrian Pottery, c.1820. 20.5 cm wide.*

Poor, Henry Varnum (1888-1971). American artist, ceramic designer and decorator, born in Chapman, Kansas. Poor studied economics and art at Stanford University in California and later at the Slade School of Fine Art, London, where he was influenced by Cubist art in R.*Fry's First Impressionist Exhibition at the Grafton Gallery in 1910. He subsequently studied at the Académie Julian in Paris. On his return to America in 1912, he taught at Stanford and in the Mark Hopkins Art Institute in San Francisco. Poor turned from painting to the design and decoration of pottery in 1923, first exhibiting in New York later that year. After 1933, he worked less often in ceramics. An oval earthenware plate painted with a nude in a waterside setting was among the work exhibited by the Syracuse Museum of Fine Arts in 1938. His book on pottery, *From Mud to Immortality*, expresses his opinions on ceramic aesthetics.
Refs: 'Ceramics by Poor at the Rehr Galleries' in *Art Digest* 22 (15th December 1947); Clark & Hughto; 'Henry Varnum Poor 1888-1970' in *Craft Horizons* 31 (April 1971); *International Exhibition of Ceramic Art* (Metropolitan Museum of Art and American Federation of Arts, New York, 1928); H.V. Poor *A Book of Pottery: from Mud to Immortality* (Prentice-Hall, Englewood Cliffs, New Jersey, 1954 or 1958), and foreword in *Ceramic International Exhibition* (catalogue, Syracuse Museum of Fine Arts, Syracuse, New York, 1958).

Pope, Frank. English ceramic modeller and designer, working for *Doulton & Co. in Lambeth from his start as an assistant in 1880 until 1923. He is noted for vases boldly decorated with natural forms or, occasionally, grotesque animals applied in relief, and for vases modelled in the shape of gourds. He worked with M.V.*Marshall and H.*Simeon on the production of pieces in mottled, brown Leopard Skin stoneware c.1910. Many designs were slip-cast and issued in editions, but Pope executed a number of individual pieces.
Mark: initials F.C.P.
Refs: see Doulton & Co.

Popov, Alexei Gavrilovich (d 1850s). Russian porcelain maker, formerly a merchant engaged in trade with China. In 1811, Popov took over the factory established near Moscow in 1806 by Karl Melli. He operated it

Alexei Popov. Display cup, cover and stand painted with a view of St Basil's, Moscow, and country landscapes. Marked with AP in Cyrillic characters. 13 cm high.

until his death in the late 1850s, assisted by his son, Dmitri. The firm made a limited number of high-quality pieces for connoisseurs as well as profitable, mass-produced, brightly painted tea services for country taverns. The specialities included bowls decorated in relief with flowers and fruit, large ceremonial dishes with bright garlands of flowers and gilded eagles, often on a blue ground, and decorative tableware. Painted decoration (e.g. portraits of heroes and battle scenes developed during the war of 1812, and scenes of Russian life) was detailed and careful. A. Popov established a laboratory for the development of new colours; the firm was noted for deep blue and green grounds, a light blue, and a chestnut brown which was used in the painting of rococo shapes. A range of cups were decorated with red roses against a dark blue ground. Figures, which constituted Popov's most renowned output, at first imitated those produced at the Imperial Factory at *St Petersburg, although the firm's work in general was designed for a more specifically Russian taste than the sophisticated, cosmopolitan style of the Imperial Factory. Subsequent figures portrayed romantic characters from the St Petersburg stage or novels (e.g. St Pierre's *Paul et Virginie*), often with floral decoration on the base, and painted and finished with great care. In the 1830s and 1840s, the figures represented street vendors, dancing peasants, etc., later reflecting the struggle of serfs for freedom. A. Popov was succeeded by his children Dmitri and Tatiana, and then Dmitri's sons, Vasilii, Ivan, Aleksei and Nikolai. An English inspiration that was sometimes apparent in Popov's style (as in a copy of a Chelsea perfume bottle) has been attributed to the influence of Caroline Southee, the American wife of Nikolai Popov.
The factory was purchased in the 1860s by the merchant Zhukov, who sold it to Rudolf

Fedorovich Schroeder in 1872. The subsequent owner, Khalatov, sold the factory to Fomichev, who closed it in 1875. The moulds for plates and figures were bought by I.A.*Ikonnikov for reproduction at his factory.
Marks: usually Cyrillic monogram of AP in underglaze blue, black, or occasionally impressed. Popov's heirs used the inscription 'Popov's' in Cyrillic script.
Refs: B. Alekseev *Porcelain* (In Russian, Kuskovo, Moscow, 1958); *Catalogue of the Third International Art Exhibition* (Victoria & Albert Museum, London, 1962); *The Connoisseur* 96 (1935); Emme; Hare; Ivanova; Nikiforova; Ross; Rozenburgh; Saltykov.

Popp, Ernst. *See* Prague.

Poppelsdorf. German faience factory established in the mid 18th century at Poppelsdorf, near Bonn (Rhineland), and acquired in 1840 by Ludwig Wessel, a local glass and pottery retailer. Wessel was succeeded by his son Franz Joseph and in 1868 by his grandsons Nikolaus Joseph (d 1888) and Karl Ludwig. The firm continued trading under the name of Wessel, and its output consisted of white or cream-coloured earthenware and glazed wall plaques.
Marks incorporate the initials LW sometimes the place name.
Refs: Honey (1952); M. Weisser *Jugendstilfliesen* (Verlag J.H. Schmalfeldt & Co., Bremen, 1978).

Porcelain League of Cincinnati. *See* Cincinnati Pottery Club.

Porcelaine de Paris. *See* Clauss family.

Porcelaine Limousine, La. *See* Redon, Martial.

Porceleyne Fles, De. Dutch ceramics factory operating from the mid 17th century; the only important Delft factory to survive well into the 19th century. In operation under the Piccardt family, the business was sold in 1876 by the owner Cornelius Tulk, who had

*Frank Pope. Sauceboat made at the *Doulton & Co. Lambeth workshop and probably modelled by Pope. Marked with monogram of EB [probably Ethel Bard]. 15.5 cm high.*

worked as a painter at the factory since 1813 and continued to do so until 1885. The output consisted of plaques decorated after paintings by old masters and leading contemporary Dutch artists. Under the ownership of J. *Thooft (1876-84), the tradition of underglaze painting in earthenware was revived (1876). Thooft's aim was to revive the Dutch ceramics industry by applying industrial processes evolved in England. Helped by Tulk, he experimented with blue-painted ware (either copied from 17th-century originals or to original designs), which formed the main output from the late 1890s to emulate earlier delftware with overglaze painting on a tin glaze, to designs by A.*Le Comte (art director, 1877-1919) and other factory painters. However, Le Comte introduced other lines: Berbas lustre ware (1890), inspired by contemporary interest in Japanese styles and techniques; Jacoba ware (1897), with a red-brown body, abstract decoration and metallic glazes, which often only partially cover the piece, applied after a biscuit firing; biscuit porcelain coloured with pink, green and blue slips and decorated with incised lines filled with gold. H.W. Mauser, technical director from the mid 1890s, evolved a range of decorative tiles, matt glazed or painted in enamels, and shaped to follow the lines of the design. He also developed glazes for a line called Delftware, with white slip coating painted predominantly in blue, green, and red pigments which flowed in a transparent glaze; designs were by Leo Senf. Designers of tile mosaics included J.*Toorop. Experimentation in glazes in the early 20th century

Porsgrund. Porcelain vase painted in pale colours with bullfinches and white berries over a field of mushrooms with snails at the base. Marked Porsgrund Norge *and the artist's monogram* Th H. *30.5 cm high.*

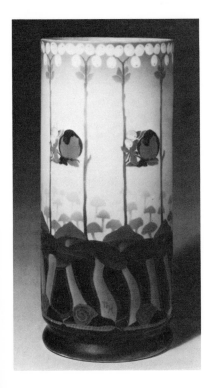

resulted in a range of high-quality *flambé* ware and gold and silver lustres. A. Labouchère entered the business in 1881, became a partner in 1884 (when the firm began trading as Thooft & Labouchère) and succeeded Thooft in 1890. The business passed to a company of shareholders in 1903, later trading as NV Koninkliche Delftsch-Aardewerkfabriek 'De Porceleyne Fles'. It is still in operation.

Marks include PICCARDT/DELFT stamped in relief; a flask (*fles*) in outline over Delft; initials T/L; Le Comte's monogram. Letters A-Z indicate the years of manufacture 1879-1904, AA-AZ 1905-1930, and BA through the alphabet from 1931.
Refs: Honey (1952); J. Ranijn *Geschiedenis van een Delftse Fabriek* (catalogue, Leeuwarden, 1970; Amersfoort, 1974); Singelenberg-van der Meer; van Straaten; E.J. van Straaten *The Revival of Dutch Ceramics 1876-1940* (catalogue, West Midlands Area Museum Service 1983).

Porsgrund. Norwegian porcelain factory, Porsgrunds Porselaensfabrik, established in 1887. The factory followed the traditional styles of other European makers in the production of hard-paste porcelain until individual lines in tableware were developed in the mid 1920s by art director N. *Gulbrandsen, who worked on functionalist principles.
    Mark: an arrow and PP, sometimes in a circle with *Porsgrund/Norge*.
Refs: Danckert; Weiss.

Portanier, Gilbert (b 1926). French artist potter, born in Cannes. Portanier studied architecture and painting at the Ecole des Beaux-Arts in Paris before going on to *Vallauris in 1948, when he established his own pottery. His work includes wall panels, dishes, vases, and sculptural pieces in painted tinglaze. He has provided designs for production as part of the *Rosenthal firm's Studio Line.
Ref: Céramique française contemporaine.

Port Arthur Pottery. Australian pottery established at the convict settlement of Port Arthur, Tasmania, in the 1830s for the manufacture of bricks, tiles and, later, flowerpots and simple utilitarian wares. After the convicts left in 1877, James Price (c.1835-1912) established a pottery there, producing bricks, pipes, tiles, flowerpots and a range of art pottery.
Ref: R. Hamilton *Port Arthur Pottery* (Launceston, 1982).

Port Dundas Pottery Co. Scottish pottery established by W.*Johnston in the partnership John Forsyth & Co. at Port Dundas, an industrial area to the north of Glasgow, in 1815 for the manufacture of stoneware. The title Port Dundas Pottery Co. was adopted by Johnston and Forsyth at a new pottery built nearby in 1821. The output of salt-glazed stoneware consisted mainly of chemical storage jars, spirit bottles, etc., a range of domestic ware, and firebrick. After its sale in 1826, the pottery traded as James Murray & Co. until its closure in 1833. The site then became a soapworks.
    Johnston transferred the Port Dundas Pottery Co. to a new pottery which he had built in East Milton Street by 1828. Under new owners Robert Cochran, James Couper

and Johnston's former partner, John McCall, briefly in 1835, and subsequently George Duncan (d 1841), succeeded by his wife Helen, the pottery continued production of a range of saltglaze, including thrown waterpipes. J.*Miller, manager from the 1840s and partner in the Port Dundas Pottery Co. from 1856, modernized and enlarged the works, introducing steam power for throwing and other processes, and reducing the number of firings necessary for dipped ware. He introduced a light-coloured glaze in the 1850s for use on beer bottles, etc. His other developments include a process of printing marks, labels, etc., on the stoneware body without the need for a previous biscuit firing. Miller's output consisted of cooking pots, storage jars, spirit bottles and barrels, some with lavish decoration; caneware or brown-glazed teapots, earthenware, cream jugs, sugar bowls, etc.; pharmaceutical ware. A separate company, the Crown Filter Co., established 1874 in part of the works, made a wide range of charcoal water filters in sizes holding from 36 to over 136 litres. Some were adapted to withstand extremes in climate and sold for ships' use or exported to Australia, New Zealand, America, India and the Far East. The filters were produced, many with rich decoration applied in relief, until the closure of the entire works in 1930.
    Marks: impressed, painted or printed, include PORT DUNDAS/GLASGOW POTTERY.
Ref: Jewitt.

Portland Pottery Ltd. *See* Ridgway Potteries Ltd.

Portmeirion Potteries. *See* Gray, A.E., Ltd.

Portneuf ware. Earthenware, including bowls, with stamped or stencilled decoration, sometimes applied with a sponge (*see* sponged ware), imported into Canada between c.1840 and c.1920 and associated with the town of Portneuf, near Quebec city. Decorative motifs included a variety of flowers, (harebells, convolvulus, fuchsia, daisies, thistles, etc.), animals (deer, rabbits, cows, goats, partridges, turkeys, peacocks, robins and other birds), or rosettes and other stylized shapes. The colours were bright—pinks, blues, greens, mauve, rust, browns and yellows. The ware was unmarked, but a number of border designs, together with the painted or printed patterns with which they sometimes occur, suggest that the ware was produced in Scotland, e.g. at *Bo'ness.
Refs: Collard; G. Cruickshank *Scottish Spongeware* (Scottish Pottery Studies, No 1, privately published, Edinburgh, 1982); R. Finlayson 'Mystery of the Lost Potteries' in *Canadian Collector* Vol I No 3 (1966); Jewitt; McVeigh; *Portrait Pottery and Other Early Wares* (Don Mills, Canada, 1972).

Portobello Pottery. Scottish pottery established, after the discovery of suitable clay in 1767, at Portobello (then called Brickfield), by the land's owner, architect and developer, William Jameson (d 1814). In 1790, the pottery advertised bricks and tiles, pipes, chimney cowls, brown ware and creamware. Cookson & Jardine, tenants in 1796, introduced white stoneware, while Jameson retained the production of brick and tiles.

Thomas Rathbone (d 1836), formerly manager or foreman at the *Bo'ness Pottery (c.1800), leased the works, 1810, in the name of his brother-in-law Thomas Yoole, who had been the tenant for two years previously, and the firm then traded as Thomas Rathbone & Co. He produced quantities of creamware and stoneware, which included a range of figures based on local characters, fishwives, highlanders, soldiers and sailors; models of birds, domestic animals, lions in creamware with splashes of underglaze colour; inscribed presentation pieces for christenings, birthdays and other family occasions. Until the 1830s, the creamware was characterized by a yellowish glaze, relatively free from crazing; afterwards the ware became gradually whiter. Low temperature pigments provided a fairly varied palette for decoration, often of stylized flowers. In the early 19th century, pink lustre was first used in narrow bands.

Rathbone owned the pottery from 1822. He was succeeded by Rathbone Brothers and, later, Samuel Rathbone, until the closure of the works in 1851. The pottery re-opened on a reduced scale in 1856.

In 1826, the brothers, Hugh and Arthur Cornwall, took over nearby premises (occupied from 1820 by George Morrison) for the manufacture of stoneware, mainly brown saltglaze, occasionally with white sprigged decoration. The pottery continued under various owners until the 1960s.
Refs: Fleming; McVeigh.

Port Richmond Pottery Co. *See* Jeffords, J.E., & Co.

Poskochin, Sergei. Russian earthenware maker working 1817-42 at a factory established earlier in the 19th century at the village of Morye in the province of St Petersburg. Poskochin's products were of high quality and resembled those of the *Kiev-Mezhegorye factory, including coloured earthenware bodies and agate ware, as well as copies of English creamware of the 18th century and glazed adaptations of Wedgwood blue jasper ware showing hunting scenes, etc. He produced a variety of pieces: vases, clock cases, *chinoiserie* figures with moving limbs, tongues and heads, and figures representing armed knights, seated men, shoe sellers, Falstaff, etc., as well as a range of table and heat-resistant kitchen wares. His decoration included painting in enamel colours with designs of flowers and insects; lavish gilding; lustre glazes; flowers; classical figure groups or hunting scenes in relief, and relief plant designs with additional touches of colour. The factory won a prize at the first exhibition of Russian factories in 1829. Poskochin sold the business to Countess Golenischeva-Kutusova in 1842. After a break in production, a similar output was resumed in 1845 and continued by several tenants under the ownership of Baron Korf, 1851-87, with considerable loss in quality. After 1887, only porcelain was produced.

Marks incorporate the name Poskochin in Cyrillic characters; Poskochin's name was retained in an oval mark used by Goleni-scheva-Kutusova, who also marked the work with her own name.
Refs: Bubnova; Lukomsky; Rozembergh.

Possil Pottery Co. *See* Nautilus Porcelain Co.

Pössneck. German porcelain factory established at Pössneck, Thuringia, in 1800 by Tobias Albert (d 1826), formerly a porcelain painter at Volkstedt, and later owner of the *Gera factory. In 1804, Albert sold the works to Albrecht Wilhelm Ernst Conta (d 1819), a physician in Pössneck, and porcelain manufacturer Christian Gotthelf Böhme. The firm made everyday tableware as well as ornamental pieces and novelties. The work was predominantly in classical shapes, with landscapes in iron red or black, medallions containing views of buildings, etc., animals (e.g. deer), hunting scenes, or bunches of flowers. Borders in gold or green included a repeating motif of leaves arranged in arrowhead shape and edgings of classical inspiration. In 1814, the firm became part of a trust instigated by the *Greiner family working in Limbach, that united with porcelain factories operating in the Thuringian forest.

Böhme died soon after Conta, and his share in the business passed to Conta's heirs in 1823. The brothers Carl Hermann and Bernhard Conta took over the factory in 1836. The firm is noted for the production of *fairings, made chiefly c.1860-c.1890 and once attributed to the firm Springer & Co. in *Elbogen, Bohemia. Some small groups, intended for use as match holders, had a small patch of the surface roughened for striking. The factory remained in the hands of the Conta family until the 20th century; it began to fail in 1937 and subsequently ceased operation.

A porcelain decorating studio trading under the name of Louis Huth was in operation at Pössneck from 1894 until c.1920.

Factory marks include P or a shield bearing a mailed arm brandishing a dagger. Louis Huth marked decoration with a tall hat and H or SAXE and LH.
Refs: Danckert; Scherf; Weiss.

Poster. *See* Owens, John B.

Poterie Caffin. *See* Mérillon, Jean.

pot lids. Decorative earthenware covers produced in England from the mid 19th century for the containers of bear-grease hair dressing and, later, other toilet preparations, relishes or preserves. The lids ranged in size from under 4 cm in diameter

pot lid. A lid showing Pegwell Bay.
S. Banger, whose name appears on the shop,
was a maker of shrimp sauce.

for pots of rouge or lip salve to about 15 cm in diameter for those containing paste, etc.

The main producers included F.& R. *Pratt & Co.; Ridgway, Bates & Co., followed by *Brown-Westhead, Moore & Co.; T., J.& J.*Mayer and their successors at the Dale Hall Works, Bates, Elliot & Co.; H.G. & D.*Kirkham, buyers of engraved plates used by the Mayer brothers and Bates, Elliot & Co.; G.L.*Ashworth & Bros; Morgan *Wood & Co.; W. Smith & Co.

Although Pratt's earliest examples were printed in two colours (blue and red), and painted with extra colour, the main output of lids was transfer-printed in full colour after the arrival of J.*Austin at Pratt's by 1847. Austin's examples are characterized by the soft effect achieved with a brown key print; black, when needed in one of his designs, was made by the superimposition of blue on brown. Other firms normally used black key prints, with a harsher result. Glazes were often crazed, with consequent staining of the porous white earthenware body underneath.

The designs, of which over 400 have been identified, included scenes featuring bears, birds, dogs and other animals, portraits of the Royal family and well-known personalities, naval and military events, international exhibitions, London scenes and landmarks in Europe, the West Indies and the Far East, figure subjects, including allegorical and genre scenes, sports, children's activities, country scenes, courting couples, women at their toilet, Greek, Etruscan and Roman scenes; a series concerned with Shakespeare's work and places associated with him; flowers and fruit, and a series inspired by the Kent fishing centre of Pegwell Bay, produced by the Mayers from 1850 for pots containing shrimp paste. Some designs were used on both tableware and pot lids. Several proprietary products, particularly cold cream, toothpaste, shaving cream and some preserves, were covered with lids that bore only lettering, and some pictorial designs were accompanied by a title.

Borders, such as lines or beading were used by several firms, but a line of dots outside a thin unbroken line, or Austin's small, repeating geometrical motifs, a scroll-like decoration, and angularly twisted lines are associated with Pratt's, while the Dale Hall makers frequently used borders of small leaf motifs or *fleurs-de-lis*.

Although the peak of production occurred 1850-70, pot lids were made until the mid 20th century to satisfy the demand of collectors. Late reproductions mainly suffered from deficiencies in register and colour balance, and loss of detail due to worn plates.
Refs: H.G. Clarke *Colour-Printed Pictures of the 19th Century on Staffordshire Pottery* (London, 1924), *The Pot Lid Book* (London, 1931), *Underglaze Colour Picture Prints on Staffordshire Pottery* (London, 1949); Godden (1966b); Rhead; W. Turner *Transfer Printing on Enamels, Porcelain & Pottery* (London, 1907); Williams-Wood.

Potschappel. German porcelain factory established by Carl Thieme in 1872 at Potschappel (Saxony). The firm made art and luxury porcelain decorated by hand and, initially (but no longer), ordinary tableware. The firm now works under the name of the national Saxon porcelain factory at Dresden.

A variety of marks include LL crossed enclosing CT and topped with a crown; a bee and a hive; a group of leaves with CT. The present cypher is formed by P and T in script, with *Dresden*.
Refs: Danckert; Mankowitz & Haggar; Weiss.

Potters' Art Guilds. *See* Compton Pottery.

Potts, Anne B. (b c.1918). English ceramic modeller, trained under G.M.*Forsyth and W.*Ruscoe at the Burslem School of Art, 1933-37. Anne Potts was engaged to run the newly opened studio pottery department at *Bullers Ltd, c.1933. Her work includes figures, groups and animal models in rolled clay and, rarely, vases. She remained with the firm until shortly after her marriage in 1939. She worked at the *Fulham Pottery Ltd in the early 1940s and subsequently continued work as a modeller.

Mark: (when used) her signature, *Anne B. Potts*, incised, sometimes in a cartouche with *Made in England/by Bullers*.
Ref: Art Among the Insulators, the Bullers Studio (catalogue, Gladstone Pottery Museum, Stoke-on-Trent, 1977).

Pouchol, Paul. French painter, decorator and ceramist, a pupil of M.*Dufrêne. Pouchol exhibited at the Salon des Indépendants in 1935. He produced decorative tinglaze, including figures and large sculptural pieces, after establishing a workshop in 1942. Some work was commissioned by Süe et Mare (Compagnie des Artistes Français).
Refs: Bénézit; Faré;

Poulsen, Christian. Danish potter working at his own studio in Lyngby by the 1950s. He made stoneware bowls, vases, etc., in bold, simple shapes with a wide range of glazes in black, white, turquoise, yellowish brown and

Anne Potts. Earthenware group, Gossips, made at the Burslem School of Art, 1932.

Pouyat family. Pieces from a dessert service painted en grisaille *with a yellow ground and gilt borders of berried foliage. Made by Pouyat and Russinger, early 19th century.*

other, often delicate, shades; a grey/white glaze sometimes accompanies simple motifs carried out in red. Tea ware in brownish red stoneware, unglazed except for a lining and exterior touches of black glaze, includes stacking teapots and hot water pots.
Ref: Hiort.

Poulson, Joseph. *See* Mintons Ltd.

Poulson, Thomas. *See* Ferrybridge or Knottingley Pottery.

Pountney, John D. *See* Bristol Pottery.

Pouyat family. French porcelain manufacturers. François Pouyat (1754-1838), the owner of several clay deposits and of clay works in Haute-Vienne (at Isle, Saint-Yrieix and later Saint-Léonard); he became partner (1800) and successor (1808) of Laurentius Russinger at the Locré factory (Manufacture de la *Courtille) in Paris, where he was followed by his sons Jean-Baptiste Pouyat (1776-1849), Léonard Pouyat (d 1845) and Jean Pouyat-Duvignaud (d 1849), who formed a partnership in 1816 with the owner of a former glassworks at Fours (Nièvre), purchasing the workshop four years later. Under the direction of Léonard Pouyat until 1845, the workshop produced porcelain for decoration in Paris; it continued in operation until 1865. After the sale of the Locré works in 1823, Jean Pouyat remained responsible for sales in Paris of the work made at Fours, while Jean-Baptiste is thought to have returned in 1824 to assist his father in Limoges.

A small Limoges factory, established by François Pouyat in 1832, was enlarged under Jean-Baptiste until it employed 127 workers in 1844. Succeeded by his sons, Emile (1806-92), head of the factory from 1849 till 1883 and trained in the Locré factory, Louis (b 1809) and Léonard-Eugène (1817-76), Jean-Baptiste Pouyat made porcelain which was known for the exceptional whiteness of the paste and an even texture that was compared with marble; pieces not left in the white were enamelled and gilded, or painted under the glaze. In 1855, the firm exhibited in Paris the Ceres desert service, made in fine, white paste with trails of ivy in *intaglio*

relief on the rims (which were edged with scrolls and ears of wheat) and, at the centre of plates and on dishes, fruit in biscuit relief. P.*Comoléra, modeller of the service, provided designs for the Pouyat factory over a period of 20 years. A service in white with perforated decoration filled with translucent enamel, the work of A.-L.*Dammouse, formed part of the firm's display in the Paris Exposition, 1878. Another service, Aurore, had lacework and enamelled decoration with mauresque elements in style. Work exhibited in 1886 included pieces with barbotine landscapes as well as blue and white ware with relief ornament lavishly gilded.

Jean-Baptiste Pouyat and his sons also inherited a clayworks and porcelain workshop, established at Saint-Léonard in the early 1820s and bought by François Pouyat in 1835. In 1883, Emile and Louis Pouyat formed La Céramique S.A., taking into their firm Baron de la Bastide and his brothers, Léon (d 1895) and Alfred Lemaigre-Dubreuil, who had both married daughters of Louis Pouyat. The claymill and factory at Saint-Léonard were sold in 1904 to Léon Pommier (d 1914), and by Pommier's widow to La Société la Porcelainerie de la Haute-Vienne. W.*Guérin bought the Pouyat Limoges factory in 1911.

Marks: versions of initials J P and L in chrome green from 1851, chrome green or impressed c.1876; with *France* c.1890; *J. Pouyat* in a laurel wreath over the glaze.
Refs: Chavagnac & Grollier; d'Albis & Romanet; Ernould-Gandouet; Guillebon; Lesur (1967).

Powder Blue. *See* Moorcroft, William.

Powder Blue. *See* Wedgwood, J., & Sons Ltd.

Powell, Alfred (d 1960) and Louise. English designers and decorators, who carried out work in ceramics from c.1904 until the late 1940s. Alfred Powell, an architect, and his wife, an embroiderer and the grand-daughter of E.*Lessore, painted pottery for the *Wedgwood factory from c.1904. Also training company artists, they introduced a new style of freehand work and assisted in the re-establishment of a department for hand painting in the 1920s. Their patterns in bright enamels or platinum lustre included flowers and foliage echoing the factory's early sprigged borders, and rich, scrolled foliage, sometimes surrounding animals or birds inspired by the decorative designs of

Alfred and Louise L. Powell. Earthenware mug with blue and purple lustre made c.1920 by J.*Wedgwood & Sons Ltd. Marks include monogram of LP.

W.*Morris, pastoral scenes, etc. Alfred Powell decorated plaques in the 1930s and 1940s with designs that included a view of Barlaston Hall, and scenes of ships, animals and birds. Some of the couple's painting was carried out in their own London studios at Millwall and subsequently at Red Lion Square, Bloomsbury, where they also made vases, bowls and jugs in simple shapes decorated with lustres. They also experimented with painting on tinglaze.

Marks: heart-shaped leaf with monograms AP or LP, painted; Wedgwood ware bears factory mark.
Refs: Anscombe & Gere; Batkin; Callen; Haslam (1975, 1977); Reilly & Savage.

Powell, Edward (1862-95). Painter of ferns and butterfly subjects at the *Worcester Royal Porcelain Co. from 1878.
Ref: Sandon (1978a).

Powell, William (b 1878). Porcelain painter working for the *Worcester Royal Porcelain

Michael Powolny. Table centrepiece designed by Powolny and made at the *Wiener Keramik workshop. 20.5 cm high.

Co. 1900-50. Powell specialized in paintings of flowers and British birds.
Ref: Sandon (1978a).

Powell, William. Potter and glass cutter working in Bristol, 1816-54. After lengthy experiments at his pottery in Temple Gate to improve the body and glaze of utilitarian brown stoneware, Powell succeeded by 1835 in producing a ware with hard body and a glaze that was resistant to acid (*see* Bristol ware). His firm subsequently produced this 'improved stone ware' in huge quantities. Powell's output included filters, bottles, jars, large jugs and other kitchen ware, footwarmers, and occasionally vases. He was succeeded by his sons, and the firm became Price, Powell & Co. after its sale to Price, Sons & Co. in 1906.

Impressed marks include POWELL/BRISTOL in an oval outline; BRISTOL/TEMPLE/GATE POTTERY, from 1830.
Refs: Godden (1964); Jewitt; Oswald; Owen; Pountney.

Powers & Edmands. *See* Edmands, Barnabas.

Pownall, William. *See* Mintons Ltd.

Powolny, Michael (1871-54). Austrian sculptor and ceramist, the son of a stovemaker at Judenburg, Steiermark, trained at the Fachschule für Tonindustrie, Znaim (1891-94) and the Kunstgewerbeschule in Vienna (1894-1901). In 1897 he was a co-founder of the Vienna Secession. After working independently as a sculptor (1900-03), he founded *Wiener Keramik with B.*Löffler in 1905, selling work through the Wiener Werkstätte. Powolny is associated with white faience painted in black; he also made pieces with coloured decoration, e.g. figures of children holding garlands, bundles of fruit, etc., the child glazed and undecorated, the flowers or fruit brightly painted. Powolny was a teacher at the Kunstgewerbeschule in Vienna from 1912. He was succeeded as head of the pottery department by R. *Obsieger in 1932, but went on to run the modelling course. He retired in 1936.

Marks: monograms of MP, painted or impressed.
Refs: Neuwirth (1974a); L.W. Rochowanski *Wiener Keramik* (Vienna, 1923).

Poynter, Maude (1869-1945). Tasmanian artist potter, born in Victoria, Australia. After studying painting in England before 1914, and pottery at Kingston-upon-Thames School of Art, she returned in 1918 to Tasmania, where she established a pottery at her home near Bothwell. Producing ceramics (mainly as a hobby) until the mid 1930s, she experimented in equipment and techniques. Her work included vases and bowls, which had incised and painted flowers, landscapes, etc., or relied for decorative effect on shaded glazes.

Maude Poynter left to live in Hobart in 1935, succeeded at the Bothwell workshop by her cousin Violet Mace (1890-1968), who had joined her as a pupil and studied for a time at the Camberwell School of Art in London. Violet Mace continued the use of incised patterns (e.g. wrens deeply incised and coloured in blue on a vase dated 1926)

and coloured glazes (e.g. turquoise in 1928).

Mylie Peppin (b 1907), a pupil of Maude Poynter, concentrated on functional wares with carved or painted oxide patterns.
Ref: Graham; J. Holmes *Early Tasmanian Pottery 1920-1950* (Tasmanian College of Advanced Education, Hobart, n.d.).

Prague. Bohemian earthenware and porcelain manufacturer established in 1793 by the Prague businessman, Carl Kunerle, and Joseph Emanuel Hübel (d 1825) in partnership with Johann Wenzel Kunerle and Josef Ignaz Lange, initially for the production of creamware. By the early 19th century, their firm occupied a factory employing about 200 workers, and produced heat-resistant ware of high quality after English styles, and figures (c.1800) which include a series of apostles inspired by Meissen. However, by 1818 the business was in serious difficulties and employed only nine workers making mainly household wares. Hübel, having been bought out of the firm for a short time, recovered it with his son, who was in 1835 to let the factory to Martin Saumer and a former manager of the *Klösterle factory, Karl Wolff. Karl Ludwig Kriegel (d 1862), who became a director and succeeded Saumer in the partnership with Wolff, 1837-41, abandoned the production of creamware in favour of porcelain. The varied output included tea and coffee sets, soup tureens, toilet sets, writing sets, clock cases, paperweights and figures; painted decoration and gilding were lavish. The sculptor, Ernst Popp, was artistic director. The Vienna wholesaler Emanuel Hofmanstahl, a financial backer of the firm since 1839, became a director after removal to Smichow in 1841. The business became a joint stock company in 1852. The factory's subsequent work mainly consisted of tableware for restaurants, hotels, etc.

Marks include the initial P; *Prag* or *Prager*; *Hübel in Prag*; *K & C/Prag.*
Refs: Danckert; Meyer; Weiss.

Pratt, F.& R., & Co. Staffordshire potters. In the early 19th century Felix Pratt (1780-1859) and his brother Richard succeeded their father, William Pratt (1753-99), at the Fenton Potteries (which he had established in 1774), producing earthenware for domestic and pharmaceutical use. They produced terracotta in a fine, rich red body, frequently painted in enamel, e.g. with a range of designs after illustrations for the *Iliad* by the sculptor and designer, John Flaxman. Clock cases, a speciality, were painted all over with brightly coloured designs resembling mosaic. The firm won a silver medal from the Society of Arts in 1848 for a pair of vases 1.75 metres in height (the largest made in terracotta up to that time), which were bought by Albert, Prince Consort.

F.& R. Pratt made figures, busts and other pieces in a creamy, lightweight earthenware body, brightly decorated under the glaze and known as *Pratt ware; however, the company became particularly associated with polychrome underglaze printing (notably by J.*Austin) used in the decoration of *pot lids. Felix Edwards Pratt (1813-94), who had joined the firm in 1828, took out a patent for improvements in the manufacture of pot lids in 1847. On tea and dessert services, which were made in semi-porcelain, printed decoration was bordered with a variety of ground colours: blue, lilac, pink, magenta, maroon, and a mottled malachite green. After 1880, wide, printed bands of geometrical motifs, oak leaves, etc., were used. Plaques or flat dishes with reproductions of paintings by Thomas Gainsborough, William Mulready, Sir David Wilkie, and other artists, featured in the firm's display at the Great Exhibition (1851) together with vases, a cheese dish, a bread plate and box covers. American views were among patterns exhibited in New York (1853), Philadelphia Centennial Exhibition (1876) and World's Columbian Exposition, Chicago (1893).

F.E. Pratt and his brother, Thomas, who was works manager, succeeded their father Felix Pratt. The firm continued under the same name, merging with Cauldon Potteries Ltd (*see* Brown-Westhead, Moore & Co.) c.1925.

Marks: printed versions incorporate the name *Pratt*, or initials F.&R. P.; a backstamp of a crown with *Manufacturers to H.R.H. Prince*/*F.& R. Pratt*, or *Patronised by the Prince Consort*. Terracotta marked F.& R. PRATT FENTON impressed. Also: F.& R. PRATT & CO/ORIGINAL/ENGRAVED/PRINTINGS/MADE IN ENGLAND/AT THE/ROYAL CAULDRON/FACTORY/ *Est 1774* (1930s printed mark incorporating a crown).
Refs: H.G. Clarke *The Pictorial Pot Lid Book* (Courier Press, London, 1970); Godden (1966a); Jewitt; L.W. Watkins 'Pratt's Colour Prints on Staffordshire Ware' in Atterbury (1980); Williams-Wood.

Pratt, Henry Lark (1805-73). English painter and porcelain decorator. Pratt was apprenticed at the factory in Nottingham Road, *Derby, as a landscape painter, and worked in a style influenced by the work of D.*Lucas, but used a softer range of colours. His other subjects included animals. While employed at the factory, he also worked on the cleaning and restoration of paintings in Derby. He then worked for *Mintons Ltd, 1830-40, as a painter of landscapes and views, leaving to become an illustrator. He received a commission from the publishers Chapman & Hall to sketch stately homes in Staffordshire, Cheshire and Derbyshire. He worked freelance as a painter of pieces produced at the Minton factory from c.1861. His son, Henry Pratt (c.1840-1914), was the painter of a view of Stafenhill Ferry near Burton-on-Trent on a teapot made at *Coalport, and died in Derby.
Refs: obituary in *Staffordshire Evening Sentinel* (8th March 1873); *see also* Derby; Mintons Ltd.

Pratt & Abson. *See* Eagle Pottery.

Pratt ware. English earthenware painted, sponged or stippled with high-temperature colours from c.1790. Designs of flowers, costume details, etc., in thick orange, yellow, green, blue, purple, brown, were used on relief-decorated jugs, teapots, figures and portrait busts and other pieces. The ware is associated with F.& R.*Pratt, makers from the early 19th century, whose name is impressed on some examples, but was made by many other firms in Staffordshire, the north of England and, c.1795-c.1830, in Scotland.
Refs: Jewitt; Rackham & Read; A. Winchester 'Jasper Ware and Some of its Contemporaries' in Atterbury (1980).

Premier Pottery. *See* Koster's Premier Pottery (Adelaide).

Premier Pottery (Melbourne). Australian pottery established in Preston, a suburb of Melbourne, in the early 1930s. The initial output of small pieces included vases with the incised mark *Pamela* and the date *1934*; The pottery's range of Remued ware, an art line introduced in 1934, consisted of bowls, vases, jugs, shallow dishes, flower bowls, ashtrays, candlesticks, etc., hand-made in a hard earthenware (fired at about 1150°C) with glossy glazes, often in blended colours, or, after 1937, matt glazes. Relief ornament included eucalyptus leaves and fruit, mentioned in advertising material and frequently used. The pottery resumed production of decorative ware after a break during World War II, but had ceased operation by 1955.
Marks: *Pamela* with *1934*, incised; after, *Remued*, sometimes with a three-digit pattern number.
Ref: Graham.

Preston, Reg (b 1917). Australian potter, trained in sculpture at the Westminster School of Art, London. Preston established his own pottery in 1945. He worked in stoneware, often making lidded shapes, with rich, glassy drip glazes, or metallic effects brushed over other glazes. Preston has exhibited in Australia and overseas, and has a studio at Warrandyte, Victoria.

Prestonpans Pottery. Scottish pottery established by William Cadell in the mid 18th

*Pratt ware. Covered Toby jug with a leopard-skin jacket, made and coloured in the style associated with F. & R.*Pratt*. 26.5 cm high.*

century at Prestonpans, Lothian, for the production of creamware. The firm remained in the hands of the founder's family until 1801, when it became Anderson & Co., although the Cadells probably retained a financial interest. From 1806, it operated in the name of local businessman David Thomson (d 1819), managing partner in Anderson & Co., who continued production of transfer-printed and hand-painted ware, as well as small figures. Another partner, John Fowler, was a local brewer and distiller. David Thomson's company was succeeded by the firm of Watson & Co., under Hamilton Watson with the Newcastle potter J.J. Forster (d 1840) as manager. The pottery's output in this period included presentation jugs with sprigged and painted decoration, but mainly consisted of transfer-printed household ware. The works ceased operation c.1839 and were sold to a soap manufacturer in 1840.

Marks used by Watson: w on a raised pad of clay, and *Watson* or *Watson & Co.* printed or impressed.

Also working at Prestonpans in the 19th century were the *Bankfoot pottery, run by Robert and George Gordon, and their successor, C.*Belfield, who produced blue-printed earthenware, terracotta, smear-glazed black basalt, and jugs with relief figures painted in orange, green and brown. A small pottery, Newhall, produced coarse domestic ware.
Refs: Fleming; Hughes (1961); McVeigh.

Price, Horace H. (1898-1965). Porcelain painter working for the *Worcester Royal Porcelain Co. from 1912. Price painted fruit and flowers, both in the style developed by J.*Hadley and in the neater, carefully detailed groups of early Worcester porcelain. He became foreman of apprentices in 1945.
Ref: Sandon (1978a).

Price, Hugh. *See* Verreville Pottery.

Price, James. *See* Port Arthur Pottery.

Price, Powell & Co. *See* Powell, William.

Priestman, James. *See* Bennett, Edwin; Chesapeake Pottery.

Primavera, Atelier. Art studio of the Paris firm, Les Grands Magasins du Printemps, established in 1912 for the production of items for interior decoration. Ceramics included lamps and ornamental figures produced in quantity at a factory in Saint-Radegonde-en-Touraine (Indre-et-Loire). The shop also sold earthenware made at the *Longwy factory and, later, a wide range of ceramics by other firms and studio potters. Workshops for other decorative materials were at Montreuil-sous-Bois.
Mark: *Atelier Primavera*, as well as factory marks.

Similar studios, e.g. La Maîtrise, which was established for Galéries Lafayette by M.*Dufrêne in 1921, were attached to Paris department stores, and the Parisian furniture makers Süe et Mare (Compagnie des Artistes Français) produced ceramics designed to accompany their interior schemes.
Refs: Baschet; Dan Klein *All Colour Book of Art Deco* (Octopus, London, 1974); *Studio Year Book* (1928).

Primitif ware. *See* Rhead, Frederick Alfred.

Prince, Edward. English ceramic painter. One of the last painters to be apprenticed at the porcelain factory in Nottingham Road, *Derby, Prince worked there until its closure in 1848. He specialized in landscapes, many with warm, brown tints, influenced by the work of D.*Lucas. After working in London, Prince returned to Derby by 1865, joining the factory in King Street. Two decorative bottles painted by him were exhibited in Nottingham, 1872.

Work signed.

Refs: see Derby.

Pröschold, A.H. *See* Gräfenthal.

Prosser, Richard. *See* Minton, Herbert.

Protât, Hugues. French-born sculptor, designer and modeller working in England from the 1850s. Protât exhibited at the Paris Salon 1843-50 and moved to London, where he worked as a stonecarver and in a furniture workshop. He was subsequently, with P.E.*Jeannest and A.E.*Carrier-Belleuse, among European modellers engaged by *Mintons Ltd, for whom he worked c.1845-58. Protât taught modelling at schools of design in Hanley and Stoke-on-Trent, Staffordshire, 1850-64, also carrying out freelance work for the firm of J.*Wedgwood & Sons Ltd from c.1858. For Wedgwood, he designed and modelled the Protât vase, a *jardinière* and other ornamental pieces. Protât was a teacher of modelling at the Minton Memorial Institute c.1851-c.1863. His freelance work continued after he settled in London (c.1864), when he also worked for other Staffordshire companies, including Sir James Duke & Nephews at the Hill Pottery, Mintons Ltd (a bust of Herbert Minton, produced in parian ware), and W.*Brownfield & Sons (table centrepieces). Protât returned to France in the early 1870s.

Refs: Aslin & Atterbury; Batkin; G. Godden in Atterbury (1980); Haggar (1953); Jewitt; Reilly & Savage.

Providence Pottery, Castleford. *See* Gill, William.

Providential Tile Works. American tile factory established 1885 at Trenton, New Jersey, making glazed tiles, many with relief decoration, intended for walls and fireplaces. I.*Broome was first designer and modeller. The works also briefly produced embossed tiles with relief ornament in a shade contrasting with the ground colour, and others with underglaze decoration. Themes of relief panels included hunting, allegorical figures, etc. A landscape panel after 'February Fill Dyke' by the artist Benjamin W. Leader and another panel 'Mignon' after Jules Lefèvre were designed by T.S. *Callowhill. The firm introduced tiles with designs outlined in gold, giving the effect of *cloisonné* metal in the 1890s. It closed in 1913.

Marks: PROVIDENTIAL/N.J./TRENTON, impressed; P.T.W./T.N.J. within circle.

Refs: Barber (1976); Barnard; Kovel & Kovel; K.M. McClinton *Collecting American Victorian Antiques* (Charles Scribner's Sons, New York, 1966).

Georges Pull. Figure of a musician with coloured glazes, before 1868. Marked on the base with the name Pull. 28 cm high.

Pruden, Keen (1795-1879), and John Mills. New Jersey stoneware and brown ware potters. Keen Pruden worked at a pottery belonging to his uncle, Joseph Pruden, in Morristown before taking over management of one in Elizabethtown, Union County.

The marks ELIZ.TOWN-N.J. and ELIZ TOWN/POTERY occur on saltglaze decorated with blue, Pruden's only known pieces. He was followed before 1850 by his son, John Mills Pruden, who marked his ware J.M. PRUDEN/ELIZ-TOWN-NJ.

The firm continued under successive owners until the early 20th century.

Ref: New Jersey Pottery to 1840 (exhibition catalogue, New Jersey State Museum, 1972).

Prutscher, Otto (1880-1949). Austrian architect, jeweller and designer of furniture, silverware and some ceramics. He studied at the Wiener Kunstgewerbeschule from 1897 and became best known for his enamelled jewellery in Art Nouveau style. He designed table services for the *Augarten factory and the firm of Jos.*Böck. He also designed tiles, vases and other decorative pieces for the Wienerberger Werkstättenschule.

Mark: monogram of OP in a rectangle.

Ref: Neuwirth (1974a).

Puchegger, Anton. *See* Pfeiffer, Max Adolf.

Pugh, William. *See* Coalport.

Pugin, Augustus Welby Northmore (1812-52). English designer, architect and writer, associated with the revival of 14th-century Gothic design for application to the whole

range of interior styling. He designed ceramics for production by his friend, H. *Minton, which included encaustic and printed tiles from 1842, and tableware, garden furniture, etc., from 1848 until his death. A bread plate with a pattern of wheat, scrolled leaves and geometrical motifs, and bordered with the inscription 'Waste not, want not' was produced c.1850 by *Mintons Ltd. A blue-printed pattern in Gothic style used by Mintons is also attributed to him. Original signed watercolour drawings for some of his tile and tableware designs are in the Minton archives; most are dated 1851.

Refs: Aslin & Atterbury; S. Durant *Victorian Ornamental Design* (Academy Editions, London, 1972); P. Stanton *Pugin* (London, 1971); M. Trappes-Lomax *Pugin, A Medieval Victorian* (London, 1933).

Pull, Georges (1810-89). French potter making *Palissy ware. Self-taught, Pull achieved very close copies of Palissy's work in 1856, building himself a kiln at Vaugirard in the same year. His pieces have the relief motifs more sparingly applied than either C.J.*Avisseau or A.*Barbizet. Helped only by his son, a sculptor, he prepared his own clay and modelled, glazed and personally supervised the firing of his pieces. From c.1867, he made figures, e.g. a hurdy-gurdy player, or architectural pieces, such as mantel decoration inspired by Henri II ware. Using a light body and transparent glaze, he employed a palette of light greens, dark brown and manganese purple, with touches of blue, yellow and red. Pull also developed a range of *flambé* ware. He was succeeded by his son, Jules-Louis.

Mark: signature.

Refs: Ernould-Gandouet; Heuser & Heuser; Lesur (1971); B. Mundt *Historismus* (catalogue, Kunstgewerbemuseum, Berlin, 1973).

Purdy, Solomon. *See* Zoarite Pottery.

Raby, Edward John (b 1863). English ceramic painter, known for his flower studies. Born in Worcester, Raby trained at the local art school and at the porcelain factory, where his father, Edward Samuel Raby (b 1826), was a modeller until 1904. Flower sprays engraved and printed from E.J. Raby's drawings were issued by the *Worcester Royal Porcelain Co., until c.1896, but he is thought to have joined *Doulton & Co. in Burslem c.1892. There, Raby painted pieces ranging from miniatures to large vases (and including early Titanian ware) with arrangements of flowers – roses, wisteria, delphiniums, thistles, apple-blossom – often in bright, jewel-like enamel colours, thought to have been fired above the usual temperature. He based the studies on his own delicate watercolour sketches from life. Raby also painted birds (e.g. crows in a winter landscape on a Titanian vase, c.1920), landscapes, Italian gardens, a view of John Milton's house in Buckinghamshire, and some designs influenced by Art Nouveau. He retired in 1919.

Mark: monogram of ER on printed designs.

Ref: Sandon (1978a)

Radford, Albert (1862-1904). Potter and ceramic modeller, born in England, one of a long-established family of potters in Staffordshire. After emigrating to America in the early 1880s, he worked at potteries in Baltimore, Maryland, and Trenton, New Jersey, winning an award from the Pennsylvania Museum & School of Industrial Design for work carried out at Trenton. He founded a short-lived firm in Broadway, Virginia, c.1890, completing his first firing in 1891. While working at a pottery in Tiffin, Ohio, from c.1893, he established a workshop, the Radford Art Pottery, which was incorporated in 1895, and from the following year produced jasper ware with fine-grained body, containing English clay, tinted light blue, royal blue, light or dark grey, or olive green. After being cast or turned, the ware was decorated with white clay cast from models made by Radford to his own designs or occasionally after Wedgwood originals. The output included boxes, small trays, fern dishes, flowerpots, covered jars, dishes, bowls, jugs, cheese covers and butter dishes. Radford moved c.1900 to Zanesville, Ohio, where he worked as a modeller for S.A. *Weller and then became general manager of the *Zanesville Art Pottery until the autumn of 1901. He subsequently worked as a designer for J.B.*Owens, whose pottery introduced a 'Wedgwood' line of art ware in 1903. In the same year, he started the A. Radford Pottery Co., building a workshop which was purchased a few months later by the *Arc-en-Ciel pottery. The jasper ware was fired at a lower temperature than the work at Tiffin, with decoration, in general, moulded and painted in coloured slip, but a few pieces had patterns applied in light clay. Tan, pink and grey were frequent body colours, sometimes appearing as reserves surrounded by a coating, e.g. in dark brown or grey, which was brushed on to give a textured surface. Glazed ware was made experimentally. The company worked in Clarksburg, West Virginia, from 1904, with Radford as general manager until his death shortly afterwards, and A.*Haubrich as head of the decorating department. In addition to domestic ware, the output included art lines: Ruko, which resembled Weller's Louwelsa and the Loy-nel-Art made by J.W.*McCoy; Radura, matt-glazed, often in green, but also blue, red, yellow, brown, mauve, tan, etc., Thera, matt-glazed with decoration painted in slip; Velvety Art Ware, coloured pink, green, blue or purple and hand-painted. In 1912, the firm sold equipment records and goodwill to the *Brush-McCoy Pottery, while another company occupied the building.

Marks: the best Tiffin pieces were stamped RADFORD/JASPER; THERA, RADURA, RUKO moulded or impressed on Clarksburg ware.

Radford's grandson, Fred W. Radford, started the production of jasper ware in 1971, using early moulds and clay formulae; the pieces are marked as reproductions.
Refs: Evans; Jervis; Kovel & Kovel; Lehner; E. Purviance 'American Art Pottery – A. Radford Pottery Company' in *Mid America Reporter* (November 1972); F.W. Radford *A. Radford Pottery: His Life and Works* (privately printed, Columbia, S. Carolina, 1973).

Radford, Edward Thomas (c.1860-1937). English potter. Radford worked for J.

*Wedgwood & Sons Ltd from 1873, ending his apprenticeship in 1880. He subsequently worked for the *Linthorpe pottery until 1886, then *Burmantofts, and for *Doulton & Co. in Lambeth, before returning to Wedgwood. He was the first thrower employed by *Pilkington's Tile & Pottery Co., where he worked from 1903 until his retirement in 1936. He was responsible for the design of many forms which he made at Pilkington's, eventually marking pieces with his initials, E.T.R.
Refs: Batkin; Cross; Godden (1966a); Lomax; Reilly & Savage.

Rai. *See* Mokubei.

Railway Pottery, Stoke-on-Trent. *See* Fielding, S., & Co. Ltd.

Rainforth, Samuel. *See* Hunslet Hall Pottery.

Rainham Pottery Ltd. *See* Roeginga Pottery.

raku. Low-fired earthenware made of an open body (one with large pores) containing particles of already fired clay (grog). The ware has been made in Japan since the 16th century and was intended by its original makers, the *Raku family, for tea-ceremony use. Tea jars, water containers, flower vases, incense boxes and primarily tea bowls (often with small foot ring) are hand-built and sometimes carved or scraped before the application of glazes, often in many thin layers which flow irregularly over the body, sometimes leaving almost half of the shape uncovered (makugusuri or 'curtain glaze'). Kuro (black) raku has thick, brown-tinged iron or lead glazes, aka (red) raku a deep orange-toned body and transparent glaze, and the rarer white raku is thickly coated with white glaze; yellow and green glazes also occur. The effect may be treacly and glossy or thin and permeable. Pieces often rely on the glazes for decorative effect, but inlaid or applied patterns occur. The body, thick, uneven and low-fired in a single-chamber kiln, is especially favoured in the making of teabowls for its tactual quality and low conductivity of heat.

Branch kilns included that of the *Ohi family. Raku ware inspired many kilns and individual potters, e.g. Kenzan, *Dohachi II, whose pieces were unglazed and had painted decoration.

The making of raku ware introduced B.*Leach to ceramics, and the ware, which he described as a 'conscious return to the direct and primitive treatment of clay' has attracted many artist potters.
Refs: Feddersen; Fournier; Hannover; Jenyns (1971); Koyama; B. Leach *A Potter's Book* (Faber, London, 1940); Munsterberg; Sanders.

Raku family. A line of Japanese potters, the makers of *raku ware, working in Kyoto and descended from Chojiro (1516-92), the son of a Korean tile maker. The line used the family name of Tanaka until 1868 and the studio name Kichizaemon. After the late 1860s they used the name Raku (enjoyment). Tanaka Sojiro (1755-1834), noted for the making of black raku teabowls under the guidance of the teamaster Ryoshin,

followed his father as head of the family in 1770. He became a monk in 1811, taking the name Ryonyu, and was succeeded in 1834 by his son Tannyu (1795-1854), who, while teaching the techniques of mixing glazes at Wakayama, made a group of *Kishu wares which he called Kairakuen; he later made Raku ware at Nakayama and retired to become a monk in 1845. Tanaka Keinyu (1812 or 1817-1902), adopted son of Tannyu, retired in 1871, succeeded by his son, Tanaka Konyu (1857-1932) and collaborated with him in organizing the celebration of Chojiro's tricentenary. Konyu retired in 1918 or 1919 to become a monk, succeeded by his eldest son Tanaka Sokichi (1887-1944), who worked under the artistic name Shonyu. He was employed by the Sen family of teamasters and from 1935 to 1942 published a magazine devoted to the study of tea. His work was influenced by other wares, e.g. *Bizen, *Shino, *Oribe, *Hagi and *Karatsu. Subsequent Raku potters produced many copies of the work of Chojiro and his near contemporary Koetsu (1558-1637), a maker of similar teabowls. Kichizaemon Raku, head of the family in the 1960s, has documented the family's history.
Refs: R. Castile *The Way of Tea* (Weatherhill, New York and Tokyo, 1971); Jenyns (1971); Kichizaemon Raku 'Chojiro and Nonko (Donyu)' in *Sekai Toji Zenshu* Vol VII (Zanho Press and Kawade Shobo, Tokyo, 1955-58); Roberts.

Rakusen Asai. *See* Tokoname.

Rakusen Ohashi. *See* Wazen.

Rakusui. Japanese potter, Okuda Bunshiro, working in Nagano, *Shigaraki, under the art name Rakusui. By the late 19th century, his family workshop employed a staff numbering between 20 and, at busy periods, about 50, on the production of tea jars, stores, oil jars, basins for water, a range of bowls, and other household ware, with white, green and transparent glazes. Acid jars, with the brown glaze introduced by Rakusui before 1878 for pickling and preserving vessels, became a staple product of the area.
Ref: Cort.

Rakuzan or **Izumo ware.** Japanese pottery made at Izumo from the 17th century. The ware includes tea vessels, notably bowls in Korean style, and later ware lavishly painted in the manner of *Ninsei ware.
Refs: Jenyns (1971); Munsterberg.

Ram, Plateelbakkerij. Dutch pottery established at Arnhem in 1920 by the director N.H. van Lerven (1875-1945), the maker and decorator of pottery designed by T.H. *Colenbrander, who carried out his ceramic research in the Ram workshop. In 1924, the business was re-formed under the direction of van Lerven and a board which, until 1927, included F.J. Mansfield, a designer for the firm and formerly at the *Rozenburg factory. The output then included simple domestic and ornamental ware and tiles. Colenbrander's designs went out of production in 1931. The works ceased operation in 1945.

Marks incorporate the name RAM and *Arnhem*.
Refs: D.J. Hulsbergen 'Th. A.C.

Plateelbakkerij Ram. Dish with spiral decoration painted by R.*Sterken, after 1923. Marked Ram Arnhem. 22 cm in diameter.

Colenbrander en de Plateelbakkerij "Ram" te Arnhem' in *Bulletin* VII (Museum Boymans-van Beuningen, Rotterdam, 1956); Singelenberg-van der Meer; van Straaten.

Ramié, Suzanne (b 1905). French artist potter. She studied at the Ecole des Beaux-Arts in Lyons before going in 1936 to learn pottery techniques at Vallauris, where she established the 'Plan' studio, trading under the name 'Madoura', which she also used as a pseudonym. Working with her husband, Georges Ramié, she made rustic earthenware as well as unique pieces and limited editions, including fountains, lamps, wall panels and furniture plaques. Some pieces were made with plaited strips of clay. Wares in traditional local styles include chestnut pots and services for tea, coffee or mocha, with lead or tin glaze.
Refs: Céramique française contemporaine; Faré; Lesur (1971); S.& G. Ramié *Céramique de Picasso* (Paris, 1951).

Randall, John (1810-1910). English porcelain painter. Randall worked at Madeley, Shropshire, for his uncle T.M.*Randall, under whom he studied painting from 1828. He became known for the painting of tropical and exotic birds, using a bright palette which included yellow, orange, red and blue for the plumage, but while at Swinton also occasionally painted native British birds in a naturalistic style. The backgrounds of his paintings are characteristically stippled in grey-green, with trees and foliage faintly outlined. After leaving Swinton, Randall worked briefly in Staffordshire and then joined the Coalport factory, where he worked from 1835 until his retirement in 1881. During the 1860s he returned to a more naturalistic style in his bird studies, which often portrayed birds of prey in their natural habitats. He was unusual among the normally anonymous Coalport artists in signing a small number of plaques, which he painted in the 1870s.

Randall was a Fellow of the Geological Society in 1863; his collection of minerals and fossils, shown in the Great Exhibition (1851), was later bought for the nation. He also wrote books which include a *History of Madeley, The Clay Industries on the Banks of the Severn, The Severn Valley,* and *The Willey Country.*
Refs: Godden (1961, 1970); Jewitt; Rice; W. Turner 'Madeley Porcelain' Parts I and II in *The Connoisseur* 22 (December 1908).

Randall, Ruth Hinie (b 1898). American ceramist and teacher, born in Dayton, Ohio. She studied at Cleveland School of Art and the College of Fine Art in Syracuse University, New York, before working briefly under M.*Powolny in Vienna in 1933. She became professor of ceramics and later design and crafts at Syracuse University, where she taught from 1930 until her retirement in 1962. Her own ceramic sculpture included a bust, Madame Queen (1935), in glazed earthenware.
Refs: Clark & Hughto; R.H. Randall *Ceramic Sculpture* (Watson-Guptill, New York, 1948).

Randall, Thomas Martin (1786-1859). English porcelain maker and decorator, born in Broseley, Shropshire. After serving an apprenticeship at *Caughley 1800-03, Randall worked in *Derby. In 1813, he left for London, where he set up an enamelling workshop with R.*Robins in Barnsbury Street, Islington. The partnership, Robins & Randall, decorated porcelain bought from the Sèvres factory at the end of soft-paste production, as well as porcelain made at the *Cambrian and *Nantgarw potteries, for sale through J.*Mortlock and other London dealers, employing M.*Webster as a flower painter 1819-22. Randall painted birds, both exotic and naturalistic, landscapes, flower subjects, figures, including cupids, and studies of shells. After the partnership was dissolved in 1835, Randall established a workshop in Madeley, Shropshire, where he initially decorated Sèvres ware with birds, fruit, flowers, etc., and later produced a similar soft paste with glazes that developed from slightly green tinged to one of creamy appearance (resembling the Sèvres) glazes and later a hard, thin glaze. Randall's ground colours included pink, turquoise, apple green, and dark or light blue; his version of *bleu du roi* was usually gilded with *oeil de perdrix* or tracery patterns. Some of the pieces had moulded relief decoration. Randall employed as decorators the figure painter Philip Ballard, and fruit and flower painters Robert Bix Gray (1803-85) and William Cook (1800-76), and trained his nephew J.*Randall in the painting of exotic birds. He is said to have produced bone china in the late 1830s. After the closure of his works in 1840, Randall moved to Staffordshire, eventually working in Shelton, still as a decorator, until his retirement to Barlaston.

Work rarely marked.
Refs: Godden (1961, 1970); Jewitt, Rice; W. Turner 'Madeley Porcelain', an interview with John Randall in *The Connoisseur* 22 (December 1908).

Ranninger, Conrad K. Pennsylvania potter making slip-decorated earthenware in Montgomery County, c.1835-c.1845. A plate signed by Ranninger and dated 1838 has paper-resist decoration: the silhouettes of horse, double eagle and heart reveal a layer of brown slip surrounded by a slightly raised ground of light-coloured slip.
Ref: Barber (1970).

Raphaelesque porcelain. *See* Worcester.

Rapin, Henri (b 1873). French painter, designer, decorator, working in a variety of

media, including furniture (exhibited from c.1903). In the 1920s, Rapin designed an earthenware service, painted underglaze with flowers and decorated in relief with masks, and became artistic consultant at the Sèvres factory, 1928-34.
Refs: Années 25; Lesur (1967).

Rateau. *See* Lahens & Rateau.

Rathbone, Harold B. English potter and artist, pupil of Ford Madox Brown and closely associated with the Pre-Raphaelite movement. Rathbone established the *Della Robbia Pottery in December 1893, at Birkenhead, Cheshire, inspired by glazed terracotta made by the Della Robbia family in Florence from the 15th century. He acted as artistic director of the pottery, also modelling and designing, with particular interest in the architectural ware. With his associate, Conrad Dressler, he produced a fountain designed by T.E. Collcut for the Savoy Hotel, London.

Mark: the initial R is regarded as indicating his own work; also monogram of H.R.
Refs: Haslam (1975); B. Tattersall 'The Birkenhead Della Robbia Pottery' in *Apollo* 97 (February 1973).

Rathbone, Thomas. *See* Portobello Pottery.

Rauenstein. German porcelain factory established 1783 at the castle of Rauenstein in Thuringia, by Johann Friedrich and Christian Daniel Siegmund Greiner (*see* Greiner family) with Johann Georg Greiner (who left one year later), under a privilege granted by the Duke of Saxe-Meiningen. By 1800, the factory was run in conjunction with *Kloster Veilsdorf. Two years later the Rauenstein firm employed 42 enamel painters, who carried out a wide variety of floral decoration, including a pattern, Vieux Nyon, with garlands on black or dark blue grounds, bouquets or fluted shapes; later patterns of the mid 19th century included a flower design, Hessian Rose, and vine leaves executed in green. Figures, which formed only a small proportion of the factory's output, included animals, comedy figures similar to those made at Kloster Veilsdorf, the seasons, country girls, portrait busts, animals and mythical characters in rococo style. J.F. Greiner was succeeded in 1820 by his daughter, who sold her share to the Schalkau merchant Georg Heinrich Wirth in 1849. Wirth's son-in-law, Ernst Wilhelm Georgii, then took charge of the factory, succeeded as director in 1858 by Ferdinand Kahle from Saalfeld. Ferdinand Georgii (1847-1900), sole owner of the firm by 1881, rebuilt a factory which had been in operation at Rauenstein from 1887 until its destruction by fire in 1892 where he transferred the firm's manufacture of figures and ornamental wares in 1893. This branch was later engaged in mass production, e.g. of dolls' heads.

Marks include crossed flags and Rn or R-n.
Refs: Ducret (1962); Haggar (1960); Hannover; Honey (1952); Scherf; Ware.

Ravilious, Eric William (1903-42). English artist, designer and illustrator. Ravilious studied at schools of art in Eastbourne and Brighton before going to the Royal College of Art in London and subsequently working as a designer. He was commissioned to design printed patterns for J.*Wedgwood & Sons Ltd, which included Garden Implements, an arrangement of gardening tools with subsidiary motifs connected with gardening, intended for a jug and beakers for soft drinks (1937-38). This pattern was produced on pottery with matching textiles in 1957. He also designed an Alphabet set (1937), Persephone, arrangements of fish, fruit, etc. (1938), Christmas tableware featuring a plum pudding, holly, snowflakes, and the word 'NOEL' (1938), a series of patterns related to travel—plane, balloon, bus, train, steamship, sailing boat—(designed in 1940 and revived in the 1950s), as well as decoration for special pieces, e.g. a Boat Race goblet, coronation mugs, and a mug to commemorate the firm's removal to Barlaston in 1940. He became an official war artist in 1940 and was lost on air patrol from Iceland.

Earthenware with Ravilious's designs bears various marks mentioning him as designer and sometimes the name of the pattern or series.
Refs: Reilly & Savage; J.M. Richards in *Eric Ravilious Memorial Exhibition* (catalogue, Arts Council, 1948-49); *Wedgwood of Etruria & Barlaston* (catalogue, Stoke-on-Trent Museum & Art Gallery, 1980).

Raynaud & Cie. French porcelain manufacturers, successors to the firm of Gustave Vogt at Limoges in 1919. Martial Raynaud (1874-1952) owned a decorating workshop in Limoges from 1910 and, with his brothers Louis and Baptiste Raynaud, operated an agency with outlets in London and Berlin. Raynaud bought Vogt's two factories at Faubourg Montjovis and another Limoges works. He was succeeded in 1952 by his son André Raynaud, who subsequently modernized the buildings. The firm made fine tableware and ornamental pieces in Art Deco styles alongside traditional pieces for sale in the USA, which provided a market for a large quantity of Raynaud ware, and the output was later noted for the wide range of styles used. Production continues.

Marks include a ball bearing the initials T & V; RAYNAUD & CIE.
Refs: d'Albis & Romanet; Lesur (1967).

Rea, Daisy (b 1894). Porcelain painter working for the *Worcester Royal Porcelain Co. from 1909. She painted flowers, either in neat sprays, or in the more florid style developed by J.*Hadley, in whose workshop she had started her training. She later painted figures, working with Freda Doughty (*see* Doughty, S.D.) on the colouring of her figures of children. Rea became head of the factory's women painters.
Ref: Sandon (1978a).

Rea, Robert (b 1856). Porcelain painter working for the *Worcester Royal Porcelain Co. from 1870 until after 1909. He specialized in paintings of butterflies or feathers.
Ref: Sandon (1978a).

Rea, William J. (c.1864-1942). American potter. Rea started work, when fourteen years old, at the Mayer China Co., later managing a pottery in Ohio, and, for ten years, the Crescent Pottery (one of the

*Eric Ravilious. Earthenware vegetable tureen printed under the glaze with a design by Ravilious (c.1939) and produced by J.*Wedgwood & Sons Ltd. Made in the early 1950s, when the pattern was reissued.*

*Trenton Potteries Co. group). He was superintendent of the *Buffalo Pottery from its founding until his retirement in 1927, and developed the coloured body used in the pottery's Deldare ware.
Refs: S.& V. Altman *The Book of Buffalo Pottery* (Crown, New York, 1969); Evans.

Recknagel, Th. German porcelain manufacturers, established at Alexandrinenthal near Oeslau, in 1886, for the production of vases, bowls, dolls and dolls' heads. The Recknagel porcelain decorating workshop was in operation at Alexandrinenthal c.1930.

Marks: both the factory and decorating studio used circular marks with crossed nails at the centre, incorporating the initials RA the factory also used a shield mark.
Refs: Danckert; Weiss.

Reckston or **Rekston.** *See* Stockton Art Pottery.

Red Flame. *See* Owens, John B.

Redon, Martial. French porcelain manufacturer, working in Limoges as a partner in the firm of P.-J.*Gibus from the early 1860s. Redon remained as sole owner of the factory after Gibus's retirement in 1881. In 1886, his firm exhibited cups, plates and vases with lavish decoration. Later in the 1880s, he became better known for more utilitarian wares, e.g. the Flora service, in fine, white porcelain with narrow bands of gilding. Other services, for fish, game, or desserts, had underglaze patterns or *pâte-sur-pâte* decoration in white or coloured paste.

Martial Redon took his son Joseph into partnership soon before his own retirement in 1896. P.*Jouhanneaud and his son entered the business in 1906, when the firm became La Porcelaine Limousine. It passed in 1918 to Jouanneaud's nephew, Georges Magne, a partner from 1912. The factory closed in 1938, and the buildings were in military use

during World War II. In 1945, Alexandre Chastagnac began repairing the factory, which was again in production in the following year. He built new premises nearby in 1955.

Marks: M. REDON LIMOGES in a circle, sometimes inderlined; MR with two Ls; *Limoges/France* normally used on wares for export.
Refs: d'Albis & Romanet; Lesur (1967).

reducing atmosphere. Kiln conditions in which air intake is kept to a minimum and oxygen atoms are extracted from oxides. Copper reduces at a lower temperature than iron, to produce copper-red enamels and lustres. The colour range of celadon glazes on stoneware and porcelain results from the reduction of iron compounds.

redware. Earthenware with soft, porous body similar to the clays used for brick and tiles, and generally covered with soft lead glaze. The clay fires to varying shades of brown/red.

Red Wing Potteries. American pottery established in the 1870s as the Red Wing Stoneware Co. in Red Wing, Minnesota, making a general line of household stoneware. After undergoing changes in title and ownership in the early 20th century, the workshop, then trading as the Red Wing Union Stoneware Co., used local clay in the production of flowerpots and vases, which were decorated with birds or floral designs in the 1920s. The output of industrial art ware was extended to include mugs, bowls, trays, covered jars, candlesticks, ashtrays, etc., and (in the 1930s) pottery with matt, glossy or crystalline glazes made and marked for sale by the *Rum Rill Pottery Co. In the same period, the pottery started production of tableware in a refined clay body. The firm traded as Red Wing Potteries Inc. from 1936, and closed in 1967.

Marks: REDWING/STONEWARE (19th century); RED WING/ART/POTTERY (circular printed mark); RUM RILL, incised. Various marks after 1936 usually incorporate the name *Red Wing*.
Refs: D. Dommel 'Red Wing & Rum Rill Pottery' in *Spinning Wheel* 38 (December 1972); Kovel & Kovel; Webster.

Reed, Adam. *See* Peters & Reed.

Reed & Clementson. *See* Clementson, Joseph.

Reed, James. *See* Swillington Bridge Pottery.

Regéc. Hungarian porcelain factory established by Prince Ferdinand Brezenheim and in production by 1831. The greyish-tinged porcelain, which has at times been taken for stoneware or earthenware, was renowned for the quality of its painted decoration. The output included display pieces for the owner's family and friends, and everyday tableware.
Mark incorporates place name.
Refs: Csanyi; Danckert.

Regnauld, Victor. *See* Sèvres.

registry mark. *see* diamond mark.

Regnier, J.-M.-F. *See* Sèvres.

Regout, Frédéric or Frits. *See* Sphinx, De.

Regout, Petrus (1801-79). Dutch manufacturer working at Maastricht, where he started pottery production at De*Sphinx factory in 1836. Regout developed his firm into one of the main industrial concerns in the Netherlands, but working conditions in his factory were exposed in an enquiry in 1886-87 and caused a strike about ten years later. Regout's firm continued under his name in the late 19th century and began trading as Sphinx-Céramique after a merger in 1958.
Refs: Singelenberg-van der Meer; *Sphinx-Céramique* (commemorative publication, Maastricht, 1959); van Straaten.

Reichenbach. *See* Carstens, C.& E.

Reichenbach, Christof. *See* Pirkenhammer.

Reichmannsdorf. German porcelain factory established 1881 in Reichmannsdorf by Hermann Leube, who produced tableware, initially undecorated, then patterned in blue and gilded. Under the direction of Leube's son, Alois, from 1917, the firm produced increasing numbers of figures, including musicians, dancers in frilled and lacy costume, and harlequins, as well as model animals, clock-cases, and religious statuary, for export to Italy, Spain, North America, India and, from 1945, the USSR.
The work was marked with the initials PLR and a crown, with a cross or lion.
Also in Reichmannsdorf, the factory of F. Gottbrecht made cups, dolls' heads, etc., in porcelain from 1833, and Carl Scheidig produced domestic and ornamental wares, as well as electrical porcelain from 1864, marking the ware with a monogram of PSR below a crown.
Refs: Danckert; Scherf; Weiss.

Reid, William (d 1837). Scottish potter, making brown or white stoneware and cream-coloured earthenware at West Pans, Musselburgh, in 1797. After working briefly from a house in Musselburgh (by 1800), he established the *Musselburgh Pottery, where he remained for the rest of his working life. The firm became Wm Reid & Son, 1837-43, and was subsequently sold to the brothers Robert and Thomas Tough.
Mark: a crown, impressed or on raised pad of clay.
Refs: Fleming; Jewitt; McVeigh.

Reinacher-Härlin, Dorkas. (1885-1968). German potter, trained as an apprentice to a local potter in Besigheim (c.1912), then at the Königliche Kunstgewerbeschule in Stuttgart (1913-16), in Vienna under M. *Powolny (1916-17), at the Keramische Fachschule in Landshut (1917-19), and in Stuttgart under M. Heider (1919-24). She then taught ceramics in Cologne, 1924-29. Her individual work included figure modelling (e.g. a Nativity group, made in a coarse chamotte body, with precisely carved detail of facial features) and vases, jugs, and other vessels decorated with plant motifs in sharp, linear relief under dark glaze. Some pieces rely for effect on shape and glaze (e.g. a covered jar in a sharply stepped form with dark, glossy glaze, and a vase composed of two joined cylinders with fawn, shaded glaze). About a year after her marriage to the lyric poet Eduard Reinacher in 1932, she abandoned ceramics.

Mark: incised monogram of *dh*.
Ref: Bock.

Reinecke, Otto. German porcelain manufacturer working at Hof-Moschendorf (Bavaria) from 1878 on the production of everyday tableware. In 1894, his factory was in the hands of Kühnert & Tischer.
A variety of marks incorporate a crown and sometimes the initials PM, with *Bavaria* or *Moschendorf*/BAVARIA; trade names, e.g. REX, *Victoria*, occur.
Refs: Danckert; Weiss.

Reiss, William. German potter, working in America. Made earthenware in Wilmington, Delaware, in the mid 19th century. He worked for *Kurlbaum & Schwartz until 1855, and was a founder of the *American Porcelain Manufacturing Co.
Ref: Barber (1976).

Rekston or **Reckston.** *See* Stockton Art Pottery.

Reliance Pottery. Australian pottery established by 1895 at Dinmore, Ipswich, in Queensland. Initially producing stoneware and red earthenware for garden use, the pottery made kitchen and tableware with Rockingham or majolica glazes resembling the work of the *Dinmore Pottery, which it absorbed before 1917. Production continued until after 1918.
Ref: Graham.

relief-decorated jugs. Slip-cast jugs in fine stoneware or parian paste, associated with English ceramics of the mid 19th century, having been produced in considerable numbers from c.1830. The lavish relief ornament, especially suited for application to jugs and, occasionally, teapots and other vessels of similar shape, was often in Gothic revival style. Designs registered by C.*Meigh included a Minster jug with architectural detail in Gothic style inspired by York Minster, the related Apostle jug, with figures of the apostles standing in pointed arches, a jug with the figure of St Anne with St John the Baptist and the infant Christ, and others with figures in a frieze of arches. Jugs moulded with handles in the form of twisted vines, sometimes accompanied by a network of vines at the base, and drinking scenes with classical figures mainly date from the 1840s and 1850s. Other relief patterns included cupids with garlands of flowers, contemporary country scenes of children, gipsies, etc., portraits of Robert Burns, the Duke of Wellington, members of the English royal family, etc. Many patterns were inspired by natural forms, with jugs in the shape of a tree trunk, handles in the form of a gnarled twig or twisted stem, and trailing flowers or foliage arranged over the body of the jug. The relief patterns became less lavish in the 1860s.
The principal English manufacturers included *Mintons Ltd, W.*Brownfield, T.& R.*Boote, and *Cork & Edge, as well as Meigh. Relief jugs were also made by J.-C.*Ziegler and at *Montereau in France. American makers included E.& W.*Bennett (a tinted body patterned in white, or Rockingham-glazed ware), C.W.*Fenton's United States Pottery Co. (parian ware); also *Taylor & Speeler (makers of relief jugs with Rockingham glaze).

Remmey family. American makers of utilitarian stoneware, descendants of John Remmey (1706-62), who arrived in New York from Germany c.1731. His grandsons, John (b 1765) and Henry Remmey, operated the family pottery from 1792 until Henry's withdrawal from the business in 1800, by which time they had moved to a site next to the *Crolius family pottery on Potter's Hill. Rows of feathery motifs brushed in cobalt blue are characteristic of the pottery's decoration of stoneware. At Potter's Hill, John Remmey used a mark, J. Remmey/Manhattan-Wells, New York. Directories list him as working at the same site, by then 11 Cross Street, until 1826, and he was still a potter in 1831, living on Thomas Street.
Henry Remmey was working in Baltimore by 1817. He is mentioned as joint manager, with his son, in an advertisement issued by a stoneware pottery in 1820. Henry Remmey Jr was listed individually in the Baltimore directory of 1824 and moved to Philadelphia, where he took over an existing stoneware factory in 1827 with a partner, Enoch Burnett. He bought Burnett's share in 1831 and enlarged the pottery, later advertising 'an extensive assortment of stoneware'. His output included chemical stoneware by 1845, and he moved to a new site within two years. His former pottery passed to R.B. *Beech, 1847-51. Remmey retired by 1865, succeeded by his son, Richard Clinton Remmey (1835-1904), who made domestic

Remmey family. Salt-glazed stoneware pitcher attributed to Henry Remmey. Incised with the name LEWIS EYRE, *the inscription* KEEP ME FULL *and the date* 1838. 21.6 cm high.

ware characterized by feathery brushwork of leaf motifs, etc., painted in cobalt blue; pitchers and jars are distinctively high-necked, sometimes with bands beaded or rouletted around the neck, in the late 19th century. Bottle-shaped banks, surmounted with moulded birds, date from the mid 1880s. The pottery increasingly concentrated on the production of chemical wares and brick, which supplanted regular domestic ware. Richard Remmey marked work with his initials or name impressed, or the stamp *R.C.R./Phila.* within an octagonal outline.

Robert Henry Remmey (b 1866) worked for his father Richard and, on succeeding him in 1892, took into partnership his brother, John Bolgiano Remmey. The factory was damaged by fire in 1896 and again in the early 20th century; the firm subsequently moved to a site on the Delaware River, continuing operation as Richard C. Remmey Son Co. Robert Remmey's sons, Robert Henry Remmey Jr (b 1895), John Grauch Remmey (b 1900) and George Bickley Remmey carried on production of refractory wares and plastics exclusively by industrial methods.
Refs: Barber (1976); Clement (1947); Ketchum (1970); S. Myers *Handcraft to Industry* (Smithsonian Institution Press, Washington, 1980); Stradling; Webster.

Remued ware. *See* Premier Pottery.

Rendaiji. Japanese kiln established in 1847 for the production of *Kutani ware by *Kiku-Saburo, with the help of *Gen'emon. After improvements to the rather low-fired paste, with yellowish-green tinge, the kiln, employing about 200 workers, produced porcelain with decoration in *aka-e style or in the manner of Old Kutani ware until the 1860s.
Refs: Gorham; Nakagawa.

Rengetsu or **Otagaki** (1791-1875). Japanese poet and potter working in Kyoto under

the artistic name, Rengetsu. Born in Tajima province (Hyogo prefecture) of the Toto clan, she served as a lady-in-waiting to a Kameoka Daimyo in Tamba before returning to Kyoto for her marriage. Widowed in 1823, she became a Buddhist nun and began making hand-modelled teapots, vases, cups, water jars, etc., using relief decoration of lotus plants and inscribing her pottery with her own verses. Her work was mainly unglazed. She visited *Shigaraki and inspired other potters who included R.*Tanii.
Refs: Brinkley; Cort; Jenyns (1971); Morse; Roberts.

Renouleau, Alfred. *See* Angoulême.

Repoussé ware. *See* Doulton & Co.

resist decoration. A decorative technique in which a protective material such as wax or paper is applied to a ceramic surface underneath slip, pigment or glaze. When the piece is fired, the resisting agent burns away leaving the covered area untreated.

Rettig, John. *See* Coultry Pottery.

Reuter, Edmond G. (1845-after 1912). Ceramic decorator, born in Geneva, and working in England 1870-95. The son of a botanist, he studied floral design in Paris (1864) and visited Egypt (1868), before joining *Minton's Art Pottery Studio, where his work included a frieze of monkeys in an interlaced pattern. Reuter moved to Minton's Ltd at Stoke-on-Trent c.1874-95, becoming assistant designer under J.-F.-L.*Arnoux by 1886. In decorative work, he was chiefly a floral and figure painter. After his return to Switzerland, he worked as illuminator, calligrapher and watercolourist.

His work was normally signed.
Refs: Godden (1961); Rhead.

Revelation. *See* Perry, Mary Chase.

Reynell, Gladys (1881-1956). Australian studio potter, born in Adelaide. She studied painting privately under Margaret McPherson (later Preston) and then pottery and painting in London. She and McPherson made some wares in Cornwall and, after World War I, taught pottery at Seale-Hayne Military Hospital. On her return to Adelaide in 1919, Reynell set up a pottery at her family's vineyard; she first exhibited her ware in Adelaide in the same year. She was assisted by George Osborne, whom she later married. In 1922, the Osbornes moved to Ballarat, Victoria, where George built a kiln, made the pots and prepared glazes, and Gladys restricted herself primarily to decorating. They stopped making pottery in 1926 when George contracted lead poisoning from the glazes they used. Their small domestic earthenwares are characteristically glazed a rich cobalt blue with simple *sgraffito* or slip patterns of flowers or fruit.
Marks: REYNELLA on South Australian wares; OSREY at Ballarat.
Ref: Graham.

Rhead, Frederick Alfred (1857-1933). English potter, ceramic designer and author; born in Newcastle-under-Lyme, the son of G.W. *Rhead (1832-1908). Frederick Rhead studied at Newcastle School of Art, where

he was later a teacher. He joined *Mintons Ltd as an apprentice under L.-M.-E.*Solon by 1872, and continued to work for the firm as a decorator of *pâte-sur-pâte* pieces, 1875-77. Rhead joined the firm of J.*Wedgwood & Sons early in 1878; his *pâte-sur-pâte* and *sgraffito* decoration were included in the firm's display at the Exposition Universelle in Paris, 1878. He later worked for Bodley & Sons at the Hill Pottery, Burslem, *Brown-Westhead, Moore & Co., and other Staffordshire firms. As art director for the firm of W.*Brownfield, he continued *pâte-sur-pâte* design and decoration, including the Gladstone Testimonial Vase in 1888.

By 1896 he carried out designs for P. *Shelley, joining his firm as art director, and created a number of earthenware lines. Intarsio was hand-painted under the glaze with patterns, often in bands, that included flowers, animals, and illustrations of Shakespeare's plays (a series introduced c.1901). The pieces were often bulbous or elongated in shape and featured long, sweeping or twisted handles. This line included clock cases entitled Day & Night, Old Father Time, The Grim Reaper, Polly Put the Kettle On, etc., and a series of character teapots introduced in c.1900. Other lines were: Spano-Lustra, with *sgraffito* patterns (repeating plant motifs, lobsters in swirling water, etc.) revealing a deep reddish earthenware body under white and green slip with added lustre; Urbato, decorated with many layers of coloured slip and additional painted colours under a plain glaze, mainly in floral or abstract patterns, but also with penguins, etc.; Primitif ware with 'accidental' effects of swirling colour, and Pastello, probably a *pâte-sur-pâte* line, of which no known examples survive. Rhead also designed a range of small grotesque figures, mainly depicting fantastic animals and, in porcelain, tea and toilet sets.

He worked as a book illustrator with his brothers G.W.*Rhead (1855-1820) and L.J.*Rhead (who also designed for Shelley) and wrote several articles on pottery decoration, as well as *Staffordshire Pots and Potters* (with G.W. Rhead). He subsequently designed for Birks, Rawlins & Co. (*see* Birks, L.A., & Co.), then worked until 1929 as art director of another Staffordshire pottery and finally headed the art departments of the *Cauldon Potteries Ltd and *Worcester Royal Porcelain Co.

Rhead was a founder member of the Pottery Managers and Officials Association and, as its President, served on the National Council of the Pottery Industry. In his design work, he aimed to ally industrial techniques with good design, and to exploit the varied artistic possibilities of ceramics without relying on the revival of earlier styles, or imitating work in other materials.

His daughter Charlotte Rhead (d 1947) trained under him as a designer and his sons F.H.*Rhead and H.G.*Rhead went on to design ceramics in America.
Refs: Aslin & Atterbury; Batkin; Reilly & Savage; Rhead; Watkins *et al.*

Rhead, Frederick Hurten (1880-1942). English-born potter working chiefly in America. Born in Hanley, Rhead was apprenticed at W.*Brownfield's pottery, working for other Staffordshire factories by 1900. He assisted his father, F.A.*Rhead, in the introduction of art wares at the *Foley Potteries. After going to America in 1902, he joined W.P.*Jervis's Avon Faience Co. by 1903, and assisted in developing earthenware decorated with Art Nouveau motifs, sometimes outlined in white slip. Briefly working at the pottery of S.A.*Weller in Zanesville, Ohio, (1903-04) he developed a third line of Dickens Ware, as well as the Jap Birdimal and L'Art Nouveau ranges. While art director of the *Roseville Pottery Co. (1904-08), he designed the Della Robbia, Olympic and Aztec Art lines. In 1908, he joined Jervis at Oyster Bay, New York.

As an instructor at the University City School of Ceramics in 1910, he wrote *Studio Pottery*. He worked and, with his wife Agnes, taught at the *Arequipa Pottery (1911-13), before establishing his own pottery at Santa Barbara (Southern California), where he experimented in the use of California clays. The output of vases, garden ornaments, etc., was thrown by two assistants to Rhead's designs and decorated by him with the help of Agnes Rhead and Lois Whitcomb (who became his second wife in 1917), using a *sgraffito* technique. Rhead based many shapes on Oriental examples, particularly from the Chinese Ming or Ch'ien Lung periods, and achieved black glazes of Chinese inspiration which resulted from fifteen years of personal research. He started a magazine, *The Potter* (1916-17), with author Edwin A. Barber as writer and historical advisor, and A.A.*Robineau and W.D.*Gates, as well as Rhead himself, as specialist contributors in an effort to provide practical information for potters.

After the closure of his pottery in 1917, Rhead took charge of research at the *American Encaustic Tiling Co. until 1927. His work included a series of zodiac tiles designed by Lois Rhead, and some porcellaneous pieces. Rhead subsequently became art director at the factory of H.*Laughlin until his death. Working with the American Ceramic Society, and as First Secretary of its Art Division in 1920, he fostered the development of American studio pottery, improving the availability of technical training and information.

Most work at the Rhead pottery was marked with the emblem of a potter throwing a vase, impressed or on a paper label, sometimes with RHEAD POTTERY/SANTA BARBARA. Rhead's surname was incised with WELLER FAIENCE on some work at Zanesville.
Refs: D.E. Alexander *Roseville Pottery for Collectors* (privately published, Richmond, Indiana, 1970); Barber (1976); Clark & Hughto; Donhauser; Eidelberg; Evans; Henzke; Keen; Kovel & Kovel; *National Cyclopedia of American Biography* (1956); F.H. Rhead *Studio Pottery* (People's University Press, University City Missouri, 1910); L. & E. Purviance & N.F. Schneider *Zanesville Art Pottery in Color* (Mid-America Book Co., Leon, Iowa, 1968), *Roseville Art Pottery in Color* (Wallace-Homestead, Des Moines, Iowa, 1970), *Weller Art Pottery in Color* (Wallace-Homestead, Des Moines, Iowa, 1971).

Rhead, George Woolliscroft (1832-1908). English artist and ceramic decorator, the son of a potter called George Rhead who worked in partnership with his brother

Frederick Hurten Rhead. Earthenware vase with carved decoration and coloured glazes. 27.9 cm high.

Sampson at Stoke-on-Trent in the 1840s, and himself the father of G.W.*Rhead (d 1920), L.J.*Rhead and F.A.*Rhead. He was a teacher of art at Newcastle-under-Lyme School of Art and the Fenton Art School, as well as working for *Brown-Westhead, Moore & Co., and carrying out heraldic decoration for *Mintons Ltd.
Refs: Reilly & Savage; Watkins *et al.*

Rhead, George Woolliscroft (1855-1920). English artist, writer and ceramic designer; the son of G.W.*Rhead (1832-1908). After training at *Minton's Art Pottery Studio, where he worked with W.S.*Coleman in 1870 (often adapting designs from Japanese originals), Rhead designed work for production at the *Foley Potteries, under his brother F.A.*Rhead as art director. He also designed glass and mural decorations, exhibited paintings at the Royal Academy, 1882-96, and worked as an illustrator. He was a teacher at Putney School of Art from 1896 and subsequently director of the Southwark Polytechnic Institute.
Refs: Bénézit; Reilly & Savage; Rhead; G.W. Rhead *The Principles of Design* (Batsford, London 1905), *Modern Practical Design* (Batsford, London, 1912), *The Earthenware Collector* (Herbert Jenkins, London, 1920); Thieme & Becker; Watkins *et al.*

Rhead, Harry G. (1881-1950). Ceramic designer, working in America. He succeeded his brother F.H.*Rhead as art director at the *Roseville Pottery Co., 1908-18. His work there included the development of the lines Carnelian and Pauleo, influenced by oriental treatment of form and glazes, Donatello,

with relief scenes featuring children and trees between fluted bands at rim and base, and Mostique, with incised designs of flowers or geometrical motifs on a textured, unglazed ground. He joined the *Mosaic Tile Co. c.1920 to supervise the production of faience tiles, leaving to found the Standard Tile Co. in 1923 at Zanesville, Ohio.
Mark: signature.
Refs: D.E. Alexander *Roseville Pottery for Collectors* (privately published, Richmond, Indiana, 1970); Evans; Kovel & Kovel; L.& E. Purviance & N.F. Schneider *Roseville Art Pottery in Color* (Wallace-Homestead, Des Moines, Iowa, 1968).

Rhead, Louis John (1858-1927). English designer and illustrator, brother of G.W. *Rhead (1855-1920) and F.A.*Rhead. After studying art in Paris from 1871, and later in London, he worked for some time as a ceramic designer, following his brother Frederick from *Mintons Ltd to the firm of J.*Wedgwood & Sons Ltd in 1878. A plaque by him was included in the Wedgwood display at the Exposition Universelle in Paris, 1878. He continued occasional ceramic design during his study in London and joined Wedgwood's permanent staff for a year in 1882. He moved in 1883 to America, where he worked as a poster designer and illustrator. He returned to England in 1896.
Refs: Batkin; Thieme & Becker; Watkins *et al.*

Rheinische Porzellanfabrik, Mannheim. German porcelain factory established at Mannheim in 1900. The output, mainly everyday tableware, included reproductions of porcelain made at the Frankenthal factory, which closed in 1800. The firm is no longer in operation.
Marks include a shield bearing the initials RP/M.
Refs: Danckert; Weiss.

Rheinsberg. German faience factory established 1762 in Rheinsberg, Brandenburg, and owned 1770-1866 by Karl Friedrich Lüdicke and his family. In the 19th century, the factory produced glazed white earthenware and black basalt, following the styles of ware produced by Wedgwood, with the impressed mark, *Rheinsberg*.
Refs: Honey (1952); Hüseler; Pazaurek; Riesebieter; O. von Falke *Alt-Berliner Fayencen* (Berlin, 1923).

Rhodes, Daniel (b 1911). American ceramist, designer and teacher, born in Iowa and trained in Chicago and New York. Rhodes became known for abstract forms which he made in the 1950s. In the late 1960s, he exhibited work combining clay with a fibreglass support, a technique resulting from his own research, which made possible a wider range of forms. Rhodes taught in a number of American Colleges and became head of ceramics at Alfred University (*see* New York State College of Ceramics). His books, *Clay and Glazes for the Potter* (1957), *Stoneware and Porcelain* (1959), *Kilns* (1968) and *Pottery Form* (1976) have become standard reference works. Since his retirement to California, his work has included hollow ware.
Refs: 'Ceramics' double issue of *Design Quarterly* 42-43 (1958); 'Ceramics East

Coast' in *Craft Horizons* 25-26 (June 1966); Clark & Hughto.

Rhodes & Yates. American pottery firm, founders in 1859 of the first pottery built in Trenton, New Jersey, solely for the production of white granite and cream-coloured earthenware. The firm received a medal from the New Jersey State Agricultural Society in 1860 for their white granite. After changes in title, the company became the City Pottery (incorporated 1875) which continued for several years.

Mark: c.p. co. below shield bearing stars and stripes.
Ref: Barber (1976).

Rice, Jean Durant (d 1919). American potter. She studied under C. and L.*Volkmar in New York and with the help of Leon Volkmar established her own pottery, Durant Kilns, at Bedford Village, New York, beginning production in 1911, after experiments (including the reproduction of 16th-century Italian enamels) which started in the previous year. She designed and modelled tableware and art pottery decorated with glazes developed by Volkmar, notably in blue, aubergine, red and yellow, which often changed in shade, darkening or lightening towards the base according to the thickness of application; interiors were often glazed in a different colour. She leased a gallery in New York 1913-18, subsequently selling work through Arden studios, a New York agent. She left a life interest in the pottery to Leon Volkmar on her death. The Durant Kilns trade name remained in use until 1930.
Mark: *Durant* and a date incised.
Refs: Cox; Evans.

Richard-Ginori, Società Ceramica. Italian ceramics manufacturers established on the amalgamation of the *Doccia factory with a firm under the ownership of Giulio Richard in 1896. Richard, a ceramist from Turin, had been a partner in a porcelain factory at San-Cristoforo, Milan, became its sole owner in 1870 and traded from 1873 under the name Società Ceramica Richard from 1873. In 1887 he bought two potteries at Pisa, one of which (the San Michele factory) continued production of glazed earthenware, and ten years later he acquired a pottery at Mondovì-Carassone.

Richard's firm and Doccia combined under the title Società Ceramica Richard-Ginori and acquired further factories, which included the Rifredi factory, producers of electrical insulators in Florence (1906), one established at Livorno in 1918 and producing electrical wares (1939), and the Ortica pottery studio at Lambrate.

The firm was known for Art Nouveau porcelain (often very large pieces) in the late 19th and early 20th centuries and, later, work designed by G.*Ponti, produced 1923-38. The art director, Giovanni Garibaldi (b 1908) who worked for Richard-Ginori from 1947 designed tableware in modern style, e.g. a stacking service (1954). The firm continued to make art porcelain at Doccia and

Richard-Ginori. Coffee service decorated with bands of grey and gold, 1955.

industrial ware at Sesto Fiorentino, nearby, where there is also a company museum. Eight factories operating in Lombardy, Piemonte and Tuscany include Colonnata (established in 1735), producer of everyday ware and porcelain in the style of *Capodimonte.
Refs: L. Ginori-Lisci *La Porcellana di Doccia* (Milan, 1963); G. Liverani *Il Museo delle porcellane di Doccia* (1967).

Richardson, A.G., & Co. Ltd. Staffordshire earthenware manufacturers working at the Gordon Pottery, Tunstall, 1915-34, and subsequently at the Britannia Pottery, Cobridge. The firm made breakfast, coffee and dessert sets as well as novelty items under the trade name Crown Ducal, and in 1921 introduced a line of tea wares in plain colours applied by aerograph; this method was later used for dinner ware. Transfer and litho-printed patterns were among the other decorative techniques used; ornamental pieces were often patterned with tube-lined slip filled with coloured glazes.
Marks: AGR & CO LTD or AGR and names of the wares (e.g. *Crown Ducal, Regal,* etc.) printed.
Refs: Bunt; Cushion (1980).

Richardson, William. See Johnston, William.

Richmond. *See* Allen, Harry.

Rickaby, Thomas (b c.1795). English potter, born at Newbottle, near Sunderland, and working at Monkwearmouth, where he established the Sheepfolds Pottery in 1840. Employing his son Thomas J. Rickaby (b 1833) and seven other workers, he made brown domestic earthenware, trays, salt kits, etc., and fulfilled orders received by the *Garrison Pottery when the Garrison's production of brown ware had ceased. Rickaby, for a short time (1847-c.1850), entered into a partnership Rickaby & Blakelock; he was succeeded by his widow, who was working c.1860, and by 1865 the firm traded as T.J. Rickaby & Co. It was transferred in late 1900, after T.J. Rickaby's death, to the Bridge End Pottery.
Ref: Shaw.

Ricketts, William (1862-1930s). Porcelain painter working for the *Worcester Royal Porcelain Co. 1877-c.1933. Ricketts was a painter of flowers and, notably, fruit. His

William Ricketts (b 1899). Earthenware coffee pot modelled as a tree trunk with a cover in the form of an Aboriginal boy, 1930s. 42 cm high.

fruit paintings, characterized by clear, firm outlines and a background blurred by the admixture of two different oils in the enamel, are found on vases and other ornamental pieces. Ricketts was also a watercolour artist and exhibited work at the Royal Academy.
Ref: Sandon (1978a).

Ricketts, William (b 1899). Australian sculptor and potter. Ricketts was entirely self-taught, apart from a brief apprenticeship to a Melbourne jeweller in the early 1930s, during which time he made some small porcelain pieces. Working from 1935 at Pinara Kutata, a conservationist sanctuary which he

*William Ricketts (b 1862). Vase painted and signed by Ricketts and made at *Worcester, 1917. 22 cm high.*

established at Mount Dandenong, Victoria, he made figures of Australian Aborigines in an attempt to explore the spirit of Aboriginal mythology. These sculptures (up to three metres in length) were fired in a charcoal kiln built on his property by H.*Beck. Ricketts's work expresses a philosophy based on classical Hindu texts, especially the Vedas, which in his belief gave rise to Australian Aboriginal legends in prehistoric times. He also made bowls and covered jars, mainly with matt glazes. After visiting central Australia in the early 1960s, Ricketts established a second sanctuary, at Pitichi Ritchi, near Alice Springs. Some sculptural work is in the Museum of Applied Arts and Sciences, Sydney, and a collection of his work is preserved at Dandenong.
Ref: Sandon (1978a).

Riddle, F.H. *See* Van Briggle, Artus.

Ridgway, George (c.1758-1823). Staffordshire potter. He made earthenware in partnership with his brother Job *Ridgway until c.1800, when he moved to the Bell Works in Broad Street, Shelton, producing earthenware. His nephews, John *Ridgway and W.*Ridgway, took over the works in 1815. He was also concerned briefly in the operation of the *Belle Vue Pottery with his brother, 1806.
Refs: Godden (1972); Jewitt.

Ridgway, Job (1759-1813). Staffordshire potter, born in Chell, near Burslem. Starting at the age of thirteen Ridgway served an apprenticeship at the *Cambrian Pottery. He returned to Staffordshire briefly c.1784 and continued training at the *Leeds Pottery. After settling in Hanley, he married Mary, the sister of Elijah Mayer (*see* Mayer, E., & Son) in 1875. He was in partnership with his brother, G.*Ridgway, and W. Smith (d 1798) in a pottery firm at Shelton until the brothers separated c.1800. Job then built the Cauldon Place factory at Shelton, where he was producing earthenware from 1802. He also participated in the establishment of the *Belle Vue Pottery in 1802 and was concerned briefly, with his brother George, in its operation in 1806. He was assisted at Cauldon Place by his sons John *Ridgway and W. *Ridgway, whom he took as partners in 1808, subsequently trading as Job Ridgway & Sons. Their output was primarily for domestic use and included tableware transfer-printed with *chinoiseries* under the glaze in blue, dessert baskets with pierced decoration, etc., rarely marked, but also comprised figures and groups, e.g. a cat with a seated spaniel, marked *J. Ridgway*. From 1808, the firm made porcelain which included teasets, dessert services and ornamental pieces, often richly painted in enamel and gilded. Moulded patterns of mythical scenes, vine borders, arabesques, etc., appear in white on a blue ground, or in the case of stoneware on buff grounds. Dinner services were normally produced in earthenware or a heavy stone china body developed to compete with C.J.*Mason's patent ironstone. The firm's large export trade gave rise to such series of views as the 'Beauties of America' printed in blue.

After Ridgway's death, his sons continued in partnership until 1830, when John Ridgway remained at Cauldon Place, while

his brother operated their Bell Works, formerly occupied by George Ridgway.

The work was usually unmarked, but impressed or printed marks incorporating RIDGWAY & SONS may come from this firm after 1808.
Refs: Godden (1972); G.B. Hughes *English Pottery & Porcelain* (Lutterworth, London, 1961); Jewitt; H.C. Wedgwood *People of the Potteries* (Adams & Dart, Bath, 1970).

Ridgway, Edward John. *See* Ridgway Potteries Ltd.

Ridgway, John (1785-1860). Staffordshire potter, son of Job *Ridgway. With his brother, W.*Ridgway, he succeeded their father at the Cauldon Place Pottery, Shelton, in which the brothers had been partners since 1808, and operated the Bell Works earlier occupied by their uncle, G.*Ridgway. John Ridgway continued at Cauldon Place after breaking the partnership with his brother in 1830. He traded as John Ridgway, and later John Ridgway & Co. His output, mainly high-quality bone porcelain, but also including earthenware and ironstone bodies, comprised tea, dessert and dinner services (often lavishly gilded), jugs, washbasins, garden fountains, etc., which were among items in the firm's display at the Great Exhibition, London, 1851. Relief decoration included garlands, sprays and posies of finely modelled flowers. The firm was also known for the even application of ground colours and high quality in gilding. In 1855, Ridgway entered into a partnership, John Ridgway, Bates & Co., making porcelain, earthenwares and a fine, creamy-white parian paste, used for figures, groups and portrait busts. Ridgway became first mayor of Hanley in 1856 and retired from his pottery in 1858; the firm was eventually succeeded by *Brown-Westhead, Moore & Co. in 1862.

Marks, impressed or printed, incorporate the name or initials of the firms, often with a pattern name; Royal Arms with JR.
Refs: Godden (1972); Williams-Wood.

Ridgway, William (1788-1864). Staffordshire potter, son of Job *Ridgway. With his brother, John *Ridgway, he entered their father's firm, becoming a partner in 1808. The brothers traded as John & William Ridgway from 1814 until they dissolved the partnership in 1830. William took over and enlarged the Bell Works in Shelton, where the brothers had succeeded their uncle, G.*Ridgway, and by 1843 he controlled six factories in Hanley and Shelton, notably the Church Works in Hanley High Street. There and in part of the nearby Cobden Works, he worked with his son, Edward John (*see* Ridgway Potteries Ltd) until 1845. The output of these factories included moulded stoneware jugs, teapots, vases, candlesticks with relief decoration; earthenware jugs, tea, breakfast, dessert and toilet wares moulded in a fine, mauve-tinted body and decorated with flowers, birds, landscapes and *chinoiseries* in slightly raised enamel; earthenware encrusted with finely modelled flowers; ranges of painted and printed wares. William Ridgway made mainly utilitarian earthenware at the Charles Street Pottery, Hanley, and at the Bell Works. In 1835 a factory in Shelton High Street was acquired by

the new partnership Ridgway, Morley, Wear & Co., which was to dissolve in 1842. Ridgway continued in partnership with his son-in-law F.*Morley until 1845. The output consisted of printed earthenware and ironstone bodies for domestic use. Ridgway retired in the 1850s, succeeded at the Church Works by his son and L.J.*Abington.

Marks include Ridgway's name or initials and printed backstamps.
Refs: Godden (1972); Jewitt; Mankowitz & Haggar; Scarratt.

Ridgway Potteries Ltd. Staffordshire manufacturer of pottery and porcelain founded by Edward John Ridgway (1814-96), son of W.*Ridgway. After working in partnership with L.J.*Abington at the Church Works in Hanley, Ridgway continued the pottery alone and in 1866 built the Bedford Works in Bedford Road, Hanley. He took his sons, John Ridgway (1843-1916) and Edward Ackroyd Ridgway (b 1846), into partnership from 1870 until his retirement in 1872. The brothers traded as Ridgway, Sparks & Ridgway with Joseph Sparks (d 1878), 1873-79. The firm's output then comprised a range of earthenware, stoneware and terracotta, including jasper ware and other tinted stoneware bodies with relief or inlaid patterns, and jet ware ornamented with raised enamel in imitation of Limoges enamel ware. The firm traded under the title of Ridgways from 1879 to 1920, when it became Ridgways (Bedford Works) Ltd. Making its administrative headquarters at Ash Hall, Stoke-on-Trent, the firm traded from 1955 as Ridgway Potteries Ltd, a group which included *Booths Ltd of Tunstall, the firm of H.J. *Colclough, the factories occupied by *Adderleys Ltd in Longton and Fenton, the Cobridge earthenware firms of North Staffordshire Pottery Co. Ltd (established 1940) and Portland Pottery Ltd (established 1946), and became Allied English Potteries (*see also* Pearson, S., & Sons Ltd) in 1964.

Marks: impressed marks incorporating the names of *Ridgway* and *Abington*, with dates; R.S.R. [Ridgway, Sparks & Ridgeway] in a variety of marks, often with a pattern name; various printed marks incorporating the name *Ridgway* or *Ridgways* with name of pattern or body and sometimes *Bedford*, *Bedford Works* or *Bedford Ware*; Ridgway Potteries Ltd continued the mark, RIDGWAY, on an oblong cartouche, surmounted by a crown and *Est. 1792*, used by Ridgways (Bedford Works) Ltd; members of the group retained earlier trade names for patterns or wares in adapted marks.
Refs: Bunt; Godden (1972); Jewitt; Scarratt.

Rie, Lucie (b 1902). Studio potter, born in Vienna, where she trained at the Kunstgewerbeschule under M.*Powolny. Her work in Austria included pieces in shapes adapted from metalwork designed by J. *Hoffmann, and later simple, thinly potted bowls and cylindrical vases. Initially using splashed or brushed decoration, she changed c.1930 to glazes applied to raw clay, achieving a wide range of textural and colour effects in one firing. Lucie Rie moved in 1938 to London, where she made ceramic jewellery and buttons. Sharing her workshop with H. *Coper, 1947-58, she made tea and coffee ware, casseroles, salad bowls and other functional ware while continuing her individual work. She ceased work with earthenware after World War II, subsequently using stoneware or porcelain. All her pieces are carefully cleaned and turned after throwing, and some are eased into asymmetrical, flattened or oval shapes. In decoration, she concentrates on the interaction of body and glaze, adding only finely drawn *sgraffito* bands (from the 1940s) or inlay (1950s). She later exploited the spiral effect achieved in throwing clays in contrasting colours, e.g. in tall bottles with flaring rims. Lucie Rie is known for her achievement of vital and widely varied results with precise technical control.

Marks include monogram of LR from c.1938.
Refs: T. Birks *Art of the Modern Potter* (Country Life, London, 1976); *Ceramic Review* 72 (November, December 1981); J. Houston (ed) *Lucie Rie* (catalogue, Crafts Council, London, 1981); Neuwirth (1974a); Rose; A.C. Sewter 'Lucie Rie—Potter' in *Apollo* 59 (February 1954); Wingfield Digby.

Rieber, Josef. *See* Mitterteich.

Riedl, Josef (b 1884). Austrian modeller working in Vienna, the son of a woodcarver. In the annual winter exhibition of the Österreichischer Museum (1910-11), Riedl exhibited figures of children, sweet dishes and other pieces issued by the *Wiener Kunstkeramische Werkstätte. Later work, exhibited in 1931, included pieces of religious and mythological inspiration.
Ref: Neuwirth (1974a).

Riegger, Harold Eaton (b 1913). American artist potter. Born in Ithaca, New York, Riegger studied at the New York College of Ceramics at Alfred University until 1938 and at Ohio State University, 1938-40. He exhibited a tall stoneware vase, unglazed, with lines of ribbing encircling the shoulder and the neck, at the Syracuse Museum of Fine Arts in the late 1930s. A spiral of close, incised lines is a feature of a glazed stoneware vase, also made at Alfred, in 1944. Riegger moved to San Francisco, teaching at the California School of Fine Arts and eventually establishing a workshop in Mill Valley, where he started to make raku ware and carried out research in primitive firing techniques. He also taught at several American colleges and wrote several handbooks on aspects of ceramic craft.
Refs: Clark & Hughto; 'Ceramics' double issue of *Design Quarterly* 42-43 (1958); Donhauser, H.E. Riegger *Raku: Art & Technique* (Van Nostrand Reinhold, New York, 1970), *Primitive Pottery* (Van Nostrand Reinhold, New York, 1972).

Riemon. *See* Miyamotoya.

Riemerschmid, Richard (1868-1957). German architect and designer, trained at the Munich Academy. Riemerschmid was a founder-member of the Münchener Vereinigte Werkstätte für Kunst im Handwerk, 1897. He taught in Nuremberg, Munich and Cologne, and designed furniture, metal and other craftwork, as well as ceramics, becoming one of Germany's most prominent modern

Lucie Rie. Stoneware vase with finely speckled glaze revealing a dark body, 1960s. Marked LR impressed. 19.5 cm high.

designers. His work included a porcelain dinner service (1905) painted with floral motifs in a geometrical arrangement surrounded by a double row of leaf motifs at the rim, produced at the Meissen factory, where he was brought in as an independent designer in 1904. Riemerschmid supported the introduction of modern styles in stoneware produced in the Westerwald region, and designed wares for the R.*Merkelbach workshop in Höhr-Grenzhausen, which

*Richard Riemerschmid. Stoneware jug designed by Riemerschmid for R.*Merkelbach in Höhr-Grenzhausen before 1906.*

included mustard pots decorated with patterns made up of circular motifs and wavy lines.
Refs: Hettes & Rada; Porzellankunst.

Riese, Johann Karl Friedrich (1759-1834). German porcelain modeller known for figures, groups and medallions in neo-classical style produced in biscuit porcelain at Berlin, where he worked 1789-1834. His son and pupil, Wilhelm Riese, also worked as a modeller at Berlin and succeeded his father as chief modeller, 1834-41.
Refs: Danckert; Haggar (1960); Hannover; Honey (1952); Weiss.

Riessner, Stellmacher & Kessell. See Amphora (Bohemia).

Ring, Joseph. *See* Bristol Pottery.

Ringel d'Illzach, Jean-Désiré (1847-1916). French modeller, medallist and ceramist, born in Alsace. He studied under sculptors in Paris and Dresden and was a member of the Société des Artistes Français from 1888 and the Société Nationale des Beaux-Arts from 1904. Ringel d'Illzach worked as a modeller in C.*Haviland's rue Blomet studio and provided designs for production by E.*Müller.
Refs: Baschet; Bénézit; Heuser & Heuser.

Rippl-Rónay, József (1861-1930). Hungarian painter, engraver and ceramic designer, trained in Munich (from 1804) and Paris (from 1889). He returned to Hungary from France c.1900, afterwards producing designs for earthenware painted with flowing floral patterns produced by V.*Zsolnay.
Refs: Neuwirth (1974b); S. Szöts *Vilmos Zsolnay, Fünfkirchen* (catalogue, Jugendstilgalerie Strauch, Vienna).

Rischgitz, Edouard (1828-1909). Painter and porcelain decorator, born in France. While working in England at the *Minton factory c.1864-70, he decorated earthenware, (e.g. a *tazza* painted with a scene from Aesop's fables in imitation of majolica dated 1864, large vases with battle or hunting scenes, animals, etc., trays and small panels), and occasionally porcelain, e.g. tableware decorated with figures in landscapes in a style resembling that of E.*Lessore.
Signed examples exist.
Refs: Aslin & Atterbury; G. Godden in Atterbury (1980).

Risley, Sidney and George L. *See* Norwich Pottery.

Ristori, Tite-Henri-Clément. Italian-born sculptor and ceramist working in Marzy (Nièvre) from c.1854, first exhibiting in 1855, when he won a medal in the Paris exposition; his work included portrait busts and sculptural pieces, e.g. hounds attacking a boar. He later moved to Nevers, nearby, until 1863. Ristori's workshop produced cups decorated with arabesques in blue on a yellow ground, vases and bowls in bluish grey or blue ground, and other pieces inspired by Nevers faience (*bleu de Nevers*) of the 17th century, sometimes using perforated designs in decoration. He exhibited simple, peasant plates decorated with flowers or military emblems in the International Exhibition in London, 1862.

TR

Mark: monogram of TR with *Marzy, Nievre.*
Refs: Lesur (1971); World Ceramics.

Riverside. *See* Avon Faience Co.

Rix, Felice (b 1893). Viennese ceramist and designer, trained at the Kunstgewerbeschule there, 1913-17. She subsequently worked mainly as a textile designer at the Wiener Werkstätte, also providing many designs for ceramics, as did her sister Kitty. The work of the two sisters is mainly indistinguishable. She settled in Japan in 1925, working as a teacher in Kyoto, 1950-63. Her work includes figures and groups, animal models, vases and dishes.
Mark: initials FR.
Ref: Neuwirth (1974a).

Rix, Wilton P. English ceramic artist working at the *Doulton & Co. studio in Lambeth from 1868; art director from 1870 to 1897. After extensive research, Rix developed a range of colours which would withstand the high temperature of salt-glazing, sometimes using glazes in two or more colours to produce a mottled effect, which was popular in the 1890s. Rix was joint patentee with H. *Doulton for the technique of Marqueterie ware in 1887.
Refs: see Doulton & Co.

Robalbhen, Henri-Léon-Charles. French cæramist. Robalbhen exhibited at the Salon des Artistes Français in 1896 and collaborated with H.-A.-L.*Laurent-Desrousseaux from 1898 on stoneware in Art Nouveau styles, with relief decoration of leaves and other plant forms highlighted by the use of glossy glazes with matt, etched areas. He also carried out some barbotine painting on bowls and flasks. His work in the 20th century included a matt-surfaced bowl with plant forms in glossy relief and a bust of Flora in coloured stoneware that dates from 1906.
Mark: ROBALBHEN, incised.
Refs: Bénézit; Heuser & Heuser; Thieme & Becker; Valotaire.

Roberts, Eugene. *See* Denver China & Pottery Co.

Roberts, William. *See* White family.

Robertson, Alexander W. (1840-1925). American potter. In 1865, he started a pottery in Chelsea, near Boston, Massachusetts, making brown-glazed earthenware. In partnership, 1868-72, with his brother, H.C. *Robertson, he produced flowerpots, plain or decorated with green paint, and unglazed chemical ware. Joined by younger brother George W. and their father J.*Robertson in 1872, he established the *Chelsea Keramic Art Works, making art pottery from 1873.
Robertson settled in California in 1884 and carried out research into local clays. With Linna Irelan, he established the *Roblin Art Pottery in 1898 and worked there until 1906, meanwhile continuing his own research

Tite-Henri-Clément Ristori. Earthenware tazza with carved and painted decoration. This piece was exhibited in Paris, 1855.

into native materials. He went to the south of California with his son, F.H.*Robertson, and occupied a studio at the Los Angeles Pressed Brick Co. where his son was engaged in clay technology. In 1910, he joined the *Halcyon Pottery as director and instructor, providing the pottery with two kilns. His work there included vases, often angular in form and frequently decorated with a single lizard in full relief. He also modelled small incense burners and a range of clay whistles.

He was invited by the *Alberhill Coal & Clay Co. to carry out research on the clays obtained nearby and produced a limited amount of art pottery on an experimental basis, 1912-14, though the projected commercial output was never realized. Robertson retired in c.1915.
Mark: initials, AWR.
Refs: Barber (1976); Evans; Kovel & Kovel; Watkins (1950).

Robertson, Frederick H. (1880-1952). American potter, son of A.W.*Robertson. He worked with his father at the *Roblin Art Pottery from 1903 and moved to Los Angeles in 1906. Robertson was a clay technologist at Los Angeles Pressed Brick, a company closely associated with the *Alberhill Coal & Clay Co., and produced many pieces of pottery in the course of his experimental work. The first dated pieces were made in 1913. By 1915, he achieved lustre and crystalline glazes, for which he won gold medals in exhibitions at San Diego and San Francisco. Crystalline glazes were used on the bases of lamps which had ceramic shades inset with coloured glass. Work of this period was seldom sold commercially. Robertson became superintendent of the Claycraft Potteries Co., chemical stoneware manufacturers, soon after the firm's incorporation in 1921, concentrating largely on clay and glaze technology, while his son G.B. *Robertson, who joined the firm as his assistant in 1925, was mainly responsible for design. The Robertsons produced a wide variety of tiles, garden ware and a number of special pieces, such as lamp bases. Joining his son at the Robertson Pottery, organized in 1934, Frederick Robertson threw work which George Robertson decorated. He died soon after the pottery's closure in 1952.
Mark: initials FHR impressed on work at Los Angeles Pressed Brick; F.H.R./*Los Angeles.*
Refs: Evans; H. Stiles *Pottery in the United States* (E.P. Dutton, New York, 1941).

Robertson, George (1777-1833). Porcelain painter, born in Ayrshire and working in *Derby from c.1797. Also a painter in oils and watercolour, Robertson executed detailed landscapes, often featuring autumn colours, local scenes and nautical subjects, specializing in naval engagements and stormy seas, at the factory in Nottingham Road.
Ref: W.H. Tapp 'George Robertson, painter of Derby China' in *The Connoisseur* (November 1935).

Robertson, George B. (1907-66). American potter. He assisted his father, F.H.*Robertson, in experimental work at Claycraft Potteries Co. from 1925, concentrating mainly on design. He organized the Robertson Pottery in Los Angeles, 1934, moving the following year to Hollywood. Chiefly engaged in design and decoration, because of a skin infection aggravated by throwing, he painted underglaze designs (often inspired by actual examples of Islamic ware). His painted ware was coated with clear glaze or a crackle glaze similar to that developed by his uncle, H.C.*Robertson. He also used brightly coloured glazes in green, turquoise, blue, white, pink or *sang de boeuf*. The ware, consisting mainly of vases, plates, smoking sets and plaques, as well as buttons, was initially thrown and, later, sometimes moulded, in simple shapes, occasionally with restrained relief decoration. Robertson moved the pottery back to Los Angeles in 1940, returning three years later to Hollywood, where the works remained until its closure in 1952.
Marks: several versions of *Robertson/ Hollywood*, impressed, incised or printed; *R/Los Angeles*, printed or incised.
Refs: Evans; H. Stiles *Pottery in the United States* (E.P. Dutton, New York, 1941); *Yesterday and Tomorrow: the Story of*

*Hugh C. Robertson. Pitcher with relief decoration made at the *Chelsea Keramic Art Works, c.1878. 38 cm high.*

Robertson Ceramics (brochure published by the pottery, c.1937).

Robertson, George W. (1835-1914). American potter. He worked with his father J. *Robertson in Boston by 1859, and with him joined his brothers A.W. and H.C. *Robertson at their pottery in Chelsea, Massachusetts, in 1872, thus forming the *Chelsea Keramic Art Works. He left the firm in 1878 with J.G.*Low, with whom he remained associated until 1890. In that year, Robertson established the Chelsea Keramic Art Tile Works at Morrisville, Pennsylvania, with his brother, Hugh, and took charge of production for the firm which was formed to provide the extra capital needed for completion of the plant, trading as the Robertson Art Tile Co. The initial output consisted of glazed brick and wall tiles in a wide variety of colours. The company also produced relief tiles, including a panel modelled in low relief by Hugh Robertson after illustrations by Gustave Doré. The firm remained in operation after George Robertson's departure in 1895, and became known as the Robertson Manufacturing Co. H.T.*Mueller was employed from 1903.
Refs: Barber (1976); Barnard; Evans; Watkins (1950).

Robertson, Hugh Cornwall (1844-1908). Potter, son of J.*Robertson, born in County Durham, England. He emigrated to America with his family in 1853 and became an apprentice at the Jersey City Pottery in 1860. In 1868, he entered into partnership with his brother A.W.*Robertson in Chelsea, Massachusetts, and took part in the production of art ware from 1873. The firm traded as the *Chelsea Keramic Art Works from 1875. Robertson shared with his pupil and sister-in-law, Josephine Day, the modelling of floral sprays, which were applied to the indented surface of the body of vases, hammered before the clay was fired. He also modelled a number of stoneware plaques, generally glazed in muted blue or grey and decorated in relief, e.g. with designs after Gustave Doré's illustrations of fables by La Fontaine or portraits of Dickens, Byron, Longfellow, and other writers. He was deeply influenced by the display of oriental ceramics in the Centennial Exhibition at Philadelphia in 1876 and, after taking control of the pottery in 1884, concentrated on the rediscovery of Chinese glazes, particularly *sang-de-boeuf*. A bright red glaze, 'Robertson's Blood', was first achieved in 1885 and perfected in 1888. Other colours included deep sea green, turquoise, apple green, mustard yellow, peachblow (shaded), maroon and purple, all noted for their brilliancy. In 1886, Robertson produced a grey-white Japanese crackle glaze which was used over designs painted in blue. He normally used very simple shapes made in fine, pale stoneware, on which the glazes might show to best effect. Robertson's devotion to glaze research at the expense of commercial production resulted in the pottery's financial failure, and in 1890, with his brother George W.*Robertson, he formed the Chelsea Keramic Art Tile Works at Morrisville, Pennsylvania, but needed extra capital before production could start (for which the Robertson Art Tile Co. was formed with George Robertson as superintendent). In

1891, Hugh Robertson became manager of the *Chelsea Pottery US, established with backing from a group of Boston men. Continuing his own experimentation, assisted by his son W.*Robertson, he perfected the crackle glaze, which became a feature of his pottery's commercially successful Cracqule Ware, as well as appearing on vases with floral decoration painted by Robertson himself and others in underglaze blue. After the removal of the pottery to Dedham (*see* Dedham Pottery) in 1896, he continued work on flowing glazes, sometimes with iridescent effects, or rough bubbled surface (Volcanic) used on porcelain vases, still of simple form. Production of the Volcanic ware required the use of more than one glaze, often fired several times. Robertson received one of the highest awards at the World's Fair in St Louis, 1904, and died four years later after a long illness resulting from lead poisoning. He was succeeded as head of the firm by his son.

Marks: monogram of HCR; small square on the face of some work at Dedham Pottery.
Refs: Barber; Clark & Hughto; Eidelberg; Evans; L.E. Hawes *The Dedham Pottery* (Dedham Historical Society, 1968); Henzke; Keen; Kovel & Kovel; Nelson; Watkins (1950); J.J. Young *The Ceramic Art: A Compendium of the History and Manufacture of Pottery and Porcelain* (Harper & Bros, New York, 1878).

Robertson, James (1810-80). Potter, born in Edinburgh, the son of an employee of the Fife Pottery, where he worked before joining a pottery in Prestonpans c.1826. Robertson subsequently worked at various earthenware factories in the north of England, then emigrated with his family to New Jersey in 1853. He worked in South River, then at the shop of J.*Carr in South Amboy and, briefly, in New York before joining H.*Speeler's firm in Trenton. By 1859, he moved to manage a pottery in Boston, Massachusetts. In 1860, he became partner in the Plympton & Robertson pottery, exhibiting work in Boston in the same year, and continued as manager for the new owner when the business changed hands (by 1862). He joined his sons A.W. and H.C.*Robertson at their pottery in Chelsea, Massachusetts, in 1872, making tiles from pressed clay. The firm then traded as James Robertson & Sons before becoming the *Chelsea Keramic Art Works.
Ref: Watkins (1950).

Robertson, William (1864-1929). American potter. He worked with his father, H.C.*Robertson, on the development of Cracqule Ware at the *Chelsea Pottery US. In 1904, he suffered injury to his hands in a kiln explosion, so that he was unable to throw, model or design, but succeeded his father as manager of the *Dedham Pottery in 1908. He continued the production of dinner ware and a few novelty items. He was succeeded on his death by J. Milton Robertson (d 1966) until the closure of the works in 1943.
Refs: Evans; Eidelberg; L.E. Hawes *The Dedham Pottery and the Earlier Robertson's*

Adelaide Alsop Robineau. Covered jar with overall decoration of flowers and satyr masks executed in white porcelain and grey pâte-sur-pâte. The finial is in the form of a daisy. Robineau's mark is accompanied by the title Pastoral *and a date, 1910. 23.5 cm high.*

Chelsea Potteries (Dedham Historical Society, Dedham, Massachusetts, 1968); Kovel & Kovel.

Robineau, Adelaide Alsop (1865-1929). American potter and porcelain maker, born in Middletown, Connecticut. She taught ceramic decoration briefly in Minnesota before going to study painting in New York, where she also worked as a miniaturist and artist in watercolours, while continuing to teach. She became an active member of the *National League of Mineral Painters until she gave up overglaze painting in 1903. In 1899, she married Samuel Edouard Robineau and, with him, established a journal, *Keramic Studio* (which was later to become *Design*) in Syracuse, New York; she acted as its editor until her death. Adelaide Robineau painted underglaze decoration on porcelain hotel ware for the *Onondaga Pottery Co. Her own early designs (and those provided for use by other decorators) were naturalistic in inspiration. She gradually adopted Art Nouveau decoration c.1900 and, later, increasingly relied on the effect of coloured glazes and oriental Mayan motifs. Dissatisfied with the shapes available for decoration, she began making her own pottery, unglazed earthenware, of which she exhibited the earliest examples in 1901, and in 1903 briefly studied the production of porcelain under C.F.*Binns. She illustrated her own experimental work, mainly slip-cast, in *Keramic Studio*. At first, she attempted a commercial output, decorated e.g. with incised geometrical designs or *pâte-sur-pâte* decoration. Influenced by T.*Doat's treatise, which she first saw in 1902, and published in a translation by her husband both in *Keramic Studio*

(1903-04) and as a book, *Grand Feu Ceramics* (Keramic Studio Publishing Co., Syracuse, New York, 1905), she soon restricted her output to individual pieces in elegant shape with carved or perforated decoration, and matt or crystalline glazes, which sometimes required a number of firings. The Robineau Pottery (established c.1904 at Syracuse) produced pieces designed, thrown, modelled, carved and decorated by A. Robineau alone, e.g. the Viking Vase (1905) decorated with longships, and a vase with incised crabs at the shoulder and base (1908). Her husband mixed clays and glazes and carried out the firing. The Robineaus exhibited hand-thrown porcelain, some delicately carved and covered with matt glazes in a variety of colours, notably a shaded brown, in the St Louis World's Fair in 1904, and crystalline-glazed pieces in blue, green, yellow and light brown in Chicago later the same year. A wide range of glazes were used on porcelain doorknobs, which were sold 1905-10. By 1907, glaze colours included dark and light blue (both very variable), orange, cream and black.

The Robineaus joined the *University City Pottery (1909-11), where they worked in association with Doat. While there, Adelaide Robineau experimented with a stoneware body, though normally working with the porcelain used at Syracuse, and developed a semi-opaque glaze which remained translucent without firing to a high gloss, and was used on the elaborately carved Scarab Vase (entitled 'The Apotheosis of the Toiler'), which represented the efforts of a beetle collecting food. The vase, entirely covered with incised decoration, was included in a large display of 55 pieces exclusively by Adelaide Robineau which won the *Gran Premio* at the International Exhibition in Turin, 1911; she regarded it as her greatest achievement. She returned in 1911 to Syracuse where she worked at her own pottery until World War I. From 1920, she taught at Syracuse University, continuing her own work in porcelain, while supervising the production of low-fired earthenware by her students. She retired because of illness in 1928.

Because of her high standards in work and repeated glazing and firing of pieces that did not satisfy her, Adelaide Robineau's output remained small. F.H.*Rhead, an associate at University City Pottery, commented on its qualities in design and technique in 1917. Only two examples of eggshell porcelain are now known, although she had experimented with carved decoration on this kind of ware by late 1907 and was again doing so in 1922. The Metropolitan Museum of Art in New York held a memorial exhibition of her work in 1929.

Mark: RP (Robineau Pottery) monogram carved in a square or circle. Her work at University City also had the UC mark.
Refs: Barber (1976); Clark & Hughto; Eidelberg; Evans; Henzke; W. Hull 'Some Notes on Early Robineau Porcelains' in *Everson Museum of Art Bulletin* 22 (1960); Keen.

Robins, Richard. English porcelain painter, trained at the *Pinxton China Factory c.1800. Robins was a working partner in a London decorating workshop which he established with T.M.*Randall, 1812-25.

Refs: S.W. Fisher *The Decoration of English Porcelain* (Derek Verschoyle, London, 1954), and in *Country Life* (6th December 1956); Godden (1966a); Jewitt; W. Turner 'Madeley Porcelain' Parts I and II in *The Connoisseur* 22 (November, December 1908).

Robinson, F. *See* Derby.

Robinson, Gray & Burns. *See* Sheriff Hill Pottery.

Robinson, Harold Taylor (c.1877-1953). English ceramics manufacturer. Travelling as a representative for *Wiltshaw & Robinson from 1899, he established *Arkinstall & Son for the manufacture of porcelain novelties and souvenirs under the trade name, Arcadian. He maintained the independence of his own company while becoming a partner in Wiltshaw & Robinson, 1906-11, and merged it with *Robinson & Leadbeater, of which he had taken control.

Robinson formed a company in the name of his father J.A. (or A.J.) Robinson & Sons Ltd, with himself, his father and his brother, Hubert Alcock Robinson, as directors operating the businesses of Robinson & Leadbeater; W.H. Robinson which was established in 1901 in Longton, taken over in 1907 and merged with Charles *Ford of Hanley (users of the trade name Swan China and bought by Robinson in 1904); the Wardle Art Pottery (formerly Wardle & Co. Ltd) of Hanley from c.1910, and Ford & Pointon (*see* Norfolk Street Works). Robinson purchased the Cauldon Place works (formerly *Brown-Westhead, Moore & Co.) which he used as his headquarters in running the firm which became in 1920 Cauldon Potteries Ltd, an amalgamation of the branches of J.A. Robinson with other businesses which Robinson either controlled or had bought, e.g. F.R.*Pratt & Co. Ltd (bought c.1900), the Cobridge earthenware manufacturers Henry Alcock & Co., Grindley Hotel Ware Co. of Tunstall, G.L.*Ashworth & Bros Ltd. He later gained control of Ridgways (Bedford Works) Ltd (*see* Ridgway Potteries Ltd), Shelton, *Wedgwood & Co., Tunstall, Bishop & Stonier, Hanley, *Coalport China Co. and the *Worcester Royal Porcelain Factory. Robinson became chairman of the Royal Crown *Derby factory in 1927, and the firm remained in the control of his family until the resignation of his son Phillip Robinson as chairman of Royal Crown Derby in 1961.

Robinson also bought the firms of W.H. *Goss, and Hewitt Bros (*see* Hewitt & Leadbeater) and absorbed them into the Cauldon group as Willow Potteries Ltd (1925) and W.H. Goss Ltd (1930). After other purchases of manufacturers of sanitary ware and suppliers of clay and fuel, Robinson suffered financial losses and went bankrupt in 1932. During his bankruptcy, he became Sales Organizer of a new company formed by the amalgamation of Burslem earthenware manufacturer, George Jones, with Bishop & Stonier, operating the Crescent Pottery, Stoke-on-Trent. This firm shortly afterwards purchased Allerton's Ltd (*see* Allerton, C., & Sons), already a part of Cauldon since 1912. After merging with Cauldon, Coalport China Co. merged with George Jones & Sons, and subsequently Coalport, Cauldon,

Allerton's, Crescent and Goss China were all used as trade names for work produced at the Crescent Pottery. The Goss mark was probably discontinued by 1939; Arcadian also disappeared as a mark.

Cauldon Potteries Ltd was acquired by Pountney & Co. in 1962, and Coalport became part of the Wedgwood group in 1977.
Refs: Andrews; Godden (1964); Jewitt; Twitchett (1976); Williams-Wood.

Robinson, James. *See* Soil Hill Pottery.

Robinson, James J. English porcelain maker. Robinson trained in ceramic techniques under his grandfather S.*Hancock, with whom he stayed as a boy, and took control of the King Street porcelain factory in *Derby from Hancock's death in 1898 until the sale of the company in 1916.
Refs: see Derby.

Robinson, William. *See* Hunslet New Pottery.

Robinson & Leadbeater. Staffordshire porcelain manufacturers. The partnership of James Robinson and Edward James Leadbeater (1837-1911) working in Stoke-on-Trent at the Glebe Street works (formerly occupied by G.*Meli) from 1865, and a factory in Wharf Street from 1870. The firm specialized in parian ware, noted for the high quality of its materials and workmanship, which included vases, flower holders, jugs, comports, table centrepieces, trinket boxes, as well as figures, portraits and groups. The firm was under the control of H.T. *Robinson from the early 20th century.

Marks: R & L impressed on the back of bases of figures from c.1885; printed mark with elephant's head and *R & L Ltd* from c.1905.
Refs: Cushion (1980); Godden (1964);

Robinson & Leadbeater. Bust of General Gordon. 20 cm high.

Jewitt; Shinn; obituary in *Staffordshire Sentinel* (28th March 1911).

Robj. French retailer, the sponsor of annual design competitions from the late 1920s until 1931. Some of the prize-winning designs were produced in limited editions at the Sèvres factory. Robj commissioned small decorative pieces in porcelain for sale in the firm's Paris showrooms. Lamps, bottles and incense burners were often in the form of human figures. Statuettes in Cubist style were produced in cream-coloured porcelain with crackle glaze. Other goods included desk sets and smokers' requisites.
Ref: Klamkin (1971).

Roblin Art Pottery. American pottery established 1898 in San Francisco by Linna Irelan and A.W.*Robertson to exploit Californian clays. The main output consisted of vases in red, white or buff bodies, often unglazed, or glazed only on the interior. Glazes, when used, were made exclusively from Californian constituents. Slip-painted ware, with glazes in green, tan, grey or blue, resembled the Bourg-la-Reine ware developed at the *Chelsea Keramic Art Works. A wide variety of decorative techniques was used, including the hammering of unfired clay in preparation for relief decoration, which Robertson had developed at Chelsea. Some pieces in red clay were coated in white slip before firing to a satin finish. Linna Irelan concentrated on the modelling of decorative work which included flowers, foliage, fungi and, notably, lizards, and was often very elaborate. Some domestic articles such as bowls, mugs and pitchers were also produced. Robertson was responsible for potting and firing the ware, all of it in thrown shapes. His own work was austere in form, with decoration mainly restricted to simple lines of beading, finely wrought handles, or a glossy glaze. The pottery and stock were destroyed in the earthquake which struck San Francisco in 1906.
Marks: a bear, impressed, often with the name of the firm; RAPC, also impressed. In addition, Robertson's initials AWR, or the name, initials or spider's web mark of Linna Irelan.
Refs: Barber (1976); Evans; Kovel & Kovel.

Rochechouart. French pottery established 1837 at Rochechouart, 40 kilometres from Limoges, for the production of porcelain. The workshop was small, having only one kiln; the known output of porcelain included a vase in rococo style. Operating under Pierre Duval after its sale, c.1850, the workshop produced pottery for domestic use. It remained the property of the Duval family, who now employ about 50 workers on the making of flowerpots, after turning production over to horticultural wares in 1925.
Refs: d'Albis & Romanet; Lesur (1971).

Rockingham ware. A trade name used to describe earthenware dipped in streaked, reddish-brown or chocolate-coloured manganese glaze, a speciality of the *Swinton Pottery. The original glaze, used on a fine, white body, is said to have required three applications and firings to develop the colour and was used on jugs, cups, tea, coffee and chocolate sets, as well as *Cadogan teapots, until the closure of the pottery in 1842. The

glaze was also used as a ground colour in the decoration of porcelain, notably by I. *Baguley. The Wedgwood firm produced Rockingham ware decorated with etched or engraved patterns in the second half of the 19th century.
The original earthenware was copied widely by British potteries producing teapots, toby jugs and ornamental ware, and was made throughout the United States from c.1840, normally with a mottled effect. The similar *flint enamel ware was developed at the *United States Pottery. East Liverpool, Ohio, eventually became the principal centre of manufacture. *Taylor & Speeler were established at Trenton, New Jersey, for the production of Rockingham ware in 1852.
Refs: Barber (1976); Eaglestone & Lockett; Jewitt; Lawrence; Rice; Spargo.

Rockingham Works. *See* Swinton Pottery.

rococo. A decorative style characterized by delicate, curving asymmetrical motifs derived mainly from rock, shell, floral and leaf forms, and developed in France in the early 18th century. The style spread throughout Europe before reaching England, where it was at its height from the mid 18th century until c.1770, and America (c.1760-80). Rococo ceramics were made in faience, and toys (scent bottles, boxes, sweet dishes, etc.) were popular.
The style was revived in the decoration of English porcelain from the 1820s to the mid 19th century, e.g. at *Swinton, *Derby and *Coalport. Many figures were produced in Europe in the mid 19th century, either from 18th-century models or from new designs set on moulded scrollwork bases. Vases encrusted with single flowers and scrolled decoration, made at the *St Petersburg factory, date from c.1850.

Rodgers, Gwladys M. (b 1887). English pottery decorator, born in Bedale, Yorkshire. After studying at the Salford School of Art, Gwladys Rodgers joined the *Pilkington's Tile and Pottery Co. as a painter, mainly working on lustre patterns until 1928, when she began to concentrate on the painting of Lapis ware, becoming one of the main decorators of that line until the firm ceased to produce art wares in 1938. She won a Gold Medal for work exhibited in Paris, 1925, and became known for the liveliness and originality of her painted patterns.
Marks: R on shield in normal square mark of Pilkington artists.
Refs: Callen; Coysh (1976); Cross; Godden (1966a); Lomax.

Roeginga Pottery. English pottery established by O.*Davies and his wife G.*Barnsley after Davies's return in 1934 from a career at sea at Rainham, which was situated in a part of Kent formerly named Roeginga. Edward Baker was employed as potter, making the output of earthenware, which was painted by Grace Barnsley and fired and marketed by Oscar Davies. The pottery closed in 1939; it was sold after World War II and reopened in 1948 under the firm of Alfred Wilson Ltd. Edward J. Baker was employed by the new owners and, with his family, succeeded them. The title became Rainham Pottery Ltd in 1956.
Marks: incised R, 1938-39; RAINHAM

impressed or painted from c.1948.
Refs: Cushion (1980); Godden (1964).

Roemer & Co. *See* Mosbach.

Rogers, James. *See* Donyatt.

Rogers, John (1760-1816) and George (1763-1815). Staffordshire potters, operating the Dale Hall Pottery established in Burslem, c.1780. George Rogers was succeeded by his nephew Spencer Rogers, and the firm traded as John Rogers & Son until its purchase by James Edwards in 1842. Rogers produced high quality pearlware printed in blue patterns, often for the American market. The output also included pieces printed with sprays of flowers in enamel.
Marks: ROGERS accompanied by a circle with an arrow extending from its right side.
Refs: Coysh (1972, 1974); Coysh & Henrywood; Jewitt.

Rokubei II or Seisai (c.1797-1860). Japanese potter, successor to the pupil of *Eisen, Shimizu (or Kiyomizu) Rokubei (c.1739-99), and working under the artistic name Seisai in Kyoto from 1811. Rokubei II worked in the style of other Kiyomizu potters, later specializing in the production of blue and white porcelain in the styles of Chinese wares, mainly for everyday use; he also made other reproductions and worked on the techniques of monochrome glazes. He was succeeded on his retirement in 1838 by Rokubei III (d 1883), who made blue and white porcelain under the artistic name Shoun, but became better known for his output of teapots in earthenware, painted with crabs. Shichibei, a nephew of Rokubei II, produced enamel-painted wares in the Kiyomizu style; his wine bottles are highly regarded. The family line was continued by Rokubei IV (1842-1914), son of Rokubei III (who produced both pottery and porcelain under the artistic name of Shorin, combining underglaze blue and enamel painting on the same pieces), his son, Rokubei V (1874-1959), and Rokubei VI, who worked in Awata.
Refs: Brinkley; Gorham; Jenyns (1965, 1971); Masterpieces; Morse; Okada; Uyeno.

Römer & Födisch. *See* Fraureuth Porzellanfabrik.

Rookwood Pottery. American art pottery established 1880 in Cincinnati, Ohio, by M.L.*Nichols Storer, with financial backing from her father Joseph Longworth (d 1883), after whose estate it was named, and with administrative help from E.P.*Cranch and technical advice from Joseph Bailey Jr., the son of Joseph *Bailey Sr, who worked mainly at Rookwood from the following year until his death.
The pottery's output consisted of commercial tableware, umbrella stands, etc., as well as Nichols's own work and (until 1883) pieces for decoration outside the pottery. At first, local clay was used in several colours, some achieved by tinting, and covered with colourless or smear glazes. Until 1884, the variety of subjects for painted decoration was limited, and heavy relief designs were used. After the construction of two new buildings, the *Cincinnati Pottery Club rented the studio the Nichols had occupied in the

Rookwood Pottery. Umbrella stand, made at Rookwood in 1883. Decoration attributed to M.A.*Daly or A.R.*Valentien. 57.1 cm high.

original building. The Rookwood School for Pottery Decoration was set up briefly; teachers included C.C.*Newton, secretary and part-time decorator at Rookwood in the early 1880s, who taught overglaze and underglaze painting, and L.A.*Fry, who taught modelling and slip decoration. In 1896, students from Cincinnati Art Academy were to receive further training on joining the pottery.

The decorating department was formally organized in 1881, with A.R.*Valentien (the first decorator regularly employed) in full charge of the department from 1884. Other decorators included Laura Fry, Harriet Wenderoth (both woodcarvers), Alfred Brennan, Fannie Auckland (*see* Auckland, W.) and W.H. Breuer. Nichols, Newton and Cranch worked in individual studios. The shapes were mainly by W.*Auckland, thrower, but some pieces, including jugs, pitchers, plates, vases and tea caddies, were designed by Laura Fry. The pottery gradually came to concentrate on slip decoration. In 1883, Fry was the first to use an atomizer to apply colour. Its use was developed by M.A.*Daly to blend grounds in dark browns, reds, orange and yellow under a yellow-tinged glossy glaze. A colour scheme using blended shades of brown, orange and yellow became associated with Rookwood's Standard Ware, which featured flowers or figures painted in slip under the glaze. Joseph Bailey Sr carried out research to enlarge the range of colours and improve their compatibility with the glazes. He was replaced as superintendent by K.*Langenbeck from the winter of 1884-85 until the end of 1885. The chance discovery of the 'Tiger Eye' golden aventurine glaze (resembling the stone in colour) led to experiments in its reproduction, which were only partially successful. A glaze with smaller crystalline flecks was called 'Goldstone'.

W.W.*Taylor, administrator and partner in the pottery from 1883, initiated measures

to improve profitability. He closed the pottery school and made a careful study of sales before deciding which lines to retain or discontinue. He ceased the production of all transfer-printed ware and any designs thought not to be assured of sales, but nevertheless maintained the independence of artists and encouraged continued experimentation. By early 1885, the pottery ceased production of Cranch's designs, Fry's carved designs filled with blue on a grey ground, Fannie Auckland's stamped patterns, or Nichols's Japanese-inspired grotesques (although Japanese art continued to provide a strong stylistic influence, notably in the work of artist K.*Shirayamadani). The pottery won the gold medal at the Exposition Universelle in Paris, 1889. In the same year, Nichols turned over to Taylor her interest in the pottery, retaining a studio for her own work.

The building of a new pottery at Mount Adams started in 1891. Floral decoration was very frequent throughout the next ten years, but there were also portraits of American Indians, negroes, portraits after Old Masters, heads of animals, and landscapes. These subjects were among work carried out by younger decorators under W.P.*McDonald from c.1897. In addition to the firm's Standard Ware, the lines included: Cameo, decorated with flowers on pink and white ground under a clear glaze; Iris (introduced 1894 or 1896), with a wide range of effects, featuring blended grounds in warm grey and white with soft tones of pink, blue, green, creamy white and yellow under a glossy glaze; Sea Green, opalescent grounds, often with designs of fish; Aerial Blue, with blue-tinted glossy glaze over decoration on blended grounds in light blue and grey. A.M.*Valentien was among artists who attempted to introduce modelled pieces, and J.H.D.*Wareham, who joined the pottery in 1893, carried out relief decoration. A metalwork department in operation 1896-97 made mounts for jugs and pitchers, and fitted lamps with mounts from Japan. Again in 1899, the pottery used metalwork overlays developed by Shirayamadani.

The Valentiens were among several artists who visited Europe on study trips intended to enlarge the pottery's artistic range. A. *Van Briggle introduced matt glazes in 1901 after experimentation that started in 1896. Several styles of decoration using matt glazes included Mat Glaze Painting, Incised Mat Glaze, Modeled Mat Glaze, and Conventional Mat Glaze. Vellum, a translucent matt glaze, was perfected in 1904 and used with detailed land and seascapes painted on vases and plaques. Wall plaques had been made experimentally from 1896, and the pottery was extended to accommodate an architectural department begun under McDonald in 1902, which made tiles, mantelpieces, wall panels, fountains and exterior decorations. It was at peak production 1907-13, and lasted until the 1940s.

The custom of individual pieces being signed by decorators and dated and numbered according to shape gradually gave way to the use of moulded decoration, which could be produced at lower cost. Under J.H. Gest, vice president and director, who succeeded Taylor 1913-34, the pottery made such pieces as bookends (from 1908), candlesticks, wall sconces, flower holders, boxes, smoking or writing requisites. The Tiger

Rookwood Pottery. Earthenware bowl made at Rookwood in 1912, decorated by Charles Stewart Todd (1885-1950). 13.9 cm high.

Eye glaze was revived in 1920. The pottery closed briefly after financial failure in 1941, but reopened under the presidency of Wareham. Production of pottery was resumed by November 1941, and continued on a small scale throughout American involvement in World War II, alongside the making of electrical parts and wooden pipes in parts of the buildings.

From 1941, the pottery was owned by a scientific, educational and research foundation under the jurisdiction of the Roman Catholic Diocese of Cincinnati. Production in the 1940s included a quantity of religious figures as well as vases, candlesticks, bookends, dishes, boxes and animal models. Clocks were introduced by 1950. After moving to Starkville, Mississippi, in 1960, under the ownership of Cincinnati businessmen William F. McConnel and James M. Smith, the pottery produced a revised range of ware, cast or press-moulded and covered with coloured glazes. Operation ceased in 1967.

Marks: a variety of incised or painted marks before 1886 mainly incorporate the name *Rookwood*, at first with Nichols's initials; others include an anchor (rare, sometimes in relief) and a kiln between two rooks (occasionally printed); a monogram introduced in 1886 had a flame added above in 1887 and another each year for the fourteen years until 1900. Roman numerals were then added below the mark, starting with I in 1901. Other letters or numbers denote the body composition (impressed letters 1883-1900), shape and size, intended glaze etc. Artists or decorators added their initials incised or painted on the base of the ware.

Refs: Clark & Hughto; Eidelberg; Evans; Kovel & Kovel; Peck; H. Peck 'The Amateur Antecedents of Rookwood Pottery' in *Cincinnati Historical Society Bulletin* 26 (October 1968), 'Rookwood Pottery and Foreign Museum Collections' in *The American Connoisseur* 178 (September 1969), 'Some Early Collections of Rookwood Pottery' in *Auction* (September

1969); M. Peck *Catalog of Rookwood Art Pottery Shapes* (Kingston, New York, 1971).

Rörstrand Porslins Fabriker. Swedish pottery established in 1726 under the patronage of the Swedish royal family. Rörstrand amalgamated with the faience and porcelain factory at Marieburg, also near Stockholm, in 1782, and both factories worked together until the closure of Marieburg in 1788. Rörstrand was bought by Bengt Reinhold Geiger in 1797. By the end of the 18th century, the factory's main product was cream-coloured earthenware (*flintporslin*) decorated in underglaze blue and a variety of colours, but pieces in the style of Wedgwood basalt and jasper ware were also produced. Some English engravings provided the basis for blue- printed patterns by the 1820s, and Swedish views bordered with lacy patterns were printed in large quantities in the 1830s. Stimulated by commercial competition with *Gustavsberg, the factory produced copies of Limoges enamels, Palissy ware and, after the introduction of porcelain in 1857, parian ware and imitations of 18th-century Sèvres pieces. Ironstone and other opaque china bodies were also made, together with lead-glazed majolica resembling that developed by *Mintons Ltd. Exhibition displays included large vases with modelled decoration. Under A.*Wallander, designer from 1895 and art director two years later, the factory adopted features of Art Nouveau decoration, often using underglaze colours over relief patterns, and developed *flambé* and other high-temperature glaze effects. *Pâte-sur-pâte* designs appeared on delicate ground colours.

Rörstrand was in operation at Gothenburg from 1926 and Lidköping from 1932, taking over in 1939 another Lidköping factory (established 1910). Animal figures were modelled by Waldemar Lindström in the early 20th century. Designers, including the glass artist, Edward Hald, and Louise Adelberg, aimed at a specifically 'Swedish style', suited to modern needs, under G.*Nylund, director from 1932 until 1958 or 1959. The factory's output also includes painted decoration by the painter Isaac Grünewald in the 1940s and geometrical patterns by the Constructivist Einar Lynge-Ahlberg. K.-H. *Stalhane contributed designs for sculptural pieces, and in the 1950s tableware (including the Moka service) was designed by Hertha Bengtson (who later worked as a designer for the firm of *Rosenthal). The factory joined the *Upsala-Ekeby group in 1964.

Marks: the three crowns of Marieburg, with *Rörstrand*; early printed marks often incorporate a pattern name.
Refs: R.A. Baeckström *Rörstrand och dess tillverkningar* (Nordiska Museet, Stockholm, 1930); Borrmann; Hannover; Lagercrantz; G.H. Strale *Rörstrands Historia och Tillverkningar: 1726-1850* (Stockholm, 1879); *Three Centuries of Swedish Pottery* (catalogue, Victoria & Albert Museum, London, 1959); E. Wettergren 'Swedish Pottery: Rörstrand and Marieburg' in *Burlington Magazine* 83, 84 (1943-44); N.G. Wollin *Modern Swedish Decorative Arts* (London, 1931).

Rosanjin Kitaoji (1883-1959). Japanese potter, artist and connoisseur, born in Kyoto. Rosanjin studied ceramic techniques at Kanazawa (Ishikawa prefecture) in 1915 and settled in 1917 at Kamakura, near Tokyo, where he established his own kiln. He specialized initially in blue and white or celadon-glazed wares in Chinese styles, then increasingly expressed his admiration for established Japanese wares by imitating those of *Seto, *Shino, *Oribe, *Bizen, *Iga, *Shigaraki and *Karatsu, as well as *Kenzan. He experimented freely, notably in the decoration of low-fired wares. Recognizing the importance of tableware and serving dishes in the presentation of food, he worked to supply a Tokyo restaurant which he ran 1925-36. In 1954, Rosanjin travelled the world, exhibiting in Europe and America.

Mark: signature (not on teabowls).
Refs: Ceramic Art of Kitaoji Rosanjin: Three American Collections (catalogue, Benrido, Tokyo/Kyoto, 1964); Cort; Koyama; S.E. Lee *Tea Taste in Japanese Art* (catalogue, The Asia Society, New York, 1963); Masterpieces; Munsterberg; Okuda; Roberts; *Rosanjin* (catalogue, The Japan Society, New York, 1971).

Roschütz. German porcelain factory established 1811 at Roschütz, Thuringia, by the firm of Unger & Schilde, for the production of everyday tableware, display services, vases, etc.

Marks include a shield bearing the initial R crossed by an arrow; a circle enclosing a crown and ALTENBURG/SAXONY.
Refs: Danckert; Weiss.

Rose, John (c.1722-1841). English porcelain maker. The son of a farmer, Rose was apprenticed to Thomas Turner, proprietor of the *Caughley factory. He left to set up his own works at Jackfield in Shropshire before establishing the *Coalport porcelain works

c.1796 with partners Richard Rose and Edward Blakeway. He bought Caughley in 1799, after the retirement of Turner, and ran both factories together before transferring equipment from Caughley to Coalport in 1814. In the same year, he took over a firm established shortly before by his brother Thomas Rose in a partnership, Anstice, Horton & Rose, immediately across the canal from the Coalport works. In 1820, Rose perfected a glaze containing feldspar with small quantities of sand, china clay, soda, nitre and calcined borax, which superseded the factory's lead glaze and won his firm the Isis Gold Medal of the Society of Arts for a glaze which would avoid the harmful effects of working with lead and arsenic compounds. Rose was succeeded as proprietor by his nephew William Frederick Rose (d 1863).
Refs: Godden (1970); Honey (1948a); Jewitt; Wykes-Joyce.

Rose, William Frederick. *See* Rose, John.

Rose Noble. In Australian ceramics, this trade name appeared as a mark on miniature moulded souvenir jugs made in the 1950s and 1960s in Sydney. A series made for the Australian states included examples with an emu in low relief and coloured black alongside PERTH W.A. stamped in black.
Ref: Graham.

Roself. *See* Foley Potteries.

Rosemeade Pottery. *See* Meade, Laura.

Rosenthal, David. *See* Bimini Werkstätten.

Rosenthal. German porcelain manufacturers established by Philipp Rosenthal (1855-1937) originally as a decorating workshop. Rosenthal then went into the production of white ware for decoration in his workshop. He opened a branch in Asch, Bohemia, 1886-99 and in 1891 started production at the newly built Porzellanfabrik Philip Rosenthal & Co. in Selb, with 225 employees. The factory of Bauer, Rosenthal & Co. K.G., built in 1897 at Kronach, Oberfranken, began production in the following year; the two sites employed 1200 workers in 1905. Some services, introduced without decoration to emphasize the elegance of their shapes, were later painted under the glaze, with slender stems and heart-shaped leaves in the case of the Botticelli or Darmstadt service (shapes produced from 1902 as Botticelli and later known as Darmstadt) or a cherry design on the Donatello service (shapes introduced 1907). The Isolde service (shapes introduced 1909-29) featured low, wide cups, jugs and other hollow ware with straight sides, narrow bands of decoration with small flowers at intervals in groups of three, and delicate lines of gilding. The firm also made porcelain for industrial use, starting with electrochemical ware made from 1900 in Selb, as well as stoneware and other ceramic bodies later made at Selb.

In 1908 Rosenthal took over the firm of Thomas & Ens (established 1903 in Marketredwitz), backed the newly founded Fachschule für die Porzellanindustrie in Selb, and started at the Selb factory an art studio which was fully established two years later. The Porzellanfabrik Jacob Zeidler & Co.,

Rörstrand. Porcelain vase decorated in relief by Waldemar Lindström. Marked: Rörstrand *with three crowns and* WL. *23.5 cm high.*

Rosenthal. Plate painted with portraits against a gold-lustre ground, late 19th century. Signed by the artist, R. Volk. 25.3 cm high.

established 1866 in Plössberg, near Selb, and acquired in 1917, worked as the Rosenthal-Porzellanfabrik Bahnhof-Selb GmbH until 1971. The firm established a workshop at the Plössberg factory in 1918 for the production of figures, which in the 1920s and 1930s included theatrical characters (e.g. pierrots), costume studies, and girls posing with animals. Other factories which became part of the Rosenthal group included, in 1921, the Krister Porzellan-Manufaktur A.G., founded at Waldenburg by C.F. *Krister in 1831 for the production of tableware, coffee sets, etc., and the factory of Thomas & Co. A.G. at Sophienthal, which Rosenthal leased in 1928, and of which the firm was owner from 1936 until its resale in 1975, producing tableware and, later, refractory wares and technical ceramics. Rosenthal also took a share in the tableware manufacturers, Keramisches Werke A.G. at Neu-Rohlau, near Karlsbad, in 1923, briefly (1932-33) owned the Preßstoffwerk-Neuwerk GmbH, producers of bakelite, metal-plated porcelain and ceramics, and in 1937 bought the workshop formerly owned by J.*Haviland at Waldershof. Decoration of tablewares, etc., was carried out at Società Ceramica del Verbano, Laveno, which the firm founded and operated in conjunction with Società

Rosenthal. Coffee set with white and matt yellow glazes. Coffee pot 23.5 cm high.

Italiana in Laveno from 1924 until the Rosenthal share was sold in 1935. Rosenthal wares were also decorated at the Munich workshop of Rudi Zöllner (established 1921), which the firm owned 1932-63. The glassworks, Cristallerie Saint Louis, Münzthal (Lothringen), became part of the Rosenthal group in 1942.

Philip Rosenthal Jr (b 1916), the founder's son, joined the firm in 1950. When he became chairman in 1958, he embarked on a policy which changed the firm's image as a manufacturer of rather conservatively styled, though high-quality tableware and gained it an international reputation for aesthetically progressive, functional design in glass, cutlery, furniture and other items of interior decoration, as well as ceramics. The development of the firm's porcelain, pottery, cutlery and glass was centralized in Darmstadt in 1959.

The first designs of Rosenthal's Studio Line had already been produced in the early 1950s. An early example was the group of designs known as 2000, provided by the American designer, Richard Latham, in association with Raymond Loewy; porcelain hollow ware in tall, waisted forms with sharply looped finials, was produced 1954-78. The Studio Line was developed from 1961 as the vehicle for the firm's artistic ambitions with the aim of creating an interior environment of complementary objects. Other important Studio Line shapes and patterns have been provided by W. Gropius who, with Louis McMillen, designed the tableware shapes produced as TAC I (or the Gropius Service) and TAC II, and by the designers Tapio Wirkkala, Bjørn Winblad, Timo Sarpaneva, Raymond Peynet, H.T. *Baumann and Ambrogio Pozzi. The range has included limited editions of art pieces: the Rosenthal relief series, Rosenthal Objets d'Art, Year Plates, and Christmas Plates in the 1960s. The artists who contributed designs for these lines include Henry Moore, Eduardo Paolozzi, Victor Vasarely and Salvador Dali.

Refs: Danckert; Weiss; *Rosenthal: Hundert Jahre Porzellan* (catalogue, Kestner-Museum, Hannover, 1982).

Roseville Pottery Co. American firm established in 1890 for the production of stoneware at the works formerly used by J.B.*Owens's pottery company in Roseville, Ohio, and incorporated in 1892. Under the management of George F. Young, the firm expanded by

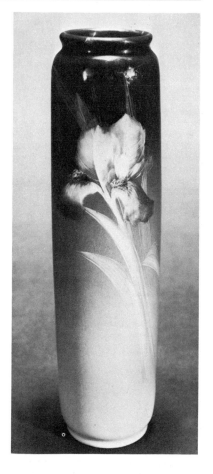

Roseville Pottery Co. Vase, painted with an iris on a green ground, c.1900. Marked in relief, Rozane ware, Royal. 37.3 cm high.

1901 to occupy one more Roseville stoneware factory and two potteries in Zanesville, although production was limited from 1910 to the Zanesville plants, one making kitchen ware and the other producing art ware ever since its introduction in 1900. The first line of art ware, moulded from native clays (and developed by R.C. Purdy in the rush to compete with the *Rookwood Pottery's Standard Ware), was hand-painted in slip with animals, flowers, portraits, etc., under the glossy glaze, against a blended, brown-toned ground. Originally marketed as Rozane, it later became available with light or dark ground and was produced until 1919 under the title Rozane Royal, which distinguished it from the other Rozane lines which followed, e.g. Azurean, with decoration painted under the glaze in blue and white slip on a blended ground of the same colours, introduced 1904; in 1905, Mongol (red glaze, usually crystalline, also called Chinese Red or Rouge Flambé) and Mara (lustre ware comparable with S.A.*Weller's Sicardo ware) both created by J.J.*Herold, and others matching introductions to Weller's range of art ware. Egypto (matt green glaze over embossed decoration) and Woodland (incised floral designs, sometimes with stippled effect on grey, yellow or brown ground) were other lines appearing in the catalogue of 1905. In the following year, the

catalogue listed Crystalis, a crystalline-glazed line, and Fudji, with stylized designs and lacking the stippling of Woodland, which it otherwise resembled. These lines were developed by G.*Fudji.

F.H.*Rhead, art director 1904-08, developed Della Robbia (introduced 1906) with incised designs, generally stylized, against a background which had been cut away to reveal a layer of contrasting clay, and sometimes embellished with coloured slips; Aztec (not listed in the catalogue until 1910) with geometrical or stylized floral patterns on buff, cream or grey ground; Olympic, transfer-printed with line illustrations of Greek myths. His brother, H.G. *Rhead, who succeeded him as art director until 1918, developed Carnelian with matt glaze on specially designed shapes 1910 (and offered in the following year with shaded colour and textured glaze), Pauleo, with red crackle glaze under metallic brown lustre (introduced 1914), Donatello (introduced 1915) with scenes showing children, in shades of green and orange/brown on white, and Mostique (introduced in the same year) with incised designs on a matt ground. The firm's next art director, F.*Ferrell, introduced many lines (at least one a year) including Sylvan decorated with owls and foliage (c.1910), Ferrella with shell decoration on mottled ground (c.1930) and, notably, Pine Cone with relief decoration of pine cones and needles, in production 1935-c.1950, though probably designed much earlier. The plant producing cooking ware was burned out in 1917 and production moved to the other Zanesville plant on Linden Avenue. By 1920, machine processes had replaced costly hand decoration of art ware, but new lines were produced even in the Depression of the 1930s. The pottery closed in 1954.

Marks incorporate the name of the pottery or ROZANE WARE and often the name of the line. Pieces marked *Olympic* also specify the subject of the decoration.
Refs: D.E. Alexander *Roseville Pottery for Collectors* (privately published, Richmond, Indiana, 1970); Barber (1976); Richard A. Clifford *Roseville Art Pottery* (Andenken Publishing Co., Winfield, Kansas, 1968); Eidelberg; Evans; W.P. Jervis *A Pottery Primer* (O'Gorman Publishing Co., New York, 1911); Kovel & Kovel; Lehner; L.& E. Purviance & N.F. Schneider *Roseville Art Pottery in Color* (Wallace-Homestead, Des Moines, Iowa, 1970); N.F. Schneider *Zanesville Art Pottery* (privately published, Zanesville, Ohio, 1963).

Rosslyn Pottery. Scottish pottery established in Fifeshire in the late 19th century, and producing earthenware with a rich, dark brown glaze, which included money-boxes in the form of farm animals (e.g. horses, sheep, sitting hens, and 'Pirley pigs'), the heads of dogs or rabbits, or in the form of chests and other items of furniture. After expansion in 1883, the pottery produced majolica and buff stoneware.
Ref: Hughes.

Roudebuth or **Roudebush**, Henry. Pennsylvania German potter making slip-decorated earthenware in Montgomery County from the late 18th century until 1816. *Sgraffito* designs included a group of five flowers surrounded by an inscription on a pie plate

dated 1811; a central device of a bird and tulips on a plate dated 1813; a more elaborate design showing a vase of flowers with a bird perched on branches above on a plate dated 1816. These plates are also signed.
Refs: Barber (1976).

Rouse, James (1802-88). English porcelain painter, the son of a gardener in Derby, where he was apprenticed at the factory of R.*Bloor in c.1815, training under W. 'Quaker' *Pegg. He went on to become the only painter employed at all three *Derby porcelain factories. His work at the Nottingham Road works included a set of three large vases painted all round with flowers and fruit. Rouse left Bloor's factory c.1826 to work briefly in Staffordshire and then from c.1833 until c.1871 at *Coalport, where he painted choice pieces for the firm's display in the Great Exhibition (1851) and the International Exhibition (1862). Much of his work was carried out on wares in Sèvres style. After working again for Staffordshire firms, he joined a company of jewellers and metalworkers in Birmingham for three or four years and worked for the firm of S. *Hancock in King Street, Derby, from 1875. His painting there included scenes of rustic figures at the centre of plates with perforated ornament. He joined the porcelain factory in Osmaston Road, Derby, in the autumn of 1882. His work included rich arrangements of flowers on dessert plates, floral panels for vases in Sèvres style, and miniatures of children on jewelled cups and saucers. Some pieces painted at Osmaston Road bear Rouse's signature. He fell ill while working on oval panels of flowers for the Gladstone service.

Rouse was known for his soft, rich arrangements of flowers, but he also painted fruit, figures (including Cupids), portraits, animals and landscapes. Rouse's sons were also porcelain painters: William Rouse (b c.1824) painted flowers at Coalport by 1841, leaving c.1860; James Rouse (born at Madeley in the early 1830s) worked at the factory in Osmaston Road; as well as landscapes, his work includes a signed portrait plaque of his father.
Refs: Godden (1970); *see also* Derby.

Rouse, Owen. *See* Jersey City Pottery.

Rousseau. *See* Saint-Clément.

Rousseau, François Eugène (1827-91). French designer, artist and retailer of glass and ceramics in Paris. Rousseau produced table services in collaboration with the firms of C.*Haviland and Barluet et Cie (*see* Creil) notably the Rousseau service decorated with designs by F.*Bracquemond after Hokusai. His own work included the modelling of tableware for decoration by Bracquemond at Creil-Montereau.
Refs: J. Bloch-Dermant *L'Art du Verre en France 1860-1914* (Denoël, Paris, 1974); Brunhammer *et al* (1976); H. Hilschenz *Glassammlung Hentriech: Jugendstil und 20er Jahre* (Kunstmuseum, Düsseldorf, 1973).

Rowe, William E. Ceramic designer, modeller and painter, working for *Doulton & Co. 1883-1939, in Lambeth. His work included a vitreous fresco panel painted with a

female portrait after Botticelli, c.1907, and stoneware vases painted with simple, stylized plant motifs against pale grounds. With H.*Simeon, he used the technical developments achieved by J.H.*Mott to create a fresh style in saltglaze for both individual pieces and large-scale production, and designed a number of pieces of Persian ware, 1919-22.
Mark: monogram of WR.
Refs: see Doulton & Co.

Royal Albert bone china. *See* Foley Potteries.

Royal Albert China. *See* Wild, T., & Co.

Royal Aller Vale & Watcombe Pottery Co. *See* Aller Vale & Watcombe Potteries.

Royal Barum Ware. *See* Brannam, Charles Hubert.

Royal Bayreuth. *See* Tettau.

Royal China. *See* Hughes, Edward, & Co.

Royal China Works, Worcester. *See* Grainger & Co.

Royal Copenhagen. *See* Copenhagen.

Royal Crown Derby. *See* Derby Crown Porcelain Co.

Royal Dux. *See* Duxer Porzellan-manufaktur.

Royal Doulton. *See* Doulton & Co.

Royal Essex Art Pottery. *See* Bingham, Edward Alfred.

Royal Grafton. *See* Jones, Alfred B.

Royal Lancastrian. *See* Pilkington's Tile & Pottery Co.

Royal Rockingham Works. *See* Swinton Pottery.

Royal Stafford or **Royal Staffordshire China.** *See* Poole, Thomas.

Royal Staffordshire. *See* Wilkinson, A.J., Ltd.

Royal Vienna Art Pottery. *See* Jones, A.G. Harley.

Royal Worcester Spode Ltd. *See* Worcester.

Rozane. *See* Roseville Pottery Co.

Rozenburg Plateelfabriek. Dutch pottery established 1883 at The Hague by the German potter Wilhelm Wolff Freiherr von Gudenburg, who had settled in the Netherlands three years before. The initial output of earthenware in the manner of early Delft gave way to vases, display plates and dishes brightly painted with asymmetrical designs of stylized flowers and other natural motifs, when von Gudenburg entered into collaboration with T.C.A. Colenbrander, artistic director of the pottery, 1884-89. Tile panels were decorated with paintings in the style

Rozenburg. A range of pieces made at Rozenburg c.1900-14. The small vase, bottom right, bears the monogram of S.*Schellink. This piece is 12.5 cm high.

associated with local artists. The business transferred to the Rozenburg estate in 1886 and in the following year became N.V. Haagsche Plateelfabriek 'Rozenburg', winning the right to use Koninklijke as part of the title in 1900. After 1889 the firm passed to a succesion of directors. The decorators included D.*Harkink, J.C.*Heytze, J.K. *Leurs, and F.J. Mansveld (1891-96), later co-director of the Plateelbakkerij *Ram. J.J.*Kok, at first artistic consultant, took over as art director in 1895 and acted as technical director from 1897. The production of light, very thinly potted earthenware, marketed as *Eierschaalporselein* (eggshell porcelain), began in 1899. The pieces were designed by Kok and the painters included S.*Schellink and R.*Sterken. The production of other decorative earthenware, tiles and tile panels continued. Some panels were designed by J.T.*Toorop c.1903. Production of a line of earthenware marketed as Juliana ware began in 1909. Kok left the firm in 1913 and production ceased in the following year. The firm was dissolved in the 1916.

Marks include von Gudenburg's initials, *WvG* and *den Haag*, 1885-89, then marks incorporating *Rozenburg, Den Haag* (the place name alone 1889-93, then with a stork from 1893, and crown, 1900-14) accompanied by the initials or signs of painters. Date letters, A in 1885 to M in 1895, were followed by year symbols.
Refs: Kunst der Jahrehundertwende und der Zwanziger Jahre (catalogue of the Karl Bröhan collection, Berlin; *Kunsthandwerk um 1900, Jugendstil-art nouveau-modern style-nieuw Kunst* (catalogue, Hessisches Landesmuseum, Darmstadt, 1973); *Rozenburg-Keramik* (catalogue, Focke-

Museum, Bremen, 1976); Singelenberg-van der Meer.

Ruaud, Jean-Baptiste. French ceramist and porcelain manufacturer. After occupying a portion of M.*Nivet's factory from 1829, Ruaud moved to the *Monnerie factory, where he remained from 1839 until his retirement in 1869. He supplied wares to cafés and restaurants, as well as making blue and white ware, and ornamental pieces which included vases with elaborately moulded scroll decoration. In his efforts to cut production costs, he introduced industrial methods, including the use of machinery in

Fernand Rumèbe. Porcelain vase with underglaze decoration in black and brown, 1925. Marked in brownish black with monogram of FR. 27.1 cm high.

making plates and other repetitive lines. In the course of research into coal firing, he developed a new process using wood and coal in 1855.
Mark: R, painted or impressed (on few pieces).
Ref: d'Albis & Romanet.

Ruko. *See* Radford, Albert.

Rumèbe, Fernand (1875-1952). French ceramist. Rumèbe started work in association with E.*Decoeur from c.1903 until the end of 1906, or a little later, when he took over Decoeur's house in Auteuil as his studio, making stoneware and porcelain painted with flowers, etc. He subsequently visited Turkey, and, in 1911, participated in several exhibitions, showing porcelain and stoneware, including tiles fired at high temperature. His decoration at this period was often inspired by the patterns of oriental carpets. He later returned to the prevailing European treatment of a variety of plant forms and geometrical designs, sometimes achieving raised effects with thickly painted slip. His work in the 1920s included pieces which resemble Chinese case glass in decoration, with an outer layer carved to expose a lighter ground colour.

Mark: painted name or initials.
Refs: Baschet; Heuser & Heuser; Lesieutre.

Rum Rill Pottery Co. American retail company based in Little Rock, Arkansas, and owned by pottery designer George Rumrill. The firm supplied designs and moulds for Rum Rill art ware produced to its own specifications by firms including the *Red Wing (in the 1930s) and *Shawnee (1941-42)

potteries, and (1938-41) the Florence Pottery under the management of L.*Gonder. The company distributed ware in a variety of coloured glazes, either matt or glossy, throughout America. Rum Rill ware includes vases, lamp bases, tableware (including luncheon sets), pitchers, covered jars, and plant pots, marked with the name of the ware. George Rumrill joined the Shawnee Pottery in the early 1940s.
Refs: Kovel & Kovel; Lehner; G. Weiss in *The Antique Trader* (5th June 1973).

Runel. *See* Sèvres.

Ruperti, Justus Christian. *See* Leeds Pottery.

Rupsch, Johann Friedrich (1775-1841) and Karl Friedrich (b 1784). Ceramic decorators working in Germany. The brothers were painters, noted for their work in underglaze blue, at Rudolszadt. Johann Friedrich Rupsch went to Klösterle in 1799 and Karl Friedrich moved to Pirkenhammer between 1806 and 1814, then to Klösterle, to Giesshübel briefly in 1817, returning to Pirkenhammer in the same year. Friedrich Rupsch, son of Johann Friedrich Rupsch (b 1801), worked as a thrower in Klösterle.
Ref: Meyer.

Ruscoe, William. English ceramist, working from c.1920. One of a family of Staffordshire potters, Ruscoe evolved rolled clay figures as a means of self-expression for his students, while teaching modelling to young potters at Burslem and Stoke-on-Trent art schools in the 1920s and 1930s. His students included

Peter Rushforth. Stoneware bottle with salt and ash glaze. 57 cm high.

James Rushton. Porcelain dish painted by Rushton for Bullers Ltd, c.1946.

A.*Potts, and Ruscoe also worked from 1941 at the studio which Anne Potts had started for *Bullers Ltd. His own simple, lively figures and groups were rolled in fireclay, often with decorative detail in white porcelain. In 1944, he moved to Exeter, where he has since worked as a teacher.
Mark: incised or painted monogram of WR from 1920 (with date from 1925).
Refs: A. Blackman 'Rolled Pottery Figures' in *Ceramic Review* 56 (March/April 1979); Cushion (1980); Godden (1964); Haslam (1977); W. Ruscoe *Sculpture for the Potter* (Academy Editions, London, 1975).

Rushforth, Peter (b 1920). Australian studio potter and teacher born in Manly, New South Wales. Rushforth studied drawing, sculpture and painting at the Royal Melbourne Institute of Technology 1946-48 and in 1950 at the National Art School in Sydney, where from 1951 he taught ceramics. He has exhibited since 1952 and established studios in the Sydney suburbs of Beechcroft and Church Point. Rushforth's work in stoneware and porcelain consists of domestic ware and decorative objects which also have a function (e.g. flower containers), all wheel thrown, and sometimes subsequently beaten or modelled, in strong, simple shapes, with a variety of glazes, including ash, feldspathic iron and saltglaze, and simple splashes of slip or glaze. His stylistic influences range from medieval English slipware to oriental pieces. He has been on study visits to Japan (*Koishibara, *Mashiko, *Kyoto), where he has exhibited, and in 1967 to Europe and the United States.
Refs: Hood; P. Thompson *Twelve Australian Craftsmen* (Sydney, 1973).

Rushton, James. English ceramic designer and decorator, working for *Bullers Ltd from 1943 after training at Burslem School of Art. He studied at the Royal College of Art on a scholarship, 1946-49, and afterwards returned to Bullers, 1949-52, while also working as a teacher of design. His early decoration was noted for its spontaneity. His later worrk includes a coffee service, in elegant forms recalling creamware, and painted over the glaze with birds, butterflies and foliage. He taught full time from 1960.
Marks: signature or initials, JR.
Ref: Art Among the Insulators

(catalogue, Gladstone Pottery Museum, Stoke-on-Trent, 1977).

Rushton, Josiah (b 1836). English porcelain painter working for the *Worcester Royal Porcelain Co. c.1852-71. Rushton was a painter of figure subjects and portraits; his work included a series 'Beauties at the Court of King Charles', vases with portraits of girls, women with children, etc., and many copies of pictures by Gainsborough, often on plaques. He exhibited at the Royal Academy in 1880.
Mark: monogram of JR with three dots.
Ref: Sandon (1978a).

Rushton, Raymond (1886-1956). Porcelain painter working for the *Worcester Royal Porcelain Co. Rushton's detailed, brightly coloured paintings of country house and cottage gardens and monochrome views of castles include a series of Royal Palace gardens. He also painted seascapes and carried out the hand colouring of printed scenes of castles and cathedral buildings desinged by H.*Davis. He retired, suffering from arthritis, in 1953.
Ref: Sandon (1978a).

Ruskin Pottery. *See* Taylor, William Howson.

Russinger, Laurentius. *See* Pouyat family.

Rustic. *See* Owens, John B.

Ryan, Mazie Theresa (1879-1946). American designer and ceramic decorator. She studied

*Mazie T. Ryan. Vase made by J.*Mayer Sr and decorated by Ryan at the *Newcomb College Pottery, c.1900-10. The design of wild tomatoes is incised and painted in blue, blue-green, yellow and buff glazes. 29.8 cm high.*

at the Sophie Newcomb Memorial College for Women, New Orleans, where she carried out decoration at the Newcomb Pottery 1898-99, and as a graduate student 1901-05. Her work included a tall, tapering vase with a 'wild tomato' design of fruiting stems around the neck, and a mug (c.1905) with carnation flowers encircling the shoulder. She later became an independent designer of pottery, as well as producing embroidery and items for interior design.

Marks: initials, MTRY, or full name in capitals, always with the initial T larger than the other letters.

Refs: Clark & Hughto; G.R. Clark *Ceramic Art: Comment and Review 1882-1978* (Dutton Paperbacks, New York, 1978); Kovel & Kovel; S. Ormond and M.E. Irvine *Louisiana's Art Nouveau: the Crafts of the Newcomb Style* (Pelican Publishing, Gretna, La, 1976).

Ryan, Thomas and Edward. *See* Clark, Nathan.

Rye, Sussex. English country pottery centre active since the 13th century near sources of clay and plentiful timber for firing. Many small potteries in the area made mainly domestic red ware for local sale, sometimes with pale slip trailed or inlaid in simple patterns under the thick lead glaze.

Incised marks incorporating the place name, *Rye,* occur on pottery made at the *Cadborough Pottery of sale further afield along the south coast and at the *Belleview Pottery by F.*Mitchell.

Refs: Brears (1971a); Lloyd Thomas (1974).

Ryonyu. *See* Raku family.

Ryosai. *See* Inoue Yoshitaka.

Ryozen (d 1841). Japanese potter, tenth in succession of a line descended from Nishimura Zengoro, who worked at Nara for six generations on the production of charcoal burners, fire boxes for tea ceremony use, and idols, in earthenware. Ryozen learned the techniques of *Raku ware and, working subsequently in Kyoto, made imitations of *Seto and *Kochi wares for the tea ceremony; some of his output was intended for everyday use. He was succeeded by his adopted son *Hozen.

Refs: Jenyns (1965, 1971); Roberts.

Ryumonji. Japanese folk pottery started in the late 16th century by Korean potters for the production of tea wares, and established after several moves at Oyamada, Kagoshima prefecture, in the 18th century. The early wares resembled those of *Osotoyama and *Koishibara, with inlaid, combed, or painted slip decoration. Celadon glazes with trails of white glaze were used in the 19th century for spouted saké bottles, etc. Ryumonji is now noted for the continued use of traditional methods and as far as possible local materials. The transparent glaze contains feldspar, silica and wood ash, and copper oxide is obtained locally for green glaze. The present output includes bowls and saké containers with trickles of brown and green glazes over a honey-coloured ground, covered dishes with white glaze poured in arcs from a swinging brush on green or brown ground, and traditional vessels for the tea ceremony.

A mottled effect produced by the application of black over white glaze in thick layers is characteristic of the area. Some large bowls have horizontal bands of simple relief decoration.

A branch established at Kumamoto in the 18th century made inkyu wares, with green splashes on a pale ground.

Refs: Jenyns (1971); Munsterberg; Okamura; Sanders.

Sabanin, Vavila Dmitrievich (d c.1874). Russian porcelain maker. After working as chemist and colour technician for his relative, A.G.*Popov, he established his own factory in 1848 or 1849 in the village of Vlasovalin in the region of Vladimir, soon moving to nearby Klimovka, where he produced table services and figures. Sabanin was briefly succeeded in 1874 by his son, who closed the factory in the following year.

Marks: '*of the factory V. Sabanin*', in Russian, or Sabanin's initials, in Cyrillic characters in blue under or over the glaze.

Refs: Ross; Rozembergh; Saltykov.

Sabrina. *See* Worcester.

Safronov, Anton Trofimovich. Russian porcelain manufacturer. At the village of Korotkaia, near Moscow, in 1830, he established a workshop which was in the hands of the *Kuznetsov family by 1851. Safronov's finer wares were decorated with flowers, or costume studies of topical figures, merchants, officials and the lower aristocracy. He also made figures of dandies and provincial ladies of fashion, as well as large quantities of everyday ware.

Mark: Cyrillic S with thickened ends (which can be confused with a mark used by the *Gardner factory) in underglaze blue.

Refs: N.V. Bulochkin 'Porcelain and Faience Sculpture' in *Russian Decorative Art* Vol III (in Russian, Moscow, 1965); Emme; Ross; Rozembergh; Saltykov.

Sahm, Bernard (b 1926). Australian studio potter, born in Sydney and trained at the East Sydney Technical College in ceramics and sculpture. Sahm studied techniques at potteries in Australia, in Germany, and under H. and M.*Davis in England. In making sculptural pieces, he aims to express a concern with various aspects of human activity and the changing values of society. Sahm taught at East Sydney Technical College, 1964-76, Sydney College of the Arts, 1977-83, and works in a studio in the Sydney suburb of Mosman.

Ref: Craft Australia No 4 (1976).

Saida. *See* Isaburo Okeya.

Saint-Amand-en-Puisaye (Nièvre). French pottery centre in Burgundy, active by the 17th century. Local potters, including the family of E.*Lion, made utilitarian stoneware with iron-bearing silicate (resulting in a colour that varied from deep red to brown) or, less frequently, wood ash, in a salt glaze. J.*Carriès worked with the Lion family from 1888 and later alone, adapting local techniques. He was followed by G.*Hoentschel, E.*Grittel, P.*Jeanneney, J.*Pointu, and P.*Pacton. Later potters working in the area included J. and N.*Pierlot at Treigny.

Refs: Céramique française contemporaine;

M. Poulet *La Poterie Traditionelle de Grès de Puisaye* (Auxerre, 1975).

Saint-Amand-les-Eaux. French porcelain factory established c.1817 at Saint-Amand-les-Eaux (Nord) by the Bettignies family, owners until 1880. The factory was exceptional in maintaining the large-scale production of soft-paste porcelain (which had been generally abandoned, e.g. by the Sèvres factory in the early 19th century). Using a thick, yellowish-white paste, sometimes in lobed shapes, the Bettignies made tableware for domestic and restaurant use, decorated with garlands, etc., in blue, in the manner of Tournai soft-paste porcelain. They also made faience painted with large red roses and leaves in a bright green based on copper oxide, or bouquets containing cornflowers and pinks in translucent colours, and white earthenware which included plates printed in series in the mid 19th century. The factory was successful in reproducing 18th-century Sèvres decorative pieces in soft-paste porcelain during their period of great popularity under Napoleon III. Imitations of other 18th-century English and French porcelains were made for decoration outside the factory.

Marks: cypher of SS flanking an A (on porcelain); *St Amand/Nord* in a circle (on cream-coloured earthenware).

Refs: Burton (1921); Ernould-Gandouet; Fontaine; Lesur (1967); Tilmans (1953).

St Anthony's Pottery. English earthenware works established c.1780 in Newcastle-upon-Tyne. Under the control, from c.1804, of Joseph Sewell and his successors, Sewell & Donkin and Sewell & Co., the works produced earthenware, including a very pale creamware. Sewell's output included woven baskets and openwork plates resembling those made by the *Leeds Pottery, and a quantity of printed ware. The firm built up a large export trade, and became known for lustre ware, e.g. jugs with moulded vines and cupids, and pink lustre decoration; silver and gold lustres were also used. Tea services composed of small pieces, sometimes with yellow ground colour and silver bands at the edges, were a speciality. Sewell & Co. ceased operation in 1878, but the works reopened 1882-1908.

Marks include *St Anthony's*, painted or impressed; SEWELL and the names of subsequent firms, impressed.

Ref: Bell.

Saint-Brice. French porcelain factory established 1825 in Saint-Brice (Haute-Vienne) by François Baignol (*see* Baignol family), who was succeeded 1840-55 by his sons Camille and Evariste. The factory was sold, then let, and passed in 1867 to the brothers Jules and Charles Berger, local potters, succeeded in 1885 by Louis Berger, who worked in partnership from 1899, trading as Berger & Cie. Michelaud Frères, owners of a Limoges decorating workshop, who bought Saint-Brice from the Berger family in 1917, specialized in luxury items, often decorated in underglaze blue.

In 1962, Georges Jammet and Henri Seignolles took over the factory from Lucien Michelaud for the production of wares to be decorated at their workshop (established 1950) in Limoges.

Marks: LUCIEN MICHELAUD/LIMOGES between two circular lines; M with LL at the centre; *Jammet Seignolles* or JS.
Ref: d'Albis & Romanet.

Saint-Clément. French faience factory established 1758 at Saint-Clément (Meurthe-et-Moselle) as a branch of Lunéville (about 12 kilometres away). In the early 19th century, under the ownership of Rousseau, the factory produced large quantities of fine white earthenware. Germain Thomas took over the factory in 1824, followed in 1840 by his three sons. After c.1867, he produced everyday ware printed with costume subjects, e.g. tourists visiting Biarritz. The factory now forms part of the Société des Faïenceries Guérin, with Lunéville.

Marks: from 1830 (rarely used) *S. Clément* in blue; sometimes (after 1850) written in a circle joined with four dots; after c.1867, printed shield over *St Clément*.
Refs: Ernould-Gandouet; Fontaine; Lesur (1971); Tilmans (1954).

Saint-Cricq-Cazaux. *See* Creil.

St George's works. *See* Worcester.

St Ives Pottery. *See* Leach, Bernard Howell.

St John Stoneware Co. Canadian manufacturers of white earthenware and ironstone china. The firm was established in 1873 with backing from Edward C. Macdonald (d 1889) and his brother, who soon took over as proprietors. The output, intended to compete with ware imported from Staffordshire, consisted mainly of undecorated tableware, but included ranges with simple decoration in enamel (maroon, pink, mauve, shades of green, buff, sometimes with touches of black), lines of gilding, a scattering of small gilt rosettes, or silver lustre used on handles and rims. Moulded tea and toilet sets were decorated with flowers, butterflies and other insects in natural colours with ribbons and ruffles in relief touched with pink or blue. Circular wall plaques were painted with landscapes, etc., at the factory, or sold for outside decoration. Other ornamental pieces included vases, small jugs, miniatures and 'St John's blue', a coloured body sprigged with decoration in white clay. The firm also advertised hotel, institutional and medical ware with initials or devices to commission.

The pottery was the main—and the longest lived—producer of white-bodied tableware to be established in Canada. After enlargement in 1888, the firm employed about 400 workers, but failed to recover after damage to the factory by fire in 1893 and ceased production by 1899.
Ref: Collard.

Saint-Léonard. *See* Monnerie factory; Pouyat family.

St Lukas. Dutch pottery established in 1909 at Utrecht by A. Enthoven and G.D.J. *Offermans, who acted as art director. The firm's pottery included lustre ware developed by Offermans, with decoration of plants,

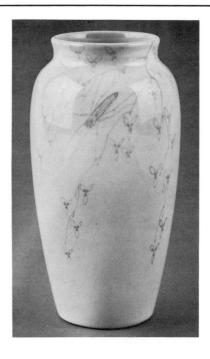

St Lukas. Vase with yellow lustre glaze and a pattern of a water spider among weed.
Mark: St Lukas, Utrecht. 18 cm high

fish, insects, and other natural forms. Decorators and designers included R.*Sterken, the silversmith, Carel Begeer (1883-1956) and C.J.*van Muijen. Jan Carel Heytze (1873-1943), art director from 1913, also concentrated on metallic and textured surfaces. The business continued under Heytze and the painter A. Seinstra (b 1877) after a temporary closure in 1923. After the firm's move to Maarssen in 1927, its output included earthenware in simple shapes with red, yellow or grey ground and decorated with horizontal stripes in black, or with stylized flowers in the same colour as the ground. Production ceased in 1930.

Marks include *St Lukas/*UTRECHT, sometimes with *Holland* or *Made in Holland* and, later, *Maarsen/Made in Holland.*
Refs: Singelenberg-van der Meer; van Straaten.

St Petersburg. Russian porcelain factory established in 1744 under the protection of Empress Elizabeth Petrovna, and under the patronage of subsequent rulers until the dethronement of Tsar Nicholas in 1917. A branch established in the reign of Tsar Paul (1796-1801) at Gatchina operated (1799-1802) with only limited success. The allied state earthenware factory, which had been established 1752 in the Neva brickworks, initially manufactured coarse-bodied earthenware with opaque glaze, and subsequently earthenware with finer, off-white body; it closed in 1802.

In this period, the St Petersburg factory produced richly decorated tableware and the newly introduced large display vases used for Imperial residences and as diplomatic gifts. Painted decoration consisted mainly of landscapes with palmettes, garlands and bouquets, laurel wreaths and, often, a scattering of flowers over the surface.

The factory was reorganized under Alexander I (1801-25) and a protective tariff imposed in 1806 on imported porcelain. D. Guryev, head of the factory throughout this reign, appointed the French master potter, Adam, as manager (1808-16) and Franz Gartenberg, formerly technologist and designer at the *Gardner factory, as experimental chemist from 1803, with the task of improving technical standards. Pierre Landel became the factory's specialist in paste and glazes and, near the end of Alexander's reign, the French painter J.-F.-J.*Swebach, the gilder Denis Moreau from Sèvres and the thrower F. d'Avignon joined the St Petersburg factory, training Russian technicians and artists as they worked.

Tableware was produced in Empire style, with elegant shapes imitating Greek, Roman or Etruscan models, sometimes with Egyptian elements in design. Decoration often took the form of narrow relief bands, and frequent motifs included eagles, lions and, swans. Gilding was lavish. The Gureyev service (begun in 1809) with gilded borders of acanthus leaves, laurel wreaths and a variety of other foliage on a magenta ground, and painted scenes showing the peoples of Russia, featured sculptural groups by S. Pimenov, which supported cups, vases and baskets. It is said that no two pieces were alike. Portraits of heroes of the war in 1812 were used on vases, plates and, especially, cylindrical cups. Black transfer printing was briefly introduced by a German workman in 1814, sometimes overpainted by hand, but was soon discontinued.

The work became heavier in style in the reign of Nicholas I (1825-55) and subjects were drawn from an increasing range of sources, e.g. French and German porcelain, oriental and Russian antiquities, and included copies of oil paintings. Some services were made with Gothic or Russian-inspired designs.

Under the Imperial ministers Prince Volkonsky and Count Perovsky, and successive directors, who were concerned chiefly with administration, the factory's production, still mainly table services and vases, also included reproductions of its own earlier designs. Modelled decoration, widely used, included in the late 1840s flowers and red coral on handles or twined around the pieces. Paul Ivanov introduced flowers and foliage modelled in high relief after Meissen models; his last piece was completed in 1851.

Flower painters included Meschtcheriakov, Golov (until the mid 19th century), A. Novikov, P. Nesterov, I. Mironov, Lifantiev, and Kornilov. In general, although painting was executed in rich, intense colours with careful detail, painted decoration became less of a speciality than relief ornament. Grounds in gold or in intense malachite green, emerald, turquoise, lapis lazuli, mauve, buff, tan, chestnut or maroon with lavish gilding completely covered the porcelain (which was noted for its dazzling whiteness), except for reserves containing paintings of flowers, birds, genre scenes, military subjects. A large vase was made in 1828 to commemorate 'the War of the Fatherland' in 1812, with portraits of Alexander I in a circular medallion flanked by female figures representing History and Glory. A service painted in the 1830s with officers and men from the Tsar's favourite regiments in

St Petersburg. Jug with moulded decoration under a pale blue glaze; the spout is in the form of a cockatoo. Printed mark of Nicholas II and date, 1897. 25.4 cm high.

accurately detailed uniform was followed by a similar service, which won a medal at the Great Exhibition in London, 1851.

In 1833, the factory opened a workshop for the production of earthenware, as well as a bronze workshop making mounts for porcelain. In the reign of Nicholas I, the principle initiated by Empress Elizabeth of using only Russian materials was broken by the importation of French clay, and the paste used in this period resembled western European porcelain, particularly that made in Limoges. A studio was devoted to the production of choice wares in 1837, and a public exhibition was held in the following year. The factory's museum, begun in 1844 to celebrate the hundredth year of operation, opened in 1845.

Under Alexander II (1855-81), the post of administrator ceased and the factory became more independent of Imperial control. The serfs had been emancipated in 1861, which affected the factory's own workforce, but also released it from the competition of private factories which had to close as their workers were freed. The porcelain was still richly gilded, with painting in white reserves on coloured grounds. Many services were made from earlier models, but introductions included tableware imitating Russian shapes formerly made in metal or wood. The factory suffered technical problems particularly with firing. Speiss, master modeller, was sent to study in England, in 1871.

Under Alexander III (1881-94), the production was varied with the use of coloured glazes and, after the Tsar's marriage to a Danish princess, with underglaze painting, in tones of grey and blue in the manner of the Royal *Copenhagen Porcelain Factory (made in large quantities in the last year of the reign). The factory continued to copy foreign porcelain in 18th-century or earlier styles and was also influenced by contemporary work from Sèvres, Limoges, etc. The Raphael service, produced for use by the

Tsar, imitated motifs from Raphael's Stanze (copied for Catherine the Great in the Hermitage). In this reign, the sale of products to private individuals was forbidden.

In the reign of Nicholas II (1894-1917), the factory continued with a varied output, adopting Art Nouveau decoration after the engagement of new artists in a reorganization of the factory. Imitations of Danish porcelain continued, using a new soft paste and a new high-temperature grey-green colour. The factory was criticized for failing to achieve any specifically Russian spirit. Painted porcelain Easter eggs were introduced, as well as vases in oriental shapes, painted in designs resembling patterns of *cloisonné* enamel. Technical improvements made possible the production of candelabra, clocks, mirror frames, furniture (e.g. stools, tables) and figures of large size. Decoration included imitations of other materials—wood, metal, stone. From 1907, a new series of sculptures, produced after P. Kamensky's designs, depicted peoples of Russia.

The factory administration underwent complete reorganization immediately after the February revolution in 1917, and was at first controlled by an executive commission and, from May, briefly directed by N.N. Pouchine. In 1918, the factory passed out of the control of the Department of Mines to the Department of Fine Arts of the Commissariat of Public Instruction, and P. Waouline was appointed commissioner. After further changes in its directors, the factory came under the Department of Academic Institutions in 1921. Despite the unsettled conditions, there was no break in production, and the factory continued to develop. Before World War I, the output had been hard-paste, soft-paste and biscuit porcelain; this was later restricted to a very highly refined paste fired at 800-900°C, glazed and fired at 1400°C, then re-fired at 600-800°C after painting.

The earlier policy of maintaining artists' anonymity was changed, and new opportunities were provided for them with support and assistance from the government. Postwar painters included: S.V.*Chekhonin; Shchekatiknina-Pototskaya (designs incorporating a hammer and sickle, with machine parts and flowers, thickly brushed); Z. Kobyletskaya (a *tête-à-tête* with cylindrical forms, painted in red and green with scenes of peaceful industrial work); N.*Suetin (many services from 1922); Mikhail Adamovich (classical architecture studies gave way to revolutionary subjects c.1919); Fresee (monochrome scenes of Moscow in blue/green); Ivachinzeva (flowers and fruit in wide brush strokes, lively colours, on cups, plates, dishes). Decorations were frequently drawn from oriental art, or represented a nationalistic expression of Russian folk-art themes in bright colours.

Modellers included Vasili Kuznetsov (b 1882), director of the modelling workshop 1914-19, who designed vases, clocks and boxes in classical style, and a number of sculptural groups on the theme of war. Natalia Danko (1892-1942), director of the modelling workshop by 1924, designed the figures, Partisan, The Awakening East, a series of women at work, sailors from the *Aurora*, and dancing peasants. A. Matveyev, sculptor, designed tableware as well as a figure of a potter (1926). Much sculptural

work was characterized by rich colouring and treatment in the Russian folk-art tradition.

The state factory exhibited abroad from 1921, participating in many European industrial exhibitions. It was renamed the Lomonosov Porcelain Factory in honour of the Russian scientist. Much of the output was redesigned by the sculptress, S. Yakovleva, who joined the factory in 1936 and collaborated on a simplification of styles with Suetin. Other designers included E. Krimmer, V. Seminov, A. Vrobyovsky, M. Mokn, I. Riznich, A. Skvortsov, L. Lebedinskaya, A. Yalskevich, L. Blak and V. Gorodetsky.

Marks from the late 18th century until 1917 consist of a crown over the Emperor's initial. Post revolutionary marks include versions of a hammer and sickle, sometimes incorporating an inscription in Russian, meaning '*for the sake of the starving*' and, later, the Cyrillic initials LFS (Leningradskij Farforowyj Savod).
Refs: Danckert; Gollerbach; Hannover; I. Rodin *The State Porcelain Factory* (Leningrad, 1938).

Saint-Radegonde-en-Touraine. *See* Primavera, Atelier.

Sakai Moitsu. *See* Kenzan.

Sakaida Kakiemon XII. *See* Kakiemon family.

Sakon family. *See* Echizen ware.

Salamander Works. Pottery established in the 1830s in New York City for the manufacture of firebrick and household earthenware, with high-quality brown glaze, sometimes over relief decoration, and flowerpots. Production moved to Woodbridge, New Jersey, and is thought to have continued until 1896.
Mark: SALAMANDER WORKS and address within double oval outline, impressed.
Ref: Barber (1976); Clement (1947).

Salmon. *See* Ziegler, Jules-Claude.

Salamander Works. Moulded stoneware pitcher with Rockingham glaze over relief decoration of masks, acanthus leaves and fruiting vines, c.1850. Incised mark: Salamander Works, N.Y. 28.5 cm high.

Salopian Art Pottery Co. Bowl with high relief decoration of fruit made at the Salopian Art Pottery in the 1890s.

Salopian Art Pottery Co. English pottery established c.1880 at Benthall, near Broseley in Shropshire, for the production of earthenware vases and plaques decorated with enamel, coloured slips, fruit and flowers moulded in relief, or incised patterns. The output also included vases in simple forms depending for decorative effect on glazes of oriental inspiration. The workshop closed c.1912.

Marks include SALOPIAN, impressed.
Refs: Godden (1964); Haslam (1975); Jewitt.

Salt, Mear, Ogden & Hancock. American firm making yellow and Rockingham-glazed ware 1841-53 at the Mansion Pottery in East Liverpool, Ohio.

Mark: name and address on a raised oval.
Refs: Barber (1976); Lehner; Ramsay.

Salt, Ralph (1782-1846). English potter working at Miles Bank, Hanley, 1812-34, as an enameller and lustre painter. Salt established the Pearl Pottery in Brook Street, Hanley, and until his retirement (c.1843) produced figures in the style of J.*Walton. His work included original figures of boys raiding birds' nests, gardeners, fops, shepherds, Dr Syntax, St Matthew, and animals, notably dogs and sheep. Titles were sometimes impressed and lustred on the piece. Salt was succeeded by Richard Booth and Williams & Willett, also makers of earthenware figures until the pottery turned to the production of ironstone china and earthenware for domestic use in 1860. His son, Charles Salt (1810-64), made parian ware, as well as earthenware figures which were similar to his father's, but less well finished.

Marks: for Ralph Salt, SALT impressed on or above a scroll; Charles Salt, SALT impressed.
Refs: Cushion (1980); Haggar (1955); Pugh; H.A.B. Turner *A Collector's Guide to Staffordshire Pottery Figures* (McGibbon & Kee, London, 1971).

Salter, Edward (b 1860). Porcelain painter working for the *Worcester Royal Porcelain Co., 1876-1902. Salter was a skilled landscape artist and also painted fish. H.*Davis was apprenticed to him in 1899.
Refs: Sandon (1978a).

saltglaze. Ware with a thin, irregular orange-peel surface texture achieved by the introduction of common salt (NaCl) into the kiln at high temperature. Chlorine is released as poisonous gas, while the sodium reacts to form a glaze on the surface of the stoneware or porcelain.

Salto, Axel (1889-1961). Danish designer and ceramic artist. Salto was among the pioneers of sculptural ceramics in Denmark. He studied languages and then painting in Copenhagen. From 1916, he illustrated books written by himself and others, helping to establish a magazine, *Klingen*, in 1917. He worked as a potter from 1923, working for *Bing & Grøndahl, N.*Krebs (1931-32) and the Royal *Copenhagen Porcelain Factory from 1934. He made simple bowls with carved relief decoration in light-coloured stoneware, with richly coloured glazes flowing over relief decoration. He also made vases, utilitarian wares and some ceramic sculptures. His experiments with the relationship between glaze and body included incisions made in the unfired body and filled with glaze to produce variations in the intensity of glaze colours, and the carving of bud-like forms and, later, fruit motifs, which provided a textured surface. He divided his own working style into three periods: grooves, budding and germinating ('It is of greater importance for an artist to create in the spirit of Nature than to reproduce its outer manifestations.') He tried to express an enjoyment of Nature than to reproduce its outer manifestations'). He tried to express an enjoyment

His designs also included book-bindings (1934), printed textiles (1944) and architectural decoration.
Refs: Beard; Hiort, Préaud & Gauthier.

Salvetat. See Sèvres.

Samson, Edmé, & Cie. French porcelain manufacturing firm established by Edmé Samson, a skilled repairer, at Saint-Maurice, near Paris, c.1845, and at Montreuil in 1864, with a decorating studio in Paris. The firm became noted for reproductions of many types of porcelain using a grey-tinged hard paste (even, in some cases, when the originals were in soft paste) and sometimes using characteristic decoration on forms that would not have been used in the originals. The firm copied German porcelains from the Höchst, Ludwigsburg, and Nymphenburg factories; imitations of Meissen figures are characterized by a glassy appearance, slight speckling in the glaze and blackening on the base. The English work of Chelsea, Bow and Worcester, Chinese export porcelains,

Axel Salto. Bowl lined with grey glaze and decorated on the exterior with an incised pattern of foliage, c.1946. Mark: three parallel lines over a circle in blue. 17.8 cm in diameter.

Edmé Samson & Cie. Porcelain tureen in the form of a cockerel, with green, yellow and aubergine glazes and ruby-coloured comb; the interior is glazed in blue. Late 19th century. 25 cm high.

three-colour Ming and K'ang Hsi wares, and occasionally Italian porcelains were among the other imitations. Soft-paste porcelain was used for small articles, boxes, etc., in the style of 18th-century French factories. Copies of the Deruta, Gubbio and other Italian maiolica centres, Moustiers, Rouen, and Delft, as well as Isnik, Hispano-Moresque and Palissy wares, were made in materials approximating to the originals. The firm continues to imitate earlier wares.

Marks include: s in varying typographical styles, according to the ware's origin.
Refs: Danckert; Ernould-Gandouet; Lesur (1967).

Samson, Thorwald P.A. Danish potter working in America from 1891 in association with L.*Ipson. He was artist and modeller at the pottery of P.*Jacobus for a year before establishing the *American Art Clay Works in 1892, continuing the pottery after Ipson's return to Denmark. After his own visit to Denmark, 1899-1902, Samson re-started the Art Clay Works, remaining there for a few months, and then began the *Norse Pottery in 1903, sharing with Ipson the entire operation of the pottery, including decoration and design as well as heavy manual work, until their move in 1904 to new premises at Rockford, Illinois, where he remained until c.1914.
Refs: Evans; Kovel & Kovel.

Samsonov Brothers. Russian potters, owners of a factory producing printed earthenware and porcelain for domestic use in the *Gzhel area, 1819-75, often using scenes with figures, etc., surrounded by floral borders, similar to those produced e.g. at the *Gardner factory.

Mark: circular painted or printed mark incorporating the Samsonov name.
Ref: Bubnova.

San Cristoforo, Milan. See Richard-Ginori, Società Ceramica.

Sanda. See Sobei Kanda.

Sanders, Herbert (b 1909). American ceramist and teacher, born in Ohio. Sanders studied at Ohio State University at Columbus, working as a graduate assistant to A.E. *Baggs in 1933, and continued to teach ceramics at the university's summer schools for three years. He received the first Ph.D. awarded for ceramics in the US from Ohio State University in 1951, and taught at San Jose State College in California from 1938, where he later established a ceramics department, remaining as professor until his retirement in 1974. Sanders is noted for his research on crystalline glazes, which he used on porcelain.
Refs: Clark & Hughto; E. Levin 'Pioneers of Contemporary Ceramic Art: Maija Grotell, Herbert Sanders' in *Ceramics Monthly* Vol 24 (November 1976); Sanders.

Sanders, John (d 1863). American potter. In the partnership Sanders & Wilson, he leased the works formerly used by J.*Vodrey at Troy, Indiana, from 1851 until the destruction of the pottery by fire in 1854. After rebuilding, the firm continued production of yellow and Rockingham-glazed earthenware. The works were in operation until c.1870.
Ref: Barber (1976).

Sandier, Aléxandre. *See* Sèvres.

Sandringham pattern. *See* Aller Vale Pottery.

sang-de-boeuf. Deep red glaze coloured by copper oxide fired in a reducing atmosphere. *Sang-de-boeuf* was known in Ming China and revived in the reign of K'ang Hsi (1662-1722). European potters sought to reproduce the colour in the late 19th century and H.C. *Robertson was noted for his work on *sang-de-boeuf* glaze in America in the 1870s. B.*Moore and *Pilkington's Tile & Pottery Co. produced good examples.

San Michele, Pisa. *See* Richard-Ginori, Società Ceramica.

Sannomata Hongama. *See* Hasami.

Sano. *See* Isaburo Okeya.

Sanyo kiln. *See* Dohachi II.

Saracen Pottery. Scottish pottery established 1875 in Possill Park, Glasgow, by Bailey, Murray & Bremner for the production of stoneware, including buff and black bodies, brown-glazed earthenware and majolica.
Teapots, jugs and other domestic pieces were impressed with the mark B.M. & Co. until c.1900.
Ref: Jewitt.

Sarreguemines. French pottery established at Sarreguemines (Moselle) in 1784; under the direction of F.-P.*Utzschneider from 1798, and the administration by A.*de Geiger from 1836, followed by his son c.1871 until 1913. Victor Jullien was employed as director until the appointment of Auguste Jaunez in 1860.
At first making low-priced earthenware, painted under a brilliant glaze, the firm soon excelled in fine decorative stoneware, introducing under the Empire a body containing

fragments of coloured clay to give the effect of a variety of stones, such as jasper, basalt, granite and especially porphyry, which they exhibited in 1806. Napoleon I commissioned garden vases imitating granite in 1810. Production also included matt stoneware with relief decoration inspired by Wedgwood: small bowls, sugar boxes, toilet sets (from c.1840) and, under Napoleon III, tobacco jars, cigar boxes and *jardinières*. The colours, initially black with white decoration (or more rarely the reverse) became more varied from the 1830s to include blue, red, yellow and brown, with reliefs in the same colour as the ground, or sometimes blacκ or brown. In the same period, the classical subjects were sometimes replaced by small everyday scenes. The colour scheme soon became restricted to shades of brown or beige, ornamented with leaves of the vine, oak or bay, and from the mid 19th century pieces in grey or beige were decorated with biblical or hunting scenes inspired by German stoneware.
The firm was noted for a variety of white earthenwares, which included vases, candleholders and plates for display, often lavishly gilded or decorated with a variety of lustre effects: platinum, copper or pinkish mauve (sometimes used on a granite ground).
Everyday ware included pots, cups, casseroles, terrines, coated with slip in pastel shades (pink, lilac, blue, green, yellow) as well as white, and garlands in relief, often picked out in black on a yellow ground, or white on blue. From c.1850, relief decoration often consisted of foliage covering the piece, or depicted a variety of scenes. Printed designs included contemporary songs, games or costumes and, from c.1840, edifying subjects (printed in black with coloured border). Large pieces were decorated with flowers *en camaïeu* in the latter half of the century. Decoration printed in blue, sometimes with touches of colour, was often inspired by Rouen faience or oriental wares.
The range of products also included painted figures (especially in the second Empire), majolica, tiles, and wall panels, sometimes with designs from Kate Greenaway.
After the inclusion of Sarreguemines in German territory (1874), the firm established two branches at Digoin and Vitry-le-François.
Marks (very varied) include U & Co, often shields, and the names of wares, and incorporate SARREGUEMINES. Majolica marks include a shield, or EMAUX DIAPRES with U&C, and the names of *Sarreguemines* and *Digoin*.
Refs: Ernould-Gandouet; Garnier; Lesur (1971); Pazaurek.

Satsuma ware. Japanese pottery made in Kagoshima prefecture (formerly Satsuma province) on Kyushu from the late 16th century at kilns founded by Korean potters. The earliest pottery of the area included heavy jars and vases with thick black glaze. A group of potters who had settled at Chosa and Sasshu became influenced by Seto wares, particularly in their making of tea bowls. Bottles made with trickle glaze over a contrasting colour on the neck from the 18th century are associated with the Tatsumonji factory, which is still in operation, having made tea ware through the 18th and 19th centuries; similar bottles were made throughout northern Kyushu, e.g. at *Koishibara and *Onda.

Satsuma ware. Earthenware vase, with enamel decoration outlined in gold, first half of 19th century. 33 cm high.

A second group settled to work at Naeshirogawa and from the mid 17th century made the white faience associated in Europe and America with Satsuma, although in Japan Satsuma ware also refers to the output of more than 56 kilns in the area (mainly surrounding Naeshirogawa). The yellow-tinged earthenware with a fine network of crackle in the glaze was gilded and enamelled in red, green, blue, purple, black and yellow. The choicest known early ware included small incense burners and boxes, wine bottles, etc., painted with diaper and key fret patterns and restrained floral designs. *Chin Jukan, followed by other potters, made pieces decorated only with carved and pierced ornament. The faience of Satsuma was introduced to western collectors at the Exposition Universelle in Paris, 1867, and brocade-patterned ware became very popular by the 1870s. Blue and white incense burners, bowls, etc., with detailed designs of Chinese landscapes and flowers were exported in the early 20th century. Other export wares included pieces with raised patterns of human figures or dragons.
Much work by the Naeshirogawa potters was later decorated in Tokyo; in addition, the enamelled ware was made in huge quantities at Kyoto, Yokohama and Tokyo for the overseas market. *Takemoto, working in Tokyo, exported pieces in Satsuma style and won a prize in the Vienna Exhibition, 1873, with work of this kind. Satsuma faience is now made at about twelve kilns, and also copied at Awata and in Mie prefecture. It has been known for pieces to be treated with tea, smoke or acid to lend an impression of age; some modern work is chalky in appearance, and lacks lustre in the enamel.
Other kilns in the area include *Ryumonji, also founded by Korean potters. A factory in operation at Shiba 1874-c.1880 produced work that was gilded and enamelled in muted

colours with figures scenes, e.g. religious festivals, and exported as Satsuma ware.
Refs: Gorham; Jenyns (1971); Koyama; Munsterberg; Okamura.

Sattler, Wilhelm. *See* Aschach.

Saturday Evening Girls' Club. *See* Paul Revere Pottery.

Saumer, Martin. *See* Prague.

Sauviat-sur-Vige. French porcelain factory established 1836 at Sauviat (Haute-Vienne) and disused ten years later. Later, the factory, let to Louis-Aimé Tharaud (son of P. *Tharaud) in 1853 and sold in 1873, produced luxury white wares under André Dupuy (d 1897), succeeded by his son Emile, who opened a decorating workshop and warehouse in Limoges, 1920. Emile Dupuy sold the factory in 1935 to Giraud (d 1968) & Brousseau (d 1967), succeeded by Giraud's family, trading as André Giraud & Cie.
Marks: LIMOGES/FRANCE and a helmet in a shield; GIRAUD/LIMOGES/FRANCE; *A. Giraud & Cie*/LIMOGES under a helmet; *Limoges/ Sauviat/1836* over a flame.
Ref: d'Albis & Romanet.

Saville, Annie. *See* Jessop, George.

Savin, Maurice-Louis (1894-1973). French painter, sculptor and ceramist. Savin learned a wide range of decorative techniques at the Ecole des Arts Décoratifs, and worked at the Sèvres factory before studying glazed earthenware in the Rhône valley. Carrying out all the production processes alone, he made tin-glazed earthenware decorated in blue and resembling delftware or Moustiers faience, and pharmaceutical pots with polychrome decoration. Savin was influenced by Italian Renaissance potters, including the Della Robbia family, making decorative panels as well as figures and portrait busts. His sculptural work included fountains, and a porcelain ceiling in the Sèvres display at the Exposition Universelle, Paris, 1937.
Mark: signature, *Savin.*
Refs: Bénézit; Faré; Lesur (1971).

Savoy China. *See* Birks, L.A., & Co.

Sawa family. *See* Fujina.

Saxbo. *See* Krebs, Nathalie.

Saywell, Roy (b 1906). English potter, working in Surrey. Saywell started work at the *Compton Pottery in 1920 as the first apprentice to join after World War I. After learning to throw, he was responsible for the extension of the pottery's main output of press-moulded garden ware to include thrown pots. He went on to manage a pottery at Brook, also in Surrey, producing domestic earthenware, and accompanied the pottery to Grayshott, when it was moved in the 1950s by Surrey Ceramic Co. Ltd, owners from 1956. He continued to specialize in the throwing of bigware.
Refs: Ceramic Review 64; Coysh (1976).

Sazerac, Bernard. *See* Angoulême.

Sazerat, Pierre-Léon (1831-91). French ceramist and porcelain manufacturer, born

in Limoges. Sazerat served his apprenticeship at Sèvres before taking over in 1852 the Touze factory (which had been established four years earlier in Limoges) in partnership with Alpinien Margaine (*see* Gibus, P.-J.). Employing about 50 workers, the firm made porcelain which included three-tiered table centrepieces, cups, vases and biscuit figures with velvety texture. Sazerat moved the firm in 1859 to new buildings in Montjovis, where he specialized in high-quality tableware and ornamental pieces. His display in the Exposition Universelle, 1867, included a vase with allegorical figures modelled by Thabard, a local sculptor. He also made earthenware painted in underglaze blue, which was first shown in Paris, 1878. His display in Limoges, 1886, comprised luxury items in porcelain, white earthenware and stoneware. He enlarged the business in partnership with clay supplier, Pierre Blondeau, from 1881. Later decoration included slip painting in Barbizon style, *grisaille* or cameos. His factory continued under his partner and successors, but was disused when bought by T.*Haviland c.1906 as a decorating workshop. It was used as a hospital in World War I and later demolished.
Marks: LS/LIMOGES/FRANCE, chrome green; L.SAZERAT/LIMOGES in a double circle; LS impressed (biscuit wares); LS/LIMOGES (earthenware).
Ref: d'Albis & Romanet.

Scandy. *See* Aller Vale Pottery.

Scarabronze. *See* Wannopee Pottery.

Scarab Vase. *See* Robineau, Adelaide Alsop.

Schachtel, Joseph. German porcelain manufacturer. He bought a small porcelain factory at Sophienau, Post Charlottenbrunn (Silesia) in 1859, at first making pipe heads. In 1866, he introduced simple, white everyday tableware. He established his own decorating workshop in 1875, and was a pioneer among German manufacturers of electrical wares. He was succeeded by his sons, Max and Eugen, in 1887. The firm ceased operation c.1920.
Marks include a monogram of JS; three *fleurs de lis* over J.S./GERMANY and a cross; an eagle with orb and sceptre over J.S.; the initials in a circle; crossed lines (resembling the Meissen sword mark).
Refs: Danckert; Weiss.

Schadow, Johann Gottfried. German ceramic modeller. Schadow worked in collaboration with court architect, Hans Christian Genelli, on the making of figures, plaques and table decorations for the Berlin factory, in the early 19th century. His work included a centrepiece for presentation to the Duke of Wellington in 1818 (now preserved at Apsley House, London) and pieces for the Generals' and the Prussian services.
Refs: Danckert; Haggar (1960); Hannover.

Schaffner, Henry (1798-1877). Swiss-born potter. After training in *Moravian communities in Europe, Schaffner went to America. He established his own pottery in Salem, North Carolina. He was succeeded by employee D.*Krause.
Ref: Bivins.

Schaller, Oscar, & Co. German porcelain manufacturers working at Schwarzenbach from 1882 on the sale of everyday wares with decoration that included onion pattern (*Zwiebelmuster*). In 1917, the factory passed to the firm of Winterling. Successors of Oscar Schaller & Co. worked from 1921 in Kirchenlamitz, Bavaria, on the production of gifts and everyday ware.
Marks, normally incorporating crossed ss, include a laurel wreath, a draped shield topped by a castle, and a circular mark topped with a crown.
Refs: Danckert; Weiss.

Scharvogel, Jacob Julius (1854-1938). German ceramist, born in Mainz, and a noted maker of Art Nouveau stoneware. He worked in Leipzig for the firm of *Villeroy & Boch, 1885-98, and was co-founder of the Vereinigten Werkstätten für Kunst und Handwerk in Munich, 1897.
At his own workshop, Münchener Kunsttöpferei, established in 1898, he made stoneware which was influenced by his studies in Paris and London, where he encountered oriental ceramics, and by 1900 made stoneware in simple shapes, with colourful, high-temperature glazes in turquoise and red, olive green, black and rust. In collaboration with T.*Schmuz-Baudiss and other designers, he made more complex shapes with relief decoration covered with brown glazes.
In 1904, Scharvogel established and headed the grand-ducal factory in Darmstadt, where until 1913 he continued his development of colourful, layered glazes. On leaving Darmstadt in 1913, he agreed not to produce pottery for three years and taught architectural ceramics in Munich, 1915-25. In 1916, he established a workshop for the production of bowls, vases, again with coloured glazes.
Marks: a bird, with SKM (Scharvogel

Jacob Julius Scharvogel. Three-handled stoneware vase in dark olive-brown and blue with light spots and grey glaze, c.1904. Marked with a phoenix and the initials SKM. 18 cm high.

Kunsttöpferei München) or alone, in a circle; at Darmstadt, EL below a crown.
Refs: Bock; Borrmann; 'Scharvogel und die Gründung der Grossherzoglichen Keramischen Manufaktur Darmstadt' in *Kunst in Hessen und am Mittelrhein* (1975).

Schaubach, Heinz. *See* Wallendorf.

Scheibe, Richard. *See* Pfeiffer, Max Adolf.

Scheibe-Alsbach. German porcelain factory established at Scheibe-Alsbach in 1834, originally as a painting workshop for the decoration mainly of tobacco pipes made and fired at Grossbreitenbach. Johann Friedrich Andreas Kister, porcelain painter, and part-owner of the factory from 1846, introduced the production of figures, which included grave ornaments, madonnas, etc. His son, August Wilhelm Fridolin Kister, sole owner from 1863, developed the output of figures, including portrait busts and animal models, as well as vases and candlesticks, from the 1860s, and table centrepieces, groups of dancers, etc., from c.1890. Modellers included G. Möller, Otto Poertzel and Felix Zeh. From 1894, the firm made figures of very high quality in earlier styles produced at Meissen. The factory later continued production of rococo figures and groups, as well as toys and dolls' heads, now operating as part of the Lichte group.

Marks include K.P.F. and K.P.M. over crossed lines; s superimposed on crossed lines.
Refs: Danckert; Scherf; Weiss.

Scheid, Karl (b 1929) and Ursula (b 1932). German studio potters. Karl Scheid was apprenticed to a potter in Stuttgart before training in the Darmstadt Werkkunstschule, arts, 1949-52. He worked in England, 1952-53, before sharing a workshop with B.*Kuhn in Lottstetten, Baden. He established his own studio (1956) in Düdelsheim, Frankfurt, where he worked from 1958 with Ursula Scheid (*née* Duntze), who also trained in Darmstadt. Karl Scheid's early work was influenced by that of L.*Rie in England. With his wife, he makes vases, bottles, bowls,

Edwin and Mary Scheier. Stoneware bowl with matt iron oxide glaze inside and glossy brown glaze on the exterior, before 1949. 14.9 cm high.

Karl Scheid. Stoneware vase made at Düdelsheim, 1957.

etc., in stoneware or porcelain, all thrown, but sometimes assembled from more than one component (e.g. double-walled bowls). Some pieces are very delicate in appearance with smooth or carefully carved surfaces, others more heavily built, and the Scheids' work is noted for the wide range of form and glaze, achieved with great precision and control. Glazes are generally soft in colour and often matt, but bold effects are achieved with layers of glaze, wax resist and contrasting touches, say of iron glaze on the rim of a bottle covered with crackled celadon glaze.

Marks: a spiral, stamped in relief; versions of a monogram of HH (the Haus Hosset in Düdelsheim) sometimes with *Scheid*; UD monogram of Ursula Duntze, with *Scheid*.
Refs: Bock; E.& H. Hohe 'Die Keramische Werkstatt K. und U. Scheid' in *Keramos* 40 (1968); Klein.

Scheidig, Carl. *See* Gräfenthal; Reichmannsdorf.

Scheier, Edwin (b 1910) and Mary. American potters. Born in New York City, Scheier studied at the New York School of Industrial Arts. After working as a merchant seaman, he joined the Federal Arts Project, eventually becoming field supervisor for crafts for the southern states. He toured the United States with a puppet show before establishing a pottery at Glade Spring, Virginia, with his wife, Mary Goldsmith, whom he married in 1935. The couple made use of fine red clay which they had discovered in the area. They

went in 1938 as teachers of ceramics to the University of New Hampshire, where their work included a glazed stoneware coffee pot and cups, which won an award in the Twelfth Ceramic National Exhibition (1947) at Syracuse as the best entry suitable for mass production. In 1945 the Scheiers took part in a programme of teaching ceramic techniques to Puerto Ricans. After their retirement from the University of New Hampshire in 1950, they continued their pottery, moving to Oaxaca, Mexico.
Refs: Clark & Hughto; E. Levin 'Pioneers of Contemporary American Ceramics: Laura Andreson, Edwin and Mary Scheier' in *Ceramics Monthly* 24 (May 1976); R. Randall 'Potter Looks at Scheier Pottery' in *Design* 47 (January 1946).

Schellink, Samuel (1876-1958). Dutch painter and draughtsman, born in Utrecht. Schellink trained at the *Rozenburg factory from 1892 and became known for his painting of the firm's eggshell ware. When production ceased at Rozenburg in 1914, he became an art dealer. He worked at *Amphora (Oegstgeest) and the *Goedewaagen pottery after 1918.

Mark: initials with a small s inside the lower curve of another.
Refs: Scheen; Singelenberg-van der Meer; van Straaten.

Schenck, Frederick. Ceramic modeller working in England c.1870-c.1890. After working briefly for Wedgwood, 1872-73, he joined the firm of G.*Jones; his work included a pilgrim bottle with *pâte-sur-pâte* decoration and modelled figures seated on the shoulders, c.1885.
Refs: Batkin; Jewitt; Reilly & Savage.

Scherf, Louis and Albert. *See* Lichte.

Scheurich, Paul (1883-1945). German modeller, born in New York. Scheurich was engaged as an independent collaborator with M.A.*Pfeiffer at Meissen c.1920. He created twelve models for the factory within the following year. He later completed designs for M.A. Pfeiffer at the Schwarzburger Werkstätte. He also worked for the *Nymphenburg factory and at *Berlin, where

*Paul Scheurich. Figures modelled by Scheurich, made at *Nymphenburg, c.1916.*

Schlaggenwald. Plate made at Schlaggenwald c.1927. 24.2 cm in diameter.

he designed figures in rococo style, and a table decoration, The Birth of Beauty, 1940-42, commissioned from the Berlin factory by the German Foreign Ministry. At this time, Scheurich also designed and modelled for the firm of *Rosenthal.
Refs: W. Baer *Berlin Porcelain* (catalogue, Staatliche Porzellan-Manufaktur Berlin/Smithsonian Institution Traveling Exhibition Service, Washington, D.C., 1980); Danckert; Forsyth; Ware.

Schilkin, Michael (1900-62). Russian sculptor and ceramic artist born in Leningrad and working in Finland. Schilkin worked at the *Arabia factory from 1936, and exhibited widely from 1937, winning prizes in Paris (1937), and Milan (1951). He became known for animal sculptures, initially naturalistic but later increasingly stylized, and human figures in stoneware with heavy coloured glazes. He also made large relief plaques in *chamotte*.
Refs: Aro; Préaud & Gauthier.

Schlaggenwald. Bohemian porcelain factory established 1793 at Schlaggenwald for the production of porcelain, notably coffee sets painted under the glaze in blue. The factory, in the hands of Louise-Sophie Greiner (d 1806) from 1800, subsequently underwent improvements and continued the production of coffee ware, mainly for export to Russia and Poland. Two years after his mother's death, Moritz Greiner (d 1836) sold the works to his brother-in-law Johann Georg Lippert (d 1843) and a partner, Wenzel Haas (d 1830), who employed about 30 workers and, by the 1820s, produced a full range of tableware, as well as tobacco pipes. Eusebius August Haas, a partner from 1827, succeeded his father in 1830. By the time of the first general Austrian trade exhibition in 1835, in which the factory won a silver medal, there were branches in Prague, Vienna, Linz, Temesvar and Bolzano. The workforce increased from about 110 in 1836 to 206 in 1847. The output, in pure white porcelain paste, included everyday tableware, as well as luxury items. Decoration included landscapes, portraits, flowers, etc., painted under the glaze of plates and cups, relief ornament, and printed patterns in green, blue or black. Lithophanes, some used as decoration in the base of cups, were made

1830-43. As well as vases, display plates and rococo figures, the output of ornamental pieces comprised such items as bottles, needleholders, paperweights, lamps, clock-cases and writing sets, some with openwork decoration, all lavishly painted and gilded. The factory later concentrated on mass-produced wares, decorated more simply with patterns of flowers or fruit. Lippert was succeeded in 1840 by his daughter, and his son-in-law, Johann Möhling, who sold the works to Haas. The firm traded as Haas & Czjsek from 1876.
Marks usually incorporate the place name, *Schlaggenwald*.
Refs: Meyer; Weiss.

Schlegel, Valentine (b 1925). French potter. She studied from 1942 at the Ecole des Beaux-Arts, Montpellier, and went in 1945 to Paris, where she made slip-painted tiles and began the production of thrown ware in 1950 and coiled pots in 1954. Many of her pieces were sculptural and intended to hold flowers. She began to work in plaster in 1957 and turned to leatherwork in 1973.
Ref: Céramique française contemporaine.

Schlegelmilch, Erhard and Reinhold. *See* Tillowitz.

Schleiss, Franz (b 1884) and Emilie. Austrian ceramic artist, Schleiss trained at the Kunstgewerbeschule in Vienna, 1905-09, with his wife, Emilie Simandl, a decorative artist who also studied at the Kunstgewerbeschule, 1904-08. Emilie Schleiss-Simandl designed figures, hollow ware with engraved decoration and, in 1908, porcelain with layered glazes. Franz Schleiss exhibited painted earthenware in 1908, and in the following year founded a workshop, Gmundner Keramik, in his home town. He remained there as director until 1922. The couple produced

Emilie Schleiss. Figure designed c.1913 and produced by the Vereinigte Wiener und Gmundner Keramik. 29.8 cm high.

many models for the workshop, which was amalgamated with Wiener Keramik in 1912 and afterwards operated as the Vereinigte Wiener und Gmundner Keramik. Their figures were simple, and sparsely painted on a white ground.
Franz Schleiss established a ceramic school in 1917, worked at the Münchener Werkstätte, 1926-27, and headed a workshop, again in Gmunden, from 1928. He designed dishes, vases, table services and decorative pieces for other German and Austrian producers as well as for his own workshops.
Marks: a stylized fish with the initials SG; a flowerpot with the initials GK in a rectangular outline; GMUNDNER/KERAMIK/AUSTRIA; Schleiss's own monogram, FS; the initials E.S.
Ref: Neuwirth (1974a).

Schley, Paul (1854-1942). German porcelain modeller. In 1868, he was an apprentice in his father's wood-carving workshop in Berlin, before working as a sculptor there and in Vienna. He joined the *Berlin porcelain factory in 1885, becoming *Modellmeister* from the same year until his retirement in 1920.
Mark: signature, *P. Schley*.
Ref: Porzellankunst.

Schlögl, Georg and Therese. *See* Tata.

Schmider, Georg. *See* Zell-Hamersbach.

Schmidt, David (b 1847). German-born potter working in America from c.1866, initially as a roof tiler and slate tile importer in Pittsburgh, Pennsylvania. Schmidt organized the Zanesville Roofing Tile Co. (incorporated 1896), changing the firm's name to *Zanesville Art Pottery in 1900.
Refs: Evans; Kovel & Kovel; L.& E. Purviance & N.F. Schneider *Zanesville Art Pottery in Color* (Mid-America Book Co., Leon, Iowa, 1968); N.F. Schneider *Zanesville Art Pottery* (privately published, Zanesville, Ohio, 1963).

Schmidt, Johann Christian. *See* Bayreuth.

Schmidt, Johann Jakob (1787-1862). German porcelain maker, son of a repairer at Ludwigsburg. Schmidt established a short-lived factory at Ulm, Württemberg (1827-33), for the production of tableware and ornamental pieces, which included figures resembling examples made earlier at Ludwigsburg.
Mark: *Ulm* over the initial *J*.
Refs: Danckert; Weiss.

Schmidt-Pecht, Elisabeth. German ceramist. She worked at the *Kandern pottery and in a faience factory at Zell-Hamersbach. Apart from some porcelain, she mainly made painted tin-glazed earthenware in Rococo style. After moving to Konstanz c.1900, she provided designs for pottery thrown by her brother, J.A. Pecht, and fired in kilns at Villingen. In 1910, she exhibited traditional shapes with decoration of flowers and spirals scratched through green, red or white slip to show the red body underneath.
Ref: Neuwirth (1974b).

Schmidt-Reuther, Gisela (b 1915). German studio potter born in Sobernheim. After training at the state ceramics school in Höhr-Grenzhausen, 1934-36, and as a sculptor in Frankfurt, 1936-37, she worked at the state majolika factory, *Karlsruhe, 1937-40, again studying sculpture (1940-44) in Berlin. She taught for a year in Trier before rejoining the ceramics school in Höhr-Grenzhausen as a teacher in 1945. Her stoneware consists of figures and animal models shaped in hollow forms or, more recently, figures that are mainly two-dimensional in effect, cut and modelled out of curved sheets of clay. Occasional pieces are left unglazed, but many are painted in coloured slip before glazing to emphasize the interplay of light and shade.

Mark: s in a circle or circular monogram of GSP incised.
Refs: Bock; U. Gertz in *Deutsche keramische Kunst der Gegenwart* (Cremer, Frechen, 1968).

Schmidt-Tummeley, Werner (b 1920) and Annemarie (b 1919). German potters. Annemarie Schmidt-Tummeley was an apprentice potter in Düsseldorf, 1945-48, and subsequently trained with her husband in Höhr-Grenzhausen. In 1949 they established a workshop in the craft community founded by architect Stefan Thiersch on the island of Juist. Their work consists of stoneware, mainly functional, thrown by Annemarie, with glazes, often in several layers, developed by her husband. Form and glaze are closely related, e.g. a crystalline glaze with complicated visual effect accentuating the curve of a globular bottle, vases and small boxes with sharply curving shapes encircled by ledges of clay which throw heavy shadows on the light, matt surface.

Marks: JUIST incised; raised or impressed monogram of ST in a rectangle.
Refs: Bock; Klinge.

Schmuz-Baudiss, Theodor Hermann (1859-1942). German painter and ceramist, born in Herrnhut, Saxony, and trained in Munich 1879-90. He later studied ceramics at the Diessen pottery, Ammersee, c.1896. In 1897, he was a co-founder of workshops in Munich, for whom he provided designs. Schmuz-Baudiss was also a designer for Swaine & Co in *Hüttensteinach, 1901-02, and then at the *Berlin factory, where he was art director 1908-26, also teaching in the Kunstgewerbeschule. He was noted for underglaze painting of landscapes, views,

Theodor Schmuz-Baudiss. Covered sauceboat from the Ceres service, first produced in 1912. This example dates from 1920. Marks include TSB and a blue sceptre. 14 cm high.

etc., on tile panels, plaques and display plates, and designed the Berlin factory's Ceres service. Other tableware designs included a tea service patterned with broom and the Bulgarian royal arms, and Pensée—a service delicately painted with pansy flowers (1902). Under his direction, the factory's palette of underglaze colours was increased with subtle, translucent shades, applied with an aerograph to provide smooth ground washes. The contours and shading were added before cooling of the piece from a first firing.

Mark: monogram of TSB.
Refs: Danckert; Haslam (1977); Porzellankunst; Weiss; *Werke um 1900* (catalogue, Kunstgewerbemuseum, Berlin, 1966).

Schneider, Paul. *See* Gräfenthal.

Schneider-Döring, Siegfried (b 1923) and Juscha (b 1919). German studio potters. Juscha Schneider-Döring studied ceramics 1935-39 at art school in her native Hamburg and then gained practical experience in East Prussia, Hamburg, and Landshut, before working in a Mecklenburg tile factory, 1944-45. At first in Rendsburg (1950) and eventually in Bad Oldesloe (1958), she established a workshop with her husband, who had studied the techniques of pottery under S.*Möller, 1947-50. The couple make domestic ware, as well as a number of individual pieces. Siegfried Schneider-Döring painted hollow ware in the 1950s, later concentrating on tiles with detailed patterns of fish, crustaceans, sea anemones, shells, plants, etc.; his wife makes thrown stoneware vases and bowls, sometimes with incised decoration or slightly distorted in shape, for which she has developed glazes inspired by Sung dynasty wares, while avoiding the use of oriental forms.

Mark: incised monogram of *Sd.*
Ref: Bock.

Schneller & Postbichel. *See* Papa.

Schnier, Jacques. *See* Walrich Pottery.

Schney. German porcelain factory established 1781 at Schney (Bavaria) for the production of porcelain, which included everyday wares, coffee cups, rustic figures, and tobacco pipes. Painted decoration, mainly of very high quality, was carried out by independent decorators.

Porcelain tableware was also produced by H.K. Eichhorn, employing about 100 workers from 1837.

Marks include: s in underglaze blue or enamel; *Schney* incised from 1830; PFS from the mid 19th century; s with a cross on everyday ware, impressed from 1910.
Refs: Danckert; Scherf; Weiss.

Schoelcher, Marc. French porcelain maker, born at Fessenheim (Haut-Rhin). In 1798, Schoelcher took over a Paris factory (Fabrique du comte d'Artois), started in 1771, and rented a showroom on the Boulevard des

Italiens in 1804. He abandoned production, concentrating on decoration from 1810. His output, much of which was exported, was noted for its luxurious finish and lavish gilding, sometimes with a damask effect of matt and shining gold forming a ground to decoration in reserves; other ground effects were marbled or scale-patterned. Schoelcher copied oil paintings on a variety of pieces, e.g. Poussin's *Moses Saved from the Water,* David's *Death of Socrates* (on vases) and Raphael's *Gardener* (on a plate). In 1828, with his son Victor Schoelcher (1804-93), who had worked for him since 1819, he formed a company for the sale of porcelain on the Boulevard des Italiens. They employed outside decorators and marked their ware Schoelcher et fils (often in combination with the makers' marks). The business is thought to have closed in 1834.

Marks: *Schoelcher* in red, brown or gold; *Schoelcher et fils* in purple.
Refs: Burton (1921); Chavagnac & Grollier; Ernould-Gandouet; Guillebon.

Schoenau, Carl and Edouard. *See* Hüttensteinach.

Schofield, John and William. *See* Vickers family.

Scholl, Michael, and son, Jacob. Pennsylvania potters making *sgraffito* decorated earthenware of high quality at Tyler's Port, Montgomery County, from the early 19th century. Michael Scholl was working by 1811 and his son by 1830. Two covered jars incised with floral designs through white slip, and touched with green and blue, bear the stamped mark of Jacob Scholl, a four-petalled flower. Pie plates from the pottery are characterized by a greenish tinge in the glaze; their shape is flat with a steeply curved rim. Graceful, tendril-like forms appear in the floral designs, and the inscriptions are carefully executed.
Ref: Barber (1970).

Schönwald. Bavarian porcelain factory established 1879 by J.N. Muller and working from 1898 as Porzellanfabrik Schönwald. The firm produced tableware for domestic and hotel use, noted after World War II for

Schönwald. Porcelain coffee pot, designed by Heinrich Löffelhardt, 1953.

a high standard of modern design, and has been part of the Kahla group since 1927.

Marks incorporate the initials PSAG with a coronet, orb, or shield bearing an eagle, sometimes with *Bavaria*.
Refs: Danckert; Weiss.

Schott, Margarete (b 1911). German studio potter born in Berlin. Schott studied and taught languages before training in ceramics at Starkenburg 1947-48 and in the artists' colony at Matildenhöhe, Darmstadt, 1948-51. She also studied in England, 1951-52, and on subsequent visits. Her bowls, dishes, beakers and vases are all individual pieces rather than functional wares, solidly thrown in fine stoneware or porcelain, often carved into faceted shapes. She has used a variety of glazes, mainly dark, glossy reduction glazes until recent years, and coloured or highlighted with iron or copper.

Mark: initial M impressed or in relief.
Refs: Bock; E. Lewenstein & E. Cooper *New Ceramics* (Studio Vista, London, 1974).

Schou, Philipps (1838-1922). Danish potter and porcelain manufacturer; a partner in *Aluminia A.S. and its manager from 1868. He was director of the Royal *Copenhagen Porcelain Factory from its amalgamation with Aluminia in 1884 until he retired, succeeded by his son-in-law F.*Dalgas, in 1902. He was responsible for the reorganization of porcelain production, and initiated a programme of artistic development. Inspired by the work of T.*Deck exhibited in Vienna 1872, he also studied ceramic styles in England, Holland, Belgium and France, visiting London and Antwerp with his artist, A.E. *Krog, in 1885, for study.
Refs: Bodelsen; Danckert; Weiss.

Schreckengost, Viktor (b 1906). American ceramic designer, painter and sculptor, the son of a potter, born in Sebring, Ohio. Schreckengost studied at the Cleveland Institute of Art from 1924 and, after graduation in 1929, went to study ceramics and sculpture under M.*Powolny for a year. On his return to Cleveland, he worked as a designer for R.G.*Cowan, while also teaching at the school of art. His work at the Cowan Pottery Studio included a set of porcelain punch bowls decorated with *sgraffito* designs of buildings, street signs, ships, water, stars, etc., in bright blue slip, commissioned by Eleanor Roosevelt for the governor's mansion in Albany, New York, and produced commercially soon before the closure of Cowan's pottery. Schreckengost subsequently produced his own ceramic sculpture, showing the influence of his time spent in Vienna in such pieces as Spring (a lamb jumping over the back of a pouncing lion, made in 1938) until he turned to political satire in The Dictator (a Roman Emperor with attendant cherubs representing Hitler, Mussolini, Stalin and Hirohito, 1939) and Apocalypse '42 (Hitler, Hirohito and Mussolini leaping the northern hemisphere on a flaming horse). Meanwhile, he designed ceramics for industrial production. He reorganized production at the Limoges China Co. (*see* Sterling China Co.), introducing dinner ware in a smooth, modern style; his Old Virginia Fashion ware was decorated with a series of scenes in blue, brown and mauve with green rim and copper edging.

Schreckengost later carried out similar work for other Ohio firms. He won the C.F. Binns Medal of the American Society for outstanding contributions to the ceramic field in 1939. After World War II, he led the department of Industrial Design at Cleveland Art Institute and worked for some time as designer and art director for a Cleveland toy manufacturer. He developed a new technique, carving pots out of blocks of dry clay, in the early 1950s. He also carried out many architectural commissions, including terracotta pieces for a building in Cleveland Zoo, and in 1958 won the Gold Medal of the American Institute of Architecture.
Refs: The Animal Kingdom in American Art (Everson Museum of Art, Syracuse, New York, 1978); Clark & Hughto; D. Grafly 'Viktor Schreckengost' in *American Artist* 13, No 5 (May 1949); Lehner; 'New Designs for Mass Production' in *Design* Vol 37 (November 1935); J. Stubblebine & M. Eidelberg 'Viktor Schreckengost and the Cleveland School' in *Craft Horizons* 35 (June 1975).

Schreiber & Betz. See Phoenixville Pottery.

Schreyögg, Georg. See Karlsruhe.

Schrezheim. German pottery established at Schrezheim, near Ellwangen, Württemberg, by wine merchant J.B. Bux (d 1800) who was succeeded by his daughter until 1833 and then her son, Franz Heinrich Wintergerst. The output included jugs, helmet ewers, mugs, and coffee pots in reddish brown body with blue-tinged glaze, painted under the glaze in blue, often with manganese, green and yellow, or with the addition of brown, clear yellow, purple and bright red enamels. In the 19th century, earlier rococo-style moulds were used for the production of yellow or brown lead-glazed wares. Porcelain was also made. The firm failed financially in 1852, but production continued until the 1860s. The buildings were destroyed by fire in 1872.

Mark: a sprig of box in the form of an arrow-head.
Refs: Haggar (1960); Hannover; Honey (1952); Pazaurek; Riesebieter; Stoehr.

Schuchard, Georg. German potter working at Magdeburg from 1799. As sole owner of his factory from 1806, Schuchard made creamware in English styles, succeeded by his family until 1865.

Marks: name or initials, impressed.
Ref: Honey (1952).

Schulz & Co. See Gotha.

Schumann, Carl. See Arzberg.

Schumann & Schreider. See Schwarzenhammer.

Schwab, Friedrich, & Co. See Gotha.

Schwanthaler, Franz (1760-1820). German porcelain modeller working at *Nymphenburg in the early 19th century, followed by his son.
Refs: Danckert; Weiss.

Schwarzburger Werkstätten. See Pfeiffer, Max Adolf; Unterweissbach.

Schwarzenhammer. German porcelain factory established by the firm of Schumann & Schreider at Schwarzenhammer, near Selb, in 1905 for the production of tableware. The firm specialized in pieces with openwork decoration.

A variety of marks incorporate the place name or *Sch* and often *Bavaria*.
Refs: Danckert; Weiss.

Schweinfurt, John George (1826-1907). German-born potter, working in New Market, Virginia, from 1850. He produced domestic earthenware, toys, banks, inkwells, flowerpots, etc., with floral decoration, and became noted for miniature jugs, pitchers and other household articles. Schweinfurt normally used a clear lead glaze, sometimes coloured with iron oxide or, occasionally, used over a covering of slip spattered with manganese or iron oxide; olive green and orange variations in tint were produced in the brown glaze by changes in the atmosphere of the kiln.
Ref: Wiltshire.

Schwetz, Karl (b 1888), **Schwetz-Lehmann,** Ida (b 1883). Austrian ceramic modellers, trained at the Kunstgewerbeschule in Vienna from 1904. Karl Schwetz interrupted his training for a year's military service in 1910, but exhibited models of deer in the following year. He later modelled pieces for the *Augarten factory. Ida Schwetz-Lehmann, whom he married in 1912, exhibited figures, vases and other decorative pieces in the winter show of the Oesterreichisches Museum in 1910 and 1911, and designed pieces for production by F.*Schleiss in Gmunden. With H.*Johnova and R.*Neuwirth, she established and worked for the *Keramische Werkgenossenschaft (1911). Her models included figures, groups and portrait busts, for Augarten and the Wiener Werkstätte, as well as her own firm.

Marks: *Ida Lehmann* or *I Schw.L.*;
KSCH.
Ref: Neuwirth (1974a).

Scott, George. Staffordshire-born potter, who left England for America by 1846 and settled in Cincinnati. After working as a dealer in ceramics, he established a pottery (1854) in which he was assisted by his wife, also a potter, and produced stoneware, yellow and Rockingham-glazed earthenware. Scott later produced white granite and cream-coloured earthenware, which included printed tableware and toilet sets. He was succeeded by his sons, who operated the firm until c.1900, trading from 1889 as George Scott & Sons.
Refs: Barber (1976); Lehner; Webster.

Scott Brothers. English earthenware manufacturers operating a factory at Southwick on the outskirts of Sunderland (Tyne & Wear). After working as a manager of the High Pottery (established c.1720 at Newbottle, to the south-west of Sunderland, for the production of brown earthenware), Anthony Scott I (1764-1847) established a pottery at Southwick in 1788, entering with his father, Henry Scott (d 1829), into a partnership which traded as Atkinson & Co. until his retirement in 1841. Scott worked in partnership with his sons Henry (1799-1854) and Anthony II (1802-82); William (b 1816) and

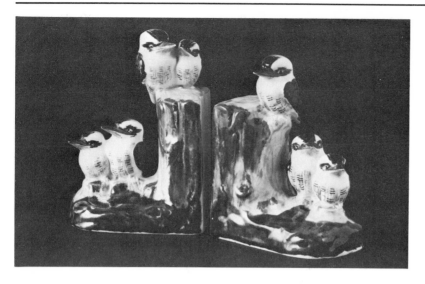

Grace Seccombe. A pair of glazed earthenware bookends in the form of kookaburras perched on tree trunks, c.1940. 14 cm high.

Thomas Pearson Scott (1800-64), also his sons, worked for the firm without becoming partners. Anthony Scott II continued to trade alone as Scott Brothers & Co., despite his brother's death; his son Anthony Scott III was sole owner of the pottery from his father's retirement in 1878.

The Southwick Pottery produced high-quality earthenware (much of it for export to European countries including Germany and, in later years almost exclusively, Denmark), which comprised dinner services, tea and breakfast sets, and sets of bowls or jugs in assorted sizes, as well as frog mugs, loving cups, smokers' accessories, Sunderland lions (figures), religious plaques, etc., in bodies including brown earthenware, creamware, and white earthenware. Pieces were sold for decoration at the *Wear Pottery, and bought from T.*Fell & Co. and the *Maling family. Transfer printing occurred in a wide variety of designs: Broseley and Willow pattern, and others of oriental inspiration; a range of views (Haddon Hall, and a series of marine views, Arabia); floral designs (Hawthorn, Iris, Ivy); bird subjects, pastoral, classical, sporting, travel scenes, etc. Jugs, ewers and mugs characteristically have flower sprays printed in black near the rim on either exterior or interior. The output included great quantities of pink lustre ware (*see* Sunderland). Special lines of coffee ware, trays, etc., made under the direction of Thomas Pearson Scott were printed, by a secret process which he had developed c.1830, with woven canework, a paisley pattern, or Mosaic design, all in dark colours. Jasper ware was made in the mid 19th century.

The pottery, then employing about 150 workers, was modernized after centenary celebrations in 1888, but failed to survive financial difficulties and a decline in business, finally closing in 1896 (after a temporary closure in 1893).

The name of *Scott* or *Scott Bros*, sometimes with the initials PB and a number, appears as an impressed or printed mark on a range of earthenware distinguished by its dark chocolate brown body, lined on the interior with white slip and decorated on the outside with transfer printing, often in primrose yellow over the glaze. The patterns were often based on *chinoiseries*, but also included military men of the early 19th century. The shape, decorative subjects and style of mark suggest a date between c.1810 and c.1840. This ware has been associated, probably incorrectly, with a firm, Scott Brothers, working in the late 18th century at Portobello, near Edinburgh.

Marks known to have been used by the Scott family in Sunderland include: *A. Scott & Co. Scott, Southwick; S. & Sons; S.B. & Co.; Scott Brothers; A. Scott & Sons; S. & S.*
Refs: Jewitt; McVeigh; Shaw.

Scovel, Elizabeth J. *See* Nashville Art Pottery.

Scrivener, R.G., & Co. *See* Norfolk Street works.

Scudder, Moses. *See* Huntington Pottery.

Seacombe Pottery. *See* Goodwin, John.

Seaham Harbour Pottery. *See* Dawson, John.

Sears, Kate B. *See* Lenox, Walter Scott.

Seba ware. Japanese pottery made at the Yamazaki and Kamijo kilns in Seba, Nagano prefecture, both of which were active in the 19th century and ceased operation by the 1920s. Their output consisted of water storage jars, saké bottles, wide bowls resembling a helmet in shape (kabuto bachi), and other domestic wares, often with bluish-white (namako) glaze applied over brown or black glazes. The kilns supplied a wide area extending over the Koshinetsu and Kanto regions.
Ref: Mizuo.

Sebright, Richard (1868-1951). English porcelain painter working for the *Worcester Royal Porcelain Co. from the 1890s to the late 1940s. He was among the factory's outstanding fruit painters, working from natural specimens and from detailed studies in watercolours of ripe fruits. He was also a skilful flower painter.
Ref: Sandon (1978a).

Sebring Pottery Co. American pottery manufacturers making decorated tableware in various earthenware and white granite bodies at the American Pottery Works, established 1887 at East Liverpool, Ohio, by Frank Sebring. The pottery moved to Sebring, Ohio (a town founded by the Sebring family in 1898). The firm's later products included porcelain and semi-porcelain.

Marks: name of the pottery, usually mentioning the material (*semi-vitreous porcelain*, etc.).
Refs: Barber (1976); Kovel & Kovel; Lehner.

Seccombe, Grace (c.1880-1956). English-born potter, working in Australia. Grace Seccombe made realistic figures painted in natural colours of the country's animals – budgerigars, opossums, koalas, kookaburras – either free-standing or on the rims of bowls, etc., working at a studio in Eastwood, Sydney, from the 1920s until the 1930s.
Mark: name incised.
Ref: Graham.

Secession or **Sezession.** A group of artists and architects including, notably, J.*Hoffmann, Gustav Klimt, K.*Moser and J.M. Olbrich, who seceded from the Viennese Akademie der bildenden Künste in reaction against its conservative attitudes and formed an organization which they called the Wiener Sezession. They built offices and exhibition rooms where they showed the work of non-Austrian designers such as Charles Rennie Mackintosh and his associates in Glasgow. The group was influential until the 1920s in the development of Austrian decorative arts since its members provided designs in a variety of media including textiles, furniture, metalwork and ceramics. Hoffmann and Moser went on to establish the Wiener Werkstätte.
Ref: R. Weissenberger *Die Wiener Secession* (Vienna, 1972).

Secessionist ware. *See* Mintons Ltd.

Seddon, Ralph. English potter. Seddon went from Staffordshire to manage the *Wear Pottery at Southwick, Sunderland, and built his own works, St Bede's Pottery, at Richmond Street, Monkwearmouth, for the production of white earthenware, mainly for sale in London. He also sold pieces, including frog mugs, to T.*Snowball for decoration. Seddon died by 1883, succeeded by Francis and Henry Seddon, who traded briefly as Seddon Brothers. St Bede's Pottery then passed to Snowball, but closed in 1885.
Ref: Shaw.

Sedgley, Walter. English porcelain painter working for the *Worcester Royal Porcelain Co., 1889-1929. Sedgley became apprenticed as a painter in 1891. His work included roses in the style developed by J.*Hadley, and he taught this flower-painting technique to other artists. He also painted a variety of subjects, including birds and, notably, Italian garden scenes.
Marks: signatures, *Seeley* or *J. Walters* on hand tinting of printed patterns.
Ref: Sandon (1978a).

Sefton & Brown. *See* Ferrybridge or Knottingley Pottery.

Seger, Hermann August (1839-93). German ceramic chemist, trained in Berlin from 1859 and Rostock until 1868. He was editor of *Notizblatt*, a ceramics journal, 1872-76. Seger carried out research (1878-90) at the Berlin factory, where he worked with chemist Albert Heinecke on the development of a soft porcelain paste (in imitation of Japanese examples), which was marketed as *Seger-porzellan*. The new formula allowed Seger to enlarge the palette of colours in use at Berlin, formerly blue and green. He also developed reproductions of Chinese *sang-de-boeuf* glazes in 1884, using a varied range of firing temperatures, and achieved a crackle glaze applied in two layers. His research resulted in techniques for glaze analysis, and in 1886 Seger cones (slim tetrahedrons of ceramic material used as indicators of kiln temperature by the degree to which they fuse, and thus bend, at known heat levels). Seger's own examples showed temperatures at intervals of 20° from 1150° to 1850°C. His pupils Kramer and Hecht extended the range to 600-2000°C. Seger published his findings on all technical aspects of preparing, glazing and firing clay in *Gesammelte Schriften*, which appeared in America in 1902.
Mark: *Sgr.P* with the Berlin sceptre mark on *Segerporzellan*.
Refs: A.G. Bleininger (ed.) *The Collected Works of Hermann August Seger* (Euston, Pennsylvania, 1902); Danckert; Haslam (1977).

Seifu Yohei (1803-61 or 1806-63). Japanese porcelain maker, born in Kanazawa. A pupil of *Dohachi, he was the first of a line of three potters of the same name working in Gojozaka, Kyoto, and established his kiln between 1818 and 1830. He made porcelains (and some faience) using a pure white paste and refined, Chinese-inspired shapes. His

Hermann Seger. Vase made in Segerporzellan *at the *Berlin factory in 1907.*

decorative techniques included painting under the glaze in blue or blue and red, delicate low-relief patterns of plants and flowers, and enamel painting in nishiki-de (brocade style). Seifu made wares with monochrome glazes, notably red, which he achieved by painting pigment on the biscuit porcelain before applying a colourless glaze. He achieved fine ivory and celadon effects. Yohei Seifu II (1844-78) made only porcelain, and Yohei Seifu III (1851-1914) was noted for white ware, celadons and pieces painted under the glaze in red.
Refs: Brinkley; Jenyns (1967); Munsterberg; Roberts; Uyeno.

Seignolles, Henri. *See* Saint-Brice.

Seiji-sha. Japanese porcelain company established in 1880 at Arita by Tsuji Katsuzo, formerly head of the *Koran-sha factory, who joined with several associates to produce porcelain which was initially intended for export to Europe and America, but was also marketed in Japan. The firm adopted industrial methods and imported machinery. Pieces exhibited in Tokyo in the early 20th century included unglazed vases in fine white paste with delicate relief decoration, and enamelled wares. Trumpet-necked vases, pedestal lamps and plaques in coarser paste were principally for export.
Refs: Brinkley; Burton (1921); Hannover; Jenyns (1967).

Seixas, David G. American manufacturer of light-bodied earthenware in Philadelphia at what was described in *Niles' Register* (1817) as the only white-ware pottery in the United States. His pottery was listed in the city directories for 1818-22. It probably operated under a manager brought in by Seixas, who is known to have had other business involvements, between 1813 and 1824.
Refs: Barber (1976); S. Myers *From Handcraft to Industry* (Smithsonian Institution Press, Washington, D.C., 1980).

Selle, Ferdinand. *See* Burgau.

Seltmann, Christian (1870-1921). German porcelain manufacturer, working from 1911 in Weiden on the production of everyday tableware for hotels, gifts and heat-resistant cooking ware, and employing about 200 workers. He was succeeded by his sons Wilhelm, who left the firm in 1935, and Heinrich, who in 1939 bought a factory established in the 1890s at Krummenaab, Upper Palatinate, and producing table services, coffee sets, gifts. In 1940, Heinrich Seltmann bought the Erbendorf factory, established 1923 for the production of everyday tableware and services. The firm, then known as Porzellanfabriken Christian Seltmann GmbH, merged with the Königliche Privat-Porzellanfabrik *Tettau in 1958 (which brought the workforce to about 3,500) and continued the output of services, table settings, coffee sets, hotel ware, heatproof utensils for cooking.
Marks: most marks used at Weiden incorporate *Seltmann* or *CS* and the place name. A crown and *Erbendorf/Bavaria*.
Refs: Danckert; Weiss.

Seltmann, Johann. German porcelain manufacturer working at Vohenstrauss, Upper

Palatinate, from 1901. Seltmann made tea, coffee, mocha sets, and gift ware.
A variety of marks incorporate Seltmann's name or initials and sometimes the place name.
Refs: Danckert; Weiss.

semi-porcelain, semi-vitreous porcelain, hotel china. In American ceramics, a hard, white body developed by the mid 1880s, fired at a high temperature and resembling porcelain, though not translucent. *See also* ironstone.

Senelle. *See* Longwy.

Senf, Leonardus, Johannes or Leon (1860-1940). Dutch painter and earthenware designer, trained at the Polytechnische School in Delft. Senf also studied under A.*Le Comte. He worked 1878-1925 at De*Porceleyne Fles, where he became head of the decorating department and contributed to the revival of blue-and-white wares in the style of Delft, and to the development of polychrome earthenware, as well as the pottery's Jacoba line and Nieuw Delft tiles.
Marks: a diamond containing a dot in each angle; a monogram of LS.
Refs: H.E. van Gelder 'Leon Senf, Ceramist 1879-1929' in *Jaarboek Nederlandsche Ambachts- & Nijverheidskunst* (1929); Scheen; Singelenberg-van der Meer; van Straaten.

Senior, James Wraith (1854-1909). English potter. Senior worked at the *Leeds Pottery from 1865 and subsequently at other potteries in the Hunslet district, before establishing his own workshop for the production of boots and other miniature pieces in earthenware. In 1884, he started the Hunsletesque Co., which later became known as the Leeds Art Pottery, making slipware and hand-painted tiles, influenced in style by *Burmantofts. Senior's works moved to *Leathley Lane Pottery in 1890, then increasing the range of output to include majolica. Senior, with some employees, reopened a works near Leeds as the Woodlesford Art Pottery, making the same kinds of ware, until its closure c.1896. Senior later established a workshop in Hunslet, where he made reproductions of Leeds Pottery creamware, sold through a local antique dealer, W.W. Slee (*see* Slee's Leeds). J.T. *Morton joined the firm briefly in 1907, leaving soon after the death of Senior, who was succeeded by sons George Wraith Senior (who had joined the firm in 1908 and retired in 1957), and James Senior. Senior's sons specialized in elaborately pierced creamware.
Refs: Coysh (1976); Jewitt; Lawrence.

Serapis-Fayence. *See* Wahliss, Ernst.

Sergent, Thomas-Victor. French potter, who, like G.*Pull and V.*Barbizet, made *Palissy ware, 1870-85, in Paris. He exhibited at the international exhibitions in Vienna (1873) and Paris (1878). His work resembled Palissy's closely in composition, but he used thicker, more glossy glazes without crazing.
Mark: T.S.
Refs: Heuser & Heuser; Lesur (1971).

Serré, Georges (1889-1956). French artist potter. Born in Sèvres (Hauts-de-Seine), he

Georges Serré. Stoneware bowl in coarse clay with a lotus design in low relief, pre 1934. Mark: GS *monogram. 21 cm in diameter.*

worked at the Sèvres factory from his apprenticeship in 1903 until 1914. In Saigon from 1916, he was influenced by Chinese wares and Khmer art. He taught ceramics from 1918. After his return to Sèvres in 1922, Serré established a studio in rue Brongniart where, encouraged by E.*Lenoble and E.*Decoeur, he began to make porcelain, as well as thick stoneware decorated with geometrical designs, deeply incised and sometimes picked out in sombre oxide colours or highlighted by the flow of the glazes. The shapes were severe: cylindrical, or flaring at the rim. Serré also produced small sculptural pieces in stoneware designed by contemporary artists.

Mark: impressed signature or initials GS.
Ref: Céramique française contemporaine.

Sesto Fiorentino. *See* Richard-Ginori, Società Ceramica.

Seto. The foremost ceramic centre in central Japan, the hilly region containing the town of Seto in Owari province (now Aichi prefecture) and centring on a triangular area with Nagoya, Shinano and Akatsu on its west, north and east corners. In Japan, all ceramics initially, and later those made in the Kujiri district of neighbouring *Mino province (Shino, Oribe) were referred to as Seto ware.

The production of glazed stoneware began at Seto in the Kamakura period (1185-1338). European collectors associate the area with grey or brown-bodied stoneware with brown or opaque, yellowish white crackled glazes, occasionally painted with iron or copper oxide, both tea and domestic wares, in shapes inspired by Sung Chinese temmoku and celadon wares. This tradition continued in Mino when the industry largely transferred there in the late 16th and early 17th centuries.

Potteries remaining in the Seto area include a group at Minami Shintani, Ibara district, producing tea bowls, vases with raised designs under green glaze, brown-glazed figures of birds, small plates in the shape of a fish, kitchen utensils. In the Meiji period, they made mortars, rouge cups, etc. The output of useful wares flourished in folk kilns at sites extending from Seto-no-Hora to Kita-Shindaki making mainly stoneware including ishi-zara, plates used in inns and houses. Large and small sizes were thickly potted in stoneware made from Seto clay, with soft, translucent glaze, yellowish grey and crackled; designs in cobalt blue or iron

black include birds, e.g. crane, trees and flowers, willows, wisteria, animals, fish, human figures, landscapes, occasionally calligraphy. Uma no me zara ('horse-eye' plates), edged with a repeating pattern of roughly semicircular motifs drawn in iron oxide with swirls of the brush and each resembling a rolling eye, were made from the early 19th century to the fall of the Tokugawa regime. Also associated with Seto are aburazara (rape oil plates)—these are flat plates placed inside lamps to catch oil drips—which were made until kerosene lamps replaced oil lamps in the late 19th century. Originally square, they became circular (about 15 cm across) in coarse, greyish clay with creamy glaze and patterned with plants, birds, landscapes, human figures.

Other products of the Seto folk kilns include food bowls painted with pine, bamboo, grass, flowers and other plant motifs; tableware with a pattern of vertical stripes in blue, red and brown; saké bottles; amberglazed storage jars, and a wide variety of useful items, often highly decorated with a brushed pattern called e Seto (picture Seto). The pieces are generally small in size, for urban sale, in contrast with the predominantly larger wares of *Tokoname on the coast to the south of Nagoya, which were primarily made for the surrounding farming community. Most of the folk kilns turned to porcelain production when it was introduced to Seto in the 19th century, but the stoneware output still continued. Equally, individual

Seto. Vase with enamelled decoration on a celadon ground, late 19th century. Marked with Seto Kawamoto *in blue. 35 cm high.*

potters or small groups withstood the industrial expansion of the Meiji period. A kiln at Seto-no-Hora continues to the present day making utility stoneware, some of it decorated.

The *Ofuke kiln at Akazu made wares for the princes of Owari. Similar wares were made at Kujiri, Ohira and the Sobokai kiln, which started at Nagoya castle c.1630, closed, and reopened in 1805. Also near Nagoya were *Inuyama and Horaku (*see* Toyosuke).

Porcelain production at Seto, developed in the early 19th century by Tamikichi *Kato, with the approval of the local authorities, restored profitability to the local stoneware kilns, which had been suffering competition from porcelain made in Hirado and Arita. By the early 20th century, a large porcelain industry had developed. The area produced mainly blue and white ware noted for its high quality, with delicate, elegant painting of landscapes or birds and flowers. Nanga painters were among the decorators. Export wares, which made up a large part of the output from the 1860s, were decorated with European smelt, of lower quality than the Chinese cobalt previously used. The potters included other members of the Kato family; Sosendo Jihei (d 1865) and many of his pupils; Shentoen Hansuke.

The porcelain also included pieces with enamelled decoration, e.g. copies of *Kutani ware (some with a forged Kutani mark). *Cloisonné* enamelling on porcelain was inspired by the discovery in 1870 of specimens of enamelled copper in the collection of a local feudal lord, deposed two years earlier. Experiments carried out at Nagoya, using a base of thin copper as well as porcelain, resulted in the brief production of large vases and dishes of enamelled copper for export to Europe; from c.1870, enamelled porcelain, looking like *cloisonné* metal (except that the enamel was fired at too low a temperature for a good polish to be obtained) was exported to Europe. These wares were shown in the Exposition Universelle in Paris, 1878. Some porcelain wares resembled bronze or corroded iron with storks, dragons, flowering branches painted in gold to look like inlaid precious metal.

Local potters were briefly inspired by Chinese wares c.1894; copies of *flambé* glazes were followed by the production of eggshell porcelain.
Refs: Brinkley; Burton (1921); Gorham; Hobson; Jenyns (1967, 1971); Mizuo; Morse; Munsterberg; Sanders.

Severn ware. *See* Chesapeake Pottery.

Sèvres. French national porcelain manufacture, established under royal privilege at Vincennes (Val-de-Marne) and later under the patronage of Louis XV. A factory built at Sèvres (Hauts-de-Seine) was in production from 1756. Production was impaired by the Revolution, but recovered under the Consulate and Empire.

A.*Brongniart, administrator from 1800 until his death in 1847, influenced the factory's technical progress throughout the 19th century, establishing aims that were directed more towards technical perfection, than industrial success. Brongniart reorganized the factory's staff, retaining the sculptor Boizot as head of the modelling department, with Lagrenée as principal painter and van

Sèvres. Double-walled vase, with leaves, florets and strapwork in blue against a perforated ground, on a gilt metal base, 1846. Printed with Louis Philippe's monogram. 55 cm high.

Spaendonck as chief flower painter, and called in contemporary artists as designers and consultants. He discontinued soft-paste porcelain in 1804 and introduced a new hard paste, developing a wider range of enamel colours and varied effects of matt or brilliant gilding. His chemists were Desfossé (1807-14) and Runel (1814-46).

The factory received a regular State subsidy from 1801, and Napoleon took Sèvres (together with the Gobelins tapestry works) under Imperial patronage in 1806, with the principal aim of commemorating his exploits on lavish pieces for the furnishing of Imperial palaces and for presentation as diplomatic gifts. At his instigation the production of services was renewed, each consisting of many pieces with designs surrounded by a lavish border on a coloured ground. They included the Service des Batailles, Service de l'Empéreur, Quartiers Généraux (1807-10), Cabaret Egyptien and several services on an Egyptian theme. Other Napoleonic themes (Entry into Berlin, Bivouac à Wagram, Trophées d'art de l'armée de l'Italie, portraits and trophies) were also executed on large vases. Porcelain tables, which reflect the factory's technical achievement, were decorated on mythological themes (Pompeian Table of Seasons), heroic subjects (Table des Maréchaux de l'Empire, c.1808 by Charles Percier and J.-B. *Isabey), but also included work tables painted with flowers, birds, etc., often mounted in bronze. Porcelain columns included one commemorating Austerlitz, 1808. Many of the artists were independent, living in Paris and working in their own studios (*chambrelinage*). Painters included Marie Jacquotot, figure painter and consultant artist, 1801-42, J.-F.-J.*Swebach, and the Dutch flower painter Jean van Os (d 1808).

Much stock was sold to alleviate financial problems in 1813 and quantities of the old soft paste were sold after the plunder of the factory by the Prussians in 1815. Ware sold in the white at these and subsequent sales was decorated over a period of almost 40 years in England and elsewhere.

After the Restoration, fewer commissions were carried out, but the kings continued to order display services. The then-forbidden Napoleonic subjects were replaced by subjects representing a love of nature or a search for knowledge – a tendency which had earlier been expressed c.1806 in services decorated with views, e.g. the port of Flushing, royal palaces of Bavaria, and especially the Service Encyclopédique which depicted scenes of working life *en grisaille* surrounded by a white and gold frieze. Later subjects included Deeds of the Bourbons, Apotheosis of Henri IV, Louis XIV and the great men of his circle, and Vues Historiques de France. Careful, detailed catalogues like the Service de l'Histoire et de la Topographie des Départements have each scene underlined with a didactic inscription (in this case, relating heroes to places). Landscape subjects also showed details of flora and fauna: Service des Oiseaux d'Amérique; Service de la Chasse; Service Forestier (trees of the world); Service des Productions de la Nature. Other services showed views from romantic lithoprints: Petites Vues de France; Vues d'Europe; Vues hors d'Europe.

Huge vases and porcelain tables were decorated with similar, historical, mythological, and religious scenes. Oil paintings were still copied, as well as miniatures on medallions and portraits on cups. The painters included Madame Ducluzeau (figure painter 1807-48) who, like Marie Jacquotot, excelled in copies of oil paintings, Charles Develly (painter of animals and landscapes 1813-48), Antoine-Gabriel Willermet (head of painting and gilding studios 1825-48), J.-M.-F. Regnier (sculptor, modeller 1826-48), J.-P.-M. Dieterlé (artist 1840-52 and head of art department, 1852-55).

Technical achievements of this period included advances in firing and the introduction of slip-casting, 1816. Lithophanes were made 1827 (before their manufacture at Berlin), and *pâte-sur-pâte* began by 1850, to be later developed by L.-M.-E.*Solon, his apprentice A.-L.*Dammouse, A.-T. Gobert (figure painter 1849-87), Charles Ficquenet (1864-81), E.*Escallier-Légérot (1874-88), Auguste Rodin (briefly) and T.*Doat. Underglaze brown colours were introduced in 1838, and *flambé* glazes were rediscovered in 1848 (but not reliably reproduced until the 1880s). A school of painting was briefly opened in 1820, and studios of glass (operating until 1852) and metal enamelling (until 1872) were created.

Brongniart was briefly succeeded by Jacques-Joseph Ebelmen (joint administrator from 1845) until his death in 1852. The factory came under the control of the ministry of agriculture and commerce after 1848. Ebelmen revived the production of soft paste, engaging Vital Roux in the preparation of pastes (1848-56) and appointed Louis Robert as head of the painting and gilding workshops, 1848-71. His modellers were Nicolle, Peyre and Dieterlé.

The physicist Victor Regnauld was director of the factory from 1852 until his retirement in 1870; he, like Brongniart, concentrated on technical improvements, mainly in porcelain, and invented a method (using compressed air) of keeping large vases in shape while they dried. Eggshell porcelain with lacy openwork decoration was used for light, footed cups of oriental inspiration. The designers Dieterlé and Nicolle (Dieterlé's successor as chief artist, 1856-71) devised low, wide forms for tableware. Large vases continued to form an important part of production and the factory advertised some 200 shapes in 1855. The range of overglaze colours increased, and successive chemists Salvetat (1846-80), Charles Lauth (head of the factory 1879-89) and Georges Vogt (1880-91) introduced a palette of *couleurs de demi-feu* which could withstand the heat needed to fire further decoration. Research was also concerned with high-temperature glazes and coloured pastes imitating marble and other stones.

Regnauld instituted a department for the study of all branches of ceramics, to encourage French production of terracotta, faience and all types of glazed or enamelled earthenware in the face of foreign competition. This research department and the production in other branches of the manufacture of garden and architectural ware helped to revive interest in earthenware and stoneware until it was discontinued c.1870.

Stylistically, the factory looked to the past: its own 18th-century models and Renaissance styles, etc. However, contemporary life was recorded in decoration for the first Exposition Universelle, 1855. A commission set up by the Third Republic after the Franco-Prussian War condemned the factory's artistic achievement.

F.*Bracquemond briefly took over as head of painting and gilding when Robert became head of the factory in 1871, followed 1872-81 by Louis Barré, flower painter from 1844. In his new position, Robert attempted to retrieve the factory's artistic reputation, initiating the Prix de Sèvres in 1875 to attract modellers. The prize went to Lemare, Mayeux and Joseph *Chéret. The factory moved in 1876 to new buildings on land given by Napoleon III in the Parc de Saint-Claude.

On his appointment to the revived post of art director (1875-87), A.E.*Carrier-Belleuse brought with him his pupil, Auguste Rodin (1879-82); they produced vases of the elements, seasons, night/day, etc. Albert Gobert succeeded Carrier-Belleuse 1887-91, and Joseph Chéret acted as his assistant in 1886.

The chemist Charles Lauth took over as director in 1879, when Robert became honorary administrator. With the help of Vogt, he developed a *pâte nouvelle*, which resembled

Chinese porcelain, in 1884, and a new soft paste in 1889.

T.*Deck, director from 1887 until his death, continued his own research, also improving the soft paste and introducing *grosse porcelaine* during his term of office. A cool reception of the factory's display in the Exposition Universelle of 1889 caused changes which included a division into artistic and technical branches. Deck was succeeded by Baumgart (1891-1909) with Vogt as technical director. Aléxandre Sandier, as head of the artistic side from the 1890s until 1908, instigated the development of new forms drawn from nature or, later, pieces decorated with allegorical, often stylized relief ornament, commissioning a number of outside artists, e.g. H.*Guimard, who designed shapes for the use of newly perfected crystalline glazes (these effects were achieved only accidentally up to 1900, when examples were exhibited on vases). The factory's very varied output ranged from such large pieces as fireplaces or fountains to ashtrays, candlesticks and other small items, as well as table and ornamental wares. Sandier also re-created interest in biscuit figures, which until 1895 had been mainly a continuation of 18th century models, portraits, busts and allegorical figures or groups. A new biscuit paste was developed by Vogt and Lauth in 1885. The series of figures for table decoration Jeu d'écharpe, modelled by A.*Léonard and inspired by the dancer Loie Fuller, was shown in the Exposition Universelle of 1900.

Study workshops for faience, stoneware and glass were organised in 1893. A new stoneware body developed for the 1900 Exposition was used for architectural decoration

Sèvres. Stoneware vase with crystalline glazes painted in lavender, slate grey, olive green and buff. Signed by the decorator, Charles Pihan, printed with the factory's oval mark, and dated 1917. 44 cm high.

Sèvres. Porcelain group modelled by Théodore Rivière, entitled Carthage and portraying Sarah Bernhardt as Flaubert's Salammbô, 1920. Signed Théodore Rivière and stamped with factory marks. 55 cm high.

as well as for vases and small sculptures; the factory introduced a series of forms named after French cities and decorated in Art Nouveau style. A new soft-paste formula introduced in 1907 was the equal of hard paste in modelling and firing, without losing the fine effect of the colours used to decorate the earlier soft paste. Its development was followed by that of kaolin soft paste in 1911, and silica soft paste in 1925.

E.*Carrière briefly succeeded Sandier as artistic director in 1908, and was himself followed in the same year by painter Edmé Conty (until 1918), the decorator Leclerq Bouché (1918-29, Léonard Gébleux (1920-27) and Maurice Gensoli (b 1892), decorator 1921-27 and head of the decorating workshop 1927-59. Decoration moved from predominantly plant forms to feature human and animal figures. The factory's display in the Exposition Internationale des Arts Décoratifs et Industriels Modernes in Paris, 1925, included monumental wares (decorative panels, fountains, richly enamelled sculptures, etc.) and items for interior decoration in a range of ceramic bodies (including porcelain) and a number of newly created items (pipes, chess sets, buttons, flagons) that were strictly geometrical in form and relief decoration. The factory's stylistic consultants were H.*Rapin, J.*Mayodon (1934-39) and E.*Decoeur (1939-48), who is regarded as one of the main inspirations for the post-war revival of artistic creativity at Sèvres, with his new designs for cups and vases, intended to exploit the effects of coloured glazes.

Under the direction of S. Gauthier (1964-76), the factory began a close association with the world of contemporary art, calling on established designers to create a wide range of new ornamental and utilitarian

forms dictated by their own stylistic inclinations. The factory continues to employ hand-throwing of forms, which are finished by turning; sculptural pieces are moulded, and very delicate or complicated shapes may be slip cast. The lithographic process, in limited use at Sèvres from the early 19th century, is now more extensively used for the printing of some grounds or portions of decoration, but many pieces are hand-painted. Gilding is often transfer-printed and hand finished.

Marks include *Manufacture Impériale* SÈVRES, sometimes with an eagle (1804-12); LL crossed (1814-24); CC crossed (1824-30); *fleur-de-lis* followed by a circular mark with SÈVRES at the centre, and subsequently monograms of LP. Under the Second Republic, the Second Empire and the Third Republic, the initial s was used with a number. 20th-century marks also incorporate s or SÈVRES and from 1941 a version of LL crossed.

Refs: Auscher; E. Baumgart *La manufacture de Sèvres à l'exposition universelle de 1900* (Paris, 1900); M. Brunet *Les marques de Sèvres* (Paris, 1953); M. Brunet & T. Préaud *Sèvres des origines à nos jours* (Fribourg, 1978); C. Dautermann *Sèvres* (New York, 1969); Chavagnac & Grollier; Garnier; A. Granger *La céramique industrielle* (Gauthier-Villars, Paris, 1905); G. Lechevallier-Chevignard *La manufacture de porcelaine de Sèvres* (Paris, 1908); T. Préaud *Sèvres Porcelain* (Smithsonian Institution Press, Washington D.C., 1980); A. Sandier & G. Lechevallier-Chevignard *Formes et décors modernes de la manufacture nationale de Sèvres* (Paris, n.d.); P. Verlet, S. Grandjean & M. Brunet *Sèvres* (Paris, 1953).

Sewell, Joseph; **Sewell & Co.; Sewell & Donkin.** See St Anthony's Pottery.

Seyler, David. See Kenton Hills Porcelain Inc.

Seynie, La. See Honoré, François-Maurice.

sgraffito decoration. Decorative designs scratched or cut through a layer of slip before firing to reveal clay of a contrasting colour.

Sharp, Samuel. See Derby.

Sharpe, Thomas (d 1838). English potter making earthenware at Swadlincote, Derbyshire, near Burton-on-Trent, from 1821. He produced kitchen ware including yellow-glazed milkpans and baking dishes in a hard earthenware body, brown-glazed teapots and transfer-printed ware, much of which was exported, notably to Canada, through an agent in Montreal.

The firm, trading as Sharpe Brothers & Co. from 1838 and as a limited company from the 1890s, continued the production of tableware with transfer-printed decoration, kitchen ware (in ironstone china advertised as Derbyshire Ironstone), relief-decorated tea and coffee pots and jugs with brown or mottled glazes, and household stoneware. Sanitary ware became the pottery's main output by c.1900.

Marks: THOMAS SHARPE or T. SHARPE impressed; monogram of SB & Co in a wreath

formed half of ivy and half of an oak branch, with SHARPES PATENT.
Refs: Collard; Godden (1964); Jewitt.

Shaw, George. See Holmes Pottery.

Shawnee Pottery. American factory established in 1937 at the works formerly occupied by the *American Encaustic Tiling Co. in Zanesville, Ohio, for the production of low-priced domestic ware, which was sold through stores, including McCrory, Sears and F.W. Woolworth. The work was often produced to the designs of customers e.g. G.*Rumrill, although the firm also employed its own designers from 1938. Production ceased in 1961.
Marks: arrowhead with profile of Shawnee Indian; the name, *Shawnee*.
Refs: Kovel & Kovel; N. Schneider 'Shawnee Pottery' in *Times Recorder* (Zanesville, 16th and 23rd October, 1960).

Shawsheen Pottery. See Dahlquist, Edward.

Sheepfolds Pottery. See Bridge End Pottery; Rickaby, Thomas.

Sheerer, Mary G. (1865-1954). American ceramic decorator and teacher; born in Kentucky. She studied drawing, painting and china decoration at the Cincinnati Art Academy and the Art Students' League before joining the art department of the Sophie Newcomb Memorial College in New Orleans, where she had spent some time in her youth, eventually becoming professor of ceramics and drawing. From 1898, she designed shapes for the Newcomb Pottery, while encouraging students to work out their own ideas freely in decoration, with the emphasis on originality and careful craftsmanship. The pieces were thrown by

*Mary Sheerer. Vase made at the *Newcomb College Pottery, 1898. 26 cm high.*

J.*Meyer for decoration by the students and employees of the pottery. Mary Sheerer was also responsible for the supervision and approval of work carried out for sale. Chairman of the art division of the American Ceramic Society, 1924-27, she became a Fellow in 1931, and acted as a delegate on the Hoover Commission to the Exposition Internationale des Arts Décoratifs et Industriels Modernes in Paris, 1925. She returned briefly to the Newcomb Pottery in 1931, the year of her retirement from the college, afterwards settling in Cincinnati.
Marks: initials MS or MGS within a label-shaped outline, incised.
Refs: F. Adams *Two Decades of Newcomb Pottery Pieces from 1897-1917* (exhibition catalogue, Newcomb College, New Orleans, February 1963); Barber (1976); Clark & Hughto; Donhauser; Eidelberg; Evans; Henzke; Keen; Kovel & Kovel; S. Ormond & M.E. Irvine *Louisiana's Art Nouveau: the Crafts of the Newcomb Style* (Pelican Publishing, Gretna, Louisiana, 1976).

Shelley, Joseph Ball (1836-96). Staffordshire manufacturer of earthenware and porcelain, formerly a lawyer's clerk. He joined his stepfather Samuel Hartshorne at the Dresden Works in Stafford Street, Longton, by 1858, briefly entering a partnership with James Adams and H.*Adams (1861-62) at the same pottery. Shelley joined the firm of H.*Wileman as a representative in 1862, and became partner with Wileman's son James at the Foley China Works (see Foley Potteries) in 1872, taking over as proprietor of the firm's porcelain production in 1884. He continued to trade as Wileman & Co. after James Wileman's retirement in 1892 and was succeeded by his son P.*Shelley.
Refs: Andrews; Bunt; Watkins *et al.*

Shelley, Percy (1860-1937). Staffordshire manufacturer of earthenware and porcelain, born in Longton. On joining his father J.B. *Shelley in 1881, Percy Shelley extended the *Foley Potteries' output (until then mainly monochrome printed porcelain) to include, by the early 1890s, display plates painted with landscapes, game and fish, as well as a variety of tea, breakfast and dessert sets and decorative pieces for the table. He employed such artists as R.J.*Morris to create new designs and engaged F.A.*Rhead as art director, followed by Walter *Slater. Percy Shelley set out to improve the quality of paste and finish. He increased the firm's export trade, and thus enabled it to survive diminished sales in Britain during World War II. In sole control of the company after his father's death, he ensured the firm's immediate financial success with the introduction of popular ranges of toilet ware, nursery sets, household ware, souvenir or commemorative pieces, and a number of ornamental lines, alongside bone china tea and coffee ware, and earthenware dinner services. He retired from the business in 1932. He was for many years a member of the National Council for the Pottery Industry.
The firm, trading under Percy Shelley's sons and grandsons as Shelleys from 1925 and Shelley Potteries from 1929, became known as Shelley China Ltd in 1965. With the subsidiary Shelley Electric Furnaces Ltd, it was taken over in 1966 by Allied

Obadiah Sherratt. Model of Polito's Menagerie, c.1820.

English Potteries (see Pearson, S., & Sons Ltd), and the name Shelley China Ltd became the property of the Doulton Group on Doulton's amalgamation with Allied English Potteries. The factory, renamed the Montrose Works, was turned over to the production of Royal Albert china (see Wild, T., & Co.).
Refs: Andrews; Bunt; Watkins *et al.*

Shepard, Elihu H. (c.1795-1876). American potter. Shepard purchased land which contained large deposits of kaolin clay at Kaolin, Missouri, and started the production of cream-coloured earthenware there in 1852, making vases, pitchers and tableware. Under the management of an English potter, the factory made imitations of majolica with sponged decoration.
Ref: Barber (1976).

Sheriff Hill Pottery. English pottery established near Gateshead, south of the River Tyne, before 1773 for the production of earthenware, including dairy and household ware, as well as painted, sponged or gilded pieces. Robinson, Gray & Burns, proprietors in the late 19th and early 20th centuries, made dishes and mugs for local sale, and vessels for use at a nearby lead works. The pottery closed on the death of the last partner, Burns, in 1909.
Refs: R.C. Bell *Tyneside Pottery* (Studio Vista, 1971); Jewitt.

Sherratt, Obadiah (1775-c.1846). Staffordshire potter, working at Burslem from c.1810; he moved from Hot Lane to Waterloo Road in 1828. Sherratt made earthenware figures and groups in a vigorous style resembling that of J.*Walton (though usually without the background of flowering branches). The figures, each original in design, were boldly modelled and enamelled in bright colours (blue, green, yellow, orange, red, brown, black). Many are on a table-like base, with four or six feet, and labelled in capital letters, often in a cartouche on the base. Sherratt's subjects included: Polito's Menagerie; Bull Baiting; Romulus and Remus; The Death of Munrow; The Sacrifice of Isaac; Ale Bench; Tee Total; Who Shall Ware the Breches;

The Roran Lion; The Duke of Wellington. Sherratt was succeeded by his widow and son, and the business ceased operation in the 1850s.
Refs: Haggar (1955); H.A.B. Turner *Collector's Guide to Staffordshire Pottery Figures* (McGibbon & Kee, London, 1971).

Sherriff, James (b c.1825). Porcelain painter working for the Worcester firm of Kerr & Binns. Sherriff specialized in flower subjects. His son, also James Sherriff (1848-85) was a painter of flowers and grasses for the *Worcester Royal Porcelain Co.
Ref: Sandon (1978a).

Sherwin, James. Australian potter working at Hobart, Tasmania, from c.1831 on the production of jars and cooking ware. Few marked pieces survive, but they are the earliest known pieces made in Tasmania.
Ref: Graham.

Sherwin & Cotton. Staffordshire tile manufacturers working 1877-1930 in Hanley. The firm's output included majolica tiles decorated with flowers, animals (e.g. a stag series c.1890), and portrait tiles in relief flooded with glaze (*émaux ombrants*) e.g. by G. *Cartlidge. The firm took out a patent for indentations cut in the reverse of tiles for more effective fixing.
Mark: Staffordshire knot in a double triangle; SHERWIN & COTTON, incised or impressed on reverse of tiles and plaques.
Refs: Barnard; Godden (1964); Lockett (1979).

Shigaraki ware. Japanese pottery of ancient origin made in the area surrounding Nagano in Shiga prefecture. Using coarse, reddish-brown clay, the potters initially produced unglazed stoneware, but developed glazes from the 17th century, using combinations of clay, feldspar and wood ash to produce various glaze effects: transparent (for plates, bowls), red (pickling jars, etc.), black (tea jars), brown or, with the addition of colouring agents, a celadon colour (using copper green and ash from rice straw), and without the iron content of true celadon glazes) and blue (containing cobalt oxide, feldspar and wood ash). Tea jars were often decorated with long drips of glaze. A white, Hagi-type glaze introduced by a Seto potter in the late 18th century was sometimes striped with green copper glaze, at first on presentation wares, but eventually in common use for jars and saké bottles. A reddish-brown glaze containing iron was used for common wares.
Nagano, which took the lead in developing new glazes and production methods, was unusual in producing large wares, such as well heads, and tea jars (up to about 80 cm high) with various glaze effects: brown, splashed at the shoulder with black; white striped with green; cobalt blue; green. The jars were distributed widely throughout Japan, often for the decoration of tea houses; some were for official use, and Nagano held exclusive rights to their sale in the tea-growing area of Uji.
The area's production grew in the 19th century: the five kilns active in 1810 increased to 26 in 1871. Those outside Nagano at that time were at Maki and Chokushi to the north, where the traditional output consisted of

small pieces glazed in copper green, cobalt blue, black, brown or white, and Eda, Koyama, Hosowara, Damura (now Ogawade) and Shimmura to the south, as well as Kinose.
Chokushi village, with 20 potters working 15 kilns at the height of production c.1900, used veins of fine, white clay from Mount Gonin. The output included a vase for use on a Buddhist altar, with globular body and trumpet-shaped neck, thrown in two pieces and luted together with slip. Kinose village produced mainly lamps and oil plates, saké flasks and religious vessels; three or four kilns were in operation in the early 20th century. Koyama became known mainly for the production of teapots, especially with landscape decoration, dipped in white slip and painted with mountains, clouds, birds, sails, pine trees, and a hut, in iron brown and copper green. Other designs included a 'green bamboo' pattern with white and brown slips over a chrome green glaze, and a slip-coated pot painted in underglaze blue. The style influenced potters in Akashi, *Kasama and *Mashiko to the north, and Noma in *Kyushu. Pieces were also supplied from Koyama as greenware to Nagano potters. Coarse wares made at Koyama included stoves and grates.
Individual makers of small wares emerged in the early 19th century as the area became less isolated from urban culture, especially that of Kyoto. The artists included *Rakusui, *Tanii Rijuro, and *Takahashi Toemon. A ceramic school was in operation from 1831. Local production had developed a degree of specialization by the 1870s to the extent that potters employed labourers to carry out heavy tasks and obtained clay and wood from suppliers. Sanitary wares became an important part of the area's output. Electrical machinery, introduced c.1920, included clay processors, and an electric wheel for use with plaster moulds. However, a reaction to industrial methods occurred in the 1920s, with an awakening of interest in *mingei wares, especially teapots.
The Shigaraki producers' trade association, formed 1895 and reorganized 1902, established a model factory (1903) in Nagano. In operation until 1927, the factory ran a training programme and introduced influences from outside the area under various directors: the first, a potter from *Kutani, introduced decoration in gold and enamel colours; Endo Heikichi, the second director, trained in Kyoto, specialized in underglaze blue painting and introduced techniques used in Kyoto for the making of special pieces for exhibition in Europe and America. However, Okuda Mijokichi (1880-1930) returned the emphasis in part to local traditions, especially in the making of large pieces associated with Nagano, his home town. The factory's main output consisted of useful wares (ink bottles, chemical wares) and vases, flowerpots, etc., for export to south-east Asia.
In the 20th century, the area has become known for the production of hibachi, with splashed blue-white glaze (namako), as well as vases, figures, etc. Ishihaze, a peaked surface effect caused by the presence of partly fired grains of silicon contained in the clay, is characteristic of Shigaraki wares. The area supports about 100 kilns.
Refs: Cort; Koyama; Jenyns (1971); Mizuo; Morse; Sanders.

Shigeba. *See* Nyudo.

Shigejiro. *See* Unrinin Banzo.

Shigekichi Urano. *See* Kenzan.

Shimmura. *See* Shigaraki ware.

Shinjo. Japanese folk pottery established c.1841 on the edge of Shinjo city, Yamagato prefecture. Initially making porcelain, the kiln later specialized in domestic ware, including large jars and three-legged cooking pots. It is noted for the streaked blue-white (namako) iron glaze frequently occurring on wares of the Tohoku region. Similar work was carried out at Shinmachi, Tsuruoka city, where a folk kiln operated in the early 19th century, but *Hirashimizu is the only other kiln active in the prefecture today.
Refs: Mizuo; Munsterberg.

Shinmachi. *See* Shinjo.

Shinnick, William M. *See* Mosaic Tile Co.

Shino ware. Japanese stoneware made from the 1570s in *Mino. There were kilns at Ogaya (where the most important kilns were at Mutabara, Kamashita and Naka), Onada, Gotomaki and Kujiri as well as in the region of Shimoishi. The ware, made from white clay, was characterized by thick feldspar glazes, warm in effect; it was generally light in colour and often irregular or distorted in shape, with corners sometimes fluted with a bamboo tool. Initially tea ware, it included from the 16th century: bowls, plates and other tableware, tea bowls, deep serving bowls, saké bottles, incense boxes, flower vases, water droppers, inkstones, etc. Pieces most commonly have decoration of plants and natural forms derived from the surrounding mountainous rural area, (birds, etc.) or abstract patterns, drawn in iron under the white glaze, giving a faint rose tinge. Grey Shino was covered with slip from the iron-rich clay commonly found in the region, through which patterns were incised (or had patterns trailed in slip from the same clay) before glazing. A reducing atmosphere in firing resulted in a mouse-grey colour. Red Shino, rose Shino and pieces made with contrasting clays, as in agate ware, also occur. In Japan, Shino was thought of as Seto ware until the 18th century, when it became associated in name with Shino Soshin (1440-1522), a connoisseur of incense for the tea ceremony. It predates *Oribe ware, also made in Mino. Makers include the *Kato family, and *Arakawa Toyoso.
Refs: Fujioka; Jenyns (1971); Mikami; Munsterberg.

Shiraishi. Japanese pottery established near Kurume in Saga prefecture by the border of Fukuoka prefecture, initially for the production of porcelain, but soon making earthenware with brick-coloured body. From the mid 19th century, the potters used a red glaze of raku type, adding amber, green and occasionally dripped white glazes, producing colourful lidded jars, cooking utensils and other domestic ware. Unglazed earthenware cups in reddish brown body are regarded as typical examples of *mingei wares.
Refs: Munsterberg; Okamura.

*Shirayamadani Kataro. Vase made at the
Rookwood Pottery. 26.7 cm high.

Shiraiwa. *See* Naraoka.

Shirayamadani Kataro (1865-1948). Ceramic artist born in Japan. While visiting America, Shirayamadani was asked to join the *Rookwood Pottery where he worked 1887-1915 and 1925-48. His painting, characterized by spontaneous, fluent brushwork, included a design of daffodils on a vase (1890) and dahlias on a narrow-necked jug under shaded brown/green/black glaze (1895). He also designed many shapes for the pottery and carried out relief decoration, e.g. a vase (1901) with a carved design of geese in white and tan against a matt green glaze; also a moulded inkwell and pen tray (1906) in the form of a waterlily pad and flower with matt blue-green and green glazes. He spent the years 1915-25 in the Far East, mainly Japan.

Mark: signature (Japanese).
Refs: Clark & Hughto; Eidelberg; Evans; Kovel & Kovel; Peck; K.R. Trapp 'Japanese Influence in Early Rookwood Pottery' in *Antiques* 103 (January 1973).

Shirobokov, Dipedri & Borisov. Russian firm making earthenware at Gorodische in the province of Tver c.1844-c.1854. As well as earthenware in local pink clay, the factory made white ware in simple forms for domestic use. Printed decoration included views of the St Petersburg district or scenes from fables at the centre of plates, etc., rimmed with wide floral bands. Cream-coloured ware in a soft tone was printed overall with a delicate, lacy design.

Mark: the firm's name in an oval wreath over the place name.
Ref: Bubnova.

Shodai. Japanese pottery centre established at Tatsunohara, Kumamoto prefecture,

c.1620 by potters from *Agano. Two remaining kilns ceased operation in the early 20th century. The workshops produced wares for the local feudal lord, and (after 1806) utensils sold locally for the storage and preparation (but not cooking) of food – water storage jars, squat, sometimes square-shouldered saké bottles, etc. – adapting Korean stoneware techniques to Japanese taste, and using a red, rough clay body and amber (ame) glaze with runs or trails of blue-white (namako) glaze. The traditional glaze effects continue on everyday domestic ware, at a kiln built at Fumoto after World War II.
Refs: Jenyns (1971); Munsterberg; Okamura.

Shonsui wares. In Japanese ceramics, a group of porcelains imported from China to Japan in the 17th century and possibly later, and widely imitated in Japan in the 19th century. Shonsui wares included tea bowls, incense boxes (often in the shapes of fruit or birds), water jars, saké flasks, double-gourd bottles, and cups, dishes and jugs which are often dented or distorted into asymmetrical shapes. Characteristically the porcelain paste is pure white, fully glazed to the rim (which is often edged in brown), and well finished with high foot rims. Decorative designs, carefully painted in underglaze blue, included landscapes, animals, human figures, and plant forms, notably the combination of pine, bamboo and plum, against a ground more or less covered with geometrical patterns. Some pieces were decorated with sketchily written columns of poetry invoking good fortune, and the name of the ware is derived from a characteristic inscription on the base of many pieces, which reads 'Go rodaiyu Wu Shonsui made' in Japanese and is probably a trademark.

Japanese imitations in the 19th century stem from Arita, the Owari district of Seto (by Tamikichi *Kato and his successors), Kokoriku (near Kutani) and the potters *Mokubei, *Dohachi II, *Shuhei, *Hozen, *Wazen and *Chikuzen.
Refs: Jenyns (1967); Mitsuoka 'Blue and white and enamelled wares of the T'ien Ch'i period' in *Sekai Toji Zenshu* Vol 11 (Zanho Press & Kawade Shobo, Tokyo, 1955-68).

Shonyu. *See* Raku family.

Shorin. *See* Rokubei II.

Shorter, Arthur Colley Austin (1882-1963). Staffordshire earthenware manufacturer. In 1916, with his brother John G. Shorter, he became director of the firm of A.J.*Wilkinson Ltd, in which their father Arthur Shorter had been a partner. The firm took over the nearby Newport Pottery Co. by 1920, and the brothers became directors of Shorter & Son Ltd, successors in 1905 to Shorter & Boulton, makers of majolica, mainly for export, at the Copeland Street works, Stoke-on-Trent, from 1879 and eventually part of the Crown Devon Group. Colley Shorter built up the Wilkinson company by careful marketing, promoted the Bizarre ware designed by C.*Cliff, who became his second wife in 1940, and with her travelled extensively on sales trips abroad.
Refs: see Wilkinson, A.J., Ltd.

shot enamels. *See* Worcester.

Shoza Kutani (1816-83). Japanese ceramist and porcelain decorator working on *Kutani ware. Shoza learned decorative techniques under *Gen'emon and *Miyamotoya and worked as a porcelain painter based in his native Terai, Nomi County, from the early 1840s. He developed a rich, decorative style, using decorative and detailed polychrome enamel designs painted in reserves against a ground of red, embellished with gold and silver, which became known as Shoza-fu (Shoza style) or saishiki kinran (coloured kinran). In his own research, he achieved a new manganese pigment (noto gosu) and a rich, deep red, and made improvements in he coloured glazes of Old Kutani ware; he also studied and made use of the pigments from Western countries that became available in Japan after 1868.
Ref: Nakagawa.

Shufflebotham, Arthur. English ceramic decorator. Shufflebotham worked in Bristol before joining the *South Wales Pottery, where he remained c.1908-c.1915. He is noted for his sketchy painting of fruit and flowers with free, wide brush strokes.
Refs: see South Wales Pottery.

Shuhei Ogata (1783-1839). Japanese studio potter, the younger brother of *Dohachi II. He was apprenticed at the *Hozan kiln in Awata. Shuhei later specialized in unglazed teapots in the manner of *Mokubei, tea bowls made in stoneware, covered in a fine, creamy crackle glaze, and decorated in underglaze blue, red-enamelled aka-e and kinrande porcelains. All his wares were carefully made. Shuhei's pupils included *Mimpei, who worked with him at *Agano c.1830 and invited him to *Awaji, where he opened a kiln in 1834.
Refs: Fujioka; *Genshoku Nihon no Bijutsu* [Colour Reproductions of Japanese Art] (30 vols, Shogakukan, Tokyo, 1967); Gorham; Jenyns (1967); Morse; Okuda; Roberts.

Shuntai (1799-1878). Japanese potter, Kato Soshiro, working in Kyoto, as the last of a line of potters with the character 'shun' in their artistic names. In the 1830s, he revived production of *Ofuke wares at Akazu, near Nagoya castle. He went to live in Mino (1851), where he opened a kiln at Imao. He later returned to Akazu and made wares painted in brown and white slip for the prince of Owari. His work included imitations of Seto, Takatori, Shino, Oribe, Tamba, Karatsu and mainland Korean wares, as well as porcelain with underglaze blue or *aka-e decoration.
Refs: Fujioka; Jenyns (1971); *Nihon no Toji: Tokyo Kokuritsu Hakubutsukan Zuhan Mokuroka* [Japanese Ceramics: Illustrated catalogue of the Tokyo National Museum] (Tokyo National Museum, 1966); Roberts.

Sicard, Jacques (1865-1923). French potter. Sicard studied the techniques of iridescent glazes during a long association with C. *Massier. He travelled to America in 1901 and was subsequently employed on the creation of an art line called Sicardo ware for S.A.*Weller. Taking care to guard the secrets of his technique, he produced individual pieces with his French assistant, Henri

Gellie. His painted designs of flowers, foliage, freely curving lines, stars, etc., were carved out in ochreous slip, coloured with metallic compounds, which achieved a lustrous finish when fired in a reducing atmosphere. The ground, in shades of green, blue, pink, crimson or purple, with blended tints resembling those of an opal stone or iridescent glass, had already undergone firing on the pieces, all thrown or hand-modelled in simple, fluid shapes, before the decoration was painted on. Leaving the Weller pottery in 1907, Sicard returned to work in the south of France, but the stock of his ware remained on the market until after 1912.

Mark: personal signature, SICARD; the ware was marked with versions of SICARDO/WELLER.

Refs: Barber (1976); Clark & Hughto; Eidelberg; Evans; Henzke; Keen; Kovel & Kovel; L.& E. Purviance & N.F. Schneider *Weller Art Pottery in Color* (Wallace-Homestead, Des Moines, Iowa, 1971).

Sicardo ware. *See* Weller, Samuel A.

Siimes, Aune (1909-64). Ceramic artist working in Finland and trained in Helsinki. In 1932 she joined *Arabia where she designed porcelain bowls, vases, etc. The pieces, slip-cast and decorated with stripes or chequered patterns in coloured slip, were very thin and translucent.
Ref: Aro.

Sika, Jutta (1877-1964). Austrian designer, born in Linz and trained 1897-1902 at the Kunstgewerbeschule in Vienna. Her work included tableware designs for the firm of J.*Böck in simple, original shapes, e.g. a coffee pot, with flat wing-shaped handles pierced by circular holes. She taught in Vienna, 1911-33.
Mark: monograms of JS in a rectangular outline.
Ref: Neuwirth (1974a).

Silcock, James. English potter born in Derbyshire and trained in Staffordshire. Silcock was working in Australia by 1879, when he was employed in the development of the *Lithgow Pottery for a colliery company founded eight years earlier in Lithgow Valley, New South Wales. He extended their output of bricks and pipes to include high-quality domestic ware. He was manager and eventually proprietor of the pottery established by R.*Turton on the outskirts of Newcastle, New South Wales. James Silcock made fine wares with white clay newly discovered at Lithgow, and a selection of his pots was shown in the Sydney International Exhibition, 1879. His diary provides documentary information on the life and skills of an Australian potter in the 19th and early 20th centuries.
Refs: Cooper; I. Evans *The Lithgow Pottery* (Sydney, 1980); J. Kalokerinos in *Pottery in Australia* Vol 12 No 2 (1973).

Silicon ware. *See* Doulton & Co.

Simeon, Harry. English ceramic modeller and designer, working for *Doulton & Co. in Lambeth 1894-1936. His work included jugs decorated with foliate patterns under ivory-toned saltglaze, and designs exploiting a mottled brown 'Leopard Skin' effect.

*Jacques Sicard. Earthenware plaque moulded in low relief with a bust of the Madonna and finished with plum and green lustre. Designed for S.*Weller, 1900-07. 23 x 16.5 cm.*

Simeon collaborated on the design of a series of vases, bowls and plaques (1919-22), closely resembling Islamic pottery in colour and pattern, and marketed as Persian ware. Simeon also designed models for a series of Tobyware jugs, 1924-30, and painted a series of tall vases with stylized animals, flowers, etc., in coloured glazes, sometimes with tube-lined outlines. In the early 1920s he designed earthenware or stoneware plaques, decorated, e.g., with a squirrel in the twigs of a fruiting oak, fish and seaweed, or, again, a bird among flowers.
Mark: initials HS.
Refs: see Doulton & Co.

Simmance, Eliza or Elise. English pottery decorator and designer. Trained at the Lambeth School of Art, she was employed by

Harry Simeon. Display plate painted by Simeon at the Lambeth Workshop. Marks include Pinder, Bourne & Co., Burslem, *impressed, and* HS, *painted. 39 cm in diameter.*

*Doulton & Co. in Lambeth, where her early work included finely incised foliage patterns surrounding panels by other artists. After c.1900 she decorated only individual pieces. She specialized for a time in painting arrangements of fruit and flowers in coloured slip built up in layers to produce a low-relief design. In the 1890s, inspired in some designs by the work of the Glasgow School, her work shows some elements of Art Nouveau, but her own style developed in freedom from c.1900 into a confident, stylized portrayal of natural forms. Her large output is noted for its variety and originality, and she was accomplished in many of the studio's decorative techniques, including carved, incised and applied relief ornament, as well as slip painting, and took part in the decoration of Silicon ware. In addition to her own work, Elise Simmance provided designs for execution by junior artists.

Marks: *e* at centre of large S, or ES monogram.
Refs: see Doulton & Co.

Simmen, Henri (1880-1969). Flemish-born ceramist, formerly an architect, working in France. Simmen studied pottery under E. *Lachenal and then established his own studio in Meudon, producing salt-glazed stoneware with buff body painted in brown with gilded highlights, or with crackle glazes painted in enamel. After travel in the Far East following World War I, he returned to France and continued his work in stoneware, relying for decorative effect on subtly coloured glazes, sometimes used over designs in low relief. His salt-glazed wares usually

*Eliza Simmance. Vase decorated with beaded panels of foliage in green and milky blue by Simmance at the *Doulton & Co. Lambeth workshop. 41 cm high.*

have geometrical patterns in black and brown highlighted with gold. Simmen's wife, who was Japanese, carved mounts in ivory and other materials for his pots.

Marks: *H. Sim* incised or painted signature.
Refs: Baschet; Haslam (1977); Lesieutre.

Simms, B.C. *See* Thompson, C.C., Pottery Co.

Simpson, Anna Frances (1886-1930). American ceramic decorator. After studying for an art diploma at the Sophie Newcomb Memorial College for Women, New Orleans, until 1906, Fanny Simpson remained as a prolific decorator at the Newcomb Pottery until her death. The Museum of Fine Arts, Houston, Texas, mounted a memorial exhibition in 1931.
Refs: R. Blasberg 'Newcomb Pottery' in *Antiques* 94 (July 1968); Clark & Hughto; Evans; Henzke; Kovel & Kovel; S. Ormond & M.E. Irvine *Louisiana's Art Nouveau: the Crafts of the Newcomb Style* (Pelican Publishing, Gretna, La, 1976).

Simpson, John (1811-84). English painter and ceramic decorator. Simpson trained at the porcelain factory in Nottingham Road in his home town of *Derby. He moved to Stoke-on-Trent c.1837, and worked for *Mintons Ltd until c.1847. There, he painted figures, landscapes and portrait plaques. From 1847, he taught porcelain painting at Marlborough House, London. Simpson also worked as a miniaturist and exhibited at the Royal Academy, 1847-71.
Refs: Aslin & Atterbury; *see also* Derby; Mintons Ltd.

Simpson, W.B., & Sons. English firm of interior decorators working in London 1870-c.1900. The firm decorated panels and, less

W.B. Simpson & Sons. Pair of tiles painted in yellow and brown, c.1880. 39.4 cm x 15.2 cm.

often, individual tiles bought in the biscuit from *Maw & Co. and probably *Mintons Ltd. The patterns were normally hand-painted under or over the glaze; transfer-printed designs were sometimes used. An early project, chimney decoration, was shown in the International Exhibition at South Kensington, London, 1871. Commissions included tiles or panels for the South Kensington Museum, the Criterion Theatre, Piccadilly, in 1874, the Lady Chapel of St Mary Redcliffe's Church, Bristol (in association with Maw & Co. and 12 panels designed by H. Walter Lonsdale for the Bute Tower of Cardiff Castle with scenes of figures in neo-classical style illustrating the life of Elijah. Panels illustrating the Book of Kings were bordered with *pâte-sur-pâte* designs of animals.
Marks (accompanying the manufacturer's mark): initials of the firm in an oval outline sometimes embossed on the back of tiles; monogram used on the face of panels.
Ref: Barnard; Lockett (1979).

Simpson, W.E. *See* Buffalo Pottery.

Sinceny. French faience factory in operation at Sinceny (Aisne) from 1728, noted for high-temperature painting in Rouen style and later enamels painted by workers from Strasbourg in the 18th century. The factory continued in the 19th century, making pieces sparsely decorated with lines and initials in blue on the rim; also a spotted ground with blue filets and sometimes polychrome roses. Utilitarian ware included brown earthenware lined with turquoise. After the closure and sale of the factory in 1864, it was reopened by a firm making wine measures and finally used for the manufacture of hard-paste porcelain by the firm of Moulin père et fils.
Refs: Brunhammer *et al* (1976); Ernould-Gandouet; Lesur (1971).

Singer-Schinnerl, Susi (b 1895). Austrian ceramist, born and trained in Vienna, where she attended the Kunstschule für Frauen und Mädchen, 1909-15, and joined the Wiener Werkstätte; there her work included figures, groups, portrait busts, vases and other pieces. In 1925, she established her own workshop in Grünbach am Schneeburg.
Marks: initials S.S. or S SS/MADE IN/ AUSTRIA.
Ref: Neuwirth (1974a).

Sipiagin, Nikolai, and son, Vsevelod. Russian porcelain manufacturers. In the late 1820s, Nikolai Sipiagin took over the factory, where he worked for a short time. His son, Vsevelod, reopened the factory in 1850 and produced decorative pieces, e.g. mugs in the form of Cossacks' heads, wearing caps and red hoods, and everyday ware, before letting the factory to the peasant Timofei Vasilievich Turku in 1855, and I.A.*Ikonnikov ten years later.
Marks: Cyrillic S; variants of '*Of the factory of V.N. Sipiagin*' in underglaze blue on ordinary ware and in gold on finer pieces, 1850-65.
Refs: Nikoforova; Ross; Rozembergh.

Sitte, Julie (b 1881) Austrian ceramic modeller, trained at the Kunstgewerbeschule in Vienna, 1906-13. She specialized in vases,

Sitzendorf. Mirror frame of modelled flowers and cupids, with holders for three candles below. 82 cm long.

animal models and other decorative pieces in a variety of earthenware bodies, often with stylized flowers or foliage in relief.
Marks include a signature, J. SITTE.
Ref: Neuwirth (1974a).

Sitte, Olga. Austrian ceramic modeller, working in Vienna. Her work, which included many models of dogs, foxes, lambs, and other animals, was produced by Wiener Keramik and later the Vereinigten Wiener und Gmundner Keramik workshops. She died before 1920.
Marks include *O. Sitte, Olga Sitte* and a monogram of OS.
Ref: Neuwirth (1974a).

Sitzendorf. German porcelain factory established in 1850 by William Liebmann, who was succeeded by 1896 by the firm of Alfred Voigt. The initial output of tableware was extended in the late 1850s to include figures and groups, notably imitations of models by the Meissen factory, and from 1880 pieces with lacework decoration. The firm continues to make ornamental ware, much of it for export, trading as VEB Sitzendorfer Porzellanfabrik.
Marks: crossed lines in the form of H; versions of a crown over S, crossed by the same arrangement of lines.
Refs: Danckert; Scherf; Weiss.

Sivad, H. *See* Davis, Harry.

Skeaping, John Rattenbury (1901-80). English sculptor, artist and designer, born in Essex. Skeaping studied in London until 1920. In 1926, he modelled the first of a series of fourteen animals, ten of which were put into production by the firm of J.*Wedgwood

& Sons Ltd in black basalt or creamware, with a variety of matt and coloured glazes. The figures included bison, a range of deer, kangaroos, sea lions, tigers, monkeys and bears. Some of them were produced throughout the 1930s and there was a re-issue of the most simple models in 1959, with tan/grey glaze. Skeaping also won a competition in 1930 with the design of a vase to commemorate the birth of Josiah Wedgwood.
Refs: Batkin; Reilly & Savage.

Skellern, Victor (1909-66). English ceramic designer and decorator, born in Fenton, Staffordshire. Skellern joined the design department of J.*Wedgwood & Sons Ltd in 1923 and studied at the Royal College of Art in London, graduating in 1933. He succeeded J. Goodwin as art director of the Wedgwood factory in 1934 and instituted technical developments, such as litho printing. He collaborated with N. Wilson on designs for new bodies and glazes, and himself created new shapes for the firm's tableware. His commemorative work for the firm included black basalt vases buried with the foundation stone of the factory in Barlaston (1938) and a mug for the firm's bi-centenary. He also carried out many patterns for tableware, e.g. printed woodland animals, before his retirement in 1965.
Refs: Batkin; Reilly & Savage.

Skinner, George and William. *See* Stafford Pottery.

Skopin. Russian pottery centre in a coal-mining area south of Ryazan, active since the 12th century and concentrated on the town of Skopin from its foundation (under the name of Ostrozhok) in the 16th century. The Skopin potters supplied surrounding villages over an increasing area with bowls, jars, dishes and other household articles in coiled and thrown earthenware, known as sinyushki, with a bluish-black tinge which developed in firing the local light-coloured clays. The ware, durable and reasonably priced, was sold as far away as Rostov and Tajanrogby by the early 19th century. The craftsmen continued to work at home in the traditional way, with the men making jars, jugs and bowls, helped by their children, while the women made smaller items, e.g. toy whistles, which were used by travelling sellers of the pottery to cry their wares.

By the early 20th century, many workshops, including that of F.*Ovodov, were making figures and such display pieces as kvass jugs (which were made in the shape of a wheel with a hollow centre intended to hold ice wrapped in a cloth for cooling the drink, kvass); often the jugs were made with the spout in the form of a snake held by a skopa (the local bird of prey, from which the town derives its name) with its wings spread on the jug's broad, patterned neck. Jugs also occur in the form of a centaur, the two-headed Imperial eagle, or the skopa. Other pieces included candlesticks in the form of a dragon, or a violinist seated on a stool and wearing a top hat (which held the candle). Intricate pieces were made in units, and from the 17th century the unfired clay was decorated with stamped motifs (usually passed from generation to generation in families) or carved with a pen-knife or wooden tool.

Victor Skellern. Teacup, saucer and plate with the pattern, Black Asia, designed by Skellern in 1956 and made at the Wedgwood factory. Plate, 27 cm in diameter.

Although the display ware had sold well to visitors from Moscow and St Petersburg, pottery-making died out in Skopin at the outbreak of World War I. However, I. *Maximov, M.*Tashcheyev and Dmitry Zholobov (*see* Zholobov Pottery) were among craftsmen who resumed production in 1934, joining the Skopin ceramics co-operative, which produced large quantities of the local household ware. With support from the local Industrial Arts Institute, the cooperative acquired a new factory building and equipment; the workshop was directed by master potter Mikhail Pelyonkin, who taught young potters. The ware has been exhibited in the USSR and other countries since 1949.
Ref: Ovsyannikov.

Slater, Eric (b 1902). English ceramic designer. Eric Slater worked for nearly two years for the North Staffordshire Railway Co., spending time in the firm's drawing office. On beginning work for the firm of P.*Shelley in 1919, he started training in design at the Burslem and Hanley art schools. Working under his father, Walter *Slater, from whom he was to take over as art director at the Shelley Potteries in 1937 or 1938, he designed a number of patterns in traditional styles (e.g. Archway of Roses for the Queen Anne shapes) before creating shapes influenced by Art Deco and Cubism in his designs in 1930 for the Vogue and Mode ranges of bone porcelain tea and coffee wares, which featured conical forms and triangular handles, with a variety of decorative patterns often based on geometrical motifs. His Regent shape (registered in 1933) was characterized by tall, inward curving sides on hollow ware, and handles in the form of a circle supported by a curved strip of clay (like one of the handles of a pair of scissors). Patterns were floral or geometrical, and the line was exhibited among other examples of the firm's tea ware at the British Industries Fair, 1933. The shape Eve was a narrower version of Mode, with hollow, rather than solid, triangular handles.

Eric Slater provided all except one of the designs for Shelley's display in the exhibition 'Britain Can Make It' in 1946; he joined the firm's Board of Directors in the same year. His later style moved from the modernistic influence of the 1930s towards *sgraffito* or resist patterns of leaves or simple scrolled motifs with cross-hatched lines or dotted areas, mainly on lightly curved bowls or other simple shapes. Examples were shown in the Festival of Britain (1951) and in a display of students' work selected for the Burslem School of Art Centenary (1953).
Refs: Dowling; Watkins *et al*.

Slater, John (1844-1914). English ceramic chemist and decorator, born in Derby, the youngest son of Joseph *Slater. He trained at the Stoke-on-Trent School of Design and became an apprentice at *Mintons Ltd under L.*Arnoux. He won first prize for china painting two years running at the Hanley Exhibition, also receiving an honourable mention with work shown in the International Exhibition in London, 1871. John Slater succeeded his brother Albert as art director of *Pinder, Bourne & Co. in 1867 and continued to work for the firm under H. *Doulton. He was responsible for the selection and training of young artists from local art schools, whom he encouraged to develop individual skills, following the policy set by Doulton in Lambeth. He introduced lustre decoration on earthenware, developing a wide range of colour effects, and during research in the 1880s devised the decorative techniques used in the company's Spanish ware and *chiné* ware (which was extensively produced at the Lambeth studio). He carried out research into the transfer printing of earthenware by photographic means by 1883, and patented methods of ceramic decoration using a gelatin print obtained from a photographic negative in 1889. Other experimental work by Slater centred on pastes related to parian ware, the development of ground colours such as Rose du Barry, topaz, turquoise, shaded colours and a vellum effect. He also patented an improved joint for sanitary fittings.

Slater was responsible for designing some of the stained glass produced by Doulton's from the late 1880s to the early 20th century and collaborated with several of the company's Lambeth designers especially on the Faience, Impasto and Silicon wares. With J.C.*Bailey, he persuaded Henry Doulton to allow experiments in the decoration of bone china bought from Burslem manufacturers, and eventually to include bone china in the firm's output. Slater developed the paste and glazes for Holbein and Luscian wares, and worked with W.G. *Hodkinson on the *pâte-sur-pâte* decorative technique for Lactolian ware. With Charles *Noke, who succeeded him as art director on his retirement in 1914, he carried out early work in the development of *flambé* glazes. While working for Doulton, Slater built up a collection of the company's work, which was sold in 1919 to John Shorter, its Australasian agent, and presented in 1932 to the Sydney Technological Museum.

John Slater's eldest brother, William, was one of the last apprentices at the porcelain factory in Nottingham Road, *Derby, before its closure in 1848. He moved to the Hill Pottery with his father. His work there included a lavishly painted level produced by Sir James Duke & Nephews for the laying of the foundation stone of the Wedgwood Institute, Burslem, by W.E. Gladstone in 1863. He later worked at Mintons, subsequently as art director to H.*Adams & Co. and, at the end of the 19th century, worked for R.H.& S.L.*Plant. George Slater, second son of Joseph, worked at Mintons in the 1880s; he is also thought to have carried out some *chiné* ware decoration for Doulton & Co.

Albert Slater was a flower painter at Mintons before becoming a designer and manager of the art department at Pinder, Bourne & Co. He left in 1867 to join Minton Hollins & Co. as designer, remaining for over 30 years. His elder son, Walter *Slater, worked under his uncle at Doulton's Burslem factory, and the younger, Frederick, became a modeller at the *Belleek factory.

Refs: Watkins *et al*; *see also* Doulton & Co.; Mintons Ltd.

Slater, Joseph (1812-96). English ceramic decorator, the son of William *Slater (d 1864). He continued to work at the porcelain factory in Nottingham Road, *Derby, after serving his apprenticeship there as designer, crest painter and gilder. After the factory's closure in 1848, he worked at the Hill Pottery under S.*Alcock. He then joined Mintons as a foreman in the painting and majolica departments, 1856-75, but left to work for *Brown-Westhead, Moore & Co.

His son, John *Slater (with brothers, Albert, William and George) also worked for Mintons.

Refs: Watkins *et al*; *see also* Derby.

Slater, Walter (c.1865-1938). English ceramic artist, nephew of John *Slater. Initially trained at *Mintons Ltd, Walter Slater joined *Doulton & Co. in Burslem as an apprentice, c.1885. Praised by Charles *Noke for

the delicacy and fine composition of his flower painting, he helped in the artistic development of Luscian and Lactolian wares. He also decorated pieces of Hyperion and, notably, Spanish wares. In 1905, he succeeded F.A.*Rhead as art director at the *Foley Potteries, where he introduced a new series of Intarsio earthenware (produced 1911-13), using the techniques of Rhead's earlier series, but with patterns of stylized blossoms, foliage and arabesques in a colour scheme which employed yellows, pinks and bright green, in contrast with the earlier deep colours. The shapes included some from Rhead's series, but were in general simpler and comprised vases, bowls, *jardinières*, covered jars and clock-cases. Other lines of pottery included Cloisello ware (jugs in assorted sizes and later some commemorative pieces bordered with a Grecian pattern in underglaze blue, with a white daisy in relief against a blue-patterned ground); Surrey Scenery (small vases printed with views after Birkett Foster in black on a gold ground); Flamboyant ware, with bright red high-temperature glazes, the result of Slater's own experiments.

Slater also supervised the development of fine bone porcelain. Oleander (tea ware formed of overlapping leaves and produced from 1912 in plain white bone porcelain) was one of the range of shapes devised under his direction. For other shapes, he designed patterns which were often oriental in inspiration, e.g. Ashbourne, an Imari-style floral pattern in red, blue and gold, used on traditional English shapes and in production 1913-35. He handed over gradually to his son E.*Slater and died soon after his retirement in 1938. His younger son, Kenneth, also worked for the Shelley family before emigrating to Canada.

Refs: Watkins *et al; see also* Doulton & Co.

Slater, William (c.1784-1864). English ceramic decorator, born in Normanton, Derby. After serving an apprenticeship at the *Pinxton China Factory, where he continued to work until the factory's closure, Slater worked for R.*Robins and T.M.*Randall and then, until 1848, at the porcelain factory in Nottingham Road, *Derby. He left Derby to join *Davenport's, where he remained until his death. Slater was a noted painter of fruit and insects, and a skilful gilder; his work included the painting of crests and heraldic devices.

His son, also William Slater (c.1807-65), was apprenticed at the Derby factory, where he worked as a gilder and painter before going on to Davenport's as designer and manager, 1833-65. A younger son, Joseph *Slater, also started as an apprentice at Derby.

Refs: Lockett (1972); Scarratt; *see also* Derby.

Slee's Leeds. Reproductions of the *Leeds Pottery's creamware made by J.W.*Senior and his successors at Hunslet and sold by Leeds antique dealer, W.W. Slee. The original figures, made at the Leeds Pottery from the 1790s in creamware (some painted under the glaze) but more often in pearlware, were skilfully potted. The faces of human figures were characteristically snub-nosed and had receding chins. The figures stood on deep, hollowed plinths, glazed on the inside. The

subjects include the Seasons and the Elements, Venus and Neptune, Mars, Minerva, Bacchus, Andromache, the poet Milton, Sir Isaac Newton, Prince Rupert, musicians and several groups of figures and domestic animals, including horses. In 1913, Senior's firm advertised a selection of figures including Bacchus, Air, a group of sheep, a horse, and a bust of Shakespeare. Reproductions of the Leeds Pottery's Pratt ware included jugs decorated with sporting and military reliefs, as well as portraits. The main production of creamware included elaborately pierced vases, flower holders, plates, dishes and table decorations. Some pieces were patterned with lustre. Senior's catalogue describes the firm's work as a revival of the Leeds Pottery manufacture made with moulds and patterns obtained from the old works. His creamware has a greyish tinge and is subject to crazing. Close reproductions were also made by other Leeds potters and J.T.*Morton, who had worked with Senior, but Senior's firm was the one closely associated with Slee.

Refs: Godden (1966a); Jewitt; Lawrence; P. Walton *Creamware and other English Pottery at Temple Newsam House, Leeds* (1976).

slip-glazes. Glazes with a high content of clay, sometimes, mainly composed of very fusible clay, such as that in *Albany slip.

smear glaze. A slight glaze which results from the presence of glaze materials in the kiln when firing occurs. The effect may be unintentional, but was used to provide the sheen of *parian ware.

Smith, Derek. British-born potter working in Australia. Smith studied at colleges of art in Loughborough and Leicester in England. He taught at the National Art School, Sydney, then set up and managed (1973-75) a pottery studio at the Sydney branch established by *Doulton & Co. in an attempt by the company to recreate in Australia an art studio similar to the one in Lambeth in the 19th century. Smith subsequently worked in his own Sydney studio, the Blackfriars Pottery, until 1983. His work includes domestic stoneware in shapes based on simple cylinders, spheres and cones and decorated in enamels. Smith also makes unique pieces, as well as fulfilling architectural commissions.

Mark: signature on individual pieces.

Ref: Janet Mansfield (ed) *The Potter's Art* (Cassell, Sydney, 1981).

Smith, James and Jeremiah. *See* Cadborough Pottery.

Smith, John. *See* Foley Potteries.

Smith, Sampson (1813-78). Staffordshire potter working at Longton in 1846, when he was a decorator. By 1851, he was making figures, including models of dogs. In 1859, he moved to the Sutherland works in Barker Street, Longton, where he made ornamental jugs, tea and breakfast sets, and other wares for the home and export markets, as well as a wide variety of figures. Figures identified with Smith or the factory include a Toby-jug portrait of Gladstone sitting against a tree stump holding an axe, and other Toby jugs; many topical personalities, such as Robert

Burns, Cardinal Manning, Disraeli, Napoleon, the Duke of Wellington, and legendary
characters such as Dick Turpin or The
Squire's Daughter; illustrations of events,
e.g. the siege of Sebastopol; models of cottages, churches, and other buildings, and
notably dogs. Smith was eventually among
the largest manufacturers of flatbacks and
other figures in earthenware decorated with
bright colours. His moulds continued in use
at his factory until 1912; about 60 discovered
in 1948 form the basis of attribution for
Smith's work. The firm, having become a
limited company in 1918, moved to new
premises c.1934.

The work was sometimes marked SS
(1846-60); SS LTD (from 1860); figures were
occasionally marked with Smith's name in
relief.
Refs: Jewitt; Pugh; H.A.B. Turner *A
Collector's Guide to Staffordshire Pottery
Figures* (McGibbon & Kee, London, 1971);
K. Woolliscroft *Sampy* (catalogue of an
exhibition at the Gladstone Pottery
Museum, 1976).

Smith, Thomas C. American potter, formerly
architect. Smith became manager of a pottery owned by W.*Boch and his brother, and
in 1857 invested in the firm, which traded
as the *Union Porcelain Works from 1861,
when he took over ownership. After a visit
to France, he continued the production of
bone china only briefly before beginning the
manufacture of hard paste. He employed
decorators from England and Germany for
the introduction of decorated ware.
Ref: Barber (1976).

Smith, T.T. *See* Volkmar, Charles.

Smith, William. *See* Stafford Pottery.

Smith, Willoughby. American potter, producing slip-decorated pie plates, jars, flowerpots, etc., in red earthenware from 1864 at a
pottery which had been established in 1784
at Womelsdorf, Pennsylvania.
Mark: name and *Womelsdorf* impressed
with type or metal die.
Ref: Barber (1976).

Smith, Fife & Co. American porcelain manufacturers working in Philadelphia by 1830,
when they exhibited two porcelain pitchers
in the Franklin Institute. The partners may
have been employees of W.E.*Tucker,
whose output their known work resembles.
Pitchers and dishes made of hard-paste
porcelain, moulded, decorated and gilded in
the manner of Tucker's wares (but in creamy-
tinged paste, because of the relatively high
content of bone ash, rather than the bluish
tinge of Tucker's paste) formed part of a gift
made for presentation by their backer, Jason
Fennemore, a Philadelphia merchant.
Mark: firm's name in red, under the glaze.
Refs: Barber; Clement (1947); S. Myers
Handcraft to Industry (Smithsonian
Institution Press, Washington, D.C., 1980).

Snel, E. *See* Mertens, Konrad.

Snowball, Thomas (b 1830). English potter
and ceramic decorator, born in Southwick,
Sunderland. Snowball was apprenticed as a
painter at the *Wear Pottery, becoming
head of the pottery's decorating department

in the 1840s. He established the High Southwick Pottery, a small brown ware works,
c.1850, and the Sheepfolds Warehouse, a
gilding and lustre studio, some time later.
Snowball initially bought printed ware for
embellishment at his decorating workshop,
but later bought ware in the white for printing by his brother Ralph Snowball (b 1832),
who worked with him for more than 35 years,
and was among the last Sunderland potters
to maintain the techniques of painting and
finishing mottled pink lustre. After the closure of Snowball's business in 1885, printing
plates and other equipment were bought for
use at the *Deptford Pottery.
Ref: Shaw.

Snowden, C.E. *See* Bridge End Pottery.

Sobei Kanda (d 1828). Japanese ceramics
manufacturer. A merchant in Sanda (Settsu
province, now Osaka and Hyogo prefectures), Sobei established a factory at Mino-
wamura c.1788, employing potters and
decorators from Arita and Kyoto for the
production of porcelain delicately painted in
light underglaze blue and sometimes also in
enamel. After discovering suitable rock
locally in 1801, he began producing celadon
glazes in a bright, pure green, which became
a speciality of the factory by 1806. In paste,
Sobei's celadon wares resemble Chinese
Lung Ch'uan porcelain; the style also re-
flects a Chinese influence, and perforated
decoration was used, with red-firing paste
showing at unglazed portions. Sobei's factory continued until the mid 19th century.
Refs: Burton (1921); Gorham; Hobson;
Jenyns (1967).

Sobei Kobayashi. *See* Kinkozan.

Società Ceramica. *See* Richard-Ginori,
Società Ceramica.

Société Céramique, Maastricht. *See*
Sphinx, De.

Sodeshi kiln. *See* Fujina.

soft-paste porcelain. A general term for
porcelain pastes developed in Europe from
the 16th to late 18th centuries in simulation
of oriental porcelain. The material contains
white clay mixed with a grit or flux (e.g.
bone ash or talc), and fired at earthenware
temperatures (often about 110°C). The paste
is translucent and the glazes which were
used provided an excellent base for enamel
painting.

Soil Hill Pottery. Yorkshire pottery established 1770 at Ovenden, near Halifax, for
the production of earthenware from local
red clay, which was used throughout the
pottery's operation. The output consisted of
domestic ware, including dishes, large bowls,
and cooking vessels, garden pots, and decorative pieces, e.g. knife boxes, candle holders,
puzzle jugs, cradles, thrown or slab-built
and decorated with white slip (also from
clay dug locally). The pottery was owned
from 1857 by James Robinson (d 1861), a
potter at nearby Bradshaw Lane, but still
worked by the Catherall family, descendants of the founder, until the late 1860s.
Robinson was succeeded as owner by another
Bradshaw Lane potter and afterwards by a

local farmer, who employed Jonas and Ellis
Crabtree as managers in the 1870s, before
the pottery's closure in 1877.

John Kitson (d 1892) reopened the Soil
Hill works in 1883 and continued production,
followed by his widow Hannah Kitson with
their children. Isaac Button (*see* Button
family), owner from 1897, and his successors
included in their output *sgraffito* ware and
large preserving pots; some pieces were sold
for decoration by the purchaser and then
glazed and fired at the pottery. After a temporary closure in 1965, the pottery resumed
production, making garden ware and drainage pipes.
Marks: I BUTTON SOIL HILL POTTERY
HOLMFIELD, impressed from c.1947 until
Button's retirement (1965).
Refs: Brears (1971a); Lawrence.

Solon, Albert L. Ceramist, born in England,
the son of L.-M.-E.*Solon. He trained as a
ceramic engineer and became an apprentice
in an English tile factory before going to
California. During his directorship of the
*Arequipa Pottery, 1913-16, he widened the
range of glazes, introducing high-quality
reproductions of glazes used on Persian
faience, notably a transparent turquoise
blue. In 1916, Solon went to teach at what is
now California State University, San Jose.
After 1921, he produced tiles in the firm
Solon & Schlemmel at San Jose.
Refs: Evans; Jervis.

Solon, Léon Victor (1872-1957). English
ceramic designer, painter and author, son of
L.-M.-E.*Solon. He studied at Hanley
School of Art and the South Kensington
Schools until c.1896 and was subsequently
employed by *Mintons Ltd from 1896, as art
director and chief designer 1900-09. Solon
specialized in decoration inspired by European Art Nouveau styles, often with stylized
floral patterns outlined in trailed slip, or
moulded to produce the same effect, and
filled with coloured glazes. With J.W.*Wadsworth, he designed Secessionist ware: matching water jugs and basins, *jardinières* and
pedestals, plates, etc., with bold decorative
designs from Viennese examples, produced
in large quantities from 1902 until c.1914.
Solon also used his bold, simple style, new
to the decoration of tiles, in the design of
wall panels with figures (reminiscent of the
work of Alphonse Mucha) in a variety of
techniques, including printing or hand painting, again with coloured glazes enclosed in
raised outlines. Like his brothers, A.L.*Solon
and Paul Solon, he worked in America,
becoming a designer for the *American Encaustic Tiling Co. 1912-25. As an interior
decorator, Solon undertook the colouring of
sculpture and architectural details in the
Museum of Fine Arts, Philadelphia, and the
Rockefeller Centre, New York. His work
includes hand-painted plaques in the style
developed at Mintons. He won a Gold Medal
for the Applied Arts from the American
Institute of Architects.
Refs: Lockett; *Studio Year Book* (1906).

Solon, Louis-Marc-Emmanuel, or **Miles**
(1835-1913). Porcelain modeller and decorator; ceramic historian. Solon, born in
Montauban (Tarn-et-Garonne), trained as
an illustrator in Paris and subsequently
worked at the *Sèvres factory, where he

L.-M.-E. Solon. Pierced plate with pâte-sur-pâte *decoration by Solon. Made at Mintons Ltd, c.1900. Signed* L. Solon. *24 cm in diameter.*

sometsuke. Large dish painted in pale blue with peacocks among peonies and chrysanthemums, late 19th century. 63.8 cm in diameter.

began his experiments in *pâte-sur-pâte*. He continued independent research, backed by Paris art dealer and designer, Eugène Rousseau. After moving to England in 1870, Solon started work at *Mintons Ltd; he married the daughter of J.-F.-L.*Arnoux, the firm's art director. Continuing his research, using the firm's parian porcelain paste, he decorated vases, trays, plaques, etc. in *pâte-sur-pâte*, and built up a studio where he trained decorators to carry out the preparatory tasks for completion of his original, and normally unique, designs. His pupils included A.*Birks, T.*Mellor, F.H.*Rhead, H.*Sanders. Working from careful drawings, Solon himself painted the figures and the intricate portions of each pattern, allowing each layer of slip to dry before the application of the next. His subjects included cupids, cherubs, and maidens clad in filmy drapery; sources of inspiration range from the Renaissance through 17th and 18th-century French and Italian painting and engraving, the work of Ingres and John Flaxman, to Victorian ephemera (e.g. greeting cards). He wrote accounts of his work and methods, published 1895 and 1901, descriptions of English porcelain, stoneware of the Low Countries and Germany, French faience, and a pottery bibliography (published in 1910). After his retirement from Mintons in 1904, Solon worked independently decorating plaques with *pâte-sur-pâte* or incised patterns. His son, L.V.*Solon, also worked at the Minton factory.

Marks: early work in France signed *Miles*; initials or signature.
Refs: Aslin & Atterbury; Godden (1961); G. Godden in Atterbury (1980).

Soma wares. Japanese stoneware made at several kilns in Somakori, Iwaki province (Fukushima prefecture) from the mid 17th century. The ware was hand built in a coarse grey, brown-speckled body, usually with thin translucent glaze over the device of a rearing horse from the crest of the Soma clan painted in brown, or in blue or in white slip. The design is thought to have originated from

a drawing by the painter Kano Naonobu (1607-50) at the request of Soma Yoshitsune, for whom the kilns were founded. Designs comprising several horses also occur. The ware, including cups and bowls with an indented side, was sold on the open market from the 19th century. The range of the output then extended, and pieces were produced from c.1920 with splashes of red on the speckled ground. The kilns now working were built c.1870. At Ohiri, about twenty families of potters continue the production of utilitarian ware.
Refs: Jenyns (1971); Mizuo.

sometsuke. In Japanese ceramics, blue and white porcelain. White biscuit ware was painted with cobalt blue (gosu) and covered with a transparent glaze. The technique originated in Yuan-dynasty China, with the *Ching-tê-chên kilns as the main producer. It has been used in Japan since its introduction by Korean potters in the early Imari period. A technique known as usu-ruri, in which the decorated areas are coated with carbon ink, and the other side of the vessel is dipped in a thin solution of blue pigment, is associated with Nabeshima. Sometsuke ware with added enamel decoration in yellow, green, purple, black and other colours, often with gold or silver, and known as some-nishiki, was introduced at *Arita in the 17th century and exported to Europe.
Ref: Living National Treasures.

Someya ware. Japanese domestic pottery, high-fired and glazed only with accidental effects of ash in the kiln, made at Ueda, Koshinetsu district. The peak of production is thought to have occurred in the late 18th century, but the kiln was in operation until 1933. The pieces are known for strength and simplicity in form.
Ref: Mizuo.

Sontag & Söhne Gmbh. See Tettau.

Soon. See Wells, Reginald.

Sorau. German porcelain factory, Sorau SARL, established at Sorau, Brandenburg, in 1888, producing everyday tableware. Also in Sorau, the C.& E.*Carstens porcelain

factory started in 1918 on the production of fine tableware for domestic use.
The Sorau factory marked work with an anchor and the initials PS.
Refs: Danckert; Weiss.

Soudbinine, Séraphin (1880-1944). Artist potter born in Nijni Novgorod, and working in France. Soudbinine was inspired by the work of his teacher, Rodin, and became interested in ceramics while visiting the Morgan Collection at the Metropolitan Museum in New York. After returning to France, he made stoneware and porcelain, thrown or modelled and mainly unique pieces (vases and bottles), seeking to achieve the high standards of Chinese and Japanese ceramics. He used brilliant monochrome or thick, white crackle glazes, and brown glazes contrasting matt and glassy finishes.

Marks: six-winged seraph's head; the signatures *Séraphin* or *Soudbinine*. Some pieces also marked UNIQUE.
Refs: Années 25; Baschet; Céramique française contemporaine; Lesieutre.

Soufflé ware. See Taylor, William Howson.

South Hylton Pottery; South Shields Pottery. See Fell, Isaac.

Southern Porcelain Manufacturing Co. American pottery and porcelain factory established in 1856 at Kaolin, South California, by William Farrar, a stockholder of the United States Pottery Co. (see Fenton, C.W.) with a nucleus of workmen taken with him from Bennington, and J.*Jones as manager. D.W. *Clark assisted (1857-58) with technical problems arising out of the use of local clays. The firm made various kinds of earthenware, white granite, and blue and white hard-paste porcelain by 1858. Toilet, table and other domestic wares echo the styles of the United States Pottery. In the Civil War, the factory made telegraph insulators and, until the early 1860s, earthenware water pipes. Jugs in white ware and porcelain with relief decoration were made in large numbers from c.1860. The factory closed after a fire in

Séraphin Soudbinine. Vase in porcellaneous stoneware. Marked with winged seraph's head surrounded by SERAPHIN. *19.1 cm high.*

1863 or 1864, but a new company formed in 1865 operated until the late 1870s, when the land and buildings were sold to a clay-mining firm.

Mark: *SP Company/Kaolin/SC* within a shield.

Refs: Barber (1976); Spargo; Stradling.

South Wales Pottery. Welsh pottery established by William Chambers at Llanelly (Dyfed) in 1839 for the production of white and cream-bodied earthenwares in a wide range including tea, table and toilet wares with sponged or transfer-printed decoration, some for export to North America, and, before the late 1850s, figures and portrait busts, including a bust of John Wesley after E.*Wood (1759-1840). Later, the firm acquired printing plates from the *Cambrian and *Ynysmedw potteries. Bone porcelain lithophanes were introduced in the 1850s; tinted bodies and parian ware were made experimentally and for a brief period. Hand-painted pieces were decorated e.g. by A. *Shufflebotham in the early 20th century. The last owners, Guest & Dewsbury, were in production 1877-1921.

Marks include w. CHAMBERS JUNIOR/SOUTH WALES/POTTERY impressed (1840-55 under the management of Chambers); S.W.P. under Chambers and his successors *Coombs & Holland* until 1858; *Llanelly*, stencilled.

Refs: P. Hughes *Welsh China* (catalogue, National Museum of Wales, Cardiff, 1972); D. Jenkins *Llanelly Pottery* (DEB Books, Swansea, 1968); Jewitt.

Southwick Pottery. *See* Scott Brothers.

Sowter, Robert, & Co. *See* Mexborough.

Sozan. *See* Suwa Yoshitake.

Sozen II. Japanese potter, Gen Asao, working in Kyoto. In 1944, Sozen accepted a government appointment to preserve the production of unka ware, earthenware formed by coiling and polished smooth with a pebble before very low firing at 600-900°C. The characteristic surface pattern of cloud (un) and flower (ka) results from carbon impregnation at points of contact between the closely stacked pots during firing in a smoky reducing atmosphere; it may also be achieved by rubbing the pots after firing with vegetable oils, while the clay is still sufficiently hot to burn the oil which it absorbs. Sozen uses a variety of clays, including white or yellow, which contrast with the dark patterns on simple, elegant shapes.

Ref: Sanders.

Spano-Lustra. *See* Foley Potteries; Rhead, Frederick Alfred.

Sparkes, John. *See* Doulton & Co.

Sparks, Joseph. *See* Ridgway Potteries Ltd.

Spaulding, Jessie R. *See* Lonhuda Pottery.

Spechtsbrunn. German porcelain factory established at Spechtsbrunn, Thuringia, in 1911 for the production of everyday tableware and decorative pieces.

Mark: *Spechtsbrunn*, below a crown and R.

Refs: Danckert; Weiss.

Speck, Paul. *See* Karlsruhe.

Speeler, Henry. German-born potter working in America. Speeler was employed at the *Harker Pottery in East Liverpool, Ohio, and was then a dealer in ceramics. He was a partner in the firm, *Taylor & Speeler in 1850s, and in 1860 built a factory later known as the *International Pottery in Trenton, New Jersey, for the production of white ware. He traded there from 1868 as Henry Speeler & Sons. The firm exhibited yellow and Rockingham-glazed ware in the Centennial Exhibition at Philadelphia in 1876, and was later bought by Edward Clark and J.*Carr.

Ref: Barber (1976).

Speight, George (b c.1809). Ceramic decorator, born in Yorkshire and employed from 1826 at the *Swinton Pottery, where his work included signed plaques showing three bereaved children in a scene entitled 'The Mother's Grave' (which he was later to repeat on a plate with lavish gilding, when working as an independent decorator); a Madonna and Child; a view of Derwent Water. He also signed the decoration of a tray depicting 'Earl Strafford occupied in dictating his defence to his secretary' after Van Dyck. Although he was best known for the painting of figures, Speight also painted flowers and studies of shells. He is thought to have painted landscapes with figures, and heraldic devices on the dessert service made at Swinton for King William IV. Speight left Swinton for Shelton in Staffordshire between 1839 and 1841, and subsequently carried out decoration for the firm of Ridgways. He is thought to have worked independently while regularly employed earlier at the Rockingham works, and returned by 1857 to Swinton, where he was still working as a decorator in 1865.

Mark: signature.

Refs: Godden (1972); Jewitt; Rice; D.G. Rice *Illustrated Guide to Rockingham Pottery & Porcelain* (Barrie & Jenkins, London, 1971).

Spencer, Edward. *See* Upchurch Pottery.

Sphinx, De. Dutch pottery established as a glassworks at Maastricht by P.*Regout in 1834 and making painted wares from 1836. The firm's output of soft earthenware soon changed to creamware, much of it transfer-printed. Regout also produced blue, yellow and black wares and some pieces with painted decoration. His firm underwent considerable expansion. He organized the Aarde-werkfabrieken van Petrus Regout with his four sons in 1870, and the sphinx mark was adopted in 1879. In 1896 the firm took over a pottery established five years earlier in Maastricht by Frederik Regout (1858-1937). It became NV de Sphinx v/h Petrus Regout & Co in 1899 and opened a wall-tile factory in Limmel, 1902. The main output consisted of services, domestic ware and decorative pieces. The factory produced a coronation plate designed by E.*Lion-Cachet in 1898. Other work included a set of pieces with austere shapes simply decorated in green and yellow with geometrical motifs designed by C.J.*van der Hoef (1902), and commissioned by the group of decorative artists

De Woning, established under J.*Eisenloeffel. The painter Edmond Bellefroid took charge of a design department established in the late 1920s, producing tea wares etc., in modern style. In 1958, the business merged with the Société Céramique (manufacturers of domestic and ornamental ware established at Maastricht in 1859 by Guillaume Lambert & Cie) and became Sphinx-Céramique.

Marks include a sphinx with *Petrus Regout & Co* or N.V. DE SPHINX and the place name, MAASTRICHT; the name SPHINX, ROYAL SPHINX/MAASTRICHT, surmounted by a crown. A face, with the initials G and O forming the eyes and an A nose, over the pottery's name, is probably a dealer's mark.

Refs: Singelenberg-van der Meer; *Sphinx-Céramique 100* (commemorative catalogue, Maastricht, 1959); van Straaten.

Spiegel, Isaac. American potter. Spiegel worked for J.*Hemphill at the American China Manufactory before establishing his own pottery c.1837 in Kensington, Philadelphia, for the manufacture of earthenware, taking over some moulds and equipment on the closure of Hemphill's factory. As well as domestic ware, he made some ornamental items, e.g. miniature barrels, openwork card trays and Rockingham-glazed figures. He retired in 1855, succeeded by his son, Isaac, who made firebrick and tiles in the late 1850s and afterwards included in his output such decorative ware as Rockingham-glazed figures of lions and dogs until 1879. A second son, John Spiegel, took over the business in 1880, subsequently making decorated biscuit ware with floral designs moulded and applied, as well as supplying vases and plaques for painting by amateur decorators. He eventually abandoned ceramics and turned to the processing of chemicals for pharmaceutical purposes.

Ref: Barber (1976).

Spinner, David (1758-1811). Pennsylvania potter, working at Milford in Bucks County, the son of a farmer who had arrived in Bucks County from Zurich in 1739. Spinner signed pieces of slipware dated between 1801 and 1811 which include a number of pie plates decorated with spirited *sgraffito* designs of figures standing or on horseback (notably in hunting scenes), soldiers, and musicians. Painted slip decoration was used less successfully and mainly depicted large flowers. Spinner also made domestic ware. The pottery closed at his death.

Ref: Barber (1970).

Spode, Josiah (1755-1827). Staffordshire manufacturer of earthenware and porcelain, son and successor of Josiah Spode (1733-97). After establishing a London warehouse for his father's firm, Spode became his father's partner and inherited his factory at Stoke-on-Trent in 1797, leaving the London branch in the hands of his eldest son William Spode and partner William Copeland. Spode continued the manufacture of well-finished tableware transfer-printed in blue with a wide range of patterns including Italian views from c.1800 (many after Merigot's *Views of Rome and its Vicinity,* published 1796-98); an Indian sporting series from c.1810 (adapted from Williamson's *Oriental Field Sports* and *Wild Sports of the East,* published from 1805); the Caramanian series of Near Eastern views by 1809; various designs of oriental inspiration (e.g. Willow, India, Two Birds, Hundred Antiques); architectural patterns, and a variety of other subjects, e.g. Milkmaid, Woodmen, Waterloo. Some patterns were printed in outline for colouring by hand.

Spode introduced porcelain, probably not before 1815, and is credited with developing the formula which became standard for English bone china, replacing a proportion of the china clay used in the firm's porcelain paste with bone ash. The bone china body was used for a variety of tableware, vases, comports, match holders, etc. The firm made porcelain containing natural feldspar from 1821. Painting was carried out by H.*Daniel, who ran a decorating department at the factory until c.1820.

Decorations included *famille rose* and japan patterns, coats of arms, and designs containing birds and flowers, notably a peacock pattern (from a Ch'ien Lung design) produced c.1813-1960s; the Cabbage pattern (with small flowers and a large pinnate leaf), also introduced c.1813, is still in production. The firm also made brown or green-glazed earthenware (e.g. Cadogan teapots, plates) and cream tableware decorated with botanical patterns, views, illustrations of Aesop's fables, etc., as well as at least twelve versions of a pattern entitled Tumbledown Dick. The firm also made tea ware, candlesticks, decorative pieces in stone china, black basalt and other fine stonewares.

Spode was succeeded by his son, also Josiah Spode (d 1829), and in 1833 W.T. *Copeland bought the factory, stock and equipment, together with the Spode family's share in the London warehouse. The firm then traded under Copeland's name, reverting to the title Spode (as Spode Ltd) in 1970.

Marks incorporate *Spode* until 1833; *Copeland* after 1833. Later marks may give both names, or *Spode* from 1970.
Refs: R. Copeland *Spode's Willow Pattern* (Studio Vista/Christies, London, 1980); D. Drakard & P. Holdway *Spode Printed Ware* (Longman, London & New York, 1983); A. Hayden *Spode & his Successors* (Cassell, London, 1925); S.B. Williams *Antique Blue & White Spode* (B.T. Batsford, London, 1943).

sponged ware. Inexpensive domestic earthenware brightly decorated in one or more shades of blue, pink, green, brown, purple and yellow applied with a firm sponge over the glaze (or occasionally in underglaze blue) in patterns of blotches, whirls, or bands, and used alone or with hand painting, often flowers, fruit, birds, cottages, or, rarely, transfer printing. Sometimes the sponge was cut into a simple geometrical shape, e.g. a star. Sponged patterns were normally used on white granite or earthenware, mainly for export to North America in the mid 19th century. Makers include many English and Scottish potters, who seldom marked this class of ware. Identified makers include the *Fife Pottery, the *Links Pottery and *Bo'ness in Scotland, the Adams family (in Tunstall and Greenfield), the Llanelly Pottery. Pieces made and marketed in America as Spatter ware have splashier decoration applied with a soft, coarse sponge. (*See also* Portneuf ware.)

Refs: Bell; Collard; G. Cruickshank *Scottish Spongeware*, (privately published, Edinburgh, 1982); C. Roberts & B. Lyon *Bo'ness Potteries: an Illustrated History* (catalogue, Falkirk Museums, 1977).

Springer & Co. *See* Elbogen; Pössneck.

Spuler, Erwin (1906-64). German sculptor, modeller and painter, born in Augsburg. Spuler trained in art and modelling in Stuttgart, 1923-24, and Karlsruhe from 1926. He worked from 1931 as an independent artist at the Staatliche Majolika Manufaktur *Karlsruhe later also teaching in the local technical high school. His early work included decorative plaques on which the image (often a portrait of a woman in a dreamy, reflective pose) was carved in relief, coated in white slip and then painted in high-temperature colours under a frit glaze of variable thickness which softened the effect of the colours. Spuler also made small clay figures and, in the 1950s, vases with painted decoration of facial features, oval dishes, etc.

Painted mark: *ESp.*
Refs: Bock; N. Moufang and A. Totti *Erwin Spuler – Ceramiche e disegni* (Galleria d'arte Totti, Milan, 1954).

Stabler, Harold (1872-1945). English designer and craftsman. Stabler studied at art school in Kendal, Cumbria, at first as a cabinet-maker and then in metalwork, which he taught at Keswick School of Industrial Art (c.1898-99), and subsequently at the Liverpool University Art School's department of metalwork. In London, he was a teacher at the Sir John Cass Technical Institute from c.1906 and headed the Institute's Art School 1907-37; he was also an instructor at the Royal College of Art 1912-26, and served on the first council of the Design & Industries Association in 1915. Stabler installed a kiln at his Hammersmith studio and, with his wife, P.*Stabler, designed and made ceramic figures and groups (e.g. a bull ridden by two children and garlanded with flowers, dated 1914 and later produced in stoneware by *Carter, Stabler & Adams), decorative features for architectural and garden use (e.g. a Harpy Eagle, his own design), enamels

Josiah Spode. Feeding bottle printed in underglaze blue, c.1810.

Harold Stabler. Two children, decked with flowers, riding a bull, c.1910. Impressed marks include Harold Stabler Hammersmith London. *33 cm high.*

and jewellery. He was a partner in Carter, Stabler & Adams from its inception in 1921 and acted as the firm's artistic consultant. He designed coffee ware and ranges of tiles depicting waterbirds (relief designs of buildings or heraldic devices, etc.) and introduced designs by students of the Royal College of Art (e.g. hunting and sporting designs in the 1920s by artist Edward Bawden). His Fighting Cock in stoneware with blue and brown glaze, shown in the Royal Academy's Arts and Crafts Exhibition 1924, was among the first reproduced on the introduction of slip-casting at the pottery in 1930. He had ceased active participation in the firm for some years before the inclusion of some of his designs in a tile exhibition jointly arranged by the Victoria & Albert Museum and the Council for Art & Industry in 1938.

Marks include HAMMERSMITH, painted with the title of the figure or group; STABLER HAMMERSMITH LONDON, impressed with a date; at Carter, Stabler & Adams, HAROLD STABLER in a rectangle, moulded.
Refs: Anscombe & Gere; Coysh (1976); Hawkins; F. MacCarthy *A History of British Design* (Allen & Unwin, London, 1979).

Stabler, Phoebe (d 1955). English sculptress, modeller and designer. Working with her husband H.*Stabler at their studio in Hammersmith, London, Phoebe Stabler

made ceramic figures, including a salt-glazed figure of a seated boy. She designed figures of Picardy Peasants (1911) which were produced from 1913 by *Doulton & Co. and marketed in competition with figures cast by *Carter, Stabler & Adams under the same title. Her Madonna of the Square (1913), produced by Doulton, closely resembles a figure made in large quantities at the Poole Pottery throughout the 1920s and entitled The Lavender Woman. Other figures were produced by both firms, the *Ashtead Potters Ltd, and, in the 1930s, at *Worcester. As well as the numerous figures which were taken into regular production at Poole, *Carter & Co. made large pieces of architectural ware designed by the Stablers, e.g. war memorials for Rugby School (1922), featuring a group of St George and the dragon (of which a cast version made by Carter, Stabler & Adams was shown in the British Institute of Industrial Art Exhibition of contemporary work at the Victoria & Albert Museum in London, 1922, the International Exhibition in Paris, 1925, and the British Empire Exhibition in London, 1924) and for the city of Durban (c.1925).

Phoebe Stabler's sister, textile designer Minnie McLeish (1876-1957), provided for Carter, Stabler & Adams designs including sailing boats on tiles (early 1920s) and a robin sheltering under flowers, Robin in the Rain (late 1920s).
Mark: PHOEBE STABLER, impressed.
Refs: Callen; R. Haggar *Recent Ceramic Sculpture in Great Britain* (Tiranti, London, 1946); Hawkins.

Staddon, Enoch. *See* Torquay Terra-Cotta Co.

Stadler, Heinrich. *See* Mosbach.

Stadtlengsfeld. German porcelain factory established at Stadtlengsfeld, Thuringia, in 1889. The factory made everyday tableware, tea and coffee sets. The firm now operates as VVB-Keramik, with a branch at Stadtlengsfeld-Rhön.

A variety of marks include FELDA CHINA/GERMANY; FELDA/RHON, with an aeroplane; an aeroplane with STADTLENGSFELD.
Refs: Danckert; Weiss.

Staehr-Nielsen, Eva (b 1911). Danish ceramic artist, associated with N.*Krebs at the Saxbo pottery. She designed stoneware vases and jars with coloured glazes and, sometimes, decoration carved in relief.
Refs: Hettes & Rada; Préaud & Gauthier.

Staffel, Rudolph (b 1911). American studio potter. Staffel was born in San Antonio, Texas, and studied in New York and, from 1931, at the Art Institute of Chicago. He taught ceramics at the Arts & Craft Club on New Orleans from 1937, also working part-time with P.E.*Cox, and then taught at the Tyler School of Art, Philadelphia, from 1940 until his retirement in 1976. In the 1950s, he was invited to produce a set of dinner ware in porcelain. Inspired by the translucency of the material, he began to develop forms with which he could exploit the play of light, enjoying the exacting nature of work with porcelain and its risk of high losses. Staffel builds and throws forms, incising the porcelain or building it up with

small pieces of clay to vary the thickness, and makes pieces with small strips of paste.
Refs: Clark & Hughto; M. Cochran *Contemporary Clay: Ten Approaches* (Dartmouth College Hanover, New Hampshire, 1976); *International Ceramics 72* (Victoria & Albert Museum, London, 1972); L. Nordness *Objects: USA* (Viking, New York, 1970); P.& R. Winokur 'The Light of Rudolph Staffel' in *Craft Horizons* 37 (April 1977).

Stafford Pottery. Pottery operating at Stockton-on-Tees, Durham, in the 19th century. A local builder, William Smith, established the Stafford Pottery at Thornaby, South Stockton c.1825 for the production of earthenware, initially brown household ware made from local red-brown clay. He took into partnership the Staffordshire potter, John Whalley, in 1826, with George Skinner (d 1870) and his brother William Skinner in 1829; the firm traded as William Smith & Co. until 1855. The output consisted of domestic white earthenware, transfer-printed creamware and pearlware, and the early brown earthenware. Wares were marketed in Germany and the Low Countries. Printed patterns for tableware included a series of Roman views; a castle set in parkland with equestrian figures; fruit and flowers. Other decorative techniques included designs painted over or under the glaze of cream earthenware, trailed or feathered slip, mocha patterns; some printing was carried out in purple lustre. In 1848, the then partners were prevented from marking their wares with the name WEDGWOOD or WEDGEWOOD, which they had used e.g. on nursery plates and other copies of work by J.*Wedgwood & Sons Ltd.

George Skinner took control of the pottery, trading as George Skinner & Co. in partnership with Whalley 1855-70, and subsequently as Skinner & Walker, with his manager Ambrose Walker until 1880. The firm operated as Ambrose Walker & Co.

*Eva Staehr-Nielsen. Stoneware jar made by Staehr-Nielsen and glazed by N.*Krebs at the Saxbo Pottery, 1954. 35.5 cm high.*

until 1893, and closed soon after becoming the Thornaby Pottery Co. in 1905.

Marks: the firm's initials, W.S. & Co., S.& W., etc., sometimes with STAFFORD POTTERY; also W.S. & Co's/WEDGEWOOD or WEDGEWOOD; W.S. & Co./ QUEEN'S WARE/STOCKTON; S.& W./QUEEN'S WARE/STOCKTON.
Refs: Grabham; Jewitt; Hurst; Lawrence; Towner (1957); Williams-Wood.

Staffordshire dogs. Chimney ornaments, usually made in pairs, produced in large numbers in the 19th century in Staffordshire and elsewhere in England. Examples made before the 1850s often have a rock or grassy base. The dogs portrayed include Maltese or King Charles Spaniels seated, often without a stand (comforter dogs), some with a painted gold chain hanging from the collar, or carrying a basket or barrel. The incised decoration representing the dog's coat seen in early press-moulded examples was replaced in the late 19th century by painted details—black noses and eyebrows, and small gilt stars, arrowheads, etc., over the body. Poodles (increasingly produced after c.1850), greyhounds, gundogs, hounds and dalmatians were also made in earthenware or bone porcelain, often enamelled and gilded. 20th-century models were slip cast and sometimes fitted with glass eyes. The makers include S.*Smith and *Kent & Parr.
Ref: H.A.B. Turner *A Collector's Guide to Staffordshire Pottery Figures* (McGibbon & Kee, London, 1971).

Staffordshire portrait figures. White earthenware commemorative figures produced from c.1840 in great quantities. Many came from small factories and pieces were usually unmarked. The figures depicted historical and literary subjects as well as commemorating contemporary personalities and events. Many figures portrayed members of the Royal family; also statesmen, authors, theatrical personalities and the characters they acted, religious leaders, sportsmen, prize fighters and criminals. Models of buildings commemorate events that took place there, or notable inhabitants.

Though associated with Staffordshire potteries, the figures were also made in Scotland, where the makers depicted fishwives and other local subjects. The characteristic colouring combines underglaze pigments, deep blue or black, with enamel colours and often gilding. While very popular in England, the figures were also exported, e.g. to Canada.
Ref: Pugh.

Stahl, Albert, & Co. *See* Volkstedt-Rudolstadt.

Stalhane, Karl-Harry (b 1920). Swedish ceramist. He specialized in stoneware, inspired by Sung Chinese wares, and his designs for the Rörstrand factory include tall, slender vases which rely for decorative effect on the relationship between shape and rich glazes. In the course of experiments with clays of the Lidköping district, he developed brownish black, greenish grey and some bright shades of red in glazes. As well as individual stoneware pieces, he designed utilitarian porcelain for use in hotels, etc. He taught at the school of applied arts in Gothenburg.
Refs: Beard; Lagercrantz; Préaud & Gauthier; *Three Centuries of Swedish*

Pottery (catalogue, Victoria & Albert Museum, London, 1959).

Stangl, J. Martin (d 1972). American potter. As technical superintendent of the *Fulper Pottery from 1911, Stangl introduced new, high-quality glazes in an extensive range. He left the Fulper Pottery briefly between 1915 and 1920 to develop a range of industrial art pottery which was introduced c.1917 by *Haeger Potteries. Stangl bought the Fulper firm in 1930 and continued limited production of art ware until 1935, afterwards concentrating on the manufacture of dinner services, and making figures after 1940. Industrial art ware and gift ware were also made under Stangl's name from the mid 1940s (the name of the firm was formally changed to Stangl Pottery Co. in 1955). The company went out of business in the mid 1970s.
Refs: Evans; Kovel & Kovel; *Stangl: A Portrait of Progress in Pottery* (privately published by Stangl Pottery Co., New Jersey, 1965).

Stanley, Jack (1905-72). Porcelain decorator working for the *Worcester Royal Porcelain Co., 1919-33. Stanley studied flower painting under E.*Phillips and figure subjects and still-life painting under W. Hawley. He trained as a modeller under F.M.*Gertner. Stanley's painting included portraits after Meissonnier and Frans Hals; he also designed printed patterns for hand tinting, and afterwards painted early models (dogs) by D. *Lindner.
Ref: Sandon (1978a).

Stanley Works, Longton. See Plant, R.H.& S.L., Ltd.

Star China Co. See Paragon China Ltd.

Star Encaustic Tile Co. American tile manufacturers founded in 1882 as successors to the Pittsburgh Encaustic Tile Co. which had been established in 1876. Under the English potter Samuel Keys, manager of both firms, who had been experimenting in the production of encaustic tiles from 1867, Star Encaustic made unglazed tiles for floors and fireplaces in a variety of shapes and colours. The firm was still operating in 1914.
Mark: initials S.E.T.Co. impressed.
Refs: Barber (1976); Barnard; Kovel & Kovel.

Statham, W.N. (1863-1940). English porcelain painter; chief landscape artist at the factory in Osmaston Road, *Derby, in the late 19th century. Statham's landscapes often feature streams edged by trees. After leaving the Derby factory, he ran a photography business and sold porcelain in his home town, Matlock. Statham wrote a history of Matlock church, and worked for a time as a teacher.
Refs: see Derby.

Steel, Thomas (1771-1850). English porcelain decorator noted for his fresh, naturalistic treatment in painting fruit, but also a skilful painter of flowers and insects. After training in his home county, Staffordshire, Steel joined the porcelain factory in Nottingham Road, *Derby, in 1815. His work included studies of fruit arranged on slabs of marble, characterized by the soft, plump look of

*Thomas Steel. Plaque painted by Steel for *Mintons Ltd, c.1840.*

individual fruits with reflected colours, the paints blended with a finger while still wet. Flowers, notably roses, are painted with highlights in sharp contrast with the dark ground colours. Steel painted many dessert services with lavish gilt borders; he also painted and signed many plaques. He worked at the *Swinton Pottery after 1826 and by 1830 with his son E.*Steele. Pieces identified as his work include a signed plaque, dated 1830, a tray with an arrangement of white grapes (a subject at which Steel excelled), and a table top painted with fruit at the corner. At the *Minton factory, where he was working in 1831, he painted a large vase with flowers on green ground. Steel subsequently worked at *Davenport's. He died in Stoke-on-Trent.

His sons, Edwin, Horatio and Thomas Steele, were all apprentices at the Derby factory. Horatio remained there until the factory's closure in 1848; his work included panels of flowers, birds and insects painted on a service made in the early 1840s for Queen Victoria. Thomas Steele was a landscape painter who went from Derby to *Coalport (c.1835-45), where he died at an early age.
Mark: the father signed his work *Thomas Steel.*
Refs: Aslin & Atterbury; Bemrose; Eaglestone & Lockett; S.W. Fisher *The Decoration of English Porcelain* (Derek Verschoyle, London, 1954); Jewitt; Rice; *see also* Derby.

Steele, Edwin (1804-71). English porcelain painter, son of T.*Steel. Edwin Steele was apprenticed at the factory in Nottingham Road, *Derby, and worked with his father from the late 1820s at the *Swinton Pottery. He was among the painters who developed a more formal style of flower painting than the earlier naturalistic manner associated with W.*Billingsley and his followers. He painted flowers on plates with borders of moulded primrose leaves, and baskets of fruit on vases dating from 1830 or before.

His work also included flowers painted on a copy of the Swinton Pottery's Rhinoceros vase. He later worked in Staffordshire and, probably, Bristol.
Some work signed.
Refs: Rice; *see also* Derby.

Stepanov, Dmitry. Russian earthenware decorator. After studying at the academy of fine arts in St Petersburg, he worked as an engraver of designs for transfer printing 1817-53 at the *Kiev-Mezhegorye factory, where he also taught drawing and engraving from 1844. His work, which included a view of a house at Obukhovka belonging to V.V. Kapnist, the writer of a poem that was incorporated in the design, and scenes of Kiev, Mezhegorye, Gatchina, etc., showed a special talent for integrating printed decoration with form.
His signature appeared on many of the factory's printed designs.
Ref: Bubnova.

Stephan, Peter (b c.1796). Porcelain modeller, born in Stoke-on-Trent, Staffordshire, and employed at the *Coalport factory on the modelling of relief-decorated services, centrepieces, vases, inkstands, etc., from c.1830 to the early 1860s. He was working in Derby in 1870. His wife, Susanna, born at Madeley, Shropshire, c.1871, was also a modeller; she made flowers for the decoration of baskets, brooches, etc., and marked her work SS/DERBY incised. She was still working in the early 1860s.
Refs: Bradley; Godden (1970); Haslem.

Stephen, James P. *See* Greenwood Pottery Co.

Stephen, Walter Benjamin (1876-1961). American potter. While working as a stonemason in Tennessee, Benjamin discovered a source of clay with which he and his mother began to experiment, making small figures and boxes. They set up a small workshop, operating as Nonconnah Pottery, and made pottery decorated with early American scenes, e.g. wagon trains, buffalo hunting, applied in light clay.

After the death of his parents in 1910, Walter Stephen moved (by 1913) to a site near Mount Pisgah, North Carolina, and entered into a brief partnership (lasting until 1916) to build a kiln and a shop. Having resumed experiments in 1920, Benjamin opened the Pisgah Forest Pottery in 1926; he produced vases, candlesticks, teasets, jugs and other domestic ware in a vitrified body with a range of glazes that included turquoise, maroon, pink, green, yellow, ivory and brown. Crystalline glazes in ivory, silver, etc., were also used. Work continued after Stephen's death.
Marks: name, *Stephen* or *W.B. Stephen*; after 1921, *Pisgah Forest*, sometimes with a potter at his wheel in relief.
Ref: Kovel & Kovel.

Stepney Bank Pottery, Stepney Pottery or **New Pottery.** English earthenware works established in the late 18th century at Ouseburn, Newcastle-upon-Tyne. Head & Dalton, proprietors of the works (then called the New Pottery) in 1801, were succeeded by John Dalton & Son, who named the works Stepney Bank Pottery. Successive owners,

Dryden, Cookson & Basket, 1816; Davies, Cookson & Wilson, 1822; Dalton, Burn & Co. or Dalton & Burn, 1833-44; Thomas Bell & Co. in the late 1840s; G.R.Turnbull made printed wares until the 1870s, when the pottery was taken over by John Wood & Co., who advertised white and coloured and all types of brown earthenware, and later printed earthenware (which had a wide range of delicately printed patterns on classical or oriental themes), as well as gas reflectors and lamp tops. The pottery was in operation until 1912.

Marks: TURNBULL/STEPNEY, impressed; J. WOOD/NEWCASTLE, impressed, sometimes used with one of several oval printed marks incorporating *J.Wood/Stepney Pottery/ Newcastle-upon-Tyne*, and the pattern name, e.g. *Albion*.
Refs: see Newcastle-upon-Tyne.

Sterken, Roelof (1877-1943). Dutch decorative artist. Sterken painted ceramics made at the *Rozenburg factory (1894-1904), *Haga (until 1907), De *Kroon (1908), *Amphora (Oegstgeest, 1909), *St Lukas (until 1913), and the *Ram pottery (from 1923).

Mark: initials, R.S.
Refs: Scheen; Singelenberg-van der Meer; van Straaten.

Sterling China Co. American manufacturers established by Frank and Frederick Sebring in 1900 at the new town of Sebring, Ohio, for the production of porcelain. The firm

*James Stiff & Sons. Stoneware vase in the style of H.*Barlow, c.1880. 23.5 cm high.*

produced dinner ware, tea sets and small services for desserts in porcelain, but was soon trading as the Limoges China Co. and discontinued porcelain manufacture in favour of semi-porcelain.

V.*Schreckengost reorganized production and restyled the factory's output of dinner ware, producing designs for Old Virginia Fashion ware, made 1942. The firm's name was changed to the American Limoges China Co. in 1949. The factory ceased operation before its sale in 1955.

Marks incorporate *Sterling China* until c.1902, and later with the name of a line, LIMOGES or SEBRING; *American Limoges, Sebring, Ohio.*

Another firm trading as the Sterling China Co. has been in operation from 1917 at Wellsville, Ohio, marking work with its office address, East Liverpool. The output includes kitchen and tablewares in semi-porcelain.
Refs: W.C. Gates Jr & D.E. Ormerod 'The East Liverpool Pottery' in *Historical Archaeology* Vol 16, 1-2 (Society for Historical Archaeology, 1982); Lehner.

Steubenville Pottery Co. American firm in operation c.1880-c.1960 at Steubenville, Ohio. The company produced white granite, including decorated tableware and toilet sets, and introduced an opaque, semi-vitreous body, cream-coloured and very light in weight, named Canton China, which was used in making vases, *jardinières*, and toilet sets or sold plain for painting by amateurs.

A variety of marks often incorporate *Steubenville* or give the name of line, or pattern.
Refs: Barber (1976); Lehner.

Stevens, Alfred (1817-75). English painter, sculptor and designer. Stevens studied in Italy 1833-42 and then worked as a teacher at the Government School of Design in Somerset House, London, 1845-47, and chief designer to the iron founders Hoole & Co. in Sheffield, 1850-57. He designed earthenware, including tin-glazed ware produced by the *Minton factory, where he was employed as a designer c.1859-c.1861.

Ornamental pieces inspired by Italian Renaissance styles in both shape and decoration were shown in the International Exhibition in 1862 and continued in production until 1864.
Refs: Aslin & Atterbury; S. Beattie *Alfred Stevens* (Victoria & Albert Museum, London, 1975); Wakefield.

Stevenson, Sharp & Co. *See* Derby.

Stiff, James, & Sons. London manufacturers, noted for the production of stoneware and architectural terracotta. In 1840, James Stiff took control of a Lambeth pottery established in the mid 18th century, probably for the production of delftware. The works became known as the London Pottery and expanded greatly by the late 19th century. The output consisted mainly of utilitarian stoneware: household jugs, preserving jars, bottles, barrels and kitchen ware. Electrical, chemical and drainage ware, water filters and containers were produced in brown saltglaze. Some water filters were elaborately decorated with figures or heraldic motifs, sometimes with Gothic elements in style,

*James Stinton. Porcelain vases made at the *Worcester factory and painted by Stinton with pheasants, 1910. 20 cm high.*

but the pottery also produced simpler versions, capable of purifying water in large quantities. Cream-bodied stoneware dipped in yellow glaze (from c.1850) largely replaced salt-glazed ware for use in jugs, jars, etc. by c.1875. Decorative stoneware jugs, vases etc., included copies of pieces made at the nearby *Doulton & Co., marked with a D.

The firm's terracotta, buff or red in colour and fired at a temperature high enough to result in a very durable product, was relatively low in price and included statuary, garden ornaments and vases, as well as architectural decoration, chimneypots, etc. The firm also used a highly porous body in the production of cells, plates, porous pots, etc.

The pottery, situated beside the Thames, which facilitated the transport of supplies and allowed an extensive export trade, employed about 200 workers; it was taken over by Doulton & Co. in 1913.

Marks include J. STIFF & SONS, impressed.
Refs: Blacker (1922b); Jewitt.

Stijl, De. Association of painters, designers and sculptors active 1917-31 in Holland. The artist and writer Theo van Doesburg published a magazine *De Stijl* in which the group expressed aims in design which included a greater abstraction and a rejection of decoration, accompanied by the use of primary colours and geometrical forms; machine-production was encouraged. The group's ideals, with those of the *Deutscher Werkbund, also formed part of the *Bauhaus teaching.
Refs: A.H. Barr Jr *De Stijl* (catalogue, Museum of Modern Art, New York, 1953); H.L.C. Jaffé *De Stijl: 1917-1931* (Amsterdam, 1956).

Stinton family. English porcelain painters working in *Worcester. John Stinton (1829-95) specialized in landscapes containing small groups of figures, and worked for Grainger & Co., c.1846-95. Of his five sons, three were painters at Worcester.

John Stinton Jr (1854-1956) started work

at the Grainger factory in 1889 and moved to the Royal Porcelain factory where he worked until his retirement in 1938. He painted a variety of cattle subjects, including Highland cattle in landscapes from 1903, and views of castles, e.g. Chepstow, Ludlow and Kenilworth, for the central decoration of plates. He was also an artist in water-colours.

Walter Stinton (d 1950) was a painter of landscapes for Grainger's and E.*Locke before joining an engineering firm at Droitwich.

James Stinton (1870-1961) painted game, especially pheasant and grouse, for Grainger & Co. and then the Royal Porcelain Co. until his retirement in 1951. His work is found on coffee services, at the centres of plates and on vases, etc.

Arthur Stinton (1878-1970), the eldest son of John Stinton Jr, worked for Grainger & Co. after 1889, and then as a decorator of glass. His sister, Kate (1880-1955), and brother, Harry Stinton (1883-1968), were also painters. Harry Stinton studied at the National Art Schools in South Kensington, London, and trained under his father at the Royal Porcelain factory from 1896. He followed his father's style in painting scenes with cattle, but in a palette which contained more purple. He also carried out water-colours of cattle, gamebirds, sheep and land-scapes in the early 20th century. He retired from the factory in 1963.

Charles Stinton was working for Flight, Barr & Barr by 1819 and continued until the firm closed. He specialized in painting birds and flowers.
Refs: Chaffers; Sandon (1978a, 1978b).

Stockton Art Pottery. Californian pottery, established as the Stockton Terra-Cotta Co. in 1890 for the production of piping for drains, stoves, etc., and firebrick. Decorative ware in semi-porcelain, introduced in 1894 under the supervision of Scottish potters Thomas S. Blakey (d 1897) and his son John, included teasets with ivy patterns moulded in relief, and vases, etc., with glossy glazes and gilded decoration. The company failed in 1895 and resumed production in the following year as the Stockton Art Pottery, next door to the previous works. Rekston, a line of art ware painted in slip against a shaded brown ground (which had been introduced in 1895 as Reckston by the original firm) was the main output, but other ornamental pieces were made from 1897 in brown, ochreous yellow, green and blue, used singly or in mottled effects. Yellow-firing clay from California, generally moulded, was used to make the *jardinières*, pedestals, umbrella stands, vases, pitchers and bowls included in the lines. Further financial difficulties caused the firm's closure in 1900. The succeeding Stockton Brick & Pottery Co., formed in 1901, made sewer pipes as well as brick, but failed to resume production of art ware.

Marks: circular device containing initials SAPC within STOCKTON CALIFORNIA impressed sometimes with REKSTON; MARIPOSA POTTERY/STOCKTON/CALIFORNIA also occurs, painted in slip under the glaze.
Refs: Barber (1976); Evans; Kovel & Kovel.

Stofflet, Heinrich. Pennsylvania potter making slip-decorated earthenware in Berks County in the early 19th century. A pie dish,

signed and dated 1814, is decorated with a *sgraffito* design of a vase and flowers.
Ref: Barber (1970).

Stoltenberg-Lerche, Hans (1867-1920). Norwegian artist and designer of bronze, jewellery, enamels and glass, as well as ceramics, born in Düsseldorf of German and Norwegian parents. He trained as a painter and worked for two years in a German ceramics factory. After travelling in Italy, he studied (1886-88) in Paris under the painter Eugène Carrière and exhibited in Paris, 1895-1912. On a visit to Italy in 1900, he began work as a sculptor in bronze. His ceramics were shown in the Norwegian pavilion at the International Exhibition of Modern Decorative Art, Turin, 1902 and in the Milan Exhibition of 1906. He made lively, contorted shapes with decoration based on natural forms (crustacea, insects and other animals, flowers, etc.) using *sgraffito* designs, bright enamels, or metallic lustre.
Ref: Borrman.

Stomfa. Hungarian faience factory, probably established in the 1780s and working until the mid 19th century. Joseph Putz, proprietor in the early 19th century, and once thought to have been the factory's founder, made wares in traditional local styles; surviving examples are dated 1810 and 1817.
Mark: ST.
Ref: Csanyi.

Stone, Charles Arthur (1866-1936). Bristol-born painter, working in Australia from c.1885. After employment in Queensland potteries (including the Albion works established by G.*Fischer), he established his own works, the Bristol Pottery, in Coorparoo, south of Brisbane, c.1894, and by 1905 produced a variety of white earthenware bodies as well as brown-glazed and red earthenware. Under the control of his son, Roy Stone, the output was extended to include art pottery, and in 1937, the firm acquired the Chelsea Art Pottery (trading from the early 1930s to 1935), renaming it the Balmoral Pottery. Stone's was then the only firm making art pottery in Queensland. The varied output of household and decorative wares in the 1930s expanded after World War II to include vases, animal figures and sculptural pieces. The firm traded under the name of Charles A. Stone until 1956, when it changed hands, later ceasing operation.
Ref: Graham.

Stone, John Hurford. *See* Legros d'Anisy, François-Antoine.

stoneware. Pottery fired to temperatures over c.1250°C. The material is more fully vitrified than earthenware, with a porosity not exceeding 5%, and the glaze and body are partly fused together. Stoneware glazes are often based on feldspars or wood ash, with low oxide content, and fire between 1200°C and 1350°C (mainly 1260-1310°C).

Stratton, Mary Chase. *See* Perry, Mary Chase.

Strauss, L. *See* Volkstedt-Rudolstadt.

Streamline tableware. *See* Adams, John.

Strebel family. *See* Arzberg.

Strebelle, Olivier (b 1927). Belgian ceramist and sculptor, working in Antwerp. He is noted for ceramic sculptures made after World War II.
Refs: Hettes & Rada; World Ceramics.

Stroganov Institute. Russian art school in Moscow, with a pottery established in 1865 under the direction (from the 1890s) of the ceramic chemist from the *Gzhel area, G.Y. Monakhov, who experimented with crystalline glazes, which he used on vases in simple shapes. The students carried out individual research, while producing large earthenware dishes and vases, strongly influenced in style by the popular revival in Russian art, e.g. a plate with turquoise, dark blue and white glazes contained within raised outlines in a pattern of small flower motifs and scrolled leaves.

Mark: monogram of Cyrillic initials of Stroganov Institute in a circular outline.
Ref: Bubnova.

Strütz, Johann Heinrich. *See* Nuremberg.

Stuart, Ralph (c.1877-1945). Ceramic artist, working in Staffordshire potteries and then, in America, at the *Onondaga Pottery Works. In 1903, he joined the *Buffalo Pottery where he eventually took charge of

*stoneware. Tin-mounted stoneware jug, with brown glaze, designed by Paul Wynand and made by R.*Merkelbach at Grenzhausen, c.1910. Marked R. Merkelbach Grenzhausen Paul Wynand.*

the art department and remained, with a short break for service in the Canadian army during World War I, until 1942. Stuart was noted for his lively, detailed paintings of wildlife (under the glaze or in enamel). He devised the decoration (often figure subjects) for Deldare Ware, and the sailing scenes of Abino Ware, and was the sole designer until 1925 of crests and devices for tableware commissioned by businesses and institutions. His later work included a service for Thanksgiving, decorated with harvest scenes and a turkeycock (1937). His wife, Anna Delaney (c.1883-1967), was also employed as a decorator at the Buffalo Pottery.

Mark: R. STUART.

Refs: S.&V. Altman *The Book of Buffalo Pottery* (Crown Publishers Inc., New York, 1969); Evans; Kovel & Kovel.

studio pottery. Hand-crafted wares created by an individual, or a small number of potters working in studio conditions (*see* artist potters).

Sturt Crafts Centre. Australian crafts centre, now comprising six production workshops, founded in 1941 by the educationalist, Winifred West. The pottery workshop was established at Sturt in Mittagong, to the south of Sydney in 1953, by I.*McMeekin. L.*Blakeborough, C.*Levy and G.*Pigott also worked at Sturt. Since the early 1960s, there has been a training programme run with the help of visiting potters, and the workshop functions as a community of professional craftsmen, producing pottery for daily use and using local raw materials to make attractive, functional wares.

Suetin, Nikolai (1897-1954). Russian Suprematist artist. Suetin was a pupil of K. *Malevich and designed porcelain for the *St Petersburg factory in the early 1920s, with forms and decoration closely related to Suprematist painting. His work included a writing set, architectural in inspiration with an inkwell that is cuboid in form and stands on a base made up of square and rectangular slabs laid on a quarter-circle of clay. Some of his designs for painted decoration were based on prints or paintings by Malevich, e.g. a pattern of triangles, rectangles, a square and a circle for a cup and saucer, after Malevich's lithograph for a book jacket in 1920. By the 1930s his work included human figures, mainly workers and peasants portrayed in grey or black silhouette.

Ref: Russisches Porzellan (information sheet, Badisches Landesmuseum, Karlsruhe, n.d.)

Süe et Mare. *See* Primavera, Atelier.

Suhl. Prussian porcelain factory established in 1861 by the Schlegelmilch family, under the name of Erdmann Schlegelmilch. This factory closed during World War I.

Marks normally incorporate the initials ES or *Suhl*, the most commonly used being a swallow with ES in an oval mark; a circular mark containing a hen, and a crown with ES and the date of foundation also occur.

The family established another Suhl factory in 1869, under the name of Reinhold Schlegelmilch, and moved it to Tillowitz (Silesia) during World War I. The firm of

Nikolai Suetin. Pieces from a porcelain service designed by Suetin and made at St Petersburg, 1930.

Karl Schlegelmilch started in 1881 at Mäbendorf, near Suhl. The Schlegelmilch family made tea and coffee sets, nursery ware, table servers and household items as well as ornamental pieces which were mainly for export. Much of the decoration was transfer-printed.

Marks include a bird in an oval, a hen in a circular shield or a crown, with the founder's initials, E.S.; the place name and the date 1861 were added.

Refs: Danckert; Scherf; Weiss.

Sukehachi. *See* Hagi ware.

Summerly's Art Manufactures. *See* Cole, Henry; Mintons Ltd.

Sunburst. *See* Owens, John B.

Sunderland. Pottery centre on Wearside in the north-east of England. Workshops near Sunderland made brown and white earthenware from the 18th century, but the area is associated with lustre-decorated earthenware made from the early 19th century to the 1880s and much exported c.1820-c.1860. The characteristic pink lustre was obtained by the use of gold oxide over a light-coloured body or glaze, sometimes with a mottled effect achieved by splashing the surface with oil resist before application of the lustre. Similar speckled pink lustre was also used at Bristol and in Staffordshire, but such pieces are often sold as Sunderland ware. The output included dinner services, teasets, jugs and bowls in sets of twelve, plaques, figures, model animals, frog mugs, tiles, etc. Many of the pieces were decorated with transfer-printed patterns in black, less often in blue or green, including verses and views of local or topical interest, notably the Wearmouth Bridge, a cast-iron construction with a span of over 78 metres that was opened in 1796 and figures in various views on marked pieces made at the *Wear Pottery, *Garrison Pottery and by J.*Dawson, *Dixon, Austin &

Co. and *Scott Bros. Other patterns commemorated the battles of Camperdown (1797), Trafalgar, and the Nile and other naval subjects, and the Crimean War; portraits represented Napoleon, John Wesley, Garibaldi, etc. Transfer printing was often combined with washed or enamel colours, bordered with pink lustre. The patterns on sets of bowls occasionally represent months of the year. Figures often portrayed religious, pastoral or topical subjects; models of dogs were usually in white, splashed with pink or copper lustre, Sunderland lions were in a white or brown body.

Sunderland ware, produced with popular appeal at moderate prices, is noted for spontaneity in design. The local potteries in general produced a varied output, ranging from lustre ware with decoration in silver as well as pink or copper lustre to brown earthenware for kitchen use.

Refs: M.A. Buckmaster 'English Lustre Ware, Copper, Silver and Gold' in *The Connoisseur* 4 (November 1902); G.B. Drury in *Antique Dealer and Collector's Guide* (May 1950); A. Hayden 'Some Sunderland Mugs' in *The Connoisseur* 9 (June 1904); Jewitt; V. Ritson in

Sunderland. Rectangular plaque with pattern printed in black enclosed in a border of pink and copper lustre. Marked with Dixon & Co., *impressed. 23 cm across.*

Sunderland Echo (9th, 10th May 1928); Shaw; *Sunderland Echo* (21st, 23rd May and 4th, 11th June 1934).

Sunderland lustre. *See* Newcastle-upon-Tyne.

Sunflower Pottery. *See* Elton, Sir Edmund Harry.

Sung glaze. *See* Doulton & Co.

Sunstone. *See* Pilkington's Tile & Pottery Co.

Sureda, Bartolomeo. *See* Buen Retiro; Moncloa, La.

Surrey Ceramic Co. Ltd. *See* Saywell, Roy.

Süs, Wilhelm. *See* Karlsruhe.

Sussex Rustic Ware. *See* Belleview or Bellevue Pottery.

Sutherland Pottery. *See* Beardmore, Frank, & Co.

Suwa Yoshitake or **Sozan** (1852-1922). Japanese potter, born and trained in Kanazawa Working under the artistic name Sozan, he made ceramics in Tokyo and then returned to Kanazawa where he took part in improving the standards of *Kutani ware and became director of the industrial school. In Kyoto from 1900, he worked at the *Kinkozan kiln and subsequently established his own kiln at Gojozaka. He travelled frequently to Korea in the course of research (starting c.1912) in Koryo wares. His work included imitations of Kutani and Koryo wares, as well as Chinese wares of the Sung dynasty.
Refs: Jenyns (1967); Roberts; Uyeno.

Swab, Friedrich, & Co. *See* Morgenroth & Co.

Swadlincote. *See* Ault, William.

Swaine, Robert and William. *See* Hüttensteinach.

Swan Hill Pottery. *See* Carr, James.

Swann, John. *See* Alexandria Pottery.

Swansea. *See* Cambrian Pottery; Glamorgan Pottery.

Swebach, Jacques-François-Joseph (1769-1823). French porcelain decorator, born in Metz (Moselle). Swebach worked in Paris, initially with his father, François-Louis-Swebach, (with whom he shared the pseudonym Fontaine), then under Michel Duplessis. Swebach was chief painter (1802-13) at the *Sèvres factory, where he painted landscapes and military subjects, working on services, e.g. 67 plates painted with views of Egypt *en grisaille* from sketches by Vivant Denon for the Service Egyptien. In 1815, he went to St Petersburg, where he continued to paint military subjects until his return to France in 1820.
His son, Bernard-Edouard Swebach (1806-70), was a painter of landscapes, battles and historical scenes at Sèvres and several Paris factories. He travelled to Russia, 1818-20.

Mark: sw (at Sèvres).
Refs: Bénézit; Guillebon.

Swillington Bridge Pottery. Yorkshire pottery established on the River Aire at Woodlesford, near Leeds, in 1791. Benjamin Taylor was proprietor from 1833, in partnership until the early 1840s with James Reed (also his partner in the *Ferrybridge Pottery and in *Mexborough) and briefly with his son Samuel Taylor until the pottery's closure c.1845. The output of domestic earthenware included creamware with a sea-green tinge in the glaze, enamel painted with floral sprays, pearlware with blue-dashed decoration on the rim and, from the 1820s, ironstone china with transfer-printed patterns (e.g. Willow Pattern) in blue. As well as inexpensive kitchen ware with bands of colour, the pottery made earthenware decorated with raised bands of ribbing painted blue or green. Mocha ware, slipware and black glazed earthenware were also made.
Marks on blue-printed ware include versions of a crown and often incorporate the name of the body, e.g. OPAQUE GRANITE CHINA or IRONSTONE.
Refs: Godden (1971); Grabham; Lawrence; Towner (1957).

Swinton Pottery or **Rockingham Works.** Yorkshire pottery established c.1754 at Swinton, near Rotherham, on land belonging to the Marquis of Rockingham, and operated 1785-1806 by Greens, Bingley & Co. The pottery produced creamware and fine earthenware with coloured glazes or transfer-printed decoration, generally similar to the work of the *Leeds Pottery, and developed the characteristic glaze of *Rockingham ware from the inferior brown glazes that were widely used. Tea and dessert services formed the main product before the introduction of porcelain, when ornamental ware became a greater part of the output.
J.*Brameld traded with his sons William and Thomas as Brameld & Co. from 1806 until their bankruptcy in 1826, and the pottery, then known as the Rockingham Works remained under the control of the Brameld family, with further backing from the Earl Fitzwilliam, until its closure in 1842. Tea, coffee and chocolate sets and jugs were among the output of cream-bodied earthenware covered with Rockingham glaze; *Cadogan pots were normally brown glazed, though some examples were glazed in green

or, occasionally, in other colours. Leaf dishes, moulded jugs, vases, dessert services, garden seats and some purely ornmental pieces (e.g. a model of Conisbrough Castle) were glazed in a rather light shade of green. Decorative techniques used on the creamware body included enamel painting of named flower specimens on dessert plates, the use of rich colours (blue, green or red) and lavish gilding with painted panels of romantic landscapes, etc., transfer printing with landscapes, pastoral scenes or *chinoiseries*, normally in blue (other colours included green, beige and black), and pierced ornament. An earthenware of exceptional whiteness (chalk body) was developed, but produced only briefly.
The pottery's output of fine stoneware included mainly cane-coloured, but occasionally black basalt, tea and coffee ware; pieces sometimes have handles decorated with a horse's tail and ending in the form of a hoof. Soft-paste porcelain with fine, translucent body containing Cornish stone and clay, and bone ash, was in full production in 1826, and comprised table services, baskets, comports, vases, trinket sets, thimbles, inkwells, brooches, etc., which after 1830 were usually decorated in revived rococo style. Relief ornament was in general lavish – scallops, shell edging, gadroons, and scrolls, but in general less ornate than on some of the pieces made at *Coalport and Grainger's *Worcester factory or by S.*Alcock & Co. Gilded patterns included lacework, vine leaves and grapes, and seaweed motifs. Some examples of flower-encrusted ware made at Coalport have been wrongly attributed to the Rockingham Works, although the high-relief flowers applied at Swinton were in general much smaller than those of Coalport. Among the firm's special items was the Rhinoceros vase; a later version has panels painted with flowers by E.*Steele.
The firm renamed the pottery the Royal Rockingham Works after receiving commissions from several members of the English Royal family, including an order from King William IV for an elaborate dessert service consisting of 200 pieces. The firm also produced trays painted e.g. with T.*Steel's studies of fruit. Bedposts, table legs, pillars and architectural ornament in porcelain and earthenware around a strengthening core were produced in small quantities after the granting of a patent in 1838. Figures, biscuit or glazed and enamelled, generally stand on a solid plinth with a small circular aperture in the base, and include theatrical and pastoral subjects, children, peasants, dogs, sheep and other animals, which have incised on the base a number below 136, with the factory mark; there is no number on portrait busts.

Swinton Pottery. Pieces from a Rockingham tea and coffee service, made at Swinton c.1835, with moulded decoration of leaves. Marked with a griffin in puce.

After the financial failure of the Bramelds in 1842, I.*Baguley established a decorating studio in a portion of the works, where he continued the use of the brown Rockingham glaze on jugs, tea and coffee pots, breakfast services and drinking vessels, as well as carrying out painted decoration and gilding. He was succeeded by his son Alfred until 1865. Another part of the works was briefly occupied by the firm P. Hobson & Son, which produced earthenware in 1852.

Marks: BRAMELD impressed (sometimes with *J. Mortlock & Co.*); BRAMELD embossed on oval garland; ROCKINGHAM/WORKS/ BRAMELD impressed; griffin marks from the crest of the Fitzwilliam family in red to 1830, afterwards puce or purple.
Refs: A.& A. Cox 'The Rockingham Dessert Service for William IV' in *The Connoisseur* 188 (February 1975); Cox; Eaglestone; Lockett; Lawrence; D.G. Rice *Illustrated Guide to Rockingham Porcelain* (Barrie & Jenkins, London, 1971).

Sylvan. *See* Brush-McCoy Pottery.

Syracuse China Corporation. *See* Onondaga Pottery Co.

Tachikui. Japanese folk pottery centre in Hyogo prefecture, active in the production of *Tamba ware from the mid 18th century to the present day. The kilns at Tachikui village, which in the 1960s numbered about thirteen, made a wide range of domestic stoneware with white, black or brown glazes, notably small jars and bottles with brown or black glaze trickled over a light ground, saké bottles with designs in black or blue on brown glaze, and long-necked jars for pepper and for wine. In 1835, Masamoto Naosuke made bottles for oil painted with a crane or other designs after the Tamba-born painter Okyo (1733-95).

Imitations of *Bizen ware made later in the 19th century included flower vases; many tea jars and bowls closely resembled *Seto ware. Since a visit from B.*Leach in the 1930s, the potters have been influenced by his work, and the spouts and handles of some pieces are made by means of European techniques. Much work has been produced for sale through Osaka and Tokyo, and some exported.
Refs: Gorham; Jenyns (1971); Okuda, Koyama & Hayashiya (eds) *Nihon no Toji* (Toto Bunka Co., Tokyo, 1932); Sanders.

Tachinami Monzaemon (1821-1902). Japanese potter, also named Okuda Shinsei, born in Nagano, *Shigaraki. He followed his family's tradition in throwing tea jars and other large pieces, such as well-heads. He also made ornamental animal models. Tachinami eventually established a pottery at Seba in the mountains near Nagano, where he worked for 20 years. His influence spread to makers of Matsumoto ware.
Ref: Cort.

Taffet. *See* Angoulême.

Taft, James Scholly (1844-1923). American art potter. With his uncle, James Burnap, Taft established the Hampshire Pottery Co. at Keene, New Hampshire, in 1871. The firm made flowerpots and earthenware for domestic use and, shortly afterwards, stoneware. In 1874, they bought a pottery at Myrtle Street, Keene, where plant containers, etc., and brown-glazed teapots were made in red earthenware by 1896, while the production of stoneware for domestic use continued at the original works. With the English potter, Thomas Stanley, as superintendent of the Hampshire Pottery from 1879, the firm introduced majolica tableware and vases in a hard, white body covered with dark glazes, enlarging the works to increase production in 1822. They also made a small quantity of underglaze-decorated ware. Under the artistic direction of Wallace L. King, the firm produced plates, dishes, dressing table sets, etc., in a semi-porcelain body with a pink-tinged ivory matt surface, transfer-printed with views associated with places in the southern and eastern US, where they were sold as souvenirs; a jug decorated with a flying witch was made for sale at Salem, Massachusetts. Other souvenir items were covered with blue, red-brown or olive green glazes. From 1904, the firm produced a wide variety of matt glazes which were used on a line of art pottery which included vases, bowls, lamps and clock cases, initially in earthenware and later in semi-porcelain. Taft ceased production in 1915, selling the pottery in 1916 to George M. Morton, an employee of W.H.*Grueby, who continued in operation until 1917, and from 1919 until the pottery's closure in 1923. In this period, production of art ware was increased, and white tableware for hotel and restaurant use, as well as mosaic floor tiles, were made (1919-21).

Early majolica was often unmarked. Marks on white ware usually incorporate the name of Taft and the pottery, and *Keene, New Hampshire*, in red; later art ware was often marked *Hampshire Pottery*, impressed.
Refs: Barber (1976); Evans; Kovel & Kovel; Watkins (1950).

Taillandier, P. Porcelain decorator working for a short time from 1894 at the porcelain factory in Osmaston Road, *Derby, where he was an assistant to D.*Leroy. Taillandier is thought to have been related to a flower painter at the Sèvres factory. His work included classical or romantic figures, notably winged cherubs.
Mark: signature.
Refs: see Derby.

Taira. *See* Echizen ware.

Taizan. In Japanese ceramics, the artistic name adopted in 1760 by a line descended from the 17th-century potter Tokuro Takahashi and working in Awata until 1894. Each successive head of the family took the name Taizan Yohei. The fifth generation made porcelain, notably celadon ware, as well as pottery in the early 19th century, and supplied blue-glazed ware to the Imperial court, 1801-20. The family was noted for the introduction of a fine mazarine blue, used both for the painting of patterns and as a ground for patterns in gold. Taizan Yohei VI was joined at his kiln by *Bizan, 1820-38, and made lavishly enamelled pieces for use at the court, 1830-43. Some of his patterns were designed by Keibun Matsumura (1779-1843) and Toyohiko Okamoto (1773-1845), leading Kyoto painters of the Shijo school. He was

Taizan. Vase painted in enamel colours and gold. Marks include Taizan, impressed, and the date, 1877. 38 cm high.

succeeded by the seventh generation until 1853. Yohei VIII, working until 1870, began the export (continued by his successors) of the family's enamelled ware, either polychrome on a matt yellow ground, or in red and blue. Yohei IX, the last head of the line, was noted for enamelled decoration in red, lavishly gilded.
Refs: Brinkley; Jenyns (1965, 1971); Roberts.

Tajimi. *See* Mino.

Takada Toyokawa-cho. *See* Takemoto Hayata.

Takahashi Toemon. Japanese potter working in Koyama, *Shigaraki, in the Tempo era (1830-44). Using fine, iron-rich clay, he made cups with incised patterns of flowers and landscapes for the sencha tea ceremony, which he impressed with the seal Shunsai. His grandson Takahashi Rakusai continued his work, becoming an Important Intangible Cultural Property in 1964.
Ref: Cort.

Takato ware. Japanese pottery made at Takato in Nagano prefecture from the establishment of a clan kiln by a potter from *Mino in 1813. The kilns, which increased in number under private management from

1841, mass-produced many vessels for use in the processing of silk and specialized in the use of streaked blue-white namako glaze. The Marusen kiln worked from the Meiji period (1868-1912) and was the last to close in 1960.
Ref: Mizuo.

Takatori wares. Japanese pottery made in Fukuoka prefecture under the patronage of the Kuroda clan, initially by Korean craftsmen who settled at Takatori after Hideyoshi's invasion of Korea in the late 16th century. After several moves, the makers established kilns at *Koishibara, where they produced wares in the Takatori tradition from the mid 17th century. The pieces are simple and elegant and many were produced for the tea ceremony after the endorsement of Takatori wares by the teamaster Kobori Enshu (1579-1647). Fine-textured grey or brownish clay was used for cylindrical tea jars and pieces in globular or gourd shapes, with glazes in many shades of brown with patches of light-coloured glaze. Other potteries continued the traditions in *Nishishinmachi and the nearby *Nishiyama kiln. An official kiln, opened at Sarayama, Sue town, by the seventh head of the Kuroda clan for the production of porcelain in the late 18th century, reopened under the supervision of an office started by the 11th clan lord in Sue (1860) to control local ceramic manufacture. Potters and decorators invited from Kyoto, Seto and the Hizen area were engaged on the mass-production of porcelain until the closure of this kiln c.1870.
Refs: Jenyns (1971); Koyama; Kozuru; Okamura; Yanosuke Miwa 'Takatori Ware' in *Sekai Toji Zenshu* Vol 4 (Sanho Press & Kawade Shobo, Tokyo, 1955-56).

Takeda Shuhei. *See* Kasugayama kiln; Minzan.

Takemoto Hayata (1848-92). Japanese potter, working primarily in his native Tokyo. He joined the Seto potter Ryokichi in making *Satsuma wares, as well as a staple output of brick and earthenware pipes, at a kiln established at Takada Toyokawa-cho. Takemoto carried out research into glazes, specializing in the black finishes used on Sung Chinese wares, including mirror black, as in raven's wing (with green sheen), hare's fur (streaked), and moss (dappled effects). His work won high regard among contemporary tea masters. He was receptive to European methods, pioneering the use in Japan of a vertical round kiln of French origin, and also employed traditional Japanese techniques in the execution of some westernized designs, but in the International Exhibition in Vienna, 1873, won a prize for an incense burner in Satsuma style.
Refs: Gorham; Jenyns (1967); *Nihon no Bijutsu* [Japanese Art] 41 (Shibundo, Tokyo, from 1960); *Nihon Bijutsu Zenshu* [Collection of Japanese Fine Art] 6 (Bijutsu Shuppan-sha, Tokyo, 1969); Roberts; Uyeno.

Takeuchi Ginshu (d 1913). Japanese potter, a maker of *Kutani ware and a pupil of *Hachiroemon. He pioneered the application of European ceramic techiques in Kutani, after their introduction in Arita c.1870.
Refs: Jenyns (1965); Roberts.

Talashkino. Artists' colony at Talashkino, formed to foster an interest in Russian folklore and organized by Princess Maria Tenicheva, the patroness of a radical group headed by Sergei Diaghilev. In 1887, inspired by similarly motivated workshops set up by Elena Polenova at Trocadero and the Mamantovs at *Abramtsevo, Princess Tenicheva founded an institute of decorative arts, where young peasants learned a variety of crafts while engaged in projects such as a folk theatre and the building of a church in traditional style. Some work was designed by Princess Tenicheva, who also took part in the establishment of a museum of decorative arts. The craft school was intended to encourage the pupils' artistic initiative within the framework of traditional styles. The pottery made there included animal and bird figures partly covered with coloured glazes. Brightly coloured pots with patterns resembling embroidery were exhibited in Paris, 1906-07. The decoration of mugs, beakers, etc., was often incised in geometrical patterns; in the case of animal jugs, the fur, features and other details were scratched or carved in relief. The artists included S.V.*Chekhonin, who made his own pots as well as decorating pottery blanks.
Ref: Rheims.

Talbot family. French stoneware potters working at La *Borne. Members of the family included Jean-Pierre Talbot (1767-1822) and his brother Jacques-Sébastien (1769-1824), who made crucifixes and pitchers or other household pieces decorated with birds, human figures, etc. J.-S. Talbot's daughter, Marie (1806-60), made jugs, fountains, calvaries, writing sets, as well as naive figures, e.g. courting couples under a tree, and bottles in the form of figures, or grotesque portraits, using grey-bodied stoneware. Jean-Pierre was succeeded by his son, Milliet-François Talbot (1802-90), and his granddaughter Marie-Louise Chameron (1846-1923), who made jugs, figures and plaques influenced by the modern style, and decorated the work of her father and son. Jean Talbot (1809-73), brother of Marie, used a characteristic border decoration of many circles centred on a dot, and made sketchy little figures with their hair drawn back. He used decoration stamped or applied on thrown forms, such as jugs with faces and tricorne hats, masks, and tobacco jars in the form of soldiers. He was followed by a son, also Jean Talbot (1844-1915). Aléxandre Talbot (1875-1956) started the use of moulds for jugs, bottles with bearded heads, and figures of the Virgin Mary, in 1914.
A relative, Leclerc-Alphonse Talbot (1882-1957), worked at La Borne d'En Bas, and his pieces include a bottle with the mark *'fait a La Borne/chez/Talbot/Alphonse/le 21 janvier/1944'*. Jean Talbot (b 1931) continued his family's work.
Refs: Ernould-Gandouet; Lesur (1971); Céramique française contemporaine.

Talmours. *See* Discry.

Tamba ware. Japanese stoneware of ancient origin, made in the former province of Tamba (Hyogo prefecture). Production extends from the Kamakura period (1185-1333) to the present day and has preserved a long tradition of the use of techniques developed

by Korean potters. The ware was initially glazed only with accidental effects resulting from ash in the kiln but after the organization of the workshop in *Tachikui village in the mid 18th century, red-brown and black glazes came into use. Similar wares were also made at Kamaya, possibly from the late 16th century, until 1934; fragments found at the site indicate the production of a wide range of bottles, and pots for tooth dye. The modern wares have glazes predominantly in black or rich shades of brown. Some pieces are splashed with yellow, and there is a group of unglazed ware painted in enamel with simple, bold designs. A wide range of decoration included a coating of light slip with dark painted designs of a lobster, etc., or marbled with a darker colour in sumi nagashi (inkflow) effect; incised designs; leaf impressions; white slip trailed through a bamboo tube to inscribe verses on the back of saké bottles; drip glazes.
Refs: Gorham; Jenyns (1971); Okuda, Koyama & Hayashiya (eds) *Nihon no Toji* (Toto Bunka Co., Tokyo, 1932); Sanders.

Tamikichi. *See* Kato Tamikichi.

Tams, James. *See* Greenwood Pottery Co.

Tams, John, & Son Ltd. Staffordshire earthenware manufacturers established in the early 19th century and working from c.1875 at the Crown Pottery in Stafford Street, Longton, formerly occupied by J.*Broadhurst. The firm specialized in government measures, mugs and jugs, advertised in 1886, together with 'printed and decorated dinner and toilet ware of all kinds in white and ivory bodies', novelties, modelled flowers, vases and household wares. The firm, operating as John Tams Ltd from 1912, continues to the present day.
A variety of printed marks normally incorporate the initials JT or the name *Tams*.
Refs: Jewitt; Godden (1964).

Tanaka family. *See* Raku family.

Tanaka Gozaemon. See Nyudo.

Tanii Rijuro (1806-91). Japanese potter born in Nagano, *Shigaraki. Tanii was noted for his experimentation with glazes. The subjects of his research included an underglaze blue associated with Kyoto potters, copper red and, notably the mottled sea cucumber (namako) glaze that came into use on the charcoal stoves (hibachi) which were to make up a large part of the output of Shigaraki. Tanii also studied the poetry and ceramics of *Rengetsu and, after visiting Kyoto, returned to work in her style at Shigaraki, using a fine, dark clay. He was followed by four generations of potters who used his artistic name, Naokata.
Ref: Cort.

Tanzan. In Japanese ceramics, the name assumed by a family of potters (starting with Tanzan Yoshitaro) in 1869 who worked at Nakanocho, Awata, from the early 1850s. Using a close-textured body and soft creamy glaze, the Tanzan family made *Awata wares under the patronage of Prince Shorein. Decoration consisted of flowers, foliage, birds and other animals, predominantly in

Millicent Taplin. Bone china coffee pot with a pattern, Kingcup, designed by Millicent Taplin for J.*Wedgwood & Sons Ltd in 1948.

soft, natural colours (russet, dark brown, etc.). The kiln also used lace patterns, scroll work and diaper patterns in relief built up in slip, resembling the warabi-de (or fern scroll) decoration associated with *Hozan. Mottled, marbled, tortoiseshell, moss agate and 'dead leaf' glaze effects, a speciality of the kiln, were often used in combination with warabi-de. Much of the output was exported to Europe and America until the 1880s.
Ref: Jenyns (1971).

Taplin, Millicent. English ceramic decorator and designer of patterns. She started work as a painter for J.*Wedgwood & Sons Ltd in 1927 and became head of the firm's painting department in 1956. She specialized in sparing, delicate patterns of flowers, sometimes adapted from 18th-century originals, and often used platinum lustre in her work. She painted a number of the unique pieces created by N.*Wilson. With V.*Skellern, she designed a lithograph pattern of strawberry plants (Strawberry Hill), which won the Design of the Year Award from the Council of Industrial Design in 1957.
Refs: Batkin; Reilly & Savage; *Wedgwood of Etruria & Barlaston* (catalogue, City Museum and Art Gallery, Hanley, 1980).

Tashcheyev, Mikhail. Russian potter working at *Skopin; a member of the cooperative of craftsmen responsible for the revival of local craft in the 1930s. He was descended from a local family of potters who had, in the early 20th century, introduced jugs in the form of centaurs, probably Greek in inspiration.
Ref: Ovsyannikov.

Tata. Hungarian faience factory working briefly at Tata 1758-62 and revived in 1768 by workers from *Holitsch. Under the direction of Georg and Therese Schlögl from the late 18th century, the factory continued the staple output of tableware, often in forms derived from metalware, until a temporary closure in 1824. It reopened in new buildings, headed until 1867 by Moses Aaron Fischer, who was joined by his son Karoly in

1850. The Fischers also decorated porcelain bought in the white from *Herend and from Bohemian factories, mainly imitating the styles of decoration used at Herend. The Viennese firm of Hardmuth bought the factory from K. Fischer and a partner, Nobel, in 1870, switching production to oven tiles.

Marks include TOTIS, TATA, and then M.A.FISCHER UND SOHN; under K. Fischer, TATA C. FISCHER and FISCHER KAROLY, TATA. Herend marks appear on some porcelain.
Refs: Csanyi; Danckert.

Tataro. Japanese pottery centre to the east of Takeo in Saga prefecture, traditionally making iron-glazed *Karatsu ware and active to the present day. Using a rough, thick clay body, the workshops produced water jars, bowls, bottles, vases, hand-warmers, funerary urns and other pieces, some very large, by a method of combined coiling and throwing. The glaze is dark, with lighter markings achieved in firing with ash from rice straw.
Ref: Okamura.

Tatenoshita. Japanese kiln thought to have been established for the lords of Soma in the early 18th century at Nakamura, Fukushima prefecture. The output included a wide variety of domestic ware, notably large storage jars, resembling Tsutsumi wares in technique, initially made as a profitable line alongside wares for the Soma clan. Production continues.
Ref: Mizuo.

Tatler, Elijah (1823-76). English-born ceramic decorator, son of the flower painter, Thomas Tatler. Tatler worked at the *Copeland factory and, after going to America as head of C.*Cartlidge's decorating department from c.1848. He painted a view of New York harbour on a doorplate, a series of birds after Audubon on doorknobs, escutcheons and other decorative hardware. Tatler returned to England soon after 1850 and subsequently worked briefly in Toronto before joining the decorating staff of Taylor & Davis in Trenton, New Jersey. Work in Trenton included a toilet service with American views, vases, cups and saucers with paintings of birds taken from nature, and a plaque with an Oriental scene entitled Byron's Dream. Shortly before his death, Tatler established a decorating workshop in Trenton, which was continued by his son.
Ref: Barber (1976).

Tatsumonji. In Japanese ceramics, the centre of a group of kilns set up by Koreans making *Satsuma ware, influenced by *Seto ware, with running glazes over a contrasting ground glaze. The kiln started in the 17th century and continues to the present day. It is particularly associated with the making of tea wares.
Ref: Jenyns (1971).

Taubenbach. German porcelain factory established by Carl Moritz and in operation at Taubenbach (Thuringia) from 1848 until the 1930s. The firm produced tableware, vases, figures and toys, and became noted for painted decoration, including bright, peasant-style patterns, with gilding, on coffee sets.

Mark: M and *Taubenbach* arranged in a

circle around the monogram initial C containing a T; a similar mark without the place name but incorporating *Qualität*; a circular mark with CARL MORITZ TAUBENBACH on a band surrounding a crown over MC and *Taubenbach*.
Refs: Danckert; Scherf.

Tauch, Edgar. *See* Walrich Pottery.

Taucher, Konrad. *See* Karlsruhe.

Tavernier, André. *See* Auxerre.

Tavernier family. *See* Arthé, Faïencerie de.

Taylor, Benjamin. *See* Swillington Bridge Pottery.

Taylor, James. *See* Old Cumnock Pottery.

Taylor, Joseph Wilson. Yorkshire potter working in the Leeds area. With his brothers, Charles (d 1885) and James, he succeeded his father, George Taylor, as a partner in the *Hunslet New Pottery in the mid 1860s, joining his uncle Samuel, who died shortly afterwards, in 1866. Subsequently working with his brother Charles at the New Pottery, J.W. Taylor was also a tenant of Petty's *Hunslet Hall Pottery from 1861 until its closure in 1881, proprietor of *Leathley Lane Pottery from 1867 and its owner in 1871, and briefly ran the *Leeds Pottery in 1881.
Refs: Grabham; Jewitt; Lawrence.

Taylor, Nicholas. Yorkshire potter. In 1893, Taylor rented the *Denholme Pottery, where he had been employed for at least two years, and returned after a brief absence to establish his own small works, also in Denholme (1898). He produced a range of thrown wares, including mugs and puzzle jugs decorated with trailed slip. He left the Denholme Pottery in 1907 and subsequently worked at Burton in Lonsdale, as a thrower at the *Littlethorpe Pottery, at *Castleford, and in Kent. He established a works at Ogden, near Halifax, for the production of earthenware, specializing in marbled ware, and painted pieces resembling the work of *Carter, Stabler & Adams, but died soon after starting the pottery.
Refs: Brears (1971a); Lawrence; J. Walton 'Some Decadent Local Industries' in *Halifax Antiquarian Society Transactions* (1938).

Taylor, Robert Minton. English potter. Taylor was a partner in *Minton, Hollins & Co. (1863-68) and in 1869 began his own manufacture at the Robert Minton Taylor Tile Works in Fenton, but was prevented by an injunction from using the name Minton on his tiles. From 1875, he was manager of the *Campbell Brick & Tile Co.

Marks: R.M.T.; F.T.W. (Fenton Tile Works); or *Robert Minton Taylor/Tile Works/Fenton near/Stoke on Trent.*
Refs: Barnard; Lockett (1979); Wedgwood & Ormsbee; *see also* Mintons Ltd.

Taylor, William. Porcelain painter working for Flight, Barr & Barr in *Worcester by 1819. Taylor specialized in painting flowers. He continued under the later firm, Kerr & Binns.

Another flower painter named William Taylor (b c.1828) worked for Kerr & Binns

from c.1845 until after 1870. His subjects included wild flowers of Australia.
Refs: Chaffers; Sandon (1978a, 1978b).

Taylor, William Howson (1876-1935). English artist potter. Taylor studied at the Birmingham School of Art, where his father, E.R. Taylor, was the Principal, and carried out experiments in ceramics at Edgbaston. He established a workshop, the Ruskin Pottery, at a site in West Smethwick which he bought in 1898 and began commercial production in 1901. Normally using local clay, he also developed a white body containing china clay and calcined flint, which he used for high-fired pieces inspired by Chinese pottery of the Sung and Ming periods. Taylor was primarily interested in glaze effects, with which he decorated rather heavily potted vases, bottles, small bowls, small trays for butter or sweets, cups, egg cups, candlesticks, buttons, and cuff links, sometimes adding silver mounts. His work included Soufflé ware, glazed with cloudy, shaded effects in a single colour or combination of colours; the tones ranged from dark blues and greens shading to turquoise and apple green, purple to pink and mauve, mottled pale green running to a darker green, bright yellow to sharp green, and also included greys and celadons. Lustres in a wide variety of colours included lemon yellow or orange, sometimes over painted decoration in green or brown; pearl, sometimes blistered in texture, was often used with a blue-green glaze.

Taylor produced high-fired wares in a range noted for its variety in texture, colour and pattern, often at a financial loss and subsidized by his other wares. Many were mottled or flecked, such as shaded beige and grey spotted with red, green streaked with black and purple, red and purple flecked with black; the use of copper salts achieved a scattering of bright green spots in *flambé* glazes. Taylor's range included matt and crystalline glazes by c.1929; blue crystalline glazes sometimes have a frosted appearance. All the pottery's work was carried out under Taylor's close supervision. He carefully guarded the secrets of his glazes and destroyed all his notes and materials shortly before he died. Production ceased late in 1933, but the firing and glazing of stock continued until 1935. Taylor closed the workshop only two months before his death.

Robert Minton Taylor. Earthenware wall tile with relief-moulded decoration, 1869-75.

W. Howson Taylor. Vase with speckled and shaded glaze in red and green on a cream ground. Impressed mark, Ruskin, England, 1925. *15.8 cm high.*

Marks: from 1899, RUSKIN (formal permission for use of the name was obtained in 1909); Taylor's name until c.1903; a pair of scissors (signifying 'tailor') painted under the glaze or, occasionally, incised until c.1920, rarely afterwards. Most pieces are dated.
Refs: Anscombe & Gere; Coysh (1976); Haslam (1975).

Taylor, William Watts (1847-1913). American businessman who was administrator of the *Rookwood Pottery. Born in Opelousa, Louisiana, Taylor moved to Cincinnati with his family as a boy. He joined his father's business as a clerk in 1865 and remained there until he took over management of the Rookwood Pottery in 1883. He initiated an increase in production efficiency, developing new art lines that sold well, eliminating those which proved unprofitable, and stopped the output of transfer-printed ware. Taylor also restricted the pottery's retail outlets to one per city, closed the decorating school and insisted on the improvement of clay bodies. Taking responsibility for the supervision of workers (in 1884), control of purchasing, correspondence, technical experiments and approval of the designs for new shapes, Taylor established the company's profitability by 1886 and made good all its early losses by 1889. He took over as president of the company in 1890 after the retirement of M.L.*Nichols Storer.
Refs: see Rookwood Pottery.

Taylor & Davis. *See* Tatler, Elijah.

Taylor & Speeler. American pottery established 1852 at Trenton, New Jersey, by James

Taylor & Speeler. Buff stoneware pitcher with flint enamel glaze, 1852-56. Impressed mark: Taylor/Speeler/Trenton/N.J. *28.6 cm high.*

Taylor and H.*Speeler, for the production of yellow and Rockingham-glazed earthenware, the first made in the area. The firm also produced white earthenware and, from c.1855, granite ware, trading from the same period as Taylor, Speeler & Bloor. The pottery was subsequently taken over by the firm, Fell & Thropp, manufacturers of cream-coloured earthenware and white granite, in which J.H.*Brewer became a partner.

Marks used by Fell & Thropp include the arms of New Jersey, a tiger's head, and a version of the British arms, all incorporating F.&T. Co.
Ref: Barber (1976).

Taylor, Ask & Co. *See* Low Pottery.

Taylor, Goodwin & Co. *See* Goodwin, John (d 1875); Trenton Pottery Co.

Taylor, Smith & Taylor Co. American pottery established in 1899 at East Liverpool, Ohio. The original partners, John N. Taylor (*see* Knowles, Taylor & Knowles) and Charles A. Smith were joined by Taylor's sons, Homer J. and William L., with Joseph Lee, and the firm then traded as Taylor, Lee & Smith, producing earthenware, ironstone china and, primarily, semi-porcelain for domestic use. In 1900, the firm moved to a new factory in Chester, West Virginia, across the Ohio River from East Liverpool. The title became Taylor, Smith & Taylor on Lee's withdrawal in 1901, and was retained after a brief closure of the firm and reorganization in 1906 under William L. Smith and his son. The pottery continued its output of semi-porcelain tableware, toilet sets and wares for hotels and restaurants. In the late 1930s, the dinner wares Lu-Ray and Vislosa, both in coloured body, were popular lines. The factory operated as a subsidiary of the Anchor Hocking Corporation from the early 1970s until its closure late in 1981.

Marks: TAYLOR/LEE & SMITH/PORCELAIN

(1900-01); a griffon on three circles enclosing the initials TST (1901-c.1930).
Refs: Barber (1976); W.C. Gates & D.E. Ormerod 'The East Liverpool Pottery District: Identification of Manufacturers and Marks' in *Historical Archaeology* Vol 16, Nos 1-2 (Society for Historical Archaeology, 1982); Lehner.

Taylor's Pottery. *See* Hunslet New Pottery.

tea ceremony or **cha-no-yu** (Japanese, 'hot water for tea'). The ritual connected with the drinking of tea, which originated in China, developed in Japan into a system of etiquette directed towards spiritual training. The rules were listed by the teamaster Sen no Rikyu in the late 16th century. Teamasters were regarded as arbiters of behaviour and taste, and influenced Japanese ceramics by their own requirements in the choice of vessels, but also by themselves making pottery and by their patronage of certain kilns in their search for appropriate wares. Production of tea wares in Japan (which still continues) began in the 16th century in *Seto with imitations of imported pieces from China and Korea. Simple, irregularly formed vessels in muted colours were favoured, e.g. examples of *Iga, *Karatsu and *Mino wares. *Raku ware was made almost exclusively for tea-ceremony use. There was a distaste for apparent sophistication in tea-ceremony wares that has influenced modern studio potters in the west.
Refs: R. Castile *The Way of Tea* (Weatherhill, Tokyo/New York, 1971); Fujioka *Tea Ceremony Utensils* (Weatherhill/Shibundo, New York/Tokyo, 1973); Jenyns (1971); Tanaka *The Tea Ceremony* (Kodansha, Tokyo; New York, 1973).

Teco pottery. *See* American Terracotta & Ceramic Co.

Teichert, Carl (d 1871) and Johann Friedrich Ernst (1832-86). German manufacturers. Carl Teichert established a workshop at Meissen in 1857 for the production of tiled stoves, using a method developed at the Meissen porcelain factory by G.H. Melzer and patented in 1855. In the early 19th century, his firm began the production of tableware after gaining authorisation to make porcelain using the shapes and some patterns of the Meissen factory. The Carl Teichert factory continued operation until 1930, when the rights to reproduce Meissen's onion pattern (*Zwiebelmuster*) were sold to Lorenz Hutschenreuther (*see* Hutschenreuther family). Ernst Teichert acted as works manager for his brother until 1868, when he established his own tileworks in Cologne. He opened another Cologne factory for the production of porcelain, succeeded by his son, Christian, who immediately switched production to tiled stoves.
Refs: Danckert; Weiss.

Teinitz. Bohemian factory established c.1793 by Count Franz Josef von Wrtby (d 1830) for the production of earthenware the output also included copies of English creamware, jasper ware with white reliefs of leaves, roses and eventually figure subjects on blue or red grounds. At the trade products exhibition in Prague in 1828, the factory's display of creamware included a plate painted with mythological scenes, and was praised for the white, smooth glaze, as well as the quality of painted and printed decoration. The owner was succeeded in 1830 by Johann Karl von Lobkowitz. The firm exhibited only useful wares 1839-45, and ceased operation in 1866.
Ref: Meyer.

Teixeira de Mattos, Joseph Henri (1856-1908). Dutch sculptor born in Amsterdam. He designed sculptural pieces made at the *Haga and *Amstelhoek factories.
Refs: Scheen; Singelenberg-van der Meer; van Straaten.

Telkibanya. Hungarian factory established in the 1830s by Prince Bretzenheim for the production of porcelain. The factory failed in the 1840s and lay idle until its revival in 1860, when a brief period of porcelain manufacture was replaced by the production of creamware.
Marks: the place name or, 1860-89, the name of the owner, *Julius Fiedler*.
Ref: Csanyi.

temmoku or **tenmoku glazes.** Near-black oriental glazes, including 'hare's fur', 'oil spot' and other effects, which may also break to an iron-red in rims or relief ornament. Temmoku glazes are used on stoneware fired in a reducing atmosphere. Black glazes for earthenware are coloured with iron, cobalt and manganese, or mixtures containing copper.

Temperance Hill Pottery. *See* Walker, Samuel or George.

Tennozan kiln. *See* Matsushiro.

Teplitz, Fachschule. Ceramic trade school established at Teplitz, Czechoslovakia, in 1874, and under the direction of painter and architect, Robert Stübchen Kirchner, from the following year. The school produced animal figures, stoneware masks, and vases with crustaceans in high relief and coloured with high-temperature glazes in shades of dark blue and grey. The chemist R. Seiffert developed crystalline glazes, which were used on an earthenware body fired at relatively high temperatures.

Marks include *K.K./Fachschule/Teplitz*, and a monogram of FST, both impressed.
Refs: Hettes & Rada; Neuwirth (1974b).

Terao Myoun kiln. *See* Matsushiro.

terracotta. Unglazed earthenware fired at a low temperature and varying in colour from buff to rich red or brown, depending on the clay from which it is made. A rich red was sometimes obtained by spraying the ware with ferric chloride before firing.
Ornamental terracotta by J.*Wedgwood & Sons Ltd (18th century) was still in production for display at the Great Exhibition in 1851.

Much work by Blanchard & Co., produced without artificial colouring, was bought for decoration in the Etruscan style by T.*Battam who worked with a dark oil-based pigment. Other English manufacturers of terracotta were *Mintons Ltd, F.& R.*Pratt, the firm of W.T.*Copeland, the Doulton & Co. workshop in Lambeth (where the work of G.*Tinworth was notable), *Pinder, Bourne & Co., and the *Watcombe Pottery (vases, etc., decorated by Battam).
In America, moulded ornamentation in terracotta designed by architects was produced for use by builders.
Refs: Aslin & Atterbury; Atterbury & Irvine; Blacker (1922a); Jewitt; Lloyd Thomas (1974, 1976); Rhead; Wakefield.

Tettau. German porcelain factory established at Tettau (Upper Franconia) in 1794 by W.H.I. Greiner who had formerly worked at Kloster Veilsdorf with a privilege from King Wilhelm II of Prussia. Greiner was succeeded by his sons, Georg Christian Friedemann who had been his partner, and Balthasar Greiner. Using a greyish or yellow-green tinged paste, the firm made services, tea, coffee and chocolate sets, often with floral painting and noted in the early 19th century for very careful finish. Some pieces, ribbed in shape, were painted in purple monochrome. From 1852, the factory was under the control of Ferdinand Klaus, who increased the output for export. The factory burned down in 1897 and was rebuilt by Sontag & Söhne GmbH. A joint stock company organized in 1915 started production of electrical porcelain in 1920. The factory is still in operation. The nearby Neu-Tettau factory, established 1904 and run by Gerold & Co., produces figures, animal groups, vases and other decorative pieces.
A variety of marks include the initial T; a lion holding a banner or shield bearing a T, sometimes with *Königl. pr.* or *priv. Tettau* or a trade name (e.g. DAISY/TEA SET, or ROYAL BAYREUTH). Marks of the Gerold factory usually incorporate the name *Neu-Tettau* or the firm's title.
Refs: Danckert; O. Dees *Die Geschichte der Porzellanfabrik zu Tettau* (Saalfeld, 1921); Haggar (1960); Honey (1952); Scherf; Weiss.

Tharaud, Camille (1878-1956). French ceramist born in Limoges. Tharaud opened an optical and photographic shop, meanwhile developing his interest in geology. On his return from war service in 1918, he became a potter and, two years later, reopened the factory of Louis Tharaud in rue du Calvaire, Limoges, established in 1854 and abandoned in 1884. His display in the Paris Exposition des Arts Décoratifs, 1925, included designs by M.*Goupy, using high-temperature decoration, for which Tharaud was to become noted. Subsequently, H. Rapin, an artistic consultant at Sèvres, created many shapes which Tharaud's firm decorated. Tharaud employed about 70 workers, including 35 painters in high-temperature colours, on the production of vases, dishes and toys, as well as decorative panels. Tharaud was assisted by his son-in-law, Albert Goumot-Labesse, who became head of production before leaving to start his own decorating workshop in 1948. Tharaud was succeeded by his widow and children until the factory's closure in 1968.

Tharaud employed a technique in which he first glazed an unfired surface, then painting on another glaze containing coloured oxides. He fired them at 1410°C in a wood-burning kiln, at first in a reducing atmosphere to improve the colour of the body, and then under full oxidization to bring out the glaze colour. The method could be made to achieve a wide range of browns, deep blue, lilac, grey, pink, emerald, yellow, rust.
Marks: LEMOVICE; *C. Tharaud.*
Ref: d'Albis & Romanet.

Tharaud, Pierre (1783-1843). French porcelain maker, born in Limoges. He was apprenticed at the *Baignol factory as a thrower in 1798 and joined the firm of F. *Alluaud in 1803. He also worked for the brothers *Darte in Paris, and returned to Limoges c.1813, taking over a porcelain factory in 1817. His work exhibited in Paris in 1819 included round and oval baskets, table centrepieces, large, graceful vases, etc., all left in the white in order to emphasize the quality of paste and form. He produced classical pieces with gold decoration (1823-27) in a new factory which he had established in 1822. He was succeeded by his widow until her retirement in 1865, when the firm passed to the *Pouyat family.
Refs: d'Albis et Romanet; Ernould-Gandouet; Weiss.

Theiss, Stephen. Belgian-born potter working in America from 1848. He was employed as a ceramic designer and modeller by C.W. *Fenton from 1850 until the closure of the United States Pottery in 1858. With other workmen, including T.*Frey, Theiss briefly formed a joint stock company to make similar wares at West Troy, New York.
Ref: Spargo.

Thesmar, André-Fernand (1843-1912). French landscape painter and craftsman; born in Chalon-sur-Saône (Saône-et-Loire). He executed *cloisonné* and *plique-à-jour* enamels, using precious metals, then developing a technique using translucent enamels with gold *cloisons* on Sèvres soft-paste porcelain, working at Neuilly (Seine) in 1892

and exhibiting his work from 1895. Thesmar also worked as a ceramic decorator.
Mark: painted monogram.
Refs: Bénézit; Brunhammer *et al* (1976); Haslam (1977).

Thiem, Otto. *See* Pfeiffer, Max Adolf.

Thieme, Carl. *See* Potschappel.

Thiirsland, Jens. *See* Kähler Ceramics.

Thoma, Hans. *See* Karlsruhe.

Thomas, Chauncey R. *See* Bragdon, William Victor; California Faience.

Thomas, Germain. *See* Saint-Clément.

Thomas & Co. *See* Rosenthal.

Thomas & Ens. *See* Rosenthal.

Thomason, James. *See* Bloor, Robert.

Thompson, C.C., Pottery Co. American pottery established in 1868 at East Liverpool, Ohio, as C.C. Thompson & J.T. Herbert. The firm became C.C. Thompson & Co. in 1870, when it was run by a partnership of Josiah Thompson (d 1889), his sons C.C. and J.C. Thompson, and B.C. Simms. The firm was incorporated in 1889 as the C.C. Thompson Pottery Co. and opened a decorating workshop in 1890. One of the largest American producers of yellow and Rockingham-glazed wares, the firm also made white ironstone (from the early 1880s) and other bodies. The pottery ceased operation in the late 1930s.

The ware was marked with THE C.C.T.P.CO over a griffon; alternatives usually incorporate the firm's initials, T, or *Thompson*, or indicate line or pattern.
Refs: Barber (1976); Lehner; F.W. McKee *A Century of American Dinnerware Manufacture* (privately published, 1966).

Thomsen, Christian (1860-1921). Danish sculptor and ceramic modeller, working for the Royal *Copenhagen Porcelain Factory, 1898-1921. He made covered boxes and other pieces, as well as figures, which included peasants, townsfolk and animals.

Monogram of *Chr.T.*
Refs: Porzellankunst.

Thomson, David. *See* Prestonpans Pottery.

Thomson, James. *See* Derby.

Thomson, John. *See* Annfield Pottery.

Thooft, Joost (1844-90). Dutch potter. In 1877, he entered a partnership with members of the Piccardt family, establishing a small production of blue-painted earthenware at

Bertel Thorwaldsen. Porcelain figure, made by *Bing & Grøndahl from a model by Thorwaldsen, 1860-1900. The figure was produced in several sizes; this one is 35 cm high.

De *Porceleyne Fles, with A.*Le Comte as art director. A. Labouchère was his partner from 1884. Thooft ceased active participation when he fell ill in 1885.
Refs: see Porceleyne Fles, De.

Thorwaldsen, Bertel or Alberto (1770-1844). Danish sculptor noted for his studies of mythical or allegorical subjects. His designs were produced in porcelain by the Royal *Copenhagen Porcelain Factory and *Bing & Grøndahl, and a set of seasons on medallions was among work made in parian ware by the *Chesapeake Pottery.
Ref: Bénézit.

Tiffany, Louis Comfort (1848-1933). American artist and interior designer, noted for jewellery, metalwork, glass and furniture designs and as an outstanding exponent of American Art Nouveau. Having initially bought lamp bases from the *Grueby Faience Co. for use with glass shades, he began secret experiments in pottery production at the studios in Corona, New York, by 1898. He exhibited three pieces with 'old ivory' glaze at the Louisiana Purchase International Exhibition at St Louis in 1904 and marketed ceramics in limited quantities after the opening of the new Tiffany & Co. building in New York (September 1905). The pottery was issued through the Corona studios and Tiffany & Co. under the same trade name as his glass—Favrile (hand-made). The pottery was, in fact, frequently cast (rather than

Fernand Thesmar. Porcelain vase painted in transluscent enamels. 9.5 cm high.

L.C. Tiffany. Earthenware vase produced by the Tiffany Studios in New York, after 1905. 27 cm high.

hand-thrown) in a fine white clay, and fired at a very high temperature. The shapes were very closely related to the decorative themes, e.g. the lips of vases were often formed by petals or leaves. A wide variety of native plants were represented, although some pieces had abstract ornamentation. Moulds were in some cases made from natural plant specimens hardened with lacquer. The glazes, initially in light yellow with shadings of old ivory, and later in green (from c.1906), red or blue, accentuate the form by gathering in crevices. Matt, crystalline and iridescent effects were achieved, and some pieces were coated with bronze from 1910. Although Tiffany ceramics were not commercially profitable, production continued until 1919. Tiffany fostered public interest in ceramics by exhibiting the work of prominent American ceramists, A.A.*Robineau and, in 1901, French studio potters, including A.*Delaherche, P.-A.*Dalpayrat, T.*Doat and A.*Bigot.

Marks: monogram of LCT, incised; *P.C.Tiffany, Favrile Pottery* or *Bronze Pottery* etched in glaze.
Refs: Barber (1976); S. Bing *La Culture Artistique en Amérique* (1896); Clark & Hughto; Eidelberg; Martin P. Eidelberg 'Tiffany Favrile Pottery, a New Study of a Few Known Facts' in *The Connoisseur* 169 (September 1968); Evans; Henzke; Kovel & Kovel; R. Koch *Louis C. Tiffany, Rebel in Glass* (Crown, New York, 1964), *Glass, Bronzes, Lamps* (Crown, New York, 1971).

tiger-eye. *See* crystalline glaze.

Tile Shop, The. *See* Bragdon, William Victor.

Till, Reginald. English ceramic designer, employed by the Poole potteries, *Carter & Co. and *Carter, Stabler & Adams in the production of glazed wares at East Quay and tiles at Hamworthy. He started work at Poole in 1923, immediately after studying at the Royal College of Art, where he had been inspired by the 15th-century maiolica of the Della Robbia family, and his designs had attracted the attention of H.*Stabler. He designed the firm's stand at the Ideal Home Exhibition in 1927, and experimented with a technique in which stencil designs were sprayed on tiles. He devised a setting in Moorish style with stencilled tiles for a stand at the Building Trades Exhibition in 1930, which was later installed in the showroom at the East Quay Works. Till also used tube-lined decoration, especially on non-slip tiles for swimming pools.
Ref: Hawkins.

Tillowitz. German porcelain factory established at Tillowitz, Silesia, Poland, in 1852 under the protection of the Count of Frankenburg. The factory was owned and managed by Erhard Schlegelmilch in 1894 and remained in operation well into the 20th century.

A factory established at Tillowitz in 1869 by Reinhold Schlegelmilch produced high-quality porcelain tablewares.

Faience and other earthenwares were produced at Tillowitz by Johann Degotschon from 1804.

Marks of the porcelain factories sometimes incorporate the place name. A shield bearing three rectangles is recorded for the E. Schlegelmilch factory in the early 20th century; Schlegelmilch used a wreath topped by a star and other marks containing the initials RS, sometimes with *Poland China/Made in Poland*. Degotschon used the marks *T, Tb* or *Tillowitz*.
Refs: Cushion (1980); Danckert.

tin glaze. A glaze which is made opaque by the addition of tin oxide. Tin glazes are ancient in origin and were used, e.g., in Assyria by the 8th century BC.

Tin-glazed earthenware, mainly painted with coloured oxides, but also decorated in relief or, as a later development, with painted enamels, is the material of *maiolica, *faience (produced notably in France, Germany and Scandinavia), Dutch Delft, and English delftware. These wares were made extensively until the 17th and early 18th centuries, but the technique of tin glaze was not one which lent itself readily to mass-production. The painting of oxide pigments on a dry, powdery glaze that had been applied to biscuit ware was costly, kiln losses were high, and the soft earthenware bodies made for a comparatively bulky, fragile ware. Tin-glazed wares were largely superseded by cream-coloured earthenware during the 18th century, except in rural areas and as a medium for individual artists.

Maiolica, developed in Spain and then Italy, was painted with patterns in lustre notably at Deruta and Gubbio in the 16th century. Copies of ware made by the Della Robbia family were among the early tin-glazed wares imitated by U.*Cantagalli. Lustre wares provided inspiration for W. *De Morgan, who rediscovered the process of lustre painting after research in the 1870s.

tin glaze. Bowl made in Milan, late 19th century. Lorentz, Milano *incised on the base.*

A.*Metthey, who worked on tin glazes before he went over to white earthenware with clear glaze is regarded as a pioneer in the revival of painted tin-glazed ware and was followed by a number of artist potters. The Swedish painter, Isaak Grunewald, used tin-glazed ware made at Rörstrand, for his Cubist/Functionalist paintings on vases. Other painters of tin-glazed ware included V.*Bell and D.*Grant, using wares produced by R.*Fry and the Omega workshops, Picasso and, later, G.*Portanier working at Vallauris. The French ceramic sculptors P.*Pouchol, G.*Carbonnel and G.*Jouve used tin-glazed ware as a medium for modelling.
Refs: A. Caiger-Smith *Tin-glaze Pottery* (Faber, London, 1973); W. Gaunt & M.D.E. Clayton-Stamm *William De Morgan* (Studio Vista, London, 1971); C. Piccolpasso *Three Books of the Potter's Art* ed. R. Lightbown & A. Caiger-Smith (Scolar Press, London, 1978).

Tinworth, George (1843-1913). English sculptor and modeller. The son of a London wheelwright, Tinworth initially worked for his father, studying modelling in the evenings at the Lambeth School of Art. He entered the Royal Academy Schools in late 1864 and first exhibited at the Academy in 1866. He assisted in the first commission given by H.*Doulton to students of the Lambeth Art School, modelling in terracotta (to designs

*George Tinworth. Salt-glazed group of frogs and mice, Hunting, modelled by Tinworth for *Doulton & Co., c.1884-86. 12.1 cm high.*

by John Sparkes) the heads of potters, and female heads representing their native countries, for the façade of an extension to the Lambeth Pottery in 1864. He began regular work at the pottery in 1866, at first modelling terracotta medallions after Greek and Sicilian coins and later designing and modelling decorative reliefs for stoneware vases. He worked with newly thrown clay, incising foliate patterns and applying relief ornament, which included spiral bands, often intricately interlocked or frilled. A jug exhibited in 1874 was decorated with scenes from Christ's Passion, separated by niches holding single, related figures from the Old Testament. Tinworth also executed a relief for the reredos in York Minster and became noted for terracotta plaques in high relief, as well as statuary fountains and occasionally pulpits or fonts for churches and private chapels. Although most of his work was religious in inspiration, he also modelled small figures of boy musicians, and animals engaged in human occupations, e.g. mice watching Punch and Judy, a set of mouse musicians, and frogs playing cricket, canoeing, or going to the races. Some of the small figures were designed as chess pieces. Other articles included an oval mirror frame decorated with a low-relief portrait of a girl with flowing hair, holding a hand mirror, c.1905. Tinworth was employed at the Doulton factory until his death.

Mark: incised monogram of GT.
Refs: see Doulton & Co.

Tirschenreuth. German porcelain factory established 1838 in Bavaria by Heinrich K. Eichhorn, who had in the previous year purchased a porcelain factory at Schney. August Bauscher (*see* Bauscher Brothers) was a partner for a time until 1880. The firm, which made tableware, was taken over in 1927 by Lorenz Hutschenreuther (*see* Hutschenreuther family).

Marks include a shield with the initials PT; a crown with OBERPFALZCHINA/BAVARIA; TIRSCHENREUTH/*1838* across a shield in an oval mark with HUTSCHENREUTHER GRUPPE/GERMANY.
Refs: Danckert; Weiss.

Titanian ware. *See* Doulton & Co.

Tittensor, Charles (b 1763). Staffordshire potter, a partner in a small pottery at Hanley by 1802 and working from the following year with his brother John. Tittensor worked in the firm Tittensor & Simpson (1807-13), and then (1815-25) as sole proprietor of a works in Queen Street, Shelton, where he made earthenware, including figures in a style resembling that of J.*Walton. The subjects, ranging from country people standing against a bocage to cherubs holding urns or columns (and often on a tiered rectangular base), were painted in bright enamel colours (with strong blue, yellow and orange often prominent) and frequently stood on a base coloured with translucent green.
Mark: TITTENSOR, impressed.
Refs: Haggar (1955); H.A.B. Turner

Harry Tittensor. Figure, The Mermaid, modelled by Tittensor for Doulton & Co., produced 1918-36.

A Collector's Guide to Staffordshire Pottery Figures (McGibbon & Kee, London, 1971).

Tittensor, Harry (1886-1942). English ceramic artist, noted for his painting of figure subjects. He was apprenticed at *Doulton & Co. in Burslem from 1900 and trained at Burslem School of Art, where he was later to become a teacher. He painted vases with classical, literary and genre subjects, decorated examples of Rembrandt ware, and assisted in the artistic development of Holbein and Titanian wares, and the company's output of modelled figures. After leaving Doulton & Co. in 1925, Tittensor worked as a painter in oil and watercolour and taught at various schools of art.
Refs: see Doulton & Co.

Tobe. Japanese ceramic centre to the south of Matsuyama on the island of Shikoku. A long-established production of stoneware was followed in the 1770s by the making of porcelain, initially white and later painted in cobalt blue under the glaze, with landscapes, bamboo, maple leaf, flower and lattice patterns. Paper stencils, introduced in the late 19th century to replace hand painting, were still in use in the late 1940s. The ware was mass-produced for sale in Japan and countries of S.E. Asia. Recently, studio potters have started to produce vases and tableware.
Refs: Munsterberg; Okamura.

Toby jugs. Jugs made in earthenware representing a man, usually holding a jug of beer and a pipe or glass, and wearing a three-cornered hat; made from the mid 18th century, by many potters. Similar jugs represent 'Bluff King Hal', 'Hearty Goodfellow' (standing), and Admiral Howe. Makers of Toby jugs included J.*Walton, also the producer of a female version, Martha Gunn, who

represents a bathing-machine attendant, and wears a tricorne hat with Prince-of-Wales feathers on the brim; also E.*Wood and, in the 20th century, Doulton & Co., Lambeth, and *Wiltshaw & Robinson in the 1920s.
Ref: D. Eyles 'Good Sir Toby' in Haggar (1955).

Todaya Tokuji or **Kyokuzan** (d 1883). Japanese potter, born in Kanazawa and making *Kutani ware. He was the son of Todaya Tokuemon (1792-1873), who had studied decoration under *Mokubei and worked at the *Kasugayama kiln. Using the artistic names Kyokuzan or Saiunro Kyokuzan, and marking his work with those seals, Todaya Tokuji worked with his father at the *Minzan kiln. He started work on his own account at about the time of his father's death, subsequently producing mainly utilitarian porcelain with *aka-e decoration and marked with a seal, Mukaiyama.
Refs: Jenyns (1965); Nakagawa; Roberts.

Toft, Charles (1831-1909). Staffordshire potter and designer. Toft trained in his home town of Stoke-on-Trent, and in the 1850s modelled figures and busts for production in parian ware by Kerr & Binns in *Worcester (e.g. a bust, possibly of Sir Walter Scott, signed *C. Toft fecit*, c.1855) and *Mintons Ltd (e.g. a bust of the Duke of Wellington, dated 1853). Toft also carried out designs for the *Bristol Pottery in 1854. He is best known for the design of Henri II ware at Mintons in the 1860s and 1870s, and is recorded as a pupil of L.-M.-E.*Solon in the technique of *pâte-sur-pâte*. Toft taught at the Birmingham School of Art in the late 1860s, also designing metalwork for the Birmingham firm of Elkington & Co. As chief modeller for J.*Wedgwood & Sons Ltd, 1872-89, he worked, among other things, on a medallion portrait of W.E. Gladstone,

Toby jug. Jug depicting Martha Gunn, made in Yorkshire, c.1800. 27.5 cm high.

Charles Toft. Jug made by Toft for *Mintons Ltd. 23.5 cm high.

a vase representing 'Peace and War' for the firm's display in the Exposition Universelle in Paris (1878), models adapted from designs by W.*Crane, a self-closing jug lid. In 1899, Toft established a small factory at Stoke-on-Trent, where he made rustic wares, including earthenware with lacy decoration in brown and white slip.

Marks include TOFT on reproductions of St Porchaire ware.
Refs: Aslin & Atterbury; Batkin; Reilly & Savage; Sandon (1978a); Cleo Witt 'Good Cream Colour Ware—The Bristol Pottery 1786-1968' in *The Connoisseur* (September 1979).

Tokoname. Japanese pottery centre about 32 kilometres south of *Nagoya. Tokoname, one of the Six Ancient Kilns, was most active from the Heian (781-1184) to Muromachi (1338-1568) periods in the production of large storage jars, plates, cinerary urns, etc., for a rural market. In the 19th century, the area was known for reddish brown, unglazed stoneware (Shudei ware), flower-pots and saké bottles, sometimes decorated with incised patterns of birds or trees. Other decorative effects included a partial coating of black lacquer, or the sharkskin effect of small drops of black enamel. The output is now restricted to drainage ware, tiles and other industrially produced ware, apart from the work of studio potters, including Rakusen Asai, who continue the production of unglazed ware, in fine-grained red clay (obtained locally), which they burnish with metal tools before wood firing.
Refs: Jenyns (1971); Mizuo; Sanders.

Tokuji. *See* Todaya Tokuji.

Tokuzan (1755-1837). Japanese potter and Buddhist priest. Tokuzan worked in Tokyo

on the production of pottery resembling *raku ware, for which he used coarse clay from *Shigaraki.
Marks: inscription, stamped, later engraved.
Ref: Roberts.

Tomimoto Kenkichi (1886-1963). Japanese potter and printmaker, born in Nara prefecture. He studied architecture in Tokyo, graduating in 1909, a year after his first visit to England, where he returned in 1911 after completing a study trip to India. Tomimoto worked in Japan with B.*Leach from 1912, becoming joint successor with Leach to the title of Kenzan VII. He established his own pottery at his birthplace, Ando, in 1915. His work was initially inspired by Korean Yi dynasty pottery. He later produced porcelain inspired by Chinese wares and painted in underglaze blue or enamels with delicate landscapes, birds or flowers. He developed an exceptionally pure white paste.

Tomimoto visited Japanese ceramic centres at Seto, Kyoto and Shigaraki to study large-scale production methods, etc., c.1919 and paid a further visit to Shigaraki in 1929, making teapots and stoves decorated in iron and copper pigments with a version of the landscape ('country road, narrow road') that he had first used early in his pottery making. Having worked for a time in Tamagawa, he moved to Shoshigaya, Tokyo, in 1927, and Kyoto in the 1940s. He initiated the ceramics section of the Nitten Academy in 1934, and began the Shinsho Craft Association for the encouragement of young potters in 1947. In 1949, he established a ceramics department at the municipal college of fine art at Kyoto, where he became professor in 1950 and college principal in 1958. Tomimoto was also one of the leaders of the folk art movement (*see* mingei ware). In 1955, he was designated Holder of the Technique for Enamelled Porcelain, which made up a large proportion of his later output, and for which he developed a lavish style using gold and silver. He received the Order of Cultural Merit in 1961.
Refs: Cort; Jenyns (1965); Koyama; Leach (1966); Living National Treasures; Masterpieces; Miller; Okada; Roberts; Sanders.

Tominosuke Miyazaki. *See* Kenzan.

Tomlinson, William. *See* Ferrybridge or Knottingley Pottery.

Tomimoto Kenkichi. Earthenware bowl painted in enamel colours. Late 19th, early 20th century.

Toneo Kikuyama. *See* Iga ware.

Toorop, Jean Theodoor or Jan (1858-1928). Ceramist, decorator and designer, born in the East Indies and working in Holland as a designer of tile-panels in relief for De *Porceleyne Fles and *Rozenburg.
Marks include the initials J.T.
Refs: Scheen; Singelenberg-van der Meer.

Tooth, Henry. English artist and pottery manager. After apprenticeship to a butcher, Tooth worked as a theatrical scene painter in London in the 1860s. He was employed as manager at the *Linthorpe Pottery (1879) on C.*Dresser's recommendation, despite his lack of any experience in ceramics other than work at a brickworks at the age of 14 years. He spent some months gaining experience in Staffordshire potteries before completing the journey to Middlesbrough from his home on the Isle of Wight. At Linthorpe, he successfully organized the expansion of the output; he also designed glaze effects with the help of H. Venables, manager of the clay department. Meanwhile, he worked as an artist, carrying out freelance contracts in Middlesbrough. In partnership with A.*Ault from 1882, Tooth established the *Bretby Art Pottery in 1883. His own company, Tooth & Co., continued the pottery from 1887 until 1933.

Mark: monogram of initials, HT.
Refs: Blacker (1922a); *Christopher Dresser 1834-1904* (catalogue, Fine Art Society, London, 1972); J.R.A. Le Vine *Linthorpe Pottery: an Interim Report* (Teesside Museums and Art Galleries Service, 1970); Haslam (1975); Lloyd Thomas (1974).

Top Pottery. Yorkshire pottery established 1790 in Rawmarsh by William Hawley (*see* Hawley family). The pottery made earthenware, including decorative jugs and loving cups painted overglaze with flowers, portraits, etc., and commemorative inscriptions, also using some modelled ornament, e.g. a dog on the handle of a jug painted with hounds. Hawley was succeeded by his wife Elizabeth and their sons. Elizabeth Hawley is thought to have made domestic ware and tiles, carrying on some export trade to Australia. The later output included transfer-printed ware. George Hawley went on to run the *Low Pottery and subsequently the *Northfield Pottery, leaving his brother Abraham to manage the Top Pottery, which closed after its sale in 1858.
Mark: HAWLEY impressed.
Refs: Grabham; Jewitt; Lawrence.

Torksey, Lincolnshire. *See* Walker, Samuel or George.

Torquay Terra-Cotta Co. English pottery established at Hele Cross on the outskirts of Torquay, South Devon, in 1875, with the aim of promoting terracotta as a ceramic art. Using fine-textured clay which fired to a light orange-red, the pottery produced slip-cast, and in some cases turned, ewers, bottles, jugs, butter coolers, toilet trays and other domestic items, as well as vases, spill jars, candlesticks, tobacco jars, etc., all carefully finished. The pottery's figures included reproductions of work by contemporary sculptors, moulded and undercut by hand, small, finely finished portrait busts, and models of birds. Vases in classical shapes were painted with detailed mythological scenes on light slip, or underglaze flower studies by Alexander Fisher, painter and decorator, whose son was also employed at the pottery before becoming a designer of metalwork. Other artists included H.A. *Birbeck. By 1882, the firm advertised decoration in slip, underglaze pigments or enamel, and naturalistic painting of plant forms, etc.

In the 1890s the pottery produced a wide range of glazed ware including pieces with flown glazes shading e.g. from purple, green or blue to white, that were imitated by other Torquay potters until the 1920s. *Sgraffito* designs of flowers were used under an amber glaze.

After its closure c.1904-c.1908, the pottery reopened under the Torquay Pottery Co. for the production of glazed wares printed with rustic landscapes, fishing boats, roses and other flowers on shaded grounds of slip, and birds with bright plumage, notably kingfishers. Moulded pieces included Toby and other portrait jugs, but most of the output was thrown. A blue ground was used after World War I, with simple, brightly painted decoration. The firm later concentrated on small novelty items, including containers for Devon Violets perfume, and closed in 1939. The proprietor, Enoch Staddon, began the production of souvenir ware at his home near Torquay at the end of World War II.

Mark: monogram of TTC, impressed; TORQUAY impressed; the firm's full name, printed.
Ref: Lloyd Thomas (1978).

Tortat, J. *See* Besnard, Ulysse.

Totoki. A line of potters starting with the third son of Korean potter Sonkai, founder of the first *Agano kiln, who went with two of his sons to establish the *Yatsushiro kiln, leaving his wife, son-in-law and third son, Totoki Magozoemon, in Agano. Both parts of the family remained under the patronage of local feudal lords.

Totoki Hosho, the fifth generation, became known for hand-modelled pieces. He was encouraged by the feudal lord of the Agano kilns to study in Tokyo and from 1804 in Kyoto. He made imitations of *raku ware on his return to Agano.

Totoki VIII worked as the last official potter at Agano Sarayama. His work included slab-built pieces.
Ref: Kozuru *Agano & Takatori Wares* (Kodansha, 1982).

Tough, Robert and Thomas. *See* Musselburgh Pottery.

Toussaint-Bougon, Pierre-Louis. *See* Chantilly.

Towne, Louis, H. *See* American Art Clay Works.

Townley. *See* Townsend, Edward.

Townsend, Edward (1904-78). Porcelain painter working for the *Worcester Royal Porcelain Co. from 1918. Townsend specialized in the painting of fruit, but also painted studies of birds, fish, cattle and particularly sheep. He became assistant foreman of the painters under H.*Davis, with a break for war service, 1942-47, and succeeded Davis as foreman 1954-71.

The pseudonym, *Townley*, appears on his tinting of printed outline patterns of the 1920s and 1930s.
Ref: Sandon (1978a).

Townshend, Henry James (1810-90). English painter and designer, initially trained as a surgeon; born in Taunton, Somerset. His work was exhibited at the Royal Academy 1839-66. Townshend executed designs for wood engravings and etchings as well as ceramics. Work produced by *Mintons Ltd included the Hop Story jug (1846) commissioned by H.*Cole, and a jug depicting coaching and rail travel, c.1847. Parian figures included the infant Neptune, shown in the Great Exhibition, 1851.
Refs: Aslin & Atterbury; Godden (1968); Shinn.

Toyosuke. (c.1788-1858). Japanese potter and lacquer artist, born in the Seto region. A kiln founded by his family at Horaku, near Nagoya, made red and black *raku wares, including tea bowls with painted decoration of cranes, etc., in 1820. Oki Toyosuke introduced a method of applying decorative lacquer to glazed pottery (1830), making ware known as Toyosuke ware or Horaku ware, and adapted the technique to porcelain decoration in 1844.

By the 1880s, the kiln was making sweet dishes, vases, boxes and other domestic articles in a fawn-coloured body, lined with an opaque crackled glaze and painting of sprays or baskets of flowers, or splashes of green enamel, and partially covered on the outside with black or dark green lacquer with coloured designs, silvered or gilded. The output also included figures for household shrines.
Refs: Audsley & Bowes; K. Herberts *Das Buch der ostasiatischen Lackkunst* (Econ-Verlag, Düsseldorf, 1959); Munsterberg; Roberts; B. von Ragué *Geschichte der Japanischen Lackkunst* (Walter de Gruyter & Co., Berlin, 1967); T. Yoshino *Japanese Lacquer Ware* (Japan Travel Bureau, Tokyo, 1959).

Tozan. *See* Ito Tozan.

Traditional Poole. *See* Carter, Truda.

transfer printing. A decorative method in which an engraved print is made on paper, with which it is transferred to a ceramic surface, glazed or unglazed. The process was in use from the mid 18th century in England, at first on glazed wares, and was adopted in other countries in response to export from England in large quantities. Transfer-printed porcelain was made at Bow (1756) and *Worcester (1757), and printing in underglaze blue began by 1759. The Liverpool decorators, Sadler & Green, in partnership from 1763, were specialists in transfer printing, and there were departments in many Staffordshire factories devoted to blue printing by the 1780s. The process was widely used in Swansea, Yorkshire (notably at the *Leeds Pottery), in the north-east of England, and in Scotland.

In the related process, bat printing, first used in Staffordshire c.1777, a flexible sheet (bat) of glue or gelatine was used to transfer a pattern in oil from a copper engraving to glazed ware. Colour was dusted on the oil before firing.

Patterns, initially mainly *chinoiseries*, of which the firm of J.*Spode was an important producer, began to include European elements in design in the early 19th century, e.g. floral borders surrounding a Chinese scene; later there were mixed patterns with perhaps Egyptian, Oriental and Western motifs occurring in the same central pattern. Within the period c.1815-35, large export markets opened in North America, Europe, India and other countries. The patterns in production included views from engravings by contemporary artists. Borders were often floral, and a border pattern would be used to provide a link between the pieces of a service with a range of central patterns.

Gold printing had been introduced c.1810, and other underglaze colours (black, green, red, purple, brown and yellow) were in use by the 1820s, though printing was normally restricted to monochrome in order to keep down costs of production. Transfer printing was also used to reduce the cost of hand painting by providing underglaze guidelines for painting in enamel colours. Polychrome printing was developed in Staffordshire by F.& R.*Pratt in the 1840s. The patterns for mass-production became increasingly standardized; Willow pattern and the similar Broseley pattern (used by *Davenport, J.*Rogers & Son and J.*Wedgwood & Sons) and the floral Asiatic Pheasants pattern were notable. The Copyright Act (1842) restricted the use of patterns which were registered either by manufacturers or by the artists (whose prints were protected once published). Scenes showing mountain landscapes with water, trees, architectural features and sometimes figures became popular. They were sometimes titled, but were often not based on the places named in the title.
Refs: Coysh & Henrywood; Lockett (1972); C. Williams-Wood *English Transfer-Printed Pottery & Porcelain* (Faber, London, 1981).

Trenton China Co. American firm incorporated in 1859 for the manufacture of porcelain, as well as chemicals and clay products, in Trenton, New Jersey. The firm later made a speciality of tableware with vitrified body, sold plain or decorated. The factory closed in 1891.

Mark: TRENTON CHINA. CO/TRENTON, N.J., impressed.
Ref: Barber (1976).

Trenton Potteries Co. American pottery combine formed in 1892 by the merging of five manufacturers of sanitary ware in Trenton, New Jersey:

The Crescent Pottery Co. which had been established in 1881 by the partnership W.S. Hancock and C.H. Cook for the production of cream-coloured and white granite wares, becoming one of the city's leading producers by c.1890.

The Delaware Pottery, started in 1884, making equipment for plumbers, pharmacists and jewellers, and experimenting in the

Trenton Potteries Co. Porcelain urn painted in enamel colours, one of four made for the St Louis World's Fair, 1904. 141 cm high.

production of Belleek ware, with the assistance of William Connelly (d 1890), a former employee of the Belleek factory.

The Empire Pottery, established in 1863 by C.*Coxon in partnership, and operated from 1883 by Alpaugh & Magowan, who produced porcelain and decorated tableware in a white granite body, while specializing in sanitary earthenware.

The Enterprise Pottery, established for the manufacture of sanitary ware by 1880; and the Equitable Pottery. A later firm, the Ideal Pottery, was also part of the group.

Marks incorporate T.P. CO. and a star, with a number at the centre indicating the manufacturing company (1, Crescent; 2, Delaware; 3, Empire; 4, Enterprise; 5, Equitable). The name of the Ideal Pottery appears in the centre of the star, rather than a number. The potteries also used individual marks.
Ref: Barber (1976).

Trenton Pottery Co. American firm incorporated 1865 for the production of earthenware at Trenton, New Jersey. By 1870 it had been purchased by J.*Goodwin (d 1875) in a partnership trading as Taylor, Goodwin & Co. until 1872.
Mark: T.P.CO./CHINA printed in black.
Ref: Barber (1976).

Trent Tile Co. American tileworks established as Harris Manufacturing Co. 1882 in Trenton, New Jersey, trading shortly afterwards as the Trent Tile Co. With I.*Broome as designer and modeller (1883-86), succeeded by W.W.*Gallimore, the company made glazed tiles, panels and, later, soda

water fountains with modelled decoration, as well as tiles with high-relief decoration glazed and sand-blasted to achieve the satiny surface marketed as 'Trent finish'. They also made floor tiles for the Roman Catholic cathedral in Trenton, designed by C.B. *Upjohn, 1938.
Mark: TRENT, impressed.
Refs: Barnard; Kovel & Kovel; K.M. McClinton *Collecting American Victorian Antiques* (Charles Scribner's Sons, New York 1966).

Trentvale Pottery. Short-lived American firm established in 1901 at the California Pottery, which had produced yellow and Rockingham-glazed earthenware at East Liverpool, Ohio, until 1900. The firm's work included lines of art ware resembling *Rookwood Pottery's Standard range, and earthenware with dark blue glaze giving the effect of black over the red body. The works reopened in 1902 after a brief closure, but did not resume the production of art ware.
Refs: Evans; Jervis.

Trent works, Stoke-on-Trent. *See* Jones, George.

Tressemanes, Emilien. *See* Vogt, John.

Trethan, Therese (b 1859). Austrian ceramic designer, working in Vienna, where she was born. She studied at the Kunstgewerbeschule, 1897-1902, and exhibited tableware and tea and coffee sets produced by the firm of J.*Böck at the Austrian museum's winter shows in 1902-03 and the following year. In 1905, she started work for the Wiener Werkstätte.
Marks: a monogram of TT, sometimes enclosed in a circle.
Ref: Neuwirth (1974a).

Triller, Ingrid (b 1905) and Erich (b 1898). Swedish studio potters making stoneware at their own workshop near Stockholm from 1935. Their work is simple in form, with fine, richly coloured glazes inspired by Chinese wares.
Ref: Lagercrantz.

Tripp, Antoine. *See* Annecy.

Trojan ware. *See* Belleview or Bellevue Pottery.

Troxel, Samuel. Pennsylvania potter working in Upper Hanover, Montgomery County c.1823-1833. Montgomery's work included a fluted dish decorated with *sgraffito* design of a vase containing flowers, with an inscription and the date 1823, several pie plates featuring the American eagle in the decorative designs, and a large *jardinière* with incised bands of leaf-shaped ornament, flowers, and raised, crimped clay, dated 1828.
Ref: Barber (1970).

Tsuboya. Japanese pottery established on the island of Okinawa by Korean makers of *Satsuma ware in the 17th century. Some ware was made for the Okinawan royal household, but the output consisted mainly of domestic ware and such items as hip flasks, vases, cinerary urns. Temmoku glazes were frequently used. Pieces were decorated with

slip, either dipped or trailed, inlaid motifs, relief applied or incised, painted under or over the glaze with abstract designs. Production continues to the present day.
Refs: Munsterberg; Okamura.

Tsuchiya family. A line of Japanese potters working at *Fujina and descended from Zenshiro (d 1786), who made copies of *Rakuzan ware. The second generation, Tsuchiya Masayoshi (d 1821) worked under the patronage of Lord Matsudaira Fumai of Matsue, who permitted him use of the artistic name Unzen.
Refs: Brinkley; Mizuo.

Tsuji family. *See* Koran-sha.

Tsunezaemon. *See* Mimpei.

Tsutsumi ware. Japanese folk ware made at Tsutsumi, near Sendai, in Miyagi prefecture. A ceramic centre of ancient origin, Tsutsumi maintained an output of tiles and then, in medieval times, a variety of unglazed earthenwares. An industry starting with the production of black roof tiles in the early 17th century developed with the establishment of an official kiln in 1684, which later made kitchen wares for general sale locally. Tsutsumi ware (the name given to the ware from c.1897) included large storage jars with a white rice-bran ash glaze (nuka-jiro) trickled over a black glaze (kurogusuri). Useful ware was mass-produced. Only the Hariu kiln remains in full operation, although pipes are still made in the area.
Refs: Mizuo; Munsterberg.

tube-lining. The decoration of ceramics with thin outlines of slip, which are trailed on the surface to contain coloured glazes which form the pattern. W.*Moorcorft used trailed-slip outlines in the decoration of hollow ware from the late 1890s, and the technique was extensively used for tiles. A similar effect can be achieved with the use of moulded outlines.
Ref: Lockett (1979).

Tucker, Thomas (1812-90). American porcelain maker; younger brother of W.E. *Tucker. He joined William Tucker's factory as an apprentice in 1828 and remained as superintendent under J.*Hemphill after his brother's death. He leased the factory from Hemphill for some months in 1837, but carried on production long enough to amass stock for a shop which he opened in Philadelphia, afterwards selling ware imported from Europe. He sold the contents of the shop in 1841 and entered the cotton business. Design books, which he kept in considerable detail, contain over 140 standard patterns for tableware and vases. They are preserved in the Philadelphia Museum of Art.
Refs: Barber (1976); Clement (1947); P.H. Curtis in *Ceramics in America* (conference report, Henry Francis du Pont Winterthur Museum, Winterthur, Delaware/University Press of Virginia at Charlottesville, 1972); James; Jervis; Ramsay.

Tucker, William Ellis (d 1832). Pioneer American porcelain manufacturer. While working as a teacher, Tucker also decorated imported porcelain at a china store owned

William E. Tucker. Porcelain pitcher made by Tucker at the United States Pottery in Philadelphia, 1827-28. 24.1 cm high.

until 1823 by his father Benjamin Tucker, a Quaker schoolmaster and businessman in Philadelphia. After attending lectures at the Franklin Institute of Pennsylvania and talks given by his father on science in industry and the applied arts, he became interested in the formulation of a porcelain paste, carrying out experiments from 1821. He worked as a merchant of dry goods from 1823 and first attempted production of creamware in 1825 and porcelain the following year. He went briefly into partnership with John Bird and bought a feldspar quarry near Wilmington, Delaware, in 1827. Tucker purchased blue clay from Mutton Hollow, New Jersey, and was later (1831) to lease kaolin beds in West Chester, Pennsylvania. His early work, produced 1826-31 at a former waterworks in Philadelphia, was white or gilt, and then decorated with butterflies, flowers or landscapes (some after river scenes drawn by Thomas Birch in 1824) painted only in charcoal, brown or sepia. With Thomas Hulme of Philadelphia briefly in partnership from 1828 until late 1829, the firm traded as Tucker & Hulme, China Manufacturers. Decoration took the form of flowers and fruit, painted over the glaze in bright colours, or simple bands of gilding. In partnership with J.*Hemphill in 1831, Tucker built a new factory in Philadelphia, which Tucker & Hemphill operated as the American China Manufactory. By the time of Tucker's death, the factory was producing a wide range of table, household and decorative ware, but the firm seems to have specialized in jugs and pitchers, which closely followed European styles of the time. His brother, T. *Tucker, who had joined the business in 1828, remained as superintendent until 1837 under Hemphill.

Tucker's porcelain was rarely marked. Known marks included, initially, *William Ellis Tucker/Manufacturer/Philadelphia; Tucker & Hulme/China Manufacturers/Philadelphia/1828* or *Tucker & Hulme/* MANUFACTURERS/*Philadelphia 1828.*
Refs: Barber (1976); Clement (1947); P.H. Curtis in *Ceramics in America* (conference

report, Henry Francis du Pont Winterthur Museum, Winterthur, Delaware/University Press of Virginia at Charlottesville, 1972); James; Jervis; Ramsay.

tulip ware. American slipware made in Pennsylvania by immigrant German potters, who settled in America in the 17th and 18th centuries. Stylized tulips were among the characteristic subjects in decoration.
Ref: Barber (1970).

Tulk, Cornelius. *See* Porceleyne Fles, De.

Tumanov, Stepan. Russian ceramic chemist. Tumanov experimented from 1918 to develop ceramic paints which became unobtainable after the Revolution, because earlier potters either destroyed secrets or fled with them, and none could be imported. He had discovered the formulae for three colours by the end of 1919 and a gilding technique by 1927. He later owned the USSR's biggest china paint factory at Dulevo.
Ref: Ovsyannikov.

Tunnicliffe, Pascoe. *See* Ashby Potters' Guild.

Tunnicliffe, Robert. *See* Pilkington's Tile & Pottery Co.

Tunstall, John. *See* Chesapeake Pottery.

Turner, Joseph. *See* Bell, John.

Turner, Nathaniel. *See* Jersey City Pottery.

Turton, Robert. Potter, born in Chesterfield, Derbyshire, and working in New South Wales, Australia, from c.1851. He established the production of bricks and drainage ware at Waratah, a suburb of Newcastle, in the mid 1850s, extending his output in 1866 to include salt-glazed ware for household use, which comprised thrown jars, jugs, mugs, and flowerpots, decorated with moulded relief patterns. He was working in partnership with his son Francis Turton by 1872. J.*Silcock became manager and later proprietor of Turton's works.

In the early 20th century, a firm, Turton & Co. Ltd (later Turton Ltd), operated a brickworks at East Maitland, New South Wales, where salt-glazed decorative ware (e.g. figures of dogs) was made in a light, white body.

20th century mark: TURTON LTD/MAITLAND.
Ref: Graham.

Tuscan China Works, Longton. *See* Plant, R.H.& S.L., Ltd.

Tustin, Sidney (b 1913) and Charles. English potters employed at the *Winchcombe Pottery. After joining the pottery in 1927, Sidney Tustin was officially apprenticed 1930-34, and worked there (with a break during World War II) until his retirement in 1978. Sharing a workshop with E.*Comfort, he threw small jugs, bowls, egg cups and dishes, butter coolers, jam pots, etc. His brother, Charles, joined the pottery in the early 1930s, and became apprenticed 1935-39 as a thrower of beakers and small pots, using a kick wheel. After conscription (1940-46), he remained at the pottery until 1954.
Refs: see Winchcombe Pottery.

Tuxedo Pottery Co. *See* Phoenixville Pottery.

Twigg, Joseph (d c.1843), sons Joseph (d 1860s), John (d 1877) and Benjamin, and grandson, Daniel. Yorkshire potters. Joseph Twigg, formerly manager of the Old Pottery at Swinton, established the Newhill Works at Wath-upon-Dearne in 1809 for the production of earthenware, remaining proprietor until his death. The early work was influenced in style by the *Swinton Pottery. After the purchase of moulds, transfer plates and other equipment in the sale of the *Don Pottery's stock (1835) the pottery produced plates with a moulded pattern of thistles under green glaze, and included Italian scenes among the transfer-printed patterns. Sponged ware was also produced. Twigg was succeeded by the firm of Coulter, Dibb & Co. (1867-71) and the pottery closed c.1873 after further changes in ownership, although bricks were made there briefly until 1876.

Twigg's sons Benjamin, Joseph and John followed the *Brameld family as operators of the *Kilnhurst Old Pottery in 1839, and became owners in 1853, trading as Joseph Twigg & Brothers. John Twigg's son, Daniel, was manager from 1877 until his retirement in 1884.

Marks: TWIGG/NEWHILL, impressed, 1822-66; TWIGG in an oval, impressed c.1820-40; TWIGG'S, impressed; *see also* Kilnhurst.
Refs: Grabham; Jewitt; Lawrence.

Tyne Main Pottery. English pottery established on the south bank of the River Tyne at Newcastle in 1831. Under proprietors Richard Davies & Co. (1831-44), R.C. Wilson (1844-51) and D. McGregor (1852-53), the works produced white, printed and lustre ware, often for export to Norway.

Marks include DAVIES or DAVIES & CO, impressed.
Ref: Bell.

Tyne Pottery. *See* Fell, Isaac.

Uhlstädt. German porcelain factory established 1837 at Uhlstädt by Carl Alberti for the production of everyday wares. The present-day factory, successor to Alberti's, is nationally owned.

Printed marks: monogram of CA

Sidney Tustin. Black-glazed jug with pattern in trailed slip, made by Tustin at the Winchcombe Pottery, late 1920s or 1930s.

surmounted by a coronet, sometimes with UHLSTÄDT in a cartouche; monogram of UP. *Refs:* Danckert; Weiss.

Ulysse. *See* Besnard, Ulysse.

underglaze colours. *See* high-temperature colours.

Unicorn Bank, Longport. *See* Davenport's.

Union Française, L'. French porcelain manufacturers established at Saint-Genou (Indre) in 1930 for the production of tableware, gifts, smokers' requisites, etc.
    Mark: a triangle, rounded at the corners, containing *L'uf* and FRANCE PORCELAINE. *Refs:* Danckert; Weiss.

Union Porcelain Works. American porcelain factory in Greenpoint, New York, bought initially as an investment by T.C.*Smith, from the firm of W.*Boch, in 1863. On his return from a visit to Europe, where he observed porcelain production, Smith enlarged the Greenpoint Works, bought a quarry to provide him with feldspar, imported Cornish kaolin, and started production of the machinery and tools needed in porcelain manufacture. He produced soft-paste porcelain door furniture, hardware trimmings, vases and dishes until 1865, when he began to market exclusively hard-paste porcelain, in the white and then decorated, at first experimentally, from 1866. Most of the output consisted of mass-produced lines, but Smith's Union Porcelain Works also produced art ware, for which it became nationally known, using only original designs. Painting on plates and plaques by the decorator, J.M. Falconer, included views of Centennial buildings. K.*Müller, who joined the firm as chief designer and modeller in 1874, was responsible for parian statuettes, the Century vase and other special or commemorative pieces. The output included

*Union Porcelain Works. The Century vase, designed by K.*Müller, 1876. 55 cm high.*

*University City Pottery. Porcelain vase by E.*Diffloth with beige glaze and green crystalline spots. Printed circular mark, American Woman's League UC 1910 and painted monogram of ED. 12.7 cm high.*

mugs with relief decoration highlighted with enamel, angular vases with oriental designs in embossed gilding and enamelled jewels, and table services with underglaze blue decoration outlined in gold; an oyster plate was made c.1880 in a style adapted from Palissy ware. By c.1891, the works produced porcelain tiles with underglaze decoration for uses in which the ability to withstand heat was important, and with overglaze painting for walls, mantelpieces, etc. Large tile panels in the company's office were decorated with scenes of Egyptian pottery-making. Smith was succeeded in 1900 by his son C.H.L. Smith, an engineer, who concentrated on machine production of domestic, hotel and institutional tablewares, hardware trimmings, electrical insulators, etc., as well as tiles. C.H.L. Smith died in the 1920s, and the Union Porcelain Works closed soon afterwards.

Marks: the head of an eagle holding s in its beak, impressed on porcelain from 1876, or in underglaze green from 1877; other marks incorporate the firm's name. *Refs:* Barber (1976); J. Brown & D. Ment *Factories, Foundries and Refineries. A History of Five Brooklyn Industries* (Brooklyn Rediscovery/Brooklyn Educational & Cultural Alliance, 1981).

United States Potters' Association. *See* Brewer, John Hart.

United States Pottery. *See* Gager, Oliver A.

United States Pottery Co. *See* Fenton, Christopher Webber.

University City Pottery. Ceramics department of the American Woman's League, a business operating from 1907 in University City, near St Louis, Missouri, for the education and general advancement of women. Under

the joint sponsorship of the Lewis Publishing Co. of St Louis and the American Woman's League from 1908, members of the league enrolled in a programme of correspondence courses, and those who showed conspicuous ability were invited to study as honours students at University City. Schools of education, languages, journalism, photography, and artistic and business subjects were planned. The school of ceramic art operated under the direction of T.*Doat, who began its organization in 1909. His associates included Edward Gardner Lewis, founder of the league, and his wife Mabel, both potters who worked at University City, A.A.*Robineau, and F.H.*Rhead who, as pottery instructor, was assisted in the course by Edward *Dahlquist and E.*Diffloth. 300 students learned the techniques of overglaze painting on porcelain through a correspondence course, and about thirty others at University City; the ceramics department had a maximum of thirty correspondence students and about ten in University City. Although students were allowed to specialize

University City Pottery. Porcelain vase with brown-speckled ochre and celadon crystalline glaze, initialled by Mabel Lewis, c.1910. 17 cm high.

in such techniques as decorating or throwing, they were encouraged to train in the entire process of ceramic production. The correspondence course in ceramics dealt with the preparation of clay and glazes, throwing, hand building, mould making, glazing and firing, with the help of photographs. Half of the profits from sales of honours students' work was used in the upkeep of the pottery. Using native clays, the pottery was noted for the high quality of porcelain produced there, and the wide range of glazes, all fired at a high temperature, which included matt and glossy surfaces, crackle, *flambé* and crystalline effects. Styles were dominated by the work of Doat and Mrs Robineau; some forms had been developed by Doat in France, e.g. a gourd shape on which *flambé* or crystalline glazes were used. Lower-fired ware, made under Rhead's guidance, was simply and freely decorated, sometimes with incised designs. When the American Woman's League failed in 1911, Doat continued production, with W.V.*Bragdon as chemist, and the pottery was reorganized in 1912, finally ceasing operation by early 1915.

Various marks, including UP impressed; several containing initials UC; circular mark WOMAN'S INDUSTRIAL CORP/*University City, Mo.* containing GLENMOOR POTTERY; *University City, Mo.* often impressed.
Refs: Brunhammer *et al* (1976); Clark & Hughto; Eidelberg; Evans; 'The American Woman's League, Its Plan and Purpose' in *Everybody's Magazine* (December/January 1908-09); L. Kohlenberger 'Ceramics at the People's University' in *Ceramics Monthly* (November 1976); Kovel & Kovel; S. Morse *The Siege of University City: The Dreyfus Case in America* (University City Publishing, St Louis, 1912).

Uno Soyo (b 1888). Japanese potter, trained until 1908 in the municipal laboratory of ceramic art in Kyoto. He specialized in blue-glazed wares resembling Chinese Kuan wares of the Sung dynasty.
Refs: Masterpieces; Roberts.

Unrinin Banzo (1836-1900). Japanese potter, born in Kinose and mentioned in 1872 as the only maker of porcelain in *Shigaraki*. He carried out research with copper red glazes in the mid 19th century, achieving success in 1868, and made thinly potted saké bottles, sauce bottles, plates, lamps, teapots, etc., with applied relief decoration. He was succeeded at his workshop by his son Shigejiro and spent the last years of his life in Kyoto.
Ref: Cort.

Unrin'in Bunzo. *See* Hozan.

Unterchodau. Bohemian factory established in 1811 for the production of creamware by mine owner Franz Miessel after the discovery of porcelain clay on his estate, Unterchodau. The only known example of the factory's early work is a holy water stoup. Miessel sold the factory in 1834 to Johann Dietl, also a mine owner, and Johann Hüttner, formerly a painter at *Schlaggenwald. The factory's early porcelain dates from the period 1835-45. Biscuit busts of the Empress Maria Anna, and of Archbishop A. Schreutz von Notzing bear the impressed mark *Chodau*. Cups were painted with landscapes or flowers. The firm also made lithophanes in the late 1830s.

The factory was sold in 1845 to Moses Porges von Portheim, who installed his sons Ignaz and Gustav as managers. The output, then chiefly porcelain, included many figures, often comic or sentimental. Some of the firm's vases were decorated with flowers in relief, and such pieces as oil lamps and writing sets were lavishly painted with flowers and gilded ornament. Useful wares, a large part of production, were also painted and embellished with burnished gilding. Shapes, in general low and rounded, resembled those made by the *Haidinger brothers.

In 1872, the Portheim family sold their business interests, and the porcelain factory was immediately re-sold to the firm of Haas & Czjzek of Schlaggenwald for the production of hotel ware, which was exported to Austro-Hungary, the Balkans, Scandinavia, the Netherlands, Great Britain, the United States, Egypt and the Middle East. Production continued, and in 1928 the owners were Olga, Baroness Haas-Hassenfels and Felix Czjzek von Smidaich.
Ref: Meyer.

Unterweissbach. German porcelain factory established 1882 at Unterweissbach, Thuringia and working under the title, Älteste Volkstedter Porzellanfabrik. After producing decorative wares under the firm Mann & Porzelius, the factory was taken over in 1908 by M.A.*Pfeiffer, who operated it as the Schwarzburger Werkstätten and commissioned designs from such established artists as E.*Barlach, G.*Marcks, P.*Scheurich, and Otto Thiem. The firm continues production of a wide range of figures as part of VEB Vereinigte Zierporzellanwerke *Lichte.

Marks: under *Pfeiffer,* U; monogram of AP below a crown; a fox with *Schwarzburger Werkstätten für Porzellankunst*. U below a crown with VEB UNTER/WEISS/BACH
Refs: Danckert; Scherf; Weiss.

Upchurch Pottery. English pottery established in 1913 by S. Wakely at Rainham, Kent. The pottery sent a display to an exhibition of British decorative arts in Paris, 1914. Much of the early work, consisting of vases, etc., in simple shapes with soft-coloured matt glazes, was designed by Edward Spencer (co-founder in 1903 of the Artificers' Guild) and sold through the guild's retail outlets. The workshop closed in 1961.
Mark: UPCHURCH, impressed.
Refs: Cushion (1980); Godden (1964); Haslam (1975).

Upjohn, Charles Babcock (1866-1953). American ceramic designer and potter. Upjohn worked for S.A.*Weller from 1895, and then as designer and modeller at the *Cambridge Art Pottery from 1900. He returned to the Weller Pottery in 1902 and continued the design of a second line of Dickens ware (which he had briefly introduced at the pottery in 1900). He established his own firm, the C.B. Upjohn Pottery Co. in Zanesville, Ohio, 1904, but sold it the following year after financial failure. Upjohn subsequently worked as designer at the *Trent Tile Co., and taught in the education department of Columbia University, 1916-40.
Mark: signature or monogram on designs (probably not made at his own pottery).
Refs: Evans; Kovel & Kovel; Lehner; N.F.

Schneider *Zanesville Art Pottery* (privately published, Zanesville, Ohio, 1963).

Upsala-Ekeby. Swedish ceramics group, centred on a factory established 1886 at Upsala, which produced porcelain from 1918. The firm produced tableware resembling that of *Rörstrand and *Gustavsberg in style. From the mid 1950s, the firm has been known mainly for simple, functional design, with simple, striking decorative motifs, or relying on plain colours for decorative effect. The large staff of designers works under the direction of Marianne Westmann.

Potteries at Gävle (established 1850 for the production of tableware and decorative pieces and making porcelain from 1910), and Karlskröna (established 1918 for the production of everyday ware in porcelain) are also part of the group.

Marks: monogram of UE in a circle; circular marks containing the names and symbols for *Karlskröna* and *Gefle* (Gävle) with *Upsala Ekeby*.
Refs: Beard; Danckert; Lagercrantz; Weiss.

Urbato. *See* Rhead, Frederick Alfred.

Urbino service. *See* Petri-Raben, Trude.

Ushinoto kiln. Japanese kiln established in Tottori prefecture in the Tempo era (1830-44), and producing saké and vinegar bottles, tea bowls, storage jars and a variety of bowls with iron or white slip decoration and transparent, black or green glazes. Through the efforts of Shoya Yoshida (1898-1972), a doctor in the San'in district and instigator of the region's folk-craft movement, as well as local folk-craft cooperatives in Tottori and Takumi, Ushinoto was revived as a folk kiln in the 1920s, after an interruption in production, and has since made tableware to modern designs.
Ref: Mizuo.

Ushkov factory. Russian factory producing earthenware and porcelain in the province of Perm (1842-61) under the owner, G. Ushkov. The output included a basin in earthenware, skilfully painted with a bouquet of flowers, now preserved in the state historical museum.
Mark: owner's name.
Refs: Bubnova; N.N. Serebryannikov *Porcelain and Faience of the Urals in the 19th Century* (Perm, 1926).

Utopian. *See* Owens, John B.

Utzschneider, François-Paul (1771-1844). Bavarian-born potter who worked in France from the outset of the Revolution, after studying ceramic techniques in England. He became director of the factory at *Sarreguemines in 1798, succeeded in 1836 by his son-in-law, A.*de Geiger.
Refs: Ernould-Gandouet; Lesur (1971).

Vale China. *See* Colclough, Herbert J.

Valentien or **Valentine,** Albert R. (1862-1925) and Anna Marie (1862-1947). American ceramic artists. Albert Valentien studied at the Art Academy in his home town, Cincinnati, Ohio, and in Europe. He joined T.J. *Wheatley's class in the decoration of Cincinnati faïence (1879), and himself taught

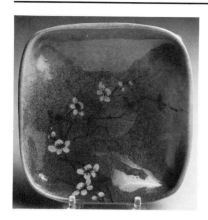

Anna Marie Valentien. Dish with decoration by A.M. Valentien, made at the *Rookwood Pottery, 1883. 15.6 cm square.

underglaze painting in the following year. He was the first artist regularly employed on the staff of the *Rookwood Pottery (1881), soon taking charge of the decorating department. In 1887, he married a fellow Rookwood decorator, Anna Marie Bookprinter, an artist, also born in Cincinnati. The couple travelled to France, where Anna Marie studied under Auguste Rodin and Antoine Bourdell; she afterwards attempted to introduce sculptural pieces at Rookwood, but only a few were produced. Albert Valentien painted vases, plates, etc., with simple, naturalistic designs in underglaze slip, showing flowers, leaves, berried twigs, rushes and fungi, sometimes with birds; a vase dated 1885 is painted with an owl perched on a pine branch. Anna Marie Valentien also painted flowers and other plant forms, as well as modelling relief decoration, e.g. a

Albert R. Valentien. Covered jar designed and made at the *Rookwood Pottery by W. *Auckland in 1885, with painted decoration by Valentien. 19 cm high.

female figure moulded on the rim of an ashtray (1901). The couple left Rookwood in 1905, moving two years later to San Diego, California, where Albert Valentien carried out a commission to paint the native wildflowers, grasses and trees of California, a task which continued over the following ten years and was echoed in the decoration of pottery modelled by Anna Marie Valentien, painted by her husband in San Diego, and possibly produced in association with a banker, J.W. Sefton Jr, owner of a pottery in the city.

Marks: initials, ARV; Bookprinter's monogram and intials AMB or AMV.
Refs: Clark & Hughto; Evans; Kovel & Kovel; Peck.

Vallauris (Alpes-Maritimes). French pottery centre of ancient origin producing lead-glazed domestic earthenware, generally with a greyish-tinged body. Pieces characteristic of the local wares include a cooking pot with the lid hollowed to hold wine for adding to the contents.

The number of potteries increased sharply in the late 19th century and at that time included workshops run by C. *Massier and other members of his family, and the *Foucard-Jourdan pottery. J. *Lenoble studied ceramic techniques in the area when visiting the south of France for his health in the 1920s. Among the many potters who later settled at Vallauris were S. *Ramié and her husband (who produced the work of P. *Picasso at the Madoura Pottery), J. *Derval and G. *Portanier.
Refs: Céramique française contemporaine; Lesur (1971).

Val-sous-Meudon. French pottery established at Val-sous-Meudon (Seine-et-Oise) under the direction of Mittenhoff & Mourot, 1802-07. As well as fine stoneware, the firm made white earthenware, some hand-painted under the glaze with garlands, country scenes or Napoleonic emblems in brown *camaïeu*. The factory was also known in the early 19th century for garden vases made in fine yellow earthenware. The firm moved to rue de Menilmontant in 1807.

Marks include VAL-SOUS-MEUDON/*1807* and the name of the firm or MM, crossed, in a double oval line.
Refs: Ernould-Gandouet; Fontaine; Lesur (1971).

van Beek, Jan Bontjes. *See* Bontjes van Beek, Jan.

Van Briggle, Artus (1869-1904). American painter, pottery decorator and artist potter, born in Ohio. While studying painting at Cincinnati Art Academy from c.1886, Van Briggle also worked as a decorator of dolls' heads and as an apprentice under K. *Langenbeck at the Avon Pottery. A decorator at the *Rookwood Pottery from 1887, he travelled to Europe in 1893 on a painting scholarship granted by the pottery. He studied at the Académie Julian under Jean-Paul Laurens and Benjamin Constant, with clay modelling as part of his sculpture course, and studied painting in Italy, 1894. On his return to Cincinnati in 1896, Van Briggle worked as a painter, continued decoration of Rookwood wares, and carried out his own attempts to reproduce Ming-dynasty

Artus Van Briggle. 'Lorelei' vase with matt turquoise glaze, c.1905. Marked with the double A of the workshop, and Van Briggle, Colo Spgs. 27 cm high.

Chinese matt glazes in a small kiln at home, achieving some success by 1898. By the beginning of the 20th century, Van Briggle had also developed a luminous turquoise glaze and a Persian-inspired shaded pink. His decoration, still executed in underglaze colours, began to include the painting of figures, strongly influenced by Art Nouveau.

Suffering from tuberculosis contracted in his boyhood, Van Briggle moved to Colorado in 1899 and continued research, using local materials and working in a laboratory at Colorado College, assisted by a friend on the college staff. He achieved a successful matt glaze in 1901 and established his own studio in the same year, with backing from M.L. *Nichols Storer. He began the Van Briggle Pottery Co. in 1901, the year before his marriage to artist Anne Louise Gregory (1868-1929), and expanded the pottery, employing a staff of 14 by 1903. He designed and modelled vases, and occasionally plates, with relief decoration of plant forms and sometimes animals, achieving a close relationship between decoration and form which was emphasized by his use of monochrome matt glazes. He incorporated human figures in such designs as the Lady of the Lily (1901), Lorelei, Despondency (both exhibited in Paris, 1903), the Siren of the Sea (exhibited St Louis, 1904) and a toast cup made in 1900.

Van Briggle, his wife, or employees working to their designs, made models for pieces moulded in limited numbers, carefully hand finished and covered with smooth, fine-textured glazes in colours which ranged from greys, greens and pinks to yellows, browns and black; a matt blue, 'turquoise Ming', has been in use to the present day, and 'Persian Rose', in tones of pink and maroon, until 1969. Glaze was applied to biscuit clay, often with an atomizer and sometimes in two colours. Metal mounts and settings of precious or semi-precious stones from Colorado also occur.

Van Briggle was succeeded by his widow as president of the firm. A new pottery was built in his memory in 1908 on West Uintah Street, Colorado Springs, under the supervision of F.H. Riddle, foreman for Van Briggle during his illness, with Anne Van Briggle, who remarried in 1908, as art director. The output included tiles for exterior and interior use, wall fountains, garden ornaments, flowerpots, novelties and commercial ware, as well as art pottery. The introduction of new glazes continued, e.g. iridescent glaze c.1909, a brown and green glaze used c.1922-35, and white 'moonglow', in use c.1946. The pottery increasingly moulded wares in large quantities after bankruptcy and reorganization in 1913, and following its sale in 1919 made only industrial art ware. However, many of Van Briggle's own designs continued in production, and a vase supported by a female figure designed by Van Briggle was introduced c.1925.

On the sale of the pottery building in West Uintah Street to Colorado College in 1968, production transferred to South 21st Street, Colorado.

Marks: double A in rectangle or trapezoid incised, from the outset of work in Colorado. Until c.1920, many pieces were dated. Colorado Springs, often abbreviated, sometimes followed the mark after 1905, and USA 1922-29. *Original* denotes a hand thrown piece, *Hand carved* incised decoration, and *Hand decorated* slip painting. Designer's initials occasionally appear, 1904-20; code numbers I, II and III, used in first three years, are thought to indicate the designer. A line of ware with glossy or flowing glazes, marked *Anna Van Briggle*, and made from 1950s, bore only the AA mark after 1965.
Refs: B.M. Arnest (ed) *Van Briggle Pottery* (Fine Arts Center, Colorado Springs, 1975); Barber (1976); D. McGraw Bogue *The Van Briggle Story* (privately published, 1968); Clark & Hughto; Eidelberg; Evans; Henzke; Keen; R. Koch 'The Pottery of Artus Van Briggle' in *Art in America* 52 (June 1964).

Vance Faience. American pottery firm established 1880 at Tiltonville, Ohio, by James Gisey for the production of Rockingham and yellow-glazed earthenware. After several changes in ownership, the first in the early 1880s, the factory (rebuilt in 1894) was acquired by businessmen J. Nelson Vance, J.D. Cuthbertson and Charles W. Franzheim for the production of art ware. In operation from

H.C. van de Velde. Stoneware vase, made in Höhr-Grenzhausen to a design by van de Velde, 1903.

early 1901, at first carrying out extensive experimentation, the company produced a variety of wares, notably jugs in various sizes, with a range of glazes that included matt green, orange brown, and blue and white, from a design by D.*Greatbach originally executed with Rockingham glaze in Bennington. The name of the company was changed in 1902 to the *Avon Faience Co.
Marks: *Vance/F. Co* impressed.
Refs: Barber (1976); Evans; Kovel & Kovel; Lehner.

van Conta, Georg. *See* Hüttensteinach.

van de Bosch, Jacob. *See* Binnenhuis.

Vandemarcq, Amédée. *See* Alluaud, François.

van der Hoef, Christian Johannes (1875-1933). Dutch sculptor, graphic artist and designer. Van der Hoef supplied strictly classical designs for *Amstelhoek from 1894 before joining *Haga as designer in 1902. A member of 't *Binnenhuis, 1903. Services were produced to his designs, with geometrical decoration, at the *Zuid-Holland pottery in 1904. He was also the main designer for *Amphora at Oegstgeest c.1910-20 where his patterns included fan-like geometrical motifs in blue, brown or black on a white ground (vase), feathery motifs in black, red, brown on white (covered jar).

Marks include monograms of CJH and the signature *C J-v-d Hoef.*
Refs: Cooper; Scheen; Singelenberg-van der Meer; E.D. van Straaten *The Revival of Dutch Ceramics 1876-1940* (catalogue, West Midlands Area Museum Service, 1983).

van der Vet, Johannes or Jan (1879-1954). Dutch painter and pottery decorator, born at The Hague. Van der Vet trained at *Rozenburg, where he worked 1894-1904, and subsequently joined the Dortsche Kunstpotterij, a small workshop operating 1903-08 in Dordrecht. He worked initially in the style of Rozenburg and then painted geometrical patterns. In 1907 he established a craft shop in Haarlem.
Mark: monogram of JV.
Ref: Singelenberg-van der Meer.

van de Velde, Henry Clemens (1863-1957). Belgian painter, architect and, from 1893, decorative designer, trained in Antwerp and Paris. Van de Velde was, with A.W.*Finch, among the painters of an avant-garde Brussels group, Les Vingt. His lecture *Le Déblaiement d'Art* (1894) was published as a brochure for the group's galleries. He was influenced by the English Arts & Crafts movement and is regarded as a pioneer of Art Nouveau and the Modern Movement.

He settled in Germany in 1898, after exhibiting designs in applied arts at Dresden in the previous year, which resulted in many design commissions. In 1901, he was invited by Wilhelm Ernst, Grand Duke of Saxe-Weimar-Eisenach, to help in the reform of schools of applied art. He conducted a seminar in Weimar (1902-14) which later developed into the Kunstgewerbeschule. His pupils included O.*Lindig. His ceramic designs included stoneware vases with figured glaze effects for the R.*Hanke workshop in Höhr-Grenzhausen (1902), a porcelain tea service (1905) with moulded rims painted in

C.J. van der Hoef. Figure of a spitting cat in white earthenware, made in Gouda and bearing van der Hoef's monogram, early 20th century. 34 cm high.

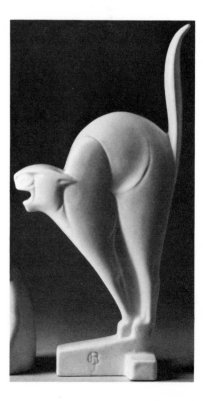

underglaze blue and gilded, commissioned by the Meissen factory, and designs for the Bürgeler Kunstkeramische Werkstätten. Van de Velde left Germany at the outbreak of World War I, lived in Switzerland from 1915, and retired there in 1947 after working in Holland and Belgium.

Marks include impressed monogram.
Refs: Henry Van de Velde zum 100 Geburtstag (Würtembergischer Kunstverein, Stuttgart, 1963); Rheims.

van Gelder, Johanna C. (b 1891). Dutch potter born in Gouda and trained in Rotterdam and (1914) at *Goedewaagen, where her work was fired. She established her own workshop, 't Potteke, at Ellecom 1915-19. After her marriage in 1919, she lived near Dordrecht. From 1927 she designed painted wares for production, e.g. by *Amphora.
Mark: the initials JVG or, from 1919, JVR arranged in the angles of a Y, with HET POTTEKE.
Ref: Singelenberg-van der Meer.

van Ham, Johannes Cornelis or Jan (b 1892). Dutch potter and ceramic decorator. Van Ham worked as a painter at the *Zuid-Holland factory from 1904, afterwards working at *St Lukas. He was among the founders of De *Vier Paddenstoelen in 1920 and remained as the firm's designer until 1939, when he continued work there alone. He sold the factory in 1942 and concentrated for a time on painting, but later returned to pottery. He also provided designs for production at the *Zenith Pottery in the 1920s.
Marks: signature and, after 1945, *'t bolwerk* over a curved line.
Refs: Eretentoonstelling Jan van Ham (Kunstliefde, Utrecht, 1972); *Keramiek van Jan van Ham* (Galerie Acquoy, Acquoy, 1979); Scheen; Singelenberg-van der Meer; van Straaten.

van Lerven, N.H. *See* Ram.

van Loon, Staats. *See* Belding, David.

van Mieg, Ludwig. *See* Pirkenhammer.

van Muijen, Cornelis Jacobus (1886-1971). Dutch potter and ceramic decorator, trained in The Hague. He worked at *Rozenburg (1899-1901) and the *Zuid-Holland factory, going to Purmerend in 1904 and *St Lukas 1909-13. He was a co-founder of De *Vier Paddenstoelen in 1920 and established the Duinvoet works at The Hague in a partnership three years later for the production of simple domestic ware in strong colours. His firm went into liquidation in 1927.
Marks: the initials VM; those of Duinvoet incorporate the pottery's name.
Refs: Scheen; Singelenberg-van der Meer; van Straaten.

van Os, Jean. *See* Sèvres.

van Recum, Johann Nepomuk. *See* Grünstadt.

*Gertrud Vasegaard. Stoneware vase painted in blue under a transluscent glaze, designed by Gertrud Vasegaard for *Bing & Grøndahl, 1952. 36 cm high.*

Vassalo, Antonio. *See* Worcester.

Vauquelin. *See* Nast, Jean-Népomucène-Herman.

van Spaendonck. *See* Sèvres.

van Wickle, Jacob. *See* Morgan, James.

Vasekraft. *See* Fulper Pottery.

Vasegaard, Gertrud (b 1913). Danish potter, trained in Copenhagen 1930-32. After working for A.*Salto for one year, she shared a studio with her sister, L.*Munch Petersen, on the island of Bornholm until 1935, continuing there alone until 1948, and working as designer for *Bing & Grøndahl, 1945-59.
Her work includes a teaset with hexagonal teapot and cups without handles (1958) still in production at Bing & Grøndahl and stoneware bowls decorated under clear glazes with linear patterns or bands of colour on a white engobe. Her daughter, Myre Vasegaard (b 1936), is also a ceramic artist, working in her own studio from 1959 after four years spent at Bing & Grøndahl.
Gertrude Vasegaard marked her work with a monogram of VG.
Ref: W. Hull *Danish Ceramic Design* (catalogue, Museum of Art, Pennsylvania State University, 1981).

Vausse, Faïencerie de. French faience factory established in the late 18th century at the former priory of Vausse (Yonne) by Joseph-Adrien Dumortier (1742-1803), born in Tournai and director of *Ancy-le-Franc from the 1770s until 1792. Using a pink body similar to that later used at the Domaine des *Cornes, the factory made tableware, many pieces decorated with revolutionary emblems. Modelled wares included holy-water stoups, bottles and figures, often religious in theme, e.g. Virgin and Child. The factory's colours included a blue of high quality; decoration *en camaïeu*,

used especially on pharmacy ware, was accompanied by distinctive touches of yellow and orange.
A relative of Dumortier, Charles-Bernard-Bonaventure Foulnier, followed him as director of the factory c.1798, when he left to found a second factory at Ancy-le-Franc. Foulnier again succeeded Dumortier as director of Ancy-le-Franc in 1803. The lease of Vausse passed to Nicolas-Edmé Petit (d 1834), initially in partnership with Jacques-Philibert Lapipe (d 1810), mayor of nearby Etivy. Petit made pharmacy jars painted with vine leaves and grapes. Under the Empire, decoration was predominantly in grey, blue, and a rusty green. As sole owner from c.1816, Petit returned to earlier forms, which included oval tureens and dishes decorated in Rouen style, and made efforts to improve the colours used in painting, because of competition from his friend Jean Philippot at the Domaine des Cornes, c.1825. The output during the Restoration period consisted primarily of such religious pieces as holy-water stoups. Painters included P. *Peigney. Petit's son, Céléstin, a doctor of medicine, succeeded him and went into partnership in 1855 with Philippot, who took over the factory and equipment in 1858, while the Petit family retained Vausse as their home.
Marks include V; Peigney's initials, P.P., and a date, *1850*.
Refs: Huillard; Lesur (1971).

Velten-Vordamm. German stoneware and faience factory working in the 20th century. Under the direction of Hermann Harkort in the 1920s, the pottery produced tableware in designs commissioned from established artists. The shapes and decorations were often based on geometrical motifs. Patterns, hand painted by about 100 employees, also include simple flowers or figures executed in a few brush strokes.
T.*Bogler acted as art director, 1925-26; his own designs were simple, with restrained linear decoration. His successor was W. *Burri, 1926-31. H.*Bollhagen joined the pottery 1927-30.
Refs: Bock; Haslam (1977).

Velvety Art Ware. *See* Radford, Albert.

Venetian. *See* Brush-McCoy Pottery; Owens, John B.

Verdier, Isidore. *See* Auvillar (Tarn et Garonne).

Vereinigte Werkstätten für Kunst im Handwerk. Craft workshops established 1897 in Munich by artists who included R.*Riemerschmid and T.*Schmuz-Baudiss, for the production of their designs in furniture, metalwork, ceramics, etc.

Mark: printed monogram of VW in a rectangular outline.
Ref: Haslam (1977).

Vermeren-Coché. Théodore. *See* Brussels.

Verreville Pottery. Scottish pottery established 1770 in Glasgow, originally for the manufacture of flint glass (which continued until 1820) and later also producing a range of earthenware. John Geddes, the owner from 1806, brought in European potters and artists to teach ceramic techniques to Scottish workers and in 1817 introduced the manufacture of bone china, which was used for the making of biscuit and enamelled figures, woven twig baskets of the type made at *Belleek, and decorative pieces with modelled flowers painted in enamel colours accompanied by painted patterns of butterflies and other insects. Geddes and his son went into partnership with Alexander Kidston, trading as Geddes, Kidston & Co. from 1827 until 1834, when Kidston bought the Geddes shares and entered into a partnership with Hugh Price. He later introduced potters and decorators from English factories and made improvements to the plant. The pottery then produced high-quality table and ornamental ware, much of it for export, until it was taken over in 1847 by Robert Cochran (d 1869), who concentrated on the output of utilitarian semi-porcelain and ceased the production of bone china in 1856, a year before his purchase of the *Britannia Pottery. He ran both potteries until his death, when he was succeeded by his son. The Verreville Pottery was demolished after its closure in 1918.

Marks (when used) incorporate the initials of Cochran's firm, impressed.
Refs: Blacker (1922a); Jewitt.

Vet, Klaas (1876-1943) and Jacob (1880-1924). Dutch potters. The brothers established a pottery in Purmerend, 1903-06, for the production of new styles in Dutch faience.

*Vereinigte Werkstätten für Kunst im Handwerk. Porcelain vase designed by T.*Schmuz-Baudiss c.1899 and manufactured by Swaine & Co. in Hüttensteinach for the Munich Workshops. 16.5 cm high.*

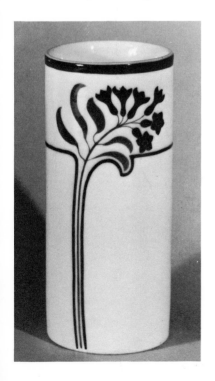

Klaas Vet was a modeller at De *Distel and designed vases and dishes made at the Arnhemsche Fayencefabriek, started with his brother in 1907 in the partnership Jb Vet & Co. Their work resembled that of the *Zuid-Holland and *Rozenburg potteries. With W.P.*Hartgring as a decorator from 1917, the output included pieces with delicate line paintings of stylized flowers and butterflies on a white ground under matt glaze. The firm also made domestic ware. Klaas Vet left after his brother's death and established the *Gelria pottery, in partnership, 1926-31. He took over a pottery, De Hoop, established 1931 in Arnhem to make and sell earthenware in modern styles and in operation until 1942. The Arnhemsche Fayencefabriek was revived under Klaas Vet's firm, with Cornelis Vet (b 1908) as a partner. The firm dissolved when Klaas Vet died, but the factory continued under Cornelis for two years.

Marks: at De Hoop, the pottery's name; the Arnhemsche Fayencefabriek marks incorporate a cockerel and *Arnhem.*
Refs: Singelenberg-van der Meer; van Straaten.

Vickers family. A family of potters making earthenware in Pennsylvania, descended from Thomas Vickers, an English Quaker, who settled in the 1680s in New Jersey, where he worked as a blacksmith. His grandson Thomas Vickers (c.1720-93) moved from Bucks County to Chester County, Pennsylvania, in 1775, and one of his great-grandsons, also Thomas Vickers (1757-1829), by 1796 established the Caln Pottery at East Caln township, near Downington in Chester County, where he was joined by three of his children, John, Ziba and Isaac. Ziba Vickers worked with his father from 1808, succeeded John as a partner in 1814 and remained until 1817. He was in Lionville in 1842.

Sherds found at the Caln Pottery site suggest a widely varied output, including yellow, black or green-glazed ware and earthenware decorated with slip or splashed with manganese dioxide. In 1809, the firm, trading as Thomas Vickers & Son, advertised for employees to produce fine creamware, which they had developed after experimenting with local clay deposits.

John Vickers (1780-1860) married Abigail Paxson in 1803 and worked with his father Thomas at East Caln until 1814. He then moved to a farm in West Whiteland township, Chester County, where he made pottery from 1817. He sold the business in 1822, a year later buying land at Lionville in Uwchlan township, where he founded a pottery which worked for 50 years under four generations of his family. After the closure of the Caln Pottery in about 1820, Thomas Vickers moved to join his son at Lionville in 1823.

Paxson Vickers (c.1816-65) joined his father John at the Lionville pottery in 1835, succeeded him, and was followed in the pottery on his own death by his widow Ann, *née* Lewis (d 1882). His son, John Vickers, who was working at the pottery in 1868, ran it under his own name in 1873. The pottery was in the hands of the brothers John and William Schofield, c.1880, and sold 1885 by the Vickers family after a decline in business. The output included lead-glazed, slip-decorated pie plates, figures with flint

enamel glaze, jars with *sgraffito* designs, jugs and other domestic ware.
Marks: TV, or, 1806-28, JV, incised.
Refs: Barber (1970, 1976); James.

Victoria Pottery. Scottish earthenware pottery established in the mid 19th century at Pollokshaws, Glasgow, by David Lockhart and Charles Arthur, makers of tableware and of chimney ornaments that were sparsely decorated with black and red enamel and touches of gilding. The firm traded as David Lockhart & Co. after Arthur's retirement in 1865, and as David Lockhart & Sons from 1898. The pottery ceased operation in 1953.
Marks: L&A impressed; DL & Co and DL & SONS, impressed.
Ref: Hughes (1961).

Vieillard, Jules (d 1868). French earthenware and porcelain manufacturer. At the end of his partnership with D.*Johnston in 1844, Vieillard established a new earthenware factory in Bordeaux the following year, remaining as its director until the year of his death. He concentrated on the production of tableware and included in his output some pieces of enormous size, e.g. a plate 1.3 metres in diameter now preserved at the Sèvres museum. In 1850, he introduced hard-paste porcelain and ironstone china. The factory soon moved away from the English influence in style that remained from Vieillard's period with David Johnston & Co. He acquired moulds and models from the Chantilly factory, together with the rights of manufacture. While retaining some printed patterns used by Johnston (e.g. weeping willow), he introduced new floral patterns, versions of patterns by the designer Jean Berain (c.1639-1711), and views of local *châteaux*, the Médoc wine harvest, traditional dances, country parties, etc., executed in an increasingly hard blue or green, pink or, later, violet. The firm also made small objects, e.g. cups and match holders, with a chequerboard pattern in coloured slip.

After Vieillard's death, the firm continued under his sons Charles (d 1893) and Albert (d 1895), who were forced by declining sales to put the production of everyday earthenware into the hands of a consortium, although they retained full control of the firm's artistic output. From 1875, they made lamps, vases, *jardinières*, etc., with Isnik or Japanese patterns featuring birds, butterflies and interlaced designs enamelled in the *cloisonné* manner introduced by Amédée de Caranza, who had briefly worked at *Longwy. Printed decoration, while not completely abandoned, declined in finish and quality. The firm went into liquidation after the deaths of Charles and Albert Vieillard.

Marks, printed or impressed, often incorporate the name of Vieillard's firm and *Bordeaux* or the initial B. They include a motif of three crescents interlocked, and some are mock-oriental in appearance.
Refs: Ernould-Gandouet; Lesur (1971).

Vienna Porcelain Factory. *See* Wiener Porzellanmanufaktur.

Vier Paddenstoelen, De. Dutch pottery established 1920 in Utrecht by J.C.*van Ham, K.*Mertens, C.J.*van Muijen and E. Snel

for the production of domestic and ornamental earthenware. Mertens and Snel left
during the first year to establish a pottery at
Velsen. Van Ham remained as designer and
van Muijen (until 1923) as technical director.
The pottery produced wares decorated in
green, yellow, orange and blue, often against
a grey or mauve ground. Van Ham sold the
pottery in 1942 to a former pupil, who moved
it to Elst and continued in operation until
1944.

Marks: in the first three years of
operation, a rectangle with UTRECHT/
HOLLAND, containing four toadstools
(*paddenstoelen*) and, in 1920, the initials
of the partners, MHM and S. When in sole
control, van Ham used a sketchier version
of the mark and a similar rectangle with H
in place of each toadstool.
Refs: Haslam (1977); Singelenberg-van der
Meer; van Straaten.

Vierthaler, Ludwig (1875-1967). Sculptor,
designer and ceramist. Vierthaler worked
for L.C.*Tiffany in New York, 1893-95, and
in the early 20th century joined the designer,
Bruno Paul, at the Vereinigte Werkstätten
in Berlin. He taught in Munich, where he
was a metalworker and designer at the Kunst-
Metall-Werkstätten Eugen Ehrenböck &
Ludwig Vierthaler. He moved to Hanover in
1910 and from 1914 provided ceramic designs
for E. Teichert at *Meissen, for *Rosenthal,
and for the Majolika-Manufaktur *Karlsruhe.

Marks: initials, monogram or signature.
Ref: Haslam (1977); *Rosenthal Hundert
Jahre Porzellan* (catalogue, Kestner
Museum, Hanover, 1982).

Vieux Nyon. See Rauenstein.

Villeroy & Boch. A German firm of pottery
manufacturers established in 1836 to co-
ordinate the operation of factories owned
by N. Villeroy and Jean-François Boch (*see*
Boch Frères) at Vaudrevanges (Wallerfangen), in operation 1778-1931, at Mettlach
in the Saar basin, Schramberg (acquired in

*Villeroy & Boch. Wall plaque portraying a
woman in a large, feathered hat. 86.5 cm
in diameter.*

*Villeroy & Boch. Vase painted with daffodils
in colour on a petrol blue ground, bearing
marks of the Mettlach factory. 40.5 cm high.*

1883 and sold in 1912) and the main Boch
factory at Sept-fontaines. The output of
stoneware, introduced at Mettlach in 1842,
included mugs and other lines exported to
America from c.1860 until the end of the
19th century. Art pottery with inlaid decoration in contrasting clays was known as
Mettlach ware. The partnership also made
transfer-printed creamware 1856-1948 at a
newly established factory in Dresden, and at
Schramberg, as part of a wide range of utilitarian and decorative wares, which also
included mosaic tiles (from 1850). In 1866,
Eugen Boch established a floor-tile works
in Mettlach. He was succeeded in 1869 by
his son, René Boch; a younger son, Edmund, eventually became head of the entire
Mettlach operation. Tiles were also made at
Dresden and in a factory at Merzig which
the firm absorbed in 1879. The firm was later
to lease the *Karlsruhe factory, 1914-20.

The firm also owned a glassworks at Wald-
gassen (1843) and a porcelain factory at
Tournai (1851-91).

Marks include a monogram of VB with
Mettlach Abbey, a square frame containing
a diagonal cross and VB/M in an octagon at
the centre, a circular mark with Mercury
looking over the name *Villeroy & Boch* and
Mettlach, Wallerfangen or *Sept-fontaines*;
VB/s and a spruce tree within an octagonal
outline.
Refs: Haggar (1960); Honey (1952); Pelka;

Porzellankunst; T. Thomas *Villeroy & Boch
Keramik vom Barock bis zur Neuen
Sachlichkeit* (Munich, 1976).

Vinta. *See* Foley Potteries.

Vion, Désiré. *See* Gille.

Vista Alegre. Portuguese porcelain factory
established under royal protection in 1824
by José Ferreira Pinto Basso, whose family
still retains control. The output consisted of
household and decorative wares.

Marks include VA (surmounted by a crown
until royal patronage was lost in 1840) and
sometimes also incorporate the place name
and *Portugal*.
Refs: Danckert; Weiss.

Vitry-le-François. *See* Sarreguemines.

Vodrey, Jabez. English potter working in
America from 1827, when he was a partner
in establishing a pottery in Pittsburgh, for
the manufacture of fine earthenware. Vodrey
was master potter for the *Lewis Pottery
Co. from 1829. He subsequently closed the
Lewis pottery and, taking workmen with
him, went to continue the production of
yellow and Rockingham-glazed wares at the
*Indiana Pottery Co. in Troy, 1839-46. He
moved to East Liverpool, Ohio, in 1847,
establishing a pottery, Woodward & Vodrey,
in the following year. Taking on more partners, he rebuilt the works after a fire in 1849
and made yellow and Rockingham-glazed
ware, followed after the company's failure
in 1857 by his sons, who traded as Vodrey &
Brother. The Vodrey Pottery Co., incorporated in 1896, made white granite and
semi-porcelain.

Marks: the Vodrey Pottery Co. used
versions of two lions supporting a shield, or
two flags with an eagle and a range of other
marks, mainly incorporating the firm's
monogram or initials.
Ref: Barber (1976).

Vogt, Gustave. *See* Raynaud & Cie.

Vogt, John (1815-1906), Charles (d 1886)
and Gustave (1849-1937). Porcelain manufacturers. John Vogt, born in Lübeck (Schles-
wig-Holstein), one of a family of porcelain
and glass retailers, established an import
house in New York, 1840, later opening an
agency and porcelain decorating studio
(where he employed 42 workers in 1864) in
Limoges. He was joined in the New York
branch by his son, Charles Vogt, and his
nephew, Frederic Dose (d 1908), trading in
1865 as Vogt & Dose; the firm also had a
decorating workshop in New York. His
second son, Gustave Vogt, took over the
Limoges agency by 1870 and went into
partnership with Emilien Tressemanes, a
porcelain salesman, in the early 1880s. They
made high-quality white ware for the expanding American market at two small factories
purchased in 1891 in Faubourg Montjovis.
In the same year they were commissioned
by a retailer in Washington to produce a
service for President Harrison. Their output
included pieces with festoons and beaded
decoration, and such items as trays and
candleholders. Dose took over the New
York branch in 1886, succeeded by Gustave
Vogt, who brought his son Charly into the

firm as New York manager while he remained as sole proprietor in Limoges after the retirement of Tressemanes in 1907. He sold the factories to M.*Raynaud in 1919, and the New York branch of the firm closed in 1931.
Ref: d'Albis & Romanet.

Vogt, Pichenot. *See* Loebnitz, Jules.

Vogue. *See* Brush-McCoy Pottery.

Voigt, Hermann. German porcelain manufacturer working at Schaala, near Rudolstadt, Thuringia, from 1872, on the production of figures, and other decorative wares. The factory is no longer in operation.
Marks include H.V. on the leaves of a bunch of grapes, printed.
Refs: Danckert; Weiss.

Volkmar, Charles (1841-1914) American painter and artist potter. Volkmar studied art in his home town, Baltimore, Maryland, becoming known as an etcher by 1859. He went to Europe by 1862, studied painting in Paris and worked as a painter of enamels and landscapes in oils and watercolours. Volkmar returned briefly to America in 1875, but then lived in Montigny-sur-Loing (Seine-et-Marne), and worked as a decorator for a French potter, while learning pottery techniques. He subsequently worked for T.*Deck and became an apprentice in the firm of D.*Haviland, where he learned the technique of barbotine decoration. On his return to America in 1879, he established a

Charles Volkmar. Vase in red earthenware, painted under the glaze in slip, c.1881. 31.7 cm high.

Leon Volkmar. Vase made at the Durant kilns, c.1925. 33 cm high.

kiln at Greenpoint, and made tiles decorated under the glaze. In 1882, he went to Tremont, New York, where he established a pottery and showroom, producing vases, tiles and plaques. The ware, moulded or thrown, usually in cream-coloured clay, was decorated in applied relief or, when thoroughly dry but not yet fired, with slip painted on by Volkmar himself or by an assistant following his designs, which were frequently pastoral scenes showing ducks, geese or cattle near water. The palette consisted of yellow, orange, red, pink, browns, greens, blues, and black, against grounds which were mainly in orange, brown or blue. Labour at the pottery was shared by Volkmar and his assistants, with pottery processes and decorating carried out in separate departments.
Volkmar moved to Menlo Park, New Jersey, in 1888 and, in partnership with J.T. Smith, established the Menlo Park Ceramic Co. for the production of tiles and architectural ceramics for interior use. The company also provided terracotta panelling with high relief decoration in Italian Renaissance style, which was enamelled to match marble wainscoting in the Rockefeller mansion in New York. Volkmar decorated tiles with opaque enamels to tone with onyx, marble, etc., or in old gold or old ivory shades; some patterns suggested by lines of low relief were covered with two-toned glazes in muted shades. After attempting to organize another company to continue the production of tiles in Menlo Park, he established the Volkmar Ceramic Co. in Brooklyn, New York, making tiles, plaques and hollow ware in white earthenware with subjects from American history painted under the glaze in cobalt blue. Working at Corona, New York, in partnership (1895-96) with the artist Kate Cory, he continued the production of plaques painted with historical buildings and personalities in blue. Subsequently alone, at first working under the trade name Crown Point, Volkmar

developed colour effects in underglaze painting, using only American clay for vases, lamp bases, etc. Crown Point ware exhibited in New York City in 1900 was noted for the richness of its colour and the quality of its forms and glazes; a semi-matt glaze was developed.
Volkmar worked as a ceramic consultant, a teacher of pottery techniques and underglaze decoration, and continued work for the Salmagundi Club which included decorated fire-place tiles in the late 1870s and the firing of a yearly consignment of 24 mugs decorated by members of the club for sale at auction from 1899.
In 1902, his son, L.*Volkmar joined him. They established the Volkmar Kilns at Metuchen, New Jersey, in 1903 and taught classes in modelling and ceramic techniques at the pottery, also making art ware, at first with glossy as well as semi-matt glazes, and tiles, panels and plaques. In 1905, Charles Volkmar changed from earthenware to a hard porcelain paste, which he glazed in a reducing atmosphere in a wood kiln. He made vases in increasingly simple forms, relying on the depth and richness of glazes, which were often dark in colour, sometimes flowing over another shade or used with a pale, muted colour on the interior of the piece. He used underglaze decoration, e.g. landscape painting on tiles, and sometimes painted in a succession of layers, each fired in turn.
Charles Volkmar continued work alone from 1911, when his son left to work with J.D.*Rice.

Marks: monogram of CV, 1879-88; VOLKMAR raised within an impressed rectangle, briefly used, 1895, then VOLKMAR & CORY, impressed. CHAS. VOLKMAR within rectangle, impressed, *Crown Point* impressed, or V incised or in relief. *Volkmar Kilns/Metuchen, N.J.,* stamped.
Refs: Barber (1976); Clark & Hughto; Eidelberg; Evans; Henzke; Jervis; Keen; Kovel & Kovel; C. Volkmar 'Hints on Underglaze' in *Keramic Studio* 1 (May 1899).

Volkmar, Leon (1879-1959). American studio potter and teacher of ceramics; born in France, where his father C.*Volkmar worked until 1879. After studies lasting from 1898 to 1900, he joined his father at Corona, New York, in 1902, then worked as a teacher, before the establishment of the Volkmar Kilns in the following year at Metuchen, New Jersey. He taught ceramics at his father's pottery and was head of the newly formed pottery school in the Pennsylvania Museum School of Industrial Art. In 1910, he joined his former pupil, J.D.*Rice, in founding a pottery at Bedford Village, New York, beginning production of tableware, vases, etc., in 1911. Volkmar was responsible for glaze research (achieving browns, black, aubergine, yellow, copper reds and blues) and the finishing of all work. In his individual pieces, he concentrated on the achievement of simple forms with fine colour and texture. Volkmar inherited an interest in the pottery on Mrs Rice's death and exercised his right of purchase in 1924,

using the name Durant Kilns until 1930. In
1937, he won a bronze medal at the Paris
Exposition for work which was primarily
cream earthenware, influenced in style by
Near Eastern pottery. He also undertook
teaching at Columbia University and the
University of Cincinnati.

Mark: v, similar to that used by father,
but usually with incised date.
Refs: Barber (1976); Cox; Eidelberg;
Evans; Kovel & Kovel.

Volkstedt-Rudolstadt. Thuringian porcelain
centre. A factory established in 1762 by G.H.
Macheleid was in the hands of Rudolstadt
businessmen Wilhelm Greiner and Karl
Holzapfel after 1797. It then passed to
Greiner, Stauch & Co. (1815-60), followed
by Macheleid, Triebner & Co. and various
partnerships under Triebner's name (1861-
98). K.*Ens, proprietor in 1898, was followed
in his own firm by Paul, Anna and Augusta
Ens, who were operating their factory as a
branch of *Sitzendorf in 1949. The Macheleid and Triebner firm passed to Mann &
Porzelius (1899-1936). Richard Eckert &
Co. (established 1895), maker of porcelain
figures and other ornamental wares, merged
with Mann & Porzelius in 1930, but continued
in operation using the monogram mark of
AV [Ältester Volkstedter] under a crown
registered (together with others) by Mann &
Porzelius in 1915-16.

The firm of Ens & Greiner, established
1837 in Lauscha, moved to Volkstedt-
Rudolstadt in 1897. Ernst Bohne Sohn produced ornamental porcelain in Rudolstadt
from 1854 until 1945, when the firm was
succeeded by Albert Stahl & Co. L. Strauss
& Sohn also made luxury wares from 1882 in
Rudolstadt and operated from 1894 as the
New York and Rudolstadt Pottery S.A. The
partnership Beyer & Bock, operators of a
painting workshop from 1853, made everyday porcelain from 1890, marking their
wares with a coronet over the initial B, or BB
crossed with a crown, and sometimes
Volkstedt.

Muller & Co. made figures and other
ornamental ware from 1907, with a break in
production during World War II, and from
1950 operated a branch in Seedorf (Württemberg). Their marks incorporate the initials
or monogram MV. Other firms established
in the area in the 20th century were Acker-
mann & Fritze, art porcelain manufacturers

*Max von Heider. Vase designed at the
workshop of von Heider and his sons at
Schongau am Lech, c.1900, produced by
Utzschneider & Co. at Sarreguemines.*

from 1908; Herzinger & Co, decorators,
working from c.1925; that of Alfred Hanika,
making gilded porcelains and modelled
flowers from 1932 until after World War II;
Rudolf Kämmer, producer of decorative
stoneware 1945-53 in Rudolstadt and subsequently flowered porcelain in the style of
*Meissen at Volkstedt.
Refs: Cushion (1980); Danckert; Weiss.

Volpato. Italian porcelain manufacturer,
Giovanni Trevisan, who established a factory in Rome, 1785. He was succeeded briefly
in 1803 by his son Joseph, who died within
some months. Volpato's widow continued
the business with the help of modeller Fran-
cesco Tinucci, whom she married. The firm,
known for reproductions in biscuit porcelain
work by the sculptor Canova, closed in 1831.
Mark: G. VOLPATO ROMA.
Ref: Danckert.

von Heider, Maximilian (b 1839) and sons
Hans (1867-1952), Fritz (b 1868) and
Rudolf. German potters. Maximilian von
Heider studied in Munich, where he was
born, and in Stuttgart and Cologne, before
working as a potter in Munich. He established
a workshop in Schongau, Bavaria, by the
mid 1890s. In the late 19th and early 20th
centuries, assisted by his sons, Maximilian
von Heider produced a wide range of stoneware, including pieces with painted or relief
decoration (cast or hand-modelled), and a
range of drip and figured glazes which he
had himself developed. Lustre effects were
brightly coloured when thickly applied, but
were sometimes diluted with turpentine to
achieve a reddish violet colour. The workshop's output included utilitarian ware,
ornamental pieces, and wall fountains, tile
panels and fireplaces in a style strongly influenced by Art Nouveau.

Hans von Heider became a teacher at the
Kunstgewerbeschule in Magdeburg, 1901-05,
going on to teach in Stuttgart.

Fritz von Heider trained as a painter in
Munich and Karlsbad before joining the
Schongau workshop, and exhibited his first
ceramics in 1897. He specialized in painting
animal subjects e.g. panther, fox, swans
(often in greyish blue or white on a reddish
background) and designed pieces for production at the workshop. He taught at the
Magdeburg Kunstgewerbeschule, c.1900.

Rudolf von Heider was a sculptor and
ceramist, working with his father before
teaching (1903-13) at the Kunstgewerbeschule
in Elbefeld.

Marks: versions of a shield incorporating
the initials *vH*, impressed.
Refs: Bock; Bormann; Thieme & Becker.

von Schauer, Anton Ritter. *See* Wiener
Emailfarbwerk Schauer & Co.

Voulkos, Peter (b 1924). American ceramist. Voulkos was born of a Greek family
in Montana and studied painting at Montana
State University, changing in his last year to
ceramics, which he studied in California.
He became known for pots and jars thrown
in bold shapes, sometimes with resist patterns
in slip under matt glazes, and concentrated
on functional wares. He established the
teaching of ceramics at the Otis Art Institute
1954 in Los Angeles and subsequently shared
the running of the department. At this time
he began experimenting with form, com-
posing his pots out of separate elements and
dealing with them as mass, rather than containers of space. He also began to make
sculptural pieces. Voulkos went on to teach
at the University of California at Berkeley
in 1959. He began working with metal as his
main medium in 1962, but he returned to ceramics in the early 1970s with the decoration
of a series of 200 plates, using techniques
such as carving, adding pellets of porcelain
and hammering.
Refs: C. Brown 'Peter Voulkos' in *Craft
Horizons* 16 (October 1956); Clark &
Hughto; E. Levin 'Peter Voulkos: A
Retrospective' in *Artweek* (18th March
1978); *Peter Voulkos: Sculpture* (Los
Angeles County Museum of Art, 1965); J.
Melchert 'Peter Voulkos: A Return to
Pottery' in *Craft Horizons* 18 (September-
October 1968); R. Slivka *Peter Voulkos: A
Dialogue with Clay* (New York Graphic
Society, New York, 1978).

Voysey, Charles F. Annesley (1857-1941).
English architect and designer of furniture,
textiles, carpets, tapestries, wallpapers,
metalwork and ceramics. He trained under
the architect J.P. Seddon and was later influenced by A.H. Mackmurdo. He designed
tiles for *Pilkington's Tile & Pottery Co.,
which included examples entitled Tulip
Tree, Fish and Leaf, Bird and Lemon Tree,
and Vine and Bird.
Refs: Lockett (1979); *see also* Pilkington's
Tile & Pottery Co.

Vrubel, Mikhail (1856-1910). Russian artist
and ceramist; trained as a painter under Ilya
Repin. Vrubel designed and decorated
earthenware in the ceramic workshop at
*Abramtsevo, and became anxious to revive
the techniques of tinglaze. He joined in a

*Volkstedt-Rudolstadt. A group of card players
made in Volkstedt by Richard Eckert & Co.,
late 19th century. Marked with EC and crossed
swords in underglaze blue. 27 cm high.*

project to build a cathedral as a communal effort, using tiles and porcelain mosaic on both exterior and interior. Vrubel's own architectural work included a brown lustre-glazed lioness's head for a gate, and stove-tiles, tile panels (e.g. Princess Dream for a Moscow hotel) and fireplaces (e.g. Mitula Salyavinovich and Volga in 1890-1900). He also created a series of sculptures, tiles and panels on fairy tale themes (e.g. Snow Maiden, Sadko) or portraits (e.g. head of an Egyptian woman). Many of the tiles were shaped to follow the lines of the design rather than break it up into squares. Vrubel's work, which also included vases and dishes, was often glazed with metallic lustre effects in a wide range of shimmering colours to accentuate the forms.
Refs: Bubnova; Ivanova.

Vsevolojsky & Polivanov. Russian porcelain manufacturers working near Moscow for some years from c.1813. The firm produced a small quantity of decorated ware, and the factory was acquired in the late 1820s by N.M.*Sipiagin.
    Marks: initially a monogram featuring Cyrillic v; later the owner's name, *Vsevolojsky*.
Ref: Rozembergh.

Vyse, Charles (d 1968). English potter and sculptor. Vyse trained as a modeller at the Hanley School of Art, subsequently working in Staffordshire potteries. In 1919, he established a London studio in Cheyne Row, Chelsea, where he worked with his wife, Nell, who carried out modelling (especially of flowers) and decoration, while Charles Vyse was also responsible for mould-making and firing. From the outset, the Vyses made figures and groups, realistically modelled and often coloured, depicting such subjects as The Balloon Woman, The Tulip Girl, a nymph riding a seahorse, a girl holding a lamb as she rides a fawn (entitled Folies Bergères), all signed *C. Vyse, Chelsea*. Vyse and his wife also experimented with glazes, e.g. wood ash on stoneware, and succeeded in reproducing Chinese Sung glazes in the late 1920s. From that time they made pieces that were in many cases copies of T'ang and Sung wares. Others were painted

with abstracts or figure subjects influenced by Cubist or Vorticist painting.

Mark: Vyse's name incised or *CV/Chelsea*.
Refs: F. Stoner in Atterbury (1980); I. Bennett in *Encyclopedia of Decorative Arts* (ed.) Philip Garner (Phaidon, Oxford, 1978).

Wächtersbacher Steingutfabrik. German pottery established in 1832 at Schlierbach (Hesse) for the production of white or cream earthenware, etc., mainly with transfer-printed decoration.
Refs: Honey (1952); Pelka; *Werke um 1900* (catalogue, Kunstgewerbemuseum, Berlin, 1966).

Wackerle, Josef (1880-1959). German sculptor, designer and ceramist who trained as a woodcarver in Partenkirchen before studying at the academy in Munich 1904. He was art director 1906-09 at *Nymphenburg, where he made figures with underglaze decoration from c.1905. Wackerle taught at the Kunstgewerbemuseum, Munich, 1917-22. His designs for the Berlin porcelain factory included figures, e.g. Masked Lady (c.1911), and groups after Meissen models. He also designed a large table service produced in 1912.
Refs: Danckert; Ware; *Werke um 1900* (catalogue, Kunstgewerbemuseum, Berlin, 1966).

Wadsworth, John William (1879-1955). English ceramic designer, working at the Minton factory. With L.V.*Solon, he designed 'Secessionist' ware from 1902. He succeeded Solon as art director, 1909-14, and again held the post, 1935-55. Wadsworth

Wächsterbacher Steingutfabrik. Stoneware vase with printed pattern in blue and white, c.1912. Marked with a shield. 34 cm high.

*John Wadsworth. Jug, Secessionist ware, designed by Wadsworth with L.V.*Solon and produced by *Mintons Ltd, with a design of plants in brown and violet against celadon and streaked blue grounds. Minton factory marks, date code for 1902. 35.5 cm high.*

Charles Vyse. Stoneware bowl, shallow with a small footring, and painted in black under a purplish-brown glaze, c.1931. Incised mark, cv. 15.2 cm in diameter.

*Josef Wackerle. Figures of smokers modelled by Wackerle, made at *Nymphenburg, by 1925.*

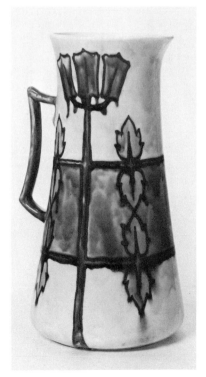

was art director for the *Worcester Royal Porcelain Co. from 1915. He was put in charge by the receiver during the company's financial problems in August 1930, but in the same month joined the firm of Maddock, makers of granite ware, primarily for the American market, in Stoke-on-Trent, returning to Worcester, 1933-35.
Refs: Studio Year Book (1906); Sandon (1978a).

Wagenfeld, Wilhelm (b 1900). German Functionalist architect and designer. He became director of the metalwork department at the *Bauhaus in 1929, but concentrated on the design of glass and ceramics from c.1931. In 1937 he designed a service for *Rosenthal and further designs for tableware were produced in porcelain at *Fürstenberg and, after World War II, by *Rosenthal for whom he worked as a freelance designer, 1952-55.
Ref: Danckert; *Rosenthal Hundert Jahre Porzellan* (catalogue, Kestner-Museum, Hanover, 1982); *Wilhelm Wagenfeld 50 Jahre Mitarbeit in Fabriken* (catalogue, Kunstgewerbemuseum, Cologne, 1973).

Wagner, Gottfried. *See* Arita.

Wagner, Theodor. *See* Gräfenthal.

Wahliss, Ernst (1836-1900). Austrian retailer and producer of ceramics. He opened a store in Vienna in 1863, with branches in London (1888) and Berlin (1896), and in 1897 took over the *Amphora factory at

Ernst Wahliss. Vase, an example of Serapis Fayence, designed by Karl Klaus 1910-1911 and produced by Wahliss. 29.4 cm high.

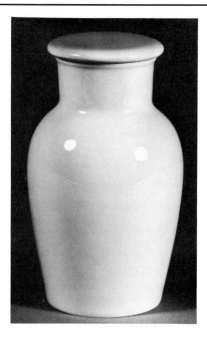

Wilhelm Wagenfeld. Porcelain tea jar by Wagenfeld, made in Fürstenberg, 1934.

Turn-Teplitz for the production of porcelain, which included the porcelain flowers formerly made at Amphora by Reissner, Stellmacher & Kessel. He exhibited work in the style of the Royal *Copenhagen factory's wares at the winter show of the Österreichisches Museum, 1899-1900. Wahliss was succeeded by his sons, Hans and Erich, who exhibited their own products and Zsolnay's Eosin ware at the Österreichisches Museum in the winter of 1902. The Wahliss firm's porcelain was painted on white or coloured grounds. From 1905, the brothers traded under the name Alexandra Porcelain Works Ernst Wahliss. The owner in 1907 was Gerhard Martin Wahliss, and the output included a variety of useful and ornamental wares in earthenware as well as porcelain of high quality. Figures, groups and portrait busts from designs originally produced by the Wiener Porzellanmanufaktur were a speciality. The firm made painted earthenware sold as Serapis-Fayence from 1911. The firm became Ernst Wahliss A.G. in 1925. Its ceramic production has since ceased.

Marks include shields, topped by coronets and usually incorporating the initials EW with TURN and WIEN; a floral mark also occurs, and Serapis wares bore a rectangle with curved sides containing SERAPIS/WAHLISS.
Refs: Danckert; Neuwirth (1974a, 1974b).

Wainwright, John. *See* Low Pottery.

Wainwright, Samuel (1747-1824). Yorkshire businessman. Wainwright was a partner in the *Leeds Pottery by 1781. His son, also Samuel Wainwright, became a potter living at the Leeds works in the 1820s, and a partner with William Hartley Jr and J.C. Ruperti when the pottery was sold in 1830. Samuel Wainwright Jr stayed on as manager until his death from cholera in 1834.
Refs: Lawrence; *Leeds Mercury* (25th

October 1834); *Yorkshire Gazette* (24th May 1824).

Waka Kitei. *See* Kameya family.

Wakasugi kiln. Japanese kiln founded by *Honda and a local tile-maker called Hayashi, with clan support, at Wakasugi village in 1811. The kiln was the first to produce *Kutani ware in Nomi county. Semi-porcelain for domestic use was normally painted in a free, simple style, although some pieces have carefully detailed patterns. The decoration included *aka-e executed by *Yujiro, Chinese-inspired scenes in underglaze blue, patterns of flowers, fruit and other plant forms imitating Ko Kutani, and some work in Imari style. Some enamelling was carried out over flowers, etc., in relief. The kiln operated as Wakasugi Tokisho (Wakasugi ceramics centre) under the control of the clan's district magistrate from 1816, and the ware was adopted for official clan use three years later. In 1820, control passed to the Bureau of Local Products, and the kiln operated under Hachibei, with Yujiro as chief potter. After fire damage in the 1830s, a new kiln was built near to a source of clay in the nearby village of Yahata, where utilitarian blue and white ware was produced on an industrial scale. The collapse of the clan system was followed by closure of the kiln, which was abandoned in 1875.
Refs: Jenyns (1951); Nakagawa.

Wakely, S. *See* Upchurch Pottery.

Walker, Ambrose. *See* Stafford Pottery.

Walker, Casandia Ann. *See* Della Robbia Pottery.

Walker, F.W. *See* Beaver Falls Art Tile Co.

Walker, James. English potter. After working as chief technician of the *Architectural Pottery Co., Walker left in 1861 to establish a pottery at East Quay, Poole, for the production of floor tiles. He sold the works to J.*Carter on his bankruptcy in 1873, remaining as an employee of Carter until 1876.
Refs: Coysh (1976); Hawkins; Jewitt.

Walker, Samuel or George (c.1785-c.1880). English porcelain maker, noted for his technical skill in potting and the building of kilns. He assisted W.*Billingsley in the development of porcelain pastes at Torksey, Lincolnshire, until 1808, and married Billingsley's daughter in 1812. He worked for Barr, Flight & Barr in *Worcester until 1813, at the *Nantgarw China Works until 1814 and again 1817-20, and at L.W.*Dillwyn's factory in Swansea, 1814-17. At Swansea, experiments by Walker resulted in a bone porcelain with greenish translucency and a glassy soft paste containing soaprock, an ingredient of early Worcester porcelain; he went on to develop from this porcelain one with a brownish translucency and a slightly pitted glaze (known as 'trident' paste, because a pair of tridents occur in the mark). In their second period of experiments at Nantgarw, Billingsley and Walker succeeded in making a porcelain that resembled in quality the soft paste used at Sèvres, but their research failed to reduce the high cost due to excessive kiln losses. The moulds and equipment used at

Nantgarw were bought by J.*Rose, who entered into a seven-year partnership in 1820 with Billingsley and Walker to produce porcelain at *Coalport.

In the 1830s, Walker emigrated to America, where he established the Temperance Hill Pottery at West Troy, New York, for the production of Rockingham-glazed ware, mainly teapots, pitchers and toys. He is also thought to have continued his research into colours, glazes and bodies, and developed a method of printing on unfired clay.
Refs: Barber (1976); Sandon (1978b); Twitchett (1980).

Wall, Gertrude Rupel (1881-1971). American potter and ceramic teacher. With her husband, J.A.*Wall, she established the *Walrich Pottery in 1922. After the pottery ceased operation in 1930, she taught ceramics, e.g. summer courses for the University of California at the *Halcyon Art Pottery until 1932, when she had to retire through illness.
Mark: monogram of GR.
Refs: W.F. Dietrich *The Clay Resources and the Ceramic Industry of California* (bulletin of the California State Mining Bureau, Sacramento, 1928); Evans; Kovel & Kovel.

Wall, James A. (1877-1952). English-born potter, employed by *Doulton & Co. before working in America. In 1922 with his wife, G.R.*Wall, he established the *Walrich Pottery, where he was responsible for preparing clay bodies, slips and glazes, as well as throwing and making moulds. After the failure of the pottery in 1930, he worked on the manufacture of porcelain insulators for the Westinghouse Co. in Emeryville, California, and later in San Francisco, firing the work of art school students.
Refs: W.F. Dietrich *The Clay Resources and the Ceramic Industry of California* (bulletin of the California State Mining Bureau, Sacramento, 1928); Evans; Kovel & Kovel.

Wallace, James, & Co. *See* Newcastle Pottery.

Wallander, Alf (1862-1914). Swedish painter, sculptor and modeller. Wallander was trained at the technical school in Stockholm 1877-78 (where he was later to teach) and the Academy, 1880-85, before working as a painter in Paris. His work included genre paintings,

Alf Wallander. A porcelain cachepot designed by Wallander and made at the Rörstrand factory, c.1900. 19 cm high.

figure studies in pastels and later, landscapes, portraits and flower painting. Wallander's designs for ceramics, glass, furniture, etc., made him a leading exponent of Art Nouveau in Swedish applied arts. He was a designer from 1895 and art director in 1900 at the *Rörstrand factory, where he remained until 1914. His work included porcelain with relief decoration painted under the glaze in soft colours. He used naturalistic designs of thistles, poppies, iris, chrysanthemums, pine branches, rowan and other plant forms to decorate bowls and vases. The sea was also a frequent theme in his decoration.
Refs: Bénézit; Porzellankunst.

'Wall body'. *See* Worcester.

Wallendorf. German porcelain factory established in 1764 by Johann Wolfgang Hamann in association with his brother, his son, Ferdinand Friedrich Hamann and Johann Gottfried and Johann Gotthelf Greiner. The output, mainly of tea, coffee and chocolate sets, cups made for export to Turkey, tankards, tureens, desk sets, etc., also included pieces with fine relief decoration of wickerwork or woven trellis with flowers, fruit and leaves. Painted decoration included flowers and birds, patterns in purple on smooth-surfaced or ribbed jugs, etc., silhouettes bordered in gold and black by J.J.H.*Haag, and pieces with blue and black grounds with polychrome painting in reserves. Figures and groups, made in large quantities, include copies from *Meissen, costume studies and representations of rural or provincial life; some are difficult to distinguish from those made at Limbach and Volkstedt, because unmarked. The factory, leased to Friedrich Christian Hutschenreuther and his son-in-law, Herman Keiser, in 1829, was sold on the death of Hamann's successor in 1833 to a partnership of the Hutschenreuther family, Kämpfe, Sonntage and the Heubach family. Work was increasingly mass-produced from the 1850s and much was sent for decoration by Sonntag & Sons at Geiersthal. Kämpfe & Heubach, joint proprietors by 1897, formed a joint stock company. Production was interrupted during World War I, but revived in the 1930s under Heinz Schaubach, working under the title Schaubach Art, and the factory was nationalized in 1953.
Marks include w sometimes with a crown; *Wallendorf* SCHAU/BACH/KUNST with a crown and flanked by scrolls.
Refs: Danckert; Haggar (1960); Hannover; Honey (1952); Weiss.

Walley, William Joseph (1852-1919). American ceramist, the son of a potter in East Liverpool, Ohio. Walley travelled to England before 1862, learning pottery techniques at *Mintons Ltd until the early 1870s. After his return to America, he attempted the production of art ware at Portland, Maine, from 1873, and at Worcester, Massachusetts in 1885, but the ventures failed. In 1898, he bought a disused red ware pottery at West Sterling, Massachusetts, where he worked mainly alone, making vases, bowls, jars, mugs, lamp bases, candlesticks, paperweights, etc., from local red clay. Walley valued the ideal of work created by hand by one artist. He produced mainly thrown

shapes, sometimes with moulded relief decoration, but cast some pieces, e.g. paperweights in the form of turtles, etc. He used glazes, both matt and glossy, in shades of red, brown and, frequently, green.
Mark: WJW impressed.
Refs: Evans; Kovel & Kovel; Watkins (1950).

Wallmann, J. *See* Bindesbøll, Thorvald.

Walrath, Frederick E. (d 1920). American studio potter and teacher of ceramics. A pupil of C.F.*Binns, Walrath won a bronze medal for work shown by the New York State School of Ceramics at the St Louis World's Fair in 1904. He taught at the Mechanics' Institute in Rochester and at Columbia University, New York, and exhibited work regularly, without apparently producing a commercial output. In making earthenware vases, covered jars, etc., he frequently used formalized floral decoration carried out in matt glazes, with emphasis on flowing matt and crystalline glazes on simple shapes. Walrath succeeded P.E.*Cox as ceramist at Newcomb College Pottery in 1918 and worked there until his death.
Marks: *Walrath Pottery* incised; emblem of four arrows.
Refs: Eidelberg; Kovel & Kovel.

Walrich Pottery. American art pottery established 1922 in Berkeley, California, by J.A.*Wall and his wife, G.R.*Wall, and named after their son, Richard. The output included vases, bowls, candlesticks, lamp bases, paperweights, bookends, plaques and tiles, often slip-cast, but sometimes press-moulded, hand-built or thrown in a variety of bodies, both earthenware and porcelain. Glazes, notably in shades of blue, matt, semi-matt or glossy, were compounded by James Wall. Sculptors engaged to work on figures and portrait busts included Edgar Tauch and Jacques Schnier. Work ceased in 1930.

Frederick E. Walrath. Tobacco jar with a painted design in matt glazes, made at Walrath's pottery c.1910. 17.1 cm high.

Marks: WALRICH incised or impressed, monogram of WP, moulded or on a paper label.
Refs: W.F. Dietrich *The Clay Resources and the Ceramic Industry of California* (bulletin of the California State Mining Bureau, Sacramento, 1928); Evans; Kovel & Kovel.

Walters, Carl (1883-1955). American artist and studio potter, born in Fort Madison, Iowa. Walters studied painting in Minneapolis (1905-07) and in New York (1908-11). After his marriage in 1912, he lived in Portland, Oregon, exhibiting his painting frequently until his return in 1919 to New York, where he began experimenting in ceramics and concentrated on the achievement of an Egyptian blue glaze. He established a studio in Cornish, New Hampshire, in 1921, at first producing painted earthenware, and moved in the following year to Woodstock, New York. He turned to ceramic sculpture, exhibiting his earliest pieces in the Whitney Studio Club, New York. His work mainly consisted of figures of animals recalling ancient Egyptian, Persian and Chinese pieces, with painted decoration of rosettes, stripes, dots, cross-hatching, etc., over the surface, but also included human figures.
Refs: The Animal Kingdom in American Art (Everson Museum of Art Syracuse, New York, 1978); E. Brace 'Carl Walters' in *Creative Art* 10 (June 1932); Clark & Hughto; W. Homer 'Carl Walters, Ceramic Sculptor' in *Art in America* 44 (Autumn 1956); *International Exhibition of Ceramic Art* (American Federation of Arts and the Metropolitan Museum of Art, New York, 1928).

Walton, John. Staffordshire potter working in Burslem, c.1806-c.1835. By 1818, Walton owned a colour works and an earthenware factory. He was known for a range of earthenware figures, characteristically backed

John Walton. Group of children quarrelling over a flowered hat. Impressed marks, Walton (SR). 20 cm high.

by a flattened tree with leaves in groups of six arranged around a bright flower, and painted in heavy, opaque enamel, which was often applied with a stiff brush to produce a streaked or stippled effect. Early figures often stand on mounds of dark green splashed with brown, or a square base painted with a marble pattern; some later pieces have an oval panel framed in blue at the front of the base. The subjects, often inspired by contemporary porcelain figures, included classical, religious and military subjects, sportsmen, rustic groups and animals. Walton's output also included Toby jugs, and jugs portraying other characters. He was followed by other potters making figures in a similar style (e.g. C.*Tittensor, R.*Salt, O.*Sherratt) and succeeded at his pottery by George Hood, producer of earthenware figures in Burslem, Hanley and Tunstall.
Mark: WALTON in a scroll on the back of the base of figures.
Refs: Haggar (1955); H.A. Turner *A Collector's Guide to Staffordshire Pottery Figures* (McGibbon & Kee, London, 1971).

Waly. French pottery making faience at Waly (Meuse) from the mid 19th century. Jean-Baptiste Carpentier (d 1822), son of the founder, built a new factory, Bel-Air, in 1771, just outside the village, where he produced white or brown-glazed earthenware for domestic use. His faience was decorated with figure subjects, *chinoiseries*, flowers, heraldic emblems, etc., in sombre high-fired colours, predominantly grey, black, a pure blue, and olive green, in contrast with the bright colours of Les *Islettes. A deep poppy red was introduced in the later years of the factory's operation. Plates and dishes are rather deep; other pieces included soup and salad bowls, cups, saucers, jars, and small figures. Carpentier was succeeded by relatives of his widow, whose family name was Mangin. By 1866, the workshop produced only yellow earthenware for domestic use. It was still in operation in the 1870s.
The site of the original factory, bought in 1771 by the local council, remained largely unused until a part was reopened by Carpentier, to increase production, in 1822. This workshop remained in operation until 1852.
Marks include MANGIN-BRICHARD/A WALY-MEUSE.
Refs: Lesur (1971); Ernould-Gandouet; Tilmans (1954).

Wannopee Pottery. American pottery established in 1887 as the New Milford Pottery Co. in New Milford, Connecticut, and operating after reorganization in 1892 as the Wannopee Pottery. At first making ordinary white earthenware and semi-porcelain, the firm introduced Duchess ware with mottled glazes. A blue-glazed ware, often with gilded decoration was used for umbrella stands, *jardinières*, spittoons, pitchers, etc. From 1895, pitchers were made in semi-porcelain with relief bands of leaves at the top and base and cameo portrait medallions showing, e.g. Mozart, Beethoven, Napoleon or McKinley. Clock cases in large or small sizes became a speciality of the firm. A line introduced in 1901 was in the form of lettuce leaves (some pieces moulded from heavily veined cabbage leaves) covered in pink or pale green glazes. At about the same time, the firm introduced a range of art ware designed by manager

Peter and Francis Warburton. Creamware figure, c.1800.

A.H. Nobel and entitled Scarabronze in forms derived from ancient Egyptian vases and characterized by a smooth metallic glaze in the colours of aged copper; Egyptian figures and characters were painted on the surface in slip containing metallic colours. Scarabronze was made in a local red clay, while the clay for other lines was largely imported. Production ceased in 1908.
Marks incorporate the name WANNOPEE, or the initials of New Milford Pottery Co., sometimes specifying the material (semi-opaque, porcelain etc.); a scarab impressed for Scarabronze; LETTUCE LEAF, trade mark.
Refs: Barber (1976); Evans; Kovel & Kovel; Watkins (1950).

Warburton, Jacob (1741-1826). Staffordshire potter. Like his parents, John Warburton (1720-61) and Anne, *née* Daniel (1713-98), Jacob Warburton was a decorator and manufacturer of cream-coloured earthenware in Cobridge. He became one of the founding partners in the *New Hall works and in 1813 took over the share bequeathed to him by his son P.*Warburton in the company which had purchased the New Hall estate in 1810.
Refs: Holgate; Jewitt; Stringer; Towner (1957).

Warburton, Peter (1773-1813) and Francis. Staffordshire potters, sons of J.*Warburton, born in Cobridge. Peter Warburton produced cream-coloured earthenware at Bleak Hill, Cobridge, for a time in partnership with his brother. Francis Warburton left in 1802 to establish a creamware pottery in the former priory at La-Charité-sur-Loire (Nièvre); he later retired through illness, and the factory

Warne & Letts. Salt-glazed stoneware jar, a rare example with the firm's full mark and the date, 1806. 31.8 cm high.

passed to another proprietor, but closed in 1812. Peter Warburton continued production at Bleak Hill, and became a partner in the joint stock company which purchased the *New Hall estate in 1810. In the same year, he took out a patent for the transfer printing of ceramics and glass with precious metals. His own output of earthenware was of high quality and rich cream in colour, with a yellowish glaze.

Two harvesting figures for the decoration of serving stands for the table, made c.1800, bear an impressed mark, P. & F. WARBURTON. Francis Warburton used LA CHARITE (impressed) on his white ware made in France.
Refs: Godden (1964); Jewitt; Lesur (1971); Rhead; Towner (1957).

Warburton, Samuel. *See* Leeds Pottery.

Wardle, John; **Wardle & Wilkinson.** *See* Denaby Pottery.

Wardle & Co. Ltd. *See* Robinson, Harold Taylor.

Wareham, John Hamilton Delaney (1871-1954). American pottery designer and decorator, born in Grand Lodge, Michigan. Wareham studied at Cincinnati Art Academy, and worked at the *Rookwood Pottery from 1893 until the year of his death. His work included relief decoration of poppy seed-pods on a moulded vase (1901) with red, green and purple matt glazes. Wareham succeeded W.P.*McDonald as head of the decorating department, and his interest in Chinese ceramics encouraged the use of new glazes developed by the pottery's chemist, Stanley Burt, with whom he developed the Wax Mat line, with a soft, waxy surface, c.1930. He became vice president of the firm and took over direction of architectural projects, eventually taking over as president in 1934.
Mark: versions of initials or monogram.
Refs: Clark & Hughto; Kovel & Kovel; Peck.

Warne & Letts. American stoneware makers working at Cheesequake, Madison, New Jersey (then a part of South Amboy), by 1800 and in operation until the 1820s. Thomas Warne (1763-before 1813) owned the site, which passed via his son, James Morgan Warne, and widow, Mary, to his father-in-law, J.*Morgan Jr, in 1815. The Warne family was related by marriage to a Joshua Letts. The pottery produced a wide range of domestic stoneware. Decoration was normally limited to stamped designs and tooled bands encircling the piece, but a jar attributed to the pottery with three American warships (suggesting a date c.1813) incised freehand on the sides provides an early example of this type of decoration.
Marks: T.W.J.L; T. WARNE CO SOUTH AMBOY; WARNE & LETTS or WARNE, AMBOY; MADE BY J.LETTS. SOUTH AMBOY. Vessels with distinctive bands of impressed decoration bear the stamped inscription LIBERTY FOREV above WARNE & LETTS *1807* S.AMBOY N.JERSEY.
Refs: Clement (1947); Stradling; Webster.

Wartha, Vincse. *See* Zsolnay.

Wärtsilä combine. *See* Arabia.

Warwick China Co. American factory organized 1887 in Wheeling, West Virginia, for the production of dinner, tea and toilet sets in semi-porcelain.
Marks: helmet with crossed swords, name of the pottery and SEMIPORCELAIN; WARWICK/SEMI/PORCELAIN; WARWICK/CHINA.
Ref: Barber (1976).

Washington Pottery. American pottery operated by brick manufacturer John Mullowny in Philadelphia from 1810. As well as bricks, it produced tea and coffee pots, pitchers, etc., in red, yellow or black-glazed earthenware, advertised in 1810 as Washington ware. The pottery was sold in 1815.
Refs: Barber (1976); S. Myers *From Handcraft to Industry* (Smithsonian Institution Press, Washington D.C., 1980).

Watcombe Pottery. Devonshire pottery established by the Watcombe TerraCotta Co., which was formed in 1869 to exploit a deposit of red clay near St Marychurch, Torquay. In 1871, local workers under the guidance of potters from Staffordshire began production of high-quality terracotta, mainly slip-cast, which included tea services, household articles, plaques, figures and architectural ornament. A glossy turquoise enamel was used to highlight decoration, to protect, say, handles from wear, and as a lining. Touches of blue or white enamel or matt black glazes, and black transfer-printed borders were also used. Relief decoration took the form of garlands of flowers, leaves, classical figures, portrait medallions, etc., separately moulded and applied in pale or tinted clay. Most early figures were classical in theme, some taken from contemporary sculpture and parian statuary.

Decorative techniques extended to include *sgraffito* patterns, with paler body showing through dark slip, sometimes combined with painting in enamels. Examples of work shown in the Exposition Universelle in Paris, 1878, included pieces that were wholly or partially glazed.

After ceasing production 1883-84, the pottery was reopened by Evans & Co., with an emphasis on contemporary subjects, e.g. figures in contemporary dress, many of them commissioned for advertisement. Oil paintings of flowers, birds, landscapes, seascapes and children were carried out on plaques, which were also sold for painting by amateurs. Slip-painting became a part of regular production in the mid 1880s on shapes which were often Oriental in inspiration. The subjects, including birds, fish, flowers and foliage, were painted on the red body or a thin engobe after the first firing. The piece was then glazed and sometimes gilded. Thrown ware, introduced in the 1890s, included a range of jugs and vases in a white body with streaked green glaze and a line with *sgraffito* designs of scarabs and other Egyptian motifs in white slip over a red body, introduced briefly in 1900. Majolica with bright glazes, moulded in a white body, and a line with streaky, variegated glazes on a red body were introduced after glaze research started in the 1890s. The firm also decorated bone porcelain bought from the firm of W. *Brownfield, possibly to fulfil commissions. After its purchase by Hexter, Humpherson & Co. in 1901, the firm became part of the combined Royal Aller Vale & Watcombe Potteries and afterwards made a wide range of useful and ornamental pieces that are difficult to distinguish from the output of the *Aller Vale pottery, including ware with *sgraffito* rhymes or proverbs accompanied by the Scandy *fleur-de-lis* motif, c.1914.

After a closure during World War I, the pottery was taken over by the Mid-Devon Trading Co. and concentrated on wares decorated with *sgraffito* mottoes, or a pattern of regularly placed spots of slip. The pottery finally closed in November 1962.

Marks incorporate *Watcombe Torquay*. A circular mark with "WATCOMBE" SOUTH DEVON surrounding a woodpecker in a branch was transfer printed or impressed in the last quarter of the 19th century.

Watcombe Pottery. Figure of a cat, off-white with brown paws and a brown hat, which bears the motto, MEW-SICK. *25.5 cm high.*

Refs: Coysh (1976); Jewitt; Lloyd Thomas (1978).

Waterloo works. *See* Boote, T.& R., Ltd.

Waterside Pottery. *See* Bateson family.

Watson & Co. *See* Prestonpans Pottery.

Watt, Linnie. English pottery designer and decorator; a regular exhibitor at the Royal Academy. While working for *Doulton & Co. in Lambeth, 1875-90, Linnie Watt specialized in rustic scenes and figures slip-painted on earthenware.
Marks: signature *L. Watt*, with the *W* superimposed on the *L*.
Refs: Atterbury & Irvine; Callen; Eyles (1975).

Watts, John (c.1786-1858). English potter. Watts worked in London as foreman and manager of a pottery in Vauxhall Walk, Lambeth, and with J.*Doulton became a partner in the pottery; their firm traded as *Doulton & Watts from 1820 until Watts's retirement in 1853.
Refs: Blacker (1922b); Eyles (1975); Jewitt; Rhead.

Watts, Mary Seton. *See* Compton Pottery.

Wax Mat. *See* Wareham, John Hamilton Delaney.

Wazen, or **Eiraku** (1823-96). Japanese potter, twelfth in the line of descent from Nishimura Zengoro (*see* Ryozen) and successor to his father, *Hozen, whose styles he adapted and developed. Wazen went in 1853 to Omuru, where he worked from 1855 on the revival of a kiln used by the 17th-century potter, Ninsei (*see* Ninsei ware). In 1858, at the invitation of the local bureau of industry and the lord of Kaga, he established a kiln at Yamashiro with his brother-in-law, Nishimura Sozaburo (1843-76), and a partner, Rakusen Ohashi, in an effort to revive the production of *Kutani wares. Spending six years at Yamashiro, he made porcelain and some faience in the style of Ninsei ware. Wazen is noted for his designs predominantly in red and gold (*aka-e, *gosu aka-e, and akaji kinga—gold patterns on a red ground outside the piece, red on white on the interior). He was also skilful in polychrome enamels with gold (*kinrande), and worked in underglaze blue. While in Kyoto, he introduced orimonde (woven-pattern style) decoration, carried out in various colours with gold and silver through coarse cloth laid on the surface of the piece. His work at Yamashiro was continued by pupils who included Okura Seishichi (1845-1918). Wazen rejoined his brother, who had returned to Kyoto after one year, and adopted Eiraku as his family name, using his father's inscription and the mark Ko Kutani in gold. He opened a factory at Okazaki (Aichi prefecture) in partnership with Rakusen Ohashi (1871), but eventually settled at Abura-koji, Kyoto, where he died, succeeded by his son Tokuzen Eiraku (Zengoro XIII), who had worked with him from c.1875, and Rakusen Ohashi.
Refs: Brinkley; Gorham; Hannover; Jenyns (1965); Koyama; Morse; Munsterberg; Nakagawa; Uyeno.

Wear Pottery. English pottery working from the 18th century on a site adjoining that of the *Scott Brothers' works at Southwick, Sunderland. The pottery made only brown earthenware until it was taken over in 1803 by Samuel Moore (1775-1844) and his brother-in-law, Peter Austin (1770-1863), trading as Samuel Moore & Co. Moore's son, Charles (1799-1852), took over management by 1831, establishing a branch, the *Bridge End Pottery, by 1844. T.*Snowball was head of the Wear Pottery's decorating department in the 1840s. George Storey Moore (b 1824) was a partner by 1847 and succeeded his uncle Charles as proprietor in 1852. The firm's output of brown and white earthenwares included decorative flowerpots, jugs, bowls, mugs, frog mugs, hollow balls, etc., printed with views of the Wearmouth Bridge, as well as a range of dinner ware. Lustre decoration was used, but many jugs, mugs, and bowls made by the Moores have edging and ground decorated with lines of red, blue or green. Pierced dishes and baskets edged with a wicker pattern have scenes of birds, etc., painted at the centre in pink lustre. Transfer-printed decoration included a wood-grain pattern on vases with handles in the form of dragon heads, and plaques with polychrome designs. Later dinner services were printed in blue with ships, flowers, birds, a group of vases, etc., bordered with key patterns.
The Sunderland lawyer R.T. Wilkinson, who took over the pottery in 1861, employed R.*Seddon as manager, and rebuilt the works, installing modern equipment. In the late 1860s, there were about 180 employees. After a further change in management in the early 1870s, the output was mainly restricted to dinner services. The pottery closed in 1882, and was demolished in the following year.
Marks include the names of the Moore firms, impressed, and a number of printed marks incorporated S.M. & CO. with a pattern name, e.g. *Asiatic Pheasants, Key Border, Sea Flower, Wild Rose, Reindeer.*
Refs: W.D. John & W. Baker *Old English Lustre Pottery* (Ceramic Book Co., Newport, Monmouthshire, 1962); Shaw.

Weatheriggs Pottery. English pottery established 1855 at Clifton, near Penrith in Cumbria, and run from 1865 by the Schofield family. John Schofield (d 1917) joined his brother Jeremiah there in the 1860s and ran the pottery until his death, succeeded by his widow (until 1937) and son, Arthur Schofield (d 1952). The output included red earthenware storage jars, lined and rimmed with lead glaze, until the 1930s, together with earthenware for domestic and dairy use, slip-decorated salt kits, money boxes (some topped with a modelled hen) and other special pieces with slip trailing and *sgraffito* inscriptions. Concentric lines of slip were trailed on decorative wares as they turned on the wheel, with other parts of the pattern added freehand; salt kits dating from the 1920s and after have SALT trailed in slip below the opening. Later wares for the local tourist market also included flowerpots, bowls, mugs and jugs. Agate ware was also produced. The pottery passed to Harry Thorburn, an employee from 1916. Under a new owner, it became the last of the traditional English country potteries still in operation.
Refs: Brears (1971a, 1974).

Weaver, Abraham. British-born potter, making slip-decorated earthenware in Nockamixon, Pennsylvania 1828-44. *Sgraffito* pie plates included one with a design of a turtle dove perching on a conifer twig, tulip flowers and the inscription: *Abraham Weaver Nockamixon Township Bucks County May 4th AD 1828 'When this you see Remember me'.*
Refs: Barber (1976).

Weaver, James (b c.1839). Porcelain painter working for the *Worcester Royal Porcelain Co. 1853-70 and subsequently for W.T. *Copeland. His early painting included cornflowers, grasses and insects. Weaver died in the 1890s.
Ref: Sandon (1978a).

Weber, Rolf (b 1907). German studio potter. He was apprenticed as a potter 1922-25, before teaching at the school for applied arts in Breslau, and then studied in Berlin. In 1937, he established a workshop in Sommershausen, near Kassel, where he was a teacher 1931-39. He produces beakers, jugs, bowls, vases, etc., in simple shapes in stoneware, (introduced 1957) with silk matt glazes, often with blue, green or brown crystalline effects. He also makes sculptural pieces, but is known for his paintings in brightly coloured glazes on plaques about 60 cm square that were intended for use as table tops or wall decoration.

Mark: four lines arranged to form a stylized w, impressed, or painted signature.
Refs: Bock; *Deutsche keramische Kunst der Gegenwart* (Cremer, Frechen, 1968).

Webster, Eric A. (b 1885). English ceramic artist. Webster was apprenticed under H. *Betteley at the *Doulton & Co. factory in Burslem, 1910, as a painter of landscapes, flowers and birds, and remained with the firm until 1962. He was among early artists concerned with the painting of figures, eventually training junior artists, and from 1925 headed a department specializing in the painting of model animals.
Refs: see Doulton.

Webster, Moses (1792-1870). English porcelain decorator, noted for his paintings of flowers. After serving an apprenticeship at the porcelain factory in Nottingham Road, *Derby, Webster briefly joined R.*Robins and T.M.*Randall in London, c.1817, where he decorated Nantgarw porcelain. At *Worcester in 1821, Webster is thought to have studied painting under T.*Baxter. He returned briefly to Derby and worked on a service (c.1825) made for John Trotter, with painted flowers and five panels in chrome green on the border. He left to succeed John Keys, the son of S.*Keys Jr, as a drawing teacher in Castle Street, Derby. He is noted for bouquets of full-blown flowers painted in free, spontaneous brushstrokes.
Refs: Sandon (1978b); *see also* Derby.

Wedel, Wilhelm. *See* Gräfenthal.

Wedgwood, Josiah, & Sons Ltd. Staffordshire pottery established in 1759 in Burslem by Josiah Wedgwood I (1730-95) and controlled by his family until it became a public company in 1967. In 1773, the firm completed a move to a new factory opened in Etruria in 1769. Wedgwood's work had become known for its high quality and variety. Tableware in a fine cream-coloured earthenware, marketed as Queensware from 1766, was produced in simple shapes recalling those of silverware, with painted borders of floral motifs, abstract patterns or edgings derived from the decoration of Greek pottery. Transfer printing (in blue from c.1805) followed less closely the neo-classical style with which Wedgwood's wares were associated. The output of jasper ware had been extended from the initial medallions and plaques to include hollow ware in the 1780s.

Wedgwood's son, Josiah II, was succeeded on his death in 1841 by his sons Josiah III, who was a partner from 1823 until his retirement in 1842, and Francis, who became a partner in 1827 and was in full control of the company 1842-70. Francis went into a brief partnership with J.*Boyle and, from 1846, Robert Brown (d 1859), a Shelton earthenware manufacturer. He then took into partnership his sons Godfrey (1859), Clement Francis (1863) and Lawrence (1865).

Under the art direction of Godfrey Wedgwood, the company produced a commercially successful range of ornamental wares. A parian paste, which had been produced c.1846, was marketed as Carrara Ware. Figures and busts were in regular production from early 1849, initially, in some cases, from moulds used for the casting of black basalt. Some models were produced in both bodies until the late 19th century. The Carrara paste was coloured either throughout or on the surface from 1850, and experiments with glazed parian in the early 1860s followed similar research carried out at the Royal *Worcester factory and at *Mintons Ltd. The production of Carrara Ware continued until the 1890s. Some models bear the signature of A.E.*Carrier-Belleuse. In basalt, vases with applied patterns of vines and leaves embellished with gilding were made c.1875.

The firm's modellers included Thomas Greatbach, who worked for Wedgwood 1844-64, E.*Keys, employed 1845-53, and Henry Brownsword (c.1825-92), who had been with the firm as an apprentice in 1838 and a modeller, 1852-62, before starting to work in close association with E.*Lessore as a painter and designer. C.*Toft joined the firm as principal modeller (working mainly on jasper ware) in 1877, and H.*Protât worked as a freelance designer.

Lessore was employed as decorator and designer from 1860 and about two years later began working from a London studio, where he produced designs and sometimes prototypes for production in the factory. He experimented with lustre decoration from 1865.

Following a commission by the firm in 1867, W.*Crane designed and decorated several vases and three trays. Later, he designed a table centrepiece and the border for a chess table, which was exhibited in London, 1871.

Wedgwood's majolica, produced in large quantities from the early 1860s until the

J. Wedgwood & Sons Ltd. Kettle from a pearlware tea and coffee service painted in blue, red and green on a brown cell-patterned ground, c.1815.

1890s (and some wares with green glaze are still in production) was made in a white body. The plain-coloured glazes included green, brown and blue. Some shapes for majolica ware were designed by C.*Dresser, who also provided designs for tableware and toilet sets, probably from the mid 1860s.

The firm's majolica ware also included a line marketed as Vigornian Ware which was acid-etched outside the factory, by a Stoke-on-Trent firm of glass engravers, with patterns of birds, butterflies, trees, flowers and other plant forms on blue or brown glazes. Mottled glaze effects were also used, and some elaborately modelled pieces were painted with coloured glazes. A line called Argenta ware called was produced with relief decoration of flowers, animals, and other natural motifs, often in Japanese-inspired style, with brightly coloured majolica glazes on pale grounds. *Emaux ombrants* were modelled by R.J.*Morris from c.1863, and in 1872 the factory acquired designs, moulds and glaze formulae from the executors of A.*du Tremblay.

Pâte-sur-pâte decoration was briefly used (1877-79), in an art department working under the supervision of T.*Allen, by F.A.*Rhead, using Carrara slip. Some pieces combine low-relief decoration by Toft and other modellers with *pâte-sur-pâte* decoration. Rhead also experimented with slipware. The main examples of barbotine ware made at the factory were by the artist, S. Bateman, who painted landscapes and nautical subjects on vases, tiles and plaques in thick slip, c.1883-88.

Other art wares produced in Allen's department included limited series with painted or printed decoration, trailed slip or lavish gilding, in shapes adapted from Japanese wares and a wide range of other sources. The French St Porchaire pottery inspired Henri II ware, which developed from experiments in the early 1860s and appeared in the firm's display at the World's Columbian Exposition in Chicago, 1893. Pieces made by T.*Mellor included vases, tea ware and a trinket set.

James Rhodes, a decorator and designer, worked at the factory from 1885 until at least 1923, and developed a range of slip-

wares, some with *sgraffito* decoration. New lines included Golconda, made in bone china with raised patterns of flowers and foliage in pink, ivory and gold; Auro Basalt with raised and gilded ornament against a black ground; Magnolia ware, in red body, and painted with flowers in light slip under a Rockingham glaze of varying thickness. W.*Burton, who joined the firm 1887-93, worked on the development of glazes and bodies; vellum wares were introduced c.1890.

H.*Barnard, a decorator of bone china, jasper ware, majolica and stoneware, developed pierced, trailed and *sgraffito* slip decoration on art wares. He worked in the firm's tile department, 1899-1902. Tiles with printed decoration had been made for a short time in the early years of the Etruria factory in the 1870s, but production had been mainly restricted to ornamental plaques and friezes (in majolica and *émaux ombrants* in the 1860s and early 1870s) until the resumption of tile production from c.1875 until the early 20th century. The factory produced a wide variety of patterns, many transfer-printed, though its output was smaller than that of the major tile manufacturers, such as *Maw & Co. or Mintons. Block printing on tiles followed its introduction for the decoration of dessert wares in 1876. The firm established a tile department 1882-1902, also decorating tiles made outside the factory.

By the mid 19th century, tableware was mainly transfer-printed. A variety of all-over patterns based on *chinoiserie* views, floral studies, etc., were used over the slightly flawed body of ordinary wares. 'Best patterns', initially flown (*see* flown blue), were generally large flower designs, used on pearlware. Decorative plates, influenced by oriental styles, were decorated in relief with prunus blossoms, bamboo leaves, insects, birds, and similar motifs with coloured glazes on a cream ground, sometimes with angular patterns perforated at the rim. New designs for tableware were produced in Allen's studio from 1878. Experiments with lithography had begun in 1863, initially in imitation of oil painting. The production of painted and printed landscapes and views extended in the 1880s to include limited editions of commemorative dishes, plates and jugs, some for export to America, in Queensware, or, less frequently, cream earthenware or bone china.

Lawrence, Cecil and Francis Hamilton Wedgwood entered into a new partnership agreement in 1891 and the firm became a limited company in 1895. J.*Goodwin, who had been a designer at Etruria from 1892, became the firm's art director 1904-34, at first working under Cecil and Frank Wedgwood. Some of his tableware designs are still in production. Two shapes, one inspired by Rouen faience, were commissioned by the French retailer, Georges Rouard, with whom the firm had entered into a sales agreement at the time of the opening of the Wedgwood showroom in Paris in 1902.

Goodwin built up a staff of painters and gilders working in traditional techniques. In Goodwin's studio, James Hodgkiss was concerned in the development of a powder blue glaze which was used for a decorative range with printing, gilding and lustre decoration derived from oriental wares. D.*Makeig-Jones started to design tablewares under Hodgkiss before the introduction of her Fairyland Lustre.

J. Wedgwood & Sons Ltd. Brass-mounted oil lamp, printed and painted with sunflowers against a terracotta ground with scale borders, 1882. 45 cm high overall.

A.*Powell, working with his wife in their London studio from the previous year, had offered designs for production at the Wedgwood factory in 1903. He started a school of freehand painting at Etruria by 1914. His pupils included M.*Taplin, who subsequently worked at the factory as decorator and designer. She was later to design lithographic reproduction in the late 1940s and 1950s and to run the firm's studio for the painting of porcelain and earthenware by hand. Inspired in the early 1920s by tin-glazed wares, the Powells designed the lustre-painted lines, Rhodian (1920), consisting of jars, vases, dishes, bowls and trays, and Persian (1926), which both had decoration in Islamic style. In the 1920s and 1930s, G.*Barnsley decorated wares which were made at the factory and subsequently sent back for firing. D.*Grant and V.*Bell in 1932 received an independent commission for a painted dinner service, which they carried out on ware made at Etruria. Later freelance artists, who provided designs for the firm's regular production, included E.*Ravilious.

Arthur Dale Holland (1896-1979), a painter specializing in flower studies, fish and game, worked for the firm 1910-35 and again in the early 1940s. His work also included the painting of figures and a line of

basalt in the early 1920s with inlaid decoration.

V.*Skellern, who had joined the firm in 1923, succeeded Goodwin as art director, 1934-65. He collaborated with the designer and technician, N.*Wilson, on the introduction of the Alpine Pink tableware, made in tinted bone china and launched commercially in 1936, as well as a number of new glazes. Other coloured bodies introduced in the 1930s included Champagne and Honey-buff variations of cream-coloured earthenware, and a grey bone china paste. Wilson developed layered bodies in two colours, which became a staple output of the firm. The designer, K.*Murray designed painted decoration for tableware in traditional shapes, as well as the shapes for cylindrical, tapering or stepped jugs, mugs, vases and bowls for which he is best known. Some of his designs have *sgraffito* lines of decoration and are occasionally referred to as 'Keith Murray slipware'.

Figures, which had not been a prominent part of the firm's output since the production of Carrara Ware, took on greater importance with the issue of animal models by J.R.*Skeaping in the 1930s. They were generally made from individual designs by independent artists, and production was interrupted by the outbreak of World War II. Figure-making was started at Barlaston in 1940. A.*Machin was engaged as a full-time modeller, providing over 20 figures and a number of other designs, such as chess men, and relief decoration for jasper ware. Freelance designers included the animal sculptor, Alan Best, who provided figures of athletes, and two animal models; Louis Richard Garbe (1876-1957), formerly Professor of Sculpture at the Royal College of Art and a modeller for *Doulton & Co. in the 1930s, provided designs for two figures of cupids and a siren, produced in 1941; D.*Lindner provided the design for a pair of bookends representing a reclining girl, c.1934. The Norwegian artist Erling Olsen (b 1903) modelled decorative lamps, bookends, vases and other Art Deco earthenware for production with soft-coloured, sometimes matt, glazes c.1935, afterwards joining the *Haeger Potteries as a designer.

Soon after the bicentenary celebrations for Josiah Wedgwood I in 1930, Josiah Wedgwood succeeded Francis Hamilton Wedgwood as Managing Director. He re-organized the firm, increasing efficiency to combat the effects of the Great Depression, and took the decision to build a new factory at Barlaston, which was planned by Wilson and Thomas Wedgwood, and began production of earthenware in 1940, and bone china and jasper ware at the end of World War II. The Etruria factory closed in 1950. Under Josiah Wedgwood V in the 1950s, the firm began a great expansion both in production and sales; in 1980 about 2,500 people were employed, and the Barlaston factory was regarded as among the largest and most modern in the world, combining advanced technological development with traditional processes. Arthur Bryan, who had joined the firm in 1947, took over as Managing Director in 1963 and became Chairman of the re-organized company in 1967. By 1980, the Wedgwood company headed a group which included William Adams & Sons Ltd of Tunstall, R.H. & S.L. Plant Ltd, Susie

Cooper Ltd (from 1966), Coalport China Ltd (1967), Johnson Bros (Hanley) Ltd (1968), J.& G. Meakin, W.R. Midwinter, A.J. Wilkinson Ltd (1970), Crown Staffordshire, Mason's Ironstone (1973), the Californian firm of Franciscan Tableware (1979), and Enoch Wedgwood (Tunstall) Ltd (1980), as well as glass manufacturers, metal-working firms and retail companies. *Refs:* Batkin; H.M. Buten *Wedgwood and Artists* (Philadelphia, 1960), *Wedgwood Counterpoint* (Philadelphia, 1962), *Wedgwood ABC but not middle E* (Philadelphia, 1964), *Wedgwood Rarities* (Philadelphia, 1968); D. Buten & P. Pelehach *Emile Lessore 1805-1876. His Life and Work* (Philadelphia, 1979); U. Des Fontaines *Wedgwood Fairyland Lustre* (Sotheby Parke Bernet, London, 1975); Forsyth; Godden (1961, 1974 a, b); Hughes (1959); Jewitt; A. Kelly *Decorative Wedgwood* (London, 1965); M. Klamkin *The Collector's Book of Wedgwood* (Newton Abbot, 1965); Lockett (1979); Mankowitz & Haggar; *Modern Wedgwood* (catalogue for the firm's bicentenary, 1930); Reilly & Savage; Rhead; Shinn; Wakefield; *Wedgwood of Etruria and Barlaston* (catalogue, City Museum & Art Gallery, Stoke-on-Trent, 1980); C.V. Wedgwood *The Last of the Radicals* (London, 1957); J. Wedgwood *Essays and Adventures of a Labour M.P.* (London, 1924), *Memoirs of a Fighting Life* (London, 1960).

Wedgwood, Ralph. *See* Ferrybridge or Knottingley Pottery.

Wedgwood & Co. Staffordshire pottery manufacturers, successors of *Podmore, Walker & Co. at two factories in Tunstall from the mid 19th century. The firm made toilet sets, tableware, etc., for sale in England, Europe and America, specializing in transfer-printed ironstone china and painted, jewelled or gilded decorative wares. It was incorporated as a limited company 1910-65 and subsequently traded as Enoch Wedgwood (Tunstall) Ltd, becoming part of the Wedgwood group (*see* Wedgwood, J., & Sons Ltd) in 1980.

Marks include WEDGWOOD & CO, sometimes with the material, e.g. *ironstone china*; the head of a unicorn with collar and chain over the firm's name on a ribbon. *Refs:* Godden (1964); Jewitt; *Wedgwood of Etruria & Barlaston* (catalogue, City Museum & Art Gallery, Stoke-on-Trent, Staffordshire, 1980).

Wegner, Andreas Franz. German modeller working at *Meissen from 1802, known for portrait busts (e.g. Napoleon). *Ref:* Danckert.

Weingarten. German porcelain factory established 1882 for the production of everyday ware and luxury items. The firm produced vases with crystalline glazes c.1900 by the sculptor, Carl Kornhas. The factory is no longer in operation.

Marks include the initials of the founder, Adolf Baumgarten; monogram of CKW in a square; the initials PW. *Ref:* Danckert.

Weinlaubdekor. *See* Meissen.

Weir, John. *See* Bell, John.

Weiss, Emil Rudolf. *See* Karlsruhe.

Weiss, George Veit. *See* Crailsheim.

Weller, Harry A. (d 1932). American potter. Weller learned ceramic techniques at the pottery of his uncle, S.A.*Weller, and worked as manager of a branch of his uncle's firm. In 1908-09, he briefly operated the pottery formerly occupied by C.*Nielson in Zanesville, making *jardinières*, umbrella stands, etc., with matt green or glossy glazes, under the title H.A. Weller Art Pottery. Weller returned to his uncle's firm and became president in 1925.
Refs: Evans; Kovel & Kovel; N.F. Schneider in *Times Recorder* (Zanesville, 4th February 1962).

Weller, Samuel A. (1851-1925). American potter. From 1872, Weller produced umbrella stands, *jardinières*, flowerpots and hanging baskets in red earthenware in his home town, Fultonham, Ohio. He moved the pottery to Zanesville in 1888, and to a new plant nearby two years later. He acquired the *Lonhuda Pottery in 1894, transferring its operations to his own works in 1895 and, in the ensuing year of partnership with W.A.*Long, developed his own production of slip-painted art ware, closely resembling Lonhuda ware and the contemporary Rookwood Standard ware, and sold as Louwelsa. This line, in production 1895-1918, consisted of vases, *jardinières*, etc., made by jigger and jolley, dried and sprayed with background colour (mainly orange blending with shades of brown) from an atomizer. Patterns of fruit, flowers or portraits (often of American Indians) were then painted on in coloured slips, chiefly in lighter shades of the background colours, and green, and covered with a clear, glossy glaze. The title was derived from the name of Weller's daughter, Louise, and his own initials. Variations introduced

Samuel A. Weller. Matt-glazed vase with moulded decoration of a frog and a snake, c.1905. 19.7 cm high.

by 1897 included Turada, designed by Weller himself, with lacy decoration inlaid in white, orange or blue slip against darker grounds of black, brown or dark blue under a glossy glaze, and the first line of Dickensware with a solid ground of dark brown, blue or green and slip-painted flowers designed by C.B. *Upjohn. Two later versions of Dickensware were to follow: one brightly painted with subjects that included characters from Dickens within *sgraffito* outlines (high gloss or matt glaze), the third with relief figures and, on the reverse side, a black disc bearing an inscription identifying the scene shown (after a Cruikshank illustration) or sometimes a portrait of Charles Dickens. This Dickens line was attributed to F.H.*Rhead, who in his short stay at the pottery also developed the lines Jap Birdimal (earthenware with designs of birds, trees, animals, Japanese figures, landscapes, geometrical motifs, etc., outlined in piped white slip, usually against a ground of blue or grey and filled in with a slip of contrasting colour under a glossy glaze) and L'Art Nouveau (relief figures framed with flowers and foliage on semi-matt ground of pink and grey) – both resembling work he had carried out at the *Avon Faience Co. Eocean (or Eosian) ware—of which the third Dickens line was a decorative variant—was painted in slip with flowers, fruit, birds, fish, figure subjects on blended grounds, generally in blue, grey and soft green, inspired by Rookwood's Iris. It was included in Weller's extensive display at the World's Fair in St Louis (1904) as well as Sicardo ware, thrown or modelled by hand and decorated with lustre on iridescent grounds in shades of purple, green and brown, developed by J.*Sicard, who joined the pottery in 1901, and Aurelian with brushed background and decoration in brighter shades of yellow, red and brown than Louwelsa, which it otherwise resembled. An Aurelian vase signed by T.J.*Wheatley

dates from 1898, and the line continued in production until 1910. Auroro, a crackle ware with aquatic or floral designs in slip on mottled grey or pink background, was produced by 1904. One version, Auroral, painted with fish on a green ground, followed Rookwood's Sea Green ware; others were entitled Aurora and Auroso.

Designers employed by the pottery included G.*Fudji, designer of a line marketed as Fudzi, which resembled his Woodland and Fudji lines developed at the *Roseville Pottery Co.; F.L.*Ferrell, artist of the Louwelsa line until 1905; A.*Haubrich, who worked on Louwelsa and Eocean 1897-1903 before joining the pottery of A.*Radford (also an employee of Weller in the early 19th century).

Weller maintained rivalry with the Roseville Pottery and, for a time, the company owned by J.B.*Owens, with the constant expansion of his range of art ware. Because of the commercial nature of his output, shapes were generally moulded in quantity, and designs were used for more than one kind of ware (e.g. decoration of poppy flower and seed heads painted under glaze and outlined in piped slip on a plate signed by F.H. Rhead was also adapted for use on mugs and condiment sets). Although the many new lines introduced after 1910 required increasingly little individual decorative work, J.*Lessell, art director 1920-24, introduced some hand-decorated wares, including LaSa with metallic lustre, usually in a tree design, on a silvery background representing

Samuel A. Weller. Dickensware stoneware vase painted with a bust of Chief Hollow Horn Bear in pastel colours with incised detail. 35 cm high.

Weingarten. Porcelain vase designed by Carl Kornhas and made at the Weingarten factory c.1900. 15.3 cm high.

water and sky; another (Lamar) featuring trees was painted over the glaze against a deep red ground.

The business, incorporated in 1922, employed about 600 workers at the time of its greatest output. When Weller was succeeded as president by his nephew H.*Weller in 1925, the firm owned three factories producing art pottery, garden ornaments and kitchen ware. As a result of the economic depression in the 1930s, two of the plants closed in 1936. The firm ceased operation in 1948 and was dissolved in 1949.

Marks: LP impressed within a shield on Lonhuda Faience produced in partnership with Long. *Weller*, impressed, often with the name of the line (but decoration and mark sometimes differ). After 1915, *Weller* alone, incised, impressed or moulded. Pieces of Sicardo and LaSa were often signed on the face. *Weller/Rhead/Faience*, incised, occurs on Jap Birdimal ware.
Refs: Barber (1976); M. Benjamin *American Art Pottery* (privately published, Washington, D.C., 1907); Evans; Jervis; Kovel & Kovel; Peck; L.& E. Purviance & N.F. Schneider *Weller Art Pottery in Color* (Wallace-Homestead, Des Moines, Iowa, 1971).

Reginald Wells. Stoneware model of a cart horse, with brown-speckled pale beige glaze, 1930s. 14.5 cm high.

Wells, Reginald (1877-1951). English sculptor and (from c.1909) artist potter. Wells made earthenware at the Coldrum Pottery, near Wrotham, Kent, using a brownish glaze and sometimes white slip decoration reminiscent of that on 17th-century Wrotham ware. He subsequently worked in Chelsea (c.1910-24) and, later at Storrington, Sussex, where he made stoneware inspired by Chinese pottery. The glazes used on his vases, etc., included a matt blue and a greyish white, containing borax and sometimes crackled in imitation of Chün or Yüan wares.

Marks include *Coldrum* with *Wrotham* or *Chelsea*, Well's signature, his initials arranged in the angles of a Y, and the mark SOON in a rectangle.
Refs: Rose; *The Studio* (December 1925); Wingfield Digby.

Wemyss ware. *See* Fife Pottery.

Wennerberg, Gunnar. Swedish ceramic designer; artistic director of the *Gustavsberg factory in the early 20th century. He started

the production of pottery decorated with simple *sgraffito* floral patterns. He also designed pieces for the Kosta glassworks near Karlskröna.
Refs: Haslam (1977); Préaud & Gauthier.

Western Pottery Manufacturing Co. *See* Denver China & Pottery Co.

West Riding Pottery. *See* Ferrybridge or Knottingley Pottery.

Wetlach, Carl. *See* Durlach.

Wetmore, Samuel & Co. *See* Huntington Pottery.

Wewerka, Hans. *See* Merkelbach, Reinhold.

Whalley, John. *See* Stafford Pottery.

Wheatley, Thomas Jerome (1853-1917). American potter. Wheatley worked as a decorator at the *Coultry Pottery in 1879 and taught a small class in underglaze decoration, while continuing his own experiments. He formed a brief partnership with Coultry for the production of underglaze faience, entering into litigation over the ownership of a number of vases which were among the assets. Wheatley claimed discovery of the technique of decorating Cincinnati faience (which he called American Limoges) and patented his method in 1880, despite its close resemblance to that already used by M.L.*McLaughlin, with slip painted on a damp clay body.

Wheatley established his own pottery (1880) in Cincinnati, at first carrying out all the processes himself and within a few months taking on other decorators. The pottery's output of vases, which were varied in shape and, in some cases, relatively large, was mainly made in local yellow clay and painted with flowers, etc., in coloured slip under a glossy glaze. Wheatley left his company, which then traded as *Cincinnati Art Pottery, in 1882.

After working as a decorator in the late 1890s for S.A.*Weller, he returned to Cincinnati c.1900 and established the Wheatley Pottery Co. in 1903, making a variety of art ware, including relief-decorated pieces with matt glazes in dark green, yellow or blue; some vases covered with green glaze resembling the work of W.H.*Grueby, or with crackled or mottled effects. Wheatley also made architectural ware, e.g. panels and mantel decoration, and garden ornaments. He rebuilt his pottery after damage by fire in 1910, continuing up to his death, by which time garden ware, tiles and chimneypots had become the main output. He was succeeded by his associate, Isaac Kahn, who moved the pottery to larger premises and expanded the range of garden ware and increased production of architectural ware.

The pottery traded as the Wheatley Tile & Pottery Co. after its purchase by a nearby tile company in 1927 and closed in the 1930s.

Marks: signature, *T.J. Wheatley*, or, from 1880, *T.J. Wheatley & Co*; initials T.J.W. & CO. (all incised). Work at the Wheatley Pottery Co. bore a paper label printed with a monogram of WP within a circle.
Refs: Barber (1976); Evans; Jervis; Kovel & Kovel; 'Wheatley Pottery Co.' in *Antiques* (June 1966).

Wheatley Tile & Pottery Co. *See* Cambridge Art Tile Works.

Wheeler, L.D. American potter. In partnership with Asa Hill, Wheeler made pottery buttons moulded or pressed from plastic clay in two grades, red clay with light brown glaze or white body with mottled glaze, at Norwalk, Connecticut, before 1850, and by 1853 made knobs for doors, furniture and shutters. He was succeeded by his son and son-in-law E.*Wood until the destruction of his pottery by fire in 1865.
Refs: Barber (1976); Watkins (1950).

Wheeling Pottery Co. American pottery established in 1879 at Wheeling, West Virginia, for the production of granite ware, sold in the white or decorated. Charles Craddock, a Staffordshire artist previously working for Mintons Ltd, was employed from 1882, later becoming head of the firm's decorating department. In 1889, the pottery amalgamated with La Belle Pottery, started in 1887 by the same company and making a semi-porcelain marketed as Adamantine China. E.M.*Pearson, general manager, became the company's president in 1890. A thinly potted porcelain paste sold as Cameo China and painted in blue and gold, or other colours, was introduced in the early 20th century.

A firm, the Wheeling Potteries Co., was organized in 1902-03, as a combination of the Wheeling, *La Belle, Riverside and *Avon Faience potteries, all in the Wheeling area, under the management of Charles W. Franzheim, president of the company. The Wheeling and La Belle factories continued the production of cream-coloured earthenware, ironstone china and semi-porcelain until their closure in 1907. The Riverside Pottery made sanitary ware, and the Avon Faience works continued the production of art ware until 1905. The company was dissolved in late 1908.

Wheeling Pottery Co. marks include a globe with an eagle and STONE CHINA, a lion and unicorn with ROYAL IRONSTONE CHINA/

T.J. Wheatley. Pilgrim flask, press-moulded in a heavy cream body, painted in slip, slightly raised. Marked T.J. Wheatley and J. Rettig [the decorator] with 1879. 33 cm high.

WARRANTED, and a variety of marks incorporating the firm's name or initials, or the name of the body.
Refs: Barber (1976); Evans; Kovel & Kovel.

Wheelock, Arthur Washburn. *See* Norse Pottery.

Whitaker, John. English porcelain modeller. Whitaker was apprenticed in 1818 as a modeller and figure maker at the porcelain factory in Nottingham Road, *Derby, where his grandfather had also been a modeller. Whitaker succeeded S.*Keys Jr as foreman of the figure modellers in 1830, and became superintendent of the modelling department in 1842. Haslem lists eighteen figures modelled by him between 1830 and 1847, and mentions a peacock as outstanding.
Refs: Eaglestone & Lockett; Haslem; Shinn; *see also* Derby.

Whitcomb, Lois. *See* Rhead, Frederick Hurten.

White, Frederick J. (1838-1919). English-born potter. White worked with his father, also a potter, in their home town of Bristol. He settled with his family at the Courtenay or Cortney Bay Pottery, New Brunswick, in 1863. He returned (1875-92) to help run the Baptist Mills Pottery in Bristol, and subsequently in America carried out research in Colorado clays at Denver and worked in local stoneware potteries. With his son, Francis G. White (1869-1960), he established his own works at Denver in 1894 for the production of household earthenware (including jugs, teapots, and bowls) in local buff-firing clay. Art ware, introduced 1909, included vases, lamps and *jardinières* with grainy, semi-matt glaze (sold as Gray Ware or Denver Gray Ware), or a variety of other monochrome glazes, many of which were developed at the pottery. Another art line was thrown in agate ware with swirling patterns of differently coloured clays. Shapes were in general very simple, and decoration was restricted to occasional impressed lines of beading, although a slip-painted line was also produced. After the introduction of art ware, the company traded as the Denver Art Pottery, moving to other sites in the city to allow expansion c.1911, in 1915 and, under the management of Francis White, in 1921. Francis White retired in the 1950s.
    Marks (when used) include *Denver*, incised, often with initial w enclosed in D; occasionally *White* or *Denver*, impressed.
Refs: Denver News (19th March 1960); *Denver Post* (30th May 1954, 18th March 1960); *Denver Times* (18th February 1919); Evans.

White, George. English ceramic decorator, noted for his painting of figure subjects, including classical or literary scenes, and realistic portraits. After training at art schools in South Kensington and Lambeth, London, he worked for *Doulton & Co. in Burslem 1885-1912, painting many vases, of which some examples were shown at the World's Columbian Exposition in Chicago, (1893).

His subjects included scenes in the style of Watteau or Pre-Raphaelite painters. White executed portraits on porcelain of H.*Doulton and some of the Burslem factory employees.
Refs: see Doulton & Co.

White, Joseph (1799-1870). English-born stoneware manufacturer, the son of a Bristol potter (also Joseph White). He trained under J.D. Pountney at the *Bristol Pottery at first as an apprentice turner in 1814. In partnership with his brother James, White started the Baptist Mills Pottery in Bristol for the production of Rockingham and black-glazed earthenware teapots, decorative stoneware jugs, and cooking and storage vessels in stoneware with a leadless glaze that was advertised as 'impervious to acids'. By 1855 the brothers had retired from their pottery, which was continued by White's son, also Joseph.
    After the departure of his second son, William D. White (1833-74), for the west coast of America in 1858, Joseph White emigrated with his wife, daughters and sons, James A. White (1841-1928) and F.J.*White, to New Brunswick, buying (in 1863) a small pottery at Crouchville, Courtenay or Courtney Bay (now East Saint John), where he continued production of the wares that he had made in Bristol, including glazed stoneware, selling as far afield as Montreal. His output also included hanging baskets and flowerpots, some decorative tiles, vases, etc., in earthenware, as well as tobacco pipes; some flowerpots were made in agate ware. After White's death, Frederick J. and briefly William continued the pottery with their brother James, who worked there alone from 1875 until the pottery's bankruptcy in the late 1880s. Joseph White's grandson, James Foley, was later to found the Canuck Pottery at Labelle, Quebec, in the 20th century.
Refs: Collard; Evans; Pountney.

White family. A family of American potters making stoneware in New York. The firm's founder, Noah White (c.1793-1865), born in Thetford, Vermont, moved to Utica, New York State, in 1828, and worked in the stoneware works founded by Justin *Campbell, buying that and the nearby pottery operated by *Brayton, Kellogg & Doolittle in 1839. With his sons, William and Nicholas A. White (d 1886), and working as Noah White & Sons from 1849, he made jugs, jars, butter crocks, etc., with ovoid bodies, decorated simply in cobalt blue. The works were expanded to include the manufacture of firebrick in the 1840s. William White left the pottery in 1856 to establish his own pottery in Illinois. In 1863, William N. White (d 1877), son of Nicholas, succeeded his grandfather in the Utica firm, which then traded as Noah White, Son & Co. The wares became increasingly refined in decoration and finish; the shapes were more commonly cylindrical (rather than ovoid). Bird motifs were frequently used, as well as the traditional flower patterns, which became increasingly naturalistic in treatment. A price list of 1860 offered jugs, churns, pitchers, spittoons, chamber pots, flowerpots, cream and butter pots, preserve jars, beer bottles, inkstands and stove tubes, as well as furnace and fire bricks. The plant, known as the Central

New York Pottery, was expanded in the 1870s, and the range of distribution increased. Work from the early 1880s is characterized by the deep colour of the blue used in decoration, which is firmly drawn and often elaborate. Some large pieces were decorated with peacocks. Noah White's son-in-law, potter William Roberts, moved c. 1849 to Binghampton, New York, where he made stoneware. His pottery shared many features of decoration with the Utica works, including birds perched on a floral spray trailed in slip. Nicholas A. White's son, Charles, became a partner in his father's business in 1882 and took over the running of Roberts's pottery in a partnership, White & Wood. He afterwards became sole proprietor of his family's Utica works, in 1886, trading as Charles N. White Clay Products until his retirement in 1909. The pottery expanded its range of refractory wares and introduced beer mugs, sometimes lidded in metal, and other moulded pieces in European styles by German designer Hugo Billhardt, with relief decoration in blue, brown and green depicting hunting, drinking scenes, etc. The production of stoneware ceased in 1907, and the firm closed at the time of Charles White's retirement.
    Marks: impressed marks incorporate the firm's names and address.
Refs: Barber (1976); Ketchum (1970); Stradling; Webster.

White Granite. *See* ironstone.

Wibsey Pottery. Yorkshire pottery working near Bradford from the 18th century until c.1840. Using local clay, the works produced brown salt-glazed stoneware, mainly cups, mugs and cooking vessels, sometimes with simple, incised patterns, lead-glazed earthenware for domestic use, and, in the 20th century, drainage pipes.
Refs: Lawrence; H.J.M. Maltby 'Wibsey Pottery' in *The Connoisseur* 83 (April 1929).

Wienerberger Werkstättenschule für Keramik. Training workshop built 1919-21 at the Wienerberger Ziegelfabriks- und Baugesellschaft [brick and tile factory] in Vienna, which had already begun the production of art stoneware early in the 20th century. The school was run by R.*Obsieger from its completion until 1932 and exhibited work to designs by Obsieger, H.*Bucher, O.*Prutscher, M.*Powolny and other artists. The output consisted of display plates, relief plaques, vases, figures and groups, as well as ovens, fountains and interior fittings.
    Mark: the initial w with a flame in an irregularly hexagonal outline.
Refs: Neuwirth (1974a, 1974b).

Wiener Emailfarbwerk Schauer & Co. Viennese workshop established by Anton Ritter von Schauer in 1900 for the production and marketing of enamel colours and the firing of painted porcelain and earthenware. In 1907, the firm also produced vases, lamps, figures, groups and other decorative pieces. Schauer was the sole proprietor after the death of his partner in 1932. The workshop also produced bronzes, silver and gold.
    Mark: seated man working in front of a furnace.
Refs: Neuwirth (1974a, 1974b).

Wiener Keramik. Figure designed by Emil Meier for Wiener Keramik, c.1908.

Wiener Keramik. Austrian ceramic workshop established 1905 in Vienna by M.*Powolny and B.*Löffler and trading in association with the Wiener Werkstätte until 1911. The workshop made decorative tiles for a commission in 1907 and supplied ceramic fittings for the Palais Stoclet in Brussels 1905-11. The output included boxes, vases, etc., in white earthenware, painted in black with geometrical patterns or flowers in outline on relief garlands, designed by artists such as J.*Hoffman, D.*Peche and Powolny, who was primarily known for spirited figures of children modelled in earthenware. Portrait figures, animal models and some other pieces were painted in bright colours. The models were mainly the work of Powolny and Löffler; other artists included the designer Fritz Dietl, E. Meier, R.*Obsieger, and F.*Schleich. In 1912, the workshop merged with that of F.*Schleiss in Gmunden to become Vereinigte Wiener und Gmundner Keramik. The joint firm was reorganized in 1918 and worked under the title, Gmundner Keramik GmbH. from the following year.

Marks: a monogram of WK, over six spots arranged in a triangle and flanked by *Lö* and Powolny's monogram, all surrounded by a rectangle; GK with a potted plant, also in a rectangular outline.
Ref: Neuwirth (1974a, 1974b).

Wiener kunstkeramische Werkstätte Busch & Ludescher. Viennese art pottery established in 1908, when Heinrich Ludescher and Robert Busch took over the firm of their employers A.*Förster & Co. Ludescher left in the following year. The firm produced decorative ware in earthenware and glazed or biscuit porcelain, specializing in figures and groups, sculptured vases, clock-cases, bowls and other decorative pieces. The artists

included Busch, G.*Dengg, B.*Emmel, and A.*Puchegger.

Marks: the initials WKW with an insect and three small shields in a circle; WKW in a triangular mark.
Ref: Neuwirth (1974a, 1974b).

Wiener Porzellanmanufaktur. The Vienna Porcelain Factory was established in the early 18th century by Claudius Innocentius Du Paquier (d 1751) under the patronage of the Emperor and with help from the municipality of Vienna. In the late 18th century under the direction of Konrad von Sorgenthal (d 1805), and with the modellist and miniaturist Antonin Grassi (1755-1807) as art director from 1790, the factory had built a reputation for tableware with very lavish gilding and detailed painting, of which some examples were inspired by the discovery of the frescoes at Pompeii and by Raphael's grotesques, and others copied from the work of painters, e.g. peasant scenes by David Teniers II and Angelica Kauffmann's mythological scenes. Painted grounds imitated a wide range of textures, including mosaics. Some pieces were decorated with *chinoiseries* in gold relief against black or red grounds imitating lacquer. The factory then employing about 400 workers, also produced household ware simply bordered with cobalt blue.

The earlier painted figures in the style of Meissen were superseded by unglazed sculptural pieces modelled by Grassi and his pupils Elias Hutter and Johann Schaller in neoclassical style. The Birth of Venus (1842), a nude figure arising from a shell, is among the last examples made in the factory. The production of table decorations ceased in 1802, although some figures from a biscuit series made in 1767 were later reproduced with enamelled decoration. Vases as well as figures were made in biscuit porcelain, and lithophanes were made by the mid 19th century.

Wiener kunstkeramische Werkstätte Busch & Ludescher. Earthenware group glazed in cream and black. Impressed with a monogram. 25 cm high.

Wiener Porzellanmanufaktur. Porcelain platter painted by Joseph Nigg with flowers which include a peony, geraniums and a pink rose, 19th century. 24 cm high.

The artistic policy determined by von Sorgenthal was maintained by his successor, Mathias Niedermeyer, who remained as manager until 1829. Franz Caucig succeeded Grassi as art director, 1807-28. The factory completed a service for presentation to the Duke of Wellington by the Emperor of Austria to commemorate the defeat of Napoleon. The decoration included portraits of classical heroes painted on shapes designed by Hutter.

Plaques were richly painted in the 1820s with flowers by artists who included Joseph Nigg, Joseph Fischer and Ferdinand Gesswald. Joseph Cloos painted puzzle pictures, usually on presentation cups, in which the initial letters of the flowers in his composition spelled out a name. Views of towns and castles were introduced and souvenir cups decorated with the Hungarian coat of arms,

Wiener Porzellanmanufaktur. Pot-pourri and cover made in the 19th century with the factory's shield mark in blue. 24 cm high.

patron saints and inscriptions in Hungarian were produced for sale in Hungary.

Despite a programme of technical innovation which included the replacement of kilns, simplified gilding processes and the introduction of chrome green as a ground colour, the factory went into financial decline, and production ceased in 1863. Liquidation followed by order of the Emperor.

600 moulds for tableware and figures were sold to the De Cente factory, a manufacturer of stoves and heat-resistant ware in Vienna-Neustadt, which subsequently ceased operation. E.*Wahliss acquired these moulds for his own production in 1900. Others were used by the *Herend factory.

In the 19th century, marks included versions of the factory's 18th century mark, a shield with two bars; also a two-barred triangle and a circular mark containing K.K. PORZ. MANUF, with the shield at the centre.
Refs: Danckert; R. Ernst *Wiener Porzellan des Klassizismus: Sammlung Bloch-Bauer* (Vienna, 1925); O. von Falke *Deutsche Porzellanfiguren* (Berlin, 1919); J. Folnesics & E.W. Braun *Geschichte der K.K. Wiener Porzellan-Manufaktur* (Vienna, 1907); Honey (1952); Weiss.

Wiener Werkstätte. Craft workshops founded in Vienna, 1903, by J.*Hoffmann, K. *Moser and F. Wärndorfer. Close associations established with *Wiener Keramik and F. *Schleiss on the production of ceramics were maintained after the opening of a ceramic workshop in 1913. Artists including D.*Peche, G.*Baudisch-Wittke, H.*Bucher, L.*Calm-Wierink, M.*Flögl, I.*Gador, E.*Kopriva, B.*Kuhn, K. and F.*Rix, S. *Singer-Schinerl, J.*Sitte and V.*Wieselthier produced a wide variety of domestic and ornamental wares. The workshops closed in 1932.

Marks usually incorporate a monogram of ww or sometimes stylized flowers.
Refs: Neuwirth (1974a, 1974b).

Wieselthier, Valerie or Vally (1895-1945). Austrian-born potter and ceramic sculptor. Vally Wieselthier studied at the Wiener Kunstgewerbeschule 1914-20 under artists including J.*Hoffmann, K.*Moser and M.*Powolny. During her work with the Wiener Werkstätte from 1912, she was influenced in style by D.*Peche. She also modelled figures for the Augarten factory and for Jos.*Bock. Her work was exhibited in 1925 at the Exposition des Arts Décoratifs in Paris, and in 1928 in America, where she settled the following year, joining the Contempora Group in New York, and doing designs for the *Sebring Pottery Co. Imaginative, humorous pieces made at her New York studio were influential in the development of ceramic sculpture in America. Vally Wieselthier stressed the importance of experimental work in pottery, an art she considered close to the human instincts and, when executed with meticulous care and deep feeling, capable of increasing the happiness of people's lives.

Marks: monogram of vw; full signature.
Refs: The Animal Kingdom in American Art (Everson Museum of Art Syracuse, New York, 1978); E.L. Cary in *Critical Comments on the International Exhibition of Ceramic Art* (American Federation of Arts,

New York, 1928); Clark & Hughto; Donhauser; Neuwirth (1974a, 1974b); 'The Pottery of Vally Wieselthier' in *Design* 31 No 6 (November 1929).

Wild, T., & Co. Staffordshire porcelain manufacturer working at the Albert Works, established in 1894 by Thomas Clark Wild, who was succeeded by his family. The firm built up a large export trade with outlets in North America, Australia, New Zealand and Africa. Wild's occupied St Mary's Works, Longton, from 1905 for the production of ware marketed as Royal Albert China, and the firm, under the control of Thomas and Frederick Wild from 1914, traded as Thomas C. Wild & Sons Ltd, 1917-c.1972. The output included tea and coffee sets, dinner services and table decoration. The firm became part of the Royal Doulton Group, and occupied the Shelley Potteries works (*see* Shelley, P.) for the production of Royal Albert China.

Printed marks incorporate a crown, ROYAL ALBERT CHINA, and sometimes the initials TCW.
Refs: Bunt; Cushion (1980); Godden (1964); Jewitt.

Wildblood, Heath & Sons Staffordshire porcelain manufacturers, operating the Peel Works, Longton. In 1887, Richard Vernon Wildblood took over the production of porcelain and fine earthenwares which had been started by the previous occupants of the factory, Webb & Walters, and replaced the earlier output of coarse earthenware. Wildblood, in a partnership Wildblood & Heath from 1889, and trading as Wildblood, Heath & Sons Ltd from 1899, produced hotel and institutional tableware, decorated with crests, badges, etc., as well as a small number of topographical pieces with views, and in 1920 advertised ornamental miniatures with coats of arms, etc. The firm ceased operation in 1927.

Printed marks incorporate a crown, the initials W.H. & S. and sometimes a label CLIFTON CHINA.
Refs: Andrews; Cushion (1980); Godden (1964); Jewitt.

Wilde, Fred H. *See* Arequipa Pottery.

Wildenhain, Frans (b 1905). Artist potter, born in Leipzig, Germany. After serving an apprenticeship as draughtsman and lithographer, Wildenhain specialized in pottery while at the Bauhaus (1924-25), under G. *Marcks, subsequently gaining his M.A. at the Kunstgewerbeschule at Halle-Saale. He took charge of the pottery department at the Folkwang School workshops in Essen-Ruhr, afterwards teaching in Halle-Saale. With his wife, M.*Friedlander, he went to Holland in 1933, establishing a workshop in Putten. He moved to Amsterdam in 1941, then to England, and in 1947 to America, briefly joining his wife at her workshop in Guerneville, California. His work is bold and simple in shape, with decoration (often featuring curved leaves, sea shells or the movement of water) closely allied to form. He said: 'I use technical and professional skills, inventing my own technique—the one which I consider meaningful to me. What counts is vision.' His sources include the folk tales of Germany, Mexico, etc., and contemporary

Japanese work. Wildenhain became professor of pottery and sculpture at the School for American Craftsmen at the Rochester Institute for Technology in New York from 1950 until his retirement in 1975, and received a Guggenheim fellowship for his work in relating ceramics to architecture.
Refs: 'Ceramics' double issue of *Design Quarterly* 42-43 (1958); Clark & Hughto; Donhauser; R.H. Johnston *Frans Wildenhain* (Rochester Institute of Technology, New York, 1975); F. Wildenhain in the catalogue of his retrospective exhibition (State University of New York, Binghampton, New York, December 1974).

Wildenhain, Marguerite. *See* Friedlander, Margarete.

Wileman, Henry (1798-1864). English pottery manufacturer. A dealer in glass and Staffordshire ceramics in London, Wileman was the owner of the *Church Gresley Pottery until his death. In the 1850s, he became the partner of John King Knight at the *Foley Potteries, trading there under his own name from 1856, and built the adjoining Foley China Works in 1860. He was succeeded by his sons James F. and Charles J. Wileman, who split the works in 1866 into units producing earthenware and porcelain respectively. James Wileman, proprietor of both works after his brother's retirement in 1870, relinquished control of the China Works in 1884, leaving them to be run by J.B.*Shelley, his partner since 1872, but managed the earthenware production until his retirement in 1892.

Marks: the Wilemans' marks include their name or initials, or incorporate the trade name FOLEY.
Refs: Andrews; Bunt; Godden (1964); Jewitt; Watkins *et al.*

Wilkes, Edward R. *See* Moore, Bernard.

Wilkins, Liza. *See* Della Robbia Pottery.

Wilkinson, A.J., Ltd. Staffordshire pottery manufacturers operating several factories in the Burslem area from the late 19th century. The firm took over the Central Pottery in 1885, making white granite ware for export to America, some decorated with gold lustre, and subsequently the Churchyard Works in 1887, and the Mersey Pottery c.1900, also working the Royal Staffordshire Pottery. The firm was purchased in 1894 by Edmund Leigh and Arthur Shorter, brother-in-law of A.J. Wilkinson. Still trading under the name of Wilkinson, it was controlled from 1916 by A.C.A.*Shorter and his brother, who took over the nearby Newport Pottery by 1920. As well as traditional designs in tableware for domestic and institutional use, the firm produced table services, toilet sets, vases, rose bowls and other ornamental pieces designed by J. Butler and strongly influenced in style by Art Nouveau, e.g. the ranges Oriflamme and Rubaiyat. Later, the production of earthenware and semi-porcelain bodies was extended to include stoneware, e.g. ribbed vases with glossy glazes. A decorative line, Tibetan ware, was decorated with bright enamel and trickled gold lustre; some pieces are marked with the signature of C.*Cliff, decorator, designer, and from

1930, the firm's art director. In 1929 the company's Newport works turned over to the large-scale production of Clarice Cliff's Bizarre ware, which was heavily promoted on the market. The firm cooperated with E.*Brain & Co. on the experimental production of tableware and other stock pieces with patterns, some printed and hand-finished, which were carried out on earthenware at the Newport works to designs by contemporary artists. Tableware sets were issued in limited editions of twelve; the pieces made by Wilkinson's (with the exception of some plaques by Frank Brangwyn) were marked *Produced in Bizarre by Clarice Cliff*, and the artist's signature was accompanied by the company mark, date and copyright.

Although the lines of Bizarre shapes – Biarritz, Odelin and Bon Jour continued to sell well, and less extreme versions of the Conical shapes were produced with open handles, the demand for Bizarre ware declined by the late 1930s, and more traditional patterns were used in decoration. During the period of restrictions on the production of decorated ware in World War II, the Bizarre workshop closed (1941), the Newport factory was annexed as a Ministry of Supply depot, and the decorators transferred to Wilkinson's other works. Small quantities of ware in a shape with toothed edge and simple banded decoration were made for export. In the 1950s, apart from the painted Crocus pattern, and some services marketed as Clarice Cliff's Dinnerware, the company mainly used traditionally inspired printed decoration of pastoral, literary and floral

Willets Manufacturing Co. The only known pair of candlesticks made in Belleek ware by Willets, c.1895-1905. 21.6 cm high.

designs on tableware. Commemorative portrait jugs depicting e.g. Winston Churchill, Lord Montgomery, and coronation ware were also produced. The sale of the company to W.R.*Midwinter Ltd was completed in 1965.

Marks incorporate the firm's name, *Wilkinson's* or *A.J. Wilkinson Ltd* and a crown or the Royal Arms, sometimes with the name of the body, e.g. *Royal Semi-Porcelain*, and *Royal Staffordshire Pottery*. (Bizarre marks: *see* Cliff, C.)
Ref: Clarice Cliff (catalogue, L'Odeon, London, 1976); Godden (1964).

Willard, W.F. *See* Gay Head Pottery.

Willermet, Antoine-Gabriel. *See* Sèvres.

Willets Manufacturing Co. American ceramics manufacturer working from 1879 at a factory built in 1853 at Trenton, New Jersey for the production of Rockingham ware and ordinary domestic earthenware, and later making porcelain hardware trimmings. Under the brothers, Joseph, Daniel and Edmund R. Willets, the firm made sanitary ware, earthenware and granite ware for domestic use, dinner services and toilet sets with underglaze decoration, and porcelain for sale to outside decorators. W.*Bromley assisted in the introduction of Belleek ware, which included picture frames with modelled flowers, as well as the shapes derived from marine life initiated by the *Belleek factory. The firm also produced thinly potted porcelain, similar to that made at Worcester, in shapes derived from Isnik wares, heavily gilded, with openwork decoration, etc.

Marks include a lion and unicorn with a shield bearing the initial w; a monogram; a snake twisted into a w, with WILLETS and

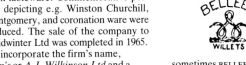

sometimes BELLEEK; versions of a globe, incorporating W.M. CO.
Ref: Barber (1976).

Williams, Joseph (b c.1805). Porcelain painter working for the *Worcester Royal Porcelain Co. in the 1850s. His work in the 1860s and 1870s included animal subjects, rustic figures in the style of Birkett Foster, and copies of such paintings as Turner's *Fighting Temeraire*.
Ref: Sandon (1978a).

Williams & Willet. *See* Salt, Ralph.

Willmore, F.R. *See* Columbian Art Pottery Co.

Willott, Ralph. *See* Longpark Pottery.

Willow Potteries Ltd. *See* Robinson, Harold Taylor.

Willumsen, Jens Ferdinand (1863-1958). Danish artist and ceramist. After working as a painter, 1881-85, Willumsen travelled in Europe, also making a study of Middle-Eastern bas reliefs. He stayed for a time (1890) in Pont-Aven (Finisterre), where he worked with his friend, P.*Gauguin, and exhibited work in the Salon des Indépendants, 1891-92. He began to experiment with stoneware in 1891 and returned to Denmark in 1894, establishing a workshop and kilns near his home in Hellerup. He was among the first Danish artists to work in stoneware, but also used terracotta and porcelain in making figures, vases and jugs. He became known for the use of richly coloured glazes. Willumsen was art director for *Bing & Grøndahl, 1897-1900, and exhibited the factory's ceramics at La Libre Esthétique, Brussels. Some of his work was fired at the workshop of H.A. Kähler (*see* Kähler Ceramics).

His son, Bode Bertel W. Willumsen (b 1895), also worked as a potter and painter.
Refs: Bénézit; Hiort.

Wilson, Alfred, Ltd. *See* Roeginga Pottery.

Wilson, David. Staffordshire earthenware manufacturer. In 1802 Wilson took over the Church Works, Hanley, which had until the previous year been under the control of his brother Robert, successor to the firm of Neale & Co. David Wilson continued the production of creamware and pearlware, often well painted with country scenes in enamels. Figures were carefully modelled and enamelled, and their glaze strongly tinged with blue. Classical figures adapted from 18th century originals were sometimes decorated with lustre (e.g. a mounted Hussar attributed to Wilson and preserved in the British Museum). Wilson's firm operated until c.1820. Joseph Mayer (*see* Mayer, E., & Son) later purchased the works, which he let in 1832 to his cousin William Ridgway.

Marks include WILSON impressed.
Refs: Haggar (1955); Jewitt.

*Jens F. Willumsen. Porcelain vase modelled with deer and, on the other side, a boy bathing, made by *Bing & Grøndahl, 1898. 40 cm high.*

Wilson, Norman (b 1902). English ceramic chemist and designer, the son of Stephen Wilson, a potter in Fenton. Norman Wilson studied at the North Staffordshire Technical College in the 1920s. After visiting Canada in 1925, he joined J.*Wedgwood & Sons Ltd in 1927, when the factory was modernized. He worked on the development of monochrome glazes and ranges of matt or satin glazes. His developments in clay bodies include Alpine pink (a tinted bone china paste), a red stoneware and a basalt body in copper, bronze and Royal Blue. He also introduced tableware (which was to be produced in great quantities) in two layers of clay, the inner layer cast inside a pre-formed outer one in contrasting colour: Wintergreen (celadon-coloured and cream) was launched in 1936 and revived in 1954; others were Summer Sky (mauve-blue and white) which was reissued in 1954, and Harvest Moon (champagne and ivory).

With Thomas Wedgwood (a director of the firm from 1933), Wilson planned the Barlaston factory, which began earthenware production in 1940. After war service, he became the firm's Production Director until his retirement in 1963, and acted as Joint Managing Director from 1961. He designed tableware, including the Barlaston shape (1955), and throughout his employment designed experimental pieces, based on Chinese or Korean originals, mainly thrown, but sometimes cast to his own design. Some unique pieces were also designed by K.*Murray. Wilson finished them with a variety of glazes, including hare's fur, and aventurine effects. He also developed a grey glaze which appeared tan-coloured breaking to grey when used over a terracotta body, as in the re-issues of figures by J.*Skeaping in the 1900s. Wilson returned from retirement to design the firm's commemorative mug for the Investiture of the Prince of Wales in 1969.
Refs: Batkin; Reilly & Savage; *Wedgwood of Etruria and Barlaston* (catalogue, City

Museum & Art Gallery, Hanley, Staffordshire, 1980).

Wilson, Samuel. English ceramic artist, working for *Doulton & Co. in Burslem 1880-1909, and noted for his landscapes, hill and valley views with deer or cattle, fish and game studies, hunting and sporting scenes. *Refs: see* Doulton & Co.

Wilson, Samuel. *See* Indiana Pottery Co.

Wiltshaw & Robinson. Staffordshire manufacturer of earthenware and porcelain operating the Carlton Works, Stoke-on-Trent, from c.1890. The firm specialized in decorative items: vases, teapots, water jugs, as well as such pieces as biscuit boxes and others for mounting in silver. In 1902 they advertised crested porcelain. H.T.*Robinson, salesman for the firm, was a partner by 1906, but J.F. Wiltshaw was sole proprietor in 1911. The firm was known for lustre decoration by 1920 and soon developed a range of 12 colours, including mother-of-pearl, various shades of orange, turquoise, black and a rich red. The output included animal models, Toby jugs and female figures from the mid 1920s. After suffering financial difficulties, Wiltshaw & Robinson merged with Birks, Rawlins & Co. (*see* Birks, L.A., & Co.) in 1932, and have since made lavishly decorated vases, coffee sets, etc., with gilding and enamelled relief work as well as lustre decoration. Tableware included pieces in the form of leaves or flowers, and others with relief ornament and floral patterns. After World War II, the range of models included a series of cars.

Printed marks incorporate the trade mark *Carlton Ware*, and sometimes W & R/STOKE ON TRENT.
Refs: Andrews; Bunt; Cushion (1980); Godden (1964); Jewitt.

Winchcombe Pottery. Gloucestershire pottery at Greet, near Winchcombe, making earthenware flowerpots, washing pans and other domestic and dairy utensils from the early 19th century until 1916, under the title Beckett's Pottery. The site was put to farm use from 1916 until its revival as the Winchcombe Pottery by M.*Cardew, who rented the works in 1926 for the production of slipware in quantities large enough to allow sale at a reasonable price for domestic use: cider jars, jugs, large bowls, etc., covered in yellowish lead glaze, which ranged in effect from rich brown, when used over red clay, and yellow (over white slip) to dark brown (over black slip), with further variations according to the colour of the clay contained in the glaze itself, and the conditions of firing; a quantity of copper oxide was sometimes added to give a green colour. Black slip was used increasingly in the 1930s either painted or as the ground for *sgraffito* designs. Cardew employed E.*Comfort, S. and C.*Tustin and, from 1936, R.*Finch, who remained as manager during Cardew's absence at Wenford Bridge, Cornwall, in 1939. Finch later purchased the pottery, which operated on a reduced scale under wartime restrictions in the early 1940s and reopened in 1946 after a break in production. Stoneware, fired experimentally from 1952, became the main output in 1959. The production of slipware continued until 1964.

Mark: circle containing monogram of WP, impressed.

Refs: Michael Cardew (collection of essays, Crafts Advisory Committee, London, 1976); M. Coleman 'Ray Finch's Workshop' in *Crafts* (September, October 1974); R. Finch 'Workshop Organization: Winchcombe Pottery' in *Ceramic Review* 3 (May, June 1970); T. Hennell 'The Potter' in *The Countryman at Work* (Architectural Press, London, 1947).

Windisch, Christophe. *See* Brussels.

Wingender, Charles and William. German-born brothers, trained as potters in the Rhineland stoneware region and working in America from the late 19th century. The brothers possibly worked for Richard C. Remmey (*see* Remmey family), before acquiring their own works (c.1894) in Haddonfield, New Jersey, where they made mugs, pitchers and ornamental flowerpots in a body resembling the stoneware used in Germany, although containing exclusively American clays. They produced original work designed by William Wingender, using techniques and decorative patterns which they had learned in Germany, and capturing the spirit of contemporary and earlier high-quality Rhenish stoneware. Among their output was a salt-glazed *jardinière* with relief decoration of vines and gnomes between bands of fern leaves; borders of beading and a stamped egg-and-dart design stood out in the greyish brown of the stoneware body against a cobalt blue ground; the pedestal was elaborately decorated with lions' heads, portrait medallions of warriors, etc. Relief decoration on mugs depicted the destruction of the Roman army led by Quintus Varus in 9 A.D., adapted from a traditional German design. The pottery was continued by later generations of the Wingender family, but by the 1930s mainly produced plain flowerpots.

Marks include CW & BRO. impressed; address and name, impressed.
Refs: Barber (1976); Stradling; Webster.

Winter, Edward and Thelma Frazier. *See* Cowan, R. Guy.

Winter, Mathias. *See* Papa.

Winter & Co. *See* Elbogen.

Wirkkala, Tappio. *See* Bryk, Rut.

Wirth, Georg Heinrich. *See* Rauenstein.

Wolfe, George. *See* Mason, Miles.

Wolff, Johann Adalbert (1867-1948). Modeller of lithophanes at Elbogen, and 1908-15 at Pirkenhammer, where his work included a portrait of Franz-Joseph I, a nativity, and a series of 12 decorative designs for beer jugs. While at Lessau 1923-30, he modelled a transparent portrait of President Masaryk. Some pieces signed *J. Wolff*.
Ref: Meyer.

Wolff, Karl. *See* Prague.

Womelsdorf, Pennsylvania. In American ceramics, the site of an earthenware pottery established in 1784 and run in the 19th century by Josiah Beck, who made kitchen ware with slip decoration. The pottery was sold in 1864 to Willoughby Smith, maker of flowerpots.

Mark: *Willoughby Smith/Wumelsdorf* [sic], stamped, in 19th century.
Ref: Barber (1976).

Wood, Beatrice (b 1894). American artist potter, born in San Francisco. In Paris, she studied art briefly at the Académie Julian, then trained for the stage at the Comédie Française. She joined the French Repertory Theater on her return to New York, also contributing to the avant-garde publications of Marcel Duchamp, whom she met in 1916. Beatrice Wood became interested in ceramics, especially lustre wares, in 1938, joining a pottery class in Hollywood. She subsequently studied under G.*Lukens at the University of California and with G. and O.*Natzler. Following Duchamp's precept that rules are fatal to the progress of art, she adopted an independent attitude towards traditional preconceptions and produced very varied work, which ranges from functional pieces to unconventional forms decorated with vivid, exotic colours, and fantasy figures. Associated since its foundation in 1946 with the Happy Valley School of the Theosophical Society, on whose property she set up her home and studio, Beatrice Wood remained active in ceramics.
Refs: 'Beatrice Wood Ceramics' in *Arts & Architecture* 64, 1947; R. Bryan 'The Ceramics of Beatrice Wood' in *Craft Horizons* 30 (April 1970); 'Ceramics by B. Wood' in *Arts & Architecture* 63 (1947); 'Ceramics' double issue of *Design Quarterly* 42-43 (1958); Clark & Hughto; E.R. Hapgood 'All the Cataclysms: a brief survey of the life of Beatrice Wood' in *Arts Magazine* 52 (1977); D. Hare 'The Lustrous Life of Beatrice Wood' in *Craft Horizons* 38 (June 1978).

Wood, Enoch. American potter, descended from a Staffordshire family of potters. Wood worked as a mould maker at the pottery of C.W.*Fenton until 1853 and then for L.D. *Wheeler at South Norwalk, Connecticut, buying a half-interest in the pottery in 1857 or 1858. After serving in the army of the north in the Civil War, he became superintendent of a pottery at Perth Amboy, New Jersey, initially making agate ware and then producing pitchers, toby jugs, etc., with Rockingham glaze.
Refs: Barber (1976); Watkins (1950).

Wood, Enoch (1759-1840). Staffordshire potter, working in Burslem. He was the son of modeller and block cutter Aaron Wood (1717-85), and began the production of earthenware with his cousin, Ralph Wood (1748-95), before forming a partnership Wood & Caldwell, which lasted from 1790 until, in 1818, he bought out his backer, James Caldwell (1760-1838), and started work with his sons as Enoch Wood & Sons, the title retained by the firm up to its closure in 1846. Wood was noted for the production of earthenware figures (many backed with

Enoch Wood (1759-1840). Busts of the Emperor Alexander I of Russia, c.1800, and John Wesley, dated 1832. 27.5 cm, 24 cm high.

bocage) and busts, characterized by fine modelling and a wide palette of enamel colours, as well as gold and silver lustre. The subjects of his figures ranged from religious and allegorical themes to Greek and Roman mythology, e.g. Bacchus and Ariadne. Some creamware figures made by Wood & Caldwell, including Faith, Hope, Charity, Sadness and Fortitude, bear the impressed mark of the *Wedgwood factory, and were probably commissioned by Wedgwood. Busts made by Wood include portrayals of John Wesley, the Revd George Whitfield, Plato, Homer, Shakespeare, Voltaire, Rousseau, Handel, George Washington, George III, the Goddess Minerva, and a life-size self portrait. In jasper ware and black basalt, Wood followed Wedgwood's styles, sometimes very closely, and moulds discovered at his factory in Fountain Place in the 1880s have exact counterparts in the relief decoration of Wedgwood's ware. A remarkable Descent from the Cross, modelled by Enoch Wood in 1777, at the age of 17 or 18, was later produced in jasper ware. Wood's creamware included fruit baskets made from strips of clay, and he experimented with porcelain.

Monochrome transfer printing, introduced at the Wood & Caldwell factory in the 1790s, became an important part of the firm's output, and Enoch Wood & Sons produced great quantities of earthenware printed with a large range of English views: named cathedrals, castles, or mansions, covering the centres of plates and rimmed with flowers and vines inside a narrow, twisted edging; English cities, taken from contemporary engravings, bordered by flowers and scrollwork alternating with six medallions; London Views, rectangular scenes, often featuring the Regent's Park, surrounded by grapes and vine leaves. The firm's American views, often bordered with shells and flowers,

were adapted from American prints of views and historic events (e.g. Lafayette at Washington's Tomb, a Pilgrim Fathers series, and the defeat of the British at Lake Champlain in 1814). Wood was among the largest exporters of Staffordshire earthenware to the US. Views of European, Asian and African countries also provided subjects for printed series. As well as a vivid, dark underglaze blue, the firm used lustre or enamel in decoration.

Wood became known as 'The Father of the Potteries'. He amassed a collection of English earthenware, which by 1816 included representative pieces from the mid 17th to late 18th centuries and was eventually dispersed to museums; in 1835 Wood presented part of his collection to the King of Saxony.

A variety of marks, impressed, moulded, incised or printed, normally incorporate the firm's name: WOOD & CALDWELL, ENOCH WOOD & SONS, or from 1840 E. & E. WOOD, sometimes adding BURSLEM, or occasionally a trade name for the body, e.g. SEMICHINA.
Refs: Collard; Coysh & Henrywood; G.W. Elliot 'Enoch Wood, Potter & Antiquary' in *Journal of the Northern Ceramic Society* Vol II (1975-76); F. Falbuder *The Wood Family of Burslem* (E.P. reprint, 1972); E.B. Larsen *American Historical Views on Staffordshire China* (revised edition, Garden City, New York, 1950); *A Representation of the Manufacture of Earthenware* (booklet published by E. Wood & Sons, 1927); S. Shaw *History of the Staffordshire Potteries* (Hanley, 1829); Towner (1957); H.A.B. Turner *A Collector's Guide to Staffordshire Pottery Figures* (McGibbon & Kee, London, 1971).

Wood, E.M. *See* Della Robbia Pottery.

Wood, George (d 1811). English potter. Wood worked in French earthenware factories before establishing his own pottery for the production of white earthenware at *Forges-les-Eaux (Seine-Maritime) in 1797. He was in partnership with his son-in-law, Pierre-Nicolas Ledoux, who succeeded him. The firm made white earthenware, decorated in basketwork relief, exhibited at Rouen in 1802. Painted decoration included brightly coloured, naive battle scenes or landscapes showing a house by a tree, or painted marbling in brown recalling the branches of trees. Transfer-printed designs depicted current events, including the appearance of the first giraffe in France, 1827.
Refs: Ernould-Gandouet; Lesur (1971).

Wood, Isaac. English modeller, a member of the Wood family of Burslem. Wood worked at the *Nantgarw Pottery and left with W. *Billingsley and S.*Walker for Swansea, where he worked as a modeller for T. and J.*Bevington, and became manager when the *Cambrian Pottery reverted to L.W. *Dillwyn in 1824. His work included a series of small rams in biscuit porcelain dating from 1817-18, among the few pieces of por- porcelain known to have been produced by the Bevingtons.
    Mark: initials, IW.
Refs: P. Hughes *Welsh China* (National Museum of Wales, Cardiff, 1972); Jenkins.

Wood, John, & Co. *See* Stepney Bank Pottery.

Wood & Caldwell. *See* Wood, Enoch (1759-1840).

Wood & Sons. Staffordshire manufacturers of earthenware, ironstone bodies, etc., established in 1865 at Burslem by Absalom Wood in partnership with his son T.F. Wood. The firm issued many reproductions of patterns earlier used by E.*Wood, but designers later followed contemporary styling in adopting simpler shapes and patterns in tableware. The firm traded as Wood & Sons (Holdings) Ltd from 1954.
    Printed marks normally incorporate the firm's name (*Wood & Son* to c.1907, *Wood & Sons* thereafter) with the body (*Royal Semi Porcelain, Ironstone China,* etc.) and a crown or the Royal Arms. A mark depicting a casserole or tureen containing a flower and leaves, with WOOD'S WARE across the belly is flanked by *Enoch 1794* and *Ralph 1750* (used from c.1917).
Refs: Bunt; Cushion (1980); Godden (1964); Watkins *et al.*

Woodall, William. *See* Macintyre, James.

Woodhead, Davison & Cooper. *See* Manor House Pottery.

Woodhouse, Violet. *See* Della Robbia Pottery.

Woodings, Norman (b 1902). English ceramic artist, apprenticed under R.*Allen in 1916 at the *Doulton & Co. factory in Burslem, where he worked until 1967. Woodings was a painter of birds, flowers, fruit and, occasionally, seascapes, before he joined a

department concerned with the painting of modelled figures. He was eventually responsible for creating the styles and colour schemes of all the company's new figures.
Refs: see Doulton.

Woodland. *See* Brush-McCoy Pottery; Roseville Pottery Co.

Woodlesford Art Pottery. *See* Senior, James Wraith.

Woodman, Stanley. English ceramic designer. After training at the Macclesfield School of Art in Derbyshire, where he later taught, and at the Royal College of Art in London, he worked as an artist and then joined *Doulton & Co. in Burslem as a designer 1938-57. He was noted for the recreation of early tableware designs, but worked in modern as well as traditional styles.
Refs: see Doulton.

Woodward, William. American artist and designer; he studied with his brother Ellsworth Woodward at Rhode Island School of Design, and then went to study in Paris. He became an instructor in drawing and painting at Tulane University, 1883, took charge of drawing and design at Tulane School of Architecture, and was appointed professor of painting at Newcomb School of Art in 1890. Woodward established the *New Orleans Art Pottery in 1886 and, on its failure in the following year, for five years headed a group of advanced students in ceramic decoration from the Newcomb and Tulane colleges, working as the Baronne Street Pottery or Baronne Street Venture at the former pottery premises. In 1895, the Woodward brothers persuaded the Sophie Newcomb Memorial College to establish a pattern class and sell the students' work (*see* Newcomb College Pottery).
Refs: see Newcomb College Pottery.

Woodward & Vodrey. *See* Vodrey, Jabez.

Woodworth, F. *See* Nichols & Alford.

Woolf, Sydney. *See* Mexborough.

Woolf family. *See* Australian Pottery.

Worbey, Alexander. Australian potter working in Kangaroo Valley, near Hobart, Tasmania, by 1882 on the production of coarse wares as well as teapots, basins, jugs and jars, some with brown glaze and mainly for a local market. Moulded decoration included grapevines. Worbey was in Hobart in 1887, but it is not known whether he was then still working in Kangaroo Valley.
Ref: Graham.

Worcester. A centre for English porcelain production from the establishment of the Worcester Porcelain Co. by Dr Wall and William Davis in 1751 at Warmstry House. The firm specialized in the production of tea and dessert wares in a porcelain paste containing Cornish soapstone, often painted with oriental patterns and *chinoiseries* under the glaze in blue. Transfer printing was introduced over the glaze in c.1755 and under the glaze about five years later. The factory became known for high-quality

ground colours: yellow, green, turquoise, claret and, notably, a deep underglaze blue which was often painted in a diaper pattern of scales, with flowers, insects, birds, etc., painted in reserves. Production continued after Dr Wall's retirement (1774), and in 1783 the banker Thomas Flight (d 1800) purchased the works, which were operated by J.*Flight and his brother John, who received a Royal Warrant in 1789.
    After John Flight's death, his brother was joined by Worcester businessman M.*Barr and the firm traded as Flight & Barr, 1792-1804. Early in this period, the porcelain paste, while still containing Cornish soapstone, grew to approach hard paste. The firm made replacement pieces for earlier Worcester services and continued the production of the Blind Earl pattern (low-relief sprays of rosebuds and foliage derived from a Meissen motif c.1760 and named after the Earl of Coventry, who lost his sight in 1780), the Queen Charlotte or Catherine Wheel pattern (also dating from c.1760, with spiral stripes in red and blue, of Chinese inspiration), the Kylin pattern (also from the Dr Wall period, with radiating segments enclosing the Chinese mythical kylin and tables with plants), and other early decorative designs. Sprays of flowers were sometimes used on spirally fluted forms for tea services. Newly designed pieces became increasingly sumptuous and included elaborate table centrepieces. Subjects for painting included named botanical specimens, studies of large flowers in panels, bands of hope, etc., panels of feathers e.g. by T.*Baxter, landscapes and printed scenes. The painter J.*Pennington, chief artist at the factory, painted portraits and rustic scenes.
    Under the partnership Barr, Flight & Barr, with Barr's son, also Martin, a member

Worcester. Tusk-shaped vase decorated in browns, greens and gold, made at the Royal Porcelain factory, c.1873. 20.3 cm high.

from 1804, the firm received another Royal Warrant in 1807.

W.*Billingsley and S.*Walker joined the factory 1808-13, initially to work on the elimination of firing problems, and in 1809 they entered into an agreement with Barr to develop a more translucent paste. The work of the period included two-handled cabinet cups and other shapes inspired by French porcelain. All pieces were wheel-thrown and turned, rather than moulded, and relief decoration was normally restricted to handles and finials. Painted subjects included shells (by c.1810), used on a wide range of shapes; landscapes, often with ruins; animals, sporting scenes, and portraits. Flowers, tropical birds, feathers etc., treated in naturalistic style, began to supersede Imari and other Japanese-inspired patterns. Flower-painting was rich and the blooms were often portrayed in bunches or in vases. A dessert service with azure ground for the Earl of Coventry (1811) was painted with flowers and bronze-coloured crests. Bat printing was introduced for classical scenes with Roman figures, rustic groups, cupids, shells (sometimes overpainted by hand), and views. A shade of salmon ('Barr's orange') and a rare marbled effect featured among the grounds used.

The partnership of Flight with Martin Barr's two sons, Martin and George Barr, who succeeded their father in 1813, traded as Flight, Barr & Barr. The work was noted for its excellent finish and craftsmanship. Every piece was hand decorated. Commissioned services ranged from simple floral subects within classical borders to rich studies of shells, feathers, flowers, birds, and land-

Worcester. Shell-shaped wall pocket, 1880. 28.5 cm long.

scapes. The design of some services combined decoration of different types (e.g. shells, flowers, feathers and landscapes divided among the pieces). Pieces derived from Etruscan shapes were often painted with classical figures. Painters included Baxter and his pupils, W.*Doe, M.*Webster, T.*Lowe, and S.*Cole.

Ornamental wares included small vases in pairs, inkwells, desk sets, candlesticks and large pairs of ornate vases. Handles were made in the form of twisted snakes and eagles' heads. The wares were embellished with hard, bright mercury oxide gilding (used from c.1790), and sometimes small beads of clay, each separately modelled by hand, arranged in lines of beading and enamelled white to represent pearls. New ground colours were introduced in the 1820s, when the range included Saxon green, pink, fawn, straw and garnet, as well as a fine underglaze blue. Armorial services were commissioned by English and other aristocratic families, including the Russian Emperor; a service for Lord Amherst on his appointment as Governor General of India; and for William IV (who had already ordered a service as Duke of Clarence) a service with heraldic decoration on blue ground, 1831, and one with green ground and crest for the Imam of Muscat.

Bone china was introduced in 1830. New shapes included cups with handles in the form of a butterfly's wings, cottages in Gothic style for use as pastille burners or night lights, pin trays, baskets, and miniature vases, water cans, candlesticks, baskets, etc. Joseph Flight's share in the company passed equally to Martin & George Barr in 1840. They then sold out to the Chamberlain partnership.

Robert Chamberlain, a porcelain painter and formerly an apprentice at the Worcester Porcelain Co., had set up a decorating workshop at Diglis, to the south of the city, c.1786. There, he decorated porcelain bought from *Caughley and the Worcester factory, selling his work as Chamberlain's Worcester. He began the production of his own porcelain c.1792 and his output in the early 19th century included a wide range of decorated porcelain following the styles of Barr, Flight Barr. His firm's amalgamation in 1840 with Flight, Barr & Barr resulted in the firm Chamberlain & Co., working at the enlarged Diglis factory under the control of Walter Chamberlain, John Lilly and Fleming St John (partners in Chamberlain & Co.). Martin and George Barr retained an interest in the firm, but did not participate in its running. The firm produced encaustic tiles, c.1840-48. Chamberlain and Lilly traded briefly from 1850 with another partner, W.H.*Kerr, who then went into partnership with R.W.*Binns. After Kerr's retirement in 1862, the firm continued as Worcester Royal Porcelain Co., a joint stock company formed by Edward Phillips, later at Derby, William Litherland, and lesser shareholders Martin Abell, Peter Hardy, Alexander Clunes Sheriff, Wm Thompson Adcock, Richard Palmore and Thomas Southall, with Binns as a director in charge of the artistic side of production until his retirement in 1897. Artists formerly employed by Kerr & Binns included W.B.*Kirk, J.*Sherriff, modellers of a number of parian figures and busts, and painters D.*Bates, J.*Rushton and W.*Taylor, J. and T.S.*Callowhill,

J.*Hopewell, G.*Hundley and J.*Williams. J.*Hadley joined the firm during this period.

The firm used a grey-tinged parian paste in the production of classical and literary figures, often in pairs, e.g. Joy and Sorrow, Liberty and Captivity, which continued for a long time in production. Modelling was of high quality. Ivory porcelain, a development of parian paste with warm, ivory colour and luscious glaze, was introduced at the International Exhibition (London, 1862) and became a speciality of the factory. A range known as Raphaelesque porcelain was delicately modelled for figures, busts and relief-decorated pieces, and tinted in Raphaelesque colours in the style of 18th-century Capodimonte porcelain. Many figures were made in the normal porcelain paste, including earlier Kerr & Binns designs.

Exhibition displays and commissions for presentation services were important in raising the prestige of the firm. A dessert service for Queen Victoria (painted in shaded enamel on a turquoise ground by T.*Bott with designs inspired by Raphael's work in the *logge* of the Vatican) was among the firm's display in the International Exhibition (1862). In 1863, Worcester Corporation ordered a tête-a-tête service for the Princess of Wales decorated en grisaille on rose-coloured panels with Royal portraits and groups of amorini taking part in the Marriage of Cupid and Psyche. A service made two years later for the marriage of the Earl of Dudley and shown at the Paris Exhibition in 1867 was painted with classical portraits by T.S. Callowhill, against a diaper of drops of turquoise enamel and burnished gold; the factory became famous for such jewelled porcelain, made with droplets of enamel, often raised in layers during repeated firings.

New stylistic influences emerged in the exhibitions in Paris (1867) and Vienna (1873). Ivory porcelain provided an ideal medium for Japanese decorative styles, which had been assimilated by the factory's artists, notably James Hadley, by the early 1870s. A series of Hadley's vases modelled in low relief to represent Japanese porcelain manufacture and gilded by T.S. Callowhill, shown in London (1871 and 1872) and Vienna (1873), were praised in the *Art Journal* of November 1872 for capturing the spirit of Japanese art without slavish imitation. The display in the Viennese exhibition included enamel painting by Bott in Limoges style; after his death in 1870, similar work was carried on by T.J.*Bott and T.S. Callowhill. Pieces designed under Renaissance Italian and Persian influences, and perforated ware (a speciality associated with G.*Owen) also featured in the Vienna display, for which Worcester was awarded joint first prize in its class with Minton's. A huge display in the Exposition Universelle, Paris (1878) included vases and services continuing the same range of styles, with the addition of experimental marbled faience resembling Japanese namako-glazed ware, a line of dark green porcelain with gilded patterns, and a dessert service painting of exotic birds recalling the time of Dr Wall. Later stylistic influences included examples of Indian art in the South Kensington Museum (now the Victoria & Albert Museum), the French Renaissance, Louis XIV and Empire styles.

In the development of useful ware at this time, the factory used a glazed parian paste, (resembling the work of the *Belleek factory) or bone china, and evolved a heavy, opaque earthenware for domestic and institutional use, which was marketed as Crown ware or later vitreous ware. Printing in gold was introduced c.1870.

Painters employed at the time included: J. Bradley, O.H.*Copson, A.*Gyngell, A. *Hill, C.*Palmere, E.J.*Raby, R.*Rea, W.*Taylor, J.*Weaver.

The factory's relief-modelled ware included centrepieces and stands with figures in country or garden settings (e.g. squabbling children and the lovers they grow up into); child figures, frequently modelled by J. Hadley, were often constructed as candlesticks, or held baskets. Hadley was also the modeller of vases in the form of hands. Other figures included series of water-carriers of various nationalities, craftsmen, allegorical representations of nations, historical characters, etc.

In the 1890s, the factory began to exploit colour effects in the decoration of porcelain, such as Coral Ware (1893), the iridescent effects of shot enamels (1894), prismatic colours resembling L.C.*Tiffany's glassware (1894), and pink porcelain, shaded with aerograph spray, a development of stained ivory porcelain. Sabrina ware, produced 1894-1930 and developed using the parian paste, was painted after an initial firing with a resist that varied in thickness according to the depth of colour required, and then impregnated with salts of cobalt, chrome green or copper green in an acid solution. During the subsequent firing, the salts produced cloudy colour effects containing spots of light – the technique produced unique pieces, as the result could not be fully controlled.

Simple patterns were applied to the less expensive wares by an early method of lithographic printing from 1890. Lithographic portraits of the Mayor and Mayoress of Worcester by Raby were used on a commemorative plate in 1896.

Principal artists included: C.*Baldwyn, H.*Chair, G.*Cole, W.*Hall, W.*Hawkins, G.*Houghton, G.*Johnson, J.H.*Lewis, E.J.*Phillips, W.*Ricketts, E.*Salter. Some of the painters marked their work with initials before the use of signatures was commonly permitted c.1900.

Under William Moore Binns, who succeeded his father as art director in 1897, the elaborate vases were superseded by simpler shapes. Biscuit barrels and other small pieces were made for mounting by Birmingham silversmiths.

The collector and benefactor Charles William Dyson Perrins became director in 1891 and provided considerable financial backing from 1898. He was the company's chairman from 1901. The factory absorbed other Worcester works, *Grainger & Co. in 1902, and the firm established by James Hadley in 1905, taking on a number of their artists.

Principal painters of the early 20th century included: R.H. and W.H.*Austin, H.*Davis, W.*Jarman, W.*Powell (b 1878), R.*Sebright, W.*Sedgley, and members of the *Stinton family.

The production of large vases continued and some earlier shapes were brought back into use. Parian paste was still used for ornamental wares, except for pieces decorated with cobalt blue, which were made in bone

Worcester. Figure of a nymph draped in green with bronze patina and gold edges, made at the Royal Porcelain factory, 1893. About 54 cm high.

china. Everyday wares were made in bone china or, until 1918, the vitreous body, with floral border patterns, or transfer-printed in blue with Willow Pattern, Royal Lily, or Broseley Dragon designs. A porcelain paste ('Wall body', named after Dr Wall) with green translucency, was developed shortly before World War I. The firm's simpler vases were painted in reserves and bordered with bands or stylized patterns in gold. Under J.*Wadsworth, art director from 1915, such patterns as spots in red or green on a black ground were introduced by 1920. Vases and bowls made in a Crownware body with underglaze painting of castles, ships, etc., and finished with pearl or gold lustre were introduced c.1924.

Principal painters, many of whom left in the depression of the 1930s when work was in short supply, included: H.*Ayrton, W. *Bagnall, E.*Barker, W.*Bee, K.*Blake, A.*Lewis, T.G.*Lockyer, G.*Moseley, H. H.*Price, D.*Rea, R.*Rushton, J.*Stanley and E.*Townsend.

Davis painted two services for Prince Ranjitsinji, one with views of the Prince's Sussex home, the other from photographs of his palace in India. The Austin brothers carried out a series of flowers and birds of Australasia. Many services had been made earlier in the 20th century for the Australian

market, including one painted by Reginald Austin with birds of paradise. Urged by Dyson Perrins, who was to purchase the factory in 1934, the firm issued a series of work painted with fabulous birds in the style used at the time of Dr Wall; George Johnson specialized in this painting. Also, octagonal plates in limited editions were painted with Audubon's North American birds on coloured grounds.

New ranges of figures launched in 1931 include historical, military and naval subjects by the modeller F.*Gertner. Other figures were designed by the freelance modellers, Freda Doughty (*see* Doughty, S.D.), D. *Lindner and P.*Stabler. The Maltese artist Antonio Vassalo specialized in the modelling of small flowers for ashtrays, pin boxes, etc., continuing a tradition in Worcester porcelain from the late 18th century. Flowers by Vassalo were also used for the decoration of bird figures by Dorothy Doughty in the 1930s. The company had established a research department in 1913, where scientific porcelain was developed for the government's war effort. In 1938, a small laboratory was set up for the development of fireproof porcelain, and research to replace the materials previously imported from Germany.

Tablewares were simply decorated, with cottages and views, and the company continued production of fine wares and figures for sale in the USA. The factory also made equipment for radar, radio and, from 1944, sparking plugs.

The film *The Doctor Ordered Clay*, which was on general distribution in 1950, outlined the firm's history, and showed artists Doris Lindner, F. Gertner and H. Davis at work on the firm's first limited-edition equestrian statuette. Ayrton was filmed at his painting.

After becoming a public company in 1954, the Worcester Royal Porcelain Co. has continued its own traditional style alongside contemporary designs, while Royal Worcester Ltd (established 1958) acts as a holding company for other firms making ceramics for use in industry, especially electronics, including the Palissy Pottery Ltd, and an earthenware factory at Stoke-on-Trent, bought in 1958. In 1961, a factory was established in Jamaica to make 'Island Worcester'. It has since been taken over by the Jamaican government. After merging with Spode in 1978, the main firm has traded as Royal Worcester Spode Ltd.

The firm of E.*Locke also worked in the city of Worcester, but remained independent of the Royal Porcelain Co. The St George's works of David Wilson Barker, making garden ornaments, horticultural ware and bricks by 1872, was purchased by J.*Carter, but the St George's Tileworks which Carter then opened at Barker's brickworks had ceased by 1892.

An extensive range of the firm's products is permanently on display at the Dyson Perrins Museum at the works in Worcester.

Marks: FB or *Flight & Barr* with crown; BFB or *Barr, Flight & Barr* with crown; FBB or *Flight, Barr & Barr* with crown; the standard mark of Kerr & Binns was a circle containing the initial w in each quarter, with a crescent at the centre partially enclosing *51*; versions of the Kerr & Binns mark, topped by a crown and sometimes containing a c at the centre rather than a

crescent were adopted by the Royal Porcelain Co. In the late 19th century the firm adopted a system of added dots, circles or letters to indicate the year of manufacture. Chamberlain's marks incorporate the company's name and sometimes *Worcester*.
Refs: Barrett (1953); Barrett & Thorpe; Binns (1865, 1897); S.W. Fisher *Worcester Porcelain* (Ward Lock, London, 1968); Godden (1961); R.L. Hobson *Worcester Porcelain* (Quaritch, London, 1910); Jewitt; Sandon (1978a, 1978b); F. Severne Mackenna *Worcester Porcelain* (F. Lewis, Leigh-on-Sea, Essex, 1950).

Worthington, Humble & Holland. *See* Herculaneum.

Wrecclesham. *See* Harris family.

Wren, Denise K., *née* Tuckfield (1891-1979). Studio potter, born in Western Australia. Denise Wren moved to England with her family when nine years old. She studied design at Kingston-upon-Thames School of Art, 1907-11, under the designer, Archibald Knox, and learned to make coiled pots, which were fired at a nearby flowerpot works. She taught herself to throw, establishing a studio at Kingston in 1911. With her husband, the writer Henry Wren, she designed and built a pottery at Oxshott, Surrey, where she lived and worked 1919-78, concentrating on the effects produced in firing relatively unrefined materials. Starting in 1919, she devised a series of high-temperature coke kilns suitable for individual potters (to whom the plans were made available the last); a salt glaze kiln was completed in 1963. During the 1920s and 1930s, she helped to arouse public interest in hand-made pottery by exhibiting widely and with books, *Handcraft Pottery* (1928) and *Finger-built Pottery* (1932).

Mark: initials D.K.W. and a wren in flight.
Refs: Ceramic Review 59 (September, October 1979), 76 (July, August 1982); Rose.

Denise Wren. Slab-built stoneware group of an elephant with two riders in grey and buff clays. 24 cm long.

Wright, Samuel. *See* Minton, Herbert.

Wrisbergholzen. German faience factory established in the 1730s by Baron von Wrisberg. From 1816 to 1826, it was under the direction of L.-V.*Gerverot (1747-1829), succeeded c.1826 by H.W.C. Huck, until its closure in 1834. The output was painted in high temperature colours: pale blue, manganese and yellow.
Mark: monogram of WR, with painter's mark (letters or numerals).
Refs: Haggar; Hannover; Honey (1952).

Wunderlich Ltd. Australian firm established in 1887 in Sydney by Ernest and Alfred Wunderlich, who were joined in Australia by their brother Otto in 1900. At first working as importers, e.g. of French tiles, the brothers eventually made their own manufacture of terracotta tiles by 1916 and tobacco jars, money boxes and small decorative pieces, also in terracotta, marked WUNDERLICH/TILES. In 1941, the firm helped to revive production at the *Calyx Porcelain and Paint Co. Ltd, making table and utility wares for the armed forces.
Refs: Forty Years of Wunderlich Industry (Wunderlich Ltd, Sydney, 1927); Graham.

Wynand, Paul. *See* Merkelbach, Reinhold.

Yamamoto Hikoemon. *See* Matsuyama.

Yamamoto Yoshitome. *See* Yokyo.

Yamazaki kiln. *See* Seba ware.

Yanagi Moneyoshi. *See* mingei ware.

Yarraville Pottery. Australian pottery in operation from 1880 at Melbourne as successor to the Footscray Pottery (*see* Chesterfield Pottery Co.). The works was among the few to attempt production of porcelain (including breakfast sets with gilded decoration) in Australia in the 19th century. The pottery showed household ware at the Centennial Exhibition, Melbourne, in 1888 and production continued until c.1900.
Ref: Graham.

Yatsushiro ware. Japanese pottery of Korean inspiration originally made at a kiln founded at Naraiki by potters from *Agano in the 17th century. The kiln was moved (1658) to Mount Hirayama, where tea ware was made for the Hosokawa clan. The body, rich in iron and fired brown at the foot, was covered with a pearly grey glaze. Decoration of cranes and clouds (unkaku), bamboo, pine, prunus blossom, etc., was inlaid or brushed in white slip, with occasional use of black or underglaze blue. Some pieces had vertical cord marks. The wares were made by descendants of the kiln's founder until 1892.
Refs: Brinkley; Hobson; Jenyns (1971); Koyama; Sato.

yellow ware. American earthenware for kitchen and table use, made in pale body with yellow transparent glaze. It was made in large quantities, generally under industrial conditions, from c.1830 until the end of the 19th century.

Yeoman Pottery. London pottery established by C. Fraser *Hamilton, in collaboration

with W. Staite *Murray at 18 Yeoman's Row, Kensington, in 1915 or 1916, and working until 1920. Firing an up-draught gas kiln, Hamilton produced earthenware painted on an engobe of white slip, which was subject to crazing. Pieces made at the Yeoman Pottery were exhibited in London in 1919 and the following year.

Mark: *Yeoman* incised in an arc.
Refs: M. Haslam 'Some Vorticist Pottery' in *The Connoisseur* 190 (October 1975).

Yeomans, Charles (b 1870). English ceramic artist, son of an employee at the *Pinder, Bourne & Co. factory in Nile Street, Burslem. He joined *Doulton & Co. in 1883 as an apprentice under John *Slater and was known for his painting of landscapes, fruit and flowers, either under the glaze or in enamel. Yeomans retired in 1936, but returned to work for Doulton's, 1939-51.
Refs: see Doulton.

Yeremina, Tatyana. *See* Artistic Ceramics Cooperative.

Ymagynatyf Pottery. London pottery in operation in Chelsea, c.1922-39. The ware was marked with the impressed or incised initials of members of the Shuffrey family, who made studio pottery: KM, HM or KE.
Ref: Godden (1964).

Ynysmedw Pottery. Welsh pottery established near Swansea at the site of a brickworks and initially for the production of firebrick in 1840. The Williams brothers, proprietors, also made buff terracotta and produced earthenware table services, tea and toilet sets with painted or printed decoration from c.1850. The printing plates were sold to the *South Wales Pottery c.1859. The pottery itself passed to the owners of the South Wales Pottery in 1870 and closed after some years.
Marks incorporate YNYSMEDW POTTERY (and variations in spelling of name), YMP or YP; L & M (owners, Lewis & Morgan).
Refs: Cushion; P. Hughes *Welsh China* (National Museum of Wales, Cardiff, 1972); Jewitt; A. Smith *Liverpool Herculaneum Pottery* (Herbert Jenkins, London, 1970).

Yohei. *See* Seifu.

Yokkaichi. *See* Banko ware.

Yokyo or **Yoko** (1753-1817). Japanese potter Yamamoto Yoshitome, formerly a doctor, working in Kaga. Initially making pottery as a hobby, he made raku ware resembling that of the *Ohi family.
Ref: Roberts.

Yoole, Thomas. *See* Portobello Pottery.

York China Manufactory. *See* Hirstwood, Haigh.

Yosabei II or **Chowaken** (d 1845). Japanese potter working in Kyoto. He succeeded his father, Yosabei, who had made simply decorated faience at a workshop in Gojo-zaka

from the early 19th century. Chowaken opened the Iseya studio in Gojo-zaka, where he made raku-style ware. He went into partnership with Waka Kitei (*see* Kameya family) and Kitei's nephew, Kumakichi or Furoken Kamefu, for the production of porcelain with decoration in underglaze blue and enamelled colours. His successor produced pottery with enamelled and gilded patterns.
Refs: Brinkley; Roberts.

Yoseimon. *See* Mori family.

Yoshidaya. Japanese kiln established, among early efforts to revive ceramic production at *Kutani, by the painter and scholar Den'emon Toyota (1752-1827), whose family traded as brewers of saké under the company name of Yoshidaya. Operating briefly on the site of the 17th-century kiln at Kutani in the early 1820s, the workshop moved in 1825 or 1826 to Etchudani, Yamashiro. Under the management of *Miyamotoya the kiln produced a wide range of domestic ware, including saké bottles, vases, and a variety of bowls and dishes, using a stoneware body made from local clays. The decoration of birds, flowers, landscapes, etc., predominantly in yellow, green and dark blue glazes, was executed by *Gen'emon and others. Despite the patronage of the Kaga clan in the period after the founder's death, the kiln ceased operation in 1831 before being reopened by Miyamotoya in 1835.
Refs: Jenyns (1967); Mitsuoka; Nakagawa.

Young, George F. (1863-1920). Manager of *Roseville Pottery Co. from 1885 and later principal owner. When he retired in 1918, his son became general manager of the firm.
Refs: Evans; Kovel & Kovel; *see also* Roseville Pottery.

Young, James Radley (1867-1933). English painter and ceramic designer. Born in Macclesfield, Cheshire, Young studied painting and modelling at Sheffield School of Art. In 1893, he joined his half-brother Edwin Page Turner in employment at *Carter & Co., where he became head of the design department. He left the firm c.1901 to start a pottery at Haslemere, Surrey, where he used a wood-burning kiln in the production of pieces with lustre glazes, and decoration incised through cream-coloured slip. Young continued freelance design for Carter & Co. and returned to work at Poole in 1904. During World War I, he formed a department for the production of domestic ware, including a line of bowls, dishes and conical vases in a greyish tile-clay body, mainly unglazed, occasionally with a smear glaze, and painted with loops and zig-zags in brown. The range was later continued by *Carter, Stabler & Adams in a finer, buff body. Young was attracted to the appearance of hand-production, and discouraged his assistants from removing from their work throwing lines and the marks of their fingers. His department also produced glazed ware striped in blue, or decorated with small flower sprigs in two or three colours. Young had independently developed his own lustre glazes, which were used at Poole, and with A.*Eason introduced tin glazes. He provided designs for Carter's tileworks, and was mainly engaged on tile painting from c.1920. With a

Yoshidaya. Earthenware vase, painted in green, aubergine and yellow, 1875-1900. 43 cm high.

short break for war work in 1917-18, he remained at the Poole potteries until shortly before his death.
Ref: Hawkins.

Young, William, & Sons. English-trained potter, William Young, working in America with his sons William, Edward and John. He claimed to be the first manufacturer of both

William Weston Young. Creamware dessert dish with sepia monochrome, probably by Young. Inscribed Marino *(a casino belonging to the Earl of Charlemont), and bearing the impressed mark* SWANSEA. *21 cm high.*

cream-coloured earthenware and porcelain in Trenton, New Jersey. The firm rented a Trenton pottery in 1853, at first making Rockingham and yellow-glazed earthenware, and introduced creamware in late 1854 or early 1855; the work included pitchers with relief decoration depicting the Babes in the Wood, and a small vase. The Young family established the Excelsior Pottery Works in new buildings in 1857. The firm's founder, William Young, was succeeded by his sons on his retirement in 1870. Their display of earthenware, porcelain, door furniture and other items of hardware won a bronze medal in the Philadelphia Centennial Exhibition (1876). The Young brothers later manufactured domestic earthenware, white granite and semi-porcelain, ornamental porcelain and sanitary ware. Dinnerware and toilet sets with underglaze decoration became a speciality.

Marks: an eagle, or 1858-79 a lion and a unicorn supporting a coat of arms over the initials, WYS.
Ref: Barber (1976).

Young, William Weston. English ceramic decorator and manufacturer. Young, a surveyor, painted a small quantity of earthenware, 1803-06, at the *Cambrian pottery, mainly with shells, birds, butterflies and other insects drawn from nature in the manner of natural history illustration. He also carried out decoration independently, using his own muffle kiln. Young helped W.*Billingsley and S.*Walker with financial loans during both their stays at *Nantgarw, and in 1814 with arrangements for the transfer of their venture to the Cambrian Pottery. He became one of the proprietors of the Nantgarw China Works in 1820, and engaged T.*Pardoe to decorate the remaining stock, which he sold at auction in 1821 and 1822.

Marks: (rare) YOUNG PINXIT, or YOUNG *f*.
Refs: Atterbury (1980); *see also* Cambrian Pottery.

Yozaemon. *See* Bizan.

Yugetsu. *See* Minzan.

William Young & Sons. Pitcher, an early example of porcelain made in New Jersey and the only known piece signed by William Young, c.1853. 27.9 cm high.

Yujiro (ɑ c.1830). Japanese potter and decorator of *Kutani ware, working at the *Wakasugi kiln soon after its establishment in 1811, he specialized in *aka-e enamelled decoration and was noted for the bold, spontaneous quality of his painting. He became chief potter after the kiln's reorganization in 1820. His pupils included *Isaburo.
Refs: Gorham; Jenyns (1965); Nakagawa.

Yumachi kiln. *See* Fujina.

Yunotsu kiln. *See* Dohei Imai.

Yusetsu Mori (1808-81). Japanese potter, woodcarver and merchant, born in Kuwana, Mie prefecture. After his rediscovery of the formulae used in making *Banko ware, he acquired Rozan's seal and stamp, and revived production. His own work was carried out only in faience with a finely crackled glaze. His decoration in underglaze blue, with red and green enamels, included floral designs or diaper patterns surrounding landscapes or illustrations of fables in medallions. He was succeeded by his son, who modelled wares in a strong, light body in white, buff, grey, black or chocolate brown clay, biscuit or smear-glazed, with delicate designs in white slip.
Refs: Feddersen; Jenyns (1971); Munsterberg; Roberts.

Yusupov, Prince Nikolai Borisovich (1751-1831). Russian porcelain maker. After working as director of the Imperial porcelain factory at *St Petersburg, 1792-1802, he established a porcelain workshop on his estate at *Archangelskoye in 1814, where painters, some of them former Sèvres employees, decorated porcelain which included imported work from Limoges and the Sèvres factory with landscapes, flowers, monograms, etc., sometimes copying illustrations from works in Yusupov's library. Tea and coffee services with miniature portrait medallions against a gold ground were a speciality of the studio. Gilding was in general lavish, and many pieces were lined with polished gold. Yusupov produced work to supply the needs of his own household and for presentation as gifts, never for sale. The workshop closed at his death. Its output was marked with Archangelskoye in Cyrillic characters, or Archangeski in gold, sometimes alongside a Sèvres mark. The signature or monogram of Lambert, a French artist employed at the workshop, sometimes accompanies the mark Aπ in underglaze blue, with a date (1831) in overglaze red.
Refs: Bubnova; Ivanova; A. Popoff 'The Francis Gardner & Other Russian Porcelain Factories' in *The Connoisseur* 96 (August 1935); Ross; Rozembergh; Weiss.

Zane Pottery Co. American pottery firm, formerly *Peters & Reed and operating as the Zane Pottery Co. from 1921. Reed was succeeded by H.S.*McClelland as president on his retirement in 1922. After enlargement, the pottery produced a wide range of garden ornaments and flowerpots. Production of Peters & Reed art wares was continued and new lines were added, including Crystaline, with semi-matt glaze in orange and green; Sheen, semi-matt glaze in four colours; Drip, with glaze trickling from the rim of the piece over a glaze in a contrasting colour; and a matt glaze sold as Powder Blue. The red body was superseded by white earthenware in 1926. McClelland's family, who inherited the pottery on his death, continued operations until 1941, when the factory was sold to L.*Gonder.
Mark: monogram of ZP Co over ZANE WARE/MADE IN USA, impressed.
Refs: Evans; Kovel & Kovel; Lehner.

Zanesville Art Pottery. American art Pottery established by D.*Schmidt as the Zanesville Roofing Tile Co. in 1896 and trading as the Zanesville Art Pottery Co. from 1900. After ceasing the manufacture of roofing tile, it produced kitchen ware, tea and coffee pots, and underglaze decorated umbrella stands, *jardinières* and pedestals. A.*Radford was employed as general manager in 1901. Art pottery, introduced by 1904 and shown at the St Louis World's Fair, included by 1908 a line sold as La Moro or Lamora vases in a variety of shapes, painted with flowers, etc., in slip under a rich, glossy glaze, or in light colours with a matt ground. The pottery, rebuilt after fires in 1901 and 1910, was purchased by S.A.*Weller in 1920.
Marks include LA MORO, impressed.
Refs: Evans; Kovel & Kovel; Lehner; L.& E. Purviance & N.F. Schneider *Zanesville Art Pottery in Color* (Mid America Book Co., Des Moines, Iowa, 1968); N.F. Schneider *Zanesville Art Pottery* (privately published, Zanesville, Ohio, 1963).

Zdekauer, Moritz. *See* Altrohlau.

Zeh, Felix. *See* Scheibe-Alsbach.

Zeh, Scherzer & Co. Porcelain manufacturers working at Rehau (Bavaria) from 1880. The firm opened a school of apprentices for the production of industrial wares and was associated 1924-26 with the Elster Studios of Mülhausen. The output included table services, tea and coffee sets, and decorative wares.
A wide range of marks usually incorporate the firm's name or initials and sometimes BAVARIA.
Refs: Danckert; Weiss.

Zeiller, Paul. *See* Lichte.

Zeisel, Eva. Hungarian-born designer working in America. In the early 1940s, she collaborated with the Museum of Modern Art, New York, in the development of a table service produced by the Castleton China Co. in New Castle, Pennsylvania, in simple, functional styles and undecorated.
Ref: World Ceramics.

Zell. German factory established by J.F. Lenz in 1806 for the production of cream-coloured earthenware and other pale-bodied wares in the styles of creamware made in England by the *Leeds Pottery and J.*Wedgwood & Sons Ltd. The factory produced porcelain 1846-67. It continues in operation in the hands of the Lenz family.
Marks include ZELL, impressed, and a shield bearing the initials JFL.
Refs: Danckert; Haggar (1960); Honey (1952); Weiss.

Zell-Hamersbach. German manufacturers of porcelain and stoneware established in 1820 by Georg Schmider. The firm made table and domestic wares. Porcelain production ceased in 1940.
Marks incorporate the name or initials of the founder with ZELL or ZELL-AM-HAMERSBACH.
Refs: Danckert; Weiss.

Zengoro family. *See* Hozen; Ryozen; Wazen.

Zenith, Plateelbakkerij. Dutch pottery, originally a pipe factory at Gouda, which produced useful and decorative earthenware from 1919. Patterns of flowers and animals were used under a glossy transparent glaze by artists who included J.C.*van Ham. The subsequent output included enamel-painted and (from 1924) matt-glazed wares. In the early 1930s, vases and other pieces were introduced in Art Deco shapes, initially with monochrome glazes and later with decoration in orange, brown and other colours. Blue and white wares were produced from 1935.
Marks: ZENITH/GOUDA; on blue-painted delftware, a coronet over a monogram of ZG.
Refs: L. Roest 'Vijftig jaar ceramiek, een nieuwe ontwikkeling van een oud bedriff' in *Mededelingenblad Vrienden van de Nederlandse Ceramiek* 46 (1967); Singelenberg-van der Meer; van Straaten.

Zerbst. German faience factory established c.1720 at Anhatt, and making cream-coloured or white earthenware in the 19th century, when the owners were August Fuckel from 1806 and G.I. Thorschmidt from 1932 until the factory's closure in 1861.
Marks: (when used) Z or ZERBST, impressed.
Refs: Haggar (1960); Hannover; Honey (1952).

Zhadin family. Russian potters working from the early 18th century at Rechitsa in the *Gzhel area. The family established a workshop, employing about 50 workers by 1850, and in operation until 1917. They produced tableware, mainly with printed designs, notably overblown flowers inspired by decoration used at the *Gardner factory. Zinaida Zhadina, a descendant of the founders, became chief technician at the factory started by the *Artistic Ceramics

Zell-Hamersbach. Stoneware jug, c.1820.

Cooperative, which she joined straight from school at its beginning in 1934.

Mark: FABRICK ZHAIDIN (1850-65).
Refs: Bubnova; Ovsyannikov.

Zholobov Pottery. Russian workshop producing earthenware at *Skopin. In the early 20th century, the pottery produced display pieces including candlesticks in the form of a tavern violinist, and a two-headed Imperial eagle. The workshop also introduced the use of pottery figures of animals (e.g. a long-maned lion with a paw resting on a ball) for use as an advertisement outside the potter's house. The owner made a Kvass jug in the form of a two-headed eagle holding a violin and bow in its claws; he also made for his own roof tiles depicting a bear playing a concertina, soldiers, a wood-owl, viper, sheep, cockerel, etc., no two alike. His son, Dmitry Zholobov, was among the potters responsible for reviving the crafts in the 1930s.
Ref: Ovsyannikov.

Ziegler, Jules-Claude (1804-56). French stoneware potter, born in Langres (Haute-Marne). Ziegler was initially a painter (his work included the cupola of La Madeleine), until failing eyesight forced him to give up. After studying the technique of stoneware on a visit to Germany, he carried out designs for Sèvres (1838-42) including an Apostle jug (1842) and established a pottery at Voisinlieu (Oise) 1839-44, at first employing about 16 workers. His workshop produced saltglaze with a brownish body decorated in relief with flowers, foliage and fruit (especially grapes taken from nature, or motifs of oriental or Egyptian origin. The forms were graceful and relaxed. Ziegler published lithographs of his designs in 1850, and became Curator of the Museum at Dijon and director of the Ecole des Beaux-Arts there. Despite the short life of his pottery, Ziegler's development of stoneware influenced the work of Mansard, an employee who succeeded him, before establishing his own stoneware pottery, also in Voisinlieu, which lasted until 1856. Ziegler's pottery also inspired the *Loc Maria firm, de la Hubaudière, makers of stoneware pieces decorated with grapes; and the Paris stoneware potter, Salmon, who produced Gothic clock-cases, as well as baskets with relief weaving, c.1850.

Ziegler's marks (infrequently used) include initials, J.Z.
Refs: Bénézit; Céramique française contemporaine; Ernould-Gandouet; Lesur (1971); Thieme & Becker.

Ziegler family. *See* Nagymarton.

Zoarite Pottery. American domestic earthenware and tiles made by the Society of Separatists of Zoar, a community organized in 1819 at Zoar, Ohio, by a group of German Protestants led by Joseph Baumler, who had emigrated from Württemberg two years earlier. The society became a corporation in 1832, when its members numbered about 500. It disbanded in 1896 or 1898, dividing the property equally among the surviving members. Roof tiles, made c.1820 to the 1840s, were moulded from local clay with lines of fluting and sometimes simple patterns incised or impressed with initials and a date.

Potters of the group made simple earthenware for household use in a variety of body and glaze colours—buff, brown, black, but often using a red body. Solomon Purdy, a potter making slipware and red earthenware in 1820 at Putnam, Ohio, worked with the Zoarites before he was listed as making stoneware at Atwater, Ohio, c.1850

Mark: ZOAR; the name S.PURDY also occurs, with ZOAR.
Refs: Lehner; Ramsay; L.G.G. Ramsay (ed) *The Complete Encyclopedia of Antiques* (Hawthorne Books, New York, 1968); Stradling; Webster.

Zoroku (d 1878). Japanese potter, Mashimizu Jutaro, working in Gojo-zaka from 1849, after studying under Waka Kitei (*see* Kameya family). His faience was of high quality and resembled the work of other Kyoto potters in style. Zoroku also made porcelain with celadon glazes. The making of tea jars and cups for the Imperial Palace earned him the name of Sogaku in 1864. He was succeeded by his son.
Ref: Brinkley.

Zsolnay. Hungarian factory established in 1862 at Pécs (Fünfkirchen) for the production of creamware by Ignaz Zsolnay, who had trained at a creamware factory and glassworks in Lukafa. Despite initial backing from his father, Ignaz Zsolnay was unsuccessful in running the factory, which passed in 1865 to his brother, Vilmos Zsolnay (d 1900). The main output of earthenware, at first in traditional styles for everyday use, was extended to include decorative pieces patterned with Turkish and Persian motifs, and shapes were sometimes also derived from Pre-Columbian, Peruvian and Chinese ceramics. The yellowish earthenware body was fired at relatively high temperatures.

Zsolnay. Jardinière painted with cockerels and a chicken among flowers, late 19th century. 38 cm high.

An experimental workshop under the direction (1893-1910) of the Hungarian ceramic chemist Vinsce Wartha (1844-1914), who was also on the staff of Budapest University, developed a rich, red iridescent glaze, marketed as Eosin and exhibited in the winter of 1899-1900 in Vienna, on which etched decoration was highlighted with gold lustre. Vases with lustre decoration, for which the factory became known in the mid 1890s, were sometimes made in the winged shapes associated with Hispano-Moresque ware, and another group of vases was made

Zsolnay. Pitcher with spout formed as a leaf and handle modelled as a standing woman. Vase painted with aubergine lustre ground, decorated with fruit and foliage modelled in high relief. Both marked with firm's medallion in relief. 44 cm and 31 cm high.

Zsolnay. Earthenware vase in Peruvian-inspired form in pale pink, blue and claret on a puce ground, c.1885. 38 cm high.

in folded shapes influenced by contemporary designs in lustred glass, with decoration in shades of green, yellow and blue. J.*Rippl-Rónay provided designs for vases c.1900. Vilmos Zsolnay's children, Terés and Júlia, and their relative Laszlo von Mattayasovszky-Zsolnay also worked as decorators and designers. After a visit to the factory at this time, W.*Crane described iridescent glazes, and designs painted in white slip in black glaze which became iridescent when fired. Dishes were painted with flowers and landscapes in red, green and blue. Some pots were in the form of animals (e.g. a coiled snake) or surrounded by animals modelled in high relief. Under the control of Zsolnay's son, Miklós (1857-1922), who had joined the firm in 1874 and succeeded his father as director in 1900, porcelain was introduced and figure production began. Mattayasovszky-Zsolnay became art director, 1922-38. The factory continues in operation, having worked from 1949 as a nationalized concern, Porzelángyár Pécs.

Marks: z.w. or z.v.pecs, sometimes with *Zsolnay*. From 1878, five towers (from the place name, Fünfkirchen); the towers enclosed in a shield from c.1903 above ZSOLNAY PECS.
Refs: W. Crane *An Artist's Reminiscences* (1907); Csanyi; Neuwirth (1974b); I. Pataky-Brestyánsky *Modern Hungarian Ceramics* (Corvina, Budapest, 1961); S. Szöts *Vilmos Zsolnay, Fünfkirchen* (catalogue, Jugendstilgalerie Strauch, Vienna).

Zuid-Holland, Plateelbakkerij, N.V. Dutch ceramics factory established 1898 in Gouda by the firm of E. Estié & Co., owners until 1905. The firm made decorative pieces with hand-painted floral patterns. Decorators and designers including D.*Harkink and E. van der Werff who worked at the pottery from 1898 until 1924, J.H.*Hartgring (until 1928), and L. and J.*Muller (until 1964), developed a decorative style similar to that of *Rozenburg factory, painting against dark grounds, usually green. Muller's mainly functional ware consisted of simple forms with matt, white glaze, often decorated with geometrical motifs. Muller's work was made in a separate department established by the factory. T.C.A.*Colenbrander was employed as decorator 1912-13, and C.J.*Lanooij was art director, 1902-03. Glazes developed by D. Harkink in 1909 were used on Rhodian and Damascus lines of earthenware. W.P. *Hartgring introduced a transparent matt glaze. C. de Lorm designed services, one in creamy-white, matt glazed ware in simple, gently curving shapes (1925), and a later service (1927) with rounded shapes in a harder body, glossy white glaze and, in some editions, bands of black in a harder body. The firm added Koninklijke to its title in 1930, and achieved considerable commercial success with the introduction of wares decorated with flowers in relief in 1938. After the death in 1954 of the director, W.A. Hoyng, whose family had owned the factory from its sale in 1905, the quality of the output deteriorated. The factory ceased operation in 1964.

Marks usually incorporate drawings of the Gate of Lazarus in Gouda, often with the name of the firm or the place name; others contain the designers' initials or the name of the ware, e.g. *Damascus.* A system of date cyphers indicates years from 1918 to 1932. *Refs:* R. Hagerman 'De Plateelbakkerij Zuid-Holland' in *Gouda Aardewerk in Heden en Verleden* (catalogue, Gouda, 1976); Singelenberg-van der Meer; van Straaten.

Zuniart. *See* Brush-McCoy Pottery.

Zwing, De. *See* Mertens, Konrad.

Plateelbakkerij Zuid-Holland. Wall plate painted in shades of grey with green and brown on a yellow ground, edged in black. Marked Zuid-Holland, Gouda, Breetveld. 42.5 cm in diameter.

Reference
Abbreviations

Andrews   S. Andrews *Crested China* (Springwood Books, Milestone Publications, London, and Hayling Island, Hants, 1980).

Années 25   *Les Années '25* (catalogue, Musée des Arts Décoratifs, Paris, 1966).

Anscombe & Gere   I. Anscombe & C. Gere *Arts and Crafts in Britain and America* (Academy Editions, London, 1979).

Aro   P. Aro *Arabia Design* (Kustannososakeyhtiö Otava, Helsinki, 1958).

Aslin & Atterbury   E. Aslin & P. Atterbury *Minton 1789-1910* (catalogue, Victoria & Albert Museum, August-October, 1976).

Atterbury (1979)   P. Atterbury (ed) *Antiques: Encyclopaedia of the Decorative Arts* (Octopus Books, London, 1979).

Atterbury (1980)   P. Atterbury (ed) *English Pottery & Porcelain* (Peter Owen, London, 1980).

Atterbury & Irvine   P. Atterbury & L.K. Irvine *The Doulton Story* (catalogue of an exhibition at the Victoria & Albert Museum, Royal Doulton Tableware Ltd, Stoke-on-Trent, 1979).

Audsley & Bowes   G.A. Audsley & J.L. Bowes *Keramic Art of Japan* (Henry Sotheran & Co., London, 1881).

Auscher   E.S. Auscher *History and Description of French Porcelain* (Cassell & Co., London, 1905).

Balston   T. Balston *Staffordshire Portrait Figures of the Victorian Age* (Faber & Faber, London, 1958).

Barber (1976)   E.A. Barber *The Pottery & Porcelain of the United States* (1893) and *Marks of American Potters* (1904); reissued in one volume (Feingold & Lewis, New York, 1976).

Barber (1926)   E.A. Barber *Tulip Ware of the Pennsylvania-German Potters* (1926; reissued Dover Publishing Inc., New York, 1970).

Barnard   J. Barnard *Victorian Ceramic Tiles* (Studio Vista, London, and New York Graphic Society, Greenwich, Connecticut, 1972).

Barrett (1951)   F.A. Barrett *Caughley & Coalport Porcelain* (F. Lewis, Leigh-on-Sea, 1951).

Barrett (1953)   F.A. Barrett *Worcester Porcelain and Lund's Bristol* (Faber & Faber, London, 1971).

Barrett & Thorpe   F.A. Barrett & A.L. Thorpe *Derby Porcelain* (Faber & Faber, London, 1971).

Baschet   Books published by Baschet et Cie, Paris (n.d.):
                        Les Styles Empire et Restauration (text by Sylvia Chadenet)
                        Le Style Second Empire (text by Philippe Jullian)
                        Le Style Louis XVI (text by Philippe Jullian)
                        Le Style Louis XV (text by Mabille)
                        Le Modern Style (text by Laurence Buffet-Challié)
                        Le Style 1925 (text by Yvonne Brunhammer)

Batkin   M. Batkin *Wedgwood Ceramics 1846-1959. A New Appraisal* (Richard Dennis, London, 1982).

Battersby (1969a)   M. Battersby *Art Nouveau* (Paul Hamlyn, Feltham, Middlesex, 1969).

Battersby (1969b)   M. Battersby *The Decorative Twenties* (Studio Vista, London, 1969).

Battersby (1971)   M. Battersby *The Decorative Thirties* (Studio Vista, London, 1971).

Beard   G. Beard *Modern Ceramics* (Studio Vista, London, 1969).

Bedford   J. Bedford *Yesterday's Junk Tomorrow's Antiques* (Macdonald & Janes, London, 1977).

Bell   R.C. Bell *Tyneside Pottery* (Studio Vista, London, 1971).

Bemrose   G. Bemrose *19th Century English Pottery and Porcelain* (Faber & Faber, London, 1952).

Bénézit   E. Bénézit *Dictionnaire critique et documentaire des peintres, sculpteurs, dessinateurs et graveurs* Paris, 1976).

Berges	R. Berges *From Gold to Porcelain—The Art of Porcelain and Faience* (Thomas Yoseloff, New York, 1963).
Binns (1910)	C.F. Binns *The Potter's Craft* (Constable & Co. Ltd, London, and Van Nostrand Co., New York, 1910).
Binns (1865)	R.W. Binns *A Century of Potting in the City of Worcester* (London, 1865; second edition, Quaritch, London, 1871).
Binns (1897)	R.W. Binns *Worcester China* (Quaritch, London, 1897).
Bivins	J. Bivins *The Moravian Potters in North Carolina* (University of North Carolina Press, Chapel Hill, North Carolina, 1972).
Blacker (1911)	J.F. Blacker *Nineteenth Century Ceramic Art* (London, 1911).
Blacker (1922a)	J.F. Blacker *The ABC of English Nineteenth Century Pottery & Porcelain* (Stanley Paul & Co., London, 1922).
Blacker (1922b)	J.F. Blacker *The ABC of English Salt-Glaze Stoneware* (Stanley Paul & Co., London, 1922).
Bloch-Dermant	J. Bloch-Dermant *L'Art du Verre en France, 1860-1914* (Denoël, Paris, 1974).
Bock	G. Reineking v. Bock *Keramik des 20 Jahrhunderts, Deutschland* (Keyser, Munich, 1979).
Bossaglia	R. Bossaglia *Art Nouveau: Revolution in Interior Design* (Orbis, London, 1973; first published by Istituto Geographico De Agostino, Novara, 1971).
Bradley	H.G. Bradley (ed) *Ceramics of Derbyshire 1750-1975* (published by author, London, 1978).
Brears (1971a)	P.C.D. Brears *The English Country Pottery* (David & Charles, Newton Abbot, 1971).
Brears (1971b)	P.C.D. Brears *Farnham Potteries* (Phillimore & Co. Ltd, Chichester, Sussex, 1971).
Brears (1974)	P.C.D. Brears *The Collector's Book of English Country Pottery* (David & Charles, Newton Abbot, 1974).
Brinkley	F. Brinkley *Japan: Its History, Arts & Literature* Vol III (T.C. & E.C. Jade, London and Edinburgh, 1904).
Brongniart	A. Brongniart *Traité des arts céramiques ou des poteries considérés dans leur histoire, leur pratique et leur théorie…deuxième edition, revue, corrigée et augmentée de notes et d'additions, par Alphonse Salvetat* (Paris, 1844).
Brosio	V. Brosio *Porcellane e Maioliche Italiane dell'ottocento* (A. Vallardi, Milan, 1980).
Brunhammer	Y. Brunhammer *La faïence française* (Editions Charles Massin, Paris, 1959).
Brunhammer *et al* (1976)	Y. Brunhammer *et al Art Nouveau Belgium/France* (catalogue Rice University and National Art Institute, Chicago, 1976).
Bubnova	E. Bubnova *Old Russian Faience* (parallel texts in English and Russian, Iskusstvo, Moscow, 1973).
Bunt	C.E.G. Bunt *British Potters & Pottery Today* (F. Lewis, Leigh-on-Sea, 1956).
Burton (1904)	W. Burton *English Earthenware & Stoneware* (London, 1904).
Burton (1906)	W. Burton *Porcelain—A Sketch of its Nature, Art & Manufacture* (London, 1906; reprinted E.P. publishing, 1972).
Burton (1921)	W. Burton *A General History of Porcelain* (Cassell, London, 1921).
Callen	A. Callen *Angel in the Studio* (Astragal Books, London, 1979).
Camart *et al*	J.P. Camart *et al L'Art de la Poterie en France de Rodin à Dufy* (Musée Nationale de Céramique, Sèvres, 1971).

Céramique française contemporaine	*Céramique française contemporaine* (catalogue, Musée des Arts Décoratifs, Paris, 1981).
Chaffers	W. Chaffers *Marks & Monograms on Pottery & Porcelain* (London, 1863, and subsequent editions).
Charles	R. Charles *Continental Porcelain of the 18th Century* (Ernest Benn, London, 1964).
Chavagnac & Grollier	X. de Chavagnac & A. de Grollier *Histoire des manufactures françaises de porcelaine* (Paris, 1906).
Cherny	N.V. Cherny *Verbilki Porcelain* (in Russian, Moscow, 1970).
Chompret	J. Chompret, J. Blanch, J. Guerin, P. Alfassa *Repertoire de la faïence française* 1 volume de texte et 5 volumes de planches (Paris, 1935).
Clark & Hughto	G. Clark & M. Hughto *A Century of Ceramics in the United States 1878-1978* (E.P. Dutton, New York, 1979).
Clement (1944)	A.W. Clement *Our Pioneer Potters* (privately published, New York, 1947).
Collard	E. Collard *19th Century Pottery & Porcelain in Canada* McGill University Press, Montreal, 1967).
Cooper	E. Cooper *A History of World Pottery* (second edition, B.T. Batsford Ltd, London, 1981).
Cort	A. Cort *Shigaraki, Potters' Valley* (Tokyo, 1979).
Cox	W.E. Cox *Pottery & Porcelain* (Crown, New York, 1964).
Coysh (1972)	A.W. Coysh *Blue-Printed Earthenware 1800-1850* (David & Charles, Newton Abbot, 1972).
Coysh (1974)	A.W. Coysh *Blue & White Transfer Ware 1780-1840* (David & Charles, Newton Abbot, 1974).
Coysh (1976)	A.W. Coysh *British Art Pottery* (David & Charles, Newton Abbot, 1976).
Coysh & Henrywood	A.W. Coysh & Henrywood *Dictionary of Blue & White Printed Pottery* (Antique Collectors' Club, Woodbridge, Suffolk, 1982).
Cross	A.J. Cross *Pilkington's Royal Lancastrian Pottery & Tiles* (Richard Dennis, London, 1980).
Csanyi	K. Csanyi *Geschichte der Ungarischen Keramik, des Porzellans und ihre Marken* (Verlag des Fonds für bildende Künste, Budapest, 1954).
Cushion (1974)	J.P. Cushion *Animals in Pottery & Porcelain* (Studio Vista, London, 1974).
Cushion (1976)	J.P. Cushion *Pottery & Porcelain Tablewares* (Studio Vista, London, 1976).
Cushion (1980)	J.P. Cushion *Handbook of Pottery & Porcelain Marks* (Faber & Faber, London, 1980).
d'Albis *et al*	J. d'Albis *et al Céramique Impressioniste: L'Atelier Haviland de Paris-Auteuil 1872-1882* (Société des Amis de la Bibliothèque Forney, Paris, 1974).
d'Albis & Romanet	J. d'Albis & C. Romanet *La porcelaine de Limoges* (Sous le Vent, Paris, 1980).
Danckert	L. Danckert *Manuel de la porcelaine européene* (revised edition, Office du Livre, Fribourg, 1980).
Deck	T. Deck *La faïence* (Paris, 1887).
Dennis (1971)	*Doulton Stoneware and Terracotta 1870-1925* (catalogue, Richard Dennis, London, 1971).
Dennis (1973)	*William Moorcroft and Walter Moorcroft 1897-1973* (Richard Dennis, 1973).
Dennis (1974)	*Charles Vyse: Figures and Stoneware Pottery* (Richard Dennis, London, 1974).
Dennis (1975)	*Doulton Pottery from the Lambeth and Burslem Studio 1873-1939* (Richard Dennis, London, 1975).
Donhauser	P. Donhauser *History of American Ceramics* (Kendall Hunt Publishing Co., Dubuque, Iowa, 1976).

Dowling	H.G. Dowling *A Survey of British Decorative Art* (F. Lewis Ltd, London, 1935).
Ducret (1940)	S. Ducret *Deutsches Porzellan und Deutsche Fayencen im Wien, Zurich und Nyon* (Geneva, 1940).
Ducret (1945)	S. Ducret *Zürcher Porzellan des 19 Jahrhunderts* (Zurich, 1945).
Ducret (1958)	S. Ducret *Die Zürcher Porzellanmanufaktur und ihre Erzeugnisse, im 18 und 19 Jahrhundert* (Zurich, 1958-59).
Ducret (1962)	S. Ducret *Porcelaine de Saxe et autres manufactures allemandes* (Fribourg, 1962).
Ducret (1965)	S. Ducret *Fürstenberger Porzellan* (Brunswick, 1965).
Ducret (1973)	S. Ducret *Würzburger Porzellan* (Brunswick, 1973).
Eaglestone & Lockett	A.E. Eaglestone & T.A. Lockett *The Rockingham Pottery* (David & Charles, Newton Abbot, 1973).
Eidelberg	M. Eidelberg 'Art Pottery' in *The Arts & Crafts Movement 1876-1916* (ed) R.V. Clark (Princeton University Press, 1972).
Ell	D. Ell (ed) *Australian Antiques. First Fleet to Federation* (Sydney, 1977).
Emme	B. Emme *Russian Art Porcelain* (in Russian, Moscow and Leningrad, 1950).
Ernould-Gandouet	M. Ernould-Gandouet *La Céramique en France au XIXe siècle* (Gründ, Paris, 1969).
Evans	P. Evans *Art Pottery of the United States* (Charles Scribner's Sons, New York, 1974).
Eyles (1970)	D. Eyles (ed) *Sir Henry Doulton* (Hutchinson, London, 1970).
Eyles (1975)	D. Eyles *The Doulton Lambeth Wares* (Hutchinson, London, 1975).
Eyles (1980)	D. Eyles *The Doulton Burslem Wares* (Hutchinson, London, 1980).
Eyles and Dennis	D. Eyles and R. Dennis *Royal Doulton Figures: Produced at Burslem 1890-1978* (Royal Doulton Tableware, 1978).
Faré	M. Faré *La céramique contemporaine* (Compagnie des Arts Photomécaniques, Paris and Strasbourg, 1953).
Feddersen	M. Feddersen *Japanische Kunstgewerbe* (Brunswick, 1960).
Fishley Holland	W. Fishley Holland *Fifty Years a Potter* (special publication, *Pottery Quarterly*, 1958).
Fleming	J.A. Fleming *Scottish Pottery* (Jackson & Co., Glasgow, 1923; reprint, 1973).
Fontaine	G. Fontaine *La céramique française* in the series *Arts, styles et techniques* (Larousse, Paris, 1946).
Forsyth	G.M. Forsyth *Twentieth Century Ceramics* (1936).
Fournier	R. Fournier *Illustrated Dictionary of Practical Pottery* (Van Nostrand Reinhold Co., New York, 1977).
Fujioka	Fujioka Ryoichi *Shino and Oribe Ceramics* (Kodansha International/Shibundo, Tokyo, New York and San Francisco, 1977).
Furnival	W.J. Furnival *Researches on Leadless Glazes* (published by the author, 1898; republished McGibbon & Kee, London, 1961).
Garnier	E. Garnier *La porcelaine tendre de Sèvres* (Paris, 1908).
Gilhespy	F.B. Gilhespy *Derby Porcelain* (Spring Books, London, 1961).
Godden (1952)	G.A. Godden *19th Century English Pottery & Porcelain* (London, 1952).
Godden (1961)	G.A. Godden *Victorian Porcelain* (Herbert Jenkins, London, 1961).
Godden (1963)	G.A. Godden *British Pottery and Porcelain 1780-1850* (Arthur Barker, London, 1963).

Godden (1964)	G.A. Godden *Encyclopaedia of British Pottery and Porcelain* (Herbert Jenkins, London, 1964).
Godden (1966a)	G.A. Godden *Illustrated Encyclopedia of British Pottery and Porcelain* (Herbert Jenkins, London, 1966; reissued Barrie & Jenkins, 1980.
Godden (1966b)	G.A. Godden *Antique China & Glass under £5* (Arthur Barker, London, 1966).
Godden (1968)	G.A. Godden *Minton Pottery & Porcelain of the 1st Period 1793-1850* (Herbert Jenkins, London, 1968).
Godden (1969)	G.A. Godden *Caughley & Worcester Porcelains 1775-1800* (Herbert Jenkins, London, 1969).
Godden (1970)	G.A. Godden *Coalport & Coalbrookdale Porcelains* (Herbert Jenkins, London, 1970).
Godden (1971)	G.A. Godden *The Illustrated Guide to Mason's Patent Ironstone China and the Related Ware* (Barrie & Jenkins, London, 1971).
Godden (1972)	G.A. Godden *Ridgway Porcelains* (Barrie & Jenkins, London, 1972).
Godden (1974)	G.A. Godden *British Pottery, an Illustrated Guide* (Barrie & Jenkins, London, 1974).
Godden (1980)	G.A. Godden *Guide to Mason's China & the Ironstone Wares* (Antique Collectors' Club, Woodbridge, Suffolk, 1980).
Gorham	H.H. Gorham *Japanese & Oriental Ceramics* (Charles E. Tuttle & Co., Rutland, Vermont, and Tokyo, 1971).
Grabham	O. Grabham 'Yorkshire Potteries, Pots & Potters' in *Yorkshire Philosophical Society Transactions* (1916).
Graham	M. Graham *Australian Pottery of the 19th and early 20th Century* (David Ell Press Pty, Hunters Hill, New South Wales, 1979).
Greer	G.H. Greer *American Stonewares, the Art & Craft of Utilitarian Potters* (Schiffer Publishing Ltd, Exton, Pennsylvania, 1981).
Guillebon	R. de Plinval de Guillebon *Paris Porcelain 1770-1850* translated by R.J. Charleston (Barrie & Jenkins, London, 1972).
Haggar (1950)	R.G. Haggar *English Country Pottery* (Phoenix House, London, 1950).
Haggar (1952)	R.G. Haggar *The Masons of Lane Delph* (Lund Humphries, London, 1952).
Haggar (1953)	R.G. Haggar *A Century of Art Education in the Potteries* (1953).
Haggar (1955)	R.G. Haggar *Staffordshire Chimney Ornaments* (Phoenix House, London, 1955).
Haggar (1960)	R.G. Haggar *Concise Encyclopaedia of Continental Pottery and Porcelain* (André Deutsch, London, 1960).
Haggar & Adams	R. Haggar & E. Adams *Mason Porcelain and Ironstone* (Faber & Faber, London, 1977).
Hakenjos (1974)	B. Hakenjos & E. Klinge *Europäische Keramik des Jugendstils, Art Nouveau, Modern Style* (Hertjens-Museum, Düsseldorf, 1974).
Handley-Read	*Victorian & Edwardian Decorative Art* (catalogue of the Handley-Read Collection, Royal Academy, London, 1972).
Hannover	E. Hannover *Pottery & Porcelain—A Handbook for Collectors. Vol I European Earthenware and Stoneware; Vol II The Far East; Vol III European Porcelain* (ed) Bernard Rackham (Edward Benn Ltd, London, and Charles Scribner's Sons, New York, 1925).
Hare	R. Hare *The Art and Artists of Russia* (Methuen & Co., London, 1965).
Haslam (1975)	M. Haslam *English Art Pottery 1865-1915* (London Antique Dealers' Club, 1975).
Haslam (1977)	M. Haslam *Marks & Monograms of the Modern Movement* (Lutterworth Press, Guildford, 1977).
Haslam (1978)	M. Haslam *The Martin Brothers, Potters* (Richard Dennis, London, 1978).

Haslem	J. Haslem *The Old Derby China Factory* (George Bell & Sons, London, 1876).
Hayden	A. Hayden *Spode and his Successors* (Cassell, London, 1924).
Henzke	L. Henzke *American Art Pottery* (Nelson, Camden, New Jersey, 1970).
Hettes & Rada	K. Hettes & P. Rada *Modern Ceramics* (Spring Books, London, 1965).
Heuser & Heuser	*Französische Keramik zwischen 1850 und 1910, Sammlung Maria & Hans-Jurgen Heuser, Hamburg* (Prestel-Verlag, Munich, 1974).
Hillier	B. Hillier *Art Deco* (Dutton, New York, 1969).
Hiort	E. Hiort *Modern Danish Ceramics* (Jul. G. Göellerups Forlag, Copenhagen, 1955).
Hobson	R.L. Hobson *Handbook of the Pottery & Porcelain of the Far East* (British Museum, London, third edition, 1948).
Holgate	D. Holgate *New Hall and its Imitators* (Faber & Faber, London, 1971).
Honey (1927)	W.B. Honey *Later Chinese Porcelain* (Victoria & Albert Museum, London, 1927).
Honey (1945)	W.B. Honey *The Ceramic Art of China and Other Countries of the Far East* (Faber & Faber, London, 1945).
Honey (1947)	W.B. Honey *German Porcelain* (Faber & Faber, London, 1947).
Honey (1948a)	W.B. Honey *Old English Porcelain* (Faber & Faber, London, 1948).
Honey (1948b)	W.B. Honey *Wedgwood Ware* (Faber & Faber, London, 1948).
Honey (1952)	W.B. Honey *European Ceramic Art* (Faber & Faber, London, 1949-52)
Honey (1962)	W.B. Honey *English Pottery & Porcelain* (A.& C. Black, London, fifth edition, 1962).
Hood	K. Hood, W. Garnsey & D. Thompson *Australian Pottery* (Melbourne, 1972).
Howe	H. Howe *Historical Collections of Ohio* (C.J. Krehbiel & Co., Ohio, 1902).
Hughes & Hughes	G.B. & T. Hughes *English Porcelain & Bone China* (The Macmillan Co., New York, 1955).
Hughes (1959)	G.B. Hughes *English & Scottish Earthenware* (Lutterworth, London, 1961).
Hughes (1977)	G.B. Hughes *The Country Life Collectors' Pocket Book of China* (Country Life, Feltham, Middlesex, 1977).
Huillard	P. Huillard *La faïence en Bourgogne auxerroise 1725-1870* (Paris, Larousse, 1960).
Hurst	A. Hurst *Catalogue of the Boynton Collection of Yorkshire Pottery* (Yorkshire Philosophic Society, 1922).
Hüseler	K. Hüseler *Deutsche Fayence* (Anton Hiersemann, Stuttgart, 1958).
Ivanova	E. Ivanova *Russian Applied Art Eighteenth to Early Twentieth Century* (Aurora Art Publishers, Leningrad, 1976).
Jaquemart	A. Jaquemart *Histoire de la Céramique. Etude descriptive et raisonnée de poteries de tous les temps et tous les peuples* (Paris, 1873).
James	A.E. James *The Potters & Potteries of Chester County* (Chester County Historical Society, Chester, Pennsylvania, 1945).
Jenkins	E. Jenkins *Swansea Porcelain* (D. Brown & Sons Ltd, Cowbridge, Glamorgan, 1970).
Jenyns (1951)	S. Jenyns *Later Chinese Porcelain* (Faber & Faber, London, 1951).
Jenyns (1965)	S. Jenyns *Japanese Porcelain* (Faber & Faber, London, 1965).

Jenyns (1971)	S. Jenyns *Japanese Pottery* (Faber & Faber, London, 1971).
Jervis	W.P. Jervis *The Encyclopedia of Ceramics* (Blanchard, New York, 1902).
Jewitt	L. Jewitt *The Ceramic Art of Great Britain* (first published, 1878; revised edition, 1883; new edition revised by G.A. Godden and published by Barrie & Jenkins, London, 1972).
John	W.D. John *Swansea Porcelain* (Ceramic Book Co., Newport, Monmouthshire, 1958).
Kahle	K.M. Kahle *Modern French Decoration* (G.P. Putnam's & Sons, New York, 1930).
Keen	K.H. Keen *American Art Pottery 1875-1930* (Delaware Art Museum, Wilmington, 1978).
Ketchum (1970)	W.C. Ketchum *Early Potters & Potteries of New York State* (Funk & Wagnalls, New York, 1970).
Ketchum (1971)	W.C. Ketchum *The Pottery & Porcelain Collector's Books* (Funk & Wagnalls, New York, 1971).
Klamkin (1971)	M. Klamkin *The Collector's Book of Art Nouveau* (David & Charles, Newton Abbot, 1971).
Klamkin (1973)	M. Klamkin *American Patriotic and Political China* (Charles Scribner's Sons, New York, 1973).
Klein	A. Klein *Moderne Deutsche Keramik* (Darmstadt, 1956).
Klinge	E. Klinge *Deutsche Keramik des 20 Jahrhunderts* (catalogue, Hetjenmuseums, Düsseldorf, 1975).
Kovel & Kovel	R. & T. Kovel *The Kovels' Collector's Guide to American Art Pottery* (Crown, New York, 1974).
Koyama	Koyama Fujio *The Heritage of Japanese Ceramics* (Weatherhill, New York, and Tankosha, Tokyo, 1973).
Lane	A. Lane *French Faïence* (Faber & Faber, London, revised edition, 1970).
Lawrence	H. Lawrence *Yorkshire Pots & Potteries* (David & Charles, Newton Abbot, 1974).
Leach (1966)	B. Leach *Kenzan and his Tradition* (Faber & Faber, London, 1966).
Lehner	L. Lehner *Ohio Pottery & Glass* (Wallace-Homestead, Des Moines, Iowa, 1978).
Lesieutre	A. Lesieutre *Art Deco* (Paddington Press, London, 1974).
Lesur (1967)	A. Lesur *Les porcelaines françaises* (Tardy, Paris, 1967).
Lesur (1971)	A. Lesur *Les poteries et les faïences françaises* (Tardy, Paris, 1971).
Lise	G. Lise *Le Porcellane* (Electa Editrice, Milan, 1975).
Litchfield	F. Litchfield *Pottery & Porcelain* (Macmillan, New York, 1925).
Living National Treasures	*Living National Treasures of Japan* (catalogue of the Museum of Fine Arts, Boston; Art Institute of Chicago; Japanese American Cultural & Community Centre, Los Angeles, 1983).
Lloyd Thomas (1974)	D.& E. Lloyd Thomas *Victorian Art Pottery* (Guildart, London, 1974).
Lloyd Thomas (1978)	D.& E. Lloyd Thomas *The Old Torquay Potteries* (Arthur H. Stackwell, Ilfracombe, Devon, and Guildart, London, 1978).
Lockett (1972)	T.A. Lockett *Davenport Pottery & Porcelain 1784-1887* (David & Charles, Newton Abbot, 1972).
Lockett (1979)	T.A. Lockett *Collecting Victorian Tiles* (Antique Collectors' Club, Woodbridge, 1979).
Lomax	A. Lomax *Royal Lancastrian Pottery 1900-1938* (published by the author, Bolton, 1957).
Lukomsky	G. Lukomsky *Russisches Porzellan, 1744-1923* (Berlin, 1924).
Madsen (1956)	S.T. Madsen *Sources of Art Nouveau* (George Wittenborn, New York, 1956).
Madsen (1967)	S.T. Madsen *Art Nouveau* (Weidenfeld & Nicolson, London, 1967).

Mankowitz	W. Mankowitz *Wedgwood* (Dutton, New York, and Barrie & Jenkins, London, 1953).
Mankowitz & Haggar	W. Mankowitz & R. Haggar *Concise Encyclopedia of English Pottery & Porcelain* (André Deutsch, London, and Hawthorn, New York, 1957).
Masterpieces	*Masterpieces of Japanese Art* (Bunka Kinyu Kuraba, 1949).
McClinton	K.M. McClinton *Art Deco* (Clarkson N. Potter, New York, 1972).
McVeigh	*Scottish East Coast Potteries 1750-1840* (J. Donald, Edinburgh, 1979).
Meyer	H. Meyer *Böhmisches Porzellan und Steingut* (Leipzig, 1927).
Mikami	Mikami Tsugio *The Art of Japanese Ceramics* (translated by Ann Herring in the Heibonsha Survey of Japanese Art, Vol 29 (Weatherhill, Tokyo and New York, 1972).
Miller	R.A. Miller *Japanese Ceramics* (Tuttle Toto Shuppansha, Rutland, Vermont and Tokyo, 1960); based on Japanese text entitled *Nihon no Toji* by Okuda Seiichi, Koyama Fujio and Hayashiya Seizo (Toto Bunka Co., Tokyo, 1954).
Minamoto	Minamoto Hoshu *An Illustrated History of Japanese Art* (Hoshino Shoten, Kyoto, 1935).
Mitsuoka	Mitsuoka Tadanari *Ceramic Art of Japan* (1949).
Mizuo	Mizuo Horoshi *Folk Kilns I* (Kodansha International, Tokyo, New York and San Francisco, 1981).
Morse	*Morse Catalogue of the Morse Collection of Japanese Pottery* (Boston Museum of Fine Art in association with Cambridge Riverside Press, 1901).
Munsterberg	H. Munsterberg *The Ceramic Art of Japan* (Charles E. Tuttle, Rutland, Vermont, 1964).
Myers	L. Myers *The First Hundred Years* (Poole Pottery Ltd, 1973).
Nakagawa	Senshaku Nakagawa *Kutani Ware* (Kodansha, Tokyo, New York and San Francisco, 1978).
Nance	M. Nance *The Pottery and Porcelain of Swansea and Nantgarw* (Batsford, London, 1942).
Naylor	G. Naylor *The Arts and Crafts Movement* (Studio Vista, London and New York, 1971).
Neuwirth (1974a)	W. Neuwirth *Wiener Keramik* (Klinkhardt & Biermann, Brunswick, 1974).
Neuwirth (1974b)	W. Neuwirth *Österreichische Keramik des Jugendstils* (Prestel Verlag, Munich, 1974).
Newmann	E. Newmann *Bauhaus & Bauhaus People* (Van Nostrand Reinhold, London, 1971).
Newton	C.C. Newton 'Early Days at Rookwood Pottery', manuscript in the Cincinnati Historical Society, edited and included in *The Bulletin of the American Ceramic Society* 18 (November 1939).
Nikiforova	L. Nikiforova *Russian Porcelain in the Hermitage Collection* (Aurora Art Publishers, Leningrad, 1973).
Okada	Y. Okada *Pageant of Japanese Art* (Tokyo, 1952).
Okamura	Kichiemon Okamura *Folk Kilns II* (Kodansha International, Tokyo, New York and San Francisco, 1981).
Okuda	Okuda Seiichi (ed) *Toho Tokiji Shusei* (catalogue, Institute of Oriental Ceramics, Tokyo, 1932).
Oliver	A. Oliver *Victorian Staffordshire Figures, a Guide for Collectors* (Heinemann, London, 1971).
Orange	J. Orange *Bizen-Ware with a Catalogue of the Later Collection* (1916).
Osgood	C. Osgood *The Jug & Related Stoneware of Bennington* (Charles E. Tuttle, Rutland, Vermont, 1971).
Oswald	A. Oswald, R.J.C. Hildyard and R.G. Hughes *English Brown Stoneware 1670-1900* (Faber & Faber, London, 1982).
Ovsyannikov	Ovsyannikov *Russian Folk Arts and Crafts* (Progress Publishers, Moscow, c.1970).

Owen	H. Owen *Two Centuries of Ceramic Art in Bristol* (London, 1873).
Paton	J. Paton *Jugs, A Collector's Guide* (Souvenir Press, London, 1976).
Pazaurek	G.E. Pazaurek *Deutsche Fayence—und Porzellan-Hausmaler* (Karl W. Hursemann, Leipzig, 1925).
Peck	H. Peck *The Book of Rookwood Pottery* (Crown, New York, 1968).
Pelka	O. Pelka *Keramik der Neuzeit* (Leipzig, 1924).
Penkala	M. Penkala *European Pottery* (Charles E. Tuttle, Rutland, Vermont, 1960).
Pevsner	N. Pevsner *Pioneers of Modern Design* (Pelican, London, 1960).
Plath	I. Plath *Decorative Arts of Sweden* (Charles Scribner's Sons, New York and London, 1948).
Porzellankunst	*Porzellankunst* (catalogue, Sammlung Karl H. Bröhan, Berlin, 1969).
Pountney	W.J. Pountney *The Old Bristol Potteries* (J.W. Arrowsmith, Bristol, 1920).
Préaud et Gauthier	T. Préaud & S. Gauthier *Ceramics of the Twentieth Century* (Phaidon/Christie's, Oxford, 1982); translation of *La Céramique, art du XXe siècle* (Office du Livre, Fribourg, 1982).
Pugh	P.D.G. Pugh *Staffordshire Portrait Figures* (Barrie & Jenkins, London, 1970).
Quénioux	G. Quénioux *Les Arts Décoratifs Modernes* (Librairie Larousse, Paris, 1925).
Quimby	I.M.G. Quimby *Ceramics in America* (Winterthur Conference Report, 1972; The University Press of Virginia, Charlottesville, 1973).
Rackham	B. Rackham *Catalogue of Herbert Allen Collection of English Porcelain* (HMSO, London, 1923).
Rackham & Read	B. Rackham & H. Read *English Pottery* (London, 1920).
Rackham & Read	B. Rackham & H. Read *English Pottery: Its Development from Early Times to the End of the Eighteenth Century* (London, 1924).
Ramsay	J. Ramsay *American Potters & Pottery* (Tudor Publishing Co. New York, 1947).
Reilly & Savage	R. Reilly and G. Savage *The Dictionary of Wedgwood* (Antique Collectors' Club, Woodbridge, Suffolk, 1980).
Reynolds	E. Reynolds *Collecting Victorian Porcelain* (London, 1966).
Rhead	G.W. Rhead *British Pottery Marks* (Scott, Greenwood & Sons Ltd, London, 1910).
Rhead & Rhead	G.W. & F.A. Rhead *Staffordshire Pots & Potters* (Hutchinson, London, 1906; reprinted E.P. Publishing, Wakefield, West Yorkshire, 1977).
Rheims	N.M. Rheims *Age of Art Nouveau* (Thames & Hudson, London, 1966).
Riano	J.F. Riano *The Industrial Arts in Spain* (South Kensington Museum Handbook, London, 1879).
Rice	D.G. Rice *Rockingham Ornamental Porcelain* (The Adam Publishing Co., London, 1966).
Rice & Stoudt	A.H. Rice & J.B. Stoudt *The Shenandoah Pottery* (Shenandoah Publishing House Inc., Strasburg, Virginia, 1929).
Riff	A. Riff *Art Populaire de France* (Strasbourg, 1960).
Robert	M. Robert *Les poteries populaires et les potiers de Limousin et de la Marche du XIIIième siècle à nos jours* (Paris, 1972).
Roberts	L.P. Roberts *A Dictionary of Japanese Artists* (Weatherhill, Tokyo and New York, 1976).
Rose	M. Rose *Artist Potters in England* (Faber & Faber, London, 1955).

Ross	M.C. Ross *Russian Porcelains* (University of Oklahoma Press, Norman, 1968).
Rozembergh	F. Rozembergh *Les marques de la porcelaine russe, période impériale* (Paris, 1928).
Saltykov	A.B. Saltykov *Russian Ceramics* (in Russian, Moscow, 1952).
Sanders	H.H. Sanders *The World of Japanese Ceramics* (Kodansha International, Tokyo and New York, 1967).
Sandon (1978a)	H. Sandon *Royal Worcester Porcelain from 1862 to the Present Day* (Barrie & Jenkins, London, third edition, 1978).
Sandon (1978b)	H. Sandon *Flight & Barr Worcester Porcelain, 1783-1840* (Antique Collectors' Club, Woodbridge, Suffolk, 1978).
Sato	Sato Masahiko *Kyoto Ceramics* (Weatherhill, New York, and Shibundo, Tokyo, 1973).
Savage	G. Savage *Eighteenth Century English Porcelain* (New York, 1952; new edition, Spring Books, London, 1964).
Scarratt	W. Scarratt *Old Times in The Potteries* (privately published, 1906).
Scheen	P.A. Scheen *Lexicon Nederlandse beeldende Kunstenaars 1750-1950* (The Hague, 1969-70).
Scherer	C. Scherer *Das Fürstenberger Porzellan* (Berlin, 1909).
Schmutzler	R. Schmutzler *Art Nouveau* (New English Library, London, and Abrams, New York, 1970).
Schwartz & Wolfe	M.D. Schwartz & R. Wolfe *A History of American Art Porcelain* (Renaissance Editions, New York, 1967).
Shaw	J.T. Shaw (ed) *Sunderland Ware. The Potteries of Wearside* (fourth edition, County Borough of Sunderland Publications, 1973).
Shinn	C.& D. Shinn *The Illustrated Guide to Victorian Parian China* (Barrie & Jenkins, London, 1971).
Singelenberg-van der Meer	M. Singelenberg-van der Meer *Nederlandse Keramiek en Glasmerken 1880-1940* (De Tidjstroom, Lochem, 1980).
Spargo	J. Spargo *The Potters & Potteries of Bennington* (Houghton Mifflin, Boston, Massachusetts, 1826; reissued Dover, New York, 1972).
Spencer	R. Spencer *The Aesthetic Movement. Theory and Practice* (Studio Vista, London, 1972).
Stoehr	A. Stoehr *Deutsche Fayenzen und Deutsche Steingut* (Richard Carl Schmidt, Berlin, 1920).
Stradling	D.& J.G. Stradling *The Art of the Potter* (Main Street and Universe, New York, 1977).
Stringer	G.E. Stringer *New Hall Porcelain* (Art Trade Press, London, 1949).
Sugimura	Sugimura Tsuno and Ogawa Masakata *The Enduring Crafts of Japan* (Walker and Weatherhill, New York and Tokyo, 1968).
Thieme & Becker	U. Thieme & F. Becker *Allgemeines Lexicon der bildenden Künstler von der Antike bis zur Gegenwart* (Leipzig, 1970).
Tilmans (1953)	E. Tilmans *Porcelaines de France* (Editions de Deux-Mondes, Paris 1953).
Tilmans (1954)	E. Tilmans *Faïence de France* (Editions de Deux-Mondes, Paris, 1954).
Timms	P. Timms *Australian Pottery 1900 to 1956* (Shepparton, 1978).
Towner (1957)	D.C. Towner *English Cream-Coloured Earthenware* (Faber & Faber, London, 1957).
Towner (1963)	D.C. Towner *The Leeds Pottery* (London, 1963).
Turner	W. Turner *The Ceramics of Swansea & Nantgarw* (London, 1897).
Twitchett (1976)	J. Twitchett & B. Bailey *Royal Crown Derby* (Barrie & Jenkins, London, 1976).

Twitchett (1980)	J. Twitchett & B. Bailey *Derby Porcelain* (Barrie & Jenkins, London, 1980).
Uyeno	Uyeno Naoteru (ed) *Japanese Art & Crafts in the Meiji Era* (English adaptation by Richard Lane for Pan Pacific Press, Tokyo, 1958).
Valotaire	M. Valotaire *La céramique française moderne* (G. Van Oest, Paris and Brussels, 1930).
Van Lemmen	H. Van Lemmen *Tiles, a Collector's Guide* (Souvenir Press Ltd, London, 1979).
van Straaten	E.J. van Straaten 'Aardewerknijverheid in Nederland 1876-1940' in *Mededelingenblad Vrienden van der Nederlandse Ceramiek* 94-95 (1979).
Vogt	Gustav Vogt *La porcelaine* (Quantin, Paris, 1893).
Wakefield	H. Wakefield *Victorian Pottery* (Herbert Jenkins, London, 1962).
Walcha (1963)	O. Walcha *Meissner Porzellan* (Dresden, 1973).
Ware	G.W. Ware *German and Austrian Porcelain* (Lothar Woeller Press, Frankfurt-am-Main, 1951).
Warren	G. Warren *Art Nouveau* (Octopus, London, 1972).
Watkins (1950)	L.W. Watkins *Early New England Potters & Their Wares* (Harvard University Press, Cambridge, Massachusetts, 1950).
Watkins (1959)	L.W. Watkins *Early New England Pottery* (Old Sturbridge Village, Sturbridge, Massachusetts, 1959).
Watkins *et al*	C. Watkins, W. Harvey, R. Senft *Shelley Potteries* (Barrie & Jenkins, 1980).
Webster	Donald Blake Webster *Decorated Stoneware Pottery of North America* (Charles E. Tuttle, Rutland, Vermont, 1971).
Wedgwood & Ormsbee	J. Wedgwood & H.O. Ormsbee *Staffordshire Pottery* (Putnam, London, 1947).
Weiss	G. Weiss *Ullstein Porzellanbuch* (Ullstein, Berlin, 1967).
Weisser	M. Weisser *Jugendstielfliesen* (J.H. Schmalfeldt & Co., Bremen, 1978).
Whiter	L. Whiter *Spode, A History of the Family, Factory and Wares from 1733-1833* (Barrie & Jenkins, London, 1970).
Williams (1931)	I.J. Williams *Catalogue of Welsh Porcelain in the National Museum of Wales* (Cardiff, 1931).
Williams (1932)	I.J. Williams *Nantgarw Porcelain* (National Museum of Wales, Cardiff, 1932).
Williams-Wood	C. Williams-Wood *Staffordshire Pot Lids & Their Potters* (Faber & Faber, London, 1972).
Wiltshire	W.E. Wiltshire III *Folk Pottery of the Shenandoah Valley* (E.P. Dutton & Co., New York, 1975).
Wingfield Digby	G. Wingfield Digby *The Work of the Modern Potter in England* (John Murray, London, 1952).
Woodhouse	C. Patten Woodhouse *The World's Master Potters* (David & Charles, Newton Abbot, 1974).
World Ceramics	R.J. Charleston (ed) *World Ceramics* (Paul Hamlyn, London, 1968).
Wykes-Joyce	M. Wykes-Joyce *7000 Years of Pottery & Porcelain* (Peter Owen Ltd, London, 1958).
Ziegler	J. Ziegler *Etudes céramiques* (Mathias, Paris, 1850).

Picture Credits

Monochrome

Monochrome pictures are reproduced by courtesy of the following:

Ashmolean Museum, Oxford 206b

Paul Atterbury 289b

Berlin, Kunstgewerbemuseum, 19b, 36a, 78a, 86a, 88c, 94a, 96b, 100a, 100b, 109a, 141a, 177b, 179a, 186b, 195a, 199a, 204b, 240a, 259b, 270a, 285a, 295a, 298a, 319a, 343c

Bing & Grøndahl Copenhagen Porcelain Ltd 53b, 95a, 121a, 122b, 190a, 236a, 280a, 327b, 357a

Boston, Museum of Fine Arts 19a, 170b

Bristol, City Museum 61a

The Brooklyn Museum, New York 334a

Cameron Books, London 53a, 72b, 77a, 99a, 101b, 102b, 103b, 105a, 124b, 126a, 174a, 197a, 218a, 225a, 330a, 341a, 359a

Ceramic Review 118a, 233a, 250a, 289a

Christie, Manson & Woods Ltd, London 9a, 17b, 42a, 51a, 52a, 63b, 71b, 85c, 97c, 101a, 104b, 113a, 145a, 173b, 194a, 196b, 212a, 221a, 242a, 263c, 267b, 272a, 288a, 291a, 308a, 313a, 321a, 329b, 338a, 340a, 349a, 352c, 358b, 360a, 361a, 362a, 365b, 366a

Christie's, New York 16a, 17a, 44b, 47a, 50a, 134b, 149a, 173a, 207b, 208a, 226a, 234a, 248b, 253b, 256b, 309b, 334c, 345a, 351c, 354d

Christie's Amsterdam 337b

Cincinnati Art Museum 10a, 18a, 27a, 32b, 79a, 80a, 81a, 90a 96a, 133a, 134b, 181b, 209a, 243a, 243b, 252a, 280b, 284a, 284b, 305a, 336a, 336b, 352b

Cologne, Kunstgewerbe Museum 16c, 26a, 35b, 101c, 235a, 260b, 263b

Copenhagen, Museum of Decorative Arts 48a, 132a, 316a

The Dartington Hall Trust 180b

Edinburgh, National Museum of Antiquities Scotland 41a, 83c, 169a

Adrian Forty 129a

Galerie Louise Leiris, Paris 260a

Ghent, Museum voor Sierkunst 16b, 97b

Hamburg, Museum für Kunst und Gewerbe, photographs Rheinländer Photoatelier 45b, 102c, 198a, 217a, 288b, 302a, 313c

Karlsruhe, Badisches Landesmuseum 23a, 25b, 27b, 34a, 38b, 44c, 48b, 52b, 53c, 54a, 117a, 122a, 123a, 135a, 135b, 154a, 158a, 161a, 164a, 168a, 178b, 186c, 193a, 201b, 204a, 210a, 213a, 220a, 222a, 237c, 279b, 296b, 296c, 297b, 298b, 301a, 320a, 337a, 339a, 342b, 343b, 344a, 344b, 351a, 354a, 364a

Klinkhardt & Biermann 37a, 38a, 55c, 69a, 121b, 130b, 142b, 186a, 219b, 262a

Lancaster, City Museum 207a

Manchester City Art Gallery 92a

Minton Museum, Royal Doulton Ltd 21a, 211a

The Newark Museum 62a, 83b, 146a, 148a, 198b, 241a, 296a, 325c, 332a, 333a, 341b, 345b, 347a, 356a, 363b

Princeton University, The Art Museum 205a, 258a, 276a, 307a, 328, 334a

Phillips, Son & Neale 21b, 33a, 33b, 33c, 39a, 44d, 45a, 55a, 55b, 56a, 59b, 59c, 72a, 82a, 83a, 84a, 89a, 94b, 117b, 131a, 132a, 138a, 142a, 151a, 151b, 156a, 159a, 164b, 176a, 180a, 181a, 189b, 195b, 209b, 211b, 214b, 217b, 220b, 222c, 225b, 230a, 230b, 238a, 251a, 253a, 255a, 255b, 256a, 262a, 264a, 264b, 265a, 268b, 269a, 277c, 282a, 286b, 304b, 308b, 308c, 318b, 320b, 329a, 336c, 340b, 343d, 346a, 347b, 354b, 363b

Royal Doulton Tableware, Information Dept 36b, 114a, 115a, 245c, 328b

Smithsonian Institution, National Museum of American History, Washington 15a, 40b, 63a, 91b, 93b, 118b, 156b, 205b, 212b, 221b, 222a, 232a, 240b, 246a, 250a, 275a, 281a, 286c, 289c, 292b, 351b

Sotheby & Co. 14a, 23a, 40a, 44a, 48c, 57a, 76a, 88b, 93a, 137a, 160a, 168b, 188a, 192a, 200a, 216b, 220c, 237b, 248c, 259a, 266a, 286a, 292a, 293c, 297a, 303a, 342a, 365a

Sotheby's Belgravia 25a, 28a, 32a, 34b, 49a, 50b, 50c, 58a, 66b, 67a, 68a, 74a, 74b, 85a, 85b, 88a, 89b, 92b, 97a, 99b, 100c, 103a, 104a, 112a, 115b, 120a, 134a, 139a, 153a, 153b, 169b, 184a, 191a, 191b, 192b, 206a, 214a, 215b, 236b, 237a, 244a, 245a, 245b, 261a, 263a, 279a, 294a, 302b, 304a, 309a, 313b, 315b, 318a, 322a, 325b, 343a, 350a, 352a, 363a, 366a

Stoke on Trent, City Museum and Art Gallery 35c, 66a, 68b, 87a, 93c, 98a, 123b, 128a, 143a, 145c, 160b, 172a, 215a, 216a, 228b, 267a, 273a, 293a, 305b, 310a, 315a, 317a, 324a, 325a, 333b, 346b

Sydney, Museum of Applied Arts and Sciences 32c, 57b, 102a, 124a, 127a, 157aa, 201a, 203a, 210b, 248a, 277b, 300a

Victoria & Albert Museum, London 35a, 46c, 59a, 65a, 71a, 91a, 109b, 130a, 136b, 144a, 145a, 150a, 163a, 170a, 177a, 178a, 182a, 185a, 228a, 239a, 249a, 254a, 268a, 277a, 328b, 330b

York, City Art Gallery 58b, 152a, 189a, 293b

Colour

Colour pictures, identified here by entry name, are reproduced by courtesy of the following:

Ashmolean Museum, Oxford: Arita.

Bing & Grøndahl Copenhagen Porcelain Ltd: Krohn.

Cameron Books, London: Cox; (photography Donna Thynne) Billington, Cantagalli, Carter, Cooper, Franck, Gustavsberg, Heubach, Kanjiro, Ponti, Powell, Richardson.

Christie's, Amsterdam: Ram.

Christie's, Geneva: Buthaud, Gallé, Rozenberg, Zsolnay.

Cincinnati Art Museum: Morgan.

Editions Graphiques, London: Amphora, Massier, Solon, Tharaud.

Royal Doulton Ltd: barbotine, Barlow, Noke, Tittensor, Vyse.

Smithsonian Institution: Clark.

Tulane University: Meyer.

Werner Forman Archive: Awaji.

Erratum
The following marks should appear in the Adams & Co. entry on page 9: